CIVIL LIBERTIES
AND HUMAN RIGHTS

Third Edition

Helen Fenwick, BA, LLB
Reader in Law
University of Durham

Cavendish
Publishing
Limited

London • Sydney

Third edition published 2002 by Cavendish Publishing Limited

This edition reprinted 2006
by Routledge-Cavendish
2 Park Square, Milton Park, Abingdon, Oxon, OX14 4RN
Simultaneously published in the USA and Canada
by Routledge-Cavendish
270 Madison Avenue, New York, NY 10016

Routledge-Cavendish is an imprint of the Taylor & Francis Group

© Fenwick, Helen   2002
Reprinted   2004, 2005, 2006

Printed and bound in Great Britain by
Biddles Ltd, King's Lynn, Norfolk

British Library Cataloguing in Publication Data
A catalogue record for this book is available from the British Library
Library of Congress Cataloging in Publication Data.

ISBN 10: 1-85941-493-1
ISBN 13: 978-1-85941-493-4

For Paul, Clare, Daniel and Patrick

PREFACE

This is an interesting and exciting time to be writing a book of this nature – and completing this third edition has been rather like writing a new book – due to the constant changes in the legal landscape in this field. It is also a time at which the academic specialising in civil liberties feels immensely under pressure – partly due to the need to try to keep an eye on so many disparate developments and partly because the parameters of the academic discipline are changing as one writes. So many areas of law have now been found to have a human rights dimension that the academic civil libertarian can no longer – if this was ever possible – have a fairly clear idea as to where the boundaries of this subject lie. A fairly arbitrary choice is all that is currently possible.

This book was nearing completion in October 2001 when the Human Rights Act 1998 (HRA) had been fully in force for one year. It was therefore written at a time of unprecedented change in the human rights field in Britain. It reflects the resulting redirection of academic debate in that field that is now occurring. The argument about the merits of adopting a 'Bill of Rights' has now moved on and instead is focusing on the new issues arising from the reception of the Convention into domestic law, particularly the extent to which the Convention rights can be afforded real efficacy in the face of a number of recent legislative measures including the Terrorism Act 2000, the Regulation of Investigatory Powers Act 2000 and the Police and Criminal Justice Act 2001. The Anti-Terrorism, Crime and Security Bill 2001 raises similar concerns.

There is a danger that the HRA will be utilised in Parliament and outside it to give the impression that such statutes have undergone a process of human rights auditing, thereby stifling political discourse and obscuring the rights-abridging effects of the legislation. In order to declare such statutes compatible with the Convention rights, it appears likely that reliance is being placed on a minimalist interpretation of the Convention. Further, the effects of the HRA may be marginalised and such an interpretation may go unchallenged due to the reduction or exclusion of judicial scrutiny in the ordinary courts which tends to accompany the creation of new statutory frameworks for the use of coercive State power. Thus this book seeks to make the argument that at the very beginning of the HRA era the danger of a decrease in State accountability and the creation of merely empty or tokenistic guarantees is apparent.

But this book also seeks to chart an intriguing parallel and partly opposed development. In a number of spheres the judiciary are showing signs of a preparedness to utilise the HRA not only to curb executive or legislative, but corporate power. Currently, this is especially true of the provision of protection for personal information – the creation of 'privacy rights' against the press. In so far as, in other words, certain private companies increase their profits by invasion of privacy, the courts are finding methods, under the impetus of the HRA, of curbing their activities. This is one respect in which it may be said that the judges are showing signs of seeking to fashion a 'Bill of Rights' out of the Convention rights. In other common law areas less receptivity to such development is apparent where Convention values are not found to coincide happily with common law ones. In relation to uses of coercive State power, especially in the immigration context, the judges have at times utilised the HRA to scrutinise executive decisions much more intensively than they felt themselves able to do previously. In contrast, the effect of the HRA in the terrorist and criminal justice context, has been muted and patchy. This is due, this book argues, partly to continuing judicial deference in the national security context and partly to judicial determination to cling to their traditional common law-based fondness for retaining the maximum discretion for the judiciary.

The above remarks are intended to indicate the main themes of the third edition of this book. It seeks to encapsulate, at this very early point in the post-HRA era, the interaction that is occurring between the Convention rights and repressive legislation, between the rights and the common law and indeed between the rights and a more developed version of themselves – a Bill of Rights. If the HRA is to be utilised to create a Bill of Rights, judges will have to look beyond the often meagre and untheorised Convention jurisprudence in doing so.

I must acknowledge the contribution of all the people who helped in formulating the ideas expressed in this book. My thanks are due to Professor Colin Warbrick, who aided me in writing the first edition by offering helpful criticism of a very early draft of Chapter 3 and as a source of information in relation to the first part of Chapter 2. My thanks are also due to Gavin Phillipson of the University of Durham for his valuable help in researching material for a number of chapters. I have drawn on certain of my articles as indicated at various points.

The main body of the text was completed by July 2001, but it was possible to add some later material in November 2001.

The book is dedicated with love and affection to Paul, Clare, Daniel and Patrick.

Helen Fenwick

Durham

December 2001

CONTENTS

PART I

Contents

PART II

PART III

PART IV

PART V

TABLE OF CASES

TABLE OF UK STATUTES

NATIONAL LEGISLATION FROM OTHER JURISDICTIONS

TABLE OF EC LEGISLATION

PART I

THEORIES OF RIGHTS AND THEIR LEGAL PROTECTION IN THE UK

In many Western Democracies, the rights of citizens are enshrined in a constitutional document sometimes known as a Bill or Charter of Rights. As Chapters 1 and 3 will explain, the rights protected under such a constitutional document are often given a special status; in a number of countries they are entrenched. Until the inception of the Human Rights Act 1998 (HRA), the UK had no similar charter of rights. In 2000, the HRA afforded further effect to the European Convention on Human Rights. But even under the HRA, the rights are not entrenched. Traditionally, in order to discover which freedoms are protected and the extent of that protection, it has been necessary to examine the common law, statutes and the influence of treaties to which the UK is a party, especially the European Convention on Human Rights.

Certain particular characteristics of the UK Constitution have determined and, even under the HRA, will continue to determine, the means of protecting fundamental freedoms in the UK. The doctrine of the supremacy of Parliament means that constitutional law can be changed in the ordinary way – by Act of Parliament. As every student of constitutional law knows, Parliament has the power to abridge freedoms that in other countries are seen as fundamental rights. It follows from this that all parts of the law are equal – there is no hierarchy of laws and therefore constitutional law cannot constrain other laws.

Further, there is no judicial review of Acts of Parliament. If, for example, a statute is passed containing a provision which in some way limits freedom of speech, a judge must apply it, whereas in a country with an entrenched Bill of Rights the law might be struck down as unconstitutional. However, there were, prior to the inception of the HRA, two possible constraints on this process. If the judge considered that the provision in question is at all ambiguous, he or she could interpret it in such a way that freedom of speech was maintained, by relying on the European Convention on Human Rights. Further, if the domestic provision came into conflict with an EU provision, the judge could decide to 'disapply' it, unless the conflict could be resolved. Thus, parliamentary sovereignty has suffered some limitation. Where the EU does have an impact, it can provide a protection which may broadly be said to remove certain fundamental freedoms, or aspects of them, from the reach of Parliament, at least while the UK is a member of the EU.

Civil liberties thus have traditionally been defined as residual, not entrenched as in other countries: they are the residue of freedom left behind after the legal restrictions have been defined. Thus, it was often said that civil liberties in the UK were in a more precarious position than they were in other democracies, although this did not necessarily mean that they were inevitably less well protected: some Bills of Rights offered only a theoretical protection to freedoms which was not reflected in practice. These constitutional arrangements have not been fundamentally changed by the HRA, as Chapter 4 indicates. Under the HRA, a judge will not be able to declare a statutory provision invalid because it conflicts with a Convention right protected by the Act.

That is the constitutional background to the HRA. It is still of great significance since it is crucial in the development of civil liberties in this country and because the HRA has been greatly influenced by the domestic constitutional traditions. This Part will seek to show that although the HRA is of immense constitutional significance, it has not brought about a fundamental constitutional transformation. This notion of transition forms the main theme in this Part.

Chapter 1 will offer an indication of the theoretical basis of rights and liberties and of the distinction between them, seeking to demonstrate that a shift from liberties to rights has occurred. Chapter 2 will undertake analysis of the treaty which has been afforded further effect in domestic law so that it may – depending on the stance of the judiciary under the HRA, come to act, in effect, as a UK Bill of Rights – the European Convention on Human Rights. Chapter 3 will consider the nature and adequacy of the traditional domestic arrangements which protected fundamental freedoms only as liberties and will consider the extent to which the Convention influenced the domestic protection of civil liberties in the pre-HRA era. Chapter 4 will consider the nature of the instrument that has, in a sense, received the Convention into domestic law – the HRA.

The Act was introduced by the Labour Government in 1997 on the basis that rights were, finally, to be 'brought home'.[1] There were expectations at that time that the HRA would revive the civil liberties tradition – there was a sense of a break with the erosions of liberty of the past.[2] But, in 2001, only one year after the Act came into force, the Labour Government is already proposing a derogation from one of the most fundamental freedoms – the right to liberty – in order to aid in combating terrorism. The legislation passed after the HRA, which is considered in this book, including the Terrorism Act 2000 and the Regulation of Investigatory Powers Act 2000, is in some respects more authoritarian than legislation passed in the pre-HRA years.

Thus, one aim of this book is to consider the impact which the HRA could have in enhancing the protection for liberty, and at the same time to examine the danger that the Convention rights are being minimised and undermined in Parliament and in the courts. There is the possibility that in Parliament, the rights might become merely empty guarantees which cast a legitimising cloak over rights-abridging legislation and executive action.[3] This book will argue that since the Convention has been received into domestic law, it should be afforded a genuine efficacy since the alternative would be likely to lead to a *decrease* in State accountability and an obscuring of political discourse as to the nature of State power and countervailing civil rights. In other words, the fact that we now have a document that looks something like a Bill of Rights, in the tradition of other democracies, should not blind us to the traditional concerns of the executive which are especially pressing at the present time.

---

1   See *Bringing Rights Home: Labour's plans to incorporate the ECHR into UK Law: A Consultation Paper,* December 1996 (1997) and the White Paper, *Rights Brought Home,* Cm 3782, October 1997; see also Straw, J and Boateng, P (1997) 1 EHRR 71.

2   See Cooke, 'The British embracement of human rights' (1999) EHRLR 243; Feldman, D, 'The Human Rights Act and constitutional principles' (1999) 19(2) LS 165.

3   This danger was pointed out by Gearty, CA, in 'Terrorism and human rights: a case study in impending legal realities' (1999) 19(3) LS 367, p 379.

CHAPTER 1

THE NATURE OF RIGHTS AN~

This book is intended to provide an analysis of the legal protectio~ in the UK.[1] The term 'civil liberties' will be used to denote the broa~ referred to as civil and political rights as they are recognised in th~ ~o provide a coherent analysis, a theoretical position will be outlined fro~ ~nount an internally consistent critique of the state of civil liberties in the UK to~ ~nis chapter will therefore aim to outline such a position in order to provide an account of a method of deriving rights from more general political theory and criticisms of this derivation; consideration of the nature of these rights and of methods of resolving conflicts between individual rights and the claims of society; and analysis of what we may be requiring of others when we assert a right or liberty.[3] Broadly, the position adopted will tend to reflect the particular brand of political liberalism expounded by John Rawls and Ronald Dworkin, in so far as their theories converge. Perhaps it should be noted at this point that the liberal conception of rights which will be discussed differs significantly from the tradition which views rights as naturally inherent in the human person.[4] By contrast, as will be seen, liberals start by devising a general political theory from which they then seek to derive a series of rights.

1 WHERE DO RIGHTS DERIVE FROM?

The liberal conception of rights can be seen to owe its antecedents to the school of so called social contractarians which found perhaps its earliest advocate in the writings of John Locke.[5] Locke imagined an actual social contract between individuals and the State at the setting up of civil society in which citizens, in order to secure the protection of their property, handed over certain powers (most importantly, a monopoly of coercive force) to

---

1   General reading which will be referred to throughout this book: Bailey, SH, Harris, DJ and Jones, BL, *Civil Liberties: Cases and Materials*, 4th edn, 1995; Feldman, D, *Civil Liberties and Human Rights in England and Wales*, 1st edn, 1993; 2nd edn 2001; Robertson, G, *Freedom, the Individual and the Law*, 7th edn (for background), 1993; Ewing, KD and Gearty, CA, *Freedom Under Thatcher*, 1990; Thornton, P, *Decade of Decline: Civil Liberties in the Thatcher Years*, 1989 (for background); Sieghart, P, *Human Rights in the UK*, 1988; Whitty, N, Murphy, T and Livingstone, S, *Civil Liberties Law*, 2001; Klug, F, Starmer, K and Weir, S, *The Three Pillars of Liberty: Political Rights and Freedoms in the UK*, 1996; Gordon, R and Wilmot-Smith, R (eds), *Human Rights in the UK*, 1997; Clayton, R and Tomlinson, H, *The Law of Human Rights*, 2000; Lord Lester of Herne Hill and Pannick, D, *Human Rights Law and Practice*, 2000; Fenwick, H, *Civil Rights: New Labour, Freedom and the Human Rights Act*, 2000.

2   The term 'civil and political rights' is used in contradistinction to the term 'economic and social rights' to denote first generation rights – those which have long been recognised in the Western democracies from the time of the French and American Declarations of the 'Rights of Man' in the 18th century.

3   General reading: the literature is immense, but the following are of particular importance. Simmonds, NE, *Central Issues in Jurisprudence*, 1986, provides a brief but extremely lucid introduction to relevant jurisprudential issues. Substantive texts: Rawls, J, *A Theory of Justice*, 1973; Dworkin, R, *Taking Rights Seriously*, 1977, and *A Matter of Principle*, 1985; Hart, HLA, *The Concept of Law*, 1961, and *Essays in Jurisprudence and Philosophy*, 1983; Waldron, J (ed), *Theories of Rights*, 1984.

4   For a modern exposition of the Natural Law School, see Finnis, J, *Natural Law and Natural Rights*, 1980.

5   Locke, J, *The Second Treatise of Government*, 1698.

ent in return for the guarantee of certain rights to 'lives, liberties and estates'. us introduced the idea, which is still central to liberalism today, that the riding purpose of the State is the securing and protection of its citizen's basic liberties. The idea of the social contract is thus clearly an immensely potent one and it is John Rawls's revival and radical revision of the idea in his *A Theory of Justice* (1972) which has almost single-handedly transformed the face of political theory; as HLA Hart has commented, rights-based theories have replaced utilitarianism[6] as the primary focus of attention.[7] Robert Nozick, a right-wing critic of Rawls whose work *Anarchy, State and Utopia* (1974) mounts a sustained attack upon Rawls's theory, has written: 'Political philosophers now must either work within Rawls's theory or explain why not'.[8]

Rawls imagines not an actual, but a hypothetical social contract taking place in what he terms 'the original position'. The essential feature of this position is that the contractors (Rawls's men) are devising amongst themselves the outlines of 'the foundation charter of their society' whilst behind 'the veil of ignorance'. The men are ignorant not only of what will be their positions in the future social hierarchy, but also of their skills, weaknesses, preferences and conceptions of the good life – whether, for example, they will be strict Muslims or humanist academics. Since none of the contractors knows what mode of life he will wish to pursue, he is bound (if he is rational) to choose a tolerant society and one which guarantees him the rights necessary to pursue any individual goals he may in future choose. In other words, the men will wish to put in place the means whereby they will, in future, be able to pursue their goals rather than adopting structures which might in future prevent them from doing so. Thus, almost any conception of the good life will require, for example, freedom from arbitrary arrest, the right to a fair trial and freedom from inhuman treatment. In addition, the man who will become the Muslim might in *future* wish to restrict freedom of speech on religious matters but, at *present*, self-interest dictates that he consider the possibility that his conception of the good life might necessarily include the exercise of freedom of speech. Thus Rawls's men adopt, *inter alia*, 'the first principle', stating that 'each person is to have an equal right to the most extensive, total system of equal basic liberties compatible with a similar system of liberty for all'.[9] These basic liberties are identical with any familiar list of civil and political rights.

Although similar to Rawls in political outlook, Ronald Dworkin offers a theoretical construct which derives rights in a different manner and indeed has criticised Rawls' theory, arguing that a *hypothetical*, unlike an *actual*, contract provides no grounds for binding actual people to its terms.[10] Dworkin attempts to derive rights from the premise, which he hopes all will agree to, that the State owes a duty to treat all of its citizens with equal concern and respect – a premise which he argues persuasively is the deep assumption underlying Rawls's use of the contract device. Dworkin is not concerned with defending rights from despotic and repressive governments and indeed he sees no need to protect – by designating them as rights – those individual interests which the *majority*

---

6   See discussion below, p 7.

7   See Hart's comments on this phenomenon generally in 'Between utility and rights', in Cohen, M (ed), *Ronald Dworkin and Contemporary Jurisprudence*, 1984.

8   Nozick, R, *Anarchy, State and Utopia*, 1974, p 183.

9   For this reference and a brief summary of the theory, see *op cit*, Rawls, fn 3, pp 11–15.

10 *Op cit*, Dworkin, fn 3, Chapter 6.

would like to see protected, since these will in any case be ensured by the democratic process which he assumes as a background to his theory. Dworkin's particular concern is to justify the protection of *unpopular* or minority rights – or those whose exercise may on occasion threaten the overall well being of the community – because such rights would potentially be put at risk if their validity were to be determined through a democratic vote.

Clearly, the institution of democracy and most familiar sets of political policies, such as seeking the economic betterment of the majority, seem to be satisfactorily explained by an underpinning utilitarianism.[11] Dworkin hypothesises that the great appeal of utilitarianism is owed at least in part to its appearance of egalitarianism through its promise to 'treat the wishes of each member of the community on a par with the wishes of any other',[12] taking into account only the intensity of the preference and the number of people who hold it. This appeal is evinced in the utilitarian maxim: 'everybody to count for one, nobody for more than one.' Dworkin finds, however, that raw utilitarianism betrays this promise, since it fails to distinguish between what he denotes external and personal preferences. For example, if the question of whether homosexual acts should be permitted in private between adults were to be decided by a majority vote (*preference maximisation*), homosexuals would express their personal preference for freedom to perform those acts. Certain heterosexuals, however, would vote against allowing this freedom, because their external preference is that homosexuals should not be free to commit such acts.

Thus, resolution of the question could be affected by the fact that certain citizens think that the homosexual way of life is not deserving of equal respect; a decision would therefore have been made at least partly on the basis that the way of life of certain citizens was in some way contemptible. If the government enforced this decision through the use of coercive force (the criminal law), it would clearly have failed in its central duty to treat its citizens with equal concern and respect. In other words, utilitarianism – and therefore democracy – has an in-built means of undermining its own promise of equality. Since for Dworkin protecting this promise of equality is the central postulate of political morality, he finds that homosexuals should be granted a right to moral autonomy which cannot be overridden even by a majority decision making process.

Opposition to the liberal conception of human rights

Utilitarianism

Utilitarianism has historically been generally hostile to the idea of rights, most famously to the notion of natural and inalienable human rights as set out, for example, in the American Declaration of Independence, which was characterised by Jeremy Bentham as

---

11 Utilitarianism is a major political philosophy. The original conception of utilitarianism espoused by Jeremy Bentham saw the aim of government as being to promote the greatest happiness of the greatest number of people (see Burns (ed), *Collected Works of Jeremy Bentham*, 1970). A more recent and fashionable version states that an ideal society is one in which there is the maximum amount of preference satisfaction (see, generally, Smart, C and Williams, *Utilitarianism: For and Against*, 1973). References in the text will be to this latter version, known as 'preference utilitarianism'.

12 *Op cit*, Dworkin, fn 3, p 275.

merely so much 'bawling upon paper'.[13] The opposition of utilitarians to the notion of *natural* rights sprang mainly from their legal positivism – their belief that a legal right only exists if there is a specific 'black letter' provision guaranteeing it. But in general, since utilitarianism sets out one supreme goal of happiness or, in its more modern version, preference maximisation, it would clearly follow that rights under utilitarianism can have only a contingent justification. In other words, they are to be respected if they help bring about the goal of maximum satisfaction of preferences, but not otherwise. It may seem odd to postulate an opposition between utilitarianism and human rights bearing in mind that JS Mill combined utilitarianism with a passionate belief in the desirability of free expression and civil rights generally. It should be noted, however, that Mill's arguments for free speech depend essentially on a belief that allowing free speech will, in the long term, have good effects – such as increasing the likelihood that the truth will be discovered – rather than on a belief that free expression is a good in itself or something to which human beings are entitled without reference to its likely effects. A utilitarian, confronted with a situation in which infringing a right would undeniably benefit society as a whole, would have no reason to support the inviolability of the right; for example, he or she would find it hard to explain why criminal suspects should not be tortured if it were proved that reliable evidence would be derived thereby, leading to increased convictions, deterrence of crime and substantial consequential benefit to society. A further variant of the theory which has sometimes been termed 'rule utilitarianism', however, states that the goals of utilitarianism can best be reached by constructing rules which it is thought will, in general, further the goal of happiness or 'preference maximisation' and then applying these rules to situations as absolutes rather than considering in each individual situation what can best further the goal (for discussion, see Smart and Williams, above, fn 11). Such rules could, of course, consist, at least in part, of a set of human rights. In relation to the example of torture given in the text, a rule utilitarian could plausibly maintain that a general rule of humane treatment of citizens is likely to lead to the greatest happiness. In deciding whether to torture an individual suspect, this would mean that instead of considering whether in this case overall utility would be increased thereby, the State should apply the rule of humane treatment, even if in the particular case it would lead to a decrease in utility. It can be seen that for rule utilitarians, the good (the goal of preference maximisation or greatest happiness) is prior to the right, in opposition to Rawls's clearly expressed conviction that the right (a system of just entitlements of citizens) is prior to any conceptions of the good – the substantive moral convictions by which individuals will live their lives.

Marxism

The former socialist bloc of States – the Soviet Union and Eastern Europe – was the driving force behind the international recognition of economic, social and cultural rights. This was at least partly due to the fact that there is a measure of hostility within Marxist thought to civil and political rights.[14] Such hostility exists mainly because Marxism advocates establishing a State which, far from being neutral amongst its citizens' varying

---

13 Bentham, J, 'Anarchical fallacies', in Bowring, J (ed), *Collected Works of Jeremy Bentham*, 1843, p 494.
14 See, eg, Marx, K, *On the Jewish Question*, 1843.

conceptions of the good and guaranteeing them the liberties necessary to pursue their private goals, instead imposes a particular conception of the good upon society. Since it regards the protection of this conception (the achievements of the revolution) as the supreme value and duty of the State, the exercise of liberties which threaten this achievement can be justifiably curtailed; hence the consistently poor record of the former Soviet bloc States and Communist China on such civil rights as freedom of speech. A theoretically related, but more moderate critique of the Western liberal conception of human rights can be found in the writings of the so called communitarians.[15]

Critical Legal Studies

The Critical Legal Studies movement (CLS) attacks the whole liberal conception of law as neutral, objective and rational. It seeks to expose the value judgments, internal inconsistencies and ideological conflicts which it sees as concealed under law's benevolent exterior of impartial justice.[16] Since the whole structure of legally guaranteed human rights is a creature of the liberal conception of law, the CLS attack fastens by extension onto the liberal notion of rights. Mark Tushnet, for example, has made four main criticisms of the liberal theory of rights in what he calls 'a Schumpeterian act of creative destruction'. He asserts that rights are: first, unstable – that is, meaningful only in a particular social setting; secondly, they produce 'no determinate consequences if claimed'; thirdly, 'rights talk ... falsely converts into empty abstractions ... real experiences that we ought to value for their own sake'; and fourthly, if conceded a dominant position in contemporary discourse, rights threaten to 'impede advances by progressive social forces'.[17] It would be inappropriate to attempt a detailed refutation of the CLS position here.[18] Perhaps the most important weakness in its critique of rights is that, as many writers have pointed out,[19] it offers no guidance whatsoever as to how the interests of vulnerable minorities are to be protected without the institution of legal rights.

2 WHAT IS MEANT BY A RIGHT?

The preceding section has set out, in a very basic manner, some of the more influential liberal theories concerning the means of deriving a system of rights from a more general moral theory. In this section, two aims will be pursued. First, an attempt will be made to shed some light on what one can be taken to mean, in general terms, when one asserts a right; secondly, a brief explanation will be given of Hohfeld's exposition of a right as an umbrella term, covering a number of more precisely delineated claims.

---

15 See, eg, Sandel, *Liberalism and the Limits of Justice*, 1982.

16 Unger, R, *The Critical Legal Studies Movement*, 1986.

17 Tushnet, M, 'An essay on rights' (1984) 62(18) Texas L Rev 1363.

18 For a general critique of the CLS attitude to rights see, eg, Price, 'Taking rights cynically' [1989] CLJ 271.

19 *Ibid*. See also eg, Rhodes, 'Feminist critical theories' (1990) 42(3) Stanford L Rev 634–38.

Distinguishing moral and legal rights

The endeavour to distinguish legal from moral rights involves a central issue in jurisprudence, namely, the relationship between law and morality, on which there is a vast literature and a number of clearly defined schools of thought. Only the barest indications of the various positions on this tendentious issue are possible here.

Legal positivism

Clearly, from a common sense point of view, if X makes a claim that she has a right to Y and there is no clear, black letter law giving her such a right, she must be taken to be asserting that she has a strong *moral* claim to Y and (probably) that this claim ought to be given *legal* force through the enactment of a specific legal right. The above point of view is – very crudely – that put forward by the school of jurisprudence known as legal positivism, whose central insistence is that there is no *necessary* connection between law and morality.[20]

Natural law

To a member of the natural law school in its traditional form,[21] by contrast, the question of whether X's claim to Y was moral or legal would be decided not empirically, by consulting the statute book, but rather by examining the normative claim made by her. If her claim was supported by an abstract notion of justice, then a measure purporting to deny the claim would not be accepted as a valid law since it would be unjust. The approach sounds extreme, but was employed during the Nuremberg trials as the underlying justification for what might otherwise have been seen as the retrospective criminalisation of those who committed their crimes under the Nazi laws thought valid at the time.

Dworkin's theory

The views of Ronald Dworkin[22] provide a middle ground between these two theories – a 'third theory of law'.[23] His theory is highly complex, but in essence is more inclusive than the positivist theory; recognising black letter legal rights,[24] it insists that the law may contain *further* rights which have never yet been recognised by a statute or in any judicial

---

20   For a full discussion of this issue, see Hart, HLA, 'Positivism and the separation of law and morals', in *Essays in Jurisprudence and Philosophy*, 1983.

21   For the classical exposition of this theory see Aquinas, '*Summa theologica*', in d'Entreves, P (ed), *Selected Political Writings*, 1970.

22   For an exposition of Dworkin's account of the relationship between law and morality, see his theory of judicial adjudication in Chapters 2–4 of *Taking Rights Seriously*, in which his theory is cast mainly in the form of a critique of legal positivism. For a fuller development of the theory, see *Law's Empire*, 1986.

23   The term was coined by Mackie, 'The third theory of the law', in Cohen, M (ed), *Ronald Dworkin and Contemporary Jurisprudence*.

24   Note that in *Law's Empire* Dworkin seems to discard any reliance on recognising 'black letter' law by some means reminiscent of Hart's rule of recognition and comes to a position in which law is entirely a matter of interpretation. For criticism of this position see, eg, Simmonds, NE, 'Imperial visions and mundane practices' [1987] CLJ 465 and Cotterell, R, *The Politics of Jurisprudence*, 1989, pp 172–81.

decision. Thus, X could correctly claim she had a right to Y, on Dworkin's account, if (a) the right would be consistent with the bulk of existing law and (b) it would figure in the best possible interpretation of the area of law concerned. By this, Dworkin means that the relevant past judicial decisions would be most satisfactorily justified by showing them all to have been concerned with protecting the right at issue, even if previous individual judgments did not explicitly recognise its existence. Such a claim might well, of course, be controversial, but it is precisely this that is at the root of Dworkin's disagreement with the positivists: finding out what the law is, he argues, will require not merely an empirical test of the law's *pedigree* (does it emanate from the right body?), but rather a complex inquiry which will, as he puts it, carry the lawyer 'very deep into moral and political theory'.[25]

If one is convinced by Dworkin's ingenious argument, the existence of a legal right can be adduced through interpretation (at least in common law jurisdictions). Alternatively, a right could, in any event, be given clear explicit protection so that its legal status was not a matter for controversy.

The strength of a right: conflicts with other claims

If a legal right is conceded to exist, it must next be asked what is and should be the nature and strength of the protection thereby given. The right may come into conflict with the claims of society, such as that a certain standard of morality should be upheld. Clearly, in resolving such a conflict, a judge will inevitably draw upon his or her background political theory. If, for example, a judge in the European Court of Human Rights, who is a utilitarian by conviction, has to consider a convincing demonstration by a defendant government that the particular application of the right to free speech claimed by the applicant will, on balance, make society worse off as a whole, he or she will be inclined to find for the government and allow the infringement of the right. Such infringement will, of course, be more readily allowable if the right is framed or has developed in such a way as to be open-ended in scope with in-built exceptions.

Both Dworkin and Rawls have argued persuasively against making rights vulnerable to utilitarian considerations in this way. The idea that '[e]ach person possesses an inviolability founded on justice that even the welfare of society as a whole cannot override'[26] lies at the centre of Rawls's political thought. The idea of such inviolable rights may seem extreme, but is in fact accepted by all civilised countries in the case, for example, of torture. It is not thought to be a sound argument for a government to assert that it is justified in torturing certain of its citizens on the grounds that it can increase the general welfare thereby. The acceptance of this principle is attested to by the non-derogability of the right to freedom from torture in all international human rights treaties including the European Convention on Human Rights (Art 15(2)).

Dworkin has addressed the specific question as to the means of understanding a legal right in an adjudicative context in some detail. Earlier, the distinction between moral and legal rights was discussed. Here it should be noted that Dworkin also distinguishes

---

25 *Op cit*, Dworkin, fn 3, p 67.
26 *Op cit*, Rawls, fn 3, p 3.

between rights that have 'trump' status and those that do not. He gives as an example of the latter a legal right to drive either way on a two-way road: such a right is a 'weak' legal right, because it is not an important human interest which is likely to be denied to certain groups through the influence of external preferences. It follows that such a right could justifiably be overridden by the government (through making the road one-way) if it thought it in the general interest to do so. By contrast, his conception of the strength of 'trump' rights leads to his insistence that an assertion of (for example) a right to free speech held by citizens 'must imply that it would be wrong for the government to stop them from speaking, even when the government believes that what they say will cause more harm than good'.[27]

It can be seen, then, that Dworkin gives us a very clear prescription for the approach that a judge should take in weighing strong or 'trump' rights against the general welfare of society. He roundly condemns the idea that a judge, in adjudicating upon a right or a government in framing it, should carefully weigh up the right of the citizen against the possible adverse social consequences, accepting that it is sometimes preferable to err on the side of society, sometimes on the side of the individual, but on the whole getting the balance about right. 'It must be wrong', he argues, to consider that 'inflating rights is as serious as invading them'. For to *invade* a right is to affront human dignity or treat certain citizens as less worthy of respect than others, while to *inflate* a right is simply to pay 'a little more in social efficiency'[28] than the government *already* has to pay in allowing the right at all. Thus, for Dworkin, if one asserts a 'trump' right, ordinary counter-arguments about a decrease in the welfare of society as a whole are simply irrelevant.

In what circumstances, then, may a strong individual right be overridden? Dworkin has argued[29] that there are three general justifications for infringement and these appear to be generally accepted by liberal thought.

Competing rights

First, there is the situation in which there is a clear competing individual claim, so that the exercise of the original right will directly infringe the competing right. The paradigmatic example of such a collision of individual rights arises where one individual uses his right of free speech to prejudice the fair trial of another. Another is where one incites violence against the other, thus infringing his right to security of the person. In such cases, since both rights are, as it were, from the same class of 'strong' rights, they will compete on equal terms, but it may nevertheless be possible to resolve the conflict by undertaking a balancing act based on proportionality. In the case of prejudice to a trial, this could be done by physically removing the trial from the area affected by the speech in question. If such avoidance of conflict was impossible, a determination might be made as to the damage inflicted on each right if the other was allowed to prevail. In the case of incitement to violence, the damage inflicted if free speech was allowed to prevail might be almost irretrievable, since the group affected might be placed at great risk for a period

---

27   *Op cit*, Dworkin, fn 3, p 191.
28   *Ibid*, p 199.
29   *Ibid*, p 200.

of time. In contrast, the damage to free speech created by avoidance of the risk might be of a lesser nature, although undesirable: the speech could be uttered in another form or another forum, so that its meaning was not lost, but it was rendered less inflammatory. Alternatively, utterance of the speech could be delayed until the situation had become less volatile. The words advocating immediate violence might be perceived as outside the area of protected speech and so might be severed from the accompanying words which could be permitted.

The right is not really at stake

The second situation in which rights may be overridden is one where the values protected by the right are not at stake in this particular situation. In other words, it may be argued that most rights have a 'core', the invasion of which will constitute an actual overriding of the right, but they also have a 'penumbra' – an area in which the value the right protects is present only in a weaker form.[30] An invasion of the penumbra may be said to constitute only an *infringement* of the right and may therefore be more readily justified. The argument that commercial speech should not be afforded the same protection as other kinds of speech would appear to rest precisely on the argument that it is in the penumbra of free speech;[31] by contrast, political speech is clearly in the 'core' of free speech.[32]

A real risk to society

The third situation justifying infringement is one in which the exercise of a right may pose a real danger to society. In such instances, liberals are unwilling to take danger to mean danger to some abstract attribute to society, such as its moral health,[33] but rather insist that the danger must ultimately amount to a threat to some concrete aspect of its citizens' well being. Thus, typically, liberals are hostile to characterising the likelihood of shocking or offending citizens as a concrete harm justifying the suppression of the right of free speech. Dworkin's own, perhaps rather unrealistically stringent test, is that the 'risk to society' justification for overriding rights is only made out if the State demonstrates 'a clear and substantial risk' that exercise of the right 'will do great damage to the person or property of others'.[34] It seems unlikely that governments would be prepared to accept such a test; the criterion laid down, for example, by the European Court of Human Rights

---

30 This view is not attributed to Dworkin, although he does accept that there will be situations in which the core value of the right will not be at stake. Dworkin has comprehensively rejected Hart's theory of statutory construction and application of the rules from past cases based around the notion of a core of certainty and a penumbra of uncertainty (for Hart's position, see *The Concept of Law*; for Dworkin's critique, *op cit*, fn 3, Chapters 2–4). Dworkin argues that the areas of a rule which form the core and those which fall in the penumbra, can only be elucidated through a judge's interpretation, which will carry him or her far from the specific words of the statute.

31 Judgment of US Supreme Court, *Bolger v Youngs Drug Products Ltd* (1983) 103 Ct 2875, 2880–81.

32 The House of Lords appeared to recognise the central importance of free political speech in their recent decision that neither local nor central government could pursue an action in defamation: *Derbyshire CC v Times Newspapers* [1993] 1 All ER 1011.

33 Eg, see the attacks by Hart, 'Social solidarity and the enforcement of morality', in *Essays in Jurisprudence and Philosophy*, and Dworkin, 'Liberty and morality', in *op cit*, fn 3, on Lord Devlin's view that society may justifiably use the criminal law to enforce a shared morality.

34 *Op cit*, Dworkin, fn 3, p 204.

for curtailing the right of free expression as set out in Art 10 does not even approach Dworkin's prescription either in stringency or clarity; instead, it has adopted the somewhat weak and uncertain phrase, 'a pressing social need'.[35] Dworkin's rights analysis should not, therefore, be taken as a description of the way rights and liberties are *actually* treated in the UK and under human rights treaties, but rather as an ideal against which the reality of such 'rights' protection can be measured.

Distinguishing rights and liberties

Having given an account of what may, in general terms, be meant by an assertion of a right in the liberal tradition, we may now turn to an analysis of the more specific claims that the assertion of a right may entail and employ this analysis to make a few general remarks about the nature of 'rights' protection in the UK.

Hohfeld's analysis

One of the more influential attempts to analyse closely the nature of a right was made by the American jurist Wesley Hohfeld.[36] Hohfeld attempted to demonstrate the way that claims of rights in everyday language can in fact be broken down into four more specific claims. First, if it is claimed that X has a right proper or 'claim right' to A, then this means that persons, generally or particularly, are under some specific corresponding duty to ensure that X has access to A. Secondly, X may be said to have an immunity as against a particular person or body; this means that they are disabled from interfering with the exercise by X of the interest (A) protected by the immunity. Thirdly, if X has only a liberty (what Hohfeld calls a privilege) to do A, this far weaker claim merely means that X does no wrong in exercising his liberty – the rights of others are not thereby infringed. However, no one has a duty to allow him to exercise A or to assist him to exercise it. Fourthly, X may have a power to do B, such as to sell his property. This last category is not particularly relevant to the subject of civil liberties.

Hohfeld applied to the reality of 'rights' protection

Hohfeld's explanation is a useful analytical tool; it can be seen by utilising it that Dworkin is advocating that rights be set out as a series of immunities – areas of entitlement which even democratically elected governments are disabled from interfering with. The US Constitution and its Amendments represent such a list of immunities. In applying Hohfeld's theory to 'rights' protection in the UK, it can be seen that it endows the commentator with the ability to distinguish between the different forms of protection offered towards different freedoms. The commentator must now apply these analytical tools to the Human Rights Act 1998 in order to find that a very significant break with the traditional findings as to rights protection in the UK has occurred.

If Dworkin's analysis is used, all rights in the UK are 'weak' since, even under the Human Rights Act 1998, all are at least theoretically subject to infringement by

---

35 See *Handyside v UK* (1976) 1 EHRR 737. For further discussion of this test, see Chapter 5, p 229.

36 Hohfeld, W, *Fundamental Legal Concepts as Applied in Judicial Reasoning*, 1920, particularly pp 35–41.

Parliament. Under Hohfeld's view, the picture is more mixed. It becomes clear that, traditionally, most freedoms in the UK were merely liberties; one did no wrong to exercise them, but there was no positive duty on any organ of the State to allow or facilitate them. For example, the Public Order Act 1986 nowhere placed upon chief constables a duty to ensure freedom of assembly and speech. Nevertheless, some of our entitlements clearly had and have the quality of Hohfeldian claim rights in that they are protected by a positive correlative duty. For example, arrested persons have the right of access to a solicitor while in police custody as guaranteed by s 58 of the Police and Criminal Evidence Act 1984. Equal treatment in certain contexts is provided for under domestic and EU instruments. However, even when a citizen holds a right, there were – under domestic law – no *legal* guarantees that the legislation providing the positive protection would not be repealed. Similarly, a citizen enjoying a liberty could not be certain that legislation would not be introduced into a previously unregulated area, thus destroying or limiting that liberty.

When the Human Rights Act 1998 came fully into force, however, in October 2000, many of our Hohfeldian liberties became rights in Hohfeldian terms since, as Chapter 4 explains, public authorities have been laid under a positive duty to respect them and will act unlawfully if they do not (s 6(1)), unless the only possible reading of contrary primary legislation is that the right must be infringed. It will become much less likely that legislation will be introduced which would have the effect of limiting the rights protected under the 1998 Act, since such legislation might eventually be declared incompatible with the guarantees of those rights (s 4). Further, when the legislation was introduced, the relevant minister would have to declare that a statement of compatibility could not be made (s 19), which would be politically embarrassing. Similarly, existing legislative protection for a right recognised under the Act would be unlikely to be repealed, since the repealing legislation could not be accompanied by such a statement and, moreover, a citizen might bring an action at Strasbourg challenging the failure to make domestic provision to deliver the right (s 7). Thus, in Hohfeldian terms, the 1998 Act itself does not provide a set of immunities since it can be overridden by primary legislation, while in Dworkinian terms the rights remain 'weak'. As indicated, the guarantees of the rights are not absolute; the deterrents against infringing them are ultimately political ones. But the Act clearly represents a dramatic shift in rights protection in the UK, away from residual freedoms towards positive rights.

CHAPTER 2

THE EUROPEAN CONVENTION ON HUMAN RIGHTS

1 INTRODUCTION[1]

The European Convention on Human Rights was conceived after the Second World War as a means of preventing the kind of violation of human rights seen in Germany during and before the war. However, it has not generally been invoked in relation to large scale violations of rights, but instead has addressed particular deficiencies in the legal systems of the Member States, who on the whole create regimes of human rights in conformity with it. Drafted in 1949 by the Council of Europe, it was based on the United Nations Declaration of Human Rights,[2] and partly for that reason and partly because it was only intended to provide basic protection for human rights, it appears today as quite a cautious document, less far reaching than the International Covenant on Civil and Political Rights.[3] Nevertheless, it has had far more effect on UK law than any other human rights treaty due to its machinery for enforcement, which includes the European Court of Human Rights with the power to deliver a ruling adverse to the governments of Member States. Moreover, the Court insists upon the dynamic nature of the Convention and adopts a teleological or purpose-based approach to its interpretation which has allowed the substantive rights to develop until they may cover situations unthought of in 1949. Had it been a more radical document, the Convention might have been self-defeating because it might have failed to secure the necessary acceptance from Member States, both in terms of ratifying various parts of it, such as the right of individual petition, and in terms of responding to adverse judgments.

Although the European Court of Human Rights may rule against the governments of Member States, its approach – which is reflected throughout the machinery for the supervision of the Convention – is not ultimately coercive. A persuasive or consensus-based approach is evident at every stage through which an application may pass. A friendly settlement may well be reached before the case comes before the Court; even if it does not, and the case reaches the stage of a final ruling adverse to the government in question, the government is in effect free to determine the extent of the changes needed in order to respond, although the possibility of future adverse rulings at Strasbourg may exercise an influence on its decision. This approach is also reflected in the doctrine of the 'margin of appreciation' which has been developed by the Strasbourg authorities. This doctrine, to which we will return below,[4] involves allowing the domestic authorities a

---

1   General reading: see Merrills and Robertson, *Human Rights in Europe*, 3rd edn, 1993; Van Dijk, P and Van Hoof, F, *Theory and Practice of the European Convention on Human Rights*, 3rd edn, 1998; Beddard, *Human Rights and Europe*, 3rd edn, 1980; Fawcett, *The Application of the European Convention on Human Rights*, 2nd edn, 1987; Jacobs, *The European Convention on Human Rights*, 1975; Nedjati, *Human Rights under the European Convention*, 1978; Harris, D, O'Boyle, K and Warbrick, C, *Law of the European Convention on Human Rights*, 2nd edn, 2002; Dickson and Connelly, *Human Rights and the European Convention*, 1996; Farran, S, *The UK Before the European Court of Human Rights*, 1996; Janis, M, Kay, R and Bradley, A, *European Human Rights Law*, 2nd edn, 2000; Clayton, R and Tomlinson, H, *The Law of Human Rights*, 2000.

2   The Declaration was adopted on 10 December 1948 by the General Assembly of the UN.

3   1966.

4   See p 34–37.

degree of discretion in deciding what is needed to protect various public interests in their own countries, even though such interests have an impact on protection for Convention rights. The use of this doctrine allows evasion of conflict over very sensitive issues between Strasbourg and the Member State. Clearly, its use may lead at times to an acceptance of a lower standard of human rights than some liberal critics would advocate,[5] but some commentators have suggested that it can be an appropriate influence on the dealings between Strasbourg and democracies with generally sound human rights records.[6]

When examining the substantive rights, they may be said to fall into two groups: Arts 2–7, covering the most fundamental human rights and containing, broadly, no express exceptions,[7] or narrow express exceptions; and Arts 8–12, which may be said to cover a more sophisticated or developed conception of human rights and which are subject to a broad range of express exceptions. Thus, under Arts 2–7, argument will tend to concentrate on the question of whether a particular situation falls within the compass of the right in question, whereas under Arts 8–11 it will largely concentrate on determining whether the interference with the guarantee can be justified (Art 12 only contains one exception, but of a very broad nature). There is an enormous amount of overlap between the Articles and it may be found that weaknesses or gaps in one can be remedied by another, although the Convention will be interpreted as a harmonious whole.[8] It will also be found that invocation of a substantive right in order to attack a decision in the national courts on its merits may sometimes fail, but that a challenge to the *procedure* may succeed under one of the Articles explicitly concerned with fairness in the adjudicative process – Arts 5, 6 and 7.[9] The rights and freedoms are largely concerned with civil and political rather than social and economic matters; the latter are governed by the 1961 European Social Charter and the 1966 International Covenant on Economic, Social and Cultural Rights.[10]

The Convention has grown by way of additional protocols so that it now creates a more advanced human rights regime based on Arts 2–14 with the First Protocol[11] in

---

5   See below, fns 98 and 124.

6   See Gearty, C, 'Democracy and human rights in the European Court of Human Rights: a critical appraisal' (2000) 51(3) NILQ 381, esp p 387.

7   Article 6 provides that trial judgments should be pronounced publicly except where, *inter alia*, the interest of morals, public order or national security demand otherwise but the primary right – to a fair hearing – is not subject to these exceptions.

8   Van Dijk and Van Hoof, *op cit*, fn 1, Chapter II.

9   This point is developed below; see pp 58–60. See Gearty, C, 'The European Court of Human Rights and the protection of civil liberties: an overview' [1993] CLJ 89 for argument that the Convention as a whole is largely concerned with *procedural* rights.

10   (1965) Cmnd 2643; see Harris, *The European Social Charter*, 1984. The charter does not have a system of petitions. On an international level, the UK is also party to the 1966 International Covenant on Economic, Social and Cultural Rights, Cmnd 6702. It is not enforceable as regards the UK by individual petition.

11   Cmnd 9221. All the parties to the Convention except Switzerland are parties to this Protocol, which came into force in 1954.

conjunction with the Fourth,[12] Sixth[13] and Seventh[14] Protocols. The very significant Protocol 12 was opened for ratification in November 2000.[15] The UK has not yet ratified the rights contained in the Fourth and Seventh Protocols, and at present does not intend to ratify the Twelfth Protocol, suggesting that although there is a measure of harmony between the basic Convention regime and the UK legal system, this is not the case as far as aspects of the more advanced regime is concerned.

In considering the operation of the Convention in practice, it should be remembered that it was not intended to mimic the working of a domestic legal system. Thus, individuals could not, until recently, take a case directly to the European Court of Human Rights in Strasbourg[16] and, in fact, it is a feature of the Court that it hears very few cases in comparison with the number of applications made.[17] However, its jurisprudence has had an enormous impact, not merely through the outcome of specific cases, but in a general symbolic, educative and preventive sense. Its function in raising awareness of human rights was of particular significance in the UK since, until the enactment of the Human Rights Act, no equivalent domestic instrument had the role of doing so. Since the Human Rights Act has afforded the Convention further effect in UK law, its interpretation, the values it encapsulates and the development of the control machinery have become of even greater significance. An understanding of the workings of the Convention is now crucial since the jurisprudence is now being very frequently relied on in the domestic courts.

The enormous increase in the number of applications from the UK since the early days of the Convention suggests that before the Human Rights Act was enacted, it was seen as a guardian of human rights by UK citizens, although to an extent it held out a promise that it could not fulfil. The immensely slow and difficult route to Strasbourg discouraged applicants from using it. It is still a slow and cumbersome route owing to the number of applications, despite improvements in the mechanisms for considering them.[18] The fact that an application may take, at present, five years to be heard is perhaps one of the main deficiencies of the Convention enforcement machinery.[19] This chapter

---

12 Cmnd 2309. It came into force in 1968; the UK is not yet a party. It contains rights relating to the field of immigration law, which have raised governmental concerns regarding the nature of the obligations created and the Government has indicated that it does not intend to ratify it at present: see the White Paper, *Rights Brought Home: the Human Rights Bill*, Cm 3782, 1997, paras 4.10–4.11. It is, however, considering the possibility of future ratification with reservations: the *Home Office Review of Human Rights Instruments* (amended), 26 August 1999. See below, p 135.

13 (1983) 5 EHRR 167. It came into force in 1985. The UK is now a party to it and it is included in the Human Rights Act, Sched 1. See below, Chapter 4, p 135.

14 (1984) 7 EHRR 1. It came into force in 1988. The UK is not a party but proposes to ratify imminently: see the White Paper, *Rights Brought Home: the Human Rights Bill*, Cm 3782, 1997, paras 4.14–4.15, and the *Home Office Review of Human Rights Instruments* (amended) 26 August 1999. Note that the other Protocols are concerned with the procedural machinery of the Convention.

15 See Chapter 4, p 135 and see below, p 85.

16 Now that the Eleventh Protocol is in force, individuals have the right to take a case directly to the Court; see below, pp 22–27.

17 Eg, in 1991, the Commission registered 1648 applications; it referred 93 cases to the Court, which gave judgment in 72. European Court of Human Rights, Survey of Activities 1959–91.

18 Eg, new procedures were introduced under the Eighth Protocol including a summary procedure for rejecting straightforward cases.

19 The *average* time is a little over four years: see 'Reform of the control systems' 15 EHRR 321, p 360, para 7. See further below, pp 22–27.

therefore devotes some time to explaining that process and the highly significant part which was, until recently, played in it by the European Commission on Human Rights,[20] before going on to consider the substantive rights.

2 THE SUPERVISORY PROCEDURE FOR THE CONVENTION

Reform of the procedure recently occurred, stemming from a recommendation of the Parliamentary Assembly of the Council of Europe that the Commission and the Court should be merged into one body – the single Court. It was proposed[21] that the new Court would come into operation in 1995 and that there would be a transitional period from 1995 to 2000 during which the old Commission and Court would hear cases already referred to them while new cases would be referred to the new Court. The new arrangements governing the control mechanism[22] are contained Protocol 11[23] which has had a radical effect on the Convention procedure. Its most significant reform was to set up the single Court,[24] which now sits full time in place of the Court and Commission (under Art 19). Now that the Court and Commission have merged, it may be argued that the authority of the Convention will increase because its jurisprudence will no longer be influenced by the decisions of an administrative body; the control system has become, in this respect, more akin to that of a domestic legal system. Below, the original arrangements for the Convention are considered and compared with the new arrangements under Protocol 11. Although the Commission has been abolished, it has had a considerable influence on the Strasbourg jurisprudence. Moreover, the role it carried out has now, in essentials, been taken over by the Court. Therefore, for both reasons, it is still of importance to understand the role and functioning of the Commission.

Originally, under Art 19, the Convention set up the European Commission on Human Rights (hereafter referred to as 'the Commission') and the European Court of Human Rights (hereafter referred to as 'the Court'). Thus, the machinery for the enforcement of the Convention is impressive compared to that used in respect of other human rights treaties, particularly the 1966 International Covenant on Civil and Political Rights, which, as far as the UK is concerned, has been enforceable only through a system of assessment of national reports.[25]

---

20 See further Bratza, N and O'Boyle, M, 'Opinion: the legacy of the Commission to the new Court under the 11th Protocol' (1997) EHRLR 211.

21 Recommendation 1194 adopted on 6 October 1992 by the Parliamentary Assembly of the Council of Europe.

22 See 'Reform of the control systems' (1993) 15 EHRR 321. For comment, see Mowbray, A [1993] PL 419.

23 Protocol 11 came into force on 1 November 1998 under Art 5 of the Protocol, which provides that it comes into force one year after it has been ratified by all the Member States. See (1994) 15 HRLJ 86. The merger procedure was completed in November 1998 when the Commission was abolished. For discussion see, eg, Schermers, H, 'The Eleventh Protocol to the European Convention on Human Rights' (1994) 19 EL Rev 367, p 378 and (1995) EL Rev 3; Lord Lester of Herne Hill QC, 'The European Convention in the new architecture of Europe' [1996] PL 5.

24 See 'Reform of the control systems' (1993) 15 EHRR 321.

25 The Optional Protocol to the Covenant governs the right of individual petition; but it has not been ratified by the UK. For comment on the general efficacy of the reporting system see (1980) HRLJ 136–70.

The role of the Commission evolved over time. It was conceived of as an advisory body which provided assistance for the Committee of Ministers (see below), composed of the Foreign Affairs Ministers of each State, who had the key role in supervising the Convention. The idea of an independent body interfering in the use of governmental powers in relation to their own citizens gained gradual acceptance, and the Commission became less of an administrative and more of a judicial body, giving Opinions on the law, albeit without the ability to take binding decisions except in relation to inadmissibility (see below). Broadly, creation of the Commission represented a compromise: it was thought too controversial merely to allow citizens to take their governments before the Court. There was a feeling that an administrative body might be more sympathetic to Member States' cases and the Member State might feel less on trial than in the Court.[26] Therefore, the Commission was created as an administrative barrier between the individual and the Court and was used as a means of filtering out a very high proportion of cases, thus considering far more cases than the Court. This might seem a strange device: European Community lawyers would be horrified at the idea of creating a European Commission to keep cases out of the European Court of Justice; they would feel that for justice to be done, the individual's case must be considered by the Court itself rather than by an administrative body reaching its decisions in secret.[27] Nevertheless, in human rights matters, the Commission has been until recently viewed as an acceptable and useful device. That view recently underwent a change which led to the proposal for merger of the Commission with the Court; we will return to this matter below.

The role of the European Commission on Human Rights

The main role of the Commission was to filter out cases as inadmissible, thereby reducing the work load of the Court. However, it also had another role: it tried to reach a friendly settlement between the parties and could give its opinion on the merits of the case if it was not intended that a final judgment should be given. It could also refer the case to the Court or the Committee of Ministers[28] for the final judgment. As explained below, parts of this role have been taken over by the Court.

The Commission consisted of one member for every Member State.[29] The members were elected by the Committee of Ministers[30] and their period of service was managed with a view to ensuring that the membership would change constantly.[31] The members of the Commission (who were unsalaried) were not government representatives; Art 23

---

26   See Janis, Kay and Bradley, *op cit*, fn 1, p 27.

27   The Commission's sessions were held *in camera* (old Art 33).

28   For the composition and functioning of this body see below, pp 24–25.

29   Under (old) Art 20, no two members of the Commission could be nationals of the same State.

30   Under (old) Art 21, the members of the Commission were elected by the Committee of Ministers by an absolute majority of votes, from a list of names drawn up by the Bureau of the Consultative Assembly and this procedure was followed as far as it was applicable when a State became a party to the Convention and when vacancies had to be filled.

31   Under (old) Art 22, the members of the Commission were elected for a period of six years and could be re-elected. However, of the members elected at the first election, the terms of seven members chosen by lot expired at the end of three years. In order to ensure that, as far as possible, one half of the membership of the Commission was renewed every three years, the Committee of Ministers could decide that the term of office of a member to be elected should be for a period other than six years but not more than nine and not less than three years.

provided that they served 'in their individual capacity'.[32] In the UK, members tended to come from within the Civil Service, thus raising some doubt as to their neutrality. Apart from the criterion contained in Art 23, members of the Commission were, in practice, expected to display high moral integrity, have a recognised competence in human rights matters and have substantial legal experience.[33] The Commission decided by a majority of votes (old Art 34) and the President had the casting vote.[34] As it was a part time body which usually only sat for about 14 weeks a year, it tended to build up a backlog of cases, thus contributing to the long delay in dealing with applications.

The role of the Commission came under review for a number of reasons. It was barely able to deal with the number of applications it received and, as States which used to be part of the Soviet Union or Yugoslavia became signatories to the Convention, this problem was exacerbated. Such countries do not have as developed a system for protection for human rights as the old Member States and so tend to use the Convention as a means of developing such protection. Thus, although a two-tier system involving two part time bodies may have been an acceptable control mechanism when the Convention was drawn up, it became much less appropriate. Moreover, although the notion of involvement of an administrative body in dealing with cases may have been acceptable in 1950, it arguably detracted from the authority of the Convention.[35]

The European Court of Human Rights[36]

The Court has increased enormously in standing and efficacy over the last 30 years, partly due to its activism and creativity in interpreting the Convention and its willingness to find that Member States have violated the rights of individuals. It has been pointed out that an explosion in the number of cases it considered occurred in the 1980s as lawyers in the different European countries realised that it held out the possibility of a remedy for their clients and also of bringing about important legal change.[37] It may be considered the European constitutional court as far as human rights matters are concerned.

As originally set up, however, the Court did not bear a great resemblance to a domestic supreme or higher court in a number of respects. In particular, individuals could not take a case directly to it and its role was restricted due to the likelihood that the European Commission on Human Rights might find a case inadmissible. When Protocol 9 came into force,[38] the individual or a group of individuals was added to the bodies who

---

32 The members usually held other posts in their own countries as university professors, legal advisers or judges. They were aided by the lawyers on the staff of the Commission.

33 Protocol 8 required that members 'must either possess the qualifications required for appointment to judicial office or be persons of recognised competence in national or international law'.

34 The Commission drew up its own rules of procedure (old) Art 36.

35 For discussion see (1987) HRLJ 8.

36 For discussion of the role of the Court in interpreting the Convention see Gearty, 'The European Court of Human Rights and the protection of civil liberties' [1993] CLJ 89. The Court's constitution and jurisdiction were governed by the Convention Arts 19–56, but under Protocol 11 these Articles were replaced by a revised Section II of the Convention (Arts 19–51).

37 See Harris, O'Boyle and Warbrick, *op cit*, fn 1, p 648.

38 On 1 October 1994, for the 13 States which consented to it. Under Protocol 9, Art 48, as amended, an individual could refer a case to the Court only after it had been screened by a panel of three members of the Court. If it did not raise a 'serious question affecting the interpretation or application of the Convention' and did not for any other reason warrant consideration by the Court, the panel could decide that it should not be considered by the Court.

could refer a case to the Court, under amendments to (old) Arts 44 and 48. The UK was not one of the consenting parties. Protocol 9 was repealed by Protocol 11, which now governs the ability of individuals to refer cases to the Court (Art 34).

Under the previous arrangements, if an application was found inadmissible by the Commission, the case would not reach the Court, as explained below. If it was found admissible, but a friendly settlement was reached, the Court might not have been required to decide on the application of the Convention. Thus, the question of admissibility and the mechanism allowing for a friendly settlement were crucial within the system for enforcing the Convention. The possibility of avoiding the Court's involvement meant, it is argued, that a lower standard of human rights than that allowed by the Convention tended to be maintained, especially in the older decisions of the Commission. From November 1998, under Protocol 11, the admissibility and the examination of the merits with a view to reaching a friendly settlement were undertaken by the Court. This reform was generally seen as likely to represent a more satisfactory arrangement, since a judicial as opposed to an administrative body is now making the key decisions. Nevertheless, since the admissibility criteria remain unchanged under Protocol 11, as indicated below, current criticism of them is still applicable.

Terms of membership of the Court, governed now by Arts 19–24 of the Convention (previously by Arts 38–43), are intended to ensure that the judges will act independently of their own governments. Under Art 20 (previously Art 38), each Member State will send to the Court[39] one judge, who must be 'of high moral character and must either possess the qualifications required for appointment of high judicial office or be jurisconsults of recognised competence' (Art 21). Rule 4 of the Rules of Court[40] provides that judges may not engage in 'any political or administrative or professional activity which is incompatible with their independence or impartiality or with the demands of a full time office'. However, this does not mean that a judge may not have served within the government and, in fact, UK judges have at times come from the Foreign and Commonwealth Office's Legal Advisers department which is responsible for defending the government in Strasbourg. The judges tend to serve for substantial periods of time, but under the Protocol 11 reforms, the initial period of office has been shortened, since they are initially elected for six rather than nine years. The Court will not have the same composition for all that time, because the terms of certain members expire earlier than those of others.[41]

The form of the Court was governed by (old) Art 43 which provided that it would consist of a Chamber composed of seven judges.[42] Like the Commission, it used to sit

---

39 A list of persons is nominated by the Members of the Council of Europe and they are then elected by the Consultative Assembly. Under Art 22 (previously 39), each member shall nominate three candidates, of whom two at least shall be its nationals. Countries which are not yet parties to the Convention may have judges on the Court as have Hungary, Czechoslovakia, Poland and Bulgaria with representatives from Estonia, Latvia and Lithuania expected.

40 The European Court of Human Rights Rules of Court (4 November 1998).

41 Under (old) Art 40, the members of the Court were elected for a period of nine years. The period is now six under Art 23(1). They may be re-elected. However, of the members elected at the first election, the terms of four members shall expire at the end of three years and the terms of four more members shall expire at the end of six years chosen by lot. The Consultative Assembly may decide, before proceeding to any subsequent election, that the term or terms of office of one or more members to be elected shall be for a period other than six years, but not more than nine and not less than three years.

42 The names of the judges are chosen by lot by the president before the opening of the case. The judge who is a national of any State Party concerned will sit as an *ex officio* member of the Chamber.

temporarily.[43] Its hearings will continue to be public,[44] although the Court deliberates in private.[45] Its decisions will continue to be taken on a majority vote.[46] The Court has jurisdiction under Art 32 (previously Art 45) of the Convention to consider all cases which raise issues as to the interpretation and application of the Convention.

Under the Protocol 11 reforms, the Court sits in Committees of three judges, Chambers of seven judges and in a Grand Chamber of 17 judges (Art 27). Chambers designate Judge Rapporteurs to examine applications. The Plenary Court does not perform a judicial function; it elects its President and Vice President for three year terms and sets up Chambers, constituted for three years.[47] Under Art 43, a party to a case may request that it be referred to the Grand Chamber within a period of three months from the date of the judgment of the Chamber. A panel of five judges from the Grand Chamber will accept the request if it raises a serious issue regarding the interpretation of the Convention or an issue of general importance. This procedure should represent a further significant improvement brought about by the Eleventh Protocol since it seemed anomalous that a human rights Convention should make no provision for appeals. In general, adoption of the Eleventh Protocol has brought about quite radical changes in the role of the Court, changes that have not been welcomed wholeheartedly by some critics.[48]

The Committee of Ministers

The Committee was not set up by the Convention; its composition and functions are regulated in the statute of the Council of Europe (Arts 13–21). The Committee consists of one representative from the government of each Member State of the Council of Europe, usually the Minister for Foreign Affairs.[49] The Committee is, therefore, a political body which, as indicated below, was nevertheless performing a judicial role prior to the Protocol 11 reforms. Like the creation of the Commission, this was the result of a compromise; it was thought when the Convention was drafted that a Court of Human Rights with full compulsory jurisdiction would be too controversial and would therefore be unacceptable to all Member States.

The Committee of Ministers used to have a decision making function. The Committee received a Report from the Commission giving its opinion on the merits of an application. If there was no move by the Commission within three months to bring the case before the Court, the Committee would take the final decision (old Art 32). Oddly, the Convention was silent as to when a case should go to the Court and when to the Committee of Ministers; the matter appeared to be in the discretion of the Commission. In practice, non-contentious cases were usually referred to the Committee. They included those cases which did not raise significant Convention issues and/or those which raised issues which

---

43 It used to sit for about 80–90 days a year (see (1993) 15 EHRR 322, p 327).
44 Under (new) Art 40.
45 Rule 22(1).
46 Rule 23 of the Rules of the Court.
47 Rule 25(1).
48 See, eg, Schermers, H, 'The Eleventh Protocol to the European Convention on Human Rights' (1994) 19 EL Rev 367, p 378.
49 If an alternative is nominated, he or she should also be a member of the government (Art 14).

concerned established Convention case law. A sub-Committee would be appointed to examine the case which decided by a two-thirds majority.[50] If it decided that there had been a violation, it would make suggestions as to the measures to be taken by a certain period and if they were not taken, it published the report. This was a sanction: a degree of humiliation would be expected to flow from the declaration by all the Foreign Ministers of the other Member States that a certain State had violated international human rights norms. Also, ammunition would thereby be offered to the Opposition parties in the particular State. In practice, if the Commission had given its opinion that a violation had occurred, the State in question usually took measures to address the violation and the Committee did not have to give judgment.

It may be noted that the position of the individual applicant before the Committee was very weak; he or she had no right to appear or to make representations. The individual was in an equally weak position before the Court, but the role of the Commission before the Court allowed the individual's interests to be represented in a way which did not occur before the Committee.

Like the Commission, the decision-making role of the Committee was viewed with increasing dissatisfaction, and under the Protocol 11 reforms, the Committee's adjudicatory function was removed, although it continues to discharge a role in supervising the execution of the Court's judgments.

The right of complaint: inter-State applications

Under Art 33 (previously Art 24) any Contracting Party may refer to the Commission, through the Secretary General of the Council of Europe, any alleged breach of the provisions of the Convention by another Contracting Party. The violation in question may be against any person; it need not be a national of the complainant State. Further, it can be an abstract application: one that does not allege a violation against any specified person but concerns incompatibility of a State's legislation or administrative practices with the Convention. There have been 19 inter-State applications so far, but more than one complaint has sprung from the same situation; only six situations have, in fact, given rise to complaints.[51] Thus this right has not proved effective; generally, States prefer not to sour their relations with other States if no interest of their own is involved. Therefore, inter-State complaints have had a much less significant impact on human rights in the Member States than the individual's right of petition.

The right of complaint: individual applications

Art 25 (now Art 34), widely viewed as the most important article in the Convention since it governs the right of individual complaint, enables citizens of Member States to seek a

---

50 In *Huber v Austria*, Report of 8 February 1973, D & R 2 (1935) and the *East African Asians* cases (1973) 3 EHRR 76, the Committee could not obtain a two-thirds majority as to the determination whether there had been a violation of the Convention; its resolution in both cases was to take no further action on the applications.

51 See Van Dijk and Van Hoof, *op cit*, fn 1, p 43.

remedy for a breach of Convention rights by petitioning the European Court. Under Art 34, the Court (previously the Commission) can receive petitions from any person, non-governmental organisation or group of individuals claiming to be the victim of a violation of one or more of the rights set forth in the Convention. Prior to the Protocol 11 reforms, the right of petition arose only if the State allegedly responsible for the violation had declared (as the UK had) that it recognised the competence of the Commission to receive such petitions (Art 25). Under the reforms, this qualification no longer appears in the relevant Article – Art 34.

The individual need not be a national of the State in question, but must be in some way subject to its jurisdiction. The Court has established that the applicant must have been personally affected by the particular violation; it is not possible to bring an abstract complaint.[52] Therefore, an application alleging that Norwegian abortion legislation conflicted with Art 2 (guaranteeing protection of life) failed because the applicant did not allege that he had been personally affected by it (*X v Norway*).[53] However, there are two exceptions to this principle. First, the application can have a mixed nature: it can be partly abstract so long as there has been some personal impact on the applicant. In *Donnelly v UK*[54] the complaint concerned the allegation that the applicants had been tortured during their detention in Northern Ireland. They also wanted a full investigation of the whole system of interrogation employed by the security forces. It was found that so long as the applicants had been *affected*, a more wide ranging review was possible in the public interest, and the complaint was admissible on that basis. Secondly, a potential victim may make a complaint if the circumstances are such that the complainant is unsure whether or not he or she is a victim of a violation of a Convention right. This was found to be the case in a complaint concerning the possibility that the applicants' telephones were being tapped (*Klass v Federal Republic of Germany*)[55] where, by virtue of the very nature of the action complained of, it was impossible for the applicants to be certain that they had been affected.

Individual applications – procedure

The process of making a complaint is a long drawn out one and extremely cumbersome despite some improvement to it undertaken in 1990 under the Eighth Protocol. Despite the Protocol 11 reforms, there are still a very large number of hurdles to be overcome which arise, in particular, from the question of admissibility. In essentials, the procedure remains the same, although the role of the Commission has been removed. A number of stages can be identified.

Pre-complaint

Before lodging the application, it must appear that:

(a) *prima facie*, a violation of one or more of the rights or freedoms contained in the Convention has taken place. This refers to Arts 2–14 and, as far as the UK is concerned, the First and Sixth Protocols;

---

52 *Klass v Federal Republic of Germany* (1978) 2 EHRR 214.
53 Appl 867/60, 4 YB 270, 276; see also *Vijayanathan v France* (1992) 15 EHRR 62.
54 Appl 5577–82/72, Yearbook XVI.
55 Judgment of 6 September 1978 A 28 (1979–80); 2 EHRR 214 (see (1980) 130 NLJ 999).

(b) the available domestic remedies have been exhausted (Art 35);

(c) the application has been made within six months of the final decision of the highest competent court or authority (Art 35(1)).

These questions will be considered at the stage of determination of admissibility, so they will not be discussed now, but chronologically, they arise before the question of admissibility and it should be borne in mind that prima facie they must be fulfilled before the complaint can be set in motion. Whether they are fulfilled will be determined by a Chamber of the Court.[56] It is worth noting that of 34,297 applications submitted to the Commission up to December 1996, only 3,458 were ultimately declared admissible.[57]

Registration of the complaint

Registration merely means that an application is pending before the Court; it has no bearing on admissibility. The Court Registry (previously the Secretary to the Commission) will open a provisional file on the complaint. The Court may indicate a preliminary view of admissibility to the complainant. This may imply that the complaint had better be withdrawn. This practice is open to criticism since it may appear to the applicant that the application is inadmissible although its admissibility has not been fully considered. It is an additional means of cutting down on the very large number of applications.

Determination of the admissibility of the complaint

Determining the question of admissibility was the Commission's main function and it is still the main method of filtering out applications. Under the current arrangements, when an application is made, it is assigned to a Chamber of the Court which designates a Judge Rapporteur to examine it.[58] Having given it consideration, the Judge refers it to a Committee or to a Chamber.[59] Under a new 'fast track' procedure the Committee can decide, by a unanimous vote only, that the application is inadmissible.[60] If so, the decision is not subject to appeal.[61] If it does not so decide, it refers the application to the Chamber for the decision on admissibility and the consideration of the merits.[62]

The complaint must satisfy the admissibility conditions as follows:

(a) The application must not constitute an abuse of the right of complaint.[63] This condition is not often used; it concerns either the aim of applicant – it may appear that the case is obviously being brought for political propaganda purposes – or his or her conduct.

(b) Under Art 35(1)(b), the matter must not be the same as a matter already examined.[64] This means that unless it contains relevant new information, the complaint must not

---

56 Article 29(1).
57 Noted in Van Dijk and Van Hoof, *Theory and Practice of the ECHR*, p 45: figures from European Commission on HR Survey of Activities and Statistics, 1996.
58 Rule 49(1).
59 Rule 49(2)(b).
60 Article 28 and Rule 53(3).
61 Rule 53(3).
62 Article 29(1).
63 Article 35(3) (previously Art 27(2)).
64 Previously Art 27(b).

concern a matter 'which is substantially the same as a matter which has already been examined by the Court or has already been submitted to another procedure or international investigation or settlement or contains no relevant new information'.[65] The limitation in respect of complaints submitted to another international organ has not, in practice, been of significance; no UK complaints have been rejected on this basis. This is mainly because the UK has not accepted the individual right of complaint to the UN Covenant on Civil and Political Rights. The limitation in respect of previous complaints made to the Court (previously the Commission) refers to substantially similar applications. If the same applicant makes a complaint, new *facts* are needed if it is not to be rejected.[66]

(c) The application must not be incompatible with the provisions of the Convention.[67] This provision encompasses a number of aspects. Incompatibility will occur if:

- the application claims violation of a right not guaranteed by the Convention. This includes the substantive rights of s 1 (Arts 2–14) and, as far as the UK is concerned, the First and Sixth Protocols. However, it may be that the right in question does not appear in the Convention, but that if the claim is not granted, violation of one of the Convention rights might then occur; the right claimed may thereby acquire indirect protection;

- the application claims violation of a right which is the subject of a derogation (Art 15) or reservation (Art 64) by the relevant Member State.[68] Thus, the right does appear in the Convention, but the State in question is not, at present, bound to abide by it. A reservation is made when a State ratifies the Convention, while a derogation may be made if an emergency arises, thus suspending part of the State's Convention obligations. Some rights, as will be seen, are non-derogable, because they are viewed as particularly fundamental;

- the applicant or respondent are persons or States incompetent to appear before the Commission. An application from an individual can only be directed against those States which are Contracting Parties. Further, the complaint must be directed against an organ of government, not against individuals.[69] However, the violation of the Convention by an individual may involve the responsibility of the State. The State may have encouraged the acts in question or failed to prevent or remedy them. Thus, the condition will be fulfilled if the State is in some way responsible for the alleged violation. This is an aspect of the phenomenon known as *Drittwirkung*, which means that human rights provisions can affect the legal relations between private individuals, not only between individuals and the public authorities;[70]

---

65 Article 32(2)(b).

66 *X v UK* (1981) 25 DR 147.

67 Article 27(2).

68 These provisions are discussed below, pp 87–89.

69 See, eg, *Nielsen v Denmark* (1988) 11 EHRR 175.

70 See Van Dijk and Van Hoof, *op cit*, fn 1, Chapter 1, Part 6. For commentary on *Drittwirkung*, see Alkema, 'The third party applicability or *Drittwirkung* of the ECHR in protecting human rights', in *The European Dimension*, 1988, pp 33–45.

- the application is aimed at the destruction or limitation of one of the rights or freedoms guaranteed by the Convention and therefore conflicts with Art 17. The intention is to prevent an applicant claiming a right which would enable him or her to carry out activities which ultimately would lead to the destruction of the guaranteed rights. Therefore, the Commission rejected the application of the banned German Communist Party due to its aims (*Kommunistische Partei Deutschland v Federal Republic of Germany*).[71] This provision suggests that the Convention adopts a teleological view of freedom; in other words, freedom is valued instrumentally as something which will lead to benefit for society as a whole, rather than as being a good in itself.

(d) Domestic remedies must have been exhausted.[72] In brief, this means that the applicant must provide *prima facie* evidence of exhaustion of remedies. The burden then shifts to the State to show that a remedy was reasonably ascertainable by the applicant, that the remedy does exist and has not been exhausted and that the remedy is effective. The requirement that domestic remedies must have been exhausted refers to: the 'legal remedies available under the local law which are in principle capable of providing an effective and sufficient means of redressing the wrongs for which (the Respondent State is said to be responsible'.[73] If there is a doubt as to whether a remedy is available, Art 35 (previously Art 26) will not be satisfied unless the applicant has taken proceedings in which that doubt can be resolved.[74] This generally means that judicial procedures must be instituted up to the highest court which can affect the decision but also, if applicable, appeal must be made to administrative bodies. However, the applicant only needs to exhaust those possibilities which offer an *effective* remedy, so if part of the complaint is the lack of a remedy under Art 13, then the application is not likely to be ruled inadmissible on this ground.[75] A remedy will be ineffective if, according to established case law, there appears to be no chance of success,[76] and the Court will decide whether a remedy did in fact offer the applicant the possibility of sufficient redress. If there is a doubt as to whether a given remedy is able to offer a real chance of success, that doubt must be resolved in the national court itself.[77] Until recently, the Court viewed judicial review as a sufficient remedy,[78] but this is no longer necessarily the case, as explained below.[79] If it can be said that the State practice complained of is a repetition of one that is in breach of Convention, but tolerated by the State authorities, it may be argued that taking the proceedings available would be ineffective.[80]

---

71 Appl 250/57, Yearbook I (1955–57), Vol 6, p 222.
72 Article 35(1) (previously Arts 26 and 27(3)).
73 *Nielsen v Denmark* Appl No 343/57; (1958–59) 2 YB 412 , p 412.
74 *De Vargattirgah v France*, Appl 9559/81.
75 *X v UK* (1981) Appl 7990/77; 24 D & R 77.
76 Appl 5874/172, Yearbook XVII (1974). See *H v UK* 33 D & R 247(1983) (Counsel's opinion as to inefficacy sufficient). Cf *K, F and P v UK* 40 D & R 298 (1984).
77 *Spencer v UK* (1998) 25 EHRR CD 105.
78 See *Vilvarajah and Four Others v UK* (1991) Judgment of 30 October 1991; Appl 12 (1991).
79 See below, p 84.
80 *Akdivar v Turkey* (1997) 23 EHRR 143, paras 66–67.

The application must have been submitted within a period of six months from the date on which the final national decision was taken (Art 36(1)). Time runs from the decision taken by the last national authority that had to be used and after the point when the decision has been notified to the applicant; ineffective remedies will not be taken into account in assessing the point from which time runs.

(e) The application must not be manifestly ill-founded (Art 35(3), previously Art 27(2)). Previously, this admissibility condition afforded a very significant power to the Commission. Formally, the Commission was not empowered to act judicially and therefore it was not intended that it should come to a judgment on the merits of the application. Yet, when it made a determination as to manifest ill-foundedness, it was pronouncing on the merits because it was determining whether or not a *prima facie* violation had taken place. Thus, this condition created an extension of the role of the Commission behind the cloak of merely determining admissibility: it was, in fact, in a number of instances taking the *final* decision on the merits.

Under the current procedure, the Committee or a Chamber of the Court finds this condition unfulfilled if the facts obviously fail to disclose a violation. In theory, this ground should only operate if the ill-founded character of the application is clearly manifest. It has been said that 'the task of the Commission is not to determine whether an examination of the case submitted by the applicant discloses the actual violation of one of the rights and freedoms guaranteed by the Convention but only to determine whether it includes any possibility of the existence of such a determination'.[81] In practice, the Commission went further: the ill-founded character of the application was not always as manifest as this would imply. This was clear from the Commission's voting procedure: it was not necessary to have unanimity on this condition; a bare majority was sufficient. Under the current arrangements it is necessary to have unanimity if a Committee declares the application inadmissible,[82] but a majority if a Chamber does so. Although it is more satisfactory that the decision is being taken judicially, it is arguable that it should have been necessary to have unanimity or a two-thirds majority as to a finding of manifest ill-foundedness by a Chamber, even though a bare majority suffices in respect of the other conditions.

The examination of the application and friendly settlements under Art 38(1)(b)

If the application is declared admissible, the Court places itself at the disposal of the parties under Art 38(1)(b) with a view to securing a friendly settlement between the parties. If both parties are willing, they can reach a friendly settlement straight after the application has been declared admissible.[83] The settlement is a compromise; its danger is that it could aid in maintaining lower standards of human rights in particular States than the Convention allows although, under Art 38(1)(b), the settlement should be on the basis of the respect for human rights accorded by the Convention. This may mean that, if the State Party in question is prepared to pay compensation and the victim is willing to

---

81 *Pataki*, Appl 596/59, Yearbook III (1960).

82 Rule 53(3).

83 If a friendly settlement is reached, the Commission will draw up a report stating the facts and solution reached. Up to the end of 1996, 324 friendly settlements had been reached.

receive it, the Court may nevertheless continue the examination of the application if the respect for human rights under the Convention demands that it should do so (Art 37(1)). In other words, the Court should have regard to its general purpose of improving human rights protection and not just the particular interest of the victim. By this means, it could prevent further applications from the same State alleging the same violation. In fact, this power is rarely invoked.[84] If the application is declared admissible and no friendly settlement is reached, it is examined under Art 38(1)(a).

Under the old procedure, if no settlement was reached, the Commission would state its Opinion as to the alleged violation in the Report to the Committee of Ministers.[85] The Report generally only went to individual applicants if the Court considered it. After having declared the application admissible, the Commission could still, after further examination, declare it inadmissible.[86]

The judgment of the Court

Prior to the Protocol 11 reforms, the Court could not hear a case unless it had gone through all the Commission's procedure and a report had gone to the Committee of Ministers. The fact, as mentioned above, that the individual in question could not refer the case to Court[87] did not seem odd at the inception of the Convention, when the right of individual petition in itself seemed controversial. However, it came to seem increasingly anomalous, and provided part of the impetus for reform. The Commission was likely, however, to bring the case before the Court and did bring the vast majority of cases once it had found them admissible. In exercising its discretion as to bringing a case before the Committee of Ministers or the Court, the Commission, as indicated above, was influenced by its nature. In general, a difficult question would go to the Court while, if the Commission was unanimous that no breach had occurred, it would go to the Committee. The trend was to refer far more cases to the Court in relation to the number of cases declared admissible.

The Court was not bound by the Report of the Commission. The function of the Commission was 'to present to the Court the issues in the case and all the relevant information which we ourselves have obtained concerning the case'.[88] The Court could disagree with points of the Commission's decisions; it could consider admissibility again and then reject the application as inadmissible. In other words, the Court was no more bound by the Commission on admissibility than it was on opinion. It was arguable that this procedure did not maintain equality between the parties, because a negative decision

---

84   *Tyrer v UK* (1978) 2 EHRR 1.

85   (Old) Art 31 provided that if a solution was not reached, the Commission would draw up a report on the facts and state its opinion as to whether the facts found disclosed a breach by the State concerned of its obligations under the Convention. The opinions of all the members of the Commission on this point could be stated in the report.

86   (Old) Art 29. At this stage, if it was to be rejected, it had to be rejected unanimously. In such a case, the decision would be communicated to the parties.

87   Under (old) Art 48, the following could bring a case before the Court: the Commission; a High Contracting Party whose national is alleged to be a victim; a High Contracting Party which referred the case to the Commission; a High Contracting Party against which the complaint has been lodged. But Protocol 11 gave the individual the right to seize the Court under Art 34.

88   *Lawless*, A 1 (1960–61), p 360; (1961) 1 EHRR 15.

on admissibility would never come before the Court, while a positive one would.[89] However, in practice, the Court tended to agree with the Commission on admissibility. Nevertheless, this and other aspects of the proceedings before the Court and Commission did involve a duplication of function which was time consuming and so supported the argument for abolition of the Commission.

Under the current procedure, the proceedings before the Chamber of seven judges will consist of a written stage, followed by a hearing.[90] The Chamber may appoint one or more of its members to conduct the initial examination. The arrangements are characterised by their flexibility: within the Rules, the Court is free to decide on a procedure which can be tailored to the nature of a particular application[91] and this may include visiting a particular place, such as a prison. An on-the-spot inquiry can be conducted by a delegate of the Court. The Court can also order a report from an expert on any matter. After this initial stage, the Chamber will normally conduct an oral hearing if there has been no oral admissibility hearing.

The applicant used to be in a weak position in the hearing. Previously, he or she did not have any right to take part in the proceedings; after a change in the rules of procedure in 1982, an applicant could be heard as a person providing clarification. Under the current Protocol 11 procedure, each of the parties can address the Court; in practice, hearings take half a day and each party is given 45 minutes to make oral submissions. If a violation appears to be established, the State must attempt to demonstrate that the case falls within an exception to the right in question. The Court is not bound by its own judgments.[92] Nevertheless, it usually follows and applies its own precedents unless departure from them is indicated in order to ensure that interpretation of the Convention reflects social change.

The procedure before the Court may conclude before the judgment on the merits if the State settles. However, the Court does not have to discontinue the procedure; it can proceed in the interests of the Convention and may give a declaratory judgment even though the State is now willing to settle. The judgment does not state what remedial measures should be taken; it is up to the State to amend its legislation or make other changes in order to conform with the judgment. Thus, a response may well be in doubtful conformity with the Convention.[93] The Court is not ultimately a coercive body and relies for acceptance of its judgments on the willingness of States to abide by the Convention. Under Art 45, reasons must be given for the judgment of the Court and if the judgment does not represent in whole or in part the unanimous opinion of the judges, any judge shall be entitled to deliver a separate opinion. Under (old) Art 52, the judgment of the

---

89 See *Van Oosterwijck v Belgium*, Judgment of 6 November 1980, A 40; (1980) 3 EHRR 557. The Court disagreed with the Commission's decision that the application was admissible; the Court held that local remedies had not been exhausted; thus the Court's decision was not on the merits.

90 Under Art 55, the Court shall draw up its own rules and determine its own procedure.

91 See Rule 42(2).

92 Rule 51, para 1 of the Rules of the Court. See Feldman, D, 'Precedent and the European Court of Human Rights', Law Com Consultation Paper No 157 (1999), App C.

93 The Contempt of Court Act 1981 may be said to represent such a response to the ruling that UK contempt law violated Art 10 in that it preserved common law contempt, which appears, especially since the decision in *AG v Times Newspapers Ltd* (see Chapter 5, p 228–29), to give insufficient weight to freedom of speech.

Court was final,[94] but now under Art 43 it can be referred to the Grand Chamber 'in exceptional cases' for judgment. Under Art 44, the judgment of the Grand Chamber is final, while a judgment of a Chamber will become final when the parties declare that they will not request referral to the Grand Chamber, where after three months no such request has been made or where the panel of the Grand Chamber rejects the request. Under Art 46, the judgment of the Court is binding on the State Party involved.

The Court can award compensation under Art 41. The purpose of the reparation is to place the applicant in the position he would have been in had the violation not taken place. It will include costs unless the applicant has received legal aid. It can also include loss of earnings, travel costs, fines and costs unjustly awarded against the applicant. It can also include intangible or non-pecuniary losses which may be awarded due to unjust imprisonment or stress.[95]

Supervision of the judgment by the Committee of Ministers

Under Art 46, the Committee is charged with supervising the execution of the Court's judgment. This includes both the judgment on the merits and on compensation. The Committee notes the action taken to redress the violation on the basis of information given by the State in question. If the State fails to execute the judgment, the Committee decides what measures to take: it can bring political pressure to bear including suspension or even, as a final sanction, expulsion from the Council of Europe. Doubts have been raised over the fitness of the Committee to oversee one of the key stages in the whole Convention process, namely the implementation of national law to bring it into line with the findings of the Court.[96] It is apparent that a rigorous analysis of the changes that the offending State has made in its law would be desirable, to ensure that the judgment is fully implemented and to make future similar breaches of the Convention by that State impossible. The Committee would not *prima facie* appear to be capable of carrying out such a quasi-judicial role and, indeed, it appears that in practice the Committee usually merely notes the receipt of the State's explanation of the changes it has made without any attempt to conduct the kind of analysis which it is suggested should be undertaken.

The question of the full implementation of a judgment of the Court arose in *Olsson v Sweden* (No 2).[97] The applicants complained that despite a previous judgment of the Court to the effect that a violation of the Convention had occurred, the Swedish authorities had continued the practice, which was contrary to the Convention. However, the Court found that the fresh complaint raised a new issue and that therefore, the question as to whether the State had fulfilled its obligations under Art 53 by implementing the judgment did not arise. Thus, this judgment avoided addressing the

---

94 As noted above, this is no longer the case under Art 43 of the Convention.

95 Eg, in the *Young, James and Webster* case (1981) Judgment of 13 August 1981, Appl 44; (1981) 4 EHRR 38, pecuniary and non-pecuniary costs were awarded: the Court ordered £65,000 to be paid. See further Chapter 4, p 174.

96 See Leuptracht, P, 'The protection of human rights by political bodies', in Nowak, M, Steurer, P and Tretter, H (eds) *Progress in the Spirit of Human Rights*, Strasbourg, 1988, pp 95–107.

97 A 250. Note that a similar issue arose in *Christie v UK* (No 21482/93, 78-A DR 119) which was, however, found inadmissible by the Commission.

Art 53 issue. However, it is suggested that the Court should be able to rule on the question whether measures introduced to implement its own judgment are sufficient. If it became clear that it could do so, one of the main concerns regarding the procedure for supervising its judgments would be addressed, although there seems to be a case for also requiring more of the Committee in terms of analysing the measures taken to implement the judgment. The role of the Committee under (old) Art 53 was retained under Protocol 11, reflecting the view that its authority has played a part in persuading States to adopt measures implementing the judgment of the Court.

The doctrine of the 'margin of appreciation'[98]

The European Court of Human Rights has stated that the role of the Convention in protecting human rights is subsidiary to the role of the national legal system[99] and that since the State is better placed than the international judge to balance individual rights against general societal interests, Strasbourg will operate a restrained review of the balance struck. Under this doctrine, a degree of discretion will be allowed to Member States as to legislative, administrative or judicial action in the area of a Convention right. However, Strasbourg will finally determine whether such action is reconcilable with the guarantee in question.

The doctrine of the margin of appreciation conceded to States was first adopted in respect of emergency situations,[100] but it was allowed to affect the application of all the Articles although it has a particular application with respect to para 2 of Arts 8–11. It has now reached the stage where it can be said that it permeates the Convention jurisprudence. In different instances, a wider or narrower margin of appreciation has been allowed. The width allowed depends on a number of factors including the aim of the interference in question and its necessity. If a broader margin is allowed, Strasbourg review will be highly circumscribed. For example, the minority in the *Sunday Times* case[101] (nine judges) wanted to confine the role of Strasbourg to asking only whether the discretion in question was exercised in good faith and carefully and whether the measure was reasonable in the circumstances. A narrow margin conceded to the State means that a rigorous or intensive review of the proportionality between the aim of an interference and the extent and nature of the interference will be undertaken. This occurred in the *Sunday Times* case; it was held that Strasbourg review was not limited to asking whether the State had exercised its discretion reasonably, carefully and in good faith; it was found that its conduct must also be examined in Strasbourg to see whether it was compatible with the Convention.

---

98 For general discussion of the doctrine, see McDonald, RJ, 'The margin of appreciation in the jurisprudence of the European Court of Human Rights', *International Law and the Time of its Codification*, 1987, pp 187–208; Van Dijk and Van Hoof, *op cit*, fn 1, p 82 *et seq*; O'Donell, 'The margin of appreciation doctrine: standards in the jurisprudence of the European Court of Human Rights' (1982) 4 Human Rights Q 474; Morrisson, 'Margin of appreciation in human rights law' (1973) 6 Human Rights J 263. See further fn 124, below.

99 *Handyside v UK* A 24, para 48 (1976).

100 See the *Lawless* case, Publ ECHR B 1 (1960–61), p 408; (1961) 1 EHRR 15.

101 Series A 30 (1979); 2 EHRR 245.

Although the doctrine is well established, it has not been applied very consistently. Therefore, it is not always easy to predict when each approach will be taken, but a number of relevant factors may be identified. The nature of the right in question may be relevant. The doctrine is particularly applicable to the Arts 8–11 group of rights since it is used in determining whether an interference with the right is justifiable on grounds of one of the exceptions contained in para 2 of these Articles. Within this group, Art 10 may be viewed as particularly fundamental.[102] Also, the particular instance will be considered: does it concern, for example, a very significant need for free expression since there is a strong public interest in the subject matter? The presence of such factors may predispose the Strasbourg authorities to conduct a wide ranging review. Such review also tends to be applicable under Arts 2[103] and 3,[104] although it may be narrowed where the State claims that the demands of national security justify the measures sought to be challenged under these Articles.[105] On the other hand, in considering the imposition of positive obligations placed on the State, a broad margin will be allowed.[106]

The nature of the restriction is significant. Some restrictions are seen as more subjective than others. It is therefore thought more difficult to lay down a common European standard and the Court and Commission have, in such instances, shown a certain willingness to allow the exceptions a wide scope in curtailing the primary rights. For example, Art 10 contains an exception in respect of the protection of morals. This was invoked in the *Handyside* case[107] in respect of suppression of a booklet aimed at schoolchildren which was circulating freely in the rest of Europe. It was held that the UK Government was best placed to determine what was needed in its own country in order to protect morals and, therefore, it could make an initial assessment of those requirements, which would then be considered for compatibility with Art 10 by Strasbourg.

The Court and Commission consider that in certain sensitive matters, most notably national security,[108] States are best placed to determine what is needed within their own particular domestic situation. Thus, emergency situations and the invocation of threats to national security invite deference. In *Council of Civil Service Unions v UK*[109] the European Commission, in declaring the Unions' application inadmissible, found that national security interests should prevail over freedom of association even though the national security interest was weak while the infringement of the primary right was very clear: an absolute ban on joining a trade union had been imposed. It is worth noting that the ILO Committee on Freedom of Association had earlier found that the ban breached the 1947 ILO Freedom of Association Convention. However, in general, if a restriction is very far-reaching, the Strasbourg authorities may be prepared to make a determination as to the need to impose it which differs from that of the State Party in question.[110]

---

102 See, eg, the judgment of the Court in *Autronic AG v Switzerland* (1990) 12 EHRR 485.

103 *McCann, Farrell and Savage v UK* (1995) 21 EHRR 97, A 324, Council of Europe Report.

104 *Soering v UK*, Judgment of 7 July 1989, A 161; (1989) 11 EHRR 439.

105 *Kröcher and Möller v Switzerland* No 8463/78, 34 DR 25.

106 See *Plattform 'Ärzte für Das Leben' v Austria* (1988) 13 EHRR 204.

107 (1976) 1 EHRR 737.

108 See *Leander v Sweden* Series A 116, para 67 (1987).

109 No 11603/85, 50 DR 228 (1987); 10 EHRR 269.

110 See, eg, *Golder*, Judgment of 21 February 1975; A 18. Discussed p 60.

The high (or low) point of deference was perhaps reached in *Brannigan and McBride v UK*,[111] in which the European Court of Human Rights upheld a derogation entered by the UK after the decision in the case of *Brogan and Others v UK*.[112] The Court found that 'a wide margin of appreciation [on the question] of the presence of an emergency ... and on the nature and scope of derogations necessary to avert it [should be allowed]'.[113]

The Court is greatly influenced by general practice in the Member States as a body and will interpret the Convention to reflect such practice so that a State which is clearly out of conformity with the others may expect an adverse ruling. However, where practice is still in the process of changing and may be said to be at an inchoate stage as far as the Member States generally are concerned, it may not be prepared to place itself at the forefront of such changes, although it will weigh the lack of a consensus against the degree of detriment to the applicant.[114] Thus, the notion of common standards strongly influences the doctrine of the margin of appreciation. Where a common standard, or a trend towards such a standard, cannot be discerned among Member States, greater deference to particular State practice is shown.[115] For example, the lack of a uniform standard was the key factor in the ruling in *Otto-Preminger Institut v Austria*.[116] The decision concerned the seizure of film likely to offend religious feeling. The European Court of Human Rights found that the film would receive protection under Art 10, but that its seizure fell within the 'rights of others' exception. In considering whether its seizure and forfeiture was 'necessary in a democratic society' in order to protect the rights of others to respect for their religious views (under Art 9), the Court took into account the lack of a uniform conception within the Member States of the significance of religion in society and therefore considered that the national authorities should have a wide margin of appreciation in assessing what was necessary to protect religious feeling. In this instance, the national authorities had not overstepped that margin and therefore, the Court found that no breach of Art 10 had occurred. Similarly, in *Wingrove v UK*[117] the Court found that the English common law offence of blasphemy was sufficiently clear and precise. The Court further found: 'there is as yet not sufficient common ground in the legal and social orders of the Member States of the Council of Europe to conclude that a system whereby a State can impose restrictions on the propagation of material on the basis that it is blasphemous is in itself unnecessary in a democratic society and incompatible with the Convention.'[118]

On the other hand, where a principle has received general acceptance in the Member States and, in particular, where it is closely linked to the notion of democracy, the Court will afford a narrow margin only. For example, in *Socialist Party and Others v Turkey*,[119] the

---

111 Series A, 258-B (1993).

112 Judgement of 29 November 1988 (1989) Series A 145-B (1988); 11 EHRR 117. See further Chapter 13, p 793.

113 Para 207.

114 *Rees v UK* (1986) 9 EHRR 56, A 106.

115 See *Rees v UK, ibid* at para 37.

116 Series A 295-A; (1994) 19 EHRR 34.

117 (1996) 24 EHRR 1.

118 Paragraph 57.

119 Judgment of 25 May 1998 (App No 20/1997/804/1007), (1999) 27 EHRR 51, paras 41, 47, 50.

Court found that the dissolution of the Socialist Party of Turkey had breached Art 11 since: 'there can be no democracy without pluralism ... It is of the essence of democracy to allow diverse political programmes to be proposed and debated ... Taking these matters into account ... In determining whether a necessity existed, the Contracting State was found to possess only a limited margin of appreciation ...' The picture is more confused where a principle may be said to have received some general acceptance within the Contracting States and where the Court itself appears to have espoused it in the past, but where it cannot clearly be said that a common standard can be found. Such confusion appears to underlie the remarks in *Cossey v UK*[120] of Judge Martens in his dissenting Opinion: 'this caution [in allowing a wide margin of appreciation based on a strict application of the common standards doctrine] is in principle not consistent with the Court's mission to protect the individual against the collectivity[121] ... in this context [of legal recognition of gender reassignment] there simply is no room for a margin of appreciation.' Thus, even within the Court there is disagreement as to the interferences which fall within the margin conceded to the State. In the only decision of the Court finding a violation of the freedom of assembly guarantee of Art 11, *Ezelin v France*,[122] two of the partly dissenting judges considered that the interference in question fell within that margin,[123] although the majority found that the State had exceeded it.

As the discussion suggests, the margin of appreciation doctrine may tend to undermine the Convention and its growth has therefore attracted criticism. Van Dijk and Van Hoof have written of it as: 'a spreading disease. Not only has the scope of its application been broadened to the point where in principle none of the Convention rights or freedoms are excluded, but also has the illness been intensified in that wider versions of the doctrine have been added to the original concept.'[124] As mentioned at the beginning of this chapter, the doctrine may sometimes be appropriate as part of a general consensus-based approach to the supervision of the Convention. However, an arbitrariness is evident in its application, a theme which is pursued below and at a number of points in this book.

3 THE SUBSTANTIVE RIGHTS AND FREEDOMS

In what follows, an outline will be given of the scope of the Articles covering the substantive rights and freedoms. In the case of Arts 3, 5, 6 and 8–11, much more detailed treatment of decisions which are relevant to particular areas of UK law will be undertaken when those areas of domestic law are considered.

---

120 A 184 (1990).
121 Paragraph 5.6.3.
122 A 202-A (1991).
123 Judges Ryssdal and Pettiti, pp 26 and 28–30.
124 Van Dijk, P and Van Hoof, F, *The Theory and Practice of the European Convention on Human Rights*, 1st edn, 1990, p 604. For further discussion of the doctrine see O'Donell, 'The margin of appreciation doctrine: standards in the jurisprudence of the European Court of Human Rights' (1982) 4 Human Rights Q 474; Morrisson, 'Margin of appreciation in human rights law' (1973) 6 Human Rights J 263; Jones, T, 'The devaluation of human rights under the European Convention' [1995] PL 430; Mahoney, P, 'Marvellous richness or invidious cultural relativism?' (1998) 19 Human Rights LJ 1.

Article 2: Protection of life

(1) Everyone's right to life shall be protected by law. No one shall be deprived of his life intentionally save in the execution of a sentence of a court following his conviction of a crime for which this penalty is provided by law.

(2) Deprivation of life shall not be regarded as inflicted in contravention of this Article when it results from the use of force which is not more than absolutely necessary:

(a) in defence of any person from unlawful violence;

(b) in order to effect a lawful arrest or to prevent the escape of a person lawfully detained;

(c) in action lawfully taken for the purpose of quelling a riot or insurrection.

The right to life can be viewed as the most fundamental of all human rights. Its significance receives recognition under all human rights' instruments[125] and its vital importance is recognised under UK common law.[126]

Scope of the right

Article 2 provides non-derogable protection of the right to life.[127] This might seem straightforward – governments are enjoined to refrain from the wanton killing of their subjects – but aside from that instance, it is not a straightforward matter to determine what the guarantee under Art 2 encompasses. The Court has said: 'the first sentence of Article 2 enjoins the State not only to refrain from the intentional and unlawful taking of life, but also to take appropriate steps to safeguard the lives of those within its jurisdiction.'[128] Thus, while the State must not order or empower its agents to kill its subjects, except within the specified exceptions, it also has further responsibilities under Art 2 to protect the right to life by law. But clearly, it is difficult to pinpoint the stage at which it may be said that the responsibility of a State for a person's death is so clear, the causal potency between the State's action or omission and the death so strong, that it is possible to find that the right to life has been violated.[129]

Decisions under Art 2 have not yet entirely clarified this issue, but they do suggest that two, usually distinct duties are placed on the national authorities, although their scope is unclear. First, as indicated, Art 2 places the public authorities under a duty not to take life except in certain specified circumstances. This duty covers intentional, officially sanctioned killings (executions, deliberate killing to save life) and unintentional killings (where the risk of killing is taken by using lethal force in a riot situation). Where State

---

125 Although in, eg, the US and India, the right is protected only on a 'due process' basis. Deprivation of life can occur, but it must be in accordance with the due process of the law.

126 It is recognised in the crimes of murder, manslaughter and infanticide. The deliberate killing of another human being is viewed as requiring to be marked out from other crimes by means of the mandatory life sentence penalty. See further Chapter 3, pp 108–09. For an early response of the UK courts to Art 2 under the HRA see Chapter 12, p 733. For a full discussion, see Clayton and Tomlinson, *op cit*, fn 1, Chapter 7.

127 See Art 15(2). Derogation is not allowed in times of emergency or war; derogation is only possible in respect of death resulting from acts of war themselves.

128 *LCB v UK* (1998) 27 EHRR 212, para 36.

129 See further Sieghart, *The Lawful Rights of Mankind*, 1986, Chapter 11.

agents do take life, the obligation to protect the right to life by law requires that 'there should be some form of effective official investigation'.[130] This requirement was found to be breached in *Jordan, Kelly, Arthurs, Donelly and Others v UK*[131] in respect of the killing of eight IRA members by the SAS in 1987. Secondly, Art 2 places a positive obligation on the State authorities to protect the right to life by law. This positive obligation may take a number of forms. It requires that reasonable steps be taken in order to enforce the law in order to protect citizens (*X v UK and Ireland*).[132] It was held in *W v UK*[133] that these measures will not be scrutinised in detail. Clearly, the State may not be able to prevent every attack on an individual without an enormous expenditure of resources.[134] Therefore, the Convention will leave a wide margin of discretion to the national authorities in this regard, although the State will be under some duty to maintain reasonable public security.[135] Where State agents' actions are very closely linked to the preservation of a known individual's life as, for example, the actions of police officers are during a hostage situation, the State will be under a positive obligation not only to seek to preserve life, but also to act reasonably in so doing. The need to preserve life in the immediate situation would appear to override the general duty to maintain State security and prevent crime. These notions seem to underlie the findings of the Commission in *Andronicou and Constantinou v Cyprus*.[136] Article 2 was found to have been violated by Cypriot police when, in attempting to deal with a siege situation in which a hostage had been taken, they fired a number of times at the hostage taker, killing the hostage. The number of bullets fired reflected, it was found, a response which lacked caution.

Similarly, situations may arise in which, while State agents do not directly take life, the State is responsible for creating a life-threatening situation. Where the State has directly created such a situation, its responsibility will arguably be greater. In *LCB v UK*,[137] the applicant had contracted leukaemia; her father had been present during British nuclear tests on Christmas Island. She complained of a breach of Art 2 since the State had not advised her parents to monitor her health. In deciding that no breach had occurred, the Court found, taking into account the information that was available at the time, that the State had done all it was required to do to prevent an avoidable risk to her life. Had the information regarding the risk been available at the time, the decision might well have gone the other way, implying that the Court is prepared in principle to hold the State responsible in such instances.

Such an instance may be distinguished from a situation created by others, or by natural causes but in which it may be said that the State still has some responsibility. The positive obligation may entail the taking of appropriate steps to safeguard life[138] where

---

130 *McCann v UK* (1995) 21 EHRR 97, para 161.

131 (2001) *The Times*, 18 May.

132 Appl 9829/82 (not published).

133 Appl 9348/81, 32 D & R (1983), p 190.

134 It was accepted in *Osman v UK* (1998) 29 EHRR 245 that the obligation to protect the right to life had to be interpreted 'in a way that does not impose an impossible or disproportionate burden on the authorities' (para 116). In that instance, the police had failed to take measures to prevent a murder taking place despite very strong indications that the victim was in imminent danger. See further below, on the Art 6 issue in the case, p 60.

135 Appl 7145/75, *Association X v UK* (1978) Appl 7154/75; 14 DR 31.

136 (1996) 22 EHRR CD 18.

137 (1998) 27 EHRR 212.

138 *X v UK*, No 7154/75, 14 D & R 31 (1978), p 32.

State agents do not themselves unintentionally take life and/or the State itself has not created the life-threatening situation, but the breadth of this duty is unclear. It seems that it will include the provision of adequate medical care in prisons[139] since, in this instance, the State is directly responsible for the welfare of citizens during their imprisonment. However, it is unclear how far the individual should have a right to secure the expenditure of resources so that the State can save or preserve his or her life. The State may bear some responsibility in a number of instances. For example, a person might die due to poor housing conditions after repeated pleas for re-housing, or due to deficiencies in health care such as a lack of a vaccination programme or poor implementation of the programme,[140] or to exposure to bacteria in certain parts of a hospital while suffering from a condition weakening the immune system. Road traffic regulations and their implementation engage the State's responsibility; life might be put at risk, for example, due to a failure to impose a particular speed limit in poor driving conditions.

The Court is proceeding cautiously in relation to the State's positive obligations under Art 2. It has shown some reluctance to read Art 2 so widely as to cover such situations, although there are indications that this stance may be changing. In *Guerra v Italy*,[141] it was said that the time may be ripe for 'the court's case law on Article 2 ... to start evolving, to develop the respective implied rights, articulate situations of real and serious risk to life or different aspects of the right to life'.

In *LCB v UK*, the Christmas Island case mentioned above,[142] the State had a direct responsibility for the lives in question and the expenditure of resources to meet it would not have been burdensome, whereas in relation to the provision of housing of a certain standard, the responsibility is less direct and immediate, and the impact on resource allocation much greater. The issue of imposing a speed limit in particular conditions raises questions of the directness of the responsibility. Drivers would be expected to drive in accordance with the road conditions. Moreover, there would be no direct relationship between those State agents involved in traffic control and those affected. The obligation to provide health care in order to save life and to regulate hospitals in such a way as to protect life has, however, been recognised.[143]

It is unclear how far Art 2 places States under an obligation to seek to ensure the continuance of life where the individual involved, or those acting on his or her behalf, wish it to end. The Commission has found that passively allowing a person to die need not attract criminal liability in order to satisfy Art 2.[144] This might apply to allowing a handicapped baby or a patient in a persistent vegetative state to die.[145] However, a

---

139 *Simon-Herald v Austria*, App 430/69 CD 38 (the application was declared admissible and a friendly settlement was later reached).

140 See *Association X v UK* (1978) Appl 7154/75; 14 DR 31.

141 (1998) 26 EHRR 357, p 387.

142 *LCB v UK* (1998) 27 EHRR 212, para 36.

143 *Scialacqua v Italy* (1998) 26 EHRR CD 164 and *Erikson v Italy*, App 37900/97, 26 October 1999.

144 *Widmer v Switzerland*, No 20527/92 (1993) unreported.

145 The position under British law seems to be that failing to intervene to save the life of a handicapped baby may be acceptable in some circumstances: see *Arthur* (unreported), discussed by Gunn and Smith [1985] Crim LR 705; *Re B (A Minor)* [1981] 1 WLR 1421, CA. Allowing a patient in a persistent vegetative state to die will be acceptable if it can be said, objectively, to be in his or her best interests because no improvement can be expected (*Airedale NHS Trust v Bland* [1993] AC 789, HL). See further Chapter 12, pp 732–33.

breach of Art 2 would probably be found where a positive act had occurred in order to end life.

The question has arisen in the context of national legislation on abortion whether the foetus can fall within the interpretation of 'everyone', but it has been determined that even if the foetus is protected, its right to life will be weighed against the mother's life and physical and mental health.[146] In *Paton v UK*[147] it was found by the Commission that Art 2 applies only to persons who have been born. Had the Commission found otherwise, all national legislation in the Member States permitting abortion would have been in breach of Art 2, since abortion even to save the mother's life would not appear to be covered by any of the exceptions. *H v Norway*[148] clarified the position. The Commission found that the lawful abortion of a 14 week foetus on social grounds did not breach Art 2. It took this stance on the basis that since the State Parties' laws on abortion differ considerably from each other, a wide margin of discretion should be allowed. It appears that the abortion laws within the Member States probably comply with Art 2, although in *Open Door Counselling v Ireland* the Court left open the possibility that Art 2 might place some restrictions on abortion.[149]

Exceptions

A very significant express exception to Art 2, limiting the scope of para 1, is in respect of the death penalty, which also includes extradition to a country where the death penalty is in force.[150] Protocol 6 has now removed the death penalty exception and it was ratified by the UK on 27 January 1999. It may be possible to challenge use of the death penalty in countries which have not ratified Protocol 6 under other Convention rights, such as Art 3.[151]

Generally, the para 2 exceptions are reasonably straightforward and are aimed mainly at unintentional deprivation of life. This was explained in *Stewart v UK*,[152] which concerned the use of plastic bullets in a riot. It was found that para 2 is concerned with situations where the use of violence is allowed as necessary force and may, as an unintended consequence, result in loss of life. On this basis, the use of plastic bullets was found to fall within its terms. However, paras 2(a), (b) and (c) also cover instances where the force used was bound to endanger life and was intended to do so, but was necessary in the circumstances. Thus, national laws recognising the right to use self-defence are, in principle, in harmony with para 2(a). Clearly, the State can use lethal force where absolutely necessary in order to quell a riot. But, the necessity will be carefully scrutinised: State agents must act with caution in resorting to lethal force.[153]

---

146 *X v UK*, Appl 8416/78; 19 D & R (1980), p 244.

147 (1981) 3 EHRR 408. It has been argued that a woman's right to an abortion must therefore have been impliedly accepted: Rendel, M (1991) 141 NLJ 1270.

148 No 17004/90 (1992) 73 DR 155.

149 Eur Ct HR, Judgment of 29 October 1992; (1992) 15 EHRR 244. For comment, see (1992) 142 NLJ 1696.

150 Appl 10227/82, *X v Spain* D & R 37 (1984), p 93.

151 See *Soering*, below, p 46–47 in relation to Art 3.

152 Appl 10044/82; D & R 39 (1985); (1985) 7 EHRR 453; see also *Kelly v UK* (1993) 16 EHRR 20, in which the European Commission found that the use of force to prevent future terrorist acts was allowable. For criticism of the decision in *Kelly*, see (1994) 144 NLJ 354.

153 A breach of Art 2 was found in *Gulec v Turkey* (1999) 28 EHRR 121: gendarmes had fired into a crowd to disperse it; less forceful means could have been used.

Also, in certain circumstances, the State can sanction the use of force with the intention of killing. It can do so, however, only when such force is absolutely necessary for the fulfilment of one of the para 2 purposes. This issue was considered by the Commission in *Kelly v UK*,[154] in which a young joyrider was shot dead by soldiers in Northern Ireland when he tried to evade an army checkpoint. It was found that the application was manifestly ill-founded, since the use of force was justified. However, it can be argued that this finding does not represent a strict application of a strict proportionality test. Kelly was apparently shot in order to prevent him escaping, but it would not appear that it was 'absolutely necessary' to shoot to kill in the circumstances, since it might well have been possible to arrest him later.

The Court addressed the question of the strictness of the 'absolutely necessary' test in *McCann, Farrell and Savage v UK*,[155] the first judgment of the Court to find a breach of Art 2. The case concerned the shooting by SAS soldiers of three IRA members on the street in Gibraltar. The UK argued that this was justified on the basis that they apparently had with them a remote control device which they might have used to detonate a bomb. The Court found that para 2 primarily describes situations 'where it is permitted to use force which may result, as an unintended outcome in the deprivation of life', but that para 2 would also cover the intentional deprivation of life. However, the use of force must be no more than absolutely necessary for the achievement of one of the para 2 purposes and the test of necessity to be used was stricter than that used in respect of the test under paragraph 2 of Arts 8–11. The main question for the Court was the extent to which the State's response to the perceived threat posed by the IRA members was proportionate to that threat. The Court found that the use of force could be justified where 'it is based on an honest belief which is perceived for good reason to be valid at the time but which subsequently turns out to be mistaken. To hold otherwise would be to impose an unrealistic burden on the State and its law enforcement personnel.' Following this finding, the Court found that the actions of the soldiers who carried out the shooting did not amount to a violation of Art 2.

However, the organisation and planning of the whole operation had to be considered in order to discover whether the requirements of Art 2 had been respected. The Court focused on the decision not to arrest the suspects when they entered Gibraltar. This decision was taken because it was thought that there might have been insufficient evidence against them to warrant their charge and trial. However, this decision subjected the population of Gibraltar to possible danger. The Court considered that taking this factor into account and bearing in mind that they had been shadowed by the SAS soldiers for some time, the suspects could have been arrested at that point. Further, there was quite a high probability that the suspects were on a reconnaissance mission at the time of the shootings and not a bombing mission. This possibility, the possibility that there was no car bomb or that the suspects had no detonator, was not conveyed to the soldiers and since they were trained to shoot to kill, the killings were rendered almost inevitable. All these factors were taken into account in finding that the killing of the three constituted a use of force which was more than absolutely necessary in defence of persons from

---

154 Appl 17579/90; (1993) 16 EHRR CD 20; 74 D & R 139 (1993).
155 (1995) 21 EHRR 97, A 324, Council of Europe Report.

unlawful violence within the meaning of para 2(a) of Art 2. The State had sanctioned killing by State agents in circumstances which gave rise to a breach of Art 2.

This was a bold decision which departs from the stance taken in *Kelly*. It emphasises that a strict proportionality test must be used in determining issues under para 2 of Art 2. Applying this test, it would appear that where an alternative to the deliberate use of deadly force exists, it should always be taken. It would therefore seem that the use of such force to effect an arrest would never be justified except where, in the circumstances, there was near-certainty that the suspect would kill if allowed to escape. This might apply, for example, in situations where hostages had been taken and threats against them issued. It would also apply in circumstances similar to those arising in *McCann*, but where no opportunity for apprehension had previously arisen and where there was a stronger likelihood that a bomb might be about to be detonated. In such instances, of course, both sub-paras (a) and (b) of Art 2(2) would be in question and it therefore appears that the McCann judgment leaves little room for the operation of sub-para (b) independently of sub-para (a) *McCann* and *Kelly* make clear the partially subjective nature of the judgment as to when the use of deadly force is 'absolutely necessary'. Article 2 itself does not make it clear whether the phrase 'absolutely necessary' is to be treated objectively or subjectively. On its face it is unclear whether Art 2 would be breached where the person using such force honestly believed, due to a mistake, that it was necessary, although in actuality it was not. In such a case, Art 2 would not be breached if there were also reasonable grounds for believing that such force was necessary. It may be noted that this stance is not in accord with UK law, which allows the use of force, including deadly force, so long as an honest (not necessarily reasonable) belief is formed that force is required,[156] and the force used is in proportion to the circumstances as the defendant believed them to be.[157] Thus, an objective test is only used in relation to the question of the proportionality between the apparent circumstances and the force used.[158]

Article 3: Freedom from inhuman treatment

No one shall be subjected to torture or to inhuman or degrading treatment or punishment.

The right to freedom from torture or inhuman or degrading treatment or punishment is recognised in international human rights Treaties[159] and in many, although not all, domestic human rights instruments.[160] The right is also protected by specific Conventions, the United Nations Convention Against Torture and Other Cruel, Inhuman or Degrading Treatment or Punishment 1984[161] and the European Convention for the Prevention of Torture and Inhuman and Degrading Treatment or Punishment 1987.[162]

---

156 *Williams* [1987] 3 All ER 411.

157 *Owino* [1995] Crim LR 743.

158 This seems to have been the basis of the decision of the House of Lords in *Clegg* [1995] 2 WLR 80, which concerned a killing of a joyrider by a soldier in Northern Ireland.

159 Article 5 of the Universal Declaration and Art 7 of the ICCPR.

160 For discussion of this right as recognised in other jurisdictions, see Clayton and Tomlinson, *op cit*, fn 1, Chapter 8, esp pp 412–29.

161 Cmnd 9593, 1985; it came into force in 1987 and it was ratified by the UK in December 1988.

162 Cm 1634, 1991; it was ratified by the UK in June 1988. For discussion, see Evans and Morgan, *Preventing Torture: A Study of the European Convention for the Prevention of Torture*, 1998.

Torture is a crime under international law.[163] Thus, there is strong international recognition of the fundamental values enshrined in this right.

Article 3 contains no exceptions and it is also non-derogable. Thus, on the face of it, once a State has been found to have fallen within its terms, no justification is possible.[164] However, it has been suggested that the exceptions to Art 2 must be taken as applying also to Art 3 since, if the State in certain circumstances may justifiably take life, it must be justifiable *a fortiori* to inflict lesser harm on citizens in the same circumstances.[165] This may be correct, but clearly it is not intended to be taken to mean that all the exceptions to Art 2 apply to all forms of Art 3 treatment. The Art 2 exceptions suggest elements of immediacy which would be applicable to severe wounding but not usually to, for example, the form of torture, severe beating of all parts of the body to extract information, which occurred in the *Greek* case.[166] Similarly, State laws allowing wounding by private individuals in self-defence would not appear to be in breach of Art 3 so long as they were in accord with para 2 of Art 2. The Court has made it clear that the use of forms of Art 3 treatment in order to extract information, even in order to combat terrorism, is unjustifiable.[167] However, it might be argued that if life can be taken in order to save life (for example, in a hostage situation where no other course is available), or as a punishment in the form of execution, Art 3 treatment used in extreme circumstances in order to obtain information to save life (the classic ticking bomb in one of a large number of crowded shopping centres, or an atomic device placed somewhere in Central London) might be viewed as justifiable if effective where no other course was available and where it was otherwise inevitable that large numbers of people would be killed.

The responsibility of the State extends beyond prohibiting the use of Art 3 treatment by State agents. It includes a duty to ensure that individuals within their jurisdiction are not subjected to Art 3 treatment by other individuals.[168] It also includes an obligation not to deport a person who needs medical treatment to a country where he will not receive it.[169] The State also has a positive obligation to carry out an effective investigation into allegations of breaches of Art 3.[170]

In determining the standard of treatment applicable below which a State will be in breach of Art 3, a common European standard is applied, but also all the factors in the situation are taken into account.[171] The Court has found that such factors include: 'the nature and context of the treatment, its duration, its mental and physical effects and, in some instances, the sex, age and state of health of the victim.'[172] Thus, it does not connote

---

163 See *R v Bow Street Stipendiary Magistrate ex p Pinochet Ugarte (No 3)* [1999] 2 WLR 827.

164 *Ireland v UK* (1978) 2 EHRR 25.

165 See Harris, O'Boyle and Warbrick, *op cit*, fn 1, p 56.

166 (1969) Yearbook XII 1, p 504, Com Rep; CM Res DH (70) 1.

167 *Tomasi v France* (1992) 15 EHRR 1.

168 In *A v UK* (1999) 27 EHRR 611, a violation of Art 3 was found since the law had failed to protect a child from excessive chastisement by his stepfather.

169 In *D v UK* (1998) 24 EHRR 423, a violation of Art 3 was found since the UK proposed sending D back to the West Indies after he had contracted AIDS, where he would not receive appropriate treatment for his condition.

170 *Aksoy v Turkey* (1996) 23 EHRR 533; *Selmouni v France* (2000) 29 EHRR 403.

171 The *Greek* case (1969), Yearbook XII 186–510.

172 *A v UK* (1998) 27 EHRR 611, para 20.

an absolute standard and, in its application, it allows for a measure of discretion. It is clear that, in order to determine this issue, *present* views must be considered rather than the views at the time when the Convention was drawn up. The three forms of treatment mentioned represent three different levels of seriousness. Thus, torture, unlike degrading treatment, has been quite narrowly defined to include 'deliberate inhuman treatment causing very serious and cruel suffering'.[173] In a number of cases, there has been a finding of torture against Turkey. In *Aksoy v Turkey*,[174] the applicant had been stripped naked, his arms had been tied behind his back and he had then been hung from his arms. In *Aydin v Turkey*,[175] the rape of a young girl by a military official was found to amount to torture; the other forms of ill treatment to which she was subjected, including beating for an hour, also amounted to torture. In *Selmouni v France*,[176] the Court found that beatings and humiliation in custody amounted to torture rather than inhuman or degrading treatment, bearing in mind the fact that 'the increasingly high standard being required in the area of protection of human rights and fundamental liberties correspondingly and inevitably requires greater firmness in assessing breaches of the fundamental values of democratic societies'.[177]

Clearly, treatment which could not come within the restricted definition of torture could still fall within one of the other two heads, especially the broad head – 'degrading treatment'. In order to characterise treatment as inhuman, it must reach a minimum level of severity.[178] Physical assault,[179] the immediate threat of torture,[180] and interrogation techniques causing psychological disorientation[181] have all been found to amount to inhuman treatment.

Treatment may be both inhuman and degrading, but degrading treatment may not also amount to inhuman treatment.[182] Degrading treatment is treatment that is grossly humiliating.[183] Degrading punishment does not inevitably include *all* forms of physical punishment, although it can include certain forms of corporal punishment, including caning,[184] which have been found not to amount to torture or inhuman punishment. Corporal punishment which could be said to be of a 'normal' type may be distinguished, it seems, from degrading corporal punishment.[185] Thus, the mere fact that physical

---

173 *Ireland v UK* (1978) 2 EHRR 25.

174 (1996) 23 EHRR 553.

175 (1997) 25 EHRR 251. See also *Salman v Turkey*, Judgment of 27 June 2000 (beatings in custody with rifle butts and sticks amounted to torture).

176 (2000) 29 EHRR 403.

177 *Ibid*, para 101.

178 *A v UK* (1998) 27 EHRR 611, para 20.

179 *Ireland v UK* (1978) 2 EHRR 25.

180 *Campbell and Cosans v UK* (1982) 4 EHRR 293.

181 *Ireland v UK* (1978) 2 EHRR 25.

182 *Tyrer*, Judgment of 25 April 1978, A 26; (1978) 2 EHRR 1.

183 *Greek* case (1969) 12 YB 1.

184 *Tyrer*, Judgment of 25 April 1978, A 26; (1978) 2 EHRR 1. In *Warwick v UK*, Eur Comm HR Report of 15 June 1986, the Commission considered that corporal punishment in schools amounted to degrading treatment.

185 *Costello-Roberts v UK*, Judgment of 25 March 1993; A 247-C (1993). It may be noted that the School Standards and Framework Act 1998 has abolished corporal punishment in the independent sector; it had already been abolished in the State sector.

punishment is administered will not, without more, necessarily involve a breach of Art 3 and nor will the mere threat of such punishment.[186]

A number of cases have arisen concerning the position of detainees. It is now clear that if a person enters police custody in a sound physical condition but, on release, is found to have sustained injuries such as bruising, the State must provide a plausible explanation.[187] In determining whether a particular treatment, such as solitary confinement, amounts to a violation of Art 3, a number of factors must be taken into account. These will include the stringency and duration of the measure,[188] the objective pursued – such as the need for special security measures for the prisoner in question[189] or the fear of stirring up discontent among other prisoners[190] – and the effect on the person concerned. The applicant will need to submit medical evidence showing the causal relationship between the prison conditions complained of and his or her deterioration in mental and physical health. If the adverse treatment has been adopted as a result of the claimant's own unco-operative behaviour, it is probable that no breach will be found.[191]

Art 3 has been interpreted widely as to the forms of treatment it covers, which include some not readily associated with the terms it uses. It could probably be used, for example, in relation to involuntary medical intervention such as sterilisation or Caesarean section,[192] and, as indicated below, racial discrimination can amount to degrading treatment. Article 3 has been used to bring rights within the scope of the Convention which are not expressly included. Thus, Art 3 could be invoked in relation to discriminatory treatment on the basis of race and possibly on the basis of sex or sexual orientation, because such treatment can be termed degrading according to the Commission in the *East African Asians* cases.[193] This possibility could help to compensate for the weakness of the Art 14 guarantee against discrimination which does not create an independent right.[194]

Other rights which otherwise would not be recognised under the Convention include the right to remain in a certain country. Violation of Art 3 may occur because of the treatment a person may receive when returning to his or her own country having been expelled or refused admission. It will have to be clearly established that the danger of such treatment is really present. The question arose in *Soering v UK*[195] whether expulsion to a country (the US) where the applicant risked the death penalty would be compatible with Art 3 because it would subject him to conditions on Death Row likely to cause him acute mental anguish. Of course, since Art 2 specifically excludes the death penalty from

---

186 *Campbell and Cosans*, Judgment of 25 February 1982, A 48; (1982) 4 EHRR 293.

187 *Tomasi v France* (1992) 15 EHRR 1; *Ribbitsch v Austria* (1992) 21 EHRR 573.

188 Complete sensory isolation is likely to amount to Art 3 treatment: *Ensslin, Bader and Raspe v Germany* (1978) 14 DR 64, p 109.

189 In *Kröcher and Möller v Switzerland* D & R 34 (1983); (1984) 6 EHRR 345 it was found that harsh conditions imposed to ensure security may not constitute a violation of Art 3.

190 Appl 8324/78, *X v UK* (not published) (the ability to encourage other prisoners to acts of indiscipline was taken into account).

191 Appl 9907/82, *M v UK* D & R 130 (1983) (dangerous behaviour of detainee taken into account in considering conditions).

192 See *X v Denmark* (1983) 32 DR 282.

193 (1973) 3 EHRR 76.

194 See below, pp 85–86.

195 Judgment of 7 July 1989, A 161; (1989) 11 EHRR 439. For discussion, see *Schabas* (1994) 43 ICLQ 913.

its guarantee, the possibility of its use cannot in itself create a violation of Art 3 because that would render those words of Art 2 otiose (assuming that the State in question had not ratified Protocol 6). The Convention must be read as a whole. However, the Court found that the manner and circumstances of the implementation of the death penalty could give rise to an issue under Art 3. The Court held that it had to consider the length of detention prior to the execution, the conditions on Death Row, the applicant's age and his mental state. Bearing these factors in mind, especially the very long period of time spent on Death Row and the mounting anguish as execution was awaited, it was found that expulsion would constitute a breach of Art 3. (In response to this ruling, the UK and the US agreed to drop the charges to non-capital murder and then extradite the applicant.)

The principle laid down in *Soering* was followed in *Chahal v UK*.[196] Originally an illegal immigrant, Mr Chahal obtained leave to remain in Britain indefinitely in 1974. In 1984, he visited the Punjab for a family wedding and met the chief advocate of creating an independent Sikh State. Later, he was arrested by Indian police and allegedly tortured. He escaped from India and became the founder of the International Sikh Youth Federation in the UK. In 1990, he was arrested after a meeting at a Southall temple. The Home Office accused him of involvement in Sikh terrorism and decided to deport him on national security grounds. He sought asylum on the ground that he would be tortured if sent back to India and applied to the European Commission, alleging *inter alia* a breach of Art 3. The Court found that since there were strong grounds for believing that Mr Chahal would indeed have been tortured had he been returned to India, a breach of Art 3 had occurred.[197]

For a breach of Art 3 to be established in the context of deportation or extradition cases, there must be a clear risk of ill treatment; a 'mere possibility' will be insufficient. In *Vilvarajah and Four Others v the UK*,[198] the applicants, Sri Lankan Tamils, arrived in the UK in 1987 and applied for political asylum under the UN Convention of 1951 Relating to the Status of Refugees, contending that they had a well founded fear of persecution if returned to Sri Lanka. The Home Secretary rejected the applications and the applicants sought unsuccessfully to challenge the rejection by means of judicial review. The applicants were then returned to Sri Lanka where, they alleged, four of them were arrested and ill-treated. They claimed that their deportation constituted breaches of Arts 3 and 13 of the European Convention. The Court considered whether the situation in Sri Lanka at the time the applicants were deported provided substantial support for the view that they would be at risk of Art 3 treatment. The Court determined that the general unsettled situation in Sri Lanka at the time did not establish that they were at greater risk than other young male Tamils who were returning there; it established only a possibility rather than a clear risk of ill treatment. No breach of Art 3 could therefore be established.[199] Arguably, this decision suggests that although an Art 3 issue may arise in asylum cases, the Convention cannot be viewed as a substitute for an effective domestic means of determining refugee claims. (It should be noted that Art 8 issues may also arise in some immigration claims; this possibility will be discussed below.)

---

196 (1997) 23 EHRR 413.

197 The Art 5 issue is considered below, p 56.

198 (1991) 14 EHRR 248, A 215.

199 See further on the outcome of the Tamils' asylum claim, Chapter 15, p 936. For comment on this case, see Warbrick, C, *Yearbook of European Law*, 1991, pp 545–53.

Soering is a very broad decision. The approach taken in the judgment may mean that a State would infringe the Convention whenever it facilitated the breach of a Convention Article by another State. However, in general, liability arises under the Convention only where a breach has already occurred, not where it is merely probable. An exception was made to that rule in *Soering* in view of 'the serious and irreparable nature of the alleged suffering risked'.[200] Thus, the *Soering* facilitation principle may apply only where the State receiving the individual in question is likely to subject him or her to treatment amounting to serious and irreparable suffering. This would include treatment in breach of Arts 3 and 2 (such as State execution without trial) and probably 5 and 6 (imprisonment without trial). Possibly, it might also include deportation leading to the probability of treatment in breach of Arts 6[201] or 7 in the receiving State which would then be likely to result in the execution or imprisonment of the individual. For example, if an individual committed an act in his or her own State before leaving for another State – a Party to the Convention – and the act committed was then criminalised with retrospective effect, the second State might act in breach of Art 7 if it extradited the individual in order to face charges and the possibility of imprisonment under the new law.

Article 3 is considered further in relation to police and immigration law.[202] Relevant issues are also raised in Chapters 16 and 17, dealing with aspects of discrimination.

Article 4: Freedom from slavery, servitude and forced or compulsory labour

(1) No one shall be held in slavery or servitude.

(2) No one shall be required to perform forced or compulsory labour.

(3) For the purpose of this Article the term 'forced or compulsory labour' shall not include:

    (a) any work required to be done in the ordinary course of detention imposed according to the provisions of Article 5 of this Convention or during conditional release from such detention;

    (b) any service of a military character or, in case of conscientious objectors in countries where they are recognised, service exacted instead of compulsory military service;

    (c) any service exacted in case of any emergency or calamity threatening the life or well-being of the community;

    (d) any work or service which forms part of normal civic obligations.

Article 4 provides a guarantee which is largely irrelevant in modern European democracies, although it is conceivable that as States with less developed human rights regimes become signatories to the Convention, it might prove to be of value. Owing to its restrictive wording, it has not proved possible to interpret Art 4 in such a way as to allow it to cover rights unthought of when it was conceived.

It is necessary to distinguish between slavery and servitude under Art 4(1) and forced or compulsory labour under Art 4(2). Slavery denotes total ownership, whereas servitude denotes less far reaching restraints; it is concerned with the labour conditions and the

---

200 Judgment of 7 July 1989, A 161, para 90.
201 See *Soering*, A 161, para 113.
202 See Chapter 13, p 852–53 and Chapter 15, p 956 and 964.

inescapable nature of the service. Article 4(1) contains no express excepti non-derogable.

Article 4(1) has not generated much case law and the few cases which brought have failed. Article 4(2) is not concerned with the total situation of th concerned; it covers the compulsory character of services which will us ally be temporary and incidental to the claimant's main job or total situation. Forced or compulsory labour has been held to denote the following: 'first that the work or service is performed by the worker against his will and, secondly, that the requirement that the work or service be performed is unjust or oppressive or the work or service itself involves avoidable hardship.'[203] Most of the case law arises in the area of professional obligations arising from certain jobs. For example, a German lawyer complained of having to act as unpaid or poorly paid defence counsel. The Commission rejected the complaint on the basis that if a person voluntarily chooses the profession of lawyer, aware of this obligation, then he can be taken to have impliedly consented to fulfil the obligation.[204] This argument will apply if the obligations are a normal part of the profession. Less emphasis was placed on the implied consent of the applicant in *Van der Mussele*,[205] which also concerned compulsory legal aid work. The Court took the view that the mere fact that the applicant had impliedly consented to the obligation was only a factor to be considered; it was not decisive. It decided that looking at all the factors, including the small amount of time devoted to such work – only 18 hours – and the fact that such work enabled the obligation under Art 6(3)(c) (if necessary to have free legal advice) to be fulfilled, no breach had occurred.

Article 5: Right to liberty and security of person

(1) Everyone has the right to liberty and security of person. No one shall be deprived of his liberty save in the following cases and in accordance with a procedure prescribed by law:

(a) the lawful detention of a person after conviction by a competent court;

(b) the lawful arrest or detention of a person for non-compliance with the lawful order of a court or in order to secure the fulfilment of any obligation prescribed by law;

(c) the lawful arrest or detention of a person effected for the purpose of bringing him before the competent legal authority on reasonable suspicion of having committed an offence or when it is reasonably considered necessary to prevent his committing an offence or fleeing after having done so;

(d) the detention of a minor by lawful order for the purpose of educational supervision or his lawful detention for the purpose of bringing him before the competent legal authority;

(e) the lawful detention of persons for the prevention of the spreading of infectious diseases, of persons of unsound mind, alcoholics or drug addicts or vagrants;

---

203 *X v Federal Republic of Germany* Appl 8410/78 (1980); D & R 216, p 219.
204 *X v FRG*, Appl 4653/70; (1974) 46 CD 22.
205 Judgment of 23 November 1983, A 70.

(f) the lawful arrest or detention of a person to prevent his effecting an unauthorised entry into the country or of a person against whom action is being taken with a view to deportation or extradition.

(2) Everyone who is arrested shall be informed promptly, in a language which he understands, of the reasons for his arrest and of any charge against him.

(3) Everyone arrested or detained in accordance with the provisions of para 1(c) of this Article shall be brought promptly before a judge or other officer authorised by law to exercise judicial power and shall be entitled to trial within a reasonable time or to release pending trial. Release may be conditioned by guarantees to appear for trial.

(4) Everyone who is deprived of his liberty by arrest or detention shall be entitled to take proceedings by which the lawfulness of his detention shall be decided speedily by a court and his release ordered if the detention is not lawful.

(5) Everyone who has been the victim of arrest or detention in contravention of the provisions of this Article shall have an enforceable right to compensation.

Although Art 5 speaks of liberty *and* security as though they could be distinguished, they are not treated in the case law as though there is any significant distinction between them. The use of the term 'security' does not appear to add anything to the term liberty. The guarantee refers to protection from deprivation of physical liberty, not to protection for physical safety.[206] The presumption embodied in the Article is that liberty and security must be maintained. However, it then sets out the two tests which must be satisfied if it is to be removed. First, exceptions are set out where liberty can be taken away; secondly, under paras 2–4, the procedure is set out which must be followed when a person is deprived of liberty. Thus, if the correct procedure is followed, but an exception does not apply, Art 5 will be breached, as, conversely, it will if an individual falls within an exception but, in detaining him or her, the correct procedure is not followed. It will be found that a number of successful applications have been brought under Art 5 with the result that the position of detainees in Europe has undergone improvement. It should be noted that Art 5 is concerned with total deprivation of liberty, not restriction of movement, which is covered by Art 2 of Protocol 4 (at the time of writing, the UK is not yet a party to Protocol 4.)

In general, the case law of the Court discussed below suggests that the circumstances in which liberty can be taken away under para 5(1)(a)–(f) will be restrictively interpreted, although the instances included are potentially wide. Article 5(1) not only provides that deprivation of liberty is only permitted within these exceptions, it also requires that it should be 'in accordance with a procedure prescribed by law'. In *Winterwerp v Netherlands*,[207] the Court found that this meant that the procedure in question must be in accordance with national and Convention law, taking into account the general principles on which the Convention is based, and it must not be arbitrary. In *Chahal v UK*,[208] the applicant complained, *inter alia*, that he had been detained although there had been no court hearing. The Home Office decided to deport him on national security grounds, but

206 *X v Ireland* (1973) 16 YB 388.
207 Judgment of 24 October 1979, A 33; (1979) 2 EHRR 387.
208 (1997) 23 EHRR 413.

he applied for asylum. He was then imprisoned for over six years. He applied to the European Commission on Human Rights, alleging, *inter alia*, a breach of Art 5, which guarantees judicial control over loss of liberty. The Court found that a breach of Art 5 had occurred, since his detention should have been subject to scrutiny in court. It had been considered by an advisory panel, but that did not provide sufficient procedural safeguards to qualify as a court.

5(1)(a): Detention after conviction

This exception covers lawful detention after conviction by a competent court. Thus, the detention must flow from the conviction. This calls into question the revocation of life licences because, in such instances, a person is being deprived of liberty without a fresh conviction. In *Weeks*,[209] the Court considered the causal connection with the original sentence when a life licence was revoked after the applicant was released. The Court accepted a very loose link between the original sentence and the revocation of the life licence on the basis that the sentencing judge must be taken to have known and intended that it was inherent in the life sentence that the claimant's liberty would hereafter be at the mercy of the executive. The Court declined to review the appropriateness of the original sentence.

5(1)(b): Detention to fulfil an obligation

This exception refers to deprivation of liberty in order to 'secure fulfilment of an obligation prescribed by law'. This phrase raises difficulties of interpretation and is clearly not so straightforward as the first form of such deprivation permitted under para 5(1)(a). It is very wide and appears to allow deprivation of liberty in many instances without intervention by a court. It might even allow preventive action before violation of a legal obligation. However, it has been narrowed down; in *Lawless*,[210] it was found that a specific and concrete obligation must be identified. Once it has been identified, detention can in principle be used to secure its fulfilment.

The obligation includes a requirement that specific circumstances, such as the possibility of danger to the public, must be present in order to warrant the use of detention. A requirement to submit to an examination on entering the UK has been found to be specific enough.[211] Moreover, it must be apparent why detention rather than some lesser measure is needed to secure compliance with the obligation. Thus, the width of Art 5(1)(b) has been narrowed down by the use of restrictive interpretation in line with furthering the aims of the Convention.

---

209 Judgment of 5 October 1988, A 114; (1987) 10 EHRR 293.
210 Report of 19 December 1959, B 1 (1960–61) p 64; Judgment of 1 July 1961, A 3 (1960–61); (1961) 1 EHRR 15.
211 *McVeigh, O'Neill and Evans v UK* (1981) Report of 18 March 1981, D & R 25; (1981) 5 EHRR 71.

5(1)(c): Detention after arrest but before conviction

This provision refers to persons held on remand or detained after arrest. Article 5(3) requires that in such an instance, a person should be brought 'promptly' to trial; in other words, the trial should occur in *reasonable* time. The part of 5(1)(c) which causes concern is the ground – 'arrest or detention to prevent him committing an offence'. This is an alternative to the holding of the detainee under reasonable suspicion of committing an offence; arguably, the two should have been cumulative. This ground would permit internment of persons even if the facts which showed the intention to commit a crime did not, in themselves, constitute a criminal offence. In *Lawless*,[212] the Court narrowed this ground down on the basis that internment in such circumstances might well not fulfil the other requirement in Art 5(1)(c) that the arrest or detention would be effected for the purpose of bringing the person before a competent legal authority. This interpretation was warranted because all of Art 5 must be read together.

A level of suspicion below 'reasonable suspicion' will not be sufficient; in *Fox, Campbell and Hartley*,[213] the Court found that Art 5(1)(c) had been violated on the basis that no reasonable suspicion of committing an offence had arisen, only an honest belief (which was all that was needed under s 11 of the Northern Ireland (Emergency Provisions) Act 1978). The only evidence put forward by the Government for the presence of reasonable suspicion was that the applicants had convictions for terrorist offences and that when arrested, they were asked about particular terrorist acts. The Government said that further evidence could not be disclosed for fear of endangering life. The Court said that reasonable suspicion arises from 'facts or information which would satisfy an objective observer that the person concerned may have committed the offence'. It went on to find that the Government had not established that reasonable suspicion was present in justifying the arrests in question. The Court took into account the exigencies of the situation and the need to prevent terrorism; however, it found that the State Party in question must be able to provide some information which an objective observer would consider justified the arrest. It was found that the information provided was insufficient and therefore a breach of Art 5 had occurred. This ruling suggests that in terrorist cases, a low level of reasonable suspicion is required and this test was applied in *Murray v UK*.[214] The Court found that no breach of Art 5(1)(c) had occurred, even though the relevant legislation (s 14 of the Northern Ireland (Emergency Provisions) Act 1987) required only suspicion, not reasonable suspicion, since there was some evidence which provided a basis for the suspicion in question.

5(1)(d): Detention of minors

This provision confers far reaching powers on national authorities with regard to those under 18 years of age. This has led the Court to interpret the term 'educational purpose' restrictively. In *Bouamar v Belgium*,[215] it was found that mere detention without

---

212 Above, fn 100.
213 Judgment of 30 August 1990, A 178; (1990) 13 EHRR 157.
214 (1994) 19 EHRR 193.
215 Judgment of 29 February 1988, A 129; (1988) 11 EHRR 1.

educational facilities would not fulfil Art 5(1)(d)); there had to be educational facilities in the institution, and trained staff.

5(1)(e): Detention of non-criminals for the protection of society

This sub-paragraph must, of course, be read in conjunction with para 5(4) – all the persons mentioned have the right to have the lawfulness of their detention determined by a Court. The width of para 5(1)(e) was narrowed down in the *Vagrancy* cases, in which the question arose of the current application of the term 'vagrant'.[216] The term had been applied to the applicants who had, therefore, been detained. The Court considered whether the applicant was correctly brought within the ambit of the term in the relevant Belgian legislation, but it refused to conduct a more than marginal review of municipal law; the question of the interpretation of national law was separated from the application of the Convention. However the Court did then turn to the Convention and conduct a far reaching review of the meaning of 'vagrant' in accordance with the Convention on the basis of a common European standard; it then found that the applicants had not been correctly brought within that term. Thus, ultimately, the margin of appreciation allowed was narrow. This stance prevents too wide an interpretation of the application of the categories of para 5(1)(e).

In *Winterwerp v Netherlands*,[217] the Court found that the detention of the mentally disordered or handicapped could be justified only where there was reliable medical evidence of the mental disorder; it must be of a type justifying compulsory detention; the condition in question must persist throughout the period of detention. In *Kay v UK*,[218] a breach of Art 5(1)(e) was found since the first of these conditions had not been complied with; *current* medical information had not been considered.

5(1)(f): Detention of aliens and deportees

The importance of this provision is that the Convention does not grant aliens a right of admission or residence in Contracting States, but para 5(1)(f) ensures that an alien who is detained pending deportation or admission has certain guarantees; there must be review of the detention by an independent body[219] and the arrest must be in accordance with national law.[220] The nature of the measures taken, including the period of detention before review, must ensure that the detention is not arbitrary.[221] Also, because the lawfulness of the detention may depend on the lawfulness of the deportation itself, the lawfulness of the deportation may often be in issue.[222]

---

216 *Vagrancy* cases, Judgment of 18 June 1971, A 14.

217 (1979) 2 EHRR 387.

218 (1998) 40 BMLR 20.

219 In *Chahal v UK* (1996) 23 EHRR 413 review by the immigration advisory panel procedure was found to be sufficient to guard against arbitrariness.

220 In *Bozano v France* (1986) 9 EHRR 297, a French deportation order was found to be invalid under national law since it was – in effect – a disguised extradition order. A violation of Art 5(1)(f) was found.

221 *Guzzardi v Italy* (1980) 3 EHRR 333; *Amuur v France* (1996) 22 EHRR 533.

222 *Zamir v UK*, Report of 11 October 1983; 40 D & R 42 (1983).

Safeguards of paras 2–4: general

Paragraphs 2–4 reiterate the principle that the liberty of the person is the overriding concern; if one of the exceptions mentioned in para 5(1) applies, the safeguards of sub-paras 2–4 must still be complied with. If they are not, the deprivation of liberty will be unlawful even if it comes within the exceptions. Paragraphs 2–4 provide a minimum standard for arrest and detention.

Promptly informing of the reason for arrest

Paragraph 5(2) provides that a detainee or arrestee must be informed promptly of the reason for arrest. This information is needed so that it is possible to judge from the moment of its inception whether the arrest is in accordance with the law so that the detainee could theoretically take action straight away to be released. All the necessary information – the factual and legal grounds for the arrest – need not be given at the point of arrest; it can be conveyed over a period of time, depending on the circumstances. A period of two days between the arrest and the conveying of the information has been found not to breach Art 5(2).[223] The Commission's view is that this information need not be as detailed and specific as that guaranteed by para 6(3) in connection with the right to a fair trial.[224]

In *Fox, Campbell and Hartley v UK*,[225] the applicants, who were arrested on suspicion of terrorist offences, were not informed of the reason for the arrest at the time of it, but were told that they were being arrested under a particular statutory provision. Clearly, this could not convey the reason to them at that time. At a later point, during interrogation, they were asked about specific criminal offences. The European Court of Human Rights found that Art 5(2) was not satisfied at the time of the arrest, but that this breach was healed by the later indications made during interrogation of the offences for which they had been arrested. Clayton and Tomlinson comment that this finding was 'an unacceptable dilution of a basic guarantee'.[226]

In *Murray v UK*,[227] soldiers had occupied the applicant's house, thus clearly taking her into detention, but she was not informed of the fact of arrest for half an hour. The question arose whether she was falsely imprisoned during that half hour. The Court found that no breach of Art 5(2) had occurred in those circumstances. Mrs Murray was eventually informed during interrogation of the reason for the arrest and although an interval of a few hours had elapsed between the arrest and informing her of the reason for it, this could still be termed prompt.

Both these decisions were influenced by the terrorist context in which they occurred and provide examples of the Court's tenderness to claims of a threat to national security made by governments of Member States. In both, a very wide margin of appreciation was allowed. It would appear that both were influenced by the crime control consideration of

---

223 *Skoogstrom v Sweden* (1981) 1 Dig Supp para 5.2.2.1.
224 It was determined in Appl 8828/79, *X v Denmark* D & R 30 (1983), p 93 that para 5(2) does not include a right to contact a lawyer.
225 Judgment of 30 August 1990, A 182; (1990) 13 EHRR 157.
226 *Ibid*, p 498.
227 (1994) 19 EHRR 193.

allowing leeway to the police to resort to doubtful practices in relation to terrorist suspects and both exhibit, it is suggested, a lack of rigour in relation to due process. Such lack of rigour might be acceptable if there was a real connection between a failure to give information to suspects and an advantage to be gained in an emergency situation, since the principle of proportionality would then be satisfied. However, in Mrs Murray's case, for example, once she was in detention and her house in effect sealed off from the outside world, it is not clear that telling her of the fact of the arrest could have created or exacerbated the unsettled situation. Thus, the Court has allowed some departure from the principle that there should be a clear demarcation between the point at which the citizen is at liberty and the point at which her liberty is restrained.

Promptness of judicial hearing

Article 5(3) confers a right to be brought promptly before the judicial authorities; in other words, not to be held in detention for long periods without an independent hearing. It refers to persons detained in accordance with Art 5(1)(c) and therefore covers both arrest and detention, and detainees held on remand. The significance of Art 5(3) rests on its strong link to the purpose of Art 5 itself.[228] There will be some allowable delay in both situations; the question is, therefore, what is meant by 'promptly'. Its meaning was considered in *Brogan v UK*[229] in relation to an arrest and detention arising by virtue of the special powers under s 12 of the Prevention of Terrorism (Temporary Provisions) Act 1989. The UK had entered a derogation under Art 15 against the applicability of Art 5 to Northern Ireland, but withdrew that derogation in August 1984. Two months later, the *Brogan* case was filed. The applicants complained, *inter alia*, of the length of time they were held in detention without coming before a judge, on the basis that it could not be termed prompt. The Court took into account the need for special measures to combat terrorism; such measures had to be balanced against individual rights. However, it found that detention for four days and six hours was too long. The Court did not specify how long was acceptable; previously, the Commission had seen four days (in ordinary criminal cases) as the limit.[230] Following this decision, the UK Government ultimately chose to derogate from Art 5 and this decision was eventually found to be lawful by the European Court of Human Rights.[231]

The question whether detainees on remand have been brought to trial or released in a reasonable time has also been considered. The word 'reasonable' is not associated with the processing of the prosecution and trial, but with the detention itself. Obviously, if the trial takes a long time to prepare for, there will be a longer delay, but it does not follow that detention for all that time will be reasonable. In the *Neumeister* case,[232] the Court rejected an interpretation of 'reasonable' which associated it only with the preparation of the trial. Thus, continued detention on remand will be reasonable only so long as the reasonable suspicion of para 5(1)(c) continues to exist. But, grounds for continued

---

228 See *Bozano v France* (1986) 9 EHRR 297; *Assenov v Belgium* (1999) 28 EHRR 652; *T v Malta* (1999) 29 EHRR 185.
229 Judgment of 29 November 1988; (1989) 11 EHRR 117; A 145.
230 *X v Netherlands* (1966) 9 YB 564.
231 *Brannigan and McBride v UK* (1993) 17 EHRR 594.
232 Judgment of 27 June 1968; (1979–80) 1 EHRR 91.

detention other than those expressly mentioned in para 5(1)(c) could be considered, such as suppression of evidence or the possibility that the detainee will abscond. However, it is clear from *Letellier v France*[233] that such dangers must persist throughout the period of detention; when they cease, specific reasons for continued detention which have been properly scrutinised must be apparent. Once the accused has been released on bail, Art 5(3) does not apply, but Art 6(1) does, as will be seen later. The question of a reasonable time for preparing for the trial can also be considered under Art 6(1).

There is no absolute right to bail under Art 5(3), but the authorities must consider whether bail can achieve the same purpose as detention on remand.[234] It is also clear that detention after demand of an excessively large sum for bail will be unreasonable if a lesser sum would have achieved the same objective.[235]

Review of detention

Article 5(4) provides a right to review of detention, whatever the basis of the detention. The detainee must be able to take court proceedings in order to determine whether a detention is unlawful. This is an independent provision: even if it is determined in a particular case by the Commission that the detention was lawful, there could still be a breach of Art 5(4) if no possibility of review of the lawfulness of the detention by the domestic courts arose. The review must be by a court and it must be adequate to test the lawfulness of the detention. This requirement was found not to have been satisfied by judicial review proceedings or by habeas corpus in *Chahal v UK*:[236] neither procedure provided a sufficient basis for challenging a deportation decision.

Article 5(4) was in issue in the a number of cases against the UK regarding discretionary life sentences, and it was found that there had to be an element in the sentence which, of its nature, was reviewable.[237] Thus, a mandatory life sentence arguably consisting wholly of a punitive element would be unreviewable since no relevant circumstance could have changed.[238] In the *Weeks* case,[239] the sentence contained a security element and therefore allowed review of the applicant's progress. In *Thynne, Wilson and Gunnel v UK*,[240] the sentence consisted of both a punitive and a security element. When the punitive element expired, a judicial procedure for review of the sentence should have been available because there was then something to review; if it had been purely punitive, there would not have been. Thus, in both cases, a breach of Art 5(4) was found. Section 34 of the Criminal Justice Act 1991 clarified the position of discretionary lifers,[241] but the secretive procedure for tariff fixing may still raise issues

---

233 A 207 (1991).

234 *Wemhoff*, Judgment of 27 June 1968; (1968) 1 EHRR 55.

235 *Neumeister*, Judgment of 27 June 1968; (1979–80) 1 EHRR 91.

236 (1997) 23 EHRR 413.

237 *Wynne v UK* (1994) 19 EHRR 333.

238 *Ibid*.

239 (1987) 10 EHRR 293.

240 Judgment of 25 October 1990, A 190; (1990) 13 EHRR 666. For comment, see Richardson, 'Discretionary life-sentences and the ECHR' [1991] PL 34.

241 On the UK response in the Criminal Justice Act 1991, s 34 (see, now, Crime (Sentences) Act 1997, s 28) see: Fitzgerald, 'The Criminal Justice Act 1991: preventative detention of the dangerous offender' [1995] EHRLR 39.

under Art 5(4) and Art 6.[242] This is also the case in respect of the power of the Home Secretary to detain young offenders at her Majesty's pleasure.[243]

Article 5(4) also applies to remand prisoners. It was found in *De Jong, Baljet and Van de Brink*[244] that it grants to a person on remand a right of access to a court after the decision (in accordance with Art 5(3)) to detain him or prolong detention has been taken. It also allows access to the files used in coming to the decision on remand.[245]

Compensation

Paragraph 5(5) provides for compensation if the arrest or detention contravenes the other provisions of Art 5.[246] This provision differs from the general right to compensation under Art 50[247] because it exists as an independent right: if a person is found to have been unlawfully arrested under domestic law in the domestic court, but no compensation is available, he or she can apply to the European Court of Human Rights on the basis of the lack of compensation. As far as other Convention rights are concerned, if a violation of a right occurs which is found unlawful by the national courts, but no compensation is granted, the applicant cannot allege breach of the right.

Article 5(5) is considered at a number of points in this book, but most extensively in Chapter 12.

Article 6: Right to a fair and public hearing

(1) In the determination of his civil rights and obligations or of any criminal charge against him, everyone is entitled to a fair and public hearing within a reasonable time by an independent and impartial tribunal established by law. Judgment shall be pronounced publicly but the press and public may be excluded from all or part of the trial in the interest of morals, public order or national security in a democratic society, where the interest of juveniles or the protection of the private life of the parties so require or to the extent strictly necessary in the opinion of the court in special circumstances where publicity would prejudice the interests of justice.

(2) Everyone charged with a criminal offence shall be presumed innocent until proved guilty according to law.

(3) Everyone charged with a criminal offence has the following minimum rights:

   (a) to be informed promptly, in a language he understands and in detail, of the nature and cause of the accusation against him;

   (b) to have adequate time and facilities for the preparation of his defence;

   (c) to defend himself in person or through legal assistance of his own choosing or, if he has not sufficient means to pay for legal assistance, to be given it free when the interests of justice so require;

---

242 See *Watson v UK* [1997] EHRLR 181.
243 *Hussain and Singh v UK* (1996) 21 EHRR 1.
244 Judgment of 22 May 1984, A 77, pp 25–26; (1984) 8 EHRR 20.
245 *Lamy v Belgium* (1989) 11 EHRR 529.
246 See the reference to Art 5(5) in HRA, s 9(3).
247 Appl No 6821/74, *Huber v Austria* 6 D & R 65 (1977), p 65.

    (d) to examine or have examined witnesses against him and to obtain the attendance and examination of witnesses on his behalf under the same conditions as witness against him;

    (e) to have the free assistance of an interpreter if he cannot understand or speak the language used in court.

Article 6 is one of the most significant Convention Articles and the one which is most frequently found to have been violated. This is partly due to the width of Art 6(1), which may cover numerous circumstances in which rights are affected in the absence of a judicial hearing. This may mean that even where a substantive claim under another Article fails, the Art 6(1) claim succeeds because the procedure used in making the determination affecting the applicant was defective.[248] In order to appreciate the way it operates, it is crucial to understand the relationship between paras 1 and 3. Paragraph 1 imports a general requirement of a fair hearing applying to criminal and civil hearings which covers all aspects of a fair hearing. Paragraph 3 lists minimum guarantees of a fair hearing in the criminal context only. If para 3 had been omitted, the guarantees contained in it could have arisen from para 1, but it was included on the basis that it is important to declare a minimum standard for a fair hearing. In practice, then, paras 1 and 3 may often both be in question in respect of a criminal charge.

Since para 3 contains *minimum* guarantees, the para 1 protection of a fair hearing goes beyond para 3. In investigating a fair hearing, the Commission is not confined to the para 3 guarantees; it can consider further requirements of fairness. Thus, if para 1 is not violated, it will be superfluous to consider para 3 and if one of the para 3 guarantees is violated, there will be no need to look at para 1. However, if para 3 is not violated, it will still be worth considering para 1. It follows that although civil hearings are expressly affected only by para 1, the minimum guarantees may also apply to such hearings too.

Article 6(1): Fair hearing

Field of application

The term 'criminal charge' has an autonomous Convention meaning. The question of what is meant by 'a criminal charge' has generated quite a lot of case law. 'Charge' has been described as 'the official notification given to an individual by the competent authority of an allegation that he has committed a criminal offence'.[249] The proceedings in question must be *determinative* of the charge. Therefore, proceedings *ancillary* to the determination of the charge do not fall within Art 6.[250]

Offences under criminal law must be distinguished from those arising only under *disciplinary* law. In order to determine whether, whatever the classification of an 'offence' in national law, it should be viewed as criminal in nature, the Court will consider the nature of the offence and the nature and severity of the penalty the person is threatened

---

248 Eg, in *Mats Jacobson v Sweden* (1990) 13 EHRR 79, the applicant was prevented from making changes to his property. His substantive claim under Art 1 of Protocol 1 failed, but his Art 6(1) claim succeeded, since he was allowed no adequate access to a court to challenge the prohibition.

249 Judgment of 15 July 1982, *Eckle* A 51; (1982) 5 EHRR 1, p 33.

250 See, eg, *X v UK* (1982) 5 EHRR 273 (appointment of a legal aid lawyer was found to fall outside Art 6).

with.[251] In *Campbell and Fell v UK*,[252] the Court had to consider whether prison discipline could fall within Art 6(1) as the determination of a criminal charge. The applicants, prisoners, were sentenced to a substantial loss of remission. This was such a serious consequence that the procedure in question could be considered as of a criminal character, but the Court considered that not all disciplinary offences in prison which in fact had an equivalent in the ordinary criminal law would be treated as of a criminal character. In general, disciplinary offences will not be viewed as criminal since they are a matter of concern to the particular profession, not a matter regulated by the law in general.[253]

'Regulatory' offences are also, in general, viewed as matters that relate to a specific group rather than to persons in general.[254] But, classification of a petty offence as 'regulatory' rather than criminal will not be decisive for Art 6(1) purposes; Strasbourg may yet determine that the offence is of a criminal character.[255] Otherwise, by reclassifying offences, the State in question could minimise the application of the Convention.

The term 'civil rights and obligations' also has an autonomous Convention meaning and therefore cannot merely be assigned the meaning of 'private' as understood in UK administrative law. Thus, the meaning of 'civil rights and obligations' does not depend upon the legal classification afforded the right or obligation in question by the national legislator; the question is whether the content and effect of the right or obligation (taking into account the legal systems of all the contracting States) allows the meaning 'civil right' or 'civil obligation' to be assigned to it.[256] This wide provision allows challenge to decisions taken in the absence of legal procedures in a disparate range of circumstances.[257] The civil right must have some legal basis as established in the State in question, but assuming that there is such a basis, Art 6 may apply to immunities or procedural constraints preventing the bringing of claims to court.[258]

In *Tinnelly v UK*,[259] the Court found that a clearly defined statutory right aimed at freedom from discrimination should be viewed as a civil right. Strasbourg may be moving towards a position in which 'all those rights which are individual rights under the national legal system and fall into the sphere of general freedom ... must be seen as civil rights'.[260] Clearly, this question remains a problematic one. It is clear that the must be a dispute between the parties, but the extent to which this is the case is not entirely settled. In *Fayed v UK*[261] it was found that although, strictly, there was no legal basis for

---

251 *Campbell and Fell*, Judgment of 28 June 1984, A 80; (1985) 7 EHRR 165; *Garyfallou AEBE v Greece* (1999) 28 EHRR 344, para 33; *Lauko v Slovakia* [1999] EHRLR 105, para 56.

252 Above, fn 251.

253 *Wickramsinghe v UK* [1998] EHRLR 338.

254 See *X v UK* (1998) 25 EHRR CD 88.

255 *Özturk*, Judgment of 21 February 1983, A 73; (1984) 6 EHRR 409.

256 Judgment of 16 July 1971, *Ringeisen v Austria*, A 13, p 39; (1971) 1 EHRR 455.

257 Eg, *O v UK* (1987) 10 EHRR 82 concerned a decision to terminate access to a child in care although no legal procedure was in place allowing consideration of its merits.

258 See *Osman v UK* (1998) 5 BHRC 293; *Fayed v UK* (1994) 18 EHRR 393.

259 (1998) 27 EHRR 249.

260 *Bentham v UK*, B 80, para 10 (1983), dissenting opinions of Mr Melchior and Mr Frowen.

261 (1994) 18 EHRR 393.

the action and so no dispute to trigger Art 6, Art 6 applied to blanket immunities preventing access to a court.

A right of access to a court

Besides the procedural guarantees, Art 6(1) has been found to provide, impliedly, a right of access to a court whether the domestic legal system allows access to a court in a particular case or not. The right is not absolute, but restrictions must not impair the essence of the right.[262] Restrictions must have a legitimate aim and be proportionate to the aim pursued. The test is, therefore, the same as that used in respect of that under para 2 of Arts 8–11.[263] In *Osman v UK*[264] the Court found, controversially, that the immunity of the police from actions in negligence breached this right of access to a court.[265] Other public policy based immunities have subsequently been found not to breach this right,[266] in pursuit of what may arguably be termed a retreat from *Osman*, and not all other constraints will do so.[267]

Once it has been determined that a particular instance falls within Art 6(1), it must be determined whether the claim in question is covered by the right of access to a court. It seems that, for example, Art 6(1) does not confer a right of appeal to a higher court.[268] It may include access to legal advice and, by implication, legal aid. These issues arise in relation both to access to a court hearing and the *fairness* of the hearing. In the very significant decision in *Golder*,[269] it was found that a refusal to allow a detainee to correspond with his legal advisor would be contrary to Art 6(1), since in preventing him even initiating proceedings, it hindered his right of access to a court. In other words, the right of access to a court must be an *effective* one.

Access to legal advice in order to obtain access to a court may not always imply a right to legal aid. The circumstances in which it will do so were considered in *Granger v UK*.[270] The applicant had been refused legal aid and so did not have counsel at appeal; he only had notes from his solicitor which he read out, but clearly did not understand. In particular, there was one especially complex ground of appeal which he was unable to deal with. In view of the complexity of the appeal and his inability to deal with it, legal aid should have been granted. It was found that paras 6(1) and 6(3)(c) should be read together and, if it would be apparent to an objective observer that a fair hearing could not take place without legal advice, then both would be violated. *Granger* was concerned with

---

262 *Tinnelly and McElduff v UK* (1998) 27 EHRR 249; *Fayed v UK* (1994) 18 EHRR 393.

263 See *Fayed v UK* (1994) 18 EHRR 393, para 67. See below, pp 66–67.

264 (1998) 5 BHRC 293.

265 The decision was severely criticised by Lord Browne-Wilkinson in *Barrett v Enfield London LBC* [1999] 3 All ER 193 on the ground that there was no immunity, but in fact no right to make a claim at all. See also the criticisms of Lord Hoffman in 'Human rights and the House of Lords' (1999) 62 MLR 159.

266 See *Z and Others v UK*, App 28945/95 (2001) *The Times*, 31 May; the case resulted from a decision of the House of Lords in *X v Bedfordshire CC* [1995] 2 AC 633 that P could not bring an action in negligence against the local authority.

267 In *Fayed v UK* (1994) 18 EHRR 393, the Court found that a limitation on the ability of the applicants to take legal proceedings to challenge the findings of a governmental inquiry into the applicants' business affairs did not constitute an unjustified denial of access to a court.

268 *Belgian Linguistic* cases, Judgment of 23 July 1968, A 6; (1968) 1 EHRR 252.

269 Judgment of 21 February 1975, A 18.

270 Judgment of 28 March 1990, A 174.

the fairness of the hearing rather than with the ability to obtain access to a court at all. However, in some instances, a person unable to obtain legal aid would be unable to obtain legal advice and therefore might be unable to initiate proceedings. In such instances, access to a court would be the main issue.[271] But, in civil proceedings, legal aid is not fully guaranteed, as it is in Art 6(3); circumstances have been accepted in which legal aid can be denied.[272]

An independent and impartial tribunal established by law

All courts and tribunals falling within Art 6 must meet this requirement. The tribunal must be established by law[273] and be independent of the executive.[274] Factors to be taken into account will include the appointment of its members, their terms of office, and guarantees against outside influence.[275] Impartiality is judged both subjectively and objectively.[276] In other words, actual bias must be shown, but also the existence of guarantees against bias.[277] The decision in *McGonnell v UK*[278] left open the question whether a judge having both legislative and executive functions could be viewed as independent and impartial. In a number of cases against the UK, military discipline as exercised by way of courts- martial has not been found to satisfy the requirement of impartiality.[279]

Hearing within a reasonable time

The hearing must take place within a reasonable time. These are the same words as are used in Art 5(3), but here, the point is to put an end to the insecurity of the applicant who is uncertain of the outcome of the civil action or charge against him or her rather than with the deprivation of liberty.[280] Thus, the ending point comes when the uncertainty is resolved either at the court of highest instance or by expiry of the time limit for appeal. In determining what is meant by 'reasonable', fairly wide time limits have been applied so that in some circumstances, as much as seven or eight[281] years may be reasonable. The Court has approved a period of nearly five years[282] and the Commission a period of seven and a half.[283] It will take into account the conduct of the accused (which may have

---

271 See *Airey v Ireland* (1979) 2 EHRR 305; *Aerts v Belgium* [1998] EHRLR 777.

272 In *Andronicou and Constantinou v Cyprus* (1998) 25 EHRR 491 it was found that *ex gratia* assistance was sufficient.

273 *Zand v Austria* (1978) 15 DR 70 (this means law emanating from Parliament, although aspects of the judicial organisation may be delegated to the executive).

274 *Benthem v Netherlands* (1985) 8 EHRR 1.

275 *Bryan v UK* (1995) 21 EHRR 342.

276 *Fey v Austria* (1993) 16 EHRR 387; *Pullar v UK* (1996) 22 EHRR 391.

277 *Remli v France* (1996) 22 EHRR 253.

278 (2000) 8 BHRC 56.

279 See *Findlay v UK* (1997) 24 EHRR 221; *Hood v UK* (2000) 29 EHRR 365, Judgment of 25.2.97; see also *Coyne v UK*, Judgment of 24.10.97, RJD 1997-V 1842; *Cable and Others v UK*, App No 24436/94 (1999) *The Times*, 11 March.

280 See, generally, Van Dijk and Van Hoof, *op cit*, fn 1, pp 446–47.

281 In *Vernillo v France* 12 HRLJ 199, seven and a half years in respect of civil proceedings was not found too long owing to the special responsibilities of the parties.

282 *Buchholz*, Judgment of 6 May 1981, A 42.

283 Report, 12 July 1977, in *Haase* D & R 11 (1978), p 78.

contributed to the delay) and the need for proper preparation of the case, bearing in mind any special circumstances such as those which might arise in child care cases. In order to determine how long the delay has been, the point from which time will run must be identified. In criminal cases, it will be 'the stage at which the situation of the person concerned has been substantially affected as a result of a suspicion against him'.[284] In civil cases, it will be the moment when the proceedings concerned are initiated, not including pre-trial negotiations.[285]

Other aspects of fairness

Apart from access to legal advice and the other minimal guarantees of Art 6(3), what other rights are implied by the term a 'fair hearing'? It has been found to connote equality between the parties,[286] and in principle, entails the right of the parties to be present in person,[287] although criminal trial *in absentia* does not automatically violate Art 6: the right can be waived[288] and does not normally extend to appeals.[289] The hearing should be adversarial[290] in the sense that both parties are given an opportunity to comment on all the evidence that is adduced.[291] A refusal to summon a witness may constitute unfairness,[292] as may a failure to disclose evidence.[293] The court must give a reasoned judgment.[294] These and further significant aspects of fairness are discussed further at relevant points in the following chapters, especially Chapter 14.[295]

Article 6(2): The presumption of innocence in criminal cases

Paragraph 2 'requires *inter alia* that when carrying out their duties, members of a court should not start with the preconceived idea that the accused has committed the offence charged; the burden of proof is on the prosecution and any doubt should benefit the accused. It also follows that it is for the prosecution to inform the accused of the case that will be made against him so that he may prepare and present his defence accordingly and to adduce evidence sufficient to convict him.'[296] It follows from the presumption of innocence that the court must base its conviction exclusively on evidence put forward at trial.[297] Thus, a conviction based on written statements which were inadmissible

---

284 *Neumeister*, Judgment of 27 June 1968; (1979–80) 1 EHRR 91.

285 Report of 7 March 1984, *Lithgow v UK*, A 102 (1986) p 120; (1986) 8 EHRR 335.

286 *Neumeister*, Judgment of 27 June 1968; (1979–80) 1 EHRR 91; *De Haes and Gijsels v Belgium* (1997) 25 EHRR 1.

287 *Colloza v Italy*, Judgment of 12 February 1985, A 89 (1985); *Zana v Turkey* (1998) 4 BHRC 242.

288 *Colloza v Italy*, Judgment of 12 February 1985, A 89 (1985).

289 *Ekbatani v Sweden* (1988) 13 EHRR 504, cf *Monnell and Morris v UK* (1987) 10 EHRR 205.

290 *Ruiz-Mateos v Spain* (1993) 16 EHRR 505.

291 *Mantovanelli v France* (1997) 24 EHRR 370.

292 *X v Austria* Appl No 5362/72, Coll 42 (1973), p 145.

293 *Edwards v UK* (1992) 15 EHRR 417 (it was found that the hearing in the Court of Appeal remedied this failure). In *Rowe and Davis v UK* (2000) 30 EHRR 1, the failure of the prosecution to make an application to the trial judge to withhold material caused a breach of Art 6. Review of the material later by the Court of Appeal could not remedy the breach.

294 *Hadjianastassiou v Greece* (1992) 16 EHRR 219, para 33.

295 See pp 900–06. Also, for further discussion, see Ashworth, A, 'Article 6 and the fairness of trials' [1999] Crim LR 261.

296 Judgment of 6 December 1988, *Barbéra, Messegué and Jabardo*, A 14 6(2) (1989) p 33. See also *Salabiaku v France* (1988) 13 EHRR 379.

297 *X v Federal Republic of Germany* D & R 17 (1980), p 231.

breached para 6(2).[298] This provision is very closely related to the impartiality provision of para 6(1).

The expectation that the State bears the burden of establishing guilt requires that the accused should not be expected to provide involuntary assistance by way of a confession. Thus, the presumption of innocence under para 6(2) is closely linked to the right to freedom from self-incrimination which the Court has found to be covered by the right to a fair hearing under para 6(1) (*Funke v France*).[299] In *Murray (John) v UK*,[300] on the other hand, the Commission did not find that para 6(1) had been breached where inferences had been drawn at trial from the applicant's refusal to give evidence. The Court also found no breach of Art 6 due to such drawing of inferences in the particular circumstances of the case, taking into account the fact that 'the right to silence' could not be treated as absolute, the degree of compulsion exerted on the applicant and the weight of the evidence against him.[301] However, the Court did find that Art 6(1) had been breached by the denial of access to a lawyer since such access was essential where there was a likelihood that adverse inferences would be drawn from silence. In *Saunders v UK*,[302] the Commission found that the applicant's right to freedom from self-incrimination had been infringed in that he had been forced to answer questions put to him by inspectors investigating a company takeover or risk the imposition of a criminal sanction. The ruling of the Court was to the same effect, taking into account the special compulsive regime in question for Department of Trade and Industry inspections.[303]

*Sub-paragraphs 6(3)(a), (b) and (c): time, facilities and
legal representation in criminal cases*

These sub-paragraphs are closely related due to the word 'facilities' used in sub-para (b). Sub-paragraphs (b) and (c) may often be invoked together: (c) in respect of the assignment of a lawyer, and (b) in respect of the time allowed for such assignment. It is not enough that a lawyer should be assigned; he or she should be appointed in good time in order to give time to prepare the defence and familiarise herself or himself with the case.[304] Both sub-paragraphs also arise in relation to notification of the right of access to legal advice and it has been held that an oral translation of the requisite information is insufficient.[305] As has already been noted in relation to *Granger*, the legal advice provisions must be read in conjunction with the right to a fair trial. A lawyer must be assigned if, otherwise, an objective observer would consider that a fair hearing would not occur. In *Poitrimol v France*[306] the Court stated: 'Although not absolute, the right ... to be effectively defended by a lawyer, assigned officially if need be, is one of the fundamental features of a fair trial.' In furtherance of the notion of providing effective legal

---

298 *Barbéra* [1987] 3 All ER 411.

299 (1993) 16 EHRR 297.

300 (1996) 22 EHRR 29. For comment, see *Munday, R* [1996] Crim LR 370.

301 *Murray (John) v UK* (1996) 22 EHRR 29. See also *Averill v UK* (2001) 31 EHRR 36.

302 No 19187/91 Com Rep paras 69–75.

303 *Saunders v UK* (1997) 23 EHRR 313. See further Chapter 13, p 855.

304 *X and Y v Austria* Appl 7909/74; 15 D & R 160 (1979).

305 *Kamasinski*, Report of 5 May 1988, para 138; (1991) 13 EHRR 36.

306 (1993) A 277-A; (1993) 18 EHRR 130.

representation, it has been found that para 6(3)(c) does not merely import a right to have legal assistance, but rather it includes three rights:[307]

(a) to have recourse, if desired, to legal assistance;

(b) to choose that assistance;

(c) if the defendant has insufficient means to pay, for that assistance to be given it free if the interest of justice so require.[308]

6(3)(d): Cross-examination in criminal cases

The Strasbourg case law has left a wide discretion to the national court[309] as to the interpretation of the first limb of para 6(3)(d) – the right to cross-examine witnesses – and so has deprived this right of some of its effect. This right would seem to be specific and unambiguous in its guarantee that witnesses against the defendant must be at the public hearing if their evidence is to be relied on. It would therefore seem to outlaw hearsay evidence. The Court has, however, shrunk at times from a straightforward assertion that this is the case.[310] The second limb – the right to call witnesses and have them examined under the same conditions as witnesses for the other side – obviously allows for a wide discretion as it only requires that the prosecution and defence should be treated equally as regards summoning witnesses.[311] So, conditions and restrictions can be set so long as they apply equally to both sides. This provision relates to the concept of creating equality between parties; it is closely related to the fair hearing principle and therefore, will apply in civil cases too.

Art 6 is considered at various points in this book, and extensively in Chapters 13 and 14, especially in relation to its impact on pre-trial procedures.

Article 7: Freedom from retrospective effect of penal legislation

(1) No one shall be held guilty of any criminal offence on account of any act or omission which did not constitute a criminal offence under national or international law at the time when it was committed. Nor shall a heavier penalty be imposed than the one that was applicable at the time the criminal offence was committed.

(2) This Article shall not prejudice the trial and punishment of any person for any act or omission which, at the time when it was committed, was criminal according to the general principles of law recognised by civilised nations.

---

307 From *Golder*, Judgment of 21 February 1975, A 18; see also *Silver v UK*, Judgment of 25 March 1983, A 61, (1983) 5 EHRR 347.

308 *Pakelli*, Judgment of 25 April 1983, A 64.

309 See, eg, *Asch v Austria* (1991) 15 EHRR 597.

310 Such an assertion was made in *Kostovski v Netherlands* (1989) 12 EHRR 434 and *Windisch v Austria* (1990) 13 EHRR 281. However, these decisions were not followed in *Isgro v Italy* (1991) Case 1/1990/192/252. For further discussion of this right, see [1993] Crim LR 261–67.

311 Appl 4428/70, *X v Austria* (1972) Yearbook XV, p 264.

Article 7 contains an important principle and it is, therefore, non-derogable, although it is subject to the single exception contained in para 2. It divides into two separate principles:

(a) the law in question must have existed at the time of the act in question for the conviction to be based on it;

(b) no heavier penalty for the infringement of the law may be imposed than was in force at the time the act was committed.

As far as the first principle is concerned, this also means that an existing part of the criminal law cannot be applied by analogy to acts it was not intended for.[312] Allowing such extension would fall foul of the general principle that the law must be unambiguous, which is part of the principle that someone should not be convicted if he or she could not have known beforehand that the act in question was criminal. In order to determine whether these requirements have been met, the Strasbourg authorities are prepared to interpret domestic law,[313] although normally they would not be prepared to do so. Although it will be cautious in this respect, the Commission must take note of an allegedly false interpretation of domestic law. *Harman v UK*[314] concerned unforeseeable liability for contempt of court. It had not previously been considered to be contempt if confidential documents were shown to a journalist after being read out in court. The Commission declared the application admissible, but meanwhile a friendly settlement was reached.

Article 7 was found to have been breached in *Welch v UK*.[315] Before the trial of the applicant for drug offences, a new provision came into force under the Drug Trafficking Offences Act 1986, making provision for confiscation orders. This was imposed on the applicant, although the legislation was not in force at the time when he committed the offences in question. It clearly had retrospective effect and was found to constitute a 'penalty' within Art 7(1). In *SW v UK and C v UK*[316] the applicants claimed that marital rape had been retrospectively outlawed and that therefore, their criminalisation for forced sexual intercourse with their wives created a breach of Art 7. Their convictions were based on the ruling of the House of Lords in *R*,[317] which removed the marital exemption. The Court found that the anticipated reform of the law undertaken in R was almost inevitable and that therefore, the applicants should have foreseen that their conduct would be found to be criminal. Thus, no breach of Art 7 was found.

Paragraph 7(2) provides an exception which appears to arise if a person is convicted retrospectively for an offence recognised in other countries, but not the one in question at the material time. This exception is potentially quite wide; it is not restricted to war crimes and could cover any deeply immoral conduct generally recognised as criminal in national laws.[318] The law in civilised countries which are not Member States can be taken into account in determining the applicability of the exception.

---

312 Appl 1852/63, *X v Austria* (1965) Yearbook VIII.

313 This was determined in *X v Austria*, above, fn 312.

314 Appl 10038/82; Decision of 11 May 1984; 38 D & R 53 (1984).

315 A 307-A; (1995) 20 EHRR 247.

316 (1995) 21 EHRR 404. For comment on the ruling, see Osborne, C (1996) 4 EHRR 406.

317 [1991] 4 All ER 481; [1991] 3 WLR 767; [1992] Fam Law 108; [1992] Crim LR 207, HL.

318 See, generally, Beddard, 'The rights of the criminal under Article 7 ECHR' (1996) ELR 3.

General restrictions on the rights and freedoms contained in Arts 8–11

These Articles have a second paragraph enumerating certain restrictions on the primary right. The interests covered by the restrictions are largely the same: national security, protection of morals, the rights of others, public safety. As indicated above, the State is allowed a 'margin of appreciation' – a degree of discretion – as to the measures needed to protect the particular interest.[319]

To be justified, State interference with Arts 8–11 guarantees must be prescribed by law, have a legitimate aim, be necessary in a democratic society and be applied in a non-discriminatory fashion. In most cases under these Articles, Strasbourg's main concern has been with the 'necessary in a democratic society' requirement; the notion of 'prescribed by law' has been focused upon to some extent, but always with the result that it has been found to be satisfied. The 'legitimate aim' requirement will normally be readily satisfied; as Harris, O'Boyle and Warbrick point out, the grounds for interference are so wide that 'the State can usually make a plausible case that it did have a good reason for interfering with the right'.[320] The provision against non-discrimination arises under Art 14 and it is potentially very significant.[321]

The 'prescribed by law' requirement means that the restriction must be in accordance with a rule of national law which satisfies the Convention meaning of 'law'. Also, the law on which the restriction is based is aimed at protecting one of the interests listed in para 2; in other words, the restriction falls within one of the exceptions. Interpreting 'prescribed by law' in *Sunday Times v UK*,[322] the European Court of Human Rights found that 'the law must be adequately accessible' and 'a norm cannot be regarded as a "law" unless it is formulated with sufficient precision to enable the citizen to regulate his conduct'. This finding has been flexibly applied; for example, in *Rai, Allmond and 'Negotiate Now' v UK*,[323] the Commission had to consider the ban on public demonstrations or meetings concerning Northern Ireland in Trafalgar Square. The ban was the subject of a statement in the House of Commons and many refusals of demonstrations had been made subsequent to it. The Commission found that the ban was sufficiently prescribed by law: 'It is compatible with the requirements of foreseeability that terms which are on their face general and unlimited are explained by executive or administrative statements, since it is the provision of sufficiently precise guidance to individuals ... rather than the source of that guidance which is of relevance.'[324] In *Steel and Others v UK*[325] the Commission introduced a very significant qualification: 'The level of precision required depends to a considerable degree on the content of the instrument, the field it is designed to cover, and

---

319 See above, pp 34–37.
320 *Law of the European Convention on Human Rights*, 1995, p 290.
321 See below, pp 85–86.
322 A 30, para 49 (1979).
323 81-A D & R 46 (1995).
324 *Ibid*, p 152. The power in question arose from the Trafalgar Square Regulations 1952 SI 1952/776 para 3 made under the Parks Regulation (Amendment) Act 1926. The Act allowed the Secretary of State to 'make any regulations considered necessary ... for the preservation of order ...' in the parks.
325 (1998) 28 EHRR 603.

the number and status of those to whom it is addressed'.[326] Although the term 'margin of appreciation' was not used, this finding appears to allow the Member State a certain leeway in relation to the 'prescribed by law' requirement.

The Court has interpreted 'necessary in a democratic society' as meaning that: 'an interference corresponds to a pressing social need and, in particular, that it is proportionate to the legitimate aim pursued'.[327] Thus, in the particular instance, it can be said that the interference is necessary in the sense that it is concerned with a particular restriction such as the protection of morals, and in the particular case, there is a real need to protect morals – a pressing social need – as opposed to an unclear or weak danger to morals. Further, the interference is in proportion to the aim pursued; in other words, it does not go further than is needed, bearing in mind the objective in question.

But, the doctrine of proportionality is strongly linked to the principle of the margin of appreciation: the Court has stated that the role of the Convention in protecting human rights is subsidiary to the role of the national legal system[328] and that since the State is better placed than the international judge to balance individual rights against general societal interests, Strasbourg will operate a restrained review of the balance struck. The notion of a margin of appreciation conceded to States permeates the Art 8(2), 9(2), 10(2) and 11(2) jurisprudence, although it has not influenced the interpretation of the substantive rights.

Art 8: Right to respect for privacy

(1) Everyone has the right to respect for his private and family life, his home and his correspondence.

(2) There shall be no interference by a public authority with the exercise of this right except such as is in accordance with the law and is necessary in a democratic society in the interests of national security, public safety or the economic well-being of the country, for the prevention of disorder or crime, for the protection of health or morals or for the protection of the rights and freedoms of others.

Article 8 seems to cover four different areas, suggesting that, for example, private life can be distinguished from family life. However, the case law suggests that these rights usually need not be clearly distinguished from each other.[329] There will tend to be a clear overlap between them; for example, it is often unnecessary to define 'family', because the factual situation might so obviously fall within the term 'private'. The inclusion of the wide (and undefined) term 'private' means that rights other than those arising from the home, family life and correspondence may fall within Art 8.

It should be noted that Art 8 only provides right to respect for private life, etc. Thus, the extent of the respect required can vary to an extent in view of the various practices in the different States. In contrast to Art 10, finding that a claim is covered by para 1 is not a

---

326 Paragraph 145. The Commission based these findings on the judgments of the Court in *Chorherr v Austria* Series A 266-B, para 23 (1993) and in *Cantoni v France*, para 35 (1996) (not yet published).

327 *Olsson v Sweden*, A 130, para 67 (1988).

328 *Handyside v UK*, A 24, para 48 (1976).

329 In *Mialhe v France* (1993) 16 EHRR 332 it was made clear that the four aspects of private life tend to constitute overlapping concepts.

simple matter: attention cannot merely focus on the exceptions. The negative obligation – to refrain from interference – is central,[330] but a number of requirements to take positive action have been accommodated within Art 8. Clayton and Tomlinson posit a number of different forms of such positive action.[331] The first arises where the applicant suffers from State inaction.[332] In *McGinley and Egan v UK*,[333] the Government was engaging in activities inherently dangerous to the health of the applicant. It was found that Art 8 requires that effective procedures should be in place to ensure that all the relevant information was made available.

Secondly, the State may be found to be under a duty to act positively to prevent an interference with the Art 8 guarantees by another private individual. The pollution cases mentioned below[334] provide examples in which it was found that the State had a duty to act to prevent or curb the pollution and to ensure that information regarding the dangers was available. Thirdly, the positive obligation may require a positive act by private persons.[335] The question of the extent to which positive obligations are recognised under Art 8 is pursued further in this book, especially in Chapter 10.[336]

But clearly, there will be limitations. In *Botta v Italy*,[337] it was found that although a positive obligation might arise in the circumstances, a fair balance had to be struck: the obligations did not extend to providing a disabled person with access to the beach and sea distant from a holiday residence. In *Barreto v Portugal*,[338] no breach was found where each family was not provided with its own home or where a landlord could not recover the possession of rented accommodation.

Respect for private life

In *Niemietz v Germany*,[339] the Court said: 'It would be too restrictive to limit the notion [of private life] to an "inner circle" in which the individual may live his own personal life as he chooses and to exclude therefrom entirely the outside world not encompassed within that circle. Respect for private life must also comprise to a certain degree the right to establish and develop relationships with other human beings.' As Harris, O'Boyle and Warbrick observe: 'this extends the concept of private life beyond the narrower confines of the Anglo-American idea of privacy, with its emphasis on the secrecy of personal

---

330 See, eg, *Gul v Switzerland* (1996) 22 EHRR 93, para 38.

331 *The Law of Human Rights*, 2000, pp 822–24.

332 The transsexual cases in which applicants have argued that they should be allowed to have their birth certificates changed to indicate their current gender (discussed in Chapter 12, pp 743–44) provide an example; those against the UK have failed. The finding of a breach in *B v France* (1992) 16 EHRR 1 occurred since the Court took into account the fact that the applicant was likely to be asked to reveal her birth certificate more often than in the UK.

333 (1998) 27 EHRR 1.

334 See the cases of *Guerra v Italy* (1998) 26 EHRR 375 and *Lopez Ostra*, (1994) 20 EHRR.

335 In *Hokkanen v Finland* (1994) 19 EHRLR 139 it was found that a private data collection firm must grant access to its records.

336 See p 538–541.

337 (1998) 26 EHRR 241.

338 (1996) 26 EHRLR 214.

339 (1992) 16 EHRR 97, A 251-B, para 29 (1992).

information and seclusion.'[340] Thus, 'private life' appears to encompass a widening range of protected interests, but this development has been accompanied by a reluctance of the Court to insist on a narrow margin of appreciation when considering what is demanded of States by the notions of 'respect' for private life and by the necessity of interferences with privacy.

Respect for the privacy of personal information clearly falls within the notion of private life, but the Court has approached this aspect cautiously, tending to be satisfied if a procedure is in place allowing the interest in such control to be weighed up against a competing interest. Thus, in *Gaskin v UK*,[341] the interest of the applicant in obtaining access to the files relating to his childhood in care had to be weighed up against the interest of the contributors to it in maintaining confidentiality, because this interference with privacy had a legitimate aim under the 'rights of others' exception. It was held that the responsible authority did not have a procedure available for weighing the two. Consequently, the procedure automatically preferred the contributors and that was disproportionate to the aim of protecting confidentiality and therefore could not be 'necessary in a democratic society'.

The opposite result was reached, but by a similar route, in *Klass v FRG*,[342] brought in respect of telephone tapping. It was found that although telephone tapping constituted an interference with a person's private life, it could be justified as being in the interests of national security and there were sufficient controls in place (permission had to be given by a minister applying certain criteria including that of 'reasonable suspicion') to ensure that the power was not abused. In the similar *Malone* case,[343] however, there were no such controls in place and a breach of Art 8 was therefore found, which led to the introduction of the Interception of Communications Act 1985. A similar path was followed in *Leander v Sweden*[344] in respect of a complaint that information about the applicant had been stored on a secret police register for national security purposes and released to the navy so that it could vet persons who might be subversive. The applicant complained that he had had no opportunity of challenging the information, but the Court found that as there were remedies in place, albeit of a limited nature, to address such grievances, Art 8 had not been breached because the national security exception could apply. Again, in *Harman and Hewitt v UK*[345] a breach of Art 8 was found as there was no means of challenging the secret directive which had allowed the storage of information on the applicants. In *Murray v UK*,[346] the taking of a photo of the applicant after arrest at an army centre was found to constitute an interference with her Art 8 right to respect for her private life. The notion that personal information should remain private even outside obviously private spaces was strongly indicated in *Niemietz v Germany*.[347]

---

340 *Law of the European Convention on Human Rights*, 1995, p 304.

341 (1990) 12 EHRR 36.

342 (1978) 2 EHRR 214; see also *Ludi v Switzerland* (1993) 15 EHRR 173.

343 Report of 17 December 1982, A 82; (1984) 7 EHRR 14. See below, pp 670–71.

344 Judgment of 26 March 1987, A 116; (1987) 9 EHRR 443. See also to similar effect *Ebchester v UK* (1993) 18 EHRR CD 72.

345 (1992) 14 EHRR 657.

346 (1994) 19 EHRR 193; cf *Friedl v Austria* (1995) 21 EHRR 83.

347 (1992) 16 EHRR 97. The case concerned a search of a lawyer's office.

Protection for personal information may be regarded as part of the 'core' of the concept of privacy, but as the Court has made clear in a number of decisions, aspects of relations with others will also fall within the concept. The Court has made it clear that the choice to have sexual relations with others falls within Art 8. In this sphere, is it suggested that the Court has gradually abandoned its initially cautious approach. In *Dudgeon*,[348] the Northern Ireland prohibition of homosexual intercourse was found to breach Art 8: clearly, there had been an interference with privacy; the question was whether the interference was necessary in order to protect morals. It was found unnecessary since the prohibition had not in fact been used in recent times and no detriment to morals had apparently resulted. Northern Ireland amended the relevant legislation in consequence,[349] allowing intercourse between consenting males over 21. However, this case concerned a gross interference with privacy since it allowed the applicant no means at all of expressing his sexual preference without committing a criminal offence. In 1984,[350] the Commission declared inadmissible an application challenging s 66 of the Army Act 1955, which governs conviction for homosexual practices in the armed forces, on the basis that it could be justified under the prevention of disorder or protection of morals clauses.[351] This stance has now been abandoned, and the Court has taken a much more interventionist stance in relation to the sexual autonomy of homosexuals.[352]

Respect for the home

In this area, the Strasbourg authorities have adopted a cautious attitude and tend to practise only marginal review of the justification of restrictions. At the core of the right to respect for the home is the right to occupy the home and a right not to be expelled from it. Thus, a violation of Art 8 was established in *Cyprus v Turkey*[353] which concerned occupying forces expelling citizens and making their return to their homes impossible. This was a very clear violation of the right. A contrasting result was reached in *Buckley v UK*.[354] A gipsy, who had lived in her home for five years without planning permission, was still entitled to respect for her home – the concept was not found only to cover homes lawfully established. However, no violation of this right was found where planning permission for retaining the applicant's caravan on her own land was refused. The refusal was partly based on the planning authority's policy in controlling the sites on which gipsies could live. The Court found that a wide margin of appreciation should be allowed

---

348 Judgment of 22 October 1981, A 45; (1982) 4 EHRR 149.

349 Homosexual Offences (Northern Ireland) Order 1982. See also *Norris v Ireland* (1991) 13 EHRR 186 which followed *Dudgeon*.

350 *B v UK* 34 D & R 68 (1983); (1983) 6 EHRR 354; A 9237/81.

351 The charges had involved a soldier under 21. Note that the Select Committee on the Armed Forces Bill 1990–91 recommended that s 66 should be replaced (para 41, p xiv). See, now, *Smith and Grady v UK* (2000) 29 EHRR 493 in which it was found that the ban breached Art 8. The ban is no longer being applied; see Chapter 16, pp 1056–57.

352 See Chapter 16, pp 1056–57 for discussion of *Lustig-Prean v UK* (1999) 29 EHRR 548 in which it was found that the army ban breached Art 8 (see also Chapter 12, pp 738–41); and *Sutherland v UK*, App No 25186/94 [1997] EHRLR 117, in which an application regarding the age of consent for homosexual relations (8.9.1999) was postponed since the Government assured the Commission that the Sexual Offences (Amendment) Bill would proceed equalising the age of consent (see, now, Sexual Offences (Amendment) Act 2000 s 1).

353 (1976) 3 EHRR 482.

354 (1997) 23 EHRR 101.

to the Member State and that such margin had not been exceeded since pro
safeguards were in place which allowed for the weighing up of the interests involv
interest of the applicant in her traditional lifestyle in a caravan and the interest of the
planning authority in regulating the use of the land in the area for the benefit of the local
community.

So, the concept of the home is quite broad, although it does not cover a future home
which is not yet built.[355] Further, the right to respect for the home does not include a right
to a home; nor does it extend to providing a decent home,[356] nor to providing alternative
accommodation.[357] Interference can arise due to a direct interference such as a seizure
order,[358] or to the use of a Compulsory Purchase Order threatening the actual home.[359]

The concept does not cover merely proprietorial rights; it includes the ability to live
freely in the home and enjoy the home.[360] The peaceful enjoyment of the home is
established as an aspect of respect of the home,[361] and this notion has been extended to
cover various forms of interference with the enjoyment of the home, such as pollution by
traffic fumes on the basis that the right implies that the home is private space to be
enjoyed free from the covert or overt blight of pollution. A number of cases have
concerned noise pollution. In *Powell v UK*,[362] a claim in respect of airport noise was
rejected on the basis that a fair balance had to be struck between the interests of the
individual and of the community. In *Lopez Ostra v Spain*,[363] a breach of Art 8 was found
after considering the fair balance to be struck, in respect of a failure to prevent a waste
treatment plant releasing fumes and smells. Failure to prevent the risk of serious
pollution was also found to breach Art 8 in *Guerra v Italy*.[364] Where applications in such
instances fail under Art 8 owing to the caution evinced in Strasbourg when dealing with
this substantive right, they may succeed under Art 6(1) if the procedure allowing
challenge to such interference is non-existent or defective.[365]

Correspondence

The case law in this area has concerned the right of a detainee to correspond with the
outside world and, in the UK, has led to a steady relaxation of the rules relating to
preventing, stopping and censoring of prisoners' correspondence.[366] In general, the
supervision *per se* of prisoners' letters is not in breach of Art 8, but particular instances,
such as stopping a purely personal letter, may be.[367] It does not have to be personal: in

---

355 *Loizidou v Turkey* (1996) 23 EHRR 513.

356 *X v Germany* (1956) 1 YB 202.

357 *Burton v UK* (1996) 22 EHRR 135 CD.

358 *Chappel v UK* (1989) 12 EHRR 1.

359 *Howard v UK* (1987) 52 DR 198.

360 *Howard v UK* (1987) 52 DR 198.

361 *Arrondelle v UK*, No 7889/77; 26 D & R 5 (1982).

362 (1990) 12 EHRR 355. See also *Baggs v UK* (1987) 52 DR 29.

363 (1994) 20 EHRR; for comment, see Sands, 'Human rights, the environment and the *Lopez Ostra* case'
[1996] EHRLR 597.

364 (1998) 26 EHRR 375.

365 See, eg, *Zimmermann and Steiner v Switzerland* (1983) 6 EHRR 17.

366 See, eg, *Silver v UK*, Judgment of 25 March 1983, A 61; (1983) 5 EHRR 347.

367 *Boyle and Rice*, Judgment of 27 April 1988, A 131.

Campbell v UK,[368] correspondence with the applicant's solicitor was read; that was a restriction on correspondence that amounted to a breach of Art 8. Supervision of correspondence during detention to an extent has also been found to breach Art 8.[369] It should be noted that an Art 10 issue may also arise in such circumstances since the detainee's right to receive or impart information is affected.[370] Searches and seizures fall within the head of 'correspondence' and, indeed, within all the rights except the right to respect for family life.[371]

Exceptions and justification under Art 8(2)

There must be an *interference* by the public authorities. But, as the discussion above indicates, this can include the failure to carry out a positive obligation. In the absence of a positive obligation, however, a failure to act would not constitute an interference.[372] Where an interference occurs, proper safeguards must be in place to protect individuals from arbitrary interfere; there must be a legal framework which satisfies the 'in accordance with the law' test and strict limits must be placed on the power conferred.[373] Where very intimate aspects of private life are involved, very particular reasons for the interference must be adduced.[374]

If the exception in respect of national security is invoked, the State may find that is relatively easy to justify the interference.[375] But where interferences, such as searches or surveillance, occur in respect of criminal activity, a higher standard will be required. Thus, judicial authorisation of searches or surveillance may be required.[376] Where a grave invasion of privacy has occurred, judicial authorisation and a warrant may not be enough.[377] This matter is pursued in Chapters 11 and 12.[378]

The head 'the economic well-being of the country' is unusual; it does not appear in para 2 of Art 8's companion Articles, Arts 9–11. A number of interferences have been found to be justified under this head.[379] In *MS v Sweden*,[380] the obtaining of access to medical records in order to assess a social security claim was found to be justified.

Justification under the heads 'for the prevention of disorder or crime' depends on the seriousness of the crime or threat to disorder, the nature and extent of the interference and the question whether a judicial warrant has been obtained. In *Camenzind*,[381] the limited

---

368 (1992) 15 EHRR 137.
369 *De Wilde Ooms* (1971) 1 EHRR 373.
370 See *Herczegfalvy v Austria* (1992) 14 HRLJ 84; (1993) 15 EHRR 437.
371 *Funke v France* (1993) 16 EHRR 297; *Mialhe v France* (1993) 16 EHRR 332; *Crémieux v France* (1993) 16 EHRR 357. For further discussion, see Chapter 11.
372 *Airey v Ireland* (1979) 2 EHRR 305.
373 *Camenzind v Switzerland*, RJD 1997-III 2880.
374 *Lustig-Prean v UK* (1999) 7 BHRC 65; *Smith and Grady v UK* (2000) 29 EHRLR 493.
375 See *Leander v Sweden* (1987) 9 EHRR 433.
376 *Funke v France* (1993) 16 EHRR 297.
377 *Niemietz v Germany* (1992) 16 EHRR 97.
378 See pp 679–82 and pp 707–08.
379 Eg *Powell v UK* (1990) 12 EHRR 355.
380 RJD 1997-IV 1437.
381 See above, fn 373.

scope of the search and the procedures in place meant that the search was proportionate to the aim of preventing crime. In *Murray v UK*,[382] the entry and search of Mrs Murray's home was not disproportionate to that aim, bearing in mind her links to terrorism.

In contrast to the stance taken under Art 10(2),[383] the exception for the protection of morals has received a restrictive interpretation. The Court has required an especially significant justification in order to be satisfied as to proportionality.[384] This exception is sometimes also raised where the exception in respect of the rights of others is invoked especially in relation to family life, where the protection of health may also be in issue. For example, in *Olsson v Sweden*,[385] the decision to take three children into care was an interference with family life. However, it could be justified as being for the protection of the health and the rights of the child.

Article 9: Freedom of thought, conscience and religion

(1) Everyone has the right to freedom of thought, conscience and religion; this right includes freedom to change his religion or belief and freedom, either alone or in community with others and in public or private, to manifest his religion or belief, worship, teaching, practice and observance.

(2) Freedom to manifest one's religion or beliefs shall be subject only to such limitations as are prescribed by law and are necessary in a democratic society in the interests of public safety, for the protection of public order, health or morals or for the protection of the rights and freedoms of others.

The right under Art 9 of possessing certain convictions is unrestricted. Restrictions are only placed on the *expression* of thought under Art 10, and the manifestation of religious belief in Art 9(2). Of course, in general, unless thoughts can be expressed, they cannot have much impact. However, Art 9 provides a valuable guarantee against using compulsion to change an opinion[386] or prohibiting someone from entering a profession due to their convictions. In the latter instance, Art 17 (which allows restrictions where a person's ultimate aim is the destruction of Convention rights)[387] might, however, come into play if someone of fascist or perhaps communist sympathies was debarred from a profession.

Freedom of religion will include the freedom not to take part in religious services, thus particularly affecting persons such as prisoners, but it may also include the opposite obligation – to provide prisoners with a means of practising their religion. However, in such instances, Strasbourg has been very ready to assume that restrictions are inherent in the detention of prisoners or are justified under para 2. For example, in *Huber v Austria*,[388] broad 'inherent limitations' on a prisoner's right to practise religion were accepted.

---

382 (1994) 19 EHRR 193.
383 See Chapter 6, pp 278–79.
384 See *Norris v Ireland* (1988) 13 EHRR 186 and *Dudgeon v UK* (1981) 4 EHRR 149.
385 (1988) 11 EHRR 259.
386 Such action would normally also involve a violation of Art 3.
387 See below, p 89.
388 (1971) Yearbook XIV, p 548.

Similarly, in *X v Austria*,[389] the Commission found no violation in respect of a refusal to allow a Buddhist prisoner to grow a beard. It is arguable, however, that inherent limitations should not be assumed in relation to a right which admits express exceptions.

Article 10: Freedom of expression

(1) Everyone has the right to freedom of expression. This right shall include freedom to hold opinions and to receive and impart information and ideas without interference by public authority and regardless of frontiers. This Art shall not prevent States from requiring the licensing of broadcasting, television or cinema enterprises.

(2) The exercise of these freedoms, since it carries with it duties and responsibilities, may be subject to such formalities, conditions, restrictions or penalties as are prescribed by law and are necessary in a democratic society in the interests of national security, territorial integrity or public safety, for the prevention of disorder or crime, for the protection of health or morals, for the protection of the reputation or rights of others, for preventing the disclosure of information received in confidence or for maintaining the authority and impartiality of the judiciary.

Article 10 obviously overlaps with Art 9, but it is broader, since it protects the means of ensuring freedom of expression; even if the person who provides such means is not the holder of the opinion in question, she or he will be protected. The words 'freedom to hold opinion' used in Art 10 cannot be distinguished from the phrase 'freedom of thought' used in Art 9. There is also an obvious overlap with Art 11 which protects freedom of association and assembly.

Scope of the primary right

The stance taken under Art 10 is that while almost all forms of expression will fall within the primary right, all expression is not equally valuable. It was found in *X and Church of Scientology v Sweden*[390] that commercial speech is protected by Art 10, but that the level of protection should be less than that accorded to the expression of political ideas, thereby implying that political speech should receive special protection. In *Markt Intern Verlag v FRG*,[391] the Court found: 'the European Court of Human Rights should not substitute its own evaluation for that of the national courts in the instant case, where those courts, on reasonable grounds, had considered the restrictions to be necessary,' an extreme statement of the extent to which Strasbourg should defer to the national decision. It appears to have been affected by the fact that the Court was dealing with commercial speech which it views as of much less significance than political speech.[392] As Harris, O'Boyle and Warbrick put it in *Law of the European Convention on Human Rights*:[393] 'The privileged position of political speech derives from the Court's conception of it as a central feature of a democratic society ...'

---

389 Appl No 1753/63 (1965) Yearbook VIII, p 174.

390 Appl No 7805/77 (1979); YB XXII.

391 In *Markt Intern Verlag v FRG*, Series A 165, para 47 (1989).

392 See the statements regarding the significance of political speech in *Lingens v Austria* (1986) 8 EHRR 103; *Jersild v Denmark* (1994) 19 EHRR 1; *Oberschlick v Austria* (1997) 25 EHRR 357.

393 1995 p 397.

The motive of the speaker may be significant; if it is to stimulate debate on a particular subject, Art 10 will be more readily applicable.[394] The Court has stressed that Art 10 applies not only to speech which is favourably received, but also to speech which shocks and offends. In *Jersild v Denmark*,[395] the Commission accepted that this may include aiding in the dissemination of racist ideas. In this instance, the applicant had not himself expressed such views; his conviction had arisen due to his responsibility as a television interviewer for their dissemination. This factor was also taken into account by the Court in finding that the conviction constituted an interference with freedom of expression in breach of Art 10.[396] The television programme in question had included an interview with an extreme racist group, the Greenjackets; such interviews were found to constitute an important means whereby 'the press is able to play its vital role as public watchdog' and therefore strong reasons would have to be adduced for punishing a journalist who had assisted in the dissemination of racist statements by conducting the interview, bearing in mind that the feature taken as a whole was not found by the Court to have as its object the propagation of racist views. The Court pointed out that the racist remarks which led to the convictions of members of the Greenjackets did not have the protection of Art 10.

There is some evidence that the Court is reluctant to intervene in instances which may not be perceived as constituting a direct interference with freedom of expression by the domestic authorities. If, as in *Glasenapp v Federal Republic of Germany*,[397] the interference can be seen as in some way indirect or as largely concerned with another interest, it may find that the Art 10 guarantee is inapplicable. The case concerned a German schoolteacher who had written a letter to a newspaper indicating her sympathy with the German Communist Party. This was found to be contrary to legislation controlling the employment of people with extreme political views and her appointment as a teacher was revoked. Her claim that this constituted an interference with her freedom of expression failed since the Court characterised the claim as largely concerned with a right of access to the civil service rather than with freedom of speech. In *Bowman v UK*,[398] restrictions imposed on persons spending money in support of parliamentary candidates was found to be a disproportionate interference with freedom of expression. In *Ahmed v UK*,[399] the Court upheld restrictions preventing certain local government officers holding political office. The Court took into account the need to protect the rights of others to effective political democracy which was answered by seeking to ensure the neutrality of local government officers.

Article 10 includes an additional guarantee of the freedom to receive and impart information. However, the seeking of information does not appear to connote an obligation on the part of the government to make information available; the words 'without restriction by public authority' do not imply a positive obligation on the part of the authority to ensure that information can be received. So, the right is restricted in

---

394 See *Thorgeir Thorgeirson v Iceland* (1992) 14 EHRR 843.

395 (1992) 14 HRLJ 74; see also the *Open Door Counselling and Dublin Well Woman Centre Ltd* case (1992) 15 EHRR 244 (below, p 77).

396 (1994) 19 EHRR 1.

397 (1986) 9 EHRR 25. See, to the same effect, *Kosiek v FRG* (1987) 9 EHRR 328.

398 (1998) 25 EHRR 1.

399 (1998) 5 BHRC 111.

situations where there is no willing speaker. Article 10 is not, therefore, a full freedom of information measure.[400] In fact, the freedom to seek information was deliberately omitted from Art 10 – although it appears in the Universal Declaration of Human Rights – in order to avoid placing a clear positive obligation on the Member States to communicate information.

A number of aspects of Art 10 and its impact on domestic law are discussed extensively in Part 2.

Restrictions and exceptions

Mediums other than written publications can be subjected to a licensing system under Art 10(1) and because this restriction is mentioned in para 1, it appears that a licensing system can be imposed on grounds other than those outlined in para 2, thereby broadening the possible exceptions. This is discussed further in Chapter 6.[401] Any such exceptions must, of course, be considered in conjunction with the safeguard against discrimination under Art 14: for example, if the State has a monopoly on a medium, it must not discriminate in granting air time to different groups.

The restrictions of Art 10(2) are wide and two, 'maintaining the authority of the judiciary' and 'preventing the disclosure of information received in confidence', are not mentioned in Art 10's companion Articles, Arts 8, 9 and 11. The first of these exceptions was included bearing in mind the contempt law of the UK, but it was made clear, in the well known *Sunday Times* case,[402] that in relation to such law, the margin of appreciation should be narrow due to its 'objective' nature. In other words, what was needed to maintain the authority of the judiciary could be more readily evaluated by an objective observer than could measures needed to protect morals. The case in question concerned reporting on a matter of great public interest – the Thalidomide tragedy – and therefore, only very compelling reasons for preventing the information being imparted could be justified. It was held that because Art 10 is a particularly important right and the particular instance touched on its essence, a breach could be found; in response, the Contempt of Court Act 1981 was passed. The 'rights of others' exception may also receive a narrow interpretation – at least in cases of defamation against a public body or person where the applicant was acting in good faith and was attempting to stimulate debate on a matter of serious public concern.[403]

A very different approach was taken in the *Handyside* case[404] arising from a conviction under the Obscene Publications Act 1959 and concerning the more subjective nature of the 'protection of morals' exception. The applicant put forward certain special circumstances – that the prohibited material in question was circulating in most other countries and so suppression could not be very evidently necessary in a democratic society – but such circumstances were barely discussed. A wide margin of appreciation

---

400 This was supported in the *Gaskin* case (1990) 12 EHRR 36 (see above, p 69): the Art 10 claim failed on this basis.

401 See pp 277–78.

402 Judgment of 26 April 1979, A 30; (1979) 2 EHRR 245 (discussed in full in Chapter 5, pp 228–30).

403 See *Thorgeir Thorgeirson v Iceland* (1992) 14 EHRR 843; *Castells v Spain* (1992) 14 EHRR 445; *Schwabe v Austria* (1992) 14 HRLJ 26.

404 Judgment of 7 December 1976, A 24; (1976) 1 EHRR 737. See further Chapter 6, p 279.

was left to the national authorities as to what was 'necessary'. One possible reason for this was that the authority of the judiciary is a more objective notion than the protection of morals and this may have led to a variation of the necessity test. A similar approach was taken in *Müller v Switzerland*,[405] the Court stating: 'it is not possible to find in the legal and social orders of the Contracting States a uniform European conception of morals. By reason of their direct and continuous contact with the vital forces of their countries State authorities are in a better position than the international judge to give an opinion on the exact content of these requirements.'

The lack of a uniform standard was also the key factor in the ruling in *Otto-Preminger Institut v Austria*.[406] The decision concerned the showing of a satirical film depicting God as a senile old man and Jesus as a mental defective erotically attracted to the Virgin Mary. Criminal proceedings for the offence of disparaging religious doctrines were brought against the manager of the Institute which had scheduled the showings of the film. The film was seized by the Austrian authorities while criminal proceedings were pending. The European Court of Human Rights found that the seizure of the film could be seen as furthering the aims of Art 9 of the Convention and therefore it fell within the 'rights of others' exception. In considering whether the seizure and forfeiture of the film was 'necessary in a democratic society' in order to protect the rights of others to respect for their religious views, the Court took into account the lack of a discernible common conception within the Member States of the significance of religion, and therefore considered that the national authorities should have a wide margin of appreciation in assessing what was necessary to protect religious feeling. In ordering the seizure of the film, the Austrian authorities had taken its artistic value into account, but had not found that it outweighed its offensive features. The Court found that the national authorities had not overstepped their margin of appreciation and therefore decided that no breach of Art 10 had occurred. This decision left a very wide discretion to the Member State, a discretion which the dissenting judges considered to be too wide.

The stance taken in *Otto-Preminger* and in *Müller* echoes the view expressed in *Cossey v UK*[407] that where a clear European view does emerge, the Court may well be influenced by it, but it also suggests a particularly strong reluctance to intervene in this very contentious area. The margin of appreciation in respect of the protection of morals will not be unlimited, however, even in the absence of a broad consensus. The Court so held in *Open Door Counselling and Dublin Well Woman v Ireland*,[408] ruling that an injunction which prevented the dissemination of any information at all about abortion amounted to a breach of Art 10. This accords with the view expressed in *B v France*[409] that what can be termed the common standards principle is only one factor to be taken into account and must be weighed against the severity of the infringement of rights in question.

The exception in respect of confidential information overlaps with others, including national security and the rights of others, but a situation could be envisaged in which a disclosure of information did not fall within those categories and could therefore be

---

405 (1991) 13 EHRR 212.
406 (1994) 19 EHRR 34.
407 (1990) 13 EHRR 622.
408 (1992) 15 EHRR 244.
409 (1992) 13 HRLJ 358.

caught only by this extra exception. This might arise in respect of a disclosure by a civil servant which did not threaten national security or any person's individual rights, such as that made in the *Tisdall* case.[410]

Actions in respect of both prior and subsequent restraints on freedom of expression may be brought under Art 10, but pre-publication sanctions will be regarded as more pernicious and thus harder to justify as necessary (*Observer and Guardian v UK*).[411] In relation to post-publication sanctions, criminal actions will be regarded as having a grave impact on freedom of expression, but civil actions which have severe consequences for the individual may also be hard to justify. In *Tolstoy Miloslavsky v UK*,[412] the European Court of Human Rights considered the level of libel damages which can be awarded in UK courts. Libel damages of £1.5 m had been awarded against Count Tolstoy Miloslavsky in the UK in respect of a pamphlet he had written which alleged that Lord Aldington, a high ranking British army officer, had been responsible for handing over 70,000 people to the Soviet authorities without authorisation, knowing that they would meet a cruel fate. The Count argued that this very large award constituted a breach of Art 10. Was the award necessary in a democratic society as required by Art 10? The Court found that it was not, having regard to the fact that the scope of judicial control at the trial could not offer an adequate safeguard against a disproportionately large award. Thus, a violation of the applicant's rights under Art 10 was found.

Article 11: Freedom of association and assembly

(1) Everyone has the right to freedom of peaceful assembly and to freedom of association with others, including the right to form and to join trade unions for the protection of his interests.

(2) No restrictions shall be placed on the exercise of these rights other than such as are prescribed by law and are necessary in a democratic society in the interests of national security or public safety, for the prevention of disorder or crime, for the protection of health or morals or for the protection of the rights and freedoms of others. This Article shall not prevent the imposition of lawful restrictions on the exercise of these rights by members of the armed forces, of the police or of the administration of the State.

Assembly

The addition of the word 'peaceful' has restricted the scope of para 1: there will be no need to invoke the para 2 exceptions if the authorities concerned could reasonably believe that a planned assembly would not be peaceful. Thus, assemblies can be subject to permits so long as the permits relate to the peacefulness of the assembly and not to the right of assembly itself. However, a restriction of a very wide character relating to peacefulness might affect the right to assemble itself and might therefore constitute a violation of Art 11 if it did not fall within one of the exceptions.

It should be noted that freedom of assembly may not merely be secured by a lack of interference by the public authorities; they may have positive obligations to intervene in

---

410 See Chapter 7, p 338.
411 (1991) 14 EHRR 153.
412 (1995) 20 EHRR 422.

order to prevent an interference with freedom of assembly by private individuals, although they will have a very wide margin of appreciation in this regard.[413] It has been held in respect of the guarantees of other Articles that States must secure to individuals the rights and freedoms of the Convention by preventing or remedying any breach thereof. If no duty was placed on the authorities to provide such protection, then some assemblies could not take place.

It will be argued in Chapter 9 that the freedom of assembly jurisprudence under Art 11 is cautious. In finding that applications are manifestly ill-founded, the Commission has been readily satisfied that decisions of the national authorities to adopt quite far reaching measures, including complete bans, in order to prevent disorder are within their margin of appreciation.[414] The Court has also found 'the margin of appreciation extends in particular to the choice of the reasonable and appropriate means to be used by the authority to ensure that lawful manifestations can take place peacefully'.[415]

Association

'Association' need not be assigned its national meaning. Even if a group such as a trade union is not an 'association' according to the definition of national law, it may fall within Art 11. The term connotes a voluntary association, not a professional organisation established by the government. It should be noted that it is only with respect to trade unions that the right to form an association is expressly mentioned, albeit non-exhaustively. Such a right in respect of other types of association is clearly implicit – a necessary part of freedom of association.

The question whether freedom of association implies protection against compulsory membership of an association was considered in *Young, James and Webster*.[416] It was found that a measure of freedom of choice is implicit in Art 11; this amounts to a negative aspect of the right to join a trade union and is not therefore on the same footing as the positive aspect, but it is still a part of freedom of association. The Court left open the question whether a closed shop agreement would always amount to a breach of Art 11; in this instance, the possibility of dismissal due to refusal to join the union was such a serious form of coercion that it affected the essence of the Art 11 guarantee. It seems that the closed shop practice may be a violation of Art 11 where there is legislation allowing it, even if the body enforcing it is not an emanation of the State (an example of *Drittwirkung*). It may be noted that the degree of freedom of choice under Art 11 is limited; it does not appear to include as a necessary component the freedom to choose between unions.[417]

The right to join a trade union involves allowing members to have a union that can properly 'protect the interests of the members'. So, a union must have sufficient scope for this, although this need not mean a right to strike; this right can be subject to the

---

413 Appl 1012/82, *Plattform 'Ärzte für das Leben' v Austria* D & R 44 (1985); (1988) 13 EHRR 204 (it was not arguable that Austria had failed in its obligation to prevent counter-demonstrators interfering with an anti-abortion demonstration).

414 See *Christians against Racism and Fascism v UK* No 8440/78, 21 DR 138; *Friedl v Austria* No 15225/89 (1995) 21 EHRR 83.

415 *Chorherr v Austria* Series A 266-B, para 31 (1993).

416 Judgment of 13 August 1981, A 44; (1981) 4 EHRR 38.

417 *Sibson v UK*, A 258; (1993) 17 EHRR 193.

restrictions of the national legislature.[418] Moreover, extra restrictions may be placed on certain groups of employees under the second sentence of para 2 and these do not expressly need to be 'necessary'. However, the purposes of the Convention imply that they should, indeed, be necessary.

Article 12: The right to marry and to found a family

Men and women of marriageable age have the right to marry and to found a family, according to the national laws governing the exercise of this right.

Article 12 contains no second paragraph setting out restrictions, but it obviously does not confer an absolute right due to the words 'according to the national laws' which imply the reverse of an absolute right – that Art 12 may be subject to far reaching limitations in domestic law. The reference to national laws also accepts the possibility that legal systems may vary among Contracting States as to, for example, the legally marriageable age. However, this does not mean that the Convention has no role at all; it may not interfere with national law governing the exercise of the right, but may do so where it attacks or erodes its essence. If a person was denied the right to marry due to limited mental faculties or health or poverty, the essence of the right would be eroded assuming that he or she was capable of genuine consent. However, where erosion of the essence of the right arises from the national rule that only persons of the opposite sex can marry, it may be acceptable. In *Rees*,[419] a woman who had had a gender re-assignment operation complained that she was unable to marry. It was held that there was no violation of Art 12 because the State can impose restrictions on certain men and women due to the social purpose of Art 12 which is concerned with the ability to procreate; marriages which cannot result in procreation may, therefore, fall outside its ambit. This interpretation was supported on the ground that the wording of the Article suggests that marriage is protected as the basis of the family; thus, Art 12 is aimed at protecting the traditional biological marriage. In other words, what appeared to be a clear interference with the essence of the right could be found not to be so under this restricted interpretation. Therefore, preventing the marriage of persons not of the opposite biological sex was not found to breach Art 12. This ruling was followed in *Cossey*[420] on the ground that changes in social values did not indicate a need to depart from the decision in *Rees*.

The principle that the Convention will not interfere with national laws which only regulate the *exercise* of the right to marry is also subject to exceptions. If a person is, in general, free to marry, but in particular circumstances will suffer detriment flowing solely from the fact of being married, Art 12 may be breached. Thus, the right to marry may include placing no sanction on marriage, such as sacking a person when he or she marries. But if a priest is sacked when he ceases to be celibate, that would not seem to constitute a breach since he has, in a sense, chosen freely not to marry.

The right to divorce or dissolution of marriage is not included under Art 12[421] so that the State need not provide the means of dissolving a marriage although, in some

---

418 Judgment of 6 February 1976, *Schmidt and Dahlström v Sweden*, A 21 (1976); 1 EHRR 632.
419 Judgment of 17 October 1986, A 106; (1986) 9 EHRR 56.
420 Judgment of 27 September 1990, A 184; (1990) 13 EHRR 622.
421 *Johnstone*, Judgment of 18 December 1986, A 112; (1987) 9 EHRR 203.

circumstances, Art 8 may be relevant. It seems that the State need not provide s
as the right has been deliberately left out of the Convention, and although the Co.
is subject to an evolutive interpretation (in other words, changes in social conditi
be taken into account), that will not apply to a right which has been totally omitted.

In accordance with the general Convention policy of reluctance to impose positive
obligations on States, the right to found a family does not include an economic right to
sufficient living accommodation for the family: it denotes an interference with the ability
to found a family and thus prevents the non-voluntary use of sterilisation or abortion.
Article 3 (and conceivably Art 2)[422] would probably also apply. The national laws are
again allowed to regulate the enjoyment of this right, but they must not erode its essence.
However, it might be argued that inherent limitations on the right in certain situations
may be allowed because restrictions are not enumerated under Art 12, and therefore such
limitations would not create a conflict with the general Convention doctrine governing
inherent limitations which tends to reject such limitations where the restrictions are
enumerated. However, it was found in *Hamer*[423] that prisoners do have the right to marry
under Art 12; inherent restrictions are possible, but they must not affect the essence of the
right. The applicant had two years to wait; that did affect the essence of the right and
therefore led to a breach of Art 12. In contrast, in *X v UK*,[424] it was found that denial of
conjugal visits to a detainee was not a violation of Art 12 since the Article grants the
general right to found a family; it does not grant that that possibility should be available
at any given moment.

The Protocols to the Convention

The First, Fourth, Sixth, Seventh and Twelfth Protocols to the Convention add to it a
number of substantive rights. Only the First and Sixth Protocols have so far been ratified
by the UK.

First Protocol

Article 1

> Every natural or legal person is entitled to the peaceful enjoyment of his possessions. No
> one shall be deprived of his possessions except in the public interest and subject to the
> conditions provided for by law and by the general principles of international law.
>
> The preceding provisions shall not, however, in any way impair the right of a State to
> enforce such laws as it deems necessary to control the use of property in accordance with
> the general interest or to secure the payment of taxes or other contributions or penalties.

The property Article of the First Protocol echoes Art 12 in allowing the national
authorities considerable freedom to regulate the exercise of the primary right. The case
law has supported this; it was determined in *James and Others*[425] that the margin of

---

422 See above, p 41.
423 Report of 13 December 1979; D & R 24 (1981).
424 Appl 6564/74; D & R 2 (1975).
425 A 98; (1986) 8 EHRR 123.

appreciation open to the legislature in implementing social and economic policies should be a wide one.[426] Thus, in this area, the Strasbourg authorities have adopted a cautious attitude to this right and tend to practise only marginal review of the justification of restrictions. As mentioned above, claims of interference with property may fail under Protocol 1, Art 1, but succeed under Art 6, where a defective procedure has authorised the interference.[427]

In *Sporrong and Lonroth v Sweden*,[428] the Court found that while a wide margin of appreciation should be allowed to the Member State in respect of prohibitions affecting the applicants' properties due to planning regulations, that margin had been exceeded since procedural safeguards were not in place which allowed the applicants to seek a reduction of the time limits on the prohibitions. A fair balance between their interests and that of the community in general had not been struck. The fair balance is the key matter under Art 1. It must be clear that there has been a weighing up of the interests involved: the interest of the applicant in the peaceful enjoyment of possessions, and the interest of the community in regulating the use of the land or possessions for the benefit of the local community.

Article 2

No person shall be denied the right to education. In the exercise of any functions which it assumes in relation to education and to teaching, the State shall respect the right of parents to ensure such education and teaching in conformity with their own religious and philosophical convictions.

The UK is a party to the First Protocol, but has made the following reservation to Art 2: '(in view of certain provisions of the Education Acts in force in the United Kingdom, the principle affirmed in the second sentence of Article 2 is accepted by the United Kingdom only so far it is compatible with the provision of efficient instruction and training and the avoidance of unreasonable public expenditure.'

The right guaranteed under the first sentence of Art 2 can be exercised by the child or the parent;[429] if one parent loses custody to the other, that parent ceases to be able to exercise the right.[430] The right in question is expressed negatively; therefore, it guarantees an equal right of access to the educational facilities that are already available. However, this implies that some facilities should be available but leaves the State a wide margin of appreciation in respect of the provision.[431] In the *Belgian Linguistic* cases,[432] it was held that Art 2 does not require the Contracting States to provide a particular type of education: it implies the right of persons to 'avail themselves of the means of instruction existing at a given time'.

426 See further Harris, O'Boyle and Warbrick, *op cit*, fn 1, p 516; Clayton and Tomlinson, *op cit*, fn 1, pp 1301–20.
427 *Mats Jacobson v Sweden* (1990) 13 EHRR 79. See above, p 58, fn 248 and associated text.
428 (1982) 5 EHRR 35.
429 *Campbell and Cosans v UK* (1982) 4 EHRR 293, para 40.
430 *X v Sweden* (1977) 12 DR 192.
431 See further Wildhaber 'Right to education and parental rights', in Macdonald, Matscher and Petzold (eds), *The European System for the Protection of Human Rights*, 1993; Clayton and Tomlinson, *op cit*, fn 1, pp 1357–66.
432 Judgment of 23 July 1968, A 6; (1968) 1 EHRR 252.

Article 3

The High Contracting Parties undertake to hold free elections at reasonable intervals by secret ballot, under conditions which will ensure the free expression of the opinion of the people in the choice of the legislature.

Article 3 provides an undertaking (not formally expressed as a right) which is clearly central to a democratic society.[433] However, it does refer to a right that individuals can invoke.[434] Article 3 does not imply an absolute right to vote, but that elections should be held at regular intervals, should be secret, free from pressure on the electorate and the choice between candidates should be genuine. It does not confer a right to a particular form of electoral system.[435]

Further Protocols

Articles 1 and 2 of the Sixth Protocol abolish the death penalty except in time of war or the threat of war. The Fourth and Seventh Protocols cover, broadly: freedom of movement (Protocol 4), the right of an alien lawfully resident in a State to full review of his or her case before expulsion, rights of appeal, compensation for miscarriages of justice, the right not to be subjected to double jeopardy and sexual equality between spouses as regards private law rights and responsibilities (Protocol 7). They are discussed in Chapter 4, as are the plans for their implementation in national law.[436] A new Protocol on Minority Rights was recommended to the Committee of Ministers in 1993, but it has not been adopted.[437] Protocol 12 provides, very significantly, a free standing right to equality which is discussed further in Chapter 16.[438]

The other Protocols, including the most recent, Protocol 11, are concerned with the procedural machinery of the Convention. These other procedural Protocols were abolished when Protocol 11, discussed above,[439] came into force.

4 ADDITIONAL GUARANTEES TO THE PRIMARY RIGHTS

Article 13: The right to an effective remedy before a national authority

Everyone whose rights and freedoms as set forth in this Convention are violated shall have an effective remedy before a national authority notwithstanding that the violation has been committed by persons acting in an official capacity.

---

433 For discussion, see Clayton and Tomlinson, *op cit*, fn 1, Chapter 20.
434 *Mathieu-Mohin v Belgium* (1987) 10 EHRR 1, para 50.
435 *Liberal Party v UK* (1980) 21 DR 211 (it could not be read with Art 14 to confer a right to a system of proportional representation on the basis that the lack of such a system discriminated against the Liberal Party).
436 See further p 135.
437 See 14 HRLJ 140.
438 See p 985.
439 See pp 20 and 32.

In *Leander v Sweden*[440] it was found that 'the requirements of Art 13 will be satisfied if there exists domestic machinery whereby, subject to the inherent limitations of the context, the individual can secure compliance with the relevant laws'. This machinery may include a number of possible remedies. It has been held that judicial review proceedings will be sufficient. In *Vilvarajah and Four Others v the UK*,[441] the applicants maintained that judicial review did not satisfy Art 13 since the English courts could not consider the merits of the Home Secretary's decision in this instance, merely the manner in which it was taken. In holding that the power of judicial review satisfied the Art 13 test, the Court took into account the power of the UK courts to quash an administrative decision for unreasonableness, and the fact that these powers were exercisable by the highest tribunal in the UK. Thus, no violation of Art 13 was found. However, more recently, in *Smith and Grady v UK*,[442] the Court said of the concept of Wednesbury unreasonableness: 'the threshold at which the ... Court of Appeal could find the Ministry of Defence policy irrational was placed so high that it effectively excluded any consideration by the domestic courts of the question whether the interference with the applicants' rights answered a pressing social need or was proportionate to the national security and public order aims pursued, principles which lie at the heart of the Court's analysis of complaints under Art 8 of the Convention.[443] This is not the last word on the matter. It is arguable that judicial review may provide a sufficient remedy in respect of breaches of Art 1, Protocol 1 especially where a large element of policy making concerning social and economic matters is at issue.[444] This matter is pursued further at various points in this book.[445]

Article 13 does not contain a general guarantee that anyone who considers that his or her rights have been violated by the authorities should have an effective remedy; it can only be considered if one of the substantive rights or freedoms is in question. The words do not and cannot connote a requirement that there should be domestic machinery in place to address any possible grievance. The words 'are violated' of Art 13 do not mean that the violation must have been established before the national courts because clearly it could not have been – if it could, that would suggest that an effective remedy *did* exist. They mean that a person should have an arguable claim; there will be no breach of Art 13 if the complaint is unmeritorious – in other words, if it is clearly apparent that no violation of the Convention has taken place. Even if no violation of the other Article is eventually found, it can still be argued that the national courts should have provided an effective means of considering the possible violation. Moreover, a claim may eventually be held to be manifestly ill-founded and yet arguable. This is an odd result but, in principle, it is what the case law appears to disclose. In *Klass*,[446] it was found that 'Art 13

---

440 Judgment of 26 March 1987, A 116; (1987) 9 EHRR 443. Note that if such machinery exists, but is of doubtful efficacy, a challenge under Art 6(1) may be most likely to succeed (*de Geouffre de la Pradelle v France* (1993) HRLJ 276).

441 Judgment of 30 October 1991, A 215.

442 (2000) 29 EHRR 493.

443 *Ibid*, para 138.

444 See the decision of the House of Lords in *Alconbury* [2001] 2 All ER 929; (2001) 151 NLJ 135 (apart from the Art 1 issues, the matter concerned the application of Art 6 under the Human Rights Act).

445 See in particular Chapter 4, p 143.

446 Judgment of 6 September 1978 A 28; 2 EHRR 214.

must be interpreted as guaranteeing an effective remedy before a national authority to everyone who claims that his rights and freedoms under the Convention have been violated'. In *Plattform 'Ärzte für das Leben'*[447] it was found that the claim must be arguable. Thus, Art 13 can be invoked only if no procedure is available which can begin to determine whether a violation has occurred. In theory, then, there could be a breach of Art 13 alone and in that sense, it protects an independent right. In practice, case law tends not to follow this purist approach, and if no violation of the substantive right is found, it is likely that no violation of Art 13 will be found either (as it may be argued occurred in the *Ärzte für das Leben* case).

In the *Klass* case, it was determined that phone tapping did not breach Art 8 since it was found to be in the interests of national security. The applicants claimed that Art 13 could be considered on the basis of their assertion that no effective domestic remedy existed for challenging the decision to tap. The Court accepted that the existing remedy was of limited efficacy: it consisted only of the possibility of review of the case by a parliamentary committee. Nevertheless, it found that in all the circumstances, no more effective remedy was possible. Thus, the Court allowed the doctrine of the margin of appreciation to resolve the difficulty which arose from the fact that the tapping was done in order to combat terrorism in its attack on democracy but the means employed, which included the suspension of judicial remedies, might well be termed undemocratic.

Article 14: Prohibition of discrimination

> The enjoyment of the rights and freedoms set forth in this Convention shall be secured without discrimination on any ground such as sex, race, colour, language, religion, political or other opinion, national or social origin, association with a national minority, property, birth or other status.

Article 14 does not provide a *general* right to freedom from discrimination, only that the rights and freedoms of the Convention must be secured without discrimination. Thus, if discrimination occurs in an area which is not covered by the Convention, such as most contractual aspects of employment, Art 14 will be irrelevant. Thus, Art 14 remains of limited value since it is not free standing and does not cover social and economic matters lying outside the protected rights. But, these weaknesses will eventually be addressed by Protocol 12, which will provide a free standing right to freedom from discrimination in relation to rights protected by law.[448] The protection from discrimination under Protocol 12 will render Art 14 redundant. However, at present, the UK Government has not ratified it and, strangely for a Labour Government committed to anti-discrimination policies, it does not currently intend to do so.[449]

However, Art 14 is not the only Convention vehicle which may be used to challenge discriminatory practices. Not only may discrimination be attacked though the medium of one of the other Articles, most particularly Art 3,[450] but the Convention may be of particular value as a source of general principles in sex discrimination cases before the

---

447 (1988) 13 EHRR 204.
448 For further discussion of the draft Discrimination Protocol, see Moon, G (2000) 1 EHRLR 49.
449 See further Chapter 16, p 965.
450 *East African Asians* cases (1973) 3 EHRR 76.

European Court of Justice.[451] An applicant may allege violation of a substantive right taken alone and also that he or she has been discriminated against in respect of that right. However, even if no violation of the substantive right taken alone is found and even if that claim is manifestly ill-founded, there could still be a violation of that Article and Art 14 taken together so long as the matter at issue is covered by the other Article. This was found in *X v Federal Republic of Germany*:[452] 'Article 14 of the Convention has no independent existence; nevertheless a measure which in itself is in conformity with the requirement of the Article enshrining the right or freedom in question, may however infringe this Article when read in conjunction with Article 14 for the reason that it is of a discriminatory nature.' In this sense, the Court has granted more autonomy to Art 14 than appeared to be intended originally.[453]

This ruling allowed more claims to be considered than the 'arguability' principle applying under Art 13. For example, in *Abdulaziz, Cabales and Balkandali*,[454] the female claimants wanted their non-national spouses to enter the UK and alleged a breach of Art 8, which protects family life. That claim was rejected. But a violation of Art 14 was found because the way the rule was applied made it easier for men to bring in their spouses. It was held that: 'Although the application of Art 14 does not necessarily presuppose a breach [of the substantive provisions of the Convention and the Protocols] – and to this extent it is autonomous – there can be no room for its application unless the facts at issue fall within the ambit of one or more of the rights and freedoms.' In response to this ruling, the UK Government 'equalised down', placing men and women in an equally disadvantageous position as regards their non-national spouses.

Under Art 14, discrimination connotes differential treatment which is unjustifiable. The differential treatment may be unjustifiable either in the sense that it relates to no objective and reasonable aim, or in the sense that there is no reasonable proportionality between the means employed and the aim sought to be realised.[455] In *Abdulaziz*, the aim was to protect the domestic labour market. It was held that this was not enough to justify the differential treatment because the difference in treatment was out of proportion to that aim. The outcome in this case illustrated the limitations of Art 14 which it shares with all anti-discrimination measures: it is concerned only with procedural fairness and can only ensure equal treatment which may be unjustifiable. Unjustifiable equal treatment is, however, unlikely to occur when the group in question is comparing itself with the dominant group since the dominant group will ensure, through the democratic process, that it does not experience a lower standard of treatment. However, where, as in *Abdulaziz*, the differentiation is occurring within a non-dominant group, the way is opened for equally poor treatment. This can be averted only by comparing the group as a whole with the dominant group. However, this argument was rejected by the European Court of Human Rights, which found that the treatment was not racially discriminatory.

---

451 See, eg, *Johnstone v Chief Constable of the RUC* [1986] ECR 1651.

452 Appl 4045/69 (1970) Yearbook XIII.

453 For comment on the increasing autonomy of Art 14, see Livingstone, S, 'Article 14 and the prevention of discrimination in the ECHR' (1997) 1 EHRR 25.

454 A 94; (1985) 7 EHRR 471.

455 *Geïllustreerde Pers NV v Netherlands* D & R 8 (1977).

5 RESTRICTION OF THE RIGHTS AND FREEDOMS

The system of restrictions

As the discussion of the substantive rights demonstrated, all the Articles except Arts 3, 4(1) and 6(2) are subject to certain restrictions, either because certain limitations are inherent in the formulation of the right itself,[456] or because it is expressly stated that particular cases are not covered by the right in question, or because general restrictions on the primary right contained in the first paragraph are enumerated in a second paragraph (Arts 8–11). Certain further general restrictions are allowed under Arts 17, 15 and 57 (previously 64). In considering the restrictions, Art 18 must also be borne in mind. It provides that the motives of the national authority in creating the restrictions must be the same as the aims appearing behind the restrictions when the Convention was drafted.

Article 15: Derogation from the rights and freedoms in case of public emergency

(1) In time of war or other public emergency threatening the life of the nation any High Contracting Party may take measures derogating from its obligations under this Convention to the extent strictly required by the exigencies of the situation, provided that such measures are not inconsistent with its other obligations under international law.

(2) No derogation from Art 2, except in respect of deaths resulting from lawful acts of war or from Arts 3, 4 (para 1) and 7 shall be made under this provision.

(3) Any High Contracting Party availing itself of this right of derogation shall keep the Secretary General of the Council of Europe fully informed of the measures which it has taken and the reasons therefore. It shall also inform the Secretary General of the Council of Europe when such measures have ceased to operate and the provisions of the Convention are again being fully executed.

Article 15 allows derogation in respect of most, but not all of the Arts. Derogation from Art 2 is not allowed except in respect of death resulting from lawful acts of war, while Arts 3, 4(1) and 7 are entirely non-derogable. Apart from these exceptions, a valid derogation requires the State in question to show that there is a state of war or public emergency and, in order to determine the validity of this claim, two questions should be asked. First, is there an actual or imminent exceptional crisis threatening the organised life of the State? Secondly, is it really necessary to adopt measures requiring derogation from the Articles in question? A margin of discretion is allowed in answering these questions because it is thought that the State in question is best placed to determine the facts, but it is not unlimited; Strasbourg will review it if the State has acted unreasonably. However, the Court has not been very consistent as regards the margin allowed to the State.[457] In general, if a derogation is entered, it must first be investigated and if found invalid, the claims in question will then be examined.

---

456 Eg, Art 14, which prohibits discrimination, is inherently limited because it operates only in the context of the other Convention rights and freedoms.

457 See pp 34–37.

The UK entered a derogation in the case of *Brogan*[458] after the European Court of Human Rights had found that a violation of Art 5, which protects liberty, had occurred. At the time of the violation, there was no derogation in force in respect of Art 5 because the UK had withdrawn its derogation. This might suggest either that there was no need for it or that the UK had chosen not to derogate despite the gravity of the situation which would have justified derogation.[459]

However, after the decision in the European Court, the UK entered the derogation, stating that there was an emergency at the time. This was challenged as an invalid derogation,[460] but the claim failed on the basis that the exigencies of the situation did amount to a public emergency and the derogation could not be called into question merely because the Government had decided to keep open the possibility of finding a means in the future of ensuring greater conformity with Convention obligations.[461] The fact that the emergency measures had been in place since 1974 did not mean that the emergency was not still in being. However, it may be argued that a State's failure to enter a derogation need not preclude the claim that a state of emergency did exist. If, whenever a State perceived the possibility that an emergency situation might exist, it felt it had to enter a derogation as an 'insurance measure' this would encourage a wider use of derogation, which would clearly be undesirable.

In the *Greek* case,[462] the Commission was prepared to hold an Art 15 derogation invalid. Greece had alleged that the derogation was necessary due to the exigencies of the situation: it was necessary to constrain the activities of communist agitators due to the disruption they were likely to cause. There had been past disruption which had verged on anarchy. Greece, therefore, claimed that it could not abide by the Articles in question: Arts 10 and 11. Apart from violations of those Articles, violations of Art 3, which is non-derogable, were also alleged. The Commission found that the derogation was not needed; the situation at the decisive moment did not contain all the elements necessary under Art 15.

Article 16: Restriction on the political activity of aliens

Nothing in Articles 10, 11 and 14 shall be regarded as preventing the High Contracting Parties from imposing restrictions on the political activity of aliens.

Since Art 16 applies to Arts 10 and 11, it implies that restrictions over and above those already imposed due to the second paragraphs of those Articles can be imposed on aliens in respect of their enjoyment of the freedoms guaranteed, as far as their political activity is concerned. This does not mean that aliens have *no* safeguard of freedom of expression, association or assembly; restrictions can be imposed only if they relate to political activities. Through its effect on Art 14, Art 16 affects all the rights in the Convention, since

---

458 Judgment of 29 November 1988; (1989) 11 EHRR 117; A 145 (1989).

459 See Chapter 13, pp 793–94.

460 *Brannigan and McBride v UK* (1993) 17 EHRR 539.

461 It may be noted that the derogation has now been withdrawn due to the inception of the Terrorism Act 2000, s 41 and an amendment was made to the Human Rights Act, Sched 3, Part 1, by order, accordingly: Human Rights Act (Amendment) Order (2001) SI 2001/1216; in force from 1 April 2001.

462 Report of 5 November 1969, Yearbook XII.

it means that the national authorities can discriminate in relation to aliens as far as any of the Convention rights are concerned. Article 16 has, therefore, been greatly criticised as creating consequences which 'hardly fit into the system of the Convention'.[463] The fact that discrimination as regards the protection afforded to Convention rights is allowable, would not, however, preclude claims that the substantive rights – other than those arising under Arts 10 and 11 – had been violated.

Article 17: Destruction of Convention rights

> Nothing in this Convention may be interpreted as implying for any State, group or person any right to engage in any activity or perform any act aimed at the destruction of any of the rights and freedoms set forth herein or at their limitation to a greater extent than is provided for in the Convention.

Article 17 prevents a person relying on a Convention right where his or her ultimate aim is the destruction or limitation of Convention rights. Article 17 is dealt with on the issue of admissibility, but it can be looked at a later stage too. Its 'restriction' applies to all the rights and freedoms. In general, if Art 17 is violated, this may well mean that one of the other restrictions on the freedom in question applies too; thus, Art 17 is of importance only when it appears that some measure allows evasion of a Convention guarantee in a manner not covered by the other restrictions. Thus, Art 17 must be read in conjunction with all the articles as allowing for a new exception. This is of particular importance where the guarantee in question is subject to few or no restrictions.

Making a reservation: Art 57

Article 57 provides that a State can declare when signing the Convention that it cannot abide by a particular provision because domestic law then in force is not in conformity with it. This may be done when the Convention or Protocol is ratified. The Court will review the reservation in order to see whether it is specific enough: it should not be of too general a nature.[464] The UK has only entered a reservation in respect of Protocol 1.[465]

6 CONCLUSIONS

It is clear that in one sense, the Convention has been astoundingly successful in creating a standard of human rights which is perceived by so many Europeans as relevant and valuable despite the fact that almost half a century has passed since it was created. The enormous and continuing increase in the number of petitions in the late 1980s, during the 1990s and post-2000 suggest that its potential has only recently been understood. Its influence is likely to increase now that a number of Eastern European States have become

---

463 See Van Dijk and Van Hoof, *op cit*, fn 124, p 410.
464 In *Belilos v Switzerland* (1988) EHRR 466 it was found that the reservation did not comply with Art 64 because it was too general.
465 See above, p 82.

signatories to it. Although it was only intended to create a minimum standard of human rights, it has succeeded in revealing basic flaws in UK law in relation to, for example, the decision to maintain or renew the detention of life prisoners.[466]

At the same time, its ability to bring about change in the laws and practices of Member States must not be exaggerated. Arguably, the Convention may be termed a largely procedural charter in the sense that a challenge to a flawed procedure is more likely to succeed under it than a claim that a substantive right has been violated.[467] Further, it may be argued that the machinery for the enforcement of the Convention is wholly inadequate, particularly in the face of a government unashamedly prepared to breach it for long periods of time.[468] This chapter spent some time dwelling on the stages through which an application will pass if it is pursued all the way through the system. The process means that if an application which is ultimately successful takes five years before the final decision, the individual affected may have to suffer a violation of his or her rights for all that time, although an interim remedy may be available under Rule 39 where the Chamber or its President considers that it should be adopted in the interest of the parties or of the proper conduct of the proceedings. Usually, such a remedy would be granted where there is an immediate risk to life or health, in death penalty cases[469] or in deportation or extradition cases.[470] There is no formal mechanism available, such as an interim injunction, to prevent the continuing violation, but a Rule 39 request is normally complied with. Now that the Court and Commission have merged, some of the overlapping stages, such as the dual consideration of admissibility, have disappeared, although the question of admissibility itself still arises. If the admissibility stage were eliminated, the workload of the single Court would increase enormously, although the quality of decision making in some individual cases might be improved. The process is still likely to be lengthy, especially as it is expected that the number of petitions will increase enormously due to the accession of Eastern European Member States.

If a petition comes before the European Court of Human Rights, it may decide that no violation has occurred due to its invocation of the margin of appreciation. If, however, it declares that a breach has indeed occurred, the violation may well subsist for some years while the Member State concerned considers the extent to which it will respond. Eventually, a measure may be adopted which may still represent a violation of rights, but of a less pernicious nature.[471] A challenge to such a measure would have to go through the same lengthy process in order to bring about any improvement in the protection afforded in the Member State to the right in question.

---

466 See, eg, *Thynne, Wilson and Gunnel v UK*, Judgment of 25 October 1990; (1990) 13 EHRR 666, discussed above, p 56.

467 See, eg, *Mats Jacobson v Sweden* (1990) 13 EHRR 79, above, p 58.

468 The UK Government is quite frequently slow to respond to an adverse ruling, and when the response comes, it may be inadequate. See Chapter 11, pp 670–71.

469 *Ocalan v Turkey*, 30.11.99.

470 *Soering v UK* (1989) 11 EHRR 439.

471 The response of the UK Government to the ruling in *Malone v UK* (1984) 7 EHRR 14 which was to place telephone tapping on a statutory footing (under the Interception of Communications Act 1985) may be an example of an inadequate implementation of a ruling since the Act does not require independent authorisation of intercept warrants even in cases unconcerned with national security. The position under the legislation which will replace the 1985 Act – the Regulation of Investigatory power as Act 2000 Part 1 – is, in essentials, the same. (See further Chapter 11, pp 670–76.)

Thus, it may be concluded that reliance on the Convention has tended to produce only erratic, flawed and weak protection of freedoms in the UK. However, as argued at the beginning of this chapter, the solution does not appear to be adoption of a more coercive process since that might lead to open conflict with Strasbourg and perhaps, ultimately, withdrawal of some State Parties from the Convention. It was intended that the twin problems of the slow procedure and inadequate enforcement would be addressed by the reception of the Convention into UK law under the Human Rights Act. The framework of the HRA, as the means of affording the needed further effect to the Convention in domestic law, is considered in Chapter 4. It will be asked whether, in terms of efficacy, it can fairly be said that the rights have now been 'brought home'.

CHAPTER 3

METHODS OF PROTECTING CIVIL LIBERTIES IN THE UK: THE BILL OF RIGHTS DEBATE FORESHADOWING THE HUMAN RIGHTS ACT

1 INTRODUCTION

The premise behind the adoption of Bills of Rights all over the world is that citizens can never be fully assured of the safety of their fundamental civil and political rights unless those rights are afforded protection from State interference. It is thought that such protection can be achieved by enshrining a number of rights in a Bill of Rights, affording it some constitutional protection and entrusting it – in effect – to the judiciary on the basis that a government cannot be expected to keep a satisfactory check on itself; only a source of power independent of it can do so. Democracies across the world that have adopted a Bill or Charter of Rights have entrusted its application largely to the judiciary on the basis that among such sources of power, they are best placed to ensure the delivery of the rights to citizens. Dworkin has argued that under a Bill of Rights, a government is not free to treat liberty as a commodity of convenience or to ignore rights that the nation is under a moral duty to respect.[1]

In the UK, however, it was thought until relatively recently that the unwritten constitution recognising residual liberties, as maintained by Parliament and the judiciary, provided a sufficiently effective means of ensuring that power was not abused.[2] Residual liberties were, however, vulnerable to invasion: the doctrine of parliamentary sovereignty meant that Parliament could legislate in an area of fundamental rights, thereby restricting or even destroying them.[3] The judiciary could also invade liberties in developing the common law, while unless a right could be said to be recognised by the common law, public authorities could invade it without relying on statute, the prerogative or common law rules.[4]

The argument that residual liberties were ineffective and that the change to a rights-based approach should be brought about gathered momentum during the 1970s and 1980s and gained ascendancy in the 1990s. This change of view was clearly traceable to the development and influence of international human rights law,[5] especially the impact of the European Convention on Human Rights. The argument was further fuelled by the invasions of liberty that occurred under the Conservative Governments from 1979–97. It was argued that the traditional checks on government power could now be seen as insufficiently effective. These two developments were, it is suggested, interlinked; as Hunt argues: 'no single factor has been more significant in exposing this gap between theory [the traditional account of domestic constitutional arrangements] and practice than the international dimension which [over the last 25 to 30 years] domestic constitutional practice has been forced to accommodate.'[6]

---

1 Dworkin, R, *A Bill of Rights for Britain*, 1990, p 23.
2 See Jennings, WI, *The Approach to Self-Governance*, 1958.
3 Thus, freedom of assembly was severely restricted in the 1990s and beyond; see Chapter 9, pp 427–32.
4 See *Malone v MPC* [1979] Ch 344, p 372.
5 See further Hunt, M, *Using Human Rights Law in English Courts*, 1997.
6 *Ibid*, p 1.

This view of the record of those Conservative Governments, viewed from the perspective offered by international human rights law, was used to support the introduction of the Human Rights Act 1998 (HRA),[7] which came fully into force on 2 October 2000. The HRA receives the European Convention on Human Rights into UK law, thereby providing the UK with an instrument that, while arguably not amounting to a 'Bill of Rights' in the modern sense,[8] provides a new and very significant protection for human rights and freedoms. The HRA comes as close to creating a Bill of Rights as the UK has ever come.

This chapter begins by considering the traditional methods of protecting civil liberties in the UK: the changes that are being brought about under the Human Rights Act must be placed in that context. Clearly, while the inception of the Human Rights Act is intended to provide a new and effective means of protecting certain fundamental rights, it does not entail an abandonment of the *traditional* methods of protecting liberties; it may provide a means of strengthening them. Moreover, existing established rights and existing rights to bring proceedings are preserved by s 11 of the Human Rights Act; therefore, all the existing methods of protecting civil liberties already developed under the law are still highly relevant. Indeed, as explained below, they will provide the usual forum in which arguments relating to civil liberties are put forward in the post-Human Rights Act era, based either on the Convention and/or on established common law principle. The chapter goes on to consider some of the arguments that were put forward, especially in the 1990s, as to the need to enact a Bill of Rights, and as to the disadvantages of taking that step. Finally, it indicates the choices that had to be taken when the Human Rights Act was enacted, against the background of the preceding debate. Chapter 4 goes on to consider the Human Rights Act itself.

2 METHODS OF PROTECTING CIVIL LIBERTIES IN THE UK

The democratic process as the guardian of civil liberties

It has traditionally been thought that Parliament provides a means of allowing the will of the people to influence the government towards the maintenance of liberty[9] through free elections and secret ballots and aided by the operation of a free press. It can react to the needs of civil liberties by providing specific legislative safeguards and, in so doing, can take into account the views and expertise of a range of groups. Moreover, it will govern according to the rule of law, which will include the notion that it will accept certain limits on its powers based on normative ideals.[10]

---

7   The HRA received royal assent on 9 November 1998.
8   See below, pp 133–34.
9   See, eg, Dicey, *The Law of the Constitution*, 1959, pp 189–90; Hume, *Political Discourses*, 1906 (first published 1752), p 203.
10   See, eg, Wade, W and Bradley, A, *Constitutional and Administrative Law*, 1985, pp 99–100.

However, commentators such as Ewing and Gearty, evaluating governments in the 1980s, argued that these traditional checks were insufficiently effective as methods of curbing the power of a determined and illiberal governing party: 'Mrs Thatcher has merely utilised to the full the scope for untrammeled power latent in the British Constitution but obscured by the hesitancy and scruples of previous consensus-based political leaders.'[11] In particular, it is clear that when the government in power has a large majority, as the Thatcher Government had, it may more readily depart from traditional constitutional principles if it is minded to do so, because Parliament is likely to be ineffective as a check on its activities. Even where the governing party does not have a large majority, it can still introduce legislation abridging basic freedoms, especially where the main opposition party sympathises with its stance. As this book indicates at a number of points, the Major Government exemplified this tendency. The Thatcher and Major Governments introduced very little legislation protective of civil liberties except where they were forced to do so by a ruling of the European Court of Human Rights, an EC Directive or a ruling of the European Court of Justice. In short, the dangers of the doctrine of parliamentary sovereignty in terms of threatening fundamental liberties became more apparent during the Conservative years of 1979–97. While it is important not to allow the record of those Conservative Governments to distort debate as to the efficacy of the democratic process in protecting civil liberties, it is also important to bear in mind the lessons which have been learnt as to the constitutional weaknesses which those governments exposed.

Government secrecy and executive discretion

Parliament's ability to create a check on government has, as Birkinshaw points out,[12] been hampered by the lack of a Freedom of Information Act in scrutinising the actions of ministers. This lack meant that the government could choose what and how much to reveal in response to opposition questions and therefore – as the *Ponting* case[13] made clear – was able to present a selective picture of events. Until 2000, Britain did not have a Freedom of Information (FoI) Act, unlike other democracies, and, following the tradition of secrecy, Parliament until recently saw no need to enact one.[14] Although FoI legislation is now in place, there are grounds for arguing that its impact in terms of enabling Parliament to play an effective role may be limited, as Chapter 7 argues.[15]

Moreover, as this book will indicate at a number of points,[16] decisions affecting civil liberties are frequently taken not under parliamentary scrutiny, but by ministers and officials exercising discretionary powers. The exercise of such powers may receive more scrutiny in other jurisdictions. For example, the Australian Government has accepted that there should be a parliamentary committee charged with scrutiny of the Australian Security Service.[17] In the UK, in contrast, when the Security Services Bill 1989 was

---

11 Ewing, KD and Gearty, CA, *Freedom under Thatcher*, 1989, p 7.
12 See Birkinshaw, P, *Freedom of Information*, 1996, Chapter 3.
13 *Ponting* [1985] Crim LR 318. See further Chapter 7, pp 338–39.
14 See Chapter 7, pp 379 *et seq*.
15 See pp 379–95 for discussion of recent developments in this area.
16 See, in particular, Chapter 11.
17 See the Australian Security Service Intelligence Organisation Amendment Act 1986.

debated, the government refused an amendment which would have subjected MI5 to scrutiny by a Select Committee.[18] It continues to be the case that questions about the operation of MI5 and MI6 will not be answered in Parliament. Clearly, matters which are hidden from the public and from opposition MPs may tend to evade the checks arising from the democratic process, such as they are.

Opposition complicity in curtailing liberties

Aside from these issues, which have become particularly pressing over the last two decades, it may also be questioned whether the Westminster Parliament by its nature provides an effective forum for taking the protection of civil liberties into account in passing legislation. A number of writers[19] have noted that Parliament at times displays a readiness to pass emergency legislation which may go further than necessary in curtailing civil liberties and which is apt to remain on the statute book long after the emergency is over. MPs, whether in government or out of it, tend to respond in an unconsidered fashion to emergencies, apparent or real. Governments wish to be perceived as acting quickly and decisively, while members of the Opposition parties, mindful of their popularity, may not wish to oppose measures adopted in the face of scares whipped up by some sections of the media. Such reactions were seen in relation to the original Official Secrets Act 1911, passed in one day with all-party support in response to a spy scare. The far reaching s 2, which was never debated at all, remained on the statute book for 78 years. Similarly, the Birmingham pub bombings on 21 November 1974 led, four days later, to the announcement of the Prevention of Terrorism Bill,[20] which was passed by 29 November virtually without amendment or dissent.

In the 1990s, Parliament quite frequently showed a marked readiness to accept claims that a number of proposed statutory measures would lead to the curbing of terrorist or criminal activity. Although such measures were likely to represent an infringement of civil liberties, they did not in general encounter determined criticism from the opposition. During the last Conservative years, Labour in opposition under Blair took a stance that could hardly be viewed as civil liberties-oriented. A number of political scientists have observed that in the 1990s, there was a general policy convergence, with the front-benchers of the Labour and Conservative Parties closer on many issues than at any point since the 1970s.[21] In the civil liberties context, two key examples were provided by the opposition impact on the Criminal Justice and Public Order Act 1994 and the Police Act 1997. Many pressure groups protested against the 1994 Bill: it probably attracted more public opposition than any other measure during the Conservative years in government 1979–97, apart from the 'Poll tax'. But, despite protests against the Bill and the far-reaching nature of many of the new provisions, it went through Parliament relatively intact. As ATH Smith observes: 'Presumably for fear of being seen to be soft on crime ... the Labour Party declined to oppose the Bill on Second Reading, leaving the serious

---

18 That position remained unchanged despite the enactment of subsequent legislation relating to the accountability of the intelligence Services: see Chapter 11, pp 649–62.

19 Eg, Robertson, G, *Freedom, the Individual and the Law*, 1993, p 506; Walker, C, *The Prevention of Terrorism in British Law*, 2nd edn, 1992, Chapter 4, p 32.

20 HC Debs Vol 882 Col 35.

21 Seldon, A, 'The consensus debate' (1994) 14 Parliamentary Affairs 512.

opposition to the Bill to the Peers. Given the target of [the public order aspects] of the Act and the social make-up of their Lordships' House ... the prospects of serious opposition were negligible.'[22]

As Chapter 11 explains, the Liberal Democrats took the lead in proposing the more far-reaching amendments to the 1997 Police Bill.[23] The Labour Party initially supported the proposals in the Bill to allow the police self-authorising powers to place bugging devices on property. Their stance was modified only after a government defeat on this matter in the Lords and severe criticism from various quarters. Jack Straw, the Shadow Home Secretary, finally agreed with Michael Howard on a compromise which would ensure that in certain serious cases the police had to seek authorisation from a judicial committee.[24] This compromise was criticised in many quarters as providing only marginally more protection for civil liberties.

The debate in the House of Commons on the Prevention of Terrorism (Additional Powers) Act 1996, which was guillotined, failed to consider in depth either the efficacy of the measure in terms of curbing terrorist activity or its likely impact on civil liberties. The debate provided, in microcosm, a good instance of the debasement and impoverishment of parliamentary criminal justice debate in the mid-1990s. The Labour Party supported the proposals partly on the narrow ground that they represented only a small increase on the extended police powers which were included in the Criminal Justice and Public Order Act 1994 and which were not challenged on grounds of principle at the Committee stage of that Bill.[25] Thus, issues as to the real value of these powers fell to be asked only by Labour backbenchers and, owing to pressure of time and the stance of the leadership, they could not be pressed home.

Examples can be found to support the other side in this debate. It is generally agreed that the democratic process worked well in creating the Police and Criminal Evidence Act 1984,[26] and it is fair to say that it had at least some impact, as suggested above, on the Police Act 1997. It might be argued that the 1994 Act was a product of special parliamentary conditions which are unlikely to recur: a particularly illiberal Home Secretary piloted it through Parliament and the Shadow Home Secretary supported its key provisions. However, subsequent developments suggest that similar conditions continued throughout and beyond the late 1990s.

The change of government in 1997, when Labour came to power after 18 years of Conservative rule, heralded the introduction of two key pieces of liberal legislation – the Human Rights Act 1998 and the Freedom of Information Act 2000. Nevertheless, the prevailing stance on both government and opposition benches remains a largely anti-liberal one. For example, the first significant counter-terrorist measure passed under the New Labour Government, the Criminal Justice (Terrorism and Conspiracy) Bill 1998, strongly resembled the 1996 Act in terms both of its content and of the parliamentary process it underwent. The Bill was rushed through both Houses in two days in the wake

---

22 Smith, ATH [1995] Crim LR 19, p 27.

23 See p 693.

24 See, now, s 91(1) of the Act.

25 Straw, J, HC Deb 2 April 1996 Col 221.

26 See Zander, M, *The Police and Criminal Evidence Act 1984*, 1995, p xi: '... there can be no denying that the whole exercise was an example of the democratic process working.'

of the Omagh bombing on the basis that the powers were needed immediately for operational reasons. In fact, no immediate action occurred in reliance on the new powers. The two central measures enhancing State power introduced in the first term of the Blair Government – the Terrorism Act 2000 and the Regulation of Investigatory Powers Act 2000, showed, it will be argued in this book, even less respect for human rights than measures such as the Police Act 1997. The stance of the Labour Government is indicated at various points in the following chapters. It will be contended that the consensus which some commentators viewed as 'shaping the politics of the 1990s'[27] is continuing post-2000. At the present time, it is argued, the Conservative opposition under Duncan-Smith has adopted a stance which is more authoritarian and even less civil rights-minded than the Labour Government. It seems clear that the Conservative approach has remained unchanged after the General Election in 2001. It may be argued, then, that there has been little effective opposition in the Commons on human rights matters from the mid-1990s onwards and, at present, little prospect of any.

The House of Lords

The fact that the UK possesses a Second Chamber was sometimes used as an argument against the introduction of a Bill of Rights. The argument ran on these lines: other countries adopted Bills of Rights for a variety of reasons – either because they were at a stage in their development when human rights were particularly at risk, or because of a particular feature of their constitution, such as the lack of a second legislative chamber[28] to keep a check on the lower House;[29] their experience is not, therefore, analogous to that in the UK. But it must be questioned how far a second chamber can protect civil liberties. The House of Lords has had some successes, notably its influence on the incorporation into the Police and Criminal Evidence Act 1984 of a provision with clear potential to safeguard the liberty of the citizen – s 78.[30] As mentioned above, the Lords also passed amendments to Michael Howard's Police Bill in 1997 allowing for judicial authorisation of bugging warrants. Crucial amendments to the Terrorism Act 2000, which narrowed the definition of terrorism in cl 1, were passed in the Lords.[31] However, the powers of the Lords to thwart the wishes of the Commons are limited. Section 2 of the Parliament Act 1911 makes various provisions for presenting a Bill for the royal assent against the opposition of the Lords. When a Bill has been passed by the Commons in two successive sessions and it is rejected for a second time by the Lords, it can be presented on its second rejection for the royal assent. The very existence of this power means that the need to invoke it is unlikely to arise because the Lords will wish to avoid the need for the Commons to use it.[32]

Prior to the reform of the House of Lords, begun in 1999, the Lords were generally circumspect in using their powers; when they opposed a Bill sent up by the Commons,

---

27 Dutton, D, *British Politics since 1945*, 2nd edn, 1997, p 155.
28 New Zealand, which adopted a Bill of Rights in 1990, has no second chamber.
29 This view was put forward by Lord McCluskey in his 1986 Reith lectures.
30 House of Lords, *Hansard*, 31 July 1984, Cols 635–75. See Chapter 14, pp 880 *et seq*.
31 See Chapter 8, pp 402–03.
32 The House of Lords will, however, on occasion use its powers of suspension fully as it did in relation to the Trade Union and Labour Relations (Amendment) Bill 1974–75.

they tended to propose amendments at the Committee stage rather than vote against the second reading, and they followed the convention that amendments at the Committee stage should not re-open matters of principle already accepted by the Commons. The Lords rarely insisted on their amendments to a government Bill. O Hood Phillips has observed[33] that there was almost a convention that the Lords would not return a government Bill to the Commons for reconsideration more than once.[34] Hereditary peers (over 750 of them) formed the majority of those entitled to sit in the Lords and ensured the continuance of a Conservative majority. Although many of them were not regular attenders, they were occasionally brought in to secure the passage of Conservative legislation which the regular attenders might be inclined to reject.[35] Their voting rights were abolished in 1999 as the first part of the Labour reform of the Lords.[36] The partially reformed House of Lords currently sees itself as having greater credibility than its predecessor and, as a result, is more interventionist.[37] Clearly, the fully reformed House may take the same or a more radical view.[38] The Lords may, therefore, become more effective in civil liberties terms. Their activism may be enhanced by the HRA since, as explained below, when Bills are introduced into the Lords, they are accompanied by a statement of compatibility with the Convention rights.[39] Thus, the Lords now have a set of standards by which to measure the impact of the legislation in question on human rights.

Conclusions

It may be concluded that Parliament has demonstrated that it is willing to move quickly to cut down freedoms, but it is, at the same time, slow to bring in measures to protect them, because civil liberties issues tend to be perceived as difficult to handle and as doubtful vote-winners. It may even be the case that the governing party would like to bring forward legislation on a civil liberties issue, such as introducing legislation making discrimination on grounds of sexual orientation unlawful, but be hesitant to do so because of its controversial nature.[40] This received parliamentary wisdom has meant that

---

33 See Hood Phillips, O, *Constitutional and Administrative Law*, 7th edn, p 148.

34 Lord Hailsham said in March 1976 in relation to the Trade Union and Labour Relations (Amendment) Bill that opposition had exhausted their powers in sending the Bill back once to the Commons and so had discharged their duty.

35 This occurred in May 1988 in relation to the introduction of the Community Charge (Poll tax).

36 The House of Lords Act 1999 removed the automatic right of hereditary Peers to sit in the House of Lords. An 'interim' House of Lords of 90 members, elected by the Peers, is currently sitting, until the reform is completed.

37 See Lord Cranborne, HL Deb 22 February 2000 Cols 151–52 and Cols 163–64. The Lord Privy Seal stated in the House Magazine on 27.9.99 that the new House of Lords will 'be more legitimate because its members have earned their places and therefore more effective ...'. In the Committee stage of the Criminal Justice (Mode of Trial) Bill in the Lords, the first amendment put down was a 'wrecking' amendment which was carried by the Lords and resulted in the immediate withdrawal of the Bill (HL Deb 20 Jan 2000 Col 1246 *et seq*).

38 See the Wakeham Report of the Royal Commission published in January 2000, *A House for the Future*, Cm 3534 (available on the web: http://www.official-documents.co.uk/document/cm45/4534/4534.htm). The report suggested a mainly appointed House of 550 with a minority of elected representatives; the Government is pledged to act on the proposals: HL Deb 7 March 2000 Col 912.

39 Human Rights Act, s 19; see Chapter 4, pp 152–53.

40 See further Chapter 16, pp 1052 *et seq*.

measures protecting civil liberties are vulnerable to under-funding,[41] and, this book will argue, in the case of the Human Rights Act, to the undermining impact of later legislation.

Under the HRA, the Westminster Parliament is still dominated by the executive and still has an untrammelled power to introduce rights-abridging legislation throughout the UK.[42] In this context, it cannot yet be said that radical constitutional reform which would genuinely constrain the power of the Westminster executive has occurred. Thus, in so far as it can be said that Parliament has shown itself to be ineffective in protecting civil liberties, it may be argued that a need for a further means of protection has been demonstrated. But such protection, under the HRA, need not be sought wholly or mainly outside Parliament. The HRA creates mechanisms which would allow Parliament to be more proactive in protecting civil rights, as explained below. But, as indicated at a number of points in this book, an optimistic or complacent attitude towards the impact of the HRA, in terms of enhancing the traditional protection offered to such rights by Parliament, would probably be misplaced. At least in the early years of the HRA, it seems probable that Parliament may accept quite readily that when Bills are presented to parliament and are declared to be compatible with the Convention rights under s 19 of the HRA,[43] this means that a process of human rights auditing has already occurred and that therefore, concerns about the effect on human rights of the provisions in question can be allayed.[44]

It is clearly pertinent to ask whether the democratic process can be trusted to safeguard civil liberties in the context of the doctrine of parliamentary sovereignty. The further question that this book will address is whether the Human Rights Act can be expected to provide the effective protection for fundamental rights that has not been achieved through the operation of the democratic process, bearing in mind the fact that parliamentary sovereignty remains intact. As indicated, the influence of the HRA on that process in a *direct* sense will also be a significant theme.

Rules and judicial interpretation: current relevance of the traditional constitutional position

Residual liberties

The influential constitutional writer AV Dicey expressed the traditional view of rights as follows: 'most foreign constitutions have begun by declarations of rights ... On the other hand, there remains through the English constitution that inseparable connection between the means of enforcing a right and the right to be enforced which is the strength of judicial legislation ... Englishmen whose labours ... framed the completed set of laws and institutions we call the constitution, fixed their minds more intently on providing

---

41 Bodies such as the Equal Opportunities Commission may be under-funded, provision of legal aid may be cut without much (or any) public outcry.

42 See p 134. The Government can, of course, use the Parliament Act procedure in order to get its legislation through the Lords, as it did in respect of the Sexual Offences (Amendment) Bill 2000, and it may be that it will have to resort to this in future if the Lords tend to refuse to accept the conventional restraints in which they previously acquiesced.

43 See below, pp 152–54.

44 See further Chapter 8, pp 409–12.

remedies for the enforcement of rights ... than upon any declaration of the rights of man ...'[45] The Diceyan tradition holds that the absence of a written constitution in the UK is not a weakness, but a source of strength. This is because the protection of the citizen's liberties is not dependent on vaguely worded constitutional documents but, rather, flows from specific judicial decisions which give the citizen specific remedies for infringement of his or her liberties. It follows from the Diceyan thesis that judges will be concerned to construe legislation strictly against the executive if it conflicts with fundamental liberties arising from the common law.[46]

Dicey regarded one of the great strengths of the British Constitution as lying in the lack of broad discretionary powers vested in the executive. Citizens could only be criminalised for clear breaches of clearly established laws and such laws also governed the extent to which individual freedoms could be infringed. Where there was no relevant law, citizens could know with absolute confidence that they could exercise their liberty as they pleased without fear of incurring any sanction.

Parliamentary sovereignty is central to the Diceyan thesis. One of its significant aspects is the position whereby, unless international treaties are incorporated into domestic law, they cannot have legal effect, domestically. This aspect derived from the supremacy of Parliament over the executive: since the making of a treaty is an executive act, any attempt by the courts to afford domestic effect to its provisions would mean undermining that supremacy. Thus, traditionally, the judiciary adopted a 'dualist' approach to such treaties; they represented a system of law external to the domestic one and not part of it. This approach entailed a resistance to any use of unincorporated international law before domestic courts.

Central aspects of Dicey's thesis are, however, unconvincing as an analysis of UK contemporary legal culture, for a number of reasons. The Diceyan view of the law as imposing only narrow and tightly defined areas of liability is no longer representative, given the prevalence of broadly drawn offences such as those arising under counter-terrorist legislation or under the Criminal Justice and Public Order Act 1994. The view that the judges will construe rules strictly against the executive is also problematic, especially in relation to the use of quasi- and non-legislation authorising interference with civil liberties. Many such rules, including the Home Office Guidelines relied on by the police until 1997 in using surveillance devices, remain on a non-statutory basis for many years; they therefore receive no parliamentary scrutiny and little or no judicial scrutiny either. When such rules *are* placed on a statutory basis, as they were under the Interception of Communications Act 1985, the Security Services Act 1989 and the Intelligence Services Act 1994, judicial scrutiny of their operation is, typically, largely ousted. This tradition was continued by the New Labour Government under the Terrorism Act 2000 and the Regulation of Investigatory Powers Act 2000, as this book will point out, and significant aspects of these schemes are found in Codes of Practice and statutory instruments. The result is that there have been and will continue to be a number of significant areas of executive action which are largely closed to judicial scrutiny.

---

45   Dicey, AV, *Introduction to the Study of the Law of the Constitution*, 10th edn, 1987, p 198; see also p 190.
46   See, eg, *Waddington v Miah* [1974] 2 All ER 377, HL.

The following discussion indicates the inadequacies of Dicey's account in a number of further respects. In particular, it indicates the extent to which the European Convention on Human Rights was used as an interpretative tool and became a source of values relied upon in the development of the common law in the 1990s.

Judicial protection for liberties outside administrative law

Under the traditional view of the constitution, the judges will interpret common law doctrines so that fundamental freedoms are protected.[47] Street, in *Freedom, the Individual and the Law*, argues: 'our judges may be relied on to defend strenuously some kinds of freedom. Their emotions will be aroused where personal freedom is menaced by some politically unimportant area of the executive.'[48] Ewing and Gearty have argued, however, that the first half of the 20th century saw a marked judicial reluctance to protect such freedoms.[49] Consideration of key decisions in the latter half of the 20th century also suggests that there did not seem to be a clear conception, shared by most members of the judiciary, of their role as protecting liberties. For example, during the miners' strike in 1984–85, striking miners shouted abuse at miners going in to work guarded by police; the working miners claimed that such action was unlawful, and it was found that although no obvious legal pigeon-hole, such as assault, could be found for it owing to the circumstances, it could be termed 'a species of private nuisance' and injunctions against the striking miners were, therefore, granted.[50] The use of common law contempt in the *Spycatcher* litigation provides a further example.[51]

On a number of occasions, the judiciary interpreted uncertain areas of the common law, such as breach of the peace, very broadly, to some extent undermining the safeguards for liberties provided by statutes covering equivalent areas. Where an attempt has been made in a statute to seek to ensure that a particular freedom is protected, as is the case in s 4 of the Obscene Publications Act 1959 and s 5 of the Contempt of Court Act 1981, it may be found that the common law begins to take on a role which undermines the statutory provisions. This can be said of the common law doctrines of contempt and conspiracy to corrupt public morals.[52] It is noticeable that when the judges are enjoined in a statute to take account of a value such as freedom of expression – as they are under s 5 of the Contempt of Court Act 1981 – they are more likely to adopt a rigorous approach than when dealing with a wide and uncertain power arising at common law.[53] Ewing and Gearty have argued that, for this reason, a Bill of Rights would be undesirable since the

---

47   See *Entinck v Carrington* [1765] 19 State Tr 1029.

48   Street, *Freedom, the Individual and the Law*, 1982, p 318.

49   See Ewing, KD and Gearty, CA, *The Struggle for Civil Liberties*, 1999.

50   *Thomas v NUM* [1985] 2 All ER 1.

51   *AG v Newspaper Publishing plc* [1988] Ch 333; [1987] 3 All ER 276; [1988] 3 WLR 942, CA. See further Chapter 5, pp 246 and 249.

52   See further Chapter 6, p 293.

53   Contrast the approach to freedom of speech taken in *AG v English* [1983] 1 AC 116 in relation to s 5 of the 1981 Act, with that taken in *AG v Newspaper Publishing plc* [1988] Ch 333 in relation to common law contempt; also the approach to the Public Order Act 1986 taken in *Reid* [1987] Crim LR 702 with that taken to breach of the peace in *Moss v McLachlan* [1985] IRLR 76. See Chapter 5, pp 238 and 246 and Chapter 9, pp 459 and 495–96 respectively.

people need Parliament to protect them from the judges, not merely the judges to protect them from Parliament.[54]

From the perspective of the 1980s, it can be said that when a commentator in the common law tradition, such as TRS Allan, sought to defend the record of the common law in protecting fundamental rights,[55] a rather ironic pattern emerged. Allan contended that the case law showed support for civil liberties; he quoted from cases which purportedly supported his contention – and then found himself apologising for the inadequacies of the Lords' approach. Having cited *Wheeler v Leicester CC*[56] as an instance of the sturdy defence of free speech, he conceded that Lord Roskill did not use free speech grounds at all, while Lord Templeman did, in general terms, but unfortunately 'failed to address the level of principle demanded by the freedoms at issue'.[57] When he turned to the *Spycatcher* litigation, he was forced to concede from the outset that the speeches are 'disappointing'. Having praised Lord Keith for affirming the general freedom to speak, he then went on to admit that his Lordship failed to injunct only because 'all possible damage to the interests of the Crown had already been done' and that he was 'unwilling to ... base his decision on any considerations of freedom of the press'.[58]

As this book will indicate, a number of 20th century decisions showed similar characteristics. Judicial activism in the 1990s, however, led to a number of significant decisions protective of liberty. They were influenced by International Human Rights law, and more specifically by the European Convention, in the sense that the judiciary began to demonstrate a strong inclination to show that the common law had long recognised the values encapsulated in the Convention. By so doing, they avoided the difficulties, discussed below, of determining the precise status of the European Convention in domestic law, while allowing for the infusion of such values into the common law.

The decision of *Derbyshire v Times Newspapers*,[59] which has been acclaimed as 'a legal landmark',[60] provides an important example of this tendency. The House of Lords found, without referring to Art 10 of the European Convention, that the importance the common law attached to free speech was such that defamation could not be available as an action to local (or central) government.[61] In the House of Lords, Lord Keith said: 'I find it satisfactory to be able to conclude that the common law of England is consistent with the [freedom of expression] obligations assumed under [the Convention].'[62] Butler-Sloss LJ said in the Court of Appeal: 'I can see no inconsistency between English law upon this subject and Article 10 ... This is scarcely surprising, since we may pride ourselves on the fact that freedom of speech has existed in this country perhaps as long, if not longer than ... in any other country in the world.'[63]

---

54 Ewing and Gearty, *op cit*, fn 11, pp 270–71.

55 Allan, TRS, 'Constitutional rights and common law' (1991) OJLS 453–60.

56 [1985] AC 1054; [1985] 2 All ER 1106, HL.

57 Allan, *op cit*, fn 55, p 459.

58 Allan, *op cit*, fn 55, p 460.

59 [1993] AC 534; [1993] 1 All ER 1011; [1992] 3 WLR 28, HL.

60 See Laws, J (Sir), 'Is the High Court the guardian of fundamental constitutional rights?' [1993] PL 67.

61 *Derbyshire* was followed and its principle extended in *Goldsmith and Another v Bhoyrul and Others* [1997] 4 All ER 268; (1997) *The Times*, 20 June. It was found that a political party cannot sue in libel, although individual candidates would be able to.

62 [1993] AC 534, p 551.

63 [1992] 3 WLR 28, p 60.

While it might be argued that the decision appears to support the Diceyan thesis, it could also be said, more convincingly, that this explanation does not account for the recognition of Convention values in the common law. Hunt argues that: 'the supposed identity of common law and ECHR is surely a modern manifestation of the ancient myth that judges are not law-makers ... [it is hard to deny that the courts are] developing the common law, extending it to cover rights and interests not previously valued by a conservative common law which privileged above all property-based or personal liberty interests.'[64] In the later seminal decision in *Reynolds v Times Newspapers Ltd*,[65] also in the field of defamation, the influence of the Convention was more overt. The House of Lords found that qualified privilege could apply to a publication where the media could establish that the information promulgated was matter that the public had a right to know. Lord Nicholls of Birkenhead found that this conclusion was firmly based on established common law principle. Lord Steyn gave more weight to Convention-based arguments in finding that: 'it is necessary to recognise the "vital public watchdog role of the press" as a practical matter'. In support of this argument, he relied on *Goodwin v UK*.[66]

But, while an attachment to free speech values that is arguably consonant with the value it is accorded at Strasbourg, is clearly evident in these decisions, this book discusses a number of decisions taken in the mid to late 1990s affecting equally fundamental rights, in the fields of public protest,[67] police powers and fair trial rights,[68] which took a very ungenerous approach to rights and liberties. The reasons for the adoption of such an approach are discussed further in the relevant chapters. But, it is suggested here that while the decisions on fair trial rights do reflect Convention values, to varying degrees, they also assert an allegiance to the dualist approach, which was not evident in *Derbyshire*. The public protest decisions, it is argued, go even further in that direction.

Thus, it can be said that over the last three decades, the judiciary did not develop a coherent approach to the protection of civil rights and liberties, although the influence of the European Convention on Human Rights became very marked, especially in the field of freedom of expression, in the 1990s. The dualist approach became 'in reality a matter of degree'.[69] But the difference of degree was sometimes quite remarkable.

Judicial review

It may be said that, before the 1990s, when fundamental human rights became an increasingly significant factor in judicial review, the judiciary maintained the classic dualist position in judicial review despite the acceptance of Convention values in other

---

64 Hunt, *op cit*, fn 5, p 186.

65 [1999] 4 All ER 609.

66 (1996) 22 EHRR 123, p 143, para 39.

67 Examples of such decisions discussed in this book include: the Divisional Court and House of Lords decisions in *DPP v Jones and Lloyd v DPP* [1999] 2 AC 240; [1997] 2 All ER 119 (for comment, see Fenwick and Phillipson, 'Public protest, the Human Rights Act and judicial responses to political expression' [2000] PL 627) *DPP v Moseley, Woodling and Selvanayagam*, Judgment of 9 June 1999; reported [1999] J Civ Lib 390, (Chapter 9, pp 465 *et seq* and p 514, respectively).

68 *Khan* [1996] 3 WLR 162; *Chalkley* [1998] 2 Cr App R 79.

69 Hunt, *op cit*, fn 5, p 41.

areas of the law. This was on the basis that to do otherwise would be to break down the traditional divide between review and appeal. And even within a strict review jurisdiction, strong deference was shown to executive decision making in the politically important areas of executive action. The reluctance of judges to intervene in such areas, including those of public security or deportation, was evident in a number of decisions. Those in *Secretary of State for the Home Department ex p Northumbria Police Authority*[70] and *Secretary of State for the Home Department ex p Hosenball*[71] showed this tendency to a particularly marked degree. Thus, traditionally, the doctrine remained fundamentally limited in that as long as a minister appeared to have followed a correct and fair procedure, to have acted within his or her powers and to have made a decision which was not clearly unreasonable under the traditional *Wednesbury* test, the decision had to stand regardless of its potentially harmful impact on civil liberties. The fact that basic liberties were curtailed in, for example, the *GCHQ*[72] case did not, in itself, provide a ground for review. In other words, the courts were confined to looking back at the method of arriving at the decision rather than forward to its likely effects. In cases which touched directly on national security, so sensitive were the judges to the executive's duty to uphold the safety of the realm, that they tended to define their powers even to look back on the decision as almost non-existent.[73]

A new development in the stance the judiciary was prepared to take when an administrative decision infringed human rights was evident in *Secretary of State for the Home Department ex p Brind*.[74] The change was explained by Lord Bridge. He rejected the argument that State officials must take the European Convention on Human Rights into account in exercising discretionary power, and thus the possibility of extending the role of the Convention in domestic law by importing it into administrative law was rejected. He made it clear that although the courts would presume that ambiguity in domestic legislation should be resolved by arriving at an interpretation in conformity with the Convention, it did not follow that where Parliament had conferred an administrative discretion on the executive without indicating the precise limits within which it had to be exercised, it could be presumed that it had to be exercised within Convention limits. It had been argued that to import such a principle must have been the legislature's intention, but the House of Lords considered that this would be an unwarranted step to take, bearing in mind that Parliament had chosen not to incorporate the Convention. Thus, the decision in *Brind* reaffirmed the accepted principle that the Convention should be taken into account where domestic legislation was ambiguous. It also determined that State officials were not bound by the Convention in exercising discretionary power.[75]

---

70 [1989] QB 26; [1988] 2 WLR 590; [1988] 1 All ER 556, CA.

71 [1977] 1 WLR 766; see further Chapter 15, pp 951–52. Further examples of decisions taking an ungenerous approach to human rights discussed in this book include the Divisional Court decisions in *DPP v Jones and Lloyd v DPP* [1997] 2 All ER 119, *DPP v Moseley, Woodling and Selvanayagam*, Judgment of 9 June 1999; reported [1999] J Civ Lib 390, (Chapter 9, p 466 and p 514); *Chalkley* [1998] 2 Cr App R 79 (Chapter 14 p 892).

72 *Council of Civil Service Unions v Minister for Civil Service* [1985] AC 374; [1985] 3 WLR 1174; [1984] 3 All ER 935, HL (the Prime Minister's decision struck directly at freedom of association).

73 See *Secretary of State for Home Affairs ex p Stitt* (1987) *The Times*, 3 February.

74 [1991] 1 AC 696; [1991] 1 All ER 720; [1991] 2 WLR 588, HL (political speech was directly curtailed); [1990] 1 All ER 469, CA.

75 It may be noted that the then Conservative Government subsequently accepted that State officials exercising such powers should comply with the Convention: HL Deb 559 WA 7 December 1994 Col 84 and WA 9 January 1995 Vol 560 Col 1.

Lord Bridge, reflecting the view of the majority, accepted nevertheless that where fundamental rights are in issue, they will affect the review of the exercise of such power. He said:

> ... we are entitled to start from the premise that any restriction of the right of freedom of expression requires to be justified and nothing less than an important competing public interest will be sufficient to justify it. The primary judgment as to whether the particular competing public interest justifies the particular restriction ... falls to be exercised by the Secretary of State ... But we are entitled to exercise a secondary judgment by asking whether a reasonable Secretary of State on the material before him could reasonably make that primary judgment. 76

Thus, where fundamental human rights were in question, the *Wednesbury* test had to be refined. This argument was applied and taken further in *Ministry for Defence ex p Smith and Others*.[77] The case concerned the legality of the policy of the Ministry of Defence in maintaining a ban on homosexuals in the armed forces. The applicants, homosexuals who had been dismissed due to the existence of the ban, applied for review of the policy. Their application was dismissed at first instance in the Divisional Court and the applicants appealed. Rejecting the argument of the Ministry of Defence that it had no jurisdiction to review the legality of the policy in question, the court applied the usual *Wednesbury* principles. This meant that it could not interfere with the exercise of an administrative discretion on substantive grounds save where it was satisfied that the decision was unreasonable in the sense that it was beyond the range of responses open to a reasonable decision maker. But, in judging whether the decision maker had exceeded that margin of appreciation, the human rights context was important: 'the more substantial the interference with human rights, the more the court will require by way of justification before it will be satisfied that the decision was reasonable.'[78] The Court rejected the argument of the Ministry of Defence that a less exacting test than applying *Wednesbury* principles of reasonableness was required. Applying such principles and taking into account the support of the policy in both Houses of Parliament, it could not be said that the policy crossed the threshold of irrationality. The concept of proportionality, as considered by the Master of the Rolls in this instance, was not viewed as a separate head of challenge, but merely as an aspect of *Wednesbury* unreasonableness.[79]

The significance of this decision lay in the meaning attributed to the word 'reasonable'; it denoted only a decision which was 'within the range of responses open to a reasonable decision-maker'.[80] But, the decision maker was required to take account of human rights in appropriate cases and she had to have a more convincing justification the

---

76 [1991] 1 All ER 720, p 723.

77 [1996] 1 All ER 257; [1996] ICR 740. See also *Secretary of State for the Home Department ex p McQuillan* [1995] 3 All ER 400; (1994) *Independent*, 23 September, in which Laws J's approach was expressly followed. Sedley J was unable to find for the applicant due to the particular statutory framework in question.

78 [1996] 1 All ER 257, p 263. See also *Bugdaycay v Secretary of State for the Home Dept* [1987] AC 514, p 531. For comment, see Fordham, M, 'What is anxious scrutiny?' [1996] JR 81.

79 For further argument as to the notion of proportionality, see Himsworth [1996] PL 46; his argument that the notion of proportionality as a separate head of review remains a possibility rests on an examination of *Ministry of Agriculture, Fisheries and Food ex p Hamble* [1995] 2 All ER 714.

80 *Ibid.*

more her decision was likely to trespass on those rights. That decision, however, remained primarily one for the decision maker. The courts would only intervene if the decider had come up with a justification which no reasonable person could consider trumped the human rights considerations – a position which was akin to classic *GCHQ* irrationality.[81] However, *Smith* did require a variable standard of review, depending on the human rights context.

A further, linked, factor of significance in *Smith* was the determination as to which policy considerations were to be allowed to override rights and which were not. It appeared that in making this determination, easily satisfied criteria were adopted. The policy factors were not required to satisfy a test such as that of a 'pressing social need',[82] since satisfying a lesser test nevertheless brought the decision within the range of responses open to a reasonable decision maker. This decision echoed that of Lord Bridge in *Brind* in relation to determinations as to overriding individual rights as guaranteed in the European Convention on Human Rights.[83]

In 1993, Sir John Laws, in an important article,[84] suggested a method of developing judicial review so that it could afford greater protection to liberties. His persuasive thesis is still of relevance in the post-HRA era since it can be used as a tool in order to measure the change brought about in judicial review in the pre-HRA era and by the HRA. He – in effect – anticipated the effect of the HRA, but, as indicated below, it appeared that, initially at least, most of his fellow judges were not prepared to do so. The main thrust of the thesis was, briefly, as follows. He proposed that review could develop such that in a case in which the exercise of discretion could have an adverse impact on fundamental rights, a two-stage test would be imposed by the courts. With respect to the first stage, the thesis noted that the courts have imposed an insistence on decision makers that their power may be used only for the purpose for which it was granted to them, the courts being the final arbiter of the nature of that purpose. As part of this attribution of purpose, the courts have consistently imposed on decision makers the presumption that power is granted to be exercised in a rational, not a capricious manner. It was proposed that a rather more stringent presumption could be imposed – namely, that no statute's purpose could include interference with fundamental rights embedded in the common law and that such interference would only be allowed if it was demonstrated that reading the statute to permit such interference was the only interpretation possible.[85] This was the

---

81   Fenwick, H and Phillipson, G, *Sourcebook on Public Law*, 1997 (2nd edn, 2002), p 803.

82   See below, p 109.

83   See fn 74, above.

84   Laws [1993] PL 59–79.

85   Laws adverts to the fact that an argument very similar to his was rejected in the *Brind* case. However, he considers that this was because the submission made in that case was that their Lordships should make such a presumption (in this case that free speech would not be infringed) under Art 10 of the ECHR. He argues that this is a mistaken approach as it amounts to an attempt to incorporate the ECHR through the back door, which the courts rightly resist since it offends against constitutional principles. Instead, he urges that the correct approach would be to argue that the norms implicit in the ECHR are already reflected in the common law – an approach which gains some support from the House of Lords decision in the *Derbyshire* case [1993] AC 534; [1993] 1 All ER 1011; [1992] 3 WLR 28, HL – and that it is the importance consequently attached by the common law to fundamental rights which provides a justification for the presumption that statutes do not intend to override them.

first stage of the test. This approach was uncontroversial in assuming that power is only granted on the understanding that it will be exercised rationally – indeed, this could be said to be a basic requirement of formal justice. By contrast, to assume that power is never granted to infringe basic liberties is to make a substantive claim – and until the late 1990s, the courts were not prepared to make it. Preparedness to impose such a presumption in all cases implied the kind of unified, purposeful determination to protect civil liberties which most commentators failed to perceive in the judiciary during most of the 1980s and 1990s.[86]

This aspect of the thesis, concerning statutory interpretation in relation to fundamental human rights, found expression in a number of decisions in the immediate pre-HRA era. In this sense, s 3 of the Human Rights Act (see Chapter 4 below) was prefigured in certain decisions that recognised common law rights which cannot be abrogated except by express words or necessary implication – where there is only one way of reading the legislation in question. These include, so far, the rights of access to the courts,[87] to free speech,[88] and to basic subsistence.[89] These decisions are discussed further in the relevant chapters in this book.[90] The rule of construction in these instances was described in one of the most significant of these decisions, *Ex p Simms*,[91] by Lord Hoffman, as follows:

> Parliamentary sovereignty means that Parliament can if it chooses legislate contrary to fundamental principles of human rights ... But the principle of legality means that Parliament must squarely confront what it is doing and count the political cost. Fundamental rights cannot be overridden by general or ambiguous words ... because there is too great a risk that the full implications of their unqualified meaning may have passed unnoticed in the democratic process ... In this way the courts of the UK, though acknowledging the sovereignty of Parliament, apply principles of constitutionality little different from those which exist in countries where the power of the legislature is expressly limited by a constitutional document.[92]

In *Ex p Witham*,[93] Laws J found that the power of the Lord Chancellor to prescribe court fees was not based on sufficiently precise words to allow him to deny the right of access to a court by preventing an applicant on income support from issuing proceedings for defamation.

The second aspect of Laws' proposed thesis was as follows: in the pre-HRA era, the courts insisted that relevant considerations should be taken into account when making a

---

86 See, eg, Oliver, D, 'A Bill of Rights for the United Kingdom', pp 151, 163; Ewing and Gearty, *op cit*, fn 11, generally and pp 64, 111, 157–60, 270–71 for particular criticisms of anti-libertarian judicial decisions and attitudes; Lester, A, 'Fundamental rights: the United Kingdom isolated?' [1984] PL 46.

87 *R v Lord Chancellor ex p Witham* [1998] QB 575. But cf *R v Lord Chancellor ex p Lightfoot* [2000] 2 WLR 318. For comment on the first instance decision [1998] 4 All ER 764, see Elliott, M, 'Lightfoot: tracing the perimeter of constitutional rights' [1998] JR 217.

88 *R v Secretary of State for the Home Dept ex p Simms* [1999] 3 All ER 400, CA; [1999] 3 WLR 328, HL.

89 *R v Secretary of State for Social Security ex p Joint Council of Welfare of Immigrants* [1996] 4 All ER 835; *Lord Saville ex p A* [1999] 4 All ER 860.

90 See Part II, pp 210–11; Chapter 15, pp 932–33

91 *R v Secretary of State for the Home Dept ex p Simms* [1999] 3 All ER 400, CA; [1999] 3 WLR 328, HL.

92 [1999] 3 All ER 400, p 412.

93 [1998] QB 575.

decision, but held that the weight to be given to those considerations was entirely for the decision maker to determine. Sir John Laws argued that, on principle, while this might be a reasonable approach when the matter under consideration involved such issues as economic policy, this was far from the case where fundamental rights were at stake, since it meant that the decision maker would be free 'to accord a high or low importance to the right in question, as he chooses' which 'cannot be right'. He argued that the courts should therefore insist that the right could only be overridden if an 'objective, sufficient justification'[94] existed so that the infringement was limited to what was strictly required by the situation. While such a development would undoubtedly have been welcome, in terms of the protection afforded by judicial review to liberties in the pre-HRA era, two objections were inescapable. The first was simply that there appeared to be no compelling reason to suppose that such a concept of proportionality (as a separate head of challenge rather than as merely an aspect of *Wednesbury* unreasonableness)[95] would not remain waiting in the wings as merely a theoretical possibility prior to the introduction of the HRA.[96] The possibility of its development as a separate head of review was first floated in the *GCHQ* case. Variable enthusiasm by the judiciary to develop it was evident after that decision. The decision in Smith clearly failed to reflect Laws' thesis, although it gave an appearance of doing so. The Laws approach was applied in order to reach an outcome protective of individual rights in *Cambridge HA ex p B*[97] in which Laws J himself was presiding; his decision was immediately overturned by the Court of Appeal.[98] In contrast to that decision, the decision in *R v Lord Saville ex p A*[99] arguably prefigured the introduction of the proportionality test under the HRA and was consistent with that of Laws in *Ex p B*. The Court of Appeal subjected the decision not to afford anonymity to witnesses in the 'Bloody Sunday' inquiry to anxious scrutiny and went on to find that the inquiry had acted irrationally in so doing since it had failed to attach sufficient importance to the right to life.

It was a notable feature of the *Ex p B* case that the Court of Appeal took a wholly different approach from Laws J, a fact which led one commentator, Mallender, to question whether judicial review, which is of course supposed to represent the practical application of the rule of law, was in fact offending against the doctrine by virtue of its increasing uncertainty.[100] Mallender went on to find that in fact, on a more general jurisprudential level, both approaches 'reveal an intention to give effect to recognisably legal values' which restrain the discretion of both of them. Nevertheless, it was clear that since the two courts differed so markedly as to which (legal) matters were (a) relevant and (b) determinative of the matter in hand, it was apparent that the rapid development of this area of law was likely to entail a period of considerable uncertainty as to the content and scope of its core principles.

---

94 *Op cit*, fn 84, p 14.
95 See, eg, the remarks of Taylor LJ in *Ex p United States Tobacco* [1992] 1 QB 353, p 366, to which Laws adverts.
96 For discussion of other proposals for the development of judicial review, see Jowell, J and Lester, A, 'Beyond *Wednesbury*: substantive principles of judicial review' [1987] PL 369.
97 [1995] TLR 159; [1995] WLR 898, CA.
98 [1995] 1 WLR 898.
99 [1999] 4 All ER 860.
100 Mallender, R, 'Judicial review and the rule of law' (1996) 112 LQR 182–86.

The second objection to Laws' thesis was that, even if such a head of challenge had been developed prior to the introduction of the HRA, the really crucial factor would have been the criteria the courts had decided to use to determine which policy considerations were to be allowed to override rights and which were not. If easily satisfied criteria had been adopted – a contingency which appeared likely – then the increased judicial protection offered to basic liberties might have turned out to consist rather more of theory than of substance. As indicated below, this will be a crucial issue under the HRA.

This discussion of judicial review in the immediate pre-HRA era indicates that it is possible to identify a common law tradition of upholding fundamental rights in certain limited, but central areas. It may be noted that that development is very clearly continuing in the HRA era.[101] The decisions considered, together with a number of others of a similar nature,[102] reaffirm, it is suggested, the value of judicial review as a means of ensuring that some harmony between UK executive practice and the standards laid down by the European Convention on Human Rights is achieved, and this was the case even in the pre-HRA era. Murray Hunt has argued that a common law tradition of developing human rights that reflected those enshrined in international human rights treaties was well established.[103] Where, however, a statute uses specific words abrogating human rights,[104] and therefore it is necessary to argue that the decision was unreasonable, the limitations of the Wednesbury doctrine, albeit refined by reference to the human rights context, persisted. The decision in *Smith* may be said to demonstrate the limitations of judicial review in this respect. The reception of the European Convention on Human Rights into UK law under the HRA means that proportionality has been established as a separate head of review where the Convention guarantees are in issue, since the need for the administrative decision or measure in question has to be considered in relation to its impact in terms of the those guarantees.

Judicial review has already shown its potential to play a much greater part in the protection of human rights in the UK in the areas of activity affected by EU law.[105] In such areas, the merits of the decision will be relevant and express words used in a statute will not overcome EU provisions.[106]

Conclusions

Two points seem to emerge from the above discussion. First, in the pre-HRA era, the judiciary did not seem to be united around a clear conception of their role. No compelling

---

101 See *Secretary of State for the Home Dept ex p Daly* [2001] 3 All ER 433; [2001] UKHL 26, HL. The case concerned the examination of legal correspondence between a prisoner and his solicitor. The applicant claimed that he should be able to be present while his correspondence was being read. The House of Lords upheld his claim on the basis that the policy was disproportionate to the aim in view. Lord Steyn said: 'it is of great importance ... that the common law itself is recognised as a sufficient source of the confidential right to confidential communication with a legal advisor for the purpose of obtaining legal advice' (para 30).

102 See, eg, *Secretary of State for Social Security ex p Joint Council for the Welfare of Immigrants* [1996] 4 All ER 385; *Secretary of State for the Home Dept and Another ex p Norney and Others* (1995) *The Times*, 6 October.

103 Hunt, *op cit*, fn 5.

104 See *Lord Chancellor ex p Lightfoot* [2000] 2 WLR 318.

105 See *Secretary of State for Employment ex p EOC* [1994] 2 WLR 409, HL.

106 For the view that the direct influence of the Convention in the UK due to its significance as a source of general principles of EU law is not confined only to those areas of activity affected by EU law: see Beyleveld, D, 'The concept of a human right and incorporation of the ECHR' [1995] PL 577.

evidence emerged of a common understanding that they should form a bulwark to protect the citizens' liberties against the burgeoning power of the executive. While decisions in the field of free speech suggested an acceptance that Convention values were recognised as common law principles, decisions in the areas in which the common law had traditionally taken a non-rights-based stance, public order and exclusion of physical evidence unlawfully obtained, showed a persistence of that tradition. Secondly, even in the area in which a clear acceptance of the role of the common law in protecting fundamental human rights was present – judicial review – the courts seemed to lack the determination to continue pushing the limits of the doctrine outwards in order to ensure greater protection. They stopped short of introducing a full proportionality test.

It may be persuasively argued that since the judiciary had no 'textual anchor for their decisions' and had to 'rely on an appeal to normative ideals that lack any mooring in the common law',[107] it is unsurprising that common practice as regards fundamental freedoms did not emerge. Dawn Oliver points out that what has been termed the 'ethical aimlessness' of the common law – its lack of a sense of clear direction – means that because the judiciary as a body has no clear conception of the way the law should develop, they have not framed any set of 'guiding principles or priorities where civil and political rights clash with public interests'.[108] Thus, the judges in general showed, at times, uncertainty as to the weight to afford to a particular liberty, while the more executive-minded amongst them could take advantage of this uncertainty to grant it little or no weight. These tendencies meant that debate as to the principles underlying civil liberties was stifled and only the most obvious instances of their infringement received attention – where very basic rights were in question.

In the years immediately preceding the coming fully into force of the HRA, there was, as indicated, an emergence of common law rights going well beyond those rights, particularly to property, that the common law had traditionally recognised. However, it is arguable that without a constitutional document such as the ECHR, with its accumulated jurisprudence, to give them substance and depth, they might have remained at an uncertain and early stage of development, especially as there was some reluctance on the part of the judiciary to import ECHR principles and a preference for relying on a coincidence between such principles and those apparently already embedded in the common law.

Now that the judges have a 'textual anchor' in the form of the European Convention on Human Rights, applied domestically under the HRA, it is nevertheless unlikely that common practice among them will be evident; as this book will indicate, clear differences of approach were already emerging in the first year after the HRA came fully into force. This is unsurprising: judges in the US Supreme Court and in the European Court of Human Rights differ very widely as to their conceptions of liberty. However, it seems unarguable that the introduction of the Convention is achieving an increase in unity amongst domestic judges; while different judges will give different weights to rights and freedoms, at the very least all will be certain about when they have to be taken into

---

107 Justice William Brennan of the US Supreme Court in Hart, *Lectures on Jurisprudence and Moral Philosophy*, p 12, 24 May 1989.
108 Oliver, *op cit*, fn 86, p 151.

account. In particular, it is clear that the structure of judicial reasoning is changing under the HRA.[109]

In relation to both the key points indicated, it may plausibly be argued that in the last century, the judiciary as a body were not able to construct for themselves a clear justification for increasing their powers over government, although signs of judicial activism in the 1990s suggested that some of them considered that they should do so. The reception of the European Convention on Human Rights into domestic law, which may be viewed as a public statement from the nation as a whole of the importance that they attach to human rights, has given the judges a clearer mandate to develop a domestic human rights jurisprudence.

The influence of the European Convention on Human Rights in the pre-HRA era

Under Art 1 of the European Convention on Human Rights, the Member States[110] must secure the rights and freedoms to their subjects, but they are free to decide how this should be done.[111] Each State decides on the status the Convention enjoys in national law; there is no obligation under Art 1 to allow individuals to rely on it in *national* courts. In some States, it has the status of constitutional law;[112] in others, of ordinary law.[113]

In the pre-HRA era, rulings of the European Court of Human Rights led to better protection of human rights in such areas as prisoners' rights,[114] freedom of expression[115] and privacy.[116] But, as an *external* force, the influence of the Convention was limited. In contrast to the influence of European Union law, discussed below, the influence of the European Convention was, and is, procedurally rather than substantively limited. As pointed out in Chapter 2, the effect of a ruling of the European Court of Human Rights is dependent on the government in question making a change in the law. The UK Government may be able to minimise the impact of an adverse judgment by interpreting defeat narrowly,[117] by avoiding implementation of a ruling,[118] or by obeying the letter of

---

109 See Chapter 4, esp pp 140–48.

110 Currently, the Western European members are: Albania, Andorra, Austria, Belgium, Cyprus, Denmark, Finland, France; Germany, Greece, Iceland, Ireland, Italy, Liechtenstein, Luxembourg, Malta, The Netherlands, Norway, Portugal, San Marino, Spain, Sweden, Switzerland, Turkey, UK. Eastern European members: Bulgaria, Croatia, the Czech Republic, Estonia, Georgia, Hungary, Latvia, Lithuania, Macedonia, Moldova, Poland, Romania, Russia, Slovakia and Slovenia and Ukraine. The numbers increased owing to the disintegration of the Soviet Union and Yugoslavia. Application for membership is being considered from Belarus.

111 This was affirmed by the Irish Supreme Court in *The State (Lawless) v O'Sullivan and the Minister for Justice*; see Yearbook of the Convention on Human Rights Vol II (1958–59), pp 608–22.

112 Eg, Austria.

113 This includes Belgium, France, Italy, Luxembourg and Germany.

114 Eg, *Golder*, Eur Court HR, A 18, Judgment of 21 February 1975.

115 *Sunday Times*, Judgment of 26 April 1979; (1979) 2 EHRR 245. See further Chapter 5, pp 228–29.

116 Eg, *Gaskin v UK* (1990) 12 EHRR 36. See further Chapter 10, p 601. See further Farren, S, *The UK before the European Court of Human Rights*, 1996.

117 As in *Golder*, fn 114, above.

118 *Brogan, Coyle, McFadden and Tracey v UK* (1988) 11 EHRR 117 (Case No 10/1987/133/184–7). The Government refused to implement the ruling, entering a derogation under Art 15. See further Chapter 2, p 88 and Chapter 13, pp 801–03.

the Article in question, but ignoring its spirit.[119] The impact of the Convention was, and is, diminished since the process of invoking it, considered in Chapter 2, is extremely cumbersome, lengthy[120] and expensive.[121] It may not become less so despite the changes which have occurred under the Eleventh Protocol, including merger of the European Court and Commission of Human Rights.[122] Under the Human Rights Act, litigants may still take cases to Strasbourg as a last resort, but, as Chapter 2 demonstrated, while the system of the long trek to Strasbourg (starting with the exhaustion of domestic remedies) remains substantially, as at present, only the most exceptionally determined and resourceful litigants are likely to pursue it.[123]

In the UK, prior to the introduction of the Human Rights Act, the Convention had no domestic binding force. Until 1997, successive UK Governments considered that it was not necessary for the Convention to be part of UK law; they always maintained that the UK's unwritten constitution was in conformity with it. Thus, until 2000, a UK citizen could not go before a UK court and simply argue that a Convention right had been violated. Nevertheless, *before* the HRA came fully into force, the influence of the Convention was rapidly becoming more significant in domestic law through rulings in UK courts and in the European Court of Human Rights. As indicated below, the Convention also had an increasing significance in human rights-related rulings of the European Court of Justice. It may be said that the Convention was encroaching steadily on UK law from every direction[124] and that its direct domestic reception under the HRA was merely the culmination of that process.[125]

The discussion above regarding the influence of human rights values in the common law demonstrated that the courts in a number of significant decisions tended to prefer to refer to common law principle rather than explicitly to the Convention in respect both of statutory interpretation and the development of the common law. However, in both respects, a strand of thinking became very evident to the effect that the Convention itself should be explicitly relied upon. It had an impact through domestic courts in the pre-HRA era in the following ways.

The domestic impact of the ECHR in the pre-HRA era: statutory construction

It became a general principle of construction that statutes would be interpreted if possible so as to conform with international human rights treaties to which the UK is a party, on the basis that the government is aware of its international obligations and would not intend to legislate contrary to them.[126] A legal presumption developed that 'Parliament

---

119 *Abdulaziz, Cabales and Balkandali v UK* (1985) 7 EHRR 471. To implement the ruling, the UK 'equalised down'. See further Chapter 2, p 86.

120 The Commission used to make over 3,000 provisional files a year. The average petition took five years and nine months between 1982–87 if it went all the way through the system – four years before the Commission, nearly two before the Court (15 EHRR 321, p 327). Petitions can take nine years. At present, the average time is four years and the Court has 5,000 cases pending.

121 Legal aid is not available until after the complaint has been held admissible by the Commission.

122 See Chapter 2, pp 22–24.

123 See Chapter 2, pp 20–30.

124 For the argument that the extent of such encroachment has been exaggerated, see Klug, F and Starmer, K [1997] PL 223.

125 See esp pp 114 and 210.

126 See the judgment of Lord Brandon of Oakbrook in *Re M and H (Minors)* [1990] 1 AC 686; [1988] 3 WLR 485, HL, p 498; [1990] 1 AC 686.

does not intend to act in breach of international law' (*per* Diplock LJ in *Saloman v Commissioners of Custom and Excise*),[127] so that a reading of the relevant legislation that did not create a breach of rights would be adopted by the courts if such a reading was possible. However, as Lord Brandon of Oakbrook made clear in *Re M and H (Minors)*,[128] the English courts were under no duty to apply the Convention's provisions directly: 'While English courts may strive where they can to interpret statutes as conforming with the obligations of the UK under the Convention, they are nevertheless bound to give effect to statutes which are free from ambiguity even if those statutes may be in conflict with the Convention'. Thus, quite a strong protection against legislative encroachment on civil and political rights, especially those arising under the Convention, became increasingly available. Other international human rights treaties to which the UK is a party, including the International Covenant on Civil and Political Rights, had much less influence, as indicated below.[129]

The interpretation of ambiguous provisions in conformity with the Convention thus left it great scope to influence domestic law even before the introduction of the HRA.

The domestic impact of the ECHR in the pre-HRA era: influence on the common law

Lord Scarman, in *AG v BBC*,[130] considered that the Convention could also influence the common law. He said that where there was some leeway to do so, a court which must adjudicate on the relative weight to be given to different public interests under the common law should try to strike a balance in a manner consistent with the treaty obligations accepted by the government: 'If the issue should ultimately be ... a question of legal policy, we must have regard to the country's international obligation to observe the Convention as interpreted by the Court of Human Rights.' This approach was endorsed by the House of Lords in *AG v Guardian Newspapers (No 2)*,[131] Lord Goff stating that he considered it to be his duty, where free to do so, to interpret the law in accordance with Convention obligations. Similarly, in *Chief Metropolitan Magistrates' Court ex p Choudhury*,[132] Art 10 was taken into account in reviewing the decision of the magistrates' court not to grant summonses against Salman Rushdie and his publishers for the common law offence of blasphemous libel.

The need to take the Convention into account was emphasised even more strongly by the Court of Appeal in *Derbyshire CC v Times Newspapers Ltd*,[133] Ralph Gibson LJ ruling that where a matter 'was not clear [by reference to] established principles of our law ... the court must ... have regard to the principles stated in the Convention'. Butler-Sloss LJ put the matter even more strongly: 'where there is an ambiguity or the law is otherwise unclear or so far undeclared by an appellate court, the English court is not only entitled but ... obliged to consider the implications of Article 10.' As indicated above, the House of Lords considered that in the particular instance, the common law could determine the

---

127 [1967] 2 QB 116, p 143.
128 [1988] 3 WLR 485, p 498; [1990] 1 AC 686, HL.
129 See also p 17. See further Clayton, R and Tomlinson, H, *The Law of Human Rights*, 2000, pp 89–103.
130 [1981] AC 303, 354; [1980] 3 WLR 109, p 130, HL.
131 [1990] 1 AC 109, p 283.
132 [1991] 1 QB 429; [1991] 1 All ER 306.
133 [1993] AC 534; [1993] 1 All ER 1011; [1992] 3 WLR 28, HL.

issues in favour of freedom of speech[134] and that therefore, recourse to the Convention was unnecessary, but the guidance offered by the Court of Appeal was still of value where the common law was uncertain. That guidance suggested that judges had no choice as to whether to consider the Convention where the law was ambiguous[135] or – and this did appear to be a new development – where it was not yet settled in an appellate court. It may, therefore, have been the case that all areas of the common law which were not clearly settled in the House of Lords and which affected Convention rights, were expected to reflect Convention principles even before the HRA came into force. Thus, some disregard for the classic dualist stance became apparent in the common law.

The influence of European Union law

It is clear that membership of the European Community has had a dramatic impact on civil liberties in the UK in the last three decades. This is despite the fact that, clearly, EU law is concerned more with social and economic than civil rights. Where EU law protects civil rights, this may not be its primary purpose. Although Community law is intended to create social benefits in addition to economic benefits, social benefits may be conceived of as a by-product of, or adjunct to, economic integration.[136]

The influence of the Convention in EU law became increasingly important due to acceptance of the principle enunciated in *Amministrazione delle Finanze dello Stato v Simmenthal*[137] and *Nold v Commission*,[138] namely, that respect for fundamental rights should be ensured within the context of the EU. The Convention has come into a closer relationship with EU law as the process of European integration has continued. The influence of European Union human rights law will increase, especially now that the Amsterdam Treaty has come into force.[139] The doctrine of respect for fundamental rights, as guaranteed by the European Convention and as resulting from the constitutional traditions common to Member States, is now embodied in Art F(2)(6)(2) of the Treaty on

---

134 [1993] 1 All ER 1011. For comment, see Barendt, E, 'Libel and freedom of speech in English law' [1993] PL 449.

135 See further on this point (1992) MLR 721.

136 This is exemplified in the case of harmonisation of a minimal level of employment protection provisions in order to create a 'level playing field' of competition for employers in the Single Market. See, eg, Nielsen and Szyszczak, *The Social Dimension of the European Community*, 2nd edn, 1993, pp 15–18; Hoskyns, 'Women, European law and transnational politics' (1986) 14 Int J Soc Law 299–315.

137 Case 106/77 [1978] ECR 629.

138 [1974] ECR 481.

139 The Treaty came into force in 1999. It extends a number of existing rights under EU law and amends the Social Charter, which lays down minimum rights for workers in the Community countries. The Conservative Government failed to ratify it, but in the Agreement annexed to the Protocol on Social Policy in the Treaty of Maastricht the other Member States recorded their agreement to 'continue along the path' laid down in it. The Labour Government has withdrawn the opt out.

European Union.[140] But although Art F2 states that the EU will respect fundamental rights as recognised by the Convention, the ECJ, in Opinion 2/94 (28 March 1996),[141] held that the EU cannot accede to the Convention, on the ground that an amendment to the Treaty of Rome would be required in order to bring about this change, since it would go beyond the scope of Art 235. Under the Treaty of Amsterdam, Art F1, voting rights of Member States who fail to observe the principle embodied by Art F(2)(6)(2) can be suspended. The EU Charter of Fundamental Rights, although not of binding force, will aid in the interpretation of EU law.[142]

EU law has already had an important impact, as this book will demonstrate, in the areas of sex discrimination,[143] data protection[144] and freedom of movement.[145] Where national measures come within the scope of Community law, they must comply with the human rights standards it maintains.[146] As this book indicates at a number of points, EU human rights law is increasingly becoming a powerful force both in terms of the protection offered by the ECJ, and of its domestic implications.[147]

The result of these developments is that, in all the Member States, implementation of EU measures in national law is clearly subject to respect for the Convention rights, although an individual cannot make an application to Strasbourg against the Union alleging that the Union has violated the Convention. Even though formal accession of the Union to the Convention has not yet occurred, the Convention will control Union conduct. Thus, the decision of the ECHR in *Rees*[148] was relied upon by the ECJ in deciding, in *P v S and Cornwall CC*,[149] that transsexuals fall within the Equal Treatment Directive. This was found on the basis that the Directive is simply the expression of the principle of equality, which is one of the fundamental principles of European law.

It is therefore probable that, as the influence of the Convention on EU law becomes more significant and the impact of EU law becomes greater in the UK, the Convention may also have more influence. EU law can, of course, have direct effect in UK courts and can even override a UK statute.[150] The ability of Parliament to infringe rights under the

---

140 For enforcement of the Convention by this means, see Craig, P and De Burca, G, *European Law: Text and Materials*, 2nd edn, 1998.

141 (1996) *The Times*, 16 April.

142 The Charter, published in May 2000 (available from the European Commission website and from the website of the House of Lords Select Committee on the European Parliament) contains those rights recognised under the European Convention on Human Rights together with a number of new social rights, including the right to strike, guarantees of maximum working hours, worker consultation and trade union membership. The rights could, potentially, bind the EU institutions. Certain Member States and the European Commission proposed that the Charter should be included in the Treaty of Nice in December 2000. Britain considers that the Charter should not become part of the Treaty, and therefore have binding effect, but should have a merely declaratory status. At present, in July 2001, this is the position. See for discussion, Wicks, E [2001] PL 527.

143 See, eg, *Marshall (No 2)* [1993] 4 All ER 586. See further Chapter 16, p 1046.

144 The Data Protection Act 1984 derived from the European Convention for the Protection of Individuals with regard to the Automatic Protection of Data, 17 September 1980. See further Chapter 10, p 598.

145 See Chapter 15, pp 946–48.

146 See, eg, *R v Secretary of State for the Home Dept ex p Adams* [1995] All ER (EC) 177.

147 See further Betten, L and Grief, N, *EU Law and Human Rights*, 1998; Neuwahl, N and Rosas, A, *The EU and Human Rights*, 1995; Jacobs, F, 'Human rights in the EU: the role of the ECJ' [2001] 26(4) ELR 331.

148 (1986) 9 EHRR 56.

149 [1996] ECR I-2143; [1996] 2 CMLR 247; [1996] All ER(EC) 397. See further Chapter 16, pp 988–89.

150 See *Factortame Ltd v Secretary of State for Transport* [1991] 1 All ER 70, HL.

Human Rights Act, as discussed below, is therefore subject to the ability of the judiciary to disapply domestic law which is incompatible with EC law. The position is as set out in the leading case *Elliniki Rasdio Phonia Tiles Rassi AE v Dimotiki Etaria*:[151] 'as soon as any [national] legislation enters the field of application of Community law, the [ECJ] as the sole arbiter in this matter, must provide the national court with all the elements of interpretation which are necessary in order to enable it to assess the compatibility of that legislation with the fundamental rights – as laid down particularly in the European Convention on Human Rights – the observance of which the Court ensures.' Thus, any national law within the field of application of EC law can be assessed as to its compliance with the Convention rights. In particular, where a Member State is seeking to carve out an exception to the general principles of EC law, the review of the European Court of Justice is most intensive. But, as a matter of EU law, the Convention rights are not directly justifiable since they are not free standing rights. The position under *Elliniki* was not, therefore, changed by Art F(2)(6)(2). The domestic courts can disapply legislative provisions which appear to conflict with EC law as interpreted in reliance on those rights. Certain Convention principles may therefore come to be of limited binding force in the UK as forming part of EU law. However, the potential impact of the Convention in the UK by this means has not as yet been fully realised.[152]

3 THE 'BILL OF RIGHTS' DEBATE

Introduction[153]

The question, canvassed over the last 30 years, whether the UK should incorporate the European Convention on Human Rights into domestic law in order to act – in effect – as a substitute for a Bill of Rights, initially gained impetus due to the UK's acceptance of the right of individual petition under the European Convention on Human Rights. It rapidly came to seem anomalous to some that the Strasbourg judges should have the power to rule on the compatibility of UK law with Convention rights, while domestic judges had

---

151 [1991] ECR I-2925.

152 See further on this issue, Van Dijk and Van Hoof, *op cit*, fn 1, Chapter 8; Clapham, *Human Rights and the European Community: A Critical Overview*, 1991; Schermers, HG (1990) 27 CMLR 249; Grief [1991] PL 555; Coppel, J and O'Neill, A [1992] 29 CMLR 669; Foster, N (1987) 8 HRLJ 245; Lenaerts (1991) 16 ELR 367; O'Leary, S, 'Accession by the EC to the ECHR' (1996) 4 EHRR 362.

153 General reading: Lord Scarman, *English Law – The New Dimension*, 1974; Wallington, P and McBride, J, *Civil Liberties and a Bill of Rights*, 1976; Bailey, SH, Harris, DJ and Jones, BL, *Civil Liberties: Cases and Materials*, 4th edn, 1995, Chapter 1; Jaconelli, J, *Enacting a Bill of Rights*, 1980; Zander, M, *A Bill of Rights*, 4th edn, 1997, Sweet & Maxwell; Dworkin, R, *A Bill of Rights for Britain*, 1990; Ewing, KD, *A Bill of Rights for Britain*, 1990; Feldman, D, *Civil Liberties and Human Rights*, 1993, Chapter 2; 'Do we need a Bill of Rights?' (1976) 39 MLR 121; 'Should we have a Bill of Rights?' (1977) 40 MLR 389; 'Britain's Bill of Rights' (1978) 94 LQR 512; 'Legislative supremacy and the rule of law' [1985] CLJ 111; 'Incorporating the Convention' (1990) 25 LAG, April; 'Fundamental rights: the UK isolated?' [1984] PL 46; Craig, PP, *Public Law and Democracy in the United Kingdom and the United States of America*, 1990; Waldron, J, 'A rights-based critique of constitutional rights' (1993) 13 OJLS 18; Adjei, C, 'Human rights theory and the Bill of Rights debate' (1995) 58 MLR 17; Oliver, D, 'A Bill of Rights for the United Kingdom', in *Government in the United Kingdom*, 1991; Lester, A, 'The judges as law-makers' [1993] PL 269.

no such power. The idea that a dissatisfied litigant could leave the House of Lords to seek 'better' justice abroad was obviously distasteful to many domestic judges.

In 1968, Anthony Lester QC proposed the incorporation of the European Convention on Human Rights into national law[154] and the Charter '88 Group[155] among others brought the issue into prominence during the late 1980s and the 1990s. But some judges[156] and academic writers remained opposed to the reception of the Convention into domestic law or unconvinced[157] of the value of so doing, as did a number of politicians, including most Conservative MPs and right-wing commentators generally.[158] Nevertheless, support for the adoption of a 'Bill of Rights' grew among lawyers, academics and politicians[159] during the 1980s and 1990s prior to the introduction of the Human Rights Act 1998 under the Labour Government.

The political history of the debate

Britain was the first Member State to ratify the European Convention,[160] despite some strong feeling against it in Cabinet, particularly from Lord Chancellor Jowitt. The government at the time recognised that it was politically necessary to accept the Convention, but Jowitt described it as 'so vague and woolly that it may mean almost anything. Any student of our legal institutions must recoil from this document with a feeling of horror '[161] However, the Government did not, at that time, accept the right of individual petition or the jurisdiction of the European Court and there was no question of incorporation of the Convention into domestic law. When the Government[162] eventually accepted the right of individual petition in 1966, there appears to have been little realisation of the significance of this move, but it was unsurprising that it should be followed by a call for enactment of the Convention into domestic law – though without being directly enforceable.[163] The call for a 'Bill of Rights' was taken up by Lord Lambton (Conservative) in 1969, who sought leave to introduce a '10 minute rule' Bill 'to preserve the rights of the individual' – in other words, to curb the power of the Labour Government in such areas as freedom of speech and education. There was little support for the Bill and it was rejected.

---

154 Lester, A, *Democracy and Individual Rights*, 1968, pp 13–15. For the view that the Convention did not need to be formally adopted into UK law since it was already part of it and could be directly relied upon in domestic courts, see Beyleveld, *op cit*, fn 106.

155 Charter '88 advocated enshrining civil liberties by means of a Bill of Rights, but it did not put forward a text. See Stanger, N (1990) 8 Index on Censorship 14.

156 Eg, Lord McCluskey in his 1986 Reith Lectures.

157 See, eg, Ewing and Gearty, *op cit*, fn 11, p 273 *et seq*; Waldron, J (1993) 13 OJLS 18, pp 49–51; Loughlin, *Public Law and Political Theory*, 1992, esp pp 220–27.

158 The official policy of the Conservative Party has been opposed to a Bill of Rights: see Conservative Research Department Brief, *Civil Liberties*, 1990. See below for full discussion, pp 119–20.

159 See Zander, M, *A Bill of Rights?*, 1997, Chapter 1; Lord Scarman, *English Law – The New Dimension*, 1974, Parts II and VII; see also Robertson, *op cit*, fn 19, Chapter 12; Lester, *op cit*, fn 86; Lord Lester [1995] PL 198, note 1; Barendt, E, *Freedom of Speech*, 1987, pp 329–32.

160 In March 1951.

161 CAB 130/64 xcA034022; for comment, see Lester, *op cit*, fn 86, pp 50–55.

162 The Labour Government headed by Harold Wilson.

163 In 1968, from Mr Anthony Lester QC. His suggestion was that a Constitutional Council should be set up with powers to preview legislation and advise Parliament of potential conflict with the Bill of Rights.

From the 1970s onwards, growth of support for a UK Bill of Rights became apparent outside the ranks of the Conservative Party, although certain senior Conservatives displayed some such support when in opposition. Labour, which toyed with the notion in 1975, opposed it before and during the 1992 General Election, eventually decided to espouse it as official policy in 1993, while there was a long history of Liberal and Liberal Democrat support for it. It is notable that the years of Thatcherism eventually led the main party of opposition to accept the need to receive the Convention into domestic law. The chequered history of the debate which follows suggests two things: first, that there was a general and increasing consensus for some time that the European Convention on Human Rights should be incorporated into domestic law, and that this course should be taken as opposed to enacting a UK Bill of Rights; secondly, that although support for 'a Bill of Rights' was concentrated in the centrist and centre-left parties, it was not confined to them.

Conservative opposition

In 1969, Mr Quintin Hogg MP published a pamphlet, *New Charter*,[164] in which he stated: 'Parliament has become virtually an elective dictatorship. The party system makes the supremacy of a government like the present, automatic and almost unquestioned.' The solution, he thought, was to make the European Convention on Human Rights enforceable in domestic courts. Mr Hogg was opposition Front Bench Spokesman on Home Affairs and the pamphlet was published by the Conservative Political Centre, but the views were stated to be the author's own and not the Party's. However, in 1970, as Lord Chancellor, he spoke against a Bill of Rights proposed by Lord Arran,[165] although he did not state that he was against all Bills of Rights. In 1975, when Labour was in power, he wrote four letters to *The Times* advocating a written constitution entrenching individual rights.[166] Also in 1975, Sir Keith Joseph published a pamphlet entitled Freedom under the Law[167] giving his view that a Bill of Rights was needed to curb the power of Parliament.

In August 1976, Sir Michael Havers (Shadow Attorney General) gave an indication that the official view of the Conservative Party was tending towards incorporation of the European Convention when he advocated such a move in a letter to the *Daily Mail*, and, in a report entitled *Another Bill of Rights?*, the Society of Conservative Lawyers supported this proposition. In 1978, Mr Leon Brittan, opposition Front Bench Spokesman on Devolution, moved an amendment to the Scotland Bill at Committee stage which would have made the European Convention effective in Scotland. The move was opposed by the Government on the ground that the question was too important to be decided in such a context; and the amendment was defeated by 251 votes to 227.[168]

When the Conservative Party came to power in 1979, it made no move to incorporate the Convention, despite some backbench interest.[169] In 1980, the Government opposed

---

164 Conservative Political Centre, No 430.
165 House of Lords, *Hansard*, Vol 313 Col 243, 26 November 1970. Lord Arran had moved the Second Reading of his Bill.
166 In May 1975.
167 Published by Conservative Political Centre.
168 House of Commons, *Hansard*, Vol 943 Col 580.
169 107 Conservative MPs signed a motion in June 1984 calling for incorporation of the Convention.

Lord Wade's Bill of Rights Bill in the Commons, as it did Lord Scarman's Bill in 1988, which was passed in the Lords, and Sir Edward Gardner's 1989 Bill incorporating the European Convention. An indication of future official Conservative policy was given by Margaret Thatcher in a letter to Bernard Crick[170] on 26 May 1988:

> The government considers that our present Constitutional arrangements continue to serve us well and that the citizen in this country enjoys the greatest degree of liberty that is compatible with the rights of others and the vital interests of the State.

This view was reiterated in 1990[171] and remained the official view of the Conservative Party in the 1997 General Election. In debate on the Human Rights Bill in 1997, however, the Conservative opposition abstained on Second Reading. The Conservative Party website[172] greeted the coming into force of the Human Rights Act by attacking it; William Hague (then the leader of the Conservative Party) stated: 'I believe that to influence our law through our elected representatives is itself a right. It is threatened by this bad law.' The Conservative manifesto for the 2001 General Election did not, however, state that, if elected, a Bill would be introduced to repeal or amend the Human Rights Act. Therefore, although it is clear that if the Conservatives under Major had taken office in 1997 they would not have introduced a measure similar to the Human Rights Bill, they appeared to have accepted, reluctantly, that repeal of the HRA would be controversial and perhaps politically damaging. Under Duncan-Smith, however, they currently favour repeal.

The Liberals and the Liberal Democrats

The Liberal Party was strongly associated with the movement to introduce a Bill of Rights. The Liberal Peer, Lord Wade, who had in 1969 initiated a four hour debate in the House of Lords on the question of the protection of human rights, moved a further debate in 1976 in the Lords on a new Bill designed to incorporate the European Convention into UK law. It provided that the Convention would prevail over subsequent legislation unless the legislation specifically provided otherwise. Lord Harris, the Secretary of State at the Home Office, said that the Government could not form a view until there had been wide public discussion of the issue. The House gave the Bill an unopposed second reading. When Lord Wade's Bill was debated again in 1977[173] and referred to a Select Committee, the Committee recommended that if a Bill of Rights were enacted, it should be the European Convention, but said that they had not reached agreement on the desirability of enacting such a Bill. Lord Wade moved an amendment, which was carried, to introduce a Bill of Rights to incorporate the Convention. He introduced his Bill again in 1978 and in 1981; each time it passed the Lords and was eventually debated in the Commons in 1981, although no second reading was secured. Lord Scarman, who has been one of the most influential supporters of adoption of a Bill of Rights, made a very significant contribution to the debate in his Hamlyn lecture in 1974 in which he concluded that certain human

---

170 Founder member of Charter '88.
171 Conservative Research Department Brief, *Civil Liberties*, 1990.
172 www.conservatives.com.
173 House of Lords, *Hansard*, Vol 379 Col 973.

rights should be rendered inviolate by entrenched laws protected by a Bill of Rights. In 1988, he failed to get a Bill through the Commons – although it passed the Lords – which provided that no minister, bureaucrat or public body should do any act which infringed the rights set out in the European Convention. In accordance with his long-standing support for the reception of the Convention into domestic law, Lord Scarman spoke in favour of the Human Rights Bill on Second Reading in the House of Lords in 1997.[174] The Liberal Democrats continued to favour adoption of the Convention before, during and after the 1992 and 1997 General Elections.[175]

The change in the Labour position

In a House of Commons Debate on the Bill of Rights question in 1975,[176] Dr Shirley Summerskill, Labour Minister of State at the Home Office, said that the Government was not 'committed against a Bill of Rights', but that the question required further consideration. In 1976, the Labour Government published a discussion document which had been prepared by the Human Rights sub-Committee chaired by Mrs Shirley Williams, recommending the adoption of the European Convention on Human Rights into national law. Just before its publication, the Home Secretary, Mr Roy Jenkins, indicated that he was moving in the direction of favouring incorporation,[177] and in 1976, the Attorney General, Mr Sam Silkin, also gave such an indication.[178] That the Government was taking this question very seriously was apparent from the composition of the Working Party which drew up the Discussion Document 'Legislation on Human Rights', published by the Home Office in 1976. Senior civil servants from a large number of different departments were involved. The document was intended only to be descriptive and explanatory: no firm conclusion on the issue was reached and official Labour party policy did not change as a result.

In 1991 and 1992, however, Labour officially opposed adoption of a Bill of Rights on the ground that government reforms would be endangered if power were transferred from government to the judiciary. The then Shadow Home Secretary, Mr Roy Hattersley, disassociated his party from Charter '88. He wrote: 'the only method of restraining the excesses of a bad government is to replace it with a good one.'[179] However, in a speech to the Fabian Society Conference on 6 January 1990, he explained more fully Labour's proposed alternative method of protecting civil rights: 'The commitment to a series of detailed and specific Acts of Parliament – each one of which establishes rights in a specific area – is a much more practical way of ensuring the freedoms we propose.' This view was encapsulated in the Labour Party Charter of Rights 1990.[180]

However, after Labour lost the General Election of 1992 and Mr Hattersley resigned as Shadow Home Secretary, John Smith, the new leader of the party, announced a change in

---

174 House of Lords, *Hansard*, Col 1256, 3 November 1997.

175 *Partners for Freedom and Justice*, Liberal Democrat Federal White Paper No 2 (1989).

176 The motion was put forward by Mr James Kilfedder (Ulster Unionist) House of Commons, *Hansard*, Vol 894 Col 32, 7 July 1975.

177 In a speech to the Birmingham Law Society on 12 February 1975. In 1976, at a conference organised by the British Institute of Human Rights, he left no doubt that he was in favour of incorporation.

178 In the MacDermott lecture at Queen's University, Belfast.

179 See *The Guardian*, 12 December 1988.

180 *The Charter of Rights: Guaranteeing Individual Liberty in a Free Society*, Labour Party document, 1990.

policy in March 1993 after the Labour Party Conference and committed the party to incorporation of the European Convention using the device of a 'notwithstanding' clause for protection and with a view to the eventual adoption of a home-grown Bill of Rights. When Tony Blair took over the leadership of the party after John Smith's death, he supported the policy of incorporation, as did the new Shadow Home Secretary, Jack Straw.

On 11 January 1994, the Labour MP Mr Graham Allen introduced a Private Members' Bill, the Human Rights No 3 Bill, which proposed incorporation of the European Convention on Human Rights with the First Protocol and the creation of a Human Rights Commission. It embodied many of the previous Labour Party proposals. It received a first reading in the Commons but did not progress to a second reading. In December 1996, the Labour Party issued a Consultation Paper on the matter entitled *Bringing Rights Home: Labour's Plans to Incorporate the European Convention on Human Rights into UK Law*.[181] The paper proposed incorporation of the Convention with the First Protocol and the creation of a Human Rights Commission; it also promised review of the possibility of ratifying later Protocols. It left it unclear whether such ratification would also imply that later Protocols would subsequently be incorporated into UK domestic law. It also promised that, in future, consideration would be given to the possibility of introducing a tailor made UK Bill of Rights. After the 1997 General Election, the Labour Government committed itself in the Queen's Speech to introducing a Bill incorporating the 'main provisions' of the Convention. The Human Rights Bill, receiving the 'main provisions' of the Convention into domestic law, was introduced into Parliament in October 1997.

Central arguments in the debate

Introduction

Broadly, rightists and leftists among academics and politicians tend to be opposed to Bills of Rights. As indicated in Chapter 1, certain groups on the left, in the UK and abroad, tend to view civil rights with hostility. Under the theory put forward by a number of writers on the left, such instruments merely focus progressive attention on 'negative rights' which foster only formal equality since in practice, they may be used by the powerful to consolidate their power over the weak.[182] At the same time, this theory finds that such attention is directed away from 'positive rights' which would lead to substantive equality through the redistribution of economic resources.[183] The liberal view has been indicated in Chapter 1; it is generally sympathetic to the notion of civil rights,[184] and is now supportive of the HRA. The remarkable increase in liberal and centre-left support for adoption of a UK 'Bill of Rights'[185] is – at least in part – attributable to the fact

---

181 Straw, J and Boateng, P, *A Consultation Paper*, 1997.

182 See further McColgan, A, *Women under the Law: The False Promise of Human Rights*, 2000 (Pearson Education).

183 See Tushnet, M, 'An essay on rights' (1984) 62 Texas L Rev 1363; Herman, D, 'Beyond the rights debate' (1993) 2 Social and Legal Studies 25.

184 This is not intended to imply that all liberals support the adoption of a Bill of Rights in the UK; as discussed below, a number of liberals are reluctant to trust the judges to give full weight to its provisions. For an attack on such adoption from a liberal point of view see Allan, 'Bills of Rights and judicial power – a Liberal's quandary' 16(2) OJLS 337–52.

185 For a full account see Zander, M, *A Bill of Rights?*, 1997, Chapter 1.

that one party was in power for 18 years and, in particular, to the effect on civil liberties of the Thatcher and Major Governments.

The 'Bill of Rights' debate will be considered here as a background to the discussion of the Human Rights Act itself, which follows. Clearly, the debate has now moved on; it is concerned less with the merits of receiving the Convention into domestic law, than with the response of public authorities, particularly the judiciary, to it. However, consideration of a key argument against reception of the Convention – the argument from democracy – is illustrative of the choices that were made when framing the Human Rights Act. The further questions as to the role of the HRA in providing improved protection for civil liberties and human rights concern the nature, status and enforcement of the Convention, and these questions are addressed in the next section.

In the mid-1990s, there was a consensus among most academic commentators that the traditional methods of providing protection for civil liberties were insufficiently effective, but no clear agreement as to the means which should be adopted in order to provide further protection. A degree of suspicion and distrust was often aroused at the notion of effecting such protection by means of a Bill of Rights which may have found its roots in the traditional view that Bills of Rights are high sounding documents which are ineffective in practice, but dangerous because they create complacency as to liberty and that, moreover, they are the marks of a primitive, undeveloped legal system. In 1776, Bentham described declarations of rights as merely so much 'bawling upon paper'. Dicey wrote that there is 'in the English constitution an absence of those declarations or definitions of rights so dear to foreign constitutionalists', but that this was a strength rather than a weakness because such rights may be constantly suspended, whereas the suspension of the English Constitution 'would mean with us nothing less than a revolution'. Lord Hailsham has said: 'show me a nation with a Bill of Rights and I will show you a nation with fewer actual human rights than Britain because the escape clauses are used, often quite ruthlessly.'[186] It has also been suggested that the notion of liberty and of the need to protect it must emanate from a source outside the Bill of Rights; Judge Learned Hand has written: 'Liberty lies in the hearts and minds of men and women; when it dies there no constitution, no law, no court can save it.'

More recently, the argument that Bills of Rights *per se* are ineffective or actually inimical to the protection of liberty, has tended to give way to the argument that although some independent restraint on the excess or abuse of power is needed, it would be dangerous or pointless to enact a Bill of Rights because it would not be wise to trust UK judges with such a significant power:[187] they would invoke the exceptions in order to interpret it in an executive-minded manner, thus perhaps emasculating the freedoms it was supposed to protect. Commentators such as Lee, Ewing and Gearty argued that it would be dangerous to trust to a Bill of Rights and that there was too great a tendency to regard one as a panacea for all that was wrong with civil liberties in the UK.[188] Ewing and Gearty considered that genuine constraints on the power of the Prime Minister were needed and that a Bill of Rights would merely amount to a cosmetic change. It was

---

186 House of Lords, *Hansard*, Vol 369 Cols 784–85.

187 Eg, Ewing and Gearty, *op cit*, fn 11, pp 262–75; Lord McCluskey (the Solicitor General for Scotland under the Wilson Labour government) in his 1986 Reith Lectures, Lecture 5.

188 Lee, *Judging Judges*, p 166; Ewing and Gearty, p 275.

further argued that whether or not UK judges could be trusted with a Bill of Rights, the whole notion of endowing an unelected group with a considerable area of power removed from the reach of the legislature is incompatible with democratic theory.[189] Allan, for example, argues that '[entrenched] Bills of Rights are singularly undemocratic'.[190]

Ceding power to unelected judges

Whether or not it is acceptable in a democracy that unelected judges should wield the power of a Bill of Rights partly depends on its authority and the availability of review of legislation. The most contentious possibility arises when, as in the US, judges are empowered to strike down legislation in conflict with the Bill of Rights, which is also given a higher authority than other statutes by being entrenched, so that no possibility of correction of judicial decisions by subsequent legislation arises, except in so far as provided for by the method of entrenchment. The argument from democracy has the greatest force only if a Bill of Rights can prevail over subsequent inconsistent legislation. It obviously has much less force if a form of parliamentary override clause prevents it from so doing. This is the case in Canada where the Charter of Rights is protected by a so called 'notwithstanding clause' – subsequent legislation can only override it if the intention to do so is clearly stated in the legislation. The perpetrators of the argument against trusting the judges did not always make clear whether they opposed both of these possibilities or only the first. It is obviously a crucial distinction as, in the second, Parliament clearly still retains ultimate power over the law. Introduction of a notwithstanding clause merely requires candour if rights are to be interfered with, which, as Dworkin has commented, 'is hardly incompatible with democracy'.[191]

However, the argument that a fully entrenched Bill of Rights *would* be incompatible with democracy should not be too readily conceded. Such an argument seems to proceed from the premise that any restriction upon the freedom of legislative bodies – even those designed to protect fundamental rights – is undemocratic. A true partisan of democracy ought also to be opposed to UK membership of all international human rights treaties, since the basic premise of all of these is that certain rights of citizens should be placed beyond the power of the majority to infringe them. The contrary notion, that there should be no limits on the power of the majority, can be defended only by reference to a rather crude form of preference utilitarianism[192] and arguably amounts to an impoverished conception of democracy. Such a conception could provide no reason why, for example, the majority should not authorise the internment, torture and summary execution of all terrorist suspects if it was clear that this would end terrorist attacks and thus immeasurably benefit the mass of the people. Those who insist that Parliament's power should be untrammeled presumably do not think that it should use its powers in this way and their conviction that it should not do so can only be justified by a belief that there must be limits on what the majority can inflict on even profoundly anti-social individuals

189 Waldron, J, 'A rights-based critique of constitutional rights' (1993) 13 OJLS 18.
190 'Bills of rights and judicial power – a Liberal's quandary' [1996] 16(2) OJLS 337–52.
191 Dworkin, *op cit*, fn 1.
192 See Chapter 1, pp 7–8 for discussion of utilitarianism.

and minorities. Thus, it may be assumed that there is general acceptance of this fundamental conviction which lies behind every Bill of Rights. Those who remain opposed to entrenched rights usually profess not to be hostile to the idea of human rights *per se*, but to be concerned with other issues.

Thus, one respected commentator, Jeremy Waldron, in setting out what could be termed the 'argument from controversy',[193] is concerned not so much that the majority should have unlimited power, but that any particular formulation of rights will inevitably be controversial and that entrenching it amounts to a permanent disabling of those who hold a contrary view about which rights should be protected. Thus, he asks rhetorically: 'Are the formulations of one generation to be cast in stone and given precedence over all subsequent revisions?' Three objections to this position are apparent. First, to characterise a Bill of Rights as setting formulations 'in stone' seems to exhibit a failure to take cognizance of the immense diversity of interpretations which can be extracted from a broadly worded document such as the European Convention,[194] and the way in which such interpretations can develop to reflect changes in popular attitudes.[195] The fact that one document – the American Constitution – has been found at different times to support both black slavery and positive discrimination in favour of black people provides clear evidence to support this argument.

The second objection is that the 'controversy' thesis determinedly ignores the reasonable degree of consensus that exists around many basic rights. For example, when discussing the possibility of protecting the right to participate in democracy, Waldron argues that democratic procedures themselves cannot be entrenched, because 'People disagree about how participatory rights should be understood ...'. Noticeably, however, he fails to mention the near-complete agreement on the fundamental right of universal adult suffrage. This point leads on to the third objection to the 'controversy' thesis, namely that, paradoxically enough, its own implications are contrary to democracy.[196]

---

193 This term is used because the fact of controversy as to the favoured list of rights lies at the heart of Waldron's argument against entrenched rights. 'A rights-based critique of constitutional rights' (1993) 13 OJLS 18.

194 Waldron's objections seem all the more strange in that *prima facie* they do not seem to take account of those adjudicatory theories which explain the vital part that both the judges' moral and political convictions and the mass of shared assumptions and understanding in a particular society play in the interpretation of texts. (For an extremely lucid and accessible exposition of the above point, see Simmonds, N, 'Between positivism and idealism' [1991] CLJ 308.) However, Waldron does mention such theories in several places (eg, pp 41–43) where he states that his objection is not so much that judges should be able to interpret and modify citizens' rights, but that democratic institutions should be disabled from doing so. But once Waldron has conceded the point that judges can radically amend the meaning of texts, his point about setting rights in stone is lost. The reason why democratic institutions should be disabled from interference with some fundamental rights is discussed in the text below: pp 126–27.

195 It is indeed arguable that judges can more readily respond to marked changes in the moral climate than politicians. Eg, the judiciary, in response to a growing consensus that the marital rape exemption was indefensible, abolished the immunity of husbands at a time when there were no indications that Parliament was prepared to make time for legislation (*R* [1991] 4 All ER 481).

196 A further paradox in Waldron's argument, the existence of which he concedes (p 46), is that if the majority vote in a referendum for an entrenched Bill of Rights they must, on his argument, be allowed to have one. Clearly, the only way to prevent the majority from entrenching a Bill of Rights would be to have an entrenched law forbidding the entrenchment of laws. This would obviously be impossible on its own terms. Since, as Dworkin notes (*op cit*, fn 1, pp 36–37), opinion polls reveal that more than 71% of the population favour an entrenched Bill of Rights, Waldron's argument appears to be self-defeating.

The refusal to disable the majority by entrenchment of rights includes, as just noted, a refusal to entrench democracy itself. This refusal in effect means that Waldron will not deny the right of the majority of the day to destroy democracy by disenfranchising a group such as all non-whites or even voting democracy itself out of existence, thereby denying it to future generations. Since, by contrast, a Bill of Rights is ultimately concerned with preserving a worthwhile democracy for the future, it can be persuasively argued that entrenched basic rights show more respect for democratic principles than do the advocates of retaining the untrammeled power of the majority of the day.[197] Entrenchment of the Convention under the HRA was not contemplated by the Labour Government and would probably be possible in the UK system only by means of a written constitution . Such a task would almost certainly not be undertaken without a referendum; if the people considered such a settlement desirable, they would in effect be expressing their will to be ruled by an unelected body within certain defined areas as the price of curbing elected power.

The argument against endowing the judges with power under an entrenched Bill of Rights should also be considered in the light of the experience of America. The most striking feature of the American system is the power of the Supreme Court to render inoperative acts of the elected representatives of the people (first asserted in *Marbury v Madison*).[198] This power seems alien to UK jurists, but the justification offered for it is that the legitimacy of judicial review of legislation derives not from electoral accountability, but from the particular positions of the judges within the constitution. The classic statement of this theory is that of Alexander Hamilton in *Federalist #78*:

> The executive not only dispenses the honours but holds the sword of the community. The legislature not only commands the purse but prescribes the rules by which the duties and rights of every citizen are to be regulated. The judiciary, on the contrary, has no influence over either the sword or the purse; no direction either of the strength or of the wealth of society. [Thus it will be] the least dangerous to the political rights of the Constitution.[199]

It could also be noted in this context that the UK has a constitutional precedent in the shape of the House of Lords for allowing an unelected body to influence legislation. The notion is not therefore entirely foreign to the UK system. Of course, this is not a complete analogy: the House of Lords has a much more limited role in this respect than judges under an entrenched Bill of Rights would have had.

If a Bill of Rights is unentrenched, as in Canada, the argument from democracy loses some of its cogency but fastens instead on the question of policy making under the Bill of Rights. A Bill of Rights would inevitably contain open-textured provisions which would have to be interpreted and that interpretation would often involve political choices. An obvious example is the choice before the European Court in the *Young, James and Webster* case[200] concerning the question of the closed shop. Ought judges – although finally

---

197 Such a view is of course endorsed by a number of legal philosophers and civil libertarians. See Dworkin, *op cit*, fn 1; the view also clearly underpins his general political philosophy: see, eg, 'Liberalism', in *A Matter of Principle*, 1985. See also Hart, HLA, *Law, Liberty and Morality*, 1963 and Lester, *op cit*, fn 154.

198 (1803) 5 US (1 Cranch) 137.

199 Mentor (ed), *The Federalist Papers*, 1961, pp 464, 465. See also Bickel, *The Least Dangerous Branch: The Supreme Court at the Bar of Politics*, 1962.

200 Eur Court HR, A 44, Judgment of 13 August 1981; (1981) 4 EHRR 38. See Chapter 8, p 413 for discussion of the decision.

subject to Parliament under an unentrenched Bill of Rights – be given a much broader policy making role or ought politicians to be the sole arbiters of such questions? Clearly, many questions which would have to be determined by the judges in applying the provisions of a Bill of Rights would lie rather in the moral than the political arena because civil rights are rights claimed against public authorities,[201] not against particular political parties. Nevertheless, it has been argued by such opponents of a Bill of Rights as Lord McCluskey that an Act of Parliament, arrived at after full consideration of the issues involved and the likely effects and covering specific areas, is a better way to protect, for example, the right to privacy than a Bill of Rights containing a provision such as 'Everyone has the right to privacy' followed by certain exceptions.

It was argued by the Labour Party in 1990[202] that rather than introducing a Bill of Rights, more certain protection would be assured by creating a number of statutes, each of which would cover one area of civil liberties. However, the introduction of such protection by this means would be time consuming and might therefore be unlikely to find a place in a legislative programme mainly concerned with social and economic issues. The lack of legislation passed over the 18 years of the Conservative Governments from 1989–97 with the sole or main intention of protecting a particular liberty supports this argument. The legislation that was passed – the Contempt of Court Act 1981; the Equal Pay (Amendment) Regulations; the Data Protection Act 1984 – was Europe-driven.[203] There has clearly been a lack of legislation passed to protect civil liberties which has been enacted without such coercion; in particular, the UK, unlike other jurisdictions, has failed so far to enact a Privacy Act. If the party of government tends to abjure its policy making role in these areas, it may be argued that the only alternative is enactment of a Bill of Rights which would largely hand such a role to the judges. Even assuming that Parliament is prepared to legislate in these areas, it can still be argued that a Bill of Rights is of value as providing a remedy which is more flexible and comprehensive than a statute and which can adapt to changing social conditions more readily. Moreover, specific pieces of legislation can have the protection they offer to liberties eroded by subsequent legislation through the operation of the doctrine of implied repeal; the protection gained is therefore more precarious than that offered by a Bill of Rights enjoying greater constitutional protection, even if only due to a convention of respect for it.

Readiness of the domestic judiciary to use rights-based reasoning

It was also argued that the judges had already shown how they would acquit themselves under a Bill of Rights and that the results were not promising.[204] For example, the Privy Council, in considering questions arising from Commonwealth Bills of Rights, sometimes

---

201 Or against private individuals where a public authority bears some responsibility for failure to protect a right. See the discussion of *Drittwirkung*, Chapter 2, p 28.

202 See *The Charter of Rights: Guaranteeing Individual Liberty in a Free Society*, Labour Party document, 1990.

203 The Contempt of Court Act 1981 was passed in response to the judgment of the European Court of Human Rights in *Sunday Times*, Judgment of 26 April 1979, A 30; (1979) 2 EHRR 245. The Data Protection Act derived from the Convention for the Protection of Individuals with regard to the Automatic Processing of Data (17 September 1980) and the Equal Pay (Amendment) Regulations from the Council Directive (75/117/EEC) of 10 February 1975.

204 Ewing and Gearty, *op cit*, fn 11, p 274.

gave certain guarantees of rights a very restrictive interpretation. In *AG v Antigua Times Ltd*,[205] the Privy Council found that a constitutional guarantee of freedom of speech was not infringed by Antiguan legislation requiring a licence from the Cabinet and a large deposit as a surety against libel in order to publish a newspaper. However, the Privy Council appeared more recently to have adopted a more liberal approach. In *Guerra v Baptiste*,[206] the Privy Council had to consider delay in carrying out an execution. Guerra was convicted of murder in the Republic of Trinidad and Tobago and sentenced to death. In 1989, he appealed against his sentence, but the appeal was not heard until October 1993. The Privy Council took into account the decision in *Pratt v AG for Jamaica*[207] in which it was found that where a State wishes to retain capital punishment, it must accept the responsibility of ensuring that execution follows as swiftly as possible after sentence, allowing a reasonable time for appeal and consideration of reprieve. If the appeal procedure allows the prisoner to prolong appellate proceedings over a period of years, the fault lies with the appeal procedure, not with the prisoner. In *Pratt*, it was found that a reasonable target would be to complete the hearings within approximately one year and to carry out the sentence of death within two years. In the present instance, there had been substantial delay amounting to nearly five years between sentence and the point at which the sentence was to be carried out. The fact that problems were created by the shortage of court resources did not justify the delay. Such problems had also been a factor in the *Pratt* case. It was, therefore, found that the sentence must be commuted to one of life imprisonment. This decision and that in *Pratt* suggested that UK judges were quite capable of adopting a generous approach to a Bill of Rights.[208] Thus, there was some basis for the argument that the judges would take decisions applying the Convention under the Human Rights Act which would not emasculate it owing to adoption of a narrow and technical approach.

As indicated above, however, certain decisions of UK judges applying the Convention could be criticised as adopting traditional, limiting methods of interpretation. In *Brind* (in the Court of Appeal) and in *AG v Guardian Newspapers*,[209] judges applied the principles of the European Convention and then proceeded to uphold the restrictions in question. On the other hand, as discussed above, in *Derbyshire CC*[210] the Court of Appeal relied on Art 10 to produce a result protective of freedom of expression. The decisions in *Ex p Witham*[211] and *Ex p Simms*,[212] considered above, relied on fundamental human rights standards in, it is suggested, a creative and dynamic fashion.

Moreover, where an international treaty has been incorporated into domestic law, the English courts have shown a willingness to adopt a broad teleological approach. In *The*

---

205 [1976] AC 16.

206 (1995) *The Times*, 8 November.

207 [1993] 3 WLR 995. Bailey, Harris and Jones (*op cit*, fn 153) comment that this decision would not be open to the usual criticism that traditional methods of interpretation would be used in determinations under a Bill of Rights (p 18).

208 Roberts considers that a purposive approach has continued to be evident in interpretations of Bills of Rights from Commonwealth jurisdictions: 'The Law Lords and human rights: the experience of the Privy Council in interpreting Bills of Rights' [2000] EHRLR 147.

209 [1987] 3 All ER 316. See also the *Brind* case [1991] 1 AC 696.

210 [1992] 3 WLR 28; see further above, p 114; HL ruling: [1993] 1 All ER 1011.

211 [1998] QB 575.

212 [1999] 3 All ER 400.

Hollandia (concerning provisions of the Hague-Visby Rules, which have been incorporated into UK law) Lord Diplock said that such provisions 'should be given a purposive rather than a narrow literalistic construction, particularly wherever the adoption of a literalistic construction would enable the stated purpose of the international Convention ... to be evaded ...'[213] It should also be noted that UK judges have adapted remarkably quickly to the demands of EU law as it affects fundamental rights and have been prepared to take decisions and make pronouncements upholding such rights which were probably unthinkable when the European Communities Act 1972 was passed.[214] Lester makes a forceful point in support of this proposition in his comments on the way that the courts have dealt with the task of applying broadly worded EU directives on sex discrimination, provisions which a legal traditionalist would term 'so vague and woolly that they might mean almost anything'. He considers that: 'English judges have interpreted and applied these general principles in a manner which recognises their fundamental nature and which gives full effect to their underlying aims,' and from this he concludes that: 'Those sceptics who doubt the ability of British judges to protect the fundamental rights of the [European] Convention should consider their impressive record in translating the fundamental rights of Community law into practical reality.'[215]

Possible models for the protection of the Convention

As indicated above, the constitutional status of Bills or Charters of Rights varies from jurisdiction to jurisdiction. Such instruments may have no special status or they may be afforded (or may acquire) some special protection from express or implied repeal which may, at its highest, involve their entrenchment.[216] Thus, a variety of models was available to choose from in considering the model to be used in order to protect the Convention. The choice arrived at, which is discussed in Chapter 4, was extremely significant, in terms of the allocation of power between the judiciary, Parliament and the government.

The terms 'entrenchment' and 'protection' which will be used below require explanation because both may encompass a number of possibilities. 'Protection' will be used to refer to any means of giving a statute a special status without seeking to entrench it in any sense of that word. 'Entrenchment' refers to requirements of form or manner or restrictions as to substance. A requirement of form denotes the need to use a particular form of words if a subsequent enactment is to repeal a former one, rather than simply allowing the normal rules of implied repeal to operate. A requirement of manner refers to the manner in which legislation is passed if it is to repeal a previous enactment. Examples of such a requirement would include the use of a two-thirds majority in the parliamentary body if a particular piece of legislation is to be repealed or amended. A restriction as to substance refers to the most stringent form of entrenchment: no method of repealing the legislation in question is provided in it. Parts of the German Basic Law are entrenched in this manner and, therefore, they can never be amended or repealed unless a break with the existing legal order occurs in Germany.

---

213 [1983] 1 AC 565, p 572.
214 Eg, *Secretary of State for Employment ex p EOC* [1994] 2 WLR 409, HL.
215 Lester, 'Fundamental rights' [1984] PL 70–71.
216 See Jaconelli, *Enacting a Bill of Rights*, 1980, for a full discussion of this issue.

Thus, a requirement of 'form' may be termed weak entrenchment since it is the weakest possible form of entrenchment available. A requirement of manner may be referred to as semi or partial entrenchment, while a restriction as to substance may be referred to as full entrenchment. Bearing this in mind, it may be found that s 2(4) of the European Communities Act 1972 has been treated as imposing a requirement of form and possibly of manner. Arguably, unless Parliament declares in an Act of Parliament that it intends to override Community law, such law will prevail over subsequent inconsistent domestic legislation. However, since no means of overriding Community law is provided for in the 1972 Act, it may even be the case that if Parliament made such a declaration, the courts would not give effect to it. In that case, there would be no means of escaping from the impact of Community law except by withdrawing from the EU.

The most common requirements of manner – such as, that legislation repealing the Bill of Rights will not be valid unless passed by a 75% majority – are incompatible with democracy if that concept is understood to connote simple majoritarianism. A Bill of Rights protected in this manner could be preserved against the wishes of the majority of the elected representatives in the legislature, so long as that majority was less than 75%. A restriction as to substance is most obviously incompatible with democracy, unless one takes the view, which is based on a different argument,[217] that full entrenchment of Bills of Rights, or at least certain fundamental provisions in them, is essential in order to maintain a healthy democracy.

In many jurisdictions, Bills of Rights are afforded a higher status than other legislation. Owing to the operation of the doctrine of parliamentary sovereignty, this possibility would be constitutionally controversial in the UK. However, the status of EU law in the UK provided a precedent for adopting the course of partially entrenching the Convention. Section 2(4) of the European Communities Act 1972 provides: 'any enactment passed or to be passed ... shall be construed and have effect subject to the foregoing provisions of this section ...' 'The foregoing' are those provisions referred to in s 2(1) giving the force of law to 'the enforceable Community rights' there defined. The words 'subject to' suggest that the courts must allow Community law to prevail over a subsequent Act of Parliament. This does not, of course, mean that the European Communities Act itself cannot be repealed. It may follow that Parliament has partially entrenched s 2(1) of the European Communities Act by means of s 2(4) imposing a requirement of form (express words) on future legislation designed to override Community law. In *Secretary of State for Transport ex p Factortame*[218] in the Court of Appeal, Bingham LJ said that where the law of the Community is clear:

> ... whether as a result of a ruling given on an Article 177 reference or as a result of previous jurisprudence or on a straightforward interpretation of Community instruments, the duty of the national court is to give effect to it in all circumstances ... To that extent a UK statute is not as inviolable as it once was.

This finding was confirmed in the House of Lords.[219]

---

217 See above, p 124.
218 [1989] 2 CMLR 353.
219 [1989] 2 WLR 997.

There was also the possibility of using a so called 'notwithstanding' clause. The Human Rights No 3 Bill introduced by the Labour MP Mr Graham Allen in January 1994 would have adopted this method of protection for the Bill of Rights. The civil rights group Liberty has supported this possibility,[220] as have some other commentators.[221] Based on the model of the Canadian Charter, the clause would state that subsequent legislation would only override the Convention if the intention of doing so were expressly stated in such legislation. Under a 'notwithstanding' clause, the judiciary would not be required to strike down legislation without a mandate from the democratically elected government. If that government did not include the clause in any legislative provision which subsequently was found to infringe the Convention, the government could impliedly be taken to be mandating the judiciary, by its omission, to strike down the offending legislation. Thus, although under such a model the judiciary are required to render Acts of Parliament inapplicable, a role which the domestic judiciary might find constitutionally problematic, they are not required to act against the wishes of the democratically elected government. Dworkin has observed, in relation to such a clause, that: 'In practice this technically weaker version of incorporation would probably provide almost as much protection as [formal entrenchment].'[222] However, this model accepts the possibility which clearly arises that future governments might come to use the clause more frequently. A government might be uncertain whether a particular measure would be in breach of the rights, but decide that a 'notwithstanding' clause should be used on insurance grounds. It is possible that use of such a clause might prove ultimately to be quite an ineffective protective device.

More effective protection for constitutional rights can be achieved by full entrenchment. Constitutions throughout the world adopt a number of different forms of entrenchment of codes of rights. The constitution of the US can be amended only by a proposal which has been agreed by two-thirds of each House of Congress or by a convention summoned by Congress at the request of two-thirds of the States. The proposed amendment must then be ratified by three-quarters of the States' legislatures. The amendment procedure itself – Article V of the Constitution – can be amended only by the same method. It was generally thought that if a Bill of Rights had been introduced containing a provision that it could not be repealed except in accordance with some such procedure, the courts would not have given effect to it. Parliament might have legislated expressly contrary to it and the possibility of unwitting implied repeal would have remained. If it had been found that a later provision would not admit of a construction in accordance with its guarantees, it was thought that judges would probably apply the later provision, thereby repealing the right in question to the extent of its inconsistency. Authority for this can be found in the *dicta* of Maughan LJ in *Ellen Street Estates Ltd v Minister of Health*[223] to the effect that Parliament cannot bind itself as to the form of future enactments. However, De Smith suggests that Parliament could redefine itself so as to preclude itself as ordinarily constituted from legislating on a certain matter. The argument is based on the redefinition of Parliament under the Parliament Acts: if Parliament can

---

220 See Klug, F and Wadham, J [1993] PL 579.
221 See, eg, Dworkin, *A Bill of Rights for Britain*, pp 24–29. The Labour Party supported this position at its conference in 1993, but had changed its position by 1996, as its 1996 consultative document reveals.
222 *Dworkin, op cit*, fn 1.
223 [1934] 1 KB 590, p 597.

make it easier for itself to legislate on certain matters, it could equally make it harder, thereby entrenching certain legislation. This analogy has, however, come under attack from Munro[224] on the ground that the Parliament Act procedure introduces no limitation on parliamentary sovereignty. The analogy of EC law would arguably support De Smith's proposition and authority is also available from other constitutions; in *AG for New South Wales v Trethowan*,[225] the Privy Council upheld the requirement of a referendum before a Bill to abolish the upper House could be presented for the royal assent. Although, as De Smith argues, this decision may be of limited application as involving a non-sovereign legislature, it does suggest that a class of legislation exists for which it may be appropriate to delineate the manner and form of any subsequent amendment or repeal. The South African case of *Harris v Minister of the Interior*[226] is to similar effect. Dicey has argued that the Bill of Rights could be entrenched within a written constitution since it would be untenable to espouse 'the strange dogma, sometimes put forward, that a sovereign power such as the Parliament of the United Kingdom, can never by its own act divest itself of authority'.[227] The point cannot be regarded as settled.

Thus, a proposal of the Labour Government that the Convention should be fully entrenched would have been constitutionally controversial and – possibly – impossible without a written constitution. However, the government did not put forward such a proposal and there was by no means agreement between supporters of the domestic incorporation of the Convention that it would have been desirable.

Chapter 4 considers the model of protection that was chosen for the Convention, in the Human Rights Act.

224 Munro, C, *Studies in Constitutional Law*, 1999.`
225 [1932] AC 526.
226 (1952) (2) SA 428.
227 Dicey, AV, *An Introduction to the Study of the Law of the Constitution*, 10th edn, 1987, p 68.

THE HUMAN RIGHTS ACT 1998

1 INTRODUCTION[1]

This chapter, which considers and analyses the Human Rights Act and certain early, very significant decisions taken under it, is intended to provide a framework for the discussion of the impact of the Act, which pervades the whole book. The discussion will cover the central aspects of the Act, but will then go on to examine more closely a number of the areas in which the Human Rights Act is ambiguous and uncertain.

The Green Paper, *Bringing Rights Home*,[2] concluded: 'We aim to change the relationship between the State and the citizen, and to redress the dilution of individual rights by an over-centralising government that has taken place over the past two decades.' This aim was to be achieved by means of the European Convention on Human Rights as afforded further effect in domestic law under the Human Rights Act 1998. The Act came fully into force on 2 October 2000. The Convention thus received into domestic law creates a transformation in constitutional terms in the sense that it provides positive rights in place of negative liberties. Since, traditionally, the constitution recognised only negative liberties as opposed to positive rights, the judicial focus of concern always tended to be on the content and nature of the restrictions in question rather than on the value and extent of the right. In other words, despite proud traditions of upholding certain fundamental rights, constitutional inadequacy became, inevitably, apparent. This approach will no longer be appropriate. Below, various approaches to the Convention are considered as the basis for allowing a subtle infusion of Strasbourg principles into UK law.

The codification of the rights of citizens, regarded by Dicey as endangering liberty, has occurred. A cultural change from complacency regarding liberty to a consciousness of rights is under way. While the Diceyan tradition demanded a basis in law for interference with liberties by public authorities, this demand is clarified and confirmed in respect of interferences with the guarantees.[3] It obliges public authorities, in particular the police, not only to discharge duties such as the duty to keep the peace, but to uphold human rights. It asks the judiciary to consider matters such as the 'quality' of law, not merely its formal existence.[4] It asks them to examine the necessity in a democracy of interfering with a right, the proportionality of the means used with the aim in question, and, if necessary, it asks them to inform Parliament that on one or more of these matters it has

---

1   See generally on the Human Rights Act: Wadham, J and Mountfield, H, *The Human Rights Act*, 1999 (useful guide); Pannick, D and Lord Lester of Herne Hill QC, *Human Rights Law and Practice*, 1999; Hunt, M, *Using Human Rights Law in English Courts*, 1997; Singh, R and Hunt, M, *A Practitioner's Guide to the Impact of the Human Rights Act*, 1999; Grosz, Beatson and Duffy, *Human Rights: The 1998 Act and the European Convention*, 2000; Clayton, R and Tomlinson, H, *Human Rights Law*, 2000; Fenwick, H, *Civil Rights: New Labour, Freedom and the Human Rights Act*, 2000, Chapter 2; Klug, F and Starmer, K [2001] PL 654; McGoldrick, D, 'The HRA in theory and practice' (2001) 50(4) ICLQ 901.

2   Straw, J and Boateng, P, *Bringing Rights Home: Labour's Plans to Incorporate the ECHR into UK Law: A Consultation Paper*, 1997.

3   See Chapter 2, esp p 66.

4   See Chapter 11, p 680.

breached the Convention. These are bold, imaginative constitutional changes. However, such boldness had limits, which are reflected in the Human Rights Act.

A seminal constitutional decision involving a choice between judicial and parliamentary checks on executive power, and therefore as to the allocation of power, had to be taken regarding the choice of model for the enforcement of the Convention. The choice made was, as indicated below, to leave the ultimate task of curbing executive power to Parliament; judicial rulings remain (at least theoretically) subject to primary legislation. The Human Rights Act therefore seeks to reconcile a transfer of power to the judiciary with parliamentary sovereignty. It is readily apparent, then, that there is a contradiction between the liberal aim of affording the Convention rights efficacy in domestic law in order to aid in reversing the effects of the over-centralisation of power, and the aim of preserving the key feature of the constitution which gave rein to that power. This contradiction gives rise to one of the central themes explored throughout this book – the search for a means of giving efficacy to the rights in the face of hostile primary legislation, particularly Labour legislation.

It is important to point out that although the Convention contains a list of rights that look very similar to those contained in a number of Bills or Charters of Rights, the Human Rights Act does not create a Bill or Charter of Rights in the way that the Canadian Charter or the US Amendments to the Constitution can be said to constitute a Bill of Rights, since those rights have the force of 'ordinary' law and also, in different respects, have a higher status than such law. Further, unlike the German Basic Law or the US Amendments, the Human Rights Act can simply be repealed or amended like any ordinary statute and it is, therefore, in a far more precarious position.

The Human Rights Act (HRA) is modelled on the New Zealand Bill of Rights which uses a rule of construction under s 6 to the effect that a court is obliged, wherever an enactment can be given a meaning that is consistent with the rights and freedoms contained in the Bill of Rights, to prefer that meaning to any other meaning.[5] In so far as one expects a Bill of Rights to demonstrate a strong commitment to human rights, demanding, if necessary, constitutional changes to provide such protection, the HRA, like the New Zealand Bill of Rights, does not have the characteristics of a Bill of Rights.

The HRA does *not* 'incorporate' the Convention rights into substantive domestic law, since it does not provide that they are to have the 'force of law', the usual form of words used when international treaties are incorporated into domestic law. [6] Instead, under s 1(2) of the HRA, certain of the rights discussed in Chapter 2 are to 'have effect for the purposes of this Act'. They are, according to the Lord Chancellor, a form of common law (since they are non-statutory) and, in that sense, they are part of domestic law.[7] But if this is correct, it is nevertheless clear that they differ strongly from common law doctrines in general, since they are accompanied by a strong interpretative obligation under s 3. These comments must be qualified further: it should be pointed out that, as indicated below,[8]

---

5   For discussion as to the use of this model, see Taggart, 'Tugging on Superman's cape: lessons from the experience with the New Zealand Bill of Rights' [1998] PL 266; Butler, A, 'Why the New Zealand Bill of Rights is a bad model for Britain' [1997] OJLS 332; Schwartz, H, 'The short and happy life and tragic death of the New Zealand Bill of Rights' [1998] NZLR 259.

6   See, eg, the Carriage of Goods by Sea Act 1971, s 1(2).

7   HL, Third Reading, Col 840, 5 February 1998.

8   See p 156.

the rights *are* in a sense incorporated into domestic law when asserted against public authorities or when the issue in question, which relates to a Convention right, falls within the scope of EC law. As explained below, the effect of the failure, technically, to incorporate the rights may not be of much practical significance except when it is arguable that relevant primary legislation is incompatible with one or more of the rights.

2 THE CHOICE OF RIGHTS

The rights protected under the HRA

The rights given this new and subtle legal status are, under s 1(1) of the HRA, Arts 2–12 and 14 of the Convention, Arts 1–3 of the First Protocol and Arts 1 and 2 of the Sixth Protocol as read with Arts 16–18 of the Convention. The rights are set out in Sched 1 of the HRA; further Protocols could be added by the Secretary of State, by order, under s 1(4). Equally, rights could be removed and any other amendments to the Act could be made, by the same route in order to 'reflect the effect, in relation to the UK, of a Protocol'. This choice of rights is significant. It is arguably a serious deficiency of the international record of the UK in human rights matters that it has not ratified all the Protocols; therefore, the most satisfactory course would have been their inclusion in the rights protected.

The Government has reconsidered the question of incorporating the Fourth and Seventh Protocols. It has decided at present to ratify the Seventh Protocol,[9] but has not yet decided to ratify the Fourth, which would require changes to immigration legislation or the entry of a reservation.[10] The question of extending the scope of the Convention in this way is of particular significance in relation to the Anti-Discrimination Protocol, Protocol 12, which will provide a guarantee of freedom from discrimination extending beyond the civil rights' arena.[11] At the present time, the Government has not yet ratified it[12] and clearly is not therefore at present minded to include it in Sched 1.

The omission of Art 13 is particularly significant. The idea behind it is that the function of that Article will be carried out by s 8 of the HRA (see below) and that its inclusion might have encouraged the judiciary to provide new remedies, going beyond those that could be provided under s 8. Possibly, Art 13 could have been utilised in an attempt to create new free standing causes of action between private parties – direct horizontal effect. As indicated below, ss 6 and 7 seek to ensure that the creation of the new action under the HRA confines it to use against public authorities. Arguably, the Art 13 jurisprudence can, however, be taken into account by the judiciary under s 2 of the HRA.[13]

---

9   This will require legislative change to certain family law principles creating inequalities between husband and wife.

10 See Home Office Review of Human Rights Instruments (amended), 26 August 1999.

11 See Chapter 2, p 83 and Chapter 16, p 985.

12 It was opened for signature in November 2000.

13 See Grosz, Beatson and Duffy, *op cit*, fn 1, para 1-06; see also Feldman, 'Remedies for violation of Convention Rights under the HRA' [1998] EHRLR 691.

Deficiencies and limitations of the Convention

It must be asked why the decision was made in the Human Rights Act to provide protection for parts of the European Convention on Human Rights, as opposed to introducing a tailor-made UK Bill of Rights or incorporating the International Covenant on Civil and Political Rights. In taking this course, the Labour Government followed a long tradition of favouring the Convention over other instruments. The overwhelming majority of human rights Bills considered by Parliament have simply advocated incorporation of the European Convention on Human Rights[14] into UK law. The House of Lords Select Committee on a Bill of Rights was unanimous on the question of creating a tailor-made Bill of Rights: 'To attempt to formulate *de novo* a set of fundamental rights which would command the necessary general assent would be a fruitless exercise.'[15] Starting from scratch and developing a Bill of Rights for the UK would have been a burdensome task because the political parties (and the various pressure groups) would have had great difficulty in reaching agreement on it, while the process of hearing and considering all the representations made by interested parties would have been extremely lengthy. Zander argued[16] that it was politically and psychologically easier to incorporate the Convention, since it was already binding on the UK internationally and both major parties have accepted the jurisdiction of the European Court of Human Rights and the right of individual petition.[17] A key argument put forward by supporters of the Convention was that the advantage to be gained by adopting the course of creating a home-grown Bill of Rights would have had to be weighed up against the possible detriment caused if the jurisprudence of the European Court of Human Rights had been seen as less directly applicable. The British judiciary might have felt that they had lost the 'anchor' of the authority of the Court and the constraint of the need to apply a reasonably uniform European standard of human rights.

Arguments against relying on the Convention are based partly on its defects of both form and content, which have often been criticised.[18] It is a cautious document: it is not as open textured as the American Bill of Rights, and contains long lists of exceptions to the primary rights – exceptions which suggest a strong respect for the institutions of the State. Perhaps the most outstanding examples of inadequacy are the limited scope of Art 14[19] and the dangerous potential of Art 17.[20] From today's perspective, the 50 year old Convention looks very much like a creature of its period,[21] with its provision against slavery and its long lists of exceptions to certain fundamental rights. Its out-of-date feel

---

14 This reference to incorporation of the Convention refers to Arts 1–18 and the First Protocol – the course advocated by the House of Lords Select Committee on Human Rights in 1978.

15 Report of Select Committee, HL Paper 176, June 1978.

16 Zander, M, *A Bill of Rights?*, p 83.

17 It may be noted that under the changes made by Protocol 11, the right of individual petition can no longer be withdrawn; see Chapter 2, p 26.

18 See, eg, Hewitt, P, *The Abuse of Power*, 1982, pp 232–40; Gearty, C [1993] CLJ 89.

19 Article 14 provides a guarantee of freedom from discrimination, but only in the context of the substantive rights. See further Chapter 2, pp 85–86.

20 It was used by the Commission to allow the banning of the German Communist party: *Kommunistische Partei Deutschland v Federal Republic of Germany*, Application 250/57 Yearbook I (1955–57), Vol 6, p 222.

21 The Convention was drafted in 1949 and based on the United Nations Declaration of Human Rights. The Declaration was adopted on December 10 1948 by the General Assembly of the UN.

has led a number of commentators to echo the plea put forward some years ago by Tomkins and Rix for 'a document of principle for the 1990s and not a document of exceptions from the 1950s'.[22] It might appear that the present structure of the Convention is simply not adequate to the task of bringing about far reaching reforms and thereby fulfilling the constitutional role which a number of commentators have enthusiastically mapped out for it.[23] As Feldman puts it, the Convention rights are 'by no means a comprehensive basis for a modern system of protection for [individualistic and public] values'.[24] The far more thorough South African Bill of Rights, which covers certain social, economic and environmental rights, provides an example of such a system. The pressure group Liberty's *Manifesto for Human Rights* proposed that a domestic Bill of Rights could be drawn up, based on the Convention, but using more up-to-date language and addressing certain of the inadequacies indicated and considered in Chapter 2.[25] In particular, Liberty criticised the lack of minimum conditions for detention outside Art 3, and the lack of a right to jury trial. It has also been pointed out that the Convention contains no specific rights for children.[26]

The decisions of the European Court of Human Rights documented in this book suggest, however, that the Convention is sufficiently open-textured to be able to cover circumstances not envisaged when it was created[27] and to adapt to changing social values. For example, although a right of access to legal advice in police custody is not expressly included, the Court has – in effect – read one into Art 6, arising in a number of circumstances.[28] The Convention, with its associated jurisprudence, comes close to comprising a modern 'document of principles' thanks largely to the enterprise of the Court, which has insisted upon the dynamic nature of the Convention and has adopted a teleological or purpose-based approach to interpretation which has allowed the substantive rights to develop.[29] But those principles cannot always be sought in the outcomes of applications. The traditional approach of the doctrine of precedent in UK courts will not, therefore, always be appropriate to the development of the domestic jurisprudence.

The Human Rights Act can nevertheless be criticised on the basis that the opportunity was lost to include certain social and economic rights,[30] including some of those protected under the International Covenant on Social, Economic and Cultural Rights. The dynamic approach of the Strasbourg Court can only marginally address the failure to provide second or third generation rights under the HRA, although, as Chapter 2 pointed

---

22 'Unconventional use of the Convention' (1992) 55(5) MLR 721, p 725. See also Ashworth, A, 'The European Convention on Human Rights and English criminal justice: ships which pass in the night?', in Andenas, M (ed), *English Public Law and the Common Law of Europe*, 1998, p 215.

23 See, eg, Feldman, D, 'The Human Rights Act 1998 and constitutional principles' (1999) 19(2) LS 165; Lord Lester of Herne Hill QC, 'First steps towards a Constitutional Bill of Rights' (1997) 2 EHRLR 124.

24 *Op cit*, Feldman, p 170.

25 National Council for Civil Liberties 1997. See also the Bill drawn up by the Institute for Public Policy Research: Constitution Paper No 1, 'A British Bill of Rights', 1990.

26 Fortin, J, 'Rights brought home for children' (1999) 62 MLR 350.

27 See, eg, *Soering v UK*, Judgment of 7 July 1989, A 161; (1989) 11 EHRR 439.

28 See Chapter 13, pp 861–63.

29 See: Van Dijk, P and Van Hoof, F, *Theory and Practice of the European Convention on Human Rights*, 3rd edn, 1998.

30 See Ewing, KD and Gearty, CA, 'Rocky foundations for Labour's new rights' (1997) 2 EHRLR 149.

out, there are signs of a change of approach in this respect.[31] It therefore remains legitimate to attack the Human Rights Act as an instrument which has not enshrined such rights, which has instead selected and elevated 'first generation' civil rights, ignoring the social and economic ones which might have given those civil rights some substantive rather than formal value.[32] That argument could now, however, be utilised to press for introducing second generation rights to future Protocols to the Convention,[33] for including Protocol 12 in Sched 1 and for giving consideration to the reception of other unincorporated treaties into domestic law. As Ewing puts it: 'the HRA provides a valuable template for other international treaties ...'[34] The inadequacies of the HRA also provide an argument for giving further effect to the European Social Charter 1961 in domestic law,[35] and for affording binding effect to elements of the recently published EU Charter of Fundamental Rights, which includes a number of social and economic rights.[36] The Charter contains those rights recognised under the European Convention on Human Rights together with a number of new social rights, including the right to strike, guarantees of maximum working hours, worker consultation and trade union membership.

3 THE LEGAL STATUS OF THE CONVENTION UNDER THE HUMAN RIGHTS ACT

The form of entrenchment for the Convention most favoured by a number of commentators was by means of a so called 'notwithstanding clause'. As indicated in Chapter 3, this means entrenchment by means of a requirement of form. Therefore, as suggested earlier in this chapter, it is not open to the objections which would be and are levelled at the adoption of a requirement of manner or a restriction as to substance. However, this model was not used for the Human Rights Act, although the constitutional protection it has received bears some similarities to the use of a 'notwithstanding clause'. Of course, there is nothing in the Human Rights Act to prevent Parliament from including a 'notwithstanding' clause in legislation, a possibility which is considered further below, at p 146.

In considering the model chosen, it is worth bearing in mind that the need to introduce further forms of protection might become apparent in future, at least for key Convention rights. Liberty has suggested that certain rights may be viewed as more fundamental than others and, therefore, might be entrenched while others might be

---

31 See Chapter 2, p 40.

32 See further Ewing, KD, 'Social rights and constitutional law' [1999] PL 104.

33 With a view to adding such Protocols to Sched 1 to the HRA 1998.

34 Ewing, *op cit*, fn 32, p 110.

35 Liberty campaigned for this possibility at the time when the Human Rights Bill was proposed but at the present time, the Labour Government has shown no interest in it. See further Ewing, KD, 'Social rights and human rights: Britain and the Social Charter – the Conservative legacy' (2000) 2 EHRLR 91.

36 The Charter was published in May 2000 (available from the European Commission website and from the website of the House of Lords Select Committee on the European Parliament). The rights could, potentially, bind the EU institutions. Britain considers that the Charter should not become part of the Treaty, and therefore have binding effect, but should have a merely declaratory status and, at the present time, it merely has such a status.

afforded less protection.[37] The Labour Party proposals in the 1996 consultative document were partly based on the New Zealand model. As indicated above, the New Zealand Bill of Rights 1990 was disabled from overriding pre-existing legislation and was subject to express or implied repeal by future enactments. This model was also adopted for the Canadian Bill of Rights 1960.

The interpretative obligation under s 3[37a]

Under s 3 of the Human Rights Act 1998, which partly reflects the proposals in Labour's Consultation paper on the matter,[38] the Convention[39] receives a subtle form of constitutional protection. The key provision in creating this form of protection for the Convention under the Human Rights Act is s 3(1), which reads: 'So far as it is possible to do so, primary and subordinate legislation must be read and given effect in a way which is compatible with the Convention rights ...' Section 3(2)(b) reads: 'this section does not affect the validity, continuing operation or enforcement of any incompatible primary legislation; and (c) does not affect the validity, continuing operation or enforcement of any incompatible subordinate legislation if ... primary legislation prevents the removal of the incompatibility'. Significantly, s 3(2)(a) makes it clear that the obligation imposed by s 3 arises in relation to both previous and subsequent enactments.

Primary and secondary legislation

Section 21(1) defines 'primary legislation' to include Measures of the General Synod of the Church of England and, most significantly, Orders in Council made under the royal prerogative. Thus, executive power as well as parliamentary sovereignty are preserved under the HRA.[40] This is clearly an anomalous provision, since it renders individual rights subordinate to powers which may be used to infringe them and which cannot claim legitimacy derived from the democratic process.

Subordinate legislation covers Orders in Council not made under the royal prerogative, orders, rules, regulations, bylaws or other instruments made under primary legislation *unless* 'it operates to bring one or more provisions of that legislation into force or amends any primary legislation'. The last provision is significant, since it means where provision is made under primary legislation for amendment by executive order, subject to the negative, or even the affirmative resolution procedure, the amendment, which will almost certainly have received virtually no parliamentary attention, will still be able to override Convention provisions. This is of particular importance in relation to the

---

37   See Klug, F and Wadham, J, 'The democratic entrenchment of a Bill of Rights: Liberty's proposals' [1993] PL 579.

37a For further discussion see Elliott, MC, 'Fundamental rights as interpretative constructs: the constitutional logic of the HRA', in Forsyth, C (ed), *Judicial Review and the Constitution*, 2001, Hart.

38   *Bringing Rights Home: Labour's Plans to Incorporate the ECHR into UK Law*. See Straw and Boateng (1997) 1 EHRR 71. For discussion, see Lyell, N (Sir) (1997) 2 EHRR 132; Wadham, J (1997) 2 EHRR 141; Ewing, *op cit*, fn 30.

39   The term 'the Convention' will be used to refer to the Convention rights currently included in Sched 1 to the HRA 1998.

40   For discussion of the effect of treating this exercise of prerogative powers as primary legislation, see Squires, N, 'Judicial review of the prerogative after the HRA' [2000] 116 LQR 572–75.

Terrorism Act 2000 and the Regulation of Investigatory Powers Act 2000, since a number of gaps were left in the provisions, to be filled in this manner.[41]

The nature of the s 3 obligation: interpretative techniques

It is clear from s 3 that the Convention will have, in one sense, a lower status than ordinary statutes in that it will not automatically override pre-existing law. But, most significantly, s 3 demands that all statutes should be rendered, if possible, compatible with the Convention rights. Therefore, by imposing this interpretative obligation on courts, the rights become capable of affecting subsequent legislation in a way that is not normally possible.[42] If legislation cannot be rendered compatible with the rights, a declaration of incompatibility can be made under s 4;[43] Parliament may then modify the offending provisions under s 10.[44] This subtle form of protection avoids entrenchment and therefore creates a compromise between leaving the protection of rights to the democratic process and entrusting them fully to the judiciary.

Use of this model for the Convention places protection for human rights very much at the mercy of judicial interpretation of statutes. More liberal-minded judges may be prepared to find that most, if not almost all statutory provisions, even if unambiguous, can be modified through interpretative techniques in order to achieve harmony with the Convention. The requirement to construe legislation *'so far as it is possible to do so'* consistently with the Convention (emphasis added) makes it clear that such a stance best reflects the intention of Parliament, although it may also be pointed out that since Parliament has enacted s 4, it clearly contemplated some limits on what could be achieved by means of s 3. There is also the question whether using very bold interpretative techniques has democratic legitimacy.

Clayton and Tomlinson suggest that the domestic courts can obtain assistance in dealing with the new rule of construction by taking into account four interpretative techniques: the rule of construction cases;[45] the rules used to construe statutes in relation to EC law; the doctrines of reading in and reading down and the rule of construction in New Zealand.[46] The possibilities offered by such techniques are considered below and at various points in this book.

The response of the House of Lords in *Pickstone v Freemans*[47] to EU law provides a model to be used in this situation. The House of Lords found that domestic legislation – the Equal Pay Amendment Regulations – made under s 2(2) of the European Communities Act appeared to be inconsistent with Art 119 of the Treaty of Rome. It held that despite this apparent conflict a purposive interpretation of the domestic legislation would be adopted; in other words, the plain meaning of the provision in question would be ignored and an interpretation would be imposed on it which was not in conflict with

---

41 See Chapter 8, p 408 and Chapter 11, esp p 699.
42 For extensive consideration of this point, see Clayton and Tomlinson, *op cit*, fn 1, Chapter 4.
43 See below, pp 149 *et seq*.
44 See below, pp 151–52.
45 Eg, *Clarke v General Accident Fire and Life Assurance Corp plc* [1998] 1 WLR 1647.
46 Clayton and Tomlinson, *op cit*, fn 1, p 156.
47 [1988] 3 WLR 265.

Art 119. This was done on the basis that Parliament must have intended to fulfil its EU obligations in passing the Amendment regulations once it had been forced to do so by the European Court of Justice. The House of Lords followed a similar approach in *Litster v Forth Dry Dock Engineering*.[48] Lord Lester has observed: 'the courts will need where possible to read provisions into ambiguous or incomplete legislation.'[49]

The courts could look to the interpretation of the rule of construction in New Zealand – s 6 of the Bill of Rights, set out above – for some guidance. It has been found: 'a consistent meaning is to be preferred to any other meaning. The preference will come into play only when the enactment can be [given such a meaning]. This must mean, I think, can reasonably be given such a meaning. A strained interpretation will not be enough.[50] A similar approach was taken in subsequent cases,[51] prompting criticism from commentators.[52] This somewhat timid and uncreative approach arguably overlooks, it is suggested, the fact that s 6 must apply to itself. Therefore, if a meaning of s 6 is adopted which curbs the impact of the right or freedom in question, it is suggested that there has been a failure to use the rule of construction correctly. It is arguable that the meaning should have been adopted which would allow s 6 to give the right full scope, which would have meant in the above instance, refusing to read the word 'reasonably' into the section.

It is clear that the courts should not imply the word 'reasonably' into s 3.[53] They are expected to find a possible, not a reasonable interpretation, according to its wording. An opposition amendment which would have imported the word 'reasonably', was opposed by the Government.[54] However, merely adopting a generous interpretation of statutes under s 3, which would mean refusing to import the word 'reasonably', would not afford the courts much guidance in using s 3, although it is a starting point, which appears to be opposed to the New Zealand approach. It would mean 'reading in' certain words into the statute, straining the meanings of words or 'reading down' statutory provisions in order to afford them a narrow construction, compatible with the right in question.

It is suggested that in determining how far and when to adopt such techniques, a purposive, rather than simply a generous approach should be adopted and that guidance as to the use of such an approach may best be derived from other jurisdictions, including Canada and the US, rather than relying on the existing domestic purposive interpretation cases. A 'purposive' approach in this context would mean, it is argued, first adopting the interpretation of the Convention right which gave effect to the values underlying the right. So doing might mean, secondly, using the techniques considered in order to interpret the statutory provision in question with a view to determining whether so doing would yield a meaning that could achieve the purpose revealed by a consideration of

---

48   [1989] 1 All ER 1194.

49   'Interpreting statutes under the HRA', 20(3) Statute L Rev 218, p 225.

50   *Ministry of Transport v Noort* [1992] 3 NZLR 260, p 272.

51   See, eg, *Quilter v AG of New Zealand* [1998] 1 NZLR 523.

52   See Taggart, M, 'Tugging on Superman's cape: lessons from the experience with the New Zealand Bill of Rights' [1998] PL 266; Butler, *op cit*, fn 5; Schwartz, H, 'The short and happy life and tragic death of the New Zealand Bill of Rights' [1998] NZLR 259.

53   This was confirmed by the House of Lords in *R v A* [2001] 2 WLR 1546 by Lord Steyn, para 44.

54   Vol 313, HC Deb Col 421, 3 June 1998.

those values. A leading decision on s 3 is the House of Lords' decision in *R v A*.[55] It is suggested that the Lords used an extremely bold interpretative technique – that of reading words into the legislative provision in question in order to render it compatible with Art 6. Although this may be what s 3 demands, it is arguable that in so doing, they in fact went beyond using interpretative techniques and – in effect – rewrote the legislation. The decision is discussed further below.

Certain parts of the existing law may, as they stand, be incompatible with the Convention. Examples may include ss 5 and ss 14A and C of the Public Order Act 1986.[56] Under s 3, the possibility of impliedly repealing such provisions has been ruled out, but unless they admit of no interpretation compatible with the Convention right(s) in question (in this instance, Arts 10, 11 and 6) they could be made to conform with it. The outcome would often be the same as that which would have been achieved had implied repeal occurred. If ambiguity, or any other loophole allowing the courts to achieve compatibility cannot be found in a provision incompatible with a Convention right, the right itself will be disapplied to the extent of its incompatibility with that particular statutory provision, at least until and if amending legislation is passed, under s 10 (see below) – in effect, a reversal of the normal rules of implied repeal.

But the early signs are that the judiciary are prepared to take an extremely vigorous stance when interpreting existing law in the light of Convention provisions. The findings of the House of Lords in *R v A*,[56a] discussed below, suggest that they are prepared to ensure that the outcome which allows the Convention to prevail is achieved even if this involves a significant disregard for statutory language. Lord Lester has observed, on this point: 'Would [the courts use the incorporating measures] to go much further than the traditional position in which the courts seek to interpret ambiguous legislation so as to be in accordance with rather than breach treaty obligations undertaken by the UK? I hope and believe that they would indeed do so ...'[57]

At the Committee stage of the Bill, Lord Irvine said: 'We want the courts to strive to find an interpretation of legislation which is consistent with Convention rights so far as the language of the legislation allows, and only in the last resort to conclude that the legislation is so clearly incompatible with the Convention that it is impossible to do so.'[58] In *R v A*, the House of Lords very clearly accepted that a declaration was indeed a last resort and that s 3 could be used in an extremely creative fashion in order to avoid having to make one. The case concerned a form of rape shield law, under s 41(3)(c) of the Youth Justice and Criminal Evidence Act 1999, that prevented a woman being questioned as to an alleged previous sexual relationship with the defendant, although evidence as to the existence of such a relationship could be adduced by the defence in relation to his belief in her consent. Thus, arguably, s 41(3)(c) protected the woman's Art 8 Rights.

Lord Steyn said:

Under ordinary methods of interpretation a court may depart from the language of the State to avoid absurd consequences: section 3 goes much further. Undoubtedly a court must

---

55   [2001] 2 WLR 1546.

56   Sections 14A and C were inserted into the 1986 Act by ss 70–71 of the Criminal Justice and Public Order Act 1994.

56a See fn 55, above.

57   'First steps towards a constitutional Bill of Rights' (1997) 2 EHRR 124, p 127.

58   *Hansard*, HL Deb Col 535, 18 November 1997.

always look for a contextual and purposive interpretation: section 3 is more radical in its effect. It is a general principle of the interpretation of legal instruments that the text is the primary source of interpretation: other sources are subordinate to it ... Section 3 qualifies this general rule because it requires a court to find an interpretation compatible with the Convention rights if it is possible to do so ... In accordance with the will of Parliament it will sometimes be necessary to adopt an interpretation which linguistically will appear strained. The techniques to be used will not only involve the reading down of express language in a statute but also the implication of provisions. A declaration of incompatibility is a measure of last resort ... It is therefore possible under s 3 to read ... s 41(3)(c) [of the Youth Justice and Criminal Evidence Act 1999] as subject to the implied provisions that evidence or questioning which is required to ensure a fair trial under Article 6(1) ... should not be treated as inadmissible [emphasis added].59

A somewhat more cautionary note was sounded regarding the application of s 3 in *Donoghue v Poplar Housing and Regeneration Community Assoc Ltd and the Secretary of State for the Environment*.[59a] Lord Woolf said that s 3 'does not entitle the court to legislate; its task is still one of interpretation but interpretation in accordance with the direction contained in s 3'.[59b] He went on to say that the most difficult task of the courts is that of distinguishing between interpretation and legislation.

In the early months of the HRA, the lower courts took an approach to s 3 which differed considerably from that taken in *R v A*, one that they can now be expected to reverse. A declaration of incompatibility was made by the Divisional Court in respect of four planning cases, *Alconbury*[59c], but the declaration was then reversed by the House of Lords,[60] on the basis that a close reading of the Convention jurisprudence revealed that no incompatibility arose.[61] A further early declaration was made by the Court of Appeal in relation to the system of appeals for prisoners detained on mental health grounds in *R (H) v Mental Health Tribunal, North and East London Region and Another*.[62] The Court found that s 73 of the Mental Health Act was incompatible with Art 5 since it in effect reversed the burden of proof against the detained person. The declaration was surprising in the sense that s 3 could have been used more strenuously to find that the system of appeals in such mental health cases could be viewed as compliant with the Convention.[63]

In *Wilson v the First County Trust Ltd*[64] the Court of Appeal found that s 127(3) of the Consumer Credit Act 1974 was incompatible with Art 6 and with Art 1 of the First Protocol to the Convention since it imposed an inflexible prohibition against the making of an enforcement order in an instance where a loan agreement did not contain the terms prescribed for the purposes of s 61(1) of the Act. The effect of s 127(3) was therefore to

---

59 *Ibid*, para 44.

59a [2001] 3 WLR 183; [2001] 4 All ER 604.

59b At paras 75 and 76.

59c See fn 60, below.

60 *R (on the application of Alconbury Ltd) v Secretary of State for the Environment, Transport and the Regions and other cases* [2001] 2 All ER 929; (2001) NLJ 135.

61 This point is considered further below; see pp 147–48.

62 (2001) *The Times*, 2 April.

63 This is not a comment on the merits of the judgment; it is unfortunate that the system of appeals in such mental health cases was not rendered compliant with the Convention prior to the coming into force of the HRA and the change that may now come about may be beneficial.

64 [2001] 3 All ER 229.

prevent the creditor from obtaining a judicial remedy where the loan agreement did not contain all the prescribed terms. The Court considered the possibility of finding 'some other legitimate interpretation' of the words of the section which would avoid the finding of incompatibility.[65] It said that a court is 'required [by s 3] to go as far as but not beyond what is legally possible ... the court is not required or entitled to give to words a meaning which they cannot bear'.[66] In the instance in question, the court did not think that the words would bear a Convention-friendly interpretation. Clearly, it is possible that this declaration will also be reversed in the House of Lords on the basis that Art 6 and Art 1 of Protocol 1 can be interpreted differently. It would not seem possible for the Lords to accept their interpretation as indicated by the Court of Appeal but then go on to find that the words of s 127(3) can be forced to take a Convention-friendly meaning. Clearly, the Court of Appeal considered that there are limits to what can be achieved even under s 3, although their finding is hardly consonant with that of the House of Lords in *R v A*.

The approach in *R v A* can also be contrasted with the decision of the Privy Council in *Brown v Stott*,[67] the first decision of the Law Lords under the HRA. The decision illustrates, it is suggested, the problems that may arise due to the adoption a form of 'purposive' approach and of 'reading down' Convention rights by reference to the purpose in question. The decision is discussed fully below, but a number of central findings in the decision illustrate the approach adopted. Lord Steyn found: 'national courts may accord to the decisions of national legislatures some deference where the context justifies it ... the subject [road safety] invites special regulation ... some infringements [of Art 6] may be justified.' Lord Hope said: 'the jurisprudence of the Court of Human Rights tells us ... that [in the case of a non-absolute right] the ... restriction contended for has to have a legitimate aim in the public interest. If so is there a reasonable relationship of proportionality between the means employed and the aim sought to be realised?' He found that, in relation to s 172 of the Road Traffic Act, which requires that drivers identify themselves, on pain of a fine, as driving a car at the material time, the answer to both questions, in terms of limiting the right not to incriminate oneself under Art 6(1), was in the affirmative. This decision exemplifies, it is suggested, the possibilities of undermining the Convention rights by taking a particular view as to the general purposes of the Convention and then by 'reading down' a particular right in order to do so. This approach is considered further below in relation to the notions of judicial activism and minimalism.

Clearly, 'the precise limits of the s 3 rule of construction remain controversial'.[68] But, as indicated, those limits are beginning to become apparent. Following the lead of the House of Lords in the four key decisions mentioned, *R v A, Brown v Stott, Donoghue* and *Alconbury*,[69] it is suggested that a four-stage approach will be adopted when Convention rights are invoked in relation to a legislative provision. First, whether or not a declaration of incompatibility has already been made in a lower court (or, if in a court unable to make a formal declaration, an informal finding of incompatibility), the Strasbourg

---

65 *Ibid*, para 41.

66 *Ibid*, para 42.

67 [2001] 2 WLR 817; [2001] 2 All ER 97, the Judicial Committee of the Privy Council. See, for the Scottish decision, *Stott v Brown* 2000 SLT 379.

68 Clayton and Tomlinson, *op cit*, fn 1, p 169.

69 *R (on the application of Alconbury Ltd) v Secretary of State for the Environment, Transport and the Regions and other cases* [2001] 2 All ER 929; (2001) NLJ 135.

jurisprudence will be considered afresh in order to determine whether there is, on close scrutiny, a problem regarding compatibility. That may be the end of the matter, as in *Alconbury*. Secondly, if there does appear to be a problem, it may be resolvable using accepted interpretative techniques as in *Brown v Stott*.[69a] Finally, if the use of such techniques would almost certainly mean that a declaration of incompatibility has to be made, s 3 will be used in a very creative fashion, as indicated by Lord Steyn in *R v A*, in order to avoid a finding of incompatibility unless, according to *Donoghue*, so doing would mean crossing the boundary between interpreting and legislating. Finally, if the words used are so clear that the use of s 3 cannot provide a method of finding compatibility, a declaration of the incompatibility will have to be made, as a last resort, when and if the matter reaches a court able to make such a declaration, under s 4.[70]

It is suggested that this is not an approach it is very easy to feel comfortable with. It may allow the senior judiciary too much leeway to allow their own values free rein, under the cloak of using interpretative techniques. It tends to marginalise the democratic process: if s 3 is used, even if it emasculates a legislative provision, as in *R v A*, Parliament has not been asked – under the s 4 procedure – to amend the provision. The whole process remains in the hands of the judiciary. In this sense, *R v A* has, it is contended, placed the whole carefully crafted scheme of the HRA in jeopardy. Even in these early days, the tensions inherent in the scheme have been explored and heightened, since it appears that s 3 will almost always be used to outflank s 4 and s 10. The idea, which seemed to be inherent in s 4, that declarations of incompatibility would be made, even in criminal cases, seems to have been shown to be misconceived. Clearly, it is hard to see that they could be where Art 6 is concerned: if a conviction is obtained in breach of Art 6, it is unsafe;[71] therefore, if a conviction is obtained after a declaration of the incompatibility of a relevant legislative provision with Art 6, it is likely to be viewed as unsafe, unless it could be argued that the provision had had in its effects, ultimately, no or virtually no impact on the conviction.[72]

In response to *R v A* it would seem on the face of it possible for Parliament merely to reinstate the offending provision, using words that left no leeway at all for the bold interpretation placed upon s 41(3)(c) of the Youth Justice and Criminal Evidence Act 1999. It should be noted that the House of Lords considered that the provision had provided a 'gateway' for the very creative interpretation adopted.[73] But the safest course would appear to be to reinstate the provision using a notwithstanding clause to protect it, such as 'this provision is to be applied notwithstanding the provisions of Art 6(1)'. However, the use of such a clause, which then played a part in obtaining a conviction, is open to

---

69a This approach receives support from *Donoghue v Poplar Housing and Regeneration Community Assoc Ltd and the Secretary of State for the Environment* [2001] 3 WLR 183; [2001] 4 All ER 604. The Lord Chief Justice said that 'unless legislation would otherwise be in breach of the Convention s 3 can be ignored; so courts should always ascertain whether, absent s 3, there would be any breach of the Convention (at para 75).'

70 As in *Wilson v the First County Trust Ltd* [2001] 3 All ER 229; [2001] EWCA Civ 633, although arguably, it is unclear that the Convention absolutely demanded this result.

71 *Condron v UK* (2001) 31 EHRR 1. See also *Forbes* [2001] 2 WLR 1, p 13, para 24.

72 Bearing in mind the fact that jurors do not give reasons for conviction and cannot be asked about them, it would be difficult in some instances to be sure that this was the case. But if, as in *R v A* itself, the allegedly incompatible provision concerned the admission of evidence, and ultimately the evidence was not admitted, it would be possible to say that the conviction was not unsafe.

73 *Ibid, per* Lord Steyn, para 42.

three objections. First, its use would appear to render the conviction unsafe and ensure a successful appeal. Secondly, an application to Strasbourg would be invited. Thirdly, the Government would suffer the grave international embarrassment attendant on legislating deliberately in breach of the Convention. The Government can no longer withdraw the right of individual petition[74] and, therefore, that drastic method of preventing applications is no longer available. It would be expected to react legislatively to a finding of a breach of Art 6, by removing or amending the offending provision. Its only recourse would seem to be to enter a reservation to that provision, at the same time as passing the amending legislation, accompanied by a notwithstanding clause. It would be a very dramatic move to enter a reservation to such a central guarantee – the right to a fair trial – although presumably, the reservation could be limited to the effect of Art 6(1) only in relation that specific provision. But none of this meets the first and most significant objection.

The conclusion must be, then, that, at least in criminal matters, s 3 provides the judges with more power – in terms of adopting what is in essence a legislative role – than the notwithstanding clause used in Canada does. Of course, the other side of the coin is that they can read *down* the Convention right in question – as in *Brown* – in order to avoid using s 3 or s 4. And, it is arguable that a factor determining their choice of approach is their view of the desirableness of the outcome, in social policy rather than legal terms.[75] The strength of the obligation under s 3 is not, it is suggested, without its dangers. The strong interpretative obligation on the judiciary can be viewed as a double edged sword. They must strive to find a Convention-friendly interpretation, but it is possible that in certain instances, the Convention standards will be diluted as courts adopt the least liberal interpretation of the Convention right in order to make it harmonise with UK legislation. An interpretative approach which leads to the dilution of Convention standards will be avoided only if a vigorous, activist approach is taken not only to foisting Convention-based interpretations onto statutory language, but also to ensuring that Convention standards are fully upheld by means of that interpretation and using the declaration of compatibility procedure where they cannot be, or where an irreconcilable clash of rights concerning an incommensurable moral issue is in question.[76]

The effect of s 2

In seeking to interpret statutory provisions compatibly with the Convention rights under the Human Rights Act, the domestic judiciary 'must take into account' any relevant Strasbourg jurisprudence, under s 2. Thus, they are not bound by it.[77] Section 2 creates

---

74 Protocol 11, Art 34.

75 They may favour a legislative regime that aids in the maintenance of road safety, whereas their 'common sense' may inform them that a woman who has allegedly had sex with a man on one occasion may be likely to consent to have sex with him on another. This implications of this latter issue in relation to rape shield laws is pursued in Chapter 17, pp 1066–67.

76 This very difficult issue is discussed further below in relation to judicial activism; see pp 191–92.

77 The term exhaustively covers any 'judgement, decision, declaration or advisory opinion of the Court', any 'opinion of the Commission given in a report adopted under Article 31', any 'decision of the Commission in connection with Article 26 or 27(2)' or any 'decision of the Committee of Ministers taken under Article 46'. The words 'in connection with' appear to mean that all findings which may be said to be linked to the admissibility procedure, including reports prepared during the preliminary examination of a case, could be taken into account.

quite a weak obligation, since it is open to the judiciary to consider but disapply a particular decision. It may be noted that only the Convention rights themselves are binding on public authorities, under s 6. As Chapter 2 indicated, the rights appear, in certain respects, quite out of date today. But since 1950, they have been subject to a rich and extensive jurisprudence. The domestic judiciary may view a number of the Articles as too bald and imprecise unless their interpretation at Strasbourg is taken into account. On the other hand, adoption of the Strasbourg jurisprudence may have the effect of 'reading down' the right.[78] In such instances, it may be that departure from such decisions would give a 'successful lead to Strasbourg'.[79] The Lord Chancellor explained the role of s 2 at the Committee stage in Parliament: '[s 2] would permit UK courts to depart from Strasbourg decisions where there has been no precise ruling on the matter and a commission opinion which does so has not taken into account subsequent Strasbourg case law ...'[80] At the Report stage, the Lord Chancellor further explained: 'Courts will often be faced with cases that involve factors perhaps specific to the UK which distinguish them from cases considered by the European Court ... it is important that our courts have scope to apply that discretion so as to aid in the development of human rights law ...'[81] In the course of such development, the courts would be likely to consider jurisprudence from other jurisdictions, since s 2 clearly leaves open the possibility of so doing.

It is too early yet to discern a trend in this respect. The House of Lords has shown itself very willing to consider jurisprudence from other jurisdictions,[82] but also to concentrate heavily on Strasbourg jurisprudence when it found such a course appropriate. It took the latter course in *R (on the application of Alconbury) v Secretary of State for the Environment*.[83] The Divisional Court made a declaration of incompatibility in relation to planning law provisions, finding them incompatible with Art 6 since the Secretary of State for the Environment, in determining a planning appeal, is acting in a dual capacity in both hearing the appeal and applying his or her own policy guidelines. Under Art 6, as Chapter 2 explained,[84] a person's civil rights and obligations must be determined by an independent and impartial tribunal. The minister, the Divisional Court found, cannot be viewed as independent and impartial owing to his dual role. On appeal to the House of Lords, the declaration was overturned.[85] The House of Lords found that the requirements of Art 6 can be satisfied by the possibility of judicial review. If the minister does not act impartially, his or her decision can be judicially reviewed. Therefore, a remedy is available. The House considered the question whether judicial review could be viewed as providing a sufficient remedy, bearing in mind the findings in *Lustig-Prean v UK*[86] and *Kingsley v UK*.[87] It came to the view, after extensively reviewing the Strasbourg

---

78 See *Salabiaku v France* A 141-A (1988) and see further pp 186–87, below. See also the discussion of the margin of appreciation doctrine in Chapter 2 pp 34–37.

79 583 HL 514, 515, 8 November 1997.

80 583 HL 514, 515, 8 November 1997.

81 484 HL 1270, 1271, 9 January 1998.

82 *R v A* [2001] 2 WLR 1546.

83 [2001] 2 All ER 929; (2001) *The Times*, 24 January.

84 See p 61.

85 See fn 83, above.

86 (1999) 29 EHRR 548.

87 (2001) *The Times*, 9 January.

jurisprudence in planning cases, that judicial review could now be viewed as providing a sufficient remedy, owing to the need to consider proportionality. But, it also considered that even without considering proportionality, judicial review could provide a sufficient remedy in the context in question, bearing in mind findings of that jurisprudence which suggested that a light touch review would be appropriate taking into account the complex and wide ranging policy issues involved in what is essentially a socio-economic matter. Lord Slynn found that the domestic courts should follow any 'clear and constant' Strasbourg jurisprudence except in special circumstances. Thus, the obligation under s 2 as interpreted by the House of Lords comes close to affording binding force to the jurisprudence.

The Act does not expressly mention the interpretation of the common law. But it is clear that s 2 makes the rights relevant to its interpretation since its application is not confined to statutory interpretation, but to the determination of any question, in a court or tribunal, that has arisen in connection with a Convention right. Further, since as indicated below, the courts themselves are public authorities under s 6, they would be expected to ensure, through their interpretation of the common law, that the Convention rights are not breached. As discussed below, the precise duty placed on the courts in this respect is a matter of debate. But it is clear that, where a legislative provision is not in question, but one party in the case before a court is a public authority, the court should apply s 2. In such an instance ss 2 and 6 in combination place, it is argued, an interpretative obligation on courts which is, in one sense, stronger than that created by s 3, since no provision allowing incompatible common law doctrines to override Convention rights appears in the Act. The further possibility that s 6 requires the court to apply s 2 to the common law where both parties are private bodies is considered below. It may be pointed out here that s 2 contains no words which would appear to limit its application to an instance in which one party before the court is a public authority; the limitation would arise if it was argued in such an instance that a private body does not possess Convention rights as against another private person and therefore that no question has arisen in connection with a Convention right. That argument appears to have been rejected, impliedly, by the courts in early decisions under the HRA.[88]

The position of the Scottish Parliament, the Northern Ireland Assembly and the Welsh Assembly

The devolution legislation places the Scottish Parliament, the Northern Ireland Assembly and the Welsh Assembly in a different position from that of the Westminster Parliament as regards the legal status of the Convention rights. The Welsh Assembly is not able to pass primary legislation and it is bound by the Convention under s 107(1) of the Government of Wales Act 1988. The Scottish Parliament cannot act incompatibly with the Convention under s 29(2)(d) of the Scotland Act 1998. The Executive and law officers in Scotland are also bound.[89] Under s 21 of the HRA, legislation passed by the Scottish

---

88 If it were correct, it would also counter the argument under s 3 that legislation should be construed compatible with the Convention rights regardless of the fact that both parties are private bodies. In *Wilson v First County Trust* [2001] 3 All ER 229, the Court of Appeal accepted that s 3 does indeed apply in such instances.

89 See Scotland Act, s 57. Thus, in Scotland and Wales, the Convention became binding from 1 July 1999, when the devolution legislation came into force, over a year before the HRA came fully into force.

Parliament and by the Northern Ireland Assembly is regarded as secondary legislation. Under s 3 of the Human Rights Act, any primary legislation[90] passed by the Westminster Parliament and applicable to Scotland, Northern Ireland and Wales will be binding, even if it is not compatible with the Convention. These arrangements mean that Scotland has, in effect, a Bill of Rights in the traditional sense since the Parliament is bound by the Convention and therefore cannot pass primary legislation which conflicts with it.[91] The references to 'legislation', so far and below, are to legislation emanating from the Westminster Parliament.

The 'declaration of incompatibility' and the remedial process

Section 4(2) applies under s 4(1) when a court is determining in any proceedings whether a provision of primary legislation is incompatible with a Convention right. If a court is satisfied that the provision is incompatible with the right, 'it may make a declaration of that incompatibility' – a declaration that it is not possible to construe the legislation in question to harmonise with the Convention. Section 4(4) applies to incompatible secondary legislation where incompatible primary legislation prevents the removal of the incompatibility. Again, the incompatibility can be declared. Thus, s 4 may seem to come close to allowing an infringement of parliamentary sovereignty since, as Feldman observes, 'For the first time Parliament has invited the judges to tell it that it has acted wrongly by legislating incompatibly with a Convention right'.[92] But, as Feldman also notes, the court is not informing Parliament that it has acted *unlawfully*, since, as explained below, Parliament is not bound by the Convention (s 6(3)). Nevertheless, the House of Lords has made it clear, in *R v A*, as indicated above, that it views the making of a declaration as a last resort to be avoided if at all possible.

But only certain courts can make the declaration. Section 4(5) provides that this applies to the House of Lords, the Judicial Committee of the Privy Council, the Courts-Martial Appeal Court; in Scotland, the High Court of Justiciary sitting otherwise than a trial court, or the Court of Session; in England and Wales, the High Court or the Court of Appeal. Under s 5(1), when a court is considering making a declaration, the Crown *must* be given notice so that it can, under s 5(2), intervene by being joined as a party to the proceedings.

A court falling within s 4(5) has a discretion to make a declaration of incompatibility. Section 4(2) clearly leaves open the possibility that such a court, having found an incompatibility, might nevertheless decide not to make a declaration of it. As indicated above, in *Wilson v the First County Trust Ltd*,[93] the Court of Appeal found that s 127(3) of the Consumer Credit Act 1974 was incompatible with Art 6 and with Art 1 of the First Protocol to the Convention. The Court considered that, having found an incompatibility, it should make a declaration of it for three reasons.[94] First, the question of the incompatibility had been fully argued at a hearing appointed for that purpose. Secondly, the order required by s 127(3) could not lawfully be made on the appeal unless the court

---

90 Scotland Act 1988, s 29(2)(b) and Sched 5, and Government of Wales Act 1988, Sched 2.
91 See further Tierney, S, 'Devolution issues and s 2(1) of the HRA' (2000) 4 EHRLR 380–92.
92 Feldman, *op cit*, fn 23, p 187.
93 See fn 88, above.
94 *Ibid*, para 47.

was satisfied that the section could not be read in such a way as to give effect to the Convention rights, and that fact should be formally recorded by a declaration that 'gives legitimacy to that order'. Thirdly, a declaration provides a basis for a minister to consider whether the section should be amended under s 10(1) (see below). The Court duly went on to make the declaration. The second reason given is of particular interest, since it suggests that a court would not feel that it could make an order required by an incompatible legislative provision without making a declaration, since the order would lack legitimacy. It may be noted that lower courts, which cannot make a declaration, are being asked under the HRA to do precisely that. This finding indicates the reluctance such courts are likely to feel in this situation. This finding further suggests, as do the other reasons, that courts within s 4(5) are unlikely to find incompatibility without declaring it. In other words, the discretion under s 4(2) appears to be narrow. It is hard to imagine circumstances in which a higher court would find an incompatibility without declaring it.

Once a declaration of incompatibility has been made, the legislative provision in question remains valid (s 4(6)). Section 3 provides that the interpretative obligation does not affect the validity, continuing operation or enforcement of any incompatible primary legislation, and this is equally the case under s 4(6) if a declaration of incompatibility is made. The Convention guarantee in question will be disapplied by the court in relation to that incompatible provision. The declaration can, however, be overturned on appeal to a higher court, as occurred in *Alconbury*.[95] The Divisional Court made a declaration of incompatibility which was overturned on appeal to the House of Lords.[96] Once a declaration has been made, there will be a period of time during which the Convention right could be utilised in respect of other relevant non-incompatible provisions. The right could also be viewed as a source of principle, until and if compatibility was achieved by amendment via the s 10 procedure considered below. The Convention provision would not appear to suffer a diminution of status except, to an extent, in relation to the incompatible legislative provision itself.

During the period after the declaration, while amendment of the legislative provision was awaited as a possibility, other courts might have to consider the same issue. Presumably, owing to the doctrine of precedent, the lower courts would view themselves as bound by the declaration. The HRA leaves open the possibility – in a higher court than the one which made the declaration – of eventually finding compatibility in respect of the incompatible legislative provision itself once it was revisited in a subsequent suitable case (assuming that the original declaration had not already been overturned on appeal). In other words, a different court might take a different view on incompatibility. Possibly, in so doing, it might be aided by jurisprudential developments occurring at Strasbourg, after the initial finding of incompatibility.

If legislation is found to be incompatible with a Convention guarantee in a court that cannot make a declaration of incompatibility or in one that can, but exercises its discretion not to do so, the position is presumably broadly the same: the legislative provision remains valid and the Convention guarantee in question will be disapplied in relation to the incompatible provision. There will be less likelihood that it will be

---

95   [2001] 2 All ER 929.
96   *Ibid.*

amended until and if a declaration of incompatibility is made, although obviously it could, theoretically, be amended without waiting for a declaration.[97] Clearly, the case might not be appealed up to a court which could make the declaration. Thus, there will probably be a longer period of time during which a Convention guarantee cannot be utilised in relation to that legislative provision, than there would be once a declaration had been made. In order to avoid this period of uncertainty, the courts are using fast track procedures to resolve the issue, as in *R v A*[98] and *Alconbury*.

Since, under s 4(5), only higher courts can make a declaration of incompatibility, the pressure on courts to find compatibility is increased, especially in criminal proceedings, since otherwise a citizen will have to suffer a breach of Convention rights.[99] However, where essential, a declaration of incompatibility should be made rather than 'reading down' the Convention right in question in order to find compatibility. The declaration is likely to trigger off amending legislation by means of the s 10 so called 'fast track' procedure, which is considered below. However, it need not do so – very significantly, the declaration is non-binding. Declarations of incompatibility may ensure that domestic law is eventually brought into a state of conformity with the human rights norms embodied in the jurisprudence of the European Court of Human Rights; possibly, quite a considerable amount of repressive legislation will eventually be swept away. A future, less liberal, government wishing to restore the provisions thus removed, although not formally constrained in any way (assuming that it could command a majority in Parliament), would do so in the face of public knowledge that it was resurrecting provisions which the courts had authoritatively determined to be in breach of Britain's obligations under the ECHR and, quite possibly, also of common law principle.[100] In this sense, both the 'adverse publicity' and the 'manifest breach' types of protection discussed below[101] bestowed by a 'notwithstanding clause' have been given – albeit to a lesser degree[102] – to the rights protected by the Convention.

If a declaration is made, s 10 will apply which, in a departure from the New Zealand scheme, allows a minister to make amendments to the offending legislation by means of the 'fast track' procedure. Section 10 may also be used where a decision of the European Court of Human Rights suggests that a provision of legislation is incompatible with the Convention. Therefore, campaigning groups could lobby the government to make amendments under s 10 following any such decision. However, as indicated above, the minister is under no obligation to make the amendment(s), either after any such decision or after a declaration of incompatibility under s 4, and may only do so if he or she considers that there are 'compelling reasons for proceeding under this section'. In other words, the fact that a declaration of incompatibility has been made will not necessarily in

---

97 Since such amendment would occur outside the s 10 procedure, the normal time constraints would apply.

98 See fn 55, above.

99 This was very clearly a pressing concern in *R v A* [2001] 2 WLR 1546; the ruling was awaited not only in that case, but in a number of pending rape cases.

100 See, eg, the statements in the House of Lords in *Derbyshire CC v Times Newspapers* [1993] 1 All ER 1011 to the effect that Art 10 of the ECHR and the English common law are substantively similar.

101 See p 154.

102 Lesser, because even where no statement of compatibility had been made, the courts would not be empowered to strike down the legislation in question.

itself provide a compelling reason, although the circumstances in which it is made may do so.

Schedule 2 provides two procedures for making a 'remedial order' which must, under s 20, be in the form of a statutory instrument. Schedule 2, para 2(a) and para 3 provide for a standard procedure whereby the minister must lay a draft of the Order before Parliament, together with the required information – an explanation of the incompatibility and a statement of the reasons for proceeding under s 10 – for at least 60 days, during which time representations can be made to the minister. It must then be laid before Parliament again and does not come into effect until it is approved by a resolution of each House within 60 days after it has been laid for the second time. The emergency procedure under Sched 2, para 2(b) and para 4 follows the same route, apart from the very significant provision for allowing the minister to make the order before laying it before Parliament. Thus, the amendment can be made outside the full parliamentary process which would be required for primary legislation, but otherwise the responsibility for amending primary legislation remains firmly in parliamentary hands, retaining 'Parliament's authority in the legislative process'.[103]

Declarations as to the compatibility of new Bills with the Convention rights

Under s 19(a) of the HRA, a Minister must state that any future Bill is compatible with the Convention or that while unable to make such a declaration, the Government nevertheless wishes to proceed with the Bill. When the relevant minister has made a declaration of compatibility under s 19(a), its effects may be viewed as *additional* to the duty the courts are already under, arising from s 3(1), to ensure that the legislation is rendered compatible with the guarantees if at all possible. The Lord Chancellor has said: 'Ministerial statements of compatibility will inevitably be a strong spur to the courts to find the means of construing statutes compatibly with the Convention.'[104]

It may be said that in one respect, s 19 bears comparison with a 'notwithstanding clause', but there is the very significant difference that, as discussed, the judiciary are not empowered to strike down legislation which contains no such clause, but which is inconsistent with the Convention. Further, s 19 does not expressly provide for the possibility that the Government deliberately *wishes* to achieve incompatibility with the Convention. It merely leaves open the possibility or – in practice – the strong probability that the legislation, or at least certain of its provisions, are incompatible. There is no procedure within the HRA allowing the Government or Parliament to declare that the judiciary should not strive to achieve compatibility even when dealing with almost certainly incompatible provisions. But s 19 resembles a 'notwithstanding clause' in the sense that a government that intends to introduce measures which are probably or certainly rights-abridging must be open about the fact.

All legislation passed since the obligation to make a statement of compatibility came into force[105] has been accompanied by a declaration of its compatibility with the

---

103 Ewing, K, 'The Human Rights Act and parliamentary democracy' (1999) 62(1) MLR 79, p 93.

104 Lord Irvine [1998] PL 221.

105 The obligation to make a statement of compatibility came into force on 24 November 1998, under the HRA 1998 (Commencement) Order 1998 SI 1998/2882.

Convention rights, under s 19. But this need not mean that all such legislation is in fact compatible: the mere fact that a declaration is made does not mean that it can be assumed that compatibility was in fact achieved. A court might reach the conclusion that compatibility was not achieved where one or more of the following three factors were present. First, a declaration under s 19 might be made and challenged in Parliament. The opposition parties might argue that the legislation had not achieved compatibility, but their amendments might be defeated due to the large majority of the Government. It could hardly be said of such legislation that Parliament was satisfied that compatibility had been achieved, and arguably a court might, therefore, be expected to view such legislation with suspicion. It could be said that the s 19 procedure had been undertaken in an attempt to mislead Parliament and that therefore, it might need to be disregarded in favour of imposing a Convention-friendly interpretation on the legislation in accordance with s 3.

Secondly, a court might take the view that Parliament had been misled into believing that the legislation was compatible. In other words, although, arguably, it can be presumed that Parliament intends to legislate compatibly with the Convention where a declaration of its compatibility is made and accepted in Parliament, it cannot be assumed that such acceptance of the correctness of the statement means that compatibility has, in fact, been achieved. A court might view the legal advice behind the declaration as flawed. It might disagree with the view expressed by the advice to the effect that there was a greater than even chance of achieving compatibility. It could be said that the legislation was inadvertently passed since it initially appeared to be compatible with the Convention, but could subsequently be viewed as having failed to achieve compatibility. More significantly, it is possible that legislation will be passed which gives an appearance of achieving compatibility only because a minimalist interpretation of the Convention has been adopted in drafting it. It is suggested that the Terrorism Act 2000 and the Regulation of Investigatory Powers Act 2000 already provide examples of such a tendency. Thirdly, legislation which was arguably compatible with the Convention when passed might become incompatible due to the effect of subsequent decisions of the European Court of Human Rights. Section 2 of the HRA requires a court to take such decisions into account 'whenever made or given'.

Thus, the s 19 procedure should, it is suggested, be viewed as the expression of an opinion based on legal advice, nothing more. The courts would be expected to satisfy their obligation under s 3 just as fully as in respect of legislation passed prior to the inception of the HRA in 1998. (It may be noted that s 19 came into force shortly after that point, not on 2 October 2000.)[106] Where no declaration was made, it could be said that the courts would be placed in a dilemma. Section 3 would still apply, but Parliament's intention could be viewed as being that the legislation in question should not be compatible with the Convention. However, if no derogation from the Convention right was sought, the dilemma could be resolved by adopting the view that Parliament could be presumed not to wish to legislate compatibly with the Convention except where it had expressly stated that such was its intention. A court could then apply s 3 as it would to legislation passed after 1950, but before 1998.

---

106 See above, fn 105.

As Chapter 13 indicates, in order to ensure that a declaration could be made, and more significantly, to ensure full compliance with the Convention in a more general sense, the Terrorism Act 2000 contained provisions that allowed the Government to abandon the embarrassing derogation from Art 5.[107] Clearly, these are early days and it would be surprising if the Labour Government, which introduced the HRA, was prepared to introduce Bills, in the first years of its operation, which could not be accompanied by a declaration under s 19. The idea behind s 19 is that governments will not be willing, in general, to introduce such Bills, although it does open the door to that possibility. In relation to Bills of Rights in general, Dawn Oliver has offered two reasons why a government would be unwilling to state openly that it was legislating in breach of a Bill of Rights.[108] First, there would be the general political embarrassment which would be caused to the government (this may be termed the 'adverse publicity' type of protection). Secondly, a declaration of intent to infringe constitutional rights would be tantamount to a declaration of the government's intention to breach its obligations under international law; this would undoubtedly provoke widespread international condemnation which would be highly embarrassing (this may be termed the 'manifest breach' type of protection).

However, it must not be assumed too readily that Bills will almost always be accompanied in future by a declaration of their compatibility with the Convention rights. The response of the Conservative Government in the 1990s to certain decisions of the European Court of Human Rights, in particular to its decision in *McCann, Farrell and Savage v UK*,[109] the first judgment of the Court to find a breach of Art 2, does not suggest that future governments would necessarily be deterred on 'manifest breach' or 'adverse publicity' grounds from using a notwithstanding clause. The same can be said of the reaction to the findings of the Court in *Jordan, Kelly, Arthurs, Donelly and Others v UK*[110] in 2001. A breach of Art 2 was found in respect of the killing of eight IRA members by the SAS in 1987. The Conservative and Unionist Parties were outraged by the verdict.

After the decision in *McCann*, Michael Heseltine, the Deputy Prime Minister, declared that the Government would not change the administrative policies or rules which had led to the deaths in question in that case; members of the Government also loudly voiced strong disapproval of the decision, and their stance was welcomed in the right wing sections of the UK press. A future government might take the view that passing a certain measure in breach of the Convention was necessary on crime control and/or anti-terrorist grounds; alternatively it might further announce its intention to seek a derogation from the relevant Article in question in order to achieve compatibility and prevent a successful challenge to the measure in the European Court of Human Rights. The hostility expressed towards the HRA in 2000 and 2001 by the Conservative Party and by right wing commentators generally suggests that these are quite strong possibilities.[111]

---

107 See p 793–94.
108 'A Bill of Rights for the UK', in *Government and the UK*, 1991.
109 (1995) 21 EHRR 97, A 324, Council of Europe Report.
110 (2001) *The Times*, 18 May; see further Chapter 2, p 39.
111 See above, p 120. The government intends to derogate from Art 5 in respect of its new counter-terrorism measures introduced in November 2001.

Conclusions

It can now be said that the rules of interpretation relating to legislation differ, depending when it was passed. Prior legislation passed before 1950 is subject to a compatible construction rule only, arising under s 3. Prior legislation passed after 1950 is subject to a 'legislative intention plus compatible construction rule'[112] since, as indicated above, Parliament can be presumed not to have intended to legislate incompatibly with the Convention. Subsequent legislation – passed after 2 October 2000 – is subject both to the general legislative intention rule and to the presumption which may be said to be embodied in the s 19 procedure; it is also subject to the compatible construction rule for the reasons given above. If no declaration of compatibility is made, subsequent legislation is arguably subject to the compatible construction rule and probably to the presumptions that affect legislation passed after 1950 but before 2 October 2000. It can be said, then, that in so far as the possibility of incompatibility arises in either prior or subsequent legislation, it will normally be dealt with by interpretation, without resorting to a declaration of incompatibility. After *R v A*[113] it can now be said with certainty that Parliament's ability to pass incompatible legislation is very narrow, owing to the strong wording of s 3. As indicated, it can even be said to be narrow where the Government appears to *wish* to pass such legislation. It may be concluded, therefore, that s 3 places the Convention in a strong position when compared with ordinary legislation, although, technically, parliamentary sovereignty is preserved. Nevertheless, a form of implied repeal or, more accurately, of temporary or even permanent disapplication of an aspect of a Convention guarantee remains a possibility, although as indicated above, the provision does not suffer repeal and still has some legal status.

However, it is also now clear that in certain respects, the Human Rights Act is in a weak position compared to, for example, the US Bill of Rights. The Human Rights Act 1998 is subject to express repeal by subsequent enactments. However, it is a constitutional truism that Parliament never uses its power to the full; for example, although theoretically able to do so, it is inconceivable at the present time that Parliament would limit suffrage to those with incomes over a certain level. The Human Rights Act may acquire such prestige that although its express repeal remains theoretically possible, it is unlikely to be undertaken. The Act of Union with Scotland 1706 and the European Communities Act 1972 arguably provide precedents for this, although admittedly, key provisions of the 1706 Act have been repealed. Complete repeal may be unlikely, but amendment and/or repeal of key sections of the HRA remains quite a strong possibility. This is a significant weakness, bearing in mind the continuing hostility of the Conservative Party to the HRA,[114] and indeed the lack of support for its values exhibited by members of the Labour government.

---

112 See Bennion, F, 'What interpretation is possible under s 3(1) of the HRA?' [2000] PL 77.

113 See above, fn 55.

114 Such hostility became ever more evident once the Conservatives had lost the 2001 General Election, owing to the change of leadership.

4 THE POSITION OF PUBLIC AUTHORITIES UNDER THE HRA

Binding effect of Convention rights

Section 6 is the central provision of the HRA. Section 6(1) provides: 'It is unlawful for a public authority to act in a way which is incompatible with a Convention right.' This is the main provision giving effect to the Convention rights: rather than incorporation of the Convention, it is made binding against public authorities. Under s 6(6), 'an act' includes an omission, but does not include a failure to introduce in or lay before Parliament a proposal for legislation or a failure to make any primary legislation or remedial order. Section 6(6) was included in order to preserve parliamentary sovereignty and prerogative power: in this case, the power of the executive to introduce legislation.

Thus, apart from its impact on legislation, the HRA also creates obligations under s 6 which bear upon 'public authorities'. Such obligations have a number of implications. Independently of litigation, public authorities must put procedures in place in order to ensure that they do not breach their duty under s 6. Guidance has been issued[115] to a number of central government departments by the Human Rights Unit (HRU) and a number of the departments have undertaken a human rights audit, reporting back to the HRU. However, beyond central government departments, practice has been very variable,[116] although certain bodies, including the police, undertook quite extensive preparation before the HRA came fully into force.[117] The Human Rights Task Force was set up by the Home Office to aid in the preparations and it has received reports from certain public authorities regarding completion of internal human rights reviews. It is clear that internal human rights reviewing and auditing in public authorities will be an ongoing process, which will intensify now that the HRA is fully in force. It is clear that the level of awareness of the implications of the HRA in the various public authorities will remain extremely variable for some considerable period.

Clearly, an exception had to be made under s 6 in order to bring it into harmony with s 3 and to realise the objective of preserving parliamentary sovereignty, but it is argued that the method adopted may not fully succeed in so doing. Section 6(2) provides: 'subsection (1) does not apply to an act if, (a) as the result of one or more provisions of primary legislation, the authority could not have acted differently; or (b) in the case of one or more provisions of, or made under, primary legislation which cannot be read or given effect in a way which is compatible with the Convention rights, the authority was acting so as to give effect to or enforce those provisions'. Thus, s 6(2)(a) creates a strong obligation requiring public authorities to do their utmost to act compatibly.

It may be noted that s 6(2)(a) applies to primary legislation only, whereas s 6(2)(b) applies also to subordinate legislation made under incompatible primary legislation. This

---

115 A number of documents have been issued by the HRU, including *Putting Rights into Public Services, July 1999; Core Guidance for Public Authorities: A New Era of Rights and Responsibilities; The Human Rights Act 1998: Guidance for Departments.*

116 See further Pleming, 'Assessing the act: a firm foundation or a false start' (2000) 6 EHRLR 560–79.

117 The Association of Chief Police Officers set up a Human Rights Working Group in November 1998; it appointed a Human Rights Programme Team in 1999. Twelve areas of police work have been selected as especially significant in HRA terms, including covert policing, discipline, hate crimes, domestic violence and public order. An audit of those areas has been undertaken in order to determine whether procedures and policies require modification.

is implicit in the use of the words 'or made under' used in the latter sub-section, but not the former. The exception under s 6 applies to legislation only (which, as indicated above, includes Orders in Council made under the royal prerogative, under s 21(1)). If a common law provision conflicts with the duty of a public body under s 6, the duty will prevail. Therefore, certain common law reforms under s 6 may occur more readily than statutory reform; as indicated above, no provision has been included in the Act allowing the common law to override the Convention or creating restrictions as to those courts which can find incompatibility between the two.

Distinguishing between public authorities and private bodies

'Standard' and 'functional' public authorities

Under s 6, Convention guarantees are binding only against 'public authorities'. Under s 6(3)(a), the term 'public authority' includes a court or under sub-s (b) a tribunal, and under (c) 'any person certain of whose functions are functions of a public nature'. Parliament 'or a person exercising functions in connection with proceedings in Parliament' is expressly excluded from the definition. This refers to the Westminster Parliament; the Scottish Parliament, the Northern Ireland Assembly and the Welsh Assembly will be public authorities.

Not only is the definition under s 6(3) non-exhaustive, it also leaves open room for much debate on the meaning of 'functions of a public nature'. The definition was explained in the *Notes on Clauses* accompanying the Bill as indicating that where a body is clearly recognisable as a public authority, there is no need to look at the detailed provisions of s 6(3)(a)–(c). Thus, the term 'public authority' includes bodies which are self-evidently of a public nature, such as the police, government departments, the Probation Service, local authorities, the Security and Intelligence Services, the BBC. They are referred to as 'standard public bodies'.

Certain bodies, which have a public and a private function, are quasi-public or hybrid bodies and, under s 6(5), are bound by the Convention rights in respect of the former function only. They are generally referred to as 'functional public bodies', the terminology used in the *Notes on Clauses* accompanying the Bill. A hospital, for example, exercises a public function in relation to NHS patients, a private one in relation to private patients. But there will clearly be room for debate as to those bodies that should be classified as standard rather than functional.[118] Classic functional bodies will include Railtrack, privatised water companies and other contracted-out services. At present, the point at which it is possible to draw a line between functional and private bodies is unclear.[119] Clearly, the distinctions between standard and functional bodies and between functional and private bodies are going to give rise to an enormous amount of litigation. But it may be argued that in principle, the courts should be prepared to take a generous stance towards both distinctions in order to draw as many bodies and functions within the direct

---

118 See Grosz, Beatson and Duffy, *op cit*, fn 1, on this point: para 4-10 *et seq*.

119 See further Oliver, 'The frontiers of the State: public authorities and public functions under the HRA' [2000] PL 476. See also for extensive discussion of the definition of public authorities, Clayton and Tomlinson, *op cit*, fn 1, pp 186–204.

scope of the HRA as possible. So doing would seem to reflect the intention underlying the Act[120] and would be consonant with the general approach taken to human rights instruments. It would also mean that the contracting out of public services to the private sector would not result in a failure of that sector to observe Convention standards in respect of such services. This is a very significant matter due to the diminution of the public sector that has occurred over the last 20 years and which is likely to continue to occur in future during Blair's second term in office and beyond it.

Dawn Oliver has, however, pointed out that a corollary of drawing as many bodies as possible into the category of standard public authorities is that they cannot also be 'victims' and therefore cannot assert rights against other public authorities, possibly resulting, if the 'State pigeon-hole becomes too full' in 'the imposition by the body politic of regulations and checks which could inhibit the development of institutions of civil society'.[121]

A variety of approaches are possible in order to determine whether a body has a public function, but the most significant one will be, it is argued, consideration of the principles deriving from judicial review case law on the question whether the decision maker is a public body.[122] Most commentators accept that this will be the primary, or at least a very significant method of answering this question,[123] although it has been argued that the judicial review cases will not be definitive, partly because the Strasbourg jurisprudence takes an autonomous approach to the nature of public bodies that differs from the judicial review approach.[124] This is a matter that is irrelevant in most contexts covered by this book. It will, therefore, be considered very briefly; an administrative law textbook will obviously provide far fuller consideration.[125] The starting point used in judicial review cases is the finding that the body is statutory or is acting under prerogative powers. But the source of a body's power is now viewed as far less significant than the public element in its functions.[126] Where a body is non-statutory, a further determining factor concerns the question whether there is evidence of government support or control for the body,[127] while a relevant, although not a conclusive factor will

---

120 The Lord Chancellor said at Second Reading of the Bill in the House of Lords: 'We ... decided that we should apply the Bill to a wide rather than a narrow range of public authorities so as to provide as much protection as possible for those who claim that their rights have been infringed'. HL Official Report Cols 1231–32, 3 November 1997.

121 'The frontiers of the State: public authorities and public functions under the HRA' [2000] Autumn PL 476, p 477.

122 See Straw, HC Deb Cols 408, 409, 17 June 1998.

123 See Clayton and Tomlinson, *op cit*, fn 1, p 194, Lester and Pannick, *op cit*, fn 1, para 2.6.3.

124 See Grosz, Beatson and Duffy, *op cit*, fn 1, para 4-04; they rely on the decision in *Chassagnou v France* (1999) 7 BHRC 151, Judgment of 29 April 1999, para 100, in which it was found that the classification of a body as public or private in national law is only a starting point. See further Bamforth, N, 'The application of the HRA to public authorities and private bodies' [1999] 58 CLJ 159. Bamforth argues that the definition under s 6(1) is out of kilter with the criteria used in judicial review for determining whether a body is a public one.

125 See, eg, Woolf (Lord) and Jowell, J, *De Smith, Woolf and Jowell Judicial Review of Administrative Action*, 5th edn, 1995; see also Pannick, 'Who is subject to judicial review and in respect of what?' [1992] PL 1.

126 This can now be said due to the influence of the finding to this effect in *R v Panel of Take-Overs and Mergers ex p Datafin* [1987] QB 815, p 838. See further Bamforth, N, 'The scope of judicial review: still uncertain' [1993] PL 239.

127 *R v Disciplinary Committee of the Jockey Club ex p Aga Khan* [1993] 1 WLR 909.

be whether it has monopoly power.[128] A further factor concerns the question whether, had the body not existed, the government would have set up an equivalent body.[129] The courts now have the task of resolving differences between these tests and the test of public function under s 6(1).[130]

If a body is subject to judicial review, it will almost certainly be a functional authority. Standard public authorities will clearly be subject to judicial review,[130a] although not necessarily in relation to all their functions.[131] A further possibility is that those bodies that are public authorities, listed in Sched 1 to the Freedom of Information Act 2000, will also be assumed to be public authorities for HRA purposes. At the points in this book at which this question does arise, most particularly in Chapter 10 in respect of media regulators and media bodies, this question is considered further.

Private acts of functional public authorities

Under s 6(5), 'in relation to a particular act, a person is not a public authority by virtue only of s 6(3)(c) if the nature of the act is private'. Since, in relation to standard public authorities, there is no need to consider s 6(3)(c), this provision refers to functional public authorities and has the effect of excluding the private acts of functional public authorities from the scope of the HRA (but see the discussion of 'horizontal effect', below). This is a very significant matter, since the private acts of standard public authorities are not excluded. Therefore, for example, assuming that acts relating to employment are private acts, an employee of a standard public authority could use the HRA directly against the authority, as explained below, while the employee of a functional public authority could not.

Thus, under the generally accepted view of s 6(3) and (5), the provisions can be said to create three categories of body in relation to the Convention rights: first, standard ('pure') public authorities which can never act privately, even in respect of matters governed by private law, such as employment relations; secondly, functional (quasi-public) authorities which have a dual function and which can act privately, and thirdly, purely private bodies which have no public function at all. It was accepted in Parliament in debate on the Human Rights Bill that this was the correct reading of s 6.[132]

Could the bodies within the categories be viewed differently, in respect of the question of the ability to carry out private acts, on the basis that s 6 does not state expressly that standard public authorities can never have a private function? In that case, the categories could consist of (a) standard bodies set up with the purpose of carrying out a wholly public function, who can nevertheless act privately in respect of certain matters; (b) bodies with several purposes, some public and some private; they could, it is suggested, operate privately in respect of *aspects* of carrying out their public functions, while they would *always* act privately respect of their private functions; (c) the third

---

128 *R v Football Assoc ex p Football League* [1993] 2 All ER 833.
129 *R v Disciplinary Committee of the Jockey Club ex p Aga Khan* [1993] 1 WLR 909.
130 See the leading findings of Woolf LCJ in *Donoghue v Poplar Housing and Regeneration Community Assoc Ltd* [2001] 3 WLR 183; [2001] EWCA Civ 595. See further *R (on the Application of Heather) v Leonard Cheshire Foundation* (2001) *Daily Telegraph*, 26 June.
130aSee Clayton and Tomlinson, *op cit*, fn 1, pp 197–98, for an extensive list.
131 *R v Jockey Club ex p RAM Racecourses Ltd* [1993] 2 All ER 225, p 246.
132 See Straw, HC Official Report Cols 409–10 (1998).

category indicated above. Under this categorisation, the prison service would have a mainly public function in respect of managing prisons and providing services in relation to prisoners, but a private function in relation to the employment of prison officers. An example of the second category would arise in respect of Railtrack, which has a public function in respect of rail safety, but might deal with ancillary matters linked to safety, including employment, which could be viewed as private. Its other, private function relates, *inter alia*, to its dealings with its shareholders and property development, and in respect of those functions it is probable that it could never act publicly.[133]

However, although it is suggested that there may be room for argument as to the categorisation of the bodies, the discussion below, and in this book in general, will adopt the former argument, since that is the intention behind s 6. It will assume, therefore, that s 6 creates three categories of bodies – standard, functional and private – and that the private acts of functional bodies are excluded from the scope of the s 6 obligation. They may not be excluded from the effects of the HRA entirely, owing to its creation of indirect horizontal effects (discussed below).

Private bodies

Private bodies are defined as such by virtue of the fact that they have no public function at all. Therefore, they are not directly bound by the Convention guarantees under the HRA. This does not mean, however, that they are entirely unaffected by them; apart from other possibilities,[134] any legislation that affects them will have to be interpreted compatibly with the Convention under s 3. This category covers, for example, individual citizens, newspapers, and other private companies, so long as they have no public function.

The division between public and private bodies is immensely significant and s 6 can be said to create an arbitrary division between the two. Bodies such as nursery schools, which have little power or desire to infringe human rights, are covered, while corporate bodies, such as Shell or media oligopolies, which may well have the ability, the will and the means to do so, are not. From this perspective, it may be said that the definition of both public and authorities does not allow the HRA to have an impact that correlates fully with the location of power in the UK. Where power exists, it may be used in a manner which infringes human rights. But the Act will be unable to address a number of instances of abuse of rights, while allowing certain powerful bodies to use it to enhance their power. For example, corporate media bodies may be able both to use the Act and to continue to rely on rights-based arguments for the enhancement of their power. The Act will not limit what has been termed 'the ability of corporate media giants to further their own commercial ends while acting in ways that run counter to maximising the provision of information upon which the claim is premised'.[135] In other words, certain powerful bodies may be able to use the Act for rights-abridging ends or in order to curb the expression of the values that underlie the Convention guarantees. For example, powerful media bodies may use their right to freedom of expression under Art 10 as a means of defending their invasion of the privacy of private citizens, protected under Art 8.

---

133 See HL Deb Col 811, 24 November 1997.
134 See the discussion of 'horizontal effect' below.
135 See Feintuck, M, *Media Regulation, Public Interest and the Law*, 1999, Part 1, Chapter 3.

Under a purposive approach, a court confronted with a large supranational company as a 'victim' of a breach of a Convention right (for example, a corporate press body invoking Art 10 against a media regulator which was itself a public authority), should take into account the values underlying Art 10 in adjudicating on the claim. This was what, it is suggested, the Supreme Court of Canada failed to do when finding that a ban on tobacco advertising infringed the free expression guarantee,[136] since the arguments underlying freedom of expression were hardly engaged by such advertising.

These criticisms could be and are levelled at Bills of Rights in general on the basis that they identify the elected government as the enemy, not recognising that the elected government can be the protector of the people, who need protection not from it, but from powerful multinational corporations. While such criticism may fail to recognise that the elected government does sometimes act as the enemy, through the agency of the police or intelligence services, it nevertheless makes a significant point which bears on the likely impact of the HRA in protecting rights threatened not by the State, but by other rights-holders. This point raises the vexed issue of 'horizontal effect'.

'Horizontal effect'

As indicated above, s 6 seeks to prevent the creation of full direct 'horizontal' effect. Thus, legal effects between private parties (for example, citizens, newspapers) may be limited to the creation of indirect horizontal effect, that is, the use of the Convention in relation to existing proceedings. In other words, it is argued that the Act will affect the legal relations between private persons and bodies although, since they are outside the scope of s 6, they will not be bound by it directly. A key concern of this book is with vertical liability – the relations between citizen and State – but the question of horizontal effect arises in certain contexts, most notably that of the assertion of privacy rights against the media, and this is considered further in Chapter 10.

In the following discussion, the term 'vertical effect' will be used to refer to the binding effect of the Convention on public authorities. 'Direct horizontal' effect would arise if private bodies were also so bound. It would mean that a private body or person claiming that her Convention rights had been breached by another private body could bring proceedings on that basis against that other body. The term 'indirect horizontal' effect will be used to refer to effects on the legal relations between private parties arising by means falling short of such a binding effect.

Statutes which affect the legal relations between private parties are affected by s 3 of the HRA and therefore, in this sense, the Act clearly creates indirect horizontal effects.[137] The position is less clear in relation to the common law. As regards the effect of s 6, this is the area of greatest uncertainty under the Act and it has therefore proved to be a focus for

---

136 *RJR MacDonald Inc v Canada* (1995) 127 DLR (4th) 1.

137 It could be argued that as private individuals do not have Convention rights against *each other*, there is no need to construe the statute in question compatibly with the rights. However, since s 3 applies to itself, it is suggested that it must not be construed in a fashion which leads to the denial of such rights where they would have been afforded to the individual at Strasbourg, bearing in mind the purpose of the HRA, to 'bring rights home'. On this point see Bamforth, N, 'The true "horizontal effect" of the HRA' (2001) 117 LQR 34. See further Chapter 10, esp pp 538–45.

academic debate.[138] The academic debate is currently polarised, Professor Wade perceiving no distinction between the obligations of private and public bodies[139] and Buxton LJ taking the stance that no horizontal effects are created.[140] Wade has argued that a citizen claiming that a private body had breached her Convention rights could claim that the court as a public authority under s 6 must afford a remedy itself for the breach.[141] She would have to find a cause of action in order to get into court.[142] However, even if this were possible (for example, a very weak claim in reliance on an uncertain area of the common law), the court would be unlikely to accept that Parliament could have intended to allow the distinction between private and public bodies under s 6 to be destroyed by this means.[143] Even if the court were prepared to find a breach of the Convention, it appears that it would be unable to afford a remedy to the litigant under s 8 of the HRA since remedies are only to be given in respect of 'acts of public authorities.'[144] Therefore, only those remedies already available under the common law could be granted. For these reasons, there are difficulties with this position.

This book takes the middle ground in perceiving the creation of indirect horizontal effect. This position has been endorsed in certain early decisions under the HRA[145] and by the majority of commentators.[146]

A litigant could argue that the court as a public authority is under a duty to interpret the common law so as to render it compatible with the Convention. A court is already under a duty to do this where the common law is unclear,[147] but the litigant could argue for an obligation in respect of the common law resembling that under s 3 in respect of

---

138 See, eg, Hunt, M, 'The "horizontal" effect of the Human Rights Act' [1998] PL 423; Graber, CB and Teubner, G, 'Art and money: constitutional rights in the private sphere?' (1998) 18(1) OJLS 61; Leigh, I, 'Horizontal rights, the Human Rights Act and privacy: lessons from the Commonwealth' (1999) 48 ICLQ 57; Wade, 'The United Kingdom's Bill of Rights', 1998, pp 62–64, and on the Convention generally: Clapham, A, Human Rights in the Private Sphere, 1993; Clapham, A, 'The privatisation of human rights' [1995] EHRLR 20; Phillipson, G, 'The Human Rights Act, "horizontal effect" and the common law: a bang or a whimper' (1999) 62 MLR 824; Buxton LJ, 'The Human Rights Act and private law' [2000] LQR 48. Clayton and Tomlinson (op cit, fn 1) provide a very full discussion of the various aspects of 'horizontal effect' that also considers the position in a variety of jurisdictions (pp 204–38). See also Hare, I (2001) 5 EHRLR 526.

139 'The United Kingdom's Bill of Rights', 1998, pp 62–63.

140 'The Human Rights Act and private law' (2000) 116 LQR 48. Wade, having set out his position in favour of full direct horizontal effect, as indicated above, fn 139, then returned to the attack, replying to Buxton in 'Horizons of horizontality' (2000) 116 LQR 217.

141 There is a strong consensus that the courts' inclusion within the definition of those bodies bound not to infringe Convention rights is the key to the horizontal effect of the Act upon the common law (above, fn 138). See also Hunt, op cit, fn 138.

142 Phillipson, op cit, fn 138, pp 828–29.

143 Hunt, op cit, fn 138, p 840.

144 For discussion of this point see Phillipson, op cit, fn 138.

145 Michael Douglas, Catherine Zeta-Jones, Northern and Shell plc v Hello! Ltd [2001] 2 WLR 992, CA; Thompson and Venables v Associated Newspapers and Others [2001] 1 All ER 908.

146 Phillipson, op cit, fn 138; Hunt, op cit, fn 138. Hunt's and Phillipson's positions differ as to the scope of the duty under s 6, but the concept of indirect horizontal effect as argued for by both has been accepted by Lord Lester and Pannick in op cit, fn 1, p 32 and by Clayton and Tomlinson, op cit, fn 1, pp 236–38.

147 See above, Chapter 3, pp 114–15.

legislation. There is, as yet, no consensus on how this point will be received,[148] although the majority view is that the HRA will at the least heighten the impact of the Convention on the common law.[149]

As Sedley LJ made clear in an important post-HRA decision,[150] once a plaintiff is in court presenting an arguable case for, for example, an injunction which would affect freedom of expression, the court clearly has a duty, under s 12(4) of the HRA (see below) to develop that action by reference to Art 10, which means also giving full weight to Art 8 as a right recognised under Art 10(2), under the 'rights of others' exception. In taking Art 10 into account, the domestic courts have also now have accepted that, as interpreted at Strasbourg, its guarantees clearly affect the relations between private parties. This point is explored further in Chapter 10. It does not mean that direct horizontal effect is created – that citizens can simply take another private person or body to court in reliance solely on a claim of breach of a Convention right. It means that once such a body is in court – which requires an existing cause of action – *and* freedom of expression is in question, s 12(4) will apply, thus creating indirect horizontal effect – the Convention rights can be made to directly affect the legal relations between private parties. This is a very significant issue, which is considered further in Chapter 8.

It would seem very strange if other Convention rights such as Art 8, protecting privacy, could be considered when freedom of expression is in question, but could not be considered when it is not. This would create such bizarre results that it is suggested that where freedom of expression is not in question (and, therefore, s 12 is not applicable) the duty of the court under s 6 must be, as indicated above, to take all the rights into account as a source of principle in relation to the common law. The scope of the courts' duty in this regard is a matter that will, no doubt, be thrashed out in a number of cases. This has been viewed as a qualified duty by Phillipson[151] and an absolute duty as argued for by Hunt.[152] However, since ss 6 and 12 are statutory provisions, they are subject to the interpretative obligation of s 3. This does not appear to be a significant matter in relation to s 12 but, as indicated by the nature of the academic debate, s 6 is far less clear. Therefore, the scope of the duty must be resolved by reference to the extent to which the Convention itself accepts horizontal effect. Since it would appear that the Convention demands that remedies should be available which can be used against private bodies,[153] not merely against the State, it is arguable that the courts' duty under s 6 in respect of the development of the common law is absolute.

The eventual impact of s 6 (as interpreted compatibly with the rights under s 3) is not a matter that can be regarded as settled; as suggested below, it is possible that eventually,

---

148 Hunt argues for an absolute duty on the courts to render the common law compatible with the Convention rights; Phillipson suggests that the obligation will be only to have regard to the Convention rights as guiding principles, having a variable weight depending on the context; Leigh considers that the HRA 'does not formally change the approach to Convention questions in the common law, although there may be a change of atmosphere post-incorporation *(ibid*, fn 138, pp 82–83).

149 This is precisely the basis of the findings in *Thompson and Venables v Associated Newspapers and Others* [2001] 1 All ER 908.

150 *Douglas, Zeta-Jones, Northern and Shell plc v Hello! Ltd* [2001] 2 WLR 992, CA.

151 See *op cit*, fn 138.

152 'The "horizontal" effect of the Human Rights Act [1998] PL 423.

153 See the discussion of *Spencer v UK* (1998) 25 EHRR CD 105; [1998] EHRLR 348 in Chapter 10, pp 540–41.

through the development of the common law, we will arrive at a position that in its *effects* is equivalent to the creation of direct horizontal effects for the rights. In other words, it is possible that, in the long term, citizens will not be deprived of a remedy in respect of a breach of their Convention rights, although the body infringing them is a private one.

Relationship between ss 3 and 6

Even where no legislation is applicable, public authorities are bound by the rights and proceedings can be brought against the authority in question for infringing them. Where legislation is applicable to a public authority, a court as itself a public authority must, in addition to its duty under s 3, seek to ensure that the Convention is adhered to and must bear in mind that it is considering the obligations of another public authority which is bound by the rights. In relation to its interpretation of the legislation itself, its duty under s 6 may add little to its duty under s 3. But other aspects of its procedure will be affected by s 6.

The relationship between ss 3 and 6 is quite complex. Both apply where legislation affects a 'public authority'. In such circumstances, it is suggested that a court should first apply s 6 and ask whether the body has, by its action or omission, breached the Convention guarantee(s) in question. If it appears that it has, the court should look to the relevant legislation to determine whether, even when the attempt is made to construe it compatibly with the Convention, it remains incompatible and therefore provides the public authority with a loophole under s 6(2). A further way of proceeding would be to consider the legislation first in relation to the public authority, affording it a Convention-friendly interpretation, and then ask whether, under such an interpretation, it appeared that the body had the power to do what it had done. If it appeared that it had not, it could be found to have acted *ultra vires*.[154] Since Convention arguments can arise by a variety of routes, as indicated below, further methods of considering ss 3 and 6 in conjunction will become apparent.

Invoking the Convention rights against public authorities

'Victims'

Section 7(1)(a) of the Act allows a person who claims that a public authority has acted or proposes to act in breach of a Convention right to bring proceedings against the public authority. Section 7(1)(b) allows a person to rely on the Convention in any legal proceedings. But in either case, the person must be (or would be) a 'victim' of the unlawful act. Section 7(7) provides: 'a person is a victim of an unlawful act only if he would be a victim for the purposes of Art 34 of the Convention if proceedings were brought in the European Court of Human Rights in respect of that act'. It was accepted in Parliament that the Strasbourg interpretation of 'victim' would be used, rather than the wider test for standing under the UK judicial review doctrine which allows pressure groups to bring actions so long as they satisfy the 'sufficient interest' test.[155] The UK

---

154 I am indebted to Gavin Phillipson for this point.

155 See the ruling of Rose LJ in *Secretary of State for Foreign Affairs ex p the World Development Movement* [1995] 1 All ER 611, pp 618–20.

group *Liberty* had argued for adoption of the latter as the test, since it is broader. But the idea behind s 7(5) is that the HRA should create symmetry with the protection for human rights provided by Strasbourg.[156] In order to obviate the possibility of circumvention of the victim test by use of judicial review outside the HRA but raising Convention points, s 7(3) provides: 'if the proceedings are brought on an application for judicial review, the applicant is taken to have sufficient interest in relation to the unlawful act only if he or she is a victim.'

The Strasbourg test is discussed further in Chapter 2.[157] It is now contained in Art 34 (formerly 25): a person (or group or non-governmental organisation) may not bring an application unless he or she has been personally affected by the alleged violation.[158] However, as Miles points out, it cannot be said that the concept of 'victim' has been interpreted consistently at Strasbourg, although it is clear that those indirectly affected may be covered.[159] There will, therefore, be substantial room for domestic litigation on this issue. But s 7(3), therefore, means that pressure groups cannot in general bring actions claiming breach of Convention rights in reliance on s 7(1)(a), although such groups may currently be able to challenge public bodies by way of judicial review, on the test of 'sufficient interest'.[160] However, when administrative action is purportedly taken under statutory powers such groups, and non-victims in general, who wish to complain about it need not rely on s 6. They can rely instead on s 3 and argue that the statute does not give powers to the executive to act incompatibly with the Convention rights unless the statute is irretrievably incompatible with them. This is possible because s 3, as indicated above, applies to all statutes and is not limited by the s 7(7) test regarding victims. This is an extremely significant matter since it greatly broadens the reach of the Convention rights, possibly in an unintended fashion.[160a]

Thus, although the definition of the bodies covered under s 6 is wide and brings a large number of them within its scope, the application of the Convention by the s 7(1)(a) route is narrowed by adopting quite a limited definition of a 'victim'. Where a non-victim wishes to complain about executive action under non-statutory powers judicial review may be available: as s 11 makes clear,[161] nothing prevents the raising of Convention points in judicial review applications based on the wider standing rules. Thus in such instances pressure groups and others may be able to raise such points outside the Human Rights Act, but not within it. A court, bound by s 6, confronted by a Convention issue in such an application, would have to consider whether to scrutinise the issues relating to proportionality or apply traditional review principles only.[162] A common law of human

---

156 See HC Official Report Col 1083, 24 June 1998.

157 For extensive discussion, see Clayton and Tomlinson, *op cit*, fn 1, pp 1484–98.

158 *X v Austria* No 7045/75, 7 DR 87 (1976); *Knudsen v Norway* No 11045/84, 42 DR 247 (1985).

159 Miles, 'Standing under the Human Rights Act: theories of rights enforcement and the nature of public law adjudication' (2000) 59(1) CLJ 133–67, p 137. She further points out that while pressure groups cannot bring actions in their own name, there are other public interest enforcement mechanisms at Strasbourg including the possibility, exceptionally, of Third Party intervention which can be used to seek to ensure that the rights are secured.

160 It may be noted that HRA, s 11 would bar the way to any narrowing of those rules.

160aSee further on this point Elliott, M, 'The HRA and the standard of substantive review' (2001) 60 CLJ 301.

161 Section 11 provides: 'A person's reliance on a Convention right does not restrict ... (b) his right to make any claim or bring any proceedings which he could make or bring apart from ss 7–9.'

162 As stated *obiter* in *Alconbury* [2001] 2 All ER 929; (2001) NLJ 135, para 53.

rights – in some respects, of a more protective nature – might continue to develop. A dual system of judicial review might arise, with more generous standing rules but weaker scrutiny, outside the HRA, while the reverse applied under s 7(1).[163] In order to avoid such a development, which would be bound to create arbitrariness, the judiciary may be minded to break down distinctions between cases based on the s 7(1) standing rules, and those outside them but raising Convention points, by relying on s 6 once an application is in court. In other words, the old standing rules may eventually prevail.

Clearly, this would be contrary to the Government's intention. The inclusion of s 7(3) was intended to avoid that possibility. Had s 7(3) not been included, a pressure group might have been able to bring an action relying on the wider judicial review standing provisions, but then obtain the stricter scrutiny available when it is argued that a public authority has breached s 6. However, such a group could seek to use s 6[164] in arguing that the development of common law rights, which could be viewed, as indicated above, in the pre-HRA era as echoing developments under the Convention, should be given an added impetus. Further, if freedom of expression was in issue, in an instance similar to those of *Brind*[165] or *Simms*,[166] s 12 providing special protection for freedom of expression (see below, p 176) would apply as well as s 3. In respect of non-statutory powers s 12 alone would apply. If so, the fact that the applicant was a non-victim would be irrelevant and an argument similar to that of Sedley LJ in the *Douglas* case[167] could be used in order to argue that, owing to the provision of Art 10(2), all the rights would be relevant under the 'rights of others' exception. Clearly, s 3 applies to s 12, and s 3 would not draw in the application of the Strasbourg test under Art 34, since Art 34 is not included in the rights referred to under s 1(1).

Actions under s 7(1)(a)

Section 7(1) provides: 'A person who claims that a public authority has acted or proposes to act in a way which is made unlawful by s 6(1) may (a) bring proceedings against the authority under this Act in the appropriate court or tribunal ...' Section 7(1)(a) thus allows a victim of a breach or threatened breach of a Convention right to bring an action against a standard public authority or a functional body acting in its public capacity[168] on that basis. The action must be brought in 'the appropriate court or tribunal' which will be determined 'by rules' (s 7(2)). Under s 7(9), the term 'rules' means: 'in relation to proceedings in a court or tribunal outside Scotland rules made by the Lord Chancellor or the Secretary of State for the purpose of this section or rules of court ...' A claim could be brought as a complaint, as an appeal, as a private law claim or counterclaim or by way of judicial review. Where actions are brought as judicial review applications, they will be

---

163 See Steyn, K and Wolfe, D, 'Judicial review and the Human Rights Act: some practical considerations' (1999) EHRLR 614.

164 On the basis that the court is a public authority. It would seem that such a group could not use s 2; since s 2 refers to the Strasbourg jurisprudence, it would draw in the 'victim' test under Art 34.

165 [1991] 1 AC 696.

166 [1999] 3 WLR 328.

167 [2001] 2 WLR 992.

168 The term 'public authority' will be used to encompass both types of body for the purposes of the rest of the discussion.

subject to the Civil Procedure Rules. But they could also be brought in the county court or the High Court where a claim for damages is made.[169]

A number of post-HRA statutes have already designated certain fora as 'appropriate tribunals'. The most significant of these is the new Tribunal set up by s 65(2) of the Regulation of Investigatory Powers Act 2000.[170] The provisions under the Immigration and Asylum Act 1999 – ss 50, 52, 54 and 55 – provide a further example. Further special rules relating to specific areas of executive action are likely to be created.

The ground of review could be on the basis of illegality in that the authority has, by its action, breached s 6 or is about to do so.[171] It is also possible that proceedings could be brought for breach of statutory duty – the duty under s 6. The possibility of creating what has been termed a 'constitutional tort' of breach of Convention rights has been left open by the HRA and by the Lord Chancellor in parliamentary debate.[172] The majority of actions brought under s 6 via s 7(1)(a) against public authorities contemplated in this book would raise purely public law issues. Thus, they could arise as a form of constitutional tort – a liability of public bodies to provide a remedy for breaching the Convention rights in the form of a new public law wrong – or by way of judicial review. The former possibility would mean that a new, free standing cause of action had arisen. The implications of both possibilities are considered below.

Section 7(1)(a) actions in the form of judicial review

Section 7(1)(a) actions might be viewed as likely to arise by way of proceedings for judicial review[173] due to the procedural exclusivity principle[174] under which private actions arise as a matter of private law, while actions raising public law issues arise by way of judicial review. The 'public law/private law' divide is an extremely complex matter which can only be touched on here. Cases raising 'public law' issues must follow the procedure which previously arose under RSC Ord 53 under the Supreme Court Act 1981[175] and is now governed by the Civil Procedure Rules. What has been termed the 'exclusivity principle' requires that litigants should not be able to avoid using judicial review by proceeding by way of a writ or an originating summons. This reasoning was based on a need to protect public authorities in the exercise of their duties, since they would be protected by the procedural limitations built into Ord 53.[176]

The public law/private law distinction has recently become less rigid,[177] but on its face it appears to lead to effects which run counter to the aims underlying the Human

---

169 HRA 1998: Rules CP5/00, March 2000, para 12.

170 See Chapter 11, pp 714 *et seq*.

171 See Craig, P, *Administrative Law*, 1994.

172 HL Deb Vol 585 Cols 853–56, 24 November 1997.

173 See, in particular, Chapter 9, p 491, Chapter 14, pp 912–14, Chapter 16, pp 1059–60.

174 The reasoning behind the 'exclusivity principle' – requiring that public law actions should proceed by way of judicial review (see *O'Reilly v Mackman* [1983] 2 AC 237, p 283) was based on a need to protect public authorities in the exercise of their duties; they would be protected by the procedural limitations built into Ord 53.

175 *O'Reilly v Mackman* [1983] 2 AC 237, pp 283–85.

176 See further Fredman, S and Morris, G, 'The costs of exclusivity: public and private re-examined' [1994] PL 69, pp 70–71 and 80–81.

177 See *Roy v Kensington and Chelsea Family Practitioner [Committee]* [1991] 1 All ER 705; *Mercury Communications Ltd v Director General of Telecommunications* [1996] 1 WLR 48.

Rights Act since it may mean that public authorities are not called to account when they breach the Convention rights; actions against public authorities brought by way of a writ could be struck out on the ground that they should have been brought by way of an application for judicial review.[178]

If the procedural exclusivity principle is found to apply to HRA actions under s 7(1)(a), which is doubtful, a number of issues will be raised.[179] It would mean that applicants would not benefit from the procedural advantages of bringing an action by way of writ or an originating summons. If proceedings were begun in this way, they would be struck out, since they should have been brought by way of judicial review. Under the Civil Procedure Rules, replacing the procedure under s 31(3) of the Supreme Court Act 1981, judicial review requires leave (now termed 'permission') and around half of judicial review actions fail at the leave stage.[180] The leave requirement is therefore controversial and has been severely criticised.[181] The Civil Procedure Rules are, of course, subject to the interpretative obligation of s 3 of the HRA and therefore, the requirement will have to be interpreted compatibly with the Convention rights, arguably taking, as indicated above, the Art 13 jurisprudence into account under s 2.[182]

Even if HRA actions are not subject to the procedural exclusivity principle, as argued below, they may be joined to an application for judicial review and where a public law remedy is sought, the claim should be brought by way of an application for judicial review. In such instances the principle, with its attendant disadvantages, would apply.

Human Rights Act claims – a new public law wrong

As indicated above, s 7(1)(a) may create a new cause of action which would not be subject to the procedural exclusivity principle. There are clear reasons, as discussed, for viewing this as the preferable alternative. It derives strong support from the parliamentary debates: '[Persons who believe that their Convention rights have been infringed] will also be able to bring proceedings against public authorities on Convention grounds even if no other cause of action is open to them.'[183] Further: 'They may [rely on the Convention rights by ... bringing proceedings under the [Act] in an appropriate court or tribunal; seeking judicial review; as part of a defence ... or in the course of an appeal.'[184] It also derives support from academic writings on the HRA. All three of the major texts published on the HRA so far have found that a new cause of action is available – a Human Rights Act claim, which is not subject to the procedural exclusivity principle.[185]

---

178 The Woolf reforms set out in Lord Woolf's Report, *Access to Justice*, 1996 were given effect under the Civil Procedure Act 1997. The Civil Procedure Rules came into force in April 1999 and the rules committee set up under the 1997 Act is currently finishing the task of revising the procedures by which applications for judicial review are made.

179 The issues raised by the principle have been the subject of a number of commentaries. See, eg, Fredman and Morris, *op cit*, fn 176, pp 70–71 and 80–81.

180 See Le Sueur, AP and Sunkin, M, 'Application for judicial review' [1992] PL 102; Law Commission Consultation Paper No 226/HC 669, *Administrative Law: Judicial Review and Statutory Appeals*.

181 See the JUSTICE-All Souls Report, *Administrative Law: Some Necessary Reforms*, 1988.

182 See p 135.

183 Lord Chancellor, 582 HL 1232, 3 November 1997.

184 The Home Secretary, 306 HC Official Report Col 780, 16 February 1998.

185 See Clayton and Tomlinson, *op cit*, fn 1, pp 1498–1501; Lester and Pannick, *op cit*, fn 1, pp 34–35 (the lack of applicability of the procedural exclusivity principle is assumed); Grosz, Beatson and Duffy, *op cit*, fn 1, p 59.

Clayton and Tomlinson argue that since s 7(3) uses the wording 'if proceedings are brought on an application for judicial review', this implies that the bringing of such proceedings is optional. They further argue that: 'the exclusivity rule would be inconsistent with the status of the HRA as a constitutional instrument. In the absence of any statutory restrictions, the courts should develop a flexible and non-technical approach in order to ensure that the safeguards provided by the Convention rights are practical and effective.' If this approach is correct, proceedings could be begun in a number of ways, not just by way of judicial review.[186]

This approach has a number of implications, as already indicated, and which are discussed further below in terms of time limits and the different positions of applicants depending whether they are raising purely HRA claims under s 7(1)(a) or mixed claims – those where the HRA claim is joined to an existing application for judicial review or to a private law claim.

The main implication of the new cause of action is that it will tend to encourage the growth of new tort actions. Assuming that litigation concerning the private functions of standard public authorities, concerning matters not tortious under existing tort law, occurs under s 7(1)(a), new areas of tortious liability will be created. Such new areas will be subject to disadvantages not arising under existing torts – the limitation period and the discretionary award of damages (see below). In an important article, Dawn Oliver argues that the creation of such new areas of tortious liability operating against public authorities may tend to lend an impetus to the creation of tortious liability against *private* bodies, arising out of existing tort actions.[187] But, if such actions tend to emerge – and as indicated below and considered further in Chapter 10, a right to privacy has already arisen from the doctrine of confidence – litigants against public authorities are likely to employ such actions in order to escape from the constraints of the HRA.

The result may be that the common law of human rights may become extremely significant; it could obtain impetus from the HRA – due to the courts' duties under ss 6, 12[188] – without being bound by its limitations. In so far as ambiguity arises as to the courts' duty under s 6 to interpret the common law compatibly with the guarantees, s 3, which clearly applies to s 6, resolves the issue in favour of the degree of horizontal effect accepted by the Convention. Where statutory torts are concerned, the same development may occur owing to the interpretative obligation of s 3. Such actions would have an even stronger spur to develop since the duty under s 3 is clear: it makes no distinction on its face between public and private bodies. Litigants taking advantage of such expanded statutory torts would also be able to escape from the constraints imposed upon tortious actions under the HRA. This issue is explored further below, and at various points in the following chapters, especially Chapter 10.

Time limits

If proceedings are brought against a public authority under s 7(1)(a), they must be brought, under s 7(5), within one year 'beginning with the date on which the act

---

186 In the county court, by issuing a claim form, in the High Court by a claim form (Civil Procedure Rules (CPR) Pt 7 or Pt 8), in the Crown Office under CPR Sched 1 r 53.

187 'The HRA and public law/private law divides' (2000) 4 EHRLR 343.

188 And, less frequently, under s 13 (see below).

complained of took place' or 'such longer period as the court or tribunal considers equitable having regard to all the circumstances, but that is subject to any rule imposing a stricter time limit in relation to the procedure in question'. The implications of the time limits relating to s 7(1)(a) proceedings are very significant. The new cause of action under s 7(1)(a), which does not depend on the judicial review rules, will be subject to the one year limit, assuming it is correct to find that the exclusivity principle does not apply. Appeals or other actions under special rules relating to specific circumstances will also be subject to the one year rule. The procedures arising under s 65 of the Regulation of Investigatory Powers Act 2000 (RIPA) would be one year under s 7(5), except in so far as the rules provide otherwise.

However, if most Human Rights Act claims under s 7(1)(a) are brought in judicial review proceedings, they will be subject to a stricter rule, since the limitation period of three months for judicial review will be applicable.[189] Thus, the time limits will create quite a severe limitation on the use of s 7(1)(a) where an HRA claim is joined to a judicial review application. But in certain circumstances, the longer period might apply; a *Pepper v Hart* statement suggests that the one year period could, exceptionally, apply: 'someone with a genuine grievance will be able to pursue it under s 7(1)(a) whether or not within the judicial review time limit.'[190] This arguable possibility would mean that while most applicants seeking review based on existing principles,[191] or on an action partly based on s 7(1)(a), would not be able to bring actions if outside the three month time limit, exceptionally, in the latter instance, applicants could originate a judicial review action even if outside that limit, but within the one year period.

Procedural and practical anomalies and limitations

On the assumptions indicated above, a number of procedural anomalies and limitations arise in relation to the HRA actions which will be considered at certain points in this book. Applicants for judicial review, as opposed to those relying on the new public law wrong, would be in different positions in a number of respects. Those raising existing principles,[192] or relying also on s 7(1)(a) alone, would be subject to the strict timing rules, although exceptionally, the one year rule might apply. But they could take advantage of the 'sufficient interest' standing test rather than the stricter 'victim' test under the HRA. They would, however, as indicated below, suffer a less intensive level of scrutiny. It is arguable, however, that applicants in the latter category, and therefore raising a mixture of Convention and common law points, would be in a complex position. In respect of the Convention, they could be subject to the stricter standing rules, but possibly to the broader time limit. In respect of the common law grounds, the reverse would be the case. It has been pointed out that these arrangements create complex procedural obstacles leading to unfairness between applicants.[193] Applicants making a claim under the new public law wrong would have to comply with the stricter 'victim' test for standing, but

---

189 CPR Sched 1 r 53.4(1). See further on a number of these matters, Supperstone and Coppel, 'Judicial review after the Human Rights Act' (1999) 3 EHRLR 301–29.

190 HC Deb Vol 314 Col 1099, 20 May 1998.

191 In particular, based on rights recognised under common law.

192 The argument would be based on established constitutional rights; see above, Chapter 3, pp 104–10.

193 Nicol, D, 'Limitation periods under the HRA and judicial review' [1999] LQR 216.

not with the three month rule. They would also be able to take advantage of the more intensive scrutiny.

In all these instances, the judicial review procedure would presumably be used once the applicant's claim is being heard. Leigh and Lustgarten have pointed out that the procedure may not be adequate as a means of determining the crucial issue of proportionality.[194] It is far less likely in judicial review proceedings, as opposed to private law actions, that discovery would be ordered or cross-examination allowed. Therefore, there are inadequacies in its fact finding role. Possibly if a perception arises among the judiciary that judicial review is simply inadequate to the task it is required to undertake under the Human Rights Act, the courts will take an activist approach in using their discretion to, for example, require cross-examination, in order to render the procedure more efficacious in protecting Convention rights, bearing in mind the duty under s 6.

These limitations of judicial review in human rights matters are likely to be very significant. But it should also be pointed out here that, in practice, some persons are virtually precluded from taking this course owing to its inaccessibility, the fact that judicial review may only be initiated in the High Court in London and the extent to which most solicitors/law centres or advisers on legal helplines have awareness of the availability or appropriateness of such review in any particular instance.[195]

Using the Convention under s 7(1)(b)

Section 7(1) provides: 'A person who claims that a public authority has acted or proposes to act in a way which is made unlawful by s 6(1) may (b) rely on the Convention right or rights concerned in any legal proceedings ...' Unlike s 7(1)(a), which appears to provide for a new cause of action against public authorities, s 7(1)(b) allows for Convention points to be raised once an action has begun under an existing cause of action, where the other party is a public authority. Therefore, s 7(1)(b) is likely to be invoked far more frequently. Under s 7(1)(b), there are a number of possible instances in which a victim can raise Convention arguments in proceedings in which a public authority is involved. In the contexts covered by this book, the Convention would frequently be invoked in criminal proceedings. It might be noted that in such instances, the 'weak' position of certain groups in seeking to rely on the rights is not as relevant as it is in relation to other methods, in particular judicial review. Questions of exclusion of evidence or abuse of process could be raised in relation to breaches of Convention rights, and these possibilities are pursued in Chapter 14.

Under s 7(1)(b), the Convention guarantees could also afford a defence in criminal proceedings in relation to common law crimes where it could be argued that a public authority had acted unlawfully under s 6. Such an argument might not be available, where statutory crimes were concerned, where it was argued that the authority had relied on incompatible primary legislation (s 6(2)(b)). But it could be raised in relation to a loosely worded statute, as Chapter 9, in particular, argues, in relation to public order law. The rights could also be used to afford a defence in common law civil proceedings where

---

194 Leigh, I and Lustgarten, L, 'Making rights real: the courts, remedies and the Human Rights Act' (1999) 58(3) CLJ 509.

195 See Le Sueur, AP and Sunkin, M, *Public Law*, 1997, Chapters 21–28, esp Chapter 21, 'Access to judicial review'.

the plaintiff was a public authority. Other existing tort actions, such as false imprisonment, which are coterminous with Convention rights (in that instance, Art 5) could be brought against public authorities under s 7(1)(b) with a view to expanding the scope of the action by reference to the right.[196] The possibilities presented by the use of tort actions are discussed at various points in this book, but most extensively in Chapter 14.[197] However, as indicated above, a litigant might not obtain an advantage by relying on s 7(1)(b) due to the discretion as to the award of damages under s 8(2) of the HRA, as discussed below. A litigant might be best advised merely to rely on the existing action, but seek to persuade the court as a public authority that the Convention principles should (if advantageous) be used to expand its scope.

Thus, where existing tort actions are coterminous with Convention rights, ss 6, 12 or 13, rather than s 7(1)(b), should be relied upon. Where a breach of a Convention right, in particular the right of respect to privacy, does not fall within an area of existing tortious liability, s 7(1)(a) should be relied upon where public authorities are concerned, but, as indicated above, the divide between public and private bodies, as between public and private law, may eventually break down.

Section 7(1)(b) could be relied upon in any judicial review action relating to civil liberties which has been begun other than by way of using s 7(1)(a) (since, in that instance, it would be redundant to rely on s 7(1)(b)). As indicated above, in such an action the claimant might seek to rely on the existing 'common law of human rights' and/or on one or more Convention rights, under s 7(1)(b). In such an application it could be argued that the action of the public authority in question was *ultra vires* on the basis that once the legislation in question was interpreted compatibly with the Convention under s 3, it did not give the authority the right to breach it as it has done. It would also appear to be possible to argue for illegality by this route (even though the applicant did not bring the action to court relying on s 7(1)(a)). But the Government sought to ensure that these possibilities would not mean that the limiting effect of the 'victim' provisions could be avoided, since s 7(1)(b) relies on that provision. A possible means of avoiding the effects of those provisions in judicial review proceedings was suggested above.

The one year time limit does not apply under s 7(1)(b); under s 22(4)(b): 'para (b) [of s 7(1)] applies to proceedings brought by or at the instigation of a public authority *whenever the act in question took place*; but otherwise that subsection does not apply to an act taking place before the coming into force of that section' (emphasis added). Where the Convention is used as a 'shield' against public authorities, therefore, pre-commencement action is covered[198]. Thus, before the Act came fully into force, public authorities were seeking to abide by it in bringing proceedings, including prosecutions, against citizens.

Remedies

Under s 8(1) a court which has found that an act or proposed act of a public authority is unlawful, is authorised to grant 'such relief or remedy or ... order within its powers as

---

196 Such actions would also, of course, be available against purely private bodies. See further Phillipson, G, 'The Human Rights Act and the common law' [1999] 62 MLR 824, esp pp 834–40, and discussion below of horizontal effects. See also Bamforth, *op cit*, fn 124.

197 See pp 912–14.

198 Following the decision of the House of Lords in *R v Lambert* [2001] 3 All ER 577, appeals against pre-commencement convictions are *not* within s 22(4)(b).

[the court] considers just and appropriate'. The term 'unlawful' clearly need not mean 'breach of a Convention guarantee' where such a breach is 'lawful' due to incompatible primary legislation or secondary legislation made under such legislation. In such circumstances, no remedy is available other than a declaration of incompatibility and the ability to make such a declaration is, as indicated, confined to certain higher courts. A litigant in a lower court or tribunal, in such circumstances, appears to be completely remediless, since even the empty remedy of a declaration is unavailable. The forum at the next level might be equally powerless. In the circumstances covered by this book, the picture is mixed as regards the ability of litigants to get into a court which can issue a declaration.[199] The litigant has little or no incentive to appeal in the hope of eventually reaching a court able to make a declaration, assuming that permission (where required) would be granted where clear incompatibility is present, especially as there is no provision requiring the Crown to bear its own costs where it intervenes in accordance with s 5(2) of the HRA. In criminal proceedings, however, the courts may take the view that to convict a defendant in breach of the Convention would be an abuse of process.[200]

It is impossible not to conclude that this aspect of the system of remedial action is inadequate to the task of providing a domestic remedy for violation of Convention rights.[201] Further, the availability of a declaration may undermine the remedy at Strasbourg. If Strasbourg were to view it as an effective remedy, which is very doubtful,[202] the availability of this 'remedy' would be likely to make the task of exhausting domestic remedies in order to take an application to Strasbourg even more difficult. In any event, if legislation is not forthcoming within the next few years to amend s 4 of the HRA with a view to allowing lower courts to make declarations, the pressure on the judiciary to find compatibility will become increasingly severe.

Assuming that a breach of the Convention is found which is not the result of incompatible legislation, all the familiar remedies including certiorari (now a quashing order), a declaration or mandamus (a mandatory order), a prohibiting order (now a prohibition) are available so long as they are within the jurisdiction of the relevant court or tribunal. Under s 8(2), damages cannot be awarded in criminal proceedings, but this obviously leaves open the possibility that they could be awarded in judicial review as well as other civil proceedings. Traditionally, the courts have been reluctant to award

---

199 Eg, an appeal from a magistrates' court to the Crown Court would require a further appeal in order to obtain a declaration. A declaration could be obtained using only one level of appeal if an appeal was by way of case stated to the Divisional Court. Appeals from the Proscribed Organisations Appeal Commission are, by leave, to the Court of Appeal in England and Wales, and to the equivalent courts in Scotland and Northern Ireland (see further Chapter 8, pp 407–08).

200 See the views of Lord Steyn in *R v DPP ex p Kebilene and Others* [1999] 4 All ER 801.

201 See Leigh and Lustgarten, *op cit*, fn 194, p 543. They conclude that rights may be less well protected than previously as a result of the HRA.

202 The applicant only needs to exhaust those possibilities which offer an *effective* remedy, so if part of the complaint is the lack of a remedy under Art 13, then the application is not likely to be ruled inadmissible on this ground: *X v UK* (1981) Appl 7990/77; 24 D & R 57. A remedy will be ineffective if according to established case law there appears to be no chance of success: Appl 5874 172, Yearbook XVII (1974). Strasbourg has not yet had the opportunity to rule on the question whether a Declaration of Incompatibility could amount to an effective remedy, since no analogous procedure exists in the Contracting States. Since it offers nothing which has previously been recognised as a remedy to the individual in question, it is suggested that there are strong grounds for considering that the system would not be viewed as offering an effective remedy.

damages in public law cases and s 8(3) of the HRA encourages the continuance of this tradition in requiring consideration to be given first to any 'other relief or remedy granted or order made', the consequences of the court's decisions and the necessity of making the award.

Under s 8(4), the court in deciding to award damages must take into account the principles applied by the European Court of Human Rights. This suggests that awards are likely to be low. The Court can award compensation under what is now Art 41.[203] The purpose of the reparation is to place the applicant in the position he would have been in had the violation not taken place. Compensation will include costs unless the applicant has received legal aid, although where only part of a claim is upheld, the costs may be diminished accordingly.[204] It can also include loss of earnings, travel costs, fines and costs unjustly awarded against the applicant.[205] Compensation is also available for intangible or non-pecuniary losses such as loss of future earnings[206] or opportunities,[207] unjust imprisonment,[208] stress or loss of personal integrity.[209] But there are two difficulties in following the principles of the European Court. One is, as Mowbray has pointed out, that the method of determining the award in any particular judgement is frequently unclear.[210] The other is that the Court, prior to the changes introduced under Protocol 11, had no independent fact finding role[211] and therefore, where it was unclear that the breach had occasioned the effect in question, it has at times refused to award compensation. This is a clear instance in which domestic courts can create higher standards than those maintained at Strasbourg, both in terms of dealing with this issue of causality and in creating a clearer rationale for awards, although they will be able to derive guidance from post-1998 decisions taken under the Protocol 11 reforms.

The use of injunctions under the HRA is discussed in Chapter 9 in the context of public protest. The discussion considers in particular the use of the Convention rights as a defence, taking into account s 12 of the HRA, which provides special protection for freedom of expression, where interim injunctions are obtained in civil proceedings against protesters – an increasingly significant phenomenon.[212] Injunctions could also be sought in certain circumstances by groups or individuals claiming that the decision of a public authority had breached the Convention. Their use would be especially appropriate in the context of public protest. As Chapter 9 points out and, as indicated below, in relation to

---

203 Previously Art 50 under the old numbering of the Articles.

204 *Steel v UK* (1999) 28 EHRR 603, para 125.

205 See as to heads of loss Burns, N (2001) NLJ 164.

206 Eg, in *Young, James and Webster v UK*, Judgment of 13 August 1981, A 44 (1981), pecuniary and non-pecuniary costs, taking such loss into account, were awarded: the Court ordered £65,000 to be paid.

207 *Weekes v UK*, A 114-A (1988).

208 In *Steel v UK* (1999) 28 EHRR 603, para 122, the three successful applicants were each imprisoned for seven hours. The Court, without giving reasons, awarded them £500 each in compensation for non-pecuniary damage.

209 See further Mowbray, A, 'The European Court of Human Rights' approach to just satisfaction' [1997] PL 647; Feldman, *op cit*, fn 13; Amos, M, 'Damages for breach of the Human Rights Act' [1999] EHRLR 178. The question of the level of damages is addressed further in Chapter 14, pp 914–15.

210 Mowbray, *ibid*, p 650.

211 As Leigh and Lustgarten point out in *op cit*, fn 194, p 529.

212 See pp 166–69. Section 12 does not apply to 'relief' in criminal proceedings.

the *International Ferries* case,[213] courts have shown deference to decisions of the police regarding public protest. However, there may well be circumstances in which a strict approach to proportionality would lead to a finding that bans or orders affecting protesters had gone further than necessary to achieve the ends in view.[214] In such an instance, issuance of an injunction would be appropriate. It may be noted that the decision at Strasbourg most in point in respect of such bans, *Christians against Racism and Fascism v UK*,[215] is a classic example of a decision which, while according with a traditionalist stance in public protest matters, would be disapplied under the activist approach. It is a relatively elderly decision of the Commission alone, in which the margin of appreciation doctrine[216] was strongly influential in leading to the conclusion that the application was manifestly ill-founded.

The remedy awarded will tend to differ, depending on whether the Convention is invoked under s 7(1)(a) or (b). If the action occurs under s 7(1)(a), the remedies normally available in judicial review proceedings may be granted and there is also the possibility that damages might be awarded. Where s 7(1)(b) is invoked, the remedy includes all those available in criminal or civil proceedings. These possibilities are considered at the relevant points in the following chapters.

5 SPECIAL PROTECTION FOR THE MEDIA AND RELIGIOUS FREEDOM?

Protecting religious organisations

The Church of England lobbied fiercely during the passage of the Human Rights Bill to be given special protection for religious freedom. The amendments to the Bill adopted in the House of Lords, which would have provided a defence where religious organisations breached human rights in the pursuance of religious belief, suggested that the Church wished to be allowed to disregard human rights values in the name of respect for religious belief, and that while protecting its own Art 9 rights, it was prepared to use them to invade the Convention rights of others.[217] The Church appeared to hope that it would be able to discriminate against persons on the ground, for example, of gender or sexual orientation in respect, *inter alia*, of employment in Church schools. Those amendments were removed in the Commons and s 13 was substituted, on the basis that Church concerns could be met without compromising the integrity of the Bill.[218] Section 13 does not allow the Church, and other religious organisations, to disregard human rights. It provides: 'If a court's determination of any question arising under this Act might affect the exercise by a religious organisation ... of [its Art 9 rights] which includes the right to freedom of religion it must have particular regard to the importance of that right.'

---

213 *R v Chief Constable of Sussex ex p International Ferries Ltd* [1999] 2 AC 418; [1999] 1 All ER 129.
214 See Chapter 9, pp 515–16.
215 Application No 8440/78 21 DR 138.
216 Application No 8440/78 21 DR 138, pp 149 and 151.
217 See 585 HL Official Report Cols 747–60, 770–90, 805, 812–13, 5 February 1998.
218 The Home Secretary, 312 HC Official Report Col 1019 (1998).

Arguably, s 13 impliedly accepts, therefore, what some commentators regard as a regrettable dislocation between human rights values and religious ones which will present judges with problems of interpretation.[219] Ian Loveland has dubbed the amendment 'a substantive obscenity'.[220]

Protecting the media

The press also lobbied for special protection. Press lobbying focused overwhelmingly upon the fear that the Act would introduce a right to privacy against the media 'through the back door', due either to judicial development of the common law in the post-HRA era, or to the probable status of the Press Complaints Commission as a public authority, itself bound to act compatibly with the Convention under s 6 of the HRA. Sometimes the basic point was missed that the Convention rights will not directly bind newspapers, since they are not public authorities.[221] The amendment became s 12, which applies 'if a court is considering whether to grant any relief [which could] affect the exercise of the Convention right to freedom of expression'. Section 12(2) provides special provision against the grant of *ex parte* injunctions, which is discussed further in Chapters 7 and 10. Under s 12(5), the term 'relief' includes 'any remedy or order other than in criminal proceedings'. Under s 12(3), no relief which, if granted, might affect the exercise of the Convention right to freedom of expression is to be granted so as to restrain publication before trial 'unless the court is satisfied that the applicant is likely to establish that publication should not be allowed.' Section 12(3) therefore affects the grant of interim injunctions generally and is discussed further in Chapter 10. Section 12(4) provides that the court must have special regard to the Convention right to freedom of expression and, in particular, to the extent to which it is about to become or has become available to the public, the public interest in its publication and 'any relevant privacy code'.[222] Section 12(4) is therefore highly relevant in actions originating under the breach of confidence doctrine, as Chapter 10 explains.

Indirect horizontal effects

In fact, media fears that a 'privacy law' would develop under the HRA were not misplaced and are currently in the process of being realised. But there is a delicious irony in the fact that it is s 12(4) that is being used, to an extent, to provide such a law with impetus. This issue is examined further in Chapter 10, but the technique being used is considered here since it is also relevant to s 13. In *Douglas and Others v Hello! Ltd*[223] Sedley LJ found that in so far as there is doubt as to the scope of the duty of the court under s 6 of

219 See further Cumper, P, 'The protection of religious rights under s 13 of the HRA' [2000] PL 254.

220 Loveland, *Constitutional Law*, 2000, p 603.

221 The definition of 'public authority' appears in ss 6(1), 6(3)(b) and 6(5)) of the Act, discussed in HL Deb Vol 582 Cols 1277, 1293–94 and 1309–10, 3 November 1997, and *ibid*, Vol 583 Cols 771–811, 24 November 1997.

222 See further on s 12(4), Griffiths, J and Lewis, T, 'The HRA s 12 – press freedom over privacy' (1999) 10(2) Ent LR 36–41. They argue that s 12(4) did not in fact provide the protection the media had hoped for, although their spokespersons believed that it had.

223 [2001] 2 WLR 992, CA (judgment of 21 December 2000).

the HRA, s 12(4) makes the matter crystal clear where interference with the right to freedom of expression is in issue. Since s 12(4) requires the Court to have particular regard to Art 10 – the right to freedom of expression – Art 10 must be applicable as between one private party to litigation and another; in other words, it has indirect horizontal effect. However, Art 10(2) is qualified in respect of the reputation and rights of others and the protection of information received in confidence. Therefore, in having particular regard to Art 10, it is also necessary to have such regard to the other Convention rights, including Art 8. Section 12(4) does not, therefore, merely give freedom of expression priority over the other rights. In weighing up the competing claims, the court also has to take the Code policed by the Press Complaints Commission into account under s 12(4)(b), as a relevant privacy code. This technique was also adopted in *Jon Venables, Robert Thompson v News Group Newspapers Ltd, Associated Newspapers Ltd, MGM Ltd*,[224] but as well as Art 8, the Arts 2 and 3 rights of the applicants were taken into account and were determinative of the issue.[225]

Thus, as indicated above, when the right to freedom of expression is in issue, indirect horizontal effects are clearly created, although an existing cause of action must be relied upon in order to get into court. Possibly, just as s 12(4) has been and will be used against the press, s 13 could be used against the Church of England or any other religious organisation. The Church is probably a functional public authority and, therefore, the question of horizontal effect may not be so relevant, depending on the circumstances of the case. Where it is unlikely to be viewed as a public authority, or where a Church group[226] is bringing an action as a victim (for example, against a media regulator in respect of an attempt to introduce religious advertising, or under the existing law of libel), s 13 would apply. But that would mean that Art 9(2) would also apply, meaning that the court would have to pay special regard to the 'rights and freedoms of others'. The right in question could be Art 10, presumably given special protection under s 12. In relation to the Church's role as an employer, an applicant could use existing anti-discrimination legislation in order to get into court. As Chapter 16 points out, the scope of such legislation is rapidly expanding and it may be found in future that it already covers discrimination on grounds of sexual orientation.[227] Therefore, once the applicant was in court arguing, for example, that he or she should not be discriminated against on that ground in respect of, say, an application for employment in a Church of England school, s 13 would be applicable and would therefore require special attention to be paid to the rights and freedoms of others. In this case they would most probably arise under Art 8 read with Art 14, or on its own; as Chapter 2 indicated, Art 8 would be applicable, depending on the specific circumstances.[228] Section 3 would obviously apply, assuming that the cause of action was based on statute (the Sex Discrimination Act 1975), but s 3 does not afford Art 9 any special prominence. The court would have to resolve the problem of determining what is meant by s 13 as distinct from s 3, if anything, when a

---

224 [2001] 1 All ER 908, HC, 8 January 2001.

225 See further Chapter 10, pp 584–85.

226 On the basis that the group itself is a private body or on the basis of the fact that, while it consists of Church representatives, it represents the Church in its private function.

227 This argument was accepted in *McDonald v MOD* [2001] 1 All ER 620, EAT, but was overturned on appeal. See further Chapter 16, p 1055.

228 See p 70. See also Chapter 16, pp 1054–58.

statutory provision is in question. It would also have to consider how to weigh up the relative force of ss 12 and 13 when opposed.

At present, it appears that s 12 has ensnared the group that lobbied for its inclusion. By a more doubtful route, the same may be true of s 13, in respect of the Church. Clearly, from a human rights perspective, this could be viewed as a welcome development, since it would mean that two bodies with, to different degrees, the ability and the evident desire to infringe the rights of others, while protecting their own, would be curbed in their ability to do so.

6 POSSIBLE RESPONSES OF THE UK JUDICIARY IN ADJUDICATING ON THE HUMAN RIGHTS ACT

There is general agreement among commentators that the response of the judiciary to the interpretation of the Convention rights will be crucial to the success of the HRA. (Of course, different views are taken as to what 'success' might mean in this context, as indicated below, and at various points in this book.) Lord Hope of Craighead, for example, has found: 'everything will depend on the ability of the judges to give effect to its provisions in a clear and consistent manner in a way which matches the intentions of the legislature.'[229] Lord Lester and David Pannick have written: 'The challenge and the opportunities for the judiciary are probably going to be the most dramatic.'[230] Clearly, judicial training will be a significant factor in relation to the performance of the judiciary.[231] But, as indicated above, in the whole discussion of the HRA, a number of areas of uncertainty have been left open; the judges, therefore, have a wide scope for the development of the law in a number of respects. The interpretation of the Convention rights will demand that they consider both the competing claims of individual rights and societal interests and conflicts between individual rights. Since they do not have much guidance as to techniques, apart from the provisions of s 2, they will have, to an extent, a free hand in using imported principles and relevant doctrines in interpreting and developing the HRA provisions and the rights themselves. The extent to which they have a discretion that they would not have if interpreting a very technical statute raises, it is suggested, a number of issues which are indicated below and considered further at relevant points in the following chapters.

The composition of the judiciary

A number of commentators have criticised the judicial appointments system,[232] and in particular the role of the Lord Chancellor in relation to it,[233] thereby making the case for

---

229 'The HRA 1998: the task of the judges' (1999) 20(3) Statute L Rev pp 185–97, p 185.

230 Preface to *Human Rights Law and Practice*, 1999. See also Martens, S, 'Incorporating the Convention: the role of the judiciary' [1998] EHRLR 5.

231 The Judicial Studies Board (JSB) held a series of 60 one day training seminars for all full and part time members of the judiciary. Magistrates' training was undertaken by Magistrates' Courts Committees. The JSB has also provided training for Chairs of Tribunals and has provided a training pack for Chairs and members of Tribunals.

232 See, eg, Fredman, S, 'Bringing rights home' (1998) 114 LQR 538.

233 See Bradley, AW and Ewing, K, *Constitutional Law*, 12th edn, 1997, p 419.

its reform in order to create a more objective and impartial system, with a view to changing the composition of the judiciary. In a response to such criticisms, the Labour Government has accepted that some reform is necessary.[234] The Judicial Appointments and Training Commission was set up in 2000; it oversees all stages of the appointments process, but has an advisory role only. In February 2001, the Lord Chancellor was criticised for soliciting funds for the Labour Party held for barristers who would thereafter be candidates for judicial appointment. Subsequently, in his statement to Parliament regarding the matter, he said that the possibility of an independent Appointments Commission – which would have an active role in the appointments process – was under consideration.

The argument for the more radical reform of the appointments system contemplated by the Lord Chancellor has a number of aspects, but centrally, it concerns the unrepresentative nature of the judiciary. Apart from the likelihood that the judges' backgrounds and experiences may differ radically from those whose rights they are considering, a matter that can have relevance in a number of circumstances, a system that – in effect – tends to exclude women from the highest office also excludes some of the most meritorious candidates, while arguably overestimating the merits of others. So far, no woman has been appointed to the House of Lords. Judges are still largely drawn from a tiny minority group: upper middle class, rich, white, elderly males who were public school and Oxbridge educated. At the present time, the House of Lords, which will often be the ultimate arbiter in the most controversial human rights cases, is all-male, with no ethnic minority representation. As positions of power in Britain are often filled by persons drawn from this group, it appears incongruous to afford them – in effect – the responsibility under the HRA of protecting the rights of minority groups, who by definition tend to be weak or unpopular. John Griffiths, in *The Politics of the Judiciary*,[235] argues that the senior judges:

> ... define the public interest, inevitably, from the viewpoint of their own class. And the public interest, so defined, is ... the interest of others in authority. It includes the maintenance of order, the protection of private property, the containment of the trade union movement.

The Griffiths argument, which is echoed by other leftist commentators, leads the left to view the domestic reception of the Convention as likely to lead to a diminution in the protection of civil liberties in the UK.[236] This may occur, in their view, for a number of reasons. In particular, it is thought that the judiciary, in the UK and abroad, cannot be trusted to protect the interests of minorities and/or unpopular groups, but will tend to protect commercial interests and the interests of those in authority. Therefore, Convention rights may be enforced by powerful bodies, including rich individuals and large corporations. Such enforcement may be to the detriment of civil liberties or to the detriment of general public interests of a social welfare nature. This is a powerful

---

234 See the Peach Report, December 1999, www.open.gov.uk/lcd/judicial/Peach/reportfr.htm. The Judicial Appointments and Training Commission was proposed: see *Access to Justice Labour Party*, 1995. See further Brazier, 'The judiciary', in Blackburn and Plant (eds), *Constitutional Reform: The Labour Government's Constitutional Reform Agenda*, 1999, p 329. See also The Rt Hon B Hale [2001] PL 489.

235 4th edn, 1991, p 327.

236 See Ewing and Gearty, *op cit*, fn 30, on Labour's plans to incorporate the Convention.

argument even to those who do not accept the conclusion which the left draws from it – that the HRA should never have been introduced.

It is not hard to find decisions made by judges under human rights documents which support the leftist thesis. For example, certain decisions under the Canadian Charter might find counterparts in the UK now that the HRA is fully in force. An example would include the use of Art 10 of the Convention to attack bans on cigarette advertising[237] or, as Chapter 6 suggests, the use of Art 10 by powerful media conglomerates against media regulators.[238]

Clearly, the causal link between the judges' backgrounds and their decisions may not be as clear as Griffiths suggests. Other variables may be present influencing particular decisions, and judges, despite similar backgrounds, sometimes display markedly differing degrees of liberalism. As Lee points out,[239] a number of House of Lords' decisions on human rights issues have been reached on a three–two majority,[240] while in others, a unanimous Court of Appeal has been overturned by a unanimous House of Lords.[241] This argument does not imply that all judges have a special facility, unknown to normal people, of rooting out in themselves all the unconscious prejudices derived from their backgrounds. Clearly, judges aspire to objectivity and impartiality, but it is obvious that sometimes they will be influenced, unconsciously or otherwise, by the interests of their class and by their experiences in general, including their sexual experiences. It is apparent, however, that despite the fact that they largely belong to a particular societal group, they do not always display attitudes which tend to be associated with that group. At the least, it is fair to say that during the Conservative years 1979–97, the judges demonstrated on the whole a greater eagerness to protect the rights of 'weak' or minority groups than did their counterparts in government. A number of highly significant decisions taken in the 1980s and 1990s relating to the rights of, for example, poorly paid women, asylum seekers or of suspects in police custody are documented in this book in which judges may be said to have acted against the interests of their class.[242] The 'judicial supremacism' controversy discussed by Loveland illustrates this tendency.[243] As he points out, a number of decisions on immigration policies taken during the second Major Government in the early-mid 1990s inflamed Conservative MPs as well as right wing commentators.[244] The argument that the judges will almost inevitably be influenced by the interests of those in authority is not, it is suggested, fully supported by the evidence.

But can it equally be said that there is a fair amount of evidence that male judges are able to overcome a lack of experience or understanding, or straightforward prejudice, based on gender and particular sexual experiences? Given the current dominance of male judges at the higher levels of the judiciary, this is a very pertinent question. Rights of

---

237 The Supreme Court of Canada struck down as an unjustifiable restriction on freedom of expression a Canadian statute prohibiting advertising: *RJR MacDonald Inc v Canada* (AG) SCC 21 September 1995.

238 See p 308; see also Part II, pp 207–08.

239 *Judging Judges*, 1989, p 36.

240 Eg *Gillick v West Norfolk and Wisbech AHA* [1986] AC 112; [1985] 3 WLR 830, HL.

241 *Mandla v Dowell Lee* [1983] 2 AC 548; [1983] 1 All ER 1062, HL.

242 *Hayward v Cammell Laird* [1988] 2 All ER 257; *Pickstone v Freemans* [1988] 3 WLR 265. See Chapter 16, pp 1019–20, Chapter 15, pp 933–34. Chapter 14, p 884.

243 *Constitutional Law*, 2000, pp 587–95.

244 See further Chapter 15, p 933–34.

especial relevance to women may often come before all-male courts under the HRA, raising fears of a lack of impartiality and understanding. In particular, Art 6 may be used to diminish the value of special protections for rape victims within the criminal justice system.[245] In Canada, the so called 'rape shield', which prevented the defence asking questions about a complainant's sexual history or reputation, was struck down by the Supreme Court under the Canadian Charter on the ground of fairness to the accused (*R v Seaboyer*),[246] although the rape shield law was reinstated.[247] In March 2001, a challenge to a law similar in certain respects to the one in Canada was considered by the House of Lords in *R v A*.[248] It may be noted that the change in the law had been campaigned for by women's groups over a long period of time, and that one of the most persuasive arguments for its introduction concerned the strong tendency of Crown Court judges to allow humiliating questions regarding the complainant's sexual history even where irrelevant to the issue of consent. Women's groups were allowed to intervene in the appeal by making written representations that the law should be retained. Further, an application was made on behalf of the Fawcett Society, a group campaigning for women's rights, to intervene on the basis that the House of Lords is insufficiently impartial to decide the case. The argument was that an all-male court might be influenced, unconsciously, by their attitudes towards sexuality and therefore would not be able to decide impartially where the balance should lie between the rights of the female complainant and the Art 6 fair trial rights of the male defendant. The House of Lords refused to accept the case made by the group and went on to find that the provision in question was not incompatible with Art 6, since s 3 of the HRA could be used in order to allow for the reading of words into the section, allowing the possibility of the admission of relevant evidence relating to a previous (alleged) sexual relationship between defendant and complainant. This was, as indicated above, an extremely activist interpretation of what s 3 requires. In reaching its decision as to the requirements of s 3, the Lords did not rehearse the relevant Strasbourg jurisprudence in any detail. Therefore, it is arguable that the legislative role being adopted was almost overt. The Art 8 rights of the complainant were not mentioned, although Art 8 concerns were considered. It is suggested that this was an instance in which the House of Lords read up the Convention right in question – and read down the domestic legislative provision – the reverse of the position the Law Lords adopted in *Brown v Stott*.[249] This approach may be termed a selectively activist one.

This example indicates the nature of the problem. It is suggested here that it is at least as hard to acquit the male judiciary of lacking understanding of women's experiences and of making decisions that appear to be tinged by sexism, as it is to acquit them of being

---

245 It is possible that the current anonymity of rape complainants in the UK might be challenged on similar grounds under Art 6 or possibly under Art 8 in conjunction with Art 14 (on grounds of equal rights to privacy).

246 [1991] 2 SCR 577; 83 DLR (4th) 193.

247 The new rape shield law (Criminal Code as amended, s 276), however, survived a human rights challenge in 2000: *R v Darrach* (2000) 191 DLR (4th) 539.

248 [2001] 2 WLR 1546. The Court of Appeal considered the possibility of incompatibility between the rape shield provision and Art 6: *R v Y (Sexual Offence: Complainant's Sexual History)* (2001) *The Times*, 13 February 2001; the House of Lords may issue a declaration of incompatibility: *R v A (Joinder of Appropriate Minister)* (2001) *The Times*, 7 March. For comment, see *The Guardian*, 19 March 2001.The provision in question is the Youth Justice and Criminal Evidence Act 1999, s 41.

249 See above, pp 144–45.

influenced by the other prejudices considered. This book seeks to provide substantiation for this argument at various points.[250] Possibly, the practice of accepting interventions from women's campaigning groups in human rights cases is an interesting development that has the potential to address this problem, to an extent. Part of a broader solution to the problem is to appoint more women to higher judicial office, especially to the House of Lords. In the case of the 'rape shield' law, the obvious solution, put forward on behalf of the Fawcett Society, was to appoint two female Law Lords in order to ensure that the decision was not taken by an all-male court. It was not expected that this would occur in this instance, but intervention aided in making the general case for reform. Reform of the appointments system may eventually change the gender make-up of the higher courts, but it may be noted that in the first 20 months of the Labour Government from 1997, the Lord Chancellor made 17 exclusively male appointments to higher judicial office.[251]

Learning lessons from the Canadian experience

In adjudication on the HRA, domestic judges are likely to refer to decisions of courts from other jurisdictions, and Canadian cases in particular are likely to be considered with some frequency,[252] although it cannot be assumed that the judiciary will invariably welcome the use of Canadian precedents.[253] Canadian judges share a similar constitutional background with UK judges and Canada has adopted the Charter of Rights and Freedoms relatively recently.

Opinions differ as to the success of the Supreme Court of Canada, as compared to that of other equivalent courts throughout the world, in upholding human rights. As well as taking the Court's jurisprudence into account in human rights cases, lessons can be drawn from the Canadian experience that are relevant to UK judges. It should be pointed out, however, that there had been judicial review of legislation in Canada since before Confederation in 1867. It has been argued that they have adjusted successfully to applying the Canadian Charter of Rights and Freedoms 1982. Professor Russell of the University of Toronto wrote in 1988 (six years after the Charter was adopted):

> In Skapinker[254] [the first Charter decision of the Canadian Supreme Court] the Court made it clear that it was prepared to take the Charter seriously, to give its terms a liberal interpretation and to strike down laws and practices of government found to be in conflict with it.[255]

Writing on two decisions in which freedom of expression was upheld under the Charter, Judge Strayer of the Federal Court of Canada has said:

> Such vague paternalistic laws had long been recognised as posing a threat to freedom of expression and they could not survive long in a country which had so recently dedicated

---

250 See, in particular, Chapter 17, pp 1064–68.

251 See (1999) 5 Legal Action, February.

252 See *R v A* [2001] 2 WLR 1546; [2001] UKHL 25, esp paras 76, 77, 100, 101. See also, *Montgomery v Lord Advocate* [2001] 2 WLR 779, p 810.

253 See *Brown v Stott* [2001] 2 WLR 817, pp 853–55, *per* Lord Hope of Craighill.

254 [1984] 2 SCR 713.

255 Russell, P [1988] PL 385, p 388.

itself to guaranteeing that freedom. One can only speculate that such laws would long since have been amended and particularised had inertia not been the line of least political resistance.[256]

In passing, it is worth noting that one of the laws in question was a provincial law dealing with film censorship which did not prescribe standards for such censorship; its counterpart can be found at present in the UK in the power of local authorities to license films, which derives from legislation passed in 1909.[257]

Decisions under the Charter have not, however, gone uncriticised from the political left: it has been said that 'the Charter is being used to benefit vested interests in society and to weaken the relative power of the disadvantaged and under-privileged',[258] referring to a decision condoning restriction of the collective bargaining power of unions in *Retail, Wholesale and Department Store Union*.[259] On the other hand, Russell has contended that the Supreme Court 'is sensitive to the left's concerns and is struggling to avoid an approach to the Charter which will give credence to them'.[260] These relatively early favourable evaluations of the impact of the Charter have received mixed support in later analysis. It has been suggested that the Charter 'has transformed the rights' agenda in Canada positively and creatively – sometimes even inspirationally'.[261] There have been, however, a number of suggestions that the record of the Supreme Court of Canada must be viewed as timorous and unflattering since it has failed to take a bold and innovative approach, one which could be viewed as showing the way forward for other such courts throughout the world.[262]

Clearly, any assessment of the record of the Supreme Court must be subject to later revision. A number of decisions of the Supreme Court are considered at various points in this book, since it will be suggested that despite the reservations expressed, they will provide a very valuable source of jurisprudence. Techniques developed by the Supreme Court in relation to the Charter will also be of relevance. The Court adopts a purposive approach 'the purpose of the right or freedom is to be sought by reference to the ... larger objects of the Charter itself, to the historical origins of the concept enshrined and, where applicable, to the meaning and purpose of [other associated rights and freedoms] ...'.[263]

The Court has also shown a strong tendency to draw upon international human rights law and to consider decisions from other jurisdictions.[264] It will be, it is suggested, valuable to adopt a similar approach to the Convention rights under the HRA, bearing in mind the meagre, under-theorised nature of much of the Strasbourg jurisprudence and the fact that it is not binding. By considering Canadian human rights jurisprudence and jurisprudence from other jurisdictions, it is arguable that the judiciary will be able to settle human rights issues in a manner that will not depend on their own personal moral

---

256 [1988] PL 347, p 359.

257 The Cinematograph Act 1909, which was concerned with the fire risk posed by films at that time.

258 (1988) 38 UTLJ 278, p 279.

259 (1986) 33 DLR (4th) 174; [1986] 1 SCR 460; for comment, see also (1987) 37 UTLJ 183.

260 *Op cit*, p 388.

261 Penner, R, 'The Canadian experience with the Charter of Rights' [1996] PL 125. See further Hogg, PW, *Constitutional Law of Canada*, 1996.

262 See Beatty, D, 'The Canadian Charter of Rights: lessons and laments' [1997] 60(4) MLR 487.

263 *R v Big M Drug Mart Ltd* (1985) 18 DLR (4th) 321, pp 395–96.

264 See Schabas, W, *International Human Rights Law and the Canadian Charter*, 1991; Hogg, *op cit*, fn 261.

outlook. As Raz puts it, the judges will have available 'distancing devices ... devices the judges can rely on to settle [such issues] in a way that is independent of the personal tastes of the judges'.[265]

Many commentators have remarked on the growing tendency of courts to refer to the human rights jurisprudence of other jurisdictions.[266] However, the legitimacy of relying on such jurisprudence has increasingly been doubted. For example, if a Canadian decision is relied upon which has itself been especially heavily influenced by jurisprudence from other jurisdictions (as has that other jurisprudence itself), could that decision be viewed as having a particular legitimacy because it reflects an accepted multinational standard of human rights? Or should it be viewed with suspicion on the basis that without looking more closely at the possible decisions that could have influenced it, it might merely reflect a selective use of jurisprudence in order to reach a desired end? It has been suggested that the invocation of foreign jurisprudence may merely obscure rather than guard against moral arbitrariness.[267] However, it is unlikely that such criticisms will lead to a reversal of such an established trend. What is needed is a deeper understanding of the use of foreign jurisprudence in domestic courts with a view to answering a number of questions, especially regarding its effect on the legitimacy of decisions. As C McCrudden argues in an important article, a systematic examination of this complex phenomenon is required so that we could 'at least understand it better'.[268]

Domestic approaches to the margin of appreciation doctrine

The part to be played by the margin of appreciation doctrine, discussed in Chapter 2,[269] in some form in the domestic courts is unclear. In the early months of the HRA, it became apparent that the judiciary were likely to continue to find that certain matters, most obviously those relating to national security, are peculiarly matters for the executive to determine. Moreover, in adjudicating on human rights cases, a domestic doctrine with some similarities to the margin of appreciation doctrine was developed, under the HRA, relying on a concept of the 'area of discretionary judgment'. The two doctrines are, however, distinct, although their effects may not always be, as explained below.

A central issue under the HRA concerns the domestic application of the margin of appreciation doctrine. Since it has probably been the key dilutant of Convention standards, as Chapter 2 indicated,[270] it is essential that UK judges and other public authorities reject it as a relevant factor in their own decision making under the Convention, although there will be instances, as indicated below, when it will be appropriate to recognise a 'discretionary area of judgement'. As indicated in Chapter 2, the doctrine is a distinctively international law doctrine, based on the need to respect the

---

265 Raz, J, 'On the authority and interpretation of constitutions: some preliminaries', in *Constitutionalism: Philosophical Foundations*, 1998, p 190.

266 See Nelken, D, 'Disclosing/invoking legal culture: an introduction' (1995) 4 SLS 435.

267 See Ghai, Y, 'Sentinels of liberty or sheep in Woolf's clothing? Judicial politics and the Hong Kong Bill of Rights' [1997] 60 MLR 459.

268 'A common law of human rights? Transnational judicial conversations on constitutional rights' (2000) 20(4) OJLS 499–532.

269 See pp 34–37.

270 See p 37.

decision making of Nation States within defined limits. Therefore, it would not appear to have any application in national law.[271] However, under s 2 of the HRA, the domestic judiciary 'must take into account' any relevant Strasbourg jurisprudence, although they are not bound by it.[272] A central concern is, therefore, the reconciliation of s 2 of the HRA with the development of the margin of appreciation doctrine, taking into account its international character.

As indicated above, s 2 creates quite a weak obligation, since it is open to the judiciary to consider, but disapply a particular decision. Only the Convention rights themselves are binding under s 6. As pointed out above, the rights appear, in many respects, quite out of date today. But, since 1950, they have been subject to a rich and extensive jurisprudence. The domestic judiciary may view a number of the Articles as far too bald and imprecise unless their interpretation at Strasbourg is taken into account.[273] But, where little or no guidance was provided by the Strasbourg jurisprudence, except in a very general sense, it would be open to the judiciary to develop their own version of the doctrine of the margin of appreciation (under a different name) based upon common law acceptance of judicial deference to Parliament and to aspects of executive power. Conversely, it would also be open to them to consider whether it is possible and desirable to avoid applying the margin of appreciation aspects of the jurisprudence.[274] While it is clear that the doctrine itself has no application in national law,[275] the obligation to disapply it may be viewed as going much further than merely refusing to import it into domestic decision making. There are some clear indications from the judiciary that they are not minded to import the doctrine wholesale into domestic law, but that they may be prepared to rely on decisions at Strasbourg which have been influenced by it. To an extent, this was the approach adopted in the leading pre-HRA case of *R v DPP ex p Kebilene*:[276] although the doctrine itself was rejected, the outcomes of applications at Strasbourg were taken into account without adverting to the influence the doctrine had had on them.[277]

---

271 As Sir John Laws puts it: 'The margin of appreciation doctrine as it has been developed at Strasbourg will necessarily be inapt to the administration of the Convention in the domestic courts for the very reason that they are domestic; they will not be subject to an objective inhibition generated by any cultural distance between themselves and the State organs whose decisions are impleaded before them.' 'The limitations of human rights' [1998] PL 254, p 258.

272 The term exhaustively covers any 'judgement, decision, declaration or advisory opinion of the Court', any 'opinion of the Commission given in a report adopted under Article 31', any 'decision of the Commission in connection with Article 26 or 27(2)' or any 'decision of the Committee of Ministers taken under Article 46'. The words 'in connection with' appear to mean that all findings which may be said to be linked to the admissibility procedure, including reports prepared during the preliminary examination of a case, could be taken into account.

273 It may be noted that this is not necessarily the case; the Strasbourg jurisprudence may have the effect of 'reading down' the right; see the discussion of *Khan v UK* (2000) 8 BHRC 310 in Chapter 14, p 906; see also *Salabiaku v France*, A 141-A (1988).

274 See Hunt, M, Singh, R and Demetriou, M, 'Is there a role for the margin of appreciation in national law after the Human Rights Act?' [1999] EHRLR 15.

275 In *R v Stratford JJ ex p Imbert* (1999) *The Times*, 21 February, Buxton LJ confirmed obiter that the doctrine had no such application. This is also the advice currently given by the Judicial Studies Board.

276 [1999] 3 WLR 372.

277 Such applications included *H v UK*, App No 15023/89 and *Bates v UK*, Appl No 26280/95.

Minimalism or activism?

Minimalism

It should now be clear that the Human Rights Act and the Convention itself leave open a great deal of leeway for diverse judicial approaches. A minimalist approach would tend to include a full reliance on the margin of appreciation aspects of the Strasbourg jurisprudence, resulting in the operation of a restrained review jurisdiction only, in determining issues covered by any 'relevant' jurisprudence. This would *not* mean openly importing the margin of appreciation doctrine into domestic decision making; rather, it would mean applying such aspects regardless of the influence it had had on them. In a sense, it would mean importing the doctrine by the back door. An example of adoption of this model in the pre-HRA era was arguably provided by *R v Khan*;[278] the House of Lords relied on an exclusion of evidence decision at Strasbourg, *Schenk v Switzerland*,[279] where a very wide margin of appreciation had been allowed, without acknowledging that this was the case. For example, it was said in the Lords in *Khan*: 'the discretionary powers of the trial judge to exclude evidence march hand in hand with Article 6(1) of the Convention ... the decision of the Court in *Schenk* ... confirms that the use at a criminal trial of material obtained in breach of privacy enshrined in Article 8 does not of itself mean that the trial is unfair.'[280] The House of Lords, therefore, appeared impliedly to reassure itself that sufficiently high standards would be maintained by following *Schenk*. But the decision in *Schenk* in fact confirms that admitting evidence obtained due to such a breach is within the margin of appreciation conceded to the national courts; it does not therefore confirm that a *domestic* practice of so doing meets nationally recognised standards of procedural justice.[281]

There appears to be at present some judicial readiness to adopt a minimalist approach under the cloak of a domestic doctrine of deference. Signs of judicial adherence to this approach were found in *Ex p Kebilene*.[282] Lord Hope said: 'This technique [the margin of appreciation] is not available to the national courts when they are considering Convention issues arising within their own countries [but] ... In some circumstances it will be appropriate for the courts to recognise that there is an area of judgement within which the judiciary will defer, on democratic grounds, to the considered opinion of [the democratic body or person] whose act or decision is said to be incompatible with the Convention.' In the context of the case, which concerned the compatibility of primary terrorist legislation with the Convention, these findings were used to justify a deferential approach. Indeed, they sought to introduce qualifications into a guarantee which on its face was unqualified. The term used by Lord Hope to describe the area in which choices between individual rights and societal interests might arise was 'the discretionary area of judgement';[283] he found that it would be easier for such an area of judgment to be

---

278 [1997] AC 558.

279 (1988) 13 EHRR 242.

280 [1997] AC 558, p 583, *per* Lord Nicholls.

281 See, eg, the decision of the Canadian Supreme Court in *R v Burlingham* [1995] 2 SCR 206.

282 [1999] 3 WLR 172. See Chapter 8, pp 411–12.

283 First coined by Pannick, D, 'Principles of interpretation of Convention rights under the Human Rights Act and the discretionary area of judgement' [1998] PL 545, pp 549–51.

recognised 'where the Convention itself requires a balance to be struck, much less so where the right [as in Art 6(2)] is stated in terms which are unqualified ... But even where the right is stated in [such] terms ... the courts will need to bear in mind the jurisprudence of the European Court which recognises that due account should be taken of the special nature of terrorist crime and the threat which it poses to a democratic society'.[284] In support of his balancing approach, Lord Hope referred to Lord Woolf's findings in *AG of Hong Kong v Lee Kwong-kut*.[285] Lord Woolf considered the Canadian approach when applying the Canadian Charter of Rights and Freedoms, art 1 of which states that the rights and freedoms which it guarantees are: 'subject only to such reasonable limits prescribed by law as can be demonstrably justified in a free and democratic society.' He said: 'In a case where there is real difficulty, where the case is close to the borderline, regard can be had to the approach now developed by the Canadian courts in respect of section 1 of their Charter.'

The approach of Lord Hope towards the development of a broad domestic doctrine of deference was therefore based on a watering down of the Convention rights since a provision equivalent to s 1 of the Charter was omitted from the basic Convention rights under Arts 2–7. A somewhat similar approach was taken in *R v Chief Constable of Sussex ex p International Ferry Traders Ltd*.[286] Lord Slynn, in a speech with which the other Law Lords agreed, found: 'the courts have long made it clear that ... they will respect the margin of appreciation or discretion which a Chief Constable has,' and, in this instance, that margin had not been exceeded. Lord Hoffman found: 'on the particular facts of this case the European concepts of proportionality and margin of appreciation produce the same result as what are commonly called *Wednesbury* principles ... in this case I think that the Chief Constable must enjoy a margin of discretion that cannot differ according to whether its source be found in purely domestic principles or superimposed European principles.' In other words, it is possible to discover, as in *Khan* and *Kebilene*,[287] that traditional notions of deference to the executive and to Parliament may be coterminous and perhaps ought to be coterminous with the expression of the margin of appreciation doctrine, or that Strasbourg principles happen to yield the same result as *Wednesbury* ones.

Under this approach, a court might ostensibly refuse to apply the margin of appreciation doctrine and yet would adopt a restrained stance in some circumstances. The court, following notions of common law restraint expressed in a manner similar to the *Kebilene* 'area of discretionary judgement' doctrine, might find that it could afford a limited interpretation to Strasbourg decisions if to do so would be in accordance with common law tradition. Obvious examples in which this stance might be taken are in respect of the exclusion of improperly or illegally obtained non-confession evidence, where the common law tradition may be termed 'amoral',[288] or in public protest

---

284 He gave the example of the ruling of the Court in *Murray v UK* (1994) 19 EHRR 193, p 222, para 47.

285 [1993] AC 951, p 966.

286 [1999] 1 All ER 129, publication on the internet at www.parliament.uk. The decision was taken in the context of EC, not Convention, law but the principles referred to were the same.

287 [1999] 3 WLR 172; discussed below and in Chapter 8, pp 411–12.

288 Zander, M, *The Police and Criminal Evidence Act 1984*, 1995, p 236. See further Chapter 14, pp 891–93.

decisions where the common law approach has not fully reflected the Convention since the focus of concern has been, broadly, on proprietorial rather than protest rights.[289]

This approach could be justified on the basis that a balance has always been struck in UK law between particular civil liberties and societal and other concerns by reference either to common law principle or parliamentary restraint. In the particular context, it is probable that that balance has been found to accord with the Convention at Strasbourg[290] (either in a specific or more general sense) even though the Convention was ratified by the UK more than 50 years ago, and therefore, there is no reason to disturb it now. On this view, the national legal system has already achieved the requisite balance within the margin it is allowed at Strasbourg. Having reviewed aspects of the balance struck by the national law, Strasbourg is satisfied with it and therefore it is necessary only to ensure that that margin is not exceeded in any particular instance.

A minimalist approach would provide a little more protection for human rights than would be provided under current judicial review principles, since the domestic courts will have to consider proportionality: an interference will be disproportionate where it goes beyond the aim in question or where little or no evidence of the need for it is advanced by the State. Where the Strasbourg jurisprudence allows different views to be taken of the need for a particular restriction, a domestic court fully applying it, including its margin of appreciation aspects, would tend to defer to the judgment of the executive. Clearly, this approach is distinguishable from that of heightened *Wednesbury* unreasonableness,[291] but it would often lead to the same outcome.[292] This approach would be most problematic where it was confronted by a clearly analogous decision at Strasbourg adopting a stance opposed to the previous general trend of UK law.[293] This may not arise very frequently, as this book indicates, but it has already arisen in the significant Privy Council decision in *Brown v Stott*,[294] a decision which, it is suggested, exemplified the minimalist approach in the sense that it required a 'reading down' of the Convention right in question.

Brown is discussed more fully in Chapter 13,[295] but the stance taken is indicated here. In *Saunders v UK*[296] it was found that, if a penalty formally attaches to silence in questioning by State agents, and the coerced statements are then used in evidence, a breach of Art 6 is almost bound to occur. Section 172 of the Road Traffic Act (RTA) 1988 makes it an offence for motorists not to tell police who was driving their vehicle at the time of an alleged offence. The coerced statement can then be used in evidence at trial for

---

289 See Gray and Gray, 'Civil rights, civil wrongs and quasi-public places' (1999) 1 EHRLR 46, and see further Chapter 9, pp 447–50, 465–74.

290 Eg, in the public order and freedom of assembly context this could be said, in a broad sense: see Chapter 9, fn 353 and associated text.

291 See *Ministry of Defence ex p Smith and Others* [1996] 1 All ER 257, p 263.

292 It might collapse into it if, in effect, a general test of 'reasonableness' rather than necessity and proportionality is adopted as Beatty suggests it has been in Canada under the Charter: see *op cit*, fn 262, p 493.

293 This occurred in *Osman v UK* (2000) 29 EHRR 245. In criticising the Strasbourg decision, Lord Hoffman has made it clear that he views the House of Lords as having a limited role in adjudicating on human rights' issues: 'Human rights and the House of Lords' (1999) 62(2) MLR 159, p 161.

294 [2001] 2 WLR 817, the Judicial Committee of the Privy Council. See, for the Scottish decision, *Stott v Brown* 2000 SLT 379; see also, for discussion, *Kerrigan* [2000] J Civ Lib 193.

295 See pp 858–60.

296 (1997) 23 EHRR 313; No 19187/91.

the RTA offence in question. In *Brown*, the Law Lords found a way of distinguishing the instant case in the particular circumstances, from *Saunders*. It was pointed out that s 172 could be distinguished from s 437 of the Companies Act 1985, the provision at issue in *Saunders* on a number of grounds, including the degree of coercion and the length of questioning. The Lords did not find that s 172 was incompatible with Art 6 and therefore it was not necessary to rely on s 6(2)(b). The Lords also used an equivalent doctrine, that of according a discretionary area of discretion to the legislature, in coming to its decision. Bearing that doctrine in mind, it was further argued that Art 6 *itself* does not expressly require that coerced statements should be excluded from evidence and that although a right to freedom from self-incrimination could be implied into it, the right had not been treated at Strasbourg as an absolute right. Following *Ex p Kebilene*, the Lords relied on decisions to that effect at Strasbourg that had been influenced by the margin of appreciation doctrine. Lord Bingham found: 'Limited qualification of [Art 6] rights is acceptable if reasonably directed by national authorities towards a clear and proper public objective and if representing no greater qualification than the situation calls for'. The objective in question was the laudable one of curbing traffic accidents. On that basis, by importing a form of balancing test into Art 6, it was found that answers given under s 172 could be adduced in evidence at trial.

While it is understandable that the Lords wished to find a method of preserving the effect of s 172, with the aim of serving an important societal interest, it is suggested that their decision will have the effect of undermining the right not to incriminate oneself in Art 6(1), in a range of circumstances. The combination of the uses of the doctrine of deference to the legislature, combined with the use of Strasbourg decisions affected by the margin of appreciation doctrine, has led, it is argued, to a decision that affords the right a lesser significance than Strasbourg has accorded it. If the intention had been to balance the rights in Art 6 against a range of societal interests, a paragraph could have been included, as in Arts 8–11, setting out the exceptions and the tests to be applied in using them. Alternatively, a general exception could have been included, as in Art 1 of the Canadian Charter. The decision not to adopt either of these courses implies that there is little or no room for the use of implied exceptions. In so far as Strasbourg has suggested that the Art 6 rights are qualified, the Lords should have considered whether adoption of that stance was due to the use of the doctrine of the margin of appreciation.

Activism

A further approach, which takes a more generous stance towards the Convention rights, may be termed activist. Such an approach might be viewed as a development from the activism shown in developing a common law of human rights in the pre-HRA era, as discussed in Chapter 3.[297] Such an approach assumes that the common law recognises and upholds fundamental human rights and that therefore, an approach which takes an activist stance towards such rights is in accordance with UK legal tradition. It is suggested that the approach taken in *Secretary of State ex p Daly*[298] exemplifies such a stance.

Although such an approach would recognise the existence of a discretionary area of judgment, it would do on carefully scrutinised grounds. Thus, the democratic quality of

---

297 See pp 102–11.
298 [2001] 3 All ER 433; HL, 23 May 2001; [2001] UKHL 26. The decision concerned rights of privacy of prisoners in respect of correspondence.

the rights-infringing rule would be considered: legislation would be treated with greater deference than executive decisions. This approach might take a more rights-affirming stance than Strasbourg in certain *selected* contexts, since common law traditions of deference were particularly apparent only in certain areas of executive decision making, areas which do not fully coincide with areas covered by the margin of appreciation doctrine.[299] Where Strasbourg activism coincided with common law activism, this approach would lead to greater protection for rights, not least because the judiciary would derive reassurance from the Convention underpinning provided for the preferred approach. Section 11 of the HRA affords recognition to the protection for fundamental rights already achieved under the common law, in providing that reliance on a Convention right does not restrict existing rights or freedoms, or a person's right to make any claim 'which he could make or bring apart from ss 7–9'. This provision may have great significance in certain contexts.[300]

But where common law tradition had diverged from Strasbourg in developing in a *less* rights-oriented manner, the HRA would provide the impetus for change, under this approach. This approach would lead to greater interference with executive decision making, and would depart, to an extent, from common law tradition in so doing. It would tend to require consideration to be given primarily to the principles developed at Strasbourg for the interpretation of the Convention rights, rather than following specific decisions, whether as to admissibility or otherwise. But, in contrast to Lord Hope's approach in *Ex p Kebilene*, it would use such principles to enhance rather than constrain the utilisation of the rights.[301]

Strasbourg has found that the purpose of the Convention is to 'maintain and promote the ideals and values of a democratic society',[302] which include tolerance of views offensive to the majority,[303] and to provide 'rights that are practical and effective' rather than 'rights that are theoretical or illusory'.[304] These concepts have not always found expression in practice, partly due to the diluting effect of the margin of appreciation doctrine. But in support of the 'activist' approach, it might be pointed out that much of the more deferential Strasbourg jurisprudence is very heavily influenced by decisions of the Commission, which, as indicated above, is not a fully judicial body[305] and, therefore, has less authority than the Court. It would be in accordance with Strasbourg principles to have regard to the balance struck between individual rights and societal interest in other

---

299 Eg, the decision of *R v Samuel* [1988] QB 615 on exclusion of evidence may be viewed as more 'activist' than the decision in the same context at Strasbourg in *Schenk v Switzerland*, A 140 (1988).

300 Where statutory provisions seek to curb reliance on the HRA, s 7, in the ordinary courts, s 11 may have a countering effect. See Chapter 11, p 713, for discussion.

301 Such an approach was evident in the Divisional Court in *R v DPP ex p Kebilene* [1999] 3 WLR 175. The Lord Chief Justice, Lord Bingham, found that the provisions in question undermined the presumption of innocence under Art 6(2) 'in a blatant and obvious way' due to the use of presumptions and the possibility of conviction on reasonable suspicion falling short of proof under the PTA, s 16A as amended. See further Chapter 8, pp 411–12.

302 *Kjeldsen v Denmark* (1976) 1 EHRR 711, p 731; see also the comments of the Court in *Socialist Party v Turkey* (1998) 27 EHRR 51 as to the need for pluralism in a democracy.

303 In *Handyside v UK* (1976) 1 EHRR 737, para 49 the Court said: '[Article 10] ... is applicable not only to "information" or "ideas" that are favourably received or regarded as inoffensive ... but also to those which offend, shock or disturb the State or any sector of the population. Such are the demands of that pluralism, tolerance and broadmindedness without which there is no "democratic society".'

304 *Airey v Ireland* (1979) 2 EHRR 305, p 314.

305 Chapter 2, pp 20–22.

European courts, and perhaps also to that struck by the International Covenant on Civil and Political Rights and in other jurisdictions, including the US or Canada. By so doing, it might be possible to determine what the outcome of a decision at Strasbourg would have been had a lesser or no margin been conceded to the State. Human rights jurisprudence from other jurisdictions will clearly prove very valuable where the Strasbourg jurisprudence is exiguous, which is frequently the case. Indeed, the domestic courts are already showing a willingness to take such jurisprudence into account.[306] Thus, activism would occur in accordance with a synthesis of Strasbourg and national constitutional. As D Beatty puts it: 'the same set of principles and analytical framework ... are used by [the judiciary] in Washington, Tokyo, New Delhi, Strasbourg, Rome, Karlsruhe ... [principles] which lie at the core of the concept of constitutional rights that allow judges to act out their role as guardians of the constitution in an objective, determinate and ultimately very democratic way.'[307]

A national court which afforded *greater* protection to the substantive rights would never exceed the margin conceded to the State unless two fundamental Convention rights came into conflict. The rejection in the Lords during debate on the Human Rights Bill of a Conservative amendment which would have required that the Strasbourg jurisprudence should be binding on the UK courts also lends support to this argument. In rejecting the amendment, the government spokesperson, the Lord Chancellor, implied that the possibility would thereby be left open of applying higher standards than those applied at Strasbourg.[308] A further Conservative amendment to the Bill, which was also rejected, sought to ensure that the domestic judiciary would be obliged to adhere to the margin of appreciation doctrine in interpreting and applying the Convention. Any domestic judge uncertain whether to disregard a Commission decision on admissibility or a deferential decision of the Court would therefore be able to find some justification under the *Pepper v Hart*[309] doctrine for so doing.

The rejection of these two amendments suggests that the legislation is not intended to place the judiciary under an obligation to afford greater weight to the Convention rights than Strasbourg has previously required, but that they are afforded a discretion to do so. It follows, it may be argued, that this approach would allow the HRA to recognise the difference between the roles of a national and an international court, and in particular the need for the latter, but not the former to take common European standards into account.

However, before accepting that activism is necessary in order to realise the full benefits of the Convention, it is essential to consider both what activism means and what its effects may be. The main concern of this book is with vertical effects in the classic arenas of State power and, therefore, it avoids the most problematic issues since activism is usually welcomed by most commentators in such arenas.[310] Indeed, as indicated

---

306 In *Albert Reynolds v Times Newspapers and Others* [1999] 4 All ER 609, the House of Lords took into account authorities from Canada, Australia and New Zealand, although in this instance they found that the Strasbourg jurisprudence was more influential.

307 Beatty, *op cit*, fn 262, p 481. This assertion of judicial objectivity would, of course, be attacked in certain quarters: see Unger, R, *The Critical Legal Studies Movement*, 1986.

308 'The Bill would of course permit UK courts to depart from existing Strasbourg decisions and upon occasion it might well be appropriate to do so and it is possible they might give a successful lead to Strasbourg.' HL Deb Col 514, 18 November 1997.

309 [1993] AC 593; [1993] 1 All ER 42.

310 See, eg, Ewing, KD and Gearty, CA, *Freedom under Thatcher*, 1989.

above, some, although by no means all, commentators look to the HRA as a means of undoing the effects in such contexts of years of untrammelled parliamentary sovereignty.[311] As this book indicates, especially in relation to State surveillance in Chapter 11, counter-terrorist and public order measures in Chapters 8 and 9, the Security and Intelligence Services in Chapter 11, such effects are readily evident.

But unbridled judicial activism might also have the effect, in certain contexts, of imposing particular moral views of on individuals and thereby infringing their Convention rights. The example of abortion was used by the Lord Chancellor in parliamentary debate in order to illustrate the possibilities which might arise. If activism was simply taken to mean a requirement to 'read up' the Convention rights and if necessary to 'read down' the domestic statute, the ideological views of particular judges might be given expression by means of the HRA. It could be argued that this is what occurred in *R v A*.[312] This could mean affording the Abortion Act 1967 as amended a very restrictive interpretation (which would not be difficult, given its apparently limited application) and reading up the right to life under Art 2. The Government would probably subsequently bring forward legislation to restore the broader application of the Act,[313] but there might be a period of time during which the social effects of the judgment were strongly apparent, bearing especially on women.

Adoption of such a stance would not, however, be warranted, since this would be an instance in which, it is argued, the principles underlying and justifying activism would not be engaged. At Strasbourg, Art 2 does not prevent abortion, since the Commission has declined to find that the foetus is protected.[314] This is not an instance where it could readily be said that had Strasbourg refused to show deference to the Member State it would have decided differently in the relevant decisions. The stance adopted, which allowed a wide margin of appreciation, appeared to be taken partly because in those decisions a conflict of rights, between Arts 8 and 2, arose. Where there is such a conflict, it may be appropriate to look at the principles underlying them, as in the apparent clash between privacy and press freedom,[315] or between freedom of expression and freedom of religion[316] in an effort to resolve the conflict at the level of principle, but where the underlying principles are probably entirely opposed, as in this instance, it would be incumbent on the judiciary to defer to Parliament, since refusing to do so would mean making a moral choice in an area of irreconcilable conflict. The term 'irreconcilable' is used to indicate that the issues in question are largely incommensurable; those taking opposing sides on the argument are unlikely to change their position whatever the

---

311 See Chapter 3, p 93–95. Some commentators, however, continue to view the allocation of any further power to the judiciary as a dangerous step and therefore consider that the protection of civil liberties should be left to Parliament; see Griffiths, 'The brave new world of Sir John Laws' [2000] March MLR 159.

312 [2001] 2 WLR 1546. This issue is considered further in Chapter 17, pp 1066–7.

313 It may be noted that if the Government brought forward such legislation, it would not need to issue a declaration of incompatibility (although it might be safer to do so to protect the legislation) since it would be overruling a precedent of the House of Lords, not the Convention guarantees themselves.

314 *Paton v UK* (1981) 3 EHRR 408; *H v Norway* No 17004/90 (1992) 73 DR 155.

315 See Emerson, C, 'The right to privacy and the freedom of the press' (1979) 14(2) Harvard Civil Rights-Civil Liberties L Rev 329, esp p 331. See further Fenwick, H and Phillipson, G, 'The doctrine of confidence as a privacy remedy in the Human Rights Act era' (2000) 63(5) MLR 660–93.

316 See Chapter 6, pp 324–45, for the argument that apparent conflicts between these freedoms are resolvable at the level of principle.

empirical evidence presented to them. To an extent, such evidence would merely be irrelevant. Where such a stark choice has to be taken, it is suggested that it is the proper role of Parliament to take it.

The proper role of activism is to uphold individual rights in the face of State interference or State neglect of the right, not to substitute judicial for State interference, in intruding on rights, even in the name of upholding competing rights. Judicial activism is justified where it results in an enhancement of the fairness and justice of public policy making, rendering public authorities accountable by reference to constitutional principle.[317] It is unjustified as a means of imposing particular views of morality on individuals. As Sir John Laws puts it, that is a matter 'upon which the judges have no special voice'.[318]

A further fear frequently expressed is that activism may seek to constrain the exercise of State power used in order to serve collective ends.[319] As this chapter indicates, the Convention, as a deeply ideological document, may be viewed as elevating individualistic, atomistic goals over socialist collective ones,[320] although the jurisprudence does not provide many examples of denial of such goals. An activist approach to it might merely be seen as exacerbating this tendency. The judiciary in other jurisdictions have often pursued what may be termed a differentiated activist approach; they may have appeared to be activist in areas with which they had sympathy, but deferential in areas with which they did not, such as trade unionism.[321] Differentiated activism may merely mean arbitrary activism. However, it may be argued that the Convention recognises collective values in the sense of seeking to underpin the democratic process[322] and of affording recognition to a wide range of public interests under para 2 of Arts 8–11. An activist judge should therefore seek to give such values full effect as key aspects of the underlying Strasbourg principles.[323] In so far as an irresolvable conflict between individualism and collectivism may nevertheless arise,[324] it is suggested that where the matter in question is one which involves a clash of moral principles and the judiciary is not well placed to assess the social and economic implications of the choice, the issue may be seen as falling within a discretionary area of

---

317 See Feldman, *op cit*, fn 23; Laws LJ, 'The limitations of human rights' [1998] PL 254.

318 Laws, *ibid*. For the view that the judiciary, and Sir John Laws in particular, are, in effect, claiming the power to determine moral and political matters, see Griffiths, 'The brave new world of Sir John Laws' [2000] 63(2) MLR 159.

319 Eg, to effect the abolition of grammar schools with a view to enhancing choice for a wider range of pupils. As is well known, the Supreme Court in the US in the 1920s and '30s used the Bill of Rights to strike down progressive employment legislation resulting from the New Deal.

320 See Ewing and Gearty, *op cit*, fn 30, but cf Feldman, *op cit*, fn 23, pp 173–78; see also review by Phillipson, G [1998] PL 538 of F Donson's chapter 'Can the common law really protect rights?' in Leyland and Woods (eds), *Administrative Law Facing the Future*, 1998.

321 See, eg, *Re Public Service Employee Relations Act* [1987] 1 SCR 313.

322 See Mowbray, A, 'The role of the European Court of Human Rights in the promotion of democracy' [1999] PL 703. See also Gearty's comments on its role in 'Democracy and human rights in the European Court of Human Rights: a critical appraisal' 51(3) NILQ 381.

323 See further Chapter 10, p 583 and Chapter 9, pp 422–26. See also Feldman, *op cit*, fn 23, pp 173–76; Mowbray, *ibid*.

324 See *Young James and Webster v UK* (1981) 4 EHRR 38.

judgment. This would be a much narrower area than that indicated by Lord Hope, by the margin of appreciation doctrine or by traditional common law deference, which, as indicated, tended in certain contexts to allow the abrogation of fundamental rights. Arguably, it would allow the boundaries of permissible activism to be delineated with reasonable clarity while still affording efficacy to the rights.[325]

The HRA itself clearly represents a choice as to the responsibility for resolving moral and political issues. Under it, judicial activism has limits; a government determined to advance collectivist goals can do so through primary legislation which cannot be struck down by the judiciary under the Act, while the response to a finding that legislation is incompatible with the Convention is in executive and parliamentary hands. This is due to the determination to preserve parliamentary sovereignty under the Act. The other side of this coin is that a government determined to push through classic civil rights-abridging legislation, such as the Terrorism Act 2000, or the Anti-terrorism Crime and Security Bill 2001, can also do so without fear of judicial 'striking down'. These dual and conflicting aspects of judicial activism and of sovereignty arise from the attempt to reconcile conflicting constitutional aims which lies at the heart of the HRA.

7 SCRUTINY OF THE WORKINGS OF THE HRA

Under the White Paper, a very significant aspect of the reception of the Convention into domestic law was to be the eventual setting up of a Human Rights Commission. The consultative paper suggested that such a Commission would probably have a number of roles which would include: providing guidance and support to those wishing to assert their rights, along the lines of the role of the Equal Opportunities Commission; instituting proceedings in its own name; scrutinising new legislation to ensure that it conforms with the Convention and monitoring the operation of the new Act.[326] Setting up such a Commission would therefore have been a significant step towards ensuring the efficacy of the Convention, in a number of respects. Unfortunately, it was not provided for under the HRA. Scotland, however, will have a Human Rights Commission,[327] as does Northern Ireland.[328] The experiment in Northern Ireland will be worth watching in this respect, and could provide a partial model for a future Human Rights Commissioner, although the Northern Ireland Commissioner has particular concerns regarding religious discrimination which are not applicable in England and Wales. Developments may be triggered by these Commissions which may increase the pressure for setting up such a body in England. The decision not to set up a Human Rights Commission, as proposed in the Green Paper,[329] created a clear weakness in the extra-judicial enforcement of the Act.

---

325 This approach appears to be in accord with that originally put forward by Pannick, *op cit*, fn 283, pp 549–51.

326 See Consultative Paper, p 11. For discussion of the role of the Commission, see Spence, S and Bynoe, I (1997) 2 EHRR 152.

327 The Justice Minister, Jim Wallace, stated that he is in favour of a Scottish Human Rights Commission: The Scottish Executive: An Open Scotland, SE/1999/51, November 1999.

328 The Belfast Agreement promised that Northern Ireland would have such a Commission. For discussion, see Harvey, C and Livingstone, S, 'Human rights and the Northern Ireland peace process' [1999] EHRLR 162, pp 168–74.

329 *Bringing Rights Home: Labour's Plans to Incorporate the ECHR into UK Law: A Consultation Paper*, December 1996 (1997). See Spencer, S, 'A Human Rights Commission', in Blackburn, R and Plant, R (eds), *Constitutional Reform: The Labour Government's Constitutional Reform Agenda*, 1999, p 395.

The presence of Commissions in the rest of the UK clearly emphasises the anomaly of failing to set up an English and Welsh one.

A Joint Parliamentary Committee on Human Rights has been set up under the Chairmanship of Professor David Feldman which will, *inter alia*, advise on legislation.[330] It is expected that it will fulfil a very valuable role. But the responsibility for the extra-judicial promotion and enforcement of the HRA is clearly fragmented. As indicated above, the Human Rights Unit and the Human Rights Task Force, set up by the Home Office, have a role in providing guidance to public authorities as to their responsibilities under the HRA, and in monitoring their progress. Further responsibility for monitoring the compliance of the key public authorities with the Convention may tend to devolve to existing bodies, all of which are bound by s 6, such as the Police Complaints Authority, the Parliamentary Intelligence and Security Committee, the Interception of Communications and Surveillance Commissioners.[331] It has been argued that the proliferation of such bodies tends to lead to the maintenance of inconsistent standards of human rights.[332] A Human Rights Commission would aid in co-ordinating the work of existing bodies with a responsibility for protecting human rights, including the HRU, the EOC, the Commission for Racial Equality and the Disability Rights Commission.

Conclusions

In considering a wide range of civil liberties and human rights, this book examines the emerging effects of the HRA in various contexts. It will argue that its impact will be immensely variable, depending on the context, but that it provides, in particular, opportunities of reversing the erosion of fundamental freedoms which occurred under Thatcher, Major, and now under New Labour in the contexts of public protest, State surveillance and suspects' rights, especially those of terrorist suspects. In the completely different context of privacy rights asserted against the media, it also offers an impetus to the developments that were already occurring in the pre-HRA era.

This book takes the stance that since the Convention has been given further effect in domestic law, it should be taken seriously, since the alternative would be likely to lead to a *decrease* in State accountability. That alternative might be more damaging than the previous constitutional position. The Convention rights might be minimised and undermined in Parliament and in the courts. In Parliament, the rights might become merely empty guarantees which cast a legitimising cloak over rights-abridging legislation and executive action.[333] Under the model termed 'minimalist', judges could duck the hard issues, purporting to review government actions under the Convention standards, but adopting a deferential stance which fails to create any real accountability. An appearance of human rights auditing might be created which was belied by the reality.

---

330 See Blackburn, R, 'A Parliamentary Committee on Human Rights', in Blackburn and Plant, *ibid*.

331 See Chapter 11 for discussion of the Commissioners; their role, under different titles, will be similar to the previous one.

332 See further Beckett, S and Clyde, I, 'A Human Rights Commission for the UK: the Australian Experience' (2000) 2 EHRLR 116.

333 This danger was pointed out by Connor Gearty in 'Terrorism and human rights: a case study in impending legal realities' (1999) 19(3) LS 367, p 379.

As Chapter 2 indicated, the Convention creates a moral structure which incorporates a set of values into UK law. Some are absolute; some have presumptive priority over competing social interests.[334] The Convention jurisprudence employs concepts recognised and developed across the world by judges who may be viewed as defending a particular set of liberal values. These may be employed in a counter-majoritarian fashion in the sense that they aid in the protection of the rights of weak and unpopular groups. But in the case of the HRA, their judicial use is subject to the possibility of using the parliamentary override. Within this compromise, previous and future erosions of liberty may be countered. And it will be crucial for the judiciary to consider other international human rights treaties to which the UK is a signatory, as well as human rights jurisprudence from other jurisdictions, since it will often be found that the same issues have arisen elsewhere. The Canadian and New Zealand jurisprudence may be of most relevance, since their Bills of Rights are of relatively recent origin and show strong similarities with the HRA. While such jurisprudence cannot merely be transplanted wholesale into the UK situation,[335] it may aid both in using the under-theorised Strasbourg jurisprudence, with its dependence on the margin of appreciation doctrine, and in encouraging the domestic judiciary to adopt a more theorised approach to human rights.[336]

But, at various points in this book, the view is taken that a narrow doctrinal legal analysis is at best incomplete and at worst, positively misleading. Thus critical analysis of, for example, the theoretical protection for individuals under the HRA or any particular enactment is of little value without an awareness of the influence of wider societal factors. There should be an awareness of how much that theoretical protection is in reality available to the underprivileged individuals who are often in most need of asserting their rights (in particular, working class black men, the most likely target of police harassment or misuse of police powers, such as stop and search). Moreover, this argument can be applied to the whole enterprise of protecting human rights under the HRA and outside it. Reliance should be placed, not only on the judiciary and on traditional legal remedies, but on the other bodies which can contribute to its success, based on the notion of seeking to afford a genuine efficacy to human rights.

---

334 The rights fall into three groups: those which are absolute: Arts 3, 4, 6(2), 6(3), 14 and First Protocol Art 3; those which are very narrowly qualified: Arts 2, 5, 6(1), 7, Sixth Protocol Art 1 (read with Art 2) and those which are materially qualified: Arts 8–12, First Protocol Art 1. See further Chapter 2, p 18.

335 See Watson, A, *Legal Transplants in Comparative Law*, 1993.

336 See the criticisms of their traditional approach advanced in Fenwick, H and Phillipson, G, 'Public protest, the HRA and judicial responses to political expression' [2000] PL 627–50.

PART II

EXPRESSION

INTRODUCTION

Part II covers a number of aspects of expression, including political expression in the form of public protest, and pornographic expression. It also covers access to official information since, without such access, some expression will be curbed or cannot occur at all. This introduction considers the justifications underlying the legal protection offered to freedom of expression, their recognition in the Strasbourg and domestic jurisprudence and the implications of the justifications for the legal restrictions on expression. The chapters contained in Part II consider the restrictions domestic law places on expression – the traditional starting point for discussion of expression in the UK – but then they go on to consider the impact of the Human Rights Act on those restrictions. In so doing, it will take account of the discussion, in Chapter 2, of the freedom of expression guarantee under Art 10 of the European Convention on Human Rights, and of a number of the other aspects of the Strasbourg jurisprudence. The main focus of these chapters will be on the changes that are likely to occur in the protection for expression under the Human Rights Act as the Strasbourg jurisprudence permeates this area of law. This part is concerned with *expression*, since that is the term used in Art 10 – a wider term than speech: Art 10 protects expression which could only very doubtfully be termed speech. However, where the expression in question consists of speech, that term will be used.

In this Part, it will be found that the right to freedom of expression comes into conflict with to freedom from manifestations of racially discriminatory views and the right to a fair trial. It has also been viewed as conflicting with the right to freedom of religion. It is apparent from the Convention jurisprudence that, where two Convention rights come into conflict, some kind of balancing act between the two needs to be undertaken.[1] Although jurisprudence in this area is very limited, it appears that the margin of appreciation becomes particularly significant here, so that States have a fairly wide discretion in resolving the conflict.[2] Domestic courts will, therefore, have an appreciable degree of latitude in determining where to strike the balance between the two interests involved. Section 12 of the HRA, which, as Chapter 4 indicated, enjoins the courts to have 'particular regard' to Art 10 when making any order which might infringe it, appears on its face to suggest a higher weighting for speech interests. Such imbalance is also *prima facie* suggested by the strength of the 'speech' jurisprudence at both the Strasbourg and

---

1 *Otto-Preminger Institut v Austria*, Series A 295-A; (1995) 19 EHRR 34, para 55. The two Convention rights in conflict there were free speech itself and – so the court found – the right to religious freedom, protected by Art 9.

2 See *Otto-Preminger Institut v Austria*, Series A 295-A; (1994) 19 EHRR 34. The restriction on Art 10 entailed by the seizure of an allegedly blasphemous film was justified by reference to the Art 9 right to freedom of religious belief. The Court applied a wide margin of appreciation, and simply said that 'the content of the film cannot be viewed as incapable of grounding' the conclusion of the national authorities that seizure was justified (para 56). Thus the test applied was reminiscent of the narrow Wednesbury standard of unreasonableness. See further Chapter 6, pp 317–19. See also *Wingrove v UK* (1997) 24 EHRR 1.

domestic levels discussed above. In *Ex p Simms*,[3] Lord Steyn referred to free speech as 'the primary right ... in a democracy' and some commentators take the view that Art 10 attracts an especially high level of protection at Strasbourg.[4]

However, save for admitting the distinction between those rights stated in absolute terms, such as Arts 3, 4 and 7 and those subject to generalised exceptions (8–11), Strasbourg has never sought to establish a hierarchy of Convention rights. Rather, where rights collide, it has advocated a careful examination of the competing claims of each in the light of all the circumstances of the case.[5] There is no indication that Parliament, in passing the HRA, intended to alter this position and create a serious imbalance between the two rights;[6] rather, it is evident that the sponsors of the amendment saw it merely as a domestic reflection of the Strasbourg approach.[7] Moreover, the un-balanced American approach is out of line with other jurisdictions and flows from factors peculiar to that jurisdiction, in particular the absolute nature of the First Amendment.[8]

Free expression justifications

All countries which have a Bill of Rights protect freedom of expression because it is perceived as one of the most fundamental rights. But why should this particular freedom be viewed as so worthy of protection? Why, as Barendt puts it, should speech which offends the majority have any special immunity from government regulation 'while there would be no comparable inhibition in restraining conduct [such as public] love-making which has similar offensive characteristics?'.[9] Four main justifications for offering protection to free speech have been offered and will be considered here in turn. In each case, an indication will be given as to the kinds of expression the various justifications will support because all the theories will not be relevant to all forms of expression. Initially, it should be noted that three of the justifications are inherently more contingent and therefore precarious than the first. These three justifications – the arguments for the opportunity to arrive at the truth through free discussion, for the necessity of free speech to enable meaningful participation in democracy and for individual self-fulfilment – all ultimately argue that speech is to be valued not for its own sake, but because it will lead to some other outcome we think desirable; thus, they may be characterised as teleological justifications. If, therefore, when considering a particular form of speech, a persuasive argument can be made out that allowing the speech is likely to achieve a result antithetical to the desired outcome, protection will no longer be justifiable. By contrast, as will be seen below, it is inherent in the first main justification for free speech – the argument for moral autonomy – that arguments about the likely effects of allowing the

---

3   [1999] 3 All ER 400, CA; [1999] 3 WLR 328, HL

4   Leigh, I and Lustgarten, L, 'Making rights real: the courts, remedies, and the Human Rights Act' (1999) 58 CLJ 509, p 524 and n 79.

5   See the views of Lord Steyn and Lord Cooke in *Reynolds v Times Newspapers* [1999] 4 All ER 609, pp 631 and 643.

6   An amendment providing that a court should 'normally' give precedence to Art 10 over Art 8 was rejected (HC Deb Vol 315 Cols 542–43, 2 July 1998).

7   See, eg, the speech of Jack Straw on new cl 12: HC Deb Vol 315 Cols 535–39, 2 July 1998.

8   See below, p 211.

9   Barendt, E, *Freedom of Speech*, 1987, p 1.

particular speech are not relevant to the question whether the justification applies – although clearly, such arguments may still be relevant in deciding whether the speech should nonetheless be abrogated.

The argument from moral autonomy

This argument was outlined in Chapter 1 as one of the most powerful justifications for human rights in general and so will only briefly be rehearsed here. Ultimately, whether the particular argument used is Rawls's hypothetical social contract[10] or Dworkin's basic postulate of the State's duty to treat its citizens with equal concern and respect,[11] this justification for free expression is centred around the liberal conviction that matters of moral choice must be left to the individual. In either case, the conclusion reached is that the State offends against human dignity,[12] or treats certain citizens with contempt if the coercive power of the law is used to enforce the moral convictions of some upon others. The argument perhaps has a more common and conspicuous application with regard to sexual autonomy and so is often disregarded in arguments about free speech.[13]

The justification is less contingent than the others, as mentioned above, because any restriction on what an individual is allowed to read, see or hear, clearly amounts to an interference with her right to judge such matters for herself. Thus, the argument consistently defends virtually all kinds of speech and other forms of expression,[14] whereas the arguments from truth and democracy[15] will tend to have a somewhat less comprehensive range of application. Since the argument also sets up freedom of speech as a strong 'trump' right,[16] or as part of the individual's claim to inviolability,[17] the right in both cases overrides normal utilitarian arguments about the benefit or detriment to society of the particular form of speech under consideration.[18] By contrast, the justifications from democracy and truth both set out goals for society as a whole and, therefore, would seem reasonably to allow abrogation of speech in the interests of other public concerns which may be immediately and directly damaged by the exercise of speech. As Barendt puts it, in discussing the argument from truth: 'a government worried that inflammatory speech may provoke disorder is surely entitled to elevate immediate public order considerations over the long term intellectual development of the man on the Clapham omnibus.'[19]

---

10 See Chapter 1, p 6.

11 See Chapter 1, pp 6–7.

12 Barendt makes the point, however, that unlimited speech may also assault human dignity (*op cit*, fn 9, pp 16–17). This argument is considered in relation to pornography below: Chapter 6, pp 271–74.

13 Barendt, eg, comments (*op cit*, fn 9, p 16) that the 'general freedom to moral autonomy [is] perhaps without much relevance to free speech arguments'.

14 It also covers material which could only doubtfully be classified as speech, eg, photographic pornography.

15 See below, p 270.

16 Ronald Dworkin's phrase; see Chapter 1, p 12.

17 The idea is Rawls's; see Chapter 1, p 11.

18 For a discussion of justifications allowing strong rights to be overridden, see Chapter 1, pp 12–14.

19 *Op cit*, fn 9, p 10.

The argument from truth

The most famous exposition of this argument is to be found in JS Mill's *On Liberty*.[20] The basic thesis is that truth is most likely to emerge from free and uninhibited discussion and debate. It is worth noting that this is a proposition about a causal relationship between two phenomena – discussion and truth – which of course has never been conclusively verified. However, its general truth is taken as virtually axiomatic in the Western democracies and forms the basic assumption underpinning the whole approach of reasoned, sceptical debate which is the peculiar hallmark of Western civilisation. Nonetheless, the crude assumption that more free speech will always lead to more truth has been attacked by certain feminist writers, who consider that the free availability of pornography leads not to the revelation of truth, but to the creation of false and damaging images of women or, more controversially, that pornography actually 'constructs the [sexist] social reality of gender'[21] – a claim which will be examined in detail in Chapter 6.

It appears that Mill envisaged his argument as applicable mainly to the expression of opinion and debate, but it can equally well be used to support claims for freedom of information, since the possession of pertinent information about a subject will nearly always be a prerequisite to the formation of a well-worked-out opinion on the matter. However, *prima facie*, it may be thought that the theory does not immediately make it clear when we need to know the truth about a given subject. Thus, it could be argued that a delay in receiving certain information (owing, for example, to government restrictions) would not greatly matter, as long as the truth eventually emerged. In response to this, it may be argued that if truth is valued substantively – a position most would assent to[22] – then any period of time during which citizens are kept in ignorance of the truth or form erroneous opinions because of such ignorance, amounts to an evil, thus giving rise to a presumption against secrecy. If, alternatively or in addition, knowledge of the truth is valued because of its importance for political participation, then clearly it will be most important to know the information at the time that the issue it concerns is most likely to affect the political climate. This rationale would thus provide a strong argument against the propensity of UK governments to attempt to conceal political secrets until revelation would no longer have a damaging effect on their interests.[23]

Clearly, whether truth is valued instrumentally – for example, as essential to self-development – or as a good in itself, some kinds of truths must be regarded as more important than others.[24] Thus, in the context of a collision between free speech and privacy rights, the small intrinsic value of knowing the facts about (say) a film star's sexual life juxtaposed with the implausibility of the notion that such information would enable more effective political participation or individual growth, provides reasonable

---

20 Mill, JS, *On Liberty*, in Cowling, M (ed), *Selected Writings of John Stuart Mill*; Everyman, 1972.

21 MacKinnon, C, *Feminism Unmodified*, 1987, p 166.

22 Mill, as a utilitarian, would probably not see truth as inherently valuable, but rather as a very important means of ensuring the overall welfare of society.

23 As seen, eg, in the so called 'Thirty Year Rule' now contained in the Public Records Act 1958. See below, Chapter 7, pp 371–72.

24 It is outside the scope of this work to attempt a full scale normative inquiry into the relative value of different truths. A commonsensical consensus approach is all that is employed in the text, where it is suggested only that the mere satisfaction of curiosity without more is of a relatively low value compared to the ending of a deception.

grounds for favouring the privacy interest in such a case. By contrast, revelations about corruption amongst prominent politicians will arguably not only have a more important part to play in the formation and development of individuals' general opinions, they will also play a vital role in enabling informed contribution to be made to the political process. Thus, a compelling argument for favouring free speech in this situation is readily made out. We will return to this argument in Chapter 10.

The argument from participation in a democracy

Barendt describes this theory as 'probably the most attractive of the free speech theories in modern Western democracies' and concludes that 'it has been the most influential theory in the development of 20th century free speech law'.[25] The argument, which is associated primarily with the American writer Meiklejohn,[26] is simply that citizens cannot participate fully in a democracy unless they have a reasonable understanding of political issues; therefore, open debate on such matters is essential. In so far as democracy rests upon ideas both of participation *and* accountability, the argument from democracy may be seen to encompass also the function which a free press performs in exposing abuses of power,[27] thereby allowing for their remedy and also providing a deterrent effect for those contemplating such wrong-doing.[28] The influence of this argument can be seen in the fact that directly political speech has a special protected status in most Western democracies.

Such speech does not, at present, have any general legal guarantee in the UK, but when the British judiciary consider the claims of free speech, they seem in general to be particularly concerned to protect free criticism of the political authorities. Thus, in the seminal House of Lords decision in *Derbyshire v Times Newspapers*,[29] Lord Keith, in holding that neither local nor central government could sustain an action in defamation, said: 'It is of the highest importance that a democratically elected governmental body should be open to uninhibited public criticism'. The fact that he based his decision on *this* justification for free speech and not on, for example, the individual right of journalists to express themselves freely, is evidence of judicial endorsement of the argument from democracy – and also, possibly, of their failure to give much consideration to other, rights-based justifications. The fact that the judiciary have mainly, or even only, this interest in mind when considering threats to free speech, helps to explain why they are so often prepared to allow speech to be overridden by other considerations. This is because this argument sees speech as a public interest and as justified instrumentally by reference to its beneficial effects on democracy, rather than seeing it as an individual right of inherent value. Therefore, clearly, it can render speech vulnerable to arguments that it should be overridden by competing public interests which are also claimed to be essential to the maintenance of democracy. Hence Margaret Thatcher's well known justification for the media ban challenged unsuccessfully in the *Brind* case:[30] 'We do sometimes have to

---

25 *Op cit*, fn 9, pp 20 and 23 respectively.
26 See, eg, his 'The First Amendment is an absolute' (1961) Sup Ct Rev 245.
27 See Blasi, V, 'The checking value in First Amendment theory' (1977) Am B Found Res J 521.
28 See Greenwalt, K, 'Free speech justifications' (1989) 89 Columbia L Rev 119, p 143.
29 [1993] AC 534; [1993] 1 All ER 1011; [1992] 3 WLR 28, HL.
30 *Secretary of State for the Home Dept ex p Brind* [1991] 1 AC 696; [1991] 1 All ER 720; [1991] 2 WLR 588, HL.

sacrifice a little of the freedom we cherish in order to defend ourselves from those whose aim is to destroy that freedom altogether.' Clearly, to a judge who sees the value of free speech only in terms of its contribution to the political process, an argument that allowing the speech in question will do more harm than good to the maintenance of democracy will always seem compelling. This is not to argue that this justification is fundamentally flawed – clearly its basic premise is correct and offers an important reason to protect speech – but rather that one should be wary of using it as the sole justification even for directly political speech.

There is, however, an argument which does see the justification as fundamentally flawed because it would appear to allow suppression of free speech by the democracy acting through its elected representatives. However, this objection may be answered by the argument that certain values, such as protection for minorities and fundamental freedoms generally, are implicit in any mature conception of a democracy.[31] Therefore, the term 'democracy' or the furtherance of democracy should not be narrowly defined to include only the decisions of the particular government in power, but should also encompass the general principles mentioned; by affording respect to such principles, democracy will ultimately be preserved. This argument would suggest that the justification would appear to have little direct relevance to sexually explicit forms of expression or blasphemous speech but, on the other hand, since freedom of expression is arguably one of the freedoms the suppression of which would undermine democracy, protection for these forms of speech can also be argued for by the justification. It should be borne in mind, however, that as this argument depends on a separate and somewhat controversial contention about the nature of democracy, it offers only an indirect defence of non-political speech.[32] Nevertheless, if the above contention is accepted, one may then conclude that the argument from democracy is actually concerned to further two values: maintenance of the democracy and effective participation in it. The two values are distinct in that although effective as opposed to passive or inert participation may help to secure maintenance of the democracy, nevertheless some of its members, while wishing to see its continuance, might not wish to participate actively in it. Thus, political speech would contribute to the maintenance of both the values, while other forms of speech would contribute only to the first, confirming what was suggested at the outset, namely that this justification argues for special protection of political speech.

The argument from individual self-fulfilment

Finally, we may turn to the thesis that freedom of speech is necessary in order to enable individual self-fulfilment. It is argued that individuals will not be able to develop morally and intellectually unless they are free to air views and ideas in free debate with each

---

31 Such a view is in fact endorsed by a number of legal philosophers and civil libertarians, and amounts to the most satisfactory reply to the charge that an entrenched Bill of Rights is undemocratic. See Dworkin, *A Bill of Rights for Britain*, 1990; the view also clearly underpins his general political philosophy, see, eg, 'Liberalism', in *A Matter of Principle*, 1985. See also Hart, HLA, *Law, Liberty and Morality*, 1963 and Lester, A, *Democracy and Individual Rights*, 1968.

32 Most commentators seem to assume that the argument from democracy has little, if any, application to pornographic material. See, eg, Dworkin, A, 'Do we have a right to pornography?' in *op cit*, p 335. Similarly, the Williams Committee did not regard the argument as pertinent to their deliberations (*Report of the Committee on Obscenity and Film Censorship*, Cmnd 7772, 1979; see below, p 270).

other. However, as Barendt notes,[33] it may be objected that free speech should not be singled out as especially necessary for individual fulfilment; the individual might also claim that, for example, foreign travel or a certain kind of education was equally necessary. On the other hand, freedom of speech represents a means of furthering individual growth which it is possible to uphold as a 'negative freedom'; other methods of furthering individual freedom would require positive action on the part of the government.

This justification is clearly rights-based and, as such, in theory at least, is less vulnerable to competing societal claims; however, it does not value speech in itself, but rather, instrumentally, as a means to individual growth. Therefore, in situations where it seems that allowing free expression of the particular material will be likely to retard or hinder the growth of others or of the 'speaker', the justification does not offer a strong defence of speech.[34] Precisely this argument has been used by feminist commentators to justify the censorship of pornography. Thus, MacKinnon asserts that far from aiding in the growth of anyone, 'Pornography strips and devastates women of credibility'[35] through the images of women it constructs in its readers' minds. The thesis which forms the basis of the UK law on obscenity – that certain kinds of pornography actually damage the moral development of those who read it by depraving and corrupting them, similarly fastens onto the argument that this kind of material achieves the opposite of the outcome which allowing freedom of expression is designed to ensure.[36] The apparent vulnerability of the argument from self-development when used to justify the protection of material which is arguably degrading[37] leads Barendt to suggest[38] that a sounder formulation of the theory is one which frames it in terms of the individual's right to moral autonomy. It is submitted that moral autonomy does provide the most persuasive defence of sexually explicit 'speech' and this argument will be developed when obscenity law is discussed. However, it will also be argued that autonomy is conceptually distinct from the notion of self-fulfilment and that nothing is to be gained by conflating the two concepts.

Implications for restrictions on expression

It is argued that the justifications considered would support the following propositions, which will be used as analytical tools to examine the soundness of the legal responses to expression considered in this Part, including those from Strasbourg. But the complex

---

33   *Op cit*, fn 9, p 15.

34   Barendt argues (*op cit*, fn 9, pp 16–17) that justifications for suppressing some forms of speech could be advanced on the basis that human dignity (the value promoted by allowing self-development) would thereby receive protection. He cites the finding of the German Constitutional Court that there was no right to publish a novel defaming a dead person as such publication might violate the 'dignity of man' guaranteed by Art 1 of the German Basic Law (*Mephisto* (1971) BVerfGE 173).

35   *Op cit*, MacKinnon, fn 21, p 193.

36   It should be noted first that pro-censorship feminists deny that their arguments have anything in common with conservative objections to pornography, eg, *op cit*, MacKinnon, fn 21, p 175, and secondly that the feminist thesis on pornography is far more complex than this. It will be explored in more detail in Chapter 6.

37   Dworkin also concludes that the argument from self-fulfilment fails to defend pornographic speech: 'Do we have a right to pornography?' in *A Matter of Principle*; he founds his defence on moral autonomy and, like the present writer, clearly regards this concept as offering a separate head of justification.

38   *Op cit*, fn 9, p 17.

issues raised by these propositions cannot possibly be considered in sufficient depth here; full treatment can be found in books dealing specifically with theories underlying freedom of expression,[39] and it may be noted that books dealing with the potential for importing free expression jurisprudence from other jurisdictions,[40] which has addressed many of the hard issues, are likely to increase in number as one of the results of the inception of the Human Rights Act.

Content and form-based interferences

As a starting point, content-based restrictions should be regarded with more suspicion than those based on *form*, since all of the free speech justifications potentially argue against such restrictions. Content-based restrictions, other than those constraining deliberate lies, prevent certain messages from ever entering the arena of debate and therefore run counter to the arguments from truth and self-fulfilment. Such restrictions prevent persons from knowing of, let alone evaluating, a particular message, thereby infringing their autonomy and, where the message is a political one, running counter to the argument from democracy. Thus, a regime committed to free speech would strongly condemn such restrictions. On this argument, a scholarly thesis arguing that the Holocaust caused far fewer deaths than is generally accepted would fall within the area of protected expression, while the handing out of leaflets and the putting up of posters by a Nazi group in a Jewish community designed to demonstrate precisely this point, might not.[41]

But the idea of seeking to ensure content neutrality (an inquiry into the validity of restrictions that completely ignores the *content* of expression) in an absolutist fashion immediately runs into some difficulties.[42] Two key problems are identified here. First, while the idea can be sustained in the example given above, it is clear that in others, the manner in which a message is conveyed may be as significant, or more significant, than the message itself.[43] The examples of symbolic protest, mime, music and art are only some of those that come to mind. The use of various techniques, such as imagery and symbolism, is not only significant, but indissociable from the message. Indeed, such techniques convey a message. In a crude sense, they are the vehicle by means of which the 'message' is conveyed, but they not only interact with it, but also convey a host of emotive and cognitive 'messages' themselves. Secondly, form-based restrictions cannot be fully divorced from content-based ones, since it is only in relation to certain contents that the issue of form is raised. Time, place and access (based on age) restrictions are less problematic, since the infringement of freedom of expression they represent may tend to

---

39　See Schauer, F, *Free Speech: A Philosophical Enquiry*, 1982; Barendt, *op cit*, fn 9; Waluchow, WJ (ed), *Free Expression: Essays in Law and Philosophy*, 1994; Campbell, T and Sadurski, W (eds), *Rationales for Freedom of Communication*, 1994.

40　A provocative and interesting forerunner of such books is Loveland, I (ed), *Importing the First Amendment, Freedom of Expression in Britain, Europe and the USA*, 1998.

41　This example is, of course, reminiscent of the famous 'Nazis at Skokie' affair. A group of Nazis wished to demonstrate, wearing Nazi uniforms and displaying swastikas, in a predominantly Jewish community. They relied, successfully, on their First Amendment right to do so, in a case that divided civil libertarians: *Collin v Smith* (1978) 578 F 2d 1197, 7th Cir; (1978) 436 US 953; (1978) 439 US 916.

42　See Feldman, D, 'Content neutrality', in Loveland, *op cit*, fn 40, Chapter 8.

43　See *Cohen v California*, (1971) 403 US 15, below, p 321.

be insignificant in relation to achieving the ultimate goals indicated by the free speech justifications.

Thus, while it is suggested that all four free speech justifications (depending on the message) would argue against content-based restrictions, they might all also be engaged by form-based restrictions. Moreover, when one examines the justifications themselves, it can be found that they will support restrictions on expression in the furtherance of non-expression values. The feminist argument in this respect is considered below. In relation to forms of hate speech, it can be argued that it is an invasion of moral autonomy and militates against self-fulfilment for someone to be *forced to witness* expression deeply offensive to her (either because it is so pervasive as to be unavoidable or because it is likely that she will encounter it unwittingly). *A fortiori* this is the case when the speech goes beyond offensiveness and becomes threatening.[44] Speech that is impliedly or expressly (so called 'fighting words') threatening or intimidatory may well impair an individual's autonomy since it has such a direct impact on her in the free ordering of her life.

It is concluded, first, that while content-based restrictions should be viewed with great caution, an engagement in the nature of the content when considering restriction is necessary, especially in terms of the impact on identifiable individuals, defined by their group status. Secondly, the argument in favour of creating simplistic distinctions between content and form is unsustainable. The extent to which the form of the expression can be said to engage the free speech justifications has to be considered. Third, while time, place and access restrictions should be rigorously scrutinised on the basis of proportionality, they are prima facie less disturbing than content or form-based ones.

Market freedom and creative freedom

The second proposition is, contrary to the US 'marketplace' model,[45] that market freedom is far from consonant with creative freedom. As Barendt puts it, in relation to US thinking: 'A market-place which few can enter does nothing for the principle that debate on public issues should be uninhibited, robust and open.'[46] Promoting market freedom will tend to mean the dominance of the media by certain conglomerates.[47] It may, therefore, lead to homogenous expression which reflects unchallenged majority viewpoints. Thus, some

---

44 As in the case of attacks on religious faith or homophobic, racist or sexist expression targeted directly at specific individuals. Examples of offensive behaviour that might readily become threatening would include putting up pornographic posters of women in the work place, sexist, homophobic or racist remarks directed at an employee, displaying an offensive symbol such as a swastika at work (see Chapter 16, pp 1007–10) or targeting persons in their homes as part of a racist campaign and, eg, putting leaflets through the door, painting racist graffiti on the house. Cf *RAV v City of St Paul, Minnesota* (1992) 112 S Ct 2538; 120 L Ed 2d 305 in which a group of racist youths burnt a home-made cross in the front yard of a black family. It was found in the Supreme Court that the Ordinance under which one of the youths was charged was overbroad and content-based: expressive conduct of this nature causing offence was protected speech under the First Amendment.

45 See Schauer, F, 'The political incidence of the free speech principle' (1993) 64 US Colorado LR 935.

46 See 'The First Amendment and the media', in Loveland, *op cit*, fn 40, Chapter 8, pp 43–44. The quotation is from *New York Times v Sullivan* (1964) 376 US 254, 270. Barendt goes on to attack the market place model on a number of further grounds; he argues that the pressures of advertisers will influence mass communication and, further, that when corporate interests determine the media agenda, and do not provide access to the means of communication for dissenters, certain ideas cannot enter the 'free' market.

47 See Feintuck, M, *Media Regulation, Public Interest and the Law*, 1999.

intervention in the market, with the free speech justifications in mind, is warranted, with a view to furthering creative freedom. Such intervention would limit cross-media ownership – the concentration of ownership in different media sectors – and would seek to protect a public service element – as opposed to the reflection of purely commercial values – in, for example, the granting of licences to broadcast and in the monitoring of output. Such an element might include requirements to broadcast at peak times programmes reflecting minority interests, experimental and original drama, investigative documentaries ('must carry' requirements).[48] Toleration of such intervention is founded on the understanding that commercial television has a dual concern which will influence its output. It must satisfy the companies who use it to advertise their products that it can deliver a mass audience, which means that it must be able to provide programming which attracts and satisfies such an audience. Therefore, unlike books, music, art, or, to an extent, newspapers, a central concern is to satisfy the advertisers. Regulation is therefore warranted in order to prevent creative freedom from being outweighed by commercial concerns.

This is a matter that is, of course, especially pertinent in relation to media regulation, but the general proposition has implications going beyond current regulatory schemes[49] and, indeed, is relevant in relation to the Human Rights Act itself.[50] The proposition covers the use of libel laws by big business,[51] rights of access to the print media,[52] interpretations of contempt law,[53] access to publicity at election times, the suppression of protest (by, for example, environmental activists) in the corporate interest.[54]

The US model

Both these propositions suggest that the US freedom of expression model should be treated with caution, although this is not to say that it should not be referred to domestically, under the HRA, as providing an extensive and rich source of jurisprudence. Under the US model, all content-based restrictions on protected speech – speech protected under the First Amendment – are self-evidently unconstitutional, as indicated below.

The US model has been strongly influenced by the 'American's characteristically profound suspicion of government and the whole-hearted belief in the socially beneficial effects of unfettered economic freedom and individual endeavor ... these traits have generated a model of the State which precludes government and courts from offering protection against significant forms of social and personal harm'.[55] The Strasbourg model, as this part will indicate, contrasts strongly with the American one in tolerating content-based restrictions that relate to the exceptions under Art 10(2).

---

48   See Chapter 6, pp 296–99 and 307–08.
49   See Chapter 6, pp 296–99.
50   See Chapter 4, p 160 and Chapter 6, pp 307–08.
51   See Wilmo, P and Rodgers, W (eds), *Gatley on Libel and Slander*, 1998, para 2.19.
52   See Chapter 10, p 560.
53   See Chapter 5, pp 223–27.
54   See Chapter 9, pp 513–15.
55   See Feldman, 'Content neutrality', in Loveland, *op cit*, fn 40, Chapter 8, p 140.

Recognition of these justifications in Strasbourg and UK expression jurisprudence

The high regard in which freedom of expression, and particularly press freedom, is held by the Strasbourg institutions was indicated in Chapter 2. The Court has repeatedly asserted that freedom of expression 'constitutes one of the essential foundations of a democratic society',[56] and that it 'is applicable not only to "information" or "ideas" that are favourably received or regarded as inoffensive or as a matter of indifference, but also to those that "offend, shock or disturb"'.[57] Particular stress has been laid upon 'the pre-eminent role of the press in a State governed by the rule of law' which, 'in its vital role of "public watchdog"' has a duty 'to impart information and ideas on matters of public interest' which the public 'has a right to receive'.[58]

However, while the rhetorical attachment to free speech is always strong, it is a marked feature of the Strasbourg jurisprudence that clearly political speech, which may be seen as directly engaging the self-government rationale, receives a much more robust degree of protection than other types of expression. Barendt's contention that this is 'the most influential theory in the development of 20th century free speech law'[59] is supported by examination of the approach of UK and Strasbourg judges. As indicated above, the basic thesis is that citizens cannot participate fully in a democracy unless they have a reasonable understanding of political issues; therefore, open debate on such matters is necessary to ensure the proper working of a democracy; as Lord Steyn has put it: 'freedom of speech is the lifeblood of democracy.'[60]

Thus, the 'political' speech cases of *Sunday Times*,[61] *Jersild*,[62] *Lingens*,[63] and *Thorgeir Thorgeirson*[64] all resulted in findings that Art 10 had been violated and all were marked by an intensive review of the restriction in question in which the margin of appreciation was narrowed almost to vanishing point.[65] By contrast, in cases involving artistic speech, supported by the values of autonomy and self-development rather than self-government, an exactly converse pattern emerges: applicants have tended to be unsuccessful and a

---

56 *Observer and Guardian v UK* A 216 (1991), para 59.

57 See, eg, *Thorgeirson v Iceland* (1992) 14 EHRR 843, para 63.

58 *Castells v Spain* A 236 (1992), para 43.

59 *Op cit*, fn 9, pp 20 and 23 respectively.

60 *R v Secretary of State for the Home Dept ex p Simms* [1999] 3 All ER 400, p 408.

61 *Sunday Times v UK* A 30 (1979). The case concerned a contempt of court action brought against the newspaper in respect of revelations it published concerning the dangers of the drug Thalidomide (for discussion, see Chapter 5, pp 229–30).

62 *Jersild v Denmark* (1994) 19 EHRR 1 concerned an application by a Danish journalist who had been convicted of an offence of racially offensive behaviour after preparing and broadcasting a programme about racism which included overtly racist speech by the subjects of the documentary.

63 *Lingens v Austria* (1986) 8 EHRR 103 concerned the defamation of a political figure.

64 *Thorgeirson v Iceland* (1992) 14 EHRR 843 concerned newspaper articles reporting allegations of brutality against the Reykjavik police.

65 See the discussion of the doctrine in Chapter 2, pp 34–37.

deferential approach to the judgments of the national authorities as to its obscene or blasphemous nature has been adopted.[66]

A similar pattern may be discerned in the domestic jurisprudence: when speech supported by the arguments from self-development or autonomy rather than self-government is in question, decisions have tended to be cautious,[67] or downright draconian,[68] and accompanied by little or no recognition of these underlying values. The most lofty rhetorical assertions of the importance of free speech and the strongest determination to protect it have been evident in cases where journalistic material raises political issues, broadly defined.[69] In such cases, the courts have either overtly adopted the Strasbourg principles described above[70] or have strongly emphasised the high status freedom of speech holds in the common law, as 'a constitutional right', or 'higher legal order foundation'.[71] Earlier pronouncements to the effect that: 'The media ... are an essential foundation of any democracy'[72] have recently been emphatically reinforced by pronouncements in the House of Lords' decision in *Reynolds v Times Newspapers*[73] which afforded an explicit recognition to their duty to inform the people on matters of legitimate public interest. Press freedom in relation to political expression has clearly been recognised as having a particularly high value in UK law and Convention jurisprudence.

66 *Müller v Switzerland* (1991) 13 EHRR 212; *Gibson v UK*, Appl No 17634 (declared inadmissible by the Commission); *Handyside v UK*, A 24 (1976) (not a case involving artistic speech but where the issue was that of obscenity); *Otto-Preminger Institut v Austria* (1994) 19 EHRR 34; *Gay News v UK* (1982) 5 EHRR 123. In *Wingrove v UK* (1997) 24 EHRR 1, the Court remarked: 'Whereas there is little scope under Article 10(2) of the Convention for restrictions on political speech or on debate of questions of public ... a wider margin of appreciation is generally available to the Contracting States when regulating freedom of expression in relation to matters liable to offend intimate personal convictions within the sphere of morals or, especially, religion' (para 58). These cases are discussed in Chapter 6, pp 280, 293–94 and pp 317–20. See Harris, J, O'Boyle, M and Warbrick, C, *Law of the European Convention on Human Rights*, 1995, pp 397 and 414.

67 *Gibson* [1990] 2 QB 619. See Chapter 6, pp 293–94.

68 *Knuller v DPP* [1973] AC 435. In *Lemon* [1979] AC 617, the House of Lords held that the common law offence of blasphemy required no mental element, and that there was no defence of public interest. See further Chapter 6, pp 314–15.

69 *Reynolds v Times Newspapers* [1999] 4 All ER 609; *Derbyshire CC v Times Newspapers* [1993] AC 534; *R v Secretary of State for the Home Dept ex p Simms* [1999] 3 WLR 328. However, deference to widely drafted primary legislation (*Secretary of State for Home Affairs ex p Brind* [1991] 1 AC 696) or governmental arguments from national security (*AG v Guardian Newspapers (No 2)* [1990] 1 AC 109) has resulted in the ready upholding of restrictions on directly political speech.

70 See the approach of the Court of Appeal in *Derbyshire* [1993] AC 534 and in *Ex p Leech* [1994] QB 198, of the House of Lords in *Reynolds* [1999] 4 All ER 609, pp 621–22, *per* Lord Nicholls, pp 628 and esp 635, *per* Lord Steyn, p 643, *per* Lord Cooke and *Ex p Simms* [1999] 3 WLR 328, p 407, *per* Lord Steyn and pp 419–20, *per* Lord Hobhouse.

71 *Reynolds v Times Newspapers* [1999] 4 All ER 609, pp 628–29 (Lord Steyn). In *Ex p Simms* [1999] 3 WLR 328, p 411, Lord Steyn described the right as 'fundamental', as did Lord Hoffman, p 412.

72 *Francome v MGN* [1984] 2 All ER 408, p 898, *per* Sir John Donaldson.

73 *Per* Lord Steyn [1999] 4 All ER 609, pp 633–34; Lord Nicholls: 'freedom to disseminate and receive information on political matters is essential to the proper functioning of the system of parliamentary democracy cherished in this country' (p 621).

The theory that freedom of speech is necessary for the discovery of truth[74] has been a strong influence in US jurisprudence,[75] but not historically at Strasbourg[76] or in the UK courts.[77] The argument from self development – that the freedom to engage in the free expression and reception of ideas and opinions in various media is essential to human development[78] – has received some recognition at Strasbourg[79] and recently in the House of Lords.[80]

Free speech protection in practice[81]

In the US, the country with perhaps the greatest commitment to freedom of speech, the First Amendment to the Constitution provides: 'Congress shall make no law abridging the freedom of speech or of the press.' This stricture is not interpreted absolutely literally, but it does mean that US citizens can challenge a law on the sole ground that it interferes with freedom of expression. However, freedom of expression is not absolute in any jurisdiction; other interests can overcome it, including the protection of morals, of the reputation of others, the preservation of public order, national security and protecting the interest in a fair trial. In fact, freedom of expression comes into conflict with a greater variety of interests than any other liberty and is therefore in more danger of being curtailed. Most Bills of Rights list these interests as exceptions to the primary right of freedom of expression, as does Art 10 of the European Convention on Human Rights. This does not mean that the mere invocation of the other interest will lead to displacement of freedom of expression; it is necessary to show that there is a pressing social need to allow the other interest to prevail.[82]

Although, until the inception of the Human Rights Act, the UK had no Bill of Rights protecting freedom of expression, Art 10 of the European Convention on Human Rights was taken into account by the courts in construing ambiguous legislation on the basis, as Chapter 3 indicated, that as Parliament must have intended to comply with its Treaty

---

74 See above, pp 202–03; see further Greenwalt, K, 'Free speech justifications' (1989) 89 Columbia L Rev 119, pp 130–41 generally.

75 See the famous *dicta* of Judge Learned Hand in *United States v Associated Press* 52 F Supp 362, p 372 (1943); and of Holmes J, dissenting but with the concurrence of Brandeis J, in *Abrams v United States* 250 US 616, p 630 (1919).

76 The repeated reference by the ECtHr to freedom of expression being one of the 'basic conditions for [society's] progress' (see, eg, *Otto-Preminger Institut v Austria* (1994) 19 EHRR 34, para 49) could be seen as a reference to the justification.

77 But see recently *Secretary of State for the Home Department ex p Simms* [1999] 3 All ER 400, p 408, *per* Lord Steyn.

78 Eg, Emerson argues that the right to free expression is justified as the right of the individual to realise his character and potentialities through forming his own beliefs and opinions ('Towards a general theory of the First Amendment' (1963) 72 Yale LJ 877, pp 879–80); see also Redish, M, *Freedom of Expression*, 1984, pp 20–30 and *op cit*, Greenwalt, fn 74, pp 143–45.

79 One of the stock phrases of the European Court of Human Rights in relation the value of freedom of expression asserts that it is one of the 'essential foundations for the 'development of everyone' (eg, *Otto-Preminger* (1995) 19 EHRR 34, para 49).

80 *Per* Lord Steyn in *Ex p Simms* [1999] 3 All ER 400, p 498.

81 For comment, see Marshall, G, 'Freedom of speech and assembly', in *Constitutional Theory*, 1971, p 154; Barendt, *op cit*, fn 9; Gibbons, *Regulating the Media*, 1998; Robertson, G and Nichol, AGL, *Media Law*, 1999; Boyle, A, 'Freedom of expression as a public interest in English law' [1982] PL 574; Singh, 'The indirect regulation of speech' [1988] PL 212; Clayton, R and Tomlinson, H, *The Law of Human Rights*, 2000, Chapter 15; Lester (Lord) and Pannick, D (eds), *Human Rights Law and Practice*, 2000, Chapter 4, p 197.

82 See Chapter 2, p 67 for discussion of this point.

obligations, an interpretation should be adopted which would allow it to do so.[83] It has also, on occasion, been taken into account where there is ambiguity in the common law. Combined with the effects of certain very significant decisions at Strasbourg, Art 10 has had a greater impact on UK law than its fellow Article, Art 11. However, its impact has been variable. It has not had as much influence as might perhaps have been expected as far as the laws of obscenity and decency are concerned. As Chapter 9 explains, it has also had little effect on expression in the form of public protest. This part covers access to information which, as Chapter 7 indicates, does not appear to be covered by Art 10, although such access may be viewed as associated with expression.

Under s 3 of the Human Rights Act, the obligation to interpret legislation compatibly with Art 10, and the related Arts 9[84] and 11, will be much stronger than it was in the pre-HRA era, while the courts and other public authorities, including the police, will be bound by the Convention under s 6 to uphold freedom of expression. As Chapter 2 indicated, Art 10 provides a strong safeguard for freedom of expression in relation to competing interests, since it takes the primary right as its starting point. The content of speech will rarely exclude it from the protection of Art 10, although not all speech is included.[85] Article 10(2) demands that interferences with the primary right should be both necessary and proportionate to the legitimate aim pursued. But the interferences with expression, considered in the following chapters, have not all been subject to the same intensity of scrutiny at Strasbourg. The reasons why this is so will be considered in those chapters.

As the following chapters indicate, there are two methods of protecting the other competing interests mentioned: prior and subsequent restraints on freedom of expression. Prior restraints are generally seen as more pernicious and therefore countries with a Bill of Rights either outlaw them or keep them to a minimum. In the case of censorship, such restraints are viewed as particularly inimical to free speech, since they may operate outside the public domain and may therefore generate little or no publicity. Decisions will be taken by an administrative body, often with no possibility of challenge in the courts. On the other hand, subsequent restraints operate after publication of the article in question: the persons responsible may face civil or criminal liability. The trial may then generate publicity and the defendants may have an opportunity of demonstrating why they published the article in question. In other words, the case for allowing the speech in question is given a hearing.[86] However, the distinction between the two kinds of restraint may not be as stark as this implies. Subsequent restraints may have a chilling effect on publications; editors and others may well not wish to risk the possibility of incurring liability and may therefore themselves take the decision not to publish without reference to any outside body. In the case of prior restraints granted by the courts, usually injunctions, the case in favour of publication will normally be heard.

---

83 See further Chapter 3, pp 108–10.

84 See Chapter 2, pp 73–74.

85 In *Jersild v Denmark* (1994) 19 EHRR 1 it was assumed that the actual racist utterances of racists in a broadcast were not protected. In *Janowskki v Poland* (1999) 5 BHRC 672 it was found that insults to civil servants acting in their public capacity were protected, although the interference was found to be justified.

86 See Barendt, E, 'Prior restraints on speech' [1985] PL 253.

When one turns to consider UK law in this area, one confronts a mass of common law and statutory restrictions on freedom of expression and on expressive activities associated with it such as marches or demonstrations. Traditionally, in order to determine how far freedom of expression was protected, it was necessary to consider the width of these restrictions in order to determine how much of an area of freedom was left within which expression could be exercised. The Human Rights Act has altered that position in the sense that the media and citizens generally should be able to rely on the Art 10 guarantee, against public authorities. Therefore, domestic freedom of expression should be determined by the scope of the Art 10 protection, bearing in mind the duty of national courts, discussed in Chapter 4, to disapply the margin of appreciation doctrine. The extent to which the judiciary take an activist or minimalist approach to that doctrine in relation to expression will be of particular significance, since Strasbourg has applied a review of very varying intensity in this context. The development of the domestic law, whether by way of legislation or the common law, is still highly significant, since all of it will have to be tested more directly against Art 10.

It will be found that the law in this area has developed in an incoherent fashion. A willingness to accept the values of freedom of expression,[87] rather than relying strongly on those that traditionally attracted protection, especially proprietorial rights, became apparent in the 1990s, as Chapter 3 indicated. But where expression came into conflict with those values that had traditionally gained acceptance, such as maintaining public order, such values remained in the ascendant. The lack of a consistent pattern was arguably due to the lack of a free expression clause against which the other interests had to be measured. The emphasis of these chapters has to be on the judges' concern to strike a balance between free expression and a variety of other interests in the pre-HRA era, and the impact of Art 10 on the stance adopted. A pervasive critical theme will be the exposure of the judges' readiness to allow freedom of expression to be restricted on uncertain or flimsy grounds. It will be found in certain contexts that some of the interests identified by judges as justifying such restrictions would not qualify as sufficient grounds for outweighing the right of free expression under the liberal conception of rights outlined in Chapter 1. In such contexts, the impact of Art 10 will, therefore, be of especial significance. In others, it will become apparent that domestic law already satisfies Art 10 requirements.

In considering UK law it will be argued that, outside the public order or anti-terrorist context, statutes in this area give, in general, greater protection to freedom of expression than does the common law and that during the 1980s and 1990s it came particularly under threat, partly, but not exclusively, through common law developments, although, as indicated above, there were also a number of recent important judgments favouring freedom of speech. A theme which runs through this part concerns the extent to which the common law has undermined statutory safeguards for freedom of speech. This is a matter of especial significance under the Human Rights Act, since inconsistent common law provisions can be disregarded when applying the guarantee under Art 10 to a public authority. As Chapter 4 explained, incompatible common law provisions do not enjoy the protection afforded to statutory ones.

---

87 See the House of Lords' decisions in the *Derbyshire* case [1993] AC 534; [1993] 1 All ER 1011; [1992] 3 WLR 28 and in *Ex p Simms* [1999] QB 349, considered above in Chapter 3, p 108.

This is not to argue that no English statute will have to be modified by interpretation now that Art 10 has been given further effect in UK law under the Human Rights Act. The strong interpretative obligation of s 3 means that the doctrine of precedent need not be adhered to in ensuring that a public authority satisfies Art 10. In examining the statutory provisions considered in this Part, it will become apparent that some of them, especially in the field of public protest, provide extremely wide powers intended to protect other interests. It must, however, be remembered that they were framed by a Parliament which had no legal brake upon its powers; it did not have to have regard to a written constitution forcing it to take freedom of expression into account. Thus, at times, it has been prepared to frame laws which, if fully enforced, would severely damage freedom of expression. Post-2000, as Chapter 4 argues, new legislation affecting freedom of expression is, and will almost invariably be accompanied by a statement of its compatibility with the Convention, but this does not mean that incompatibility will not be found. Further, the statement may be issued on the basis of an interpretation grounded in a minimal version of the Convention. It is suggested that this is true of parts of the Terrorism Act 2000, discussed further in Chapters 8 and 9, in relation to its effect on freedom of expression.

But pre- and post-Human Rights Act legislation affecting freedom of expression shares the same characteristic: the laws are not usually fully enforced; if they were, the consequent clash between the media and the government would bring the law into further disrepute. Thus, although by examining the provisions of these statutes an indication of the 'balance' Parliament had in mind may be gained, other more nebulous factors, including the influence of powerful media bodies, must also be taken into account. Such factors may not apply in relation to public protest, and one of the concerns of this part is to reveal the different emphasis placed on expression arising as protest rather than as an aspect of media freedom.

But the main concern of this part is to evaluate the change in this 'balance' which may occur under the Human Rights Act and to consider the extent to which such a change reflects the theoretical justifications underpinning various aspects of freedom of expression. The extent to which such justifications are likely to play a part in determining the resolution of the conflict between expression and a number of societal and individual interests, under the Human Rights Act, will form a central theme.

CHAPTER 5

RESTRAINING FREEDOM OF EXPRESSION UNDER THE LAW OF CONTEMPT

1 INTRODUCTION[1]

This chapter is essentially concerned with two interests which are frequently perceived as being in conflict: the interests in protecting the administration of justice and in media freedom. The protection of the administration of justice is a general aim which is not concerned solely with protecting the right of the individual to a fair trial, although it may have that effect. Domestically, the interest in the administration of justice has been protected by the law of contempt. A number of aspects of contempt law are discussed below, including its use in curbing pre-trial discussions and publicity in the media which might influence those involved in forthcoming proceedings, threats to justice in the long term sense, and requirements to disclose journalistic sources. It is apparent that, *prima facie*, contempt law creates interferences with the guarantee of freedom of expression under Art 10. The interference may be justified where it has the legitimate aim of 'maintaining the authority and impartiality of the judiciary' under para 2. This phrase may be taken to cover the preservation of the integrity of the administration of justice, including the rights of litigants. Since contempt law has a role to play in preventing prejudice to proceedings or deterring the media from causing such prejudice, it may be viewed as a means of protecting Art 6 rights,[2] although the main responsibility for providing such protection falls on the trial judge.[3] Viewed as exceptions to Art 10, such rights fall within the rubric 'the rights of others' in para 2, as well as that of 'maintaining the authority of the judiciary'. (Since court proceedings may bring an individual to the attention of the media, with the result that details of their personal lives are revealed, the guarantee of respect for privacy under Art 8 may also be relevant; the implications of this possibility are discussed in Part III, Chapter 10.) Contempt law therefore comes into conflict with free expression, either on the basis of protecting general societal interests or other individual rights. Article 6 is not engaged where the threat is to the administration of justice in a general or long term sense. Similarly, the use of contempt law to require the disclosure of sources would not normally engage Art 6, although it clearly does create an interference with the Art 10 guarantee, and moreover one which is viewed at Strasbourg as particularly serious, as indicated below.

But the notion that free speech and the administration of justice are likely to come into conflict should be examined further. This part began by arguing that one of the most

---

1   General reading: for a historical overview, see Fox, *The History of Contempt of Court*, 1927; Arlidge, A and Eady, D, *Contempt of Court*, 1982 (for background); Goodhart, AL, 'Newspapers and contempt of court in England' (1935) 48 Harv LR 885; Sufrin, B and Lowe, N, *The Law of Contempt*, 1996; Miller, CJ, *Contempt of Court*, 1999; Barendt, E, *Freedom of Speech*, 1987, Chapter 8; Robertson, G, *Media Law*, 1999, Chapter 6; Arlidge, A and Smith, ATH, *Arlidge, Eady and Smith on Contempt*, 2nd edn, 1999; Barendt, E and Hitchens, L, *Media Law: Cases and Materials*, 2000, Chapters 12, 13, 14; Clayton, R and Tomlinson, H, *The Law of Human Rights*, 2000, Chapter 15; Marshall, G, 'Press freedom and free speech theory' [1992] PL 40; Laws LJ, 'Problems in the law of contempt' (1990) CLP 99; Naylor, B [1994] CLJ 492; Laws LJ (2000) 116 LQR 157.

2   See Chapter 2, pp 57–63.

3   See the comments of Simon Brown LJ regarding the differing roles of the judge in contempt proceedings and at trial: *AG v Birmingham Post and Mail Ltd* [1998] 4 All ER 49.

influential justifications for free speech arises from the part it plays in furthering democratic values. Speech which, under strict scrutiny, undermines the fairness of a trial can be viewed as attacking such values rather than upholding them. Chapter 10 argues that the conflict between speech and privacy is more apparent than real since, as Emerson puts it, the rights are 'mutually supportive in that both are vital features of the basic system of individual rights'.[4] It is suggested that, to an extent, this may also be said of free speech and fair trials. In a democracy, free speech serves the ends of justice since the free debate of conceptions of justice may allow for the inclusion of a variety of views within the process of justice which will therefore enhance its moral authority.[5] Thus, if one of the justifications for speech is that it supports the fairness of trials by scrutinising justice, as an aspect of the 'open' justice principle, speech which, on careful scrutiny, creates unfairness may legitimately be restricted since it undermines that central justification. In other words, freedom of speech has a key role as an essential aspect of a fair system of justice, but speech which affects the impartiality of a hearing may undermine public confidence in the role of the courts and the administration of justice, and can therefore undermine its key role.

Further, it is a central tenet of a democracy that justice should not be arbitrary and, therefore, the State has a duty to ensure that all have equal access to justice. As Chapter 1 indicated, rights are premised on the notion that the State has a duty to treat all its citizens with equal concern and respect. That notion underlies, it is argued, both free speech and fair trials. If the fair trial of an individual is arbitrarily affected by media coverage, since that individual is accused of a crime which has caught public attention, the State has failed to secure equal access to justice. Therefore, restrictions on such coverage may be justified on the basis that free speech which creates such an interference undermines an aspect of its own underlying rationale.

In many such instances, no sufficient competing aspect is available in order to found the argument that the restrictions are unjustified, since the speech in question may be trivial and sensationalist, motivated solely by profit-making concerns. The fact that newspaper coverage constitutes 'speech' should not be allowed to obscure the failure of some sensationalist coverage of certain cases to participate in almost all the justifications for affording speech primacy over competing interests. Moreover, the guarantee under Art 10 is most strongly engaged, not only when those justifications, especially the argument from democracy, are at stake, but when the promulgator of the speech is also observing the duties and responsibilities which accompany the exercise of the freedom.[6] Such responsibilities include that of avoiding the invasion of the interests protected under para 2 in a manner which is unnecessary in a democratic society and which is motivated and determined merely by market considerations. Thus, it may be concluded that careful differentiation must be maintained between speech which conflicts with the underlying aims of both free speech and justice, and speech which furthers those aims.

But the argument regarding the harmony between the furtherance of the ends of both justice and speech may break down, it is suggested, where the dominant conception of

---

4   Emerson, C, 'The right to privacy and the freedom of the press' (1979) 14(2) Harvard Civil Rights-Civil Liberties L Rev 329, p 331.

5   See further Allan, TRS, 'Procedural fairness and the duty of respect' [1988] 18 OJLS 497, esp pp 507–10.

6   Article 10, para 1.

justice is itself arguably flawed and an instance arises, related to a specific trial, which is especially illustrative of that flaw. In other words, it provides a strikingly paradigmatic example, which may not soon be repeated. For example, the percentage of convictions for rape is extremely low. In a rape trial, the fact that a defendant had a number of rape convictions, or had been acquitted of rape on numerous occasions, would not normally go before the jury. If a newspaper, which was campaigning for improvement in the conviction rate for rape, disclosed such facts pre-trial, as part of its campaign, and, in particular, as part of an argument that rape convictions should be disclosed to the jury, it might seek to justify its publication on the basis that it would influence debate as to conceptions of justice in such trials and might therefore serve the ends of both free speech and justice. The interest in the *efficacy* of speech as well as in its justifications in a formal sense could be relied on in an effort to outweigh the argument that the use of this particular trial in order to give bite to the campaign had undermined the principle of equal access to justice.

This example illustrates the difficulty of formulating a general principle of harmony between the interests involved. But, as a general proposition, subject to exceptions, it is suggested that the idea of antinomy between free speech and fair trials is misconceived. If these underlying ideas are taken into account, they provide a means of analysing domestic and Convention rules for their legitimacy in terms of the harmony between free speech and the administration of justice identified here. Where they fail to promote such harmony, reforms will be suggested. It will be argued that the Convention jurisprudence has gone somewhat further than domestic jurisprudence in recognising such harmony, bearing in mind the central aim of the Convention, which is to protect and promote democratic values. However, in certain instances, it will be suggested that the influence of the margin of appreciation doctrine has led to failures in this respect.

The central concern of this chapter is the probable impact of the Convention under the Human Rights Act on aspects of domestic contempt law. It will indicate that the domestic development of the law of contempt has been quite strongly influenced by the Strasbourg jurisprudence. While the common law afforded supremacy to the administration of justice, Strasbourg aided in the creation of a shift in favour in freedom of expression. Nevertheless, despite the influence of the Convention, this chapter will contend that domestic contempt law fails to satisfy Art 10 in certain respects. It will also be argued that, as currently administered, it fails to protect the administration of justice and, in some respects, to meet the demands of Art 6. The response of UK contempt law to findings at Strasbourg and the judicial domestic interpretations of the Convention have not shown a sufficient appreciation, it will be argued, of its key underpinning values. In particular, the extent to which the apparent conflict between Arts 10 and 6 may be resolvable at the level of principle has largely gone unrecognised. These failings are revealed, it will be contended, by testing contempt law and practice directly against Convention standards under the Human Rights Act.

2 PREJUDICING PROCEEDINGS

A central area of contempt law is that which is concerned with publications potentially interfering with the course of justice in civil or criminal proceedings. Media bodies may incur liability for contempt due to potentially prejudicial reporting of and discussion of, or relating to, pending proceedings. This form of contempt is therefore intended to limit the freedom of the media to report on or comment on issues arising from, or related to, the administration of justice. Such restriction answers to a genuine public interest in ensuring that justice is properly administered and is unaffected by bodies who are unlikely to judge the merits of a case fairly. If, for example, a large number of tabloids, in pursuit of a newsworthy story, take the view that a defendant is guilty, they may slant stories and pictures so that they seem to give that impression and such coverage may affect the jury. If so, the conviction will have been influenced by the partial views of a certain group of people who do not have all the evidence available to them and are influenced by concerns other than the concern to ensure fairness in decision making. If a trial seems to have been prejudiced by unfair reporting, a successful appeal may be brought on that basis,[7] but this method only creates a remedy for the defendant; it does not deter the media from such behaviour in future. No one would argue that this is a desirable method of preventing prejudice to the administration of justice, since it may allow the factually guilty to be acquitted or the innocent to be convicted.

In seeking to avoid such interferences with the course of justice while also affording protection to the freedom of the press, States have chosen to adopt either a *preventive* or a *neutralising* model,[8] or a mixture of both. Both models seek to ensure fair hearings, but the former seeks to do so by curbing media freedom to an extent, the latter by insulating the hearing from potentially prejudicial publications, while leaving media freedom largely intact. Under the preventive model, the State seeks to prevent the publication of potentially prejudicial material while allowing non-prejudicial reporting of proceedings and of discussion relating to them. This model has traditionally been used in the UK. Under the neutralising model, the emphasis is placed on dealing with the potential effects of prejudicial material, by means of procedural devices aimed at ensuring the impartiality of the jury. Such devices include the use of strong directions to the jury, jury challenges, changing the trial venue, stays, and sequestration of the jury. If neutralising measures fail, the remedial measure of acquittal may be the last resort. Since the First Amendment provides an unqualified guarantee, the emphasis in the US has been on neutralising measures rather than on sanctions intended to deter the media from publishing potentially prejudicial material.[9] In *Nebraska Press Association v Stuart*[10] the Supreme Court held that adverse publicity before a trial would not necessarily have a prejudicial effect on it and that therefore, a prior restraint would not be granted. Barendt, commenting on this decision, argues that subsequent restraints might therefore also be unconstitutional; thus, a conviction might not be obtained in respect of an already

---

7 See the successful appeal on this basis in *Taylor* (1993) 98 Cr App R 361, CA (for discussion, see below, p 236).

8 See Cram, I, [1998] EHRLR 742.

9 See *Knapp* (1990) 114 L Ed 2d 763 on the detailed questioning of jury members; see Chesterman (1997) 'OJ and the dingo: how media publicity for criminal jury trials is dealt with in Australia and America' 45 Am Jo Comp Law 109 and *Cram* [1998] EHRLR 742 on the US neutralising approach generally. As the most extreme neutralising measure, a conviction may be quashed and a retrial ordered. In *Shepherd v Maxwell* (1966) 384 US 333, a re-trial was ordered because of the extensive media coverage. For comment on *Shepherd v Maxwell*, see Grant, A, 'Pre-trial publicity and fair trial' (1976) 14 Osgoode Hall LJ 275. The neutralising measure of sequestration of the jury was used in the trial of OJ Simpson in 1995 and attracted widespread criticism in the UK.

10 (1976) 427 US 539.

published article which created a risk of prejudicial effect.[11] Therefore, witnesses' statements may be obtained pre-trial, while assertions of guilt or confessions and hearings to determine the admissibility of evidence[12] may all be made public. The use of procedural devices such as delaying the trial, or changing its venue, as an alternative to restraining the media, are not always very effective, leaving open the possibility that defendants may appeal against conviction and obtain an acquittal owing to the publicity. Certain US commentators therefore favour adoption of the preventive approach used in Britain.[13]

When Canada adopted the Charter of Rights and Freedoms in 1982, the Supreme Court considered that the common law stance of affording the fairness of trials priority over free speech had been changed by the Charter and that therefore, adherence to a neutralising rather than a preventive model had become appropriate. The Court found that a ban on pre-trial publication should only be ordered when 'alternative measures', such as jury sequestration, could not prevent the risk of prejudice.[14] In contrast, Australia has adopted a stance more akin to that of domestic common law, although somewhat less restrictive of freedom of expression.[15]

It is argued below that, contrary to the view which some commentators have taken,[16] Strasbourg has on the whole adopted a preventive rather than a neutralising approach and that therefore, the Convention under the Human Rights Act, unlike the Canadian Charter, does not demand a radical change in the stance of UK law, in this context. Moreover, bearing in mind the arguments outlined above, regarding the underlying harmony of values between free speech and the fair administration of justice, it is argued that the preventive is, in general, to be preferred to the neutralising model since much speech which, under close scrutiny, creates prejudice to trials runs counter to its own underlying justifications, while at the same time the quality of justice may be affected by using neutralising measures.[17] It must be pointed out, however, that the preventive model may become unworkable owing to current technological changes, particularly the use of the internet and the proliferation of websites, a point which will be developed further below. Bearing these points in mind, the central argument will be that while radical change is unnecessary in this area of contempt law, certain reforms are necessary in order to meet, in full, the demands both of media freedom and the administration of justice, as recognised under the Convention, but interpreted domestically under the Human Rights Act.

---

11 Barendt, E, *Freedom of Speech*, 1987, p 228.

12 *United States v Brooklier* (1982) 685 F 2d 1162; *Re Application of Herald Co* (1984) 734 F 2d.

13 See Krause (1996) 76 Boston UL Rev 357.

14 See *Dagenais v Canadian Broadcasting Corpn* (1995) 120 DLR (4th) 12, p 37. For comment, see Horwitz, 'Jury selection after *Dagenais*: prejudicial pre-trial publicity' (1996) 42 CR 220.

15 For discussion of the Australian approach, which contrasts it with that adopted in the US, see Chesterman (1997) 45 Am Jo of Comp Law 109. In Australia, contempt cannot be committed until proceedings are pending: *James v Robinson* (1963) 109 CLR 593.

16 Mann, FA has written: 'In a potentially wide variety of cases the European Court may assume a revising function and impose continental standards or, perhaps one should say abuses, upon this country which, in the name of freedom of the press and discussion are likely to lower English usages by the substitution of trial by media for trial by courts' (1979) 95 LQR 348, p 352.

17 This point has been made by Chesterman (1997) 45 J Comp Law 109 and by Krause (1996) 76 Boston UL Rev 357. Clearly, devices such as delaying the trial may mean that defendants will spend longer in custody; the stress of victim-witnesses may be increased; memories of the relevant events may fade.

The Strasbourg stance

Under Art 10, an interference with the guarantee of freedom of expression can be justified if it is prescribed by law, has a legitimate aim and is necessary in a democratic society. Proceedings against a media body for contempt in respect of its coverage of a forthcoming or ongoing action, or of issues impliedly or expressly linked to it, may be justified if they have the legitimate aims of protecting the 'rights of others' and/or of 'maintaining the authority and impartiality of the judiciary'. The 'rights of others' exception covers Art 6 rights. The 'authority' of the judiciary refers to the acceptance of the courts as the proper forums for the settlement of disputes.[18] The term 'impartiality' refers to the preservation of confidence in the courts by persons engaged in dispute settlement and the public in general.[19] This exception was apparently included in the Convention at the instigation of Britain precisely to cover contempt of court.[20] The other European signatories have no clearly comparable law, although laws regulating pre-trial publicity are common.

As indicated, this form of contempt law can be viewed as protecting the right to a fair trial, together with the societal interest in preserving the integrity of the administration of justice. It can be argued, therefore, that where this other 'strong' right is at stake, Strasbourg would accept that free speech must be more readily compromised, unless in the particular instance the speech would in fact further the ends of justice.[21] But resolving these matters under the Convention is not entirely straightforward owing to the particular approach it adopts, which is influenced by its own structural constraints. This approach is revealed by a consideration of the stance taken at Strasbourg to claims that Art 10 has been violated by prosecutions of journalists in respect of publications bearing upon legal proceedings in the line of authority stemming from *Sunday Times v UK*,[22] *Worm v Austria*[23] and *News Verlags v Austria*.[24]

The *Sunday Times* case is discussed in full below. The State argued that the interference with freedom of expression could be justified since it served the legitimate aim of preserving the authority and impartiality of the judiciary. The stance adopted by the Court in finding a breach of Art 10 was explicable on the basis that the interest in protecting such authority or, at a more general level, the administration of justice, was very weak: little threat could be discerned since the litigation in question was dormant. Although, as an aspect of its application of the requirements of proportionality, the Court took the view that the strong free speech interest outweighed the slight impact on the administration of justice, a more satisfactory way of viewing the case is, it is argued, to say that the speech in question engaged strongly in the debate as to the proper ends of justice, but no countervailing considerations regarding equal access to justice or the creation of unfairness genuinely arose. In contrast, in *Worm*, the interference with the

---

18 *Chorherr v Austria* (1994) 17 EHRR 358.
19 *Fey v Austria* (1994) 16 EHRR 387; *Worm v Austria* (1998) 25 EHRR 454, p 473.
20 See the Joint Dissenting Opinion in *Sunday Times v UK* (1979) 2 EHRR 245, p 285, para 2.
21 See the discussion as to when 'strong' individual rights may be infringed in Chapter 1, pp 12–14.
22 (1979) 2 EHRR 245.
23 (1997) 25 EHRR 557; (1998) 25 EHRR 454.
24 (2001) 31 EHRR 8.

freedom of speech guarantee had a link with the Art 6 guarantee. An article evincing a belief in the guilt of the defendant had led to the conviction of the applicant owing to its potential influence on the criminal proceedings. It was viewed as undermining the presumption of innocence which is guaranteed under Art 6(2). The State argued that the prosecution had the legitimate aims of preserving the authority and impartiality of the judiciary and the 'rights of others'. No breach of Art 10 was found. This was an instance in which it could more readily be argued that the speech ran counter to the underlying speech-supporting rationales. But, it is also suggested that the Court conceded a margin of appreciation to the State in failing to scrutinise in detail the question whether prejudice to the proceedings was genuinely likely to arise. Similarly, in *BBC Scotland v UK*,[25] the effect of a broadcast on specific proceedings was taken into account under the 'rights of others' exception and the need for the interference was not subjected to a strict scrutiny. Had it been, it is possible that a breach of Art 10 might have been found, bearing in mind the lack of direct references to the case.

In contrast, in *News Verlags v Austria*,[26] which concerned a somewhat weaker Art 10 claim, the 'rights of others' exception was invoked, but the application succeeded. The case concerned the prosecution of the company for the publication of a photograph of a right wing extremist, B, who was accused of sending letter bombs as part of a political campaign. The text accompanying the photograph accused him of being the perpetrator of the attacks. The applicant company complained that court decisions prohibiting it from publishing the photograph in the context of reports on the criminal proceedings against it, violated its right to freedom of expression. The case turned on the proportionality of the interference with the aims pursued which were to protect the rights of others and the authority of the judiciary. The Court subjected this question to a detailed review, while conceding a narrow margin of appreciation to the State. It took into account the possible effect on the Art 6(2) rights of B. But it also took account of the facts that he had sought publicity as a Nazi activist and that the offences in question had a political background and were 'directed against the foundations of a democratic society'.[27] Reiterating the significance of the essential function of the press in a democratic society, the Court pointed out that its duty to inform the public extends to reporting and commenting on court proceedings and noted the consonance of its discharge of such a duty with the requirement under Art 6(1) that hearings should be public. The injunctions restricted the choice of the newspaper as to its presentation of reports. The Court in particular took account of the fact that although objection was taken only to the picture in conjunction with the adverse comments, the injunction created an absolute prohibition on publishing a picture of B with or without such comments. The Court concluded on that basis that there was no reasonable relationship of proportionality between the interference and the aims pursued.

It may be argued that the intensity of the review undertaken in this instance was due partly to the special circumstances of the case, especially the fact that as a right wing

---

25 (1998) 25 EHRR CD 179.

26 (2001) 31 EHRR 8; (2000) 9 BHRC 625.

27 Paragraphs 54 and 55.

extremist, B had himself sought publicity for his views in the past. The stance taken may also be indicative of the more interventionist stance the Court has tended to take in the last few years, discussed in Chapter 14.[28] But the key point was that the photograph alone was unlikely to cause prejudice to the proceedings and yet the effect of the injunction was to prohibit any publication of the photograph, even if accompanying a fair and accurate factual report of the proceedings. The injunction, therefore, had the potential to curb both free speech and, indirectly, the openness of the proceedings, since such a report was found to be consonant with that aspect of Art 6(1). Thus, the Court made explicit, in a partial sense, the consonance between Arts 10 and 6. That line of argument could, as indicated, have been taken further and the broader harmony between the aims of free speech and the protection for the administration of justice could have been clearly indicated.

Given the tendency of the Court to view its approach to the interests of freedom of expression and the administration of justice as 'the balancing of competing interests'[29] where a claim raising these issues arises under Art 10, it is arguable that the stance taken would have differed had the Austrian Court refused to grant the injunction and B had brought a claim to Strasbourg, arguing for a violation of Art 6(2). In *Ribemont v France*[30] an application brought on the basis of a violation of the Art 6(2) guarantee owing to the effect of a publication succeeded once the violation was found since, apart from provisions allowing for the exclusion of persons from a hearing in certain circumstances (see below), Art 6 is not qualified. In other words, where a matter comes to light in the form of an Art 10 claim, the Court's reasoning follows the contours of that Article which require it to afford presumptive primacy to freedom of expression and to regard the administration of justice as an exception to that right. It is perhaps inevitable, then, that the two interests will be viewed, broadly, as competing. Where the same issues arise in the form of an Art 6 claim, there can be no balancing of competing interests except as regards the requirements of a public hearing in Art 6(1). The choices thereby apparent, embedded in the moral framework of the Convention, inform us that Art 6 takes precedence over Art 10. But if the harmony between these interests argued for in this chapter is to be recognised, the domestic courts are not required to adopt the same stance. In any event, as argued below, the means – mainly actions for contempt – of allowing for the recognition of these interests in domestic law would not require them to do so.

These differences of approach to Art 10 claims are not explicable simply by reference to the question whether the 'rights of others' exception can be said to be at stake in any particular instance. It is necessary also to consider the role played by the margin of appreciation doctrine. The *Sunday Times* case established that the interference with freedom of expression represented by curbing media freedom to comment on a forthcoming action or on issues linked to it must answer to a pressing social need.[31] Where, as in that instance, the interference is aimed – broadly – at the protection of the

---

28 See pp 900–01.

29 Paragraph 56, relying on the judgment in *Bladet Tromsø and Stensaas v Norway* (2000) 29 EHRR 125; (1999) 6 BHRC 599.

30 (1995) 20 EHRR 557. The Court found that Art 6(2) had been breached by a statement made by the French Minister of the Interior and senior police officers at a press conference in which they named the applicant as involved in a murder.

31 (1979) 2 EHRR 245, para 62.

administration of justice, but has only a very indirect and uncertain justification in terms of protecting litigation, the review of the existence of such a need is likely to be intense. But where the interference appears to be strongly linked to the preservation of Art 6 rights, it may be less intense and the interference may be found to be justified, as in *Worm* and *BBC Scotland v UK*. The margin of appreciation conceded was narrow in the *Sunday Times* case, since the Court took the view that the notion of the authority and impartiality of the judiciary is an objective one which can, therefore, be closely scrutinised. But, in contrast, as Chapter 4 pointed out, where two rights are viewed as in conflict, the Court tends to afford a wide margin of appreciation.

It may be concluded, therefore, that where a conflict between free speech and a fair trial arises at Strasbourg as an Art 6 claim, the Convention does not adopt the stance that the two strong individual rights can be balanced against each other. Where a direct threat to the fair trial of an individual arises, the guarantee under Art 6 will prevail, since it is not materially qualified. Where, in contrast, the issue arises as part of an Art 10 claim, the Art 6 issue will be considered as an exception to it, and the individual right at stake will be afforded recognition by this means, together with the general interest in 'maintaining the authority of the judiciary'. Where *both* exceptions are at stake, Strasbourg review may tend, as indicated, to be less intense, although where harmony between the primary right and the exceptions can be discerned in terms of their underlying values, this will affect the intensity of the review, as in *News Verlags*. But where the interference cannot be viewed as directly protecting the interests of specific individuals in fair proceedings, as in the *Sunday Times* case, although its operation clearly directly infringes the individual freedom of expression of specific journalists, the free speech principle will prevail, unless the interference answers to a pressing social need. Under the Strasbourg rhetoric, therefore, regarding competing interests, some recognition of the consonance between the values underlying them is evident despite the obscuring effect of the margin of appreciation doctrine.

Approaches to the domestic impact of the Convention under the Human Rights Act

A court, adjudicating on an action for contempt against a media organ will be bound by all the Convention rights under s 6 of the Human Rights Act (HRA) and must ensure that, in particular, Arts 10, 6 and 8 are satisfied. It must also interpret the Contempt of Court Act 1981 compatibly with the Convention under s 3. But, the discussion above has indicated that the impact of the Convention on this area of domestic contempt law is likely to be far from straightforward. It is not enough to argue merely that the Convention will demand a shift towards freedom of expression, since such an argument would fail to appreciate its much wider and more varying demands, and the relationship between those demands and the role played by the doctrine of the margin of appreciation.

In so far as, traditionally, domestic contempt law favoured the protection of the administration of justice over the protection of freedom of expression, it failed to strike a balance which is consistent with the Convention. The domestic inquiry has always begun by considering the law governing the interference with the negative liberty of expression. The domestic courts have traditionally been preoccupied with the administration of justice rather than with individual rights to free speech. This approach was modified in the pre-HRA era under the Contempt of Court Act 1981, which was a response to the finding at Strasbourg[32] that common law contempt had failed to afford sufficient weight to freedom of expression, as explained below. The approach adopted will now require further modification under the HRA, but the structure of domestic decision-making need not fully follow the Strasbourg model since Art 10 and, in some instances, Art 6 issues will normally arise during a contempt action[33] rather than as aspects of an Art 10 claim. Article 6 issues will also be raised during a criminal trial or on appeal as part of an argument that the jury or others would be or had been affected by the publication of prejudicial journalistic material.

As argued above, although the overturning of a conviction or a stay of proceedings can be used as a remedy where there has been a violation of Art 6 rights because of a publication, it would be more satisfactory to use preventive measures where the possibility of prejudice to proceedings genuinely arises. Strasbourg tends to favour such measures, as indicated, although where the connection between protecting the right to a fair trial and suppressing the speech in question is doubtful, it will subject them to an intense scrutiny. It will be argued that, at the present time, contempt law is failing to fulfil this preventive role, but that neutralising measures have not fully taken its place. Common law contempt afforded primacy to the interest in the administration of justice, but it is suggested that statutory contempt is not engaging fully with the core values underlying either free speech or the administration of justice. In particular, it will be argued that contempt law is failing to meet Art 6 demands that the relevant legislation, and executive decisions taken in relation to it, should be efficacious in protecting the right to a fair trial.[34] Its failure relates, it is argued, to the role of the Attorney General, who has the responsibility under s 7 of the Contempt of Court Act 1981 for initiating prosecutions against media bodies.[35] Theoretically, superior courts[36] can punish contempts on their own motion. This inherent power is preserved under s 7. In practice, the courts do not exercise this power in respect of publications subject to the strict liability rule (see below). A party to proceedings in a superior court could put, through counsel, the argument that a publication is prejudicial. The judge could then refer the matter to the Attorney General. This would not necessarily mean, however, that proceedings would be brought.[37]

The Attorney General can also seek an injunction to restrain a planned publication and, in this respect, can be viewed as having a limited vetting role.[38] He may also issue warnings to the media regarding coverage of cases which have attracted public attention.[39] The Attorney General is a member of the Cabinet. Theoretically, he or she acts

---

32 In the *Sunday Times* case (1979) 2 EHRR 245 (see below, p 229).

33 They might also arise in judicial review proceedings; this is discussed below, pp 225–26.

34 Such demands are those indicated in *BBC Scotland v UK* (1998) 25 EHRR CD 179. See also *Worm v Austria* (above, fn 23) or *News Verlags* (2001) 31 EHRR 8 although the laws at issue in those instances were not contempt laws.

35 Section 7 provides: 'Proceedings for a contempt of court under the strict liability rule shall not be instituted except by or with the consent of the Attorney General or on the motion of a court having jurisdiction to deal with it.'

36 In England and Wales, the House of Lords, the Court of Appeal, the High Court of Justice, the Crown Court, the Restrictive Practices Court, the Employment Appeals Tribunal, the Courts-Martial Appeal Court.

37 See *R v Taylor and Taylor* (1993) 98 Cr App R 361 (discussed below, p 252).

38 This occurred in *AG v Times Newspapers Ltd* [1974] AC 273 (see below, pp 228–29).

39 He issued such warnings in respect of the 'Yorkshire Ripper' case and in the case of Frederick and Rosemary West.

in two distinct capacities – as a member of the government and as an independent law officer. His role as law officer places him, theoretically, at a distance from the government. In practice, his impartiality may be questioned, owing to the conflict of interests which is inherent in his dual role. He may come under pressure to initiate prosecutions in cases in which the government itself has an interest. As Borrie and Lowe observe: 'in cases such as these the Attorney's role ... does smack of partisanship'.[40] Conversely, it is possible that he may be reluctant to initiate proceedings when to do so would mean bringing the government – in effect – into conflict with powerful media proprietors. Clearly, there will be variable practice between the office-holders in these respects, but this inconsistency itself has a questionable effect on the quality of justice and the protection for media freedom. As certain of the decisions discussed below indicate, it cannot be said that when the massed tabloids act, effectively, in concert in their coverage of a trial-related story, they are immune from prosecutions. But it will be argued that a reluctance to prosecute a large number of media organs simultaneously, especially those with large circulations, is evident. The result is arguably that the tendency to prosecute those parts of the press which have the most central role in furthering the values underpinning political speech is not in proportion to their tendency to affect the fairness of trials.

The Attorney General is now bound by s 6 of the HRA and, therefore, must ensure that both Arts 10 and 6 are satisfied. While it may be argued that contempt law does not directly provide a remedy where a publication has prejudiced a trial or may be about to do so, it has a link with Art 6, as indicated in the Strasbourg jurisprudence. Injunctions are infrequently granted,[41] but would be of value as a preventive measure. An injunction against one newspaper would prevent it from pursuing a story, while it might deter others from running variations on the same story, thereby preventing the greater risk of prejudice arising from a wide ranging and relentless coverage of issues relevant in a forthcoming trial. More generally, prosecutions for contempt, where Art 6 rights were violated, might have a future deterrent effect. In other words, the link between the use of contempt law and Art 6 should be given some weight in the current situation in which the judiciary do not at present use neutralising measures, such as stays, extensively.[42]

As indicated above, once a contempt action is in being, the national court is not in the same position as Strasbourg since it must rule not on whether an interference with Art 10 rights was justified, but on whether the interference should be allowed to occur at all. The part played by the margin of appreciation at Strasbourg should not be reflected, as Chapter 3 argues, in domestic decision making. In so far as, in the *Worm* case and in *BBC v Scotland*, a less intensive review was conducted where the 'rights of others' exception was in question, the domestic courts would be expected to take a different stance. Thus, where Art 6 rights appear to be at stake, detailed and rigorous review would determine whether this is in fact the case. Such a stance would be more satisfactory than that adopted at Strasbourg, since the central concern should be, it will be contended, the need to isolate the fundamental values at stake in terms of both free speech and fair trials and to tailor domestic law in order to protect them.

---

40 *The Law of Contempt*, 1996, p 485.

41 In *AG v News Group Newspapers* [1987] 1 QB 1, an injunction would have been granted.

42 See the comments of Simon Brown LJ regarding the failure to use stays in certain instances in which prejudice to proceedings was found: *AG v Birmingham Post and Mail Ltd* [1998] 4 All ER 49.

In a contempt action, the court would be bound by the Convention rights under s 6 of the HRA and, where the statutory provisions were in question, could seek to ensure that it discharged that obligation by interpreting them compatibly with the relevant guarantees. It is suggested that the domestic court could examine the effect of finding liability in terms of both Arts 10 and 6. In so doing, it is argued, it would not only escape the structural constraints of the Strasbourg approach, but might more readily recognise the underlying harmony between the two Articles.

In order to illustrate this approach, two instances will be considered taken from the cases discussed below. In the first example, based on the *Taylor* case,[43] it is assumed that all the tabloid newspapers have reported, in sensationalist and misleading terms, on a forthcoming trial which has happened to catch the public eye. They are prosecuted for contempt. (In fact, in *Taylor*, no prosecution was forthcoming, a factor which may have played a part in recent tabloid excesses.) Assuming that *prima facie* liability could be established under the 1981 Act, it must also be asked whether the creation of such liability would be unjustified under Art 10. The first question would be whether it would constitute an interference with the freedom of expression of the tabloids. Despite the lack of value of the speech, such an interference would be found, since Strasbourg rarely denies Art 10 protection to speech on the basis of its content. The interference would clearly be found to be prescribed by law – the 1981 Act. The legitimate aims in view would be the preservation of the authority and impartiality of the judiciary and of the rights of others. Those aims would probably be established, on the facts; they have been established in all the relevant claims considered at Strasbourg.

The key question would be whether the interference represented by the creation of liability would be necessary in a democratic society. In determining necessity, the proportionality of the potential interference would require careful scrutiny. This would be the point at which the domestic court would be expected to take a somewhat different stance from that taken by Strasbourg, in relation to the 'rights of others' exception, in that its scrutiny of this question should be much more intensive. Factors to be taken into account would include the extent to which the various newspapers had in fact misled readers and the ability of jurors to disregard the coverage, on strong directions from the judge. But the central importance of fair trials in a democratic society should also be considered, as should the lack of value of the speech. The question of proportionality can encompass such matters, as the decisions in *News Verlags* and *Sunday Times* demonstrated. On the facts, it is argued that a finding of liability against the newspapers under the 1981 Act would be justified under Art 10. The same result would be likely to arise if the liability was then considered from the Art 6 perspective since, on the facts, it could readily be found that the fairness of the trial had been affected and possibly that the presumption of innocence had also been undermined. The court would have discharged its duty under s 6 of the HRA. (Had it appeared that it would fail to do so if it found against the newspapers, it would then have had to examine the statutory provisions in detail for their compatibility with the Convention under s 3 of the HRA.) If, on the above facts, the Attorney General failed to bring a prosecution, it is argued that he would have failed to discharge that duty.

---

43 See below, p 236. For comment on the case and its implications within the Convention, see Borrie and Lowe, *The Law of Contempt*, 1996, pp 481–82.

The opposing result would be reached, it is argued, in a case in which certain newspapers comment on a matter of grave public importance, relating to the possibility of abuse of power in part of the executive, where no criminal trial is affected. The comment may, however, affect the ability of the Attorney General to continue a breach of confidence action with a view to suppressing debate on the matter. Publications in other jurisdictions in fact render it extremely unlikely that the rights can be preserved in any event. This example is based on *AG v Times Newspapers*,[44] which is discussed below. In this instance, the speech in question concerns a matter of great public significance while hardly affecting Art 6 rights. The interest in question, which might conceivably be viewed as falling within Art 6, concerns the preservation of the rights of one party to a civil action. (Strasbourg, however, did not view that right as engaging the 'rights of others' exception as a distinct exception when it considered the interference with freedom of expression created by the grant of an injunction on grounds of breach of confidence.)[45] The sanction of contempt of court would be, in this instance, disproportionate to the aim of preserving the authority of the judiciary since it could not in fact be preserved by that means.[46] Thus, the action would fail, since the imposition of liability on the newspapers would be unjustified.

These two examples illustrate the harmony that exists between the values underlying Arts 6 and 10. They also, it is argued, indicate the proper approach to the infusion of Convention values into this area of contempt law. Essentially, it is an approach that seeks out and protects the core values at stake in relation to both media freedom and the administration of justice. In identifying the consonance which exists between such values it differentiates sharply between speech supported by the justifications from truth, democracy or self-fulfilment, and speech which is promulgated mainly to further the ends of media conglomerates. It seeks to preserve impartiality and fairness, especially in criminal proceedings, but demands a rigorous and careful scrutiny of the possibility that unfairness may arise.

Domestic provisions: the development of the common law

This particular area of criminal contempt at common law curtailed the freedom of the media to discuss and report on issues arising from criminal or civil proceedings on the basis that those proceedings might suffer prejudice. However, it went further than was necessary to deal with very clear risks of interference with the administration of justice. The media was restricted in its reporting of issues relevant to civil or criminal proceedings which were, or were soon to be, in being. It is important to note that civil proceedings can also be prejudiced, even though usually no jury is involved, but obviously this danger may be less likely to arise. It is apparent that more weight was given to protecting the administration of justice rather than free speech, from the ease with which it was possible to satisfy the common law tests.

The elements of common law contempt consisted of the creation of a real risk of prejudice (the *actus reus*) and an intention to publish; it was therefore a crime of strict

---

44   [1992] 1 AC 191; discussed below, p 249
45   *Observer and Guardian v UK* (1991) 14 EHRR 153; discussed below, pp 360–61.
46   See pp 358–59.

liability. The *actus reus* could be fulfilled if it were shown that the publication in question had created a risk that the proceedings in question might be prejudiced; it was irrelevant whether they actually had been. This distinction was clearly illustrated by *Thompson Newspapers Ltd ex p AG*.[47] While the defendant was awaiting trial, The *Sunday Times* published his photograph and commented on his unsavoury background as a brothel keeper. This was held to amount to contempt. He was convicted and then appealed on the ground that the trial had been prejudiced by the article, but his appeal failed on the basis that jurors had not in actuality been so prejudiced. This case further illustrates the nature of the actus reus: it was not necessary to publish very damaging comments in order to create the risk in question.

At common law, there was a certain time before and a certain time after the action, known as the *sub judice* period, when there was a risk that any article published relevant to the action might be in contempt. The starting point of this period occurred when the proceedings were 'imminent' (*Savundranayagan and Walker*).[48] This test attracted much criticism because of its vagueness and width; it was obviously capable of applying a long time before the trial and it therefore had an inhibiting effect on the media out of proportion to its value. In particular, it gave rise to the restriction caused by so called 'gagging writs'. A newspaper might be discussing corruption in a company. If a writ for libel was then issued – although there was no intention of proceeding with the case – the newspaper might find itself in contempt if it continued to discuss the issues. Thus, this method could be used to prevent further comment.

The need for reform which would, in particular, address the width of the imminence test was apparent and led to the setting up of the Phillimore Committee in 1974,[49] but it might not have come about without the influence of the European Court of Human Rights. The ruling that UK contempt law had breached Art 10 arose through the decision of the House of Lords in *AG v Times Newspapers Ltd*.[50] The case concerned litigation arising out of the Thalidomide tragedy. The parents of the Thalidomide children wished to sue Distillers, the company which had manufactured the drug, because they believed that it was responsible for the terrible damage done to their unborn children. Distillers resisted the claims and entered into negotiation with the parents' solicitors. Thus, the litigation was dormant while the negotiations were taking place. Meanwhile, the *Sunday Times* wished to publish an article accusing Distillers of acting ungenerously towards the Thalidomide children. The article came close to saying that Distillers had been negligent, although it was balanced in that it did consider both sides.

The Attorney General obtained an injunction in the Divisional Court preventing publication of the article on the ground that it amounted to a contempt of court. The Court of Appeal then discharged the injunction in a ruling which weighed up the public interest in freedom of speech against the need to protect the administration of justice and found that the former value outweighed the latter: the article concerned a matter of great public interest and, since the litigation in question was dormant, it would probably be

---

47   [1968] 1 All ER 268; [1968] 1 WLR 1.
48   [1968] 3 All ER 439; [1968] 1 WLR 1761, CA.
49   See *Report of the Committee on Contempt of Court*, Cmnd 5794, 1974. For comment, see Dhavan, R, 'Contempt of court and the Phillimore Committee Report' (1976) 5 Anglo-Am L Rev 186–253.
50   [1974] AC 273; [1973] 3 All ER 54; [1973] 3 WLR 298, HL. For case notes, see Miller, CJ (1974) 37 MLR 96; O'Boyle, M (1974) 25 NILQ 57; Williams, DGT (1973) 32 CLJ 177 and Miller, CJ [1975] Crim LR 132.

unaffected by it. The House of Lords then restored the injunction on the ground that the article dealt with the question of negligence and therefore prejudged the case pending before the court. It held that such prejudgment was particularly objectionable as coming close to 'trial by media' and thereby leading to an undermining of the administration of justice: a person might be adjudged negligent by parts of the media with none of the safeguards available in court. The confidence of the public in the courts might be undermined, thus creating a long term detriment to the course of justice generally.

This ruling created a possible new test for the *actus reus* of contempt. Termed the 'prejudgment' test, it was wider than the test of real risk of prejudice, in that little risk to proceedings might be shown, but it might still be possible to assert that they had been prejudged. This test was heavily criticised by the Phillimore Committee; it had a potentially grave effect on freedom of speech because it was very difficult to draw the line between legitimate discussion in the media and prejudgment. Since it was easier to satisfy the prejudgment test than the old test for the *actus reus* of common law contempt, the Phillimore Committee considered that the *Sunday Times* ruling strengthened the case for reform. Meanwhile, the case was on its way to the European Court of Human Rights. The editor of the *Sunday Times* applied to the European Commission of Human Rights seeking a ruling that the imposition of the injunction breached Art 10 of the European Convention, and five years after the judgment of the House of Lords, the case came before the European Court of Human Rights (*Sunday Times* case).[51]

As indicated in the introduction to this Part, the Art 10 guarantee of freedom of expression is subject to exceptions to be narrowly construed. The Court found that the injunction clearly infringed Art 10(1) and that this was not a trivial infringement; the free speech interest involved was very strong, because the matter was one of great public concern. However, the injunction fell within Art 10(2) because it had an aim permitted by one of the exceptions – maintenance of the authority of the judiciary.

The next question was whether the injunction was 'necessary in a democratic society' in order to achieve the aim in question: it was not enough merely to show that the injunction was covered by an exception. In order to make a determination on this point, the Court considered the meaning of the term 'necessary'. It ruled that this did not mean indispensable, but connoted something stronger than 'useful', 'reasonable' or 'desirable'. It implied the existence of a 'pressing social need'. Was there such a need? The Court employed the doctrine of proportionality in determining the existence of such a 'need' in the circumstances: it weighed up the strength of the free speech interest in considering whether the injunction was disproportionate to the aim of preserving the authority of the judiciary. It found that although courts are clearly the forums for settling disputes, this does not mean that there can be no newspaper discussion before a case. The article was couched in moderate terms and explored the issues in a balanced way. Moreover, the litigation in question was dormant and therefore unlikely to be affected by the article. Nevertheless, the injunction created an absolute prohibition on discussion of the issues forming the background to the case. Thus, on the one hand, there was a strong free speech interest; on the other, there was a weak threat to the authority of the judiciary. If the free speech interest had been weaker, it might have been more easily overcome. The court,

---

51 Judgment of 26 April 1979, A 30; (1979) 2 EHRR 245. For case notes see Duffy, PJ, 5 H Rts Rev 17; Mann, FA (1979) 95 LQR 348; Wong, W-WM (1984) 17 NY Univ JIL and Pol 35.

therefore, concluded that the interference did not correspond to a social need sufficiently pressing to outweigh the public interest in freedom of expression. In reaching its conclusion that a breach of Art 10 had therefore taken place,[52] the Court also adverted briefly to the value of the article in furthering the aim of preserving the authority of the judiciary since 'in bringing to light certain facts it might have served as a brake on speculative and unenlightened discussion'. In other words, the speech in question served the ends of justice in a general sense.

The UK Government responded to this decision in the enactment of the Contempt of Court Act 1981 which was supposed to take account of the ruling of the European Court and was also influenced to an extent by the findings of the Phillimore Committee.[53]

The Contempt of Court Act 1981

The 1981 Act was designed to modify the common law without bringing about radical change. It introduced various liberalising factors, but it was intended to maintain the stance of the ultimate supremacy of the administration of justice over freedom of speech, while moving the balance further towards freedom of speech.[54] In particular, it introduced stricter time limits, a more precise test for the *actus reus* and allowed some articles on matters of public interest to escape liability even though prejudice to proceedings was created.

These reforms brought about under the Act will be considered below, bearing the obligation of s 3 of the Human Rights Act in mind, in terms of their ability to satisfy the Convention, in particular Art 10, interpreted domestically. In any particular instance, the *current* Strasbourg standards should be taken into account in strictly scrutinising interferences with the Art 10 guarantee. It would not be sufficient to assume that such standards will be met on the basis that the 1981 Act was introduced in order to take account of a Strasbourg ruling. In order to determine whether liability is created, the following steps must be taken, bearing those standards in mind.

The publication falls within s 1 of the Act

Under s 1, conduct will be contempt if it interferes with the administration of justice in particular proceedings regardless of intent to do so. Thus, not all publications which deal with issues touching on the administration of justice will fall within the 1981 Act. The starting point under s 1 is to ask whether the publication touches upon particular legal proceedings. In other words, if the article appears to have a long term effect on the course of justice generally, without affecting any particular proceedings, it would seem to fall outside the Act and might be considered at common law. This point will be considered below.

It is important to note that it is not necessary to show that the defendant intended to prejudice proceedings: the 'strict liability rule' under s 1 continues the position as it was at

---

52 It may be noted that the Court was divided 11–9 in reaching this determination.

53 See *Report of the Committee on Contempt of Court*, Cmnd 5794, 1974; Green Paper, Cmnd 7145, 1978.

54 For comment on the 1981 Act, see Miller, CJ [1982] Crim LR 71; Lowe, NV [1982] PL 20; Smith, JC [1982] Crim LR 744; Zellich, GF [1982] PL 343; Redmond, M [1983] CLJ 9.

common law. After establishing that the publication might affect particular proceedings, a number of other tests must be satisfied if the strict liability rule is to be established. If the publication does affect particular proceedings, but one of these tests is unsatisfied, it might still be possible to consider it at common law. It should be noted that the proceedings must be 'court' proceedings. This test includes certain tribunals in the contempt jurisdiction.[55]

The proceedings are 'active'

This test, which arises under s 2(3), is more clearly defined than the test at common law and therefore proceedings are 'active' (or sub judice) for shorter periods. Thus, the test is intended to have a liberalising effect. The starting and ending points for civil and criminal proceedings are defined in Sched 1. For criminal proceedings, the starting point (Sched 1, s 4(a–e)) is: the issue of a warrant for arrest, an arrest without warrant or the service of an indictment (or summons or an oral charge); the ending point is acquittal, sentence, any other verdict or discontinuance of the trial. The starting point for civil proceedings occurs when the case is set down for a hearing in the High Court or a date for the hearing is fixed (Sched 1, ss 12 and 13). This provision was clarified in *AG v Hislop and Pressdram*:[56] it was found that s 2(3) was fulfilled because the proceedings in question (an action for defamation) had come into the 'warned' list at the time the articles in question were published. This starting point addresses the problem of gagging writs: the mere issuance of a writ would not mean that any further comment could give rise to an action for contempt because the issue of a writ is not the starting point. The end point of the active period for civil proceedings comes when the proceedings are disposed of, discontinued or withdrawn. The precision of these provisions, which allows the media to determine with reasonable certainty the point at which a risk of liability arises, means that they can be viewed as meeting the demands of Art 10.

Surprisingly, appellate proceedings are also covered by Sched 1. The starting point occurs when leave to appeal is applied for, by notice of appeal or application for review or other originating process; the end point occurs when the proceedings are disposed of or abandoned. Section 9 of the Criminal Appeal Act 1995 provides that a reference by the Criminal Cases Review Commission to the Court of Appeal is to be treated as an appeal under the Criminal Appeal Act 1968 for all purposes, and therefore, appellate proceedings become active when such a reference is made.

These provisions are less restrictive than the previous ones under the common law, which also covered the period during which notice to appeal could be given, but the key question is why appellate proceedings are covered at all. The Phillimore Committee recommended that most appellate proceedings should not be covered.[57] Given the principles at stake, discussed above, it is suggested that the ends of justice are unlikely to be served by seeking to stifle media comment that refers specifically to appeals, since the openness of the discussion supports confidence in the quality of justice which is unafraid

---

55 Section 19 provides that 'court' includes 'any tribunal or body exercising the judicial power of the State'. See further Borrie and Lowe, *op cit*, fn 43, pp 485–91.

56 [1991] 1 QB 514; [1991] 1 All ER 911; [1991] 2 WLR 219, CA.

57 Phillimore Committee Report, para 132.

of comment. The misinformed or biased nature of aspects of such discussion would not be expected to affect the judiciary, especially the senior judiciary. Therefore, no fear of arbitrariness due to prejudice should arise. As Lord Reid said in the *Sunday Times* case: 'It is scarcely possible to imagine a case when comment could influence judges in the Court of Appeal or noble and leaned Lords in this House.'[58] Nevertheless, Channel 4 was enjoined from broadcasting a re-enactment, in the form of a dramatic 'reconstruction', of the appeal of the Birmingham Six, until after the decision on the appeal had been taken.[59] This was a doubtful decision, since it was highly unlikely that the judges would have been influenced by the programme. The injunction was therefore obtained on the basis that the public's view of the judgment of the court might have been affected by it. This justification is flawed, since it does not appear to be covered by s 2(2) of the Act,[60] and also because the public's view of that judgment and of the Appeal Court generally would be more greatly influenced, it is suggested, by the impression given that a ban was necessary in order to prevent the programme from influencing the judges.

It is probable that prosecutions in respect of contempt of appellate courts will not be brought in future. In *Re Lonhro plc and Observer Ltd*,[61] the House of Lords relied on Art 10 in finding that since the possibility that a professional judge would be influenced by media coverage of a case is extremely remote, it would be extremely hard to establish a 'pressing social need', as required by Art 10, to suppress the speech in question. This stance has now been reinforced by the inception of the Human Rights Act.

The publication creates 'a substantial risk of serious prejudice or impediment to the course of justice in the proceedings in question' (s 2(2))

This test, on its face, is probably in harmony with Convention standards as indicated in *Worm v Austria*,[62] *News Verlags*[63] and *BBC Scotland v UK*.[64] In requiring a substantial risk of serious prejudice, it might even be said to set too high a threshold: publications merely creating a risk of serious prejudice will not be covered, although it is arguable that Art 6 may demand that they should be.

The inclusion of a substantial risk of impediment may be viewed as making it clear that UK law adheres more to a preventive rather than a neutralising model in terms of seeking to ensure the fairness of trials. The more far reaching neutralising measures, such as changing the venue of the trial or delaying it, would clearly tend to have an impeding effect on it. On the other hand, the use of lesser neutralising measures, such as warnings to the jury to disregard media coverage, are matters which may properly be taken into account when considering the risk in question. In *AG v Times Newspapers*[65] it was found that jurors were able to ignore possibly prejudicial comment in newspapers. That case

---

58   *AG v Times Newspapers*, fn 50, above.

59   *In re Channel 4 Television Co Ltd* (1988) *The Times*, 2 February; [1988] Crim LR 237.

60   Since it could not have been shown that a substantial risk of prejudice to the proceedings – the appeal – would arise. Section 2(2) does not refer to a substantial risk of prejudice to the course of justice in a general sense.

61   [1989] 2 All ER 1100, HL.

62   See above, fn 23.

63   (2001) 31 EHRR 8.

64   See above, fn 25.

65   (1983) *The Times*, 12 February, DC. See also *AG v MGN* [1997] 1 All ER 456.

concerned a relatively trivial incident which happened to attract publicity because of the fame of one of the persons involved, a factor which jurors might be expected to appreciate, leading them to discount the press coverage. Recently, it has become more common for consideration to be afforded to the likelihood that the jury will be strongly directed to ignore prejudicial coverage of the trial.[66] Thus, responsibility is shifting to an extent from the media and is being placed upon judges and jurors. Perhaps, as indicated above, that shift of responsibility is not fully in accordance with the notion that the 'duties and responsibilities' of Art 10 are placed upon those exercising the right to freedom of expression it protects, that is, the media.

It should be pointed out that the s 2(2) test can be viewed as taking a preventive or deterrent stance and as going further in terms of protecting the fairness of trials than neutralising or remedial measures (acquittals, abandonment of the proceedings) do. Section 2(2) can be said to punish media bodies who have created prejudice even where – from the point of view of the *trial* judge, as opposed to the judge in the contempt proceedings – a stay of proceedings or other measures are not viewed as necessary. Section 2(2) is an objective test; it is unconcerned with the question whether prejudice has actually been caused. Moreover, as Simon Brown LJ pointed out in *AG v Birmingham Post and Mail*,[67] 's 2(2) postulates a lesser degree of prejudice than is required to make good an appeal against conviction. Similarly, it seems to me to postulate a lesser degree of prejudice than would justify an order for a stay'. He went on to conclude that where s 2(2) was satisfied, it would not follow that a conviction was imperilled or that a stay was required, but that the converse was not the case: 'I find it difficult to envisage a publication which has concerned the judge sufficiently to discharge the jury and yet is not properly to be regarded as a contempt.' Clearly, although this may be an accurate statement of the effect of s 2(2) where a particular publication creates a likelihood of prejudice to a criminal trial, the preventive or punitive effect can only occur if (a) the prejudicial effect is not the result of cumulative media coverage of issues relevant to or arising from a particular case, and (b) if contempt proceedings are actually brought. As the discussion below indicates, both these matters are problematic.

According to the Court of Appeal in *AG v News Group Newspapers*,[68] both limbs of the test under s 2(2) must be satisfied: showing a slight risk of serious prejudice or a substantial risk of slight prejudice would not be sufficient. The question to be asked under the first limb could be broken down as follows: can it be argued that there is a substantial risk that a person involved in the case in question such as a juror would (a) encounter the article, (b) remember it and (c) be affected by it so that he or she could not put it out of his or her mind during the trial? Clearly, a person cannot be affected at all by something he or she has never encountered or has forgotten about. Thus, a number of factors may be identified which will be relevant to one or more of these questions. Five such factors are identified below which, apart from the first, will also be relevant at the stage of considering whether serious prejudice has occurred. In considering them, it should be noted that Lord Diplock has interpreted 'substantial risk' as excluding a 'risk which is

---

66 See, eg, *AG v MGN* [1997] EMLR 284.
67 [1998] 4 All ER 49, pp 57, 59. See further *Mcleod* (2000) *The Times*, 20 December.
68 [1987] 1 QB 1; [1986] 2 All ER 833; [1986] 3 WLR 365, CA.

only remote',[69] a finding which arguably emasculates the sub-section.[70] In *MGN Pension Trustees Ltd*[71] it was found that the term meant 'not insubstantial' or 'not minimal' rather than weighty. If this should be taken to mean that fairly slight risks are sufficient, it is open to question as seeming not to further the policy of the Act which is to narrow down the area of liability covered by criminal contempt. However, the finding has been interpreted in other instances as effectively excluding such risks.[72] In *AG v Guardian Newspapers*,[73] Sedley LJ considered that the risk in question could not be clearly be viewed as substantial, taking into account the use of directions to the jury to disregard media comment. Collins J also took into account the effect of judicial directions on the jury in terms of neutralising any prejudice created by the publication. It was found that the test of 'serious prejudice', but not that of 'substantial risk', was satisfied. This stricter standard, which gives full weight to the limiting words of s 2(2), may be more in harmony with Art 10 than the formulation suggested by Lord Diplock, since it would exclude from liability publications that were very unlikely to create prejudice.

Obtaining a conviction under the test as currently interpreted is especially difficult where a substantial risk of serious prejudice or impediment is created by the *totality* of the news coverage rather than by the coverage of one media organ. *AG v MGN*[74] concerned the coverage of a case involving the notorious boyfriend of a soap opera actress by five tabloid newspapers, which mentioned his previous criminal record and presented a misleading picture of the incident in question. It was found that none of the articles, considered separately, reached the required threshold under s 2(2). The judge, Schiemann LJ, said that where, in such an instance, the totality of the coverage had prejudiced the trial, it might be proper to stay the proceedings. This decision reveals a weakness in the preventive model, since it means that the creation of serious prejudice to a trial by a large number of newspaper articles in combination cannot be addressed by means of contempt law where *individual* articles just fail to satisfy the strict test of s 2(2) as interpreted in *AG v Guardian Newspapers*.

Five key factors may be identified which are likely to be of significance in determining whether the s 2(2) test is satisfied in any particular instance:

(1) If an article is published in a national newspaper, it is possible that jurors and others may encounter it; however, if the publication has a very small circulation, this risk might be seen as too remote. This point was considered in *AG v Hislop and Pressdram*,[75] which concerned the effect of an article in *Private Eye* written about Sonia Sutcliffe, wife of the Yorkshire Ripper. Private Eye had published two articles making

---

69 *AG v English* [1983] 1 AC 116; [1982] 2 All ER 903; for comment, see Zellick, 'Fair trial and free press' [1982] PL 343 (especially on the question of the degree of risk); Ward (1983) 46 MLR 85; Redmond [1983] CLJ 9. It may be noted that aspects of *AG v English* were the subject of an unsuccessful application to Strasbourg: *Times Newspapers Ltd and others v UK* (1983) 8 EHRR 45, p 54. Bearing in mind the comments in Chapter 2 as to the effect of the Commission on the Convention jurisprudence, especially in its older decisions, it is suggested that this finding of inadmissibility would not be repeated today and that the decision is somewhat out of line with the generality of the jurisprudence relating to pre-trial publicity and the reporting of issues relating to litigation.

70 See Zellick, *ibid*, on this point, p 344.

71 [1995] EMLR 99.

72 See, eg, Lord Lane's comments in *AG v Times Newspapers Ltd* (1983) *The Times*, 12 February, DC.

73 [1999] EMLR 904.

74 [1997] 1 All ER 456.

75 [1991] 1 QB 514; [1991] 1 All ER 911; [1991] 2 WLR 219, CA.

serious allegations against Sonia Sutcliffe and in response she began an action for defamation. Shortly before the hearing of the action, *Private Eye* published two further articles defamatory of Mrs Sutcliffe. The Attorney General brought proceedings for contempt of court in respect of the second articles, and on appeal it was determined that as *Private Eye* had a large readership, many of whom might live in London, where the libel action was held, it could not be said that the risk of prejudice was insubstantial. In *AG v Independent TV News and Others*,[76] ITV News and certain newspapers published the fact that a defendant in a forthcoming murder trial was a convicted IRA terrorist who had escaped from jail where he was serving a life sentence for murder. It was found that s 2(2) was not satisfied, since the trial was not expected to take place for nine months, there had only been one offending news item, and there had been limited circulation of only one edition of the offending newspaper items. The risk of prejudice was found to be too small to be termed substantial.

(2) The ruling in *AG v News Group Newspapers*[77] made it clear that the proximity of the article to the trial will also be relevant to the question of risk. The Court of Appeal held that a gap of 10 months between the two could not create the substantial risk in question because the jury would be likely to have forgotten the article by the time the trial came on. Even if the article were faintly recollected at the time of the trial, it might be likely to have little impact. Similarly, in *AG v Independent TV News* and Others one of the factors founding the ruling that s 2(2) was not satisfied was that the trial was not expected to take place for nine months and therefore the risk that any juror who had seen the offending item would remember it was not seen as substantial. In contrast, in *AG v Hislop and Pressdram*, a gap of three months between publication of the article and the trial of the libel action did create such a risk. A publication during the trial is clearly most likely to create a risk. In *AG v Newsgroup Newspapers*,[78] the *Sun* published a serious allegation regarding a defendant in a murder trial at the point at which the jury had retired to consider its verdict. The murder charge was dropped, and the *Sun* was fined for contempt. Of course, this factor cannot be considered in isolation from the others: the subject matter of the publication or language used may be more likely to ensure that it is remembered even over a substantial period of time.

(3) If the case will be very much in the public eye because of the persons or issues involved (as was the case in respect of the article in *Hislop and Pressdram* concerning Sonia Sutcliffe, wife of the Yorkshire Ripper) the article is more likely to make an impact, although the mere fact that the issue attracts a great deal of media coverage will not mean that jurors will be unable to put it from their minds.

(4) The language used in the publication will clearly be relevant and will relate to the impact of the allegations made or issues raised. An article making relatively mild allegations not couched in particularly vitriolic language might have little influence and might, in any event, be blotted out by the immediacy of the proceedings. However, it is also possible that very specific pieces of information soberly conveyed, such as previous convictions of the defendant, might make even more impact than a

---

76   [1995] 2 All ER 370.
77   [1987] QB 1.
78   16 April 1999, unreported.

forceful opinion couched in more emotive language. In *AG v BBC, Same v Hat Trick Productions Ltd*[79] it was found that assumptions of the guilt of the defendants may create prejudice even though they arise within a humorous context. During a programme in the irreverent, satirical series *Have I Got News for You*, remarks were made which assumed that the Maxwell brothers were guilty of defrauding the *Daily Mirror* pensioners. The broadcast occurred six months before the trial of the Maxwells. It was found that despite the humorous context, the remarks might have been taken seriously by viewers and that therefore s 2(2) was satisfied. In *AG v Morgan*[80] an article in *The News of the World* referred to the criminal record of one of the defendants and to the criminal background of both defendants. These references were given great prominence and were repeated throughout the article. Despite the lapse of time before the trial – eight months – a substantial risk of serious prejudice was found to have been created.

(5) Photographs accompanying an article will also be relevant,[81] especially where identification is likely to be in issue at the trial,[82] or where they are used to create a misleading impression. They are also likely to increase the impact of the publication and make it more memorable. In *Taylor*,[83] a large number of tabloid newspapers had published a photograph which was taken of one of the defendants in a murder trial giving the husband of the victim a polite kiss on the cheek; it was distorted in such a way as to give the impression that it was a passionate mouth to mouth kiss and was captioned 'cheats kiss'. It was found that this was part of an 'unremitting, extensive, sensational, inaccurate and misleading press coverage' and had led to a real risk of prejudice to the trial. (This determination was not made in contempt proceedings, although it would obviously have been relevant to them, but in overturning the convictions of the two defendants.)

Having established a substantial risk that jurors and others will be influenced by the article, it will be necessary to ask whether there is a substantial risk that the effect of such influence will be of a prejudicial nature or would be likely to impede the proceedings in question. A publication which was in some way relevant to a trial might be likely to create a substantial risk that it would influence persons involved in the trial, bearing the factors identified in mind, but without leading to prejudice to it. An article published in every national newspaper in the land on the day of the trial and discussing certain issues relevant to it in a striking and interesting, but fair and impartial manner would have an influence, but not a prejudicial one. In considering whether it would be prejudicial, the two limbs of the test must be considered together: it must be shown that the language used, the facts disclosed or sentiments expressed would lead an objective observer to conclude that a substantial risk had been established that persons involved in the proceedings would be prejudiced, before going on to consider whether that effect could properly be described as serious.

---

79 [1997] EMLR 76; (1996) *The Times*, 26 July.
80 [1998] EMLR 294.
81 See *AG v Newsgroup Newspapers Ltd* (1983) *The Times*, 12 February.
82 See *R v Evening Standard Co Ltd ex p AG* (1976) *The Times*, 3 November.
83 (1993) 98 Cr App R 361, CA.

Prejudice and its seriousness can be established in a number of ways: the article (or other publication) might be likely to have the effect of influencing persons against or in favour of the defendant; it might be likely to affect either the outcome of the proceedings in question or their very existence – as where pressure is placed on one party to drop[84] or even to continue with proceedings. In *Re Lonhro plc*,[85] Lord Bridge said: '[pre-trial] it is easy to see how critical public discussion of the issues and criticism of the conduct of the parties, particularly if a party is held up to public obloquy, may impede or prejudice the course of the proceedings by influencing the conduct of witnesses or parties in relation to the proceedings. If [a jury is involved] the possibility of prejudice by advance publicity directed at an issue which the jury will have to decide is obvious.' It is assumed that lay persons are more likely to be affected by media coverage than professionals; as indicated above, it would be readily assumed that a judge would be unaffected.[86] Therefore, civil proceedings are less at risk of being prejudiced than criminal ones, except in those instances in which a jury is used.[87] But, as indicated, civil actions can be affected in other ways. Also, witnesses, especially lay witnesses, in both civil and criminal actions might be affected by media coverage. They might be deterred from coming forward[88] or they might be intimidated or influenced[89] by it.

As noted above, the proximity in time between the article and the proceedings can affect this limb of s 2(2), as can the extent to which it may be said that the trial concerns a person in the public eye. If the article is published some time before the trial, as in *AG v News Group Newspapers*, its likely effect on the minds of jurors will be lessened because it may only exist there as a faint memory: any effect it has is unlikely to be of a seriously prejudicial nature. This might be the case even though the article would have been likely to have such an effect had it been fresh in their minds. In the *Hislop* case, however, the vitriolic nature of the article did suggest that it would be likely to have a seriously prejudicial effect. The serious allegations in question were held to blacken the plaintiff's character and might well have influenced the jurors against her. The fact that Peter Sutcliffe was well known also made it more likely that the article would have an impact. However, courts will not be quick to assume that jurors are incapable of ignoring prejudicial publications. In *AG v Guardian Newspapers*[90] the publication of the fact that one unidentified defendant out of six in a Manchester trial was also awaiting trial elsewhere was not found to satisfy s 2(2), since it was thought that it would not cause a juror of ordinary good sense to be biased against the defendant.

---

84 See *Hislop and Pressdram* [1991] 1 QB 514; [1991] 1 All ER 911; [1991] 2 WLR 219, CA: this aspect of the case is discussed in relation to common law contempt, below, pp 248–49.

85 [1990] AC 154, p 209B.

86 This is the general view expressed in the relevant jurisprudence in Britain and in other common law jurisdictions. Eg, Lord Salmon said in *AG v BBC* [1981] AC 303, p 342: 'I am and always would be satisfied that no judge would be influenced by what may be said by the media.' Of course, it should be borne in mind that this stance is taken by the judges themselves.

87 In respect of defamation and in certain actions against the police.

88 See *Vine Products Ltd v Green* [1966] Ch 484, p 495.

89 See *Re Doncaster and Retford Co-operative Societies Agreement* [1960] LR 2 PC; *Hutchinson v Amalgamated Engineering Union, Re Daily Worker* (1932) *The Times*, 25 August.

90 [1992] 3 All ER 38, CA.

The test of 'impeding' proceedings is treated in a more specific fashion. It may be satisfied where the publication can be said to have led to the delay of the proceedings owing to the risk of prejudice.[91]

The article amounts to 'a discussion in good faith of public affairs or other matters of general public interest' and 'the risk of impediment or prejudice to particular legal proceedings is merely incidental to the discussion' (s 5)

Section 5 reflects the guarantee under Art 10. It affords a high value to political speech, broadly defined, and therefore reflects the value placed upon such speech at Strasbourg. If it appears that s 2(2) is fulfilled, it must next be established that s 5 does not apply. Section 5 does not, therefore, operate as a defence. If it did, it would not follow the contours of the inquiry to be conducted under Art 10. *AG v English*[92] is the leading case on s 5 and is generally considered to provide a good example of the kind of case for which s 5 was framed. After the trial had begun of a consultant who was charged with the murder of a Down's syndrome baby, an article was published in the *Daily Mail* which made no direct reference to him, but was written in support of a pro-life candidate, Mrs Carr, who was standing in a by-election. Mrs Carr had no arms; the article referred to this fact and continued: 'today the chances of such a baby surviving are very small – someone would surely recommend letting her die of starvation. Are babies who are not up to scratch to be destroyed before or after birth?' The trial judge referred the article to the Attorney General, who brought contempt proceedings against the *Daily Mail*. First, it was determined that the article did fulfil the test under s 2(2) on the basis that jurors would be likely to take the comments to refer to the trial; therefore, the assertion that babies were often allowed to die if handicapped might influence them against the consultant, Dr Arthur.

The burden then fell on the prosecution to show that s 5 did not apply. Lord Diplock adopted a two stage approach in determining this issue. First, could the article be called a 'discussion'? The Divisional Court had held that a discussion must mean the general airing of views and debating of principles. However, Lord Diplock considered that the term 'discussion' could not be confined merely to abstract debate, but could include consideration of examples drawn from real life. Applying this test, he found that a discussion could include accusations without which the article would have been emasculated and would have lost its main point. Without the implied accusations, it would have become a contribution to a purely hypothetical issue. It was about Mrs Carr's election and also the general topic of mercy killing. The main point of her candidature was that killing of sub-standard babies did happen and should be stopped; if it had not asserted that babies were allowed to die, she would have been depicted as tilting at imaginary windmills. Thus the term 'discussion' could include implied accusations.

Secondly, was the risk of prejudice to Dr Arthur's trial merely an incidental consequence of expounding the main theme of the article? Lord Diplock held that in answering this, the Divisional Court had applied the wrong test in considering whether the article could have been written without including the offending words. Instead, the Court should have looked at the actual words written. The main theme of the article was

---

91 See *AG v BBC* (1992) *The Independent*, 3 January 1992.
92 [1983] 1 AC 116; [1982] 2 All ER 903.

Mrs Carr's election policy; Dr Arthur was not mentioned. Therefore, this article was the antithesis of the one considered in the *AG v Times Newspaper*,[93] which was concerned entirely with the actions of Distillers. Clearly, Dr Arthur's trial could be prejudiced by the article, but that prejudice could properly be described as incidental to its main theme.

Thus, s 5 applied; the article did not, therefore, fall within the strict liability rule. This ruling was generally seen as giving a liberal interpretation to s 5.[94] Had the narrow interpretation of the Divisional Court prevailed, it would have meant that all debate in the media on the topic of mercy killing would have been prevented for almost a year – the time during which the proceedings in *Arthur's* case were active from charge to acquittal. (It may be noted that Dr Arthur was acquitted; therefore, the article presumably did not influence the jurors against him. That fact, however, as pointed out above, would not have precluded a finding that there was a substantial risk of serious prejudice to his trial.) Lord Diplock's test under s 5 may be summed up as follows: looking at the actual words written (as opposed to considering what could have been omitted), was the article written in good faith and concerned with a question of general legitimate public interest which created an incidental risk of prejudice to a particular case? It seems that the discussion can be triggered off by the case itself; it need not have arisen prior to it.

This ruling gave an emphasis to freedom of speech which tended to bring the strict liability rule into harmony with Art 10 as interpreted by the European Court of Human Rights' ruling in the *Sunday Times* case. However, despite this broad interpretation of s 5, the media obviously does not have *carte blanche* to discuss issues arising from or relating to any particular case during the 'active' period.

The *AG v English* ruling did not concern a direct reference to a particular case and therefore it was uncertain until the ruling in *AG v Times Newspapers*[95] whether s 5 would cover such references. The *Sunday Times* and four other newspapers commented on the background of an intruder into the Queen's bedroom, Michael Fagin, at a time when he was about to stand trial. The comments of the Mail on Sunday about Fagin, which included the allegation that he had had a homosexual liaison with the royal bodyguard and that he was a 'rootless penniless neurotic', satisfied the s 2(2) test as it was thought that they would affect the jury's assessment of his honesty. However, they fell within s 5 as they were part of a discussion of the Queen's safety, which was a matter of general public concern. In contrast, The *Sunday Times'* allegation that Fagin had stabbed his stepson could not fall within s 5, as it was irrelevant to the question of the Queen's safety, but had nevertheless been considered in detail.

Finally, it must be shown that the article was written in good faith. In *AG v Hislop* the articles in question did not fall within s 5 because it could not be said that they were published in good faith: the finding – relevant to the question of contempt at common law – that the editor had intended to prejudice the relevant proceedings – was held to be incompatible with a finding of good faith under s 5.

Section 5 clearly requires some fine lines to be drawn. Where a piece merely discusses a particular case and makes no attempt to address wider issues, s 5 will not apply (*Daily*

---

93 See above, fn 50.
94 See, eg, Robertson, *op cit*, fn 1, p 216.
95 (1983) *The Times*, 12 February.

Express case),[96] but where there is some discussion of wider issues, this will not mean that it will always apply. This issue can only be resolved by looking at the subject matter of the discussion and asking how closely it relates to the trial in question: can it be said that the risk of prejudice the publication creates is merely incidental to its main theme? In *AG v TVS Television, AG v HW Southey and Sons*[97] it was determined that a TVS programme, concerned with the possibility that Rachmanism had arisen in the south of England, but focused on landlords in Reading, which coincided with the charging of a Reading landlord with conspiring to defraud the DHSS, could not create a merely incidental risk. Similarly, in *Pickering v Liverpool Daily Post and Echo Newspapers plc*,[98] where the discussion centred on the case itself, s 5 did not apply. This issue was further considered in *AG v Guardian Newspapers*[99] and it was determined that the term 'merely incidental' should receive a wide interpretation. However, it is suggested that it would be to misunderstand s 5 to say that a discussion which arose from and concerned the case itself would never be able to take advantage of s 5 protection: s 5 impliedly accepts that the discussion, but not the risk of prejudice it creates, need not be merely incidental to the trial. Obviously, given that it will already have been shown that the article in question creates a risk of serious prejudice, it might be hard to show that the prejudice is merely incidental if the article relates largely to the case. However, it might not be impossible if the thrust of the discussion could not be said to cause prejudice, while the part which could was capable of being viewed as incidental to the rest.

Owing largely to the operation of s 5, the strict liability rule seems to have created a fairer balance than was the case at common law between freedom of speech and protection for the administration of justice. However, the uncertainty as to the application of the term 'incidental' and as to the effect of s 5 where the article focuses on the case itself means that s 5 may allow some legitimate debate in the media to be stifled and therefore, it might be argued, now that the HRA is in force, that further relaxation is needed in order to afford the high value to political speech which is accorded to it at Strasbourg. This possibility is considered further below.

The Defence of 'ignorance' under s 3

A defendant charged with the s 1 offence can seek to use s 3 as a defence. Section 3 is a true defence, since the burden of proof lies on the defendant. The publisher or distributor will not be strictly liable if, having taken all reasonable care, he or she does not know and has no reason to suspect that the proceedings are active or that the publication contains the type of material likely to give rise to strict liability under s 2. It may be noted that since the common law (see below) does not depend on the use of the active test, liability could still arise outside the statute even where, within the statute, s 3 would have been applicable.

---

96 (1981) *The Times*, 19 December.
97 (1989) *The Times*, 7 July.
98 [1991] 2 AC 370; [1991] 1 All ER 622, HL.
99 [1992] 3 All ER 38, CA.

Further restrictions on reporting of court proceedings

The general principle that justice should be openly administered is well established.[100] This principle is recognised in the Art 6 requirement that everyone is entitled to a 'fair and *public* hearing'. This Art 6 requirement is subject to a number of exceptions contained in para 1: 'the press and public may be excluded from all or part of the trial in the interests of morals, public order or national security in a democratic society, where the interests of juveniles or the protection of the private life of the parties so require or to the extent strictly necessary in the opinion of the court in special circumstances where publicity would prejudice the interests of justice'. In this respect, Arts 10 and 6 are not in conflict, since Art 10 may be said to require impliedly that restrictions on allowing journalists to attend hearings should be strictly scrutinised. Conflict is more likely to arise between the interest in open justice and the Art 8 guarantee of a right to respect for privacy. This issue is considered in Chapter 10.[101]

In general, in accordance with the open justice principle, courts are open to the public and therefore a fair and accurate factual report of the proceedings, in good faith, will not amount to a contempt. This is provided for under s 4(1) of the 1981 Act. The reverse is true of private sittings, a report of which will usually *prima facie* amount to a contempt. Section 4(1), therefore, creates an exception from strict liability in respect of proceedings held in public, so long as the other elements mentioned are present. Another way of putting this is to say that fair and accurate reports of proceedings would not fall within s 2(2) in any event: s 4(1) merely makes this explicit, in statutory form. However, a number of exceptions to the principle of openness have been created to allow the withholding of information, either temporarily or indefinitely. For example, at common law, a judge can order prohibition of a publication in order to prevent, for example, the disclosure of the identity of a witness. The leading authority is *AG v Leveller Magazine Ltd*[102] in which it was accepted that departure from the principle of openness would be warranted if necessary for the due administration of justice, and that therefore if a court made an order designed to protect the administration of justice, then it would be incumbent on those who knew of it not to do anything which might frustrate its object. All these exceptions must be considered for their compatibility with Art 10, since all clearly represent interferences with freedom of expression. In relation to reporting restrictions, as opposed to restrictions on those who may attend the hearing, a conflict between Arts 10 and 6 may arise where the restrictions are aimed at avoiding prejudice to the trial.

Postponing reporting of information

Section 4(2) of the 1981 Act provides that during any legal proceeding held in public, a judge may make an order postponing reporting of the proceedings if such action 'appears necessary for avoiding a substantial risk of prejudice to the administration of justice in those proceedings', thus creating an exception to s 4(1).[103] This might typically involve

---

100 See the comments to this effect and on the need to limit use of private hearings in *Preston* [1993] 4 All ER 638; 143 NLJ 1601.

101 See pp 547–50.

102 [1979] AC 440; [1979] 2 WLR 247, HL.

103 For comment on s 4 of the 1981 Act, see Walker, C, Cram, I and Brogarth, D (1992) 55 MLR 647.

the reporting of matters which the defence wished to argue should be ruled inadmissible. A right of appeal against such orders in relation to trials on indictment was created by s 159 of the Criminal Justice Act 1988 in order to take account of a challenge under Art 10 at Strasbourg.[104] The position of the media when a s 4(2) order is made in respect of reporting a summary trial is less clear. However, it was established in *Clerkenwell Metropolitan Stipendiary Magistrate ex p The Telegraph and Others*[105] that in such circumstances, the media have a right to be heard and must be allowed to put forward the case for discharging the order. When the applicants, publishers of national newspapers, became aware of the existence of the order, they were granted a hearing before the magistrate at which they submitted that the court had power to hear representations from them as to why the order should be discharged. The magistrate held that the court had no power to hear from anyone but the parties to the proceedings. The applicants sought a declaration that the court did have the power to hear their representations, and it was determined, relying on *Horsham Justices ex p Farqharson*,[106] that they had sufficient standing to apply for judicial review. It was found to be implicit in s 4(2) that a court contemplating use of the section should be able to hear representations from those who would be affected if an order was made. In determining whether the order should be maintained, it was found to be necessary to balance the interest in the need for a fair trial before an unprejudiced jury on the one hand and the requirements of open justice on the other. In performing this balancing exercise, the magistrate would need to hear representations from the press as being best qualified to represent the public interest in publicity.

The ruling of the Court of Appeal in *Horsham Magistrates ex p Farqharson* was to the effect that such orders should be made sparingly; judges should be careful not to impose a ban on flimsy grounds where the connection between the matters in question and prejudice to the administration of justice was purely speculative. If other means of protecting the jury from possibly prejudicial reports of the trial were available, they should be used. Moreover, it must be ensured that the ban covers only the matters in question.

This ruling was reinforced by the decision in *Central Independent Television plc and Others*.[107] During a criminal trial, the jury had to stay overnight in a hotel and in order that they could watch television or listen to the radio, the judge made an order under s 4(2) postponing reporting of the proceedings for that night. The applicants, broadcasters, appealed against the order under s 159 of the Criminal Justice Act 1988 on the basis that there was no ground on which the judge could have concluded that there was a substantial risk of prejudice to the administration of justice. Further, the judge had incorrectly exercised his discretion under the sub-section and failed to take proper account of the public interest in freedom of expression and in the open administration of justice. The Court of Appeal found that it had not been necessary to make the order as there was little, if any, evidence of a risk to the administration of justice: the previous

104 The journalist, Crook, attempted to challenge a s 11 anonymity order: *Central Criminal Court ex p Crook* (1984) *The Times*, 8 November. When the challenge failed, Crook took the case to Strasbourg.
105 [1993] 2 All ER 183; (1992) *The Times*, 22 October.
106 [1982] 2 All ER 269, CA.
107 [1991] 1 All ER 347.

reporting of the case had not suggested that reporting on the day in question would be anything other than fair and accurate. Even had there been a substantial risk, it might have been possible to adopt alternative methods of insulating the jury from the media. Where such alternative methods were available, they should be used. Accordingly, the appeal was allowed.

The emphasis in this judgment on the need to restrict reporting only where clearly necessary is in accordance with Art 10 requirements: the convenience of the jury is not a sufficient reason for invoking the sub-section, since it would not fall within one of the legitimate aims of Art 10(2). Similarly, in *Ex p The Telegraph plc*,[108] the Court of Appeal found that even where a substantial risk to proceedings might arise, this need not mean that an order must automatically be made. The court based this finding on the need to consider the two elements of s 4(2) separately; first, a substantial risk of prejudice to the administration of justice should be identified flowing from publication of matters relating to the trial and, secondly, it should be asked whether it was necessary to make an order in order to avoid the risk. In making a determination as to the second limb, a judge should consider whether in the light of the competing interest in open justice, the order should be made at all, and if so, with all or any of the restrictions sought. In the case in question, the order should not have been made, since the risk of prejudice was outweighed by the interest in open justice. In *MGN Pension Trustees Ltd v Bank of America National Trust and Saving Association*,[109] the Serious Fraud Office applied for an order postponing reporting of civil actions brought by trustees of the pension fund until after the criminal proceedings were concluded. Six newspapers opposed the application. The judge followed the steps indicated in *Ex p The Telegraph* in determining that no order would be made.

These decisions suggests a concern on the part of the judiciary to prevent a ready use of s 4(2) orders which would be prejudicial to the principle of open justice.[110] Incidentally, it is of some interest to note that this decision followed closely on that in *AG v Guardian Newspapers*[111] which concerned an article written while a ban on reporting of a major fraud trial was in force, criticising the alleged propensity of judges in such trials to impose bans. It was held that the article created too remote a risk to constitute a contempt under the strict liability rule, and Brooke J took the opportunity of re-emphasising the importance of the news media as the eyes and ears of the general public.

This approach was developed in *R v Beck ex p Daily Telegraph*.[112] Beck, who had been a social worker in charge of children's homes, was charged with offences involving sexual abuse, and owing to the number of charges, the trial was split into three. At the first trial, a s 4(2) order was made, owing to the risk of prejudice to the subsequent two trials. On appeal, the Court of Appeal accepted that there was a substantial risk of prejudice, but went on to find that the public interest in the reporting of the trial outweighed the risk. In so finding, the court emphasised the concern which the public must feel because of the particular facts of the case and the right of the public to be informed and to be able to ask

---

108 [1993] 2 All ER 971.

109 [1995] EMLR 99.

110 See also *Saunders* (the Guinness trials) [1990] Crim LR 597; *Barlow Clowes Gilt Managers v Clowes* (1990) *The Times*, 2 February, and *Sherwood ex p The Telegraph Group plc* (2001) *The Times*, 12 June.

111 [1992] 3 All ER 38.

112 [1993] 2 All ER 177.

questions about the opportunities created for those in public service to commit such offences.

These decisions suggest that the domestic courts are already taking into account the demands of Arts 10 and 6 by reference to the principles underlying those two Articles. The stance taken towards the role of journalists closely parallels that taken at Strasbourg, as indicated in the Introduction to Part II, above.

Prohibiting reporting of information

Section 11 of the 1981 Act allows a court which has power to do so to make an order prohibiting publication of names or other matters if this appears necessary 'for the purpose for which it was so withheld'. Thus, s 11 does not itself confer such a power and therefore refers to other statutes[113] and to the imprecise common law powers. The leading authority is the House of Lords' decision in *AG v Leveller Magazine Ltd*.[114] The majority found that if, in the course of regulating its own proceedings, a court makes an order designed to protect the due administration of justice, it is then incumbent on those who know of the ruling to do nothing which would frustrate the object of the ruling. At present, there are signs that a robust interpretation will be given to s 11 similar to that being taken to s 4(2): the fundamental importance of open justice will be outweighed only by a very clear detriment which answers to a general public interest flowing from publication of the matters in question – economic damage to the interests of the defendant will not suffice.[115] Nor will a concern to protect the 'comfort and feelings of the defendant'.[116] The courts may be prepared to make anonymity orders to protect the privacy of those involved in proceedings,[117] but only where the failure to afford anonymity would, under strict scrutiny, render the attainment of justice very doubtful.[118] Witnesses are placed in a somewhat different position. There is a clear public interest in encouraging witnesses to come forward and to co-operate in proceedings. Therefore, courts have shown a greater willingness to ensure the anonymity of witnesses.[119] If a court takes measures to protect the anonymity of witnesses such as sitting *in camera* or allowing the use of screens, there may be no need to make an express s 11 order.

The granting of anonymity raises a number of Convention issues. From the perspective of Art 10, anonymity clearly limits what can be reported about a case and may inhibit later reporting or discussion of any issues arising out of the case. However, such restrictions may be justifiable within the para 2 exceptions which include 'for the rights of others'. The right to respect for privacy would therefore be covered, as would

---

113 A number of statutory provisions impose restrictions such as allowing certain persons concerned in a case to remain anonymous. This is provided for in relation to complainants in rape cases under the Sexual Offences (Amendment) Act 1976, s 4, as amended, and for children under the Children and Young Persons Act 1933, s 39(1). See further Chapter 10, pp 547–50.

114 [1979] AC 440; [1979] 2 WLR 247, HL. For comment on s 11 of the 1981 Act see Walker, Cram and Brogarth, *op cit*, fn 103.

115 *Dover JJ ex p Dover DC and Wells* (1991) 156 JP 433; [1992] Crim LR 371.

116 *Evesham JJ ex p McDonagh* [1988] 1 QB 553, p 562.

117 See *H v Ministry of Defence* [1991] 2 QB 103 and *Criminal Injuries Compensation Board ex p A* [1992] COD 379.

118 *Westminster CC ex p Castelli and Tristan-Garcia* (1995) *The Times*, 14 August.

119 See *Watford Magistrates' Court ex p Lenman* [1993] Crim LR 388; *Taylor* [1994] TLR 484.

Art 6 rights. Therefore, the current emphasis on granting anonymity only on the basis that otherwise, the administration of justice would suffer, is questionable. In future, the court will be bound by Art 8; therefore witnesses, plaintiffs and defendants will be able to argue in certain circumstances that anonymity should be granted even where such administration does not clearly demand it.

While Arts 6 and 10 may come into conflict in respect of anonymity granted to the defendant, they may have similar demands in respect of anonymity granted to witnesses. Allowing witnesses to give evidence behind screens or by means of a video link clearly raises Art 6 issues, as Strasbourg has accepted.[120] But it also raises Art 10 ones. Again, argument could be raised under both Articles to the effect that any measures affording anonymity to witnesses should be strictly scrutinised. But while arguments for anonymity might prevail under Art 10 since it is materially qualified, they would be less likely to do so under Art 6.

Intentionally prejudicing proceedings

Section 6(c) of the 1981 Act preserves liability for contempt at common law if intention to prejudice the administration of justice can be shown. 'Prejudice [to] the administration of justice' clearly includes (and may solely denote – see below) prejudice to particular proceedings. Once the requirement of intent is satisfied, it is easier to establish contempt at common law rather than under the Act since it is only necessary to show 'a real risk of prejudice' and proceedings need only be imminent, not 'active'. Clearly, liability can be established at common law in instances when it might also be established under the 1981 Act, as occurred in the *Hislop* case, and also in instances when the Act will not apply because proceedings are inactive. Possibly, it might also be established where one of the statutory tests other than the 'active' requirement was not satisfied. These preliminary observations are developed below, taking Convention standards into account under the HRA. Section 3 of the HRA does not apply (except to s 6(c) itself) since intentional contempt arises at common law, but the court has a duty to ensure that that the common law is compatible with the Convention under s 6. It will be suggested, in particular, that the common law requirements should be subjected to a strict scrutiny in so far as they represent the possibility of circumventing a measure adopted specifically to meet Art 10 standards.

A publication will fall within the area of liability preserved by s 6(c) if the following three elements are present.

Intention to prejudice the administration of justice

The test for intention to prejudice the administration of justice was established in *AG v Times Newspaper*[121] and *AG v News Group Newspapers plc*.[122] It was made clear that 'intention' connotes specific intent and therefore cannot include recklessness. The test

---

120 See *Doorson v Netherlands* (1996) 22 EHRR 330.
121 [1992] 7 AC 191; [1991] 2 All ER 398; for a report of the Divisional Court proceedings see *Re AG v Observer and Guardian Newspapers Ltd* (1989) *The Times*, 9 May; for comment see [1989] PL 477. For comment on the *mens rea* issue, see Laws (1990) 43 CLP 99, pp 105–10.
122 [1989] QB 110; [1988] 3 WLR 163; [1988] 2 All ER 906.

may be summed up as follows: did the defendant either wish to prejudice proceedings or ('oblique' intent) foresee that such prejudice was a virtually inevitable consequence of publishing the material in question?[123] Thus, it is not necessary to show a desire to prejudice proceedings or that where there was such a desire, that it was the sole desire. This test is based on the meaning of intent arising from two rulings on the *mens rea* for murder: *Hancock and Shankland*,[124] *Nedrick*[125] and *Woollin*.[126]

This is a subjective test, but the Court of Appeal in *AG v Newspaper Publishing plc* (the *Spycatcher* case)[127] appeared to be asking whether or not the consequences in question were 'foreseeable', suggesting not that the defendant should actually have foreseen them, but that an objective observer would have done so. This would, of course, be an easier test to satisfy, although since, in practice, it will be necessary to infer that the defendant foresaw the consequences, the difference between the two tests may be of only theoretical importance. This argument is put forward on the basis that in general, if an objective observer would have foreseen a risk of prejudice, it will be hard for an editor to show that he or she did not, because, unlike some defendants to whom this test is applied (in other areas of criminal law), an editor must make a decision as to publication unaffected by mental incompetence (it is assumed), emotion or the need to act in the heat of the moment. Nevertheless, a concept of 'objective intent' is insufficiently distinguishable from recklessness; as it is established that recklessness will not suffice for common law contempt, intention clearly refers to subjective intent.

A number of circumstances may allow the inference of intention to prejudice the proceedings to be made, although it is suggested that the relevance of the circumstances will depend on the form of intent – desire or oblique intent – which seems to be in question. In *AG v News Group Newspapers plc*,[128] the newspaper's support for the prosecution in its columns and in funding a private prosecution allowed the inference to be made. A Dr B was questioned about an allegation of rape made against him by an eight year old girl, but eventually the county prosecuting solicitor decided that there was insufficient evidence to prosecute him. *The Sun* obtained the story and decided that it should offer the mother financial help in order to fund a private prosecution. It published various articles attacking Dr B: 'Rape Case Doc: Sun acts'; 'Beast must be named, says MP', etc. The Attorney General brought a prosecution against *The Sun* for contempt. The articles could not come within the strict liability rule because the proceedings in question – the private prosecution – were not active. The contempt alleged, therefore, arose at common law. It was found that intention could be established, either on the basis of a desire to prejudice the proceedings (presumably in order to vindicate the paper's stance) or because the editor must have foreseen that Dr B would almost certainly not receive a fair trial. The judgment would support either view, but probably favours the former: in

---

123 Moreover, although this issue has not yet arisen and may be unlikely to arise, it is necessary to show that the almost inevitable effect of the article would also have been obvious to an objective observer where it is clear that the editor did not wish to prejudice proceedings. The defence could conceivably argue that the editor in question *did* foresee that the article would almost certainly have the effect in question, but that an objective observer would *not* have come to that conclusion.

124 [1986] AC 455; [1986] 1 All ER 641; [1986] 3 WLR 1014.

125 [1986] 3 All ER 1; [1986] 1 WLR 1025.

126 [1999] 1 AC 82.

127 [1988] Ch 333; [1987] 3 All ER 276; [1988] 3 WLR 942, CA.

128 [1989] QB 110; [1988] 3 WLR 163; [1988] 2 All ER 906.

his ruling, Watkins LJ said: '... they could only have printed articles of such a kind if they were campaigning for a conviction as they clearly were.' However, if he had the latter form of intent in mind, it may be said that although the newspaper had acted reprehensibly in using its power to attempt to influence a trial it had itself become involved in, it is arguable that intent should not have been so readily established. The fact that *The Sun* was personally involved was not, it is argued, relevant to oblique intent. The proceedings were clearly not going to occur for some time; therefore, although the defendants probably foresaw some risk of prejudice to them, it was not clear that such prejudice could be said to be a virtually inevitable consequence of publication. In fact, Dr B was acquitted; the jury were clearly able to put out of their minds any influence articles may have had.

The *Sun* case may be contrasted with *AG v Sport Newspapers Ltd*[129] in which the test for intention was somewhat more strictly interpreted. One David Evans, who had previous convictions for rape, was suspected of abducting Anna Humphries. He was on the run when *The Sport* published his convictions; the proceedings were not therefore active, and so the case arose at common law. It did not appear that *The Sport* wished to prejudice proceedings. Was it foreseen as a virtual certainty that prejudice to Evans's trial would occur as a result of the publication? It was held that there was a risk of such prejudice of which the editor of *The Sport* was aware, but that such awareness of risk was not sufficient. Clearly, had the *mens rea* of common law contempt included recklessness it would have been established.

Imminence

At common law, the *sub judice* period began when proceedings could be said to be imminent (*Savundranayagan*).[130] This test would of course be readily satisfied where proceedings were active. However, it may not always be necessary to establish imminence. In *AG v News Group Newspapers plc*[131] it was held obiter that where it is established that the defendant intended to prejudice proceedings, it is not necessary to show that proceedings are imminent. In his judgment, Watkins LJ approved of David Pannick's contention that 'no authority states that common law contempt cannot be committed where proceedings cannot be said to be imminent but where there is a specific intent to impede a fair trial, the occurrence of which is in contemplation'. It was found that even if the trial of Dr B was too far off to be said to be pending or imminent, the conduct of *The Sun* in publishing stories at the same time as assisting the mother in the private prosecution could still amount to contempt. Bingham LJ concurred with this dilution of the imminence test in *AG v Sport*,[132] although in the same case Hodgson J considered that proceedings must be 'pending'. He interpreted 'pending' as synonymous with 'active', an interpretation which would have greatly curtailed the scope of common law contempt.

This point, therefore, remains unresolved, leaving the media without a clear guide as to the period during which publication of matter relevant to proceedings will be risky. If

---

129 [1991] 1 WLR 1194.
130 [1968] 3 All ER 439; [1968] 1 WLR 1761, CA.
131 [1989] QB 110; [1988] 3 WLR 163; [1988] 2 All ER 906.
132 [1991] 1 WLR 1194.

proceedings need not even be imminent, it appears that reporting of matters which may give rise to proceedings at some point in the future will be severely circumscribed. The test of imminence is itself too wide and uncertain, but would be preferable to the uncertainty on this point which was exacerbated by *AG v Sport*. It is uncertain what the alternative test contemplated by Lord Bingham could be. There cannot be an intention to prejudice something which cannot even be identified as a possibility. Thus the test at its least stringent must be that proceedings can be identified as a possibility before this head of common law contempt can be in question. This development in common law contempt may significantly curtail press freedom, since it clearly does nothing to help editors who wish to determine whether or not a publication might attract a criminal prosecution. Therefore, if a prosecution under this head was brought in the post-HRA era, it is questionable whether the interference with freedom of expression it would represent could be said to be 'prescribed by law' due to the lack of precision and therefore of forseeability present in this area of the common law. As Chapter 2 indicated, an interference must not only have a basis in law, that basis must be of sufficient quality.[133] Probably the most satisfactory method of ensuring that the requirements of quality are met would be to adopt the course suggested by Hodgson J. The 'active' test is laid down with reasonable precision and would, therefore, probably meet those requirements. Obviously, this would confine common law contempt to instances in which the statute could also be used. It would still have a role since, where intention was shown, a much higher fine would be imposed on the media organ in question. Such a development would be, it is suggested, appropriate in the post-HRA era since it would recognise that it should not be possible to circumvent a statute that had been adopted in order to meet a Strasbourg ruling.[134]

A real risk of prejudice

It must be shown that the publication amounts to conduct which creates a real risk of prejudice to the administration of justice (*Thompson Newspapers*).[135] There may be a number of different methods of fulfilling this test. In *Hislop and Pressdram*[136] it was found that the defendants, who were one party in an action for defamation, had interfered with the administration of justice because they had brought improper pressure to bear on the other party, Sonia Sutcliffe, by publishing material in *Private Eye* intended to deter her from pursuing the action. There was a substantial risk that the articles might have succeeded in their aim; had they done so, the course of justice in Mrs Sutcliffe's action would have been seriously prejudiced, since she would have been deterred from having her claim decided in a court. Counsel for *Private Eye* had argued that defamatory material which the defendant seeks to justify should not be restrained, because until it is clear that the alleged libel is untrue, it is not clear that any right has been infringed (*Bonnard v Perryman*).[137] This argument was rejected because the question of deterrence did not depend on the truth or falsity of the allegations. The possibility of justification was thus

---

133 See p 66.
134 In the *Sunday Times* case; see above, fn 51.
135 [1968] 1 All ER 268; [1968] 1 WLR 1.
136 1991] 1 QB 514; [1991] 1 All ER 911; [1991] 2 WLR 219, CA.
137 [1891] 2 Ch 269, p 289.

irrelevant. In this instance, it might also be noted that the relevant tests under the 1981 Act had been satisfied; therefore, it would seem that, *a fortiori*, common law contempt could be established, it having already been accepted that the articles had been published with the intention of putting pressure on Mrs Sutcliffe to discontinue the defamation action, thereby satisfying the *mens rea* requirement at common law.

The 'real risk of prejudice' test may also be fulfilled in certain circumstances if part of the media frustrates a court order (including orders made under s 4(2) of the 1981 Act) against another part. This highly significant extension of common law contempt arose from one strand of the *Spycatcher* litigation. In 1985, the Attorney General commenced proceedings in Australia in an attempt to restrain publication of *Spycatcher* by Peter Wright. The book included allegations of illegal activity engaged in by MI5. In 1986, after the *Guardian* and the *Observer* had published reports of the forthcoming hearing which included some *Spycatcher* material, the Attorney General obtained temporary *ex parte* injunctions preventing them from further disclosure of such material.[138] While the temporary injunctions were in force, *The Independent* and two other papers published material covered by them. It was determined in the Court of Appeal (*AG v Newspaper Publishing plc*)[139] and confirmed in the House of Lords (*AG v Times Newspapers Ltd*)[140] that such publication constituted the *actus reus* of common law contempt on the basis that publication of confidential material, the subject matter of a pending action, damaging its confidentiality and thereby probably rendering the action pointless, created an interference with the administration of justice. The case therefore affirmed the principle that once an interlocutory injunction has been obtained restraining one organ of the media from publication of allegedly confidential material, the rest of the media may be in contempt if they publish that material, even if their intention in doing so is to bring alleged iniquity to public attention. This case thus allowed the laws of confidence and contempt to operate together as a significant prior restraint on media freedom and in so doing, created an inroad into the general principle that a court order should only affect the party to which it is directed as only that party will have a chance to argue that the making of the order would be wrong.

The decision in *AG v Newspaper Publishing plc and Others*[141] seems to represent an attempt to narrow down the area of liability created by the decision in *AG v Times Newspapers Ltd*. The case arose from the reporting of the appeals in the *Ordtech* case,[142] a case which bore strong similarities to the *Matrix Churchill* case.[143] The appellants appealed against their convictions for exporting arms; public interest immunity certificates were issued, but the Court of Appeal ordered that the material covered by them, which was crucial to the appeal, should be disclosed in summarised and edited form to the appellants and their legal advisors. The order restricted the use of the material to the appeal and requested its return on conclusion of the appeal. In court, in directing return of the documents, the Lord Chief Justice indicated that breach of the order would result in the matter being referred to the Attorney General. In its report of the

---

138 For full discussion of this branch of the litigation see Chapter 7, pp 357–61.

139 (1990) *The Times*, 28 February.

140 [1992] 1 AC 191; [1991] 2 All ER 398; [1991] 2 WLR 994, HL: for comment see NLJ 173 and 1115.

141 [1997] 3 All ER 159; (1997) *The Times*, 2 May, CA.

142 See *Blackledge and Others* (1996) 1 Cr App R 326, CA.

143 See below, pp 367–68.

proceedings, *The Independent* published a small amount of material from the documents which did not also appear in the written copy of the judgment. The Attorney General brought proceedings for contempt against *The Independent*, relying on the ruling in *AG v Times Newspapers* to the effect that if a third party with the requisite intent acts to frustrate the basis on which a court has determined that justice should be administered, then it will be guilty of contempt. On behalf of *The Independent* it was argued that the *Times* case represented an extension of the law as it had previously been understood and that the court should be slow to extend the law any further since any such extension represented a further encroachment on freedom of expression and inhibited the media in its function of informing the public. The court did not accept that any conduct by a third party inconsistent with a court order was sufficient to amount to the *actus reus* of contempt: it was found necessary to show that a significant and adverse effect on the administration of justice in the relevant proceedings had occurred. The Court of Appeal used the wording of Art 10 of the Convention in finding that restraints on freedom of expression should be no wider than necessary in a democratic society, and considered that conduct which is inconsistent with a court order in a trivial way should not create the risk of a conviction for contempt. The application of the Attorney General was therefore dismissed.

This decision narrows down the area of liability created in the *Times* case, but does not affect the extension of the law it brought about. That extension may be incompatible with Art 10. Although trivial or technical breaches of court orders made against others will not attract liability, the area of liability which remains is likely to create a curb on press freedom which may be incompatible with the crucial role of the press in a free society, bearing in mind the emphasis placed upon that role in *Goodwin v UK*[144] by the European Court of Human Rights.[145] The principle laid down in the *Times* case is likely to be challenged now that the HRA is fully in force. The argument would be that the grant of such an injunction clearly creates, as a prior restraint, a grave interference with the freedom of the media. While its grant might be in accordance with the law, based on the findings in the *Times* case, and would probably have the legitimate aim of maintaining the authority of the judiciary, the effects of such an injunction would appear to be disproportionate to such an aim, since all organs of the media would – potentially – be silenced for a substantial period of time. Further, they would be at risk of incurring criminal liability, although if the newspaper against which the injunction was originally granted breached it, civil liability only would arise. Not only, therefore, would the grant of such an injunction be of doubtful compatibility with Art 10 since it allows such far reaching restrictions on media freedom, but the possibility of affecting organs of the media by obtaining an injunction against one of them would also appear to engage s 12 of the HRA. Section 12, as indicated above, does not apply to 'relief' granted in criminal proceedings, under s 12(5). But the injunction would be granted in civil proceedings, although it would potentially create criminal liability (or at least liability which, in Convention terms, has all the hallmarks of criminal liability).[146]

---

144 *Goodwin v UK* (1996) 22 EHRR 123.

145 These issues are discussed further in Chapter 7, pp 357–61, in relation to the breach of confidence issue, the other strand of the *Spycatcher* litigation.

146 *Benham v UK* (1996) 22 EHRR 293.

It is argued that the only satisfactory way of meeting the demands of s 12 would be to leave the Attorney General to seek an injunction against each media organ separately. If an injunction was granted and breached by a particular organ, it would be liable for civil contempt. It may further be noted that in any event, if the test for imminence comes to be based in future on the 'active' test, liability would not arise in a number of instances, including the one which arose in *Spycatcher*, since at the time when *The Independent* published its article, no proceedings were active.

The relationship between the 1981 Act and the common law

Common law contempt represents not only an alternative, but also, where proceedings are active, an additional possibility of establishing liability. It presents such an alternative in all instances in which proceedings are not active, assuming, of course, that the *mens rea* requirement can be satisfied, and it has proved to be of great significance in this context owing to the readiness with which it has sometimes been accepted that the common law tests have been fulfilled. The doctrine has therefore attracted criticism as circumventing the 1981 Act[147] but it may also, even more controversially, present an alternative in instances where proceedings are active, but liability under the Act cannot be established. If, as suggested above, the 'active' test replaces that of imminence in respect of common law contempt under the HRA, this would be the only significant role of common law contempt. It would open up the possibility that the Act and, in particular, the provisions of s 5, could be undermined. This is of particular significance given that s 5 was adopted to take account of the ruling in the European Court of Human Rights that UK contempt law had breached the Art 10 guarantee of freedom of speech.

Common law contempt was established in the *Hislop* case in an instance in which proceedings were active and, therefore, the relationship between the concept of good faith under s 5 and the question of intention under s 6(c) came under consideration. It appeared that a finding of intention to prejudice the administration of justice necessary to found liability for contempt at common law would probably preclude a finding of good faith under s 5. This finding seemed to obviate the possibility of proceeding at common law in appropriate instances in order to avoid the operation of s 5 – a course which would have undermined the policy of the Act as providing some safeguards for media freedom. However, the point is open to argument. It could be said that in the majority of cases, a finding of good faith under s 5 would indeed preclude a finding of intention to prejudice proceedings, but in one instance it might not. It might be shown that where a newspaper recognised a strong risk that proceedings would be prejudiced, but did not desire such prejudice (as may have been the case in *AG v Newspaper Publishing plc*), a finding of good faith might not be precluded. A publisher might argue that his or her recognition of the risk to proceedings was outweighed (in his or her own mind) by the need to bring iniquity or other matters of public interest to public attention. The good faith requirement under s 5 might cover such a situation, thereby preventing liability under statute, although it might still arise at common law. Thus, for example, the principle arising from *AG v Newspaper Publishing plc* might apply where proceedings were active and where publication of material covered by an injunction fell within s 5. In this sense, therefore,

---

147 Miller has written 'I think it is at best messy and may also be dangerous to allow the common law to outflank the Act' [1992] Crim LR 112.

common law contempt may have the ability to undermine the statutory protection for freedom of speech,[148] unless requirements similar to those under s 5 can be implied into the common law in reliance on Art 10, a matter which is discussed further below.

The possibility envisaged is unlikely to arise. However, there are other circumstances in which a prosecution at common law could succeed in an instance in which proceedings are active but prosecution under the Act fails. For example, s 5 might be irrelevant because it might be clear that the article does not concern a discussion in good faith of public affairs. However, s 2(2) might not be satisfied on the basis that, although some risk of prejudice arose, it could not be termed serious enough. In such an instance, there appears to be no reason why the common law could not be used instead on the basis that the test of showing 'a real risk of prejudice' is less difficult to satisfy. If so, it would be possible to circumvent the more stringent s 2(2) requirement. Of course, it would be necessary to prove an intention to prejudice the administration of justice. Bearing in mind the fact that the 1981 Act was introduced in order to satisfy Art 10, it is suggested that its circumvention under the common law should be resisted.

Conclusions: impact of the HRA

This overview of this form of contempt gives rise, it is argued, to the conclusion that at present, it is out of accord with Convention values and requirements in terms of both law and practice. As indicated above, a comparison between the *Taylor* and the *Spycatcher* cases[149] suggests that both statute and common law are insufficiently focused on the core values at stake. In *Taylor*, the individual's right to a fair trial under Art 6 was genuinely threatened; at the same time, the speech in question was of very little value in Art 10 terms. Yet no prosecution was forthcoming. In contrast, *Spycatcher* concerned political speech to which Strasbourg accords the highest value, while the Art 6 guarantee was hardly engaged.

A possible explanation for practice in these and other similar instances is that where speech is directly critical of a part of the executive and therefore, impliedly, of government itself, the interests of the government in stifling it are most obviously engaged. Such an instance arose in *Spycatcher* and provided an example of the failure of an Attorney General to ensure that an appearance of distance from the government was maintained. In contrast, when the trial of an obscure personage, accused of a highly publicised crime, is in question, there is little or no political advantage to be gained in seeking to prevent or punish interferences with it. But there may be quite severe political disadvantage in appearing to attack the massed ranks of the tabloids. As indicated above, it is not entirely possible to dismiss misgivings as to the ability of Attorney Generals to distance themselves fully from their political colleagues, who may have such considerations in mind.

The problems created by the willingness of newspaper proprietors to damage the fairness of trials in pursuit of competitive advantage are likely to continue so long as they

---

148 For comment on these developments in common law contempt, see Stone, 'Common law contempt' (1988) 138 NLJ 136; Halpin, A, 'Child's play in the Lords' (1991) 141 NLJ 173; McHale, J, 'Common law contempt' (1991) 141 NLJ 1115.

149 See above, pp 226–27.

view contempt actions as improbable. Certain trials such as that of the Taylor sisters, of Harold Shipman in 2000, and the trial in 2001 of the suspect charged with the murder of the television presenter Jill Dando, attract immense media coverage, which has, in the case of a number of newspapers, little connection with free speech values but is motivated merely by profit making concerns. Assuming that in the very competitive media market, one newspaper is unlikely to forgo the chance of attracting readers by its coverage of such cases, intervention by the State is essential if certain defendants are not to bear the burden created by the demands of the market. Ironically, some tabloids profess to be eager to bring particular criminals to justice. But, by their coverage of a trial, they may act in a manner which runs counter to that end since the conviction may have to be overturned. If so, the victim or the victim's relatives may be forced to suffer the consequences, not, essentially, of the pursuit of free speech interests, but of profit-related ones.

These problems could be addressed by removing the role of the Attorney General in bringing contempt proceedings. It could be discharged by a judicial committee with a clear remit to institute proceedings where there were serious grounds for fearing prejudice to a criminal trial. But wider issues must be addressed. The question of the value of contempt actions as a deterrent should be considered, as should the use of injunctions. If the law of contempt is to be used, in the post-HRA era, as a means of *preventing* prejudice, injunctions should be obtained at an early pre-trial stage, where a case is likely to attract widespread coverage. In order to satisfy Art 10, they would have to be subject to the s 5 requirements, however, which, it is argued, also require reform in order to answer to its demands.

One possibility would be to replace s 5 with a more general public interest test which clearly allows discussion of significant matters of public interest, including those focusing mainly on the particular case. Development of a form of 'public interest defence' at common law[150] is also likely through the application of the Art 10(2) test, assuming that the common law continues to have a role. As indicated above, its imprecision as regards the *sub judice* period may mean that it cannot be viewed as being 'prescribed by law'. If the current test were replaced by the 'active' test, the role of common law contempt, such as it is, might almost disappear. It should be noted that the use of the imminence test also allows the s 3 'ignorance' test to be circumvented.

In relation to reform of s 5, Miller favours the Australian approach which allows a balancing exercise between the public interest in publication and the interest in a fair trial to be carried out,[151] and which allows suppression of material where the risk it creates to a fair trial is very clear.[152] This approach, rather than the American one, would seem to accord with the demands of the Convention, although, as argued above, when closely scrutinised, the values underlying both free speech and the fairness of trials, as recognised by the Convention are not, except at a very superficial level, in conflict. Section

---

150 Section 6(b) preserves all common law defences. Support for such a defence could derive from certain Australian cases (eg, *Registrar, Court of Appeal v Willesee* [1985] 3 NSWLR 650) and from the ruling of the Court of Appeal, although not the House of Lords, in the *Sunday Times* case, especially Lord Denning's speech [1973] QB 710, p 741.

151 See Miller, CJ [1992] Crim LR 106, p 114; also Walker, S, 'Freedom of speech and contempt of court: the English and Australian approaches compared' (1991) 40 ICLQ 583.

152 Miller instances *Hinch v AG for Victoria* (1987) 164 CLR 15; see also Miller, CJ (1993) LQR 39.

5 does not, however, appear to be in accordance with those values in the sense that it accepts that a substantial risk of serious prejudice can be caused to proceedings, so long as it is incidental to the discussion. Section 5 therefore accepts that a fair trial is unlikely, a stance which seems to be out of accord with the prominence given to fairness under Art 6. Section 5 does not, therefore, satisfy the aims of a preventive model. If a preventive approach is to be continued, albeit with the adoption of certain features of a neutralising one, such as strong directions to the jury to ignore media coverage, the better solution might be to replace s 5 with a general public interest test making specific reference, on the model provided by s 12 of the HRA, to Art 10. If such reforms do not occur, s 5 may be re-interpreted to bring it more into line with the Art 10 tests. The term 'incidental' is not a particularly apt test to be used as a means of determining whether a pressing social need to interfere with the speech in question has been established. Section 5 is, in one respect, very broad – since it covers any good faith discussion of public affairs – but in another, it is very narrow, since it only prevents an interference with worthwhile speech when the risk arising from the discussion can be viewed as incidental to its main theme. The term 'incidental' could be given a broad meaning so that it covered matters that could be viewed as not absolutely central to the argument in question. Further, the term 'serious' could be read into the section before the term 'discussion' in order to seek to differentiate between discussions of matters of crucial significance and of more trivial matters. Where the discussion could be viewed as especially significant, an extremely wide meaning could be given to the term incidental. The simplest alternative of all would be to read the words 'if the tests under Art 10 would thereby be satisfied or' into the section after the word 'rule'. This would, of course, be a very bold application of s 3 of the HRA, but it is suggested on the basis of the extremely bold approach the House of Lords has shown that it is prepared to take.[153]

The use of the preventive model therefore requires review in the post-HRA era with the aim of providing effective protection to both the administration of justice and free speech. But such review must also take account of technological developments, since they may require a further shift towards a neutralising model. The internet allows for the electronic transmission of information across frontiers. The information is available to anyone in a particular jurisdiction who has access to a computer. It is also now possible to receive information from the internet via digital or satellite television or via a mobile phone. Significant litigation, covering matters of public interest, may result in the creation of a website covering the case and the background issues surrounding it.[154] In such instances, prejudicial material may be posted on the website and jurors and witnesses may access it.[155] Contact email addresses of witnesses may be posted on the site, with the result that they receive material which might influence them. The site might be created by a person in any jurisdiction; therefore, the 1981 Act could not be used. This possibility may require jurors to be warned not to access such websites. But it is suggested that, in future, this problem may become much more pressing and will require more far reaching measures to be taken, at least in high profile cases. Such measures may tend more

---

153 In *R v A* [2001] 2 WLR 1546; [2001] UKHL 25; see Chapter 3.

154 Eg, David Irving, who was involved in a defamation action brought against Penguin Books, established his own website in order to make available information regarding the trial.

155 See further Bonnington, A, 'News without frontiers: pre-trial prejudice and the internet', in Edwards and Waelde (eds), *Law and the Internet*, 1997; Walker, C, 'Fundamental rights, fair trials and the new audio-visual sector' (1996) 59 MLR 517.

towards a neutralising than a preventive model, and any reform of the 1981 Act will have to take this issue into account.

It is concluded that the present approach is anomalous and inconsistent. The preventive approach as recognised under the 1981 Act and the common law, is not achieving its objective. At the same time, a shift towards the neutralising model has occurred in a piecemeal and incoherent fashion. The most extreme method of remedying the effects of prejudicial press coverage – acquittal – is used with some readiness despite its effect upon the administration of justice, while certain lesser measures, such as the use of a *voir dire* in order to determine jury knowledge of the case,[156] or the delay of the trial, are shunned or rarely used. As argued above, such measures place burdens on the criminal justice system while having, in many instances, no genuinely beneficial consequences in terms of freedom of speech. But the question whether the use of such measures as a safeguard is warranted where contempt law is ineffective should be addressed as part of a review of this area of law. In the meantime, it is suggested that judicial reliance on the Convention and especially on its underlying principles under the HRA could address certain of the deficiencies indicated above.

3 PROTECTING JUSTICE AS A CONTINUING PROCESS

Publications which interfere with the course of justice as a continuing process, as opposed to publications which affect particular proceedings, may occasionally attract liability. The forms which a risk to justice as a continuing process might take are considered below. A key issue to be considered concerns the mental element under this form of contempt. Such publications must fall outside the Contempt of Court Act 1981, which according to s 1 is concerned only with publications which may affect *particular* proceedings. They must, therefore, arise at common law; the question is whether *mens rea* must be shown, as s 6(c) seems to provide. It could be argued that the words 'administration of justice' used in s 6(c) could be interpreted to mean 'in particular proceedings only', in which case forms of strict liability contempt may still exist at common law. Support could be found for such an interpretation on the basis that s 6(c) is concerned to demonstrate that where intention can be shown, nothing prevents liability arising at common law. Given the context in which this statement is made (appearing to present a contrast to the strict liability rule) it might seem that the area of liability preserved by s 6(c) would cover the same ground as s 1, but only in instances in which mens rea could be shown. This point is not settled: there is no post-Act authority on it.

If, on the other hand, s 6(c) covers all interferences with the administration of justice at common law, whether in relation to particular proceedings or not, it would appear to cover the form of contempt known as 'scandalising the court' (considered below) which would run counter to the ruling of the Divisional Court in *Editor of New Statesman*[157] and to some persuasive authority from other jurisdictions.[158] Nevertheless, this may be the

---

156 In *Andrews (Tracey)* [1999] Crim LR 156, the Court of Appeal re-stated its view that juries should not be questioned regarding their knowledge of the case they are to judge upon.

157 (1928) 44 TLR 301.

158 *Solicitor General v Radio Avon* [1978] 1 NZLR 225; cf *S v Van Niekirk* (1970) 3 SA 655. See Miller, *op cit*, fn 1, pp 378–79 and Borrie and Lowe, *op cit*, fn 43, pp 359–60.

more satisfactory approach, since it would be more likely to allow the UK to fulfil its Art 10 obligations under the HRA. Otherwise, common law contempt might have too wide a potential and the intention of the European Court of Human Rights in the *Sunday Times* case would not be given full effect. This would mean that liability for 'scandalising the court' would arise only where intention to interfere with the course of justice generally was shown. However, this point cannot yet be regarded as settled.[159]

It is possible to interfere with the course of justice in the long term in various ways. In *AG v News Group Newspapers* it was found that 'the purpose of the contempt jurisdiction is to prevent interference with the course of justice'. It may be argued that these comments apply where no trial or other proceeding is in contemplation. An interference might arise where a part of the media made a prejudgment on a particular issue with legal implications, although no court had made a determination on the issue or where a court had made a contrary determination. In most instances of prejudicial comment in the media, particular proceedings are soon to occur, or at least exist as a possibility in the future. Therefore, s 6(c) would apply, as would s 1, if the proceedings were active. Thus, attention focuses on the effect of the comment upon those proceedings. However, instances may arise in which no proceedings ever occur. For example, in 1997, the *Daily Mirror* published pictures of five men with the caption 'Murderers!' Proceedings against three of them for the racially motivated murder of Steven Lawrence[160] had led to their acquittal. At the time of the *Mirror's* comment, no proceedings which could be influenced by it were in being, although there were future possibilities. It was possible that the family of the victim might bring a civil action against the men for battery; thus, the *Mirror* might possibly have been found to have caused prejudice to that action. (However, since the action would have been heard by a judge only, it would have been improbable that a finding of such prejudice would have been made.) Prosecutions against two of the suspects were still possible. The suspects could, of course, have sued the *Mirror* for defamation. That might have provided them with a remedy, but it does not address the possibility that the action of the *Mirror* could be viewed as undermining the authority of the judiciary since it usurped the function of the courts. The ruling of the House of Lords in *AG v Times Newspapers*,[161] which has not been overruled, lends some support to the possibility that a sanction, other by way of a defamation action, is available in respect of 'trial by newspaper', although it may also be said that the spirit of the judgment of the European Court of Human Rights in the *Sunday Times* case[162] might be flouted if it was found that one existed.[163] At present, domestic law does not appear to recognise liability for any form of interfering with the course of justice in the long term, apart from the form discussed below. If such a form does exist in respect of prejudgments it may, as argued above, be covered by s 6(c).

---

159 In the pre-HRA era, the weight of academic opinion was to the effect that *mens rea* was not required: Borrie and Lowe (*op cit*, fn 43) consider, p 360, that the common law is left untouched by the 1981 Act in relation to publications interfering with the course of justice as a continuing process. This view is also taken by Walker, C (1985) 101 LQR 359, pp 369–70.

160 See Chapter 13, p 760.

161 [1974] AC 273; [1973] 3 All ER 54; [1973] 3 WLR 298, HL.

162 Judgment of 26 April 1979, A 30; (1979) 2 EHRR 245.

163 In *Re Lonhro plc* [1990] 2 AC 154, p 208; [1989] 2 All ER 1100 and 1116, Lord Bridge said that it was 'extremely doubtful' that the *Sunday Times* case could still be relied upon owing to the decision at Strasbourg, although that decision was not direct authority. However, he did not entirely rule out the possibility that the prejudgment test could still be used.

The form of contempt termed 'scandalising the court'[164] arose in order to protect the judicial system from media attacks. The idea behind it is that it would be against the public interest if the media could attack judges and cast doubt on their decisions – suggest, for example, that a judge had shown bias – because the public confidence in the administration of justice would be undermined. It has not been affected by the 1981 Act because there are normally no proceedings which could be influenced; any relevant proceedings will usually be concluded. If an attack on a judge occurred during the 'active' period, it would probably fall outside the Act, since any risk it created would tend to be to the course of justice as a continuing process rather than to the particular proceeding. Prosecutions are rare (and, in recent times, almost unheard of in the UK), but Lord Hailsham said in *Baldry v DPP of Mauritius*,[165] a Privy Council decision, that although it was likely that only the most serious or intolerable instances would be taken notice of by courts or Attorney Generals, nothing had happened in the intervening 80 years to invalidate the analysis of this branch of contempt put forward in *Gray*.[166] Thus, this branch of contempt law is still alive, and cannot merely be disregarded by the media.

As noted above, the weight of authority is probably to the effect that this is a form of strict liability contempt arising at common law, but this point cannot be regarded as settled. If the view taken in *Editor of New Statesman*[167] is correct, there would be no need to show an intention to lower the repute of the judge or court in question, merely an intention to publish. The *actus reus* of this form of contempt consists of the publication of material calculated to lower the reputation of a court or judge, thereby creating a real risk of undermining public confidence in the due administration of justice.

There are two main methods of fulfilling this *actus reus*. First, a publication which is held to be scurrilously abusive of a court or judge may provide the classic example of scandalising the court. The leading case is *Gray*,[168] which arose from the trial of one Wells on a charge of obscene libel in which Darling J warned the press not to publish a full account of court proceedings (because details of obscene matter might have been included). After they were over, the *Birmingham Daily Argus* published an article attacking him and referring to him as an 'impudent little man in horsehair' and 'a microcosm of conceit and empty-headedness [who] would do well to master the duties of his own profession before undertaking the regulation of another'. This article was held by the Divisional Court to be a grave contempt as it was 'not moderate criticism; it amounted to personal, scurrilous abuse of the judge in his capacity of judge'. On the other hand, in *Ambard v AG for Trinidad and Tobago*,[169] reasoned criticism of certain sentences was held by the Privy Council not to constitute contempt on the basis that 'Justice is not a cloistered virtue: she must be allowed to suffer the scrutiny and respectful, even though outspoken, comments of ordinary men'. In a more recent case, *Metropolitan Police Comr ex p Blackburn*,[170] the Court of Appeal reaffirmed this position.

---

164 For general comment on this head of contempt, see Walker, *op cit*, fn 159.
165 [1983] 2 AC 297; [1983] 3 All ER 973.
166 [1900] 2 QB 36; (1900) 69 LJ QB 502.
167 (1928) 44 TLR 301.
168 Above, fn 166.
169 [1936] AC 322; [1936] 1 All ER 704.
170 [1968] 2 All ER 319, CA.

Secondly, a publication may scandalise a court if it imputes bias to a judge – even if it does so in a moderate way – on the basis that allegations of partiality will undermine confidence in the basic function of a judge. The leading case in this area is *Editor of New Statesman*.[171] The pioneer of birth control, Dr Marie Stopes, lost a libel action and an article commenting on the case stated: '... the verdict represents a substantial miscarriage of justice (we are not in sympathy with Dr Stopes but prejudice against her aims should not be allowed to influence a Court of Justice as it appeared to influence Mr Justice Avory in his summing up. Such views as those of Dr Stopes cannot get a fair hearing in a court presided over by Mr Justice Avory.' The editor was found to be in contempt, because although the article was serious and seemingly respectful, it imputed unfairness and lack of impartiality to the judge in the discharge of his judicial duties. The most notorious instance of this variety of scandalising the court occurred in *Colsey*.[172] A moderate article had imputed unconscious bias to a judge because in making a determination as to the meaning of a statute, he might have been influenced by the fact that he had himself earlier, as Solicitor General, steered it through Parliament.

Until 1999, there were no further successful prosecutions for this form of contempt in the UK. Prosecutions may have been discouraged owing to the attacks on the *Colsey* ruling, which clearly laid itself open to the charge of amounting to an unjustified encroachment on the free speech principle.[173] In 1999, the Attorney General sought to jail a defendant, Scriven, from whom an undertaking not to scandalise the court had been obtained, but subsequently breached. The defendant had agreed not to make further accusations, including accusations of bias, against the judiciary, but in November 1999 he placed material on a website which criticised a number of judges.[174] Lawyers in the Lord Chancellor's department complained to the service provider, who closed the website down. Scriven signed an undertaking not to breach the terms of an injunction requiring him to refrain from further criticism. The material was subsequently published on a US website. Proceedings for contempt were brought against him in respect of breach of the undertaking.[175]

It will not be surprising to learn that this is an area of contempt law which has attracted particular criticism,[176] and such criticism has especial pertinence in the post-HRA era. Some critics argue that the offence of scandalising the court should be abolished altogether on the grounds that the rationale of the offence – undermining public confidence in the administration of justice – is too imprecise to justify imposing restrictions on freedom of speech. They argue that a system of justice should not be so lacking in self-confidence that it must suppress attacks on itself. Harold Laski has written: 'To argue that the expression of doubts as to judicial impartiality is an interference in the course of justice because the result is to undermine public confidence in the judiciary is to forget that public confidence is undermined not so much by the comment as by the habit

---

171 (1928) 44 TLR 301.

172 (1931) *The Times*, 9 May.

173 See, eg, Goodhart, AL (1935) 48 Harv L Rev 885, pp 903–04; (1931) 47 LQR 315.

174 *R v Hulbert* (1999) unreported; see News Report, *The Guardian*, 8 November 1999.

175 See News Report, *The Guardian*, 31 January 2001.

176 See Borrie and Lowe, *op cit*, fn 43, p 360 *et seq*; Law Commission Report No 96, *Offences relating to Interference with the Course of Justice*, pp 67–68.

which leads to the comment.'[177] It may be argued that the public will have more confidence in the judiciary if it can be freely discussed. Moreover, because no jury sits in such cases, the judicial system is in a sense prosecution and judge in the same case, thereby giving rise to a suggestion of bias. It may be asked why only judges and not, for example, politicians or members of the clergy, should receive this special protection from criticism? Why single out judges for such insulation? The position may be compared to that in America where this form of contempt is almost extinct owing to the ruling in *Bridges v California*;[178] it was held that the evil of displaying disrespect for the judiciary should not be averted by restricting freedom of expression, as enforced silence on a subject is more likely to engender resent, suspicion and contempt. This is, therefore, a further instance in which the ends of both justice and free speech would be served by curtailing or abolishing this area of liability.

On the other hand, it might be argued that an action for defamation is not a sufficient remedy where bias has been imputed to a judge because it would place him or her in an invidious position while the action was being held. More doubtfully, it might also be said that the singling out of judges can be justified on the basis that, unlike many other public figures, judges may be more reluctant to use available fora from which to reply to criticism. A compromise between these two positions could be effected by adopting the course advocated by the Law Commission – replacement of this form of liability with a narrowly drawn offence covering the distribution of false matter with intent that it should be taken as true, and knowing or being reckless as to its falsity when it imputes corrupt conduct to any judge.[179] Narrowing down the current offence and affording it much greater precision would be, it is suggested, much more in accordance with the demands of Art 10, including the 'prescribed by law' requirement. As currently conceived, it may allow for an interference with truthful and highly significant speech which may readily be viewed not only as unjustifiable in a democratic society, but also as too imprecise to form a basis for criminality.

4 DISCLOSURE OF JURY DELIBERATIONS

Section 8 of the 1981 Act provides that disclosure of jury deliberations will amount to a contempt of court, and it is clear from the ruling in *AG v Associated Newspapers Ltd and Others*[180] that this provision must be interpreted literally. In that instance, jury deliberations were not disclosed directly to the defendant newspaper, but to researchers who made a transcript of them. The paper then used the transcript in order to gather information for the article in question. It was argued on behalf of the defendants that the word 'disclose' used in s 8 is capable of bearing two meanings; it could mean disclosure by anyone, or it could mean disclosure by a member of the jury to the defendant. As Chapter 2 indicated, it was well established in the pre-HRA era that where a statute

---

177 (1928) 41 Harv L Rev 1031, p 1036.
178 (1941) 314 US 252.
179 This was the view of the Law Commission in their report (No 96), *op cit*, fn 176.
180 [1994] 2 WLR 277; [1994] 1 All ER 556; (1994) 142 NLJ 1647, HL; [1993] 2 All ER 535; (1993) 144 NLJ 195, CA.

contains an ambiguous provision, it should be construed so as to conform with the relevant Convention guarantee. On that basis, the narrower meaning should have been adopted, allowing the defendants to escape liability. However, it was found that the word 'disclose' was not ambiguous: in its natural and ordinary meaning, which Parliament clearly intended it to bear, it denoted disclosure to anyone; the defendants therefore clearly fell within its provisions. The closing up of a potential loophole in s 8 achieved by this ruling means that the important institution of the jury is largely immune from scrutiny at least as regards the manner in which it discharges its role.[181] The section does not prevent interviewing of jurors which does not touch upon their deliberations in the jury room, but such inquiries should only be undertaken with the leave of the trial court or after verdict and sentence, by the Court of Appeal.[182]

Jury deliberations are clearly a matter of very significant public interest and it is therefore argued that s 8 should have been framed much less widely. Exceptions could have been included (as they were under the clause as originally drafted)[183] which would have allowed approaches to jurors as part of academic research so long as the proceedings and jurors were not identified.[184] The only current constraint is the requirement of the Attorney General's consent to a prosecution, but even this is not necessary where proceedings are instituted on the motion of a court.

The Runciman Royal Commission on Criminal Justice recommended that s 8 should be amended in order to allow research to be conducted into the reasoning of jurors in reaching a verdict.[185] Possibly, s 8 will be found to be incompatible with Art 10 now that the Human Rights Act is in force since jurors are denied freedom of expression and informed debate on a matter of great public interest is curbed in circumstances which go beyond the exceptions under para 2. Even if it could be argued that the exception 'for maintaining the authority of the judiciary' could be said to apply, which is doubtful, the absolute nature of the section probably means that it creates an interference disproportionate to the end in view. Such a finding would be expected to prompt review of the section. It is suggested that a return to the clause originally put forward in the Contempt Bill would meet the Art 10 requirements. That clause merely prevented the naming of particular trials or jurors. It would have protected jurors without preventing proper research. The repeal and replacement of s 8 with a revised clause on those lines is warranted not only on grounds of freedom of speech, but in the interests of justice, since the results of research into the workings of the jury system might lead to reforms which would serve those interests. For example, the use of juries in serious fraud trials may be inappropriate and may not serve the interest in convicting the guilty. Research into the impact of prejudicial media coverage and into the efficacy of neutralising measures, such as directions to the jury, is also inhibited in the UK, although it has been conducted abroad in relation to US juries.[186] Such research would serve the ends of justice, since it

---

181 For consideration of the effect of the restriction see the RCCJ Report, CM 2263, 1993, p 2; see also fn 187, below.

182 *McCluskey* (1993) 94 Cr App R 216, CA. See also *Mickleborough* [1995] 1 Cr App R 297, CA.

183 See 416 HL Deb, 20 January 1981.

184 It is worth noting that the Divisional Court in *AG v New Statesman* [1981] QB 1 indicated that disclosure of jury room secrets which did not identify the persons concerned could have no adverse effects on the administration of justice.

185 Cm 2263, 1993, p 2.

186 See Simon 'Does the court's decision in *Nebraska Press Association* fit with the research evidence on the impact on jurors of news coverage?' (1978) Stanford L Rev 515.

might aid in ensuring that neutralising measures were tailored more specifically to the potential for harm in different instances. But such research has been inhibited by s 8.[187]

5 PROTECTION OF SOURCES[188]

Introduction

The protection of sources is clearly vital to the role of journalists. If sources do not believe that their identity will be protected, they will not normally contact journalists and therefore, the most potent source of information, that of a person who is, in some sense, an 'insider', will be denied to them. If sources are afraid to come forward, the result will be that the public will not be informed on matters which are frequently of grave public interest. These may relate to crime, when the source may be a person involved in, or in some way linked to, forms of criminal activity. Or, they may relate to national security; the source may be a civil servant who is activated by conscience in seeking to disclose an abuse of power by the executive. They may relate to improper practices in large commercial organisations, in which case the source is likely to be an employee, who is prepared to 'blow the whistle'. Such an employee would now have protection from dismissal under the Public Interest Disclosure Act 1998, but nevertheless is likely to want to protect her identity.

Thus, the use of and protection of sources serves a vital function in relation to the role of the media. In recognition of this, journalists view themselves as morally obliged to protect the identity of their sources, a principle which is recognised in cl 15 of the Press Commission Code.[189] Where the media exposes executive malpractice, it performs a vital constitutional role. In general, the speech generated, which relates to the matters mentioned, is of great value in a democracy and would be viewed as of the first importance within Art 10. Nevertheless, the protection it is afforded under UK law, is, it will be argued, inadequate.

Section 10 of the Contempt of Court Act

Until the inception of the Human Rights Act, receiving Art 10 into domestic law, very little formal recognition was given in UK law to the constitutional role of the press. However, an exception to this rule was afforded by s 10 of the 1981 Act which provides:

> No court may require a person to disclose, nor is any person guilty of contempt of court for refusing to disclose, the source of information contained in a publication for which he is responsible, unless it be established to the satisfaction of the court that disclosure is necessary in the interests of justice or national security or for the prevention of disorder or crime.

---

187 The Fraud Trials Committee was unable to conduct research into the experience of juries in fraud trials: *Fraud Trials Committee Report*, 1986, HMSO, para 8.10.

188 For comment on s 10, see Allan [1991] CLJ 131; Miller, CJ [1982] Crim LR 71, p 82; Palmer, S [1992] PL 61.

189 For further comment on the Code, see Chapter 10, p 552–53.

The exceptions under s 10 regarding national security and the prevention of crime answer to the exceptions to Art 10. The term 'the interests of justice' is not repeated in para 2 of Art 10, although it may be covered to an extent by the term 'the preservation of the authority and impartiality of the judiciary' and, possibly, by the 'rights of others' exception. The key issue, therefore, is whether the interpretation of the term 'necessary' is compatible with the Strasbourg view of what is necessary in a democratic society in order to further those aims.

Section 10 does not provide any new power to require a journalist to disclose the identity of a source. As Lord Diplock put it in *Secretary of State for Defence v Guardian Newspapers*,[190] the leading case: 'Section 10 confers no powers upon a court additional to those powers, whether discretionary or not, which already existed at common law or under rules of court, to order disclosure of sources of information, its effect is restrictive only.' It was also determined in that case that s 10 will apply to the disclosure of information which might reveal the identity of the source. Thus, s 10 creates a presumption in favour of journalists who wish to protect their sources, which is, however, subject to four wide exceptions, the widest of which arises where the interests of justice require that disclosure should be made. It was found in *Secretary of State for Defence v Guardian Newspapers*[191] that disclosure of the identity of the source would only be ordered where this was necessary in order to identify him or her; if other means of identification were reasonably readily available, they should be used. On the other hand, this did not mean that all other means of inquiry which might reveal the identity of the source must be exhausted before disclosure would be ordered. The term 'necessary' was found in *Re an Inquiry under the Companies Security (Insider Dealing) Act 1985*[192] to mean something less than indispensable, but something more than useful. In *Guardian Newspapers* a civil servant, who considered that Parliament was being misled as regards the arrival of cruise missiles in Britain, sent a photocopy of a memorandum regarding the timing to *The Guardian*, who published. The Secretary of State wished to discover the identity of the civil servant and sought the return of the photocopy, since it would reveal the identity. The Secretary of State, the plaintiff, claimed that the national security exception under s 10 applied on the basis that the fact of a secret document with restricted circulation relating to defence having come into the hands of a national newspaper was of great significance in relation to the maintenance of national security. The minority in the House of Lords were not convinced by this evidence, but the majority accepted it, Lord Bridge stating that any threat to national security ought to be eliminated by the speediest and most effective means possible. The identity of the source was duly discovered when the photocopy was returned and she was prosecuted.[193] The majority, therefore, took the traditional stance of failing to afford a full scrutiny to imprecise claims of a threat to national security made by the executive. However, the House of Lords did suggest that more convincing evidence would be needed in future.

The House of Lords clarified the nature of the balancing exercise to be carried out under s 10 in *X v Morgan Grampian Publishers and Others*.[194] A confidential plan was stolen

---

190 [1984] 3 All ER 601; [1985] AC 339, 347, HL.
191 [1985] AC 339.
192 [1988] 1 All ER 203.
193 See Chapter 7, p 338.
194 [1991] AC 1; [1991] 2 All ER 1, HL.

from the plaintiffs, a company named Tetra; information apparently from the plan was given by an unidentified source by phone to William Goodwin, a journalist. The plaintiffs applied for an order requiring Goodwin to disclose the source and sought discovery of his notes of the phone conversation in order to discover his or her identity. The House of Lords had to consider the application of s 10 to these facts. It found that when a journalist relies on s 10 in order to protect a source, it must be determined whether the applicant's right to take legal action against the source is outweighed by the journalist's interest in maintaining the promise of confidentiality made to him or her. The House of Lords took into account various factors in balancing these two considerations, including the threat to the plaintiffs' business and the complicity of the source in 'a gross breach of confidentiality'. Lord Bridge, with whom the other Law Lords unanimously agreed, found that the interest of the plaintiffs in identifying the source outweighed the interests of the journalist in protecting it. Goodwin refused to reveal the identity of the source and was fined £5,000 for refusing to obey the court's order.

Goodwin applied to the European Commission on Human Rights[195] which gave its opinion that the order against Goodwin violated his right to freedom of expression under Art 10 of the Convention on Human Rights. The Court found that there was a vital public interest in protecting journalistic sources, since so doing was essential to the maintenance of a free press.[196] Thus, the margin of appreciation was circumscribed by that interest. It considered that limitations placed on the confidentiality of such sources would require the most careful scrutiny. The applicant argued that 'the law as it stood was no more than a mandate to the judiciary to order journalists to disclose sources if they were 'moved' by the complaint of an aggrieved party'. Was the vital public interest in protecting sources outweighed by Tetra's interest in eliminating the threat of damage due to the dissemination of confidential material? The injunction was already effective in preventing the dissemination of such information and therefore the additional restriction on freedom of expression entailed by the disclosure order was not supported by sufficient reasons to satisfy the requirements of Art 10(2). The order was disproportionate to the purpose in question and therefore could not be said to be necessary. Tetra's interest in disclosure, including its interest in unmasking a disloyal employee, was not outweighed by the public interest in the protection of journalistic sources. A breach of Art 10 was therefore established. In order to comply with this ruling, it was arguably necessary to amend the 'interests of justice' head of s 10. The then Conservative Government stated, however, in response to the ruling, that it had no plans to amend the 1981 Act.[197] Thus, it might appear that under s 3 of the HRA, when a suitable case arises, s 10 may be found to require amendment or, more probably, re-interpretation.

However, in *Camelot Group Ltd v Centaur Communications*[198] the Court of Appeal allowed the 'interests of justice' exception under s 10 an even wider scope. The company, Camelot, runs the UK national lottery. An anonymous source sent Camelot's draft accounts to the newspaper, which published them. Camelot sought return of the documents in order to identify the source, and the paper relied on s 10. The court found

---

195 *Goodwin v UK* (1994) No 17488/90 Com Rep, *The Guardian*, 26 May 1994.
196 *Goodwin v UK* (1996) 22 EHRR 123. See also *Fressoz and Roire v France* (1999) 5 BHRC 654.
197 *Hansard* (Lords) 13 April 1996 Vol 571, Col 6147, Written Answer.
198 [1998] EMLR 1; [1999] QB 124.

that the interests of Camelot in ensuring the loyalty of its employees and ex-employees should outweigh the public importance attached to the protection of sources. In the present instance, the Court considered that in any event, there was no public interest in protecting the source. The Court of Appeal considered that in reaching this finding it was applying the same test as was applied by the European Court of Human Rights in *Goodwin*.

Clearly, the term 'the interests of justice' used in s 10 leaves room for varying interpretations. Nevertheless, the determinations as to proportionality in *Camelot* and *Goodwin* do not, it is suggested, afford equal weight to the role of the media in informing the public. Given the scope for a different interpretation, it is probable that amendment of s 10 will not be required under the HRA. However, given that the European Court of Human Rights allowed the domestic authorities a margin of appreciation (albeit circumscribed) in determining the issue of proportionality in *Goodwin*, one would have expected the domestic authorities to take an even stricter view of the issue. Camelot obtained an injunction preventing any further dissemination of its accounts. Once the injunction had been obtained against Centaur, any other newspaper which published information covered by it would have risked liability for contempt of court owing to the contempt ruling in the *Spycatcher* case, discussed above.[199] Therefore, the disclosure order might have been viewed as disproportionate to the end in view. The significance of the information itself might also have been taken into account in reaching this finding, since it concerned the accountability of a large and very profitable company engaged, at least to an extent, in funding public and community services. Significant issues of public interest are raised, it is suggested, by the question of the proportion of lottery money which is diverted to community projects, and the like, and the proportion which is straightforward profit. There is clearly an important political dimension to Camelot's activities which might not arise in respect of the activities of many private companies.

In the pre-HRA decision in *Saunders v Punch Ltd*,[200] in which an injunction had been granted to restrain use of the information in question, it was found that the interests of justice were not so pressing as to require the statutory privilege against disclosure to be overridden. In *John v Express Newspapers*,[201] this approach was followed by the Court of Appeal. As similar cases arise under the HRA it may be expected, bearing in mind the importance accorded at Strasbourg to the protection of sources under Art 10 as a vital part of the media's role, that the question of proportionality will be resolved by taking account of the effect of the use of an injunction and of attempts to obtain the information by other means.

The ruling in *Ashworth Hospital Authority v MGN Ltd*[202] indicated that a stricter approach is being taken, under the HRA, to the interests of the media in protecting sources. It was found that the jurisdiction to order the disclosure of the identity of a wrongdoer did not have to be confined to cases involving tort but should be of general application. Further it was found that the exercise of the court's jurisdiction to order disclosure was not precluded by the provisions of the 1981 Act or the Convention, but

199 See above, p 249.
200 [1998] 1 WLR 986.
201 (2000) *The Times*, 26 April.
202 [2001] 1 WLR 515 1 All ER 991, CA.

that in interpreting s 10 of the Act the court should, where possible, (a) equate the specific purposes for which disclosure of the source was permitted under s 10 with 'legitimate aims' under Art 10 of the Convention, and (b) apply the same test of necessity as that applied by the European Court. Applying that test to the instant case, it was found that the disclosure of confidential medical records to the press was misconduct which was contrary to the public interest. But the exceptional circumstances were stressed: it was said that there is a very clear need to confidentially protect a patient which should be safeguarded in any democratic society.

This ruling clearly viewed the very significant interest in preserving patient confidentiality as requiring more than merely an injunction to protect it. But in other, less significant, circumstances an injunction might be more likely to be viewed as sufficient. But it might be pointed out that if the contempt ruling in *Spycatcher* is eventually overturned in a ruling which takes full account of Art 10,[203] the use of injunctions in such circumstances may have less efficacy from the standpoint of the body seeking to prevent disclosure of the information in question. Thus, ironically, the argument against making a disclosure order on grounds of disproportionality would be affected, since the other remedy available able to meet the end in view would be less effective.

Protection of sources and counter-terrorist measures

Schedule 7 para 3(5) of the Prevention of Terrorism (Temporary Provisions) Act (PTA) 1989 provided for the production of material relating to terrorism if such production would be in the public interest. This provision was replaced by an equivalent provision under the Terrorism Act 2000, once it came into force. The Terrorism Act 2000 now makes similar provision in Sched 5. It was assumed in *Director of Public Prosecutions v Channel Four Television Co Ltd and Another*[204] that the existence of the provision means that the making of such an order precludes a s 10 defence. The potential danger of Sched 7 in terms of media freedom was shown in that case. Channel 4 screened a programme in its Dispatches series called 'The Committee', which was based on the allegations of an anonymous source (Source A) that the RUC and Loyalist paramilitaries had colluded in the assassination of Republicans. The police successfully applied under Sched 7 para 3(5) for orders disclosing information which would probably uncover the identity of Source A. Channel 4 refused to comply with the orders on the ground that to do so would expose Source A to almost certain death and it was then committed for contempt of court. It attempted to rely on the public interest provision of Sched 7 in arguing that it was in the public interest for the identity of Source A to be protected, but this was rejected on the following grounds. Channel 4 should not have given an unqualified assurance of protection to the source even though had it not done so, the programme could probably not have been made, because so doing was likely to lead to flouting of the provisions of the Prevention of Terrorism (Temporary Provisions) Act. Thus, giving such assurances could inevitably undermine the rule of law and therefore, it was held, help to achieve the very result that the terrorists in Northern Ireland were seeking to bring about. Channel 4

---

203 See above.
204 [1993] 2 All ER 517.

was therefore fined for non-compliance with the orders. In determining the amount of the fine, it was borne in mind that the defendants might not have appreciated the dangers of giving an unqualified assurance, but a warning was given that this consideration would be unlikely to influence courts in future cases of this nature.

It may be argued that this ruling fails to accord sufficient weight to the public interest in the protection of journalistic sources in order to allow the media to fulfil its role of informing the public. The comment that the assurances given to Source A as a necessary precondition to publication of this material would undermine the rule of law, ignores the possibility that undermining of the rule of law might be most likely to flow from the behaviour alleged in the programme: it might appear that nothing would be more likely to undermine the rule of law than collusion between State security forces and terrorists. The decision not to impose a rolling fine on Channel 4 or make a sequestration order may be welcomed in the interests of press freedom, but it is clear that such indulgence may be refused in future, thereby creating a significant curb on investigative journalism. Schedule 7 para 3(5) as currently interpreted may therefore also be incompatible with Art 10.

Conclusions

It is suggested that the domestic decisions discussed above reveal that the domestic courts are not affording the same weight to media freedom as that afforded at Strasbourg, as indicated in the strong judgment in the *Goodwin* case. In particular, the 'interests of justice' exception is being interpreted in a manner which affords greater weight to the right to take legal action in order to protect proprietorial rights – the right to take legal action and to the preservation of confidentiality – than to the principle of freedom of expression. This approach may require reconsideration, although the most recent decisions discussed above suggest that a change of approach – which accords greater recognition to the need to protect sources – is already occurring.

The power under the Prevention of Terrorism (Temporary Provisions) Act (now under the Terrorism Act 2000) afforded primacy to national security without explicitly providing a defence for journalists. It will have to be interpreted compatibly with Art 10, in a manner which may impliedly provide such a defence.

CHAPTER 6

RESTRAINING FREEDOM OF EXPRESSION ON THE GROUNDS OF OFFENSIVENESS, OF PROTECTING MORALITY AND RELIGIOUS SENSIBILITIES; HATE SPEECH; CENSORSHIP, LICENSING AND REGULATION OF THE VISUAL MEDIA

1 INTRODUCTION

This chapter covers a variety of forms of expression. Much of it is primarily visual and also falls outside the category of political expression. This may be said of some films, of music, opera, mime, plays, paintings, all of which are covered by aspects of the law and regulation considered below. But aspects of political expression are also covered, since some regulation of political expression is a feature of broadcasting regulation, while hate speech almost inevitably has a political message. Thus, under the Human Rights Act (HRA) 1998, the judiciary may be expected to take a different stance towards the different types of expression, which reflects the hierarchy of expression recognised within the Strasbourg jurisprudence, as the Introduction to this part indicated.[1] In any event, adoption of such a stance would be in accord with their own leanings as expressed in the recent free expression decisions in the pre-HRA era discussed in Chapter 3.[2] However, if the justifications for freedom of expression considered in the Introduction are taken into account, particularly those from truth and self-fulfilment, it is suggested that there is no convincing basis for relegating 'artistic' expression to a lowly place in such a hierarchy.

The inception of the HRA means that the UK courts are faced with the difficult theoretical problems associated with a positive right to freedom of expression as opposed to a negative liberty. This is a matter that is especially pertinent in relation to the forms of expression considered in this chapter. Instead of merely determining whether a particular statute or a doctrine of the common law applies to a factual situation, the courts must consider the weight to be given to a particular manifestation of expression, when considering the claim that an interference with it is justified. As Chapter 3 indicated, they were already going down this path in creating a common law right to freedom of expression. But they will now have to consider such a right in a much wider range of situations, and will have to grapple with the doctrinal constraints of the Art 10(2) exceptions. The use of a range of laws, such as those aimed at the protection of children, at licensing television companies, at forms of paedophile activity, at political impartiality in broadcasting, at protecting religious sensibilities may all have to be considered in relation to the freedom of expression guarantee. In other words, in instances in which, previously, the free speech argument would hardly be heard, it will often take a central place. The theorising of judgments in all sorts of areas of law that have had a largely or partly unrecognised effect on expression will begin to take place.

The judiciary will be faced with rules deriving from a range of common law doctrines and statutes, some of which are far too subjective, imprecise and broad to be sustained, if the free speech justifications are to be given weight. If the propositions advanced in the Introduction to Part II are accepted, media regulation designed to intervene in the market

---

can be defended even when it affects the content of broadcasts in terms of 'must carry' requirements designed to reflect the values of plurality and creativity. On the other hand, such regulation based on the content of broadcasts as indicated by such uncertain terms as 'taste and decency' will be in a far more doubtful position. Further, the distinctions that will be found below, based partly on the medium in question, must also be called into question.

This is a context in which it is suggested that the HRA will not have a radical impact as far as the general statutory regime governing explicit expression is concerned. It may, however, have an impact as regards specific decisions taken under that statutory regime; in relation to the common law, especially the law of blasphemy, and in relation to aspects of media regulation. The Introduction to Part II is intended to provide a theoretical framework, based on the free speech justifications, within which to view the laws that are discussed below. As the domestic HRA free expression jurisprudence begins to take form, the stance taken in relation to those propositions, which will present the judiciary with harder choices than they have previously faced, will determine its distinctive quality.

2 RESTRAINING EXPRESSION ON THE GROUNDS OF OFFENSIVENESS AND OF PROTECTING MORALITY

Law and pornography: theoretical considerations

The question as to how far sexually explicit speech deserves the same protection as other forms of expression and if it does not, how far and for what reasons it should be suppressed, has, as Barendt notes, '... almost certainly elicited more academic commentary than any other [free speech] topic'.[3] As striking as the amount of writing on the subject is the failure by academics of different persuasions to reach a consensus view. Thus, for example, AWB Simpson, a former member of the Williams Committee appointed in 1977 to review obscenity law, recalls that the law certainly did not represent such a consensus: 'Before, during and after the Committee sat, the chorus of abuse against the law continued; virtually everyone claimed that it was unworkable.'[4] In a similar vein, conservatives,[5] liberals[6] and feminists[7] have all attacked the Committee's findings and all

---

3   Barendt, E, *Freedom of Speech*, 1987, p 245.

4   Simpson, AWB, *Pornography and Politics: the Williams Committee in Retrospect*, 1983, p 80.

5   See, eg, the comments of Mary Whitehouse in *The Sunday Times* that, as a result of the Committee's report, '... we are going from a quicksand into ... a very, very mucky quagmire ...' quoted in Simpson, *ibid*, p 44; he also quotes (p 45) a *Daily Telegraph* leader which criticised the 'some would say excessively liberal principle' it endorsed.

6   See, eg, the detailed analysis in Dworkin, R, 'Do we have a right to pornography?', in *A Matter of Principle*, 1985, in which he broadly endorses the Committee's conclusions, but argues that these cannot be supported by the arguments they deployed.

7   The whole approach of the feminists is hostile to the broadly liberal stance adopted by the Committee; see, eg, Brownmiller, S, *Against Our Will*, 1975, where it is asserted that all previous value systems, including the liberal tradition, have worked against the interests of women. For explicit criticism of the Committee by a more moderate feminist, see Eckersley, R, 'Whither the feminist campaign? An evaluation of feminist critiques of pornography', 15 Int J Soc of Law 149. Eckersley dismisses Williams as having 'simply fail[ed] to register the feminist objection' (p 174).

for different reasons. In addition, even to speak of 'feminist' and 'liberal' positions necessitates a conscious simplification, because these two opposing positions, at first sight monolithic, are in fact riven by internal debate; in particular, the feminist camp displays a conspicuous lack of unanimity.[8] Nevertheless, an attempt will be made, in what follows, to outline briefly the 'core' of each stance and evaluate the strength of their arguments, both against each other and directly on the subject of the permissibility of censorship in this area.

The conservative position

The conservative position, which in the popular consciousness is probably most associated with Mary Whitehouse, finds its academic and somewhat more abstract exposition in Lord Devlin's work, *The Enforcement of Morals*, 1965. In essence, Devlin's view is that since a shared set of basic moral values is essential to society, it is as justified in protecting itself against attacks on these values (such as that mounted by pornography) as it is in protecting itself against any other phenomena which threaten its basic existence, such as violent public disorder. On this thesis, moral corruption of the individual is to be prevented in order to ensure the ultimate survival of society. By contrast, Whitehouse's concerns are presumably more with damage to individuals *per se*, a position which, as argued below, appears to reflect that taken by the case law in this area. Devlin's position, by contrast, is clearly not compatible with most existing UK law:[9] it could neither support nor even account for the existence of the public good defence in s 4 of the Obscene Publications Act 1959,[10] or indeed any similar defence: it would appear somewhat absurd to argue that material which threatened the very survival of society should be allowed to circulate freely on the grounds that it was somehow also in the public good.[11]

Devlin's position also appears to have been placed in doubt on the theoretical level by Hart's incisive critique.[12] Briefly, Hart's objections are as follows: on the more favourable reading of Devlin's position, he is not assuming, but trying to establish the truth of the proposition that a shared set of moral standards (going on Devlin's account far beyond simple prohibitions on violence, theft, etc) is an essential attribute of society. If this is the case, argues Hart, Devlin fails to establish the proposition for the simple reason that he offers no empirical evidence to support it. This leads one, Hart continues, to the suspicion that Devlin actually *assumes* the truth of the proposition and thus builds his theory on a tautology: having defined society as a system of shared beliefs he then concludes, with perfect logic but some futility, that if those shared beliefs change radically or unanimity is lost, the society has disintegrated. Devlin's position, therefore does not strike one as particularly strong.

---

8   For comments on the divisions in the feminist critique of pornography see Eckersley, *ibid*. See also Lacey, N, 93 JLS 93.

9   It may find reflection in some of the more obscure common law offences such as conspiracy to corrupt public morals and outraging public decency. The Lords, in *Knuller v DPP* [1973] AC 435; [1972] 3 WLR 143; (1972) 56 Cr App R 633, HL, a much criticised decision, arguably gave some support to the Devlin thesis. For discussion of the decision, see below, p 293.

10 For discussion of the defence, see below pp 284 *et seq*.

11 Under the 1959 Act, the defence of public good only comes into play once it has been decided that the material is likely to deprave and corrupt: *Penguin Books* [1961] Crim LR 176 (the Lady Chatterley's Lover trial). See below, p 285.

12 For a summary of Hart's critique, see 'social solidarity and the enforcement of morality', in *Essays in Jurisprudence and Philosophy*, 1983.

The liberal position

The liberal position on pornography is broadly united around general opposition to censorship in the absence of clear evidence of a concrete harm caused by its free availability.[13] However, unanimity does not exist as to the rationales for free speech most applicable to defending a liberty to read or view pornographic material. There is general agreement that Meiklejohn's argument from participation in democracy[14] is of little relevance; as Dworkin caustically remarks, 'No one is denied an equal voice in the political process ... when he is forbidden to circulate photographs of genitals to the public at large'.[15]

A variant of Mill's argument from truth[16] was avowedly the free speech justification adopted by the Williams Committee convened in 1979 to report on obscenity; although they expressed some scepticism at Mill's perhaps rather naive conviction that in a *laissez faire* market of ideas, truth would always win out,[17] they endorsed the main thrust of his theory. Interference with the free flow of ideas and artistic endeavour was unacceptable since it amounted to ruling out in advance possible modes of human development, before it was known whether or not they would be desirable or necessary. Since they also reached the conclusion that '... no one has invented or in our opinion *could* invent, an instrument that would suppress only [worthless pornography] and could not be turned against something ... of [possibly] a more creative kind',[18] they concluded that this risk of suppressing worthwhile creative art ruled out censorship of the written word. (They regarded standard photographic pornography as not expressing anything that could be regarded as an 'idea' and so as unprotected by the argument from truth.)

Ronald Dworkin has mounted a sustained attack on this rationale;[19] it rests, he contends, on the instrumental justification that allowing the free circulation of ideas is necessary to enable individuals to make intelligent and informed choices about how they want to lead their lives and then flourish in them. He finds that such an argument is unable to support its own conclusion against censorship; for, he urges, it must be accepted that allowing the free availability of pornography will 'sharply limit' the ability of some (perhaps the majority) to shape their cultural understanding of sexuality in a way they think best – a way in which sexuality has dignity and beauty. His argument appears to conclude that the justification from self-development does not argue conclusively against censorship, because of the plausible case that forbidding some pornography will for many people greatly assist in their self-development. Dworkin is surely correct when he concludes that not self-development, but the straightforward argument from *moral autonomy* amounts to the strongest case against censorship in this area. This argument simply points out that judging for an individual what will and will not be beneficial for him or her to read represents a clear invasion of the strong individual right to decide

13 See Feinberg, J, *The Moral Limits of the Criminal Law: Offense to Others*, 1985. For a brief discussion of the possible link between pornography and the commission of sexual offences, see below, p 274.

14 See above, pp 203–04 and fn 26.

15 Dworkin, R, *op cit*, fn 6, p 336.

16 See above, pp 202–03.

17 Report of the Committee on Obscenity and Film Censorship (Williams Committee), Cmnd 7772, 1979, para 5.20.

18 Ibid, para 5.24.

19 Dworkin, R, *op cit*, fn 6.

moral issues concerned with one's own life for oneself.[20] Such an invasion could therefore only be justified if a serious risk of substantial damage to the concrete well being of society was shown.[21] Since the law does not posit such a risk, censorship is unacceptable. Whether this argument also provides a convincing answer to the radical feminist objections to free access to pornography will be considered below; this position must first be sketched out.

It should finally be noted that liberals are willing to support restrictions on the outlets and public display of pornography[22] on the grounds that such restrictions do not necessarily spring from contempt for those who read pornography, but may simply reflect the genuine and personal aesthetic preferences of those who would rather not have to suffer the continual and ugly spectacle of publicly displayed pornography.[23]

The pro-censorship feminist position

The views of feminist writers on the harms pornography does, on the justifications offered for allowing its free availability and on what, if anything, the law should do about it are many and varied.[24] However, the pro-censorship feminist position on the possibility of legal control of pornography is generally equated with the views of Catherine MacKinnon and Andrea Dworkin, who framed an Indianapolis Ordinance giving rise to civil liability for trafficking in pornography or forcing it upon unwilling recipients; its constitutionality was successfully challenged on the grounds of incompatibility with the First Amendment.[25] The essence of this variant of feminist thought is that while pornography is regarded as causing harm to some individual women, by causing some individual men to perpetrate rape, battery and sexual abuse,[26] pornography causes a far more subtle and all-pervasive harm to all women. It is on the latter argument that the remainder of the discussion will concentrate.

---

20 See above, Chapter 1, p 7.

21 It is submitted that other possible justifications for abrogating speech (described in Chapter 1, pp 12–13) are not in most instances applicable here. But see below, p 274 for consideration of the possible link between pornography and sexual offences.

22 Such as, eg, the recommendations of the Williams Committee; see their 'Summary of our proposals', above, fn 17.

23 See Dworkin, R, op cit, fn 6, pp 355–58, where he broadly endorses the Williams Committee's proposals.

24 For feminist writers who take a different stance on pornography from that broadly examined here, see any of the following: the chapters on pornography in Smart, Feminism and the Power of Law, 1989, in which the author expresses distrust of using the law to control pornography; Rhode, Justice and Gender, 1989, in which the extent to which feminism has framed a puritanical ideology of sexuality and pornography is deplored: it is argued that women who find explicit depictions of, eg, bondage or anonymous sex don't 'need more sexual shame, guilt and hypocrisy, this time served up as feminism'. See also Jackson, 'Catherine MacKinnon and feminist jurisprudence: a critical appraisal' (1992) JLS, pp 195–213 for a moderate critique, particularly of MacKinnon's views on the impossibility of non-coercive heterosexual activity in contemporary society.

25 For the first instance decision, see American Booksellers Assoc, etc v Hudnitt III, Mayor, City of Indianapolis et al 598 F Supp 1316. For the (unsuccessful) appeal, see 771 F 2d 323.

26 See, eg, MacKinnon, C, Feminism Unmodified, pp 184–91.

In some of their more terse, dramatic statements, such as 'Pornography is violence against women',[27] and 'We define pornography as a practice of sex discrimination',[28] it sounds as if MacKinnon and A Dworkin regard the very existence of pornography as a concrete harm to women which goes far beyond mere offence and yet is not a physical harm. However, in the more precise explanations they offer, it seems clear that the harm is caused through the effect it has on men's view of women: 'Men treat women as who they see women as being. Pornography constructs who that is.' In other words, the argument does remain, as R Dworkin claims, 'a causal one'.[29] At this point, having posited a link between pornography and the way men treat women, the explanation draws in the more general radical feminist thesis that men have near total power over women and that consequently, 'the way men see women defines who women can be'.[30] Elsewhere, MacKinnon explains that this power is generated by the fact that men have managed to establish the total 'privileging' of their interests and perceptions and the concomitant complete subordination of women and then passed this off as reality or 'just the way things are'. MacKinnon calls the resulting illusion 'metaphysically nearly perfect'.[31] Several more moderate feminists have pointed out[32] that this view places feminism in the bizarre position of having to deny the possibility of its own existence because it entails assuming that all available modes of thought and perception are male, although masquerading as neutral. If this were true, it is hard to see how women could even come to realise that they were oppressed, let alone frame proposals for affirmative action to free themselves from male dominance. MacKinnon has indeed asserted that 'Feminism affirms women's point of view by ... explaining its impossibility',[33] but since MacKinnon herself has in fact somehow managed to construct a substantive and highly influential feminist point of view – including the analysis of pornography under consideration – this reply seems rather unconvincing. It might be thought at this point that since acceptance of the radical feminist thesis on pornography is apparently only possible if one also accepts a metaphysical theory which seems both to deny its own existence and to involve acceptance of the most comprehensive conspiracy theory ever devised, the thesis can be summarily dismissed.

This, it is submitted, would be premature. The most significant feminist point with respect to pornography is the effect it is said to have on men's view of women and therefore on the way they treat them. One does not have to accept the general radical feminist thesis in order to give *some* consideration to the proposition that pornography, through the effect it has on men, oppresses women. Consequently, the discussion will now turn to considering whether the feminist thesis can still provide a justification for restrictions on the freedom to consume pornography even if the notion of total female subordination is rejected.

---

27 The basic thesis of Dworkin, A, *Pornography: Men Possessing Women*, 1979, quoted in Simpson, *op cit*, fn 4, p 71.

28 MacKinnon, *op cit*, fn 26, p 175. The quotation given refers specifically to the Indianapolis ordinance, but equally summarises MacKinnon's analysis of pornography.

29 Dworkin, R, 'Liberty and pornography', *The New York Review of Books*, 15 August 1991, p 12.

30 MacKinnon, *op cit*, fn 26, p 172.

31 See 'Feminism, Marxism, method and the State', in Bartlett and Kennedy (eds), *Feminist Legal Theory*, 1991, p 182.

32 See, eg, Sandra Harding's introduction to MacKinnon's 'Feminism, Marxism, method and the State', in Harding, S, *Feminism and Methodology*, 1987.

33 MacKinnon, C, *Feminist Legal Theory*, p 181.

The oppression of women caused by pornography is claimed to manifest itself in the following three distinct ways. First, women are discriminated against, sexually harassed and physically assaulted in all walks of life; this constitutes a denial of their civil right to equality. Secondly, women are denied their positive liberty, their right to equal participation in the political process because of the image in men's minds constructed by pornography which 'strips and devastates women of credibility',[34] and consequently prevents women's contributions from being taken seriously. Finally, pornography 'silences' women – even their negative ability to speak is denied because they are not seen as fully human agents, but rather as dehumanised creatures who 'desperately want to be bound, battered, tortured, humiliated and killed'.[35] The argument that the State should, therefore, seek to ban pornography on the basis of furtherance of equality, just as it seeks to outlaw discrimination in employment, is developed in *Only Words*.[36]

Two points may be made in response to the above. First, this thesis attributes to men a uniformly passive and receptive attitude to all pornographic images.[37] Nowhere in a long essay on pornography[38] does MacKinnon appear to advert to the possibility that many men may completely reject the 'message' of violent misogynistic pornography, even though some may be aroused by it. Her theory thus, in effect, amounts to a profound refusal to recognise the immense difference which men's backgrounds, education and life experiences will have on their responses,[39] and more generally, the enormous variety of human responses to any given phenomena which will be found even amongst those of similar backgrounds; ultimately, her theory denies (male) free will and with it men's individual voices.[40]

The second point is that if one leaves aside the extreme idea of the total control of men over women described above, it then becomes impossible to accept the immense influence that is attributed to the consumption of pornography. The idea, for example, that pornography silences women in all walks of life remains quite simply, 'strikingly implausible'[41] perhaps precisely *because* it is so eloquently expressed and it is hard to take seriously the notion that pornography denies women the right to participate in political life. One could only accept such arguments if one regarded women as defined completely by the images of pornography; as has been seen, that argument in turn could only have

---

34 MacKinnon, *op cit*, fn 26, p 193.

35 MacKinnon, *op cit*, fn 26, p 172. Cf Andrea Dworkin's description of the view that rape law evinces of women as one in which rape is not really against a woman's will, 'because what she wants underneath is to have anything done to her that violates or humiliates or hurts her': *Pornography: Men Possessing Women*, 1979.

36 MacKinnon, C, *Only Words*, 1993. For criticism of the notion that banning pornography should be viewed as an aspect of the furtherance of equality, see Sadurski, 'On "Seeing speech through an equality lens": a critique of egalitarian arguments for suppression of hate speech and pornography' (1996) 16(4) OJLS 713.

37 Andrea Dworkin attributes a similarly monolithic character to men; consider, eg, the following description of the male sex: 'Terror issues forth from the male; illuminates his essential nature and his basic purpose' (*Pornography: Men Possessing Women*, 1979, p 74).

38 MacKinnon, 1987, Chapter 14.

39 For criticism of this characteristic failing in MacKinnon's work generally, see Jackson, above, fn 24.

40 An ironic point, since MacKinnon often talks of men 'silencing' women.

41 Dworkin, R, *op cit*, fn 6, p 14; Rhode also asks how, if women are silenced by pornography, a small group of feminists managed to mount a challenge to some of the most cherished principles of American constitutionalism and one of its most successful entertainment industries: Rhode, D, *Justice and Gender*, 1989.

force if one first accepted that men's view of women is almost wholly constructed by pornography and then could agree to the assertion that men's view of women is all that women are. The impossibility of accepting such counter-intuitive propositions means, it is submitted, that the radical feminist argument does not convincingly establish that the availability of pornography represents or causes actual infringements of the rights of women. In strict liberal theory, therefore, the argument from moral autonomy would, in the absence of competing individual rights, require that the choice as to which kinds of explicit literature to read and which to shun, remains properly with the individual. However, a number of comments may be made as to this finding. First, in contrast to many other types of speech, we have found that the only convincing argument for free speech in this area rests upon the interest in moral autonomy, unbolstered by other free speech justifications. Secondly, it seems self-evident that some invasions of autonomy – those which interfere with choices which go to the core of the individual's identity – must be more grave than invasions with respect to more peripheral areas. Interference with the individual's choice to view violent misogynistic pornographic films with no pretension to artistic expression is arguably less of an infringement of his autonomy than, say, interfering with the right of the individual to have homosexual relations. If this argument is accepted, it follows that the autonomy interest here is comparatively weak.

These two points, taken together, would suggest that the total case for protecting inartistic violent pornography is not a particularly strong one. This case must then be balanced against the risk that there may possibly be a link between pornography and the commission of sexual offences. The argument as to this link is still ongoing and it is submitted that a proper evaluation of the evidence in this area falls within the ambit of the social sciences rather than a study of civil liberties. *Some* evidence has been produced of a link, although this evidence is disputed by other studies;[42] what is clear is that there may be said to be a chance of a risk that pornography contributes towards the motivation of sex offenders. It is submitted that until a consensus on the evidential question emerges, the law is entitled, given the relative weakness of the argument for protecting violent hard core pornography, to take a pragmatic stance and allow narrow and selective censorship of at least sexual violence in films, subject to an artistic merits defence, rather than insist that pornography should be unrestricted until the hypothesised link with sex offences has been established beyond reasonable doubt. Further, the case for withdrawal of restrictions must also be balanced against the possibility that while a particular group of men may be influenced by pornography towards the commission of sexual offences, a further group may also be influenced by it towards psychologically damaging treatment of women falling short of any criminal offence. If the link discussed above were established, this further argument would come into play since it would seem strange if pornography could have a highly significant influence on one group of men but none at all on any other. Thus, this point supports the pragmatic stance advocated above, although it falls well short of accepting the general pro-censorship feminist position.

---

42 Evidence for a causal link is quoted in MacKinnon, *op cit*, fn 26, pp 184–91, while Dworkin, R, cites a recent UK study which finds against such a link: Cumberbatch, G and Howitt, D, *A Measure of Uncertainty – the Effects of the Mass Media*, 1989. The findings of this latter study were published in the Daily Telegraph, 23 December 1990. Eckersley discusses the issue (*op cit*, fn 7, pp 161–63). See also Itzen, C (ed), *Pornography: Women, Violence and Civil Liberties*, 1993, which puts forward a body of evidence supporting a causal link.

A further, distinct argument concerns the harm that may be done to the *participants* in the making of hard core pornographic films. This will depend on the nature of the pornographic industry in the particular jurisdiction. If such films portray a variety of actual sexual acts, including sado-masochistic ones, the participants may suffer psychological or even physical harm. This point is of especial pertinence to women since, typically, the female participants are subjected to sexual acts in which they are more victim than perpetrator. For example, a typical scenario might include one woman having sex with a large number of men and being 'roughed up' by them. In such circumstances, it is arguable that the woman's consent may be undermined owing to uncertainty as to what will occur, intimidation into accepting certain acts, such as anal sex, and, more generally, owing to the power disparity between the woman and the almost exclusively male directors of such films. The women participants are, typically, young and from economically deprived groups. If, for example, a woman is alone with a group of men in a house at which filming is taking place and has already been bullied and intimidated, the question whether she is continuing to give informed consent to a variety of sexual acts, which have been occurring for a period of time, begins to lose any reality.[43] If it *was* fairly clear that she was no longer giving such consent, it is hard to imagine that it would be possible, in practice, for her to seek the protection of the law, a fact of which she, and the film makers, will be aware. The film makers are under commercial pressures to push participants into accepting more extreme acts. If it appears from the nature of a film that participants may have been intimidated and subjected to actions verging on sexual abuse (owing to the circumstances, including the duration of one session), both feminists and liberals, on the arguments indicated, would unite in accepting regulation. On this argument, films depicting simulated sado-masochism or actual sexual acts would not necessarily be banned completely, but the conditions under which such filming could take place would be subject to rigorous controls, with the welfare of the participants in mind, and designed to be certain that full, informed consent had always been given. But where it was clear that such controls had not been in place, and that harm, such as psychological trauma, had occurred, censorship would clearly be warranted, except in exceptional cases owing to the strong artistic merits of the film. Where it could only be said that a risk of such harm was possible, it could be viewed as a further factor to be weighed in the balance, along with those identified above.

As a matter of interest, it is worth considering what the position would be if radical feminist scholars could somehow establish that pornography really did construct the social reality of women's identity. How would the feminist argument fare in competition with the liberal arguments for free speech? In the case of the three instrumental justifications, the arguments from democracy, truth and self-development,[44] the feminist

---

43   During the making of a documentary into the making of hard core pornographic films in Los Angeles, *Hard Core*, (broadcast on Channel 4 on 7 April 2001) the Director of the Channel 4 documentary intervened when it appeared that due to bullying and intimidation by the Director of the pornographic film, the woman participant was no longer capable of giving informed consent. She had already been subjected to painful and humiliating acts to which it appeared probable that she had not given consent. In other words, consented-to acts had verged into actions going beyond the apparent boundaries of what she had consented to beforehand. Despite her distress occasioned by painful, forceful oral sex, the Director wished to continue filming and she was told that she must next participate in a group orgy scene in which she would be the only woman. She appeared to acquiesce, but after the intervention, she, and the film crew, had to leave immediately. See further *The Times*, 9 April 2001, p 27.

44   See the Introduction to Part II, above, pp 202–05.

thesis would be able to demonstrate how, in the case of pornography, each argues for restraint on speech. They would argue that free circulation of pornography hinders, even prevents women's participation in the democratic process; it assists not in finding the truth, but in constructing false and all-pervading images of women; it does *not* assist in the healthy development of those who take advantage of its free availability: rather they become rapists, abusers, misogynists.

The one liberal defence of free speech not *explicitly* addressed by the feminist argument is the argument from moral autonomy, which it was suggested above[45] provides the only arguable defence of the right to choose to read pornography. How would this argument fare if it was shown that the basic rights to equality, political participation and speech were in reality denied to all women by the consumption of pornography? Ronald Dworkin has considered this hypothetical position, in which he does not accept that pornography causes individual men to rape and assault women, but accepts the remainder of the feminist claims. One might consider that he would conclude that the massive infringements of women's strong individual rights and the concomitant loss of their moral autonomy would clearly override the comparatively minor invasions of men's free speech and autonomy represented by restrictions on pornography. Somewhat surprisingly, however, Dworkin argues that even if it were the case that the posited harms were actually visited upon all women by pornography, still this would provide no justification for restraining its free availability.[46] Such a view places the right to consume hard core pornography over the rights of half the population to be treated with dignity and respect, to equal participation in democratic government and to free speech itself. Such a conclusion represents, it is submitted, a complete betrayal of the premise on which Dworkin's whole theory of rights is based, namely the overriding duty of the State to treat all its citizens with equal concern and respect.

3 LEGAL RESPONSES TO EXPLICIT EXPRESSION

That the above conclusions on pornography are not in general accepted by States, is revealed by the fact that almost all Bills or Charters of Rights, apart from the US Bill of Rights, contain an exception to the free speech clause which *inter alia* allows restraint on freedom of speech on the broad ground of protection of morality. The 'absolute' nature of the First Amendment, in contrast, has led the US courts to interpret the First Amendment so as to exclude obscene speech from the category of protected speech.[47] Section 14 of the New Zealand Bill of Rights protects freedom of expression, but the protection is subject to such 'reasonable limits prescribed by law as may be justified in a free and democratic society'. Such limits include the regulation of obscenity and pornography.[48] The justification borne in mind in interpreting such exceptions is the harm to be guarded against which seems to include three possibilities: the corruption of persons, particularly children as the more vulnerable; the shock or outrage caused by public displays of certain

---

45   See p 270.

46   Dworkin, R, *op cit*, fn 6, p 15.

47   See *Roth v US* (1957) 354 US 476; *Memoirs v Massachusetts* (1966) 383 US 413.

48   *Society for Promotion of Community Standards Inc v Waverley International (1988) Ltd* [1993] 2 NZLR 709.

material and the commission of sex crimes.[49] The development of UK law has been based on the avoidance of the first two possibilities mentioned, although in relation to the visual media, the third has had some influence. On the ground of causing shock, the public display of certain publications can be regulated, while others viewed as having the potential to corrupt can be prohibited entirely, either by punishment of those responsible after publication or by being suppressed or censored before publication.

The type of restraint used tends to depend on the type of publication in question because it seems to be accepted that the harm which may be caused will vary from medium to medium. The print media are subject to a far more lax regime than the visual media. Printed matter, including magazines, newspapers and books, is not subject to censorship before publication, but punishment is available afterwards if indecent or corrupting material is published. Books are less likely to be punished than magazines because it is thought that something which has a visual impact is more likely to cause harm. Thus, films and broadcasts are censored because of their visual nature and are also subject to punishment. The theatre, however, is in an odd position; it has not been censored since 1968 despite its visual impact. Possibly, this may be due to the idea that theatre audiences are more sophisticated and less likely to be affected by what they have seen than cinema audiences. As indicated below, the internet is also in an anomalous position: although it may be viewed as broadly analogous to the visual media, it is not, and, under current proposals, will not be subject to the same regime.

The likelihood that sweeping change will not occur is partly due to the Strasbourg stance in relation to explicit expression in general, indicated below. It is also due to the fact that, in practice, much of the material subject to seizure consists merely of photographs of various sexual acts and of genitals, with no conceivable artistic merit. Therefore, since the statutory regime is in most respects almost certainly within the margin of appreciation conceded to the Member State, it is unlikely that the judiciary would be inclined to bring about significant change in it, through challenging interpretation, since the result would merely be to increase the trafficking in hard core pornography. There are grounds for arguing that this change would be desirable, but decisions under the HRA hardly provide the appropriate forum for bringing it about. If radical change is to come about, due in part to the impact of the internet, it would have to be brought about by Parliament.

The Strasbourg stance

Article 10(1) specifically provides that the Article 'shall not prevent States from requiring the licensing of broadcasting, television or cinema enterprises'. It is significant that this provision arises in the *first* paragraph of Art 10, thereby providing a limitation of the primary right that on its face is not subject to the test of para 2. However, a very restrictive approach to this sentence has been adopted. It has been found to mean that a licensing system is allowed for on grounds not restricted to those enumerated in para 2; the State may determine who is to have a licence to broadcast. But in general, other decisions of the

---

49 These were the key notions of harm considered by the Williams Committee appointed in 1977 to review obscenity and indecency law (Williams Report, Cmnd 7772, 1979). Broadly, the Committee endorsed regulation of pornography with a view to preventing the second of the harms mentioned.

regulatory bodies who normally grant licences and oversee broadcasting, etc, are not covered by the last sentence of para 1 and must be considered within para 2.[50] Thus, content requirements must be considered under para 2. The preservation of a State monopoly on broadcasting must also be considered within para 2.[51]

As discussed in Chapter 2, under Art 10(2), an interference with the guarantee of freedom of expression under Art 10 can be justified if it is prescribed by law, has a legitimate aim and is necessary in a democratic society. As the Introduction to this part indicated, Strasbourg affords a very high value to freedom of expression and, in particular, views the scope for interference with political expression as very limited.[52] Even in respect of artistic expression, which appears to have a lower place in the hierarchy of expression,[53] the discussion below indicates that no decisions defending restrictions on the freedom of expression of adults can be found, except in respect of hard core pornography, or where a risk to children is also present, or in the context of offending religious sensibilities.

As the Introduction to Part II indicated, certain forms of expression which may be said to be of no value may fall outside the scope of Art 10(1) and it is arguable that, for example, material gratuitously offensive to religious sensibilities[54] or depictions of genitals in pornographic magazines intended merely for entertainment[55] may fall outside its scope. On the other hand, 'hard core' pornography has been found by the Commission to fall within Art 10(1).[56] Given the breadth of para 2, it is unnecessary to seek to draw lines between artistic erotica and forms of pornography aimed at entertainment alone, even assuming that such line-drawing has any validity.[57] The jurisprudence under Art 10 in this context, as in others, concentrates on the para 2 tests.

Interferences with explicit expression may be justified if they have the legitimate aim of providing for the protection of morals or – in certain circumstances – the 'rights of others'. The use of laws on obscenity, indecency or blasphemy against explicit expression or regulation of the media with a view to upholding 'standards of taste and decency' are matters that, potentially, could be addressed under the HRA, relying on Art 10. Specific possibilities are considered below, at relevant points. Here, the Strasbourg stance on the application of Art 10 to explicit expression is considered.

The line of authority stemming from the *Handyside* case[58] suggests that although explicit expression, including some pornographic expression, is protected within Art 10(1), interference with it can be justified quite readily in certain circumstances. It is clear that the scope of the domestic margin of appreciation is not the same in respect of all the aims listed in Art 10(2). The protection of morals would appear to be viewed as requiring a wide margin owing to its subjective nature, in contrast with the protection of

---

50 *Groppera Radio AG v Switzerland* (1990) 12 EHRR 321.
51 *Informationsverein Lentia v Austria* (1993) 17 EHRR 93.
52 See pp 209–10.
53 See pp 209–10.
54 *Otto-Preminger Institut v Austria* (1994) 19 EHRR 34.
55 In *Groppera Radio AG v Switzerland* (1990) 12 EHRR 321, it was thought that mere entertainment might not fall within Art 10(1).
56 *Hoare v UK* [1997] EHRLR 678.
57 See Kearns, P, 'Obscene and blasphemous libel: misunderstanding art' [2000] Crim LR 652.
58 Eur Ct HR, A 24; (1976) 1 EHRR 737.

the authority of the judiciary, which is seen as a more objective notion.[59] The uncertainty of the notion of the protection of morals appears in the lack of a clearly discernible common European standard.

In the *Handyside* case, the European Court of Human Rights had to consider the test of 'deprave and corrupt'. A book called The *Little Red Schoolbook*, which contained chapters on masturbation, sexual intercourse and abortion was prosecuted under the Obscene Publications Act 1959 (see below, p 281) on the basis that it appeared to encourage early sexual intercourse. The publishers applied for a ruling under Art 10 to the European Commission and the case was referred to the Court, which determined that the book fell within Art 10(1). In a famous passage, which strongly favours freedom of artistic or creative expression (the expression of information or ideas), it found: 'Freedom of expression constitutes one of the essential foundations of a democratic society, one of the basic conditions for its progress and for the development of every man. Subject to paragraph 2 of Article 10, it is applicable not only to information or ideas that are favourably received, or regarded as inoffensive but also to those that offend, shock or disturb the state or any sector of the population. Such are the demands of that pluralism, tolerance and broadmindedness without which there is no democratic society.'[60]

However, as this passage indicates, the interference could be justified under para 2. The Court then considered the protection of morals provision under Art 10(2), in order to determine whether the interference with the expression was necessary in a democratic society. It suggested that the 'protection of morals' exception refers to the corruption of individuals rather than to an effect on the moral fabric of society.[61] The Court found that the requirements of morals vary from time to time and from place to place and that the domestic authorities were therefore best placed to judge what was needed. They must 'make the initial assessment of the reality of the pressing social need implied by the notion of necessity in this context'.[62] The judgment thus accepted that domestic authorities would be allowed a wide margin of appreciation in attempting to secure the freedoms guaranteed under the Convention in this area, although this was not to be taken as implying that an unlimited discretion was granted: the power of appreciation 'goes hand in hand with a European supervision' which concerns the legislation in question – the Obscene Publications Act – and the decision applying it. The Court placed particular weight on the fact that the book was aimed at children between the ages of 12 and 18 and that it might encourage them 'to indulge in precocious activities harmful for them or even to commit certain criminal offences'.[63] Thus, the English judges were entitled to find that the book would have a 'pernicious effect on the morals' of the children who would read it. In finding that the tests under para 2 were satisfied, it was said that the fact that the book was circulating freely in the rest of Europe was not determinative of the issues, owing to the application of the margin of appreciation doctrine.

---

59 See the judgment of the Eur Ct HR in the *Sunday Times* case (1979) 2 EHRR 245; discussed in Chapter 2, p 76.
60 *Ibid*, para 49.
61 *Ibid*, para 52.
62 *Ibid*, para 48.
63 *Ibid*, para 52.

A similar stance was taken in *Müller v Switzerland*[64] in respect of a conviction arising from the exhibition of explicit paintings: the fact that the paintings had been exhibited in other parts of Switzerland and abroad did not mean that their suppression could not amount to a pressing social need. The Court took into account the fact that the paintings were exhibited to the public at large, without a warning as to their content, and that a young girl had seen them.

It is notable that the Court in *Handyside* based its justification for the protection of freedom of expression on the arguments from democracy and self-fulfilment rather than on those from truth or moral autonomy.[65] As indicated above, in the Introduction to Part II, these justifications, as instrumental arguments, are open to attack in the way that the argument from moral autonomy is not. This stance of the Court is especially relevant in the context of explicit expression since the argument may provide, as indicated above, the sole justification. (It is not suggested that this was the case in *Handyside* itself; on the contrary, on the basis of the content of the book, three of the four justifications could have applied.) In the other contexts covered by Part II, all four justifications may be present. The Court's stance may have some bearing on the cautious nature of its jurisprudence in this area, although unlike the Supreme Court of Canada, it has not explicitly addressed this issue.[66]

These two decisions give a strong indication as to the stance taken by the Court in respect of Art 10, para 2, but may be viewed as turning on their special facts, particularly the fact that children might have been affected. The thinking behind the *Handyside* decision can find some parallels from the US[67] and Canada.[68] In the US, however, there has been a greater concentration on the question whether restrictions aimed at children might impinge also on the freedom of expression of adults and on the extent to which this should be tolerated,[69] a matter which was in issue in *Handyside*, although not afforded weight by the Court.

These decisions at Strasbourg do not determine the question of the consumption of explicit material solely or mainly by a willing adult audience. That question was considered in *Hoare v UK*,[70] which concerned the possession of 'hard core' pornographic videos. The applicant had been convicted of possessing obscene material under s 2 of the Obscene Publications Act. The Commission found quite easily that the restriction on his freedom of expression had the legitimate aim of protecting morals and was not disproportionate to that aim. Owing to the nature of the material, the justifications underlying freedom of expression, referred to above, were not present, apart from the justification based on moral autonomy. In *Otto-Preminger Institut v Austria*,[71] discussed below,[72] the Court considered the question of restrictions on freedom of expression in

---

64 (1991) 13 EHRR 212. See Chapter 2, p 77.

65 See the Introduction to Part II.

66 See *R v Butler* [1992] 1 SCR 452.

67 *Ginsberg v New York* 390 US 629 (1968).

68 *Irwin Toy Ltd v AG (Quebec)* [1989] 1 SCR 927 (broad limitation on broadcast advertising aimed at children).

69 *Reno v American Civil Liberties Union* (1997) 521 US 844.

70 [1997] EHRLR 678.

71 (1994) 19 EHRR 34.

72 See pp 317–19.

respect of a film where the expression was aimed at a willing adult audience. A warning had been given and therefore viewers knew what to expect. Nevertheless, owing to the shock caused to particular religious sensibilities in the local region, it was found, in a much criticised decision,[73] that the interference could be justified despite the fact that the measure had the effect of preventing the showing of the film across the whole country. That decision can be contrasted with the findings of the Commission in the same case that Art 10 had been violated, and with those of the Commission in *Scherer v Switzerland*;[74] it was found that the conviction of the proprietor of a sex shop for showing obscene and explicit videos had breached Art 10, since access was restricted to adults and no one was likely to confront them unwittingly.

Below, the principles deriving from the stance indicated are considered in relation to the specific contexts covered.

Statutory obscenity[75]

Obscenity law operates as a subsequent restraint and is largely used in relation to books, magazines and other printed material, material posted on web-pages or videos;[76] theoretically it could also be used against broadcasts and films. The harm sought to be prevented is that of a corrupting effect on an individual. In other words, it is thought that an individual will undergo a change for the worse after encountering the material in question. The rationale of the law is thus overtly paternalistic. Of course, if all material which might appear capable of causing corruption were suppressed, a severe infringement of freedom of speech would occur. Thus, the statute which largely governs this area – the Obscene Publications Act 1959 – takes the stance that in preventing material which may deprave and corrupt, a line must be drawn between erotic literature and the truly obscene on the basis that hard core pornography does not deserve special protection.[77] This echoes the approach in America, where this form of pornography is not defined as 'speech' because it is thought that the justification for the constitutional protection for freedom of speech does not apply.[78] In fact, oddly enough, this may mean that pornography is more likely to be prohibited in the US than in the UK. Now that the HRA is in force, it is fair to say that pornography is, in a sense, in a better position in the UK than in the US since, as indicated above, it will probably fall within the range of expression protected by Art 10(1).

---

73   For an incisive critique see Pannick, D, 'Religious feelings and the European Court' [1995] PL 7.

74   A 287 (1993) Com Rep (the case was discontinued in the Court owing to the death of the applicant).

75   See, generally: O'Higgins, P, *Censorship in Britain*, 1972; Robertson, G, *Obscenity*, 1979, and (with Nichol, D) *Media Law*, 1992, Chapter 3; MacMillan, PR, *Censorship and Public Morality*, 1983; Barendt, E, *Media Law*, 1993; Baker, R, *Media Law*, 1995; Carey, P, *Media Law*, 1996; Feldman, D, *Civil Liberties in England and Wales*, 1993, Chapter 15; Bailey, SH, Harris, DJ, and Jones, BL, *Civil Liberties: Cases and Materials*, 4th edn, 1995, Chapter 5; Itzen, *op cit*, fn 42; MacKinnon, *op cit*, fn 36; Travis, A, *Bound and Gagged – A Secret History of Obscenity in Britain*, 2000.

76   In *AG's Reference (No 5 of 1980)* [1980] 3 All ER 816, CA, it was found that a video constituted an article for the purposes of the 1959 Act.

77   See, for argument on this point, Dworkin, R, 'Is there a right to pornography?' (1981) 1 Ox JLS 177.

78   *Miller v California* (1973) 413 US 15. It should be noted that under the argument from moral autonomy, it is irrelevant whether the material concerned is classified as 'speech' or not.

The idea of preventing corruption had informed the common law long before the 1959 Act; it sprang from the ruling in *Hicklin*.[79] Determining whether material would 'deprave and corrupt' was problematic, especially as it was unclear to whom the test should be applied. Two cases in 1954 showed the uncertainty of the law. In *Martin Secker and Warburg*[80] it was determined that the test applied to persons who might encounter the material in question. But at the same time, in *Hutchinson*,[81] the court held that the test should be applied to the most vulnerable person who might conceivably encounter the material and that the jury could therefore look at the effect it might have on a teenage girl. Moreover, the jury could find that something which could merely be termed shocking could deprave and corrupt.

The 1959 Act was passed in an attempt to clear up some of this uncertainty, although it failed to lay down a test for the meaning of the term 'deprave and corrupt'. The *actus reus* of the offence involves the publication for gain (s 2(1)) or having for such publication (s 1(2) of the Obscene Publications Act 1964) an article which tends, taken as a whole, (or where it comprises two or more distinct items, the effect of one of the items) to deprave and corrupt a significant proportion of those likely to see or hear it (s 1(1)). This is a crime of strict liability: there is no need to show an intention to deprave and corrupt, merely an intention to publish. Once it is shown that an article is obscene within the meaning of the Act, it will be irrelevant, following the ruling of the Court of Appeal in *Calder and Boyars*,[82] that the defendant's motivation could be characterised as pure or noble. The Act does not cover live performances on stage which fall within the similarly worded Theatres Act 1968.

'Deprave and corrupt'

This test could be applied to any material which might corrupt; it is clear from the ruling in *Calder (John) Publishing v Powell*[83] that it is not confined to descriptions or representations of sexual matters and it could therefore be applied to a disturbing book on the drug-taking life of a junkie. This ruling was followed in *Skirving*,[84] which concerned a pamphlet on the means of taking cocaine in order to obtain maximum effect. In all instances, the test for obscenity should not be applied to the type of behaviour advocated or described in the article in question, but to the article itself. Thus, in *Skirving*, the question to be asked was not whether taking cocaine would deprave and corrupt, but whether the pamphlet itself would.

This test is hard to explain to a jury and uncertain of meaning, with the result that directions such as the following have been given: '... obscenity, members of the jury, is like an elephant; you can't define it, but you know it when you see it.'[85] However, it is clear from the ruling of the Court of Appeal in *Anderson*[86] that the effect in question must be

79 (1868) 3 QB 360.
80 [1954] 2 All ER 683; [1954] 1 WLR 1138.
81 (1954), unreported. For an account of the proceedings see St John Stevas, N, *Obscenity and the Law*, 1956, p 116.
82 [1969] 1 QB 151; [1968] 3 WLR 974; [1968] 3 All ER 644; (1968) 52 Cr App R 706.
83 [1965] 1 QB 159.
84 [1985] QB 819.
85 Robertson, *op cit*, fn 75, p 45.
86 [1972] 1 QB 304.

more than mere shock. The trial judge had directed the jury that the test connoted that which was repulsive, loathsome or filthy. This explanation was clearly defective, since it would have merged the concepts of indecency and obscenity and it was rejected by the Court of Appeal on the basis that it would dilute the test for obscenity which, it was said, must connote the prospect of moral harm, not just shock. The conviction under the Act was therefore overturned because of the misdirection. The House of Lords in *Knuller v DPP*[87] considered the word 'corrupt' and found that it denoted a publication which produced 'real social evil' – going beyond immoral suggestions or persuasion.

This was quite a strict test, but it was qualified by the House of Lords in *DPP v Whyte*.[88] The owners of a bookshop which sold pornographic material were prosecuted. Most of the customers were old men who had encountered the material on previous occasions and this gave rise to two difficulties. First, the old men were unlikely to engage in anti-social sexual behaviour and therefore the meaning of 'corrupt' had to be modified if it was to extend to cover the effect on them of the material: it was found that it meant creating a depraved effect on the mind which need not actually issue forth in any particular sexual behaviour. Secondly, it was suggested that the old men were already corrupt and therefore would not be affected by the material. However, it was held that corruption did not connote a once-only process: persons could be 'recorrupted' and, on this basis, a conviction was obtained. (Interestingly, this finding suggests that there is a presumption that the 'deprave and corrupt' test is of universal application: no person or group of persons can be excluded in principle from its ambit. In this sense it differs from the test as put forward in *Hicklin*; that test applied only to those whose minds were open to immoral influences.) The test will not be satisfied if the material in question causes feelings of revulsion from the immorality portrayed. This theory, known as the 'aversion theory', derives from *Calder and Boyars*, which concerned *Last Exit from Brooklyn*; it was found that the horrific pictures it painted of homosexuality and drug taking in New York would be more likely to discourage than encourage such behaviour.[89]

The 'deprave and corrupt' test must be applied to those likely to see or hear the material in question and, therefore, the concept of relative obscenity is imported into the Act. In other words, the obscenity or otherwise of material cannot be determined merely by its consideration or analysis but, rather, will depend on the character of the consumer and, in this sense, the test presents a contrast with German obscenity law which absolutely prohibits hard core pornography, although soft core material is quite freely available.[90] It was held in *DPP v Whyte*[91] that in order to make a determination as to the type of consumer in question, the court could receive information as to the nature of the relevant area, the type of shop and the class of people frequenting it. The jury must consider the likely reader in order to determine whether the material would deprave and corrupt him or her rather than considering the most vulnerable conceivable reader. In *Penguin Books*,[92] which concerned the prosecution of *Lady Chatterley's Lover*, the selling

---

87 [1973] AC 435; [1972] 3 WLR 143; (1972) 56 Cr App R 633, HL.

88 [1972] AC 849; [1972] 3 All ER 12, HL.

89 [1969] 1 QB 151; [1968] 3 WLR 974; [1968] 3 All ER 644; (1968) 52 Cr App R 706. For comment, see Robertson, *Obscenity*, 1979, pp 50–53.

90 German Criminal Code, s 184(3).

91 [1972] AC 849; [1972] 3 All ER 12, HL.

92 [1961] Crim LR 176; see Rolph, CH, *The Trial of Lady Chatterley*, 1961.

price of the book was taken into account and the fact that being in paperback, it would reach a mass audience.

The jury has to consider whether the article would be likely to deprave and corrupt a *significant proportion* of those likely to encounter it. It was determined in *Calder and Boyars*[93] that the jury must determine what is meant by a 'significant proportion' and this was approved in *DPP v Whyte*, Lord Cross explaining that 'a significant proportion of a class means a part which is not numerically negligible, but which may be much less than half'. This formulation was adopted in order to prevent sellers of pornographic material claiming that most of their customers would be unlikely to be corrupted by it. The effect of the article as a whole on persons likely to encounter it should be considered, not merely the effect of specific passages of a particularly explicit nature. However, in *Anderson*[94] it was made clear that where the article consists of a number of items, each item must be considered in isolation from the others. Thus, a magazine which is, on the whole, innocuous, but contains one obscene item, can be suppressed, although a novel could not be.

It may be reasonably straightforward to identify a group, of whom a significant proportion might encounter the material, but it is unclear how it can then be determined that they would be likely to experience depravity and corruption as a result. The ruling in *Anderson* was to the effect that in sexual obscenity cases and normally in other obscenity cases, the defence cannot call expert evidence as to the effect that an article may have on its likely audience. Thus, the view taken in *DPP v A and BC Chewing Gum Ltd*[95] that such evidence would be admissible may be regarded as arising only due to the very specific circumstances of that case. However, it was decided in *Skirving*[96] that in cases concerned with alleged depravity and corruption arising from factors other than the sexual nature of the material, expert evidence will, exceptionally, be admissible, although the evidence can only be as to the effects of the behaviour described in the material, not as to the likely effects of the material itself. Thus, generally, where the material deals with matters within their own experience, the jury will receive little help in applying the test. However, it seems clear that a jury will be able to take into account changing standards of morality ('the contemporary standards' test from *Calder and Boyars*) in considering what will deprave and corrupt. Therefore, the concept of obscenity is, at least theoretically, able to keep up to date. The application of these tests at the present time was seen in the trial for obscenity of the book *Inside Linda Lovelace*[97] which suggested that a prosecution brought against a book of any conceivable literary merit would be unlikely to succeed. Thus, in December 1991, the DPP refused to prosecute the Marquis de Sade's *Juliette*, even though it was concerned (fictionally) with the torture, rape and murder of women and children.

The defence of public good

This defence, which arises under s 4 of the 1959 Act (as amended by s 53 of the Criminal Law Act 1977) and s 3 of the Theatres Act 1968, was intended to afford recognition to

---

93   [1969] 1 QB 151.
94   [1972] 1 QB 304.
95   [1968] 1 QB 159.
96   [1985] QB 819.
97   For comment see (1976) NLJ 126. The prosecution failed.

artistic merit. Thus it may be seen as a highly significant step in the direction of freedom of speech, acknowledging the force of a variant of the free speech argument from truth which was also used by the Williams Committee.[98] Under the 1959 Act, it is a defence to a finding that a publication is obscene if it can be shown that 'the publication of the article in question is justified as for the public good in that it is in the interests of science, literature, art, learning or of other objects of general concern'. Under the 1968 Act, the similarly worded defence which covers 'the interests of drama, opera, ballet or any other art or of literature or learning' is somewhat narrower as omitting the concluding general words. Under s 53(6) of the 1977 Act, this narrower defence applies to films. Expert evidence will be admissible to prove that one of these possibilities can be established and it may include considering other works.

It was determined in *Penguin Books* in respect of *Lady Chatterley's Lover* that the jury should adopt a two-stage approach, asking first whether the article in question is obscene and if so, going on to consider whether the defendant has established the probability that its merits are so high as to outbalance its obscenity so that its publication is for the public good. The failure of the prosecution was seen as a turning point for literary freedom and the jury allowed it to be known that the second stage of the test afforded the basis on which the novel escaped suppression. In *DPP v Jordan*,[99] the House of Lords approved this two-stage approach and the balancing of obscenity against literary or other merit.

In *DPP v Jordan*, the attempt was made to widen the test. The main question was whether the articles in question – hard core pornography – could be justified under s 4 as being of psychotherapeutic value for persons of deviant sexuality in that the material might help to relieve their sexual tensions by way of sexual fantasies. It was argued that such material might provide a safety valve for such persons, which would divert them from anti-social activities and that such benefit could fall within the words 'other objects of general concern' deriving from s 4. The House of Lords, however, held that these words must be construed *ejusdem generis* with the preceding words 'art, literature learning, science'. As these words were unrelated to sexual benefit, the general words which followed them could not be construed in the manner suggested. It was ruled that the jury must be satisfied that the matter in question made a contribution to a recognised field of culture or learning which could be assessed irrespective of the persons to whom it was distributed.

Although the test of public good has clearly afforded protection to freedom of expression in relation to publications of artistic merit, it has been criticised. It does not allow for consideration of the benefits of pornography and may be inapt as a means of considering 'new art at the cutting edge of art development'.[100] It requires a jury to embark on the very difficult task of weighing a predicted change for the worse in the minds of the group of persons likely to encounter the article, against literary or other merit. Thus, an effect or process must be imagined which, once established, must be measured against an intrinsic quality. Geoffrey Robertson has written: 'the balancing act is a logical nonsense [because it is not] logically possible to weigh such disparate concepts as 'corruption' and 'literary merit'.[101] The test seems to create an almost complete

---

98   See above, p 270.
99   [1977] AC 699.
100 Kearns, P, 'Obscene and blasphemous libel: misunderstanding art' [2000] Crim LR 652, p 654.
101 Robertson, *op cit*, fn 75, p 164.

paradox: it assumes that an individual can be corrupted, which suggests a stultifying effect on the mind and yet can also experience an elevating effect due to the merit of an article. However, such an interpretation of the test is open to two objections. First, a person could experience corruption in the sense that her moral standards might be lowered, but she might retain a sense of literary or artistic appreciation. Secondly – and this might seem the more satisfactory interpretation – the *message* of the article and its general artistic impact (through, for example, its influence on other works which followed it) might be for the public good although some individuals who encountered it were corrupted. Thus the term 'publication' in s 4 must mean publication to the public at large, not only to those who encounter the article if the test is to be workable.[102]

It should be noted that, as discussed below, the defence can be avoided by bringing a charge of indecency at common law; as *Gibson*[103] demonstrated, the merits of an obscene object may, paradoxically, prevent its suppression while the merits of less offensive objects may not.

Forfeiture proceedings

The vast majority of actions against allegedly obscene material take the form of forfeiture proceedings. Under s 3 of the 1959 Act, magazines and other material, such as videos, can be seized by the police if it is suspected on reasonable grounds that they are obscene and have been kept for gain. No conviction is obtained; if found to be obscene, the material is merely destroyed; no other punishment is imposed and therefore s 3 may operate at a low level of visibility. Seizure may mean that the safeguards provided by the Act can be bypassed: consideration is not given to the possible literary merits of such material because the public good defence is not taken into account in issuing the seizure warrant. The merits of an article can be taken into account in the forfeiture hearing in determining whether it out-balances its obscenity, but there is not much evidence that magistrates take a very rigorous approach to making such a determination. They do not need to read every item, but need only look at samples selected by the police[104] and seem, in any event, more ready than a jury to find that an item is obscene.[105] It seems, therefore, that the protection afforded by the 1959 Act to freedom of speech may depend more on the exercise of discretion by the police as to the enforcement of s 3 or on the tolerance of magistrates, rather than on the law itself. However, s 3 can be used only in respect of material which may be obscene rather than in relation to any form of pornography; it was held in *Darbo v DPP*[106] that a warrant issued under s 3 allowing officers to search for 'sexually explicit material' was bad on its face, as such articles would fall within a much wider category of articles than those which could be called obscene.

---

102 The House of Lords in *Jordan* [1977] AC 699 appeared to take this view. See also Robertson, *op cit*, fn 75, on the point (pp 168–69).

103 [1990] 2 QB 619; [1991] 1 All ER 439; [1990] 3 WLR 595, CA.

104 *Crown Court at Snaresbrook ex p Metropolitan Police Comr* (1984) 148 JP 449.

105 Bailey, Harris and Jones note (*op cit*, fn 75, p 328) that comment arose when forfeiture proceedings of an edition of the magazine *Men Only* coincided with the jury acquittal of the editors of *Nasty Tales* of the offence under s 2 ((1973) 127 JPN 82). Robertson argues (*Obscenity*, 1979, p 96) that as the hearing is before a tribunal which has already decided that the material is – at least prima facie – obscene, it is likely to have an appearance of unfairness. The Bench may be unlikely to be convinced that in effect, it was wrong in the first place in issuing the summons.

106 (1992) *The Times*, 4 July; [1992] Crim LR 56.

Statutory obscenity, the HRA and the protection of morals exception under Art 10(2)

Clearly, any prosecutions under the Act or forfeiture actions constitute interferences with the Art 10 guarantee of freedom of expression under the HRA, although subject to justification. In relation to any particular decision, the public authorities involved are bound by s 6 of the HRA to ensure that the tests under Art 10 are satisfied, while the provisions of the 1959 Act must be interpreted consistently with Art 10 under s 3 of the HRA. As Chapter 4 indicated, s 12 of the HRA does not apply to criminal proceedings. Forfeiture proceedings have the hallmarks of criminal proceedings in certain respects, although a conviction is not obtained, and therefore they may be outside the ambit of s 12.

Given the wide margin of appreciation afforded to the domestic authorities in the relevant decisions, little guidance as to the requirements of Art 10 in this context is available, especially where the material is directed at a willing adult audience. The domestic judiciary are, therefore, theoretically free to take a different stance. The decisions considered above at Strasbourg on the 1959 Act indicate that the statutory regime relating to publication of an obscene article under s 2 is broadly in harmony with Art 10 of the European Convention. Nevertheless, a specific decision might not meet the proportionality requirements, scrutinised more intensively than at Strasbourg.

The UK forfeiture regime has not itself been tested at Strasbourg. The HRA requirements may be especially pertinent in relation to forfeiture: the magistrates conducting the proceedings are, of course, bound by Art 10 and therefore would be expected to approach the task with greater rigour. In particular, it is arguably necessary to examine each item, even where a large scale seizure has occurred, rather than considering a sample of items only.[107] But since, in practice, a vast amount of material is condemned as obscene in legal actions for forfeiture, the practical difficulties facing magistrates make it possible, especially initially, that the impact of the HRA will be more theoretical than real. It seems probable that, in practice, magistrates will not examine each item and will give only cursory attention, if any, to considering the application of the somewhat elusive Strasbourg case law. However, if on occasion publishers seek to contest s 3 orders before a jury, the proportionality of the measures adopted may receive more attention. Moreover, it is arguable that Art 6 might be breached by the procedure since it could be said to lack impartiality, given that the same magistrate may sign the seizure order, and determine forfeiture.[108]

Statutory indecency[109]

The concept of indecency, as opposed to obscenity, is contained in certain statutes and also exists at common law. The idea of prohibiting indecency is, essentially, to prevent *public displays* of offensive material or the possibility that such material will impinge in some way on the general public, or a part of it. Such prohibition is aimed at protecting persons from the shock or offence occasioned by encountering certain material, rather

---

107 It was found that such sampling was acceptable in *Snaresbrook Crown Court ex p Comr of the Metropolis* (1984) 79 Cr App R 184. For discussion, see Stone, R [1986] Crim LR 139.

108 See above, fn 105.

109 See Robertson, *op cit*, fn 75, Chapter 7; Robertson, G and Nichol, AGL, *Media Law*, 1992, pp 115–24.

than at preventing moral deterioration. Therefore, except perhaps in a very broad sense, it may be said not to be aimed at the protection of morals and so might not fall within that exception to Art 10. The general lowering of moral standards or attacks on the moral fabric of society must occur – if it is assumed that it is likely to occur at all – through the medium of individual persons who are affected by encountering obscene material;[110] it would seem, therefore, that the 'moral fabric of society' would be unaffected by material which only serves to shock. However, it might be very broadly argued on a conservative view that indecent material might have a corrupting effect if it was repeatedly encountered because it might lead at each encounter to less outrage as sensibilities became blunted. In any event, the European Court of Human Rights has found that material which was, arguably, merely shocking, fell within the protection of morals exception.[111]

If the material is not obscene and is either stored with a view to sale, or offered for sale, it will not attract liability, unless the provision of s 160 of the Criminal Justice Act 1988 apply (below). Indecency is easier to prove than obscenity because there is no defence of public good, there is no need to consider the whole article and there is no need to satisfy the difficult test of deprave and corrupt. Prosecuting authorities have taken note of these distinctions and have therefore tended at times to rely on the law against indecency where, arguably, the article in question could be said to be obscene.[112] It will be seen that the existence of these two strands of law has led to some anomalies.

Meaning of indecency

The test for indecency was discussed in *Knuller v DPP*;[113] it was determined by Lord Reid to be satisfied by material which creates outrage or utter disgust in 'ordinary decent-minded people'. This statement, coupled with the general tenor of Lord Reid's comments, suggested that the level of shock would have to be fairly high. In *GLC ex p Blackburn*,[114] Lord Denning approved the simple test of 'is this indecent?' since he considered that if jurors were asked the more complex question 'will it deprave and corrupt?' they would allow very offensive articles into circulation. However, Lord Bridge wondered whether asking whether something is shocking or disgusting could be a suitable test of criminality. Sir Robert Megarry has said that 'indecency' is too subjective and emotional a concept[115] to be workable as a legal test. It seems that the test is not confined to sexual material; Lord Reid in *Knuller* considered that 'indecency is not confined to sexual indecency'.[116] This is supported by the finding in *Gibson*[117] that the use of freeze-dried foetuses as earrings on a model of a head was indecent.

Uncertainty arises as to whether the term 'indecency' denotes a relative concept: a concept which, like that of relative obscenity, depends on its context or on the nature of

---

110 For criticism of the view that preventing the lowering of the moral tone of society justifies censorship, see the introduction to this chapter, p 269.
111 *Müller v Switzerland* (1988) 13 EHRR 212.
112 This trend is reflected in Lord Denning's comments in *GLC ex p Blackburn* [1976] 1 WLR 550, p 556.
113 [1973] AC 435, p 457; [1972] 3 WLR 143; (1972) 56 Cr App R 633.
114 [1976] 3 All ER 184.
115 *A Second Miscellany at Law*, p 316.
116 [1973] AC 435, p 458.
117 [1990] 2 QB 619; [1991] 1 All ER 439, CA.

the audience or recipient. According to the ruling of the Court of Appeal in *Straker*,[118] such considerations are irrelevant: indecency is an objective quality discoverable by examination in the same way that, for example, a substance might be discovered to be a certain chemical. However, *Wiggins v Field*[119] suggests otherwise; the ruling specifically demanded that the circumstances in which the alleged indecency occurred should be taken into account. A prosecution was brought in respect of a reading of Allen Ginsberg's poem 'America' on the basis of a charge of using indecent language in contravention of a local bylaw. The Divisional Court held that if the context was considered – this was the work of a recognised poet, read without any intention of causing offence – the charge of indecency could not be supported. This stance was taken by the Court of Appeal in *AG ex rel McWhirter v IBA*;[120] it was agreed that the film in question 'taken as a whole' was not offensive, although a small percentage of it depicted indecent incidents. Thus it may be that the Straker ruling, to the effect that indecency may be treated as an objective concept, is confined to cases arising under the Post Office Act 1953, but the point cannot yet be regarded as settled. However, it is clear that the notion of indecency will vary from generation to generation and that the jury will be expected to apply current standards.[121]

The variety of specific statutory offences

The word 'indecent' is contained in a number of statutes and bylaws. Therefore, only specific areas are covered, but if no statute affects a particular area, the gap may be filled by the common law.

Taking an indecent photograph or film of a person under the age of 16 is prohibited under s 1 of the Protection of Children Act 1978, as is possessing it with a view to sale, showing it or distributing it. The only intention needed is the intention to take a photograph; whether the photograph is indecent depends on the view of the jury regarding recognised standards of propriety.[122]

No artistic merits defence is available, although the distributor of the photographs, *not* the taker of them, can seek to show that he had a 'legitimate reason' for distributing or showing the photographs or for having them in his possession. Section 84 of the Criminal Justice and Public Order Act 1994 amended the 1978 Act to add 'pseudo-photographs' of children in order to cover digitally created photographs.[123] It also amended the Act so that the storage of data on computer disk or by other electronic means capable of conversion to a photograph is covered. Section 160 of the Criminal Justice Act 1988 created an additional offence of merely possessing the indecent picture of a child without a view to sale, display or distribution. The offence under either the 1978 or the 1988 Act can be committed merely by downloading an image onto a computer;[124] automatic

---

118 [1965] Crim LR 239; this approach was affirmed by the Court of Appeal in *Stamford* [1972] 2 WLR 1055; [1972] 2 All ER 427.

119 [1968] Crim LR 50.

120 [1973] QB 629.

121 *Shaw v DPP* [1962] AC 220, p 292. This approach was accepted in *Stamford* [1972] 2 WLR 1055; [1972] 2 All ER 427.

122 *R v Graham-Kerr* (1988) 88 Cr App R 302.

123 See further Manchester, C, 'Criminal Justice and Public Order Act 1994: obscenity, pornography and videos' [1995] Crim LR 123, pp 123–28.

124 *R v Bowden* [2000] 2 All ER 418.

storage of an image on a hard disk would not amount to making a photograph or pseudo-photograph.[125] Further, it has been found that possession requires knowledge.[126]

The breadth of these offences was illustrated when the Saatchi Gallery in London was threatened with prosecution in March 2001 for showing pictures of children playing naked on the beach, taken by their mother, a professional photographer, as what one commentator called 'a celebration of the wonderment and *joie de vivre* of her children'.[127] The prosecution did not materialise, apparently on the basis that no element of lewdness was present. Similarly, when the Mapplethorpe Exhibition was shown at the Hayward Gallery in London in Autumn 1996, the Gallery took legal advice owing to the sexually explicit nature of some of the exhibits. Prosecution under the 1959 and/or under the 1978 Act appeared to be a possibility. It decided not to show three photographs, one of which was of a child.[128]

Offensive displays fall under the Indecent Displays (Control) Act 1981, which covers public displays of anything capable of being displayed,[129] but is limited in its application; it does not apply to the theatre, cinema, broadcasting (which are covered by different provisions), museums, art galleries, local authority or Crown buildings (s 1(4)). Shops which display an adequate warning notice are exempted[130] as far as adults are concerned; thus, as will be seen below, art galleries are, anomalously, more constrained in their displays than sex shops, in that they will fall within the common law on indecency and will not be able to take advantage of this exception. Mailing of sexual literature is covered by s 11 of the Post Office Act 1953; sexual literature in luggage is covered by s 49 of the Customs and Excise Management Act 1979.

In the 1970s, customs officials interpreted the term 'indecency' widely; in 1976, for example, they seized and destroyed 114,000 books and magazines and 4,000 films. It also appeared that the test was being used in an arbitrary and indiscriminate manner. For example, in 1985 books ordered by the bookshop 'Gay's the Word' were impounded, including books by Oscar Wilde and Gore Vidal. The trial was about to commence, but the proceedings were withdrawn because of the ruling of the European Court of Justice in *Conegate Ltd v Customs and Excise Comrs*.[131] It was held under Art 36 of the Treaty of European Union[132] that Britain could not apply a more stringent test – indecency – to imported goods when the equivalent in terms of domestically produced ones could circulate freely because they were not obscene. Thus, where obscenity or indecency existed as alternatives, the easier test should not be used to favour domestic goods since that would amount to arbitrary discrimination on trade between Member States contrary to Art 36. Customs officers now apply this ruling but not just to EU imports, because it would be too impracticable to apply different tests to imports from different countries. This ruling has therefore resulted in a major relaxation on censorship. Hard core

---

125 *Atkins v DPP* [2000] 2 All ER 425.

126 *Ibid.*

127 See *The Guardian*, Report, 10 March 2001, p 9.

128 See further Warbrick, 'Federalism and free speech', in Loveland (ed), *Importing the First Amendment*, 1997, pp 177–79 and 190–92.

129 For discussion of the effect of the Act, see (1982) Stat LR 31; (1981) 45 MLR 62; (1981) 132 NLJ 629.

130 Section 1(3)(b).

131 [1987] QB 254; [1986] 2 All ER 688. Figures quoted by Robertson, *Obscenity*, 1979, p 193.

132 Formerly Art 30 of the Treaty of Rome.

pornography is, however, still seized; this is justifiable under Art 36 because it would also be prohibited if disseminated internally under the Obscene Publications Act.

Anomalies have arisen from the dichotomy between the tests for indecency on the one hand and obscenity on the other in other contexts. In *Straker*,[133] obscenity charges which resulted in an acquittal were brought in respect of the sale of artistic nude studies. The defendant then sent the pictures by post to persons interested in photographic art and was prosecuted successfully under s 11 of the Post Office Act 1953. In other words, the mere fact that the articles happened to be transferred through the post meant that criminal liability could arise, although otherwise it could not have done so. The DPP has recognised the anomalies created by cases of this nature and therefore he indicated – in 1981 – that prosecutions under the Post Office Act would be confined to cases where the indecent material sent through the post was unsolicited.

Apart from statutes prohibiting the promulgation of indecent material in specific situations, the possibility also arises of using the Sexual Offences Act 1956 to prevent displays of indecency in stage plays and perhaps in the context of other live performances. A play, *The Romans in Britain*, which was staged in 1982 by the Royal National Theatre, included a depiction of the homosexual rape of a young druid priest by three Roman soldiers. Mary Whitehouse wanted to bring an action in respect of this scene, but the Attorney General refused permission as required under s 8 of the Theatres Act. Under s 2 of the Act, liability at common law could not arise in respect of a stage performance. Therefore, Mary Whitehouse invoked s 13 of the Sexual Offences Act 1956, which proscribes the procurement by one male of an act of gross indecency on another. This was arguably fulfilled by the procurement by the male director of the commission of an act of gross indecency by one actor on another. Had a female director been in charge, no prosecution would have been possible. It was determined on a preliminary ruling that *prima facie* liability might be established using this method.[134] At that point the prosecution was withdrawn; Mary Whitehouse had established the point in question and did not wish to take the risk that the prosecution would fail, as it might have done on various grounds. In particular, it was uncertain whether it could be shown that any indecency took place: it was unclear whether the actor's penis or thumb was shown in the scene. The significance of this possibility should not be over-emphasised; nevertheless, it clearly subverts the purpose of the Theatres Act, which should therefore be amended to prohibit liability arising under other statutes.

Statutory indecency, the HRA and the protection of morals exception under Art 10(2)

Prosecutions under these provisions will normally constitute interferences with freedom of expression under the HRA. The public authorities involved are bound by s 6 of the HRA to ensure that the tests under Art 10 are satisfied, while the provisions of the various statutes must be interpreted consistently with Art 10 under s 3. As Chapter 2 indicated, State interference with the Art 10 guarantee must be in accordance with the law, under

---

133 [1965] Crim LR 239; this approach was affirmed by the Court of Appeal in *Stamford* [1972] 2 WLR 1055; [1972] 2 All ER 427.
134 *The Romans in Britain*, see [1982] PL 165–67.

para 2, if it is to be justified. This requirement covers not only the existence of national law, but its quality. In *Kopp v Switzerland*[135] the Court clearly stated that the essential requirements of a national legal basis are those of accessibility and foreseeability. These requirements require precision so that, in this context, the citizen is sufficiently aware of the meaning of the term 'indecency'. It is suggested that, as currently interpreted, the term is so uncertain that there is at least room for argument that these statutory provisions do not meet the 'prescribed by law' requirement. In *Hashman and Harrup v UK*,[136] the Court found that the *contra bono mores* doctrine was too uncertain to meet this requirement, since it depended on a vague concept of anti-social behaviour. Arguably, the concept of indecency considered in *Knuller v DPP*,[137] which depends on considering whether material would disgust 'ordinary decent-minded people' is almost equally imprecise; as pointed out above, doubts have been expressed as to the suitability of such a concept as a basis for criminality.

It would, of course, be a bold domestic court that was prepared to find such a significant flaw in a large number of statutory provisions (and in respect of common law indecency, discussed below). The Commission has had the opportunity of making such a finding but has not done so,[138] although this is not conclusive of the issue. It is more likely that certain aspects of this statutory regime will be found to be disproportionate to the legitimate aim pursued, either in terms of the provisions themselves or in respect of decisions made under them. It is suggested that the provisions of s 160 of the Criminal Justice Act 1988, affecting the downloading of pseudo-photographs of persons under 16 onto a computer, presumably from a website, might be viewed as disproportionate to the aim in view. The provisions criminalise a person merely for possessing a photograph, or its equivalent, which has been created without the involvement of a child. It is hard to view the use of the criminal law in this way as proportionate, since it is unclear that morals could be protected by this means. The breadth of the offences under the Protection of Children Act was indicated by the possibility of prosecution in respect of the Saatchi Exhibition. Arguments regarding proportionality could be raised in a similar instance, especially regarding the lack of an artistic merits defence or a defence of legitimate reason applicable to the creator of the photographs, so that the taking and distributing of photographs of children by paedophiles is not distinguished from taking them for artistic or scientific purposes.

Common law offences of indecency and obscenity

Conspiring to corrupt public morals

Prosecutions for conspiracy to corrupt morals can be brought at common law, as can prosecutions for outraging public decency. Thus, common law indecency creates a much wider area of liability than is created under statute because the law is not confined to specific situations such as using the mail. In *Shaw v DPP*,[139] the House of Lords

---

135 (1999) 27 EHRR 91, paras 70–71.
136 (2000) 8 BHRC 104. See Chapter 9, p 493.
137 [1973] AC 435, p 457; [1972] 3 WLR 143.
138 *Gibson v UK*, Application No 17634.
139 [1962] AC 220; [1961] 2 WLR 897, HL; for comment, see (1961) 24 MLR 626; (1964) 42 Canadian Bar Review 561.

determined that the offence of conspiring to corrupt public morals existed on the basis that the law conferred a general discretion to punish immoral (not merely criminal) conduct which could injure the public. Thus, any subject matter which could lead others astray – although not necessarily amounting to a criminal offence – could be the subject of a prosecution if two or more persons were involved. Lord Reid, in his dissenting judgment, argued that the decision offended against the principle that the criminal law should be certain; it would be very difficult to determine beforehand what a jury would consider to fall within the area of liability created. The DPP then used this form of liability in instances where the material in question appeared to fall outside the Obscene Publications Act or added a charge of conspiracy to corrupt public morals to a charge of obscenity as an alternative in case the obscenity charge failed. The decision in *Shaw* has been especially criticised on the basis that it left it unclear whether an agreement to commit adultery could amount to a criminal conspiracy.[140]

Outraging public decency

Despite such criticism, the House of Lords confirmed the existence of the offence of conspiring to corrupt public morals and also the existence of the substantive offence of outraging public decency and conspiring to commit it in *Knuller v DPP*,[141] which concerned publication of homosexual contact advertisements. The conviction on the latter count was, however, overturned because the trial judge had misdirected the jury as to the ingredients of the offence. The House of Lords ruled that the necessary 'public' element would be present even if the indecency was not immediately visible, since it appeared on an inside page, so long as there was an express or implied invitation to penetrate the cover and partake of the lewd contents; therefore there must be a reference on the cover to the contents. Furthermore, the contents must be so offensive that the sense of decency of the public would be outraged by seeing them. Whether or not a member of the public *would* be so outraged, would be determined by reference to that section of the public likely to frequent the place where the publication in question was sold. In this respect, conspiracy to outrage public decency differs from conspiracy to corrupt public morals, which requires that the public at large must be considered. The motive in offering the article will be irrelevant, although it will be necessary to show that the defendant was aware both of the lewd nature of the material in question and that it was being placed on public sale.

Both these offences were preserved in s 5(3) of the Criminal Law Act 1977, and in *Gibson*[142] the Court of Appeal reaffirmed the ruling of the House of Lords in *Knuller* as to the ingredients of the offence of outraging public decency. The defendants were convicted of the offence after displaying in an art gallery a model of a human head with earrings made out of freeze-dried human foetuses of three to four months gestation. It may be noted that, at first instance, the jury was directed that they were entirely free to use their own standards in deciding whether the model was indecent. Argument on appeal centred on s 2(4) of the 1959 Act which provides that where a prosecution is brought in respect of an obscene article, it must be considered within the Act, not at common law, 'where it is of

---

140 See Robertson, *op cit*, fn 75, p 215.
141 [1973] AC 435; [1972] 3 WLR 143; (1972) 56 Cr App R 633, HL.
142 [1990] 2 QB 619; [1991] 1 All ER 439; [1990] 3 WLR 595; for comment, see Childs [1991] PL 20–29.

the essence of the offence that the matter is obscene'. 'Obscene' could denote something which disgusted the public or something which had a tendency to corrupt; if it carried the first meaning, the prosecution failed, as there was no suggestion that the exhibition of the earrings had a tendency to corrupt. Moreover, if the second, more restricted meaning were accepted, that would undermine the defence contained in s 4 of the Act which could be invoked if the material in question was, *inter alia*, of artistic worth. However, Lord Lane held that the words of s 1(1) were plain and clearly indicated that the restricted meaning of 'obscene' applied throughout the Act; he refused to depart from the normal canons of statutory construction.

If the defence argument on the meaning of obscene had been accepted, a greater number of publications would have fallen within the Obscene Publications Act and could have benefited from the s 4 defence, although this would also have meant extending the ambit of the Act, including the powers of seizure under s 3. As it is, the anomaly has been continued that the artistic merit of objects which more seriously breach normal moral standards – objects which may corrupt – can prevent their suppression while the merits of less offensive objects cannot. This anomaly could have been addressed not by extending the meaning of obscenity, but by introducing a defence of public good which would have applied to common law indecency. A further anomaly arises due to the exclusion from the Indecent Displays (Control) Act 1981 of art galleries which, as noted above, are actually more restricted under common law. It was found in *Gibson* that the prosecution did not have to prove an intent to outrage public decency or recklessness as to the risk of such outrage; it was only necessary to prove that a defendant had intentionally done an act which in fact outraged public decency; he could not escape liability merely because his own standards were so base that he could not appreciate that outrage might be caused. This requirement may be contrasted with the full *mens rea* required for conspiracy to corrupt public morals. In *Knuller*, the House of Lords found that the defendant must intend to corrupt morals.

Impact of the HRA

If these common law doctrines are used in the HRA era, opportunities will arise to consider whether their continued existence is justifiable, in the light of the statutory regimes with which they overlap. A court in the discharge of its duty under s 6 of the HRA could drastically curtail these offences, by reference to Art 10. These two common law offences are each aimed at a distinct mischief. Conspiracy to corrupt public morals clearly stems from the same roots as the offence under the Obscene Publications Act, rather than forming a part of the laws against indecency. Its existence is therefore perhaps even less defensible than that of conspiracy to outrage public decency, since it covers an area of liability which cannot be distinguished from that covered by the 1959 Act and is therefore most likely to allow escape from the statutory safeguards. It can exist only on the basis that its *actus reus* is the agreement between the parties rather than the risk of corruption of morals, whereas common law indecency can be distinguished from the offence under the 1959 Act on the more substantial basis that it is concerned in essence with indecency rather than obscenity.

On the other hand, it may be argued that the protection of morals answers to a more weighty public interest than the prevention of shock or outrage, and this contention is reflected in Art 10, which contains an exception expressed in terms of the former interest, but not the latter. However, when the defendants in *Gibson* applied to the European Commission alleging a breach of Art 10,[143] the application was found inadmissible, suggesting either that in the particular circumstances, the conviction might have appeared to have the effect of protecting morals, as opposed to merely preventing outrage, or that the protection of morals exception may sometimes cover material which merely shocks. It must be said that at present, the European Court has not always drawn a clear distinction between the two mischiefs: in *Müller v Switzerland*,[144] paintings found to offend morals under Swiss law fell within Art 10(2) as likely to 'grossly offend the sense of sexual propriety of persons of ordinary sensitivity'. This sounds like indecency rather than corruption, but the Court blurred the distinction between them in implying that the former would merge with the latter once a certain level of offensiveness was reached. That level may be reached, it is suggested, by speech which may best be termed 'very shocking'. The Court made it clear that speech which would merely be termed 'shocking' or 'disturbing' would not reach it. Thus, it seems that these common law offences may be viewed as having a legitimate aim under Art 10(2), although their curtailment is nevertheless warranted because of their uncertain ambit and the anomalies they create.

It may be noted that the development of the wide ranging and flexible doctrine of common law indecency and conspiracy to corrupt public morals bears some resemblance to that of common law contempt: both doctrines work in tandem with statutes which create a more precise area of liability and which provide a defence which may ensure compatibility with Art 10 of the European Convention on Human Rights. In both instances, therefore, the common law tends to undermine the safeguards for free speech provided by the statute. However, testing the use of common law indecency and obscenity against the para 2 requirements under the HRA would import into them an ingredient akin to a defence of public good, since giving consideration to the question whether their use in a particular instance was necessary in a democratic society would require giving some consideration to the content of the expression in question. Where it could be said to have clear artistic merit, a court would be expected to give that factor some weight in assessing the question of proportionality.

4 REGULATING BROADCASTING, THE INTERNET, FILMS AND VIDEOS

Introduction

This section considers the regulation of broadcasting, the internet, films and videos.[145] The regimes in place at present for each of these media differ from each other quite considerably. But they also contrast strongly with the regime in respect of books, newspapers, magazines and other printed matter. Broadcasting, films and videos are subject to regulatory schemes which are wholly statute-based, in the case of broadcasting

---

143 *Gibson v UK*, Appl No 17634.
144 (1991) 13 EHRR 212.
145 For a comprehensive treatment, see Gibbons, *Regulating the Media*, 2nd edn, 1998.

and videos, and partly statute-based in respect of films. At present, there is no State regulation of the internet, apart from the application of the ordinary law. A new regulatory regime is to be put in place for broadcasting in 2003, as explained below, which will, to an extent, also affect use of the internet.

The statutory regimes currently in place include elements of licensing, regulation by administrative bodies and censorship. The reasons behind treating broadcasting and films differently from the print media differ in a number of respects, but have a common historical basis. The stricter system of controls seems to have been adopted in answer to the view that owing to their particular impact on audiences, films, videos and broadcasting require a system of prior restraints, whereas it is now accepted that books and other printed material do not. These media are viewed as beneficial to the public in a number of respects, but are also seen as possible sources of harm. Owing to the availability of censorship, it is very unlikely that a film or broadcast could attract liability under the Obscene Publications Act;[146] nevertheless, it provides a further possibility of restraint and can also be used as a guide as to the standards censorship will observe. Thus, the regulatory regimes in place mean that the visual media are censored beyond what the law demands. The impact of the HRA in these areas is likely to be very variable and its effects will be complicated by the fact that a number of the media bodies involved are private bodies, while the administrative bodies are public authorities.

Broadcasting, telephony and computerised systems[147]

Introduction

As indicated above, broadcasting is subject to a number of special restrictions that do not apply to the print media. The print media are subject to the criminal and civil law, as already discussed, and in respect of newspapers and magazines, as Chapter 8 indicates, to a system of self-regulation. Films are subject to a stricter regime, as indicated below, but it is partly self-regulatory. The film industry is not subject to *positive* obligations regarding content, as the broadcasting media is in certain respects. Until recently, broadcasting, telecommunications and the computer industry were viewed as three separate sectors, requiring very different regulatory regimes. Telecommunications systems are not regulated as regards content; they are monitored by the 'watchdog' body – the Office of Telecommunications (OFTEL) – while the computer industry is merely regulated by the general law, like any other industry. However, the emergence of digital technology is leading to the convergence of all three sectors. The *method* of delivering output is becoming less significant. Thus, the question arises whether the regulatory model for

---

146 The Obscene Publications Act, s 1 covers these media under s 1(2) since the Broadcasting Act 1990, s 162, has brought radio and television within its ambit.

147 See, generally, Gibbons, T, *Regulating the Media*, 2nd edn, 1998, Robertson and Nichol, *op cit*, fn 109, Chapter 15; Munro, C, *Television, Censorship and the Law*, 1979; Reville, N, *Broadcasting*, 1991; Horrie, C and Clarke, S, *Fuzzy Monsters: Fear and Loathing at the BBC*, 1994; Bailey, Harris and Jones, *op cit*, fn 75, Chapter 5, Part 3; Reville, *Broadcasting: the New Law*, 1991; Barendt, E, *Broadcasting Law: A Comparative Study*, 1995; Goldberg, D, Prosser, T and Verhulst, S, *Regulating the Changing Media: A Comparative Study*, 1998; Barendt, E and Hitchens, L, *Media Law: Cases and Materials*, 2000, Chapter 8; Hitchens, L, 'Approaches to broadcasting regulation: Australia and the UK compared' (1997) 17(1) LS 40. For discussion and criticism of the Broadcasting Act 1996 see Feintuck, M (1997) 3(2) European Public Law 201.

broadcasting will continue to be appropriate in the converged environment.[148] This section must be read in the light of the implications of convergence, in particular the greater pressure towards deregulation generated by the influence of rapid technological change. As Goldberg, Prosser and Verhulst put it, 'One of the problems in much of the debate is the assumption that technological change is the only determinant of this growth [of convergence] ... this ... assumes that new technologies will always prove marketable and that different markets are shaped by technology ... we should treat with caution suggestions that the brave new world of media abundance is imminent and be slow to abandon the protections developed in the old world of a number of media outlets and services'.[149] The government proposals on this matter, which will lead to legislation in 2003, are discussed in the concluding part of this section.

Why is broadcasting subject to a particularly strict regime, one that would arguably appear intolerable if applied to the print media? Historically, the scarcity of frequencies was thought to provide a rationale.[150] However, cable and satellite television have enormously increased the number of actual and potential channels. Digital technology will further increase the number of channels available. There are far more channels available at present in the UK than there are individual newspaper titles. It is also argued, as indicated, that broadcasting is the most influential means of communication;[151] since it comes into the home and so much time is spent watching television, it has a unique impact on people and also affects children in a way that the print media normally does not. It has further been argued that regulation is necessary in order to preserve pluralism – in order to ensure that a range of views, including a variety of political ones, are heard.[152] It is probably fair to say that lack of regulation of the press in the UK has led to a predominance of right wing views. In other words, it is arguable that a significant main threat to free expression – in terms of diversity – comes not from government, but from private corporate bodies. Therefore, although there are difficulties with this argument, it provides a rationale for broadcast regulation, even in the context of a rapidly changing technological landscape, if plurality and impartiality can be ensured by this means.

The so called deregulation of independent television under the Broadcasting Act 1990, considered below, represents a movement away from governmental influence, and towards the influence of media regulators. An underlying policy objective was that of enhancing the ability of corporate bodies to maximise commercial success by furthering and developing concentrations of media power, especially in the sectors of the press and satellite broadcasting. The Act raised questions about the influence of the owners of broadcasting stations who may wish to use broadcasting as a means of exerting political influence. The Broadcasting Act 1996 further eased some of the restrictions on media ownership created by the 1990 Act, with a view to balancing 'proper commercial demands and the wider public interest which includes plurality, diversity of opinion'.[153]

---

148 See further Barendt and Hitchens,*op cit*, fn 147, Chapter 8.

149 Goldberg, Prosser and Verhulst, *op cit*, fn 147, p 296.

150 See Briggs, A, *The History of Broadcasting, Vols 1 and 2*, 1961 and 1965; Barendt and Hitchens, *op cit*, fn 147.

151 See Barendt and Hitchens, *op cit*, fn 147, pp 5–9.

152 See Feintuck, M, *Media Regulation, Public Interest and the Law*, 1999.

153 Bottomley, V, Dept of National Heritage Press Release DNH 219/96. For discussion of regulation of cross-media ownership and concentrated media ownership see Fleming, H (1997) 60(3) MLR 378; Hitchens (1994) 57 MLR 585.

The current proposals for a new Communications Act in 2003 are based, it will be argued below, on the model of deregulation put in place by the 1990 Act. This continued movement away from market regulation may have the effect of detracting from the exercise of creative freedom since small independent broadcasters may be unable to gain a foot-hold in the market, while investigative journalism (especially investigations into corporate matters) and alternative film making may be squeezed out in the pursuit of commercially safe, but bland broadcasting, such as game shows, soap operas, gardening and home decorating programmes. On this view, further movement towards privatisation of the means of communication, deregulation and the freer expression of commercial values is unwelcome.

If the familiar free speech justifications[154] are considered in the context of market regulation, the thesis can be put forward that market regulation is an essential precondition for securing the objectives inherent in those justifications. Feintuck argues that media regulators are concerned to limit 'the ability of corporate media giants to further their own commercial ends while acting in ways that run counter to maximising the provision of information upon which the claim is premised'.[155] However, the ethos underlying the regulatory regime considered below is unclear, although it could be broadly expressed as intended to be in the public interest. It is suggested that intervention cannot be assisted by the failure to identify a meaningful guiding principle for media regulation.

The subject of European competition law and European broadcasting law in general, is beyond the scope of this book, but below, indications are given as to the significance of the role of the EU in relation to broadcasting, and it may be argued that since economic integration is a central constitutional value for the EU, its regulatory agenda may bear more resemblance to that of the US, which is economics-based, than to the public interest value evident in the regimes of its Member States.[156]

The HRA may have a significant role to play in relation to media regulation in terms of providing a counter to commercial values. If the public interest has so far been defined within the regulatory regime considered below in too nebulous a manner, the Strasbourg jurisprudence would provide a means of creating greater certainty, in terms of the part to be played by media regulation in a democratic society. The jurisprudence of the European Convention on Human Rights, especially that relating to Art 10, is centrally premised on the notion that the purpose of the Convention is to 'maintain and promote the ideals and values of a democratic society'.[157] Article 10 arguments, taking such jurisprudence into account, could be raised in relation to the adjudication of any regulatory body, such as, in future, OFCOM, the new super-regulator to be created under the current proposals, discussed below, for the future regulation of broadcasting and telecommunications. All such bodies are bound by s 6 of the HRA.[158] It is at least arguable that the infusion of clear substantive values into media regulation, organised around the concept of the

---

154 See the Introduction to Part II, and see further Barendt, *op cit*, fn 3.

155 See Feintuck, *op cit*, fn 152.

156 *Ibid*, p 170.

157 *Kjeldsen v Denmark* (1976) 1 EHRR 711, p 731; see also the comments of the Court in *Socialist Party v Turkey* (1999) 27 EHRR 51 as to the need for pluralism in a democracy.

158 Most, if not all, of these bodies are likely to be classified as functional public bodies on the basis that they are acting in a public capacity: see below, Chapter 10, p 559.

public interest, could occur under the HRA. Or, the Act could play a part in allowing such an infusion to occur since it provides media regulators with a benchmarking document with its jurisprudential accretions[159] which is highly relevant to the argument that a version of media freedom informed by Strasbourg principles is not necessarily coterminous with market freedom.

The basic regulatory regime

In the 1950s, with the advent of commercial television, it was considered necessary to impose direct statutory regulation on broadcasting. Special duties were imposed on independent broadcasting to maintain standards of taste and decency and of impartiality; the responsibility for maintaining standards was given to the Independent Broadcasting Authority (IBA), established in 1954. The current regime represents an attempt to deregulate broadcasting, in the sense of enhancing market freedom, especially by affording further leeway to cross-media ownership, that is, ownership in more than one media sector. In terms of creative freedom it would be misleading to speak of 'deregulation' when the new system has led to the establishment of an overlapping and strict set of controls over broadcasting. As Gibbons puts it: '[the 1990 Act created the danger that cross-media ownership would] create pressure for more homogenised editorial positions or, as has occurred, cross-media promotion.'160

Independent broadcasting is governed by the Broadcasting Acts 1990 and 1996. Prior to the introduction of the Broadcasting Act 1990, the IBA was charged with the regulation of independent television. As part of the policy of deregulation of television, the 1990 Act set up the Independent Television Commission (ITC) to replace the IBA as a public body charged with licensing and regulating non-BBC television services.[161] The function of the ITC in this respect is similar to that of the Radio Authority (RA), which has the statutory function, under Part III of the 1990 Act, of licensing and monitoring the independent radio stations.

Public broadcasting is governed by the Royal Charter of the BBC which partly comprises a Licence Agreement.[162] The BBC operates under this Agreement and also under the terms of its Charter.[163] This includes the undertaking to comply generally with the statutory duties placed on the IBA.[164] Under these instruments, the Board of Governors of the BBC has the responsibility for maintaining standards of taste and decency and of impartiality. The current (1996) Charter and Agreement set out in more detail the obligations of the BBC as a public broadcaster operating by means of the licence fee, in particular its obligation to maintain independence. Although it is commercially

---

159 See *Sunday Times v UK* A 30 (1979); *Jersild v Denmark* (1994) 19 EHRR 1; *Lingens v Austria* (1986) 8 EHRR 103; *Thorgeirson v Iceland* (1992) 14 EHRR 843.

160 'Aspiring to pluralism: the constraints of public broadcasting values on the deregulation of British media ownership' (1998) 16 Cardozo Arts and Entertainment Journal 475, p 485.

161 For discussion of the change in regime introduced under the 1990 Act, see Jones, T, 'The deregulation of broadcasting' (1989) 52 MLR 380–88.

162 Cmnd 8233.

163 Cmnd 8313.

164 This undertaking is annexed to the Corporation's licence agreement. This includes the requirement to observe due impartiality. See Gibbons, T, 'Impartiality in the media' (1985) *Archiv für Rechts- und Sozialphilosophie*, Beiheft, Nr 28 pp 71–81.

funded, Channel 4 also has a public service remit governed by statute – s 25 of the 1990 Act. Section 106 of the Broadcasting Act 1996 established the Broadcasting Standards Commission; as discussed below, the Commission monitors BBC and independent programming. Under the proposals in the White Paper on *The Future of Broadcasting*,[165] its role will be taken over in 2003 by a new 'standards' body, OFCOM, which will have legally enforceable controls over public broadcasting for the first time.

Control over broadcasting on political grounds

Government influence over broadcasting is of enormous significance owing to the importance of broadcasting as the main means of informing the public as to matters of public interest. The openly partisan nature of the popular press means that, as suggested above, broadcasting provides the only impartial source of information for most people. The government may exert control over broadcasting by means of the statutory regimes it puts in place, and more directly by the use, exceptionally, of its censorship powers in relation to independent television under s 10(3) of the Broadcasting Act 1990 and in relation to the BBC via s 13(4) of the BBC's Licence Agreement, or through more subtle means, such as the criteria used to determine appointments to the BBC Governors.

Under the current statutory scheme, political advertising, which includes advertising by a body whose objects are wholly or mainly of a political nature, must not be broadcast by a licensed service.[166] The ITC and RA are under duties to ensure that this rule is complied with. The challenge of a sub-group of Amnesty International (a group campaigning on human rights abuses) to this ban was unsuccessful[167] on the basis that a material proportion of its objects were political, although the way that the RA had reached its decision was criticised. The possibility of a successful challenge under the HRA in similar circumstances is considered below.

Impartiality

As indicated above, the Independent Broadcasting Authority (IBA) was, prior to the introduction of the Broadcasting Act 1990, charged with the regulation of independent television. Before its abolition, it had acquired a reputation for determined resistance to government influence, largely due to its refusal to bow to political pressure in relation to Thames TV's investigation into the shooting of three IRA members on Gibraltar, *Death on the Rock*. An independent investigation into the making of the programme largely exonerated it of bias or of interference with the inquiry in Gibraltar.[168]

When the Broadcasting Act 1990 set up the ITC and the RA to replace the IBA, the 1990 Act imposed a detailed impartiality requirement on the ITC,[169] a controversial requirement that is clearly an infringement of the freedom of expression of broadcasters. The ITC was required, under the impartiality clause introduced by s 6(1)(c) of the 1990

---

165 Published 12 December 2000.
166 Broadcasting Act 1990, ss 8(1)(a) and 92.
167 *R v Radio Authority ex p Bull and Another* [1997] 3 WLR 1094.
168 Windlesham/Rampton Report on *Death on the Rock*, 1989.
169 The function of the Radio Authority is similar in this respect to that of the ITC.

Act, to set up a Code to require that politically sensitive programmes must be balanced in order to ensure due impartiality. Such programmes can be balanced by means of a series of programmes (s 6(2)); it is not necessary that any one programme should be followed by another specific balancing programme. The ITC Programme Code (last revised Autumn 1998), cl 3.3(i) makes it clear that a company cannot be heard to argue that a programme which might be said to have an anti-government bias may be balanced by programmes broadcast by other companies: the company has to achieve impartiality in its own programming. The Code also indicates in cl 3.3 that it may sometimes be appropriate to ensure that opposing views are indicated in a single programme, where it is unlikely that the subject will be considered again in the near future or where the issues are of 'current or active controversy'.

Further guidance as to the requirements of due impartiality is provided by the revised Code, which is very detailed. It states in its 'Objectives' in cl 3.1 that broadcasters do not have to be 'absolutely neutral on every controversial issue, but that they should deal even-handedly with opposing points of view in the arena of democratic debate'. Clause 3.2(i) explains that the term 'due' is significant and implies that the requirements of impartiality must be adequate to the nature of the subject and the type of programme.

The due impartiality requirement may have meant that some politically controversial programmes are not made: the expense and difficulty of setting up balancing programmes may have had a deterrent effect. In interpreting the Code, the companies may act cautiously and may interpret what is meant by 'bias' broadly. Thus, although the due impartiality provisions may seek to balance a need for impartiality against the need to protect freedom of expression, they may not achieve that balance in practice, although it can be argued that the requirement serves the ends of promoting plurality and wider debate, since the dominance of one set of views may be prevented. On the other hand, s 6 can only affect a *positive* decision to broadcast a programme dealing with a sensitive issue; there is nothing in the arrangements for the franchising of independent television and radio to affect a decision to ignore some such issues on political grounds. The franchises went to the highest bidder once a 'quality control threshold' was satisfied. Nothing was done to attempt to ensure that a political balance between franchise holders was achieved at that stage.

The impartiality requirement only affects non-BBC broadcasting, although the BBC has undertaken to comply generally with the statutory duties placed on the IBA (replaced by the ITC). However, this undertaking is unenforceable, although the BBC generally complies. Cases of doubt will be referred up the Corporation management hierarchy: producers may refer to middle management, who may seek direction from departmental heads, who may then consult the Managing Director or even the Director General. Thus censorship is largely self-imposed; the government cannot bring *direct* influence to bear. However, the Board of Governors of the BBC is appointed by the government and although they usually leave editorial matters to the Director General, they may occasionally intervene; they did so in 1985 in relation to a programme about an IRA sympathiser in Belfast, *Real Lives*, after condemnation of it by the Prime Minister – an incident which was perceived as damaging to the BBC's reputation for independence from the government.[170] On the other hand, certain incidents, such as coverage of the US

---

170 Robertson and Nichol, *op cit*, fn 109, p 484.

bombing of Libya, led to expressions of concern in the 1980s from the Conservative Party about BBC 'bias' against the government, although this may have been partly mollified by the banning of a documentary on the Zircon spy satellite project in 1987 and of a documentary on the workings of Cabinet government. Both films were eventually shown with modification, the latter by Channel 4 in 1991.[171] Generally speaking, as Gibbons points out, the 'reference up' procedure will tend to exclude the influence of the Governors, partly because thinking at the higher levels may be anticipated at the lower.[172]

Direct censorship powers

As mentioned above, the government has a direct power of censorship in relation to independent television under s 10(3) of the Broadcasting Act 1990[173] and in relation to the BBC via s 13(4) of the BBC's Licence Agreement. The power under s 10(3) is of the widest possible nature since it allows a ban on broadcasting 'any matter' or class of matter. It was invoked by the Secretary of State in 1988 in order to issue directives requiring the BBC and IBA to refrain from broadcasting words spoken by persons representing organisations proscribed under the Northern Ireland (Emergency Provisions) legislation and also Sinn Fein, Republican Sinn Fein and the Ulster Defence Association. The ban was challenged by the National Union of Journalists and others, but not by the broadcasting organisations themselves, in *Secretary of State for the Home Department ex p Brind and Others*.[174] The applicants submitted that the Home Secretary's discretionary powers were exercisable only in conformity with Art 10 of the European Convention and that in curtailing freedom of expression where there was no pressing social need to do so, the directives contravened Art 10. Article 10 had to be taken into account on the basis that when legislation confers an administrative discretion on an authority which is capable of being exercised in a way which infringes human rights as protected by the Convention, it was presumed that the intention of the enabling legislation was that the discretion should be exercised within Convention limits. As the directives did not so conform, the minister had acted *ultra vires*. The House of Lords agreed that the Convention could be used as a rule of statutory construction to resolve ambiguity in subsequent primary legislation, but disagreed with the submission that the issuing of the directives was therefore *ultra vires*, on the ground that it could not be presumed that discretionary powers were, by analogy, limited by the terms of the Convention. It was found that such a presumption would go far beyond the resolution of an ambiguity as it would assume that Parliament had intended to import the text of the Convention into domestic administrative law. As Parliament had chosen not to incorporate the Convention into domestic law this, it was found, was an unwarranted assumption.

It was further submitted that administrative action can be challenged by way of judicial review if it is disproportionate to the mischief at which it is aimed and that this

---

171 See further Fiddich, P, 'Broadcasting: a catalogue of confrontation', in Buchan and Sumner (eds), *Glasnost in Britain: Against Censorship and in Defence of the Word*, 1989.

172 Gibbons, *op cit*, fn 145, p 141.

173 The power now arises under s 10(3); previously it arose under the Broadcasting Act 1981, s 29(3).

174 [1991] 1 AC 696; [1991] 1 All ER 720; [1991] 2 WLR 588, HL; [1990] 1 All ER 469, CA; for comment see Jowell [1990] PL 149 (on the Court of Appeal ruling). For further discussion, see above, Chapter 3, pp 105–06.

particular exercise of power went further than was necessary to prevent terrorists increasing their standing. The House of Lords held that lack of proportionality was merely to be regarded as one aspect of *Wednesbury* unreasonableness, not as a separate head of challenge. The question to be asked was, therefore, whether the minister's decision was one which no reasonable minister could have made. Taking into account the fact that the directives did not restrict the reporting of information, but merely the manner of its presentation – direct speech – it was found that this ground of challenge had not been made out. The House of Lords indicated that the challenge might have succeeded had the interference been more wide ranging.

Nevertheless, the ban meant that a Sinn Fein or IRA member could not be forced to justify their policies and therefore it caused offence to the principle that flawed or evil speech is best combated by further speech.[175] Moreover, as it applied equally to historical programmes, it infringed the principle that the search for truth should override other interests except where a clear danger in allowing the speech may be shown. In its own terms, the ban may have been ineffective and self-defeating, not only because it did not appear to prevent the dubbing of the voices of Sinn Fein leaders and others by actors, but also because, ironically, in itself it publicised them, rather than denying them 'the oxygen of publicity'. Gerry Adams, the leader of Sinn Fein, was able to publicise himself in America as the man whose voice could not be heard on UK airwaves. The ban remained in place until September 1994, when it was lifted after the IRA declared the cessation of violence. Although the ceasefire broke down in 1996, the ban was not re-imposed.

Clearly, as Chapter 3 explained, the inception of the HRA has had the effect of reversing the decision in *Brind* as regards the effect of the Convention on administrative powers. If the power of censorship is invoked again, it will have to be used within Convention limits.

Censorship on grounds of taste and decency

Within Western Europe, in terms of censorship, the UK operates one of the strictest regulatory regimes for broadcasting. However, in the 1990s, the regulatory regime controlling broadcasting was confronted with the dissemination of material by methods which seemed to fall outside its compass since the expression originated outside the UK, but could be accessed from within it. Concern was raised that obscene or indecent material would be disseminated via the internet and by non-terrestrial 'foreign' broadcasters. The difficulty of attempting to regulate material when it is transmitted by these means, and the movement towards bringing such material within the regulatory regime for broadcasting, are discussed below.

Under s 6(1)(a) of the 1990 Act, the ITC must attempt to ensure that every licensed television service includes nothing in its programmes 'which offends against good taste and decency' and this echoes the similar requirement imposed on the BBC by the terms of its Charter. Clearly, these are terms which leave a good deal of leeway to broadcasters as regards their interpretation. Moreover, they invite consideration of explicit material in the

---

175 A principle which derives from Mill's argument from truth; see Part II, pp 202–03. Nevertheless, the ban was upheld at Strasbourg: *Brind and McLaughlin v UK* (1994) 18 EHRR CD 76. The margin of appreciation conceded was wide, owing to the terrorist context.

context in which it is shown, so that what might be offensive in one setting and with one particular audience in mind, would not be so in another.

The ITC published a Programme Code dealing with these matters in 1991 (revised in 1998) which attempts to strike a balance between preserving good taste and decency on the one hand and avoiding too great a restraint on freedom of speech on the other. It therefore allows sexual scenes under cl 1.5 so long as they are presented with 'tact and discretion'. Under cl 1.2(iv), which covers feature films, it sets out rules which follow the guidelines laid down by the BBFC (see below): '18' rated films may be shown, but only after 10 pm. '15' rated films should not normally start before 9 pm, while '12' rated films should not start before 8 pm. Under the family viewing policy set out in cl 1.2, the ITC accepts that a compromise is necessary between protecting children and ensuring that a wide range of programmes suitable for adults are broadcast. It does not seek to ensure that unsuitable material will never be viewed by a few children. Thus, the rules assume 'a progressive decline throughout the evening in the proportion of children present in the audience'. Further, the BBFC standards are to be regarded as minimum ones; the mere fact that a film has an '18' certificate is not to be taken as implying that it would be proper to broadcast it. Under cl 1.5, sexual scenes should not be shown until after 9 pm except in the case of nature programmes, educational programmes or where the representation is non-graphic. In such instances, approval must be obtained in advance from the licensee's most senior programme executive or the designated equivalent. Graphic portrayal of sexual violence is only exceptionally justifiable and the same approval regime obtains. Violence in general is covered by cl 1.6, which sets out a number of factors to be kept in mind, including the content of the programme schedules as a whole and the policy of family viewing time. The cl 1.6 rules are not in general very specific, but they do provide that violence should not be shown for its own sake and that ingenious, easily imitated methods of inflicting pain or injury should not be included. Clause 1.6 concludes: 'In so sensitive an area risks require special justification. When in doubt, cut.'

In some respects, these arrangements could be said to represent a slackening of restraint on what may be broadcast in the sense that the television companies no longer have to submit their controversial programmes to an outside body for preview and censorship. As the Annan Committee pointed out in 1977,[176] the old system meant that programmes might be subject to dual censorship in being considered first by the IBA and then by the company concerned. However, although such censorship is now solely in the hands of the companies themselves, the ITC has a number of sanctions to use against a company which fails to abide by the Programming Code, ranging from a requirement to broadcast an apology to the power to revoke its licence. The financial penalties available are very severe and may well tend to deter the companies from taking risks in their interpretation of what is allowed by the Code.

The role of the ITC in this respect was to an extent duplicated by the Broadcasting Standards Council (BSC), set up in 1988 to monitor the standards of taste and decency being maintained in programmes. Under s 152 of the 1990 Act, the BSC had a duty to draw up a code relating to broadcasting standards covering the BBC and independent television and radio broadcasting. The BSC seemed to work on the assumption that absolute standards could be discerned and maintained as opposed to steadily changing

---

176 Report of the Committee on the Future of Broadcasting, chaired by Lord Annan, Cmnd 6753.

ones.[177] Section 106 of the Broadcasting Act 1996 established the Broadcasting Standards Commission, which was made up of a merger of the Broadcasting Standards Council and the Broadcasting Complaints Commission.[178]

The Broadcasting Standards Commission was charged with the duty of drawing up a code in respect of programme standards under s 107 which is based on s 152 of the 1990 Act, the 'Standards Code'; it also had to draw up a code to cover matters of fairness and privacy (that Code is considered in Chapter 10). Section 108 re-enacts the former s 152. Thus, as far as independent broadcasting is concerned, a dual and overlapping system is in place imposing an onerous burden on the companies. The Commission is under a duty to monitor programmes (s 109), including BBC programmes, in relation to taste and decency, especially the portrayal of sex and violence, and to consider complaints regarding these matters (s 110). If a complaint is upheld, the BBC and independent broadcasters are under a legal obligation to publish it (s 119). The main sanction is contained in the adverse publicity.

Satellite television

The ITC Code does not apply to broadcasters who are not licence holders of the ITC. Under s 43 of the 1990 Act, a satellite service was required to hold an ITC licence if it was a 'domestic satellite service' or a 'non-domestic satellite service'. A domestic service was intended to use direct broadcasting by satellite on one of the five frequencies allocated to the UK at the World Administrative Radio Conference in 1977. A non-domestic satellite service was one which either used a lower powered satellite to transmit programmes from the UK or transmitted from outside the territory of prescribed countries, but a UK supplier dictated the service. 'Non-domestic' satellite services were not to be subject to the same regime as domestic services in the sense that they were to transmit on allocated frequencies and were to have public service responsibilities.

If a service is licensed from within an EU Member State, it must receive freedom of reception within other Member States under the EU Directive on Transfrontier Television (89/552/EEC). In *Commission of EC v UK*[179] it was found that s 43 of the Broadcasting Act 1990 applied different regimes to domestic and non-domestic satellite services and that in exercising control over certain broadcasters falling under the jurisdiction of other Member States, the UK had failed to fulfil its obligations under Arts 2(1)(2) and 3(2) of the Directive. Thus, in 1997, the distinction between domestic and non-domestic services was abolished: only one category was created – satellite television services.[180] Section 89 of the Broadcasting Act 1996 amended s 45 of the 1990 Act to allow for the immediate revocation of the licence of a satellite television service which breached s 6(1)(a) of the 1990 Act. Under Art 2a(2) of the Directive, Member States can derogate from the obligation to allow the free movement of broadcast if a number of conditions are satisfied, including the condition, under Art 22, that the programmes might severely affect minors

---

177 BSC Annual Report 1988–89 and Code of Practice 1989, p 41. For comment on the work of the BSC, see Coleman, F, 'All in the best possible taste – the Broadcasting Standards Council 1989–1992' [1992] PL 488.

178 For aspects of the work of the Commission, see below, Chapter 10, p 557.

179 Case 222/94 [1996] ECR-I 4025.

180 Satellite Television Service Regulations 1997 SI 1997/1682. Further amendment was made under the Television Broadcasting Regulations 1998 SI 1998/3196.

because of their violent or sexual content. Using the Art 2a procedure, the National Heritage Secretary has issued a number of proscription orders against satellite channels from EU Member States which beam hard core pornography into Britain. Such proscription orders are made under s 177 of the 1990 Act; so far, the question whether they breach EU law has not been addressed by the European Court of Justice.

The internet

The question of the regulation of the internet is immensely complex; it has recently been addressed in an important new book.[181] The issues raised can only be touched on here, but one of the most significant concerns its regulation in the converged environment, which is considered below. The obvious problem which arises if one considers the regulatory regime applied to broadcasting under the 1990 Act, is that the internet provides a complex global communications network which cannot be fully subject to regulation applied within the boundaries of one State. 'By creating a seamless global-economic zone, borderless and unregulatable, the internet calls into question the very idea of a nation-state.'[182]

In response to these difficulties, the UK Government has not yet sought to apply regulation to the internet based on the model for broadcasting. The regulatory model resembles that in place for the press in the sense that the ordinary criminal and civil law applies (although there are problems in applying it in practice) and any regulation is self-imposed. Such 'regulation' as there is is operated globally by various interest groups who, unsurprisingly, favour the self-regulatory model. One of the most significant is the Internet Society, based in the US.[183] However, given the convergence between broadcasting and the computer industry, of which the internet is an aspect, the Government has taken the view, as indicated below, that this model is no longer appropriate.

One of the problems arising from the possibility of access to various websites, viewed in this country and elsewhere, as most pressing is that of the ability of obscene material, especially child pornography, to – in effect – cross frontiers, evading ordinary controls. Such material is usually considered within the Obscene Publications Act or the laws relating to indecency, as indicated above,[184] as far as the internet is concerned. Section 168 of the Criminal Justice and Public Order Act 1994 added the transmission of electronically stored data to the Obscene Publication Act's definition of 'publication'. Creating a link from a UK-based web-page to another in another jurisdiction on which obscene material is posted arguably amounts to 'publication'.[185] In *Graham Waddon*,[186] the defendant was convicted of the offence under s 2(1) of the 1959 Act on the basis that he had maintained a website in the USA onto which he had uploaded obscene material from the UK. Thus the

---

181 Akdeniz, Y, Walker, C and Wall, D (eds), *The Internet, Law and Society*, 2000.

182 Barlow, JP, 'Thinking locally, acting globally' (1996) Cyber-Rights Electronic List 15 January.

183 See Akdeniz, Walker and Wall (eds), *The Internet, Law and Society*, 2000, pp 6–14.

184 See p 289.

185 See Akdeniz, Y, 'To link or not to link?' (1997) 11(2) International Review of Law, Computers and Technology 281.

186 (1999) Southwark Crown Court, 30 June; appeal dismissed 6 April 2000.

fact that the material was placed on a US-based website did not prevent the defendant from being charged and convicted of the s 2(1) offence in England.

Web-based information on a range of websites is available to any user who possesses a computer of the correct specification. Children could therefore readily gain access to such information and images, and the question of the obscenity of the material in question might therefore have to be determined by reference to that likely audience, depending on the circumstances, including the nature of the website and the likelihood that children would be able to access it. Since it is possible for information and images to be posted on a website by any person anywhere in the world, the UK obscenity regime can be evaded in the sense that a person in the UK can readily access the material; previously it would have had to be brought, physically, into the country. In practice, downloading such material will normally not be detected. While it may be possible in some instances to identify the service provider who placed the obscene matter on the site, this will be unavailing unless the person is in the UK. Thus, the availability of hard core pornography on the internet appears to undermine the provisions aimed at it when it arrives in this country or is disseminated within it by other means. This is a problem that affects a number of countries, but it is particularly pressing in the UK since it relies on an uncertain concept of obscenity and seeks to criminalise the promulgation and sale of material that would be legal in a number of other countries.[187]

Impact of the HRA and the future of communications: conclusions

In 2000, the government published a White Paper, *A New Future for Communications*,[188] which set out its vision and objectives for the 21st century. It is suggested, bearing in mind the discussion above, that a number of matters should have been addressed. It is contended that the overlapping controls over broadcasting are, put bluntly, aimed at preserving market freedom rather than creative freedom. Their tendency is to make for cautious rather than explorative and challenging broadcasting. The rationales for adopting this regulatory regime have come under challenge due to the convergence of the separate technological sectors. The use of an out of date and virtually unworkable test – of 'obscenity' – as the basis for the regulation of explicit material on the internet and as the ultimate, albeit unchallenged, standard by which to judge the suitability of films and other programmes for broadcasting, looks increasingly bizarre from a global perspective.

The era covered by the White Paper is also of course the HRA era, although the Act is not mentioned in the Paper. Nevertheless, it is suggested that the HRA is clearly relevant and that the uncertainty and weakness of the jurisprudence of the Convention relating to explicit expression does not need to deter domestic policy makers from adopting a more rigorous approach, based on the principles underlying Art 10 and also on human rights jurisprudence in other jurisdictions. As indicated above, those principles provide indications as to the policy that could be adopted in relation to providing erotic and explicit material of artistic merit aimed at a consenting adult audience.[189] In contrast, the

---

187 See further Akdeniz, Walker and Wall, *op cit*, fn 183, pp 208–12.
188 Published 12 December 2000; www.communicationswhitepaper.gov.uk.
189 See pp 279–81.

principle of non-interference with *political* expression, except in exceptional circumstances, is well established under the Convention.[190]

However, these matters are hardly addressed in the White Paper. The reforms fail to challenge accepted ideas of taste and decency and, in particular, do not address the question why videos or websites can contain explicit material that cannot be broadcast. Its key concern is to create a dynamic and competitive communications and media market. It adopts, in essentials, the current regulatory model for broadcasting, recognising the convergence environment by applying it to telecommunications as well as broadcasting and – in a superficial sense – to the internet. The proposed legislation will create one super-regulator, OFCOM, which will replace OFTEL and may also replace the BSC. OFCOM will have the responsibility for maintaining standards of impartiality and 'taste and decency'. The BBC will retain its current role, but the public service element of the ITV companies will be subject to less prescriptive regulation.

The dominant theme is the continuance of light-touch regulation, in terms of commercial freedom, which was introduced under the 1990 Act. In this sense, the proposed legislation is likely to represent a business-oriented reform. It favours corporate interests, not necessarily those of plurality and diversity. It does not address substantive media freedom issues. For example, while corporate advertising remains central to the commercial viability of independent television, political advertising will still be disallowed. Thus, in so far as groups such as Greenpeace or Amnesty might wish, *inter alia*, to criticise corporate interests, by means of such advertising, they will be unable to do so.

Journalists, film makers and groups such as Amnesty, whose advertising has been rejected,[191] could challenge media regulators, including, in future, OFCOM, directly by invoking s 7(1)(a) of the HRA. Decisions as to licensing, political advertising, adjudications regarding taste and decency and impartiality could be subjected thereby to a more intensive scrutiny. Assuming that the independent television companies are not public authorities, under s 6 of the HRA, which is almost certainly the case, they could also bring such proceedings, as 'victims' under the HRA. Proceedings under s 7(1)(a) of the HRA could not be brought *against* the independent companies, but decisions of the public service broadcasters – the BBC, Channel 4[192] – as to programming policy, etc – could be challenged directly by invoking s 7(1)(a) of the HRA, so long as the person bringing the action satisfied the victim requirement under s 7(3). The use of s 7(1)(a) would mean that such decisions would be tested more directly against Convention standards than they have been by means of judicial review. Section 12 of the HRA would be applicable. The application of the various Codes of Practice could also be challenged in such proceedings, including the new ones which may be promulgated even in advance of the legislation which is expected in 2003. Provisions of such Codes could be struck down

---

190 See pp 209–10.

191 In this instance the group – or a representative sub-group directly concerned with advertising – could be viewed as a 'victim' under HRA, s 7(3): see Chapter 4, pp 164–66 for discussion of the term.

192 Both bodies are likely to be found to be public authorities under HRA, s 6. The BBC is almost certainly a public authority, while Channel 4 probably is: both bodies have a public function in respect of their public service remit which is especially significant in the case of the BBC. Channel 4's role is governed by statute – Broadcasting Act 1990, s 25.

by the courts unless primary legislation prevented the removal of the incompatibility. Given that the detailed provisions are commonly contained in the Codes, this is a significant possibility.

Clearly, it can be said, as indicated above, that those Convention standards are themselves 'soft edged' in respect of the 'protection of morals' – they very clearly leave room for the adoption of an activist or a minimalist approach. The stance considered above might well support quite far reaching restrictions on broadcasting owing to the possibility that children might be affected, since it comes into the home. But the Strasbourg standard as regards political expression is much stricter, as the Introduction to this part indicated.[193] The use of the Convention jurisprudence on both political and, if afforded a creative interpretation, artistic expression might enable pressure to be brought to bear, tending to promote the representation of a wider range of views, including views of minority groups, in broadcasting.

It must be pointed out, however, that when the power of the owners of the television companies to influence the nature of broadcasting is compared with that of the media regulators or of the public service broadcasters, a scheme in which the powers of the latter but not the former can be challenged looks fundamentally flawed. There is clearly a mismatch between the areas in which the HRA can intervene and the location of the main influences over the medium of most significance in terms of its cultural and opinion-forming impact.

Regulation of films and videos[194]

The view of the Williams Committee on Obscenity and Film Censorship, which conducted a review of the area in 1979,[195] was that the censorship of films should continue. The Committee considered that in the light of some psychiatric evidence to the effect that violent films might induce violent behaviour, a policy based on caution was justified.[196] However, Barendt argues that the evidence that films have a very different impact from books or magazines is not strong and that the difference in treatment may be due to historical reasons: new forms of expression take time to gain the acceptance accorded to traditional mediums and are viewed with some suspicion.[197]

Films

Currently, censorship of films operates in practice on two levels: first, the British Board of Film Classification (BBFC), a self-censoring body set up by the film industry itself in 1912, may insist on cuts before issuing a certificate allowing the film to be screened or may refuse to issue a certificate at all. It was set up in response to the Cinematograph Act 1909, which allowed local authorities to grant licences in respect of the films to be shown in

---

193 See pp 209–10.
194 See generally Robertson, *op cit*, fn 75, pp 257–68; Robertson and Nichol, *op cit*, fn 109, Chapter 14; Hunnings, N, *Film Censors and the Law*, 1967.
195 Cmnd 7772, 1979. See Simpson, *op cit*, fn 4, pp 35–38.
196 Simpson, *op cit*, fn 4, p 37.
197 Barendt, *op cit*, fn 3, p 125.

their particular area; the idea was that the film industry would achieve a uniformity of decision making by local councils. Thus, it would have a guide as to whether a film would be shown and as to where to make cuts in order to achieve a wider audience. Films are classified by age: 'U' films are open to anybody as, in effect, are 'PG' (parental guidance) classified films. After that are '12', '15' and '18' certificate films. 'R18' films (restricted viewing) may be viewed only on segregated premises. An 'R18' certificate means that the BBFC considers that the film would survive an Obscene Publications Act prosecution; it will refuse a certificate if a film is thought to fall within the Act. In coming to its decision, the BBFC will take the 'public good' defence under s 4(1A) of the 1959 Act, as amended, into account. This defence is the more restricted defence under s 3 of the Theatres Act 1968; s 4(1A) provides that a film or soundtrack can be justified as being for the public good 'on the ground that it is in the interests of drama, opera, ballet or any other art or of literature or learning'. Therefore, the BBFC may grant a certificate on the grounds of artistic merit to a film which contains some obscene matter.

Of course, most film distributors have no interest in achieving only a restricted publication for a film and are, therefore, prepared to make cuts to achieve a wider circulation. Thus, the system of control may be driven largely by commercial motives: a distributor may make quite stringent cuts in order to ensure that, for example, a film receives a '15' certificate and so reaches a wider audience. The further difficulty with the availability of the R18 classification is that it may mean that the BBFC are not exploring the boundaries of obscenity in adult films in general, those that receive the 18 classification. The R18 classification may, in effect, drive a wedge between such films and the outer limits of acceptability.

The second level of censorship is operated by local authorities under the Cinemas Act 1985 which continues the old power arising under the Cinematograph Act 1909. The local authority will usually follow the Board's advice; authorities are reluctant to devote resources to viewing films and will tend to rely on the BBFC's judgment.[198] But authorities may, on occasion, choose not to grant a licence to a film regardless of its decision. Films which have been licensed but which nevertheless have been banned in some areas include *A Clockwork Orange*, *The Life of Brian*, *The Last Temptation of Christ* and *Crash*. There is no requirement of consistency between authorities and thus discrepancies have arisen between different local authority areas. It is notable that the cinema is the only art form subject to moral judgment on a local level and it may be asked why it should be so singled out. This dual system of censorship was criticised by the Williams Committee in 1979 (see below), partly on the ground of the anomalies caused by having two overlapping levels and partly due to the inconsistency between local authorities. It considered that a unified system should be adopted. In particular, it criticised a system which allowed adult films to be censored beyond the requirements of the Obscene Publications Act.

Videos

The Video Recordings Act 1984 was introduced after a campaign about the dangers posed by video 'nasties' to children. The campaign, by the *Daily Mail* and a group called the

---

198 See Holbrook (1973) 123 NLJ 701.

Festival of Light, managed to convince Parliament that legislation was necessary in order to address the problem.[199] It should be noted that the connection between violence on film and violent behaviour in children has not yet been firmly established. However, it appears to be possible that there is a greater likelihood not that children may perpetrate violence as an immediate reaction to exposure to violent films, but that they may be de-sensitised to violence in a long term sense if they watch a great deal of it.[200]

Under the Video Recordings Act 1984, the BBFC was established as the authority charged with classifying videos for viewing in the home. Videos are classified and therefore censored in almost the same way as films, and under s 9 of the 1984 Act, it is an offence to supply a video without a classification certificate, unless it is exempt on grounds of its concern with education, sport, music or religion. Under s 2(2), the exemption will not apply if the video portrays human sexual activity or gross violence or is designed to stimulate or encourage this. Section 4 of the 1984 Act requires that the BBFC should have 'special regard to the likelihood of video works being viewed in the home'. Thus, makers of videos may find that videos are censored beyond the requirements of the Obscene Publications Act. The 1984 Act places the BBFC in the position of official censors and in that role, their work has often been criticised as over-strict and arbitrary.[201]

The regime in respect of videos was made potentially more restrictive in 1994. Fears that children might be more likely to commit violence after watching violent videos[202] led the government to include a number of provisions in the Criminal Justice and Public Order Bill 1994 which was then before the Commons. Under s 90 of the Criminal Justice and Public Order Act 1994, inserting s 4A into the 1984 Act, the BBFC must have 'special regard' to harm which may be caused to 'potential viewers or through their behaviour to society' by the manner in which the film deals with criminal behaviour, illegal drugs, violent behaviour or incidents, horrific incidents or behaviour or human sexual activity. These criteria are non-exhaustive. The BBFC can consider any other relevant factor. The kind of harm envisaged, to a child or to society, is not specified and nor is the degree of seriousness envisaged. Once the Board has taken the above factors 'into account', s 4A does not prescribe the Board's response.[203]

Section 89 of the 1994 Act also amended s 2(2) in respect of the scope of exemptions. It is no longer necessary to show that the video is designed to stimulate or encourage the activity mentioned above, but only that it is likely to do so. Further, the exemptions will not apply if a video 'depicts techniques likely to be useful in the commission of offences' or 'criminal activity likely to any significant extent to stimulate or encourage the commission of offences'.

---

199 See Petley, J, *Screen*, Vol 25 No 2, p 68.

200 See further Home Affairs Committee, *Video Violence and Young Offenders*, Fourth Report (1994) HC 514.

201 See Hunnings, N, 'Video censorship' [1985] PL 214; Robertson, G, *Freedom, the Individual and the Law*, 1993, pp 263–72.

202 See further Home Affairs Committee, *Video Violence and Young Offenders*, Fourth Report (1994) HC 514.

203 See, on this issue, Manchester, C, 'Criminal Justice and Public Order Act 1994: obscenity, pornography and videos' (1995) Crim LR 123, pp 129–30.

There is a right of appeal from the decisions of the BBFC to the Video Appeals Committee, under s 4, which operates as a Tribunal. In 2000, the BBFC and the VAC came into conflict in respect of a number of explicit videos which depicted actual, rather than simulated, sexual scenes. The BBFC considered that no certificate should be issued, but, on appeal, the VAC disagreed. The BBFC sought review of the decision of the VAC: *Video Appeals Committee of the BBFC ex p BBFC*,[204] but was unsuccessful on the basis that the VAC had taken all the relevant factors into account, including any risk to children. The judgment appeared to be based on the legal view that the access of adults to explicit material should not be prevented on the basis that it might be harmful to children if it happened to come into their hands. It was thought that since the videos were to be sold in adult sex shops, the risk that they would come into the hands of children was very slight. The Home Secretary, Jack Straw, was angered by the decision of the VAC and indicated that new legislation on obscenity might be necessary.[205] The VAC has not always been so bold: it did not reverse the decision of the BBFC in relation to the video *Visions of Ecstasy*, on the basis that it was possibly blasphemous (see below).

The impact of the HRA

The stance of the BBFC is obviously influenced by the composition of the Board. But its effect on film makers has been criticised as militating against creativity. It has been suggested that a cosy relationship has developed that is insufficiently challenging – the acceptable boundaries are not fully explored in the name of artistic integrity and creative freedom.[206] Commercial judgment rather than artistic considerations dominate; the most pressing consideration is to find the widest audience, which may mean instituting cuts in order to obtain a 15 certificate. These factors lead to a heavier censorship of films in the UK than in Europe or the US.

It seems possible that the inception of the HRA could have some impact on this situation. For example, a film maker whose film was refused a classification without certain cuts, could seek to challenge the decision of the BBFC or, in the case of a video, that of the VAC, upholding the BBFC's decision. The VAC and BBFC are, assuming that they are public authorities, bound by the Convention rights under s 6 of the HRA. Therefore, they should ensure that their decisions do not breach Art 10, or any other relevant Article. The 1984 Act, as amended, must be interpreted compatibly with the Convention rights under s 3 of the HRA. Given that a number of its terms are very open-ended, there is room for a range of interpretations. The VAC is a body set up under statute with a public function in the sense of hearing appeals regarding the classification of material to be promulgated to the public; it is also subject to judicial review. It is therefore almost certainly a public authority under s 6 of the HRA. The BBFC has a public function which is also statutory in respect of providing classification certificates for videos. Its function in relation to films is not statutory, but can clearly be termed public. Had it not undertaken the classification of films, the government would have been likely to set up a statutory body.[207] It is suggested that it is probably a functional public

---

204 (2000) EMLR 850.

205 See *The Guardian*, 17 May 2000.

206 See Robertson and Nichol, *op cit*, fn 109, p 593.

207 See further Chapter 4, pp 157–9, on functional public authorities.

authority. Therefore, there are grounds for taking the view that private bodies or persons could bring an action against either body under s 7(1)(a) of the HRA, relying on Art 10. In such an action, the Court would have to give effect to s 12 of the HRA.

The stance taken by Strasbourg in relation to films likely to offend religious sensibilities was indicated in the leading decision: *Otto-Preminger*.[208] The decision is considered in detail below.[209] The film in question was not likely to be viewed by children, but was found to be offensive to religious sensibilities. The seizure and forfeiture of the film was not found to breach Art 10. Further guidance derives from the decision of the Court of Human Rights in *Wingrove v UK*.[210] This decision is also considered further below. It concerned a decision of the BBFC, upheld by the VAC, to refuse a certificate to the short, explicit film *Visions of Ecstasy*. The Court found that the decision to refuse a certificate was within the national authorities' margin of appreciation. But the film, which was to be promulgated as a short video, was viewed as offensive to religious sensibilities and as quite likely to come to the attention of children, since it could be viewed in the home.[211] No breach of Art 10 was found.

In the case of a sexually explicit or violent film, the problem would be, as indicated above, that the Strasbourg jurisprudence appears to support quite far reaching restrictions. However, where the risk of children viewing the film is very slight due to the use of age restrictions, *and* the question of offending religious sensibilities does not arise, it is suggested that the jurisprudence can be viewed as supporting the availability of even very explicit films. This contention derives from the principles underlying the jurisprudence, which, as indicated above, relate to the familiar free speech justifications, including that of self-fulfilment.[212]

It is concluded that where the question of offence to religious sensibilities does not arise, and bearing in mind the expectation that the domestic courts will not adopt the margin of appreciation doctrine, it would be consonant with the general Strasbourg freedom of expression jurisprudence to leave little scope under Art 10(2) for interferences with the freedom of expression of film makers in respect of films targeted at adults. Following this argument, it would be expected that they would be afforded an 18 certificate and, possibly, appropriate warnings would have to be posted at cinemas so that an unwitting viewer would not be offended. Different considerations would apply to *videos*, owing to the possibility that they might be viewed by children, although this argument should be considered carefully, in terms of its impact on adults. The question of the harm that might be caused should also be considered, bearing in mind the lack of evidence mentioned above regarding a connection between behaviour seen on film and actual behaviour. The mere invocation of the possibility that children might view a video should not be enough. Guidance on this matter might usefully be sought from other jurisdictions,[213] since it is not a matter that Strasbourg has inquired into in any depth. The

---

208 (1994) 19 EHRR 34.
209 See pp 317–18.
210 (1996) 24 EHRR 1.
211 See paras 61 and 63 of the judgment.
212 See pp 204–05.
213 See above, pp 278–80.

question of the validity of taking the stance adopted in *Wingrove* and *Otto-Preminger* is considered in the next section.

5 BLASPHEMY, SEDITIOUS LIBEL, RELIGIOUS AND RACIAL HATRED

Blasphemous and seditious libel

The existence of the offence of blasphemous libel[214] stems from the 17th century when it was tried in the Ecclesiastical courts. It was then thought to be a form of sedition due to the close relationship between the Church and the State. Therefore, it only protected the Anglican Church; other sects of the Christian Church such as Catholicism, or other religions, received no protection. Its basis, which derives from *Taylor's* case,[215] was that the defendant had aspersed the Christian religion. By the middle of the 19th century and in particular after the case of *Ramsay and Foote*,[216] it became clear that the basis of blasphemy had changed: it required a scurrilous attack on Christianity rather than merely reasoned and sober arguments against it. It was thought by 1950 that the offence was a dead letter.[217] However, it was resurrected in *Lemon*.[218] Gay News published a poem – 'The Love that dares to speak its name' – by a professor of English literature, James Kirkup. It expressed religious sentiment in describing a homosexual's conversion to Christianity and in developing its theme it ascribed homosexual practices with the Apostles to Jesus and made explicit references to sodomy. Mary Whitehouse obtained leave to bring a private prosecution against Gay News and the editor and publishing company were convicted of the offence of blasphemous libel.

The Court of Appeal held that the intention or motive of the defendants was irrelevant since blasphemy was a crime of strict liability. It could therefore be committed by a Christian as there was no need to show that the material had mounted a fundamental attack on Christianity (as had been thought). There was no defence of publication in the public interest; serious literature could therefore be caught. The work in question need not be considered as a whole. All that needed to be shown was that the material in question, which was published with the defendant's knowledge, had crossed the borderline between moderate criticism on the one hand and immoderate or offensive treatment of matter sacred to Christians on the other. It was only necessary to show that resentment would be likely to be aroused, not that it actually was aroused. The past

---

214 General reading: see Robertson, *op cit*, fn 75, Chapter 8, pp 236–43; Robertson and Nichol, *op cit*, fn 109, Chapter 3, pp 124–27; Bailey, Harris and Jones, *op cit*, fn 75, Chapter 9, pp 591–98; Robillard, JA, *Religion and the Law, 1984*, Chapter 2; Barendt, *op cit*, fn 3, pp 167, 260; for historical discussion of the development of blasphemy law see Kenny, CS, 'The evolution of the law of blasphemy' [1992] CLJ 127–42 and Walter, *Blasphemy Ancient and Modern*, 1990. For a discussion of the theoretical issues lying behind blasphemy law, see Feinberg, *Offense to Others*, 1985 and, in the context of possible reform, see Law Commission Report No 145, *Offences against Religion and Public Worship*, 1985.
215 (1676) 1 Vent 293.
216 (1883) 15 Cox CC 231.
217 This was Lord Denning's description of it in *Freedom under the Law*, 1949, p 46.
218 [1979] AC 617; [1979] 2 WLR 281; [1979] 1 All ER 898, HL.

requirement to show that a breach of the peace might be occasioned by publication of the material was no longer necessary. The case was considered by the House of Lords on the question of the mental element required. The judgment confirmed the Court of Appeal ruling that it was only necessary to show an intent to publish the material. This decision has been much criticised[219] as it inhibits many, if not most, juxtapositions of sexuality with aspects of the Anglican religion by writers and broadcasters. In common with other parts of the common law, it allows the Obscene Publications Act to be circumvented because it admits of no public good defence. Moreover, there are already various areas of liability, discussed above, arising at common law and under statute which could be used to prevent offence being caused to Christians.

Gay News applied to the European Commission on Human Rights on a number of grounds including that of a breach of Art 10.[220] This application was ruled inadmissible in a cautious judgment. It was found that the Art 10 guarantee of freedom of expression had been interfered with, but that the interference fell within the 'rights of others' exception of Art 10(2). Was the interference necessary in a democratic society? It was found that once it was accepted that the religious feelings of citizens may deserve protection if attacks reach a certain level of savagery, it seemed to follow that the domestic authorities were best placed to determine when that level was reached. In other words, the argument used in the *Handyside* case, that a very wide margin of appreciation was required, was again invoked.

It seemed fairly clear in the pre-HRA era that this offence was unlikely to be extended beyond Anglicanism. The Law Commission in their 1985 Report[221] concluded, rather, that it should be abolished, in finding that an offence of wounding the feelings of adherents of any religious group would be impossible to construct because the term 'religion' could not be defined with sufficient precision. The argument in favour of extension of the offence was put and rejected in *Chief Metropolitan Magistrate ex p Choudhury*,[222] a case which arose out of the publication of Salman Rushdie's *The Satanic Verses*.[223] The applicants applied for judicial review of the refusal of a magistrates' court to grant summonses against Salman Rushdie and his publishers for, *inter alia*, the common law offence of blasphemous libel. The Court of Appeal found that the expression of views in an artistic context would not prevent them from amounting to a blasphemous libel, a finding that has been criticised as revealing a 'lack of judicial awareness of the right to artistic expression and its theoretical basis ... [and an ignorance of] the autonomy of art as a specific cultural category with its own symbolic methods'.[224] But it was determined after reviewing the relevant decisions that the offence of blasphemy was clearly confined only to publications offensive to Christians. Extending the offence would, it was found, create great difficulties since it would be virtually impossible to define the

---

219 See Robertson, *op cit*, fn 75, p 242; Law Commission Report, 1985.

220 (1979) 5 EHRR 123.

221 Report No 145, Offences Against Religion and Public Worship. This was preceded by the Law Commission Working Paper No 79 of the same title (1981). See Robertson [1981] PL 295; Spencer, JR [1981] Crim LR 810; Robillard (1981) 44 MLR 556 for comment on the 1981 Working Paper. The direction reform might take is considered further below, pp 325–27.

222 [1991] 1 QB 429; [1991] 1 All ER 306, DC; for comment, see Tregilgas-Davey, M (1991) 54 MLR 294–99.

223 For discussion of Muslim and Western reactions to publication of *The Satanic Verses*, see Abel, R, *Speech and Respect*, 1994, Chapter 1 (iii).

224 See Kearns, *op cit*, fn 57, p 656.

term 'religion' sufficiently clearly. Freedom of expression would be curtailed as authors would have to try to avoid offending members of many different sects.

The applicants did not, however, rely only on domestic law; during argument that the offence should be extended, it was said that UK law must contain a provision to give effect to the Convention guarantee of freedom of religion under Art 9.[225] In response, it was argued and accepted by the Court of Appeal that the Convention need not be considered because the common law on the point was not uncertain. However, the respondents nevertheless accepted that in this particular instance, the Convention should be considered. It was found that the UK was not in breach of the Convention because extending the offence of blasphemy would breach Arts 7 and 10; the exceptions of Art 10(2) could not be invoked, as nothing in the book would support a pressing social need for its suppression. Furthermore, Art 9(1) could not be treated as absolute; implied exceptions to it must include the lack of a right to bring criminal proceedings for blasphemy where no domestic law had been infringed. Article 9 might be infringed, it was found, where Muslims were prevented from exercising their religion, but such restrictions were not in question. It should be noted that that last finding and probably the finding regarding Art 10(2) can now be said to be wrong, as a matter of Convention law, in the light of the findings in *Otto-Preminger* in the Strasbourg Court (below).

On behalf of the applicants, it was further argued that if Art 9 provided no protection for Muslims, they had suffered discrimination in the exercise of their freedom of religion and therefore a violation of Art 14 had occurred. This interpretation of Art 9, read alongside Art 14, had been rejected by the European Commission in the *Gay News* case.[226] In this case, it also failed on the ground that the envisaged extension of UK law to protect Islam would involve a violation of Art 10, which guarantees freedom of expression. Such an extension was not, therefore, warranted. It seems clear from this ruling and from statements made by Lord Scarman in the House of Lords in *Lemon*,[227] which were relied upon in the *Choudhury* case, that the judiciary are not minded to extend this offence, considering that only Parliament should do so.

The applicants also argued that the crime of seditious libel would extend to the image of Islam presented by *The Satanic Verses*. This offence at one time seemed to cover any attack on the institutions of the State, but in modern times, it has been interpreted to require an intention to incite to violence and the words used must have a tendency to incite to violence.[228] It was not, therefore, apt to cover the offence caused to Muslims by the book, which could be said to be intended to arouse general hostility and ill will between sections of the community, but not against the public authorities. This finding, which was contrary to the ruling in *Caunt*,[229] means that incitement to religious hatred is not covered by any part of the law, although attacks on Anglicanism would in most instances fall within blasphemy, while attacks on religious groups which are also racial groups would fall within incitement to racial hatred (see below, p 327).

---

225 For discussion of the particular question whether blasphemy law can be defended by reference to the rights of others to freedom of religion, see below, pp 324–26.

226 (1982) 5 EHRR 123.

227 [1979] AC 617, p 620. Lord Scarman considered that there was a case for extension, however.

228 *Burns* [1886] 16 Cox CC 333; *Aldred* (1909) 22 Cox CC 1; *Caunt* (1947) unreported, but see case note 64 LQR 203; for comment see Barendt, *op cit*, fn 3, pp 152–60.

229 (1947) 64 LQR 203.

An application was made to the European Commission on Human Rights by the applicants in *Choudhury*,[230] but it was declared inadmissible on the ground that Art 9 does not include a positive obligation on the part of the State to protect religious sensibilities. The discriminatory application of blasphemy law therefore remains a source of discontent among Muslims. Parliament had the opportunity of abolishing the offence of blasphemy in 1994 when a Bill was put forward by Lord Lester which would have achieved this. However, it was withdrawn after the government opposed it,[231] partly on the ground that no clear consensus as to the value of abolishing this offence could be discerned.

The future of blasphemy law: impact of the HRA

The Strasbourg jurisprudence

Consideration of the Strasbourg jurisprudence suggests that the inception of the HRA will not bring about reform of UK blasphemy law since such reform is not required in order to ensure harmony with Art 10 of the European Convention on Human Rights as interpreted at Strasbourg. This suggestion is borne out by the findings of the European Commission in the *Gay News* case.

But the most significant ruling is that of the European Court of Human Rights in *Otto-Preminger Institut v Austria*.[232] An order was made for the seizure and forfeiture of a film, *Das Lieberkinzil (Council in Heaven)*, which caricatured aspects of Christianity, on the basis that it disparaged religious doctrines and was 'likely to arouse justified indignation'. The film was based on a satirical play by Oskar Panizza, published in 1894. The play bases itself on the assumption that syphilis was God's punishment for man's fornication and sinfulness at the time of the Renaissance. The film begins and ends with a depiction of Panizza's trial for blasphemy in 1895 in respect of the play. It shows the performance of the play, by the *Teatro Belli* in Rome, which portrays God as a senile old man, prostrating himself before the devil. Jesus is portrayed as a mental defective and is shown attempting to kiss and fondle his mother's breasts. God, Jesus and the Virgin Mary agree with the Devil to punish the world; the Devil suggests infecting the world with a sexually transmitted disease; as his reward, he demands freedom of thought. Apart from satirising aspects of religious belief, the film explores the idea of the limitations of artistic freedom, explicitly in relation to the trial and impliedly (in the context of the trial) in the case of the play.

In an Opinion that strongly emphasised the need to protect artistic freedom, the Commission found a breach of Art 10. In considering whether the interference was necessary in a democratic society for protecting the right to freedom of religion under Art 9, the Commission took into account the role of works of art in a democratic society and relied on the observation in *Müller*[233] to the effect that 'those who create, perform, distribute or exhibit works of art contribute to the exchange of ideas and opinions which is essential for a democratic society. Hence, the obligation of the State not to encroach

---

230 *Choudhury v UK* (1991) No 17349/1990; (1991) 12 HRLJ 172.
231 555 HL Deb Cols 1891–1909, 16 June 1994.
232 (1994) 19 EHRR 34.
233 (1991) 13 EHRR 212.

unduly on their freedom of expression.' A warning was given to the public as to the nature of the film, and although access was not specifically restricted, the film was to be shown in a 'cinema of art' at a late hour. Therefore, it was unlikely that young children would be present. These factors affected the Commission's view. The Commission considered that recourse to certain artistic methods (satirisation and caricature) would not 'justify the imposition of a restriction on a work of art even if it deals with religion'.[234] Further, 'a complete prohibition which excludes the chance to discuss the message of the film *must* be seen as a disproportionate measure' (emphasis added). [235]

The Court took a strikingly different stance. The Austrian Government maintained, and the Court accepted, that the seizure and forfeiture were aimed at protecting the 'rights of others' within Art 10(2). The Court found that 'the manner in which religious doctrines are opposed or denied is a matter which may engage the responsibility of the State, notably its responsibility to ensure *the peaceful enjoyment of the right under Article 9'* (emphasis added).[236] The Court found that the responsibilities of those exercising the right under Art 10 include 'an obligation to avoid as far as possible expressions that are gratuitously offensive to others and thus an infringement of their rights and which therefore *do not contribute to any form of debate capable of furthering progress in human affairs'* (emphasis added).[237] Therefore, it might be considered necessary to prevent such expressions.

The Court took into account the lack of a uniform conception in Europe of the significance of religion in society in finding that it was not possible to arrive at a comprehensive definition of what constitutes a permissible interference. It therefore left a wide margin of appreciation to the Austrian Government in respect of assessing the extent of the interference necessary. It considered, however, that the necessity for the restriction 'must be convincingly established'. In finding that the seizure and forfeiture were necessary, the Court accepted the view of the Austrian authorities that the offensive nature of the film was not outweighed by its artistic merits and left them a wide margin of appreciation in determining the measures needed in the light of the local situation, bearing in mind the fact that the Roman Catholic religion was the dominant religion in the local region, the Tyrol. The Court did not give a specific reason for finding that the case for adopting the measures had been convincingly established, merely asserting that the Austrian authorities had not overstepped their margin of appreciation. No breach of Art 10 was therefore found.

Harris, O'Boyle and Warbrick criticised the breadth of the decision in these terms: 'It is hard to know which aspect of the majority's judgment more threatens freedom of expression interests: that outrage of people based only on knowing of, not being confronted with, certain expression provides justification for interfering with the expression, or, this being the case, that the indignation of people in a discrete geographic area is sufficient to justify the interference across the entire State.'[238] Bearing in mind the completeness of the interference, and its theoretical basis, this judgment is, it is argued,

---

234 (1994) 19 EHRR 34, para 72.
235 *Ibid*, para 77.
236 *Ibid*, para 47.
237 *Ibid*, para 49.
238 *Law of the European Convention on Human Rights*, 1995, p 402.

entirely unsatisfactory in the light of the free speech justifications discussed in the Introduction to Part II. The Court appeared to afford little weight to the value of the speech in question in terms of providing worthwhile dissent from established thought. In finding that the film did not contribute to 'debate capable of furthering progress in human affairs' it revealed a failure to understand the principle of moral autonomy which demands that citizens should be free not only to choose to view works of art, but to decide for themselves whether they have value.[239] It also showed a misunderstanding of the nature of the argument from truth, which it appeared to be referring to, in that it excluded the possibility that the film's message might in future be viewed as winning out in the market place of ideas. In other words, it allowed an interference in that free market of ideas which sought to preclude that possibility. In attacking the *manner* of the dissent from established religious ideas, the Court, in contrast to the Commission, failed to understand the nature of artistic endeavour, which often uses techniques such as satire in order to make an impact on an audience. In this respect, it disregarded its own earlier statement to the effect that 'Article 10 protects not only the substance of the ideas and information but also the form in which they are conveyed'.[240] It further failed to differentiate between taking account of the possibility that the expression in question had value, based on an understanding of the free speech justifications, and assessing that value itself.[241] Clearly, the Court possessed no special expertise allowing it to arbitrate as to the artistic worth of the film. The judgment was also unsatisfactory even in its own terms, since it failed to conduct a strict evaluation as to whether the need for such a wide ranging restriction had been convincingly established. In short, this was an unconvincing, under-theorised judgment of the Court which is unworthy of its freedom of expression jurisprudence in general. The Opinion of the Commission was, it is suggested, far more in tune with that jurisprudence.

The judgment of the Court in *Wingrove v UK*[242] applied the reasoning from *Otto-Preminger* and therefore showed very similar tendencies. Again, the decision can be contrasted with the finding of the Commission that there had been a violation of Art 10.[243] The Court had to consider whether a refusal of the BBFC to issue a certificate licensing a video, *Visions of Ecstasy*, constituted a breach of Art 10. The film depicts erotic visions experienced by St Theresa of Avila, a 16th century Carmelite nun. In the short, silent film she is depicted in a white habit suspended from a cord being erotically embraced by her own psyche, represented by a half-naked woman. That scene is intercut by scenes showing St Theresa, as part of her fantasies, kissing and embracing Christ who is fastened to the cross. She kisses his wounds and sits astride him in a manner reflecting intense arousal. The BBFC took the view that if the video had been granted a classification certificate and shown in the UK, a private prosecution for blasphemy might have been brought successfully.

---

239 See the statement to this effect in the well known free expression decision in the US: (1966) *Ginzburg v US* 463, p 498.

240 *Oberschlick v Austria* (1991) 19 EHRR 389.

241 See further Pannick, *op cit*, fn 73.

242 Opinion of the Commission: (1994) 19 EHRR CD 54. Judgment of 25 November 1996, Case 19/1995/525/611; (1996) 24 EHRR 1. For further discussion, see Ghandi, S and James, J, 'The English law of blasphemy and the European Convention on Human Rights' [1998] EHRLR 430.

243 *Wingrove v UK* (1994) 76-A DR 26.

The Court found that the restriction was prescribed by law, taking into account the fact that the BBFC was acting within its powers under s 4(1) of the Video Recordings Act 1984 and that no general uncertainty was apparent as to the definition of blasphemy formulated in the *Lemon* case. The refusal of the certificate had the aim of protecting the rights of others within Art 10(2) and was consonant with the aim of the protection afforded by Art 9 to religious freedom. In considering the necessity and proportionality of the restriction, the Court went on to find that while the margin of appreciation allowed to States would be narrow in relation to political speech, it would be wide in relation to offending 'intimate personal convictions within the field of morals or, especially, religion'.[244] It also placed strong emphasis on the fact that views hostile to Christianity could be expressed under the English law of blasphemy: 'it is the manner in which the views are advocated rather than the views themselves which the law seeks to control ... The high degree of profanation that must be attained [is] ... itself a safeguard against arbitrariness.'[245] The Court found, having viewed the video, that the decision of the BBFC that it would outrage and insult the feelings of believing Christians could not be said to be arbitrary or excessive. The national authorities had not overstepped their margin of appreciation: the exception applied and therefore no breach of Art 10 had occurred.

It is suggested that this judgment strongly resembles that in *Otto-Preminger* in revealing a strange failure in a court of human rights to understand or afford weight to the familiar free speech justifications. The judgment reveals an inability to appreciate that a *complete* ban on a film is especially difficult to defend if the principle of moral autonomy is to be given any weight. It failed to understand the value of allowing dissent, not only from established views of religious figures, but also from such views as to their proper portrayal. In placing so much emphasis on the question of the *manner* of the portrayal, it shows a readiness to stifle artistic initiative, thereby preventing the free debate of the ideas the film portrays and also preventing, or at least strongly curbing, the outgrowths in terms of further artistic exploration of similar ideas, that it might have fostered.

Domestic approaches to blasphemy law under the HRA

Where the European Court of Human Rights leaves a wide margin of appreciation to Member States in determining the extent of the exceptions to a Convention right, this could be taken to imply that, at least until a common European conception of the width of the exception emerges, States have the main responsibility for ensuring that rigorous human rights standards are maintained. It is suggested that the ease with which publications can infringe blasphemy law in the UK does not represent a maintenance of such standards and that therefore, reform of blasphemy law should be attempted, now that the HRA is in force, by domestic judges who are not trammelled by the margin of appreciation doctrine. Moreover, given the widespread criticism of the decisions in *Otto-Preminger* and *Wingrove*, and the failure to understand basic principles of freedom of expression that they reveal, there are strong grounds for arguing that the domestic courts should not follow them, but should look for guidance to the Commission in both

---

244 Judgment in draft form, p 22.
245 *Ibid*, para 60.

instances, and to courts in other jurisdictions in order to achieve a more developed understanding of those principles.

For example, in the well known judgment in *Cohen v California*,[246] the US Supreme Court found that a political view expressed in profane terms was protected by the First Amendment; it said: 'much linguistic expression serves a dual communicative function: it conveys not only ideas capable of relatively precise, detached explication, but otherwise inexpressible emotions as well ... words are often chosen as much for their emotive as their cognitive force. We cannot sanction the view that the Constitution, while solicitous of the cognitive content of individual speech, has little regard for that emotive function which, practically speaking, may often be the most important element of the overall message sought to be communicated.' These words would clearly be equally applicable to a film such as Council in Heaven, which had both an emotive and a cognitive function, or to *Visions of Ecstasy*, which had a largely emotive function.

There are at least two clear reasons why some change is needed in the current law. First, from a pragmatic point of view, the present situation, since it is perceived by Muslims as unfair, is a considerable source of racial tension: it both engenders feelings of anger and alienation in the Muslim community and, when these feelings are expressed through such activities as book burning and attacks on booksellers stocking *The Satanic Verses*, increased feelings of hostility towards Muslims in certain sections of the non-Muslim population. Secondly, from the liberal point of view broadly endorsed in this book, it is indefensible that the State should single out one group of citizens and protect their religious feelings while others are without such protection. In what follows, therefore, the question whether blasphemy law should be extended, abolished or replaced by an offence of incitement to religious hatred, will be considered from the point of view of the philosophical justifications which would support each alternative. The probable effect of each course of action on racial tension will also be briefly considered. This discussion is premised upon the argument outlined in Chapter 1 that free speech, as a strong individual right, should be infringed only if a similar individual right is threatened by speech, or if the values which lead us to support free speech are not at issue in the instant case, or if the speech carries a real risk of substantial damage to the well being of society.

When blasphemy law is considered in suitable instances under the HRA, the arguments for its abolition or extension are likely to be canvassed. Since blasphemy is a common law doctrine, the judges are, it is suggested, at liberty to abolish, extend or curtail it, under s 6 of the HRA. The argument to extend the blasphemy law to cover other faiths would clearly find support in principle if the present law is viewed as having a firm

---

246 (1971) 403 US 15, 25-6. The decision, regarding the words 'Fuck the draft' could be viewed as affected by being taken in the context of political speech. Nevertheless, lower courts have applied the words regarding emotive communication to visual expression that cannot be regarded as political expression: *Cinevision Corp v City of Burbank* 7456 F 2d 560, p 569 (concerning music) and *Birkenshaw v Haley* (1974) 409 F Supp 13 ED Mich (concerning mime).

basis in Convention values.[247] It receives strong support, it is suggested, from the decision in *Otto-Preminger* which would have to be taken into account by the domestic judiciary, under s 2 of the HRA, in a suitable case. It could be argued that since the Strasbourg Court has found that Art 9 covers a right to be free from the knowledge that expression offensive to one's religious beliefs is occurring in one's locality, and that that right further covers the a ban on such speech that covers the whole country, the reach of Art 9 has been greatly extended. Muslims could readily argue that the sale of a book or showing of a film with a theme similar to that of *The Satanic Verses*, amounts on this argument to a violation of their Art 9 rights and that a complete ban, as opposed to a very restricted sale, confined to certain localities, would therefore be warranted. Article 14 could also be invoked in conjunction with Art 9. The argument of the European Commission on Human Rights in *Choudhury*,[248] to the effect that Art 9 does not include a positive obligation on the part of the State to protect religious sensibilities, may be doubted on the basis that positive obligations have been accepted under Art 8.[249] The Art 7 problem would still have to be overcome and it is suggested that, since the decision as to the reach of rights to freedom of religion in *Otto-Preminger* is out of line with the stance in most 'civilised nations',[250] the exception under Art 7(2) could not be invoked successfully.[251]

There are practical difficulties, based on the nature of the HRA, in seeking to rely on Art 9 in relation to a bookseller or a film producer or a broadcaster. Probably, a Muslim group would not have standing (s 7(3)) under s 7(1)(a) to bring an action based on a free standing application of Art 9 and, in any event, the other party would not normally be a public authority. The 'victim' provision under s 7(3) would obviously still create a difficulty, but there would be the possibility of bringing an action based solely on Art 9 where a public authority, such as a media regulator, or the BBC, was involved. If a remedy was available, it would presumably take the form of an injunction, since the Convention cannot be used to create criminal liability. But the most obvious, and, as

---

247 For general discussion of this issue, see 'Speech, religious discrimination and blasphemy' (1989: Proceedings of the American Society of International Law, p 427 *et seq*' and, in particular, Reisman's article, pp 435–39: he makes out an elegant thesis that attempts such as Ayatollah Khomeni's, to punish and deter unorthodox references to the Koran amount to a 'claim of the right to exclusive control of major symbols of global culture and the prerogative of deciding how they are to be used artistically' (p 437). He expresses concern over 'the support lent by religious leaders in the West' to this claim and the criticism of Rushdie expressed by some of them. He warns that imposing censorship on artists or forcing them to internalise such censorship through insisting that free expression amounts to a form of religious intolerance will lead to the deterioration of the arts: creative endeavour will become a kind of 'communal Rubik cube in which a limited number of approved elements are moved feverishly round in an ever decreasing number of "new" combinations' (p 439).

248 *Choudhury v UK* (1991) No 17349/1990; (1991) 12 HRLJ 172.

249 See Chapter 10, pp 538–41.

250 The fact that, as the Court noted in *Wingrove*, para 57, 'the application of [blasphemy laws in Europe] is becoming increasingly rare and several States ... have recently repealed them altogether ...' would also support this contention. In the US, the First Amendment provides expressly that 'Congress shall make no law respecting an establishment of religion, nor prohibiting the free exercise thereof' and in *Joseph Burstyn Inc v Wilson* (1952) 343 US 495, an attempt to stop the screening of a film on the ground that it was blasphemous failed. The decision made it clear that the offence of blasphemy could not be sustained since it was entirely opposed to First Amendment principles. See also the famous 'Nazis at Skokie' decisions: *Collin v Smith* (1978) 578 F 2d 1197, 7th Cir, (1978) 436 US 953, (1978) 439 US 916; *Skokie v Nat Socialist Party* (1978) 373 NE 2d 21; it raised issues which have parallels with those in *Otto-Preminger*.

251 See Chapter 2, pp 64–66.

indicated, probably the only, vehicle existing in domestic law on which to base an Art 9 argument is blasphemy law. The result of an attempt to use the blasphemy law might end in an application for judicial review, as in *Choudhury*. A Muslim group would base their application on the ordinary standing rules, as in *Choudhury*, and then rely on s 7(1)(b) in order to argue that their Art 9 and 14 rights should be afforded recognition.

But, practical issues aside, the key issue of principle concerns the validity of the arguments that freedom of expression should give way to a right to freedom of religion that includes the right not to be offended by the promulgation of expression that offends against religious sensibilities. To evaluate the force of this argument, it is necessary first to identify which, if any, of the rationales for blasphemy law would provide support for both its continued existence and extension, and which would not. Three rationales will be considered in turn: the argument from the protection of society, the argument from preventing individual distress and the argument from the right to religious freedom. The point of view which sees blasphemy law as protecting those shared beliefs of a society which are essential to its survival[252] would not, it is submitted, support the extension of the law to cover other faiths; the law would then be protecting a whole set of conflicting beliefs and thus supporting religious pluralism, not the survival of religious conformity. It may be argued that the law should uphold religious pluralism as a shared belief, but abolition of the offence of blasphemy would do this far more simply than extension.

The argument that blasphemy laws are justified because they protect individual believers from mental anguish immediately runs into a host of problems over extension of the law. For if one is concerned to protect individuals from the mental distress which can flow from attacks on deeply held beliefs,[253] it is not readily apparent that society should not also outlaw attacks upon deeply held non-religious beliefs, such as a deep belief in the equality of the sexes.[254] But one would then arrive at a position in which the criminal law would be being used to prevent people from attacking or insulting the deep beliefs of others. Arguably, such a law would be unworkable, since it would require judgments to be made about indeterminable matters such as the depth at which a belief was held. More importantly, not only would such a law represent a major infringement of the individual's freedom of speech, offering only the prevention of distress as a justification, it would be philosophically indefensible besides. If we are really committed to the notion that free discussion is the best way to arrive at the truth,[255] it seems nonsensical to abandon that position when our most important beliefs are at stake; if anything, we should be most concerned precisely to *encourage* free discussion of our deep beliefs since, almost axiomatically, it is our deepest beliefs which we most wish to be true.

---

252 Lord Devlin is usually associated with the thesis that society may justifiably protect its shared moral beliefs through the criminal law: see his *The Enforcement of Morals*, 1965. It is arguable that the protection of society was, historically at least, one of the purposes of blasphemy law: see, eg, *Taylor's case* [1676] 1 Vent 293 in which it was said: 'For to say, Religion is a cheat is to dissolve all those obligations whereby civil societies are preserved.'

253 Note, eg, the *dicta* of Lord Scarman in *Lemon* [1979] AC 617, p 620 that 'there is a case for legislation extending [blasphemy law] to protect the religious beliefs and feelings of non-Christians'. Arguably, however, he saw protection of feelings as ultimately aimed at 'the internal tranquillity of the Kingdom'.

254 Recognising this, a number of commentators have attempted to frame definitions of 'religious belief' in which the term includes both actual religious convictions and those beliefs which hold a place in people's minds analogous to that held by religious belief. See, eg, Clements, 'Defining "religion" in the First Amendment: a functional approach' (1989) 74 Cornell LR 532.

255 For an exposition of this theory, see above, pp 202–03.

It is submitted that the only justification for continuance of the blasphemy law which could offer it even *prima facie* support is the argument from the right to religious freedom, which is protected under Art 9 of the Convention. The need to provide such protection is also viewed as falling within the 'rights of others' exception to Art 10 and, therefore, as arguably justifying the banning of publications that might offend religious sensibilities, as the Court of Human Rights found in *Otto-Preminger* and *Wingrove*. It is contended that the argument accepted by the Court that such publications infringe Art 9 is deeply flawed. In order to demonstrate this, it is necessary to consider the substantive contention that, as Poulter puts it:

> Freedom of religion is ... a valuable human right and it may be doubted whether it can be fully enjoyed in practice if the State allows religious beliefs to be vilified and insulted in a gratuitous manner.[256]

The first assertion made here, about the value of religious freedom, is of course readily conceded. However, the argument, as expressed by the Court of Human Rights, then goes on to assume that the State is under a positive duty to facilitate the full enjoyment in practice of its citizens' right to freedom of religion, taking that term to encompass a duty to prevent attacks on religion which take a certain objected-to form. This is surely a mistaken view; rather, it is submitted, the right to religious freedom is violated if one is not free to choose, express and manifest one's religious beliefs:[257] the right is not so violated simply because one is not protected from mental suffering caused by verbal attacks upon one's religion or offensive portrayals of it. As Van Dijk and Van Hoof put it in one of the leading texts: 'this decision [in *Otto-Preminger*] is mistaken. The screening of the film in no way would have limited or inhibited Roman Catholics in manifesting their religion ... a right [not to be insulted in one's religious views] is not included in Article 9 but is on the contrary inconsistent with the "pluralism indissociable from a democratic society"[258] embedded in Article 9.'[259]

Even if it were to be accepted for the purposes of argument that the religious freedom of those from Christian faiths should be protected by the blasphemy law, it is denied that this finding would be a conclusive argument for continuing or, *a fortiori*, extending the protection. If Poulter's contention, and that of the Court of Human Rights, are correct, then we are confronted by a situation in which two important individual rights – freedom of religion and freedom of speech – come into conflict with each other. In such a situation, it is surely reasonable not simply to assume that freedom of religion should override freedom of speech, but rather to attempt to weigh up which right would suffer most if the other was given precedence. If this is done, the argument runs as follows: if there was no offence of blasphemy, this might mean that on occasion some distress, perhaps acute, would be associated with the practice of one's religion, although those aware that they might suffer distress can normally take steps to ensure that they do not encounter the

---

256 Poulter, S, 'Towards legislative reform of the blasphemy and racial hatred laws' [1991] PL 371, p 376.

257 Thus, Art 18 of the Universal Declaration of Human Rights provides that: 'Everyone has the right to freedom of thought, conscience and religion; this right includes freedom to change his religion or belief and freedom ... in public or private to manifest his religion or belief in teaching, practice, worship and observance.' Both the International Covenant on Civil and Political Rights (Art 18) and the European Convention (Art 9) contain very similar provisions.

258 *Kokkinakis v Greece* A 260-A, p 18.

259 Van Dijk, P and Van Hoof, F, *Theory and Practice of the European Convention on Human Rights*, 1998, p 551.

offending publication. If there is such an offence, it might mean that use of the coercive sanctions of the law would severely damage the liberty to write creatively or speak one's mind freely on religious matters.[260] Clearly, the damage done to freedom of religion if there is no blasphemy law is far less than the damage done to freedom of speech if there is one.

In any event, the argument that regards a blasphemy law as essential because the right to religious freedom demands it, immediately runs into difficulties since it is clearly necessary to define religion. One could not follow the path described above and define religion to include secular but deeply held beliefs, as one would then be placed in the absurd position of defending secular ideas from attack by reference to a right to *religious* freedom. Nor could one overcome this difficulty by adopting a pragmatic stance and framing a statute protecting only the five major world religions. If the individual's right to religious freedom demands protection against vilificatory attacks upon her religion,[261] and since presumably members of less well known religions are as entitled to religious freedom as members of the major religions, it follows that they must also be entitled to protection against such attacks. Clearly, therefore, a satisfactory definition of religion would have to be arrived at. The difficulties of framing such a definition have already been noted. In this connection, it is also worth recalling that the UN General Assembly *Declaration on the Elimination of All Forms of Intolerance and Discrimination Based on Religion and Belief*, as one commentator notes, 'does not seek to define religion or belief'. He explains: 'This is because no definition could be agreed upon, as none could be agreed when the texts of Article 18 of the Universal Declaration and Article 18 of the ICCPR were drafted.'[262] Since, therefore, the impossibility of framing such a definition seems to be well attested to, it may reasonably be concluded that the project to extend blasphemy law to cover other faiths is fraught with difficulty.

On all these grounds, it is concluded that the argument that freedom of religion demands a blasphemy law, fails. It follows, if this view is accepted, that the abolition of the current law can readily be defended on Art 10 grounds without fear of offending against Art 9. Christian beliefs and doctrines could, therefore, be placed in the same position as Islamic or deeply held secular beliefs in that its adherents can choose to avert their eyes from distasteful portrayals of their beliefs, and to combat what they regard as untrue or unfair representations with – in their view – more truthful or more inspirational speech. In both *Wingrove* and *Otto-Preminger*, it was very unlikely that a religious adherent who might be offended would unwittingly view the film.

Abolition of the blasphemy law would tend to ease racial tension since at least it would be clear that all religions were being accorded an equal lack of protection. This would be the better solution, since it is by no means clear that extending blasphemy law would ease the problem. Indeed, it is possible that if, for example, Muslims had been able to use an extended blasphemy law to suppress *The Satanic Verses*,[263] considerable

---

260 Poulter concedes that his proposed extension of the blasphemy law (see *op cit*, fn 256, p 378 *et seq*) might well have caught *The Satanic Verses* (pp 384–85).

261 This proposition is not conceded as indicated. It is put forward by Poulter, 'Towards legislative reform of the blasphemy and racial hatred laws' [1991] PL 371–85.

262 Boyle, K, 'Religious intolerance and the incitement of hatred', in Coliver (ed), *Striking a Balance: Hate Speech, Freedom of Expression and Non-discrimination*, 1992.

263 See Poulter, *op cit*, fn 256.

resentment might well have been engendered in the non-Muslim community. The justified grievance felt by Muslims about the unfairness of the present law would, to a certain extent, be remedied if blasphemy was abolished altogether as an offence.

Incitement to religious hatred: extending the offence of incitement to racial hatred?

The International Covenant on Civil and Political Rights, to which the UK is a signatory, requires Contracting States to prohibit the advocacy of 'national, racial or *religious* hatred that constitutes incitement to discrimination, hostility or violence' (Art 20, emphasis added). In practical terms, it would be fairly straightforward to amend ss 17–23 of Part III of the Public Order Act 1986 which, as indicated below, prohibit incitement to racial hatred,[264] to include religious groups.[265] At the present time cl 38 the Anti-Terrorism, Crime and Security Bill 2001 provides for such amendation. The problem of defining religion, of course, still remains. However, since such incitement represents a far narrower area of liability than blasphemy, the danger that a wide interpretation of 'religion' would lead to the courts being overrun by claims from obscure groups is accordingly less great. Furthermore, prosecutions in this area can only be brought with the consent of the DPP, so the possibility of frivolous prosecutions being brought would be slight. The justification sometimes put forward for abrogating free speech in this area is that prohibiting the advocacy of racial hatred does not strike at the core value of free speech because neither individual self-fulfilment, nor the opportunity to arrive at the truth through free discussion, nor the chance to participate meaningfully in democracy[266] seem to be strongly threatened by such a prohibition.

Such an extension would, of course, still represent an interference with the individual's moral autonomy, since it amounts to judging both for him and his possible audience what is and is not fit for them to hear. However, the State is supposed to leave such judgments to the individual because to do otherwise would be to violate the individual's basic right to equal concern and respect[267] and it may be argued that the present situation, in which the advocacy of hatred against Muslims is allowed, while Sikhs and Jews are protected from such speech,[268] *itself* amounts to a denial of equal

---

264 For discussion of racial hatred in the context of freedom of speech, see Robertson and Nichol, *op cit*, fn 109, Chapter 3, pp 129–32; Barendt, *op cit*, fn 3, pp 161–67 and generally Cotterell, R [1982] PL 378; Dickey [1968] Crim LR 489; Gordon, *Incitement to Racial Hatred*, 1982; Leopold, P [1977] PL 389; Wolffe [1987] PL 85. For the argument that the State should seek to ban racially motivated hate speech on the basis of furtherance of equality just as it seeks to outlaw discrimination in employment, see MacKinnon, *op cit*, fn 36. For criticism of the argument, see Sadurski, W, 'On "Seeing speech through an equality lens": a critique of egalitarian arguments for suppression of hate speech and pornography' (1996) 16(4) OJLS 713.

265 The definition under the Race Relations Act of 'racial group' which will be used under the Public Order Act 1986 does not include religious groups; see *Mandla v Dowell Lee* [1983] 2 AC 548; [1983] 1 All ER 1062, HL. But discrimination on grounds of religion can be viewed as indirect racial discrimination.

266 See above, pp 203–04.

267 See, eg, Dworkin, R, *op cit*, fn 6.

268 Muslims, unlike Sikhs and Jews, are not defined as a racial, as well as religious, group. See the definition from *Mandla v Dowell Lee* [1983] 2 AC 548; [1983] 1 All ER 1062, HL, discussed below, p 1002. But prejudice against Muslims can be viewed as indirect racial discrimination; see Chapter 16, pp 1016–17.

respect for Muslims.[269] Accordingly, there appears to be an arguable case that the Public Order Act provisions should be extended to cover religious hatred: the interference with moral autonomy involved is necessary to avoid discrimination and there is an argument that the free speech interest involved is relatively weak; in addition, there are strong utilitarian arguments that such a measure would considerably ease racial tension.

The argument above is, however, predicated on the assumption that the prohibition of incitement to racial hatred under the Public Order Act does not *already* create an unacceptable infringement of freedom of speech. However, as pointed out below, it may be argued that the offences as currently conceived go beyond the mischief that they are intended to prevent. There is an argument that some provision should be available to prevent some forms of racist speech owing to its special propensity to lead to disorder and that such protection should be extended to religious groups, but it is argued that one could comfortably support the addition of incitement to religious hatred to Public Order Act offences only once they had been reformed to encompass a much more narrowly targeted area of liability.

Hate speech: stirring up racial hatred[270]

Domestic provisions

The offence of stirring up racial hatred was introduced under s 6 of the Race Relations Act 1965, in order to meet public order concerns and protect persons from the effects on others of provocative and inflammatory racist expression. The Public Order Act 1936 was amended in order to include this offence, but Part III (ss 17–23) of the Public Order Act 1986 extends its ambit. Section 18 provides that liability will arise if threatening, abusive or insulting words or behaviour are used or written material of that nature is displayed, intended by the defendant to stir up racial hatred or which make it likely that racial hatred will be stirred up against a racial group (not a religious group) in Great Britain.[271] Where intent is not shown, it is necessary to show that the accused realised that the words used might be threatening, abusive or insulting.[272] Section 18(2) catches private or public meetings (unless held in a 'dwelling'). Section 19 makes it an offence to publish threatening, abusive or insulting material, either intended by the defendant to stir up racial hatred or which make it likely that racial hatred will be stirred up against a racial group. Section 21 extends the offence to the distributing, showing or playing of visual images or sounds. Section 20 makes it an offence to stir up racial hatred in the public

---

269 It might be argued from this that all measures prohibiting incitement to racial hatred should be repealed, but this is not a practicable possibility and would involve the UK in an even clearer breach of Art 20 of the ICCPR than is currently being committed by the lack of protection for Muslims.

270 For general discussion of this offence and its background, see Bindman, G (1982) 132 NLJ 299; Cotterell, *op cit*, fn 264; Gordon, *op cit*, fn 264; Williams, DGT [1966] Crim LR 320; Leopold, *op cit*, fn 264; Wolffe, W [1987] PL 85.

271 'Racial group' is defined using the same terms as under the Race Relations Act; see Chapter 16, p 1002. The result is that, eg, hatred may be stirred up against Muslims – so long as the offence under the 1986 Act, s 5 (see Chapter 9, pp 506–08) is not committed – but not against Sikhs.

272 Section 18(5) governs the *mens rea* if it is not shown that the defendant intended to stir up racial hatred. He must intend the words, etc, to be or be aware that they might be, threatening, abusive or insulting. Awareness as used in the 1986 Act seems to mean subjective recklessness.

performance of a play, but the likelihood that hatred will be stirred up must be judged by reference to 'all the circumstances' and 'in particular taking the performance as a whole'. Therefore, the context in which, for example, a character is racially abused must be considered: where the message of the play as a whole could not be viewed as one aimed at stirring up racial hatred, the offence will not be committed. Thus, plays that explore the theme of racism in society should escape liability.

Section 22 makes it an offence to use threatening, abusive or insulting visual images or sounds in a programme, intended by the defendant to stir up racial hatred, or which make it likely that racial hatred will be stirred up against a racial group. Section 164(2) of the Broadcasting Act 1990 amended s 22 so that it covers 'programme services', including cable programme services. The offence under s 22 can be committed by the programme producer, director, the television company and any person 'by whom the offending words or behaviour are used'. This is a broadly worded offence which encourages caution in producing programmes about the problem of racism, since it can be committed without any intent on the part of the producer or the company. Programmes can only be shown if it is made clear, editorially, that the message of racists is disapproved of. Section 23 of the 1986 Act places further obstacles in the way of those producing programmes about racism, particularly historical programmes. Section 23, as amended by s 164(4) of the Broadcasting Act 1990, creates an offence of possessing racially inflammatory (threatening, abusive or insulting) material with a view, in the case of written material, to publication or distribution and, in the case of a recording, to its being distributed, shown, played or included in a programme service, intended by the person possessing it to stir up racial hatred or which makes it likely, having regard to all the circumstances, that racial hatred will be stirred up. Television researchers must be sure that historical material will be placed in a context which makes it clear that its message is disapproved of.

These offences have a number of elements in common. None of them requires a need to show that disorder was caused, or that there was an intent to cause disorder, and there is no need to show that racial hatred is actually stirred up. It is not an essential ingredient to show that there was an intent to stir up racial hatred. It is sufficient to show that hatred *might* actually be stirred up. In that circumstance, s 18 imports an element of *mens rea*, but the other sections do not, a very significant difference.[273] The offence might be committed by broadcasting or using or promulgating words or material by the methods indicated above, threatening, abusive or insulting matter which, objectively speaking, is incapable of stirring up racial hatred so long as the accused intended that it should do so. It may be noted that the s 18 offence is the only public order offence which may be committed by words alone unaccompanied by the need – as an essential ingredient – to show any likelihood that they would cause distress, since the offence could be committed by uttering words which were greeted with delight by those who heard them. But of most significance is the possibility that criminal liability can arise owing to the promulgation of material likely to stir up racial hatred unintentionally.

These offences represent a restriction based on manner rather than content due to their specific requirements. Reasoned argument of a racist nature would not incur

---

273 See above, fn 272. The other sections provide a defence – in effect, a reversed *mens rea*: the defendant could prove that he was not aware of the content of the recording/material/broadcast and had no reason to suspect that it was threatening, etc.

liability, since the racist words or material must be threatening, abusive or insulting. Further, the term 'hatred' is a strong one: merely causing offence or bringing into ridicule is not enough and nor is racial harassment. Thus, the offences are narrowly conceived; although they cover political expression, they concentrate on the *manner* of the expression. Further, it is hard to conceive that the manner – threats, abuse, insults – could itself be defended by reference to the free speech justifications discussed in the Introduction to Part II. Where the threat, etc, is thematically appropriate since it is placed within a context, such as a play or film touching on the theme or subject of racism, it will probably fall outside the area of liability, since all the circumstances must be taken into account. However, the breadth of the offences relating to broadcasting are, as suggested above, likely to deter the production of documentaries dealing with the subject of racism. This position will be greatly exacerbated if cl 38 of the Anti-Terrorism Bill becomes law. Those provisions in particular may be called into question under the HRA.

Impact of the HRA

Is expression likely to stir up racial hatred covered by Art 10(1)? In other words, would it be viewed as protected expression at all? In *Lehideux and Isornia v France*[274] it was found that if material is directed towards attacking the Convention's underlying values, it will be outside the protection of Art 10.[275] In that instance, the material supported a pro-Nazi policy. However, in *Kuhnen v FRG*,[276] Art 10 was found to cover the conviction of the applicant for advocating the reinstitution of the Nazi Party, although the interference was justified under Art 10(2). Similarly, Art 10 applied in *Glimmerveen and Hagenbeeck v Netherlands*. The applicants had been convicted of possessing leaflets which incited racial discrimination. The interference was found to be justified under Art 10(2). In that instance, Art 17 was relied upon.[277] Where racist expression is concerned, reliance on Art 17, either in addition to Art 10(2) or alone, tends to produce the same result: the interference is found to be justified and the review is not intensive.[278]

Jersild[279] concerned an application by a Danish journalist who had been convicted of an offence of racially offensive speech after preparing and broadcasting a programme about racism which included overtly racist speech by the subjects of the documentary. A breach of Art 10 was found. The interference with expression was found to be disproportionate to the aim pursued – protecting the rights of others. The Court stressed that its finding was directed to the value of enabling the media to act as a public watchdog. The news value of the programme was a matter that could be best assessed by professional journalists. The Court also considered that the mode of presenting the broadcast should be determined by journalists. Had the racists who spoke on the programme applied to Strasbourg, their own convictions would have been found to be justified under Art 10(2), if indeed Art 10(1) would have been applicable, which is doubtful.

---

274 (1998) 5 BHRC 540.

275 *Ibid*, p 558, para 53.

276 (1988) 56 DR 205.

277 (1979) 18 DR 187. See Chapter 2, p 89.

278 See *X v Germany* (1982) 29 DR 194; *T v Belgium* (1983) 34 DR 158; *H, W, P and K v Austria* (1989) 62 DR 216.

279 *Jersild v Denmark* (1994) 19 EHRR 1.

It seems to be clear that persons directly using threatening or abusive or insulting speech likely to stir up racial hatred would not obtain any benefit by invoking Art 10. But the position of those who aid in the dissemination of such speech, who do not have the purpose of stirring up racial hatred, is different. It is arguable that UK law does not draw a sufficiently clear distinction between the two groups. *Jersild* suggests that the restrictions on broadcasting in relation to racial hatred are open to challenge under the HRA since it would seem possible that if an equivalent situation arose in the UK, the presenter and producer of the programme could be convicted of the offence under s 22 of the 1986 Act. Possibly television researchers involved could also be convicted of the broader offence under s 23.

If cl 38 of the Anti-Terrorism, Crime and Security Bill 2001 becomes law, so that in all the contexts mentioned offences of stirring up religious hatred can also be committed, the effect on freedom of expression will be very significant. However, the impact of the provisions can be curbed. Prosecutions for the offences of stirring up racial or religious hatred can only be brought with the consent of the Attorney-General, which has so far been sparingly given in respect of race hatred. Since the Attorney-General is a public authority under the HRA, he or she should give careful consideration to Art 10 before giving consent. If prosecutions are brought, the courts are in the same position. They need not, as argued above, give weight to Art 9, on the ground that protection for religious freedom does not include protection against attacks on religion. The term 'hatred' should be given full weight, while the term 'insulting' should, it is argued, be interpreted as meaning – insulting to the reasonable, tolerant religious adherent rather than in relation to adherents of a particular sect (or group within a religion) which may be of an extreme nature.

Section 3 of the HRA could be relied upon, if necessary, to interpret the term 'circumstances' used in ss 19-22 of the 1986 Act, as amended by the 2001 Act. The term is used, as indicated above, in respect of material likely to stir up racial or religious hatred rather than in respect of instances where the defendant intended to do so. No 'public good' defence is included in the 1986 Act or in the current version of cl 38 of the Anti-terrorism, Crime and Security Bill 2001. But consideration of the 'circumstances' could include consideration of the extent to which the broadcast or other material was for the public good in terms of its artistic or other merit. Since this is a strained interpretation, s 3 of the HRA might need to be relied upon, in order to achieve compatibility with the demands of Art 10 in respect of a particular provision, in particular ss 22 and 23 of the 1986 Act, as amended. If there was a problem with compatibility in the particular instance s 6 of the HRA could be relied upon, to find an application of the provision in question which would allow – in effect – for the worth of the material to be taken into account,

It may be noted that the 2001 Bill was accompanied by a statement of compatibility under s 19 of the HRA. But, as Chapter 4 argues, such a statement leaves the judges free to consider compatibility afresh. It may be argued that rather than strive to ensure compatibility, a declaration of incompatibility should be made in order to mark the dangerous potential of the new provisions and to invite Parliament to think again.

6 CONCLUSIONS

The Williams Committee recommended in 1979 that the printed word should not be subject to any restraint and that other material should be restrained on the basis of two specific tests: first, material which might shock should be available only through restricted outlets; second, material should not be *prohibited* unless it could be shown to cause specific harm.[280] Clearly, these proposals would give greater weight to freedom of expression than is currently given, in that they would allow greater differentiation between the kinds of harm which might be caused by different forms of material, an emphasis on inquiring into whether harm is or could be caused by the promulgation of pornography to a willing adult audience, and in particular they could have led to the abolition of the uncertain and almost unworkable 'deprave and corrupt' test. The Committee emphasised a fundamental difference between the *prohibition* and the *restriction* of the sale of pornography and other explicit material.

These proposals found partial expression in the Indecent Displays (Control) Act 1981, the provisions under the Local Government (Miscellaneous Provisions) Act 1982 for regulating 'sex establishments' and the Cinematograph (Amendment) Act 1982, which changed the classification of films and in particular introduced the 'R18' rating. The proposal as to removing the prohibition as opposed to restriction from the written word and from much other pornographic material has not been implemented[281] and various far reaching restraints remain, including the use of forfeiture proceedings and the uncertain offence of outraging public decency, both tending to undermine the safeguards for artistic freedom contained in the 1959 Act.

It seems that, if there is to be radical reform of the law relating to obscenity, indecency and censorship, the government will have to take the initiative. As indicated, the inception of the HRA is unlikely to bring about sweeping change. The UK position in respect of restraints on freedom of speech in the name of the protection of morality does not appear to breach Art 10. In any event, the preoccupation of the domestic judiciary with the value of *political* expression and decisions such as those in *Knuller* and *Gibson* do not suggest that there is a determination on the part of the judiciary to import greater certainty and liberality into the restriction and regulation of explicit expression. Similarly, after the decisions in the *Handyside* case and in *Müller v Switzerland*,[282] it seems unlikely that there will be any UK move towards greater protection of freedom of speech in this area by recourse to the European Convention on Human Rights at Strasbourg. It may be assumed that the exception contained in Art 10(2) in respect of the protection of morals will continue to be widely interpreted because the European Court of Human Rights will continue to allow a wide margin of appreciation to Member States in this very sensitive area. However, as indicated above, there are strong grounds for expecting the domestic judiciary to take a stance under the HRA towards expression offensive to religious sensibilities which differs from that taken at Strasbourg. In so far as political expression is

---

280 See Williams Committee, *op cit*, fn 17; Simpson, *op cit*, fn 4; for commentary, see McKean, WA [1980] CLJ 10; Coldham, S (1980) 43 MLR 306; Dworkin, *op cit*, fn 77.

281 For further discussion of the Committee's position, see above, p 270.

282 See further Feingold, C, 'The Little Red Schoolbook and the European Court of Human Rights' (1978) Revue des Droits de l'Homme 21.

affected, especially by aspects of media regulation, the domestic judiciary now have the opportunity to take a more intrusive stance towards furthering the protection of such expression, under the HRA. This may be a very important development in the domestic *political* expression jurisprudence.

CHAPTER 7

OFFICIAL SECRECY AND ACCESS TO INFORMATION

1 INTRODUCTION[1]

An assertion of a right to access to information can be distinguished from an assertion of a free speech right, although the two are clearly linked.[2] This distinction receives support from the wording of Art 10 of the European Convention, which speaks in terms of the freedom to 'receive and impart information', thus appearing to exclude from its provisions the right to demand information from the unwilling speaker. Moreover, the phrase 'without interference from public authorities' does not suggest that governments should come under any duty to act in order to ensure that information is received.

There are at least three reasons why access to information is often treated as a distinct interest. First, freedom of information can be justified by reference to values that go beyond those underlying freedom of speech. It is generally accepted that the quality of decision making will improve if access to official information allows citizens to scrutinise the workings of the government and public authorities generally. Moreover, the accountability of the government to the public is increased, since pressure can more readily be brought to bear on the government regarding the effects of its policies and citizens are able to make a more informed choice at election times.

Secondly, information may be sought although it is not intended that it should be communicated to others. It is not clear that the free speech justifications considered in the Introduction to Part II would apply to such a situation, and therefore it would tend to be considered purely as an access to information or privacy issue. Indeed, in such instances, the seeker of information might well be asserting a right not merely to gain access to the information, but also to have its confidential quality maintained. Access rights under the Data Protection Act 1998 often take account of both interests, as discussed in Chapter 10, and therefore may be said to be opposed to free speech interests. Thus, it is clear that many demands for access to information are not based on an assertion of free speech interests. Thirdly, information intended to be placed in the public domain may be sought when there is no speaker willing to disclose it, or where the body which 'owns' the information is unwilling that it should be disclosed. Whether such communication of

---

1   General reading, see: Hartley, T and Griffiths, J, *Government and Law*, 1981, Chapter 13; Williams, DGT, *Not in the Public Interest*, 1965; Leigh, D, *The Frontiers of Secrecy – Closed Government in Britain*, 1980; Michael, J, *The Politics of Secrecy*, 1982; Robertson, G, *Public Secrets*, 1982; Wilson, D, *The Secrets File*, 1984; Wass, D, *Government and the Governed*, 1984, p 81 *et seq*; Birkinshaw, P, *Freedom of Information: The Law, the Practice and the Ideal*, 3rd edn, 2001; Ewing, KD and Gearty, CA, *Freedom Under Thatcher*, 1990, Chapter 6; Birkinshaw, P, *Government and Information*, 1990; Vincent, *The Culture of Secrecy, Britain 1832–1998*, 1998; Feldman, D, *Civil Liberties and Human Rights in England and Wales*, 2nd edn, 2002, Chapter 14; Bailey, SH, Harris, DJ and Jones, BL, *Civil Liberties: Cases and Materials*, 4th edn, 1995, Chapter 7; Baxter, JD, *State Security, Privacy and Information*, 1990; Shetreet, S (ed), *Free Speech and National Security*, 1991; Gill, P, *Policing Politics: Security, Intelligence and the Liberal Democratic State*, 1994; Lustgarten, L and Leigh, I, *In From the Cold: National Security and Parliamentary Democracy*, 1994; Whitty, N, Murphy, T and Livingstone, S, *Civil Liberties Law*, 2001, Chapter 7.
2   See further Barendt, E, *Freedom of Speech*, 1987, pp 167–72.

confidential information should be regarded as 'speech' or not,[3] it is clearly a necessary precondition for the production of speech and therefore can be treated as deserving of the same protection as 'speech' in that the result will be that the public will be informed and debate on issues of public interest will not be stifled. The argument that such dissemination of information will render the government more readily accountable is strongly related to the justification for free speech discussed in the Introduction to Part II,[4] which argues that it is indispensable to democracy, since it enables informed participation by the citizenry.

However, freedom of speech guarantees, including Art 10, do not tend to encompass the imposition of positive obligations and therefore, in general, are violated when a willing speaker is prevented from speaking rather than in the situation where information deriving ultimately from an unwilling speaker – usually the government – is sought, entailing the assertion of a positive right. Thus, a distinction should be drawn between gaining access to the information and then placing it in the public domain – the second situation giving rise to a free speech interest. However, these issues have tended to arise together within the legal scheme in the UK, which has traditionally protected a 'closed' system of government; it is therefore convenient to consider both within the same chapter.

As these remarks indicate, Art 10 of the Human Rights Act cannot be expected to have much impact on *access* to information, in the sense of using Art 10 to create an access right. The Freedom of Information (FoI) Act, introduced in 2000, provides for the first time a statutory right of access to official information. However, it is suggested that Art 10 can be relied upon in relation to the dissemination of information once obtained, as a means of interpreting the provisions of the new FoI Act.

Rights of access to information overlap with certain privacy interests since they may cover many situations in which a person might wish to receive information, apart from that of the individual who wishes to obtain and publicise government information. However, freedom of information is most readily associated with the demand for the receipt of information with a view to placing it in the public domain; thus the rights of the individual who wishes to receive information for his or her *private* purposes will be considered in Chapter 10.

Probably the most important value associated with freedom of information is the need for the citizen to understand as fully as possible the working of government, in order to render it accountable; one of the main concerns of this chapter is therefore with the methods employed by governments to ensure that official information cannot fall into the hands of those who might place it in the public domain, and with methods of preventing or deterring persons from publication when such information has been

---

3   The European Court of Human Rights takes the view that it should not. In the *Gaskin* case (1990) 12 EHRR 36 it viewed a demand for access to information which the body holding it did not wish to disclose as giving rise only to an Art 8 issue, not an Art 10 issue. The US Supreme Court has held that the First Amendment does not impose an affirmative duty on government to make information not in the public domain available to journalists (417 US 817). For discussion of this issue see Barendt, *op cit*, fn 2, pp 107–13.

4   See pp 202–03.

obtained. This chapter also places a strong emphasis on the choices that were made as to the release of information relating to public authorities – not only to central government – in the FoI Act 2000.

The key concern of this chapter is with the degree to which a proper balance has been and is currently being struck between the interest of the individual in acquiring information and the interest of the State and public authorities in withholding it. Clearly, there are genuine public interests, including that of protecting national security, in keeping some information out of the public domain; the question is whether other interests which do not correspond with and may even be opposed to the interests of the public are also at work. Initially, it may be said that in the UK, the area of control over government information is one in which the State's supposed interest in keeping information secret has often prevailed very readily over the individual interest in question. Frequently, the justifications put forward for preventing access to information could not conceivably be brought within one of the three justifications broadly accepted by liberal political theory as allowing the infringement of individual rights.[5]

It has often been said that the UK is more obsessed with keeping government information secret than any other Western democracy.[6] It is clearly advantageous for the party in power to be able to control the flow of information in order to prevent public scrutiny of certain official decisions and in order to be able to release information selectively at convenient moments.

The British Government has available a number of methods of keeping official information secret, including use of the doctrine of Public Interest Immunity (PII), the deterrent effect of criminal sanctions under the Official Secrets Act 1989, the Civil Service Conduct Code,[7] around 80 statutory provisions engendering secrecy in various areas and the civil action for breach of confidence. The situation of the civil servant in the UK who believes that disclosure as to a certain state of affairs is necessary in order to serve the public interest, may therefore be contrasted with the situation of his or her counterpart in the US, where he or she would receive protection from detrimental action flowing from whistle-blowing[8] under the Civil Service Reform Act 1978. A weak form of a public interest defence might have been adopted under proposals in the government White Paper on freedom of information, published in July 1993.[9] It was proposed that the disclosure of information would not be penalised if the information was not 'genuinely confidential'. But when the Labour Government introduced the Public Interest Disclosure Act 1998, crown servants involved in security and intelligence activities, or those whose 'whistle-blowing' breaches the 1989 Act, were expressly excluded from its ambit, leaving them unprotected from employment detriment.

The justification traditionally put forward for maintaining a climate of secrecy, which goes beyond protecting specific public interests such as national security, is that freedom of information would adversely affect 'ministerial accountability'. In other words,

---

5   For an explanation of these three justifications, see Chapter 1, pp 11–13.

6   Eg, Robertson, G, *Freedom, the Individual and the Law*, 1989, pp 129–31.

7   See Drewry and Butcher, *The Civil Service Today*, 1991. It should be pointed out that the Civil Service Code, which came into force on 1 January 1996, contains a partial 'whistle-blowing' provision in paras 11–12.

8   For discussion of the situation of UK and US civil servants and developments in the area, see Cripps, Y, 'Disclosure in the public interest: the predicament of the public sector employee' [1983] PL 600; Zellick, 'Whistle-blowing in US law' [1987] PL 311–13; Starke (1989) 63 ALJ 592–94.

9   *Open Government*, 1993, HMSO. See below, pp 371–73 for discussion.

ministers are responsible for the actions of civil servants in their departments and therefore must be able to control the flow of information emanating from the department in question. However, it is usually seen as essential to democracy that government should allow a reasonably free flow of information so that citizens can be informed as to the government process and can therefore assess government decisions in the light of all the available facts, thereby participating fully in the workings of the democracy. A number of groups, including the Campaign for Freedom of Information, have therefore advocated freedom of information and more 'open' government in Britain, as in most other democracies. They accept that certain categories of information should be exempt from disclosure, but argue that those categories should be as restricted as possible compatible with the needs of the interest protected, and that the categorisation of any particular piece of information should be open to challenge.

The citizen's 'right to know' is recognised in most democracies including the US, Canada, Australia, New Zealand, Denmark, Sweden, Holland, Norway, Greece and France. In such countries, the general principle of freedom of information is subject to exceptions where information falls into specific categories. Perhaps responding to the general acceptance of freedom of information, there was a shift in the attitude of the Conservative Government of 1992–97 to freedom of information in the UK in 1992: that is, the principle was accepted, but the traditional stance as to the role of the law hardly changed. The UK has traditionally resisted freedom of information legislation and, until 1989, criminalised the unauthorised disclosure of any official information at all, however trivial, under s 2 of the Official Secrets Act 1911, thereby creating a climate of secrecy in the Civil Service which greatly hampered the efforts of those who wished to obtain and publish information about the workings of government. The Freedom of Information Act 2000 signalled a break with the traditional culture of secrecy: 'the principle that communication was the privilege of the State rather than of the citizen was at last ... reversed.'[10] The Act, introduced by the current Labour Government, extends well beyond government departments. The part it may play once it is fully in force (by 2005) in introducing a climate of openness in the Civil Service, and in public authorities more generally, is one of the central concerns of this chapter.

2 OFFICIAL SECRECY

Section 2 of the Official Secrets Act 1911[11]

During the 19th century, as government departments grew larger and handled more official information, the problem of confidentiality grew more acute. Internal circulars such as the 1873 Treasury minute entitled *The Premature Disclosure of Official Information* urged secrecy on all members of government departments and threatened the dismissal of civil servants who disclosed any information; a Treasury minute issued in 1875 warned civil servants of the dangers of close links with the press.[12] The need for a further

---

10   Vincent, *The Culture of Secrecy, Britain 1832–1998*, 1998, p 321.

11   See Hooper, D, *Official Secrets*, 1987, for history of the use of s 2.

12   See Robertson, *op cit*, fn 1, p 53.

safeguard was emphasised in 1878 when one Marvin, who worked in the Foreign Office, gave details of a secret treaty negotiated between England and Russia to a particular newspaper. His motive appeared to be dissatisfaction with his job. He was prosecuted, but it was then discovered that no part of the criminal law covered the situation. He had memorised the information and thus had not stolen any document. He was not a spy and could not, therefore, be brought within the provisions of the Treason Act 1814. No conviction could be obtained and the Official Secrets Act 1889 was passed largely as a means of plugging the gap which had been discovered.

The 1889 Act made it an offence for a person wrongfully to communicate information obtained owing to his employment as a civil servant. However, the government grew dissatisfied with this measure; under its terms, the State had the burden of proving both *mens rea* and that the disclosure was not in the interests of the State. It was thought that a stronger measure was needed, and this led eventually to the passing of the Official Secrets Act 1911. It has often been suggested that the manner of its introduction into Parliament was disingenuous and misleading.[13] It was introduced apparently in response to fears of espionage and by the Secretary of State for War, not by the Home Secretary, giving the impression that it was largely an anti-espionage measure. Section 1 did deal largely with espionage, but s 2 was aimed not at enemy agents, but at English civil servants and other Crown employees. It was called, innocuously, 'an Act to re-enact the 1889 Act with amendments'. These disarming measures seem to have succeeded; it was passed in one afternoon and s 2 received no debate at all.

Section 2, which appeared to create a crime of strict liability, imposed a complete prohibition on the unauthorised dissemination of official information, however trivial. It is thought that the government clearly intended s 2 to have such a wide scope and had wanted such a provision for some time in order to prevent leaks of *any* kind of official information, whether or not connected with defence or national security.[14] It lacked any provision regarding the substance of the information disclosed so that technically it criminalised, for example, disclosure of the colour of the carpet in a minister's office. It criminalised the receiver of information as well as the communicator, although there did appear to be a requirement of *mens rea* as far as the receiver was concerned; he or she had to know that the disclosure had occurred in contravention of the Act. Thus, it afforded no recognition to the role of the press in informing the public.

There were surprisingly few prosecutions under s 2; it seems likely that it created an acceptance of secrecy in the civil service which tended to preclude disclosure. In one of the few cases which did come to court, *Fell*,[15] the Court of Appeal confirmed that liability was not dependent on the contents of the document in question or on whether the disclosure would have an effect prejudicial to the interests of the State. The eventual demise of s 2 came about owing to a number of factors, of which one appears to have been the realisation that its draconian nature was perceived as unacceptable in a modern democracy and that therefore, convictions under it could not be assured. Such a realisation probably developed in response to the following three decisions.

---

13   See *The Franks Report*, Cmnd 5104, 1972, para 50; Birkinshaw, *op cit*, fn 1, p 76.
14   See *ibid*, para 50.
15   [1963] Crim LR 207.

Aitken and Others[16] arose from the disclosure by a reporter, Aitken, that the UK Government had misled the British people as to the amount of aid the UK was giving Nigeria in its war against Biafra. The Government had suggested that it was supplying about 15% of Nigeria's arms, whereas the figure should have been about 70%. This figure derived from a government document called the Scott Report, which Aitken disclosed to the press. Aitken was then prosecuted under s 2 for receiving and passing on information, but the judge at trial, Caulfield J, clearly had little sympathy with a case seemingly brought merely to assuage government embarrassment and which disclosed no national security interest. Furthermore, the facts obtained from the Scott Report were obtainable from other sources. The judge found that a requirement of *mens rea* was needed and, moreover, effectively directed the jury to acquit in a speech which placed weight on the freedom of the press and suggested that it should prevail given the lack of a significant competing interest. He considered that s 2 should be 'pensioned off'.

Tisdall[17] also created some adverse publicity for the government owing to what was perceived as a very heavy handed use of s 2. Sarah Tisdall worked in the Foreign Secretary's private office, and in the course of her duties she came across documents relating to the delivery of cruise missiles to the RAF base at Greenham Common. She discovered proposals to delay the announcement of their delivery until after it had occurred and to make the announcement in Parliament at the end of question time in order to avoid answering questions. She took the view that this political subterfuge was morally wrong and therefore leaked the documents to the *Guardian*. However, they were eventually traced back to her. She pleaded guilty to an offence under s 2 and received a prison sentence of six months – an outcome which was generally seen as harsh.[18]

A similar situation arose in *Ponting*,[19] the case which is usually credited with sounding the death knell of s 2. Clive Ponting, a senior civil servant in the Ministry of Defence, was responsible for policy on the operational activities of the Royal Navy at a time when opposition MPs, particularly Tam Dalyell, were pressing the government for information relating to the sinking of the *Belgrano* in the Falklands conflict. Michael Heseltine, then Secretary of State for Defence, decided to withhold such information from Parliament and therefore did not use a reply to parliamentary questions drafted by Ponting. He used instead a much briefer version of it and circulated a confidential minute indicating that answers on the rules of engagement in the Falklands conflict should not be given to questions put by the Parliamentary Select Committee on Foreign Affairs. Feeling that opposition MPs were being prevented from undertaking effective scrutiny of the workings of government, Ponting sent the unused reply and the minute anonymously to the Labour MP, Tam Dalyell, who disclosed the documents to the press.

Ponting was charged with the offence of communicating information under s 2. The relevant sub-section reads:

> ... it is an offence for a person holding Crown office to communicate official information to any person other than a person he is authorised to communicate it to or a person to whom it is *in the interests of the State* his duty to communicate it. [Emphasis added.]

---

16 Unreported. See Aitken, J, *Officially Secret*, 1971.

17 (1984) *The Times*, 26 March.

18 See Cripps, *op cit*, fn 8.

19 [1985] Crim LR 318; for comment, see Brewry, G, 'The *Ponting* case' [1985] PL 203, 212 and [1986] Crim LR 491.

The defence relied on the phrase the 'interests of the State', arguing that the term 'the State' should be interpreted as 'the organised community' rather than the government. This interpretation seemed to be warranted by part of Lord Reid's judgment in *Chandler v DPP*.[20] Thus, it could be argued that it was in the interests of the nation as a whole that Parliament should not be misled and that there was a moral duty to prevent this. The word 'duty' in s 2, it was claimed, therefore connoted a moral or public duty. However, the Crown relied upon other comments of Lord Reid in *Chandler* to the effect that where national security was a factor, the government would be the final arbiter of the State's interests. The judge, McCowan J, accepted this argument, finding that the 'interests of the State' were synonymous with those of the government of the day, and he therefore effectively directed the jury to convict. Despite this direction, they acquitted, presumably feeling that Ponting should have a defence if he was acting in the public interest in trying to prevent government suppression of matters of public interest. The prosecution and its outcome provoked a large amount of adverse publicity, the public perceiving it as an attempt at a cover up which had failed, not because the judge showed integrity, but because the jury did.[21]

The decision in *Ponting* suggested that the very width of s 2 was undermining its credibility; its usefulness in instilling a culture of secrecy owing to its catch-all quality was seen as working against it. The outcome of the case may have influenced the decision not to prosecute Cathy Massiter, a former officer in the Security Service, in respect of her claims in a Channel 4 programme screened in March 1985 (*MI5's Official Secrets*) that MI5 had tapped the phones of trade union members and placed leading CND members under surveillance.[22] Section 2's lack of credibility may also have been a factor in the decision to bring civil as opposed to criminal proceedings against *The Guardian* and *The Observer* in respect of their disclosure of Peter Wright's allegations in Spycatcher: civil proceedings for breach of confidence were, in many ways, more convenient and certainly less risky than a s 2 prosecution. No jury would be involved and a temporary injunction could be obtained quickly in *ex parte* proceedings. However, the government did consider that the criminal rather than the civil law was, in general, a more appropriate weapon to use against people such as Ponting, and therefore thought it desirable that an effective criminal sanction should be available. When the government was eventually defeated in the *Spycatcher* litigation, the need for such a sanction became clearer.[23]

There had already been a long history of proposals for the reform of s 2. The Franks Committee, which was set up in response to Caulfield J's comments in *Aitken*, recommended[24] that s 2 should be replaced by narrower provisions which took into account the nature of the information disclosed. The Franks proposals formed the basis of

---

20   [1964] AC 763; [1962] 3 All ER 142, HL.

21   For comment on the decision, see Ponting, C, *The Right to Know*, 1985; Brewry, *op cit*, fn 19.

22   The Independent Broadcasting Association banned the programme pending the decision as to whether Massiter and the producers would be prosecuted. The decision not to prosecute was announced by Sir Michael Havers on 5 March 1985. An inquiry into telephone tapping by Lord Bridge reported on 6 March that all authorised taps had been properly authorised. This, of course, did not address the allegation that some tapping had been carried out although unauthorised.

23   *AG v Guardian (No 2)* [1990] 1 AC 109 (see below, pp 357–9).

24   *Report of the Committee on s 2 of the Official Secrets Act 1911*, Cmnd 5104, 1972; see Birtles, W, 'Big brother knows best: the Franks Report on section 2 of the Official Secrets Act' [1973] PL 100.

the government's White Paper on which the Official Secrets Act 1989 was based. There had been various other attempts at reform; those put forward as Private Members' Bills were the more liberal. For example, Clement Freud MP put forward an Official Information Bill[25] which would have created a public right of access to official information, while the Protection of Official Information Bill,[26] put forward by Richard Shepherd MP in 1987, would have provided a public interest defence and a defence of prior disclosure.

The Official Secrets Act 1989[27]

Once the decision to reform the area of official secrecy had been taken, an opportunity was created for radical change which could have included freedom of information legislation along the lines of the instruments in America and Canada. However, it was made clear from the outset that the legislation was unconcerned with freedom of information.[28] It decriminalises disclosure of some official information, although an official who makes such disclosure may, of course, face an action for breach of confidence as well as disciplinary proceedings, but it makes no provision for allowing the release of any official documents into the public domain. Thus, claims made, for example, by Douglas Hurd (the then Home Secretary) that it is 'a great liberalising measure' clearly rest on other aspects of the Act. Aspects which are usually viewed as liberalising features include the categorisation of information covered which makes relevant the *substance* of the information, the introduction of tests for harm, the *mens rea* requirement of ss 5 and 6, the defences available and decriminalisation of the receiver of information. In all these respects, the Act differs from its predecessor, but the nature of the changes has led commentators to question whether they will bring about any real liberalisation.[29] Other aspects of the Act have also attracted criticism: it applies to persons other than Crown servants, including journalists; it contains no defences of public interest or of prior disclosure and no general requirement to prove *mens rea*. Thus, what is omitted from its provisions, including the failure to provide any right of access to information falling outside the protected categories, is arguably as significant as what is included. The Human Rights Act may provide a means of tempering the effects of the 1989 Act. There is obviously a tension between the two statutes, since the one binds public authorities – which includes government departments – under s 6 to observe the Convention rights, including the right to freedom of expression, while the other creates criminal liability for disclosure of information whether or not the disclosure is in the public interest. Further, the 1989 Act must be interpreted under s 3 of the HRA so as to render it compatible with the Convention rights. The tension between the two was explored in the preliminary

---

25 1978–79, Bill 96.

26 1987–88, Bill 20.

27 For comment on the 1989 Act see Palmer, S, 'The Government proposals for reforming s 2 of the Official Secrets Act 1911' [1988] PL 523; Hanbury, W, 'Illiberal reform of s 2' (1989) 133 Sol Jo 587; Palmer, S, 'Tightening secrecy law' [1990] PL 243; Griffith, J, 'The Official Secrets Act 1989' (1989) 16 JLS 273; Feldman, D, *Civil Liberties and Human Rights*, 1st edn, 1993, Chapter 14.3.

28 See the White Paper on s 2, Cmnd 7285, 1978; the Green Paper on *Freedom of Information*, Cmnd 7520, 1979; White Paper: *Reform of the Official Secrets Act 1911*, Cmnd 408, 1988.

29 Eg, Ewing and Gearty, *op cit*, fn 1, p 200.

hearing in the *Shayler*[30] case (discussed below) in which it was argued unsuccessfully that s 1 of the 1989 Act is incompatible with Art 10. Below, the possible effects of Art 10 on the Official Secrets Act are indicated.

Criminal liability for disclosing information

The general prohibition on disclosing information under the Official Secrets Act 1911 was replaced by the more specific prohibitions under the Official Secrets Act 1989. Sections 1–4 of the 1989 Act (excepting the provisions of s 1(1)), which also determine the categorisation of the information, all concern unauthorised disclosures by any present or former Crown servant or government contractor of information which has been acquired in the course of his or her employment. If a civil servant happened to acquire by other means information falling within one of the categories which he or she then disclosed, the provisions of s 5 would apply. Section 7 (below) governs the meaning of 'authorisation', while ss 5 and 6 apply when any person – not only a Crown servant – discloses information falling within the protected categories.

Security and intelligence information is covered by s 1. The category covers 'the work of or in support of, the security and intelligence services' and includes 'references to information held or transmitted by those services or by persons in support of ... those services'.[31] It is, therefore, a wide category and is not confined only to work done by members of the security and intelligence services. Section 1(1) is intended to prevent members or former members of the security services (and any person notified that he is subject to the provisions of the sub-section) disclosing anything at all relating or appearing to relate to[32] the operation of those services. All such members thus come under a lifelong duty to keep silent even though their information might reveal a serious abuse of power in the security services or some operational weakness. There is no need to show that any harm will or may flow from the disclosure, and so all information, however trivial, is covered.

David Shayler, a former member of MI6, was charged with an offence under s 1(1) and s 4(1) in respect of his allegations that MI6 had been involved in a plot to assassinate Colonel Gadafy; further allegations exposed, Shayler claimed, serious illegality on the part of MI6, and were necessary to avert threats to life and limb and to personal property.[33] A preliminary hearing was held regarding the effect of the Human Rights Act on s 1(1). It was argued that since s 1(1) and s 4(1) are of an absolute nature, they are incompatible with Art 10 of the Convention, under the Human Rights Act, owing to the requirement that interference with expression should be proportionate to the legitimate aim pursued. In other words, using s 3 of the HRA in a creative fashion to seek to resolve the incompatibility would be unfruitful, since compatibility could not be achieved. This

---

30 Preparatory hearing: (2001) *The Times*, 10 October, 98(40) LSG 40; CA.

31 Section 1(9).

32 Under s 1(2), misinformation falls within the information covered by s 1(1) as it includes 'making any statement which purports to be a disclosure of such information or which is intended to be taken as being such a disclosure'.

33 *R v Shayler* (2001) 28 September, CA, see fn 30.

argument was rejected by the Court of Appeal, on the basis that avenues of complaint were available to Shayler. Assuming that this ruling is followed, Art 10 will have no impact on s 1(1). This decision is discussed further below.

Section 1(3), which criminalises disclosure of information relating to the security services by a former or present Crown servant as opposed to a member of the security services, does include a test for harm under s 1(4) which provides that:

> ... a disclosure is damaging if:
>
> (a) it causes damage to the work of or any part of, the security and intelligence services; or
>
> (b) it is of information or a document or other article which is such that its unauthorised disclosure would be likely to cause such damage or which falls within a class or description of information, documents or articles the unauthorised disclosure of which would be likely to have that effect.

Taken at its lowest level, it is clear that this test may be very readily satisfied: it is not necessary to show that disclosure of the actual document in question has caused harm or would be likely to cause harm, merely that it belongs to a class of documents, disclosure of which would be likely to have that effect. Disclosure of a document containing insignificant information and incapable itself of causing the harm described under s 1(4)(a) can, therefore, be criminalised, suggesting that the importation of a harm test for Crown servants as opposed to members of the security services may not inevitably in practice create a very significant distinction between them. However, at the next level, harm must be likely to flow from disclosure of a specific document where, owing to its unique nature, it cannot be said to be one of a class of documents.

In such an instance, the ruling of the House of Lords in *Lord Advocate v Scotsman Publications Ltd*[34] suggests that the test for harm may be quite restrictively interpreted: it will be necessary to show quite a strong likelihood that harm will arise and the nature of the harm must be specified. The ruling was given in the context of civil proceedings for breach of confidence, but the House of Lords decided the case on the basis of the principles under the 1989 Act even though it was not then in force. The ruling concerned publication by a journalist of material relating to the work of the intelligence services. Thus, the test for harm had to be interpreted, according to s 5, in accordance with the test under s 1(3) as though the disclosure had been by a Crown servant. The Crown conceded that the information in question was innocuous, but argued that harm would be done because the publication would undermine confidence in the security services. The House of Lords, noting that there had already been a degree of prior publication, rejected this argument as unable alone to satisfy the test for harm. The case therefore gives some indication as to the interpretation the harm tests may receive. This ruling affords some protection for journalistic expression concerning the intelligence services which, under the HRA, would be in accordance with the high value Strasbourg has placed on expression critical of the workings of the State and State agents.[35]

---

34   [1990] 1 AC 812; [1989] 2 All ER 852, HL; for criticism of the ruling, see Walker [1990] PL 354.

35   See *Thorgeirson v Iceland* (1992) 14 EHRR 843; *The Observer and the Guardian v UK* (1991) 14 EHRR 153.

Even taken at its highest level, the harm test is potentially very wide because of its open-textured wording. It states, in effect, that a disclosure of information in this category is damaging if it causes damage to the area of government operation covered by the category. No clue is given as to what is meant by 'damage'; in many cases it would, therefore, be impossible for a Crown servant to determine beforehand whether or not a particular disclosure would be criminal. The only safe approach would be non-disclosure of almost all relevant information; the position of Crown servants under the 1989 Act in relation to information in this category is therefore only with some difficulty to be distinguished from that under the 1911 Act. However, the fact that there is a test for harm at all under s 1(3), however weak, affirms a distinction of perhaps symbolic importance between two groups of Crown servants because the first step in determining whether a disclosure may be criminalised is taken by reference to the *status* of the person making the disclosure rather than by the nature of the information, suggesting that s 1(1) is aimed at underpinning a culture of secrecy in the security services rather than at ensuring that no damaging disclosure is likely to be made.

Section 2 covers information relating to defence. What is meant by defence is set out in s 2(4):

(a) the size, shape, organisation, logistics, order of battle, deployment, operations, state of readiness and training of the armed forces of the Crown;

(b) the weapons, stores or other equipment of those forces and the invention, development, production and operation of such equipment and research relating to it;

(c) defence policy and strategy and military planning and intelligence;

(d) plans and measures for the maintenance of essential supplies and services that are or would be needed in time of war.

It must be shown that the disclosure in question is or would be likely to be damaging as defined under s 2(2):

(a) it damages the capability of, or of any part of, the armed forces of the Crown to carry out their tasks or leads to loss of life or injury to members of those forces or serious damage to the equipment or installations of those forces; or

(b) otherwise than as mentioned in para (a) above, it endangers the interests of the United Kingdom abroad, seriously obstructs the promotion or protection by the United Kingdom of those interests or endangers the safety of British citizens abroad; or

(c) it is of information or of a document or article which is such that its unauthorised disclosure would be likely to have any of those effects.

The first part of this test under (a), which is fairly specific and deals with quite serious harm, may be contrasted with (b), which is much wider. The opening words of (b) may mean that although the *subject* of the harm may fall within (a), the level of harm can be considered within (b) since it does not fall within terms denoting harm used in (a). This could occur where, for example, there had been *damage* as opposed to 'serious damage' to installations abroad. Clearly, this interpretation would allow the harm test to be satisfied in a wider range of situations. On this interpretation, as far as disclosures concerning UK armed forces operating *abroad* are concerned, it would seem that (b) renders (a) largely redundant, so that (a) would tend to play a role only where the disclosure concerned operations within the UK. It may be noted that parts of this test are mere verbiage; it would be hard to draw a significant distinction between 'endangering' and 'seriously obstructing' the interests of the UK abroad. In fact, the overlapping of the harm tests within the categories and across the categories is a feature of this statute; the reasons why this may be so are considered below.

Information relating to international relations falls within s 3(1)(a). This category covers disclosure of 'any information, document or other article relating to international relations'. Clarification of this provision is undertaken by s 3(5), which creates a test to be used in order to determine whether information falls within it. First, it must concern the relations between States, between international organisations or between an international organisation and a State; secondly, it is said that this includes matter which is capable of affecting the relation between the UK and another State or between the UK and an international organisation. The harm test arises under s 3(2) and is identical to that arising under s 2(2)(b) and (c).

Section 3(1)(b) refers to confidential information emanating from other States or international organisations. This category covers 'any confidential information, document or other article which was obtained from a State other than the United Kingdom or an international organisation'. Clearly, the substance of this information might differ from that covered under s 3(1)(a), although some documents might fall within both categories. Under s 3(6), the information will be confidential if it is expressed to be so treated due to the terms under which it was obtained or if the circumstances in which it was obtained impute an obligation of confidence. The harm test under this category contained in s 3(3) is somewhat curious: the mere fact that the information is confidential or its nature or contents 'may' be sufficient to establish the likelihood that its disclosure would cause harm within the terms of s 3(2)(b) (which uses the terms of s 2(2)(b)). In other words, once the information is identified as falling within this category, a fiction is created that harm may automatically flow from its disclosure. This implies that there are circumstances (such as a particularly strong quality of confidentiality?) in which the only ingredient which the prosecution *must* prove is that the information falls within the category.

Given that s 3(3) uses the word 'may', thereby introducing uncertainty into the section, there is greater leeway for imposing a Convention-friendly interpretation on it. If the word 'may' is interpreted strictly, the circumstances in which it would be unnecessary to show harm would be greatly curtailed. It could then be argued that since harm or its likelihood must be shown, the harm test itself must be interpreted compatibly with Art 10. It would have to be shown that the interference in question answered to a pressing social need.[36] Depending on the circumstances, it could be argued that if, ultimately, the 'interests of the UK abroad' would be benefited by the disclosure, or on balance little affected, no pressing social need to interfere with the expression in question could be shown.

Section 4 is headed 'crime and special investigation powers'. Section 4(2) covers any information the disclosure of which:

(a) ... results in the commission of an offence; or facilitates an escape from legal custody or the doing of any other act prejudicial to the safekeeping of persons in legal custody; or

---

36 *Sunday Times v UK* (1979) 2 EHRR 737.

impedes the prevention or detection of offences or the apprehension or prosecution of suspected offenders; or

(b) which is such that its unauthorised disclosure would be likely to have any of those effects.

'Legal custody' includes detention in pursuance of any enactment or any instrument made under an enactment (s 4(6)). In contrast to s 3(3), in which the test for harm may be satisfied once the information is identified as falling within the category, in s 4(2), once the test for harm has been satisfied, the information will necessarily be so identified. As with s 2, parts of this test could have been omitted, such as 'facilitates an escape', which would have been covered by the succeeding general words.

Section 4(3) covers information obtained by the use of intercept and security service warrants. This applies to:

(a) any information obtained by reason of the interception of any communication in obedience to a warrant issued under s 2 of the Interception of Communications Act 1985, any information relating to the obtaining of information by reason of any such interception and any document or other article which is or has been used or held for use in or has been obtained by reason of any such interception; and

(b) any information obtained by reason of action authorised by a warrant issued under s 3 of the Security Service Act 1989, any information relating to the obtaining of information by reason of any such action and any document or other article which is or has been used or held for use in or has been obtained by reason of any such action.

There is no harm test under this category. Thus, in so far as it covers the work of the security services, it creates a wide exception to the general need to show harm under s 1(3) when a Crown servant who is not a member of the security services makes a disclosure about the work of those services.

Section 5 is headed 'information resulting from unauthorised disclosures or entrusted in confidence'. This is not a new category. Information will fall within s 5 if it falls within one or more of the previous categories and it has been disclosed to the defendant by a Crown servant or falls within s 1 of the Official Secrets Act 1911. Section 5 is primarily aimed at journalists who receive information leaked to them by Crown servants, although it could of course cover anybody in that position. It is also aimed at the person to whom a document is entrusted by a Crown servant 'on terms requiring it to be held in confidence or in circumstances in which the Crown servant or government contractor could reasonably expect that it would be so held' (s 5(1)(ii)). The difference between entrusting and disclosing is significant in that, in the former instance, the document – but not the information it contains – will have been entrusted to the care of the person in question.

If the Crown servant has disclosed or entrusted it to another who discloses it to the defendant, this will suffice (s 5(1)(a)(i) and (iii)). These provisions are presumably aimed mainly at the journalist or other non-Crown servant who receives the information from another journalist who received it from the civil servant in question. However, this does not apply where the information has been *entrusted* to the defendant, but has never been *disclosed* to him or her; in that case, it must come directly from the civil servant, not from another person who had it entrusted to him or her (s 5(1)(b)(ii)). The disclosure of the information or document by the person into whose possession it has come must not already be an offence under any of the six categories.

Since s 5 is aimed at journalists and potentially represents an interference with their role of informing the public, it requires a very strict interpretation under s 3 of the HRA, in accordance with Art 10, bearing in mind the emphasis placed by Strasbourg on the importance of that role.[37] In contrast to disclosure of information by a Crown servant under ss 1–4, s 5 does import a requirement of *mens rea* under s 5(2) which, as far as information falling within ss 1, 2 and 3 is concerned, consists of three elements. The defendant must disclose the information knowing or having reasonable cause to believe that it falls within one or more of the categories, that it has come into his possession as mentioned in sub-s (1) above and that it will be damaging (s 5(3)(b)). As far as information falling within s 4 and probably s 3(1)(b) is concerned, only the first two of these elements will be relevant. Under s 5(6), only the first of these elements need be proved if the information came into the defendant's possession as a result of a contravention of s 1 of the Official Secrets Act 1911. Thus, as far as disclosure of such information is concerned, the *mens rea* requirement will be fulfilled even though the defendant believed that the disclosure would not be damaging and intended that it should not be. Indeed, since the *mens rea* includes an objective element, it may be satisfied under all the categories where the defendant did not in fact possess the belief in question, but had reasonable cause to possess it.

The requirement of *mens rea*, although not as strict as may at first appear, represents the only means of differentiating between journalists and Crown servants. The test for damage will be determined as it would be if the information was disclosed by a Crown servant in contravention of ss 1(3), 2(1) or 3(1) above. A court could afford recognition to the significance of the journalistic role, as required by Art 10, by placing a strong emphasis on the *mens rea* requirement. Where a journalist appeared to be acting in the public interest in making the disclosure, it would be possible for a court to interpret the *mens rea* requirement as disproved on the basis that it would be impossible to show that the defendant knew or should have known that the disclosure was damaging to the interest in question if on one view (even if mistaken) it could be seen as beneficial to it, and that was the view that the journalist took.

Section 4 is not mentioned, because the information will not be capable of falling within s 4(1) unless the harm test is satisfied. As already mentioned, there is no harm test under s 4(3). Thus, an interesting anomaly arises: if, for example, information relating to the work of MI5 is disclosed to a journalist by a security service agent, a distinction is drawn between disclosure by the agent and by the journalist: in general, it will not be assumed in the case of the latter that the disclosure will cause harm, but if the information relates to (say) telephone tapping, no such distinction is drawn. If the journalist is then charged with an offence falling within s 5 due to the disclosure of information under s (3), both he or she and the agent will be in an equally disadvantageous position as far as the harm test is concerned. The apparent recognition of journalistic duty effected by importing the harm test under s 1(3) into the situation where a security service member discloses information to a journalist, may therefore be circumvented where such information also falls within s 4(3).

---

37   See, eg, *Goodwin v UK* (1996) 22 EHRR 123.

Another apparent improvement which might tend to affect journalists more than others is the decriminalisation of the receiver of information. If he or she refrains from publishing it, no liability will be incurred. Of course, this improvement might be said to be more theoretical than real in that it was perhaps unlikely that the mere receiver would be prosecuted under the 1911 Act even though that possibility did exist.

The fact that journalists were included at all in the net of criminal liability under s 5 has been greatly criticised on the basis that some recognition should be given to the important role of the press in informing the public about government policy and actions.[38] In arguing for a restrictive interpretation of s 5 under s 3 of the HRA, a comparison could be drawn with the constitutional role of the press recognised in America by the *Pentagon Papers* case:[39] the Supreme Court determined that no restraining order on the press could be made so that the press would remain free to censure the government.

Section 6 covers the unauthorised publication abroad of information which falls into one of the other substantive categories apart from crime and special investigation powers. It covers the disclosure to a UK citizen of information which has been received in confidence from the UK by another State or international organisation. Typically, the section might cover a leak of such information to a foreign journalist who then passed it on to a UK journalist. However, liability will not be incurred if the State or organisation (or a member of the organisation) authorises the disclosure of the information to the public (s 6(3)). Again, since this section is aimed at journalists, a requirement of *mens rea* is imported: it must be shown under s 6(2) that the defendant made 'a damaging disclosure of [the information] knowing or having reasonable cause to believe that it is such as is mentioned in subsection (1) above and that its disclosure would be damaging'. However, it is important to note that under s 6(4), the test for harm under this section is to be determined 'as it would be in relation to a disclosure of the information, document or article in question by a Crown servant in contravention of s 1(3), 2(1) and 3(1) above'. Thus, although it appears that two tests must be satisfied in order to fulfil the *mens rea* requirement, the tests may in fact be conflated as far as s 3(1)(b) is concerned because proof that the defendant knew that the information fell within the relevant category may satisfy the requirement that he or she knew that the disclosure would be damaging. The requirement that *mens rea* be established is not, therefore, as favourable to the defendant as it appears to be because – as noted in respect of s 5 – it may be satisfied even where the defendant believes that no damage will result. Once again, aside from this particular instance, this applies in all the categories due to the objective element in the *mens rea* arising from the words 'reasonable cause to believe'.

The requirement that the information, document or article is communicated in confidence will be satisfied as under s 3 if it is communicated in 'circumstances in which the person communicating it could reasonably expect that it would be so held' (s 6(5)). In other words, it need not be expressly designated 'confidential'.

A disclosure will not lead to liability under the Act if it is authorised and so it is necessary to determine whether or not authorisation has taken place. The meaning of

---

38   See, eg, Ewing and Gearty, *op cit*, fn 1, pp 196–201.
39   *New York Times Co v US* (1971) 403 US 713.

'authorised disclosures' is determined by s 7. A disclosure will be authorised if it is made in accordance with the official duty of the Crown servant or a person in whose case a notification for the purposes of s 1(1) is in force. As far as a government contractor is concerned, a disclosure will be authorised if made 'in accordance with an official authorisation' or 'for the purposes of the functions by virtue of which he is a government contractor and without contravening an official restriction'. A disclosure made by any other person will be authorised if it is made to a Crown servant for the purposes of his functions as such; or in accordance with an official authorisation.

Defences

The defence available to Crown servants arises in each of the different categories and reads:

> ... it is a defence to prove that at the time of the alleged offence he did not know and had no reasonable cause to believe that the information, document or article in question was such as is mentioned (in the relevant subsection) or that its disclosure would be damaging within the meaning of that subsection.

Belief in authorisation will also provide a defence under s 7. Thus, the Act appears to provide three defences for Crown servants: first, that the defendant did not know and had no reasonable cause to believe that the information fell into the category in question; secondly, that he or she did not know and had no reasonable cause to believe that the information would cause harm, and thirdly, that he or she believed that he had lawful authorisation to make the disclosure *and* had no reasonable cause to believe otherwise. However, it is unclear whether there are three defences or only two; the Act may be read as requiring the defendant to prove that he or she did not know that the information fell into a particular category and that it was not realised that it would cause harm. This would arise if the word 'or' which links the first and second defences is expressed conjunctively: the defendant might be able to satisfy the second requirement but not the first, and therefore would find no protection from this defence.

The first two defences may, be conflated in certain categories, largely because the second defence is intimately tied up with the harm tests and therefore, like them, operates on a number of levels. Where the harm test operates at its lowest level, only the first defence is available. Thus, a person falling under ss 1(1) or 4(3) has no opportunity at all of arguing that, for example, the triviality of the information or the fact that it was already in the public domain had given rise to an expectation that its disclosure would cause no harm at all. At the next level, under s 3(1)(b), because the test for harm may be satisfied merely by showing that the information falls within the sub-section, the second defence could be viewed as more apparent than real and could therefore be categorised along with the defence under s 1 as non-existent. However, following the argument regarding the interpretation of the harm test under this section above, this defence could be afforded some substance, under s 3 of the HRA. Under s 1(3), the second defence is extremely circumscribed. It would not necessarily avail the defendant to prove that for various reasons, it was believed on reasonable grounds before the disclosure took place that it would not cause harm. So long as the prosecution could prove a likelihood that harm would be caused from disclosure of documents falling into the same class, the harm test under the section would be satisfied and the defendant would be forced to prove that he or she had no reasonable cause to believe that disclosure of documents of that class would cause harm – a more difficult task than showing this in relation to the particular disclosure in question.

Generally, under all the other categories the harm test allows for argument under both the first and second defences, assuming that they are expressed disjunctively. However, under s 4(4), the second defence alone applies to information falling within the category under s 4(2)(a), while the first alone applies to information likely to have those effects under s 4(2)(b). This is anomalous, as it means that the disclosure of information which had had the effect of preventing an arrest could be met by the defence that it was not expected to have that effect, while information which had not yet had such an effect, but might have in future, would not necessarily be susceptible to such a defence. So long as the disclosure of the document was in fact likely to have the effect mentioned, it would be irrelevant that the defendant, while appreciating that it might in general have such effects, considered that they would not arise in the particular instance. Thus, a broader defence would be available in respect of the more significant disclosure, but not in respect of the less significant. This effect arises because, under s 4(2), the first defence is contained in the second owing to the use of the harm test as the means of identifying the information falling within the section.

Thus, it is clear that the Act is less generous towards the defendant in terms of the defences it makes available than it appears to be at first glance. Moreover, it is important to note that, although it is a general principle of criminal law that a defendant need have only an honest belief in the existence of facts which give rise to a defence, under the Act a defendant must have an honest and reasonable belief in such facts. However, as indicated, s 3 of the HRA could be used to broaden the defences in certain respects.

The Act contains no explicit public interest defence and it follows from the nature of the harm tests that one cannot be implied into it; on the face of it, any good flowing from disclosure of the information in question cannot be considered, merely any harm that might be caused. Thus, while it may be accepted that the Act at least allows argument as to a defendant's state of knowledge (albeit of very limited scope in certain instances) in making a disclosure to be led before a jury, it does not allow for argument as to the good intentions of the persons concerned, who may believe with reason that no other effective means of exposing iniquity exists. In particular, the information may concern corruption at such a high level that internal methods of addressing the problem would be ineffective. Of course, good intentions are normally irrelevant in criminal trials: not many would argue that a robber should be able to adduce evidence that he intended to use the proceeds of his robbery to help the poor. However, it is arguable that an exception to this rule should be made in respect of the Official Secrets Act. A statute aimed specifically at those best placed to know of corruption or malpractice in government should, in a democracy, allow such a defence. The fact that it does not argues strongly against the likelihood that it will have a liberalising impact. However, s 3 of the HRA could be used creatively, as indicated, to seek to introduce such a defence – in effect – through the back door.

Whether or not this is possible in respect of categories of information covered by a harm test, it appears that it is not possible in respect of s 1(1) and s 4(1). In *Shayler*[40] Judge

---

40 (2001) 28 September, CA.

Moses found that there was no need to rely on s 3 HRA since no incompatibility between Art 10 and s 1(1) arose.[41] He reached the conclusion that s 3 could be ignored in reliance on the finding of the Lord Chief Justice in *Donoghue v Poplar Housing and Regeneration Community Assoc Ltd and the Secretary of State for the Environment*;[42] he said that 'unless legislation would otherwise be in breach of the Convention s 3 can be ignored; so courts should always first ascertain whether, absent s 3, there would be any breach of the Convention'.[43] The conclusion that ss 1(1) and 4(1) were not in breach of Article 10 was reached on the basis that Mr Shayler did have an avenue by which he could seek to make the disclosures in question. There were various persons to whom the disclosure could be made, including those identified in s 12. Further, significantly, under s 7(3) of the 1989 Act a disclosure can be made to others if authorised; those empowered to afford authorisation are identified in s 12. Shayler could have sought authorisation to make his disclosures from those identified under s 21 or from those prescribed as persons who can give authorisations. Such persons or bodies now include the new Tribunal established under the Regulation of Investigatory Powers Act 2000 s 65[44] and a Minister of the Crown. Such persons could have authorised disclosure to other persons *not* identified in s 12 or prescribed.

Also, Mr Justice Moses found, a refusal of authorisation would be subject, the Crown accepted in the instant case, to judicial review. The refusal to grant authority would have to comply with Article 10 due to s 6 HRA; if it did not, the court in the judicial review proceedings would be expected to say so.[45] Mr Justice Moses went on to say 'It is not correct ... to say that a restriction [under s 1(12) and 4(1)] is imposed irrespective of the public interest in disclosure. If there is a public interest it is ... not unreasonable to expect at least one of the very large number identified [by reference to s 12 and to the bodies prescribed] to recognise the public interest and to act upon it'.[46] He went on to call the suggestion that all those so identified would not authorise the disclosure in such circumstances as far fetched. But he thought that even if the possibility might arise 'it is a step too far to say that the proportionality of this legislation must be judged in the light of the possibility that the courts themselves [in judicial review proceedings in respect of a refusal of authorisation] would countenance suppression of a disclosure which they considered necessary to avert injury to life, limb or serious damage to property even before October 2000'. Therefore he found that no absolute ban was imposed.

The Court of Appeal agreed that the interference with freedom of expression was in proportion to the legitimate aim pursued – that of protecting national security on the basis that the members of the Security Services and those who pass information to them must be able to be sure that the information will remain secret.

---

41 Paragraph 78 of the transcript.
42 [2001] 3 WLR 183.
43 *Ibid*, para 75.
44 See Chapter 11, pp 714 *et seq*. The old tribunals set up under s 7 of the Interception of Communications Act, s 5 of the Security Services Act 1989 and s 9 of the Intelligence Services Act 1994 were prescribed for this purpose under the Official Secrets Act 1989 (Prescription) Order 1990 SI 1990/200 as amended by SI 1993/847. That prescription now applies to the single Tribunal.
45 Paragraphs 25 and 26 of the Transcript.
46 *Ibid*, para 54.

The Court of Appeal also agreed that for the reasons given the absence of a 'public interest' defence in the 1989 Act does not breach the Convention. Mr Justice Moses had stated that had he found otherwise he would have considered the use of s 3 of the HRA but would have rejected the possibility put forward on behalf of Shayler, of inserting the word 'lawful' into s 1(9) so that s 1(1) would only cover the *lawful* work of the Secret Services. He also rejected the similar argument in respect of s 4. In so finding he again relied on *Donoghue v Poplar Housing and Regeneration Community Assoc Ltd and the Secretary of State for the Environment*[47] in which Lord Woolf said that s 3 does not entitle the court to legislate.[48]

This decision means that s 3 need not be used in relation to s 1(1) and s 4(1) and it is probable that the same arguments would apply if, in respect of disclosure of information falling within other categories, the defence sought to introduce a public interest defence.

The problem with Mr Justice Moses' analysis, which was accepted by the Court of Appeal, is that the means he views as available to members or former members of the Security Services to expose iniquity is so unlikely to be used. It seems, to say the least, highly improbable that such a member would risk the employment detriment that might be likely to arise, especially if he then proceeded to seek judicial review of the decision. It would appear that it would place him in an impossible position vis a vis colleagues and superiors. Both current and former members may be deterred from using this route for the simple reason that they will probably view it as inefficacious. It would probably be impossible to prove to a court that Security Service work was creating dangers to persons without adducing evidence which itself would be covered by s 1(1). The Act has been in force for over 10 years and no such member has ever availed themselves of this route, although persons other than Shayler have made or sought to make disclosures to the public at large, as this chapter reveals. One of the most important principles recognised at Strasbourg is that rights must be real not tokenistic or illusory. It is argued that the right to freedom of expression – one of the central rights of the Convention – is rendered illusory by ss 1(1) and 4(1) of the OSA in relation to allegedly unlawful activities of the Security Services – a matter of great significance in a democracy.

The argument that members of the Service and others must be able to trust each other to keep information secret would be expected to extend only to information which did not reveal illegality. Otherwise the policy of ss 1(1) and 4(1) of the OSA seems to be to promote criminal conspiracies among members of the Services or between members and informants to conceal information revealing unlawful activities.

The impact of the OSA in terms of freedom of expression is further exacerbated since no general defence of prior publication is provided; the only means of putting forward such argument would arise in one of the categories in which it was necessary to prove the likelihood that harm would flow from the disclosure; the prosecution might find it hard to establish such a likelihood where there had been a great deal of prior publication

---

47 *Ibid.*
48 *Ibid*, paras 75 and 76.

because no further harm could be caused. Obviously, once again, this will depend on the level at which the harm test operates. Where it operates at its lowest level, prior publication would be irrelevant. Thus, where a member of the security services repeated information falling within s 1 which had been published all over the world and in the UK, a conviction could still be obtained. This position is out of accord with Art 10: in such an instance, the imposition of criminal liability would be unable to preserve national security and therefore, it would be disproportionate to the aim of so doing.

If such publication had occurred, but the information fell within s 1(3), the test for harm might be satisfied on the basis that although no further harm could be caused by disclosure of the particular document, it nevertheless belonged to a class of documents the disclosure of which was likely to cause harm. However, where harm flowing from publication of a specific document is relied on, *Lord Advocate v Scotsman Publications Ltd* suggests that a degree of prior publication may tend to defeat the argument that further publication can still cause harm. However, this suggestion must be treated with care, since the ruling was not given under the 1989 Act and the link between the Act and the civil law of confidence may not form part of its *ratio*.[49] It should also be noted that s 6 provides that information which has already been leaked abroad can still cause harm if disclosed in the UK. The only exception to this arises under s 6(3), which provides that no liability will arise if the disclosure was authorised by the State or international organisation in question.

Conclusions

The claim that the Act is an improvement on its predecessor rests partly on the substance or significance of the information it covers. Such substance is made relevant first by the use of categorisation; impliedly, trivial information relating to cups of tea or colours of carpets in government buildings is not covered (except in Security Services buildings) and secondly, because even where information *does* fall within the category in question, its disclosure will not incur liability unless harm will or may flow from it. Thus, on the face of it, liability will not be incurred merely because the information disclosed covers a topic of significance such as defence. In other words, it does not seem to be assumed that because there is a public interest in keeping information of the particular type secret, it inevitably relates to any particular piece of information. However, in relation to many disclosures it is, in fact, misleading to speak of using a second method to narrow down further the amount of information covered because, as noted above, establishing that the information falls within the category in question is in fact (or may be; no guidance is given as to when this will be the case) synonymous with establishing that harm will occur in a number of instances.

Clearly, if only to avoid bringing the criminal law into disrepute, 'harm tests' which allow the substance of the information to be taken into account are to be preferred to the width of s 2 of the 1911 Act. However, although the 1989 Act embodies and emphasises

---

49 [1990] 1 AC 812; [1989] 2 All ER 852, HL. Only Lord Templeman clearly adverted to such a link.

the notion of a test for harm in its reiteration of the term 'damaging', it is not necessary to show that harm has *actually occurred*. Bearing this important point in mind, it can be seen that the test for harm actually operates on four different levels:

(a) The lowest level arises in two categories, s 1(1) and s 4(3), where there is no explicit test for harm at all – impliedly, a disclosure is of its very nature harmful.

(b) In one category, s 3(1)(b), the test for harm is more apparent than real in that it may be identical to the test determining whether the information falls within the category at all.

(c) In s 1(3), there is a harm test, but the harm need not flow from or be likely to flow from disclosure of the specific document in question.

(d) In three categories, ss 2, 3 and 4, there is a harm test, but it is only necessary to prove that harm would be *likely* to occur due to the disclosure in question, whether it has occurred or not.

Even at the highest level, where it is necessary to show that the actual document in question would be likely to cause harm, the task of doing so is made easy due to the width of the tests themselves. Under s 2(2), for example, a disclosure of information relating to defence will be damaging if it is likely to seriously obstruct the interests of the UK abroad. Thus, the harm tests may be said to be concerned less with preventing damaging disclosures than with creating the *impression* that liability is confined to such disclosures.

These tests for harm are not made any more stringent in instances where a non-Crown servant – usually a journalist – discloses information since, under s 5, if anyone discloses information which falls into one of the categories covered, the test for harm will be determined by reference to that category. The journalist who publishes information and the Crown servant who discloses it to him or her are treated differently in terms of the test for harm only where the latter is a member of the security services disclosing information relating to those services.

One of the objections to the old s 2 of the 1911 Act was the failure to include a requirement to prove *mens rea*. The new Act includes such a requirement only as regards the leaking of information by non-Crown servants; in all other instances, it creates a 'reversed *mens rea*': the defence can attempt to prove that the defendant did not know (or have reasonable cause to know) of the nature of the information or that its disclosure would be damaging. We will return to this defence below. However, under ss 5 and 6 the prosecution must prove *mens rea*, which includes a requirement to show that the disclosure was made in the knowledge that it would be damaging. This is a step in the right direction and a clear improvement on the 1911 Act; nevertheless, the burden of proof on the prosecution would be very easy to discharge where the low level harm tests of ss 1(3) and 3(1)(b) applied once it was shown that the defendant knew that the information fell within the category in question.

Under s 3 of the HRA it is strongly arguable that the Act needs to afford greater recognition to the important constitutional role of the journalist in order to bring it into line with the recognition afforded to that role at Strasbourg under Art 10. But unless s 3 is used creatively in order to create such recognition, a journalist who repeated allegations made by a future Peter Wright as to corruption or treachery in MI5 could be convicted if it could be shown first, that he or she knew that the information related to the security services and, secondly, that disclosure of that *type* of information would be *likely* to cause damage to the work of the security services, regardless of whether the particular allegations would cause such damage. In the case of a journalist who repeated allegations made by a future Cathy Massiter, it would only be necessary to show that the allegations related to telephone tapping and that the journalist knew that they did. Clearly, this would be a burden which would be readily discharged.

It may be argued – bearing in mind the scarcity of prosecutions under the 1911 Act – that the Official Secrets Acts were put in place mainly in order to create a deterrent effect and as a centrepiece in the general legal scheme engendering government secrecy, rather than with a view to their invocation. The 1989 Act may be effective as a means of creating greater government credibility in relation to official secrecy than its predecessor. It allows the claim of liberalisation to be made and gives the impression that the anomalies in existence under the 1911 Act have been dealt with. It appears complex and wide ranging partly due to overlapping between and within the categories and, therefore, will be likely to have a chilling effect because civil servants and others will not be certain as to the information covered except in very clear cut cases. It may, therefore, prove more effective than the 1911 Act in deterring the press from publishing the revelations of a future Peter Wright in respect of the workings of the security services. Thus, it may rarely need to be invoked and, in fact, may have much greater symbolic than practical value.

In considering the impact of the Act, it must be borne in mind that many other criminal sanctions for the unauthorised disclosure of information exist and some of these clearly overlap with its provisions. Sections 1 and 4(3) work in conjunction with the provisions of the Security Services Act 1989 to prevent almost all scrutiny of the operation of the security services. Even where a member of the public has a grievance concerning the operation of the services it will probably not be possible to use a court action as a means of bringing such operations to the notice of the public: under s 5 of the Security Services Act, complaint can only be made to a tribunal and under s 5(4), the decisions of the tribunal are not questionable in any court of law. In a similar manner s 4(3) of the Official Secrets Act, which prevents disclosure of information about telephone tapping, works in tandem with the Interception of Communications Act 1985. Under the 1985 Act, complaints can be made only to a tribunal whose decisions are not published, with no possibility of scrutiny by a court. Moreover, around 80 other statutory provisions provide sanctions to enforce secrecy on civil servants in the particular areas they cover. For example, s 11 of the Atomic Energy Act 1946 makes it an offence to communicate to an unauthorised person information relating to atomic energy plant. Further, s 1 of the Official Secrets Act 1911 is still available to punish spies. Thus, it is arguable that s 2 of the 1911 Act could merely have been repealed without being replaced.

A number of the provisions of the 1989 Act look increasingly anomalous in the Human Rights Act era. Although repeal of the Act is unlikely, the pressure to amend s 1(1), as the most pernicious section – in terms of its impact on State accountability – may eventually become irresistible.

Breach of confidence

Introduction[50]

Breach of confidence is a civil remedy affording protection against the disclosure or use of information which is not generally known and which has been entrusted in circumstances imposing an obligation not to disclose it without authorisation from the person who originally imparted it. This area of law developed as a means of protecting secret information belonging to individuals and organisations.[51] However, it can also be used by the government to prevent disclosure of sensitive information and is, in that sense, a back-up to the other measures available, including the Official Secrets Act 1989.[52] It is clear that governments are prepared to use actions for breach of confidence against civil servants and others in instances falling outside the protected categories – or within them. In some respects, breach of confidence actions may be more valuable than the criminal sanction provided by the 1989 Act. Their use may attract less publicity than a criminal trial, no jury will be involved and they offer the possibility of quickly obtaining an interim injunction. The latter possibility is very valuable because, in many instances, the other party (usually a newspaper) will not pursue the case to a trial of the permanent injunction since the secret will probably be stale news by that time.

However, where the government, as opposed to a private individual, is concerned, the courts will not merely accept that it is in the public interest that the information should be kept confidential. It will have to be shown that the public interest in keeping the information confidential due to the harm its disclosure would cause is not outweighed by the public interest in disclosure. Thus, in *AG v Jonathan Cape*,[53] when the Attorney General invoked the law of confidence to try to stop publication of Richard Crossman's memoirs on the ground that they concerned Cabinet discussions, the Lord Chief Justice accepted that such public secrets could be restrained, but only on the basis that the balance of the public interest came down in favour of suppression. As the discussions had taken place 10 years previously, it was not possible to show that harm would flow from their disclosure; the public interest in publication therefore prevailed.

The nature of the public interest defence – the interest in disclosure – was clarified in *Lion Laboratories v Evans and Express Newspapers*.[54] The Court of Appeal held that the defence extended beyond situations in which there had been serious wrongdoing by the plaintiff. Even where the plaintiff was blameless, publication would be excusable where it was possible to show a serious and legitimate interest in the revelation. Thus, the *Daily Express* was allowed to publish information extracted from the manufacturer of the intoximeter (a method of conducting breathalyser tests) even though it did not reveal iniquity on the part of the manufacturer. It did, however, reveal a matter of genuine

---

50 General reading: Gurry, F, *Breach of Confidence*, 1985; Bailey, Harris and Jones, *op cit*, fn 1, pp 435–52; Robertson, G and Nichol, AGL, *Media Law*, Chapter 4; Wacks, R, *Personal Information*, 1989, Chapter 3; Feldman, *op cit*, fn 27, pp 648–68.

51 See Chapter 10, pp 565–80.

52 For comment on its role in this respect see Bryan, MW, 'The Crossman Diaries: developments in the law of breach of confidence' (1976) 92 LQR 180; Williams, DGT, 'The Crossman Diaries' (1976) CLJ 1; Lowe and Willmore, 'Secrets, media and the law' (1985) 48 MLR 592.

53 [1976] QB 752.

54 [1985] QB 526; [1984] 2 All ER 417, CA.

public interest: that wrongful convictions might have been obtained in drink driving cases owing to possible deficiencies of the intoximeter.

Just as the Official Secrets Act creates a direct interference with political speech, the doctrine of confidence as employed by the government can do so too. Therefore, the use of the doctrine in such instances will require careful scrutiny, with Art 10 in mind. Since this is a common law doctrine, s 3 will not apply. But the courts have a duty under s 6 of the HRA to develop the doctrine compatibly with Art 10. The duty of the courts in relation to the doctrine of confidence under the HRA was considered by Sedley LJ in *Douglas and Others v Hello! Ltd*.[55] The case concerned private individuals, not the State, but the findings are relevant, since principles from such private cases have been relied upon by the State, as indicated below, in seeking to use the doctrine to prevent the disclosure of governmental information. He said that the jurisprudence of the Strasbourg Court and the common law 'now run in a single channel because, by virtue of s 2 and s 6 of the Act, the courts of this country must not only take into account jurisprudence of both the Commission and the European Court of Human Rights ... they must themselves act compatibly with that and the other Convention rights'.

Thus a court, as itself a public authority under s 6, is obliged to give effect to Art 10, among other provisions of the Convention, when considering the application of this doctrine. In so doing, the courts have more leeway than they do under s 3 of the HRA since no provision was included in the HRA allowing the common law to override the Convention rights. Since, in an action between the individual and the State, the vexed issue of horizontal effect does not arise,[56] this matter can be regarded as settled, since the State as employer is also presumably a public authority under s 6. Section 12(4) is also applicable where interference with the right to freedom of expression is in issue, as it inevitably will be in this context. Section 12(4) requires the Court to have particular regard to the right to freedom of expression under Art 10. Thus, s 12(4) provides added weight to the argument that in the instance in which the State seeks to suppress the expression of an individual using this doctrine, the court must consider the pressing social need to do so and the requirements of proportionality very carefully, interpreting those requirements strictly. In considering Art 10, the court should, under s 12(4)(a), take into account the extent to which the material is or is about to become available to the public and the public interest in publication. These two matters are central in breach of confidence actions. They imply that the State's task in obtaining an injunction where a small amount of prior publication has taken place – or is about to – has been made harder.

In breach of confidence actions the State, as indicated below, typically seeks an interim injunction and then, if it has obtained it, may proceed to the trial of the permanent injunction. However, s 12(3) of the HRA provides that prior restraint on expression should not be granted except where the court considers that the claimant is 'likely' to establish at trial that publication should not be allowed. Moreover, *ex parte* injunctions cannot be granted under s 12(2) unless there are compelling reasons why the respondent should not be notified or the applicant has taken all reasonable steps to notify the respondent. All these requirements under the HRA must now be taken into account in

---

55   [2001] 2 WLR 992.
56   See Chapter 4, pp 161–64.

applying the doctrine of confidence. The result is likely to be that the doctrine will undergo quite a radical change from the interpretation afforded to it in the *Spycatcher* litigation, which is considered below.

The Spycatcher *litigation*

The leading case in this area is the House of Lords' decision in *AG v Guardian Newspapers Ltd (No 2)*,[57] which confirmed that the *Lion Laboratories Ltd v Evans* approach to the public interest defence is the correct one and also clarified certain other aspects of this area of the law. In 1985, the Attorney General commenced proceedings in New South Wales[58] in an attempt (which was ultimately unsuccessful)[59] to restrain publication of *Spycatcher* by Peter Wright. The book included allegations of illegal activity engaged in by MI5. In the UK on 22 and 23 June 1986, *The Guardian* and *The Observer* published reports of the forthcoming hearing which included some *Spycatcher* material and on 27 June the Attorney General obtained temporary *ex parte* injunctions preventing them from further disclosure of such material. *Inter partes* injunctions were granted against the newspapers on 11 July 1986. On 12 July 1987, *The Sunday Times* began publishing extracts from *Spycatcher* and the Attorney General obtained an injunction restraining publication on 16 July.

On 14 July 1987, the book was published in the US, and many copies were brought into the UK. On 30 July 1987, the House of Lords decided[60] (relying on *American Cyanamid Co v Ethicon Ltd*)[61] to continue the injunctions against the newspapers on the basis that the Attorney General still had an arguable case for permanent injunctions. In making this decision, the House of Lords were obviously influenced by the fact that publication of the information was an irreversible step. This is the usual approach at the interim stage: the court considers the balance of convenience between the two parties and will tend to come down on the side of the plaintiff because of the irrevocable nature of publication. However, since an interim injunction represents a prior restraint and is often the most crucial and, indeed, sometimes the *only* stage in the whole action, it may be argued that a presumption in favour of freedom of expression should be more readily allowed to tip the balance in favour of the defendant. This may especially be argued where publication from other sources has already occurred which will be likely to increase, and where the public interest in the information is very strong.

It is arguable that the House of Lords should have been able in July 1986 to break through the argument that once the confidentiality claim was set up, the only possible course was to transfix matters as at that point. The argument could have been broken through in the following way: the public interest in limiting the use of prior restraints could have been weighed against the interest in ensuring that everyone who sets up a legal claim has a right to have it heard free from interference. A prior restraint might be

---

57 [1990] 1 AC 109; [1990] 3 WLR 776; [1988] 3 All ER 545, HL.
58 [1987] 8 NSWLR 341.
59 HC of Australia (1988) 165 CLR 30; for comment see Mann, FA (1988) 104 LQR 497; Turnbull, M (1989) 105 LQR 382.
60 *AG v Guardian Newspapers Ltd* [1987] 3 All ER 316; for comment, see Lee, S (1987) 103 LQR 506.
61 [1975] AC 396; [1975] 1 All ER 504, HL.

allowed even in respect of a matter of great public concern if the interest it protected was clearly made out, it did not go beyond what was needed to provide such protection and it was foreseeable that the restraint would achieve its objective. If it seemed probable that the restraint would not achieve its objective, it would cause an erosion of freedom of speech to no purpose. In the instant case, although the first of these conditions may have been satisfied, the other two, it is submitted, were not; the restraint should not, therefore, have been granted. Such reasoning would bring the law of confidence closer to adopting the principles used in defamation cases as regards the grant of interim injunctions.[62] If a case of this nature recurs now that the HRA is in force, such reasoning would be taken into account under s 12(4) and s 6; since relying on either section the demands of Art 10 must be met, an injunction should not be granted where it is probable that it will not be able to serve the legitimate aim in question, owing to the probability that further publication abroad, or on the internet, will occur.

The judgment of the House of Lords did nothing to curb the use of 'gagging injunctions' in actions for breach of confidence where there had not been prior publication of the material. In any such action, even where the claim was of little merit, and the public interest in publication strong, it was possible to argue that its subject matter should be preserved intact until the merits of the claim could be considered. Even in an instance where the plaintiff (the State) then decided to drop the action before that point, publication of the material in question could be prevented for some substantial period of time. The House of Lords' decision was found to be in breach of Art 10 of the European Convention on Human Rights, as discussed below, but on the ground of prior publication, rather than public interest in the material.

In the trial of the permanent injunctions, *AG v Guardian (No 2)*,[63] the Crown argued that confidential information disclosed to third parties does not thereby lose its confidential character if the third parties know that the disclosure has been made in breach of a duty of confidence. A further reason for maintaining confidentiality in the particular instance was that the unauthorised disclosure of the information was thought likely to damage the trust which members of MI5 have in each other and might encourage others to follow suit. These factors, it was argued, established the public interest in keeping the information confidential.

On the other hand, it was argued on behalf of the newspapers that some of the information in *Spycatcher*, if true, disclosed that members of MI5 in their operations in England had committed serious breaches of domestic law in, for example, bugging foreign embassies or effecting unlawful entry into private premises. Most seriously, the book included the allegations that members of MI5 attempted to destabilise the administration of Mr Harold Wilson and that the Director General or Deputy Director General of MI5 was a spy. The defendants contended that the duty of non-disclosure to which newspapers coming into the unauthorised possession of confidential State secrets may be subject, does not extend to allegations of serious iniquity of this character.

---

62 See *Bonnard v Perryman* [1891] 2 Ch 269; *Herbage v The Times Newspapers and Others* (1981) *The Times*, 1 May.

63 [1990] 1 AC 109; [1990] 3 WLR 776; [1988] 3 All ER 545, HL; in the Court of Appeal [1990] 1 AC 109; [1988] 3 All ER 545, p 594.

It was determined at first instance and in the Court of Appeal that whether or not the newspapers would have had a duty to refrain from publishing *Spycatcher* material in June 1986 before its publication elsewhere, any such duty had now lapsed. The mere making of allegations of iniquity was insufficient, of itself, to justify overriding the duty of confidentiality, but the articles in question published in June 1986 had not contained information going beyond what the public was reasonably entitled to know and in so far as they went beyond what had been previously published, no detriment to national security had been shown which could outweigh the public interest in free speech, given the publication of *Spycatcher* that had already taken place. Thus, balancing the public interest in freedom of speech and the right to receive information against the countervailing interest of the Crown in national security, continuation of the injunctions was not necessary. The injunctions, however, continued until the House of Lords rejected the Attorney General's claim (*AG v Guardian Newspapers Ltd (No 2)*)[64] on the basis that the interest in maintaining confidentiality was outweighed by the public interest in knowing of the allegations in *Spycatcher*. It was further determined that an injunction to restrain future publication of matters connected with the operations of the security services would amount to a comprehensive ban on publication and would undermine the operation of determining the balance of public interest in deciding whether such publication was to be prevented; accordingly, an injunction to prevent future publication which had not yet been threatened was not granted.

It appears likely that the permanent injunctions would have been granted but for the massive publication of *Spycatcher* abroad. That factor seems to have tipped the balance in favour of the newspapers. It is arguable that the operation of the public interest defence in this instance came too close to allowing for judicial value judgments rather than application of a clear legal rule. Without a Bill of Rights to protect freedom of speech, the Law Lords, it is suggested, showed a tendency to be swayed by establishment arguments. The judgment also made it clear that once the information has become available from other sources, even though the plaintiff played no part in its dissemination and indeed tried to prevent it, an injunction would be unlikely to be granted. This principle was affirmed in *Lord Advocate v Scotsman Publications Ltd*,[65] which concerned the publication of extracts from *Inside Intelligence* by Antony Cavendish. The interlocutory injunction sought by the Crown was refused by the House of Lords on the ground that there had been a small amount of prior publication and the possible damage to national security was very nebulous. The decision suggests that the degree of prior publication may be weighed against the significance of the disclosures in question: if less innocuous material had been in issue, an injunction might have been granted.

The Observer and *The Guardian* applied to the European Commission on Human Rights claiming, *inter alia*, that the grant of the temporary injunctions had breached Art 10 of the Convention, which guarantees freedom of expression. Having given its opinion

---

64 [1990] 1 AC 109; [1990] 3 WLR 776; [1988] 3 All ER 545, p 638; for comment, see Williams (1989) 48 CLJ 1; Cripps, Y, 'Breach of copyright and confidence: the *Spycatcher* effect' [1989] PL 13; Barendt, E, '*Spycatcher* and freedom of speech' [1989] PL 204; Michael, J, 'Spycatcher's end?' (1989) 52 MLR 389; Narain, BJ (1988) 39 NILQ 73 and (1987) 137 NLJ 723 and 724; Burnett, D and Thomas, R (1989) 16 JLS 210; Jones, G, 'Breach of confidence – after *Spycatcher*' (1989) 42 CLP 49; Kingsford-Smith, D and Oliver, D (eds), *Economical With the Truth*, 1990, chapters by Pannick and Austin; Ewing and Gearty, *op cit*, fn 1, pp 152–69; Turnbull, M, *The Spycatcher Trial*, 1988; Bailey, Harris and Jones, *op cit*, fn 1, pp 435–50.

65 [1990] 1 AC 812; [1989] 2 All ER 852, CA.

that the temporary injunctions constituted such a breach, the Commission referred the case to the court. In *Observer and Guardian v UK*,[66] the Court found that the injunctions clearly constituted an interference with the newspapers' freedom of expression; the question was whether the interference fell within one of the exceptions provided for by para 2 of Art 10. The injunctions fell within two of the para 2 exceptions: maintaining the authority of the judiciary and protecting national security. However, those exceptions could be invoked only if the injunctions were necessary in a democratic society in the sense that they corresponded to a pressing social need and were proportionate to the aims pursued.

The court considered these questions with regard first to the period from 11 July 1986 to 30 July 1987. The injunctions had the aim of preventing publication of material which, according to evidence presented by the Attorney General, might have created a risk of detriment to MI5. The nature of the risk was uncertain as the exact contents of the book were not known at that time because it was still only available in manuscript form. Further, they ensured the preservation of the Attorney General's right to be granted a permanent injunction; if *Spycatcher* material had been published before that claim could be heard, the subject matter of the action would have been damaged or destroyed. In the court's view, these factors established the existence of a pressing social need. Were the actual restraints imposed proportionate to these aims? The injunctions did not prevent the papers pursuing a campaign for an inquiry into the operation of the security services and, though preventing publication for a long time – over a year – the material in question could not be classified as urgent news. Thus, it was found that the interference complained of was proportionate to the ends in view.

The court then considered the period from 30 July 1987 to 30 October 1988, after publication of *Spycatcher* had taken place in the US. That event changed the situation: in the court's view, the aim of the injunctions was no longer to keep secret information secret; it was to attempt to preserve the reputation of MI5 and to deter others who might be tempted to follow Peter Wright's example. It was uncertain whether the injunctions could achieve those aims and it was not clear that the newspapers who had not been concerned with the publication of *Spycatcher* should be enjoined as an example to others. Further, after 30 July it was not possible to maintain the Attorney General's rights as a litigant because the substance of his claim had already been destroyed; had permanent injunctions been obtained against the newspapers, that would not have preserved the confidentiality of the material in question. Thus, the injunctions could no longer be said to be necessary either to protect national security or to maintain the authority of the judiciary. Maintenance of the injunctions after publication of the book in the US therefore constituted a violation of Art 10.

This was a cautious judgment. It suggests that had the book been published in the US after the House of Lords' decision to uphold the temporary injunctions, no breach of Art 10 would have occurred, despite the fact that publication of extracts from the book had already occurred in the US[67] and the UK. The Court seems to have been readily persuaded by the Attorney General's argument that a widely framed injunction was

---

66 (1991) 14 EHRR 153; for comment see Leigh, I, '*Spycatcher* in Strasbourg' [1992] PL 200–08.
67 The *Washington Post* published certain extracts in the US on 3 May 1987.

needed in July 1986, but it is arguable that it was wider than it needed to be to prevent a risk to national security. It could have required the newspapers to refrain from publishing Wright material which had not been previously published by others until (if) the action to prevent publication of the book was lost. Such wording would have taken care of any national security interest; therefore, wording going beyond that was disproportionate to that aim.

Thus, although the newspapers 'won', the judgment is unlikely to have a significant liberalising influence on the principles governing the grant of temporary injunctions on the grounds of breach of confidence. The minority judges in the court set themselves against the narrow view that the authority of the judiciary is best preserved by allowing a claim of confidentiality set up in the face of a strong competing public interest to found an infringement of freedom of speech for over a year. Judge Morenilla argued that prior restraint should be imposed in such circumstances only where disclosure would result in immediate, serious and irreparable damage to the public interest.[68] It might be said that such a test would impair the authority of the judiciary in the sense that the rights of litigants would not be sufficiently protected. However, following the judgment of the Lords, the test at the interlocutory stage allowed a case based on a weak argument to prevail on the basis that the court could not weigh the evidence at that stage and therefore had to grant an injunction in order to preserve confidentiality until the case could be fully looked into. As noted above, this stance can mean that the other party does not pursue the case to the permanent stage and, therefore, freedom of speech is suppressed on very flimsy grounds. Thus, a greater burden to show the well founded nature of the claim of danger to the public interest – even if not as heavy as that under the test proposed by Judge Morenilla – should be placed on the plaintiff, and such a burden would be, it is argued, more in accord with the duties of the court under ss 6 and 12 of the HRA.

The result of the ruling in the European Court of Human Rights appears to be that where there has been an enormous amount of prior publication, an interim injunction should not be granted, but that it can be when there is at least some evidence of a threat to national security posed by publication coupled with a lesser degree of prior publication. It meant that the action for breach of confidence was still of great value as part of the legal scheme bolstering government secrecy.

However, recent developments in the case of *AG v Times*[69] suggest that Art 10 is having a greater impact in breach of confidence actions than it had at Strasbourg. Tomlinson, a former MI6 officer, wrote a book, *The Big Breach*, about his experiences in MI6[70] which The Sunday Times intended to serialise. There had been a small amount of publication of the material in Russia. The Attorney General sought an injunction to restrain publication. The key issue concerned the degree of prior publication required before it could be said that the material had lost its quality of confidentiality. The Attorney General proposed the formula: 'publication has come to the widespread attention of the

---

68 He relied on the ruling to this effect of the US Supreme Court in *Nebraska Press Association v Stuart* (1976) 427 US 539.

69 [2001] EMLR 19.

70 Tomlinson was charged with an offence under the Official Secrets Act, s 1, pleaded guilty and was imprisoned for six months.

public at large.'[71] This formula would have meant that injunctions could be obtained even after a high degree of prior publication and therefore it was unacceptable to *The Sunday Times*. However, the two parties agreed on a formula: that the material had already been published in any other newspaper, magazine or other publication whether within or outside the jurisdiction of the court, to such an extent that the information is in the public domain (other than in a case where the only such publication was made by or caused by the defendants). The Attorney General, however, contended that the defendants had to demonstrate that this was the case, which meant that they had to obtain clearance from the Attorney General before publishing.

In arguing against this contention at first instance, the newspaper invoked Art 10 and also relied on s 12(4) of the HRA. It was argued that the restriction proposed by the Attorney General would be disproportionate to the aim pursued and therefore could not be justified in a democratic society. The decision in *Bladet-Tromsø v Norway*[72] was referred to, in which the Court said that it is incumbent on the media 'to impart information and ideas concerning matters of public interest. Not only does the press have the task of imparting such information and ideas, the public has the right to receive them'.[73] Taking these arguments into account, it was found at first instance that the Attorney General had to demonstrate why there was a public interest in restricting publication. No injunction was granted since it was found that he had not done so. On appeal, the same stance was taken. It was found that the requirement to seek clearance should not be imposed: the editor had to form his own judgment as to whether the material could be said to be already in the public domain. That position was, the Court found, most consonant with the requirements of Art 10 and s 12.

This decision suggests that, bearing in mind the requirements of the HRA, an injunction is unlikely to be granted where a small amount of prior publication has already taken place. It does not, however, decide the question of publication where no prior publication has taken place, but the material is of public interest (which could clearly have been said of the Wright material). Following *Bladet-Tromsø v Norway* it is suggested that an injunction should not be granted where such material is likely, imminently, to come into the public domain, a position consistent with the demands of s 12(4), which refers to such a likelihood. Even where this cannot be said to be the case, it would be consonant with the requirements of Art 10 and s 12 to refuse to grant an injunction on the basis of the duty of newspapers to report on such material. The burden would be placed on the State to seek to establish that a countervailing pressing social need was present and that the injunction did not go further than necessary in order to serve the end in view.

Confidence and contempt

Recent developments in common law contempt will allow breach of confidence a greater potential than it previously possessed to prevent dissemination of government information. While the temporary injunctions were in force, *The Independent* and two other papers published material covered by them. It was determined in the Court of

---

71 *Ibid*, para 2.
72 (1999) 6 BHRC 599.
73 Paragraph 62 of the judgment.

Appeal (*AG v Newspaper Publishing plc*)[74] that such publication constituted the actus reus of contempt. The decision therefore affirmed the principle that once an interlocutory injunction has been obtained restraining one organ of the media from publication of allegedly confidential material, the rest of the media may be in contempt if they publish that material even if their intention in doing so is to bring alleged iniquity to public attention. Such publication must be accompanied by an intention to prejudice the eventual trial of the permanent injunctions, although this only need be in the sense that it was foreseen that such prejudice, while undesired, was very likely to occur.

Thus, the laws of confidence and contempt were allowed to operate together as a significant prior restraint on media freedom and this principle was upheld by the House of Lords (*AG v Times Newspapers Ltd*).[75] Arguably, this ruling afforded insufficient recognition to the public interest in knowing of the allegations made in *Spycatcher* which should have outweighed the possibility that publication of the allegations would constitute an interference with the administration of justice. It may be that the House of Lords did not appreciate the extent to which this decision, in combination with the possibility of obtaining a temporary injunction where an arguable case for breach of confidence had been made out, would hand government an effective and wide ranging means of silencing the media when publication of sensitive information was threatened.

However, the potential of this method should already have been apparent. In 1987, the BBC wished to broadcast a programme to be entitled *My Country Right or Wrong* which was to examine issues raised by the *Spycatcher* litigation. The Attorney General obtained an injunction preventing transmission on the ground of breach of confidence (*AG v BBC*).[76] According to the Attorney General, the injunction then affected every organ of the media because of the July ruling of the Court of Appeal in *AG v Newspaper Publishing plc*[77] (this was a preliminary ruling on the *actus reus* of common law contempt which was affirmed as noted above).

It seems fairly clear that although the government eventually lost in the *Spycatcher* litigation, the decision will not have any liberalising impact as far as enhancing the ability of newspapers to publish information about government is concerned. The most pernicious aspect of breach of confidence – the ease with which interim injunctions may be obtained – remains largely unaffected by the outcome of the litigation and where such an injunction is obtained, it will affect all of the media in the sense that they probably will not wish to risk criminal liability for contempt of court. Thus, these developments in the use of the common law as a means of preventing disclosure of information provide a further means of ensuring secrecy where information falls outside the categories covered by the Official Secrets Act, or where it is thought appropriate not to invoke criminal sanctions. *AG v Guardian Newspapers* has demonstrated that temporary injunctions may be obtained to prevent disclosure of official information even where prior publication has ensured that there is little confidentiality left to be protected. Now the HRA is in force, it is probable that this development of common law contempt and confidence may be

---

74 [1992] 1 AC 191; (see further Chapter 5, p 249).
75 [1992] 1 AC 191; [1991] 2 All ER 398; [1991] 2 WLR 994, HL.
76 (1987) *The Times*, 18 December. For comment, see (1990) 10 OJLS 430, p 435; Thornton, P, *Decade of Decline*, 1989, pp 9–11.
77 [1988] Ch 333; [1987] 3 All ER 276; [1988] 3 WLR 942, CA.

found to fail to fulfil the requirements of Art 10 of the Act,[78] since the demands of proportionality are unlikely to be satisfied where the whole of the media is – in effect – restrained from publication, although it has not had a chance to argue the case for publication in the public interest.

Defence Advisory notices[79]

The government and the media may avoid the head-on confrontation which occurred in the *Spycatcher* litigation by means of a curious institution known until 1992 as the 'D' (Defence) notice system. This system, which effectively means that the media censor themselves in respect of publication of official information, can obviate the need to seek injunctions to prevent publication. The 'D' Notice Committee was set up with the object of letting the Press know which information could be printed and at what point: it was intended that if sensitive political information was covered by a 'D' notice, an editor would decide against printing it. The system is entirely voluntary and in theory the fact that a 'D' notice has not been issued does not mean that a prosecution under the Official Secrets Act 1989 is precluded, although in practice it is very unlikely. Further, guidance obtained from the Secretary to the Committee does not amount to a straightforward 'clearance'. Press representatives sit on the committee as well as civil servants and officers of the armed forces.

The value and purpose of the system was called into question due to the injunction obtained against the BBC in respect of *My Country Right or Wrong* as mentioned above. The programme concerned issues raised by the Spycatcher litigation; the BBC consulted the 'D' Notice Committee before broadcasting and were told that the programme did not affect national security. However, the Attorney General then obtained an injunction preventing transmission on the ground of breach of confidence, thereby disregarding the 'D' Notice Committee.

Some criticism has been levelled at the system: in the Third Report from the Defence Committee,[80] the 'D' notice system was examined and it was concluded that it was failing to fulfil its role. It was found that major newspapers did not consult their 'D' notices to see what was covered by them and that the wording of 'D' notices was so wide as to render them meaningless. The system conveyed an appearance of censorship which had provoked strong criticism. It was determined that the machinery for the administration of 'D' notices and the 'D' notices themselves needed revision. The review which followed this reduced the number of notices and confined them to specific areas. The system was reviewed again in 1992 (*The Defence Advisory Notices: A Review of the D Notice System*, MOD Open Government Document No 93/06) leading to a reduction in the number of notices to six. They were renamed Defence Advisory notices to reflect their voluntary nature.

---

78 Section 12 would appear to be inapplicable to contempt proceedings in such circumstances, since they are criminal: s 12(5).

79 On the system generally, see Jaconelli, J, 'The "D" Notice system' [1982] PL 39; Fairley, D (1990) 10 OJLS430.

80 (1979–80) HC 773, 640 i–v, *The 'D' Notice System*.

Public interest immunity

Discovery may be needed by one party to an action of documents held by the other in order to assist in the action or allow it to proceed. Where a member of the government or other State body is the party holding the documents in question, it may claim that it is immune from the duty to make such disclosure, asserting public interest immunity (PII), a privilege based on the royal prerogative.[81] The immunity is expressly preserved in the Crown Proceedings Act 1947, but this means that the courts have had to determine its scope. Section 28(1) of the 1947 Act, which provides that the court can make an order for discovery of documents against the Crown and require the Crown to answer interrogatories, is qualified by s 28(2), which preserves Crown privilege to withhold documents on the grounds of public interest in a variety of cases.

Certain decisions demonstrate the development there has been in determining the scope of this privilege. The House of Lords in *Duncan v Cammell Laird and Co*[82] held that documents otherwise relevant to judicial proceedings are not to be disclosed if the public interest requires that they be withheld. This test may be found to be satisfied either (a) by having regard to the contents of the particular document, or (b) by the fact that the document belongs to a category which, on grounds of public interest, must as a class remain undisclosed.[83] Crown privilege as formulated here was an exclusionary rule of evidence based on public interest and the minister was deemed the sole judge of what that constituted. In *Ellis v HO*,[84] a prisoner on remand, who was severely injured by a mentally disturbed prisoner in the prison hospital, sued the Crown for negligence. Privilege was claimed to prevent the disclosure of medical reports on his assailant and so the action had to fail. The danger clearly arose that, since the executive was the sole judge of what was in the public interest, matters embarrassing to government might be concealed. In *Conway v Rimmer*,[85] the speeches in the House of Lords revealed the degree of concern which had arisen in the judiciary as to the danger of injustice created by the use of this privilege by ministers. In that case, a police constable was prosecuted for theft. The charge was dismissed, but he was dismissed from the police force. He brought an action for malicious prosecution against his former superintendent, but the Home Office objected to the disclosure of reports relevant to the case. The House of Lords, in a landmark decision, overruled the minister's claim of Crown privilege and ordered disclosure.

This decision substituted judicial discretion for executive discretion regarding disclosure of documents. However, the judges have tended to exercise this discretion cautiously. Disclosure is unlikely to be ordered unless the party seeking it can show: first, that the material is clearly relevant to a specific issue in the case; secondly, that it will be of

---

81 See Cross and Tapper, *Cross on Evidence*, 7th edn, 1990, Chapter 12; [1942] 1 All ER 587. For a discussion of the legal and historical background see: Jacob, 'From privileged crown to interested public' [1993] PL 121; Bradley, AW, 'Justice, good government and public interest immunity' [1992] PL 514; Ganz, 'Matrix Churchill and public interest immunity' (1993) 56 MLR 564; Allan, 'Public interest immunity and ministers' responsibility' [1993] CLR 661.

82 [1942] AC 624.

83 [1942] 1 All ER 587, p 592.

84 [1953] 2 QB 135.

85 [1968] AC 910, HL.

significant value in the fair disposal of the case; and thirdly, following *Air Canada v Secretary of State for Trade (No 2)*,[86] that it will assist the case of that party. The main issue for determination in Air Canada concerned the conditions which have to be satisfied before a court will inspect documents for which PII is claimed. If the court does not inspect, it cannot order disclosure. The court considered that the documents were relevant in the case and necessary for its fair disposal. However, this did not lead the majority to find that inspection was necessary in order to determine whether non-disclosure would prevent the court from judging the issues. Instead, the majority found that the party seeking disclosure must show that 'the documents are very likely to contain material which would give substantial support to his contention on an issue which arises in the case'.[87]

After *Air Canada*, in effect, three tests had to be satisfied before disclosure could be ordered. The documents in question must be relevant to the case; they must be of assistance in disposing of it and the party seeking disclosure must show that they will assist his or her own case. As Zuckermann points out, this means that if the party seeking disclosure does not know in detail what the documents contain, he or she will not be able to satisfy the third test and the court will therefore refuse to inspect the documents to see if the second test is satisfied.[88] The second test mentioned above has received an interpretation restrictive of disclosure; the need to show that the material in question will be of *substantial* assistance to the court was emphasised in *Bookbinder v Tebbit (No 2)*.[89] Even where these three tests may be satisfied, discovery may be refused due to the nature or 'class' of the material in question even where it clearly falls outside the protected categories covered by the Official Secrets Act 1989. In *Halford v Sharples*,[90] the applicant claimed sex discrimination in that she had not been recommended for promotion, and sought discovery of documents from, *inter alia*, the police authority which had failed to interview her and the Chief Constable of her own force. The Court of Appeal found that all documents of any type relating to internal police inquiries were protected by PII and that therefore, production of the files would not be ordered. It also found that immunity from disclosure was also an immunity from use. Thus, no use at all could be made of the information contained in the documents in question, regardless of the fact that both parties were aware of their contents.

The House of Lords in *Chief Constable of West Midlands Police ex p Wiley, Chief Constable of Nottinghamshire Police ex p Sunderland*[91] considered that there was insufficient evidence to support Lord Oliver's conclusion in Neilson as to the need for a new class claim to PII. Thus, it was found that Neilson must be regarded as wrongly decided, but that did not mean that PII would never attach to police complaints documents: whether it did or not would depend on the particular contents of the document.[92] This decision emphasises that a clear case must be made out for use of a broad class claim to PII and, as far as

---

86 *Air Canada v Secretary of State for Trade (No 2)* [1983] 1 All ER 910, pp 923–25 HL(E).
87 *Per* Lord Fraser [1983] 1 All ER 917.
88 Zuckerman, AAS, 'Public interest immunity – a matter of prime judicial responsibility' (1994) 57 MLR 703.
89 [1992] 1 WLR 217.
90 [1992] 3 All ER 624, CA.
91 [1995] 1 AC 274, pp 281, 291–306; (1995) 1 Cr App R 342, HL.
92 See *Taylor v Anderton* [1995] 2 All ER 420, CA.

documents in the hands of public authorities are concerned, it is preferable that each case be considered on its own facts and not on the basis of a class claim. Moreover, it is to be welcomed in the interests of justice as going some way towards ensuring that civil actions against the police are not undermined by claims that relevant information cannot be disclosed.

One of the most controversial assertions of PII occurred in the *Matrix Churchill* case,[93] in which PII certificates were used in an attempt to suppress evidence in the trial of three directors of the company Matrix Churchill for supplying arms to Iraq in breach of export restrictions on the sale of military equipment.

Suppression appeared to be sought owing to the political embarrassment which was likely to be aroused if it was discovered that government ministers were condoning the arms sales. The trial collapsed after Alan Clark revealed in court that evidence affecting the defence was not before the court because of the certificates. The case caused a political storm and led to an inquiry under Sir Richard Scott, resulting in the *Scott Report*.[94] AAS Zuckermann[95] observed, commenting on the case, that, after *Conway v Rimmer*, ministers were relieved of the responsibility of considering suppressing evidence by way of PII certificates on the administration of justice. On this basis, the responsibility for the suppression of evidence lies with the courts, not ministers, and therefore Zuckermann does not condemn the ministerial practices revealed in the Scott Report. He ends by arguing that the courts, 'not just ministers', should be put on trial for their part in the Matrix Churchill affair. On this view, judicial responsibility for the suppression of evidence, claimed in Conway, is in a sense a double-edged sword; on the one hand it allows the judges to provide a check on the actions of the executive, but on the other it frees the executive from keeping a check on itself as regards the potential effect of a PII certificate on the administration of justice. Zuckermann assumes that the only public interest which ministers can be expected to understand and evaluate – in the light of judicial approval of 'closed' government – is the interest in secrecy. Once that interest is established, they can and perhaps should close their eyes to the likely consequences attendant on issuance of the certificate, such as the possibility that an innocent person might be convicted, even where such a possibility is self-evident due to the nature of the material sought to be suppressed (as it seems to have been in the Matrix Churchill case) and despite their knowledge of judicial timidity and reluctance to resist PII claims, especially in national security cases. Possibly, Zuckermann's understandable eagerness to condemn judicial bolstering of the 'wall of silence blocking access to public documents' has led him to accept too readily ministerial claims of inability to understand or take any responsibility for the requirements of the interests of justice so long as a public interest in non-disclosure can be made out. Possibly, he also displays a readiness to accept that ministers are seeking to act in the public rather than the government interest when a claim for suppression of evidence is made. In the light of Lord Templeman's comments in

---

93 See Leigh, D, *Betrayed: The Real Story of the Matrix Churchill Trial*, 1993; Tomkins, 'Public interest immunity after *Matrix Churchill*' [1993] PL 530; Leigh, I, 'Matrix Churchill, supergun and the Scott Inquiry' [1993] PL 630; Tomkins, A, *The Constitution Unwrapped: Government after Scott*, 1997.

94 *Report of the Inquiry into the Export of Defence Equipment and Dual-use goods to Iraq and related prosecutions* (1995–96) HC 115, 15 February 1996.

95 Zuckerman, *op cit*, fn 88.

Wiley, above, it is suggested that both ministerial and judicial responsibility for creating 'the wall of silence' should be clearly condemned.

Zuckermann's conclusions as regards the use of PII certificates generally, and as regards their use in the *Matrix Churchill* case in particular, do not harmonise with those of *Sir Richard Scott* in the Scott Report. Scott found that the government attitude:

> ... to disclosure of documents to the defence was consistently grudging. The approach ought to have been to consider what documents the defence might reasonably need and then to consider whether there was any good reason why the defence should not have them ... the actual approach ... seems to have been to seek some means by which refusal to disclose could be justified.[96]

The danger in the argument, reiterated by Lord Scarman in *Air Canada*,[97] that judges take the responsibility for considering the effect of suppression of evidence on the administration of justice, is that both judiciary and ministers succeed in shuffling off the responsibility for such suppression: the judges accept, as ministers strongly demand they should, that matters of public safety can be judged only by the executive, while ministers hide behind the fiction that the judiciary will weigh up the interest in such matters against the interest in justice. Thus, ministers are able to adopt the convenient constitutional position of demanding on the one hand that the judiciary should not look behind PII claims based on national security interests and on the other that if judges accede to such demands, they must take the responsibility for doing so. Clearly, there is a strong argument that judges should be less timid when faced with such claims, but there also appears to be merit in Sir Richard Scott's argument[98] that ministers must take some responsibility for putting them forward, bearing in mind ministerial responsibility for upholding the proper administration of justice. It is suggested that the creation of a dichotomy between ministerial and judicial responsibility in this matter, in order to ensure that the latter prevails, is unnecessary and leads to situations such as the one which arose in *Matrix Churchill*. Thus, in the light of *Matrix Churchill*, there is arguably a need for greater regulation of the issue of PII certificates which would be based on the acceptance of initial ministerial responsibility for their potential effects on justice, although the judiciary should remain the final arbiters in the matter.[99]

The argument, criticised by Sir Richard Scott, that before signing a PII certificate ministers need to do no more than satisfy themselves that documents fall into a prescribed class, may be based partly on 'entrenched conventions of public administration' including the rule that 'secrecy is in the interests of good government'. In future, this argument may become less sustainable in the face of the new culture of openness depending from the 1994 Code of Practice on Access to Government Information, as revised in 1997 (discussed below). Although the Code excludes many matters from its ambit, including categories of information which would be likely to be the subject of PII claims, it is based on the principle that responsibility for ensuring access to official information lies with departments, not with the judiciary, thus suggesting not

---

96 Section G of the *Scott Report*. See also the debate in Parliament on the Scott Report, HC Deb, 26 February 1996; HC Deb Vol 272 No 51, in particular Col 612.

97 See above, fn 86.

98 See para G18.67 of the Scott Report.

99 See further Leigh, I, 'Reforming public interest immunity' (1995) 2 Web JCL 49–71.

only that good government requires a degree of openness, but that it accepts sole responsibility for ensuring that openness is maintained. It may also be noted, in support of this point, that the duties and responsibilities of ministers set out in *Questions of Procedure for Ministers* include: '... the duty to give Parliament and the public as full information as possible about the policies, decisions and actions of the government and not to ... knowingly mislead Parliament and the public ... [and] the duty to ... uphold the administration of justice.'

The then Conservative Government responded to the Scott Report by announcing that changes would be made to the practice in respect of PII certificates issued by the government.[100] An immunity claim would be made only where a real danger to the public interest could be shown. The certificate itself would explain the harm which might be caused, unless to do so would in itself bring about the harm in question. Although these changes were expressed to apply only to government claims for immunity, it was accepted that they might apply in other instances.

Under the HRA, the use of PII certificates may have to be re-evaluated due to the demands of Art 6. If the prosecutor considers that the material is sensitive, an application to a court for a ruling to protect it on grounds of PII must be made.[101] It can be made *ex parte* with notice to the defence or, in an exceptional case, without notice. In any such application a judge, bound by s 6 of the HRA, would have to consider Art 6 requirements in respect of such disclosure. Guidelines as to the use of public interest certificates were provided in *Davis, Rowe and Johnson*.[102] However, the use of PII in that case was found to breach Art 6 by the European Court of Human Rights[103] and, therefore, they will have to be re-examined. The domestic courts will have the opportunity of doing so now that HRA is fully in force. The findings in the same context in *Fitt and Jasper v UK*[104] will be relevant. The Court said that in those instances, the judge had been able to consider the sensitive material in question and therefore was able to conduct a balancing act between fairness to the defence and to the prosecution. On that basis, no breach of Art 6 was found. Disclosure of evidence raises a number of issues under Art 6. The fair hearing requirement of Art 6(1) has been found to connote equality between prosecution and defence[105] ('equality of arms') and, where relevant material is withheld from the defence, equality is unlikely to be assured. Moreover, failure to disclose evidence may prevent the defence challenging the credibility of a witness and therefore may not be reconcilable with the Art 6 guarantees.[106] However, the Strasbourg case law has left a discretion to the national court[107] as to the interpretation of the right to cross-examine witnesses under para 6(3)(d)[108] and so has deprived this right of some of its effect. The position appears to be that the rights of witnesses to life, liberty and security, which fall within the

---

100 HC Deb Vol 576 Col 1507; HC Deb Vol 287 Col 949, 18 December 1996.

101 See Criminal Procedure and Investigations Act 1996, ss 3(6) and 7(5).

102 [1993] 1 WLR 613.

103 *Rowe and Davis v UK*; Appl No 28901/95; [1999] Crim LR 410; (2000) 30 EHRR 1.

104 [1999] EHRLR 430.

105 Judgment of 27 June 1968, *Neumeister*, A 8 (1968), para 43.

106 *Kostovski v Netherlands* (1989) 12 EHRR 434; *Windisch v Austria* (1990) 13 EHRR 281. See Chapter 11, p 709 for further discussion.

107 See, eg, *Asch v Austria* (1991) 15 EHRR 597; *Liefveld v Netherlands* (1995) 18 EHRR CD 103.

108 See Chapter 2, p 64.

Convention, should be balanced against the rights of the defendant. Measures should be available to test the evidence, while recognising the need – where relevant – to protect the witness.[109] Where the aim of the failure to disclose evidence is, however, to protect governmental interests, as in *Matrix Churchill*, it is likely that the fair trial requirement would prevail.

3 RIGHTS OF ACCESS TO INFORMATION PRIOR TO THE FREEDOM OF INFORMATION ACT[110]

Introduction

The attitude to secrecy exemplified by US freedom of information legislation, which is founded on the presumption that information must be disclosed unless specifically exempted, may be contrasted with the traditional position in the UK, which took the opposite stance. No comprehensive provision was made for such disclosure: the starting point was, as indicated above, to criminalise disclosure in certain categories of information. American freedom of information provision can, in particular, be contrasted with provision under the UK Public Records Act 1958, which is considered below. It provides a measure of access to official information, but only after 30 years or more have passed. Considering all the various and overlapping methods of preventing disclosure of official information in the UK, and bearing in mind the contrasting attitude to this issue evinced in other democracies, it is fair to say that that until 2000, the UK was being increasingly isolated in its stance as a resister of freedom of information legislation. Since virtually all other democracies had introduced such legislation, that stance was indefensible in a mature democracy. It was finally abandoned when the Freedom of Information Act 2000 was introduced.

However, even before that point, and before the Labour Government came to power in 1997, there had been certain developments under the Conservative Governments of 1989–97, especially under the Major Government, which suggested that a gradual movement towards more open government was taking place in the UK. The Data Protection Act 1984 allowed access to personal information held on computerised files. A very limited right to disclosure of information in the field of local government was created.[111] The Campaign for Freedom of Information had, from 1985 onwards, brought about acceptance of the principle of access rights in some areas of official action. It supported Private Members' Bills, as explained in Chapter 10, which allowed for rights of access to information in certain limited areas.[112] Disclosure of a range of information was decriminalised under the Official Secrets Act 1989, as indicated above.

---

109 See *Doorson v Netherlands* (1996) 22 EHRR 330.

110 See, generally, Birkinshaw, *op cit*, fn 1; *Reforming the Secret State*, 1990; 'The White Paper on open government' [1993] PL 557.

111 Part VA of the Local Government Act 1972 (introduced by the Local Government (Access to Information) Act 1985. The right allowed members of the public to inspect local authority minutes, reports and background papers and to take copies of them. However, a number of significant areas were exempt from the access right; also, council 'working parties' are exempt.

112 See Chapter 10, pp 601–02.

After the 1992 general election, the Prime Minister promised a review of secrecy in Whitehall to be conducted by William Waldegrave, the minister with responsibility for the Citizen's Charter, which would concentrate on the large number of statutory instruments which prevent public disclosure of government information in various areas, with a view to removing those which did not appear to fulfil a pressing need. It was also promised that a list of secret Cabinet committees with their terms of reference and their ministerial membership would be published. It was proposed that reform of the Official Secrets Act 1989 would be undertaken, so that disclosure of a specific document would be criminalised as opposed to disclosure of a document belonging to a class of documents which might cause harm. In fact, this reform did not take place. A White Paper on Open Government (Cm 2290) was published in July 1993 and a Code of Practice on Access to Government Information was introduced in 1994.

The Public Records Acts

The UK Public Records Act 1958, as amended by the Public Records Act 1967, provides that public records will not be transferred to the Public Records Office in order to be made available for inspection until the expiration of 30 years, and longer periods can be prescribed for 'sensitive information'. Such information will include personal details about persons who are still living and papers affecting the security of the State. Some such information can be withheld for 100 years or for ever, and there is no means of challenging such decisions. For example, at the end of 1987, a great deal of information about the Windscale fire in 1957 was disclosed, although some items are still held back. Robertson argues that information is withheld to prevent embarrassment to bodies such as the police or civil servants rather than to descendants of persons mentioned in it; and in support of this he cites examples such as police reports on the NCCL (1935–41), flogging of vagrants (1919), and decisions against prosecuting James Joyce's *Ulysses* (1924) as instances of material which in January 1989 was listed as closed for a century.[113]

However, a somewhat less restrictive approach to the release of archives became apparent in 1994. In 1992–93, a review was conducted of methods of ensuring further openness in government and its results were published in a White Paper entitled *Open Government* (Cm 2290).[114] The White Paper stated that a Code of Practice on Access to Government Information would be adopted (the Code is discussed below) and there would be a reduction in the number of public records withheld from release beyond 30 years. A review group established by Lord Mackay in 1992 suggested that records should only be closed for more than 30 years where their disclosure would cause harm to defence, national security, international relations and economic interests of the UK; information supplied in confidence; personal information which would cause substantial distress if disclosed. Under s 3(4) of the 1958 Act, records may still be retained within departments for 'administrative' reasons or for any other special reason.

---

113 See Robertson, G, *Media Law*, 1999, Chapter 10 'Public Records'.
114 The White Paper proposals in relation to public records are considered by Birkinshaw, P, 'I only ask for information – the White Paper on open government' [1993] PL 557.

The Freedom of Information (FoI) Act 2000, Part VI and Sched 8 amends the 1958 Act. Part VI amends the exemptions of Part II of the 1958 Act in respect of historical records, with a view to enhancing the ease of access to them. Section 63(1) of the FoI act reduces the number of exemptions that apply to such records. This is done in three tranches. First, exemptions are removed after 30 years in respect of a number of categories of information, including information prejudicial to the economic interests of the UK, information obtained with a view to prosecution, court records, information prejudicial to public affairs and commercial interests. Secondly, one exemption is removed after 60 years – in respect of information concerning the conferring of honours. Thirdly, a large number of exemptions under s 31 relating to various investigations and the maintenance of law and order are removed after 100 years. These modest provisions are to be welcomed, as easing the task of historians, but their limited nature should be questioned; especially, it must be asked why any absolute exemptions, in particular those relating to intelligence information, remain.[115]

The Code of Practice on Access to Government Information

Introduction

Instead of freedom of information legislation, the Major Government favoured the introduction of an unenforceable *Code of Practice on Access to Government Information*. It came into effect from 4 April 1994 as promised in the White Paper *Open Government* (Cm 2290), and it is now in its 2nd edition, as revised in 1997.[116] It may be noted that the Code is still being used and, until the Freedom of Information Act 2000 comes fully into force by 2005, it will remain the most comprehensive, albeit unenforceable, access to information measure.[117] The Code provides that non-exempted government departments will publish 'facts and analysis of the facts which the government considers relevant and important in framing major policy proposals and decisions',[118] 'explanatory material on departments' dealings with the public', and 'reasons for administrative decisions to those affected', and information in accordance with the Citizen's Charter on the operation of public services.[119] Such departments will also provide information on receipt of specific requests.

On its face, this Code exhibits a number of the features which may be found in FoI legislation abroad apart, of course, from the crucial failure to create a legally binding right of access to information. However, it will be argued that in almost every instance, where various possibilities are available, it chooses the course which disadvantages the seeker after information and undermines the principle of 'openness'. The Code is apparently

---

115 Cf the provision in respect of intelligence information held in the Public Record Office of Northern Ireland, which will no longer be subject to an absolute exemption, under FoI Act, s 64(2).

116 The amendments took into account the recommendations of the Select Committee on the PCA in its Second Report, *Second Report from the Select Committee on the Parliamentary Commissioner for Administration*, HC 84 (1995–96), *Open Government*.

117 For discussion of the Code, see Tomkins, *op cit*, fn 93, Chapter 3, pp 112–24.

118 Paragraph 3(i).

119 Paragraph 3(ii) and (iii).

based on the presumption that all useful government information will be released unless there are pressing reasons why it is in the public interest that it should remain secret. This is the general principle on which freedom of information is based. However, in relation to major policy decisions (Part I, s 3(i)) the Code only relates to information considered 'relevant' by the government. In countries which have FoI, the usefulness or relevance of documents containing information is determined by the person who seeks it rather than by government ministers or civil servants. Usefulness is not an objective quality, but depends on the purposes of the seeker which only he or she can appreciate.

Further, the Code promises only to afford release of information as opposed to documents. As the Campaign for Freedom of Information has pointed out, this is: 'a potentially overwhelming defect: the opportunities for selective editing are obvious.'[120] As pointed out in the memorandum submitted by the Campaign for Freedom of Information,[121] and endorsed in the Second Report from the Select Committee on the PCA, the information seeker will be unable to ensure that all significant parts of the document in question have been disclosed. The Select Committee on the PCA has accepted the claim that 'there will always be a possibility, whether by design or oversight, that significant aspects of a document are removed or obscured in any paraphrase'.[122] The Ombudsman considers that the access should be to documents rather than only to information. The Second Report from the Select Committee on the Parliamentary Commissioner for Administration (PCA)[123] and the First Special Report from the Public Service Committee recommended that the access under the Code should be to the documents themselves.[124] The then Conservative Government stated that documents could already be released under the Code, but considered that this would not necessarily be a helpful approach for departments dealing with Code requests.

Thus, both these limitations undermine the principle of 'openness' and add to the number of avenues available to a department which is subject to the Code to use in order to avoid complying with it in relation to sensitive information.

In other respects, it is apparent that the Major Government failed to show a serious commitment to the fundamental principles of freedom of information. As the Select Committee on the PCA pointed out, the government made little effort to publicise the Code and this may be one reason for the lack of interest shown in it by individual citizens.[125] Individual citizens who are aware of its existence may be deterred from using the Code by the charges which have been imposed for providing information, which have, in some instances, been excessive.[126]

---

120 Appendices to the Minutes of Evidence taken before the Select Committee on the PCA, session 1993–94, HC 33 (1993–94), Vol II, p 258.

121 *Ibid.*

122 See Second Report, *op cit*, fn 116, para 82.

123 HC 84 (1995–96), para 83.

124 *Public Service Committee First Special Report*, HC 67 (1996–97), para 32.

125 See further the *Second Report of the Parliamentary Commissioner for Administration*, HC 91 (1994–95), para 5.

126 See further the Citizen's Charter report on the operation of the Code, *Open Government*,1994.

Exemptions

As indicated below, a number of matters are not part of the remit of the PCA. This means that such areas are subject to no enforcement mechanism at all. The departments concerned may voluntarily release information and may respond to specific requests, but the information seeker has no means of attempting to ensure that full or any information is delivered. The Code at present excludes these areas of operation from its coverage, as it indicates in para 6, and goes even further in exempting a number of matters from the access which *are* within the jurisdiction of the PCA.

The Code sets out its purpose of extending access to official information, in Part I, but makes the access subject to a large number of exemptions, set out in Part II. The exemptions can be divided into two groups: those which are subject to a harm test and those which are not. The key exemptions within the former group cover information relating to: defence, security and international relations, internal discussion and advice, law enforcement and legal proceedings, effective management of the economy and collection of tax, effective management and operations of the public service, third parties' commercial confidence, immigration and nationality information, medical information given in confidence, information which is soon to be published or where disclosure would be premature, and research, statistics and analysis where disclosure could be misleading. The latter group includes information within the following categories: communications with the royal household, public employment, public appointments and honours, privacy of an individual, information given in confidence, information covered by statutory and other restrictions. Unreasonable, voluminous and vexatious requests, or requests requiring an 'unreasonable diversion of resources', are also exempt.

The harm tests are varied and some are more complex than others, but none of them seeks to explain what is meant by 'harm'. Thus, in relation to defence, security and international relations under para 1, part of the harm test is concerned with 'information whose disclosure would harm national security or defence' without giving any further indication as to what this might entail. However, the inclusion of harm tests narrows down the exemptions: the Code does not simply exempt, for example, information concerning the effective management of the economy from its provisions; it does so only when disclosure of such information would 'harm the ability of the government to manage the economy or where such disclosure could prejudice the conduct of official market operations or lead to improper gain or advantage' (para 6). How far it would be possible to be sure that information which did not satisfy the harm test was not being withheld is another matter. But, in theory, the harm tests are a step in the direction of disclosure. This cannot be said of information falling into the categories where it is not required that harm should be shown.

One of the key criticisms of the Code relates to the extensiveness of the list of exemptions and their breadth. Compare, for example, the confidentiality provision in the Code (para 14(a)) with the equitable doctrine of confidence. The key difference is that under the latter, before the publication of the information concerned can be actionable, the plaintiff may have to show that disclosure would cause him some kind of detriment.[127]

---

127 See, eg, the well known exposition of the doctrine in *Coco v AN Clark (Engineers) Limited* [1969] RPC 41, p 47. Some doubt has been expressed as to whether detriment is a necessary ingredient of the action (*dicta* of Lord Keith in *AG v Guardian Newspapers (No 2)* [1988] 3 All ER 545, p 640) but the orthodox view remains that it is.

Additionally, the defendant may still defeat the plaintiff's claim if he can show that publication would be in the public interest, a defence which is of quite a wide scope,[128] thus affording more recognition to freedom of speech and of information. The Code does not require the department concerned to show that any detriment would flow from the requested disclosure, nor is there any public interest exception. This provision in the Code thus affords freedom of information less recognition than the existing law.

Not only are the exemptions very broad, they are likely to give rise to grave difficulties of interpretation and, in any event, to be exploited by the department concerned. In this context, it may be noted that a survey published in March 1997[129] showed that public bodies are not meeting the standards of openness laid down in the government Code. Fifty government departments were asked for information to which the public is entitled under the Code. Eleven gave wrong or inadequate information and three refused to reply at all. Among those showing poor practice were the Legal Aid Board and the Commission for Racial Equality. The Department for Education and Employment and the Office for National Statistics were among those which refused to reply. If a department considers, on its interpretation of one of the exempting provisions, that the exemption applies, although the information seeker and Ombudsman disagree, the department cannot be compelled to release the information. No avenue of challenge to the exclusions from the Code is available.

As indicated above, the PCA's remit is, in any event, limited. Certain matters set out in Sched 3 of the Parliamentary Commissioner Act 1967 are excluded from the investigation by the PCA. These include extradition and fugitive offenders, the investigation of crime by or on behalf of the Home Office, security of the State, action in matters relating to contractual or commercial activities, court proceedings and personnel matters of the armed forces, teachers, the civil service or police. UK Governments have always resisted the extension of the Ombudsman system into these areas. Of these restrictions, those attracting the most criticism have been the exclusion of contractual and commercial matters and of public service personnel matters. The Fourth Report from the Select Committee on the PCA 1979 considered that both exclusions were unjustified. Whatever justification might be put forward for these limitations, it is hard to show that the PCA derives positive benefit from being excluded from these areas and the PCA himself has said that such exclusion from his scrutiny may not reflect Parliament's intentions.[130] Future review of the Code may consider narrowing down the exemptions from the Code, but the question would remain whether the PCA's supervision should be allowed to extend into areas from which, traditionally, he has been excluded. Obviously, as the FoI Act comes more fully into force, this question will become less significant.

---

128 See, eg, *Lion Laboratories v Evans and Express Newspapers* [1985] QB 526; [1984] 2 All ER 852, HL and *W v Egdell* [1990] Ch 359. See further Chapter 10, pp 578–79.

129 The journalists' magazine UKPG published the survey on 7 March 1997, para 9.

130 PCA Annual Report for 1988.

The role of the Parliamentary Commissioner for Administration

The White Paper describes the role of the PCA as follows:

> The Parliamentary Commissioner for Administration (PCA), the Parliamentary Ombudsman, has agreed that complaints that departments and other bodies within his jurisdiction have failed to comply with this Code can be investigated if referred to him by a Member of Parliament. When he decides to investigate he will have access to the department's internal papers and will be able in future to report to Parliament when he finds that information has been improperly withheld. The Select Committee on the PCA will then be able to call departments and ministers to account for failure to supply information in accordance with the Code, as they can now call them to account for maladministration or injustice. The Ombudsman has the confidence of Parliament and is independent of the government. Parliamentary accountability will thus be preserved and enhanced. Ministers and departments will have a real spur to greater openness and citizens will have an independent investigator working on their behalf.[131]

As indicated, the Ombudsman considers complaints that information has been improperly withheld by government departments, but no legal remedies are provided for citizens if the Code is breached. Under s 5(1) of the Parliamentary Commissioner Act 1967, the Ombudsman can take up a complaint only if the citizen has suffered injustice as a result of maladministration; both maladministration and injustice must be shown and there must be a causal link between them. These requirements were relaxed in relation to complaints relating to the Code of Practice. In relation to the Ombudsman's wider role in combating maladministrative secrecy – where the Code makes no commitment to release particular information – these requirements must, however, be met.

If a citizen fails to obtain information or full information in a non-exempt, or arguably non-exempt area, he or she can complain to an MP who will normally pass the complaint to the Ombudsman. However, challenge to refusals of information by departments via an MP to the Ombudsman is clearly unlikely to be as effective as challenge in a court. If the Ombudsman recommends that a department should reveal information and the department does not accept the recommendation, it may be called upon to justify itself before the Select Committee on the Parliamentary Commissioner for Administration. However, this will not have the same impact as if the enforcement mechanism for the Code were to be legally binding since the Committee cannot compel a department to release information. Thus, the Ombudsman has no means of enforcing his recommendations unless he takes the means of redress into his own hands by disclosing the disputed information. The first edition of the Code provided in para ix that he should not normally do this. He might be reluctant to take this course since it would probably damage relations between himself and the department in question, which would almost certainly have repercussions in relation to other aspects of his role. Thus, the Code is perhaps most open to criticism due to its lack of 'teeth'.

The grace and favour nature of this scheme is, it is contended, inappropriate in relation to freedom of information, although the recommendatory nature of the PCA may be appropriate in relation to his main function: the fact that the PCA operates informally

---

131 *The White Paper on Open Government*, Cm 2290, July 1993.

and privately has been thought to enhance his powers of persuasion.[132] The Second Report from the Select Committee concluded that the Ombudsman should not be given binding powers in relation to the FOI aspects of his role, but should maintain an integrated approach (para 119). The Committee noted that in New Zealand, the Official Information Act is enforced by an Ombudsman, but that the recommendations on disclosure were made legally binding unless vetoed by an Order in Council within 21 days. This suggests that the traditional, recommendatory approach of the Ombudsman was seen as inappropriate in relation to freedom of information. Nevertheless, the Committee rejected this model.

Since findings and recommendations made by the PCA are not enforceable in law; the adverse publicity which would be generated by a refusal to comply with a recommendation is the only sanction for non-compliance. However, research indicates that the influence of the PCA is far greater in practice than his limited formal powers might suggest. Rodney Austin notes: 'Whitehall's record of compliance with the non-binding recommendations of the ombudsman is actually outstanding; on only two occasions have government departments refused to accept the PCA's findings and in both cases the PCA's recommendations were [nevertheless] complied with.' However, Austin goes on to note that:

> ... compliance with the PCA's recommendations usually involves the payment of an *ex gratia* compensation or an apology or the reconsideration of a prior decision by the correct process. Rarely does it involve reversal on merits of an important policy decision. Governments will fight tenaciously to preserve secrets which matter to them ... there is little ground for optimism that in a crucial case the government would not choose to defy the PCA ...[133]

Criticism can also be made of the use of the MP filter in relation to Code-based complaints. Most significantly, it means that there is no direct access to the body which is supposed to play a role in policing the Code, on behalf of the citizen. Citizens who need to obtain access to the Ombudsman system may not be able to do so because having contacted an MP with a complaint, the MP may decide not to refer the complaint on to the PCA. Furthermore, MPs may appear to be hampered by their political allegiance, in contrast to the Ombudsman, who is independent. Although MPs may not know the political allegiance of a constituent who makes a complaint regarding a refusal of access to politically sensitive information and might, in any event, be uninfluenced by it, the constituent might assume that the complaint would be more forcibly pursued by an opposition MP. In some instances, MPs may have an interest in seeing that the information is withheld and therefore may face a conflict of interests. The Public Service Committee recommended that MPs should be able to make a complaint to the Ombudsman directly concerning the withholding of information by a government department without having to act through another member.[134] The then Conservative Government considered that this would involve a departure from the basic principles

---

132 See Tomkins, *op cit*, fn 93, Chapter 3, p 119.

133 'Freedom of information: the constitutional impact', in Jowell, J and Oliver, D (eds), *The Changing Constitution*, 3rd edn, 1994, p 443.

134 *Public Service Committee First Special Report*, HC 67 (1996–97), para 9.

under the Parliamentary Commissioner Act 1967 and stated that it would seek the view of the Select Committee on the PCA before responding.

Conclusions

If the PCA's ability to underpin the Code had been enhanced by making the Ombudsman's recommendations enforceable in the courts, as in New Zealand, a number of problems would still have remained. The complainant would not have been able to enforce the Code in person. Many avenues of escape from it would still have existed due to the limitations of the Ombudsman's jurisdiction. The Ombudsman might have found eventually that he was almost unable to cope with the volume of complaints under the Code and this situation would probably have been exacerbated if he had also been involved in litigation in attempting to enforce recommendations. Enhancing the role of the Ombudsman along New Zealand lines might have amounted merely to tinkering with the problems. Taking freedom of information seriously means placing it on a statutory basis, with enforcement in the courts.

4 THE FREEDOM OF INFORMATION ACT 2000

Introduction

The criminalisation of the disclosure of official information under the Official Secrets Acts discussed above may be contrasted with the position in other democracies which have introduced freedom of information legislation[135] within the last 30 years. Canada introduced its Access to Information Act in 1982, while America has had such legislation since 1967. Its Freedom of Information Act 1967 applies to all parts of the Federal Government unless an exemption applies. Exempted categories include information concerning defence, law enforcement and foreign policy. The exemptions can be challenged in court and the onus of proof will be on the agency withholding the information to prove that disclosure could bring about the harm the exemption was intended to prevent. However, although the principle of freedom of information in America has attracted praise, its application in practice has often been criticised.[136] In particular, the American business community considers that the system is being abused by persons who have a particular financial interest in uncovering commercial information. A number of reforms have been suggested since 1980 and, in 1986, a major FoI Act reform was passed which extended the exemption available to law enforcement practices.

With the example set by other democracies in mind, commentators have been arguing for a number of years that the voluntary Code should be replaced by a broad statutory

---

135 See McBride, T, 'The Official Information Act 1982' (1984) 11 NZULR 82; Curtis, LJ, 'Freedom of information in Australia' (1983) 14 Fed LR 5; Janisch, HN, 'The Canadian Access to Information Act' [1982] PL 534; for America, see Supperstone, M, *Brownlie's Law of Public Order and National Security*, 1982, pp 270–87; Birkinshaw, *op cit*, fn 1, Chapter 2.

136 For discussion of criticism in the US see Birkinshaw, *op cit*, fn 1, pp 39–40.

right of access to information, enforceable by another independent body or through the courts.[137] In particular, many commentators considered that one of the messages of the Scott Report published in February 1996 was that the UK needed an FoI Act, although it is impossible to know whether FoI could have prevented the Matrix Churchill affair.[138] The report tellingly revealed the lack of 'openness' in government: the system appeared to accept unquestioningly the need to tell Parliament and the public as little as possible about subjects which were seen as politically sensitive. It was apparent that the voluntary Code could not provide a sufficient response to the concerns which the report aroused. The Matrix Churchill affair, which led to the Scott Inquiry, would not, it seems, have come to the attention of the public but for the refusal of the judge in the *Matrix Churchill* trial to accept that the information covered by the PII certificates, relating to the change in the policy of selling arms to Iraq, could not be revealed. As the Select Committee on the PCA pointed out in its Second Report, an FoI Act would tend to change the culture of secrecy in government departments.

For the reasons given above, the general consensus was that merely placing the Code on a statutory basis was not a satisfactory course of action. The Conservative Governments of 1979–97 had no plans to enact FoI legislation. The Select Committee on the PCA recommended the introduction of an FoI Act,[139] but this proposal was rejected by the then Conservative Government.[140] The Labour Government which came into office in 1997 had made a manifesto commitment to introduce an FoI Act. The White Paper *Your Right to Know*[141] was published on 11 December 1997. The White Paper stated: 'Unnecessary secrecy in government leads to arrogance in governance and defective decision-making ... the climate of public opinion has changed: people expect much greater openness and accountability from government than they used to'.[142] A comprehensive statutory right of access to information was introduced with the inception of the Freedom of Information Act 2000.

Statutory freedom of information

Introduction

The FoI Act 2000 is the latest of the Labour Government's major measures of constitutional reform, receiving royal assent on 30 November 2000.[143] As will be

---

137 See Birkinshaw, *op cit*, fn 1; Tomkins, *op cit*, fn 93, Chapter 3, pp124–26.

138 See Birkinshaw, P, 'Freedom of information' (1997) 50 Parliamentary Affairs, p 166; Tomkins, *op cit*, fn 93, Chapter 3, pp 123–26.

139 Paragraph 126.

140 HC 75, HC 67 (1996–97).

141 Cm 3818.

142 White Paper, *Your Right to Know*, Cm 3818, 1997.

143 I am indebted to Gavin Phillipson of Durham University for an analysis of the Act on which this section is partly based. Owing to the very recent passage of the Act, there is a comparative dearth of written analysis dealing with it. The best source of detailed critical analysis of the Bill may be found on the website of the Campaign for Freedom of Information (http://www.cfoi.org.uk), which contains numerous briefing notes and press releases. None of these is on the final text of the Act, but those prepared for the House of Lords' Committee, Report and Third Reading stages are extremely useful, provided they are read alongside the Act itself, and the following analysis has relied on those notes.

indicated below, the White Paper proposed an FoI regime that would have had a radical impact.[144] Had it been implemented, not only would it have brought the UK into line with other democracies as regards its freedom of information provision, but also in a number of respects the legislation would have been more bold and radical than that in place in other countries. When the Bill appeared, it was a grave disappointment,[145] but a number of improvements were made to it during the parliamentary process. The Act that has emerged cannot be termed radical – far from it – but it shows an adherence to the principle of openness which was absent in the Bill.

In what follows, the aim is to provide an overview of the key provisions of the Act and an indication of some of the main criticisms made of it during its passage through Parliament. Two initial points should be noted: at the time of writing, the main provisions of the Act are not yet in force, and need not come fully into force for five years (s 87(3)). It is expected that the provisions will come into force over this period so as to increase its coverage of public authorities gradually, starting with central government. The other point to note is that the Act does not extend to Scotland; proposals have already been drawn up for a more liberal Scottish FoI regime, to be put in place by legislation passed by the Scottish Parliament.

Fundamentals of FoI and the 2000 Act

Rodney Austin identifies a number of common features of FoI regimes, which, together, indicate in essence how FoI legislation differs from the approach taken by the UK up until the 2000 Act.[146] As indicated above, the historical approach of the UK has been to make no comprehensive statutory provision for disclosure of official information, except under the very limited provisions of the Public Records Act 1958; the starting point instead was the criminalisation of disclosure in certain categories under the Official Secrets Acts and by virtue of numerous other statutory provisions. By contrast, the essence of FoI regimes, identified by Austin, are: the creation of public rights of access to official information; placing the determination and enforcement of those rights in the hands of 'an authority independent of government', whether the courts or an information commissioner; the extension of the basic right to information to cover 'all official information other than that specified to be exempt' (ibid). The assumption lying behind FoI legislation is that the release of information is something which is desirable in general terms, with the burden lying on government to justify refusal to release in particular cases.

The 2000 Act may be said partially to share the bases of FoI legislation identified above; as will be explained below, it will give UK citizens, for the first time, a statutory right to official information, which will extend to all such information except that which the Act defines as exempt. In terms of enforcement, there is a mixed picture: as will appear below, the right to information given by the Act is enforceable by an independent Information Commissioner, who, in the final resort, can enforce her orders through

---

144 See Birkinshaw, P, 'An "All singin' and all dancin'" affair: New Labour's proposals for FoI' (1998) PL 176.

145 See Birkinshaw, P and Parry, N, 'Every trick in the book: the Freedom of Information Bill 1999' (1999) 4 EHRLR 373.

146 'Freedom of information: the constitutional impact', in Jowell, J and Oliver, D (eds), *The Changing Constitution*, 4th edn, 2000, p 362.

invoking the courts' power to punish for contempt of court. However, the Commissioner's power to force government to disclose information will not apply to some of the information that may be released under the Act: her disclosure orders can in some cases be quashed by ministerial veto. This is perhaps the first major concern about the Act. The second is the great number and width of the exemptions it contains and the fact that many of these amount to 'class exemptions' where, in order to refuse release of the information, it is not necessary to satisfy a 'harm test', that is, show that release of the particular information requested would prejudice a particular interest, but merely that the information falls into a specified class and is, for that reason alone, exempt.

The scope of the Act

The Act covers 'public authorities'. Section 3 sets out the various ways in which a body can be a public authority. Instead of using the method adopted in the HRA, which, similarly, covers only 'public authorities' and which defines them by means of a very broad and general, non-exhaustive definition, the FoI Act takes the different route of listing a number of public authorities in Sched 1. The list is divided into two halves. First, Parts I–V list those bodies that are clearly public authorities; under s 6 of the HRA they would be standard public authorities. Second, Parts VI–VII list those bodies that are only public authorities so long as they continue to meet the conditions set out in s 4(2) and (3) – that they have been set up by government and their members appointed by central government. Such bodies would probably also be viewed as standard public authorities under the HRA. But the list is not exhaustive, since s 4(1) gives the Secretary of State the power to add bodies to the list in Parts VI–VII if they meet the conditions set out in ss 4(2) and (3), by Order. Further, s 5 provides the Secretary of State with a power to designate a body as a public authority even though it is not listed in Sched 1, and does not meet the conditions set out in ss 4(2) and (3), but which appears to him to be exercising public functions. These bodies would probably be viewed as functional public authorities under s 6 of the HRA. Under s 3(1)(b), a publicly owned company as defined in s 6 is automatically a public body; no formal designation is needed. Section 6 defines such bodies as those wholly owned by the Crown or any public authority listed in Sched 1, other than government departments.

Some public authorities are covered only in respect of certain information they hold, in which case the Act only applies to that class of information (s 7(1)). Rather disturbingly, under s 7(3), the Secretary of State can amend Sched 1 so that a particular public authority becomes one which is subject only to such limited coverage by the Act – in effect potentially drastically limiting the range of information which can be sought from that authority.

It is suggested that although the FoI follows the model of the HRA in differentiating between public authorities as indicated, and between private and public bodies, Sched 1 read with ss 3–6 does *not* provide an exhaustive list of those bodies that are public authorities for the purposes of s 6 of the HRA, although these provisions provide a useful guide. The security and intelligence services, which are presumably standard public authorities under s 6 of the HRA, are omitted from Sched 1 and therefore they are completely excluded from the Act. They meet the conditions set out in ss 4(2) and (3), but are – it is readily apparent – unlikely to be added to Sched 1, Parts VI–VII. The difference of approach between the two statutes is defensible; there may be cogent reasons why a body, such as the security service, should not provide information (although a *complete* exclusion is hard to defend), although it would be expected to observe the Convention rights in its operations.

Thus, the Act covers, in Sched 1, all government departments, the House of Commons, the House of Lords, quangos, the NHS, administrative functions of courts and tribunals, police authorities and chief officers of police, the armed forces, local authorities, local public bodies, schools and other public educational institutions, public service broadcasters. Under s 5, private organisations may be designated as public authorities in so far as they carry out statutory functions, as may the privatised utilities and private bodies working on contracted-out functions. The coverage of the Act is therefore far greater than that under the Code and it is notable that some private sector bodies may be covered, although the government made it clear in debate on the Bill that a distinction between private and public bodies in terms of their obligations under the FoI Act should be strictly maintained and that s 5 should be used only to designate bodies discharging public functions.[147] The FoI Act is clearly *not* to be extended into the realm of business. The Act has been praised for the very wide range of bodies which it covers; in comparison with FoI regimes abroad, the coverage is very generous. But it should be noted that in fact, its coverage of private bodies discharging public functions is subject to the exercise of a discretion by the Secretary of State.

The rights granted by the Act

The Act begins with an apparently broad and generous statement of the rights it confers. The Act grants two basic rights. Section 1(1) states:

> Any person making a request for information to a public authority is entitled –
>
> (a) to be informed in writing by the public authority whether it holds information of the description specified in the request [this is referred to in the Act as 'the duty to confirm or deny']; and
>
> (b) if that is the case, to have that information communicated to him.

It may be noted that the right conferred under s 1(1)(b) can cover original documents as well as 'information',[148] and in this respect the Act is clearly an improvement on the Code.

Both these fundamental rights are subject to the numerous exemptions the Act contains. In other words, broadly, where an authority is exempt from providing information under the Act, it is also entitled to refuse even to state whether it holds the information or not, although in some cases, it may only do this where stating whether it holds the information would have the effect of causing the prejudice that the exemption in question is designed to prevent. Such cases will be indicated below.

---

147 HC Standing Committee B, 11 January 2000, Col 67.
148 Section 84 defines information broadly to cover information 'recorded in any form', and in relation to matters covered by s 51(8) this includes unrecorded information.

Exemptions under the Act

Under the White Paper, certain public bodies were to be completely excluded from the Act. One was Parliament, on the ground that, as stated in the White Paper, its deliberations are already open and on the public record. The security services, including GCHQ, were also excluded on the ground that they would not be able to carry out their duties effectively if subject to the legislation. Thus, the Security Services were to be subject to a blanket agency exemption. Apart from these exemptions, there were no exempt categories of information at all held by bodies which are subject to the Act. But seven specified interests were indicated in the White Paper, which took the place of the exemptions under the Code. The test for disclosure was based on an assessment of the harm that disclosure might cause and the need to safeguard the public interest. The test was: will this disclosure cause substantial harm to one of these interests? The first of these interests covered national security, defence and international relations. Obviously, this interest covered a very wide range of information. A further five interests were law enforcement, personal privacy, commercial confidentiality, the safety of the individual, the public and the environment, and information supplied in confidence. Finally, there was an interest termed 'the integrity of decision-making and policy advice processes in government'. In this category, a different test was used: it was not necessary to show that disclosure of the information would cause substantial harm; a test of simple harm only was used. The reason for placing this information in a special category was, in the words of the White Paper: 'now more than ever, government needs space and time in which to assess arguments and conduct its own debates with a degree of privacy ... [decision making in government] can be damaged by random and premature disclosure of its deliberations under Freedom of Information legislation.' This exemption was possibly the most controversial, since it meant that the full background to a decision could remain undisclosed, tending to restrict debate and challenge to it.

Thus, the exemptions under the White Paper were relatively narrow and were subject to quite a strict harm test. They may be sharply contrasted with those that emerged under the Act which include a number of 'class' based exemptions. Nevertheless, the exceptions under the Act will be, on the whole, less wide ranging than those under the Code, taking into account the limitations of the PCA's remit. In certain respects, however, the Code is, on its face, more generous, as indicated below. In particular, the total exemption under s 21 does not appear in the Code in as broad a form,[149] and the exemption under s 35 is broader than the equivalent exemption under the Code – in para 2.

The exemptions under the Act rely on the key distinction between 'class' and 'harm-based' exemptions mentioned above. The harm-based exemptions under the Act are similar to those indicated in the White Paper: they require the public authority to show that the release of the information requested would, or would be likely to, cause prejudice to the interest specified in the exemption. But a number are class-based, meaning that in order to refuse the request, the authority only has to show that the information falls into the class of information covered by the exemption, not that its release would cause or be likely to cause harm or prejudice. It may be noted that the class exemptions can be further divided into two groups: those that are content-based, in the sense that no access to the

---

149 Paragraph 8 of the Code refers to information obtainable under existing statutory rights.

information under the FoI or any other interest is available; and others, which relate not to the content of the information, but to the process of acquiring it. These distinctions are made clear below, in the first group of exemptions considered.

The Act complicates matters further by providing that, in relation to some, but not all, of the class exemptions, and almost all the 'harm exemptions', the authority, having decided that the information is prima facie exempt (either because the information falls into the requisite class exemption, or because the relevant harm test is satisfied, as the case may be), must still then go on to consider whether it should be released under the public interest test set out in s 2. This requires the authority to release the information unless 'in all the circumstances of the case, the public interest in maintaining the exemption outweighs the public interest in disclosing the information'. It should be noted that this provision was amended in the Lords so as to require release unless the interest in maintaining secrecy *'outweighs'* the interest in disclosure. This was thought to provide greater protection for freedom of information, since it must be demonstrated that the need for secrecy is the more compelling interest in the particular case.

The strengthening of the public interest test which took place in the Lords led some Liberal Democrat peers to claim that its application to class exemptions in effect transformed them into 'harm'-based exemptions. However it should be noted that the Campaign for Freedom of Information (CFOI) emphatically rejected this view, on cogent grounds. While the application of a public interest test to the class exemptions does provide for the opportunity to balance the interest in disclosure against that in secrecy, the test is not the same as it would be if considering a harm test. As the CFOI notes, where information falls into a class exemption, and an authority objects to disclosure even under the public interest test, it will be able not only to argue that the specific disclosure would have harmful effects, *but also that the public interest would be harmed by any disclosure from within the relevant class of documents, regardless of the consequences of releasing the actual information in question.*[150] By contrast, under a prejudice test, the authority must be able first to identify that harm would be caused by releasing the *specific information* requested, and then go on to show that that specific harm outweighs the *public interest* in disclosure.

In the result, the exemptions under the Act can actually be broken down into four different categories, starting with the most absolute exemptions and moving to the least. It is helpful to consider them in the order suggested by this categorization, because the Act does not set out the exemptions in any systematic way, but rather randomly, so that class exemptions are mixed in with 'harm-based' exemptions, and 'absolute exemptions' with both. It should be noted that the following categorisation relates to categories of exemptions not necessarily to categories of information, although the two may be synonymous. The four suggested categories are as follows, and are described in order of their illiberality.

(a) 'Total' exemptions: that is, class exemptions to which the public interest test in s 2 *does not apply*. Thus, the public authority concerned only has to show that information sought falls into the exempt class, not that its disclosure would cause any harm or prejudice; and, there is no duty to consider whether the public interest in maintaining the exemption outweighs the public interest in disclosing the information.

---

150 Freedom of Information Bill, House of Lords Third Reading, 21 November 2000 briefing notes, p 10.

(b) Class exemptions to which the s 2 public interest test does apply. This is self-explanatory.

(c) Harm-based exemptions to which the s 2 public interest test does not apply. In these exemptions, the authority has to show that the release of the particular information concerned would cause or be likely to cause the relevant prejudice, but then need not go on to consider whether this prejudice outweighs the public interest in disclosure: once prejudice is established, that is the end of the matter.

(d) Harm-based exemptions to which the s 2 public interest test *does* apply. These are the exemptions under which it is hardest for the public authority concerned to resist the release of information. To do so, it must first demonstrate prejudice or likely prejudice from the release of the particular information request and then, even if prejudice is shown, go on to consider whether the public interest in forestalling that prejudice outweighs the public interest in disclosing the information under s 2.

These categories are important not only in terms of the substantive legal tests which must be satisfied before information may be withheld: they also have crucial practical consequences in terms of time limits and enforcement. As explained below, the 20 day deadline for releasing information does not apply to information released only on public interest grounds. More importantly, the Commissioner's decision to order release on such grounds can, in relation to information held by certain governmental bodies, be vetoed by ministers (see further below).

We now turn to enumerating and commenting upon the numerous exemptions the Act contains, classified in accordance with the scheme outlined above.

(a) Class exemptions not subject to the public interest test

First, there are the total exemptions – class exemptions that are not subject to the public interest test.

Most of these exemptions are fairly self-explanatory; therefore, explanation is given where necessary. Section 21 covers information that is reasonably accessible to the applicant from other sources. It should be noted that this exemption applies even if the applicant would have to pay a higher fee than that provided by the Act to obtain the information (s 21(2)(a)) so long as the information can still be viewed as reasonably accessible. If the fee is excessive, this may no longer be the case. But, in order to be reasonably accessible, the information must be provided *as of right*. The duty to confirm or deny *does* apply, so an applicant would at least have to be told whether the authority to which he applied was holding the information. This is not an exemption in the usual sense of the word – as applied to freedom of information schemes – since it is not content-based and does not deprive the applicant of access to the information in general; it merely prevents her from obtaining it under the Act itself.

Section 23(1) covers information supplied by or which relates to the intelligence and security services, GCHQ, the special forces and the various tribunals to which complaints may be made about their activities and about phone tapping. It should be noted that, as indicated above, the bodies mentioned in this exemption are not themselves covered by the Act at all. This exemption therefore applies to information which is held by *another public authority*, but which has been supplied by one of these bodies. Because it is a class exemption, it could apply to information which had no conceivable security implications, such as evidence of a massive overspend on MI5 or MI6's headquarters. The duty to confirm or deny does not apply to information in this category where complying with it would itself involve disclosure of information covered by this exemption. Bearing in mind the complete exclusion of the security and intelligence services from the Act, the use of this exemption unaccompanied by a harm test and not subject to the public interest test is likely to mean that sensitive matters of great political significance remain undisclosed, even if their disclosure would ultimately benefit those services or national security.

Section 32 covers information *which is only held* by virtue of being contained in a document or record served on a public authority in proceedings or made by a court or tribunal or party in any proceedings or contained in a document lodged with or created by a person conducting an inquiry or arbitration, for the purposes of the inquiry or arbitration. The duty to confirm or deny does not apply. Section 34 covers information where exemption from s 1(1)(b) is required for the purpose of avoiding an infringement of the privileges of either House of Parliament. The duty to confirm or deny does not apply to information in this category where compliance with it would entail a breach of parliamentary privilege.

The exemption under s 40(1) is a complex one, but essentially it covers two classes of data. The first is information which the inquirer would be able to obtain under the Data Protection Act (DPA) 1998 because it is personal information which relates to himself; the second covers personal information which relates to *others*, the disclosure of which would contravene one or more of the data protection principles or the right under the Act to prevent processing likely to cause damage or distress. The first part of this exemption is designed to ensure that the FoI Act does not give rights which overlap with those granted by the DPA; the second, to ensure that the FoI Act does not give rights which contravene the DPA.

There are a number of further total exemptions. Vexatious requests (s 14) and unduly costly requests (those where compliance would cost more than a reasonable amount, to be specified (s 12), are exempt, but the duty to confirm or deny applies. Information the disclosure of which would contravene any other Act of Parliament (for example, the Official Secrets Act 1989) or would be incompatible with any EU obligation or constitute a contempt of court (s 44) is exempt and the duty to confirm or deny does not apply to the extent that compliance with it would amount to a contravention, as described above. This exemption ensures that the FoI Act cannot be seen impliedly to repeal the numerous provisions that criminalise the release of information, but rather preserves them all.

Information the disclosure of which would be an actionable breach of confidence (s 41) is exempt and the duty to confirm or deny does not apply if compliance with it would itself amount to a breach of confidence. This exemption requires some comment. While it is expressed as an absolute exemption, with no need to show that prejudice would be caused by release of the information, and no requirement to consider the public interest in disclosure, in fact the doctrine of confidence may contain the first (that is, a need to show detriment – there are conflicting *dicta* on the matter)[151] and certainly contains the second.

---

151 See Chapter 10, p 577.

The CFOI has expressed concern that while there is clearly some need to protect genuine confidences, governments could seek to protect all information supplied by third parties simply by agreeing with the third party at the time of the communication of the information that it would be treated with confidence. The information would then become confidential, provided that it was not already in the public domain, and subject to the public interest test and, possibly, the need to show detriment.

(b) Class exemptions subject to the public interest test

The second category covers class exemptions subject to the public interest test. It will be recalled in relation to these exemptions that in practice, while the Commissioner will always have the last word on whether the information falls into the class in question, she will not always be able to enforce a finding that it should nevertheless be released on public interest grounds if the information is held by certain governmental bodies, since the ministerial veto may be used.

It is most convenient to quote the Act itself for the first of these exemptions. Under s 30(1):

> Information held by a public authority is exempt information if it has at any time been held by the authority for the purposes of –
>
> (a) any investigation which the public authority has a duty to conduct with a view to it being ascertained –
>
>   (i) whether a person should be charged with an offence, or
>
>   (i) whether a person charged with an offence is guilty of it,
>
>   (b) any investigation which is conducted by the authority and in the circumstances may lead to a decision by the authority to institute criminal proceedings which the authority has power to conduct, or
>
> (b) any criminal proceedings which the authority has power to conduct.

This exemption, together with that contained in s 35, is one of the most widely criticised provisions in the Act. It is a sweeping exemption, covering all information, whenever obtained, which relates to investigations that may lead to criminal proceedings. It represents a specific rejection of the recommendation of the MacPherson Report[152] that there should be no class exemption for information relating to police investigations. It overlaps with the law enforcement of s 31, which does include a harm test. The exclusion of police operational matters and decisions echoes the approach under s 4 of the Official Secrets Act, but unlike s 4, no harm test is included. There are certain aspects of information relating to investigations which would appear to require disclosure in order to be in accord with the principle of openness enshrined in the Act. For example, a citizen might suspect that his or her telephone had been tapped without authorisation or that he or she had been unlawfully placed under surveillance by other means. Under the Act, no satisfactory method of discovering information relating to such a possibility will exist. It is therefore unfortunate that telephone tapping and electronic surveillance were not subjected to a substantial harm or even a simple harm test.

---

152 The *MacPherson Report on the Stephen Lawrence Inquiry*, Cm 4262, 1999, proposed that all such matters should be covered by the FoI Act, subject only to a substantial harm test.

This exemption extends beyond protecting the police and the CPS. Other bodies will also be protected: it will cover all information obtained by safety agencies investigating accidents. Thus, it will cover bodies such as the Health and Safety Executive, the Railway Inspectorate, Nuclear Installations Inspectorate, Civil Aviation Authority, Marine and Coastguard Agency, environmental health officers, trading standards officers and the Drinking Water Inspectorate. It will cover routine inspections as well as specific investigations, since both can lead to criminal prosecution. Thus, anything from an inspection of a section of railway track by the Railway Inspectorate, to a check upon hygiene in a restaurant by the Health and Safety Executive could be covered. The duty to confirm or deny does not apply (s 30(3)). As the CFOI commented:

> Reports into accidents involving dangerous cars, train crashes, unsafe domestic appliances, air disasters, chemical fires or nuclear incidents will go into a permanently secret filing cabinet. The same goes for reports into risks faced by workers or the public from industrial hazards. The results of safety inspections of the railways, nuclear plants and dangerous factories would be permanently exempt. This is the information that most people assume FoI legislation exists to provide.[153]

It is particularly hard to understand the need for such a sweeping class exemption when s 31 specifically exempts information which could prejudice the prevention or detection of crime, or legal proceedings brought by a public authority arising from various forms of investigation. That exemption will ensure that no information is released which could damage law enforcement and crime detection, while we have noted above that information which could amount to a contempt of court is also exempted. The CFOI noted that the recently retired director general of the Health and Safety Executive has said publicly that the work of the HSE does not require such sweeping protection.[154] It should be noted that, where it has been decided that the information falls into the protected class, the authority must then go on to consider whether it should be released under the public interest test. Since most of the information above will not be held by a government department (see below), the Commissioner will be able to order disclosure if she thinks the information should be released under this provision, with no possibility of a ministerial veto.

The other major class exemption in this category, under s 35, has been just as criticised. It amounts to a sweeping exemption for virtually all information relating to the formation of government policy. Under s 35(1):

> Information held by a government department or by the National Assembly for Wales is exempt information if it relates to –
>
> (a) the formulation or development of government policy,
>
> (b) Ministerial communications,
>
> (c) the provision of advice by any of the Law Officers or any request for the provision of such advice, or
>
> (d) the operation of any Ministerial private office.

---

153 Freedom of Information Bill, House of Lords Committee Stage, 19 October 2000 briefing notes.
154 *Ibid.*

The duty to confirm or deny does not apply.

This exemption is presumably intended to prevent government from having to decide policy in a goldfish bowl – to protect the freeness and frankness of Civil Service advice and of internal debate within government – but, once again, it appears to go far beyond what would sensibly be required to achieve this aim. Section 36 contains a harm-based exemption which covers almost exactly the same ground: it exempts government information which would, or would be likely to, inhibit (a) the free and frank provision of advice, or (b) the free and frank exchange of views for the purposes of deliberation, or (c) would otherwise prejudice, or would be likely otherwise to prejudice, the effective conduct of public affairs. Since this covers all information whose release might cause damage to the working of government – and is framed in very broad terms – it appears to be unnecessary to have a sweeping class exemption covering the same ground. Moreover, this exemption is not restricted to Civil Service advice; it covers also the background information used in preparing policy, including the underlying facts and their analysis. As the CFOI commented:

There would be no right to know about purely descriptive reports of existing practice, research reports, evidence on health hazards, assumptions about wage or inflation levels used in calculating costs, studies of overseas practice, consultants' findings or supporting data showing whether official assertions are realistic or not.[155]

The sole, and very limited exception to this exemption appears in sub-s (2) of s 35; it applies only 'once a decision as to government policy has been taken' and covers 'any statistical information used to provide an informed background to the taking of the decision'. This was a concession made by the government fairly late in the Bill's passage through Parliament and is very limited. First, unlike most other FoI regimes, by excluding only statistical information from the exemption, it allows the *analysis* of facts to be withheld. Secondly, it only applies once a decision has been taken. Thus, where the government gave consideration to introducing a new policy but then shelved the matter without a decision, statistics used during the consideration process would, bizarrely, remain exempt.

The Act is much more restrictive in this respect than the present, voluntary Code of Practice on Access to Government Information. The latter requires both facts and the analysis of facts underlying policy decisions, including scientific analysis and expert appraisal, to be made available, once decisions are announced. Material relating to policy formation can only be withheld under a harm test – if disclosure would 'harm the frankness and candour of internal discussion'. The White Paper preceding the Bill proposed that there should be no class exemption for material in this area, but rather that, as under the Code, a harm test would have had to be satisfied to prevent disclosure. While information in this category is subject to a public interest test, it is important to note that, because, by definition it will generally be information held by a government department, if the Commissioner orders disclosure on public interest grounds, the ministerial veto will be available to override her.

---

155 Freedom of Information Bill, House of Lords Committee Stage, 19 October 2000 briefing notes, p 1.

Information intended for future publication where it is reasonable that information should be withheld until that future date is exempt (s 22), and the duty to confirm or deny does not apply to the extent that complying with it would itself entail disclosing such information. The problem with the class exemption under s 22 is its imprecision: it does not specify a period within which the information has to be intended for publication for this exemption to apply. The government repeatedly rejected amendments that would have provided that this exemption could only be relied upon if a date for publication within a short, specified period had already been fixed.

There are a number of further class exemptions. Information subject to legal privilege (s 42) is exempt. The duty to confirm or deny does not apply if compliance with it would itself breach legal privilege. Trade secrets (s 43(1)) are exempt, but the duty does apply. 'Communications with Her Majesty, with other members of the Royal Family or with the Royal Household', or information relating to 'the conferring by the Crown of any honour or dignity' (s 37) are exempt, and the duty to confirm or deny does not apply. It is unclear why it is necessary to bestow a class exemption relating to the royal household and honours and dignities, although this follows the voluntary Code of Practice.

A separate class exemption covers information obtained for the purposes of conducting criminal proceedings and a very wide variety of investigations (specified in s 31(2)) carried out under statute or the prerogative, and which relate to the obtaining of information from confidential sources.

(c) Harm based exemptions not subject to the public interest test

This third category of exemptions has only one member. There is a general, harm-based exemption under s 36 for information the disclosure of which would be likely to prejudice the effective conduct of public affairs or inhibit free and frank discussion and advice. This exemption is subject to the general public interest test with one exception: for a reason that is not readily apparent, where the information in question is held by the Commons or Lords, the public interest test cannot be considered.

(d) Harm-based exemptions which are subject to the public interest test

As harm-based exemptions, these are in one respect the least controversial aspect of the Act. But it should be noted that the Act departed from one of the most liberal and widely praised aspects of the White Paper, namely, the requirement that in order to make out such exemptions, the authority concerned would have to demonstrate 'substantial' harm. This has been changed to a test of simple prejudice, although government spokespersons attempted to deny that the change would make any difference in practice. In each case, the duty to confirm or deny does not apply if, or to the extent that, compliance with it would itself cause the prejudice which the exemption seeks to prevent.

These exemptions cover information the disclosure of which would prejudice or would be likely to prejudice: defence and the armed forces (s 26), international relations (s 27), the economy (s 29), the mental or physical health or safety of any individual (s 38), auditing functions of other public authorities (s 33), the prevention, detection of crime, legal proceedings brought by a public authority arising from an investigation conducted for any of the purposes specified in s 31(2) (above) and carried out under statute or prerogative, collection of tax, immigration controls, good order in prisons; the exercise by any public authority of its functions for any of the purposes specified in s 31(2) (above), relations between administrations in the UK (for example, between the government and the Scottish Executive) (s 28). These exemptions are relatively straightforward, although they go beyond the information covered by the Official Secrets Act.

A number of these exemptions are more contentious. Section 24 covers information the disclosure of which would prejudice or would be likely to prejudice national security. The use of the national security exemption, albeit accompanied by the harm test, may mean that sensitive matters of great political significance remain undisclosed. In particular, the breadth and uncertainty of the term 'national security' may allow matters which fall only doubtfully within it to remain secret. Had the Act been in place at the time of the change in policy regarding arms sales to Iraq, the subject of the Scott Report, it is likely that information relating to it would not have been disclosed since it could have fallen within the exception clauses. The whole subject of arms sales will probably fall within the national security exception and possibly within other exceptions as well.[156]

Under s 43, information the disclosure of which would prejudice or would be likely to prejudice the commercial interests of any person (including the public authority holding it) is exempt. The CFOI commented that under this exemption, the prejudice referred to could be caused by consumers refusing to buy a dangerous product. Thus they noted that the fact that a company had sold dangerous products, or behaved in some other disreputable manner, could be suppressed if disclosure would lead customers to buy alternative products or shareholders to sell their shares.[157] This is clearly correct; however, in the case of unsafe products, the public interest test would surely require disclosure.

Section 36 covers information which, in the reasonable opinion of a qualified person, would prejudice or be likely to prejudice collective ministerial responsibility, or the work of the Executives of Northern Ireland and Wales, or which would be likely to inhibit the free and frank provision of advice, or the free and frank exchange of views for the purposes of deliberation, or would otherwise prejudice, or would be likely otherwise to prejudice, the effective conduct of public affairs. Two main criticisms of this exemption can be made. First, the test is not a wholly objective one, but is dependent upon 'the reasonable opinion of a qualified person'. The intention behind this provision is apparently to allow a person representing the department or body in question to make the primary determination of prejudice, with the Commissioner being able to take issue with such a finding only if it is irrational in the *Wednesbury* sense. The second main objection to this section is the 'catch-all' provision covering information the release of which could 'prejudice the effective conduct of public affairs', a phrase which is so vague and broad that it could mean almost anything.

Expiry of certain exemptions

As indicated above, the Act, through amendments to the Public Records Act, provides that some of the exemptions will cease to apply after a certain number of years,[158] though

---

156 See further the Minutes of Evidence before the Public Service Committee HC 313-1 of 1995–96 QQ 66 *et seq.*

157 Freedom of Information Bill, House of Lords Committee Stage, 19 October 2000 briefing notes, p 1.

158 See p 372.

these limitations are hardly generous. The following exemptions will cease to apply at all after 30 years (s 63(1)): s 28 (inter-UK relations), s 30(1) (information obtained during an investigation), s 32 (documents generated in litigation), s 33 (audit functions), s 35 (information relating to internal government discussion and advice), s 36 (information which could prejudice effective conduct of public affairs), s 37(1)(a) (communications with royal household), s 42 (legal professional privilege) and s 43 (trade secrets and information which could damage commercial interests). The exemptions under s 21 (information accessible by other means) and s 22 (information intended for future publication) will cease to apply after 30 years where the relevant document is held in a public record office (s 64(1)). Still less generously, information relating to the bestowing of honours and dignities (s 37(1)(b)) only ceases to be exempt after 60 years, while we will have to wait 100 years before the expiry of the exemption for information falling within s 31, that is, information which might prejudice law enforcement, the administration of justice, etc.

Additionally, one of the absolute exemptions – information provided by the security, intelligence, etc services (s 23(1)) – *will cease to be absolute* after 30 years, that is, the public interest in disclosure must be considered once 30 years has expired.

Applying for information and time limits

Requests for information must be in writing (s 8) and, under s 9, a fee may be charged subject to an – as yet – unfixed maximum, which ministers indicated would probably be set initially at £10. Information requested must generally be supplied within 20 days of the request (s 10(1)). However, there is an important exception to this: where an authority finds that information is *prima facie* exempt, either because it falls within a class exemption, or the requisite prejudice is thought to be present, but then goes on to consider whether the information should nevertheless be released under the public interest test, it does not have to make a decision within the normal 20 day deadline. Instead, it must release the information only within an unspecified 'reasonable period'.

Clearly, there may be practical problems in using the Act. The citizen may have difficulty in obtaining the document he or she requires. He or she might not be able to frame the request for information specifically enough in order to obtain the particular documents needed. The request might be met with the response that 3,000 documents are available touching on the matter in question; the citizen might lack the expert knowledge needed to identify the particular document required. If so, under s 1(3), the authority need not comply with the request and can continue to postpone its compliance until and if the requester succeeds in formulating the request more specifically. Section 1(3) does not allow the authority to postpone the request until it has had a chance to obtain further information, enabling it to deal with the request.

The enforcement mechanism

The enforcement review mechanism under the Act is far stronger than the mechanism established under the Code. The internal review of a decision to withhold information, established under the Code, was formalised under the Act and the role of the Ombudsman was taken over by that of the Information Commissioner. The

Commissioner's powers will also be much more extensive than those of the Ombudsman. As indicated below, she will have the power to order disclosure of the information and can report a failure to disclose information to the courts who can treat it in the same way as contempt of court. Under the White Paper, it was to be a criminal offence to destroy, alter or withhold records relevant to an investigation of the Information Commissioner. It was also to become a criminal offence to shred documents requested by outsiders, including the media and the public. However, the two offences are omitted from the Act. No civil liability is incurred if a public authority does not comply with any duty imposed by the Act (s 56).

The rights granted under the Act are enforceable by the Data Protection Commissioner, to be known as 'The Information Commissioner'. Importantly, the Commissioner has security of tenure, being dismissible only by the Crown following an address by both Houses of Parliament. An appeal lies from decisions of the Commissioner to the Information Tribunal which is made up of experienced lawyers and 'persons to represent the interests' of those seeking information and of public authorities (Sched 2, Part II).

Under s 50: 'Any person (in this section referred to as "the complainant") may apply to the Commissioner for a decision whether, in any specified respect, a request for information made by the complainant to a public authority has been dealt with in accordance with [the Act].' The Commissioner must then make a decision unless the application has been made with 'undue delay', is frivolous or vexatious or the complainant has not exhausted any complaints procedure provided by the public authority (s 50(1)). If the Commissioner decides that the authority concerned has failed to communicate information or confirm or deny when required to do so by the Act, she must serve a 'decision notice' on the authority stating what it must do to satisfy the Act. She may also serve 'Information Notices' upon authorities, requiring the authority concerned to provide her with information about a particular application or its compliance with the Act generally.

The Commissioner may ultimately force a recalcitrant authority to act by serving upon it an enforcement notice, which (*per* s 52(1)) 'requir[es] the authority to take, within such time as may be specified in the notice, such steps as may be so specified for complying with those requirements'. If a public authority fails to comply with a Decision, Enforcement or Information Notice, the Commissioner can certify the failure in writing to the High Court, which, the Act provides (s 52(2)):

> may inquire into the matter and, after hearing any witness who may be produced against or on behalf of the public authority, and after hearing any statement that may be offered in defence, deal with the authority as if it had committed a contempt of court.

In other words, the Commissioner's decisions can, in the final analysis, be enforced just as can orders of the court. These powers are buttressed by powers of entry, search and seizure to gain evidence of a failure by the authority to carry out its obligations under the Act or comply with a Notice issued by the Commissioner (detailed in Sched 3).

Appeals

However, the Commissioner's decisions are themselves subject to appeal to the Tribunal, and this power of appeal is exercisable upon the broadest possible grounds. The Act provides that either party may appeal to the Tribunal against a decision notice and a public authority against an enforcement or information notice (s 57(2) and (3)) either on the basis that the notice is 'not in accordance with the law', or 'to the extent that the notice involved an exercise of discretion by the Commissioner, that he ought to have exercised his discretion differently' (s 58(1)). The tribunal is also empowered to review 'any finding of fact on which the notice in question was based' and, as well as being empowered to quash decisions of the Commissioner, may 'substitute such other notice as could have been served by the Commissioner'.

There is a further appeal from the Tribunal to the High Court, but on a 'point of law' only (s 59). In practice, this will probably be interpreted so as to allow review of the Tribunal's decisions, not just for error of law, but also on the other accepted heads of judicial review.

The ministerial veto of the Commissioner's decisions

The ministerial veto is another highly controversial aspect of the Act. The White Paper made no provision for such a power of veto, on the basis that to do so would undermine confidence in the regime. Such a veto clearly dilutes the basic FoI principle that a body independent from government should enforce the rights to information and since, in cases where the release of information could embarrass ministers, it constitutes them judge in their own cause, is objectionable in principle.

For the veto to be exercisable, two conditions must be satisfied under s 53(1): first, the Notice which the veto will operate to quash must have been served on a government department, the Welsh Assembly or 'any public authority designated for the purposes of this section by an order made by the Secretary of State'; secondly, the Notice must order the release of information which is *prima facie* exempt but which the Commissioner has decided should nevertheless be released under the public interest test in s 2. (By *prima facie* exempt, it will be recalled, is meant information that either falls into a class exemption or, where prejudice is required to render it exempt, the Commissioner has adjudged the prejudice to be present).

The veto is exercised by means of a certificate signed by the minister concerned stating that he has 'on reasonable grounds formed the opinion that, in respect of the request or requests concerned, there was no failure' to comply with the Act. The decision must be made at a relatively senior level. If the information is sought from a department of the Northern Irish Executive or any NI public authority, it must be exercised by the First and Deputy Minister acting together; if a Welsh department or any Welsh public authority, the Assembly First Secretary; if from a government department or any other public authority, a Cabinet minister. The reasons for the veto must be given to the complainant (s 56), unless doing so would reveal exempt information (s 57) and the certificate must be laid before Parliament or the Welsh/NI assembly as applicable.

Publication schemes

Under ss 19 and 20, public authorities must adopt 'publication schemes' relating to the publication of information by that authority. This is a significant aspect of the Act since more citizens will thereby gain access to a wider range of information. The difficulty and expense of making a request will be avoided. The scheme can be devised by the authority or, under s 20, a model scheme devised by the Information Commissioner can be used. If a tailor-made scheme is used, it must be approved by the Commissioner (s 19(1)(a)). Therefore, authorities are likely to use the model schemes, thereby avoiding the need to submit the scheme for approval. Consistency between authorities is probably desirable as promoting consistency and thereby enhancing access to information.

Conclusions

Despite its weaknesses, this is a constitutional development whose significance can hardly be over-stated. The FoI Act, enforceable by the Information Commissioner, will be a clear improvement on the Code introduced by the Major Government. Rodney Austin described the draft Bill as 'a denial of democracy'.[159] It is suggested that the improvements made to the Bill during its passage through Parliament, while still leaving it a far weaker and more illiberal measure than proposed by the widely praised White Paper which preceded it, render this view no longer accurate. In particular, the public interest test has been strengthened, and applies to most of the exemptions in the Act, including, crucially, the key class exemptions relating to investigations and to the formation of Government policy; however, as the CFOI points out, it is misleading to view this as converting class exemptions into 'harm-based' ones, since the very existence of a class exemption is based upon a presumption, built into the Act, that such information is, *as a class*, of a type which generally should not be released.

The Act does represent a turning point in British democracy by, for the first time in its history, removing the decision to release many classes of information from government and placing it in the hands of an independent agency, the Information Commissioner, and in giving a statutory 'right' to information, enforceable if necessary through the courts, to citizens. However, as seen, the Act fences round this basic right with so many restrictions that, depending upon its interpretation, much information of any conceivable interest could still be withheld. Whether this turns out to be the case in practice will depend primarily upon the robustness of the stance taken by the Commissioner, particularly in applying the public interest test to the class exemptions under the Act, where it will provide the only means of obtaining disclosure.

---

159 Austin, R, 'Freedom of information: the constitutional impact', in Jowell, J and Oliver, D, op cit, fn 146, p 237.

CHAPTER 8

FREEDOM OF ASSOCIATION

1 INTRODUCTION[1]

There is a close nexus between the freedoms of association, expression and assembly, since together they protect an interest which is vital in a democratic society – the right of citizens to form groups in order to express a view publicly that may be at variance with the official view. The linkage between association and assembly is sometimes explicitly reflected in human rights documents as it is in Art 20 of the Universal Declaration of Human Rights and in Art 11 of the European Convention on Human Rights. The right to freedom to associate with a group in order to assemble to publicise the views of the group and obtain public support lends efficacy to freedom of expression in the form of protest. Clearly, a protest or plea for support will be more effective if carried out collectively rather than individually. All free societies recognise the need, first to allow citizens to join or support groups which express a view at variance with the government view and secondly, to allow such groups to assemble in order to express their views publicly. Toleration of public protest is one of the main distinctions between totalitarian societies and democracies.

Usually, in order to make an effective public protest or demonstration, a group needs to have coherence and a structure. Thus, freedom of assembly would be emasculated were it not underpinned by freedom of association; only spontaneous meetings and marches would receive protection. Equally, freedom of association would almost cease to exist if citizens could join a group, but could not meet regularly with it. Therefore, the right to freedom of association discussed in this chapter underpins and is strongly linked to the right to the freedoms of assembly and protest, discussed in the next.

However, the two freedoms of association and assembly can be exercised entirely separately; freedom of association includes the freedom to be a member of a group that never meets but communicates with its members by other means. Equally, it includes the freedom to choose not to join a group.[2] Similarly, freedom of assembly covers the freedom to engage in an entirely spontaneous demonstration. Both freedoms partly derive their legitimacy from their close association with freedom of expression,[3] in that both protect the freedom to propagate opinions publicly, thereby fostering public debate, the search for truth and participation in the democracy.

---

1   General reading: Bailey, SH, Harris, DJ and Jones, BL, *Liberties: Cases and Materials*, 4th edn, 1995, pp 177–81; Feldman, D, *Civil Liberties in England and Wales*, 1993, pp 783–84; Walker, C, *The Prevention of Terrorism*, 1992, Chapter 5; Tomuschat, C, 'Freedom of association', in Macdonald, Matscher and Petzold (eds), *The European System for the Protection of Human Rights*, 1993.

2   See the judgment of the European Court of Human Rights in *Young, James and Webster v UK* A 44; (1981) 4 EHRR 38.

3   See Lord Denning's comments on this point in *Hubbard v Pitt* [1976] QB 142. However, in America it has been determined in the leading 'symbolic speech' case that speech and conduct can be disentangled: the one can be punished so long as the incidental restriction caused to the other goes no further than is necessary for the furtherance of the interest in question. (*United States v O'Brien* (1968) 391 US 367; for criticism, see Nimmer [1973] 21 UCLA L Rev 38–44.) See Barendt's discussion of the relationship between freedom of speech and freedom of association: *Freedom of Speech*, 1987, pp 280–98.

Association and assembly have received recognition in domestic law as negative liberties. But it is evident that association had failed to acquire the status of a common law right,[4] although the common law has recognised the freedom of association with other private individuals[5] and the autonomy of associations in relation to their control of their membership.[6] Under the Human Rights Act (HRA), the right to the exercise of this freedom was afforded clear recognition for the first time under domestic law. As Chapter 9 argues, rights of public protest and assembly under the HRA will have to be exercised in the face of an increasing mass of statutory and common law restrictions. In contrast, freedom of association is less restricted: there were few general restrictions under UK law on the freedom to join or form groups which did not constitute conspiracies.[7] However, the potential for creating quite wide ranging restrictions has been created under the Terrorism Act 2000. Such restrictions, although not directly aimed at assembly or protest, will also curtail those freedoms. It will be suggested below that while most restrictions on freedom of association are compatible with Art 11 under the HRA, counter-terrorist provisions are more problematic in the light of the Strasbourg 'association' jurisprudence.

The earlier Strasbourg jurisprudence tended to be protective of State interests,[8] but the recent 'association' jurisprudence of the Court is more interventionist. In *Socialist Party and Others v Turkey*,[9] the Court allowed only a very narrow margin of appreciation in finding that the dissolution of the Socialist Party of Turkey had breached Art 11. The Court linked the three freedoms of expression, association and assembly together in finding that democracy demands that diverse political programmes should be debated, 'even those that call into question the way a State is currently organised'. The Court did not accept that the message of the group that a federal system should be put in place which would ensure that Kurds would be put on an equal footing with Turkish citizens generally, amounted to incitement to violence. The dissolution of the party was disproportionate to the aim in view – the preservation of national security. This stance is in accordance with the Convention jurisprudence, which has quite consistently recognised the need to protect the interests of minority and excluded groups.[10]

Similar findings were made in *Sidiropoulos v Greece*[11] in respect of an association formed to promote the interests of the Macedonian minority in Greece. The Court said that one of the most important aspects of freedom of association was that citizens should be able to form a legal group with the aim of acting collectively in their mutual interest. In

---

4   See Chapter 3, p 108.

5   *Cambridgeshire CC v R* [1994] 2 FCR 973.

6   See, eg, *Cheall v Association of Professional Executive Clerical and Computer Staff* [1983] 2 AC 180. See, generally, Ewing, K, 'Freedom of association', in McCrudden, C and Chambers, G (eds), *Individual Rights and the Law*, 1994, pp 239–63.

7   For criminal or civil law purposes. See Chapter 5, pp 292–93 for consideration of the wide ranging common law offence of conspiracy to corrupt public morals. For general discussion, see Hazell, R, *Conspiracy and Civil Liberties*, 1974, Chapter 6.

8   See *Glasenapp v FRG* A 104 (1986); *Kosiek v FRG* A 105 (1986); *CCSU v UK* (1988) 10 EHRR 269.

9   Judgment of 25 May 1998 (App No 20/1997/804/1007); (1999) 27 EHRR 51, paras 41, 47, 50.

10 Such groups have included criminals: *Soering v UK* A 161 (1989); prisoners: *Ireland v UK* A 25 (1978); *Golder v UK* A 18 (1975); racial minorities: *East African Asians cases* (1973) 3 EHRR 76, *Hilton v UK* Appl No 5613/72, 4 DR 177 (1976) (no breach found on facts); sexual minorities: *Dudgeon v UK* A 45 (1982), *B v France* A 232-C (1992); political minorities: *Arrowsmith v UK* Appl No 7050/75, 19 DR 5 (1978); religious minorities: *Kokkinakis v Greece* A 260-A (1993).

11 (Chamber) (1998) available from the Court's website, www.dhcour.coe.fr.

Vogt v Germany[12] the Court held that a woman who was dismissed from her teaching post because of her membership of an extreme left wing group had suffered a violation of both Arts 10 and 11. These decisions suggest that where political associations are in question, the Court will take a strict stance, in accordance with its stance on political expression.[13] But, these decisions may be contrasted with that in *Ahmed v UK*.[14] The applicants were local government officers who were active in local politics. Regulations were introduced with a view to ensuring local government impartiality; they restricted the political activities of certain categories of local government officers; thereupon the applicants had to resign from their political parties and cease canvassing for elections. The Court found that the interference with their Art 10 and 11 rights was proportionate to the aims in view since it was intended to ensure that the traditional political neutrality of council officers was maintained. Thus, unless a countervailing Convention value is also in issue, it may be assumed that political associations will receive particular protection.

Trade unions are also expressly protected, under para 1. But a wider margin may be conceded to the Member State in respect of interference with trade union membership, where the interest at issue cannot be viewed as political.[15] Apart from political associations and trade unions, Art 11 protects groups in general that are set up in order to further the common interests of the members. But Strasbourg has taken a fairly narrow view of association; it excludes merely social groupings.[16]

The key rights protected by Art 11 include the basic right to form associations[17] and the right to autonomy of an association.[18] An association itself can exercise Convention rights, including freedom of expression (*Socialist Party and Others v Turkey*).[19] Below, the scope and content of Art 11 and the impact of the Strasbourg jurisprudence are considered in more detail in relation to particular restrictions in domestic law.

2 QUASI-MILITARY AND TERRORIST GROUPS

Military or quasi-military organisations

A number of specific statutory provisions place limits on the freedom to join or support groups that are associated with the use of violence. The most general restriction arises under s 2 of the Public Order Act 1936, which prohibits the formation of military or quasi-military organisations. Under s 2(1)(b), a quasi-military organisation is defined as 'one organised and trained or organised and equipped either for the purpose of enabling them to be employed for the use or display of physical force in promoting any political object or in such a manner as to arouse reasonable apprehension that they are organised and

---

12   (1995) 21 EHRR 205.
13   See the Introduction to Part II, p 209–10.
14   (1998) 5 BHRC 111; [1999] IRLR 188.
15   See *Gustaffson v Sweden* (1996) 22 EHRR 409.
16   *Anderson v UK* [1998] EHRLR 218. For discussion, see Chapter 9, p 491.
17   *X v Belgium* (1961) 4 YB 324.
18   *Cheall v UK* (1985) 8 EHRR 74.
19   Judgment of 25 May 1998, Appl No 20/1997/804/1007; (1999) 27 EHRR 51, paras 41, 47, 50.

either trained or equipped for that purpose'. The use of the latter words extends the ambit of this provision and means that it has the potential to catch quite a wide range of groups, assuming that they have, or appear to have, a political objective. However, not many prosecutions have been brought under this provision. The last successful one was in *Jordan and Tyndall*.[20] The defendants were both members of a fascist group called *Spearhead*. They engaged in various activities that included practising foot drill and storing sodium chloride with the probable aim of using it to make bombs. It was held that their activities satisfied the test under s 2(1)(b).

Alternatively, under s 2(1)(a) a group organised, trained or equipped in order to allow it to usurp the function of the army or the police would fall within this prohibition against quasi-military groups, thus possibly catching vigilante groups such as the Guardian Angels (a group organised with the object of preventing crime on underground railways).

If prosecutions continue to be confined to groups that are associated with violence, it may be assumed that these provisions are compatible with Art 11.

Terrorist groups

Introduction

In terms of the effect on freedom of association, there is a clear distinction between designation of a group as terrorist and the proscription of certain terrorist groups. Proscription of terrorist groups strikes directly at freedom of association although, clearly, it may be justifiable. Designation of a group as 'terrorist' indirectly undermines individual rights to freedom of association; the group can exist, but its activities and ability to organise itself are curtailed. Further, persons belonging to or associated with a terrorist (albeit, non-proscribed) group can be subjected to a regime in terms of the substantive criminal law and criminal justice provisions that is more draconian than that applying to 'ordinary' suspects. Therefore, there are strong deterrents against being a member of such a group and against being associated with it.

The Terrorism Act (TA) 2000, introduced under the Labour Government, created the possibility of a very significant extension of the definition of terrorism. Since terrorist groups can be proscribed, the freedom of association of a wide range of groups was threatened with the possibility of complete extinction or of being severely undermined. The government published a consultation paper on the future of anti-terrorism laws in December 1998.[21] It was intended to address the question of the rationale of retaining 'emergency' anti-terrorism laws in the face of the peace process[22] and, therefore, to counter the argument that the current version of the Prevention of Terrorism Act (PTA) with its various later accretions should be repealed and not replaced. The 1998 paper was based on a report prepared by Lord Lloyd of Berwick in 1996.[23] In 1995, Lord Lloyd had

---

20 [1963] Crim LR 124. For discussion, see Williams, DGT, *Keeping the Peace*, 1967, pp 222–23; Walker, M, *The National Front*, 1977, pp 39–45.

21 *Legislation against Terrorism. A Consultation Paper*, Cm 4178, 1998.

22 See the Introduction to the paper, and, in particular, para 6.

23 Lord Lloyd of Berwick's *Inquiry into Legislation against Terrorism*, Cm 3420, published in October 1996.

been asked by Michael Howard, the then Home Secretary, to consider the future of anti-terrorist legislation on the assumption that a lasting peace was achieved. He recommended in his report that a new permanent anti-terrorist law should replace the temporary provisions. The policy adopted in his report formed the background to the consultation paper and, in turn, to the Terrorism Bill 2000. When the TA came into force, it repealed the previous counter-terrorist provisions, the PTA 1989 and the Northern Ireland (Emergency Provisions) Act 1991 (EPA).[24] The new Act is far more extensive, covering a much wider range of groups; it is permanent; its main provisions will apply equally across the UK, although there are special transitional provisions for Northern Ireland.

The justification for the new provisions is that they are needed at the present time to combat the threat from three groups. The first of these comprises those Irish splinter groups opposed to the peace process.[25] The second comprises 'international terrorists'. The paper notes that across the world there has been a rise in terrorism 'motivated by religious idealism'.[26] Both these groups are already covered under the existing legislation, although not all the special provisions are applied equally to international terrorism. The threat is apparently from the new, third group, on which the case for new legislation must largely rest. This group comprises a wide and disparate range of domestic groups other than those connected with Irish terrorism, such as animal rights or environmental activists[27] and, possibly, anti-abortion groups.[28] The paper accepts that the level of violence associated with such groups is low compared with the level of IRA violence in the early 1970s. However, it argues that these groups pose a continuing threat and that other single issue groups may be set up and may use violent methods 'to impose their will on the rest of society'.[29] Thus, the paper switches the focus of concern from the need

---

24   The PTA was renewed for the last time on 15 March 2000. The EPA was renewed for the last time on 24 August 2000. The special measures it provides for Northern Ireland are provided in Part VII of the Act of 2000.

25   In the Paper the government finds: 'there are small numbers who remain opposed to peace and wedded to violence. So, even though the context is of a general movement towards lasting peace in Northern Ireland, it is too soon to be confident that all terrorism has been abandoned' (ibid, para 2.3).

26   Lord Lloyd's report draws attention to 'possible future changes in the terrorist threat' and to lives and property in the UK; changes which mirror what is happening across the world ...' (ibid, para 2.4). Examples are given of the rise of 'Islamic extremism' and the use of Sarin nerve gas on the Tokyo underground in 1995 by the Aum Shinrikyo religious cult, which killed 12 people and affected up to 5,500.

27   'The threat from some marginal but extreme elements of the animal rights movement continues to be of more concern to the Government [than Scottish or Welsh nationalist groups].' The paper notes that animal rights extremists have in the past sent letter bombs to the leaders of major political parties, attacked Bristol University's Senate House with a high explosive bomb, targeted a veterinary surgeon and a psychologist with car bombs and caused millions of pounds worth of damage. 'The shape of new counter-terrorist legislation needs to reflect the possible threat from indigenous groups too' (Chapter 2 of the paper, para 2.5). In Chapter 3 of the paper, the concerns regarding these groups are given some further substance. It is noted that in 1997 more than 800 incidents were recorded by the Animal Rights National Index (ARNI) and 'these included attacks on abattoirs, laboratories, breeders, hunts, butchers, chemists, doctors, vets, furriers, restaurants, supermarkets and other shops' which resulted in injuries, although not in deaths, and in damage done in 1997 estimated at more than 1.8 million (ibid, para 3.10).

28   The paper speculates as to the possibility that anti-abortion groups will adopt terrorist methods in the UK: 'In the United States, for example, there is an increasing tendency by individuals and groups to resort to terrorist methods. Some of those opposed to the USA's laws on abortion have bombed clinics and attacked, and, in a number of cases, killed doctors and nursing staff employed by them. Although there have been no comparable attacks in the United Kingdom, the possibility remains that some new group or individual could operate in this way in the future' (ibid, para 3.12).

29   Ibid, para 3.12.

for measures to combat a high and rising level of violence to the need to be ready to combat the possibility of violence in the future. The threat of violence from environmental, animal rights or anti-abortion activists may be a real possibility, but it has not yet materialised on anything like the scale previously thought of as necessary to justify the draconian anti-terrorist laws. Moreover, it is unclear that the ordinary criminal law would be inadequate as a response to the activities of such groups. The paper merely provides assertions rather than evidence as to the need for special counter-terrorist measures, as opposed to a more effective use of the existing criminal law. No effort is made to analyse the need for the extension of the special provisions to a very wide range of new groups. It does not, for example, draw on experience from other countries, including European ones, which are equally faced with extremist groups. The problems experienced in the US are mentioned, but no study is made of the efficacy of the means used to combat them.

The new definition of terrorism

Terrorism was defined in s 20(1) of the Prevention of Terrorism (Temporary Provisions) Act 1989 as 'the use of violence for political ends and includes any use of violence for the purpose of putting the public, or any section of the public in fear'. But this did not mean that the PTA powers applied to all activities that fell within the definition. The special powers conferred apply only to 'terrorism connected with the affairs of Northern Ireland' or (in certain instances) to international terrorism. Non-Irish domestic terrorism, that is, terrorism having its origins in the affairs of any part of the UK other than Northern Ireland, was excluded from the scope of the Act. The s 20 definition of terrorism was in fact extraordinarily wide and imprecise since the use of the word 'includes' meant that the requirement of putting a section of the public in fear was not an essential ingredient of it. The terms 'violence' and 'political ends' were undefined. Arguably, therefore, 'the use of violence for political ends' could include some public protest. It is unclear whether s 20 is confined to violence against persons. The definition might, therefore, be unworkable in practice were it not for the current qualified application of the powers. Even bearing those qualifications in mind, the definition means that the special powers could be used against a very wide range of activities so long as a connection with Northern Irish affairs or, even more vaguely (in the case of certain powers), an 'international' aspect, can be found. The definition of terrorism in the EPA was identical to that in s 20 of the PTA. The EPA did not impose any limitations on the kinds of terrorism to which it applies. But there appeared to be official agreement that in practice, the powers have only been used to combat Irish terrorism.[30]

The government stated that its proposed new definition was 'the use of serious violence against persons or property, or the threat to use such violence, to intimidate or coerce a government, the public, or any section of the public for political, religious or ideological ends'.[31] This definition was an extraordinarily wide interpretation of 'terrorism'. Clearly, it was intended to include forms of direct action adopted by environmental groups or animal rights activists. This definition was in some respects

---

30   *Ibid*, para 3.2.
31   *Ibid*, para 3.17.

wider than that under s 20, since it clearly applied to property as well as persons and covered serious disruption as well as violence. In its *application* it would also have been far wider. It was, however, narrower than that under s 20 in that it made it clear that intimidating or coercing a government, the public, or any section of the public was an essential ingredient. The definition actually adopted under s 1 of the new Act is significantly wider even than the proposed one or that under s 20. Section 1 provides, in essence, that 'terrorism' means the use or threat, 'for the purpose of advancing a political, religious or ideological cause', of action 'designed to influence the government or to intimidate the public or a section of the public' (s 1(1)(b)) which involves serious violence against any person or serious damage to property, endangers the life of any person, or 'creates a serious risk to the health or safety of the public or a section of the public, or is designed seriously to interfere with or seriously to disrupt an electronic system'. The Act will also apply wherever terrorist action takes place under s 1(4). The requirement of a threat to the established order contained in the words: 'to intimidate or coerce a government', the key limiting factor under the proposed definition, has been watered down to 'influence'. But the key point is that in its potential effect, the s 1(1) definition is far wider in practice than s 20 since the new legislation, unlike the PTA, allows the *definition itself* to determine the application of the special powers. The government assumes that such application will, owing to the decisions of police officers, the DPP and the CPS, in practice affect only the most extremist groups. But, given the lack of effective, independent control over the day to day decision making of such bodies, this is not, it is argued, a satisfactory position in civil liberties terms.

The definition was attacked in Parliament as creating a 'fatally flawed' Bill. It was also said: 'it is utterly perplexing that we should apparently be wedded to a definition that threatens to undermine so sweepingly civil liberties and the credibility of governance itself.'[32] However, the amendments put forward by the Liberal Democrats, which would have narrowed it down, were overwhelmingly defeated, Labour and Conservative MPs (with a few exceptions) voting together.[33] The limiting words of s 1(1)(b) were added as a Lords' amendment, reluctantly accepted by the government.[34]

As indicated, the new Act will apply all the special 'terrorism' offences, which were developed in the context of the PTA or EPA, to an extremely wide range of organisations. Unless and until the Home Secretary proscribes a range of domestic animal rights and environmental groups, the proscription-related offences will not apply to them. But all the special terrorist offences, which have no equivalents in ordinary criminal law, will apply, as will the special criminal justice regime for terrorists, affording them lesser rights within the criminal justice system than 'ordinary' criminals.[35] These offences and the special regime will tend to undermine freedom of association since, although it will not be an offence simply to belong to a terrorist organisation, many activities linked to it, such as organising it, will be criminalised. Further, persons will be deterred not only from joining the organisation, but also from associating themselves with it in any way.

Section 29 of the EPA made it an offence to direct 'at any level' a terrorist organisation. The maximum sentence that could be given on conviction for the offence was life

---

32 Mr Simpson MP, HC Deb Cols 399 and 394, 15 March 2000.

33 HC Deb Col 415, 15 March 2000.

34 HL Deb Col 1443–1451, 4 July 2000.

35 See further Chapters 13 and 14. For discussion see Rowe, JJ [2001] Crim LR 527.

imprisonment. The PTA contained no equivalent provision. The term 'directing' was not defined in the EPA but it clearly had the meaning of taking some authority for actions to be carried out, or playing some part in giving orders in relation to them.[36] The consultation paper noted that there have only been two convictions for this offence, pointing out that its nature means that it is difficult to get evidence to support a charge; witnesses are particularly reluctant to make statements implicating people who hold positions of authority within terrorist organisations. But where a conviction is obtained, 'it is likely to be of some significance and to have a major impact on the terrorist organisation in question'.[37] Lord Lloyd considered that the offence had been of real value. He recommended that it should be retained in permanent legislation and it should be extended to cover the whole of the UK and all forms of terrorism. The government agreed with his recommendation,[38] which is fully reflected in s 56 of the new Act. Thus, the leaders, and all with some authority within the vast range of groups within the UK which may fall within the definition, will become liable to a sentence of life imprisonment simply by virtue of their position once the Act comes into force.

Proscription

Introduction

Proscription places severe limits on freedom of association by outlawing a number of specified terrorist groups. Its use may be seen as providing a legitimate means of expressing outrage at the activities of such groups, thereby tending to prevent illegitimate expressions of public anger. It has been argued that it may discourage supporters of terrorist organisations and may signal political strength.[39] On the other hand, it has been argued that these benefits are minimal and that it is 'a cosmetic part of the PTA' which is in fact 'counter productive as it impedes criminal investigation and political discussion'.[40] Lord Jellicoe's review of the operation of the PTA doubted the value of proscription, considering that its detrimental effects in terms of constraining the free expression of views about Northern Ireland outweighed its benefits.[41] In response, a Home Office circular was issued[42] giving guidance to the police as to the proper use of ss 1 and 2, bearing in mind the possible effect on freedom of expression.

The PTA 1989[43] made it an offence under s 2 to belong to a proscribed organisation. The proscribed organisations were listed in Sched 1 to the Act. These powers were extended to Northern Ireland by virtue of s 28 of the EPA 1991.[44] 'Organisations' were

---

36 In the consultation paper the government explained: 'The offence is aimed at the strategists – those who plan campaigns and order them to be carried out, but who do not normally themselves take any part in the detailed planning or execution of the individual attacks which make up the campaign.' (*Ibid*, para 12.9.)

37 *Ibid*, para 12.9.

38 *Ibid*, para 12.10.

39 Wilkinson, P, *Terrorism and the Political State*, 1986, p 170.

40 See Walker, *op cit*, fn 1, p 64.

41 Cmnd 8803, 1983; the review did not, however, recommend deproscription, since it would create public resentment.

42 On 9 August 1983 (Current Law Statutes 1984, note to s 1(1)).

43 For commentary on the PTA provisions, see Bonner, D [1989] PL 440.

44 For commentary on the predecessor to the 1991 Act, see *Review of the Operation of the Northern Ireland (Emergency Provisions) Act 1978*, Cmnd 9222; Bonner [1984] PL 348.

widely defined as 'any association or combination of persons' (s 1(6) of the PTA). An organisation did not need to engage in terrorism itself; it was enough if it promoted or encouraged it. These arrangements are continued under the new scheme.

There have been no convictions for proscription-related offences in Britain since 1990 although, in the same period, 195 convictions were obtained in Northern Ireland. Therefore, the need to retain the power to proscribe in relation to Britain under the new legislation is unclear. However, under the Terrorism Act 2000, the current power of proscription and all the proscription-related offences are retained, and their impact is greatly extended. Section 3(1) provides: 'For the purposes of this Act an organisation is proscribed if it is listed in Schedule 2, or it operates under the same name as an organisation listed in that Schedule.' The power to add to or delete groups from the Schedule is exercised under s 3(3) by the Secretary of State, by order. Under s 3(4), the power may be exercised 'only if he believes that [the organisation] is concerned in terrorism' and, under s 3(5), it will be concerned in terrorism if it '(a) commits or participates in acts of terrorism, (b) prepares for terrorism, (c) promotes or encourages terrorism, or (d) is otherwise concerned in terrorism'. In other words, groups which do not themselves fall within the s 1 definition but which are in any way 'concerned' in terrorism can be proscribed. The addition of the term 'concerned in terrorism' makes this provision wider than that under the PTA. Parliament's approval is required for additions to, or deletions from, the list as it was under the PTA provisions.[45]

Proscribed groups

Difficult decisions will have to be taken concerning the new 'terrorist' groups (under the new definition) to be proscribed. At present, under Sched 2 of the new Act, the groups listed were already proscribed under the EPA; they will now be proscribed throughout the UK.[46] But the key issue under the new Act will be whether all or most of the other groups falling within the new definition will eventually be proscribed. There appear to be three options for the trend of proscription over a period of time. First, the current proscriptions could be retained, merely adding further Irish splinter groups if necessary. Secondly, both Irish and international groups could be proscribed, leaving domestic groups that fall within the definition unproscribed. Thirdly, all groups falling within the definition could be proscribed. This will clearly be a very significant matter; whichever option is chosen, the government is likely to leave itself open to severe criticism. Choosing the first or second would mean that while the members of certain domestic groups are, in effect, redefined as 'terrorists', the groups would remain openly able to engage in various public activities such as advertising for members, fund-raising, holding

---

45 Under the Act of 2000, s 123(4): 'An order or regulations under any of the following provisions shall not be made, subject to subsection (4), unless a draft has been laid before and approved by resolution of each House of Parliament ...'. The provisions listed include s 3(3). Section 123(5) covers cases of urgency, in which case an order may be made without approval; if so it will lapse after 40 days unless approved.

46 The following groups are listed in Sched 2: the Irish Republican Army, *Cumann nam Ban, Fianna nah Eireann*, the Red Hand Commando, *Saor Eire*, the Ulster Freedom Fighters, the Ulster Volunteer Force, the Irish National Liberation Army, the Irish People's Liberation Organisation, the Ulster Defence Association, the Loyalist Volunteer Force, the Continuity Army Council, the Orange Volunteers, the Red Hand Defenders and certain Islamic terrorist groups.

marches or possibly even putting up members to stand for elections.[47] This would seem bizarre and would aid in devaluing the concept of terrorism. Such a stance could come to undermine the whole legislation and provides an argument for returning to the qualifications of the PTA, rather than for proscribing all the new 'terrorist' groups.

Lord Lloyd recommended adoption of the third option. This option would be highly problematic in practical terms and deeply objectionable at the level of principle. The government is attracted to it since it would provide 'a mechanism to signal clearly condemnation of any terrorist organisation whatever its origin and motivation'.[48] The government also saw advantages in criminalising fund-raising activity of any kind for a particular group since that would remove the requirement to prove end use of funds. But it recognised the practical problem that changing the group's name could circumvent the provisions. It is unlikely to put this option into practice for some years.[49]

If the third option is eventually adopted, the list, if it is to have any credibility, would have to be exhaustive: it would clearly be inequitable to proscribe one group falling within the definition while failing to proscribe another which was equally within it. Given its width, the definition potentially covers a vast range of organisations. There would clearly be practical difficulties in drawing up and then maintaining an up to date list of international and domestic groups to be proscribed. The list would be of immense scope; it would probably include hundreds of names and it would quickly become out of date. Clearly, it might come to appear ludicrously broad and simply unworkable. It is likely that the list will be built up gradually, beginning with the addition of international groups.[50]

The offence under s 2(1)(a) of the PTA of belonging to a proscribed organisation was reproduced in s 11 of the TA. Under s 11(1), a person commits an offence if he belongs or professes to belong to a proscribed organisation; a maximum penalty of 10 years' imprisonment is imposed. It is notable that there is no *mens rea* requirement. There is a limited defence under s 11(2): 'it is a defence for a person charged with an offence under sub-s (1) to prove that the organisation was not proscribed on the last (or only) occasion on which he became a member or began to profess to be a member, and that he has not taken part in the activities of the organisation at any time while it was proscribed'. But it is not a defence to prove that the defendant did not know that the organisation was proscribed or that it was engaged in activities covered by ss 1(1) and 3 of the Act.

A number of objections of principle arise in respect of the application of the proscription-related offences to a wider range of groups. The key objection is that the profound impact on rights of association, expression and assembly created by making it an offence simply to belong to a certain group is justifiable only by reference to the

---

47 All these activities might in certain respects fall within the terrorist offences discussed below, but they do not in themselves either constitute offences or lead almost inevitably to liability under the proscription-related offences.

48 'The current provisions, under which only Irish terrorist groups can be proscribed, could be construed by some as indicating that the Government does not take other forms of terrorism as seriously. Furthermore a wider provision could deter international groups from establishing themselves in the UK' (the 1998 *Consultation Paper: Legislation on Terrorism,* para 4.14).

49 At the Committee stage in the House of Commons, the government said that in the immediate future it would not add domestic groups to the list; see HC Deb Col 431, 15 March 2000.

50 The explanatory notes to the Act state: 'The Government is considering which organisations involved in international terrorism might be added to the Schedule.'

serious harm it is likely to cause. The use of the very broad definition of terrorism in the TA as the basis for proscription, together with an executive exercise of discretion does not, it is argued, provide a sufficient safeguard against a broad use of these powers.[51] Further, by making it possible to proscribe a wide range of groups, the legislation potentially curtails proscription-related activities that previously would not have been conceived of as related to terrorism. For example, a group which did not itself engage in terrorism but which, for example, expressed support for the 'serious disruption' of a computer system, could be proscribed as falling within the s 1 definition.

Deproscription

Under the previous scheme, if an organisation was proscribed on insufficient grounds, there was little possibility of challenge to the order. There was no right of appeal against proscription, and judicial review, while theoretically available, was likely to be extremely limited. In *McEldowney v Forde*[52] an order was made under statutory instrument banning republican clubs or any like organisation, thus potentially outlawing all Nationalist political parties. Nevertheless, the House of Lords preferred not to intervene, Lord Diplock stating that he would do so only if proscription were extended to bodies obviously distanced from Republican views.

The new Act sets up, under s 5, a new body known as the Proscribed Organisations Appeal Commission (POAC). It is modelled on the Special Immigration Appeals Commission which also provided the model for the new tribunal set up under the Regulation of Investigatory Powers Act 2000, discussed in Chapter 11.[53] The Commission also appears to have certain parallels with the Security and Intelligence Service Tribunals, discussed in Chapter 8, which have never upheld a complaint. Under s 4, if an individual is affected by proscription, or an organisation considers that it should not be proscribed, the first step is to ask the Secretary of State to deproscribe; the Secretary of State is obliged to consider such applications within a period of time specified in regulations to be made under s 4(3). If the Secretary of State refuses to deproscribe, then the organisation or individual may appeal to the POAC as set out in s 5 and Sched 3.[54]

Under s 5(3), the Commission 'shall allow an appeal against a refusal to deproscribe an organisation if it considers that the decision to refuse was flawed when considered in the light of the principles applicable on an application for judicial review'. Clause 9 of the original Bill provided that the reference to those principles allows the appellant to raise

---

51 The proscription-related evidence provisions exacerbated these possibilities. The PTA, s 2A made it possible to convict a person of membership of a proscribed organisation on the unsubstantiated opinion of a police officer combined with adverse inferences drawn from the silence of the accused person. These highly controversial provisions, which were inserted by the Criminal Justice (Terrorism and Conspiracy) Act 1998, ss 1–4, were reproduced in the Act of 2000 in ss 108 and 9 but applied only to Northern Ireland, with the intention that they should be repealed within five years.

52 [1971] AC 632.

53 See pp 714 *et seq*.

54 It may be noted that under s 10, immunity from criminal proceedings is conferred upon a person who seeks deproscription by way of application or appeal under ss 4 or 5, either on behalf of the proscribed organisation or as the person affected. Clearly, otherwise, such a person would be discouraged from pursuing either course, or from instituting proceedings under the HRA, s 7, by the risk of prosecution for certain offences, eg the offence of membership of a proscribed organisation. Section 10 provides that evidence of anything done, and any document submitted for these proceedings, cannot be relied on in criminal proceedings for such an offence except as part of the defence case.

points concerning those rights under the European Convention on Human Rights that are 'Convention rights' under the HRA. After amendment, this provision was removed, but the Commission would be expected to apply Convention principles as a court would in judicial review proceedings, now that the HRA is in force. If the Commission finds in favour of an applicant and makes an order to that effect, this has the effect of requiring the Secretary of State either to lay a draft deproscription order before Parliament or to make a deproscription order on the basis of the urgency procedure. Such a finding is to be treated, under s 9(4)(b), as determining that 'an action of the Secretary of State is incompatible with a Convention right'. Rules may be made under s 9 providing that the POAC is the forum in which proceedings under s 7(1)(a) of the HRA can be brought. If the POAC finds against the applicant under s 5, s 6 allows a further appeal from its decision to a court, on a point of law, and – depending on the rules made – in relation to s 7 of the HRA, if leave is given by the POAC or the court in question. Under s 7, if an appeal to the POAC is successful, and an order has been made deproscribing the organisation, anyone convicted of one of the offences listed in sub-s (1)(c) in respect of the organisation, may appeal against his conviction to the Court of Appeal or Crown Court, which must allow the appeal,[55] so long as the offence was committed after the date of the refusal to deproscribe. This provision includes persons, other than members of the organisation itself, who have been convicted of proscription-related offences at a point after a refusal to deproscribe and who have already exhausted ordinary avenues of appeal.

The procedure before the POAC may be far removed from that which would be applicable in an ordinary court. Under Sched 3 para 5(1), the Lord Chancellor has the power to make rules regulating the exercise of the right of appeal to the Commission and prescribing practice and procedure to be followed in its proceedings. Its members are to be appointed by the Lord Chancellor. Three members must attend the proceedings and one must be a person who holds or has held high judicial office (within the meaning of the Appellate Jurisdiction Act 1876). Under Sched 3, the Lord Chancellor's rules may provide that proceedings may be determined without an oral hearing in specified circumstances; provision may be made regarding the burden of proof; full particulars of the reasons for proscription or refusal to deproscribe may be withheld from the organisation or applicant concerned; the Commission may exclude persons, including legal representatives, from all or part of the proceedings and permit proceedings for leave to appeal to a court under s 6 to be determined by a single member. Thus, although the procedure may appear adversarial, its procedural limitations are likely to handicap one side so greatly that the Commission may be unable to discharge its fact-finding role effectively. It may therefore prove ineffective in protecting bodies from unjustified proscription.[56]

Bearing these comments in mind, a further feature of the proceedings is significant: under Sched 3 para 8, s 9(1) of the Interception of Communications Act 1985 'shall not apply in relation to (a) proceedings before the Commission, or (b) proceedings arising out

---

55 Under s 7(2), once deproscription has occurred, if the convicted person appeals to the Court of Appeal under the Criminal Appeal Act 1968, s 1 (appeal against conviction on indictment) 'the court shall allow the appeal'.

56 For discussion of the similar limitations in respect of the new tribunal set up under the Regulation of Investigatory Powers Act 2000, see Chapter 11, pp 715, 718–19.

of proceedings to which paragraph (a) applies'.[57] Thus, the Commission may take its decision on the basis of secret intercept evidence. But, such evidence cannot be disclosed to the organisation concerned, its legal representatives or the applicant under para 8(2). Therefore, the applicant or the legal representatives would have no means of challenging it or of bringing forward other evidence which might be relevant to it; Art 8 or Art 6 arguments could not be made. A complaint or proceedings in the Regulation of Investigatory Powers Act Tribunal could not be mounted, unless on speculative grounds only.[58]

This procedure is clearly designed to keep deproscription claims, for the most part, out of the ordinary courts. The courts could have heard such claims in judicial review proceedings and could have applied Convention principles to them under ss 6 and 7 of the HRA. Recourse to a court is not, however, entirely prevented; an avenue of appeal from a decision to refuse leave is provided, and the Act does not contain an ouster clause. However, the remedy provided by the POAC may mean that judicial review of decisions to refuse leave and to refuse to make a deproscription order is found to be unavailable. Section 9 appears to be intended to keep proceedings based on s 7 of the HRA largely in the POAC, thereby, apart from the appeals procedure, preventing the ordinary courts from hearing points raised under s 7 of the HRA. Various features of the deproscription procedure raise Convention issues, which are considered below.

Requirements of the Convention under the HRA

Counter-terrorist provisions that extend to groups putting forward a wide range of political messages – using that term in the broad sense that Strasbourg has endorsed – interfere with the flow of information and ideas. Such provisions will come into conflict with the expression, association, and assembly of a very wide and divergent range of groups and persons and therefore call into question their compatibility with democratic values. Clearly, a number of the provisions above may have been of doubtful compatibility with the Convention when they were only applied in practice to certain Irish terrorist groups. But once they are applied far more widely, the issue of compatibility, on a domestic level under the HRA, becomes far more problematic. It is not possible to consider all the instances in which the new legislation may give rise to conflicts with the Convention; the focus will be on certain of its key aspects. The terrorism offences are discussed further in Chapter 9 in relation to their compatibility with the freedom of assembly and expression guarantees under Arts 11 and 10. Their potential impact, and that of the special criminal justice regime, discussed in Chapter 13, on a wide range of groups such as environmental activists, calls into question the definition of terrorism itself, for its compatibility with Art 11. Bearing in mind that many of these groups, if not all, could be viewed as political associations, it could be argued that designating some of these new groups terrorist is a disproportionate response to the threat that they pose and that the use of the ordinary criminal law would be sufficient. Further, the definition itself could be attacked on the ground of its imprecision: a group might fall foul of one of the terrorist offences without having a clear means of knowing beforehand that it could be designated a terrorist group.

---

57 This will have to be amended to refer to the equivalent provision under the Regulation of Investigatory Powers Act 2000, once that Act comes fully into force. See Chapter 11, pp 684–86.
58 See Chapter 11, pp 714 et seq.

Walker has argued in relation to the PTA and EPA provisions that *prima facie* proscription breaches Arts 10 and 11 of the European Convention on Human Rights but that, apart from exceptions contained in those Articles, Art 17 might justify it since it limits Convention guarantees to activity in harmony with its aims and this could not be said of IRA methods.[59] This Article states that the Convention is not to be interpreted so as to imply a right 'for any State, group or person to engage in any activity ... aimed at the destruction of any of the [Convention rights] or at their limitation to a greater extent than ... provided for in the Convention'. Clearly, a number of groups might be proscribed under the current provisions, taking s 1 into account, which cannot so readily be viewed as out of harmony with the aims of the Convention, and therefore the exceptions under the relevant Articles will frequently have to be relied on if compatibility with the Convention is to be found. This could be said *a fortiori* of the much wider range of persons potentially affected by the special terrorist offences which also *prima facie* breach Arts 10 and 11 of the Convention.

There are a number of possible methods of seeking to ensure that the HRA is complied with in this context. They depend mainly on court action, but, as pointed out in Chapter 4, the Home Secretary and other relevant members of the executive are bound by s 6 of the HRA to abide by the Convention. Articles 10 and 11 should therefore be taken into account in taking decisions to add groups to the list of those proscribed under the new Act. Their requirements in relation to such groups are discussed below. Since the police and the Home Secretary are subject to the Convention under s 6, judicial review could be sought of decisions taken by them under the new Act. But, as indicated above, decisions to proscribe may be found to be unsusceptible to review. The POAC itself, as a public authority, must apply the Convention rights in its adjudications and, therefore, in relation to the question of deproscription, it should take the relevant Convention rights into account. The courts will be able to apply those rights in hearing appeals from the POAC, on points of law. There would also be the possibility of considering whether the POAC provides an effective remedy for the citizen.[60] The rules made by the Lord Chancellor under s 9 with the intention that proceedings under s 7(1)(a) of the HRA are brought in the POAC would have to be interpreted compatibly with the Convention under s 3 of the HRA.

In judicial review proceedings, or on an appeal on a point of law to a court against a refusal to deproscribe, it could be argued that the POAC does not meet the requisite standards of independence under Art 13 since, *inter alia*, the Lord Chancellor appoints its members.[61] The ability of the Lord Chancellor to regulate its procedure would also be relevant. This argument would depend on the view taken of the role of the Lord Chancellor, and in particular whether it could be said that in appointing the POAC and regulating it he should be viewed as acting as part of the executive. It could also be argued that the POAC fails to comply with Art 6(1) and (3) since the applicant may be in

---

59 Walker, *op cit*, fn 1, pp 49–50.

60 As Chapter 4 points out, p 135, this possibility is open due to the *Pepper v Hart* statement of the Lord Chancellor in Parliament to the effect that although Art 13 was omitted from the rights protected by the HRA, the courts may be able to view acceptance of the need to allow an effective remedy under Art 13 as an aspect of the intention behind the Act. See HL Deb Col 477, 18 November 1997, HC Deb Col 980, 20 May 1998.

61 See *Govell v UK* (1997) 4 EHRLR 438, discussed further in Chapter 11, p 723.

such a weak position before it. Article 6 guarantees a fair hearing in the determination of a criminal charge.[62] It provides basic guarantees under Art 6(3) of a fair hearing, including the right to cross-examination and to legal representation. These requirements are discussed further in Chapters 13 and 14.[63] The POAC's appeal function might be viewed as the 'determination of a criminal charge' since proscription carries criminal implications going beyond those relating to terrorism alone. It is arguable that the POAC may not provide a fair hearing for the appellant, bearing in mind the procedure that can be followed, described above. The actual procedure followed will depend on the rules made by the Lord Chancellor; those rules will presumably be applied at the discretion of the POAC itself. But the 2000 Act suggests that the new rules should provide for various features of the proceedings, such as exclusion of the appellant from all or part of them, and the direct and secret reception of evidence from phone intercepts which may breach the requirements of fairness.[64] Depending on the procedure adopted in a particular instance it is possible that, apart from any of the other requirements of fairness, the minimal safeguards of Art 6(3) might be unobserved or not fully observed. The impartiality and independence requirements of Art 6(1) could also be raised. It is suggested that the appointments procedure for the POAC complies with the Art 6 requirements in these respects,[65] but that it is debatable whether this is the case in relation to the possibilities provided for under the Act for the determination of its procedure by the Lord Chancellor.[66]

In criminal proceedings on the new application of the special terrorist offences, the courts will have the opportunity of interpreting them, under s 3 of the HRA, compatibly with the Convention rights. They must also discharge their duty under s 6 of the HRA. The approach of the courts towards the new legislation will clearly be crucial. Traditionally, since terrorism has been viewed as threatening national security, the courts have adopted a deferential stance.[67] While a far wider range of persons and activities will be designated 'terrorist' under the new Act, it is apparent that the actions of many such persons and groups do not genuinely threaten national security, not least because the scale of their operations is likely to be small. The approach taken by the House of Lords in *ex p Kebilene*[68] to counter-terrorist provisions, particularly the findings of Lord Hope of Craighead, suggests that where national security is in issue, the judges will refuse (overtly) to apply the margin of appreciation doctrine in adjudicating on the new provisions, and yet may adopt a restrained approach. It was said in *Ex p Kebilene* in the context of the case, which concerned the compatibility of terrorist legislation with Art 6,

---

62 For further discussion as to the field of application of Art 6, see Chapter 2, pp 58–64; Chapter 11, pp 900–02.

63 See pp 854–64, 900–06.

64 See *Rowe and Davis v UK* No 28901/95; Judgment of the Court of 16/2/00; (2000) 30 EHRR 1.

65 See *Campbell and Fell v UK* A 80 (1984).

66 *Sramek v Austria* A 84 (1984) 7 EHRR 51. One of the central questions which cannot yet be answered will be the practice adopted: *Campbell and Fell v UK* A 80 (1984). See also the findings on impartiality in the context of military discipline – *Findlay v UK* (1997) 24 EHRR 221; *Hood v UK* (2000) 29 EHRR 365.

67 In *CCSU v Minister for the Civil Service* [1985] AC 374, the House of Lords accepted the government's claim that national security was at risk, without demanding that evidence should be put forward to support it. In the case of *Rehman v Secretary of State for the Home Dept v Rehman* [2001] 3 WLR 877 (judgment of the CA [2000] 3 All ER 778), the House of Lords accepted that it was for the government alone to determine whether a threat to national security, broadly defined, existed. Thus, the judiciary tends to accept government claims that such a threat is self-evident or must be taken on trust.

68 [1999] 3 WLR 172.

that a deferential approach could be justified. The approach of the courts is likely to continue to depend on the extent to which national security can be said to be at stake. Under the previous legislation, in the context of Irish terrorism, the courts tended to take an absolutist approach, readily making the assumption that considerations of national security outweighed the individual rights at stake. The courts are less likely to be deferential where national security is not an issue and therefore may show a greater willingness to take a robust approach to the new Act than they would if adjudicating on the activities of IRA terrorists. Under the current legislation, bearing in mind its width and the influence of the HRA, the approach might be more nuanced, and might depend more on the particular circumstances of each case, since the groups or the activities in question may be far more divergent from each other, and many persons who are not part of any such group may fall within the new provisions.

The notion of increasing the number of groups to be proscribed lies at the heart of the new legislation. A key issue will therefore be the compatibility of the proscription of new groups with Arts 10 and 11 since, as the Introduction to this chapter indicated, the complete outlawing of a group constitutes *prima facie* a breach of those Articles. In findings as to proscription, therefore, para 2 of those Articles will be of most relevance. As Chapter 2 indicates, State interference with the Art 10 and 11 guarantees must be prescribed by law, have a legitimate aim, be necessary in a democratic society and be applied in a non-discriminatory fashion if it is to be justified. It can probably be assumed that the exercise of the proscription power would be viewed domestically as prescribed by law since it is enshrined in primary legislation, although the 'quality' of that legislation should also be questioned.[69] In freedom of expression and association cases, Strasbourg's main concern has been with the 'necessary in a democratic society' requirement. In *Sidiropoulos v Greece*[70] the Court considered the outlawing in Greece of an association called the Home of Macedonian Civilisation, which had been formed in Macedonia. The authorities refused to register it, on the basis that it was viewed as intended to undermine Greece's national integrity, contrary to Greek law, since it intended to publicise the idea that there is a Macedonian minority in Greece. The Court indicated the stance it would take towards the aims of the State authorities – the preservation of national security and the prevention of disorder – in this context. They were found to be legitimate but the means used to further them – disallowing the registration of the group and therefore outlawing it – was found to be disproportionate to them and therefore unnecessary in a democratic society. Thus, proscription of a particular group, depending on the extent to which there was evidence that it threatens national security and public order, might be found domestically to violate these two Articles. Where, for example, an environmental activist group had been proscribed on the basis that it was encouraging another group to damage a public utility, it might be found quite readily that proscription was disproportionate to the aims in view.

The offence under s 56 of the new Act to direct 'at any level' a terrorist organisation is not confined to proscribed groups. If a minor figure in an organisation which fell within the wide definition of terrorism under s 1, but within its less serious aspects, was charged with this offence, a court which found that this interference with Art 11 was

---

69 See Chapter 11, pp 679–81.
70 (1998). Available from the Court's website, see above, fn 11.

disproportionate to the aims pursued could interpret the terms used in s 56, especially 'directing' and 'at any level' under s 3 of the HRA so as to exclude such figures from the ambit of the section. For example, taking the terms together, it could be argued that the term 'directing' qualifies 'at any level', so that only figures at some level within the *leadership* sector of the organisation are covered.

3 TRADE UNION MEMBERSHIP[71]

Freedom not to join a trade union

The European Court of Human Rights considered this issue in *Young, James and Webster v UK*.[72] In 1975, British Rail entered a closed shop agreement that made membership of a certain trade union a condition of employment. The three applicants, who were already employed by British Rail, disagreed with the political activities of trade unions; they therefore refused to join the union and were dismissed. They claimed that their dismissal on this ground constituted an infringement of Art 11 of the European Convention.

The European Court of Human Rights found that the agreement between British Rail and the unions was lawful under the Trade Union and Labour Relations Act 1974, which allowed for dismissal for refusing to join a trade union unless the refusal was on grounds of religious belief. In determining whether that provision infringed Art 11, the court considered the 'negative aspect' of freedom of association, in other words, the right not to join a group. It was found that the negative aspect was not on the same footing as the positive aspects, but that when an individual's freedom of choice in association was so abridged – where there was only one ground on which it was possible to refuse to join a union – then an interference with freedom of association had occurred since it must necessarily include freedom of choice. This did not mean that all closed shop agreements would infringe Art 11; the court was careful to confine its argument to the facts of the specific case. (The drafters of the Convention were aware of closed shop agreements operating in certain of the Member States in 1949 and therefore deliberately omitted a clause protecting an individual's right not to be compelled to join an association.) The Court did not find that the agreement was necessary under Art 11(2) but decided the case solely under para 1.

In response, UK law was changed by means of a provision inserted into s 58 of the Employment Protection (Consolidation) Act 1978 which widened the exception on grounds of religious belief to include making a dismissal unlawful if the person objected on the grounds of a deeply held conviction to being a member of a trade union (the right not to be dismissed or refused employment due to non-membership of a Trade Union is now contained in ss 137 and 152 of the Trade Union and Labour Relations (Consolidation) Act 1992). This statutory right probably ensures that domestic law is compatible with Art

---

71 For general discussion of the impact of the HRA, see Lightman, G and Bowers, J, 'Incorporation of the ECHR and its impact on employment law' [1998] EHRLR 560.

72 A 44; (1981) 4 EHRR 38; for commentary, see [1982] CLJ 256 and (1982) 15 Cornell ILJ 489.

11, in respect of the freedom not to join a union.[73] The statutory right does not, however, affect compulsory membership of professional associations. A person who suffered employment detriment as a result of refusing to join such an association could bring an Art 11 action against her employer under s 7(1)(a) of the HRA (if it was a standard public authority) or rely on Art 11 under s 7(1)(b) in any existing cause of action.

Freedom of choice between unions

The need to show a very clear curtailment of choice where the negative aspect of freedom of association is in question was affirmed by the decision of the European Court of Human Rights in *Sibson v UK*,[74] which concerned a choice between unions rather than a choice as to whether to join one at all. The applicant had resigned from his union, the TGWU, due to dissatisfaction with its decision in respect of a complaint he had made; he had then been ostracised by his workmates, who threatened to go on strike unless he rejoined the union or was employed elsewhere. He joined another union and his employer then sought to employ him at a depot some distance away; he refused this offer, resigned and claimed constructive dismissal. When this claim failed in the domestic courts, he applied to the European Commission on Human Rights, alleging a breach of Art 11. The court found that no breach had occurred: his treatment did not infringe the very substance of his freedom of association; he had not been subject to a closed shop agreement and had had the offer of continuing to work for the company without joining the union. Moreover, he had had no objection to union membership as such.

Owing to this decision, it is probable that the HRA will not have much impact on freedom of choice between unions. However, it may be argued that this decision should not be characterised as one entirely concerned with the negative aspect of freedom of association since, in order to rejoin the TGWU, the applicant would have had to resign from the second union. Therefore, the claim could be characterised as concerning the right of an employee to choose which particular union to join free from pressure from workmates or the employer. The applicant had been faced with the choice of working elsewhere or resigning from one union and joining another. It might appear that such a situation concerns a highly significant interest – the freedom to choose between associations – and that therefore, this decision is unfortunate in leaving such freedom unprotected so long as the employee retains the basic freedom not to join a union. It is instructive to note that the International Covenant on Economic, Social and Cultural Rights, unlike the European Convention, includes 'the right to join the trade union of *his choice'* (emphasis added).

Freedom to join or form a union

During the Conservative Government's period of office from 1979 to 1997, no move was made to outlaw union membership *per se* or to prevent the formation of unions in general.

---

73 In *Sigurjonsson v Iceland* (1993) 16 EHRR 462, the Court found that a pre-entry closed shop agreement was clearly out of accord with the negative right to freedom of association which it explicitly recognised as at the heart of Art 11. See also *Chassagnou v France* (1999) 7 BHRC 151 (concerning the negative right outside the context of union membership).

74 A 258; (1993) *The Times*, 17 May.

Such a move would, of course, have constituted a clear breach of Art 11. However, certain measures were taken which curtailed choice of unions or which had the effect of reducing the size of the group that retains the right to union membership. Certain bodies, such as the army under the Army Act 1955, the police under s 47 of the Police Act 1964 and certain public officials have traditionally been debarred from union membership, but this group was enlarged when civil servants working at Government Communications Headquarters (GCHQ) were de-unionised. Their challenge to the ban on trade unions was considered in *Council of Civil Service Unions v Minister for the Civil Service*[75] (the GCHQ case). The Minister for the Civil Service, the Prime Minister, Margaret Thatcher, gave an instruction issued under Art 4 of the Civil Service Order in Council to vary the terms of service of the staff at GCHQ with the effect that staff would no longer be permitted to join national trade unions. Six members of staff and the union involved applied for judicial review of the minister's instruction on the ground that she had been under a duty to act fairly by consulting those concerned before issuing it. In the House of Lords it had first to be determined whether the decision was open to judicial review. In this instance, the Prime Minister was exercising powers under the royal prerogative which were traditionally seen as unsusceptible to judicial review as deriving from the common law and not from statute. However, Lord Denning in *Laker Airways v Department of Trade*[76] seemed to have effected some erosion of that principle and, following his lead, the House of Lords determined that the mere fact of the power deriving from the prerogative as opposed to statute was not a sufficient reason why it should not be open to review.

Having made this determination, the House of Lords then found that the decision making process had in fact been conducted unfairly. Usual practice had created a legitimate expectation that there would be prior consultation before the terms of service were altered; therefore, there was a legitimate expectation that that practice would be followed which had not been fulfilled. However, the Prime Minister argued that national security considerations had outweighed the duty to act fairly; had there been prior consultation, this would have led to strikes which would have affected operations at GCHQ – the very reason why union membership had been withdrawn. In her assessment, the requirements of national security outweighed those of fairness. The appellants argued, first, that this argument was an afterthought, and secondly, that national security had not been and would not be affected, in part because the unions were offering a no-strike agreement. However, the House of Lords held that the Prime Minister was better placed than the courts to determine what was needed by national security, although it was held that there must be some evidence of danger to national security; a mere assertion that such danger existed would be insufficient. As some evidence of such a danger had been put forward, the challenge to the union ban failed.

A group from GCHQ applied to the European Commission alleging a breach of both Art 11 and of the Art 13 provision that there must be an effective remedy for violation of a Convention right.[77] They were claiming that judicial review did not afford such a remedy. Accepting that the ban infringed the applicants' freedom of association, the government

---

75 [1985] AC 374; [1985] 3 WLR 1174; [1985] 3 All ER 935; for comment, see [1985] PL 177, p 186.
76 [1977] QB 643.
77 *Council of Civil Service Unions v UK* (1987) 20 DRE Com HR 228; (1988) 10 EHRR 269.

argued that it fell within Art 11(2) because it was adopted in furtherance of the interests of national security and that the margin of appreciation allowed to Member States in that respect should be wider than in respect of the other exceptions,[78] since it should be assumed that only the domestic authorities were competent to make a determination as to the needs of national security. Therefore, once it had made a determination that national security would be affected by industrial disruption and that a no-strike agreement would be inadequate, its decision could not be questioned by an outside body. It followed that the blanket ban imposed was not disproportionate to the end in view, which was to protect national security.

The applicants argued, on the other hand, that the exception under Art 11(2) in respect of the needs of national security could not apply because the ban was out of proportion to the aim pursued; there was no sufficiently pressing need to impose it. Only if such a need could be shown could such a grave infringement of freedom be justified. No such pressing need could be shown because there had been no recent action at GCHQ and when there had been such action, the government had not reacted to it for three years, thereby suggesting that it was not over-concerned about the effect on national security. Further, the government had stated in 1981 in Parliament that action at GCHQ had not affected national security. A no-strike agreement, it was argued, would be in proportion to the requirements of national security.

The government's second argument was that the applicants fell within the second sentence of Art 11(2) which allowed restrictions to be imposed on the police, armed forces or the members of the administration of the State. It was argued that 'restriction' could include a total ban. The applicants, however, argued that the sentence should be narrowly construed; the word 'lawful' should mean that it should be interpreted in accordance with Convention limits and that, accordingly, it could not authorise a complete denial of trade union membership.

The Commission found that the ban amounted to a clear *prima facie* breach of Art 11; the question was whether it could be justified. The word 'lawful' was interpreted as meaning 'in accordance with national law'. The Civil Service Order in Council that had been made fulfilled that requirement. Could the term 'restriction' mean 'destruction'? It was found that the fact that the ban was complete did not mean that it would not be proportionate to the aim pursued, which was to protect national security, one of the exceptions contained in Art 11(2). The second sentence of Art 11 was considered. It was found that it allowed for restrictions which could not be justified under the first sentence; it was also applicable to the ban. The application was found to be manifestly ill-founded as far as Art 11 was concerned. The Commission further accepted the government's argument in relation to the alleged breach of Art 13 that judicial review afforded a sufficient remedy. Thus, the application was found to be inadmissible. Those who refused to give up their trade union membership were eventually sacked. The right to join a union was only reinstated at GCHQ in 1997 after the Labour Government came to power.

The Conservative Governments between 1979 and 1997 brought about a further curtailment of freedom of choice in union membership due to its policy of allowing non-industrial civil servants to choose only those unions which were not affiliated to the

---

78 This had been accepted in other decisions including the *Klass* case 1978 A 28; 2 EHRR 214.

Labour Party, on the ground that to do otherwise would imperil the political neutrality of the Civil Service. Thus, a non-industrial civil servant who wished to join an affiliated trade union could not do so, while a civil servant whose industrial grade became non-industrial might have to give up the membership of an affiliated union for that of a non-affiliated one. In pursuance of this policy, the Conservative Government informed the Ministry of Defence in respect of security guards in April 1992 that it would no longer be able to recognise the TGWU and GMB as their representatives due to the political affiliation of those unions.

A possibly related policy concerned the use of penalties against employees who refused offers to give up union membership. In *Associated British Ports v Palmer and Others*,[79] the Court of Appeal found that granting pay rises only to employees who were prepared to renounce their right to union representation was in breach of s 23 of the Employment Protection (Consolidation) Act 1978 which renders unlawful action taken against an employee with the purpose of deterring him from trade union membership. The government immediately responded to this decision by introducing an amendment to the Trade Union Reform and Employment Rights Bill 1993 (then at the report stage in the House of Lords) during its Third Reading in the House of Lords, allowing employers to award pay rises selectively in order to encourage employees to give up union membership.[80] On appeal, the House of Lords found in *Associated British Ports* and in *Associated Newspapers*[81] that the term 'action' did not include omissions in this context, taking the legislative history of the provision into account. This decision almost completely emasculated the protection offered under the Act. It also meant that the amendment made to the Trade Union Reform and Employment Rights Act 1993 was probably unnecessary. Deakin and Morris comment on the House of Lords' decision: 'It is possible to argue that in *Associated Newspapers* the courts have gone well beyond what even the government thought desirable or at least politically expedient in this area.'[82] The House of Lords' decision was likely to be enormously influential in deterring employees from joining or remaining in trade unions. Although the decision did not in formal terms affect the freedom to join a union, it substantively undermined it.

The current Labour Government, however, brought forward legislation to reverse the decision.[83] Employees now have the right not to be subjected to any detriment short of dismissal by any act or deliberate failure to act by his employer.[84] The position now appears to harmonise with the requirements of Art 11 and, therefore, it does not appear to be open to challenge under the HRA. However, domestic provisions regarding the right to form a union and on consultation may contravene Art 11.[85]

---

79 *The Times*, 5 May 1993.

80 On 24 May 1993, the House of Lords therefore adopted the unusual procedure of recommitment of a section to the Bill, followed by a report stage, followed by the third reading of the remainder of the Bill.

81 *Associated Newspapers Ltd v Wilson* [1994] 2 AC 454 ; [1995] 2 All ER 100.

82 Deakin, S and Morris, G, *Labour Law*, 1995, p 643. For further discussion of this area see *op cit*, Chapter 8.

83 Employment Rights Act 1999, s 17. For discussion, see Ewing, K, 'Freedom of association and the Employment Act 1999' [1999] ILJ 283.

84 Trade Union and Labour Relations (Consolidation) Act 1992, s 146, as amended by Employment Rights Act 1999, Sched 2.

85 See Lightman and Bowers, *op cit*, fn 71, p 571.

CHAPTER 9

FREEDOM OF PROTEST AND ASSEMBLY

1 INTRODUCTION[1]

It is often said that toleration of public protest is a hallmark of a democratic, free society. The logic of such a society is that it is prepared to take at least some account of the wishes of its citizens and will not wish to stray too far from the path of majority acceptance in decision making. Further, it does not impose one vision of the good life on its citizens; therefore, it tolerates and even encourages the public expression of various political visions. Public protest as a form of expression is therefore tolerated in free societies.[2] However, the public interests which may be threatened by public protest – the maintenance of order, the preservation of property, freedom of movement, respect for personal autonomy – may also be viewed as essential to democracy.[3] Thus, a tension clearly exists between the legitimate interest of the State in maintaining order on the one hand and, on the other, the protection of the freedoms of protest and assembly.

Therefore, in seeking to discover the limits of the legal acceptance of freedom of protest and assembly, and the value the law places upon it, this chapter focuses on those provisions of the criminal and civil law most applicable in the context of demonstrations, marches or meetings. The legal regime relies on the use of both prior and subsequent restraints. Prior restraint on assemblies may mean that an assembly cannot take place at all or that it can take place only under various limitations. Subsequent restraints, usually arrests and prosecutions for public order offences, may be used after the assembly is in being. Although the availability of subsequent restraints may have a 'chilling' effect, they are used publicly and may receive publicity. If an assembly takes place and, subsequently, some of its members are prosecuted for public order offences, it will have achieved its end in gaining publicity and may in fact have gained greater publicity due to the prosecutions. If the assembly never takes place, its object will probably be completely defeated.

---

1   On this topic see: Williams, DGT, *Keeping the Peace*, 1967 (excellent historical account); Brownlie, I and Supperstone, M, *Law Relating to Public Order and National Security*, 1981; Marshall, G, 'Freedom of speech and assembly', in *Constitutional Theory*, 1971, p 154; Bevan, VT, 'Protest and public disorder' [1979] PL 163; Uglow, S, *Policing Liberal Society*, 1988; Smith, ATH, *Offences Against Public Order*, 1997; Sherr, A, *Freedom of Protest, Public Order and the Law*, 1989; Ewing, KD and Gearty, CA, *The Struggle for Civil Liberties*, 1999; Ewing, KD and Gearty, CA, *Freedom under Thatcher*, 1990, Chapter 4; Bailey, SH, Harris, DJ and Jones, BL, *Civil Liberties: Cases and Materials*, 4th edn, 1995, Chapter 3; Whitty, N, Murphy, T and Livingstone, S, *Civil Liberties Law*, 2001, Part V; Feldman, D, *Civil Liberties and Human Rights in England and Wales*, 2002, Chapter 17; Waddington, PAJ, *Liberty and Order*, 1994; Clayton, R and Tomlinson, H, *The Law of Human Rights*, 2000, Chapter 16. For discussion and criticism of the Public Order Act 1986, see Bonner, D and Stone, R, 'The Public Order Act 1986: steps in the wrong direction?' [1987] PL 202; Card, R, *Public Order: the New Law*, 1987; Smith, ATH, 'The Public Order Act 1986 Part I' [1987] Crim LR 156; Gearty, CA, 'Freedom of assembly and public order', in *Individual Rights and the Law in Britain*, 1994, p 55. For discussion and criticism of the Criminal Justice and Public Order Act 1986, see Allen, MJ and Cooper, S, 'Howard's way: a farewell to freedom?' 58(3) MLR 364, p 378; Fenwick, H and Phillipson, G, 'Public protest, the Human Rights Act and judicial responses to political expression' (2000) PL 627–50.

2   See, eg, Nimmer, MB, 'The meaning of symbolic speech under the First Amendment' (1973) 21 UCLA L Rev 29, 61–62; Kalven, H, 'The concept of the public forum' (1965) Sup Ct Rev 1, p 23.

3   See Bailey, Harris, and Jones, *op cit*, fn 1, p 167.

Prior and subsequent restraints arise from a large number of wide ranging and sometimes archaic powers which spring partly from a mix of statutory provisions, partly from the common law and partly from the royal prerogative.[4] To an extent, the number of restraints available is unsurprising because the range of State interests involved is wider than any other expressive activity would warrant: they include the possibilities of disorder, of violence to citizens and damage to property. Clearly, the State has a duty to protect citizens from the attentions of the mob. The need to give weight to these interests explains the general acceptance of freedom of assembly as a non-absolute right,[5] even though it may be that violent protest is most likely to bring about change.

Most of these restraints are not aimed specifically at assemblies and protesters, but generally at keeping the peace. Nevertheless, they severely affect the freedoms of protest and of assembly. Therefore, those seeking to exercise the freedoms of protest and assembly have historically been in a vulnerable position[6] and currently they are in an especially precarious legal position since such a web of overlapping and imprecise public order provisions now exists and is constantly increasing.[7] But, for the first time, they can rely on an express recognition in domestic law of rights to protest and assemble within Arts 10 and 11 of the European Convention on Human Rights as received into UK law under the Human Rights Act (HRA) 1998. This constitutes a potentially climactic break with the traditional UK constitutional position. That position was that citizens might do anything which the law did not forbid, whereas, under the HRA, they are able to exercise rights to protest and assembly, circumscribed, as Chapters 2 and 4 explain, only in a manner compatible with specified Convention exceptions or, exceptionally, by incompatible domestic legislation.[8]

As Sedley LJ put it in *Redmond-Bate v DPP*:[9] 'A liberty, as AP Herbert repeatedly pointed out, is only as real as the laws and bylaws which negate or limit it. A right, by contrast, may be asserted in the face of such restrictions and must be respected, subject to lawful and proper reservations, by the courts.'[10] Since, as indicated, the extent of such reservations, which may undermine the right, will largely be determined by police officers and magistrates, it is important to bear in mind their obligations to abide by the Convention rights under s 6 of the HRA. Most significantly, this means that, for the first time, the constitutional duty placed personally on individual police officers[11] and magistrates to keep the Queen's Peace will be coupled with a corresponding duty to uphold public freedom of expression.

---

4   For discussion of the various offences, see Smith, JC, *Smith and Hogan Criminal Law*, 1996 (standard criminal law text), Chapter 21; Thornton, P, *Public Order Law*, 1987; Smith, ATH, *Offences Against Public Order*, 1987.

5   See the leading US case, *Hague v Committee for Industrial Organisation* (1938) 307 US 496. For further discussion, see Williams, DGT [1987] Crim LR 167.

6   See Ewing and Gearty, *op cit*, fn 1.

7   The latest provision is contained in the Criminal Justice and Police Act 2001, s 41; see below, pp 505–06.

8   HRA 1998, s 3(2).

9   [1999] All ER (D) 864; (1999) *The Times*, 28 July; see below, p 503–04 for discussion.

10   Transcript, para 15.

11   See *Humphries v Connor* (1864) 17 ICLR 1.

The focus of this chapter is on the mass of common law and statutory public order provisions, in the light of the new rights to freedom of assembly and protest. Having considered the justifications underpinning such rights, it will evaluate possible responses of the judiciary to the acceptance of the substantive values underlying public expression under Arts 10 and 11 in UK public order law. It will be argued that common law has failed to provide the recognition for the value of public protest as a form of political expression which is evident in respect of media expression. This is due, it will be contended, to the desire to protect countervailing interests, particularly proprietorial rights, but the judiciary have not made this explicit: the express balancing act which may be carried out at Strasbourg between political expression and other societal interests has not occurred in the judgments of domestic courts, often because the former value is merely afforded no recognition at all. Moreover, the guarantees of freedom of expression and peaceful assembly under Arts 10 and 11 of the Convention have hardly been adverted to in the domestic courts as aids to statutory interpretation or to resolve common law policy issues in public protest cases, as the decisions discussed below reveal. The close nexus between assembly and expression has failed to receive recognition when low level public order offences, committed in the course of, or directly through, the exercise of political protest, are adjudicated upon. The HRA may encourage a change in the judicial response, and the central theme of this chapter will concern its impact within the established context of the existing and increasing web of restrictions.

Underlying justifications

In considering the justifications underlying rights of protest and assembly it should be noted that the rights are distinguishable, although they will often be exercised together. Some protest of the symbolically or actually obstructive type, such as standing in front of grouse shooters or lying down in front of earth moving machinery, is primarily expression-based: the assembly element may not be significant. Equally, while persons may assemble in a group in order to make a more effective protest, not all groups come together in order to protest: the assembly may be of a ceremonial, albeit political nature; the Orange parades in Northern Ireland fall into this category. In such instances, the fact of assembling is significant and, although the assembly is expressing a message, it could not readily be characterised as a protest.

The individual rights to assemble and make public protest are bolstered by the interests justifying freedom of speech – furthering the search for truth, the participation of the citizen in the democracy and the exercise of autonomy. The justification based on the argument from truth[12] is present in the sense that citizens must be able to communicate with each other if debate which may reach the truth is to occur: public protest provides one means of ensuring that speech reaches a wider audience. Political speech is justified instrumentally on the basis that it allows participation in the democracy;[13] public protest is one particular and direct means of allowing such participation to occur outside election periods. Public protest is probably one of the most effective means by which ordinary citizens can bring matters to the attention of others, including Members of Parliament.

---

12 Mill, JS, *On Liberty*, 1972.
13 See Meiklejohn, 'The First Amendment is an absolute' (1961) Sup Ct Rev 245.

Ordinary citizens are unlikely to be able to gain access to the media to publicise their views; they may, for example, distribute leaflets or posters without assembling in order to do so, but such methods are probably less effective if they are not part of a public protest. A clear example was provided by the anti-poll tax marches in the 1990s. As the Introduction to Part II indicates, this justification for expression is the one most favoured by the European Court of Human Rights,[14] which has also given a very wide meaning to the concept of political expression. Therefore, allowing forms of protest suggests that a society wishes to encourage participation in the democratic process since citizens will thereby be able to signal their response to government policies, encourage changes in policy and deter the government from repressive measures. Public protest provides a direct means of allowing democratic participation to occur outside election periods. On this argument, the acceptance of the freedom to protest poses no threat to the established authorities, but rather underpins the democratic process which placed them where they are and from which they derive their legitimacy. In particular, protesters could be viewed as exercising, through the protest, a choice as to their mode of participation in political activity, a choice, which in the case of some minority groups, may not be a real one, in the sense that they may be, in effect, excluded from mainstream politics. Its exercise may also be bolstered, therefore, by arguments in favour of equality of democratic participation.

Thus, one of the most significant justifications underpinning public protest is that it provides a means whereby the free speech rights of certain groups can be substantively rather than formally exercised. Disadvantaged and marginalised groups, including racial or sexual minorities and groups following 'alternative' lifestyles, may be unable to exercise such rights in any meaningful sense since they cannot obtain sufficient access to the media. At the same time the media, particularly the tabloid press, may tend to misrepresent them. However impoverished members of such groups may be, they are able to band together to chant slogans, display placards and banners and demonstrate by means of direct action. By these means they may be able both to gain access to methods of communication through publicity and to persuade members of their immediate audience to sympathise with their stance. As Barnum puts it: 'the *public* forum may be the *only* forum available to many groups or points of view.'[15] Thus, public protest can act both as a means of access to the media and as a substitute for fair media exposure.[16] The truism that speech in general generates speech is especially applicable to speech or expression as protest.

These methods may provide the only avenue available to such groups if they wish to participate in the democracy and it is of crucial importance that they should be able to take it since, by its very nature, the democratic process tends to exclude minorities with whom the majority may be out of sympathy. Minority interests may be safeguarded only indirectly within that process, by persuading sufficient numbers of people to sympathise with causes which do not directly affect them. There is a reasonable degree of academic consensus regarding the need to protect public protest in order to safeguard minority

---

14 See *Castells v Spain* A 236 (1992), paras 42, 46; *Goodwin v UK* (1996) 22 EHRR 123.

15 Barnum, DG, 'The constitutional status of public protest activity in Britain and the US' (1977) PL 310, p 327. See also Williams, *op cit*, fn 1, p 10.

16 As indicated below (see fn 38), public protest websites may act as one such substitute.

interests:[17] while it has frequently been suggested that State regulation of the media, far from inhibiting free expression, tends to safeguard it,[18] that argument has been applied to public protest only in respect of the regulation of counter-protest. Unsurprisingly, the intense debate on these issues derives from the First Amendment jurisprudence; within the American academic community there appears to be agreement, not only that the State cannot deny a forum to those whose ideas it finds acceptable while denying it to those expressing unpopular views,[19] but also that 'equality of status in the field of ideas' or equality in the exercise of speech rights[20] requires substantive protection. Denial of a public forum for the exercise of expressive rights bears unequally on different groups: it may amount in effect to a denial of the free speech rights of certain minority groups since equal access to other means of exercising those rights will tend to be unavailable. This has also been recognised in the UK context; as Bevan has put it: '[public protest] assists the "unknowns", those who do not have the capability or resources to exercise expression through the conventional media'.[21]

A further justification for speech based on moral autonomy[22] counters public protest in one respect, since the right of a citizen to choose what she will see or hear would seem to include a right not to be forced to encounter protest which she finds offensive.[23] Article 10 of the European Convention on Human Rights protects the 'freedom of expression and the freedom ... to receive ... information and ideas ...'. This includes a right not to speak, according to the Commission in *K v Austria*,[24] and may therefore include a right not to be forced to encounter speech. In the context of public protest, this would probably depend on the duration of the protest and its probable impact on passers-by and others. It might also depend on the extent to which the protesters could be viewed as exercising, through the protest, a choice as to their mode of participation in political activity, a choice which, in the case of some minority groups, may not be a real one, in the sense that they may be, in effect, excluded from mainstream politics. Its exercise may also be bolstered, therefore, by arguments in favour of equality of democratic participation, in addition to those reliant on the values most readily viewed as underlying expressive rights. As Barendt points out, in relation to the German *Brokdorf* case,[25] freedom of assembly (protected, in Germany, by Art 8 of the Basic Law) 'enables people, especially minorities, to participate in the political process. Participation rights are not exhausted by membership of political

---

17 See, eg, Allen and Cooper, *op cit*, fn 1, p 378; Barnum, 'The constitutional status of public protest activity in Britain and the US' (1977) PL 310.

18 See, eg, Abel, R, *Speech and Respect*, 1994, pp 48–58. Abel argues, using examples of media regulation by the market, that 'State withdrawal exposes speech to powerful market forces'. See also Feintuck, M, *Media Regulation, Public Interest and the Law*, 1999.

19 See *Police Dept of the City of Chicago v Mosley* (1972) 408 US 92, pp 95–96. The case concerned an anti-racist protest by a single black protester.

20 See Karst, 'Equality as a central principle in the First Amendment', 43 University of Chicago L Rev 20.

21 Bevan, *op cit*, fn 1, p 187.

22 See Scanlon, T, 'A theory of freedom of expression' (1972) 1 Phil and Public Affairs 204; see p 201, above.

23 Cf Dworkin's distinction between display and distribution: 'Do we have a right to pornography?' in *A Matter of Principle*, 1985, pp 355–58.

24 A 255-B (1993), Com Rep, paras 45, 49.

25 (1985) 69 BVerfGE 315.

parties ... the exercise of the right enables protesters to express their personalities by their physical presence ...'.[26]

Thus justifications deriving from free speech values and from the choice as to the mode of participation in the democracy underpin freedom of assembly and public protest. Even an assembly which publicised anti-democratic views would fall within the justification from the argument from truth. But it is clear that these justifications are not equally present in relation to all assemblies or all forms of what may loosely be termed protest. Public assembly and protest occurs in various forms,[27] admittedly overlapping, ranging from the peaceful expression of a message or views to rioting and extreme violence; it can be categorised as: peaceful persuasion,[28] offensive or insulting persuasion,[29] intimidation,[30] symbolic or persuasive physical obstruction or interference,[31] actual physical obstruction or interference,[32] forceful physical obstruction[33] and violence.[34] The argument from democracy most clearly supports peaceful assemblies or marches that use speech in some form to persuade others, including the authorities, to a particular point of view. The second and third forms, which may occur by means of both speech and conduct, may be supported by the arguments from truth and democracy so long as they are not outweighed by the threat posed by the action. Since these justifications are goal- as opposed to rights-based, they would support only public protest which did not run counter to the goals in question (such as a racist protest).[35] Further, since they set out goals for society as a whole, they would seem to allow interference with speech in the interests of other public concerns which may be immediately and directly damaged by the exercise of speech. As Barendt puts it, in discussing the argument from truth: '... a government worried that inflammatory speech may provoke disorder is surely entitled to elevate immediate public order considerations over the long term intellectual development of the man on the Clapham omnibus.'[36]

The last four forms, often loosely referred to as 'direct action', cannot be termed 'speech', but may be viewed as forms of expression and as having, to varying extents, the same role as political speech. If, as in the last three, a group seeks not to persuade others, but by its actions to bring about the object in question, the democratic process may be said to have been circumvented rather than underpinned. Some forms of non-violent action may well be combined with attempts at verbal persuasion, but may also be intended in themselves to bring about the object in question or at least to obstruct others in their attempts to bring about various objects. Such action would include industrial and other forms of picketing and protests such as those of hunt or fishing saboteurs who physically obstruct the activity in question, albeit usually by non-violent means. Does

---

26 Paper given February 2000 at the Cambridge public law conference.
27 I am indebted to Gavin Phillipson, University of Durham, for suggestions as to their categorisations.
28 Eg, offering innocuous leaflets or chanting inoffensive slogans.
29 Eg, carrying racist banners, displaying pictures of dead foetuses.
30 Eg, shouting and gesturing at individuals crossing picket lines.
31 Eg, lying passively in front of earth moving machinery, conducting a vigil.
32 Eg, blowing horns during a hunt or chaining oneself to a tree.
33 Eg, resisting official attempts to remove members of a sit-in.
34 Eg, attacking counter demonstrators or police officers.
35 See *Kuhnen v FRG* No 12194/86 (1988) 56 DR 205.
36 *Freedom of Speech*, 1987, p 10.

such action fall within the justifications for freedom of protest at all? If it is non-violent, it may be lawful in itself on the principle that everything which is not legally forbidden is allowed. Sleeping in a tree in order to prevent it being cut down or throwing twigs into water to disrupt angling is not intrinsically unlawful, but if no rights-based justification protects such activity and if it impinges on the lawful activity of others, it may appear reasonable to proscribe it. Such activity could, however, be viewed as symbolic speech – message-bearing expression – and therefore as deserving of a degree of protection on that basis. It could be viewed both as obstructing the activity in question but also as calling attention to it, fuelling debate and thereby potentially activating the democratic process. However, such action is also likely to create an invasion of personal autonomy. This argument may be countered where strong justification for the direct action is put forward. An obvious example is its use by the Suffragettes in order to persuade and to draw attention to a cause of immense importance in a democracy. It is clearly questionable whether, short of violence, such protest should be placed, in the eyes of the law, in the same category as late night high street rowdiness. The same cannot be said so readily of direct action which seeks to prevent an outcome of lesser significance – such as the building of a bypass – which has been determined upon by an application of the democratic process.[37]

The fourth form of protest, persuasive physical obstruction or interference, is in a rather different position, although the line between the fourth and fifth tiers will often be hard to draw. Such action is not intended to bring about the object in question directly, but to draw attention to a cause. Of course, some direct action may exemplify both purposes. This may be said of the actions of hunt or fishing saboteurs and motorway protesters.[38]

Direct action may include, in its most extreme form, group violence intended to force others into compliance with a certain view. This would include political riots intended to overthrow the government. This would be unjustifiable in relation to a democratically elected government following the arguments above. However, some forceful action may not be intended in itself to bring about the object in question directly, but may be used as a desperate expedient to draw attention to a cause where peaceful means have failed. It may be distinguished from violent direct action, since it is still intended to bring about its object by democratic means; it may be used to draw attention to a cause and to persuade the electors and Parliament that action is necessary. Such action may be preferred to direct action due to the nature of the object in question. The history of the Suffragette movement shows that after peaceful protest had failed, forceful or violent protest was adopted.

Political riots do not present States with the dilemmas normally associated with public protest. The difficulty usually lies in determining whether a protest, which is justified by reference to the arguments above, has the potential to threaten public order.

---

37 In the case of road building, the extent to which the outcome may be said to represent an application of the democratic process is debatable, especially where the road is within the remit of the Department of Transport rather than a local council. In both instances, under the Highways Act 1980, s 258, objections may be made by those directly and indirectly affected and usually a public inquiry will be arranged and conducted by an 'independent' inspector – a civil servant in the Department of Transport – who then makes a recommendation to the Secretary of State.

38 A good example is the protest at Newbury against the A34 bypass. Between 1994 and 1998 every form of protest was used, from non-violent direct action to criminal damage; see the Newbury Bypass website: geocities.com/newburybypass/index.html.

This possibility clearly raises issues as to the scope of State duties to keep the peace and to safeguard the interests of citizens upon whom protests may impinge. Forms of direct action may infringe privacy rights and the freedom from physical attack or threats. The substance of the protest may be offensive and hurtful to others. The manner of the protest may involve intimidation, thereby potentially infringing the rights of persons to security of the person, freedom of movement and possibly to freedom of assembly. Non-violent or more vulnerable groups may require a calm public order situation in order to be enabled to make an effective protest. Protecting the freedom to protest can mean protecting powerful and well organised groups at the expense of the weak.

In a mature democracy, it would be expected that the extent to which a protest was persuasive rather than simply obstructive would tend to determine the extent of its constitutional protection, although even obstructive protest may be viewed as falling within the range of expressive rights,[39] as raising issues of association and, arguably, of participation in the democracy. The direct action forms of protest might be justified, particularly when exercised by minority groups, on the grounds that they provide a substantive means of engaging in the more *effective* means of communicating with others (since such forms are most likely to attract media attention) and of participating freely in political activity.[40] The same arguments could be applied to persuasive protest requiring a particular forum and time for its exercise. In other words, the equality principle in terms of free expression and rights to engage in political activity might be taken to demand that minorities should be allowed access to forms and places of protest going beyond the relatively innocuous or convenient. Such an argument might allow interference with forms of direct action exercised by minority groups to be considered as interferences with the freedoms of expression, assembly and association though subject to justification, although this raises the difficult issue of the relationship between equality and freedom.[41] Constitutional protection for such freedoms might be expected to override societal interests in preventing mere inconvenience or preserving decorum but, depending on considerations of proportionality, might give way to justifications based on moral autonomy, the risk of personal harm and, perhaps, economic loss. If the value of minority political participation is at stake, a protest expressing a minority viewpoint tending to marginalise a further minority might undermine any special claim it might otherwise have had to access to a particular place.[42] These are the issues with which, on the whole, the domestic courts have not had to grapple in determining public order questions,[43] but with which they are now confronted under the HRA 1998.

---

39 Such protest will be viewed as an expression of opinion according to the findings of the European Court of Human Rights in *Steel v UK* (1999) 28 EHRR 603 and *Hashman and Harrup v UK* (1999) 30 EHRR 241, both discussed below. The protests at issue in those decisions might be viewed as having both persuasive and destructive elements, but it might be argued that a protest intended by the protesters to be purely obstructive could also be viewed as the expression of an opinion; it could also lead incidentally to publicity for the cause and on that basis also could be viewed as a form of expression.

40 See Barendt's argument, above, fn 26 and associated text.

41 See Karst, *op cit*, fn 20, p 43.

42 Eg, racist groups were diverted from marching through Asian communities in Leicester in 1974 and 1979, by the imposition of conditions under the Public Order Act 1936, s 3(1). Such conditions could now be imposed under the 1986 Act, s 12.

43 As Feldman puts it: 'the central value [in UK public protest cases] is public order ...' *Civil Liberties and Human Rights in England and Wales*, 1993, p 785.

The legal response

The development of public order law

Taking the justifications underpinning public protest considered above into account and weighing them against the interest of the State and its citizens in the maintenance of public order, it is clear that some restraint on public protest is needed and is justifiable. The difficulty is that, in furtherance of the interest in public order (which in itself protects freedom of protest and assembly), the constitutional need to allow freedom of assembly in a democracy may be obscured. Historically, the UK has had no formal constitutional or statutory provision providing rights to protest and assemble. Instead, it has seen a series of often ill-considered and needlessly broad statutory responses to disorder. Thus, the activities of the followers of Mosley underpinned the Public Order Act 1936,[44] while in the period leading up to the inception of the Public Order Act 1986 there were a series of disturbances beginning with the Brixton riots in 1981[45] and continuing with the disorder associated with the miners' strike in 1984–85, probably the most significant event in British public order history. The strike largely provided the justification for the introduction of the Public Order Act 1986, although it does not appear that further police powers to control disorder were needed. The police did not seem to have lacked powers to deal with the disturbances; on the contrary, a number of different common law and statutory powers were invoked, including powers to prevent a breach of the peace, s 3 of the Public Order Act 1936, offences of unlawful assembly, of obstruction of a constable and of watching and besetting under s 7 of the Conspiracy and Protection of Property Act 1875.[46] However, the government took the view that the available powers were confused and fragmented and that there was scope for affording the police additional powers to prevent disorder before it occurred.[47] It therefore introduced a number of low level public order offences and created a cumbersome, unwieldy framework for the policing of processions and assemblies under the 1986 Act.

The late 1980s and the early 1990s witnessed some similar protests, notably the anti-poll tax demonstrations, protests against *The Satanic Verses* and against the Criminal Justice and Public Order Act (CJPOA) 1994 itself ('Kill the Bill' protests). Mass protest was not a hallmark of the 1990s, but the period did see an enormous growth in the use of direct action by a variety of groups, usually protesting about environmental and animal rights issues. These included hunt saboteurs, fishing saboteurs, motorway and bypass protesters, and veal calf protesters. The protests at Newbury, Twyford Down and Oxleas Wood against bypasses[48] and at Brightlingsea and Shoreham Ferry Port against the

---

44 For an excellent account of this period, see Ewing and Gearty, *op cit*, fn 1, 1999.

45 See the inquiry by Lord Scarman, *The Brixton Disorders*, Cmnd 8427, 1981.

46 See McCabe, S and Wallington, P, *The Police, Public Order and Civil Liberties: Legacies of the Miners' Strike*, 1988, esp Appendix 1; Wallington, P, 'Policing the miners' strike' (1985) 14 ILJ 145. During the miners' strike, over 10,000 offences were charged; see Wallington, *ibid*.

47 See: House of Commons, Fifth Report from the Home Affairs Committee, Session 1979–80, *The Law Relating to Public Order*, HC 756-1; Lord Scarman, *The Brixton Disorders*, Part VI, Cmnd 8427, 1981; Smith, ATH, 'Public order law 1974–1983: Developments and proposals' [1984] Crim LR 643; White Paper, *Review of Public Order Law*, Cmnd 9510, 1985.

48 See Bryant, B, *Twyford Down: Roads, Campaigning and Environmental Law*, 1996; 'Roads to nowhere', Green Party Election Manifesto 1997, Transport section.

export of veal calves were particularly notable. The growth in the use of direct action was arguably traceable to the perception of animal rights and environmental groups that the government's pursuit of free-market policies meant that it had little concern with environmental as opposed to commercial values.[49] Therefore, during its lengthy period in office, it was assumed that it would be unresponsive to a minority view, and peaceful protest as part of the democratic process would be ineffective. The rise in direct action suggested that the traditional aim of protest – to persuade – was being abandoned. The response of the Major Government was to introduce more draconian measures under the CJPOA 1994 aimed largely at direct action in order to suppress it.[50]

The coming into power of the Labour government in 1997 did not herald any diminution of the direct action form of protest, on the government's own analysis of its predicted prevalence.[51] The concerns of protesters against motorway development, abuse of human rights and on environmental matters, including the introduction of genetically modified crops, continued to be expressed in this form.[52] Diverse groups continued to view protest as a valuable means of drawing attention to viewpoints which tended to be excluded from what may be termed the mainstream communications market place, particularly the tabloid press. Direct action protest may indirectly generate debate and scrutiny of the issues it raises – in the media, and sometimes in the form of official inquiries. The use of direct action at Huntingdon Life Sciences against the use of animals in medical research currently provides an example of the effect of such action in terms of re-igniting serious debate on aspects of the issue.[53] Demonstrations against the impact of trading globalisation took place in London in 1999, 2000 and 2001, and human rights groups, including Amnesty, attempted to protest against the abuse of human rights in China on the occasion of the visit of the Chinese President in October 1999,[54] but were met by heavy-handed policing. Flags and banners were forced from the hands of protesters and removed from the windows of private houses. The availability of a range of other means of communication, particularly via the internet, did not appear to lead to the marginalisation of protest as a means of communicating and of participating in the democratic process. Indeed, the internet, far from providing an alternative means of communication, facilitates protest and publicises it.[55] The movement away from socialist

49 See Monbiot, G, 'The end of polite resistance', TLS, 8 March 1997; Bryant, *op cit*, fn 48.

50 For the background to the 1994 Act, which received the royal assent on 3 November 1994, see the introduction in Wasik and Taylor's Guide to the Act, 1995, p 1. For discussion of the public order offences see Smith, ATH [1995] Crim LR 19.

51 *Legislation Against Terrorism: A Consultation Paper*, Cm 4178, 1998.

52 See the Newbury Bypass website: geocities.com/newburybypass/index.html; reports of protests at Newbury, *Daily Telegraph,* 11 January 1999 and 30 April 1999; the Greenpeace website: greenpeace.org.uk/.

53 See, eg, *The Guardian,* 16 January 2001, p 7 and 22 January 2001, p 5, Radio 4's World At One, 15 January 2001 and two lengthy Channel 4 documentaries in the same week. See further www.huntingdon.com; www.vivisectioninfo.org/HLS.html;www.freezone.co.uk/ liberationmag/huntingex.htm.

54 The Home Office stated that it had not placed pressure on the Metropolitan Police to prevent demonstrators disrupting the visit of the Chinese President (national news reports 25.10.1999). A routine internal review was carried out which exonerated the police; report published on 17.3.2000. Eventually, in judicial review proceedings brought by lawyers for the Free Tibet campaign, the Metropolitan Police admitted that that the treatment of the demonstrators had been unlawful: news reports, 4 May 2000.

55 The Newbury Bypass website – geocities.com/newburybypass/index.html – for example, runs to 23 pages and has links to a mass of connected pages.

policies under New Labour and the similarities between the criminal justice policies of the two main parties, appeared to give rise to a continued perception that radical views could find no place within mainstream politics.

The response of the New Labour Government to the likelihood that the direct action form of protest would continue in evidence during its period of office mirrored that of the Major Government. It passed the Terrorism Act (TA) 2000, largely aimed, like the 1994 Act, at this form of protest, but it used the technique, as Chapter 8 explains, not of introducing new, draconian offences, but of applying the established terrorism offences to the new targets. By using the rubric 'terrorist' to denote the groups to be targeted, it sought to deflect the opposition which would have arisen had the terrorism offences merely been used overtly as a means of curbing the activities of environmental activists and the like, under a new public order Act. However, the constantly reiterated plea of government ministers to the effect that the TA is aimed only at those who are likely to undermine democracy, has not prevented the perception from arising among many protest groups that they are the target of its provisions, for the very straightforward reason that the new definition of terrorism in s 1 is not remotely confined to combating a threat to democracy, but, as Chapter 8 argues, rather connotes, quite clearly, the notion of stifling dissent.[56] The introduction of a new Terrorism Act, as the government's consultation paper preceding the Act explains,[57] can only be justified in relation to non-Irish domestic groups, including groups motivated by ideological as well as political concerns; two of the key target groups expressly mentioned are animal rights or environmental activists.

The new definition, discussed in Chapter 8, will tend to allow many activities, currently criminal, to be re-designated as terrorist. The definition now expressly covers threats of serious disruption or damage to, for example, computer installations or public utilities. The definition is therefore able to catch a number of forms of public protest. Danger to property, violence or a serious risk to safety that can be described as 'ideologically, politically, or religiously motivated' may arise in the context of many demonstrations and other forms of public protest, including some industrial disputes. The government stated in the paper that it had 'no intention of suggesting that matters that can properly be dealt with under normal public order powers should in future be dealt with under counter-terrorist legislation'.[58] But once special arrest and detention powers are handed to the police, they can be used, at their discretion, if a particular person or group falls, or appears to fall, within the new definition. Some direct action against property by animal rights or environmental activists may well fall within it. As pointed out below, some 'direct action' by such groups may be viewed as forms of expression and as having, to varying extents, the same role as political speech.[59] Some direct action, such as the destruction of genetically modified crops, may be intended both to disrupt and to draw attention to a cause. Direct action forms of protest going beyond persuasion may provide a substantive means of engaging in the more effective means of communicating with others (since such forms are most likely to attract media attention).

---

56 See Chapter 8, p 402–03.

57 *Legislation Against Terrorism: A Consultation Paper*, Cm 4178, 1998, Chapter 2.

58 *Ibid*, para 3.18.

59 Such action is likely to be already tortious or criminal but, as Chapter 4 notes, defendants can raise Art 10 and 11 arguments in defence.

To label forms of such action 'terrorist', as the new legislation does, is not only to devalue that term, but to take a stance towards forms of protest more characteristic of a totalitarian State than of a democracy.

The nature of public order law

Although the method adopted by the TA 2000 differs, as indicated, from that of its predecessors, the effect is the same: it follows the tradition they established, whereby provisions likely to affect public protest and assembly are simply added to the existing and extensive ones. A number of trends inimical to public protest are discernible, carried through from the Public Order Act 1986, to the CJPOA 1994, the Protection from Harassment Act 1997, ss 1 and 25 of the Crime and Disorder Act 1998, the TA 2000 and, at present, culminating in the Criminal Justice and Police Act 2001. Certain features of these statutes exhibit the traditional hallmarks of UK public order law, but in the more recent legislation their illiberal tendency is more greatly marked. These statutes are littered with imprecise terms such as 'disorderly' or 'insulting' or 'disruptive', all objectionable under rule of law notions since protesters cannot predict when a protest may lead to criminal liability. Reliance on the likelihood that police, magistrates or the CPS will under-enforce the law is unsatisfactory due to the likelihood that their decisions, in any particular instance, will not be subjected to independent scrutiny. Such reliance hardly provides the firm basis for the exercise of rights to assemble and to protest which one would expect to find in a mature democracy.

The more recent statutory offences tend to have the ingredients of a minimal actus reus and an absent, minimal or reversed *mens rea*.[60] This tendency contributes to the conflation of substantive offences with police powers, evident in the 1986 Act, which has recently become more marked. The CJPOA 1994 continued the trend begun by the 1986 Act of introducing a number of offences which depended on taking orders from the police and which were based on the reasonable suspicion of a police officer.[61] For example, s 60 of the 1994 Act was amended by s 25 of the Crime and Disorder Act 1998 to provide a power under s 60(4A)(a) to demand the removal of a face covering 'if the constable reasonably believes that person is wearing [it] wholly or mainly for the purpose of concealing his identity' and to create an offence punishable by one month's imprisonment of failing to remove the covering. A reasonable, if erroneous, belief is sufficient and no mens rea need be established, so that the wearing of a covering for religious reasons could be irrelevant. No defence of reasonable excuse is provided, so that, for example, it would be unavailing for a farm worker protesting against hunting to claim to wish to conceal her identity not from the police, but from her employer. This trend was strongly continued under the TA 2000.[62]

The more recent provisions affecting public protest also exhibit a tendency not only to create restrictions at the outer limits of what might be tolerated in a democratic society,

---

60 See discussion of the Public Order Act 1986, ss 14A, 14C; the Criminal Justice and Public Order Act 1994, s 69 and the Crime and Disorder Act 1998, s 1, below.

61 See the 1986 Act, ss 12 and 14. Sections 14A and C, introduced under the 1994 Act, s 70, are discussed below, as are the 1994 Act, ss 68 and 69.

62 See Chapter 8, pp 402–06 and below, pp 519–22 for discussion of the relevant counter-terrorist offences.

but to impose criminal penalties while marginalising the criminal process in dealing with disorder. Thus, s 69 of the 1994 Act allows for the conviction of the defendant due to disobedience to a ban on entering land imposed by a police officer, even if the original order was based on an error.[63] Section 3 of the Protection from Harassment Act 1997 and s 1 of the Crime and Disorder Act 1998 provide criminal penalties for disobedience to civil orders. Section 1 of the 1998 Act provides a penalty of a maximum of five years' imprisonment for failing to obey an order obtained on the civil standard of proof,[64] forbidding any form of 'anti-social' behaviour.[65] As Chapter 8 explains, s 3(4) of the TA 2000 empowers the Home Secretary to add a group to the list of those proscribed 'if he believes that it is concerned in terrorism'. There is no express requirement of reasonable belief; nor is it necessary for the group to fall within the definition of terrorism under s 1.[66] No criminal or other proceedings are necessary and there is no right of appeal to a court.[67] Not only do the proscription provisions have immense implications for the rights of the groups proscribed to association, expression and assembly, they also provide the basis for criminalising a wide range of persons who are in some way associated with such groups, including those who merely organise informal meetings at which a member of a proscribed group is speaking, regardless of the purpose of the meeting as a whole.[68]

These recently introduced statutes tend to provide a minimal recognition of a need to protect freedom of expression and assembly by including certain defences of 'reasonableness' without attempting to define the meaning of the term[69] and without making any reference to expression. Such defences stand in contrast to those provided in statutes affecting *media* freedom of expression, such as s 5 of the Contempt of Court Act 1981, s 4 of the Obscene Publications Act 1959, and s 12 of the HRA, all of which provide explicit and detailed defences, allowing, in effect, for a balancing act between protecting expression and the societal interest at stake.

Clearly, the nature of the statutory provisions is only one factor contributing to the real extent of rights to protest and assemble. The common law power to prevent a breach of the peace or to be of good behaviour arguably outdoes such provisions in terms of exhibiting many of the features just criticised, and, as indicated, judicial influence in developing and interpreting public order law has been significant. The key factor, however, continues to be the working practice of the police.[70] The police may already have developed a practice which renders a statutory power irrelevant, or they may consider that the use of the power would exacerbate a public order situation, rather than defusing it. The police may therefore tend to pick and choose among the available powers, tending to prefer familiar or very broad ones, particularly the power to prevent a breach of the peace. These factors appear to explain why certain of the far reaching

---

63 See *Capon v DPP*, Case CO/3496/97 judgment 4 March 1998, LEXIS transcript, discussed Mead [1998] Crim LR 870; considered below, pp 486–7.

64 According to the 1998 Magistrates' Courts Rules applicable to these orders.

65 Section 1(10)(b).

66 See the TA 2000, s 3(5) and Chapter 8, pp 402–03.

67 See Chapter 8, pp 404–06.

68 See further p 520, below.

69 Eg the Public Order Act 1986, ss 5(3)(c) and 4A(3)(c); the Protection from Harassment Act 1997, s 1; the Crime and Disorder Act 1998, s 3(1)(c) and s 1(10).

70 See Waddington, *Liberty and Order*, 1994.

provisions of the Public Order Act 1986, including the obligation to notify the police of a march,[71] the powers to impose conditions on marches[72] and assemblies,[73] and to ban assemblies on the basis of a reasonable belief in the risk of serious public disorder[74] have hardly been used.[75] In contrast, there is emerging evidence that the broader, less cumbersome provisions discussed below, including the recently introduced statutory powers, are being utilised against protesters. The accountability of the police has lain in this context largely in the hands of magistrates due to the dominance of summary offences and the use of binding over powers; therefore, the reality of freedom of protest has frequently been determined at that level. As Palmer puts it, 'prosecutions before magistrates' courts [which] may give rise to [frequently unreported] decisions of the Divisional Court of the Queen's Bench ... are the gauge by which the health of civil liberties in this country can be measured'.[76]

Methods of policing disorder are also significant. Developments in the law during the 1980s and 90s, which provided the police with new and extensive powers to control public protest, have been matched to an extent by developments in such methods. Equipment has become more effective; in 1981, the Home Secretary announced that stocks of CS gas, water cannon and plastic bullets would be held in a central store available to chief officers of police for use in situations of serious disorder, although only as a last resort.[77] However, CS gas has not been used to control disorder since 1981 and water cannon were withdrawn from availability in 1987.[78] The possibility that the use of forceful tactics may exacerbate public order situations has been recognised since Lord Scarman's report into the Brixton disorders in 1981.[79]

The conditions under which various weapons and tactics may be used are not defined in any statute and before the inception of the HRA it appeared that their use was subject to a very low standard of scrutiny by the courts. When a local police authority tried to prevent the Chief Constable applying for plastic bullets from the central store, the Court of Appeal declared that the Crown had a prerogative power to keep the peace which allowed the Home Secretary to 'do all that was reasonably necessary to preserve the peace of the realm'.[80] As the power is undefined, it appeared to render lawful any measures taken by the Home Secretary which can be termed 'reasonably necessary' in order to keep the peace. However, this position cannot be sustained under the HRA, since a court would be expected to examine the proportionality of the measures taken with the aim of preventing disorder.[81]

---

71 Section 11.
72 Section 12.
73 Section 14.
74 Section 13.
75 See Waddington, *op cit*, fn 1, 1994.
76 Palmer, S, 'Wilfully obstructing the freedom to protest?' [1987] PL 495.
77 Report of HM Chief Inspector for Constabulary for 1981, 1981–82, HC 463. For discussion of police riot control techniques and equipment see Waddington, *The Strong Arm of the Law*, Chapter 6.
78 See Jason-Lloyd, L (1991) 141 NLJ 1043.
79 Above, fn 45
80 *Secretary of State for the Home Dept ex p Northumbria Police Authority* [1989] QB 26; [1988] 2 WLR 590; [1988] 1 All ER 556, CA; for criticism, see Beynon [1987] PL 146 (on the Divisional Court decision); Bradley, AW, 'Police powers and the prerogative' [1988] PL 298.
81 See further Chapter 4, p 171.

Meetings on private premises

Although the emphasis of the discussion so far has largely been on meetings and demonstrations in public places, meetings held on private land or premises with the permission of the owner are, nevertheless, affected by a number of public order provisions. Under the Public Order Act 1986, still the central statute governing this area, any meeting held in wholly enclosed premises will be a private meeting (s 16), including a meeting held in a town hall, although the town hall is owned by a public body. The provisions of ss11–14A of Part II of the Public Order Act 1986, creating a statutory framework for marches and assemblies, do not cover private meetings. But the public order provisions of ss 5, 4A and 4 do apply to 'private places'. However, if the place in question is a 'dwelling', the words or behaviour must affect a person outside the dwelling. Thus, in theory, these provisions are applicable to private meetings not held in a person's home. Provisions aimed at violent disorder – ss 1, 2, 3 – apply equally to private and public places, without any qualification regarding dwellings. The counter-terrorism measures discussed below could also be used in respect of private meetings.

Aside from the powers of arrest under the provisions of Part I of the 1986 Act which, with the qualifications mentioned regarding dwellings, are available, the power of the police to enter indoor meetings is uncertain. It was generally thought that the police had no power to enter unless they were invited in. However, such a power may derive from the decision in *Thomas v Sawkins*.[82] A meeting was held in a hall to protest regarding the provisions of the Incitement to Disaffection Bill which was then before Parliament. The police entered the meeting and its leader, who considered that they were trespassing, removed one of the officers, who resisted the ejectment. In response, the leader brought a private prosecution in which he sought to show that the officers were trespassers and that therefore he had a right to eject them, in which case their resistance would amount to assault and battery. The court found that the officers had not been trespassing. Although the meeting had not constituted or given rise to a breach of the peace, the officers had reasonably apprehended a breach because seditious speeches and incitement to violence might have occurred. The police had therefore been entitled to enter the premises. This decision has been much criticised.[83] Nevertheless, it does not hand the police *carte blanche* to enter private meetings; it should mean that the police can enter the meeting only if there is a clear possibility that a breach of the peace may occur. The nature of this doctrine and the probable effect on it of the HRA is considered below. Under the Strasbourg jurisprudence, an element of immediacy is necessary.[84] Therefore, the power to enter meetings indicated in *Thomas v Sawkins* is likely to undergo limitation.

A more narrow right to enter premises which might be applicable in respect of some meetings arises under s 17(1)(c) of the Police and Criminal Evidence Act 1984. A police officer has the right to enter and search premises with a view to arresting a person for the offence arising under s 1 of the Public Order Act 1936 of wearing a uniform in connection with a political object. Furthermore, the police can enter premises in order to arrest a person for an offence under s 4 of the Public Order Act 1986. It should be noted that the

---

82   [1935] 2 KB 249.
83   See Goodhart, AL [1936–38] CLJ 22.
84   *McLeod v UK* (1998) 27 EHRR 493 RJD 1998-VII 2774. See below, p 496.

offence under s 4 (discussed below) can be committed in a private or public place, although not in a dwelling. Presumably, it could therefore be committed in a town hall. Thus, a meeting during which violence might be threatened to persons present[85] would give police officers the right to enter if they had reasonable suspicion that such could be the case. If it was thought that one of the serious public order offences under ss 1, 2 or 3 of the 1986 Act was occurring or about to occur, the police could arrest under the general arrest power of s 24 of the Police and Criminal Evidence Act 1984. We will return to this arrest power and police powers of entry to premises in Chapters 11 and 13 below.

Conclusions

Thus, the domestic focus of attention has been, and still is, on the many areas of law which delimit the residual freedom to make public protest. Clearly, it is understandable that public protest suffers greater circumscription than political expression generally, since it conflicts with a large number of societal interests and may create invasions of individual autonomy,[86] damage to property and even personal injury. But the traditional marked judicial reluctance to consider the free expression claims of public protest in a democracy provides, it will be argued, too great a contrast not only with the stance taken in Strasbourg, but with that taken by the domestic judiciary, and the House of Lords in particular, in relation to the political expression of the media.[87]

In considering public protest, Strasbourg has viewed it as a form of political expression and has therefore relied on case law in other areas of expression.[88] In contrast, in the domestic courts, 'rights' to the freedoms of protest and assembly are occasionally mentioned,[89] but their content is hardly considered; far more typically, the interest of the judgment centres on the legal content of proprietorial rights. Perhaps even more significantly, the status of Arts 10 and 11 as providing claim rights subject to exceptions which are 'necessary in a democratic society', has provided Strasbourg, as *Handyside v UK*[90] makes clear, with the opportunity of considering the hallmarks of such a society. Strasbourg is therefore able to consider what is required in terms of the necessity of an interference with public protest, both in terms of the maintenance of the democracy and of effective participation in it. In contrast, the domestic judiciary have been confined to applying the law, whether or not its restrictions go beyond those nationally and internationally deemed necessary in democracies. The UK courts have hardly participated in the ongoing debate in democracies regarding the permissible extent of such restrictions, and to an extent this is due to their inevitable preoccupation, under a constitution based on negative liberties, with the legal content of the restriction in

---

85   In general, the control of indoor meetings is the responsibility of the persons holding the meeting and to that end, a reasonable number of stewards should be appointed (Public Order Act 1936, s 2(6)) who may use reasonable force to control disorder and to eject members of the public whose behaviour does not constitute reasonable participation in the meeting.

86   In the sense that the protest must be experienced by those who may not wish to experience it. It may also interfere with individual choices as to activities and movement.

87   See *Derbyshire CC v Times Newspapers* [1993] AC 534 and *Reynolds v Times Newspapers* [1999] 4 All ER 609.

88   See, eg, *Steel and Others v UK* (1999) 28 EHRR 603, para 101.

89   See, eg, Lord Denning's comments in *Hubbard v Pitt* [1975] 3 All ER 1.

90   (1976) 1 EHRR 737.

question. As indicated above, this position has, formally, changed under the HRA. Its possible effects in this context form the central theme of this chapter.

Judicial uncertainty in applying the Convention will arise in a number of contexts, but public protest cases will present them with an especially stark choice, since the HRA provides that public authorities must not infringe Arts 10 and 11; on its face, this requirement demands a break not only with the traditional acceptance that there is no legal right to assemble or engage in public protest in the UK, but with the failure to prevent encroachment on the negative liberty. As indicated above, references to 'rights' are occasionally made, but they appear to be, loosely, to negative liberties.[91] The HRA requires more of public authorities than a mere voluntary tolerance of public protest or a recognition of freedom of assembly that can be readily abrogated,[92] and, moreover, if the judiciary, while paying lip-service to rights to freedom of protest, maintain something close to the present balance between public order and freedom of assembly, in the new era, they will fail to give it full effect.

2 RIGHTS TO ASSEMBLE AND TO PROTEST

Traditional legal recognition of freedom of assembly[93]

It is generally thought that there is a right to assemble in certain places, such as Trafalgar Square or Hyde Park, but it is a fallacy that UK law has recognised any legal right to do so.[94] Until the Convention was received into domestic law, it continued to afford virtually no recognition to rights to meet or to march. However, there are two instances in which such recognition is given. There is a very limited right to hold meetings, applying only to parliamentary candidates before a general election, which arises under ss 95 and 96 of the Representation of the People Act 1983. This right will normally be upheld even when it appears that it is being abused by a minority group: in *Webster v Southwark LBC*[95] the Labour council had wished to deny it to a National Front candidate, but the court upheld the statutory right of the group to meet. Once an election meeting is in being, the law will afford a limited protection: it is an offence under s 97 of the 1983 Act to use disorderly conduct in order to break up a lawful public election meeting and this will include meetings held on the highway.[96] This limited provision may be compared with more

---

91 It may be noted that when approval has been expressed of Lord Denning's defence of 'rights to protest', the 'right' has become a freedom: *per* Otton J in *Hirst and Agu v Chief Constable of West Yorkshire* (1987) 85 Cr App Rep 143: having quoted Lord Denning's findings with approval, he went on to say: 'the freedom of protest on matters of public concern would be given the recognition it deserves.'

92 See *DPP v Jones* [1999] 2 WLR 625. The decision is discussed in detail below, pp 465–74.

93 See Barnum, *op cit*, fn 17 and (1981) 29 Am Jo of Comparative Law 59; also Stein, LA [1971] PL 115 for discussion of the constitutional status of public protest.

94 In respect of Trafalgar Square, see *Ex p Lewis* (1888) 21 QBD 191. By statutory instrument, an application must be made to the Department of the Environment to hold a meeting in Trafalgar Square (SI 1952/776). There is no right to hold meetings in the royal parks: see *Bailey v Williamson* (1873) LR 8 QB 118.

95 [1983] QB 698; [1983] 2 WLR 217.

96 *Burden v Rigler* [1911] 1 KB 337.

general provisions from other jurisdictions making it an offence to disrupt any meeting that has not been prohibited.[97]

Further, s 43 of the Education (No 2) Act 1986 provides that university and college authorities are under a positive duty to 'ensure that freedom of speech within the law is secured for members, students and employees of the establishment and for visiting speakers'.[98] Although there may be an argument that this provision is to be welcomed as promoting free speech interests, it is somewhat anomalous, to say the least, that a right to meet arises in certain specified buildings but not in others, such as town halls, while it does not arise at all in public places such as town squares or parks. In *Caesar-Gordon ex p University of Liverpool*,[99] the University gave permission, under a number of limitations, allowing a South African speaker to speak at a meeting. Concerns were expressed about the possibility of disorder in the nearby area of Toxteth, an area with large ethnic population. The Divisional Court upheld the limiting conditions imposed which included the right to charge the organisers, the Conservative Association, for the cost of security, and a ban on publicity. Thus, quite severe limits can be placed on this right in practice.

But apart from these narrow rights, arising from specific provisions, a group which is prevented from holding an effective meeting due to the activities of other groups had no special protection.[100] A group which wished to assemble in a particular place had no right to do so, although a very limited freedom to assemble on the highway was recognised prior to the inception of the HRA, as discussed below.[101] On the other hand, the law affords great prominence to the freedom to pass and re-pass along the highway. Section 137 of the Highways Act 1980 provides that a person will be guilty of an offence if he 'without lawful authority or excuse wilfully obstructs the free passage of the highway'. It might appear, therefore, that the negative freedom to assemble is entirely abrogated so far as the highway is concerned since most assemblies will create some obstruction. However, according to *Hirst and Agu v Chief Constable of West Yorkshire*,[102] the term 'lawful excuse' refers to activities which are lawful in themselves and which are reasonable, and this was found to cover peaceful demonstrations. This decision supports the view that freedom of assembly has found some recognition as a common law principle.

Further, s 14 of the Public Order Act 1986 impliedly recognises the freedom to meet so long as the statutory requirements are complied with, and this argument may be supported by the existence of certain specific statutory prohibitions on meetings in certain places or at certain times, such as s 3 of the Seditious Meetings Act 1817 which prohibits meetings of 50 or more in the vicinity of Westminster during a parliamentary session.

---

97 See, eg, Arts 284 and 285 of the Austrian Criminal Code.

98 For discussion of this provision see Barendt, E, *Freedom of Speech*, pp 321–22; Barendt, E, 'Freedom of speech in the universities' [1987] PL 344.

99 (1990) 3 All ER 821.

100 See discussion of this point in the European Court of Human Rights in *Plattform 'Ärzte für das Leben' v Austria* (1988) 13 EHRR 204; it was found that freedom of assembly could not be reduced to a mere duty on the part of the State not to interfere; it did require the State to take some positive steps to be taken although the State was not expected to guarantee that a demonstration was able to proceed.

101 See p 467–8.

102 (1986) 85 Cr App R 143. See also *Nagy v Weston* [1966] 2 QB 561; [1965] 1 WLR 280; cf *Arrowsmith v Jenkins* [1963] 2 QB 561; [1963] 2 All ER 210; for comment, see [1987] PL 495.

Such restrictions impliedly support the existence of a general freedom to meet or march that will exist if not specifically prohibited. The decision in *Burden v Rigler*[103] that, for the purposes of s 97 of the Representation of the People Act 1983, the fact that the meeting is held on the highway will not of itself render it unlawful, also supports this view. However, it will be indicated throughout this chapter that common law recognition of freedom of assembly was patchy, limited and precarious. Therefore, the rights of freedom of expression and assembly recognised in domestic law under the effects of the HRA are of especial significance.

Rights to make public protest within Arts 10 and 11

Under s 6 of the HRA, those seeking to exercise rights of protest and assembly can rely on Arts 10 and 11 of the Convention, and any other relevant right,[104] against public authorities, in particular the police. All the legislation already mentioned and discussed below must be interpreted compatibly with those rights, under s 3, taking the Strasbourg jurisprudence into account under s 2. But, in order to evaluate the impact of the Convention, it is necessary to consider the scope and content of the Art 10 and 11 rights of protest and assembly.

Existing jurisprudence on the right to protest is scanty,[105] and very few cases deal with direct action protest, which has been analysed under Art 11[106] and, recently, Art 10.[107] Owing to the existence of Art 11, it is fair to say that until recently, Strasbourg had not developed a distinct Art 10 jurisprudence on expression as public protest. However, recent decisions, discussed below, suggest that such a jurisprudence may be developing and that Strasbourg currently views freedom of assembly simply as an aspect of freedom of expression.[108] This stance is appropriate given the deliberate adoption of the wider term 'expression' rather than 'speech' in Art 10; it also avoids the problems experienced in the US, in distinguishing between message-bearing conduct and conduct *simpliciter*. The conduct element of assemblies and protests may exclude it from Art 11 protection due to the requirement that they should be 'peaceful' and possibly this restriction should also be read into Art 10, at least in respect of *group* protest, in order to ensure the consistency and coherence of the two Articles. This does not imply that the 'assembly' element within the exercise of Art 11 rights is necessarily subordinate to the 'expression' element or that it is

---

103 [1911] 1 KB 337.

104 Article 5 may have particular applicability. See Chapter 2, pp 49 *et seq*.

105 There have been comparatively few decisions by the Court (*Plattform 'Ärzte für das Leben' v Austria* A 139 (1988); *Ezelin v France* A 202 (1991); *Steel v UK* (1998) 28 EHRR 603; *Chorherr v Austria* A 266-B (1993); *Hashman and Harrup v UK* (1999) 30 EHRR 241; (2000) 8 BHRC 104). Most of the jurisprudence consists of admissibility decisions in the Commission, finding that the application was manifestly ill founded.

106 *G v FRG* No 13079/87 (1980) 21 DR 138.

107 See *Steel v UK* (1999) 28 EHRR 603 and *Hashman and Harrup v UK* No 25594/94, 25 November 1999, [1999] EHRLR 342, (2000) 8 BHRC 104. Previously, the general tendency was to treat Art 11 as *lex specialis* in such cases, with Art 10 requiring no separate consideration *per se*, but nevertheless providing relevant principles to assist in the consideration of the Art 11 claim (see, eg, *Ezelin v France* A 202 (1991), para 35).

108 *Ezelin v France* A 202-A (1991). However, it may be noted that in his partly dissenting opinion, Judge de Meyer took the view that the two Articles were inextricably linked in their bearing on the instant situation and that there had been a violation of both (p 31).

unnecessary to distinguish between the two elements. In *Chorherr v Austria*[109] the expression of protesters appeared likely to offend some spectators, leading to an interference with their peaceful enjoyment of a parade. The interference of the State with the Art 10 rights of the protesters was justified since it had the aim of upholding freedom of assembly.

Freedom of assembly under Art 11

Article 11 is specifically aimed at freedom of assembly. Forms of public protest as examples of both assembly and expression will fall within Art 10 also. Some forms of protest, such as handing out leaflets or expressing an opinion through direct action – where the 'assembly' element of the protest may be insignificant – may be considered only within Art 10. The value of freedom of choice as to the *manner* of participation in political activity may, however, fall most readily within Art 11 which, in this instance, should not therefore be viewed simply as providing assembly rights interchangeable with expression rights under Art 10. As indicated in Chapter 8, Art 11 protects both association and assembly, and in its judgement in *Socialist Party and Others v Turkey*[110] the Court linked the three guarantees together in finding that the dissolution of the Socialist Party of Turkey had breached Art 11. The individuals affected by the interference in question could be viewed as exercising rights to participate in political activity, of a central nature in a democracy. As indicated above, such participation can occur by various means, including direct action, and is clearly not confined to activity associated only with general elections. The persons participating may be viewed as exercising a choice as to the particular manner of their participation. The close connection which the Court perceived between the freedoms of association and expression echoes the findings of Judge Harlan in the US Supreme Court in 1958: 'Effective advocacy of both public and private points of view, particularly controversial ones, is undeniably enhanced by group association, as this Court has more than once recognised in remarking upon the close nexus between the freedoms of speech and assembly.'[111]

If the argument in favour of rights of association and participation in political activity is applied to public protest, it may in certain circumstances provide a foundation for the claims of protesters that might not readily arise if Art 10 alone was relied on. As Barendt has pointed out,[112] the US Supreme Court has shown itself willing to protect rights of access to particular public places in order to hold meetings or demonstrations, in contrast to its stance in respect of the exercise of speech rights. Although this stance flows from the wording of the First Amendment which, in contrast to Art 10, refers to speech rather than expression, the argument may be of relevance in relation to 'manner' issues and have value in carving out a distinctive, or any, role for Art 11 which is not at present apparent in the recent Strasbourg public protest jurisprudence. Thus, once domestic courts begin to develop a distinctive Convention jurisprudence on public protest, it is suggested that they should question the treatment of protest as simply a form of political expression.

---

109 A 266-B (1993).

110 Judgment of 25 May 1998 (App No 20/1997/804/1007); (1999) 27 EHRR 51, paras 41, 47, 50.

111 *NAACP v Alabama* (1958) 357 US 449, p 460.

112 In 'Freedom of assembly', in Beatson and Cripps (eds), *Freedom of Expression and Freedom of Information*, 2000.

Although protest is thereby bolstered by the arguments outlined supporting the special position of such expression, there may be instances in which other arguments based on the exercise of autonomy in relation to political activity, deriving solely or mainly from Art 11, should be utilised. If protesters rely on both Arts 10 and 11, the argument that other means of communication, such as the internet, are available or that free expression justifications may not fully support rights to determine the place, manner and time of the protest, will carry less weight since each protester may be viewed as exercising rights to self-determination in choosing both to associate with a particular group and to participate in the political process in a particular manner, time and place.

Article 11 leaves a great deal of discretion to the judiciary. It is not a far reaching provision since, as explained in Chapter 2, it protects only freedom of *peaceful* assembly and since, in common with Arts 8–10, it contains a long list of exceptions in para 2.[113] In interpreting it, the UK judiciary are obliged, under s 2 of the HRA, to take the relevant Strasbourg jurisprudence into account. That jurisprudence is not, on the whole, of a radical nature, although the Court has found that the right to organise public meetings is 'fundamental'[114] and includes the right to organise marches, demonstrations and other forms of public protest. Article 11 may impose limited positive duties on the State to ensure that an assembly or a protest can occur even though it is likely to provoke others to violence; the responsibility for any harm caused appears to remain with the counter-demonstrators.[115] The acceptance of further positive duties, including a duty to require owners of private land to allow some peaceful assemblies on their property, has not yet been accepted under the Convention but remains a possibility,[116] especially, as Harris, O'Boyle and Warbrick point out,[117] in view of the growth of quasi-public places such as large, enclosed shopping centres and the privatisation of previously public places.

'Direct action' used in a symbolical sense has been found to fall within Art 11.[118] The key factor in determining whether a protest counts as a peaceful assembly appears to be whether it is violent in itself or whether any violence arises incidentally.[119] *G v FRG*[120] concerned a sit-in that had blocked the road to a US Army barracks in a protest against nuclear weapons.[121] Under the distinction suggested above,[122] the protest would be

---

113 See Chapter 2, p 74.

114 *Rassemblement Jurassien Unite Jurassienne v Switzerland* No 819/78, (1979) 17 DR 93, 119.

115 *Plattform 'Ärtze fur das Leben' v Austria* A 139 (1988), para 32; Judgment of 21 June 1988; 13 EHRR 204.

116 See *De Geillustreede Pers v Netherlands* No 5178/71, 8 DR 5 (1976) Com Rep; the Commission accepted that States may have positive obligations to uphold freedom of expression in the context of media ownership. In the US, the 'access' issue was initially resolved in favour of the property right, but now seems to be moving towards acceptance of exceptions favouring expressive rights; see Nardell, 'The Quantock Hounds and the Trojan Horse' [1995] PL 27 on *R v Somerset CCV ex p Fewings*, [1995] 1 All ER 513 for discussion of the shopping mall/'constitutional fora' cases. See further below, pp 453–54.

117 *Law of the European Convention on Human Rights*, 1995, p 419.

118 *G v Federal Republic of Germany* No 13079/87, (1989) 60 DR 256, 263. Currently, the Court views such protest as falling most readily within Art 10; see below, 440–41.

119 *Christians against Racism and Fascism v UK* No 8440/78, (1980) 21 DR 138, 148.

120 No 13079/87, (1980) 21 DR 138.

121 The protest was intended to mark the third anniversary of the NATO Twin-Track Agreement (NATO-Doppelbeschluß).

122 See p 426.

viewed as primarily symbolic, rather than obstructive, since the demonstrators blocked the road for only 12 minutes in every hour. The applicant ignored an order to leave the road, was arrested and convicted of the offence of coercion by force or threats.[123] It was found that 'the applicant's conviction ... interfered with his [Art 11] rights'.[124] However, the interference was again quite readily found to be justified. The Commission considered that the applicant's conviction for having participated in the sit-in could be viewed as necessary in a democratic society for the prevention of disorder and crime, since the blocking of a public road had caused more obstruction than would normally arise from the exercise of the right of peaceful assembly. The applicant and the other demonstrators had thereby intended to attract broader public attention to their political opinions concerning nuclear armament. However, 'balancing the public interest in the prevention of disorder and the interest of the applicant and the other demonstrators in choosing the particular form of a sit-in, the applicant's conviction for the criminal offence of unlawful coercion does not appear disproportionate to the aims pursued'. The application was dismissed as manifestly ill founded.

The Court has only found an infringement of freedom of assembly under Art 11 in one judgment, *Ezelin v France*,[125] discussed below. In two further instances, *Steel v UK*[126] and *Hashman v UK*,[127] a violation of Art 10 was found in respect of public protest and the Court therefore did not find it necessary to consider Art 11. It has been a feature of the practice that applications do not reach the Court since the Commission has readily found them to be manifestly ill founded.[128] This cautious stance largely arises from the wide margin of appreciation that has been afforded to national authorities in determining what is needed to preserve public order at local level.

Protest as expression under Art 10

The Art 10 jurisprudence relating specifically to public protest is meagre, as this chapter will indicate. However, the extensive jurisprudence on expression generally, especially political expression, is clearly applicable to public protest.[129] The *content* of speech will rarely exclude it from Art 10 protection: thus, speech as part of a protest likely to cause such low level harm as alarm or distress may be protected according to the *dicta* of the Court in *Müller v Switzerland*[130] to the effect that the protection of free speech extends equally to ideas which 'offend, shock or disturb'. The Court has repeatedly asserted that freedom of expression 'constitutes one of the essential foundations of a democratic

---

123 Under the German Criminal Code, s 240.

124 It accepted that 'the applicant and the other demonstrators had not been actively violent in the course of the sit-in concerned'.

125 A 202-A (1991).

126 In *Steel and Others v UK* (1999) 28 EHRR 603, a violation of Art 10 was found in respect of interferences with public protest.

127 (2000) 8 BHRC 104; (1999) 30 EHRR 241. Both judgments are discussed below, pp 443–44 and 493.

128 *Friedl v Austria* Appl No 15225/89 (1992) unreported; *Christians Against Racism and Fascism v UK* Appl No 8440/78; 21 DR 138 (1980).

129 *Steel and Others v UK* (1999) 28 EHRR 603.

130 (1991) 13 EHRR 212.

society', that exceptions to it 'must be narrowly interpreted and the necessity for any restrictions ... convincingly established'.[131] As the Introduction to this part indicates, it is a marked feature of the Strasbourg jurisprudence that political expression receives a high degree of protection. One of the leading works on the Convention concludes: 'It is clear that the Court ascribes a hierarchy of value' to different classes of speech, attaching 'the highest importance to the protection of political expression ... widely understood.'[132]

Prima facie all forms of protest that can be viewed as the expression of an opinion fall within Art 10 according to the findings of the Court in *Steel v UK*.[133] Thus the direct action form of protest, such as symbolic or actual physical obstruction, does fall within the scope of Art 10,[134] a finding that was reiterated in *Hashman v UK*.[135] In *Steel*, protesters who were physically impeding grouse shooters and road builders were found to be engaging in 'expression' within the meaning of Art 10. These findings are clearly of the highest significance, but, unfortunately, since they were made without the slightest attempt at explanation or justification,[136] it is impossible to ascertain with any certainty either the limits of the protection thereby extended to such protests, or whether Strasbourg views such expression as having a lower status than 'purely' expressive protest activities – carrying banners, handing out leaflets, shouting slogans, and the like. *Steel* also concerned third, fourth and fifth applicants, who had engaged in purely peaceful protests with no element of obstruction or other 'action'. Since no justification for the arrest of such purely peaceful protesters was apparent, a breach of Art 10 was found. As explained below, no breach was found in respect of the first two applicants and the Court did not scrutinise the question of proportionality very closely. This stance suggests that while actual obstruction falls within Art 10, it may have a lower status than protest in the form of pure speech.

In *Steel*, the Court drew no distinction between actual and symbolic obstruction, and has not therefore considered the means by which any such distinction might manifest itself in the assessment of the lawfulness of State interferences with these forms of obstruction. It is clear only that violent or threatening protest – which, according to the Commission, includes 'demonstration[s] where the organisers and participants have violent intentions that result in public disorder' – falls outside Art 11 and, probably, Art 10.[137]

---

131 *Observer and Guardian v UK* judgment of 26 November 1991, A 216, pp 29–30, para 59; 14 EHRR 153.

132 Harris, J, O'Boyle, M and Warbrick, C, *Law of the European Convention on Human Rights*, 1995, pp 397 and 414. The second rank is artistic speech, the third commercial speech, eg, advertising. They acknowledge that these terms may be too narrow (p 397, fn 14 and associated text). In particular, the term 'artistic' is too restrictive since it does not cover all speech, including some forms of protest, which may be said to be supported by the free speech arguments.

133 (1999) 28 EHRR 603.

134 See *Steel v UK* (1999) 28 EHRR 603, para 92: 'It is true that the protests took the form of physically impeding the activities of which the applicants disapproved, but the Court considers nonetheless that they constituted expressions of opinion with the meaning of Article 10.'

135 *Hashman* (2000) 8 BHRC 104; (1999) 30 EHRR 241 does not offer much guidance as to the scope of protection for direct action since, having found that a sanction applied to the applicants for blowing a horn with the intention of disrupting a hunt was a form of expression within Art 10, the Court went on to find that the interference was not 'prescribed by law': the domestic law – the *contra bono mores* doctrine – was found to be insufficiently precise.

136 The like finding made by the Commission in *G v FRG*, fn 120 above, similarly took the form of a bare assertion.

137 See above, fn 119.

Justifications for interferences with the primary rights

Owing to the likelihood that, as indicated, most forms of protest will fall within Art 10, and probably also Art 11, the emphasis of Strasbourg findings is on the para 2 exceptions which include 'in the interests of national security ... public safety ... for the prevention of disorder or crime ... for the protection of the ... rights of others'. Under the familiar formula discussed in Chapter 2, in order to be justified, State interference with Art 10 and 11 guarantees must be prescribed by law, have a legitimate aim, be necessary in a democratic society and be applied in a non-discriminatory fashion (Art 14). In carrying out this assessment, the domestic courts are obliged to take the Strasbourg public protest jurisprudence into account although they are not bound by it.[138]

In freedom of expression cases, Strasbourg's main concern has been with the 'necessary in a democratic society' requirement; the notion of 'prescribed by law' has been focused upon to some extent but almost always with the result that it has been found to be satisfied. The 'legitimate aim' requirement will normally be readily satisfied; as Harris, O'Boyle and Warbrick point out, the grounds for interference are so wide that 'the State can usually make a plausible case that it did have a good reason for interfering with the right'.[139] The provision against non-discrimination arising under Art 14 is potentially very significant, especially in relation to minority public protests, but so far it has not been a significant issue in the relevant freedom of expression jurisprudence.

The requirements of precision and foreseeability connoted by the term 'prescribed by law'[140] have been flexibly applied in this context; for example, in *Rai, Allmond and 'Negotiate Now' v UK*,[141] the Commission had to consider the ban on public demonstrations or meetings concerning Northern Ireland in Trafalgar Square. The ban was the subject of a statement in the House of Commons and many refusals of demonstrations had been made subsequent to it. The Commission found that the ban was sufficiently prescribed by law: 'It is compatible with the requirements of foreseeability that terms which are on their face general and unlimited are explained by executive or administrative statements, since it is the provision of sufficiently precise guidance to individuals ... rather than the source of that guidance which is of relevance'.[142] In *Steel and Others v UK*[143] the Commission introduced a very significant qualification to the requirement: 'The level of precision required depends to a considerable degree on the content of the instrument, the field it is designed to cover, and the number and status of those to whom it is addressed.'[144] Although the term 'margin of appreciation' was not used, this finding appears to allow the Member State a certain leeway in public protest

---

138 HRA 1998, s 2(1).

139 *Law of the European Convention on Human Rights*, 1995, p 290.

140 *Sunday Times v UK* A30, para 49 (1979).

141 81-A D & R 46 (1995).

142 *Ibid*, p 152. The power in question arose from the Trafalgar Square Regulations 1952 SI 1952/776, para 3, made under the Parks Regulation (Amendment) Act 1926. The Act allowed the Secretary of State to 'make any regulations considered necessary ... for the preservation of order ...' in the parks.

143 (1998) 28 EHRR 603; [1998] Crim LR 893.

144 Paragraph 145. The Commission based these findings on the judgments of the Court in *Chorherr v Austria* Series A 266-B (1993), para 23 and in *Cantoni v France* para 35 (1996) RJD 1996-V 1614.

cases in relation to the 'prescribed by law' requirement. As indicated below, that leeway was overstepped by the *contra bono mores* (contrary to a good way of life) power arising under the Justices of the Peace Act 1361, due to its imprecision.[145]

The Court tends to afford a wide margin of appreciation when reviewing the necessity of interferences with expression in the form of protest, viewing measures taken to prevent disorder or protect the rights of others as peculiarly within the purview of the domestic authorities, in contrast to its stance in respect of 'pure' speech. Therefore, expression as protest tends to be in a precarious position. The notion of a margin of appreciation conceded to States permeates the Art 10(2) and 11(2) public protest jurisprudence, although it has not influenced the interpretation of the substantive rights.

In finding that applications are manifestly ill founded, the Commission has been readily satisfied that decisions of the national authorities to adopt quite far reaching measures, including complete bans, in order to prevent disorder are within their margin of appreciation.[146] The Court has also found 'the margin of appreciation extends in particular to the choice of the reasonable and appropriate mean to be used by the authority to ensure that lawful manifestations can take place peacefully'.[147] Thus, States are typically *not* required to demonstrate that lesser measures than those actually taken would have been inadequate to deal with the threats posed by demonstrations – disorder, interferences with the rights of others and so on.

The effect of this 'light touch' review may also be seen in the tendency to deal with crucial issues – typically proportionality, but also in some cases the scope of the primary right[148] – in such a brusque and abbreviated manner that explication for the findings is either non-existent or takes the form of mere assertion.[149] Moreover, the jurisprudence is, in general, markedly under-theorised, in notable contrast to that concerning media expression. 'It is fair to say that little recognition of the distinctive value of public protest as compared to other forms of political discussion is apparent from the case law; moreover ... general principles have not played [a] great ... part in cases involving public protest.'[150] In *Steel*,[151] for example, which, as indicated, concerned interferences with the freedom of expression of five applicants, the proportionality of the arrest and 17 hour detention of the second applicant and her subsequent imprisonment for seven days on refusing to be bound over is airily determined, in a mere two sentences. The applicant was physically impeding digging equipment by sitting on the ground. The Court's

---

145 See *Hashman and Harrup v UK* (1999) 30 EHRR 241; Appl No 25594/94 (European Court of Human Rights); (2000) 8 BHRC 104.

146 See *Christians against Racism and Fascism v UK* No 8440/78, 21 DR 138; and *Friedl v Austria* No 15225/89 (1992) unreported.

147 *Chorherr v Austria* A 266-B (1993), para 31.

148 See the crucial findings in *Steel v UK* (1999) 28 EHRR 603, *Hashman and Harrup v UK* (above, fn 127) and *G v FRG* 21 DR 138 (1980) that direct action fell within the scope of Arts 10 and 11.

149 While such terse reasoning is a typical feature of the Strasbourg case law (see, eg, Dickson, 'The common law and the European Convention', in *Human Rights and the European Convention*, 1997, pp 216–17), the tendency is particularly marked in protest cases: cf, eg, the reasoning devoted to the proportionality issue in *News Verlags v Austria* (2001) 31 EHRR 8 (a case concerning media freedom discussed in Chapter 6 – six lengthy paragraphs – with that in *Steel v UK* (one paragraph).

150 See Fenwick and Phillipson, *op cit*, fn 1, pp 629–30.

151 (1998) 28 EHRR 603.

finding was that her arrest and detention was justified as necessary to prevent disorder and protect the rights of others.[152] But these grounds had scant substantiation: it was accepted that no violent incidents or damage to property had been caused by the road protesters (para 15) and the conduct of the applicant had been entirely peaceful: she had never resisted being removed from the area by security guards – so it is hard to see wherein lay the 'risk of disorder',[153] still less why it was sufficient to justify such comparatively drastic action. As for 'the rights of others', the court, rather extraordinarily, nowhere said what these 'rights' were, although presumably the judges had in mind the fact that the road builders were engaged in a lawful activity – building a road – which the protesters were disrupting. The issue of the gravity of the interference with these 'rights' was not touched upon: the road builders did have security guards, and were apparently able to carry on with their work, at the cost of some inconvenience. In neither case was the question of alternative means of protecting the road builders even adverted to, much less subjected to any analysis. In other words, one of the justificatory grounds for the interference with Art 10 rights was unsubstantiated by any real evidence; the other was subject to no analysis at all.

In *Pendragon*[154] and *Chappell*,[155] Commission cases on challenges to blanket bans[156] on assemblies at and around Stonehenge, these tendencies are even more marked. In both cases, the bans under challenge prevented Druids from holding bona fide religious ceremonies, which had been held for over 80 years during the summer solstice period. Since such bans constitute prior restraint, and in both cases resulted in the criminalisation of those engaged in purely peaceful gatherings, it might have been expected that they would have been subjected to that 'most careful scrutiny' which prior restraints in other contexts demand.[157] In *Pendragon*, the ban caught a group of Druids conducting a ceremony *near* Stonehenge; the justification for it put forward by the Chief Constable was that in the previous year, about 40 people had tried to gain access to the monument itself, during the solstice period. The Commission cited no evidence whatever to justify the assertion that the use of a blanket order – the most serious interference possible – was the *only way* of protecting Stonehenge,[158] an assertion which must be seriously open to question, given the plethora of other powers available.[159] In fact, the Commission made no inquiry at all as to whether less intrusive means could have been used: it merely

---

152 (1998) 28 EHRR 603, para 109.

153 The first applicant, it found, 'had created a danger of serious physical injury to herself and others and had formed part of a protest which risked culminating in disorder and violence': (1998) 28 EHRR 603, para 105). Neither of these factors was present in relation to the second applicant, so the reference was not only worthless, but positively misleading (though the Court did note that the risk of disorder was 'arguably less serious than that caused by the first applicant' (para 109)).

154 No 31416/96 (1998).

155 No 12587/86 (1987).

156 In *Chappell*, these were made under the National Heritage Act 1983, and the Ancient Monuments and Archaeological Areas Act 1979, in *Pendragon*, under s 14A itself.

157 *Observer and Guardian v UK* (1991) 14 EHRR 153, para 60.

158 The government simply asserted that 'the other powers in the Act did not provide adequate protection'.

159 In respect of breach of the peace, attempted or actual criminal damage, breach of conditions applied to specific assemblies (ie, to keep clear of Stonehenge), POA 1986, s 5, and possibly CJPOA, s 69, breach of an order imposed under the powers used in *Chappell*.

asserted blandly: 'it cannot be considered to be an unreasonable response to prohibit assemblies at Stonehenge for a given period.'

In *Chappell*, the Commission found that the decision to enforce a total ban 'was a necessary public safety measure, and that any implied interference with the applicants' rights under Article 9[160]... was ... necessary ... in the interests of public safety, for the protection of public order or for the protection of the rights and freedoms of others'. It may be noted that this purported determination consists of a mere assertion that the Convention tests were fulfilled. A similar finding was made in relation to Art 11. As in *Steel*, part of the justification for the restrictions was asserted to be 'for the protection of the rights and freedoms of others' although there was no mention of what these rights might be, still less any analysis of why they should outweigh the primary Convention rights of freedom of religion and assembly, exercised in a wholly peaceful manner. The dismissal of both cases as 'manifestly ill founded' indicated the Commission's view that the applications raised no serious issues of law. The specific problems these characteristics raise when attempting to 'apply' the case law to particular domestic facts are considered at various points in this chapter.

Only in *Ezelin v France*[161] did the Court take a 'hard look' at the issue of proportionality. The applicant, an advocate, took part in a demonstration against the judicial system generally and against particular judges, involving the daubing of slogans attacking the judiciary on court walls, and eventual violence. Ezelin did not himself take part in any illegal acts, but did not disassociate himself from the march, even when it became violent. He was disciplined by the Bar Association and eventually given a formal reprimand, which did not impair his ability to practice. No fine was imposed. The French Government's argument was that, 'By not disavowing the unruly incidents that had occurred during the demonstration, the applicant had ipso facto approved them [and that] it was essential for judicial institutions to react to behaviour which, on the part of an 'officer of the court' ... seriously impaired the authority of the judiciary and respect or court decisions'.[162] The argument was rejected; Art 11 was found to have been violated. In an emphatic judgment, the Court found: '... the freedom to take part in a peaceful assembly – in this instance a demonstration that had not been prohibited – is of such importance that it cannot be restricted in any way, even for an advocate, so long as the person concerned does not himself commit any reprehensible act on such an occasion.'[163]

Conclusions

The broad phrasing of Arts 10 and 11[164] will inevitably leave a great deal of interpretative discretion to the UK judiciary in considering their application to existing law. But certain conclusions can be drawn: the Court will not tolerate the arrest and detention of purely peaceful protesters, even if the protest degenerates into violence, so long as the protesters

---

160 See Chapter 2, pp 73–74; Art 9 guarantees the right to 'freedom of thought, conscience and religion', including the right 'either alone or in community in others and in public or private, to manifest [one's] religion ... in worship ... practice and observance'.

161 A 202 (1991).

162 *Ibid*, para 49.

163 *Ibid*, para 53.

164 Articles 5 and 6 may also be relevant in some circumstances.

in question have not themselves committed 'reprehensible acts'. The finding of the Court in *Steel v UK*,[165] reiterated in *Hashman v UK*,[166] that direct action protest, such as physical obstruction, does fall within the scope of Art 10[167] is of great significance, as is the finding of the Commission that protesters engaged in a 'sit-in' blocking a road are covered by Art 11.[168] It appears to be the case that Strasbourg views such expression as having a lower status than 'purely' expressive and speech-based protest activities, but a distinction has not been drawn between actual and symbolic obstruction,[169] although it may be inferred that actual obstruction might be viewed as reprehensible.

Thus, apart from violent or threatening protest, most forms of protest and assembly are within the scope of both Arts 10 and 11, although ceremonious processions and assemblies will probably be considered only within Art 11,[170] while the recent tendency is to consider forms of direct action within Art 10. All the forms of protest mentioned above, apart from the last two,[171] appear to be covered. Thus, forms of protest including those far removed from the classic peaceful assembly holding up banners or handing out leaflets engage these Articles, but interference with direct action protest can be readily justified, even where it is primarily of a symbolic nature.

Nevertheless, it is evident that the application of the above case law without more, would do little to structure the domestic judicial discretion, leaving the courts free to apply Arts 10 and 11 so that they constitute little or no check upon police discretion over assemblies and demonstrations on the ground. Whether this turns out to be the case depends crucially upon two factors: first, the attitude of the domestic courts towards the margin of appreciation doctrine and any domestic equivalent; secondly, whether they are prepared to make any use of the more fundamental principles underlying Convention jurisprudence on political expression generally.

The domestic application of Arts 10 and 11

In Chapter 4, two opposing judicial approaches were indicated to the application of the Convention, although it was pointed out that judicial reasoning cannot always be neatly pigeonholed. It is suggested below that the two approaches are of especial significance in this context, since the common law has failed to afford the protection to freedom of protest and assembly which has been evident at Strasbourg. This is not a context in which the tendency of the common law has been to achieve high standards of human rights

---

165 (1998) 28 EHRR 603.

166 (1999) 30 EHRR 241; No 25594/94 25 November 1999; (2000) 8 BHRC 104.

167 In *Steel v UK* (1999) 28 EHRR 603, para 92: 'It is true that the protests took the form of physically impeding the activities of which the applicants disapproved, but the Court considers nonetheless that they constituted expressions of opinion with the meaning of Article 10.'

168 *G v FRG* Appl No 13079/87 (1980) 21 DR 138.

169 Above, pp 439–40.

170 See *Chorherr v Austria* A 266-B (1993); see above, p 438.

171 See p 424.

protection. If the judges fail to abandon their traditional approach in favour of a more activist stance, under the impetus of the HRA, it will continue to be the case that the freedoms of protest and assembly receive less recognition in the UK than in other comparable democracies.

As commentators have agreed[172] and as the House of Lords recently stressed,[173] the margin of appreciation doctrine, as such, should not be applied by domestic courts, since it is a distinctively international law doctrine. Applying the Convention without such reliance would have two aspects. It would mean, first, refusing to import the doctrine into domestic decision making on the Convention where no Strasbourg decision was in point, and, secondly, where such a decision was in point, seeking to apply it but to disentangle the margin of appreciation aspects from it. This might mean giving consideration to the likely outcome of the case at Strasbourg had the doctrine been disregarded. However, as discussed above, the reasoning in much of the case law is quite sparse and tokenistic, the doctrine having had the effect, not of influencing a particular part of the judgment in a clear way, but simply of rendering the whole assessment quite rudimentary. Therefore, stripping away the effects of the doctrine might merely mean treating certain judgments as non-determinative of the points raised at the domestic level. Certainly, domestic courts minded to make an intensive inquiry into questions of proportionality will receive little aid from the cases described above in so doing.

Minimalism

This is a context in which the possible stances that the domestic judiciary might adopt when confronted with public order cases raising Art 10 and 11 issues are, it is argued, quite clearly opposed. A minimalist approach might be, in this context, almost indistinguishable from what might be termed a 'traditionalist' one and might yield similar results, since this is a field in which the judiciary have, since *Beatty v Gillbanks*,[174] almost invariably eschewed an activist approach. A minimalist approach could be justified on the basis that a balance has always been struck in UK law between freedom of assembly and public order by reference either to common law principle or parliamentary restraint; with only two exceptions,[175] that balance has been found to accord with Arts 10 and 11 at Strasbourg[176] and therefore there is no reason to disturb it now. Under this approach, the courts, while pronouncing the margin of appreciation doctrine

---

172 See Laws, J (Sir), 'The limitations of human rights' [1999] PL 254, p 258; Feldman, D, 'The Human Rights Act and constitutional principles' (1999) 19(2) LS 165, p 192; Pannick, D, 'Principles of interpretation of Convention rights under the Human Rights Act and the discretionary area of judgment' (1998) PL 545; Hunt, M, Singh, R and Demetriou, M, 'Is there a role for the 'margin of appreciation' in national law after the Human Rights Act?' (1999) 1 EHRLR 15, esp p 17.

173 *R v DPP ex p Kebilene and Others* [1999] 3 WLR 972, p 1043, *per* Lord Hope: '[the doctrine] is not available to the national courts ...'; see *dicta* to like effect in *R v Stratford JJ ex p Imbert* (1999) *The Times*, 21 February, *per* Buxton LJ.

174 [1882] 9 QBD 308, discussed below, p 497.

175 See the findings of the Court under Art 10 regarding the third, fourth and fifth applicants in *Steel, Lush, Needham, Polden and Cole v UK* Appl No 24838/94 (1999) 28 EHRR 603 above, pp 441–43, and *Hashman and Harrup v UK* (1999) 30 EHRR 241; (2000) 8 BHRC 104.

176 See, eg, *Chappell v UK* (1988) 10 EHRR 510; *Christians Against Racism and Fascism v UK* Appl No 8440/78 (1980) 21 DR 138; the findings as regards Steel and Lush in *Steel, Lush, Needham, Polden and Cole v UK* Appl No 24838/94 (1999) 28 EHRR 603.

inapplicable, would not take the further step of recognising and making due allowance for its influence on the cases applied. Thus, judges would rely simplistically and solely on the *outcomes* of decisions at Strasbourg – most of which are adverse to the applicants – without adverting to its influence on those outcomes. Thus, they would import its effects – 'light touch' review and therefore a 'soft-edged' proportionality standard likely to catch only grossly unreasonable decisions – into domestic decision making. Anticipation of such an approach is not unduly pessimistic: arguably it was already evident in the pre-HRA era in Convention-based reasoning.[177]

The traditionalist judge would tend to take the view that common law principle has long recognised values which are coterminous with the factors taken into account at Strasbourg in evaluating the balance in question, and that, in most instances, the outcome of cases would not differ whether freedom of expression was viewed as a common law principle or as protected under the Convention. Occasional judicial pronouncements suggest that the common law recognises legal rights to assemble and protest. In *Hubbard v Pitt*,[178] in a well known minority judgment, Lord Denning referred to 'the right to demonstrate and the right to protest on matters of public concern'.[179] Recently, Eady J found, in a decision concerning animal rights' activists, that the Protection from Harassment Act 1997 'was ... not intended by Parliament to be used to clamp down on ... the rights of political protest and public demonstration which are so much a part of our democratic tradition'.[180] The traditionalist judge might note, however, that the two decisions at Strasbourg which have found that the UK had breached Art 10 in interfering with public protest, both concerned common law doctrines. Such a judge might perhaps also acknowledge that there has been more reluctance to accept that the freedoms of protest and assembly, as opposed to media freedom of speech, are recognised as reflecting common law values[181] coterminous with Convention ones.[182]

---

177 See the recent House of Lords decision in *Ex p Kebilene* [1999] 3 WLR 972 and the earlier case of *Khan* [1997] AC 558, HL. Sedley J, in *Redmond-Bates* (1999) Crim LR 998; (1999) *The Times*, 28 July, also appeared to follow this tendency in remarking merely that the decision in *Steel* 'demonstrates that the common law [of breach of the peace] is in conformity with the Convention'.

178 [1975] 3 All ER 1.

179 *Ibid*, pp 10D and 11B.

180 *Huntingdon Life Sciences Ltd and Another v Curtin and Others* (1997) *The Times*, 11 December; (1998) 3(1) J Civ Lib 37.

181 Compare the following pronouncement of Lord Hewart CJ in finding that where a public meeting might lead others to breach the peace, the speaker could be arrested: 'There have been moments during the argument in this case where it appeared to be suggested that the court had to do with a grave case involving what is called the right of public meeting. I say "called" because English law does not recognise any right of public meeting for political ... purposes ...' (*Duncan v Jones* [1936] 1 KB 218, p 221), with these pronouncements from *Derbyshire CC v Times Newspapers* in which it was found that local (or central) government cannot sue for libel. Lord Keith said: 'I find it satisfactory to be able to conclude that the common law of England is consistent with the [freedom of expression] obligations assumed under [the Convention]' [1993] AC 534, p 551, HL. Butler-Sloss LJ said: 'I can see no inconsistency between English law upon this subject and Article 10 ... This is scarcely surprising, since we may pride ourselves on the fact that freedom of speech has existed in this country perhaps as long, if not longer than ... in any other country in the world' ([1992] 3 WLR 28, p 60, CA). Admittedly, in view of the dates of these findings, this comparison might be viewed as mischievous and unfair, since the later decisions might be said to have been reached in the 'shadow' of the Convention. But the decision of the House of Lords in *DPP v Jones and Lloyd* [1999] 2 All ER 257, discussed below, pp 465 *et seq*, could hardly be viewed as upholding the right to protest and assemble as strongly as *Derbyshire* upheld media freedom of speech.

182 The Divisional Court decision in *Jones and Lloyd v DPP* [1997] 2 All ER 119, discussed below,pp 465–6, found that there is no right to assemble on the highway, merely a voluntary toleration of such assemblies. No reference was made to an acceptance of Convention values within the common law except to say that Art 11 did not need to be referred to since the law was not ambiguous.

Since, under the HRA, the courts must take account of rights to protest as opposed to negative liberties,[183] these approaches will have to be modified in order to provide a little more protection for such rights than was provided previously. Under judicial review principles, the domestic courts must consider proportionality: a restriction will be disproportionate where there is insufficient need for it or where no evidence of such need is advanced by the State. Where different views might be taken of the need for a particular interference, such as a ban imposed on a march under s 13 of the Public Order Act 1986, a domestic court fully applying the Strasbourg jurisprudence, including its margin of appreciation aspects, would tend to defer to the judgment of the executive. Clearly, this approach is distinguishable from that of heightened *Wednesbury* unreasonableness,[184] but it would often lead to the same outcome.

The likelihood that a domestic doctrine of judicial restraint will be developed in relation to aspects of executive decision making, including the policing of public protest, derives support from the decision of the House of Lords in *Chief Constable of Sussex ex p International Ferry Traders Ltd*.[185] International Ferry Traders Ltd, who were engaged in exporting live cattle, had sought judicial review of the decision of the Chief Constable of Sussex to limit the policing of animal rights protesters at Shoreham ferry port. The Lords had to consider the discretion of a Chief Constable to deploy powers to prevent a breach of the peace against protesters and the relevance of the margin of appreciation allowed to Member States in respect of satisfying their Community obligations under the free movement of goods provisions of Art 34 of the Treaty of Rome. Lord Slynn, in a speech with which the other Law Lords agreed, found: 'the courts have long made it clear that ... they will respect the margin of appreciation or discretion which a Chief Constable has,' and in this instance that margin had not been exceeded. As to the European aspects of the case, Lord Hoffman found 'on the particular facts of this case the European concepts of proportionality and margin of appreciation produce the same result as what are commonly called Wednesbury principles ... in this case I think that the Chief Constable must enjoy a margin of discretion that cannot differ according to whether its source be found in purely domestic principles or superimposed European principles'.

The decision illustrates the attachment of the judiciary to the doctrine of deference to policing decisions, even where the application of European law might have led to a different result. Lord Hoffman's judgment above suggests that in the post-HRA era, the application of the Strasbourg public protest jurisprudence in order to determine questions of proportionality might lead to the same results as the application of the *Wednesbury* doctrine, since decisions of Chief Constables as to the needs of public order would tend to be as readily deferred to within the 'review' model as those in respect of the allocation of resources. This decision was in keeping with the only judicial review case involving a challenge to the decision of a Chief Constable to seek a ban on processions – *Kent v Metropolitan Police Comr*[186] – the most attenuated form of *Wednesbury* review was adopted, the courts affording the Commissioner a very wide margin of discretion. Courts

---

183 The Convention rights will be claim rights in the sense that they are binding on public authorities under the HRA, s 6. See Chapter 1, p 14.

184 See *Ministry of Defence ex p Smith and Others* [1996] 1 All ER 257, p 263.

185 [1999] 1 All ER 129.

186 (1981) *The Times*, 15 May.

adopting this approach would continue to apply traditional notions of deference to assessments of police officers and trial courts in respect of the possibility of disorder and the action thought necessary to avert it, interfering only if grossly disproportionate action had been taken. This would, as Lord Hoffman's *dicta* make clear, entail the type of low-intensity inquiry into the existence of a 'pressing social need' to restrict rights to protest typified by the Strasbourg case law, albeit adopted for somewhat different reasons. The issue of whether less intrusive means could have been adopted would either be ignored or treated as an issue of police expertise, to which the courts should likewise defer.

Under the HRA, this approach has now become established as a domestic version of the margin of appreciation doctrine, recognising and respecting an 'area of discretionary judgment'.[187] The application of this discretionary area in this context is likely to encourage the continuance of a deferential approach to the decisions of police officers and other bodies,[188] either on democratic grounds, or on the well established and familiar basis that the issue is one of expertise and on-the-spot discretionary decision making that should be interfered with only in cases of manifest injustice.[189]

It is contended that under both the 'minimalist' and 'traditionalist' approaches, the clear danger exists that the change brought about by the HRA in relation to protest will be cosmetic only: while the rhetoric of legal reasoning will change, the actual standards applied and the results obtained will not, or will do so only marginally. Indeed, the inception of the HRA could exacerbate the failures of the pre-HRA era as evinced in a number of the decisions discussed below;[190] executive interferences with public protest could be given an appearance of human rights auditing, but successful challenges would be as rare as ever. Thus, the executive may be able to stifle political accountability in the form of criticisms of such interferences by asserting that the courts have found that such actions do not infringe the basic Convention rights to expression and assembly. Legal protection, therefore, would not be enhanced, while political accountability would actually be hampered. Moreover, the opportunity offered, under an activist approach, of differentiating between forms of protest, such as the physical obstruction of the fuel protest in November 2000[191] and the symbolically obstructive protests in *Steel*, would be

---

187 In *R v DPP ex p Kebilene* [1999] 3 WLR 972, Lord Hope rejected any domestic application of the margin of appreciation doctrine, but went on: 'In some circumstances it will be appropriate for the courts to recognise that there is an area of judgment within which the judiciary will defer, on democratic grounds, to the considered opinion of [the democratic body or person] whose act or decision is said to be incompatible with the Convention.' See also Lord Hoffman, 'The Human Rights Act and the House of Lords' (1999) 62(2) MLR 159, esp p 161; Laws, 'Wednesbury', in Forsyth and Hare (eds), *The Golden Metwand and the Crooked Cord: Essays in Honour of Sir William Wade QC*, CUP, 1998, p 201; Pannick, 'Principles of interpretation of Convention rights under the Human Rights Act and the discretionary area of judgment' (1998) PL 545, pp 549–51; Hunt, Singh and Demetriou, 'Is there a role for the 'margin of appreciation' in national law after the Human Rights Act?' (1999) 1 EHRLR 15. In *Brown v Stott* [2001] 2 WLR 817, p 835, Lord Bingham found that a discretionary area of judgment would be accorded to the legislature and the government; in the post-HRA cases of *R v A* [2001] 2 WLR 1546 and *Wilson v First County Trust* [2001] 3 All ER 229 the House of Lords and the Court of Appeal respectively accepted that this was the case. See further Chapter 4, pp 143–44.

188 Ie, Parliament's decision to enact the relevant legislation in the first place.

189 See Fenwick, H, *Civil Rights: New Labour, Freedom and the Human Rights Act*, 2000, pp 138–39, and Ewing and Gearty, *op cit*, fn 1, pp 91–93.

190 In particular, *Winder* and *Capon*; see below, pp 484–87.

191 See Fenwick, H and Phillipson, G, 'Direct action, convention values and the Human Rights Act' [2001] LS, forthcoming.

lost. A domestic jurisprudence that in its development would call upon the underlying Convention values in order to create such a differentiation, would thus fail to come into existence.

Activism

A further possible approach, which may be referred to as 'activist',[192] would start from the premise that the reception of the Convention into UK law represents a decisive break with the past. Under this approach, judges would regard themselves as required to go *beyond* the minimal standards applied in the Strasbourg jurisprudence,[193] given that Strasbourg's view of itself as a system of protection firmly subsidiary to that afforded by national courts has led it, particularly in public protest cases, to intervene only where clear and unequivocal transgressions have occurred. Such a stance would recognise that, as a consequence, most of the cases on peaceful protest have not in fact required national authorities to demonstrate convincingly that the test of 'pressing social need' has been met. Furthermore, significantly, it would look for assistance to the general principles developed by Strasbourg.[194]

One such principle, repeated in a number of cases, is that 'the right to freedom of peaceful assembly ... is a fundamental right in a democratic society, and, like the right to freedom of expression, is one of the foundations of such a society ...'.[195] As indicated in Chapter 3 and the Introduction to Part II above, the House of Lords has demonstrated that it can take such principles seriously and give them real efficacy in the field of media freedom, even prior to the coming into force of the HRA.[196] The way is now open to domestic courts to take to heart the principle – declared by Strasbourg but not given practical effect by it – that peaceful protest has equal weight to freedom of expression generally, a freedom which is accorded 'special importance' within Strasbourg jurisprudence,[197] and now, within the common law.

Assuming that the freedom of expression dimension of public protest is given domestic recognition, following *Steel*, the principles developed in the Strasbourg and domestic media freedom jurisprudence can be utilised in protest cases, thus underpinning and guiding judicial activism. Courts will be required to consider the extent to which Convention rights should be abrogated *in a democratic society*, taking the values and hallmarks of such a society – 'pluralism, tolerance and diversity'[198] into account. Such an approach would *not* provide a charter for those bent on disrupting the

---

192 Fenwick, H, *Civil Rights: New Labour, Freedom and the Human Rights Act*, 2000, pp 502–05.

193 In the words of Judge Martens, '[the task of domestic courts] goes further than seeing that the minimum standards laid down in the ECHR are maintained ... because the ECHR's injunction to further realise human rights and fundamental freedoms contained in the preamble is also addressed to domestic courts'. ('Opinion: incorporating the Convention: the role of the judiciary' (1998) 1 EHRLR 3.)

194 See Fenwick, H, *Civil Rights: New Labour, Freedom and the Human Rights Act*, 2000, pp 502–03. As the House of Lords recently stressed: 'in the national courts also the Convention should be seen as an expression of fundamental principles rather than as a set of mere rules' (*R v DPP ex p Kebilene* [1999] 3 WLR 972).

195 *Rassemblement Jurassien v Switzerland* (1980) 17 DR 93, p 119.

196 See Chapter 3, pp 108–09, and the Introduction to Part II, pp 209–10.

197 The court referred to 'the special importance of freedom of peaceful assembly and freedom of expression, which are closely linked in this instance' (*Ezelin v France* A 202 (1991), para 51).

198 *Handyside v UK* (1976) 1 EHRR 737, para 49.

lawful activities of others. It would mean that the expressive dimension of 'direct action' protest was recognised and given due weight in legal assessment as a basic value enshrined in law. But it would also require proper analysis of the extent to which direct action which aims to disrupt the lawful pursuits of others would be permitted in a democracy governed by the rule of law. This is not the place to consider this debate at length, but it is certainly arguable that those who attempt directly to prevent such activities are in fact undermining both the democratic process (by attempting to marginalise its role in determining which pursuits are to remain lawful) and the rule of law – by attacking the basic liberty of the citizen to do that which the law does not forbid. Both of these are core values of the Convention. The clash of such values and the method of their resolution must now be made explicit in the legal discourse surrounding the limits of public protest: they must not be simply ignored or marginalised as at present in most domestic courts, or recognised in a purely tokenistic sense as in too many decisions at Strasbourg.

Under this approach courts would make a real attempt to 'strip away' or 'disapply' the effects of the margin of appreciation doctrine in applying Strasbourg jurisprudence. Thus, they would apply a more rigorous approach to proportionality than has Strasbourg, making use as indicated of underlying Convention values in the attempt to flesh out the meagre Strasbourg jurisprudence, and to construct out of it a coherent set of openly stated principles. Under the 'activist' model, then, it appears to be unlikely that justifications for judicial restraint in public protest decisions, if any, will be fully coterminous with Strasbourg restraint.

In this context, such an approach would lead to much greater interference with executive decision making. It would be in accordance with this approach to have regard to the balance struck in public protest matters in other European courts within the margin of appreciation, and perhaps also to that struck by the International Covenant on Civil and Political Rights and in the US or Canada.[199] In support of this approach, it might also be pointed out that the Strasbourg public protest jurisprudence is very heavily influenced by decisions of the Commission, which is not a fully judicial body[200] and therefore has less authority than the Court. As Chapter 2 indicates, within the Court there is disagreement as to the interferences which fall within a State's margin of appreciation,[201] and this is particularly so in the only decision of the Court finding a violation of the freedom of assembly guarantee of Art 11, *Ezelin v France*.[202] Two of the partly dissenting judges considered that the interference in question fell within that margin,[203] although the majority found that the State had exceeded it.

---

199 See, eg, *Brandenburg v Ohio* (1969) 395 US 444 in which it was found that an interference with public protest was acceptable only where incitement to unlawful action occurred. This may be compared with the decision on breach of the peace in *Nicol v DPP* (1996) 1 J Civ Lib 75 (discussed below, pp 498–99) in which such interference was permitted on the ground that it would not be unreasonable for others to react violently; no element of incitement was necessary.

200 See Chapter 2, pp 21–2.

201 Eg, in *Cossey v UK* A 184 (1990), para 3.6.5, Judge Martens, in his dissenting opinion, differed sharply from the majority in the Court in finding: '... I think that the Court should not have built its reasoning on the assumption that "this is an area in which the Contracting Parties enjoy a wide margin of appreciation" ... In this context there simply is no room for a margin of appreciation.'

202 A 202-A (1991).

203 Judges Ryssdal and Pettiti, pp 26 and 28–30.

However, the domestic judiciary may find the 'activist' approach problematic, especially in determining whether a restriction is necessary in a democratic society in an instance covered by an adverse Commission decision on admissibility. It is inevitable, at least in the early decisions under the HRA, that in such circumstances some practitioners, magistrates or judges, lacking familiarity with the Strasbourg system, will view the finding of manifest ill-foundedness in a number of Strasbourg public protest cases as virtually conclusive of the issue since on its face, it appears to mean that the case was almost unarguable.[204] This problem will be exacerbated since public protest issues are usually adjudicated on in low-level courts.

Positive obligations

The particularly thorny question of affording positive rights of access to land is likely to arise. It is now established that the right of access to the highway may include holding an assembly on it.[205] But *prima facie* assemblies on other quasi-public or private land will virtually always be trespassory, unless in the circumstances it is found that permission to hold some peaceful protests was given. Strasbourg has not yet accepted that there is a positive obligation on the public authorities to require private individuals to allow the exercise of protest and assembly rights on their land. But an activist domestic court might be prepared to uphold such a claim, thereby anticipating the stance on this matter which some commentators view Strasbourg as not unlikely to adopt.[206]

When the issue of exclusion of persons from a quasi-public place, a shopping mall, was raised before the Commission, it declared the application inadmissible, on the basis that Art 11 was not applicable, since the applicants were gathering there for a purely social purpose.[207] Clearly, had Art 11 been engaged, a different outcome might have been achieved. In the US, the courts are moving away from a position of upholding proprietorial rights and towards providing protection for expressive activity in quasi-public forums.[208] This can also be said of the Canadian and Australian courts.[209] In contrast, the traditional stance of the UK judiciary is to favour the property right when it conflicts with rights of protest. In general, they tend to uphold proprietorial rights in an abstract fashion, regardless of any real harm that may occur due to their infringement.[210] But Art 10 and 11 arguments might persuade them in future to consider the possibility of

---

204 Under Art 27(2) of the Convention, the Commission shall consider inadmissible any petition submitted under Art 25 which it considers ... manifestly ill-founded ... The Court has said: 'rejection of a complaint as "manifestly ill-founded" amounts to a decision that there is not even a prima facie case against the respondent State ...': *Boyle and Rice v UK* A 131 (1988), paras 53–54. However, Harris, O'Boyle and Warbrick, in *Law of the European Convention on Human Rights*, 1995, p 627 observe: '[the manifestly ill-founded provision] is possibly the only provision in the Convention where the Commission, in its practice, has departed from the literal and ordinary meaning of the words employed.'

205 *DPP v Jones* [1999] 2 WLR 625.

206 Harris, O'Boyle and Warbrick, *op cit*, fn 132, p 419.

207 *Anderson v UK* [1998] EHRLR 218. As the Commission implied, the outcome would probably have been different had the UK ratified Protocol 4, Art 2, which guarantees freedom of movement.

208 See *Shad Alliance v Smith Haven Mall* 484 NYS 2d 849, esp p 857.

209 See *Harrison v Carswell* (1975) 62 DLR (3d) 68 Supreme Court of Canada; *Gerhardy v Brown* (1985) 159 CLR 70.

210 See on this point Gray and Gray, 'Civil rights, civil wrongs and quasi-public places' [1999] EHRLR 46.

recognising broader access rights to quasi-public land. *DPP v Jones*[211] has already found that this is the case as far as the highway is concerned, but a large number of quasi-public places exist to which the public has limited rights of access, such as unenclosed shopping malls, parks, the grounds and forecourts of town halls or civic centres, monuments and their surrounding land or rights of way across private land.[212] At present, such rights of access would not include assemblies for the purpose of protests and demonstrations.

The issue might arise in two ways. A group seeking access to a forum for the holding of an assembly or demonstration might seek to bring an action against the relevant land-owning body if it was a public authority under ss 6 and 7(1)(a) of the HRA, claiming that a refusal to allow an assembly in a particular place had constituted an interference with its Art 10 and 11 rights. For example, it might seek judicial review of the decision of a local authority refusing it access to a park in order to hold a meeting. Where a group was charged with infringing a ban on assemblies under ss 13 or 14A of the Public Order Act 1986 (discussed below), it could raise the issue under s 7(1)(b) of the HRA.

Conflicting rights

Where, as is frequently the case, various provisions discussed below[213] are used in respect of a conflict between two groups, such as hunters and hunt saboteurs, the argument might be raised in court that those provisions should be interpreted in such a way as to protect freedom of assembly in the sense of allowing persons to engage in group activities, such as hunting, shooting or fishing, free from interference by others.[214] The provisions might appear to allow the State to discharge a positive obligation to ensure that such groups are able to assemble. This argument finds some support from the ruling in *Chorherr v Austria*.[215] The expression of protesters appeared likely to offend some spectators, leading to an interference with their peaceful enjoyment of a parade. The interference of the State with the Art 10 rights of the protesters was justified since it had the aim of upholding freedom of assembly. This argument would place the law in the position of choosing between the Art 11 rights of opposing groups or between the Art 10 rights of one group and the Art 11 rights of another. This would be the case, of course, only if the activities of hunters, fishers and the like were able to take advantage of the Art 11 guarantee. As noted above, the Commission has found that Art 11 does not cover peaceful assembly for purely social purposes[216] and it is therefore probable that it does not cover the activities in question. However, this decision is not directly in point and, in any event, the domestic courts would not be bound by it.

The group activities in question might also, or alternatively, find protection under Art 8 since, depending on the circumstances, the activities of the protesters in coming onto private land in order to protest against activities taking place there could be viewed as

---

211 [1999] 2 WLR 625.

212 See further below, p 491.

213 In particular, the Criminal Justice and Public Order Act 1994, ss 68 and 69 and the Public Order Act 1986, ss 14A and 14C.

214 See *Plattform 'Ärtze fur das Leben' v Austria* A 139 (1988), para 32; 13 EHRR 204.

215 A 266-B (1993).

216 *Anderson v UK* Case No 33689/96, (1998) 25 EHRR CD 172. This application arose from *CIN Properties Ltd v Rawlins* [1995] 2 EGLR 130.

interfering with the right to respect for private life, the home and the family.[217] The interference with the Art 10 and 11 rights of protesters under the domestic provisions could then be justified on the basis that it allowed discharge of the State obligation under Art 8 to ensure that the exercise of the rights it guarantees is not threatened by the interference of private persons.[218] The court itself would have to ensure that it did not fail to protect the Art 11 or 8 rights of the hunters or shooters,[219] if it was prepared to countenance the argument that those rights were at stake. It would then have to perform a balancing act between the exercise of two conflicting rights with very little guidance from Strasbourg, since where such a conflict arises, Strasbourg allows a very wide margin of appreciation.[220]

Procedural problems

A key factor affecting the reception of Arts 10 and 11 into UK law will be, as indicated, the model favoured by the senior UK judiciary. But there may also be procedural difficulties in bringing about statutory change. Relying on Arts 10 and 11, protesters will be able to challenge public order provisions in criminal proceedings under s 6(1)(b) and s 7(1)(b) of the HRA, or seek judicial review of public order decisions made by police or local authorities under s 6(1)(a) and s 7(1)(a). However, as Chapter 4 explains, s 6 of the HRA provides that it is lawful for a public authority to act in a way which is incompatible with Convention rights if it is authorised to do so by primary legislation. If the legislation is thought to be incompatible, the court must nevertheless apply it; the higher courts can make a declaration of incompatibility which will have no impact on the instant decision but which will probably trigger off a legislative change by ministerial amendment.[221] Public order questions are rarely adjudicated on in those courts which are able to make a declaration,[222] and some defendants would have little interest in appealing to a higher court in order to obtain the declaration since it would be of no personal benefit. However, members of some protest groups may be likely to wish to appeal test cases to the higher courts in order to obtain changes in the law. But unless they do so as defendants in criminal proceedings, this will be possible under s 7(1)(a) HRA only if they themselves

---

217 See *Spencer (Earl) v UK* (1998) 25 EHRR CD 105. The applicants complained that English law provided no remedy for the invasion of their privacy through the publication in the press of various (truthful) stories relating to the bulimia and mental health problems of Countess Spencer, including photographs taken of her walking in the grounds of the clinic. The Commission dismissed the claim as manifestly ill founded, not on the basis that the Convention did not require a remedy in such circumstances, but on the basis that such a remedy – breach of confidence – did exist in UK law, but had not been exhausted.

218 In *X and Y v Netherlands* (1985) 8 EHRR 235 the Court stated: 'these [Article 8] obligations may require the adoption of measures even in the sphere of relations between individuals.' In other words, the term 'interference by a public authority' used in Art 8 can mean 'unjustified failure to prevent interference by others'.

219 Since, as Chapter 4 points out, the court is itself a public authority under the HRA, s 6, and is itself bound to respect the Convention rights.

220 See *Otto-Preminger Institut v Austria* (1994) 19 EHRR 34. The conflict in the case between Arts 10 and 9 played a part in the concession of a very wide margin of appreciation to the State.

221 See Chapter 4, pp 151–52; the HRA, s 10(2), provides: 'If a Minister of the Crown considers that there are compelling reasons for proceeding under this section, he may by order make such amendments to the legislation as he considers necessary to remove the incompatibility.'

222 See s 4(4) and (5) of the Act which provide that no court lower than the High Court or Court of Appeal may make a declaration of incompatibility.

have been 'victims' or are likely to become victims in future, within the meaning of s 7(7) of the HRA.[223] Owing to the effect of s11 of the HRA they could, however, raise Convention points in judicial review proceedings based on the old standing rules.[224] This course would be an attractive one since executive action, under statutory powers, which breaches Convention rights is unlawful unless the Statute cannot be rendered compatible with the rights.[225]

Reform of common law powers under s 6 may occur quite readily. As Sedley LJ said in *Redmond-Bate v DPP*,[226] before the HRA was fully in force, 'it is now accepted that the common law should seek compatibility with the values of the Convention'. This finding was reinforced, in a different context, in the post-HRA decision in *Douglas and Others v Hello!*.[227] If incompatibility is found, the Convention guarantee should prevail, since no provision was included in the Act allowing the common law to override the Convention or creating restrictions as to those courts which can find incompatibility between the two.

3 LEGAL REGULATION OF MEETINGS AND MARCHES: THE STATUTORY FRAMEWORK

The Public Order Act 1986, as amended by the CJPOA 1994, put in place a cumbersome statutory framework for the policing of marches and assemblies which was much more extensive than that put in place by the predecessor of the 1986 Act, the Public Order Act 1936. The interaction between this framework and the HRA forms the central focus of the following discussion.

Advance notice of public processions

Sections 12 and 13 of the Public Order Act 1986, which allow banning or limitation of a march, are underpinned by s 11, which provides that the organisers of a march (not a meeting) must give advance notice of it to the police in the relevant police area[228] six clear days before the date when it is intended to be held.[229] This national requirement was an entirely new measure, although in some districts a notice requirement was already imposed under local regulations. It represents the first step to involving the police so that they will have an opportunity to impose conditions. It should be remembered, of course, that organisers of a sizeable march would probably have to involve the police in any event, as they might need traffic to be held up while crossing busy roads. As the main purpose of s 11 is to allow conditions to be imposed on marches that might disrupt the community, but as those are the very marches that the police would tend to know of in any event, the need for a new provision of this nature is questionable.

---

223 See Chapter 4, pp 164–66.
224 See Chapter 4, p 170.
225 See Chapter 4, p 156.
226 (1999) *The Times*, 28 July; [1999] All ER (D) 864.
227 [2001] 2 WLR 992, CA.
228 Section 11(4).
229 Section 11(5) and (6).

However, the notice requirement does not apply under s 11(1) if it was not reasonably practicable to give any advance notice. This provision was intended to exempt spontaneous demonstrations from the notice requirement, but is defective because of the use of the word 'any'. Strictly interpreted, this word would suggest that a telephone call made five minutes before the march set off would fulfil the requirements, thereby exempting very few marches. In most circumstances, even though a march sets off suddenly, it might well be reasonably practicable to make such a telephone call. However, it can be argued that the word 'any' should not be interpreted so strictly as to exclude spontaneous processions where a few minutes was available to give notice, because to do so would defeat the intention behind including the provision. If read in combination with the requirements as to giving notice by hand or in writing, it should be interpreted to mean 'any written notice' under s 3 of the HRA. If it were not so interpreted, it might be argued that s 11 breaches the guarantees of freedom of assembly under Art 11 and of expression under Art 10, since it could criminalise the organiser of a peaceful spontaneous march. Punishing the organisers of such a march by way of criminal sanctions could be viewed as disproportionate to the legitimate aim pursued – to obviate the risk of disorder – since other measures, such as limiting the numbers of persons taking part in the march or a careful choice of route could achieve the same result. In any event, giving very short notice of a spontaneous march would not give the police enough time to impose conditions and therefore the aim in question could not, in fact, be attained by that means.

Advance notice must be given if the procession is held 'to demonstrate support or opposition to the views or actions of any person or body of persons, to publicise a cause or campaign or to mark or commemorate an event'. This provision was included in order to exempt innocuous crocodiles of children from the requirement. Processions customarily held are expressly exempted.[230] The notice must specify the date, time and proposed route of the procession and give the name and address of the person proposing to organise it. Under s 11(7), the organisers may be guilty of an offence if the notice requirement has not been satisfied or if the march deviates from the date, time or route specified. If it does, an organiser may have a defence under s 11(8) or (9) that he or she either had no reason to suspect that it had occurred or that it arose due to circumstances outside his or her control.

Section 11 criminalises what may be trivial administrative errors and, although police officers will use a discretion in bringing prosecutions under it, this leaves the power open to abuse and means that potentially, at least, it could be more rigidly enforced against marchers espousing unpopular causes. At present, prosecutions under s 11 are very rarely being brought and therefore its deterrence value to organisers may become minimal.[231] For example, the organisers of a large peace march, held on the date the UN Security Council ultimatum against Iraq[232] expired, failed to comply with the notice requirements under s 11 but no prosecution was brought. However, organisers of the 'veal calves' protest at Brightlingsea in April 1995 were threatened with prosecution under s 11.

---

230 Section 11(2). Funeral processions are also covered by this exemption.
231 Waddington, *Liberty and Order*, 1994, pp 37–40.
232 Contained in SC resolution 678, 15 January.

The notice requirement in itself may have some inhibiting effect on organisers of marches, but except in that sense, it cannot readily be characterised 'an interference' with freedom of expression or assembly under the HRA since it is not a request for *permission* to hold the march. Once notice is correctly given, the march can take place, although conditions may be imposed on it, the matter considered in the next section. As indicated above, prior restraints on marches, including complete bans, have been upheld at Strasbourg, although the margin of appreciation doctrine was influential.[233] Owing to its relatively minimal impact on marches, which means that it is probably – depending on the circumstances of a particular case – proportionate to the aims pursued, the notice requirement, assuming that it exempts spontaneous marches, appears to be compatible with Arts 10 and 11.

Imposing conditions on meetings or marches

The s 12 power

Section 12 of the 1986 Act reproduces in part the power under s 3 of the Public Order Act 1936 allowing the Chief Officer of Police to impose conditions on a procession if he apprehended serious public disorder. However, the power to impose conditions under s 12 may be exercised in a much wider range of situations than the old power. It arises in one of four situations that may be known as 'triggers'. In making a determination as to the existence of one of these 'triggers', the senior police officer in question should 'have regard to the time or place at which and the circumstances in which, any public procession is being held or is intended to be held and to its route or proposed route'. Bearing these factors in mind, he or she must reasonably believe that 'serious public disorder, serious damage to property or serious disruption to the life of the community' may be caused by the procession (s 12(1)(a)).

The third phrase used is a very wide one which clearly offers police officers some scope for interpretation and may be said to render the other two 'triggers' redundant. This 'trigger' has attracted particular criticism from commentators. It has been said that 'some inconvenience is the inevitable consequence of a successful procession. 'The Act threatens to permit only those demonstrations that are so convenient that they become invisible.'[234] Bonner and Stone have warned of 'the dangers that lie in the vague line between serious disruption and a measure of inconvenience'.[235] Further, it has been noted that the term 'the community' is ambiguous. In the case of London, it is unclear whether the term could be applied to Oxford Street or central London or the whole Metropolitan area.[236] The more narrowly the term is defined, the more readily a given march could be said to cause serious disruption. Serious obstruction of traffic might arguably amount to some disruption of the life of a small area which might be said to constitute a 'community'.

---

233 Eg, *Christians Against Racism and Fascism v UK* (1980) 21 DR 138.
234 Ewing and Gearty, *Freedom under Thatcher*, 1990, p 121.
235 'The Public Order Act 1986: steps in the wrong direction?' [1987] PL 202, p 226.
236 Ewing and Gearty, *Freedom under Thatcher*, 1990, p 121.

Imposition of conditions allows police officers to cut down the cost of the policing requirement for an assembly and therefore may encourage them to interpret 'the community' or 'disruption' in the manner most likely to bring the 'trigger' into being, since the conditions then imposed, such as requiring a limit on the numbers participating, might lead to a reduction in the number of officers who had to be present. However, in answer to some of these fears, it can be noted that in Reid[237] it was determined that the 'triggers' should be strictly interpreted: the words used should not be diluted. This third 'trigger' causes particular concern under Arts 10 and 11 since it does not readily equate to any of the legitimate aims under the second paragraph of those Articles. Probably, it could cover the prevention of disorder as opposed to 'serious disorder' (the first 'trigger'); it might also cover protecting 'the rights of others', an aim which has received a broad and imprecise interpretation at Strasbourg.[238] But the police and courts would have to consider whether either of those aims applied, bearing in mind the need for a stricter approach at the domestic level.

The fourth 'trigger', arising under s 12(1)(b), consists of an evaluation of the purpose of the assembly rather than an apprehension that a particular state of affairs may arise. The senior police officer must reasonably believe that the purpose of the assembly is 'the intimidation of others with a view to compelling them not to do an act they have a right to do or to do an act they have a right not to do'. This requires a police officer to make a political judgment as to the purpose of the group in question because it must be determined whether the purpose is coercive or merely persuasive. Asking police officers to make such a judgment clearly lays them open to claims of partiality in instances where they are perceived as out of sympathy with the aims of the group in question. It should be noted that the fourth 'trigger' requires a reasonable belief in the presence of two elements – intimidation and coercion. Therefore, a racist march through an Asian area would probably fall outside its terms since the element of coercion would probably be absent. It might, however, fall within the terms of the third 'trigger'. On the other hand, a march might be coercive without being intimidatory. In Reid, the defendants shouted and raised their arms; it was determined that such behaviour might cause discomfort, but not intimidation, and that the two concepts could not be equated. In News Group Newspapers Ltd v SOGAT[239] it was held that mere abuse and shouting did not amount to a threat of violence for the purposes of intimidation under s 7 of the Conspiracy and Protection of Property Act 1875. Thus, behaviour of a fairly threatening nature would have to be present in order to cross the boundary between discomfort and intimidation.

The conditions that can be imposed under s 12 if one of the above 'triggers' is thought to be present are very wide in the case of processions: any condition may be imposed which appears necessary to the senior police officer in order to prevent the envisaged mischief occurring. The conditions imposed may include changes to the route of the procession or a prohibition on it entering a particular public place. If the march is already assembling, the conditions may be imposed by the senior police officer present at the scene who may be a constable; if the conditions are being considered some time before this point, the Chief Officer of Police must determine them.

---

237 [1987] Crim LR 702.
238 See the discussion in Steel v UK (1999) 28 EHRR 603 relating to the first and second applicants.
239 [1986] ICR 716.

The very wide discretion allowing a range of conditions to be imposed is now subject to the proportionality requirement of Arts 10 and 11, para 2. Such a requirement should now be read into the term 'necessary' under s 12 under s 3 of the HRA. The duty of the police under s 6 of the HRA means that they must seek to ensure that conditions are not imposed which go beyond the legitimate aim pursued. The interpretation of s 12 which is compatible with Arts 10 and 11 under the HRA is considered below, at pp 475–78.

The s 14 power

Section 14 of the 1986 Act allows the police to impose conditions on assemblies.[240] It was introduced in the 1986 Act as an entirely new power. Conditions may be imposed only if one of four 'triggers' under s 14(1) – identical to those arising under s 12 – is present. However, once it is clear that one of the 'triggers' is present, the conditions that may be imposed are much more limited than those that may be imposed on marches. They are confined to such 'directions ... as to the place at which the assembly may be (or continue to be) held, its maximum duration or the maximum number of persons who may constitute it' as appear to the senior police officer 'necessary to prevent the disorder, damage, disruption or intimidation'. It must be clear that the condition was communicated to the members of the march. In *Brickley and Kitson v Police*,[241] anti-apartheid demonstrators outside the South African embassy were asked to move away from the front of the embassy to a nearby street, Duncannon Street. The pickets in Duncannon Street increased and four of the demonstrators moved back in front of the embassy. The Chief Officer of Police feared that further disorder might be caused and imposed a condition under s 14 requiring the pickets to stay in Duncannon Street. This was conveyed to them over a megaphone. However, it was uncertain whether this information was actually communicated to the pickets and therefore their convictions in respect of failure to abide by the condition were quashed. The defences available if there is a failure to comply with the conditions are identical to those under s 12, as is the power of arrest arising under s 14(7).

Liability under ss 12 and 14

A member of the march or assembly will incur liability under s 12(5) or 14(5) if he or she knowingly fails to comply with a condition. An organiser[242] will incur liability under ss 12(4) or 14(4) if he or she knowingly fails to comply with the conditions imposed, although he or she will have a defence if it can be shown that the failure arose from

---

240 Under s 16, an assembly consists of 20 or more people in a public place; a public place is defined as one which is wholly or partly open to the air. Section 16 defines a public procession as one in a place to which the public have access. No further guidance is given. Presumably the procession must be moving and will become an assembly if it stops and if it consists of 20 or more people, in which case different rules will apply.

241 *Legal Action*, July 1988, p 21 (Knightsbridge Crown Court).

242 The 1986 Act does not define the term 'organiser' and there is no post-Act case law on the issue. It is submitted that on the dictionary definition of the term, stewards and others who have some role as marshals will be organisers. This contention is supported by the ruling from *Flockhart v Robinson* [1950] 2 KB 498 that a person who indicated the route to be followed should be designated an organiser as well as the person who planned the route. Thus, it appears probable that the term includes stewards as well as leaders of the assembly or march.

circumstances beyond his or her control. Thus, the *organiser* must actually breach the condition in question; he or she would not incur liability merely because some members of the march or assembly did so and therefore, where a march contains an unruly element which deliberately breaches conditions imposed, the persons involved will incur liability, but the organiser may escape it. An organiser may also incur liability if he or she incites another knowingly to breach a condition that has been imposed (ss 12(6) and 14(6)). According to the Court of Appeal in *Hendrickson and Tichner*,[243] incitement requires an element of persuasion or encouragement; moreover, following *Krause*,[244] the solicitation must actually come to the notice of the person intended to act on it. Therefore, merely assuming the position of leader of a march or assembly which is in breach of a condition would not seem to be sufficient of itself to amount to incitement. However, express or implied encouragement to bring about or continue a breach, such as leading the group in a certain forbidden direction, would amount to incitement if the leader was aware of the breach of the condition.

Effects of the HRA

The impact of the HRA on the statutory framework under the 1986 Act in general is discussed in full below.[245] Only indications as to the specific effects on ss 12 and 14 are given here. In criminal proceedings brought in reliance on these provisions, defendants can rely on s 7(1)(b) of the HRA, using the argument that in the circumstances, the interference with the freedoms of expression and assembly was disproportionate to the aims pursued. Since ss 12 and 14 confer a *discretion* on the police, it could not be said that the imposition of disproportionate conditions was unavoidable under s 6(2)(a) of the HRA. If it was argued that the police were acting to satisfy s 6(2)(b) of the HRA, it could be found that ss 12 and 14, due to their broad wording, could have been read or given effect in a way which rendered them compatible with the Convention rights (for example, by adopting a strict interpretation of the meaning of the third 'trigger' or by imposing conditions of a narrow ambit).

Prior to the inception of the HRA, the scope for challenging the conditions was very limited: there is no method of appealing from them and it was only possible to have them reviewed for procedural errors or unreasonableness in the High Court. The power to impose any condition thought necessary under s 12 is so subjective that until Arts 10 and 11 were given further effect in domestic law under the HRA, the courts had little scope for assessing the legality of the decision made,[246] although the condition must relate to the mischief it is designed to avert. However, in dealing with police action to maintain public order, the courts have been very unwilling to find police decisions to have been unlawful.[247] Applying the rule from *Kent v Metropolitan Police Comr*[248] one can infer that a challenge to a condition would almost certainly fail, although a challenge mounted

---

243 [1977] Crim LR 356.

244 (1902) 18 TLR 238.

245 See pp 474–80.

246 See, eg, *Secretary of State for Education and Science v Tameside* [1977] AC 1014.

247 See, eg, *Secretary of State for the Home Department ex p Northumbria Police Authority* [1989] QB 26; [1988] 2 WLR 590; [1988] 1 All ER 556, CA.

248 (1981) *The Times*, 15 May.

where a senior officer had evinced a belief in the existence of a 'trigger' which no reasonable officer could entertain, might succeed due to the need to show a reasonable belief in relation to the 'triggers'. No presumption in favour of freedom of assembly was imported.

This very 'light touch' review is now no longer appropriate under the HRA, since the courts will have to consider proportionality. The extent to which this will have any real impact in practice will depend on the approach adopted, as indicated above, and on the willingness of judges to examine the evidence available to the police at the time as to the likelihood that, for example, a particular group would be likely to cause disruption or disorder. Further consideration is given below to the approach to both ss 12 and 14 which might be taken under the HRA.

Imposing banning orders on marches

As indicated above, the 1986 Act for the first time gave the police the power to impose very wide ranging conditions[249] if they were thought necessary for the prevention of serious public disorder, serious damage to property or (the least grave trigger condition) 'serious disruption to the life of the community'.[250] This latter trigger attracted widespread criticism for its imprecision[251] and for decisively lowering the level and nature of risk that must be shown before conditions can be imposed. However, the 1986 Act did make some attempt to strike a balance between speech and public order interests. It provided, as did its predecessor, for the possibility of an outright ban on public processions,[252] but only if the Chief Constable reasonably believed that his powers to impose conditions on processions under s 12 (based on the same 'trigger' conditions as for assemblies)[253] would be inadequate to prevent 'serious public disorder'.

Under s 13(1) of the 1986 Act, a ban must be imposed on a march if it is thought that it may result in serious public disorder. This power is exercised as follows.

If, at any time, the Chief Officer of Police reasonably believes that, because of particular circumstances existing in any district or part of a district, the powers under s 12 will not be sufficient to prevent the holding of public processions in that district or part from resulting in serious public disorder, he shall apply to the council of the district for an order prohibiting for such period not exceeding three months as may be specified in the application the holding of all public processions (or of any class of public procession so specified) in the district or part concerned.

In response, the council may make the order as requested or modify it with the approval of the Secretary of State. It should be noted that once the Chief Officer of Police

---

249 Directions may be given as to the number of persons who may attend an assembly, its duration and location.

250 These conditions were considerably broader than the single one of anticipated 'serious public disorder' which alone could trigger the power to impose conditions upon processions under the Public Order Act 1936, s 3.

251 See, eg, Bonner and Stone, *op cit*, fn 1, p 226; Ewing and Gearty, *op cit*, fn 1, p 121.

252 Section 13.

253 Ie, serious public disorder, serious damage to property or serious disruption to the life of the community.

has come to the conclusion in question he or she must, not may, apply for a banning order. This power is exercised in respect of London by the Commissioner of Police for the City of London or the Commissioner of Police of the Metropolis. A member of the march or a person who organises it knowing of the ban will commit an offence under s 13(7) and (8) and can be arrested under s 13(10).

This reproduces the old power under s 3 of the Public Order Act 1936. Assuming that a power was needed to ban marches expected to be violent, this power was nevertheless open to criticism in that once a banning order had been imposed, it prevented all marches in the area it covered for its duration. Thus, a projected march likely to be of an entirely peaceful character could be caught by a ban aimed at a violent march. The Campaign for Nuclear Disarmament attempted to challenge such a ban after it had had to cancel a number of its marches (*Kent v Metropolitan Police Comr*),[254] but failed because of the finding that an order quashing the ban could be made only if there were no reasons for imposing it at all. The court found that the Commissioner had considered the relevant matters and, further, that CND had a remedy under s 9(3) (now s 13(5) of the 1986 Act) as they could apply to have the order relaxed.

It is arguable that the 1986 Act should have limited the banning power to the particular marches giving rise to fear of serious public disorder, but this possibility was rejected by the government on the ground that it could be subverted by organisers of marches who might attempt to march under another name. It would therefore, it was thought, have placed too great a burden on the police, who would have had to determine whether or not this had occurred. However, in making this decision, it is arguable that too great a weight was given to the possible administrative burden placed on the police and too little to the need to uphold freedom of assembly. A compromise solution – banning all marches putting forward a political message similar to that of the offending march – could have been adopted and this possibility is considered further below in relation to the effects of the HRA.

This power was being used with increased frequency up to the mid-1980s: there were 11 banning orders in the period 1970–80 and 75 in the period 1981–84[255] (39 in 1981, 13 in 1982, nine in 1983 and 11 in 1984). Interestingly, however, as Waddington has noted, there have been few bans of marches in London since the passing of the 1986 Act.[256] The power may have been used sparingly because police officers preferred to police a march known about for some time as opposed to an assembly formed hastily in response to a ban or a hostile, unpredictable and disorganised march. As Waddington has argued, such considerations may account for the police refusal to ban the third anti-poll tax march to Trafalgar Square, although such a march had previously led to a riot, and in the face of fierce pressure to ban from Westminster City Council, local MPs and the Home Secretary.[257] However, the power to ban and to impose conditions gives the police bargaining power to use in negotiating with marchers and enables them to adopt a policy of strategic under-enforcement as part of the price of avoiding trouble when a march

254 (1981) *The Times*, 15 May.
255 White Paper, (1985) Cmnd 9510, para 4.7.
256 Waddington, *op cit*, fn 1, pp 58–61.
257 Waddington, *op cit*, fn 1.

occurs. Moreover in some circumstances there may appear to be no alternative but to ban a march.[257a]

It might seem that the s 13 banning power would be in breach of Arts 10 and 11, in that the banning of a march expected to be peaceful would not appear to be justified under para 2 of those Articles in respect of the need to prevent disorder. In *Christians Against Racism and Fascism v UK*,[258] however, the applicants' argument that a ban imposed under s 3(3) of the Public Order Act 1936 infringed *inter alia* Art 11 was rejected by the Commission as manifestly ill founded, on the ground that the ban was justified under the exceptions to Art 11 contained in para 2, since there was a real danger of disorder which it was thought could not be 'prevented by other less stringent measures'. However, this is a relatively elderly decision of the Commission alone that was strongly affected by the margin of appreciation doctrine. Therefore, the domestic judiciary would be free to scrutinise the extent of the risk and the proportionality of a particular ban, bearing in mind the possibility that a particular march affected by the ban was unlikely in itself to give rise to disorder. While a ban is allowable under the Convention, it is a prior restraint and therefore should be scrutinised with especial rigour.[259] The approach that might be taken is considered further below, in conjunction with the impact of the HRA on s 14A of the 1986 Act.

Imposing banning orders on assemblies

Prior to the Public Order Act 1986, there was no statutory power at all to place prior restraints, still less a ban, upon assemblies as opposed to marches. The police had therefore dealt with outbreaks of disorder at such assemblies using their powers to arrest for breach of the peace and for specific common law[260] and statutory public order offences.[261] When s 13 of the 1986 Act was passed, no parallel power to ban assemblies was included, on the grounds, apparently, that the then Thatcher Government considered that it would represent too serious an inroad upon freedom of speech.[262]

Only eight years later, the power to ban assemblies was introduced in the CJPOA 1994 by inserting s 14A into the 1986 Act.[263] Although the power is only to ban assemblies taking place on private land, the widespread 'privatisation' of previously common land means that there is in fact little land on which demonstrations may take place without the landowner's consent which are non-trespassory.[264] The introduction of a banning power, deemed unnecessary and too draconian less than 10 years previously and not even requested by the police,[265] itself represented a decisive movement towards

---

257a Eg, in August 2001 a march of a far-right group against asylum-seekers, intended to go through Sunderland town centre to coincide with the gathering of football match supporters for an important match, was banned.

258 (1984) 24 YB ECHR 178.

259 Since the ban would affect freedom of expression, the jurisprudence under Art 10 on prior restraints could be considered. This point was stressed in *Wingrove v UK* (1997) 24 EHRR 1 by the Commission, in pointing out that scrutiny of such restraints should be especially strict.

260 Namely the offences of riot, rout, unlawful assembly and affray.

261 Eg, Public Order Act 1936, s 5: using threatening, abusive or insulting words or behaviour likely to cause, or with intent to provoke a breach of the peace.

262 'Meetings and assemblies are a more important means of exercising freedom of speech than are marches.' *Review of Public Order Law*, Cmnd 9510, 1985, pp 31–32).

263 Under s 70.

264 See further below, p 491–92.

265 See Marston and Tain, *Public Order Offences*, 1996, p 124.

authoritarianism. However, the Act compounded this trend by basing the power to ban not, as in the case of processions, upon the most grave risk – a belief in otherwise uncontrollable serious public disorder – but the least and most ill defined: anticipation of 'serious disruption to the life of the community'. In this respect, it is a much wider power than that arising under s 13.

Section 14A provides that a Chief Officer of Police may apply for a banning order if he reasonably believes that an assembly is likely to be trespassory and may result in serious disruption to the life of the community or damage to certain types of buildings and structures. Section 14A(1) provides that a Chief Officer of Police may apply for a banning order[266] if he reasonably believes (a) that an assembly is likely to be trespassory and (b) may result in serious disruption to the life of the community or damage to certain types of buildings and structures, in particular, historical monuments. The requirement of trespass is made out where the Chief Constable believes that an assembly is intended to be held on land (a) to which the public has no right of access and is likely to be held without the permission of the occupier of the land or (b) on land to which the public has only a limited right of access and the assembly is likely to exceed the limits of any permission of the landowner or the public's right of access. If an order is made, it will subsist for four days, operate within a radius of five miles around the area in question, and prohibit any trespassory assembly held within its temporal and geographical scope.[267]

Just as s 13 catches peaceful processions, the provisions of s 14A mean that assemblies that are not likely *in themselves* to cause the prohibited harm under s 14A(1) or 14A(4) may nevertheless be banned once the ban is in place, triggered by trepassory assemblies expected to cause that harm. Section 14A is backed up by s 14C (inserted into the 1986 Act by s 71 of the 1994 Act). Section 14C provides a very broad power to stop persons within a radius of five miles from the assembly if a police officer reasonably believes that they were on their way to it and that it is subject to a s 14A order. If the direction is not complied with and if the person to whom it has been given is aware of it, he or she may be arrested and may be subject to a fine if convicted. Thus, this power operates before any offence has been committed and hands the police a very wide discretion.[268]

Jones and Lloyd v DPP

This decision is considered in detail since it is the currently the leading decision on public protest and because it indicates, tellingly, that the assimilation of Art 10 and 11 values into domestic law will be especially problematic in the field of protest.

Section 14A was considered in *Jones and Lloyd v DPP*.[269] The case concerned an assembly on the route leading to Stonehenge, at a time when a s 14A order was in force. The order prohibited the holding of trespassory assemblies within a four mile radius of Stonehenge and covered the period from 29 May to 1 June 1995. While the ban was still in

---

266 Orders are granted by the local authority, with the approval of the Secretary of State.
267 Section 14A(5).
268 See further below, p 474.
269 [1997] 2 All ER 119.

force, a protest was held against it, in the form of an assembly on a road near Stonehenge, within the five mile radius covered by the ban. It was found as a fact at trial that the assembly was non-obstructive, orderly and wholly peaceful.[270] Nevertheless, the protesters were asked by the police to move on; some did, but others refused and were arrested and charged with the offence under s 14A. The main question that arose was whether the assembly in question was subject to the s 14A order. This depended on s 14A(5) of the 1994 Act which provides that once an order is in being, it operates to prohibit any assembly which is held on land to which the public has no or only a limited right of access and which takes place without the permission of the owner of the land or exceeds the limits of the permission or of the public's right of access. In this instance, the assembly was simply present on the highway, but within the relevant four mile radius. Section 14A(9) provides that 'limited' in relation to a right of access by the public to land means that their use of it is restricted to a particular purpose.

The key question was, therefore, whether the category of legitimate purposes for which the highway might be used included use of it by peaceful assemblies. Thus, the main issue that arose was whether the assembly was 'trespassory', so as to fall within the s 14A order. The question, therefore, was whether the category of legitimate purposes for which the public might lawfully use the highway included peaceful, non-obstructive assembly. The Divisional Court,[271] disagreeing with the Crown Court on the point, found that it did not.[272] The Divisional Court found that the highway was to be used for passing and repassing only and that assembling on it was outside the purpose for which the implied licence to use it was granted. In so finding, the court relied on *Hickman v Maisey*.[273] The decision concerned the defendant's use of the highway in order to gain information by looking over the plaintiff's land. The defendant was on the highway watching the plaintiff's land. It was found that the plaintiff owned the sub-soil under the highway and that the defendant was entitled to make ordinary and reasonable use of it. Such watching was held not to be reasonable; the defendant had gone outside the accepted use and therefore had trespassed.

On behalf of the respondents it was argued that any assembly on the highway is lawful so long as it is peaceful and non-obstructive, since such an assembly is making a reasonable use of the highway. The Divisional Court, however, took the view that s 14A(5) operates to prohibit any assembly which exceeds the public's limited right of access. The right of access was found to be limited to the right to pass along the highway, not to hold a meeting or demonstration on it. Such activities might be tolerated, but there could be no legal right to engage in them. Section 14A(5) was found to operate to prevent assemblies which would otherwise be permitted. Thus, since the assembly had exceeded the limited rights of access to the highway, it fell within s 14A(5) and the fact that, but for the s 14A order, it would probably have been permitted, could not affect this argument. It was also argued on behalf of the respondents that unless there was a right to hold an assembly as opposed merely to a toleration, Art 11 of the European Convention on

---

270 See p 15 of the Crown Court's judgment, cited at [1999] 2 WLR 625, p 627, *per* Lord Irvine.
271 For the Crown Court's reasoning on the point, see the speech of Lord Hutton ([1999] 2 WLR 625, p 657); the DPP appealed the point by way of case stated to the Divisional Court.
272 [1997] 2 All ER 119.
273 [1900] 1 QB 752, CA.

Human Rights would be breached. However, the court found that recourse to the Convention was unnecessary since the law in question was not ambiguous and, further, that since peaceful assemblies are normally permitted, the law was in any event in conformity with the Convention. The case was remitted to the Crown Court for a rehearing.

John Wadham of Liberty said of this decision: 'A peaceful non-obstructive gathering is a reasonable use of a public highway. To say that it is a form of trespass seems extraordinary.'[274] Nevertheless, this decision represented a reasonable interpretation of the very restrictive provisions of s 14A. No authority clearly suggests that there is a legal right to assemble on the highway since it is difficult to support an argument that assembling on the highway and remaining there for a substantial period of time is incidental to passage along it. Therefore, if the term 'right' within s 14A(1) means 'legal right', then any activity on the highway, other than passing along it, involving 20 or more people, is illegal if a s 14A order is in force. The limits of the rights to use the highway was the main question before the House of Lords when it considered the case.[275]

Despite the advent of the HRA (although it was not fully in force at the time), the Lords declined the opportunity to move beyond the traditional limited judicial perspective adopted in protest cases and to consider instead the political expression dimension of public protest. By a three to two majority, the Lords upheld the defendants' appeal. Since all those in the majority delivered substantial and quite different speeches, it is a matter of some difficulty to identify the ratio, but the key finding in common was that since *the particular assembly in question* had been found by the tribunal of fact to be a reasonable user of the highway, it was therefore not trespassory and so not caught by the s 14A order. The conduct of the protesters, according to the majority, thus had the classic character of an English negative liberty: since it was not unlawful, it was permitted, and the police had 'no right' to remove the protesters. This was the basis of the judgment, not any finding that the protesters had a positive right to peaceful protest which the police were under a corresponding duty to respect.[276] The majority, therefore, apparently found a liberty to peaceful assembly on the highway. A liberty generally is precarious for two reasons: there is no duty upon the State (or anyone else) to respect it or facilitate its exercise, and the legislature (or the judiciary through the common law) may encroach upon it at any time. The liberty identified by their Lordships shares both these enervating characteristics; what is remarkable, however, is the exceptionally precarious footing upon which its status even as a currently lawful activity rests. Not one of their Lordships was prepared to find that assemblies on the highway which were both peaceful and non-obstructive were invariably lawful. Lord Irvine stipulated that in addition, they would also have to be 'reasonable' in the eyes of the tribunal of fact,[277] without defining what

---

274 (1997) *The Times*, 24 January.

275 *Jones and Lloyd v DPP* [1999] 2 WLR 625. The following discussion is drawn in part from Fenwick and Phillipson, 'Public protest, the Human Rights Act and judicial responses to political expression' (2000) PL 627–50.

276 Lord Hutton did appear to assert this ([1999] 2 WLR 625, p 660), but his conclusion (p 666), upholds only the narrow and precarious liberty formulated by Lords Irvine and Clyde.

277 '[A] public highway [may be used] for any reasonable purpose provided the activity in question does not amount to a public or private nuisance and does not obstruct the highway by unreasonably impeding the primary right of the public to pass and re-pass: within these qualifications there is a public right of peaceful assembly on the highway': [1999] 2 WLR 625, pp 632–33.

was meant by 'reasonable' in this context.[278] Lord Clyde agreed, explicitly limiting his finding to the statement that a peaceful, non-obstructive assembly on the highway 'does not necessarily constitute a trespassory assembly'.[279] Similarly, Lord Hutton said: '... I desire to emphasise that my opinion that this appeal should be allowed is based on the finding of the Crown Court that the assembly on this particular highway ... at this particular time, constituted a reasonable use of the highway. I would not hold that a peaceful and non-obstructive public assembly on a highway is always a reasonable user and is therefore not a trespass.'[280]

Since, therefore, their Lordships explicitly contemplated that a peaceful (and non-obstructive) assembly could nevertheless be found to be unreasonable and therefore unlawful, it is in fact correct to say that they declared no liberty to hold such assemblies on the highway.[281] Rather, what the judgment upholds is a liberty to use the highway in a way which a trial court as the tribunal of fact finds to be reasonable, nothing more.[282] The lawfulness of such assemblies is thus placed in the hands of magistrates' courts.[283] The legal reasoning by which the majority reached their conclusion is no more reassuring. Clayton notes that Lord Clyde, with the minority, 'considered that the law of trespass defined the issue',[284] but it is apparent that this was also the case for Lord Irvine. Neither of their Lordships thought that they were liberalising the law in order to facilitate public protests. Their reasoning proceeded on the basis of an orthodox approach to analysis of the common law; from this, Lord Irvine deduced and stated explicitly that he was merely declaring what the law was already and had been probably since *Harrison v Duke of Rutland*[285] and certainly since *Hickman v Maisey*[286] in 1900: namely, that reasonable users of the highway include not only activities strictly related to passing and re-passing, but also those which are customary and reasonable, such as taking a sketch, stopping to talk to a friend, carol singing, and so on. He strictly based his judgment on prior authority[287] and stated explicitly that he found it unnecessary to have regard to the Convention.[288] He made no mention of any common law right to peaceful assembly and, indeed, the only principle which went to his decision[289] was that the Divisional Court's judgment would

---

278 [1999] 2 WLR 625, p 633. He added the words 'in the sense defined' after the word 'reasonable' (p 633B), but it is not clear what this refers to. It cannot mean 'reasonable' in the sense of 'not unreasonably impeding the right to pass and re-pass' since this would render otiose the separate stipulation that an assembly must be 'non-obstructive'; in any event, at an earlier point, his Lordship explicitly stated that the test of 'reasonable user' was additional to that of not impeding the public's right to pass and re-pass (*ibid*, pp 632H–633A).

279 *Ibid*, p 655.

280 *Ibid*, p 666 (emphasis added).

281 Still less did they uphold any right to assembly on the highway, as one commentator has erroneously declared: Foster (1999) 33(3) L Teach 329–36, p 330.

282 [1999] 2 WLR 625, p 667, *per* Lord Hutton.

283 The offence under s 14A is triable summarily, subject to the normal right of appeal to the Crown Court.

284 Clayton, G, 'Reclaiming public ground: the right to peaceful assembly' (2000) 63(2) MLR 252, p 257.

285 [1893] 1 QB 142.

286 [1900] 1 QB 752, CA.

287 'I conclude that the judgments of Lord Esher MR and Collins LJ are authority for the proposition that the public have the right to use the public highway for such reasonable and usual activities as are consistent with the general public's primary right to use the highway for purposes of passage and repassage': [1999] 2 WLR 625, p 631D.

288 *Ibid*, p 635.

289 His references to the Convention are expressly *obiter* only: *ibid*, p 635B.

have rendered many activities commonly carried on in the street unlawful, and 'the law should not make unlawful what is commonplace and well accepted'.[290] Lord Clyde's approach was to like effect.[291] While one commentator describes this approach as 'refreshing and positive',[292] it gives a higher place to the uncertain value of preserving accepted custom than to the supposedly fundamental human right declared in Art 11. Lord Clyde's approach differed only in that he expressly disclaimed any human rights dimension to the case at all, remarking: 'I am not persuaded that the ... case has to be decided by reference to public rights of assembly.'[293] To both of their Lordships it appeared to make no difference whether a given group of people were meeting to engage in political protest or to look at an interesting shop window; neither indicated that a magistrates' court should take into account any expressive dimension of a given assembly of people in arriving at the determination of reasonableness.

It was, therefore, only Lord Hutton who based his findings at least partly upon the broad right at stake: 'the common law recognises that there is a right for members of the public to assemble together to express views on matters of public concern and I consider that the common law should now recognise that this right, which is one of the fundamental rights of citizens in a democracy, is unduly restricted unless it can be exercised in some circumstances on the public highway.'[294] However, it is apparent from this conclusion that in his view, as in Lord Irvine's,[295] the demands of this 'right' are satisfied provided merely that an assembly on the highway is not invariably tortious. Moreover, this consideration was only one of his three reasons for his conclusion.[296]

Thus, Lord Irvine considered compatibility with Art 11[297] (strictly, *obiter*),[298] but recognised no equivalent common law right. Lord Hutton ignored the Convention, thought that there was a common law right to peaceful assembly, but gave it minimal recognition. Aside from a brief citation by Lord Hutton,[299] human rights jurisprudence on the matter from other jurisdictions played no part in the decision. By no stretch of the imagination, therefore, could human rights considerations be said to have played a leading role in the decision. Furthermore, there was no awareness of the background to the case – the unprecedented legislative attack upon the right to peaceful assembly of which s 14A was the culmination.[300] For two out of three of their Lordships, the issues

---

290 *Ibid*, p 631.

291 *Ibid*, pp 654–55.

292 Clayton, *op cit*, fn 284, p 254.

293 [1999] 2 WLR 625, p 654.

294 [1999] 2 WLR 625, p 660.

295 '... in my judgment our law will not comply with the Convention unless its starting point is that assembly on the highway will not necessarily be unlawful': [1999] 2 WLR 625, pp 634H–635A.

296 The second was the need to harmonise the civil law of trespass with the criminal law on obstruction of the highway ([1999] 2 WLR 625, p 664); his third was that the authorities themselves indicated that extensions to the lawful uses of the highway might be necessary and desirable in response to changing circumstances ([1999] 2 WLR 625, pp 660 and 664–66).

297 Lord Clyde made a glancing reference to it, but only to the fact that Art 11 laid down 'express limitations' to the right it declared! ([1999] 2 WLR 625, p 654).

298 Above, fn 289.

299 He cited *The Queen in Right of Canada v Committee for the Commonwealth of Canada* (1991) 77 DLR (4th) 385, p 394) ([1999] 2 WLR 625, pp 661–62).

300 See above, pp 464–65.

raised were to be resolved by reference to the interpretation of 19th century case law on real property.

This approach compares strikingly with that taken in the media freedom cases of *Simms*[301] and *Reynolds*,[302] decided within a few months of *Jones*. In those decisions, freedom of expression, both as a common law 'constitutional right' and as embodied in Art 10 of the Convention, was 'the starting point' of legal reasoning.[303] *Reynolds* included extensive citation and consideration of relevant Convention jurisprudence.[304] The values underpinning freedom of expression in general, and those particularly engaged by the instant case were identified; in *Simms* the demands of freedom of expression were treated as the touchstone by which the legality of subordinate legislation was to be assessed, and were found to demand a reading of it which ran clearly counter to its literal meaning.

It was common ground between all their Lordships that any users of the highway other than passage must not be incompatible with that primary use; they must therefore be peaceful and non-obstructive. The very narrow distinction which divided their Lordships was whether such other users had to be 'reasonable and usual'[305] (as the majority thought) or 'reasonable and associated with passage' (the view of the minority – Lords Slynn and Hope). The case law was clearly capable of supporting both interpretations,[306] as the ability of the majority to base their judgment on prior authority indicates.[307] In any event, regardless of the interpretation adopted of the cases, no recognition was shown of the fact that those upon which the minority principally relied – *Hickman v Maisey*[308] and *Harrison v Duke of Rutland*[309] – were 19th century authorities, not decided in the House of Lords. Nevertheless, these hundred year old findings from inferior courts were treated almost as if they were binding. Remarkably, in fact, their Lordships clearly preferred to rely on these dated authorities, even though, as the appellants pointed out, this involved rendering the civil law inconsistent with the criminal law of obstruction of the highway,[310] as interpreted in a more recent Court of

---

301 [1999] 3 All ER 400.

302 [1999] 4 All ER 609. See Chapter 3, p 104.

303 See *Simms* [1999] 3 All ER 400, p 407, *per* Lord Steyn and p 412, *per* Lord Hoffman (referring to 'fundamental rights' generally); *Reynolds* [1999] 4 All ER 609, p 629, *per* Lord Steyn.

304 (1999) 4 All ER 609, pp 621–22 (*per* Lord Nicholls), p 628 and esp p 635 (*per* Lord Steyn), p 643 (*per* Lord Cooke).

305 See, eg Lord Irvine: [1999] 2 WLR 625, p 631C.

306 For the wider view see, eg, *Hickman v Maisey* [1900] 1 QB 752, pp 757–58, *per* Collins LJ: 'in modern times a reasonable extension has been given to the use of the highway as such ... the right of the public to pass and repass ... is subject to all those reasonable extensions which may from time to time be recognised as necessary to its exercise in accordance with the enlarged notions of people in a country becoming more populous and highly civilised but they must be such as are not inconsistent with the maintenance of the paramount idea that the right of the public is that of passage'. For the narrower view see, eg, *Harrison v Duke of Rutland* [1893] 1 QB 142, p 154, *per* Lopes LJ: 'If a person uses the soil of the highway for any purpose other than that [of passage and repassage] he is a trespasser'; and Kay LJ, p 158: 'the right of the public upon a highway is that of passing and repassing over land the soil of which may be owned by a private person ... any other purpose is a trespass.'

307 See [1999] 2 WLR 625, p 665, *per* Lord Hutton. The leading text (Clerk and Lindsell, *The Law of Torts*, 17th edn, 1995, p 861) cited by Lord Slynn ([1999] 2 WLR 625, p 638) appeared to favour the majority view, although his Lordship did not take it so.

308 [1900] 1 QB 752.

309 [1893] 1 QB 142.

310 Highways Act 1980, s 137(1), provides: 'If a person, without lawful authority or excuse, in any way wilfully obstructs the free passage along a highway he is guilty of an offence ...'

Appeal decision.[311] The fact that their approach would logically have entailed the implied repeal of that authority[312] and a consequent considerable broadening in scope of the related criminal offence did not appear to be a matter of concern. So reluctant, indeed, were the minority to depart from the 19th century view of the law that they formulated a series of extremely questionable arguments against adopting the majority's view of the case law. Lord Slynn clearly misstated the possible adverse impacts which would flow from it.[313] Lord Hope made the novel proposition that where Parliament has legislated by reference to common law principles,[314] the effect of that reference is to forbid any subsequent judicial development of the common law in that area;[315] at another point, his Lordship resorted to virtual tautology, arguing that the proposed development of the law would be incompatible with the previous law.[316]

It is when the concrete, practical distinction between users which are 'reasonable and associated with passage' and 'reasonable and usual' is grasped that this dogged refusal to contemplate a modest development of the law from one formulation to another appears all the more remarkable. The narrower view apparently permits activities such as stopping to consult a map or tie a shoelace, since these are directly connected to the activity of travelling along a highway, but not activities such as carol singing, leafleting, assembly, all of which become acts of trespass. However, since *all* agreed that no use could be lawful which impeded the primary right of passage, even the majority view would not have allowed activities which caused any obstruction to passage or were otherwise unreasonable. It therefore entailed no actual *detriment* to the highway owner or anyone else. The minority were not then protecting a property owner from detrimental interference with his property. They invoked as the sole justification for the criminalisation of entirely peaceful protesters an entirely technical, abstract right: the entitlement of a highway owner to have the highway used only for activities which, as

---

311 *Hirst and Agu v Chief Constable of West Yorkshire* (1987) 85 Cr App R 143. See below, p 481.

312 In *Hirst*, the crucial issue was whether peaceful protest on the highway constituted a reasonable user, thus amounting to a 'lawful excuse' for obstruction. Glidewell LJ pointed out that, logically, 'for there to be a lawful excuse ... the activity in which the person causing the obstruction is engaged must itself be inherently lawful. If it is not, the question whether it is reasonable does not arise': (1987) 85 Cr App R 143, p 151. The court then went on to find that peaceful assembly was a reasonable user and thus constituted a lawful excuse. The minority in *Jones* simply dismissed the comparison ([1999] 2 WLR 625, pp 640 and 651). However, on the interpretation of the case law which they upheld, the activities in question in *Hirst* – protesters holding a banner and giving out leaflets – would clearly have been unlawful, as a trespass; therefore, on the logic of Glidewell LJ's argument, the decision in *Hirst* that such activities were reasonable and thus a lawful excuse would have been wrong.

313 Lord Slynn contended: 'the defendants' argument in effect involves giving to members of the public the right to wander over or to stay on land for such a period and in such numbers as they choose so long as they are peaceable, not obstructive, and not committing a nuisance': [1999] 2 WLR 625, p 639. This is clearly inaccurate: the judgment concerned the highway, not 'land' generally, and it is only reasonable and customary users that are to be allowed.

314 By relying on the notion of civil trespass, as s 14A does.

315 '... the intention of Parliament as disclosed by the language of that section was to rely upon the existing state of the law relating to trespass ... this ... makes the ... [a]symmetry [between civil and criminal law] inevitable.' ([1999] 2 WLR 625, p 651).

316 'I do not think that this broad argument can be reconciled with Lord Esher MR's statement of the law.' ([1999] 2 WLR 625, p 648).

well as being peaceful, non-obstructive, customary and reasonable, were also 'associated with passage'.[317]

This tendency to rely upon artificial legal reasoning may also be seen in the lack of any appreciation of the fact that the normative context of the decisions relied upon differed markedly from that in Jones, a tendency present equally in the majority judgments. In both Hickman[318] and Harrison,[319] the plaintiffs owned the highway in question and had brought legal action to stop activities taking place on them which were actually detrimental to them. Moreover, neither defendant was engaging in peaceful protest. By contrast, the peaceful protest which took place in Jones was presumably a matter of complete indifference to the highway authority and amounted to a political expression. At no point were these significant differences adverted to.[320] Lord Hope indeed made a point of 'stress[ing] that the purpose for which the appellants were seeking to remain where they had gathered is not material in this context'.[321] As noted above, the majority, particularly Lords Irvine and Clyde, found in favour of the defendants on the basis that their activity was no more harmful than other inoffensive activities customarily carried out on the highway, such as carol singing and queuing, which they were reluctant to stigmatise as unlawful. The contrast with leading cases on journalistic speech, such as Reynolds, discussed above, is particularly striking in this regard: in that case, the central point was to mark out discussion of important public affairs in the media, as deserving of special protection under common law and the European Convention because of its vital role in maintaining democratic society.[322]

Not only does this approach display a characteristically exaggerated attachment to the value of property rights,[323] it also exemplifies the tendency of English judicial reasoning to assume a narrow and technical basis, abstracted from any meaningful context. The property right at stake in Jones was treated, in Sunstein's phrase, as a 'purposeless abstraction',[324] unrelated to any human interests or values. As Professor Gray puts it, 'property' exists in the law as 'an abstract "bundle of rights" – an artificial construct – interposed between the possessor of land and the land itself ...'[325] There was

---

317 The idea of a highway owner actually taking legal action to protect this right, by, for example, suing a group of carol singers for 'trespass' to the highway is evidently absurd; the authors are aware of no recorded case of a highway authority suing persons who have committed such a technical trespass: see Bailey, Harris and Jones, op cit, fn 1, p 182.

318 [1900] 1 QB 752. The defendant, a racing tout, was using the highway to observe the plaintiff's race horses being trained.

319 [1893] 1 QB 142. The defendant was using the highway to disrupt grouse shooting on the plaintiff's land.

320 This tendency is a marked feature of English law on public order: Glidewell LJ in Hirst and Agu (1987) 85 Cr App R 143, a case concerning peaceful protest, applied Nagy v Weston [1965] 1 WLR 280, where the facts concerned a hot-dog stall and expressly compared the case with 'persons distributing advertising material ... outside stations'. See Bailey, Harris and Jones, op cit, fn 1, p 167.

321 [1999] 2 WLR 625, p 650.

322 Albeit that the Lords did not find that 'political speech' should automatically attract privilege as a generic class.

323 See below, fn 324 and fn 335 and associated text.

324 The phrase is taken from Sunstein, C, who uses it to describe the approach of the US Supreme Court to the First Amendment: Sunstein, C, Democracy and the Problem of Free Speech, 1993.

325 Author of the leading text, Elements of Land Law, 1993.

no recognition of the fact that, as the Supreme Court of New Jersey has put it: 'property rights serve human values. They are recognised to that end, and are limited by it,'[326] a proposition explicitly recognised also by the German Constitution.[327]

The explicit treatment of the human rights dimension by the minority was – like Lord Clyde's – one which sought its marginalisation. Both of their Lordships claimed that there was no need to advert to the Convention because there was no ambiguity in the common law[328] – this despite the fact that the House had split 3:2 on its interpretation. Both, nonetheless, made token references to it, although, as with the majority, there was no consideration of Strasbourg jurisprudence, despite the fact that a number of relevant cases were cited to their Lordships in argument – again, a sharp contrast with the approach of the House of Lords in the recent cases relating to media freedom, discussed in Chapter 3, above. Lord Slynn was plainly uninterested in the Convention: he claimed that his view of the law was not inconsistent with Arts 10 and 11 because both 'provide for exceptions to the rights created', but made no attempt even to specify those exceptions which might be relevant.[329] Lord Hope was clearly also disposed to ignore the Convention altogether,[330] preferring to take the relevant principles on free speech from a case some 90 years old.[331] Their Lordships were content with the idea that while the right to demonstrate was 'of great importance' it could simply be exercised somewhere else. Klug, Starmer and Wier,[332] noting Forbes J's similar attitude in *Hubbard v Pitt*,[333] describe this as the 'working assumption of most judges when restricting the activity of protesters' and as 'simply wrong'. As Clayton puts it: 'There is not some other place where the public have a better right. If freedom of assembly cannot be exercised in the streets, it is in effect denied.'[334] Once again, their Lordships showed no awareness of the practical realities of human rights.

The one substantive Convention argument which Lord Hope did consider was, characteristically, related to the defence of property rights. His view was that any possible restrictions on Art 11 entailed by s 14A could be justified as necessary to protect the rights of property holders to peaceful enjoyment of their possessions under Protocol 1 of the Convention.[335] Indeed, he said that a construction of Art 11 which gave a right to peaceful assembly on the highway could 'deprive' owners of 'their right to the quiet

---

326 *State v Shack* (1971) 277 A 2d 369, p 372.

327 Article 14(2) of the German *Grundgesetz* provides: 'Property imposes duties. Its use should also serve the welfare of the community.'

328 [1999] 2 WLR 625, p 640, *per* Lord Slynn and, p 651, *per* Lord Hope.

329 [1999] 2 WLR 625, p 640.

330 See the opening words of his speech: [1999] 2 WLR 625, p 641.

331 *McAra v Magistrates of Edinburgh* 1913 SC 1059, p 1073: '... there is no such thing as a right in the public to hold meetings as such in the streets ... the right of free speech is a perfectly separate thing from the question of the place where that right is to be exercised.'

332 *The Three Pillars of Liberty*, 1996, p 193.

333 [1976] QB 142: 'They are free at some other place and by legitimate means, to bring their dislike ... before the public.'

334 'Reclaiming public ground: the right to peaceful assembly' [2000] MLR 252, p 257. Similarly, Sherr notes: 'Highways are the most probable places for outdoor protests to be held ...' *Freedom of Protest, Public Order and the Law*, 1989, p 61.

335 'Every natural and legal person is entitled to the peaceful enjoyment of his possessions ...' See Chapter 2, p 81.

enjoyment of their possessions contrary to Art 1 of the First Protocol'.[336] Since his Lordship expressly drew no distinction as to the position between publicly owned highways and private ones,[337] his view entailed the novel proposition of attributing to emanations of the State (highway authorities) 'rights' under the Convention.

The decision of the police in this case to arrest and seek the prosecution of an entirely peaceful protest group lends credence to the civil libertarian and leftist thesis that enormous discretion has been placed in the hands of the police which may be used to harass marginal groups.[338] The response of the House of Lords suggests very little preparedness to restrict that discretion and indicates how far judicial attitudes currently are from a real appreciation of the importance and practical realities of the right to peaceful protest. The decision of the House of Lords has attracted favourable reviews: Barendt considers that Lords Irvine and Hutton 'formulated a broad common law right of public assembly'.[339] Another commentator describes the decision as 'the endorsement of the right to peaceful assembly ... an important vindication of a fundamental civil liberty'.[340] It is suggested, reluctantly, that such assessments are overly generous. It is contended that the concession granted by the majority was so limited and precarious, and the approach of their Lordships in general[341] so narrow and blind to the human rights values at stake, that the judgment as a whole cannot but leave a civil libertarian with a sense of strong unease, despite the fact that the outcome could have been so much worse. Gray and Gray have spoken of the manner in which, in other jurisdictions, 'the operation of the private law of trespass is inevitably and increasingly qualified by the paramountcy of human rights considerations'.[342] Such qualification was, it is suggested, barely present in the decision of the majority and stoutly resisted by the minority.

Impact of the HRA on ss 12–14A of the 1986 Act

Section 13 catches all marches once a ban is in place, not merely trespassory ones. Sections 12 and 14 can affect peaceful marches and assemblies which could disrupt the life of the community. The disruption could be caused by the size of the group or the particular circumstances applicable: it is not necessary for the group to be disorderly. The decision in *Jones* makes it clear that peaceful non-obstructive assemblies are not inevitably non-trespassory and therefore they can fall foul of s 14A, if a ban is already in place. Thus, those assemblies recognised at Strasbourg as most worthy of protection can attract liability under the statutory framework created by the 1986 Act. It would appear that this position is incompatible with Arts 10 and 11. Are there grounds for expecting a radical

---

336 [1999] 2 WLR 625, p 652.

337 *Ibid*, pp 643 and 650–51, rejecting counsel's suggestion that statutory highway authorities should be treated differently from private owners.

338 For a general survey of repressive police tactics against leftist working class demonstrations, see Bowes, *The Police and Civil Liberties*, 1966; Sherr, A, *Freedom of Protest, Public Order and the Law*, 1989, p 30 *et seq*; Ewing and Gearty, *Freedom under Thatcher*, 1990, Chapter 4.

339 Freedom of assembly', in Beatson and Cripps (eds), *Freedom of Expression and Freedom of Information*, 2000, p 3.

340 Clayton, *op cit*, fn 284.

341 The approach of the Divisional Court was in line with that taken by the minority; thus, of the seven judges who adjudicated upon this case in the two courts, a majority found against the applicants.

342 'Civil rights, civil wrongs and quasi-public places' [1999] EHRLR 46, p 100.

change in approach under the HRA? The findings of the House of Lords in *Jones* strongly suggest that the traditionally blinkered and deferential judicial approach to public protest prevails. Therefore, challenges to ss 12–14A in future may present the judiciary with a dilemma, since they will be expected to construe existing law so that it complies with the Convention, 'in so far as it is possible' under s 3 of the HRA.

In an instance such as *Jones*, or in respect of ss 12–14, the court's approach to the problem would be bound to undergo a radical change, at least in methodology. Rather than focusing primarily upon the limitations upon otherwise lawful conduct that these sections create, the starting point would be the Convention rights in issue. The court would be bound to find that a protest which was wholly peaceful fell within Art 11 and, following *Steel*, it would also find Art 10 applicable.[343] *Prima facie* interference with the right(s) would clearly have occurred, including the arrests of the defendants and any convictions sustained.[344] Having made this determination, the court would then have to consider the exceptions within para 2 of those Articles. It would be bound under s 3 of the HRA to find an interpretation of ss 12–14A which was compatible with the Convention if at all possible, but the question of what was required in order to achieve compatibility would be open to interpretation, depending on the view of the Strasbourg jurisprudence adopted.

It is suggested that there are, in fact, two contrasting lines of authority in that jurisprudence relevant to these issues. In *Steel v UK*,[345] the Court found that the interference with an entirely peaceful protest which had occurred was disproportionate to the aim of preventing disorder, and in *Ezelin v France*[346] the Court made a significant statement of basic principle:[347] 'The Court considers ... that the freedom to take part in a peaceful assembly ... is of such importance that it cannot be restricted in any way ... so long as the person concerned *does not himself* commit any reprehensible act on such an occasion.'[348] On its face,[349] this finding would prohibit the application of criminal sanctions to peaceful protesters[350] as a result of the use of blanket bans, a possibility which, as noted above, is left open by *Jones*. This possibility is also supported to an extent by the jurisprudence of the Court on prior restraint outside the context of public protest.[351] It would also prohibit the imposition of conditions which can, depending on

---

343 See above, text to fn 107.

344 Where an arrest and police detention took place but no charges were laid, or no conviction sustained, there would still be a *prima facie* violation of Arts 10 and 11, following *Steel* (1999) 28 EHRR 603: violations were found in relation to the third, fourth and fifth applicants who were arrested and detained but not tried (the prosecution adduced no evidence).

345 (1999) 28 EHRR 603. The applicants had been holding a banner and giving out leaflets outside an arms exhibition.

346 A 202 (1991).

347 Note that within the Convention system, there is no difference in weight between '*obiter* comments' and those which, in common law terms, form part of the 'ratio' of the case: see Harris, O'Boyle and Warbrick, *op cit*, fn 132, pp 18–19.

348 A 202 (1991), para 53.

349 The Crown might argue that it is inapplicable beyond its particular facts: it concerned professional disciplinary sanctions applied to a lawyer who took part in a march that became violent and disorderly, but who conducted himself peacefully.

350 It might be argued that a distinction should be drawn between protesters who take part in a peaceful demonstration which they know to be banned, arguably thereby committing a 'reprehensible act', and those who obey the ban by abandoning their proposed demonstrations, but bring proceedings to test its legality.

351 See Chapter 7, pp 358–59.

the circumstances, have an effect on an assembly almost as severe as that created by a ban. As indicated above, conditions can be imposed on peaceful assemblies where it is thought that a risk of disruption to the life of the community may arise.

On the other hand, there is a consistent line of case law from the Commission which indicates that bans – therefore, *a fortiori* the imposition of conditions – on assemblies and marches are in principle compatible with Art 11 even where they criminalise wholly peaceful protests[352] or prevent what would have been peaceful demonstrations from taking place at all.[353] The cases, particularly *Pendragon* and *Chappell*, also exhibit an unwillingness to examine the proportionality of bans to the threatened risks with any rigour.

It would therefore be open to a court inclined to a minimalist response to the HRA to follow the Commission case law on the basis that it is more directly applicable to ss 12–14A, since it deals directly with prior restraints, unlike *Steel* and *Ezelin*. On such an approach the imposition of conditions under ss 12 or 14 or of bans under s 13 would be substantively unaffected by the HRA since the police assessment of the need to impose the condition or seek the ban would be deferred to. This approach would also leave Jones substantially untouched, although it would probably require the court to engage in an inquiry not relevant to *Jones*,[354] namely to satisfy itself that there was some risk of disorder or property damage to justify the making of the original s 14A order. However, provided some evidence to this effect was produced, such a court would take the view that its sufficiency to justify the ban was a matter within the 'area of discretion' of police decision making. Such courts would thus continue to find such assemblies lawful or unlawful depending on the view of the trial court as to their 'reasonableness' in the circumstances.

A court inclined to take a more rigorous approach to its new duties under the HRA would go into the matter a little more deeply. In relation to s 13 or 14A, it could start by noting that the *effect* of a blanket ban under either of those provisions is that those organising or taking part in demonstrations caught by it can be subject to criminal penalties and hence to an interference with their Arts 10 and 11 rights even though they themselves were behaving wholly peacefully. This is apparently contrary to the statement of principle set out in *Ezelin*, above, since the arrest and conviction of such demonstrators cannot be seen to be directly serving one of the legitimate aims of preventing public disorder or ensuring public safety. It is therefore arguable that such bans always constitute breaches of Arts 10 and 11, when they catch entirely peaceful protesters, since the 'legitimate aim' test is unsatisfied. At the least it may be argued that since such bans are so repugnant to the Convention in principle, the burden should be on the authorities to show that a ban was, genuinely, the only way of dealing with the threatened disorder. The court would attribute the Commission's failure to take this approach in the

---

352 *Pendragon v UK* Appl No 31416/96 (1998); *Chappell v UK* Appl No 12587/86 (1987) (both discussed above, p 444).

353 *Christians Against Racism and Fascism v UK* (1980) 21 DR 138 is a particularly clear example. See also *Rassemblement Jurassien v Switzerland* Appl No 8191/78 (1980) 17 DR 93; *Rai, Allmond and 'Negotiate Now v UK'* 81-A D & R 146 (1995).

354 The point of law certified for consideration by the Lords in *Jones* related to whether the particular assembly fell within the s 14A order; they were not asked to consider the adequacy of the grounds for granting of the original order.

Strasbourg cases to the effects of the margin of appreciation.[355] It could also note the fact that all the cases on blanket bans are merely admissibility decisions of the Commission, which clearly have a lower status in the Convention case law than decisions of the Court[356] especially where, *prima facie*, they run counter to its decisions.

There would, therefore, be strong grounds of principle to justify a departure from *Jones*,[357] on the basis that it affords too precarious a level of protection to a fundamental right in allowing peaceful, non-obstructive protests to be interfered with, not after satisfying the rigorous standard suggested above, but merely because a magistrates' court has found the assembly to be 'unreasonable'. The question would then be how far a court wished to go in establishing a new approach to s 14A. The civil trespass finding could be modified: a court could find that if an assembly is peaceful and non-obstructive, it must *always* be termed reasonable, therefore non-trespassory, and so outside the terms of any s 14A order in force. A court could go further, and find that even obstructive assemblies are not necessarily trespassory: as noted above, the criminal law on obstruction of the highway provides for peaceful protest to constitute a lawful excuse to such conduct.

A further, more contentious possibility, might arise where a group was charged with infringing a ban imposed under s 14A of the Public Order Act 1986 in respect of land owned by a public authority. A possible recourse (apart from a challenge to the ban itself, discussed above), since *prima facie* it would appear to be trespassory, would be to argue that in the circumstances it had a constructive licence to enter the land on the basis of the demands of the guarantees under Arts 10 and 11. A failure to accept such an argument could lead, potentially, to a serious interference with those guarantees.[358] A successful claim of such access rights would mean reinterpreting s 14A(5) in order to find that rights of access to certain areas, going beyond the highway, exist for the purpose of holding peaceful assemblies. If such a claim was upheld, it would also preclude the imposition of tortious liability.

However, such an approach would still leave untouched the more fundamental objection to s 14A – that it allows for the criminalisation of purely peaceful protests through prior restraint, on the basis only of a risk of 'serious disruption to the life of the community' and civil trespass. There are two aspects to this objection: the first is to blanket bans *per se*; the second is to the use of 'serious disruption to the life of the community'[359] as the test for their imposition. A court which formed the view that

---

355 In one case, the Commission argued that such bans were justified since they were 'based on considerations designed to ensure an even application of the law in that it aims at the exclusion of any possibility for the taking of arbitrary measures against a particular demonstration' (*Christians against Racism and Fascism v UK* (1980) 21 DR 138, p 150).

356 See Harris, O'Boyle and Warbrick, *op cit*, fn 132, p 18: 'If the Court interprets the Convention differently from the Commission, the Court's view prevails,' as, they note, the Commission has accepted.

357 The break with precedent would be justified on the basis that the new interpretative approach under s 3 rendered the decision non-binding; the opinion of Lord Irvine on the decision's compatibility with the Convention was *obiter* only and made without the benefit of full argument on the point.

358 The members of the assembly would be convicted of various offences arising under s 14B, however peaceful or non-obstructive the assembly was. Its organiser could be imprisoned (s 14B(5)), as could anyone who could be proved to have incited a member of the assembly to come onto the land (s 14B(7)).

359 Such a claim could be raised collaterally as a defence to criminal proceedings (*Boddington v British Transport Police* [1998] 2 WLR 639 and HRA 1998, s 7(1)(b)). Those aggrieved by the making of a s 14A order could also challenge it directly by relying on HRA 1998, s 7(1)(a).

blanket bans *per se* were essentially incompatible with the Convention could enforce this view through a radical reinterpretation of s 14A under s 3(1) of the HRA. It would entail reading into ss 14A (5)[360] the requirement that a given assembly, as well as being trespassory and within the geographical and temporal scope of a subsisting s 14A order, also must itself pose a threat of disorder, or otherwise satisfy one of the exceptions to Art 11. Since such an interpretation would mean that s 14A effectively ceased to bestow a power to impose blanket bans and is only doubtfully necessary under the Convention, it is unlikely to be adopted.

Under s 14A, attention will therefore probably focus upon scrutiny of the risk of 'serious disruption to the life of the community'. This method could also be used to bring ss 12 and 14 into line with the Convention. Courts will be required to determine that the nature of the risk anticipated is one which would constitute one of the legitimate aims for limiting the primary rights under Arts 11 and 10. It has been pointed out that this vague and ambiguous phrase,[361] 'would appear to subsume and indeed go beyond the criteria for restricting public protest laid down in Art 11(2)'[362] of the Convention. Given the terms of these criteria, the grounds for the ban would have to be justified, either on the basis of protecting 'the rights of others' (discussed below),[363] or because the 'serious disruption' feared amounted to 'disorder' for the purposes of Art 11(2). But if it was feared merely that serious traffic congestion might occur, which could be seen as disrupting the 'life of the community', by making it more difficult for activities such as shopping and commuting from work to carry on, this would not appear to amount to 'disorder' under para 2.

Under a more subtle approach, consideration would be given to the question of the compatibility with general Convention principles of the concept of 'community' used in s 14A. As Fitzpatrick and Taylor comment, the use of the term:

> begs the question of how the 'community' in question is actually constituted ... [under] the Act ... the community ... is defined implicitly by a notionally uniform way of life of those who inhabit the ... area in question ... one result of the Act is that certain groups become socially and politically authorised to undertake practices of exclusion on the basis that it is they who represent 'the community'.[364]

Under the Act those engaging in protest – which could be seen as an 'intrinsically communal' activity – 'are constructed by [it] as being inherently in opposition to the exercise of the day-to-day rights of members of the community within which the assembly takes place'.[365]

---

360 Above, p 466.

361 The alternative ground is reasonable anticipation of 'significant' damage to historical, etc, buildings (s 14A(1)(b)(ii)).

362 Fitzpatrick, P and Taylor, N, 'Trespassers might be prosecuted: the European Convention and restrictions on the right to assemble' [1998] EHRLR 292, p 297.

363 See above, p 444.

364 Fitzpatrick and Taylor, *op cit*, fn 362, p 298.

365 Fitzpatrick and Taylor, *op cit*, fn 362. They further point out that protests, such as that at Newbury, attracted both support and opposition from the local communities: 'thus ... the intra-community factions could be simultaneously causing each other "serious disruption".' See also Gray and Gray, *op cit*, fn 210, p 51.

There is a compelling argument to the effect that this aspect of the Act is in opposition to one of the most basic values underlying the Convention, insisted upon by the Court in a number of freedom of expression judgments, although not in the context of public protest: that the key characteristics of that 'democratic society', the values of which are the touchstone by which the legality of restrictions on individual rights must be determined, are 'pluralism, tolerance and broadmindedness'.[366] An activist approach to the HRA would lead a court to recognise the concrete relevance and applicability of such constitutive values underlying the Convention, rather than the 1986 Act's 'monolithic'[367] conception of the community: the Court would thus view its duty under s 6 of the HRA as including a duty to respect and uphold pluralism and diversity within communities, and in determining whether the life of a given community will be 'seriously disrupted' by a given protest, to ascribe to that community the qualities of tolerance and broadmindedness towards the values and activities of others. Such an attitude would raise decisively the value of peaceful protest and place quite a heavy burden upon those arguing that serious disruption to the community justified prior restraint of such assemblies.

Section 13 is not open to amelioration in order to achieve compatibility with Arts 10 and 11, by way of reinterpretation of the meaning of trespass, since it provides a power to ban all marches for a period, not merely trespassory ones. However, a court confronted with the kind of situation that arose in *Christians Against Racism and Fascism*[368] under the HRA could take a hard look at the question of proportionality. The court could take the view that the geographical or temporal scope of the ban had been greater than was needed to obviate the risk of serious disorder. Or it could find that the ban need not have been imposed at all since the imposition of conditions under s 12 would have been sufficient. More controversially, it could find that the banning order applied for could have excluded the peaceful march caught by the ban. It could do this in one of two ways. Either it could be found that the duty of the Chief Officer of Police under s 6 of the HRA required him to exclude the march from the ban, where it was reasonable to expect him to know that it was imminent. It could be argued that a power to seek an order to ban all marches could be interpreted as a power to ban all *at the most*, using s 3 of the HRA creatively as the House of Lords did in *R v A*.[369] Alternatively, the words 'or any class of public procession' used in s 13(1) could be utilised to afford leeway to include potentially disruptive marches (using 'disruptiveness' as the method of defining their membership of the class) and therefore to exclude marches expected to be entirely peaceful. As indicated above, this interpretation does not reflect Parliament's intention in passing s 13. However, s 3 of the HRA allows Parliament's intention to be disregarded, since it imposes a later requirement of achieving compatibility with the Convention rights. Since, in the particular instance, the Chief Constable had failed to exclude the march from the ban, the banning order could be viewed as an interference disproportionate to the aim of preventing disorder pursued.

---

366 *Handyside v UK* (1976) 1 EHRR 737, para 49.
367 Fitzpatrick and Taylor, *op cit*, fn 362.
368 See above, p 464.
369 See Chapter 4, p 142–43.

These suggestions indicate the impact that the HRA could have on the legal framework within which marches and assemblies operate. They indicate opposing lines of thought within the Convention jurisprudence, but also demonstrate that the *Ezelin* and *Steel* line is more in tune with the Convention stance on prior restraint generally. Clearly, the stance of the House of Lords in *Jones* gives little cause for expecting a rigorous approach to the Convention jurisprudence or an understanding of Convention values. However, as Chapter 4 indicated, there are signs that decisions taken under the HRA, rather than in the period immediately before it came fully into force, show a much greater understanding and appreciation of those values.[370]

4 CRIMINALISATION OF TRESPASS AND OBSTRUCTION OF THE HIGHWAY

In order to assemble or demonstrate, protesters require access to land. But in order to create an impact, persons normally assemble in large groups. If they are on the highway, they are very likely to cause some obstruction to free passage and therefore may fall foul of the offence of obstructing the highway. Further, the tendency for public spaces to be privatised has been reinforced by the direction of UK law. Not only are there virtually no positive rights of access to forums for the holding of meetings,[371] but under the provisions discussed below, a 'creeping criminalisation of trespass'[372] has occurred, denying protesters access to private or quasi-public land on pain of the risk of arrest and conviction, not merely of incurring tortious liability. There are now a number of circumstances in which a person who merely walks onto land may incur criminal liability. A central issue, therefore, is the impact of the HRA on the creation of such liability, and on the offence of obstructing the highway when used against assemblies.

Obstructing the highway

The pre-HRA interpretation

Section 137 of the Highways Act 1980 provides that a person will be guilty of an offence if he 'without lawful authority or excuse in any way wilfully obstructs the free passage of the highway'. The only right in using the highway is to pass and re-pass along it – to make an ordinary reasonable use of it as a highway. Since obstruction of the highway is a criminal offence, it might therefore appear that all assemblies on the highway are *prima facie* unlawful since they are bound to cause some impediment to those passing by and therefore they can only take place if the police refrain from prosecuting. However, the courts seem to take the stance that not every such assembly will be unlawful; the main issue will be what was reasonable in the circumstances.

---

370 See, in particular, p 142–4.

371 See the Representation of the People Act 1983, ss 95 and 96 (providing a right for Parliamentary candidates to hold meetings at election times) and the Education (No 2) Act 1986, s 43 (providing that university and college authorities must secure freedom of speech for persons, including visiting speakers, within their establishments).

372 See Wasik and Taylor, *The Criminal Justice and Public Order Act 1994*, 1995, p 81.

In *Arrowsmith v Jenkins*[373] it was determined that minor obstruction of traffic can lead to liability under the 1980 Act. A pacifist meeting was held in a certain street which linked up two main roads. The meeting blocked the street and the organiser co-operated with the police in unblocking it. It was completely blocked for five minutes and partly blocked for 15 minutes. The police had advance notice of the meeting and the organiser was under the impression that the proceedings were lawful, especially since other meetings had been held there on a number of occasions without attracting prosecutions. Nevertheless, the organiser was convicted. This use of the Highways Act is open to criticism; it places such meetings in a very precarious position since it seems to hand a power to the police to license them, thereby seriously undermining freedom of assembly. However, in *Nagy v Weston*[374] it was held that a reasonable user of the highway will constitute a lawful excuse and that in order to determine its reasonableness or otherwise, the length of the obstruction must be considered, its purpose, the place where it occurred and whether an actual or potential obstruction took place.

The purpose of the obstruction, mentioned in Nagy, was given greater prominence in the significant decision in *Hirst and Agu v Chief Constable of West Yorkshire*:[375] it was said that courts should have regard to the freedom to demonstrate. This was found in relation to the behaviour of a group of animal rights supporters who had conducted a demonstration in a busy street. The crucial issue was whether peaceful protest on the highway constituted a reasonable user, thus amounting to a 'lawful excuse' for obstruction. Glidewell LJ pointed out that, logically: 'for there to be a lawful excuse ... the activity in which the person causing the obstruction is engaged must itself be inherently lawful. If it is not, the question whether it is reasonable does not arise.'[376] The court then went on to find that peaceful assembly was a reasonable user and thus constituted a lawful excuse.

The impact of the HRA

Following the interpretation accorded to s 137 in *Hirst and Agu*, the purpose of an assembly as a means of legitimate protest may suggest that it can amount to a reasonable user of the highway. It may be noted that this finding is consonant with the finding of the House of Lords in *Jones* in the context of s 14A of the 1986 Act. It also means that the use of s 137 against protesters is less likely or less likely to succeed unless the obstruction becomes unreasonable. Therefore, the stance taken under s 137 may be in accord with the values of Arts 10 and 11. Nevertheless, there is still the question of the reasonableness of an obstruction. The courts' approach to this question will, as indicated above, undergo a change, when protesters are charged with the offence under s 137, at least in terms of methodology: the starting point will be the Convention rights in issue. An assembly that is obstructive (due to numbers or circumstances), but wholly peaceful, will fall within Art 11 and, following *Steel*, Art 10 would also be applicable.[377] *Prima facie* interference with the right(s) would clearly have occurred; the court would therefore consider the

---

373 [1963] 2 QB 561; [1963] 2 All ER 210; for comment, see [1987] PL 495.
374 [1966] 2 QB 561; [1965] 1 WLR 280.
375 (1987) 85 Cr App R 143.
376 *Ibid*, p 151.
377 See above, p 441.

exceptions within para 2 of those Articles. It would be bound under s 3 of the HRA to find an interpretation of s 137 which was compatible with those rights.

It is suggested that, in this instance, *Steel* and *Ezelin* are most clearly applicable since s 137 does not amount to a prior restraint. The finding in *Ezelin v France*[378] that freedom of peaceful assembly cannot be restricted in any way so long as the person in question has not committed any reprehensible act[379] would be applicable, since the obstructiveness of an assembly may frequently have nothing reprehensible about it – as appeared to be the case in *Arrowsmith and Jenkins*. Further, the conviction of persons taking part in a peaceful assembly does not appear to serve one of the legitimate aims of preventing public disorder or ensuring public safety. Obstruction is not necessarily equivalent to disorder. It is therefore arguable that the use of s 137 in such an instance would constitute a breach of Arts 10 and 11 since, in relation to disorder or public safety, the 'legitimate aim' test would be unsatisfied.

The rights of others might, however, be in question, depending on the circumstances, in which case the issue would be one of proportionality. Since s 137 uses the imprecise term 'excuse', which, as indicated, has been found to mean a reasonable user, a Convention-friendly interpretation can be adopted quite readily, without needing to rely on s 3 of the HRA. It could be found that a peaceful, albeit obstructive, assembly would normally amount to a reasonable user of the highway, but that where the obstruction created a risk to safety or impinged disproportionately on the right of others to free movement[380] due to its length, it could no longer be viewed as reasonable.

Criminalising trespass

Wasik and Taylor note that 'The criminalisation of various forms of trespass in the 1994 Act ... has been vigorously opposed by those who fear that it will provide an inappropriate disincentive to group protest'.[381] As argued in the Introduction to this chapter, forms of direct action are less justifiable under rights-based arguments than other forms of protest. But the concern generated by the provisions discussed below is that over-reaction to the activities of hunt saboteurs has led to an unnecessary distortion of this area of the criminal law, to the detriment of freedom of protest.

The statutory scheme: mass trespass

Simple trespass – walking onto someone's land without permission or refusing to leave when asked to do so – has never been a crime under UK law. However, the 1986 Act created a special form of criminal trespass under s 39[382] which involved the application of a two-limb test. Under the first limb (s 39(1)), it had to be shown that two or more

---

378 A 202 (1991).

379 *Ibid*, para 53.

380 It may be noted that, as indicated above, Strasbourg has not indicated with any precision which 'rights' are in question. See above, p 444.

381 *The Criminal Justice and Public Order Act 1994*, 1995, p 81.

382 For comment on this offence, see Vincent-Jones (1986) 13 JLS 343; *Stonehenge* (1986) NCCL; Ewing and Gearty, *op cit*, fn 1, pp 125–28.

persons had come onto the land as trespassers with the common purpose of residing there for some period of time and that reasonable steps had been taken to ask them to leave on behalf of the occupier. Further, they must have brought 12 or more vehicles onto the land or threatened or abused the occupier or his agents or family or damaged property on the land. If the senior police officer believed that these conditions were satisfied, he could direct the persons to leave.

Under the second limb (s 39(2)), if they then failed to comply with the direction or came back onto the land within three months, they committed a criminal offence punishable with three months imprisonment. Section 39 was aimed at certain forms of assemblies, including animal rights activists and the 'peace convoys' which gather for the summer solstice festival at Stonehenge. As a number of commentators pointed out, it was probably unnecessary to enact this offence given the availability of civil remedies and the possibility of using powers to prevent a breach of the peace against mass trespassers or of charging them with low level public order offences.[383] It has also been suggested that the provision failed to confine itself to preventing the mischief it was created to prevent.[384] It could also be criticised as adding to the number of offences which can occur due to disobedience of police orders; it has been argued that a person should be obliged to take orders from the police only in the narrowest of circumstances.[385]

Section 39 was repealed by the CJPOA 1994 and its provisions replaced by s 61. Section 61, however, closely resembles s 39 and the changes it makes tend to have the effect of widening the offence. Under s 61, the persons in question need not have entered the land originally as trespassers; the question is whether they are trespassing, whether or not they originally entered the land as trespassers. If they did not enter as trespassers, the power to eject them only arises if there is a reasonable belief that the other conditions under s 61(1) are satisfied. The conditions under s 61(1) are similar to those under s 39(1), but the number of vehicles has been reduced from 12 to six and damage to the land itself has been included as well as damage to property on the land.

Aggravated trespass

The CJPOA 1994 also created the offence of aggravated trespass under s 68, which is aimed at certain groups such as hunt saboteurs or motorway protesters.[386] Section 68 creates a two stage test; first, it must be shown that the defendant trespassed on land in the open air and secondly, in relation to lawful activity which persons are engaging in or are about to engage in, that he did there anything intended by him to have the effect of either intimidating those persons so as to deter them from the activity or of obstructing or disrupting that activity.[387] No defence is provided and, crucially, it is not necessary to show that the activity was actually affected. This is a broadly worded provision; its impact in practice will depend on the meaning attached to the imprecise terms 'disrupt' and 'obstruct'. A great many peaceful but vociferous demonstrations may have some impact of an obstructive nature on lawful activities. It is, however, limited in its

---

383 Smith, ATH, *Offences Against Public Order*, 1987, paras 14–18.

384 Card, R, *Public Order: The New Law*, 1987, takes this view: see pp 146–48.

385 See [1987] PL 211.

386 See HC Deb Col 29, 11 January 1994.

387 Section 69(1)(a).

application in that it does not apply to demonstrations on a metalled highway, although it does include public paths such as bridleways, and it excludes most, but not all buildings.[388]

Section 68 has been used against hunt saboteurs and other protesters on a number of occasions and some of the decisions on the section have had the effect of widening the area of liability created still further. In *Winder v DPP*[389] the appellants had been running after the hunt. It was accepted that they did not intend to disrupt it by running but it was found that running after it was a more than a preparatory act and that it was close enough to the contemplated action to incur liability. The defendants could not have been charged with attempting to commit the offence[390] but, rather remarkably, the courts used the statutory test for attempts – whether the actions were 'something more than merely preparatory to the commission of the offence' – in support of their finding that the defendants had committed the actual offence,[391] thus appearing to conflate attempts to commit offences with the offences themselves. The willingness of the court to extend the boundaries of s 68 to catch such activities was all the more disturbing given that s 69 allows a direction to be given where it is suspected that the s 68 offence will be committed, a provision surely intended to cover precisely this set of circumstances. Thus, it was found that the offence under s 68 could be established if the appellants were trespassing on land in open air with the general intention of disrupting the hunt and were intending when in range to commit the acts in question with the required intention. This decision comes very close to punishing persons for their thoughts rather than for their actions.

Laws LJ's findings in *DPP v Barnard and Others*,[392] a decision that also concerned the breadth of s 68 when applied to direct action protest, showed similar tendencies, which are also found in Lord Bingham's willingness in *DPP v Capon*[393] (discussed below) to entertain the notion that mere presence on land *per se* might constitute 'doing there anything' intended to be intimidatory, obstructive or disruptive under s 68(1), a construction of the offence which could effectively remove the need to prove one if its constituent elements.[394] The decision concerned protesters against open cast mining who came onto land at an open cast site. The information against them alleged that having trespassed on land in the open air, they then, in relation to a lawful activity of open cast mining which persons were about to be engaged in on that land, did an act of unlawfully entering on that land, intended by them to have the effect of intimidating those persons

---

388 'Land' is defined in s 61(9); it does not include metalled highway or buildings apart from certain agricultural buildings and scheduled monuments; common land and non-metalled roads are included.

389 (1996) *The Times*, 14 August.

390 There is no offence of attempting to commit summary offences unless specifically provided for in the statute creating the offence: Criminal Attempts Act 1981, s 1(4).

391 'The running after the hunt was, in the undisputed circumstances of the present case, sufficiently closely connected to the intended disruption as to be, in the words of the Criminal Attempts Act 1981, 'more than merely preparatory'.

392 Before Laws LJ and Potts J (judgment of 15 October 1999); (1999) *The Times*, 9 November.

393 Below, fn 399.

394 'If the Police Sergeant had been found to have based his reasonable belief [that the s 68 offence was being committed] simply on the fact that [they] were present at the scene then ... it would be necessary ... to consider whether presence alone might be intimidatory ... obstructive ... or disruptive.' (Lord Bingham LCJ, *obiter*.)

so as to deter them from engaging in that activity, or obstructing or disrupting that activity, contrary to s 68(1). The magistrate, relying on *Winder*, found that three elements were required to establish the offence of aggravated trespass: namely, trespass, an intention to disrupt a lawful activity and an act done towards that end. The magistrate found that the allegation in the informations that the respondents 'unlawfully entered on land' alleged no more than that they had trespassed, and therefore was not capable of amounting to the second aggravating act required by the words in s 68(1): '... does there anything which is intended by him to have the effect ...' The magistrate refused an application by the prosecution to amend the informations to allege the act of 'unlawfully occupying the site in company with numerous other people' on the ground that it still would not have disclosed an offence, as occupation of the site was the act of trespass, and not an additional act aggravating that trespass. Reference to the number of people was no more than an indication that some were trespassing.

Laws LJ found that the magistrate was clearly correct in finding the original information to be defective. Proof was required of trespassing on land in the open air and of doing a distinct and overt act other than the act of trespassing which was intended to have the effects specified under sub-ss (a)–(c) of s 68(1). Unlawful occupation could equate to no more than the original trespass, but there might, he found, be circumstances where it could constitute the second act, other than trespass, required under the offence. However, a bare allegation of occupation was insufficient. It had to be supported by particulars of what the defendant was actually doing, and the occupation had to be distinct and overt from the original trespass. The proposed amendment would, he found, have disclosed an offence under s 68(1) of the 1994 Act, but it would not have been appropriate to allow the amendments; accordingly, the appeal was dismissed.

This decision suggests at first sight that when a group of protesters merely come onto land to protest about something taking place there, they do not thereby commit a criminal offence. It reiterates that the offence under s 68 consists of distinct elements, all of which must be shown to be present. But the potential blurring of the distinction between the first two to the effect that for the purposes of the offence of aggravated trespass, the occupation of land could constitute an act intended to intimidate, obstruct or disrupt, if it was distinct from a mere act of trespass, might lead to confusion as to the difference between simple and aggravated trespass. The circumstances in which an occupation of land will be viewed as distinct from a trespass on it are left unclear. The mere fact that the defendants unlawfully (that is, committing the tort of trespass) occupied the site in company with numerous other people does not necessarily mean that the offence under s 68 is made out unless the group do there anything which, in relation to others engaging in a lawful activity, is intended to have the effects mentioned in sub-ss (a)–(c) of s 68(1). If, for example, a large group walked onto land and engaged in a peaceful sit-in without making any effort to approach the persons the protest was aimed at, it is unclear that any of the effects mentioned above could be said to have occurred. The terms are ambiguous, but bearing Arts 10 and 11 in mind, they should now be interpreted more strictly under s 3 of the HRA. On the facts, the protesters' behaviour was quite closely analogous to that of the successful applicants in *Steel* in that the protest clearly constituted an expression of opinion, albeit occurring by means of action rather than speech, which was peaceful and unlikely to lead to disorder.

Directions under s 69

Far-reaching provisions under s 69 underpin s 68. Section 69(1)(a) provides that if the senior officer present at the scene reasonably believes that a person is committing, has committed or intends to commit the offence under s 68, or (b) that two or more persons are trespassing and have the common purpose of intimidating persons so as to deter them from engaging in a lawful activity or of obstructing or disrupting that activity, he can direct any or all of those persons to leave the land. Under s 69(3), if the person in question, knowing that the s 69 direction has been given that applies to him, fails to leave the land[395] or re-enters it as a trespasser within three months,[396] he commits an imprisonable offence. It is a defence for the person to show that he or she was not trespassing on the land[397] or that he or she had a reasonable excuse[398] for failing to leave the land or for returning as a trespasser.

It may be noted that s 69 is the equivalent of s 14C of the Public Order Act 1986, which was discussed above. Section 14C allows a constable to stop a person whom he reasonably believes is on her way to an assembly in an area to which a s 14A order applies, and to direct her not to proceed in that direction. The power can only be used within the area to which the order applies. Failure to comply is an offence and renders the person liable to arrest. The similarities between s 14C and s 69 mean that much of the discussion below would apply also to s 14C.

Although s 68 may not lead to the criminalisation of persons who simply walk on to land as trespassers, s 69 has the potential to do so, depending on the interpretation given by the courts to the 'reasonable excuse' defence. For example, where a person is in receipt of the direction under s 69, even though it was erroneously given (since in fact, although she was trespassing, she did not have the purpose of committing the s 68 offence), she may still commit an offence if thereafter she re-enters the land in question during the specified time. The fact that on the second occasion she was merely walking peacefully on to land in order to engage in a non-obstructive public protest would be irrelevant unless she could also produce an excuse which could be termed reasonable. Whether the erroneousness of the senior police officer's original 'reasonable belief' would amount to a reasonable excuse is left unclear.

Capon v DPP[399] made it clear that the offence under s 69 could be committed even though the offence under s 68 was not established. The defendants were videoing the digging out of a fox when they were threatened with arrest under s 68 by a police officer if they did not leave and were asked whether they were leaving the land. This exchange and question was found to be sufficient, in the circumstances, to constitute the direction necessary under s 69. Their intention in undertaking the videoing was not found to be to disrupt, intimidate or interfere with the activity in question. Despite the fact that the protesters had been peaceful and non-obstructive throughout,[400] and it was very

---

395 Section 69(3)(a).

396 Section 69(3)(b).

397 Section 69(4)(a).

398 Section 69(4)(b).

399 Case CO/3496/97 Judgment of 4 March 1998 LEXIS; considered: Mead [1998] Crim LR 870.

400 In the exchange with the officer, one said, 'I have no intention of disrupting [the hunt] ...'; another, 'We're here quite peacefully ... simply videoing what is going on' (Mead [1998] Crim LR 870, p 871).

doubtful whether the officer had directed his mind towards all the elements of the offence, including the *mens rea*,[401] it was found that there was sufficient evidence. It was further found that there was no defence of 'reasonable excuse' in the circumstances,[402] even though the protesters were still in the process of trying to find out what offence they were being arrested for[403] when they were, in fact, arrested, and genuinely believed that no direction under s 69(1) had been made against them.

The judgment consisted of a fairly orthodox exercise in statutory interpretation, coupled with a generous approach to the reasonableness of the officer's belief.[404] Since criminalisation of what will often, in Convention terms, be an act of political expression,[405] rests primarily upon the state of belief of a single officer, perhaps formed in a few moments, a court with any appreciation of the enormous discretion that this statute affords the police to interfere with political protest would have been expected to conclude both that it should construe the statute as strictly as possibly against the executive, and, further, that it should scrutinise the actions of the police officer, especially the clarity of his instructions,[406] and the findings of the trial court with particularly anxious care. Further or alternatively, the court could have found that where the defendants were in fact engaged in peaceful protest, they could plead 'reasonable excuse'; the very broad phrasing of that defence provides the most obvious means by which to import human rights values into s 69. The court, unfortunately, showed no awareness of any of these factors, engaging instead in a purely mechanistic interpretation of the law; indeed, there was no (explicit) *normativity* in its approach at all.

Under this approach, the outcome in instances similar to *Winder* or *Capon* might not differ in the post-HRA era, although the reasoning process by which it was reached would, since the value of political expression – taking that term to encompass an animal rights' protest – receive some consideration.[407] It is suggested that the decisions reveal a judicial approach that, far from engaging with the thorny issues raised by the direct action form of protest, shows a continuance of traditional, formalist reasoning, coupled with marked executive-friendly tendencies: a willingness to widen the scope of already widely drafted offences and a reluctance to interfere with the exercise of broad police discretion. Such tendencies proceeded directly, it appeared, from the evident lack of judicial recognition of the issues of principle at stake.

---

401 As Mead notes *op cit*, fn 63, p 875.

402 'The fact that the appellants were not ... committing an offence under s 68 plainly ... does not provide a reasonable excuse for not leaving the land. So to hold would emasculate the obvious intention of the section' (*per* Lord Bingham, Case CO/3496/97 (1998), transcript).

403 The first protester said, immediately before he was arrested, 'I'm not prepared to leave the land because I don't believe I'm committing any offence'; the second, 'I don't understand' (Mead [1998] Crim LR 870, p 871).

404 In particular, as Mead points out, no inquiry was made as to whether he had directed his mind towards all the elements of the offence, including the *mens rea* (*op cit*, fn 63, pp 874–75).

405 The ECHR had not delivered judgment in *Steel* at this point (judgment was delivered on 23 September 1998) and *Capon* was decided on 4 March 1998; however, the decision of the Commission, which made a like finding as to the applicability of Art 10, was delivered on 9 April 1997.

406 As Mead remarks: '... it must be very difficult to "know" within section 69(3) that a direction has been given if the police are permitted such wide and uncertain language as this' (Mead, *op cit*, fn 63, p 872).

407 *Winder* was reported in *The Times* only (above, fn 389); *Capon* not at all.

The impact of the HRA on ss 61, 68 and 69

The effect of the Convention on prosecutions brought under ss 61, 68 and 69 will be, at least superficially, quite dramatic, whether a minimalist or an activist approach is followed. As indicated above, judicial consideration of these provisions at present gives no recognition to the Convention rights at stake. By contrast, as discussed above,[408] the European Court made a clear finding in *Steel*,[409] confirmed in *Hashman*,[410] that protest which takes the form of physical obstruction nevertheless falls within the protection of Art 10 – and presumably Art 11.[411] Unless the courts simply refuse to follow this aspect of the *Steel* and *Hashman* judgments – as they could do[412] – they will be bound to find that the actions of similar protesters engage Arts 10 and 11.[413] Acceptance of such engagement would – at least in formal terms – entirely change the approach to the determination of such cases. Instead of merely undertaking a standard exercise in statutory interpretation, the courts will have to decide whether the interference with the protesters' Convention rights is justifiable under the second paragraphs of those Articles.

In the absence of further direct guidance, it is necessary both to resort to inference from the *outcomes* of direct action and other cases, and to attempt to draw conclusions from the more general Convention principles enunciated at Strasbourg. As indicated above, it appears that while there is no express statement to the effect that 'expression' in the form of direct action has a lower status than 'pure' expression, such a finding can be inferred from the case law. In *Steel* itself, the Court appeared to be readily convinced of the necessity and proportionality of the interferences with the two direct action protests complained of by the first two applicants.[414] In contrast, as discussed above, the Court in *Ezelin*[415] found that it was impossible to justify interferences with the freedom of peaceful assembly unless the person exercising the freedom himself committed a 'reprehensible act'. The first two applicants in *Steel* were both acting 'peacefully' in the sense that they were not themselves offering violence. In order to reconcile the two decisions, therefore, it

---

408 See p 441 above. The findings were that protesters who were arrested and detained after, respectively, obstructing a grouse shoot and sitting in the path of road making equipment had suffered a *prima facie* violation of Art 10.

409 (1999) 28 EHRR 603.

410 (2000) 8 BHRC 104; (1999) 30 EHRR 241.

411 The Court in *Steel* found that there was no need to consider the applications under Art 11, implying that since the matter had been resolved under Art 10, consideration of Art 11 would be otiose, as raising the same issues. It may be noted that Art 11 protects only freedom of 'peaceful' assembly; as indicated above (see fn 446) it is arguable that this restriction should also be read into Art 10, although since the words were not expressly included, it might be interpreted more broadly in relation to that Article since it potentially reduces the scope of the primary right.

412 Above.

413 Even where an arrest and detention had occurred, but no further action had been taken, an interference might be viewed as subsisting on the basis that protesters would not be able to exercise their Convention rights free from the fear of arrest and charges: see *Dudgeon v UK* (1982) 4 EHRR 149.

414 The case also concerned third, fourth and fifth applicants, who had engaged in purely peaceful protests with no element of obstruction or other 'action'. The first applicant, who had been impeding grouse shooters, was detained for 44 hours and sentenced to 28 days' imprisonment upon refusing to be bound over; the second, who had been lying down in front of digging equipment, suffered a 17 hour detention and 7 days' imprisonment. The Court found that these were 'serious interference[s]' with the applicants' Art 10 rights. However, it had little difficulty in going on to find them to be both necessary and proportionate.

415 (1991) 14 EHRR 362.

must be assumed either that *obstructive* protest, while it does fall within at least Art 10, does not constitute that class of purely 'peaceful' protest which, according to Ezelin, 'cannot be restricted in any way' or that any restriction is more readily justifiable.

It seems clear from the findings in *Steel* as to the first and second applicants, and from the Commission decision in *G v FRG*,[416] that where a protester is engaged in obstructive, albeit non-violent activity, arrest and imprisonment are in principle justifiable under the Convention. Such an acceptance does not, however, entail a finding that s 68 is Convention-compliant. Section 68 is aimed only at disruptive protesters, not at those engaged purely in verbal persuasion, and therefore the powers it provides may, depending on their interpretation, be compatible with Art 10 as interpreted in *Steel*. However, it must be recalled that in *Steel, actual disruption* had been caused by the protesters: by contrast, s 68 makes clear on its face that it is necessary only that 'acts' additional to trespass, committed with the *intention* of causing disruption, obstruction or intimidation are required to make out the offence. Thus, in cases where the protesters have engaged in action intended to be disruptive, etc, but no such disruption has actually been caused, it is doubtful whether the imposition of criminal liability could be seen as 'necessary' under the Convention. Its imposition would arguably be incompatible with *Steel* and would amount to a clear departure from the principle set out in *Ezelin*, that peaceful protest cannot be interfered with, unless the particular protesters arrested commit 'reprehensible acts'.[417]

If this argument is accepted, a significant narrowing of the area of liability generated by s 68 will be required: the offence will have to be re-interpreted under s 3(1) of the HRA so that it catches only 'acts' that actually have some disruptive, etc, effect. This would entail a clear departure from the literal meaning of the section, but it is presumably a 'possible' interpretation under s 3. On this basis, *Winder*, which allows the criminalisation of protest at a stage even further away from actual obstruction, would also have to be reconsidered and, it is suggested, overruled.

Section 69, as interpreted by *Capon*, is similarly problematic. As *Capon* made clear, s 69 allows peaceful protesters to be arrested even though in fact there was no obstruction, intimidation or disruption of others and no risk of disorder, as long as a police officer reasonably believed that such factors were present. This belief is supposed to be 'reasonable',[418] but as *Capon* vividly demonstrates,[419] the inhibiting effect of this requirement in practice can all but disappear due to the courts' marked disinclination to take issue with the judgments of police officers on the spot.[420] Therefore, it may be argued, depending on the particular circumstances, that certain s 69 'bans' may be unjustifiable under para 2 of Arts 10 and 11, bearing in mind the extent of the discretion to interfere with peaceful protest which this section vests in the police without any independent check, and the extent of the interference – in effect, a complete ban on entering the land in question, potentially lasting for three months. Since s 69 can operate

---

416 (1980) 21 DR 138.

417 Reading *Steel* and *Ezelin* together, it must be assumed that the 'reprehensible acts' mentioned in *Ezelin* included obstructive behaviour.

418 Section 69(1).

419 Above, text to fn 404.

420 (1999) 28 EHRR 603, pp 609–10, 638–39 and 647: the arrest of purely peaceful protesters (the third, fourth and fifth applicants) was found to create breaches of Arts 5(1) and 10.

as a prior restraint, Art 10 would demand that any direction given should be strictly scrutinised.[421]

Such protesters have clearly committed no 'reprehensible' acts, as *Ezelin* requires. One possible response, therefore, would be to reinterpret s 69 under s 3(1) of the HRA so as to allow for a lawful direction to be given only where in fact one of the above elements is actually present. Reasonable belief will have to be taken to mean reasonable and true belief.[422] While such a reading renders s 69 largely otiose (since s 68 would cover such a situation) it is again, a 'possible' reading under s 3(1). A further, more likely, possibility would be to find by reference to Arts 10 and 11 that the erroneousness of the senior police officer's original 'reasonable belief' should amount to a reasonable excuse. It would also be possible to find that purely peaceful protesters have a 'reasonable excuse' for not obeying a s 69 direction under s 69(4)(b). Moreover, under this view, courts will surely find that the Convention requires officers to use the clearest possible words when ordering persons to leave the land, precisely what the court failed to do in *Capon*.

That decision also raises the possibility that a direction under s 69, if it can be given in such an imprecise form, might be found in future to fail to satisfy the test denoted by the term 'prescribed by law' under Arts 10 and 11, assuming that the activity in question could be viewed as constituting the expression of an opinion so as to engage those Articles. It might well be argued that if a direction can be given in the form of a question, as in *Capon*, the term is too imprecise to satisfy that test. But, equally, the domestic court would be free to apply a doctrine of deference to the executive, whereby the nature of the direction should not be scrutinised too closely since the circumstances could be best assessed by the police officer on the ground. In the words of Lord Slynn, in the *International Ferry Traders* case,[423] the courts might show respect to 'the margin of appreciation or discretion' of the police officers in question in refusing to undertake a rigorous review of the wording of a direction. But since the courts will be forced to recognise that they are dealing with the exercise of a fundamental right under the Convention, it would be problematic to allow for its abrogation on the exceptionally flimsy grounds upheld in that case.

The discussion so far has not centred on the question of rights of access to land, except in relation to the highway, under s 14A of the 1986 Act.[424] It is now established that the 'right' of access to the highway may include holding an assembly on it. But *prima facie* assemblies on other quasi-public or private land will virtually always be trespassory, and therefore could attract liability under ss 68, 69 or 61 of the CJPOA unless, in the circumstances, it is found that express or implied permission to hold some peaceful protests was given. A large number of quasi-public places exist to which the public has limited rights of access, such as unenclosed shopping malls, parks, the grounds and forecourts of town halls or civic centres, monuments and their surrounding land or rights of way across private land. At present, such rights of access would not include assemblies

---

421 See p 475.

422 It should be noted that s 69 raises an issue distinct from that of arresting under s 68(4) on the basis of reasonable suspicion of committing the offence under s 68. Since s 68(4) requires reasonable suspicion as to the commission of an offence, it is in principle compatible with Art 5 under the exception of para (1)(c).

423 [1999] 1 All ER 129; see above, p 449.

424 See above, p 468.

for the purpose of protests and demonstrations. Strasbourg has not yet accepted that there is a positive obligation on the State to require public authorities or private individuals to allow the exercise of protest and assembly rights on their land. But an activist domestic court might be prepared to uphold such a claim in respect of a public authority, thereby anticipating the stance on this matter which some commentators view Strasbourg as not unlikely to adopt.[425] When the issue of exclusion of persons from a quasi-public place, a shopping mall, was raised before the Commission, it declared the application inadmissible, on the basis that Art 11 was not applicable, since the applicants were gathering there for a purely social purpose.[426] Clearly, had Art 11 been engaged, a different outcome might have been achieved.

In the US, the courts are moving away from a position of upholding proprietorial rights and towards providing protection for expressive activity in quasi-public forums.[427] This can also be said of the Canadian and Australian courts.[428] In contrast, the traditional stance of the UK judiciary, as indicated above, is to favour the property right when it conflicts with rights of protest. In general, they tend to uphold proprietorial rights in an abstract fashion, regardless of any real harm which may occur due to their infringement.[429] But Art 10 and 11 arguments might persuade them in future to consider the possibility of recognising broader access rights to quasi-public land.

The issue might arise in two ways. A group seeking access to a forum for the holding of an assembly or demonstration might seek to bring an action against the relevant landowning body, if it was a public authority, under ss 6 and 7(1)(a) of the HRA, claiming that a refusal to allow an assembly in a particular place had constituted an interference with its Art 10 and 11 rights. Where a group was charged with infringing s 61 of the CJPOA in respect of private or quasi-public land, its main recourse, since *prima facie* it would appear to be trespassory, would be to argue under s 7(1)(b) of the HRA that in the circumstances it had an implied licence to enter the land on the basis of the demands of the guarantees under Arts 10 and 11. A failure to accept such an argument could lead, potentially, to a serious interference with those guarantees.[430] A successful claim of such access rights would mean reinterpreting s 61 in order to find that rights of access to certain areas, going beyond the highway, exist for the purpose of holding peaceful assemblies. If such a claim was upheld, it would also preclude the imposition of tortious liability.

Similar arguments could be raised under ss 68 or 69 of the CJPOA; a group charged with aggravated trespass could argue, as a preliminary issue, that they had not trespassed since they were within the limited rights of access to the land. Upholding such a claim would mean, in effect, deeming under s 68 that an implied or constructive licence to enter

---

425 Harris, O'Boyle and Warbrick, *op cit*, fn 132, p 419.

426 *Anderson v UK* [1998] EHRLR 218.

427 See *Shad Alliance v Smith Haven Mall* 484 NYS 2d 849, esp p 857.

428 See *Harrison v Carswell* (1975) 62 DLR (3d) 68 Supreme Court of Canada; *Gerhardy v Brown* (1985) 159 CLR 70.

429 See, on this point, Gray and Gray, *op cit*, fn 210.

430 The members of the assembly would be convicted of various offences arising under s 14B, however peaceful or non-obstructive the assembly was. Its organiser could be imprisoned (s 14B(5)), as could anyone who could be proved to have incited a member of the assembly to come onto the land (s 14B(7)).

the land existed, imposed by the HRA. Any such implied licence would no doubt be highly circumscribed. For example, it would have to avoid allowing any infringement of Art 8 rights, including respect for the home. It would probably apply for a limited period and possibly only to peaceful protests, such as a sit-in.

The status of the landowning body under s 6 of the HRA would be relevant. Further, since the offences in question are statutory, the court would have to satisfy its obligation under s 3. If the landowning body was itself a standard public authority, it would clearly be bound by the Convention rights. If it was a functional body,[431] it would depend whether its public function could be said to be engaged by the claims of the protesters. As Chapter 4 indicated, s 6 of the HRA will bring a number of bodies which manage or own land within its ambit, including bodies such as Railtrack, which are classic hybrid bodies. If, for example, Railtrack bought land, perhaps by means of a Compulsory Purchase Order, in order to place railway lines across it, it would then own the land for the purpose of satisfying its public function as the manager of rail infrastructure, but such ownership would nevertheless probably be part of its private function.[432] But if it acted in order to secure the lines by, for example, placing fences round them, it would be doing so in pursuance of its statutory duty in respect of rail safety and therefore might be viewed as acting in that respect as a public authority.[433] A body exercising a private function, or a fully private body, would not be bound by s 6, but would still be affected by s 3 of the HRA. If, for example, an assembly took place, in the period to which a s 14A ban applied, on land owned by a privatised body which could not be viewed as related to the public function of that body, a court would still have to interpret s 14A(5) in order to ensure compatibility with Arts 10 and 11. If, alternatively, a person was charged with an offence under ss 61, 68 or 69 in respect of such an assembly, the court would have to ensure compatibility with those Articles in respect of the term 'trespass' in ss 61, 68(1) or 69(1).

5 BREACH OF THE PEACE, BINDING OVER AND BAIL CONDITIONS[434]

Justices and any court of record having criminal jurisdiction have a power at common law[435] to bind over persons to keep the peace. Under the Justices of the Peace Act 1361, there is also a power – the *contra bono mores* (contrary to a good way of life) power – to bind over persons to be of good behaviour. If a person refuses a binding over order, he or she can be imprisoned for up to six months. These ancient powers are of great significance in relation to direct action, demonstrations and public protest generally due

---

431 See Chapter 4, pp 157–59.

432 There was a *Pepper v Hart* statement in Parliament to this effect: 583 HL 796, 811 (24 November 1997).

433 Clearly, it does not necessarily follow in any particular circumstance that Art 10 and 11 would require that access to the land should be allowed for protesters. Both Articles contain exceptions in the interests of public safety.

434 For discussion of this power, see Grunis, A [1976] PL 16; Law Commission Paper, *Binding Over: The Issues*, 1987, Paper 103: for comment, see [1988] Crim LR 355; 'The roots and early development of binding over powers' [1988] CLJ 101–28; Kerrigan, K, 'Breach of the peace and binding over – continuing confusion' (1997) 2(1) J Civ Lib 30.

435 See the Justices of the Peace Act 1968, s 1(7) and the Administration of Justice Act 1973, Sched 5.

to the wide discretion they hand to police and magistrates. Academic writers agree that the notion of maintaining the Queen's peace continues to be the central one in public order law.[436] It has been said to express the idea that 'people should be free to act as they choose so long as they do not cause violence'.[437] This simple concept appears to be unobjectionable in civil libertarian terms, since it would not sanction interference with the freedom to protest peacefully. However, it will be argued below that this concept no longer expresses the central value underlying the doctrine of breach of the peace. In many respects, it has been replaced by a notion of freedom of action so long as serious inconvenience is not caused. The concept itself has also changed and grown in a way that has taken it some distance from the values it may originally have expressed. Since the breach of the peace doctrine has the potential to curb all forms of protest – not excluding peaceful persuasion – it is likely to come into domestic conflict with Arts 10 and 11 of the Convention.

The *contra bono mores* power

The *contra bono mores* power under the 1361 Act allows the binding over of persons whose behaviour is deemed by a bench of magistrates to be anti-social although not necessarily unlawful. This vague and broad power hands an unacceptably wide discretion to magistrates to determine the standards of good behaviour; it has been severely criticised as a grave breach of rule of law standards.[438] The power has been used in this century against those engaging in political public protest and against groups such as animal rights activists. In *Hughes v Holley*,[439] the Court of Appeal confirmed the existence of the power and its availability regardless of the lawfulness of the behaviour in question.

However, following the decision in *Hashman v UK*[440] it is probable that the doctrine will become a dead letter. The case concerned the behaviour of hunt saboteurs. One of the applicants had blown a horn with the intention of disrupting a hunt. There was no threat of violence and no breach of the peace. Blowing a horn is not unlawful. However, it was probable that he would have repeated the behaviour in question, which was found to be anti-social by the magistrates. He was therefore bound over to be of good behaviour and the binding over order was upheld on appeal. The case led to an application to the European Commission on Human Rights under Arts 10, 11 and 5; it was declared admissible under Arts 10 and 11.[441] The Court went on to find that the power was too vague and unpredictable in its operation to satisfy the 'prescribed by law' requirement under Arts 10 and 11.[442] The finding of the court in *Sunday Times v UK*,[443] that 'a norm

---

436 See, eg, Feldman, *Civil Liberties and Human Rights in England and Wales*, 1993 p 786; 'Breaching the peace and disturbing the quiet' (1982) PL 212; Williams, *op cit*, fn 1.

437 Feldman, *op cit*, fn 43, p 787.

438 Williams, G, 'Preventive justice and the rule of law' (1953) 16 MLR 417. See also Hewitt, P, *The Abuse of Power*, 1984, p 125.

439 (1988) 86 Cr App R 130.

440 (2000) 8 BHRC 104; (1999) 30 EHRR 241.

441 *Hashman and Harrup v UK* (1996) 22 EHRR CD 184.

442 Article 8 uses the formulation 'in accordance with the law', but it was established in *Silver v UK*, judgment of 25 March 1983, A 61; (1983) 5 EHRR 347 that both formulations are to be read in the same way.

443 Judgment of 26 April 1979, A 30, para 49.

cannot be regarded as a "law" unless it is formulated with sufficient precision to enable the citizen to regulate his conduct', was not satisfied. Thus, it may be assumed that, although this decision is not binding, the *contra bono mores* power is unlikely to be used now that the HRA is fully in force.

Breach of the peace

Introduction

The notion of breaching the peace is less vague and uncertain, but it has quite frequently been interpreted very broadly. If a police officer suspects that a breach of the peace is likely to be committed – for example, a march is expected to be disorderly – a person or persons can be arrested without a warrant under common law powers to prevent a breach of the peace and can be bound over to keep the peace, in other words not to continue the behaviour thought likely to lead to the breach of the peace. Thus, the march could be prevented from occurring. If the person refuses the binding over order, he or she can be imprisoned. Under s 6 of the HRA, this power is likely to be re-evaluated when applied to protesters. The tendency of the judiciary – as shown, for example, in *Piddington v Bates*[444] – to accept the finding of the police officer on the ground, is likely to undergo a change.

This flexible common law power[445] overlaps with a number of the powers arising under the 1986 and 1994 Acts and is in general more useful to the police than they are, as its definition is so vague. This vagueness means that it can be used in such a way as to undermine attempts in the statutory provisions to carve out more clearly defined areas of liability. The leading case is *Howell*,[446] in which it was determined that a breach of the peace will arise if an act is done or threatened to be done which either: harms a person or *in his presence* his property or is likely to cause such harm or which puts a person in fear of such harm. Under this definition, threatening words might not in themselves amount to a breach of the peace, but they might lead a police officer to apprehend a breach. Another and rather different definition of the offence was offered in *Chief Constable for Devon and Cornwall ex p CEGB*[447] by Lord Denning. His view was that violence, or the threat of it, was unnecessary; he considered that 'if anyone unlawfully and physically obstructs a worker – by lying down or chaining himself to a rig or the like – he is guilty of a breach of the peace'. On this view, peaceful protest could be severely curtailed. It is generally considered that the view taken in *Howell* is the correct one,[448] but the fact that as eminent an authority as Lord Denning could offer such a radically different definition of the offence[449] from that put forward in *Howell* only a year earlier, epitomises the disturbingly

---

444 [1961] 1 WLR 162.
445 For comment see 'Breaching the peace and disturbing the quiet' [1982] PL 212; Williams, *op cit*, fn 1.
446 [1981] 3 All ER 383.
447 [1982] QB 458.
448 See, eg, Thornton, *op cit*, fn 4, p 74. In *Percy v DPP* [1995] 3 All ER 124, DC, the *Howell* definition as opposed to that of Lord Denning, was preferred. Lord Denning's definition was rejected as erroneous.
449 It should be noted that breach of the peace, though arrestable, is not a criminal offence.

vague parameters of breach of the peace. The *Howell* definition in itself is extremely wide, largely because it does not confine itself to violence or threats of violence. Nor does it require that the behaviour amounting to a breach of the peace, or giving rise to fear of a breach of the peace, should be unlawful under civil or criminal law. Further, it has been recognised for some time by the courts that a person may be bound over for conduct which is not itself a breach of the peace and which does not suggest that the individual concerned is about to breach the peace, but which may cause another to breach the peace.[450] This third possibility is arguably implicit in the *Howell* definition itself and indeed is not sufficiently distinguished, within that definition, from conduct which in itself amounts to a breach of the peace. This additional possibility is of great significance in the context of public protest since it means that in certain circumstances peaceful, lawful protest can lead to the arrest and binding over of the protesters.

The width of powers to prevent a breach of the peace means that they can be used to curtail freedom of assembly in situations in which statutory powers might be inapplicable. For example, *Piddington v Bates*[451] suggested that the courts could be, at times, very unwilling to disagree with the finding of the police officer on the ground. In that case, the defendant wished to join other pickets at a printer's works but was told by police officers that only two men were to be allowed to picket each of the main entrances. The defendant then tried to push 'gently' past the police officer and was arrested for obstructing a police officer in the course of his duty. On appeal, it was held that the officer had reasonably apprehended that a breach of the peace might occur and the limiting of the number of the pickets was designed to prevent it; however, the main reason for fearing trouble was apparently merely that there were 18 pickets at the works. In effect, therefore, a condition was imposed on a static assembly, reducing its numbers to four. It is interesting to note that if that situation were to occur today, with the 1986 Act in force, the powers under s 14 allowing control of assemblies could not be used, since less than 20 people were present and even had more than 20 pickets been there, it seems probable that none of the 'trigger' conditions would have been satisfied. The case illustrates the readiness of the common law to sanction police interference with free assembly on production of what can only be described as minimal evidence of a risk of disorder.

Immediacy

Once it is accepted that an arrest may be made in respect of an apprehended breach of the peace, the question of the necessary degree of immediacy arises. When this power, in conjunction with the offence of obstruction of an officer in the execution of his duty, was used extensively during the miners' strike,[452] it was made clear that an arrest can occur well before the point is reached at which a breach of the peace is apprehended. The most notorious[453] instance of its use occurred in *Moss v McLachlan*.[454] A group of striking miners were stopped by the police a few miles away from a number of collieries; the

---

450 *Wise v Dunning* [1902] 1 KB 167; *Lansbury v Riley* [1914] 3 KB 229.

451 [1961] 1 WLR 162.

452 March 1984 to March 1985.

453 The case has attracted widespread criticism; see Ewing and Gearty, *op cit*, fn 1, pp 111–12; Newbold [1985] PL 30.

454 [1985] IRLR 76.

police told them that they feared a breach of the peace if the miners reached the pits and that they would arrest the miners for obstruction if they tried to continue. After some time, a group of miners tried to push past the police, were arrested and convicted of obstruction of a police officer in the course of his duty. Their appeal on the ground that the officers had not been acting in the course of their duty was dismissed. It was said that there was no need to show that individual miners would cause a breach of the peace, nor even to specify at which pit disorder was expected. A reasonable belief that there was a real risk that a breach would occur in close proximity to the point of arrest (the pits were between two and four miles away) was all that was necessary. (A case in Kent in which striking miners were held up over 200 miles away from their destination suggests that this requirement of close proximity may be becoming otiose.)[455] In assessing whether a real risk existed, news about disorder at previous pickets could be taken into account; in other words, there did not appear to be a requirement that there was anything about these particular miners to suggest they might cause a breach of the peace.[456] Thus, a number of individuals were lawfully denied their freedom of both movement and assembly apparently on no more substantial grounds than that other striking miners had caused trouble in the past, without having themselves provided grounds on which violence could be foreseen.

The decision in *Peterkin v Chief Constable of Cheshire*,[457] taken one year before the HRA came fully into force, takes a strongly differing stance. Peterkin, a hunt protester, had access to intelligence that told him when and where the Cheshire Hunt was to meet. He was making his way to the hunt in a convoy of vehicles carrying other protesters when he was arrested for conduct likely to cause a breach of the peace. The arresting officer said that he anticipated that Peterkin and the other protesters would enter private land, causing a serious breach of the peace. Peterkin argued that he was arrested merely for walking on a country lane, half a mile from where the hunt was taking place, and was not in sight of it at the time. He claimed unlawful arrest, false imprisonment and assault and battery against the Cheshire police on the basis that they had no legal grounds for the arrest and therefore any actions used to effect it were unlawful. In awarding damages, Manchester County Court found that there were no such grounds, since there was no apprehension or imminent threat of any breach of the peace. In requiring a clear element of immediacy, this decision, if followed, will create a strong inhibitory rule, not as to the nature of the doctrine, but as to the point at which it can be invoked. It is in accordance with the stance taken in *McLeod v UK*,[458] in which it was found that it is insufficient to find that a breach may occur at some future point, but is not immediately probable. It can be assumed that *McLeod* will be taken into account in findings as to the application of the breach of the peace doctrine under s 2 of the HRA and therefore the stance taken in *Peterkin* is likely to prevail.

---

455 *Foy v Chief Constable of Kent* (1984) unreported, 20 March. It has also been noted by Thornton, *op cit*, fn 4, pp 97–98 that the Attorney General, in a written answer to a parliamentary question tabled during the miners' strike, omitted the requirement of an imminent threat to public order.

456 The miners apparently gave a hostile reception to passing NCB coaches but this, it appears, occurred after the police had stopped them and informed them that they could not proceed. It does not appear, therefore, that it could have formed part of the basis for the police decision that a breach of the peace was to be expected.

457 (1999) *The Times*, 16 November.

458 (1998) 27 EHRR 493, RJD 19998-VII 2774, Judgment of the Court, 23 September 1998.

Provoking a breach of the peace

Cases such as *Moss v McLachlan* concerned the use of preventive powers against those who could be viewed as likely to breach the peace at some future point. An equally broad view has been taken by the courts of conduct which might provoke others to breach the peace. *Beatty v Gillbanks*[459] established the important principle that persons acting lawfully could not be held responsible for the actions of those who were thereby induced to act unlawfully. However, in *Duncan v Jones*,[460] a speaker wishing to address a public meeting opposite a training centre for the unemployed, was told to move away to a different street because the police apprehended that her speech might cause a breach of the peace. A year previously there had been some restlessness among the unemployed following a speech by the same speaker. She refused to move away from the centre and was arrested for obstructing a police officer in the course of his duty. On appeal, it was found that the police had been acting in the course of their duty because they had reasonably apprehended a breach of the peace.

The case therefore clearly undermined the *Beatty v Gillbanks* principle in that the freedom of the speaker was infringed, not because of her conduct, but because of police fears about the possible response of the audience. In the later case of *Jordan v Burgoyne*,[461] it was found that a public speaker could be guilty of breach of the peace if he spoke words which were likely to cause disorder amongst the particular audience present, even where the audience had come with the express intention of causing trouble. In *Wise v Dunning*[462] it was found that a breach of the peace would arise if there is an act of the defendant 'the natural consequence of which, if the act be not unlawful in itself would be to produce an unlawful act by other persons'. An extremely wide interpretation of this possibility was accepted in *Holmes v Bournemouth Crown Court*;[463] an anti-smoking campaigner who held up a placard and shouted anti-smoking slogans, but in no way threatened violence, was arrested on the ground that if he stayed in his position – outside the designated lobbying area at a Conservative Party Conference – a breach of the peace might arise. The finding that in arresting him, the officer had acted in the execution of his duty, was upheld on appeal.

A similar stance was taken in *Kelly v Chief Constable of Hampshire*[464] which concerned an altercation between a hunt saboteur and a huntsman, resulting in the arrest of the saboteur. According to the Court of Appeal, if a constable reasonably believes that a breach of the peace is about to occur due to a dispute, he may arrest one of the participants: he has complete discretion as to which participant to arrest, and this may even be the case where the evidence suggests that the one not arrested has committed an assault on the other.[465] In other words, the victim of the assault may be arrested to prevent a fight between the two from breaking out.

---

459 (1882) 9 QBD 308.

460 [1936] 1 KB 218; for comment see Daintith [1966] PL 248.

461 [1963] 2 QB 744; [1963] 2 All ER 225, DC. It should be noted that the case was concerned with breach of the peace under the Public Order Act 1936, s 5.

462 [1902] 1 KB 167. See also *Duncan v Jones* [1936] 1 KB 218.

463 (1993) unreported, 6 October 1993, DC; cited in Bailey, Harris and Jones, *op cit*, fn 1, p 256.

464 (1993) *The Independent*, 25 March.

465 *Obiter* comment from Lloyd LJ. The huntsman had assaulted Kelly with his whip.

In *Percy v DPP*,[466] Collins J ruled: 'The conduct in question does not in itself have to be disorderly or a breach of the criminal law. It is sufficient if its natural consequence would, if persisted in, be to provoke others to violence.'[467] Similarly, in *Morpeth Ward JJ ex p Ward*,[468] which concerned the behaviour of protesters against pheasant shooting, Brooke J stated: '... provocative disorderly behaviour which is likely to have the natural consequence of causing violence, even if only to the persons of the provokers, is capable of being conduct likely to cause a breach of the peace.'[469] Thus, the reasonableness of the shooters' behaviour or potential behaviour was not called into question. The court did not lay down a test to determine the point at which a violent reaction to provoking behaviour might be termed an unnatural consequence of such behaviour. It focused simply on the question whether the natural consequence of the behaviour in question was to provoke violence, thus leaving open the possibility that an extreme reaction from those provoked, although probably unreasonable, might be termed natural. The reasonableness of the shooters' behaviour or potential behaviour (one of the shooting party had threatened to kill a protester) was not called into question. The response of the shooters was viewed as the natural and probable consequence of the protest; the attribution of responsibility for the apprehended breach of the peace on the basis of proportionality between the provocation and the reaction was avoided.

This very wide finding received a more restrictive interpretation in *Nicol v DPP*,[470] which concerned the behaviour of fishing protesters. During an angling competition the protesters blew horns, threw twigs into the water and attempted verbally to dissuade the anglers from fishing. This provoked the anglers so that they were on the verge of using force to remove the protesters. The protesters were arrested for breach of the peace. It was found that they were guilty of conduct whereby a breach of the peace was likely to be caused since their conduct, although lawful, was unreasonable and was likely to provoke the anglers to violence. Thus, the reasonableness of the behaviour of those provoked was considered. Simon Brown LJ found that a natural consequence of lawful conduct could be violence in another only where the defendant rather than the other person could be said to be acting unreasonably, and, further, that unless the anglers' rights had been infringed, it would not be reasonable for them to react violently. It was assumed that their rights had been infringed,[471] and that as between the two groups the behaviour of the fishing protesters was clearly unreasonable. The need to show an infringement of 'rights' and the findings as to reasonableness place a limitation on the 'natural consequence' test which was not present in *Wise v Dunning*. This finding offers some clarification of the 'natural consequence' test although, since there is no right to fish, the rights referred to are unclear. The term 'liberties' rather than 'rights' would have been more appropriate. Possibly in referring to an infringement of rights Simon-Brown J was seeking to distinguish so called direct action from other forms of protest.

---

466 [1995] 3 All ER 124, DC.

467 *Ibid*, p 131.

468 (1992) 95 Cr App R 215.

469 *Ibid*, p 221.

470 (1996) 1 J Civ Lib 75. See further *Steel v UK* (1999) 28 EHRR 603.

471 The rights referred to were left unclear. There is, of course, in general no right to fish, merely a freedom to do so; fishing rights may be obtained under a contract with the landowner, but this does not appear to have been the case in this instance since the anglers were fishing in a public park.

It is unclear at present whether the test from *Nicol* or from *Ex p Ward* will prevail. Clear adoption of the *Nicol* test would go some way towards restoration of the *Beatty v Gillbanks* principle, since following it, behaviour which has as its natural consequence the provoking of others to violence will not amount to a breach of the peace unless it is also unreasonable. But, of course, the test depends upon a wide and uncertain test of reasonableness; the judiciary may well be disinclined to find that the behaviour of groups espousing minority, 'alternative' viewpoints, such as hunt saboteurs or tree protesters, while lawful, was also reasonable. This decision may well be interpreted to mean that any activities as part of peaceful protest, which may provoke those whose behaviour is the subject of the protest to use force, should be accounted behaviour likely to give rise to a breach of the peace, so long as the protesters can be said to have infringed 'rights'. The judiciary may be disinclined to find that the behaviour of groups such as hunt saboteurs or tree protesters, while lawful, was reasonable.

Adoption of the *Nicol* test in relation to protest by speech rather than by means of direct action might allow a distinction to be drawn between forceful speech calling the attention of others to arguments, issues or events, and speech which consists of an attack upon the hearers with the intent of causing extreme provocation. The crucial difference should be the verbal attack which renders the speaker directly responsible for awakening hatred and violence. Arguably, the first type of speech should never be restrained, but it may be acceptable to restrain the second when it offers extreme provocation to its hearers.[472] Sections 4, 4A and 5 of the Public Order Act 1986 (below) appear to be aimed only at the latter, deliberately provocative form of speech, although they are not confined to instances of extreme provocation. However, as seen above, the power to prevent a breach of the peace fails to distinguish at present clearly between the two situations.

Bail conditions

Binding over to keep the peace may form part of a bail condition, but bail conditions may be more specific than this. A person charged with any offence may be bailed as long as they promise to fulfil certain conditions.[473] This aspect of criminal procedure can readily be used by the police against protesters or demonstrators; they can be charged with a low level public order offence or bound over to keep the peace, thus allowing the imposition of conditions which may prevent participation in future protest. If the conditions are broken, the bailee can be imprisoned. The Bail Act 1976 requires that applications for bail should be individually assessed in order to determine whether conditions should be imposed, thereby reflecting concern that the bailing procedure should not result in any further deprivation of liberty than is necessary. Despite this, during the miners' strike there was evidence that conditions were being routinely imposed without regard to the threat posed by the individual applicant. The Divisional Court, however, found that such practices were lawful (Mansfield JJ *ex p Sharkey*).[474]

---

472 For comment on this issue see Birtles (1973) 36 MLR 587. For discussion in the context of race hatred see Chapter 6, pp 327–30.

473 See Feldman, *op cit*, fn 43, pp 835–42.

474 [1985] QB 613.

Impact of the HRA

On the basis of the decisions discussed, the breach of the peace doctrine not only fails to distinguish fully between the forms of protest referred to above, but also makes no attempt to inquire into their significance in terms of free expression. The doctrine provides no means of distinguishing between rowdy football supporters and protesters. There is no recognition of the particular need to protect the communicative rights of minority groups, on the basis that their views may find little expression within mainstream speech, or of the likelihood that the provision of such broad police powers, while neutral on their face as between collective and minority standpoints, will tend to bear disproportionately on the latter. The domestic decisions discussed here tend to exhibit an arbitrariness which fuels the general argument that these powers provide the police with an unacceptably wide discretion which is not fully held in check by the courts. Even where cases do not come to court, or where decisions to bind over are overturned on appeal, as in *Percy v DPP*[475] the detention of the defendant will have occurred on what is often a flimsy and imprecise legal basis. Within the models indicated above, what effect will Arts 10 and 11 have on the development of the doctrine of breach of the peace?

As noted above, any interference with freedom of peaceful assembly must be 'prescribed by law' according to Arts 10(2) and 11(2). These words import requirements of certainty and fair warning and therefore under the HRA, the arrest and bind over powers are likely to be reviewed by the judiciary in order to determine whether they meet these standards. The view of the Law Commission is that '... binding over falls short of what ought to be two elementary principles of criminal or quasi-criminal law. These require the law to be both certain and readily ascertainable'.[476] However, as indicated above, the actual standards connoted by the words 'prescribed by law' may not be very high, particularly where public order matters are in issue. In *Steel and Others v UK*,[477] which concerned the arrest and detention of applicants engaged in various forms of public protest, the European Commission on Human Rights took note of the findings of the Law Commission regarding certainty, but, taking account of the notion of varying levels of precision referred to above, it found that 'the concept of "breach of the peace" is sufficiently certain to comply with the notion of "prescribed by law" under Article 10 para 2'.[478] The Court found that the breach of the peace doctrine provided sufficient guidance and was formulated with sufficient precision to satisfy the requirement of Art 5(1)(c) that arrest and detention should be in accordance with a procedure prescribed by law, and that the prescribed by law requirement of Art 10 was also satisfied.[479] In *McLeod*

---

475 [1995] 3 All ER 124. The case concerned a solitary protester who trespassed at a US military base; it was found that her conduct was likely to give rise to a breach of the peace and, when she refused to be bound over, she was imprisoned. However, on appeal, the Divisional Court found that trained military personnel were unlikely to be provoked into responding to her trespass with violence.

476 Law Commission Report No 222, para 4.16. The Law Commission relied in part on the failure of these powers to meet the standards laid down by the European Convention on Human Rights.

477 (1999) 28 EHRR 603.

478 Para 148. Usually, Strasbourg will find a violation of the 'prescribed by law' requirement only where the interference has no legal basis: *Malone v UK* A 82 (1984) 7 EHRR 14; *Halford v UK* [1997] IRLR 471. But, exceptionally, in *Hashman and Harrup v UK* (2000) 8 BHRC 104, a basis in law was present but did not satisfy the requirements of this test; discussed above, p 493.

479 *Steel and Others v UK* (1999) 28 EHRR 603.

v UK,[480] the Court found that the breach of the peace doctrine was 'in accordance with the law' under Art 8. Thus, in respect of the key elements of 'prescribed by law' – legal basis, certainty and accessibility – the breach of the peace doctrine meets Strasbourg standards. Within the 'review' model it is, therefore, almost inconceivable that domestic courts would wish to import higher standards under the 'prescribed by law' rubric. Within the 'activist' model, however, this would be possible on the argument that the findings in question depended on the application of relatively low standards of precision and accessibility.

Reappraisal and reform of the doctrine of breach of the peace is more likely to occur by reference to the notion of what is 'necessary in a democratic society' within Arts 10 and 11 para 2. This issue was extensively considered by the Court in Steel, but the findings were quite strongly influenced by the doctrine of the margin of appreciation.[481] The first applicant had taken part in a protest against a grouse shoot and had stood in the way of participants to prevent them taking shots. Since this behaviour was likely to be provocative, the Court found that her arrest and detention, although constituting serious interferences with her freedom of expression, could be viewed as proportionate to the aim of preventing disorder and of maintaining the authority of the judiciary[482] and this could also be said of her subsequent detention in the police station for 44 hours,[483] bearing in mind the findings of the police or magistrates that disorder might have occurred. The Court made little attempt to evaluate the real risk of disorder, taking into account the margin of appreciation afforded to domestic authorities in determining what is necessary to avoid disorder in the particular domestic situation.[484] It may be noted that this conclusion was reached only by a five to four majority; the partly dissenting opinions of Judges Valticos and Makarczyk termed the measures taken against the first applicant, Helen Steel, 'so manifestly extreme' in proportion to her actions during the protest that a violation of Art 10 had occurred. The second applicant had taken part in a protest against the building of a motorway, placing herself in front of the earth-moving machinery in order to impede it. The Court found unanimously that her arrest also could be viewed as proportionate to the aim of preventing disorder, even though it accepted that the risk of immediate disorder was not so high as in the case of the first applicant.[485] The Court accepted the finding of the magistrates' court that there had been such a risk.

The third, fourth and fifth applicants were peacefully holding banners and handing out leaflets outside a fighter helicopter conference when they were arrested for breach of the peace. The Court found that there was no justification for their arrests at all since there was no suggestion of any threat of disorder.[486] A violation of Art 10 was therefore found in respect of those applicants. These findings draw a distinction between the first category of protest and the fourth and fifth forms – symbolic physical action and obstructive action

---

480 Above, fn 458.
481 This was acknowledged by the Court, para 101.
482 Paragraphs 104 and 107.
483 Paragraph 105. The Commission acknowledged (para 156) 'some disquiet as to the proportionality of a detention of this length' which continued long after the grouse shoot was over.
484 Paragraph 101.
485 Paragraph 109.
486 Paragraph 110.

– suggesting that interferences with protest as direct action may frequently fall within the national authorities' margin of appreciation. But, significantly, the findings also make it clear that the fourth and fifth forms constitute expressions of opinion and therefore fall within Arts 10 and 11. This was re-affirmed in *Hashman and Harrup v UK*.[487]

The stance of the Court in *Steel* in fact implies less tolerance of peaceful direct action than the stance taken in *Nicol*, since the Court required only an interference with the rights of others and the possibility of disorder in order to be satisfied regarding proportionality; no added requirement to show that the defendant rather than the other party was acting unreasonably was imposed. The dissenting minority judgments in *Steel* made an oblique reference to such a comparison in noting that the behaviour of the first applicant, albeit 'extreme', was aimed at preserving the life of an animal.[488] The findings of the Court provide little basis for curbing interference under the breach of the peace doctrine with certain forms of public protest of the direct action type, although they do require a re-structuring of the domestic scrutiny of such interference, which takes the primary right as the starting point. *Steel* clearly affords the domestic judiciary a wide discretion in interpreting the requirements of the Convention in an analogous case. In evaluating the risks posed by a protest, the courts might tend to adopt notions of deference to decisions of the executive in respect of the possibility of disorder in accordance with the tradition in such cases, and take the view that the courts should be reluctant to interfere with the decision of the police officer or magistrate (as the tribunal of fact) in question. A minimalist approach to Arts 10 and 11 would lead to a similar result. If *Steel* was simply applied regardless of the influence of the margin of appreciation, little protection would be available for most direct action forms of protest. But, following an activist approach, the domestic judiciary, faced with similar facts, but disapplying the margin of appreciation aspects of *Steel*, would find that the interference was unjustified since their review of the decisions of the police or of magistrates would be less restrained. Within this model, some interferences with freedom of expression would be allowed, where direct action was likely to provoke immediate disorder due to the degree of provocation offered, but the measures taken in response, such as the length of detention, would be much more strictly scrutinised for their proportionality with the aims pursued.

The decision in *Steel* is of most value in placing the form of protest most deserving of protection, peaceful persuasion, in a specially protected position. Therefore, it will be problematic, even within the 'review' or minimalist model, to uphold arrest or bind over decisions in such instances or in cases of the *Holmes v Bournemouth*[489] type. This would be a welcome restriction and clarification of the breach of the peace doctrine but, in terms of protecting public protest, it would achieve no more than *Nicol* has already done. Both *Steel* and *Nicol* leave open leeway for deciding when it should be found that protest, which has some provocative effect, should nevertheless be termed peaceful. In other words, in terms of the categories of protest indicated, their application to the second form of protest – insulting or offensive persuasion – is dependent on the degree of provocation. The findings in *Steel* impliedly drew a distinction in terms of reasonableness between action which is directly and physically provocative and speech which might have some

---

487 (2000) 8 BHRC 104; (1999) 30 EHRR 241.
488 Partly dissenting opinions of Judges Valticos and Makarczyk.
489 6 October 1993, unreported, DC.

provocative effect, but which could nevertheless be viewed as part of a peaceful protest. It is not clear that they simply drew a distinction between physical and verbal protest. Such a distinction would fail to take account of forms of hate speech which may be far more provocative to hearers than forms of physical obstruction such as the ones at issue in *Steel*. Thus, a minimalist approach to *Steel* would be to confine it to speech which had little provocative effect. In *Steel* itself, in respect of the successful applicants, there was no evidence that the audience in question – those participating in the fighter helicopter conference – were provoked. A traditionalist approach would be to defer to the opinion of the officer on the ground as to the likelihood that disorder would follow the provocation.

But a more activist approach would be to afford protection to insulting or offensive persuasion or symbolic direct action, following Steel, and this approach would also receive some endorsement from *Plattform 'Ärtze fur das Leben' v Austria*[490] which adopted a version of the *Beatty v Gillbanks*[491] approach. Such an approach to the decision in *Steel* was, in some respects, taken by Sedley LJ in *Redmond-Bate v DPP*[492] in the period before the HRA was fully in force. Ms Redmond-Bate and other women, a group of fundamentalist Christians, were preaching forcefully on the steps of Westminster Cathedral. A large crowd gathered, who were angered by their preaching. Fearing a breach of the peace, a police officer asked the women to desist; when they refused, he arrested them. The Divisional Court found that in the circumstances, two questions should be asked of the action of the police officer. First, was it reasonable to believe that a breach of the peace was about to be caused? Secondly, where was the threat coming from? These questions could have been answered by distinguishing the facts from those relating to the successful applications in *Steel* and bringing them, at the same time, within the rule from *Nicol*, on the basis that the women did in fact provoke their audience and could have been viewed as acting unreasonably since they continued to preach despite the growing restlessness of the crowd. It could have been said that the natural consequence of the lawful but arguably unreasonable conduct of the women was the provocation of others. Applying *Steel*, however, the Divisional Court found, in answer to both the questions posed, that there were no sufficient grounds on which to determine that a breach of the peace was about to be caused or, moreover, on which to determine that the threat was coming from Ms Redmond-Bate, bearing in mind the tolerance one would expect to be extended to offensive speech. Sedley LJ said: 'Free speech includes not only the inoffensive, but the irritating, the contentious, the eccentric, the heretical, the unwelcome and the provocative providing it does not tend to provoke violence. Freedom only to speak inoffensively is not worth having.'[493] He went on to find that the Crown Court had correctly directed itself that 'violence is not a natural consequence of what a person does unless it clearly interferes with the rights or liberties of others so as to make a violent reaction not wholly unreasonable'[494] and he emphasised that the court should make its own independent judgment of the reasonableness of the police officer's belief.

---

490 A 139 (1988), para 32; Judgment of 21 June 1988; 13 EHRR 204.
491 (1882) 9 QBD 308, discussed above, p 497.
492 (1999) *The Times*, 28 July; [1999] All ER (D) 864.
493 Transcript, para 12.
494 Transcript, para 16.

This decision simplified the tests from *Nicol* of determining which party was acting reasonably where one was provoked to violence and as to which was exercising rights. The key test put forward was one of reasonableness: a breach of the peace will occur where violence was threatened or provoked, in the sense of infringing rights or liberties, unless the provoked party acts wholly – not partly – unreasonably. Sedley LJ then categorised certain of the decisions mentioned above into those where the provoked party was reasonable or unreasonable, in order to offer some guidance on this matter. He placed *Beatty v Gillbanks* and *Percy v DPP* in the first category, but, strangely, put *Wise v Dunning* and *Duncan v Jones* in the second. In *Duncan*, there was little evidence on which to base an apprehension of a breach of the peace and it was unclear that persons provoked by the speech in question could be said to have acted reasonably. Thus, although *Redmond-Bate* applies *Steel* quite broadly, it still leaves some uncertainty as to the status of provocative speech; the test of reasonableness will be, it is suggested, no more certain in its application than the tests from *Nicol* and will therefore have some chilling effect on protest.

Indications of a more restrictive domestic approach also comes from *Bibby v Chief Constable of Essex*,[495] which is not a public protest case; it concerned the arrest of a bailiff who was seeking to seize goods. But various requirements were laid down in the findings of the Court of Appeal, which would be of significant applicability in a protest case. The threat to the peace must be real and present in order to justify depriving a person of his liberty when he is not himself at that point acting unlawfully. Following *Redmond-Bate*, the threat must come from the person under arrest, overturning *Kelly*. The other conditions confirmed those laid down in *Nicol* to the effect that the violence provoked must not be wholly unreasonable.

In the post-HRA era, a more activist approach to *Steel* would afford the substantive rights under Arts 10 and 11 greater weight in cases of persuasive or provocative speech by disallowing interferences with these forms of protest unless incitement to violence or to hatred of racial, religious or sexual groups had occurred. A presumption that it is normally unreasonable to be provoked to violence or the threat of it by speech could be imported into the doctrine, a stronger test than the one put forward by Sedley LJ. In response to the finding in *Steel* that breaching the peace is a criminal offence, it would appear that the courts will have to create a clearer distinction between conduct likely to cause a breach, allowing for a preventive arrest, and conduct actually amounting to a breach. The former could not, it seems, if *Steel* is followed on this point, lead to binding over, since no offence has been committed which would allow for this punishment. Since such preventive powers are frequently, although not exclusively, used where the arrestee may cause another to breach the peace, *Steel* might therefore herald a return to the more minimal interpretation in *Howell*, leaving the possibility of causing another to breach the peace to the statutory provisions discussed below, in particular ss 5 and 4A of the Public Order Act 1986 which cover much of the same area. Admittedly, ss 5 and 4A, unlike the breach of the peace doctrine, criminalise offensive speech *per se* without requiring a public order rationale. The 'victim' need only be distressed rather than likely to react violently. However, the nature of the language required for both provisions curtails their ambit, in contrast to the breach of the peace doctrine. Almost all the cases concerning peaceful

---

495 *The Times*, 24 April 2000.

persuasion discussed above, in which the doctrine was successfully invoked, would fall outside ss 5 and 4A, apart, probably, from *Wise v Dunning* in which abusive or insulting words or behaviour were used. The peaceful direct action cases of *Nicol* and *Percy* probably would not be covered, although they would fall within s 68 of the CJPOA, as discussed above. In other words, if the use of provocative speech requires a legal response at all, such a response should be left to those provisions which lay down a more precise test for liability than the breach of the peace doctrine.

But such determinations, which would have the effect of greatly narrowing down the doctrine, would not be fully rooted in the application of *Steel* or other analogous decisions at Strasbourg: they would have to be based largely on an appeal to a notional 'higher' standard of human rights, articulated by the general principles informing the Strasbourg jurisprudence, which might have been adhered to but for the margin of appreciation doctrine.[496] If one of the key principles at stake is the need to protect the communicative rights of minority groups, such as pacifists, animal rights or environmental activists, reliance might be placed, by analogy, on strong pronouncements of the need to protect minority rights and plurality within democracies which, as indicated above, are scattered across the Convention jurisprudence.[497]

6 CRIMINALISING PUBLIC DISORDER AND ANTI-SOCIAL BEHAVIOUR

Introduction

The criminalisation of low level forms of anti-social behaviour, begun under s 5 of the Public Order Act 1986, continued under s 154 of the CJPOA 1994,[498] and taken further under the Protection from Harassment Act 1997 and s 1 of the Crime and Disorder Act 1998, culminated for the present in s 41 of the Criminal Justice and Police Act 2001. These provisions target similar forms of anti-social behaviour which had previously been viewed as too trivial or too imprecise to attract criminal or, in most instances, civil liability. All are aimed at behaviour causing harassment, alarm or distress or, under the 1997 Act, amounting to harassment, and all are targeted at particular social problems, largely unrelated to public protest. Section 5 of the 1986 Act was aimed at the perceived problem of disturbance from football hooligans or late night rowdies; the 1997 Act at the problem of so called 'stalkers'; s 1 of the 1998 Act at anti-social neighbours. Section 41 of the 2001 Act was, however, aimed at the direct action form of protest and, in particular, at the actions of protesters against the use of animals in experiments at Huntingdon Life *Sciences*. All these provisions, due to their breadth, have a potential application to protest

---

496 Eg, the Court in *Handyside v UK* (1976) 1 EHRR 737, para 49 found, in a famous passage, that Art 10 is applicable 'not only to ideas that are ... regarded as inoffensive, but also to those which offend, shock or disturb', although in the particular instance, due to the operation of the margin of appreciation doctrine, the application failed.

497 Above, p 438.

498 Which inserted s 4A into the 1986 Act.

within all the categories indicated above,[499] probably not in all circumstances excluding the first – peaceful persuasion.

Ingredients of the offences

Threats, abuse, insults

The offences created require establishment of a minimal and imprecise actus reus. Section 5 is the lowest level public order offence contained in the 1986 Act and the most contentious, since it brings behaviour within the scope of the criminal law which was previously thought of as too trivial to justify the imposition of criminal liability.[500] It criminalises the person who 'uses threatening, abusive or insulting words or behaviour or disorderly behaviour' or 'displays any writing, sign or other visible representation which is threatening or abusive or insulting' which takes place within the 'hearing or sight of a person likely to be caused harassment, alarm or distress thereby'. The word 'likely' imports an objective test into the section: it is necessary to show that a person was present at the scene, but not that he or she actually experienced the feelings in question, although it must be shown that in all the circumstances, he or she would be likely to experience such feelings. In so showing, it is not necessary to call the person in question as a witness. In *Swanston v DPP*[501] it was found that if a bystander gives evidence to the effect that the 'victim' perceived the threatening, abusive or insulting words, then the court can draw the inference that they were so perceived. There is no need to aim the words or behaviour at a specific individual, so long as an individual can be identified and the inference can be drawn that he or she would have perceived the words or behaviour in question. It was determined in *DPP v Orum*[502] that a police officer may be the person caused harassment, alarm or distress but in such instances, Glidewell LJ thought it might be held that a police officer would be less likely to experience such feelings than an ordinary person. These two decisions enhance the ease with which this offence may be deployed, as does *DPP v Fidler*,[503] in which it was found that a person whose own behaviour would not satisfy the requirements of s 5 may be guilty of aiding and abetting this offence if he or she is part of a crowd who are committing it.

Whether the words used were insulting, etc, is a question of fact for the magistrates. The terms used must be given their ordinary meaning: *Brutus v Cozens*.[504] Following *Ambrose*,[505] rude or offensive words or behaviour may not necessarily be insulting, while mere swearing may not fall within the meaning of 'abusive'. However, threatening gestures such as waving a fist might suffice. Whether or not the words are insulting is not a purely subjective test and therefore the mere fact that the recipient finds them so will not be sufficient. The House of Lords so held in *Brutus v Cozens*[506] in respect of disruption

---

499 See p 424.
500 For background to s 5, see Law Commission Report No 123, *Offences Relating to Public Order*, 1983.
501 (1997) *The Times*, 23 January.
502 [1988] 3 All ER 449.
503 [1992] 1 WLR 91.
504 [1973] AC 854; [1972] 2 All ER 1297; [1972] 3 WLR 521, HL.
505 (1973) 57 Cr App R 538.
506 [1973] AC 854; [1972] All ER 1297; [1972] 3 WLR 521; (1973) 57 Cr App R 538, HL.

of a tennis match involving a South African player by an anti-apartheid demonstrator. Some of the crowd were provoked to violence, but the conduct of the demonstrator could not be described as insulting. The conviction of the defendant under the predecessor of s 4 was therefore overturned. The test appears to be whether a reasonable person sharing the characteristics of the persons at whom the words in question are directed would find them insulting. However, whether or not the speaker knows that such persons will hear the words is immaterial as far as this ingredient of s 4 is concerned (*Jordan v Burgoyne*).[507] It was found in *DPP v Fidler*[508] that a person whose own behaviour would not satisfy the requirements of s 5 may be guilty as aiding and abetting this offence if he or she is part of a crowd who are committing it.

Thus, taken at its lowest level, s 5 criminalises a person who displays disorderly behaviour calculated to create harassment. Section 5 was included as a measure aimed at anti-social behaviour generally, but its breadth and vagueness have given rise to the criticism that the police have been handed a very broad power.[509] The criminalisation of speech which causes such low level harm as alarm or distress may be contrary to dicta of the European Court of Human Rights in *Müller v Switzerland*[510] to the effect that the protection of free speech extends equally to ideas which 'offend, shock or disturb'.[511] Section 5, far from being confined to restraining rowdy hooligans, has been used against political speech. In the so called *Madame M* case, four students were prosecuted for putting up a satirical poster depicting Margaret Thatcher as a 'sadistic dominatrix';[512] the students were acquitted, but the fact that such a case could even be brought in a democracy is highly disturbing. This was not an isolated use of s 5 against political speech: protesters outside abortion clinics have been prosecuted[513] and, in Northern Ireland, s 5 has been used against a poster depicting youths stoning a British Saracen with a caption proclaiming 'Ireland: 20 years of resistance'.[514] Similarly, as one commentator noted when the Act was passed: 'In the context of pickets shouting or gesturing at those crossing their picket lines, the elements of this offence will usually be established without difficulty.'[515]

Further, the sheer number of prosecutions being brought under s 5 conclusively demonstrates that the police are not showing restraint in using this area of the Act. The old s 5 offence under the Public Order Act 1936, an offence with a higher harm threshold,[516] accounted for the majority of the 8,194 charges brought in connection with the miners' strike of 1984. In a survey of 470 public order cases in 1988, conducted that year, in two

---

507 [1963] 2 QB 744; [1963] 2 All ER 225.

508 [1992] 1 WLR 91; for comment see Smith, JC [1992] Crim LR 63.

509 See comment on s 5 [1987] PL 202.

510 (1991) 13 EHRR 212.

511 It should be noted that in *Brutus v Cozens* [1973] AC 854; [1972] 2 All ER 1297; [1972] 3 WLR 521; (1973) Cr App R 538, HL, Lord Reid said that the previous Public Order Act 1936, s 5 was 'not designed to penalise the expressions of opinion that happen to be disagreeable, distasteful or even offensive, annoying or distressing'. The new s 5 offence precisely does cover 'distressing' speech, but use could be made of Lord Reid's *dicta* to argue that expression of opinions *per se* should not be criminalised.

512 Thornton, P, *Decade of Decline: Civil Liberties in the Thatcher Years*, 1990, p 37.

513 *DPP v Fidler* [1992] 1 WLR 91; *DPP v Clarke* [1992] Crim LR 60.

514 Reported in *The Independent*, 12 September 1988; mentioned in Ewing and Gearty, *op cit*, fn 1, 1990, p 123.

515 Williams, *op cit*, fn 5.

516 It was similar to the offence which replaced it (the 1986 Act, s 4).

police force areas, it was found that 56% of the sample led to charges under s five. Research has also shown that during the period 1986–88, the number of charges brought for public order offences doubled and this was thought to be due not to increased unrest, but to the existence of the new offences, particularly s 5 with its low level of harm.[517]

The *mens rea* requirements of the s 5 offence may offer a degree of protection to free expression. Under s 6(4), it must be established that the defendant intended his words, etc, to be threatening, abusive or insulting or was aware that they might be. In *DPP v Clarke*[518] it was further found that to establish liability, it is insufficient to show only that the defendant intended or was aware that he might cause harassment, alarm or distress; it must also be shown that he intended his conduct to be threatening, abusive or insulting, or was aware that it might be. Both mental states have to be established independently. Thus, showing that the defendant was aware that he might cause distress was not found to be equivalent to showing that he was aware that his speech or behaviour might be insulting. Applying this subjective test, the magistrates acquitted the defendants and this decision was upheld on appeal. Using this test, it was found that anti-abortion protesters had not realised that their behaviour in shouting anti-abortion slogans, displaying plastic models of foetuses and pictures of dead foetuses would be threatening, abusive or insulting. This decision allows those who believe fervently in their cause, and therefore fail to appreciate that their protest may insult or offend others, to escape liability. It therefore places a significant curb on the ability of ss 5 and 4A to interfere with Art 10 and Art 11 rights. Persons participating in forceful demonstrations may sometimes be able to show that behaviour which could be termed disorderly and which might be capable of causing harassment to others, was intended only to make a point and that it had not been realised that others might find it threatening, abusive or insulting. Once a particular group of protesters has been prosecuted, however, and it has been found, as in *Clarke*, that others found their protest threatening, abusive or insulting, the subjective element of the mens rea will be in future readily made out, even if the instant prosecution fails. The burden imposed by the subjective test for intention or awareness is to be welcomed, since it means that an offence which strikes directly at freedom of expression and can only doubtfully be justified is harder to make out.

Section 154 of the CJPOA 1994 inserted s 4A into the 1986 Act, thereby providing a new and wide area of liability which to some extent overlaps with s 5. Section 4A of the 1986 Act criminalises threatening, abusive, insulting words or behaviour or disorderly behaviour which causes a person harassment, alarm or distress thereby. Thus, the *actus reus* under s 4A is the same as that under s 5 with the proviso that the harm in question must actually be caused as opposed to being likely to be caused. The *mens rea* differs somewhat from that under s 5, since the defendant must intend the person in question to suffer harassment, alarm or distress. Section 4A provides another possible level of liability with the result that using offensive words is now imprisonable, without any requirement (as under s 4, below) to show that violence was intended or likely to be caused. It may therefore offend against the protection for freedom of speech under Art 10 of the European Convention on Human Rights which, as pointed out above, clearly includes protection for forms of forceful or offensive speech.

---

517 Newburn, T *et al*, 'Policing the streets' (1990) 29 HORB 10 and 'Increasing public order' (1991) 7 Policing 22; quoted in Bailey, Harris and Jones, *op cit*, fn 1, pp 229–30.
518 [1992] Crim LR 60.

Section 4 of the Act covers somewhat more serious behaviour than s 5. It is couched in the same terms except for the omission of 'disorderly behaviour', but instead of showing that a person present was likely to be caused harassment, etc, it is necessary to show 'intent to cause that person to believe that immediate unlawful violence will be used against him or another by any person or to provoke the immediate use of unlawful violence by that person or another or whereby that person is likely to believe that such violence will be used or it is likely that such violence will be provoked'. One or more of these four possibilities must be present. The behaviour in question must be specifically directed towards another person. If the defendant does not directly approach the person being threatened, he or she might be unlikely to apprehend immediate violence. However, there might remain the possibility that the defendant intended his or her words to provoke others to violence against the victim. Under s 6(3), it must also be established that the defendant intended his words, etc, to be threatening, abusive or insulting or was aware that they might be.

It was found in *Horseferry Road Metropolitan Stipendiary Magistrate ex p Siadatan*[519] that 'violence' in this context must mean immediate and unlawful violence. The case arose from publication and distribution of *The Satanic Verses* by Salman Rushdie. The applicants alleged that the book contained abusive and insulting writing whereby it was likely that unlawful violence would be provoked contrary to s 4. On appeal from the decision of the magistrates not to issue a summons against the distributors of the books, Penguin Books, Watkins LJ found:

> We find it most unlikely that Parliament could have intended to include among sections which undoubtedly deal with conduct having an immediate impact on bystanders, a section creating an offence for conduct which is likely to lead to violence at some unspecified time in the future.

The finding that the violence provoked must be immediate, although not necessarily instantaneous, led to dismissal of the appeal. This strict interpretation was confirmed in *Winn v DPP*[520] and it was made plain that the prosecution must ensure that all the ingredients of the particular form of the offence charged under s 4 are present. The appellant threatened and abused a Mr Duncan who was attempting to serve a summons on him. On appeal, the ingredients of the s 4 offence were considered. It was clear from the provision of s 7(2) of the Act that s 4 creates only one offence; however, it is clear that the offence can be committed in one of four ways. Common to all four are the requirements, first, that the accused must intend or be aware that his words or behaviour are or may be threatening, abusive or insulting (s 6(3), which governs the *mens rea* requirement) and secondly, that they must be directed to another person. The offence charged included a statement of the required intention and was based on the fourth way it could be committed: that he used threatening and abusive words and behaviour whereby it was likely that violence would be provoked. The charge, therefore, required proof of a likelihood that Mr Duncan would be provoked to immediate unlawful violence and as there was no evidence to that effect, the direction to the justices was that the charge under s 4 should have been dismissed. Had the charge related to the first form of the offence – 'intent to cause that person to believe that immediate unlawful violence will be

---

519 [1991] 1 QB 260; [1991] 1 All ER 324; [1990] 3 WLR 1006.
520 (1992) 142 NLJ 527.

used against him' – it might have succeeded. It should be noted that such intent must be shown in addition to the *mens rea* under s 6(3).

The decision in *Siadatan* places a curb on the use of s 4A which might otherwise have occurred under the HRA. As it currently stands, it is clear that the ingredients of this offence relate to a much higher harm threshold than those of ss 4A and 5; therefore, although its use may on occasion be viewed as creating an interference with the Art 10 rights of protesters, the interference is likely to be proportionate to the aim pursued.

Harassment

Section 41 of the Criminal Justice and Police Act 2001 clearly draws on the ingredients of ss 5 and 4, although there are also significant differences. There are also similarities with the offences under s 14C of the 1986 Act and s 69 of the 1994 Act. Section 41 allows a constable to give any direction to persons, including a direction to leave the scene where they are outside or in the vicinity of a dwelling, if the constable reasonably believes (a) that they are seeking to persuade a person living at the dwelling not to do something that he/she has a right to do or to do something she/he is not under any obligation to do, and (b) that the presence of the persons (normally protesters) is likely to cause harassment, alarm or distress to the person living at the residence. Disobedience of a direction is an arrestable offence.

Section 41 is an offence with a minimal *actus reus*, as is apparent when it is compared with the requirements of s 5 of the 1986 Act or ss 69 and 68 of the 1994 Act. The requirement that the words or conduct should be abusive, etc, in s 5 is missing; the requirements of ss 69 or 68 that the persons in question should be trespassing and must do something intended to be obstructive or intimidatory or disruptive are also absent. But s 41 is similar to s 69 and a number of the other recent offences discussed in this chapter in that it conflates the exercise of police powers with the substantive offence. The key limiting requirement is that the persons must be outside or in the vicinity of a dwelling, although the term 'the vicinity' is open to quite a wide interpretation. The need for the introduction of this new offence must be questioned, bearing in mind that ss 5 or 4A could be used against intimidation by protesters gathered outside the home of the person targeted. The offence of harassment under the 1997 Act would also be available.

Section 1 of the 1997 Act defines harassment as a course of conduct which a reasonable person would consider amounted to harassment of another where the harasser knows or ought to know that this will be its effect; s 2 makes harassment an offence. An interim injunction, breach of which is an offence (s 3(6)) punishable by up to 5 years' imprisonment (s 3(9)), can be obtained under s 3 in civil proceedings. No definition of a course of conduct which might amount to harassment is offered. Section 1 of the 1998 Act provides a penalty of a maximum of 5 years' imprisonment for failing to obey an order obtained on the civil standard of proof,[521] forbidding any form of 'anti-social' behaviour,[522] defined under s 1(1)(a) as behaving: 'in an anti-social manner, that is to say in a manner that caused or was likely to cause harassment, alarm and distress to one or more persons' other than those of the same household as the defendant.

---

521 According to the 1998 Magistrates' Courts Rules applicable to these orders.
522 Section 1(10)(b).

The defence of reasonableness assumes especial significance in relation to the 1997 and 1998 provisions, since in contrast to the earlier ones, there is either no need to establish *mens rea* or its establishment is likely to have little inhibitory effect. Thus, the decision in *Clarke* will not have a ready application under those Acts. Sections 1 and 2 of the 1997 Act makes it a requirement of establishing the offence that the harasser knows or ought to know that the course of conduct amounts to harassment. However, since an interim injunction can be obtained under s 3 of the Act, in *ex parte* proceedings, the establishment of that state of mind would be aided in proceedings for its breach once it had been served on the defendant. Breach of such an injunction is punishable by five years' imprisonment. Therefore, although prima facie the 1997 Act imports a *mens rea* requirement, the existence of punishment on the civil standard of proof allows for its circumvention. Criminal proceedings relating to the same course of conduct, but under s 2, may also be affected, as explained below, once an injunction has been obtained. Section 1 of the 1998 Act requires no circumvention of *mens rea* requirements, since it merely abandons them. They could be re-introduced only in the form of a 'reversed' *mens rea*, under the defence of reasonableness, unless, in a public protest case, with a view to narrowing down the potential of this section to interfere with Art 6, 10 or 11 rights, a judge was prepared to import the additional *mens rea* element identified in *Clarke*.

These matters are linked to the key difference between these two recent provisions and the previous ones – their hybrid nature in allowing for criminal sanctions, including imprisonment, on the civil standard of proof for breach of an injunction or order. The 1997 Act allows for an injunction to be obtained at the instigation of the 'victim' in *ex parte* proceedings, merely on his or her affidavit. This probably explains why the 1997 Act is proving to offer a primary means of curbing various forms of protest. It provides a contrast to ss 5 and 4A of the 1986 Act, which are widely used, but not, research suggests, frequently in the context of political protest.[523] Unlike the 1997 Act, they appear, on the whole, to have been used to target those at whom they were originally aimed.

The features of the 1997 Act which have made it attractive as a measure to be used against protesters, are, it should be noted, also present in the 1998 Act in the sense that the subject of the protest can (indirectly) instigate proceedings[524] and criminal sanctions, including imprisonment, may be imposed on the civil standard.

Defences of reasonableness

These statutory provisions all provide defences of reasonableness, none of which is defined or specifically aimed at protecting expression.[525] Demonstrators shouting at

---

523 Waddington explains the reluctance to arrest in this context on the basis that it risks sparking off hostility among other protesters and can create trouble later, since the arrest may be scrutinised in court: see *op cit*, fn 1, pp 54–55. Independent records of arrests may be available since supporters of the protest may photograph them and reporters may well also be present. Records and reports of arrests may help to lead to acquittals and may fuel public criticism of the police. This would be unlikely to be the case in relation to the arrest of, eg, drunken football supporters.

524 The application for the order is made by the 'relevant authority' under s 1(1), but it may be triggered off by allegations made to the police or housing authority.

525 Under s 5(3)(c) and s 4A(3)(b) of the 1986 Act, s 1(3) of the 1997 Act and s 1(5) of the 1998 Act. It may be noted that under the 1997 and 1998 provisions, the 'defence' operates as partially reversed *actus reus*, in the sense that if the defence is proved (the burden of so doing is on the defendant), then harassment or anti-social behaviour is not established.

passers-by to support their cause, whose behaviour could readily be termed threatening or disorderly, etc, and likely to cause one of the passers-by harassment, distress or alarm,[526] will have a defence under s 5(3)(c) if they can show that their behaviour was reasonable. The Act gives no guidance as to the meaning of the term, but it was determined in *DPP v Clarke*[527] that the defence is to be judged objectively, and it will therefore depend on what a bench of magistrates considers reasonable. In that case, the behaviour of the protesters outside an abortion clinic was not found to be reasonable. The use of pictures and models of aborted foetuses appeared to contribute to this conclusion.

This decision, which would clearly also apply to charges under s 4A, and, where appropriate, to s 12(3) of the 1997 Act and s 1(5) of the 1998 Act as well, obviously does not give much guidance to protesters seeking to determine beforehand the limits or meaning of 'reasonable' protest. As a deliberately ambiguous term, it obviously leaves enormous discretion to the judiciary to adopt approaches to its interpretation in accordance with Arts 10 and 11 as interpreted in *Steel*, ranging from the minimalist to the activist. Under the former approach, it might be found that only innocuous, peaceful persuasion could be termed reasonable. Such a finding might be of value where, for example, a large number of groups were served with injunctions under s 3 of the 1997 Act since it might serve to allow differentiation between those whose peaceful persuasion had nevertheless been viewed by its target as 'harassment' and those groups which had adopted more forceful means. But a more 'activist' interpretation of this defence would have to find a basis in the general principles articulated above,[528] especially applicable in relation to protest expressing minority viewpoints. This would be a matter of significance, since such viewpoints may be unlikely to be favourably received by others. Thus, offensive words used by protesters could be found to fall within this defence on the basis that in the context of a particular demonstration which had a legitimate political aim, such behaviour was acceptable and therefore reasonable. An argument for giving such a wide interpretation to the term 'reasonable' can be supported on the basis that, as argued above, to criminalise such behaviour would arguably amount to a very far reaching curb on the freedom to protest which might be found to be in breach of Art 10 or Art 11, bearing in mind the need to interpret statutory provisions in conformity with the Convention.

Impact of the HRA

Suggestions as to the effect of the HRA on ss 5, 4A and 4 have already been made. Section 5 is the most problematic provision, as indicated. The similar offence under s 41 of the 2001 Act is also problematic in the sense that it hits directly at peaceful protest – protest that need not be abusive, etc, but is aimed only at persuading. The protesters need have no intention of causing harassment, alarm or distress so long as a constable reasonably believes that the target of the protest might experience those feelings. In catching peaceful protest, this offence comes directly into conflict with Arts 10 and 11. However, s 41 can also be viewed as protecting Art 8 rights. However, a court would be expected to consider

---

526 It is not necessary to prove that anyone actually experienced harassment, merely that this was likely.
527 Above, fn 518.
528 See above, pp 421–26.

the extent to which those rights could be said to be at stake and the proportionality of the police response, in using s 41 as opposed to a lesser measure.

The relevance of the civil standard of proof in the 1997 and 1998 Acts is likely to raise questions about the compatibility of these provisions with Art 6. At Strasbourg, the fact that national law classifies an act as non-criminal is relevant but not conclusive. In *Benham v UK*,[529] the leading case on 'criminal charge', the Court found that although the legislation in question[530] clearly did not create a criminal offence in UK law, it should be accounted criminal for Art 6(1) purposes. The proceedings against the applicant[531] had been brought by the public authorities; the proceedings had some punitive elements and the bringing of them implied fault on the part of the applicant. Further, the penalty was severe (committal to prison for up to three months).[532]

Under the HRA the national court, however, may be placed in a difficulty where s 3 of the 1997 or s 1 of the 1998 Act classifies an act as non-criminal, but Art 6 suggests that it is criminal. Anti-social behaviour orders, according to the applicable 1998 Magistrates' Courts Rules, will be made on the civil standard of proof, no legal aid is available, and under s 1(10)(b) of the 1998 Act, there is the possibility of 5 years' imprisonment if the order is breached. If, for example, a defendant in a magistrates' court raises the issue of the compatibility of an order under s 1 of the 1998 Act with Art 6, it might be necessary to stay the proceedings while the issue is dealt with on an appeal by way of case stated. Owing to the provision of s 3 of the HRA, it would appear that a national court could not merely redefine ss 1 and 2 as creating criminal offences if that involved finding that Art 6 and ss 1 and 2 were incompatible.

The extent to which the hybrid nature of s 3 of the 1997 Act has the potential to allow interferences with the Art 6, 10 and 11 guarantees was illustrated in two recent, significant decisions. In *Huntingdon Life Sciences Ltd and Another v Curtin and Others*[533] the company (HLS) obtained an *ex parte* injunction against six groups under s 3 of the Act, which prohibited conduct amounting to harassment within the terms of the Act, or entering HLS research sites. HLS was engaged in animal experimentation and was the subject of a campaign by a number of animal rights' organisations. One of the defendants, the British Union of Anti-Vivisectionists (BUAV), a peaceful campaigning group, applied to have the injunction varied so that it was not covered. Eady J found, in the *inter partes* proceedings, that the plaintiff had not provided sufficient evidence to support the claim that the defendants should be covered by the injunction. He also considered it unfortunate that the provisions of the Act were couched in such wide terms that they could appear to cover 'the rights of political protest and public demonstration which are so much a part of our democratic tradition'. This judgment clearly recognised, as the legislators did not, the general need to seek to delineate forms of anti-social behaviour sufficiently clearly so as to avoid infringing the rights in question.

---

529 (1996) 22 EHRR 293. See also *Lauko v Slovakia* (1999) 1 EHRLR 105 in which it was found that a penalty for anti-social behaviour was inherently criminal in nature.

530 The Local Government Changes for England (Community Charge and Council Tax, Administration and Enforcement) Regulations 1995, SI 1995/247, s 41.

531 In respect of default on payment of the community charge or poll tax.

532 The magistrates could only exercise their power of committal on a finding of wilful refusal to pay or culpable neglect (para 56 of the judgment).

533 (1998) 3(1) J Civ Lib 37.

The BUAV was exempted from the injunction, but the case illustrates the ease of obtaining interim injunctions against a wide range of persons and groups in these circumstances. In practice, once such an injunction is obtained, the police are likely to enforce it against a number of persons who are not covered or are only doubtfully covered by it, on the basis that they appear to be acting under the authority of, or in concert with, one of groups which are enjoined. This will commonly occur in such situations.

A rather similar situation arose in *DPP v Moseley, Woodling and Selvanayagam*.[534] One of the defendants, Ms Selvanayagam, had been served with an *ex parte* interim injunction under s 3 of the 1997 Act, which she was seeking to challenge. After she had been served with the injunction, she and the other two defendants continued to demonstrate peacefully against the fur trade, at a fur farm. They were arrested and charged with the offence under s 2 of the 1997 Act. All of them relied on the defence that the conduct was reasonable in the circumstances under s 1(3)(c), and this defence was accepted by the magistrate. He further found that the injunction was obtained only on the basis of affidavit evidence and could not as a matter of law preclude the finding of reasonableness. Therefore, he acquitted all three. On appeal, the High Court found that pursuit of a course of harassment in breach of an injunction would preclude establishing the defence of reasonableness and that the magistrate had not been entitled to go behind the terms of the injunction. The other two respondents were not named in the injunction and there was no basis for considering that they were acting in concert with Ms Selvanayagam. Therefore, they were not precluded from putting forward the defence of reasonableness. Accordingly, Ms Selvanayagam was convicted under s 2.

The most striking feature of this case is the acceptance that a central issue in a criminal trial can be predetermined in civil proceedings, particularly uncontested *ex parte* proceedings, in which the only evidence is 'on the papers'. The Act, as indicated, provides a remedy of imprisonment for breach of an injunction; there is therefore no reason why its breach should also be determinative of separate criminal proceedings. This matter clearly raises Art 6 issues; it comes close to obtaining a conviction 'on the papers' since, if an injunction has been previously obtained, the burden on the prosecution will be considerably eased. Although Strasbourg has not dealt with the precise point regarding the usurpation of the function of the criminal court by previous civil proceedings, it has made it clear in a series of cases that the use of written statements from witnesses who are not present at the trial will contravene Art 6(3)(d) except in limited, exceptional circumstances.[535] It may be said that an injunction obtained at an uncontested hearing is analogous to such statements. The use of such an injunction to predetermine a key issue in the criminal trial might also be viewed as infringing the presumption of innocence under Art 6(2) since the defendant may be confronted with an irrebuttable presumption against her. In *Salabiaku v France*[536] it was found that while Art 6(2) 'does not ... regard presumptions of fact or of law provided for in the criminal law with indifference', it permits the operation of such presumptions against the accused so long as the law in question confines such presumptions 'within reasonable limits which take into account

534 Judgment of 9 June 1999; reported [1999] J Civ Lib 390.
535 *Unterpinger v Austria* (1991) 13 EHRR 175; *Van Mechelen v Netherlands* (1998) 25 EHRR 647; *Kostovski v Netherlands* (1989) 12 EHRR 434; *Delta v France* (1993) 16 EHRR 574; *Doorson v Netherlands* (1996) 22 EHRR 330.
536 (1988) 13 EHRR 379.

the importance of what is at stake and maintain the rights of the defence'.[537] It is debatable whether the rights of the defence can be said to be preserved where no means at all of going behind an injunction is available.

Clearly, the use of injunctions as in *Huntingdon Life Sciences* and *Moseley* represents an interference with the Art 10 and 11 rights of the protesters, which must be justified under the para 2 exceptions. The fact that the injunction operates as a prior restraint is not conclusive of the issue since, as indicated above, Strasbourg has accepted that the use of such restraint may be justified in certain circumstances in public protest cases.[538] The leading case on prior restraints is *Observer and Guardian v UK*,[539] in which the Court considered the compatibility with Art 10 of interim injunctions preventing those newspapers from publishing *Spycatcher* material. The Court laid down the basic principle that: 'while Art 10 does not in terms prohibit the imposition of prior restraints on publication ... the dangers inherent in [them] are such that they call for the most careful scrutiny on the part of the Court ...'[540] These findings were based on the perishable nature of news, a relevant consideration on the facts. But there is no reason to view the stance of the Court as precluding consideration of other values which are threatened by the use of injunctions as a prior restraint on expression, bearing in mind the arguments set out at the beginning of this chapter as to the value of public protest. Injunctions may not prevent the protest completely, but they may prevent it from being effective by excluding it from the place where it will have most impact. Moreover, arguments opposed to prior restraint need not rest only on values associated with expression, but may take into account the value of rights of participation in the political process, and such arguments may be raised under Art 11. In other words, while it might be argued that the terms of an injunction under s 3 of the 1997 Act preventing protesters from demonstrating, say, outside the new detention centre for asylum seekers at Oakington, Cambridge on the anniversary of its opening, would not prevent them from distributing leaflets or holding a peaceful protest elsewhere, it would undermine the exercise of rights of effective expression and of participation in the political process.

Such arguments, where linked to Art 10, could be given added impact by invoking s 12 of the HRA in relation to the use of *ex parte* injunctions in cases analogous to *Moseley*.[541] Section 12(1) provides: 'this section applies if a court is considering whether to grant any relief which, if granted, might affect the exercise of the Convention right to freedom of expression ... (2) if the person against whom the application for relief is made (the respondent) is neither present nor represented no such relief is to be granted unless the court is satisfied ... that the applicant has taken all practical steps to notify the respondent or that there are compelling reasons why the respondent should not be notified.' Under s 12(4) 'the court must have particular regard to the importance of the convention right to freedom of expression ...'. Section 12(2) provides a strong adjuration against the use of *ex parte* injunctions which, it is suggested, is as applicable in public

---

537 See p 388, para 28.
538 See, eg, the decision of the Commission in *Christians Against Racism and Fascism v UK* Appl No 8440/78 (1980) 21 DR 138.
539 (1991) 14 EHRR 153; for comment see Leigh, I, '*Spycatcher* in Strasbourg' [1992] PL 200.
540 *Ibid*, para 60.
541 See also the discussion of injunctions more generally in Leigh, I and Lustgarten, L, 'Making rights real: the courts, remedies and the Human Rights Act' (1999) 58 CLJ 509.

protest cases as it is in those for which it was intended – injunctions against publications by the media. It may be noted that Art 10 only is referred to and therefore, as far as s 12 is concerned, the Art 11 argument would be irrelevant, an unfortunate effect of seeking to afford added weight to the Art 10 rights of one group – the media – while disregarding those of another – protesters. Section 12 may have been limited in its application to civil proceedings[542] with the intention, *inter alia*, of excluding public protest from its ambit. If so, the failure to take account of the use of injunctions and orders obtained in civil proceedings in protest cases may have led to this unintended result.

Section 12 may apply to orders made under s 1 of the 1998 Act, which potentially could also operate as prior restraints. The procedure to be followed appears to allow the grant of *ex parte* orders, but the defendant should be informed before the hearing that an application for an order has been made.[543] In a public protest case, the defendant would be likely to attend the hearing in order to raise the question of the interference with Art 10 and 11 rights which would occur if the order was made. Section 12(2) would not therefore normally be of relevance, but s 12(4) would be, and might tip the scales against the grant of an order in a protest case.

The arguments which will be raised under the HRA in relation to injunctions or anti-social behaviour orders when used in protest cases, will seek to create a clear distinction, which the architects of the 1997 Act and s 1 of the 1998 Act failed to create, between their operation in relation to those at whom they were targeted, and protesters. Under the activist model, such orders or injunctions would be subject to strict scrutiny under Arts 6, 10 and 11. The Art 8 rights, if in question, of those subject to the protest would also be relevant. Where an order or injunction was issued, the result might be that it would be carefully limited in order to answer to the strict requirements of proportionality. This can equally be said of ss 5 and 4A of the 1986 Act: a key distinction could thereby be created between their application to hooliganism and to protesters.

Public nuisance

The statutory offences discussed bear similarities with the common law doctrine of public nuisance, which has occasionally been used against public protest. This common law offence will arise if something occurs which inflicts damage, injury or inconvenience on all members of a class who come within the sphere or neighbourhood of its operation.[544] Liability for committing a public nuisance may arise by blocking the highway; however, according to *Clarke (No 2)*,[545] the disruption caused must amount to an unreasonable user of the highway in order to found such liability. Thus, once obstruction has been shown, the question of reasonableness arises. It would appear from *News Group Newspapers Limited v SOGAT*[546] that to cause a minor disruption for a legitimate purpose such as a march does not constitute an unreasonable user of the highway and will not therefore

---

542 Under s 12(5).
543 Magistrates' Courts (Sex Offender and Anti-Social Behaviour Orders) Rules 1998.
544 See Halsbury's Laws of England, 4th edn, Vol 34, para 305. For discussion of the offence see Spencer, JR [1989] CLJ 55.
545 [1964] 2 QB 315; [1963] 3 All ER 884, CA.
546 [1986] ICR 716; [1986] IRLR 337.

amount to a nuisance. It might seem that an assembly could not constitute a reasonable user of the highway under the Highways Act and yet nevertheless amount to a public nuisance. However, *dicta* in *Gillingham BC v Medway Dock Co*[547] suggest that this might, exceptionally, be possible.

Public nuisance, as a common law doctrine of a broad and imprecise nature, might not meet the requirement of 'prescribed by law' under Arts 10 and 11. Moreover, given its lack of precision and the lack of any defence of reasonableness it is suggested that, in satisfying their duty to observe proportionality under Arts 10 and 11, in pursuance of their duty under s 6 of the HRA, the police should not employ a common law offence of this width when a more precisely defined statutory offence – arising under s 137 of the Highways Act – is available. It is suggested, therefore, that this offence should not be used in future against assemblies on the highway.

Private common law remedies

Apart from control by the police, meetings and demonstrations can be prevented or curbed by private persons who seek injunctions to that end.[548] An interim injunction may be obtained very quickly in a hearing in which the other party is not represented. Even if a permanent injunction is not eventually granted, the aim of the demonstration may well have been destroyed by that time. In *Hubbard v Pitt*,[549] the defendants mounted a demonstration outside an estate agent in order to protest at what was seen as the ousting of working class tenants in order to make way for higher income buyers, thereby effecting a change in the character of the area. They therefore picketed the estate agents. The plaintiffs sought an injunction to prevent this on various grounds, including that of nuisance. At first instance, it was held that a stationary meeting would not constitute a reasonable user of the Highway and the grant of the interim injunction was upheld by the Court of Appeal, Lord Denning dissenting on the ground that the right to demonstrate is so closely analogous to freedom of speech that it should be protected.

Under the HRA, the use of such injunctions would raise a number of issues. They resemble injunctions available under s 3 of the 1997 Act. However, since they are based on the common law, s 3 of the HRA does not apply. Section 6 of the HRA does not apply directly unless the party seeking the injunction is a public authority or a private body discharging a public function. In *Hubbard*, those seeking the injunctions would not have fallen within either of those categories. But, as Chapter 4 indicated, s 6 has implications even for private parties.[550] Thus, the Strasbourg protest jurisprudence should be taken into account when considering the grant of an injunction in similar circumstances, arguably even where the common law is not ambiguous.

---

547 [1992] 3 All ER 931.

548 For discussion of such use of injunctions see Wallington, 'Injunctions and the right to demonstrate' [1976] CLJ 82. For discussion of their use in the context of labour disputes see (1973) 2 ILJ 213; Miller, *Contempt of Court*, 1989, pp 412–22.

549 [1976] QB 142.

550 See pp 161–64.

7 RIOT, VIOLENT DISORDER AND AFFRAY

Serious offences under the 1986 Act

Section 9 of the Public Order Act 1986 abolishes the common law offences of riot, unlawful assembly and affray and replaces them with similar statutory offences of riot (s 1), violent disorder (s 2) and affray (s 3).[551] Each of these offences may be committed in a public or a private place and it is not necessary that any person should actually have feared unlawful violence. Violent disorder would be most commonly used against unruly demonstrations, since it can be committed by words alone.

In order to establish an affray, it must first be shown that the defendant used or threatened unlawful violence towards another, secondly that his conduct was such as would cause a person of reasonable firmness present at the scene to fear for his personal safety and thirdly, under s 6(2), that he intended to use or threaten violence or was aware that his conduct might be violent or threaten violence. Under s 3(3), a threat cannot be made by the use of words alone. A demonstration in which threatening gestures were used might fulfil the first limb of s 3(1), but a strong argument can be advanced that it does not fulfil the second. If the gestures are part of a demonstration, it is probable that a person of reasonable firmness would not fear unlawful violence even though such a person might feel somewhat distressed. In *Taylor v DPP*,[552] Lord Hailsham, speaking of the common law offence, said 'the degree of violence must be such as to be calculated to terrify a person of reasonably firm character'. The Act, of course, refers to 'fear' as opposed to terror, but this ruling suggests that 'fear' should be interpreted restrictively.

Violent disorder is a completely new offence which was aimed in part at curtailing the activities of violent pickets. It is couched in the same terms as affray, but requires that three or more persons are involved. In order to establish violent disorder, it must first be shown that the defendant was one of three or more persons who used or threatened unlawful violence; secondly, that his conduct was such as would cause a person of reasonable firmness present at the scene to fear for his personal safety and thirdly, that the defendant himself actually used or threatened violence. The mental element under s 6(2) is the same as for affray. It may be argued that in the context of a demonstration, threatening gestures would not be termed a threat of violence. 'Violence' is a strong term which should not be watered down. In one respect, however, violent disorder is wider than affray since it may be committed by the use of words alone. If no threats are used by a defendant, he could not incur liability under s 2 even if it was found that he encouraged violence by others.[553]

Riot is the highest level public order offence created by the Act and is similar to the offence of violent disorder. However, it is narrower in that it requires that 12 or more persons who are present together use or threaten unlawful violence for a common purpose and that the defendant must actually use violence intending to do so or being

---

551 For comment on the new offences see 'Public Order Act offences' (1989) December LAG.

552 [1973] AC 964.

553 *McGuigan and Cameron* [1991] Crim LR 719; *Fleming and Robinson* [1989] Crim LR 658; cf *Caird* (1970) 54 Cr App R 499.

aware that his conduct may be violent. The requirement that the conduct of them (taken together) is such as would cause a person reasonable firmness present at the scene to fear for his personal safety is common to all three offences.

Impact of the HRA

The behaviour covered by these provisions will in general fall outside Art 11, which covers only peaceful assemblies, and possibly outside Art 10 as well. Even assuming that a disorderly assembly could be viewed as expressing an opinion and therefore as within the principle from *Steel*, the measures used against it would readily be viewed as proportionate to the aims of preserving order and public safety. However, the HRA may allow differentiation to be created between the application of these offences to protesters and to hooligans. In respect of protesters, the proportionality of the measures adopted would be considered, although, depending on the circumstances, the court might view the choice of measures as falling within the area of discretionary judgment likely to be accorded to the police.

8 COUNTER-TERRORIST POWERS

Introduction

As explained in Chapter 8 and in the introduction to this chapter, the Terrorism Act (TA) 2000 allows for the application of a number of provisions developed to combat Irish terrorism to be applied to a much wider range of targets. Since it is aimed at certain groups which put forward a political or ideological message,[554] a potential conflict with Art 10 under the HRA arises. In particular, it may be asked whether a proportionate response to the activities of a number of groups which fall within the s1(1) definition would not have been merely to use the ordinary criminal law against them, where necessary.

The offences discussed below could probably only have been introduced in the context of the threat from Irish terrorism, in some instances, as indicated in Chapter 8, at a time when the number of deaths from bomb attacks had been very high in the preceding years. At the time, MPs obviously could not know that in 2000 they would be asked to apply all these offences to groups which, in terms of their ability to create a serious threat to life and their willingness to do so, cannot be compared with the IRA. Moreover, certain of these offences appeared only in the Emergency Powers Act (applicable only in Northern Ireland), partly on the basis, as indicated above, that the threat was greatest in Northern Ireland and that without some apparently strong justification, they should not be included in the Prevention of Terrorism Act (PTA). Unless and until the Home Secretary proscribes a range of domestic animal rights and environmental groups, the proscription-related offences will not apply to them. But all the special terrorist offences

---

554 They must fulfil the other criteria of s 1(1); see Chapter 8, p 403.

and the special arrest and detention powers will apply,[555] meaning that although terrorist groups can lawfully exist, they are virtually precluded from exercising public freedom of expression.

Proscription-linked offences curbing assembly and protest

Under s 2(1)(a) of the PTA, it was also an offence to solicit support, other than money or other property, for a proscribed organisation. This is reproduced in s 12(1) and it is also an offence under s 12(2) for a person to arrange, manage or assist in arranging or managing a meeting which he knows is: '(a) to support a proscribed organisation, (b) to further the activities of a proscribed organisation, or (c) to be addressed by a person who belongs or professes to belong to a proscribed organisation.' It is an offence under s 12(3)(a) to address such a meeting in order to encourage support for a proscribed organisation or 'further its activities'. These are broadly drawn offences, although they do include a *mens rea* ingredient. Their impact on speech, association and assembly is clearly far reaching, bearing in mind the wide range of meetings, including very small, informal ones, covered. The fact that the majority of speakers at a meeting were opposed to the methods or aims of a proscribed group would not affect the liability of the organiser so long as he was aware that a speaker was a member, or professed member, of such an organisation, speaking in support of it. A meeting is defined as one at which three or more persons are present and there is no need for it to be open to the public. The maximum punishment for this offence is 10 years' imprisonment.

Restrictions on the use of badges or uniforms as signals of support for certain organisations are intended to have the dual effect of preventing communication – by those means – of the political message associated with the organisation and of tending to minimise the impression that the organisation is supported, thereby denying reassurance to its members, lowering their morale and preventing them from arousing public support. Under s 3 of the PTA 1989, it was an offence to 'wear any item which arouses a reasonable apprehension that a person is a member or supporter of a proscribed organisation'. This provision is reproduced in s 13 TA, which makes it an offence to wear an item of clothing, or wear, carry or display an article 'in such a way or in such circumstances as to arouse reasonable suspicion [that the person in question] is a member or supporter of a proscribed organisation'. Again, it is notable that no element of *mens rea* is included. The offence can be established on the basis of proof of reasonable suspicion alone and no defence is provided.

An overlapping offence arises under s 1 of the Public Order Act 1936: it is an offence to wear a uniform signifying association with any political organisation or with the promotion of any political object. Section 1 was invoked in *Whelan v DPP*[556] against leaders of a Provisional Sinn Fein protest march against internment in Northern Ireland, all of whom wore black berets while some wore dark glasses, dark clothing and carried Irish flags. It was found that, first, something must be 'worn' as apparel and secondly, that it must be a uniform. Something might amount to a uniform if worn by a number of persons in order to signify their association with each other or if commonly used by a

---

555 See Chapter 13.
556 [1975] QB 864.

certain organisation. By this means, the third requirement that the uniform must signal the wearer's association with a particular political organisation could also be satisfied. Alternatively, it might be satisfied by consideration of the occasion on which the uniform was worn without the need to refer to the past history of the organisation. It was found that the items worn could amount to a uniform; this decision therefore greatly diminished the distinction between this offence and that under the PTA. The justification for retention of the PTA provisions is therefore doubtful due to the overlap between the two offences.

Clearly, a number of objections of principle arise in respect of the application of the proscription-related offences to a wider range of groups. The key objection is that, by making it possible to proscribe a wide range of groups, the legislation potentially curtails proscription-related activities which previously would not have been conceived of as related to terrorism. Some examples are illustrative. A group which did not itself engage in terrorism but which, for example, expressed support during one of its assemblies for the 'serious disruption' of a computer system could be proscribed as falling within the definition. If, during a march, members of a group opposed to the introduction of GM crops wore badges expressing support for a proscribed environmental activist group, they would commit an offence. They would also attract criminal liability if they carried leaflets which aroused reasonable suspicion that such support was being expressed, although the leaflet was in fact that of a similar but more moderate and non-proscribed group. If a person who opposed the use of violence to further the cause of animal rights organised a meeting to express such views in private with two other people, one of whom was a member of a proscribed animal rights group, who spoke in its favour, she would commit an offence carrying a maximum penalty of 10 years' imprisonment, unless she could disprove the *mens rea* element.

Inciting terrorism abroad

The new legislation does not only act as the 'trigger' applying the old offences to a wider range of groups; it will also create new offences of inciting terrorism abroad, which apply under ss 59, 60 and 61 of the TA to England and Wales, Northern Ireland and Scotland, respectively. In the Consultation Paper, the government expressed concerns as to the effect on free speech: 'the incitement offence could be difficult in practice to prove and ... the effect of [its creation] could be to constrain freedom of expression. On the other hand ... considerable concern can be caused by ... statements ... encouraging and glorifying acts of terrorism.'[557] The government came down on the side of inclusion of the offence. Under s 59(1), 'A person commits an offence if (a) he incites another person to commit an act of terrorism wholly or partly outside the United Kingdom, and (b) the act would, if committed in England and Wales, constitute one of the offences listed in subsection (2)'. Under s 59(2), the offences are the more serious offences against the person: murder, an offence under ss 18, 23, 24, 28 or 29 of the Offences against the Person Act 1861 (OAPA) and an offence under s 1(2) of the Criminal Damage Act 1971. Under s 59(3), the penalty for conviction under this section will be the penalty 'to which he would be liable on conviction of the offence listed in subsection (2) which corresponds to the act which he

---

557 *Legislation Against Terrorism: A Consultation Paper*, Cm 4178, 1998, Chapter 2, para 4.19.

incites'. Sections 60 and 61 create equivalent provisions relating to Scotland and Northern Ireland.

In defending the introduction of the new offence, Jack Straw, the then Home Secretary, pointed out that existing legislation which has implemented various international covenants means that it is already an offence to incite anyone abroad to hijack an aircraft or to invite someone in Turkey or India to commit murder. Therefore, extending the offence to other countries, such as Japan or Australia, is logical: 'Every terrorist attack represents a violation of our democratic values ... our response must be sufficiently robust to challenge and defeat these ... activities. I think we have got the balance right.'[558] This claim is presumably based on the restriction of the offence to incitement to commit the serious offences listed. Nevertheless, it is open to question. It means that a person who encouraged another to assassinate a terrorist dictator would commit an offence punishable with a mandatory sentence of life imprisonment. The offence might also be committed during a demonstration at which words spoken denouncing such a dictator could be construed as amounting to incitement to assassinate him. Section 59 also creates doubtful distinctions between offences. Sometimes very little separates the person who commits grievous bodily harm (s 18 of the OAPA) from the person who commits serious bodily harm (s 20 of the OAPA) and this is more clearly the case where the attack need not in fact have been committed. But the s 20 offence is not listed in s 59(2). Therefore, determination that a person is subject to a penalty of a maximum of life imprisonment or to no penalty at all may rest on a very fine distinction.

Requirements of the Convention under the HRA

The offences discussed tend to strike directly at freedom of political expression, which, as indicated in the Introduction to Part II, is 'one of the essential foundations of a democratic society', so that exceptions to it 'must be narrowly interpreted and the necessity for any restrictions ... convincingly established'.[559] Such offences include those of incitement, of wearing any item that arouses a reasonable apprehension that a person is a member or supporter of a proscribed organisation, of organising a meeting at which a member of a proscribed organisation is speaking, and that of soliciting support for such an organisation. The use of these offences is *prima facie* an interference with the guarantee under Art 10 since all, including the wearing of an item, involve exercises of expression. In particular, the incitement provisions under ss 59–61 and the provision of s 12 regarding meetings afford very little recognition to the value of peaceful protest and assembly. Strasbourg, as indicated in the Introduction to this chapter, affords that value pre-eminence in a democracy.[560] Charging a member of an assembly with one of these offences would clearly, therefore, amount to an interference with the Art 10 guarantee. The domestic court would be expected to observe the same or higher standards than Strasbourg in scrutinising the need for the interference, bearing in mind the narrow

---

558 Straw, J in a *Guardian* article, 14 December 1999.
559 *Observer and Guardian v UK* A 216, pp 29–30, para 59; Judgment of 26 November 1991.

margin of appreciation afforded to States in respect of interference with political speech, especially where it concerns criticism directed at the government itself.[561]

Obviously, the view taken of the necessity and proportionality of the interference would depend on the particular circumstances behind the charging of the offence in the instance before the court. But to take the example used above of a person meeting privately with two others and hearing a member of a proscribed group: it might be problematic to find that the necessity for the interference with freedom of expression in a democratic society had been convincingly established. This offence is especially pernicious in terms of freedom of expression since the meeting in question might be entirely peaceful: liability would depend solely on the *content* of the speech of at least one of the speakers. The incitement offence under ss 59, 60 and 61 is unconfined to members of proscribed groups. Taking the example used above of charging the offence in respect of persons at a public meeting denouncing a terrorist dictator, a court which viewed the interference with freedom of expression as, in the circumstances, disproportionate to the aims in view, could take the opportunity of construing the wording of the provisions very strictly. In particular, where there was leeway to do so, on a very strict interpretation of the application of certain of the offences listed in s 59(2), it might be found that incitement merely of lesser, similar, but unlisted offences had occurred.

The most obvious and useful means of challenging the application of the new provisions will be during the criminal process itself under s 7(1)(b) of the HRA. Apart from arguments under Arts 10 and 11, the Art 6 guarantee of a fair and public hearing will provide the means whereby aspects of the criminal liability created under the TA 2000 will have to be examined. In criminal proceedings on the application of the counter-terrorist offences, the courts will have the opportunity of interpreting them, under s 3 of the HRA, compatibly with the Convention rights. They must also discharge their duty under s 6 of the HRA. The approach of the courts towards the new legislation will clearly be crucial.

Traditionally, since terrorism has been viewed as threatening national security, the courts have adopted a deferential stance.[562] While a far wider range of persons and activities will be designated 'terrorist' under the new Act, it is apparent that the actions of many such persons and groups do not genuinely threaten national security, not least because the scale of their operations is likely to be small. The approach taken by the House of Lords in *Ex p Kebilene*[563] to counter-terrorist provisions, particularly the findings of Lord Hope of Craighead, suggests that where national security is in issue, the judges will refuse (overtly) to apply the margin of appreciation doctrine in adjudicating on the new provisions, and yet may adopt a restrained approach. It was said in *Ex p Kebilene* in the context of the case, which concerned the compatibility of terrorist legislation with Art 6, that a deferential approach could be justified. The approach of the courts is likely to

---

560 See *Ezelin v France* (1991) 14 EHRR 362. On political expression generally, see *Castells v Spain* A 236, p 23, para 43; Judgment of 23 April 1992.

561 See *Incal v Turkey* (2000) 29 EHRR 449 and see the Introduction to this part, pp 209–10.

562 In *CCSU v Minister for the Civil Service* [1985] AC 374 the House of Lords accepted the government's claim that national security was at risk, without demanding that evidence should be put forward to support it. In the case of *Secretary of State for the Home Department v Rehman* [2001] 3 WLR 877, HL; [2000] 3 All ER 778, CA, the House of Lords accepted that it was for the government alone to determine whether a threat to national security, broadly defined, existed. Thus, the judiciary tends to accept government claims that such a threat is self-evident or must be taken on trust.

563 [1999] 4 All ER 801; Divisional Court [1999] 3 WLR 175.

continue to depend on the extent to which national security can be said to be at stake. Under the previous legislation, in the context of Irish terrorism, the courts tended to take an absolutist approach, readily making the assumption that considerations of national security outweighed the individual rights at stake. The courts are less likely to be deferential where national security is not an issue and therefore may show a greater willingness to take a robust approach to the new Act than they would if adjudicating on the activities of IRA terrorists. Under the current legislation, bearing in mind its width and the influence of the HRA, the approach might be more nuanced, and might depend more on the particular circumstances of each case, since the groups or the activities in question may be far more divergent from each other, and many persons who are not part of any such group may fall within the new provisions.

Article 6 provides guarantees that may come into conflict with a number of provisions of the new Act. A number of provisions under the TA 2000 may be regarded as infringing the presumption of innocence at trial. This may be due to the use of presumptions against the defendant, to the need to show reasonable suspicion only, regarding the main or only ingredient of the offence, and/or to the lack of a need to prove *mens rea*. A number of the special offences contain, as indicated above, a 'reversed' *mens rea*: the defendant has the burden of disproving knowledge or intent. Strictly, the burden of proof is unchanged but, clearly, where the prosecution has merely to prove a minimal *actus reus* beyond reasonable doubt, its burden is significantly lowered, while the presumption of innocence is undermined. Under a number of the offences under the TA discussed, including those contained in ss 12 and 13, there is no need for the prosecution to show *mens rea* and the *actus reus* of these offences tends to be minimal. For example, under s 13, the *actus reus* can consist of doing something which gives rise to reasonable suspicion that support is being expressed for a proscribed organisation. Clearly, the interpretation of these provisions in practice will depend on the attitude of the domestic judiciary. A means of narrowing down the use of presumptions was established in *R v Killen*[564] which held that, under the existing law, although the fact of possession constituted a *prima facie* case, the guilt of the accused still had to be proved beyond all reasonable doubt.

If it appeared that a certain provision of the Act was incompatible with Art 6, the court would have three main and contrasting courses of action available to it. First, it could seek to water down the Art 6 guarantee in the manner suggested by Lord Hope in *Ex p Kebilene*[565] by balancing the individual right to a fair trial against the purposes of the terrorist legislation. In so doing, it might be found that the provision of the 2000 Act could be fully or largely applied. Secondly, it could give full weight to the Art 6 guarantee in the manner suggested by the Lord Chief Justice in the Divisional Court in *Ex p Kebilene*, and could go on to find that applying the statutory provision in question would lead to unfairness at trial, based on the standards of Art 6. It could then declare that to do so would be an abuse of process. Thirdly, a court of sufficient authority could, on appeal, make a declaration of incompatibility.

564 [1974] NI 220.
565 [1999] 4 All ER 801. For discussion, see Chapter 4, pp 186–87.

9 CONCLUSIONS

Before the HRA came into force, the true boundaries of public protest were drawn, not by reference to the constitutional significance in a democracy of rights of political participation or of affording expression, through the medium of forms of protest, to a variety of viewpoints, but often arbitrarily due to the imprecision of the law and the approach frequently taken to it in low level courts or by the police. It is tempting to look forward to the use of Arts 10 and 11 in the post-HRA era in the expectation not only that the boundaries will eventually be re-drawn more precisely, but also that legal discourse in this area will no longer focus simply on disorder, but rather will seek to engage in the ongoing debate, at Strasbourg and in other jurisdictions, as to the values underlying the constitutional significance of protest and the weight they should be afforded. Whether that expectation will be fulfilled depends partly on the readiness of the domestic judiciary to disregard the outcomes of many of the public protest cases that Strasbourg has considered. But this chapter has also suggested that the impact of the HRA on public protest will be principally determined not by the Strasbourg jurisprudence it introduces, but by the prevailing and established judicial attitude to public protest, and the extent to which the judiciary are prepared to move away from it, by giving practical effect to the core values underlying the Convention. Vital, also, will be the way that the judiciary deal with the problematic issue of the margin of appreciation and its role in the jurisprudence they will have to consider.

As we have seen, reliance on the outcomes of cases at Strasbourg will provide no secure grounding for such protection – rather the reverse. The judiciary must therefore be prepared to draw upon the general principles and values underlying the Convention – free expression, pluralism, tolerance and the maintenance of diversity as essential characteristics of a democratic society – if the HRA is to provide more than a cosmetic change in approach to the protection of the right of peaceful protest.[566]

Judges within the 'activist' model may find that their decision making can be rooted in the general principles upheld at Strasbourg as underpinning the Convention rather than in its particular application. The justification for affording greater weight to communicative rights than that afforded at Strasbourg in findings under Arts 10 and 11 can be found in the need to ensure the genuine efficacy of the rights, with a view to realising the free expression and assembly objectives referred to above, especially in the case of minority groups or viewpoints. As argued, the Convention jurisprudence clearly recognises the need to protect a plurality of views in a democracy, even in the face of offence caused to the majority.[567] It would be in accordance with the Convention concept of a democratic society to refuse to place those seeking to exercise communicative rights in the same position as football hooligans and to reject a legal tradition of valuing the general societal interest in public order over the exercise of such rights. In accordance with the values of the Convention, safeguarding the interests of minorities in a democracy is not to circumvent the democratic process, but to uphold it by obviating the danger that those interests will be marginalised.

---

566 They will also, of course, be free to draw upon the rich US and Canadian jurisprudence on public protest as a basic civil right.

567 Above, pp 440–41.

If the judiciary are prepared to take this stance, the nature and structure of judicial argument in public protest cases, as well as the likely outcomes, will change radically. Although some judges are likely to tend towards approaches which have been termed 'minimalist' or 'traditionalist', the rather tokenistic changes in legal reasoning which would result might still eventually come to influence judicial attitudes. In public order cases such judges will hear, even if they are unreceptive to, arguments from counsel as to the value of this form of political expression. Once the judiciary are placed in the position of considering such value and the need nevertheless to circumscribe protest within a democracy, they may eventually come to view this matter from a broader perspective[568] and to participate in the debate which has been occurring in other jurisdictions for many years. Ultimately, in this particular area of political expression, the Act may come to have a more profoundly educative effect than in others, not only on the public, but on the judiciary.

---

568 Comparison may be made here with the manner in which the jurisprudence of the Canadian Supreme Court changed radically following the enactment of the Charter of Fundamental Rights, from orthodox 'black letter' analysis to a far more theorised and philosophical approach: see Leigh and Lustgarten, *op cit*, fn 541.

PART III

THE PROTECTION OF PRIVACY

INTRODUCTION[1]

The right to respect for privacy is now accepted as part of the domestic law of a number of countries[2] and of international human rights instruments.[3] However, the limits of the right are still unclear and a generally accepted definition of privacy has not emerged. As Raymond Wacks has observed, 'the voluminous [theoretical] literature on the subject has failed to produce a lucid or consistent meaning of [the] concept'.[4] It may be said, therefore, that privacy has become a complex and perhaps almost unworkably broad concept due to the variety of claims or interests which have been thought to fall within it.[5] The European Court of Human Rights has accommodated many disparate issues within the concept of privacy arising under Art 8 of the European Convention on Human Rights: they range from the rights of homosexuals[6] to the right to receive information about oneself.[7] As Feldman has argued, the scope of Art 8 is continuing to widen.[8]

The Convention does not attempt to define privacy,[9] but various definitions have been put forward which tend to be very broad: it has been termed 'a circle around every individual human being which no government ... ought to be permitted to overstep' and 'some space in human existence thus entrenched around and sacred from authoritative intrusion'.[10] Feldman has found that the desire for a private area in life derives its justification from personal autonomy, which is linked to the idea of 'defensible space', and from the 'idea of utility' – the idea that 'people operate more effectively and happily

---

1 See generally Wacks, *The Protection of Privacy*, 1980; Westin, AF, *Privacy and Freedom*, 1970; Bailey, SH, Harris, DJ and Jones, BL, *Civil Liberties: Cases and Materials*, 4th edn, 1995, Chapter 8; Wacks, R (ed), *Privacy*, 1993; Feldman, *Civil Liberties and Human Rights in England and Wales* (1993) 1st edn, Part 3; Markesinis, B (ed), *Protecting Privacy*, 1999; Clayton and Tomlinson, *The Law of Human Rights* (2000) Chapter 12; Eady, D, 'A statutory right to privacy' (1996) 3 EHRLR 243; Winfield, P (1981) 47 LQR 23; Yang, TL (1966) 15 ICLQ 175; Wacks, R, 'The poverty of privacy' (1980) 96 LQR 73; Seipp, D, 'English judicial recognition of the right to privacy' (1983) 3 OJLS 325; Leigh, I, 'Horizontal rights, the Human Rights Act and privacy: lessons from the Commonwealth?' (1999) 48 ICLQ 57; Grosz, S and Braithwaite, N, 'Privacy and the Human Rights Act', in Hunt and Singh (eds), *A Practitioner's Guide to the Impact of the Human Rights Act*, 1999; Wright, J, 'How private is my private life?', in Betten, L (ed), *The Human Rights Act 1998: What it Means*, 1999. Whitty, N, Murphy, T and Livingstone, S, *Civil Liberties Law: The Human Rights Era* (2001) Chapter 6. Chapter 10 is based partly on Fenwick, H and Phillipson, G, 'Breach of confidence as a privacy remedy in the Human Rights Act era' (2000) 63(5) MLR 660–93.

2 For example, the US Privacy Act 1974 and the tort or torts of invasion of privacy, the Canadian Protection of Privacy Act 1974, Art 1382 of the French Civil Code; German courts can protect privacy under s 823(1) of the Civil Code and a right to privacy arises under the German Basic Law Art 10 (albeit limited to posts and telecommunications).

3 It appears in the European Convention on Human Rights, Art 8 and the International Covenant on Civil and Political Rights, Art 17.

4 'Introduction', in Wacks, *op cit*, fn 1, p xi.

5 See Wacks, *op cit*, fn 1, Chapter 1, pp 10–21.

6 *Dudgeon* (1982) 4 EHRR 149.

7 *Gaskin* (1990) 12 EHRR 36.

8 (1997) 3 EHRLR 264.

9 See further Chapter 2, pp 67–72.

10 Mill, JS, *Principles of Political Economy*, 1970, p 306.

when they are allowed to make their own arrangements about domestic and business matters without interference from the State'.[11] Such phrases suggest that some aspects of an individual's life, which can be identified as private aspects, are of particular value and therefore warrant special protection from State intrusion. At an intuitive level, the notion that boundaries can and should be placed around such aspects of an individual's life, preventing such intrusion and thereby protecting personal autonomy, seems to be accepted as the fundamental basis of the idea of privacy[12] and underlies decisions under Art 8.[13] However, as recognised at Strasbourg, the right goes further than simply requiring that the individual should be let alone – in two respects. As indicated below, the right also encompasses positive obligations on the part of the State authorities. It also places obligations on private bodies, which can include positive obligations. In *X and Y v Netherlands*[14] the Court stated: 'these [Art 8] obligations may require the adoption of measures even in the sphere of relations between individuals.'

The disparate obligations created by this right are reflected in the different concerns of the three chapters in Part III. Chapter 10 deals with the protection of personal information from non-consensual use by public and private bodies. It particularly concentrates on invasion of privacy by the media. Chapter 11 considers State surveillance and searches of property; it covers a variety of intrusions of State agents into private life and considers the safeguards available to the individual. Chapter 12 considers protection for family and sexual life. It will be argued that in each of these contexts the Human Rights Act (HRA), which has imported the Strasbourg conceptions of privacy into domestic law, will be of great significance. The recently introduced statutes which now have a central impact in this context, the Data Protection Act 1998 and the Regulation of Investigatory Powers Act 2000, must be interpreted compatibly with the Convention rights under s 3 of the HRA. The HRA is also providing the impetus for further protection for privacy under common law and statutory developments, especially the development of the doctrine of confidence.

Theoretical considerations

If it is accepted that the value of personal autonomy underlies differing conceptions of privacy, it is necessary first to draw a distinction between what may be termed 'substantive' and 'informational' autonomy. The former denotes the individual's interest in being able to make certain substantive choices about personal life for him or herself, such as the choice to engage in certain sexual practices, without State coercion.[15] Privacy derives its value partly from its close association with personal autonomy, in the sense that freedom from interference by the authorities will foster the conditions under which autonomy can be exercised. Thus, some authoritative invasions of privacy may be said to

---

11 See *Civil Liberties and Human Rights in England and Wales,* 1st edn, 1993, pp 353–54.
12 See Seipp, *ibid,* p 333.
13 See, eg, *Leander v Sweden* (1987) 9 EHRR 433; *McVeigh, O'Neill and Evans v United Kingdom* (1981) 45 EHRR 71.
14 (1985) 8 EHRR 235.
15 Eg, over matters such as abortion and sexual activity.

lead to interference with individual autonomy. The exercise of autonomy may not be entirely dependent on establishing a state of privacy, but may at least be fostered thereby. But privacy may also be associated with self-fulfilment in the sense that protection for the private life of the individual may provide the best conditions under which he or she may flourish. In other words, self-fulfilment may be fostered if the individual is able to enjoy the benefits of the private: the dropping of the public mask, the communion of intimates, the expression of the deepest emotions.

The term 'informational autonomy', on the other hand, refers to the individual's interest in controlling the flow of personal information about herself, the interest referred to by the German Supreme Court as 'informational self-determination',[16] or as Beardsley has put it, the right to 'selective disclosure'.[17] In accordance with the views of a number of writers, it is suggested that this interest is one of the primary concerns of the law in this area.[18] The ability to exercise control in this manner also affords some protection to other values, as Feldman[19] has pointed out: 'If people are able to release [private] information with impunity, it might have the effect of illegitimately constraining a person's choices as to his or her private behaviour, interfering in a major way with his or her autonomy'.[20] Control over information thus indirectly protects substantive autonomy. Personal dignity, which must be diminished when information relating to intimate aspects of a person's life are widely published, giving rise to feelings of violation, shame, and embarrassment, is also afforded a measure of protection. Informational control also protects what Feldman identifies as the value in forming spheres of social interaction and intimacy – for example, work colleagues, friends, family, lovers – which may be seen as essential to human flourishing.[21] It is clear that the intimacy that such relationships entail is predicated upon an ability of the individual to ensure that information which may be circulated within one sphere is not, without her knowledge or consent, transferred to another sphere or the outside world. A privacy law would give legal force to that ability.

---

16   BGH, 19 December 1995, BGHZ 131, pp 322–46.

17   'Privacy: autonomy and selective disclosure', in Nomos XIII 54.

18   See Wacks, op cit, fn 1, pp 10–21; Westin, op cit, fn 1, p 7; Miller, A, *Assault on Privacy*, 1971, p 40. Ruth Gavison's definition of privacy – 'a limitation of others' access to an individual' – has three aspects: information; attention; physical access ('Privacy and the limits of law' (1980) 89(3) Yale LJ 421); see also Gross's similar definition: 'The concept of privacy' (1967) 42 NYULR 34, p 36. We consider the issue of physical access to be adequately dealt with by the law of trespass; it will be argued below that the issue of 'attention' can be addressed within an 'informational' paradigm, provided that term is conceived of with sufficient sensitivity and flexibility. Cf Wacks, op cit, fn 1, p 76 (acknowledging the point as from unpublished work by Ruth Gavison. Parent agrees ('A new definition of privacy for the law' (1983) 2 Law and Philosophy 305, p 326).

19   Feldman, D, 'Secrecy, dignity or autonomy? Views of privacy as a civil liberty' (1994) 47(2) CLP 42, p 54.

20   *Ibid*, p 51. Feldman's view is that privacy protects persons operating in a given sphere from interference within that sphere by those who are outside it. He argues that within each different sphere of existence, privacy operates in four dimensions: 'space (including access to and control over material goods), time; action; and information' (*ibid*, p 52). Chapter 10 deals mainly with 'information': control over 'space' is dealt with by the law of trespass and property and considered mainly in Chapter 11; the 'action' and 'time' categories clearly raise issues of substantive autonomy, considered in Chapter 12. As regards the attempt to bring both informational and substantive autonomy under one definition: see Parent, op cit, fn 18, pp 309 and 316 and Wacks, op cit, fn 18, esp p 79.

21   *Ibid*, pp 51–69. As Fried notes, privacy is essential for 'respect, love friendship and trust' – 'without it they are simply inconceivable' ('Privacy' (1968) 77 Yale LJ 477, p 483).

Since considerations of this nature involve an implied contrast between the public and the private, it may be helpful at this point to consider the division between the two spheres in order to come closer to examining what may be encompassed by the notion of privacy. A variety of referents may be used. The private might be viewed as a sphere which should be almost entirely unregulated by the public (law) although also delineated by it. This division, however, poses problems. It will be argued in Chapter 12 that when aspects of the private sphere – particularly family life – are regulated by law, the benefits they offer may be diminished. Thus, a broader social division between the public and the private may be suggested: arguably, the public includes State activity, aspects of the world of work, the pursuit of public interests, while the private includes the home, the family, the expression of sexuality and of the deepest feelings and emotions. Postulating such a division need not obscure the fact that these spheres are not entirely distinct, but must interact. The pursuit of the public interest will often affect and even determine some aspects of the private life of the family and the individual in terms, for example, of housing and welfare policy, while at the same time, the need to afford respect to the private will help to shape such policies.

The strength of claims that respect for individual autonomy has not been accorded may be affected, as the following chapters explain, by the nature of the obligation sought to be imposed on public authorities or private bodies, and by their potential effect on competing interests. 'Control over personal life' will be treated as covering areas as disparate as allowing a homosexual to choose to express his or her sexuality free from State interference, and enabling an individual to enjoy his or her property free from the attentions of reporters. On the one hand, the individual's privacy is invaded through the criminalisation of certain activities, while on the other he is complaining that the law does not prevent an invasion of privacy. In the former case, if the homosexual were to be prevented from expressing his sexual orientation, the government would be using its coercive powers to give effect to the moral conviction that the homosexual's way of life is contemptible. Thus, it would clearly be failing in its duty to treat its citizens with equal respect; to prevent this, under the liberal analysis of rights, the homosexual should be given a 'strong' right to sexual autonomy which would overcome any competing claims of society.

By contrast, the State, in failing to control the activities of the reporter, is not thereby giving expression to feelings of contempt for the individual's way of life; rather, it is arguably erring on the side of free expression as it collides with the interest of the individual in securing her privacy. Thus, in this case, the individual's claim is weaker in itself and, further, has to compete with a strong claim to free expression which the interest in moral autonomy does not face. Moreover, in the case of public figures claiming privacy rights against the press, the argument that views free speech as essential in order to ensure meaningful participation in a democracy has particular strength. In practical terms, this would lead one to suggest that in the case of public figures, the claims of free expression should override privacy unless it was clear that the information gained was in no way related to their fitness to carry out their public functions. In the case of a purely private figure, or of private facts unrelated to the public function of public figures, freedom of expression would still compete with the claim of privacy. However, two of the important justifications for free speech – the arguments from truth and from political participation – would be largely irrelevant so that the strength of the free expression claim would be appreciably diminished.

It may be concluded that privacy is in a weak position in so far as its ability to overcome other individual rights is concerned – where the values underpinning that other right are genuinely at stake. In contrast, where preservation of privacy may lead to upholding an individual's moral autonomy, it is more clearly evident that it should be treated as a strong individual right able to overcome various public interests.

Domestic protection for privacy

Traditionally, UK law recognised no general right to respect for privacy, although there was some evidence, as will be seen, that the judges considered this to be an evil which required a remedy. It has been argued that various areas of tort or equity such as trespass, breach of confidence, copyright and defamation are instances of a general right to privacy,[22] but it is reasonably clear from judicial pronouncements that these areas and others were treated as covering specific and distinct interests which only incidentally offered protection to privacy[23] – despite the fact that the term 'privacy' was used in a number of rulings.[24] In such instances, it can usually be found that a recognised interest such as property actually formed the basis of the ruling. Thus, prior to the inception of the HRA, UK law offered only a piecemeal protection to privacy and therefore a number of privacy interests were largely unprotected. In so far as the protection for privacy broadened in the years immediately prior to the inception of the HRA, the initiative largely came not from the courts or the government but from Europe – either from European Community directives[25] or from decisions under the European Convention on Human Rights.[26]

When Art 8 of the Convention was received into domestic law under the HRA 1998, UK citizens acquired, for the first time, a guarantee of respect for their privacy. Under ss 6 and 7(1)(a) of the HRA the right will be directly enforceable against public authorities, such as the police or the BBC, but not against private bodies, including the press. But, citizens can sue private bodies relying on existing causes of action, assuming that a cause of action covers the situation in question, and looking to the court itself as a public authority under s 6 of the HRA, and to its obligations under s 12, to develop the action by reference to Art 8. In other words, as Chapter 4 argued, the Convention rights can have indirect horizontal effect.[27] The precise nature of this effect is a complex and still unsettled matter, which is explored in Chapter 10.

---

22 See Warren and Brandeis, 'The right to privacy' (1890) 4 Harv L Rev 193.

23 See, eg, the comments of Glidewell LJ in *Kaye v Robertson* [1991] FSR 62, CA: 'It is well known that in English law there is no right to privacy ... in the absence of such a right the plaintiff's advisers have sought to base their claim on other well-established rights of action.'

24 Eg, *Prince Albert v Strange* (1848) 2 De Gex & Sm 652; *Clowser v Chaplin* (1981) 72 Cr App R 342.

25 See the section on Data Protection below.

26 For decisions against the UK, see below.

27 See pp 161–64.

CHAPTER 10

PROTECTION FOR PERSONAL INFORMATION

1 INTRODUCTION[1]

It may hardly be doubted that the lack of a tort of invasion of privacy aimed at the protection of personal information is one of the most serious lacunae in English law. Described by the Law Commission as 'a glaring inadequacy',[2] and condemned by the Court of Appeal,[3] *dicta* in a recent decision of the House of Lords[4] remarked upon '... the continuing, widespread concern at the apparent failure of the law' in this area.[5] A number of persons or bodies may acquire, store, disclose or publish personal information without the consent of the subject of it. The acquisition and use of personal information by State agents, with the purpose of preventing or detecting crime or protecting national security, is considered in Chapter 11. But the use of personal information by a range of private and public bodies for other purposes is considered here. The press is one of the worst offenders, in terms of acquiring and publishing personal information non-consensually, and therefore the use of various legal provisions against the press forms a central theme in this chapter. But it should also be pointed out that the internet represents in one sense a far greater threat to privacy, since by its nature it may render developments in the law otiose.[6] Even assuming that the developments discussed below lead eventually to a respect for personal privacy not evident at present in the publishing of a number of media bodies, especially the tabloid press, this threat may lead to a further re-evaluation of the legal approach to the protection of privacy.[7]

---

1   Reading that will be referred to in this chapter: Wacks, R, *Personal Information, Privacy and the Law*, 1993; Wacks, R, *Privacy and Press Freedom*, 1996; Markesinis, B (ed), *Protecting Privacy* (a collection of essays reviewing the concept of privacy and the law relating to it, especially in the context of personal information, in a number of jurisdictions), 1999; Younger Committee, *Report of the Committee on Privacy*, Cmnd 5012, 1972 (criticised: MacCormick, DM, 'A note on privacy' (1973) 84 LQR 23); *Report of the Committee on Privacy and Related Matters*, Chairman David Calcutt QC (Calcutt Report), Cmnd 1102, 1990; Calcutt, *Review of Press Self-regulation*, Cm 2135, 1993; National Heritage Select Committee, 'Privacy and media intrusion', Fourth Report, HC 291, 1993; Lord Chancellor's Green Paper, *Infringement of Privacy*, 30 July 1993, CHAN J060915NJ.7/93; *Privacy and Media Intrusion*, White Paper (1995) Cm 2918; Eady, D, 'A statutory right to privacy' (1996) 3 EHRLR 243; Markesinis, B, 'The right to be let alone versus freedom of speech' [1986] PL 67; Wilson, W, 'Privacy, confidence and press freedom' (1990) 53 MLR 43; Markesenis, B, 'Privacy, freedom of expression, and the horizontal effect of the Human Rights Bill: lessons from Germany' (1999) 115 LQR 47; Leigh, I, 'Horizontal rights, the Human Rights Act and privacy: lessons from the Commonwealth?' (1999) 48 ICLQ 57; Singh, 'Privacy and the media after the Human Rights Act' (1998) EHLR 712; Grosz, S and Braithwaite, N, 'Privacy and the Human Rights Act', in Hunt, M and Singh, R (eds), *A Practitioner's Guide to the Impact of the Human Rights Act*, 1999; Wright, J, 'How private is my private life?', in Betten, L (ed), *The Human Rights Act 1998: What it Means*, 1999; Elliott, M, 'Privacy, confidentiality, horizontality: the care of the celebrity wedding photographs' [2001] CLJ 231.

2   Law Commission Report No 110, *Breach of Confidence*, para 5.5. The Commission was referring specifically to the fact that 'the confidentiality of information improperly obtained ... may be unprotected'.

3   *Kaye v Robertson* [1991] FSR 62, CA.

4   *Khan* [1997] AC 558.

5   *Ibid, per* Lord Nicholls.

6   See below, p 587.

7   See further Chapter 6, pp 306–07.

Warren and Brandeis' verdict in the 19th century, 'The Press is overstepping in every direction the obvious bounds of propriety and decency ... [inflicting] through invasions of privacy ... mental pain and distress far greater than could be inflicted by mere bodily injury',[8] is alarmingly true today, over 100 years later. Anyone familiar with the output of our print media will be wearily aware of its penchant for publishing what one journalist has described as 'toe-curlingly intimate details' about the sex lives not only of celebrities, but of 'quite obscure people'.[9] Intrusive prurience is not the only complaint: Victim Support has detailed a large number of case histories in which ordinary victims of crime and their families had had their suffering markedly exacerbated by intrusive and insensitive publications in local and national newspapers describing their plight in quite needless detail, causing in some cases diagnosable psychiatric harm, making others feel forced to move from the area where the crime had been committed; causing all intense emotional distress.[10] In contrast to the position in the US, and virtually every other Western democracy, such injuries have no remedy in a privacy law in this country: a toothless Press Complaints Commission could only request the offending newspaper to print its adjudication on the matter.[11] It is frequently remarked of countries which have a privacy law, such as France and Germany, that their media does not exhibit the 'gutter' quality associated with the UK tabloid press.[12] In our cut-throat media market, the tendency of debased and lurid 'news' coverage in one newspaper to drive down the standards in another is very marked. Within this pervasive 'gutter' culture, which will influence the choices of readers, a newspaper which is unwilling to debase its standards may not survive, detracting from the diversity of opinion one would expect of a free press.

While the notion of respect for individual privacy could be said to be a clear underlying common law value,[13] it failed to find full expression, perhaps because intermittent governmental interest in the latter half of the 20th century in statutory protection for privacy distracted the courts with the chimera of possible legislative

---

8   'The right to privacy' (1890) IV(5) Harvard L Rev 193, p 196.

9   Marr, A, *The Independent*, 25 April 1996. In a recent conference speech, the editor of *The Guardian*, Alan Russbridger, listed a string of recent examples in which newspapers had published intimate details about the personal lives of celebrities, in some cases surreptitiously obtained, with either no or the flimsiest of 'public interest' justifications (Human Rights, Privacy and the Media, organised by the Constitution Unit, and the Centre for Communication and Information Law, UCL, 8 January 1999).

10 See Fourth Report of the National Heritage Select Committee on Privacy and Media Intrusion Minutes of Evidence, Appendix 24 HC 294-II (1993).

11 See below, pp 551–56 for discussion of the role of the Commission.

12 As Markesinis remarks, '... the possible extra-marital affairs of German politicians and businessmen hold little or no appeal for most readers of German newspapers.' (Markesinis, *op cit*, fn 1.)

13 See *dicta* of Laws J in *Hellewell v Chief Constable of Derbyshire* [1995] 1 WLR 804, p 807; *Francome v Mirror Group Newspapers* [1984] 1 WLR 892, in which the Court of Appeal recognised (in effect) a right to privacy in telephone conversations; *Stephens v Avery* [1988] Ch 449; *dicta* of Lord Keith in *AG v Guardian Newspapers (No 2)* [1990] 1 AC 109, p 255, 'The right to personal privacy is clearly one which the law [of confidence] should seek to protect'. In the recent decision in *Dept of Health ex p Source Informatics Ltd* [2001] 2 WLR 953; (2000) *The Times*, 21 January, Simon Brown LJ stated clearly that in cases involving personal information, 'The concern of the law [of confidence] is to protect the confider's personal privacy'. In *R v Khan* [1997] AC 558, Lords Browne-Wilkinson, Slynn and Nicholls left open the question whether English law already recognised a right to privacy.

action.[14] Quite clearly, however, no government in the past grasped this nettle, out of a fear of press hostility.[15]

In October 2000, however, the Human Rights Act 1998 (HRA) introduced Art 8 of the European Convention on Human Rights into UK law, providing for a right to respect for private life.[16] While the general view is that Art 8 will not be directly justiciable against the press or other private bodies,[17] it will be argued that its reception into UK law nevertheless provides an impetus for the notion of respect for privacy as an underlying legal value finally to find expression through the common law. The Data Protection Act 1998 (DPA) represents a further legislative development of immense significance for the protection of personal information. The Act will have a very significant impact on all bodies that process personal data, including the press, and undoubtedly the interaction between the DPA and the HRA will be complex and intriguing. Inevitably, tension will be generated by the incursion of the HRA and DPA into an area which previously was largely unregulated, being governed partly by media codes of practice partly by relatively narrow (albeit expanding) common law doctrines.

This chapter will examine the impact of the HRA on the currently available measures protecting personal information and aspects of privacy more generally, especially the doctrine of confidence. The implications of the development of protection for privacy for freedom of expression will be considered, as will jurisprudence from other jurisdictions, in particular the jurisprudence generated by the American 'private facts' tort.[18]

---

14 The Younger Committee (*Report of the Committee on Privacy*, Cmnd 5012, 1972, Calcutt Committee on Privacy and Related Matters, hereafter *The Calcutt Report* (Cmnd 1102, 1990), Review of Press Self Regulation (Cm 2135), Fourth Report of the National Heritage Select Committee in 1993, *op cit*, fn 10, all proposed the introduction of statutory measures to protect privacy, as did the Lord Chancellor's Green Paper of the same year (CHAN J060915NJ.7/93).

15 Such fear was clearly evident during the passage of the HRA itself. In response to the press outcry over the possibility that the Act would create a right to privacy, the Government introduced a specific amendment in favour of press freedom (HRA, s 12, discussed below), and repeatedly and explicitly sought to reassure the press during the Bill's debate. As Lord Ackner put it, the Lord Chancellor devoted 'a very large part of his [second reading] speech ... to trying to pour oil on ruffled waters.' (HL Deb Col 473, 18 November 1997). In fact, bearing in mind the effect of s 12(4)(b), discussed below, the government may have deceived the press as to the impact that s 12 was actually likely to have. For an example of blanket hostility from the press' representative body – the Newspaper Society – to the possible development of any privacy law in the UK, see Rasaiah, 'Current legislation, privacy and the media in the UK' (1998) 3(5) Communications Law 183.

16 As Chapter 2 explained, pp 67–72, Art 8 of the Convention provides a person with a right to respect for four different rights: 'his private and family life, his home and his correspondence'. Paragraph 2 then specifies a number of grounds permitting interference by 'a public authority' with this right.

17 See below, fn 52.

18 See below, esp p 613 for a discussion of the tort. Emphasis is placed on the American tort since, in comparison with other common law jurisdictions, the case law is particularly rich, having been generated over a considerable period of time; further, the American tort had its genesis in the Warren and Brandeis reading of a number of English decisions, including some breach of confidence cases (in particular, *Prince Albert v Strange* (1848) 2 De Gex & Sm 652; *Duke of Argyll v Duchess of Argyll* [1967] 1 Ch 302; *Pollard v Photographic Company* (1888) Ch 345), and therefore is particularly relevant to the development of a cause of action growing from the same roots.

2 POTENTIAL PROTECTION FOR PERSONAL INFORMATION UNDER THE HUMAN RIGHTS ACT

Strasbourg jurisprudence on protection for personal information

Article 8(1) provides a 'right to respect for private and family life, the home and correspondence'; para (2) states: 'There shall be no interference by a public authority with the exercise of this right' (emphasis added). There is a substantial jurisprudence on the data protection obligations of public authorities. It is clear that the actions of such bodies in the gathering, storing and use of information relating to private or family life, including photographs,[19] engages Art 8.[20] Certain categories of material, such as those relating to health[21] or sexual orientation or activity[22] are regarded as 'particularly sensitive or intimate',[23] requiring especially compelling grounds to justify interference. As Chapter 11 will indicate, surreptitious methods of obtaining information, such as telephone tapping, are seen as particularly serious breaches of Art 8.[24] The collection of personal information by the private bodies, including, in particular, the press, sometimes using surreptitious means, and its publication, is in reality only one, often highly objectionable manifestation of data collection and processing. One cannot, of course, infer the simple transposition of Convention obligations upon public authorities onto private agents. However, the Court has found[25] that Art 8 obligations may require the adoption of measures even in the sphere of relations between individuals. In other words, 'interference by a public authority' can mean 'unjustified failure by that authority to prevent interference by others'. Thus, the State may be under a positive obligation to provide legal protection for the individual, even when public authorities are not themselves responsible for an interference with the Art 8 right.

However, Strasbourg has approached the notion of an obligation to intervene between private parties with caution. It has found that, in deciding whether there is even a prima facie engagement of Art 8 in such a context, 'regard must be had to the fair balance that has to be struck between the general interest of the community and the interests of the individual'.[26] Thus, the gathering and subsequent publication of personal information by a private bodies, including the press, would not automatically engage Art 8, as such actions would if carried out by a public body. Nevertheless, the strength of the jurisprudence on interferences with personal information by public bodies indicates that the interest in being free from such intrusion is one which, in general terms, falls within the ambit of Art 8. As a leading text in the area puts it: 'the obligation of the State to

---

19   *Murray and Others v United Kingdom* (1994) 19 EHRR 193 (photographing of a person at a police station without her consent was found to be a *prima facie* violation of Art 8).

20   See, eg, *Leander v Sweden* (1987) 9 EHRR 433; *McVeigh, O'Neill and Evans v United Kingdom* (1981) 45 EHRR 71.

21   *Z v Finland* (1998) 25 EHRR 371.

22   *Lustig-Prean v United Kingdom* (1999) 29 EHRR 548; 7 BHRC 65.

23   Feldman, 'Information and privacy'; conference paper, Cambridge Centre for Public Law, Freedom of Expression and Freedom of Information, 19-20 February 2000.

24   *Kopp v Switzerland* [1998] HRCD 6 (356), para 72.

25   *X and Y v Netherlands* (1985) 8 EHRR 235.

26   *Cossey v UK* A 184, para 37 (1990).

respect private life by controlling the activities of its agents [in collecting personal information] ought to extend also to similar operations by private persons such as ... newspaper reporters'.[27]

When one turns to the case law directly on the question of the obligations of private parties to protect private information, a brief survey reveals both that it is very meagre and that there are no directly relevant successful applications. However, in order to understand quite why the Court has taken such a cautious stance, it is necessary to appreciate the significance which the margin of appreciation doctrine has had in this context. The essence of the doctrine[28] is that in assessing compliance with the Convention, the Court will afford States a certain latitude, principally in deciding what kinds of interferences with Convention rights are necessary. The margin can widen or narrow depending on the circumstances of the case, resulting in a variation of the intensity of the Court's review of the States' actions. Three principal factors influence Strasbourg in conceding a particularly wide margin of appreciation: first, where a complainant seeks to lay a positive obligation on the State; second, where the harm complained of flows from the action of a private party, rather than the State itself, so that the so called 'horizontal effect' of the Convention is in issue; third, where there is a potential conflict with another Convention right. Clearly, these factors may arise independently of each other. Or they may, as in the context under discussion, arise contiguously, thereby demanding that an especially wide margin should be allowed. In a number of the key decisions to be discussed, all three were present,[29] which may explain the somewhat unsatisfactory and misleading nature of some of the judgments given.

In *Barclay v United Kingdom*,[30] the Court accepted that a lack of a remedy in respect of the filming of a private home by reporters could in principle constitute a breach of Art 8, although on the facts no invasion of private life had occurred.[31] There is, thus, no bar in principle to the application of the Court's general approach to interferences with personal information to the actions of private bodies. *Winer v UK*[32] is often seen as indicating the contrary. The applicant complained that various aspects of his private life had been publicised in a book; he had settled a defamation case in respect of some of the statements made, but argued that he had no remedy under national law in respect of those which were truthful. His application was declared inadmissible, the Commission stating briefly that it viewed the available remedies, in particular that of defamation,[33] as satisfactory and that no positive obligation to provide further remedies in respect of the truthful statements should be imposed, bearing in mind the wide margin of appreciation to be

---

27 Harris, D, O'Boyle, K and Warbrick, C, *Law of the European Convention on Human Rights*, 1995, p 310.

28 For discussion, see Chapter 2, pp 34–37 and Fenwick, H, 'The right to protest, the Human Rights Act and the margin of appreciation' (1999) 62(4) MLR 491, pp 497–500.

29 All three were present in: *Winer v UK* (1986) 48 DR 154; *Spencer (Earl) v UK* (1998) 25 EHRR CD 105 and *N v Portugal* Appl No 20683/92, 20 February 1995; however, the third was influential only in *Winer*.

30 (1999) Appl No 35712/97 (admissibility only).

31 The property filmed was the island of Brecqhou, owned by the Barclay brothers. They had no home there, and were not present when the filming occurred.

32 (1986) 48 DR 154.

33 The remedy represented by the doctrine of confidence was not explicitly adverted to, presumably because at the time of the application it was still viewed as having only marginal application to privacy.

afforded in this area, the limitation of the Convention right to freedom of expression which such remedies would entail and the availability of a remedy in defamation. The applicant's privacy 'was not wholly unprotected'. However, the possibility was clearly left open of imposing a positive obligation on the State in an instance in which no national remedy was available. The obvious example, impliedly envisaged, would be an instance in which truthful, personal facts about an individual were published without consent and it was apparent that a defamation action had no or virtually no hope of success. In such circumstances, then, an individual might be viewed as holding a privacy right, which the State would come under a positive obligation to respect, a finding which receives some indirect support from the decision in N v Portugal.[34]

The most important decision for our purposes is Spencer (Earl) v United Kingdom.[35] The Commission dismissed as inadmissible Earl Spencer's claim that the UK Government had failed to protect him from invasions of privacy by the press[36] on the basis that he had failed to exhaust domestic remedies, namely breach of confidence. This judgment accepted that an interference with the right to respect for privacy had arguably occurred, and required a remedy, but that the doctrine of confidence would have provided one and should have been used. Had the Commission considered that the pleaded facts disclosed no arguable breach of Art 8, it would simply have so held – as the Court did in Barclay – and would not have instead decided the case on non-exhaustion of domestic remedies. It appears, therefore, to follow that Spencer, far from suggesting that Art 8 does not require the UK to develop a privacy law, was decided on the assumption that it already has one, albeit at a relatively early stage of development. As Harris et al put it in relation to the efficacy of domestic remedies for exhaustion purposes, the key issue in Spencer: 'in a common law system it [is] incumbent on an aggrieved individual to allow the domestic courts the opportunity to develop existing rights by way of interpretation'.[37] Thus, since the Commission in both Winer and Spencer could identify a remedy which, applying a wide margin of appreciation, it could view as sufficient, it found against the applicant. Had no remedy been identifiable, there are therefore grounds for assuming that the applications would have been declared admissible.

Individual decisions are not the only matters of relevance here, however. As the House of Lords recently stressed in Ex p Kebilene: 'in the national courts also the Convention should be seen as an expression of fundamental principles rather than as a set of mere rules ...'.[38] Strasbourg has found that the purpose of the Convention is to 'promote the ideals and values of a democratic society,'[39] and to provide 'rights that are

---

34   N v Portugal, Appl No 20683/92, 20 February 1995. A magazine publisher's application complaining of a breach of Art 10 after being convicted of defamation and invasion of privacy in respect of the publication of photographs of a well known businessman engaged in sexual activities was rejected as manifestly ill-founded. The Commission considered that the sanction was proportionate and necessary for the protection of the rights of others, one of which was clearly the right to protection from invasion of privacy through publication of true facts by other private individuals.

35   (1998) 25 EHRR CD 105.

36   The applicants complained of publication in the press of various (truthful) stories relating to the bulimia and mental health problems of Countess Spencer, including photographs taken of her walking in the grounds of a health clinic.

37   Harris, O'Boyle and Warbrick, op cit, fn 27, p 611.

38   R v DPP ex p Kebilene [1999] 3 WLR 972.

39   Kjeldsen v Denmark (1976) 1 EHRR 711, p 731; Socialist Party v Turkey (1999) 27 EHRR 51.

practical and effective' rather than 'rights that are theoretical or illusory'.[40] The Convention must be given an 'evolutive' interpretation'[41] which takes account of current standards in European countries,[42] in which legal protection for privacy is the norm.[43] In the context of Art 8 it has been said: 'The Court has not perceived the rights in Article 8 in wholly negative terms – the right to be left alone. Instead it has acknowledged that States must ensure ... the effective enjoyment of liberty'.[44] As suggested earlier, effective enjoyment of liberty cannot occur when persons who are constantly afraid of betraying information to the media are forced to order their choices in life as a consequence,[45] and it would appear to be a hallmark of a democratic society that it seeks to protect a person from any such curtailment of liberty.

Such principles have perhaps not received enough attention in this context; moreover, *Barclay* is a very recent case and the significance of the *Spencer* decision has only recently achieved widespread recognition,[46] perhaps due to a failure on the part of some commentators to appreciate the considerations outlined above, coupled with a tendency to concentrate on the apparently disappointing outcomes of the individual applications. Thus, a number of commentators, writing before the HRA had come fully into force, concluded that the current Art 8 jurisprudence cannot be said to require the courts to develop the common law so as to provide a remedy for non-consensual use of true but personal information. Thus, one commentator bluntly concludes: '... Strasbourg case law ... does not require a specific remedy between private individuals'.[47] Another comments: 'The still unanswered question is whether Article 8 also requires a Member State to provide a right of action against intrusions into private life by private persons ...'.[48] It is contended that this question is *not* unanswered: the cases discussed above quite strongly imply that it should be answered in the affirmative.

---

40 *Airey v Ireland* (1979) 2 EHRR 305, p 314.

41 *Johnstone v Ireland* A 112, para 53 (1986).

42 See Chapter 2, p 36; *Tyrer v UK* A 26 (1978), para 31. There are also numerous resolutions of the Council of Europe on effective protection for personal information (Nos 73(22) and 74(29)).

43 For discussion of the law in Germany, see Markesenis, B and Nolte, N, 'Some comparative reflections on the right of privacy of public figures in public places', in Birks, P (ed), *Privacy and Loyalty*, 1997; in relation to Germany, France and Italy see Chapters 2–5 of Markesenis, B (ed), *Protecting Privacy*, 1999; *The Calcutt Report*, op cit, fn 1, paras 5.22–5.28) also discusses privacy protection in Denmark and the Netherlands.

44 Harris, O'Boyle and Warbrick, *op cit*, fn 27, p 303.

45 See above, p 536.

46 One of the leading works on the Convention has no discussion at all of the issue of intrusion by the press into private life: Van Dijk, P and Van Hoof, F, *Theory and Practice of the European Convention on Human Rights*, 1998, pp 489–504; similarly the discussion of Art 8 in a recent textbook on media law makes no mention of the decision (Carey, P, *Media Law*, 1999, pp 79–81); Leigh in an article dealing with horizontality, the HRA and privacy, cites *Winer*, but not *Spencer* (1998) 25 EHRR CD 105, p 86 (*op cit*, fn 1). The decision receives some attention from Grosz and Braithwaite (*op cit*, fn 1), Singh (*op cit*, fn 1) and Wright (*op cit*, fn 1).

47 Leigh, *op cit*, fn 1.

48 Nicol, D, 'Media freedom after the Human Rights Act 1998', conference paper, fn 9 above; see also Naismith, 'Photographs, privacy and freedom of expression' (1996) 2 EHLR 150, p 156.

The 'horizontal effect' of Art 8 under the HRA

Most public authorities and a number of private bodies engage in the processing of personal information. They will therefore be subject to the provisions of the DPA 1998[49] and any other relevant statute, such as the Protection from Harassment Act 1997, and such statutes must be interpreted compatibly with the Convention rights under s 3 of the HRA, whether or not both parties concerned are private bodies.[50] In rendering such statutes compatible with the Convention, it is clear that Art 8 will be of particular relevance.

Where a body processing personal information (which includes its publication) is a public authority it could be sued directly under s 7(1)(a) of the HRA in respect of breaches of Art 8. But, it now seems fairly clear that there is no possibility under the HRA of suing *private* bodies for breach of Art 8 of the Convention under s 7(1)(a), principally because, as Chapter 4 explained, s 6 of the Act makes the Convention rights binding only upon 'public authorities'. However, since the courts, as 'public authorities'[51] themselves will have a duty not to act incompatibly with the Convention rights, this will create some role for the rights even in litigation between private parties, thus giving rise to indirect 'horizontal effect'. It now seems clear that this will not require the courts to create new causes of action in such litigation;[52] rather, the s 6(1) duty to act compatibly with the Convention rights will bite upon their adjudication of existing common law actions.

What precisely s 6(1) will require of the courts in private common law adjudication is a vexed and much discussed issue.[53] Space precludes full rehearsal of the numerous and complex arguments here; while one commentator has argued that the courts will have an absolute duty to render all private common law compatible with the Convention rights,[54] others have perceived a much more limited duty.[55] This chapter will adopt the position, as indicated in Chapter 4,[56] that the courts will not be placed under the absolute duty just mentioned, a conclusion arrived at on the basis of a number of factors: the apparent failure to incorporate the Convention rights themselves means that in the private sphere they are arguably not rights to enforce but only legal values;[57] the fact that such a duty could require courts to overturn settled common law rules and principles;[58] that it could

---

49 Unless they are excluded from its ambit: see pp 604–05.

50 Due to the effect of HRA, s 3(1) which, in covering all statutes, also covers those which create a number of rights binding private bodies.

51 Section 6(3)(a).

52 See Chapter 4, p 162. There are clear *Pepper v Hart* statements in Parliament to this effect: see HL Deb Vol 583 Col 784, 24 November 1997 and *op cit*, Vol 585 Col 841, 5 February 1998; HC Deb Vol 314 Col 406, 17 June 1998. There is also virtually unanimous agreement amongst the commentators on the point: Phillipson, G, 'The Human Rights Act, "horizontal effect" and the common law' (1999) 62 MLR 824, pp 826–28; Hunt, M, 'The horizontal effect of the Human Rights Act' [1998] PL 423, p 442; Buxton LJ, 'The Human Rights Act and private law' [2000] 116 LQR 48; Markesenis, *op cit*, fn 1, pp 72–73; Leigh, *op cit*, fn 1, pp 84–85; Singh, *op cit*, fn 1; cf Wade, W (Sir), 'The United Kingdom's Bill of Rights', in Forsyth, C and Hare, I (eds), *The Golden Metwand and the Crooked Cord: Essays in Honour of Sir William Wade QC* , 1998, pp 62–63. See also *Douglas and Others v Hello!* [2001] 2 WLR 992, discussed at pp 581–84.

53 See fn 52 above and Chapter 4, p 162.

54 Hunt, *op cit*, fn 52, pp 439–43.

55 See, eg, Leigh, I: the HRA 'does not formally change the approach to Convention questions in the [private] common law' (*op cit*, fn 1, pp 82–83). See also Feldman, D, 'The Human Rights Act 1998 and constitutional principles' (1999) 19 LS 165, p 201.

56 See pp 162–63.

57 Phillipson, *op cit*, fn 52, pp 834–37. It now appears that this is not, however, the case so far as HRA, s 3 is concerned: see *Wilson v First County Trust* [2001] 3 All ER 229, discussed in Chapter 4, p 149.

58 Phillipson, *op cit*, fn 52, pp 838–40.

'indirectly impose a very significant degree of liability on private bodies ... contrary to the general scheme of the Act and the clear intention of its sponsors.'[59] Rather, it is suggested that the courts will be obliged, when engaged in common law adjudication, to develop and apply the law by reference to relevant Convention rights, treating them as legal principles having a variable weight, depending on the context.[60]

It is suggested, however, that in the area of privacy with which this chapter is concerned, the distinction between having regard to the Convention rights and having an absolute duty to act compatibly with them when applying existing common law, may well turn out to be of little practical significance. This is because the difference between the two models would be of most practical importance when a clear imperative from the Convention clashed with a well defined pre-existing common law rule or principle. A judge accepting an absolute duty would be bound to override the common law, whereas under the weaker model, the Convention would provide only a reason for changing it. However, such a direct clash is most unlikely to occur in this area. The indeterminacy and paucity of Strasbourg jurisprudence on this aspect of Art 8 means, as explored above, that English courts will glean from it general principles and guidance, rather than clear-cut rules, which might have conflicted with the common law. While the common law doctrine of trespass currently lacks flexibility, the currently very fluid and flexible boundaries of the doctrine of confidence, discussed below, will make it unnecessary to override clear pre-existing rules of the action in order to achieve Convention-compliance. Moreover, there are strong arguments of principle which may persuade a judge treating the Convention rights only as relevant principles to afford them an especially high weight when dealing with invasions of privacy by the media,[61] or other powerful conglomerates, thus minimising the difference between the stronger and weaker models. The power of such bodies to invade privacy is arguably equal to that of the State, rendering the drawing of a sharp, formalistic distinction between the State and the private agent, whereby rights are upheld against the one but not the other, unjustified at the level of principle. Moreover, in contrast with certain instances in the private sphere in which a plaintiff might have freely agreed to a diminution of his rights by another,[62] the invasion of individual rights by certain private bodies, particularly the press, may be as involuntary as if perpetrated by the State.

---

59 Phillipson, *op cit*, fn 52, p 848; see also p 840.

60 Phillipson, *op cit*, fn 52, pp 843–44. Buxton LJ (*op cit*, fn 52) argues that the HRA will have no impact at all on private common law: the rights could not even figure as principles or values in such a context, he argues, since they 'remain, stubbornly, values whose content lives in public law' (*ibid*, p 59). This argument, it is suggested, cannot be reconciled with the findings of the Commission in *Spencer*, and the Court in *Barclay* (discussed above) that the actions of private agents can engage Art 8, requiring domestic courts, through the common law, to offer redress; nor with the approach of the House of Lords in the recent decision in *Reynolds v Times Newspapers* [1999] 4 All ER 609 where, in the context of a private defamation action, their Lordships regarded the Convention as of great importance; (see esp *ibid*, pp 621–22, *per* Lord Nicholls; *ibid*, pp 628, 635, *per* Lord Steyn). Lord Nicholls specifically stated that, following the coming into force of the HRA 1998, 'the common law is to be developed in a manner consistent with Art 10' (*ibid*, p 622); Lord Steyn observed that, with the coming into force of the HRA 1998, 'The constitutional dimension of freedom of expression is reinforced' (*ibid*, p 628). Neither of their Lordships appeared to consider the private nature of the proceedings of significance in this respect.

61 For the full argument on this point, see Phillipson, *op cit*, fn 52, pp 846–47.

62 Eg, where a schoolteacher accepted a job at a Catholic school and signed a contract which provided that s/he would not publicly deny any of the fundamental doctrines of the Catholic church. Strasbourg has quite readily accepted restrictions on Convention rights where these are said to have been voluntarily accepted by the applicant as a result of their employment: see, eg, *Ahmed v UK* (1982) 4 EHRR 125; *Stedman v UK* (1997) 23 EHRR CD 168; *Rommelganger v Germany* (1980) 62 D&R 151 (no violation of Art 10 when employee of Catholic hospital dismissed for expressing pro-abortion views).

Judicial responses to Strasbourg jurisprudence

Under the HRA, then, Art 8 should figure as a relevant, weighty principle in considering privacy complaints raised within the common law. A key factor, however, will be the response of the courts to the Strasbourg jurisprudence on that article examined above, since it is that case law, rather than Art 8 itself, which articulates the need for protection for personal information intrusion. When considering any issue under the Convention, s 2(1) of the HRA requires the domestic judiciary to take any relevant Strasbourg jurisprudence into account.[63] Since they are not bound by the case law, the courts could depart from it when so minded.

If the courts merely attempt to reach the same decisions as Strasbourg would have done, they would in effect be applying the international law doctrine of the margin of appreciation in a domestic setting. As Chapter 4 pointed out, commentators have agreed,[64] and the House of Lords[65] has stressed, that this would be wholly inappropriate. But a further and more difficult step is required: in applying Strasbourg jurisprudence under s 2 of the HRA, judges should attempt to disregard those aspects of the judgment which were attributable to the doctrine, difficult though this task will be.[66] Judges of a conservative bent, who wish to adopt a minimalist approach to the domestic application of the Convention,[67] might not take this further step or it might be merely overlooked: thus, while pronouncing the margin of appreciation doctrine inapplicable, judges could in fact rely fully on the outcomes of decisions at Strasbourg, without adverting to the influence of the doctrine on those outcomes. This indeed was the approach arguably adopted in the recent House of Lords decision in *Ex p Kebilene*,[68] and the earlier case of *Khan*.[69] This approach would be wholly mistaken, in considering the application of *Winer* and *Spencer* to domestic law: it might well lead to the assumption that the failure of both applications reflected the lack of a requirement under Art 8 to provide a remedy for non-consensual disclosures of true but personal information. As indicated below, the courts have not so far adopted a minimalist approach in this context.[70]

---

63 See Chapter 4, pp 146–48.

64 See Laws LJ, speaking extra-judicially ('The limitations of human rights' (1999) PL 254, p 258): 'The margin of appreciation ... will necessarily be inapt to the administration of the Convention in the domestic courts'; Feldman, *op cit*, fn 23, p 192: 'The doctrine will have no application in national law'; see further Chapter 4 , p 186–87; Phillipson, *op cit*, fn 52, pp 844–46.

65 In *DPP ex p Kebilene and Others* [1999] 3 WLR 972, p 1043, Lord Hope of Craighead said: 'This technique [the doctrine] is not available to the national courts when they are considering Convention issues arising in their own countries.'

66 See Phillipson, *op cit*, fn 52, pp 845–46.

67 Eg, Buxton LJ, who believes that it has no place in private common law proceedings (see fn 52 above).

68 [1999] 3 WLR 972. The decisions concerned included *H v UK* Appl No 15023/89 and *Bates v UK* Appl No 26280/95; see further Chapter 4 pp 186–7.

69 [1997] AC 558, HL; the Strasbourg decision in question was *Schenk v Switzerland* A 140 (1988).

70 See pp 581–91.

Moreover, in this area, there is no justification for replacement of the margin of appreciation doctrine with a domestic version, whereby the courts take a restrictive approach to the protection of Convention rights, in deference to the 'area of judgment' or 'discretion' of another body,[71] in this case, to Parliament's presumed intent in not enacting a law of privacy. It is quite clear that the sponsors of the HRA explicitly contemplated the creative development of the common law to protect privacy. During the debate on the Bill, Lord Irvine said: 'it must be emphasised that the judiciary are free to develop the common law in their own independent judicial sphere,' remarked that the judges were 'pen-poised' to develop a right to privacy through the common law, and contended that 'it will be a better law if [they] developed it after incorporation because they will have regard to Articles 8 and 10 [of the Convention]'.[72] The introduction of s 12 of the Act, strengthening press freedom, was clearly premised on the understanding that the Act might well drive forward the development of common law causes of action protecting privacy against the press.

Since there are, therefore, no grounds for deference to the judgment of another body in this context, and given the clear need to strip away its margin of appreciation aspects from the Strasbourg jurisprudence, an 'activist' approach to the application of such jurisprudence,[73] leading to positive development of the law in this area, would seem to be justified. The next sections consider the current state of the law in this area, examining its efficacy in protecting privacy, and looking at the effect the HRA has so far had on it.

3 REPORTING RESTRICTIONS, BROADCASTING REGULATION AND PRESS SELF-REGULATION

Introduction

Successive governments have considered that the press should regulate itself as regards protection of privacy rather than using civil or criminal sanctions. Self-discipline has been preferred to court regulation in order to preserve press freedom. In contrast, as Chapter 6 indicated, broadcasting regulation has a statutory basis and overlaps with the control exercised by the Independent Television Commission and the Radio Authority.[74] Nevertheless, the model used for broadcasting is in some respects similar to the press self-regulatory scheme.

---

71 See further Chapter 4 pp 144–5 for recent post-HRA decisions on the subject; it was pointed out that Lord Hope in *Ex p Kebilene* [1999] 3 WLR 972 said: 'In some circumstances it will be appropriate for the courts to recognise that there is an area of judgment within which the judiciary will defer, on democratic grounds, to the considered opinion of [the democratic body or person] whose act or decision is said to be incompatible with the Convention.' See also Lord Hoffman, 'The Human Rights Act and the House of Lords' (1999) 62(2) MLR 159, esp p 161; Laws LJ, 'Wednesbury', in Forsyth and Hare (eds), *The Golden Metwand and the Crooked Cord: Essays in Honour of Sir William Wade QC*, 1998, p 201; Pannick, D, 'Principles of interpretation of Convention rights under the Human Rights Act and the discretionary area of judgment' [1998] PL 545, pp 549–51.

72 HL Deb Col 784, 24 November 1997.

73 For further discussion of this term, see Chapter 4, p 189–92.

74 See Chapter 6, pp 299–300.

Certain especially sensitive information is not dealt with under these regulatory models, but is the subject of specific reporting restrictions. In some instances, these were adopted once it was clear that self-regulation could not be trusted to ensure that some newspapers would behave responsibly.[75] The media are also subject to the DPA 1998 in respect of their processing of personal information, although, as explained below, the Act does not provide a full protection against intrusion on privacy by the media.

There is an obvious tension between press self-regulation, broadcasting regulation and Art 8 of the Convention, introduced into UK law by the HRA. As discussed below, the Press Complaints Commission (PCC) and the Broadcasting Standards Commission (BSC) have powers to adjudicate upon violation of their respective privacy codes. Their adjudications will be published by offending newspapers or broadcasters and this arguably constitutes some 'respect' for private life.[76] However, when the European Commission on Human Rights considered the PCC in *Spencer (Earl) v UK*,[77] it made no suggestion that its activities could satisfy the requirement of respect for private life. Rather, it pointedly remarked: 'the PCC has no legal power to prevent publication of material, to enforce its rulings or to grant any legal remedy against the newspaper in favour of the victim.' Thus, it is reasonably clear that reliance on the PCC alone is inconsistent with the Convention principle that rights should be 'practical and effective', not 'theoretical or illusory'.[78]

As far as broadcasting is concerned, the impact of the Independent Television Commission (ITC), which has powerful sanctions at its command, as explained in Chapter 6,[79] might be viewed as providing an effective remedy for breaches of Art 8, although this is open to question since they only operate post-broadcast. Moreover, the requirement to broadcast BSC adjudications is statutory. But the press is subject to no similar constraints. Thus, it is apparent that self-regulation of the press is no longer sufficient to protect privacy. Judicial recognition of the need to provide further protection for privacy, reflecting the demands of the HRA, is already becoming apparent.[80] The self-regulatory regime described below, therefore, is likely to become increasingly marginalised by actions relying on common law liability under the impetus of the HRA,[81] as explained in the next section. The broadcasting regime is likely to be influenced by the HRA, but less radically.

---

75 The law regarding the anonymity of rape complaints was prompted by public outrage in 1986 after the *Sun* published without her consent a picture of a rape victim in the 'Ealing vicarage' rape case taken as she was leaving church. The Press Council adjudication one year later censured the *Sun* for its unwarranted invasion of privacy: *Press Council, The Press and the People* 1987, p 241.

76 See Phillipson, *op cit*, fn 52 and Wright, *op cit*, fn 1, pp 137–38.

77 (1998) 25 EHRR CD 105.

78 *Airey v Ireland* (1979) 2 EHRR 305, p 314.

79 See p 304.

80 See *Douglas and Others v Hello!* [2001] 2 WLR 992, pp 581 *et seq* below.

81 An example of such marginalisation occurred in the case of *Holden (Amanda) v The Star* unreported; see *The Guardian*, 2 July 2001; (2001) *The Observer*, 15 July and fn 124 below and associated text.

Specific reporting restrictions[82]

Wardship proceedings, the inherent jurisdiction of the court,
and the doctrine of confidence

A number of specific restrictions prevent the reporting of information relating to children. For example, under s 12(1) of the Administration of Justice Act 1960, the press cannot report any aspect of wardship proceedings,[83] although a conviction will not be obtained where a newspaper editor publishes material relating to wardship proceedings without being aware of the connection.[84] The privacy of children also receives some protection from the courts' inherent jurisdiction to protect the privacy of minors. This was confirmed in *Central Independent Television*.[85] A programme was made depicting the work of the police, which included an investigation into a man subsequently convicted of offences of indecency. The plaintiff recognised him as her husband in a trailer shown of the programme. She did not wish her daughter, aged five, who knew nothing of his convictions, to know what had occurred and therefore sought to have the programme altered so that it would not be possible to recognise her husband. The Court of Appeal refused the injunction despite accepting that it had an inherent jurisdiction to protect the privacy of minors. It found that the protection for the privacy of children would not extend to covering publication of facts relating to those who were not carers of the child in question and which occurred before the child was born.

Exceptionally, an injunction granted to protect the anonymity of a child may be extended, on grounds of the doctrine of confidence, once the child reaches 18. This was found in *Venables, Thompson v News Group Newspapers Ltd, Associated Newspapers Ltd, MGM Ltd*.[86] Jon Venables and Robert Johnson were claimants in proceedings for injunctions. In 1993 they had murdered a boy of two, James Bulger, when they were 10 years old. The murder was particularly shocking and distressing and the facts were widely publicised in the media. They were sentenced to be detained during Her Majesty's pleasure under s 53(1) of the Children and Young Persons Act 1933 (CYPA 1933), and they were placed in separate secure units. At the conclusion of their trial, the judge granted comprehensive injunctions restricting publication of further information about the two boys, with no limit of time, based both under s 39 of the CYPA 1933 (which is discussed below) and the inherent jurisdiction of the High Court to deal with children. The claimants reached 18 and wanted the injunctions to continue. The injunctions were principally designed to protect their new identities when they were released into the community.

The court had to decide whether there was jurisdiction to grant an injunction against the whole of the media in respect of an adult to protect his identity and other relevant information. That issue raised the question of the effect of the implementation of the HRA

---

82 See also Chapter 5, pp 241–45. For further discussion see Barendt, E and Hitchens, L, *Media Law: Cases and Materials*, 2000, Chapter 7.

83 See *Re X (A Minor) (Wardship: Injunction)* [1984] 1 WLR 1422 (the Mary Bell case).

84 *Re F* [1977] Fam 58.

85 [1994] Fam 192.

86 [2001] 1 All ER 908, Fam Div (High Court of Justice, Queen's Bench Division).

1998 and, in particular, the applicability of the Convention, since the proceedings were private ones. A number of newspapers made representations to the court. They pointed out that the speech of Lord Steyn in *Secretary of State for the Home Department ex p Simms*[87] supported the presumption in favour of freedom of expression. The speech of Lord Templeman in *AG v Guardian Newspapers*,[88] the judgment of Hoffman LJ in *Central Independent Television*[89] and the judgment of Munby J in *Kelly v BBC*[90] also provided support. It was not, it was argued, a question of a balancing exercise by the court, since freedom of expression had presumptive priority. The newspapers further argued that, if either of the claimants was discovered by a journalist, it should be left to the judgment of the editor whether or not to publish the information. Instances could be found, it was pointed out, where the press was asked by the court not to publish and did not do so.[91]

It was further pointed out that if injunctions were granted, they would become a precedent for the future. One example would arise if Myra Hindley were ever released. It was pointed out that the Court of Appeal in *Chief Constable of the North Wales Police*[92] had refused to grant injunctions to prevent the Chief Constable from revealing to the owner of a caravan site the past convictions of two paedophiles living on the site. The positive obligation on a public authority, in this instance, the court, to ensure proper protection of rights under the Convention, including the right to freedom of expression, was also relied on.

The key issue in the case for the injunctions concerned the grave danger to the claimants if their new identities and whereabouts became known, since threats against them had frequently been made, including threats to their lives. They were also likely to suffer serious and relentless invasions of privacy. The court found that in the light of the judgments in the *Douglas* case[93] regarding the effect of s 12(4) of the HRA it was clear that Art 10 had to be applied directly. The injunctions had been granted originally on the basis of the inherent jurisdiction of the Family Division of the High Court to protect minors, and on the statutory provisions in s 39 of the CYPA 1933. That basis no longer existed, but the court considered that the injunction could be based upon the law of confidence, taking into account the implementation of the HRA 1998. The court therefore proceeded to grant the injunctions 'against the world'. The findings as to confidence are considered below.[94] This was a very significant ruling since it provided for the anonymity of adults. However, the question whether the injunction would have been issued on grounds of the threat of a very serious invasion of privacy alone was left open. It may be noted that the injunction was varied in July 2001 to absolve internet service providers (ISPs) from liability if matter identifying Venables or Thompson were to be posted on a website accessed through ISPs without their knowledge, if they had no knowledge that the material was on the site and had taken all reasonable steps to prevent publication of the

---

87 [1999] 3 WLR 328, p 337.
88 [1987] 1 WLR 1248, p 1297.
89 [1994] Fam 192, p 203E, 204C.
90 [2000] 3 FCR 509, p 525.
91 *See Broadmoor Hospital Authority and Another v R* [2000] 2 All ER 727.
92 [1999] QB 396.
93 [2001] 2 WLR 992.
94 See pp 584–87.

banned material.[95] However, the varied injunction did not specify the steps that ISPs would be expected to take. This episode highlighted the inefficacy of the use of injunctions in the internet era.

Juveniles involved in criminal proceedings

Under s 39 of the CYPA 1933, a court (apart from a Youth Court) could direct that details relating to a child, who was a witness or defendant, including his or her name, shall not be reported and that no picture of the child should be broadcast or published. The media could make representations to the judge, arguing that the demands of media freedom outweigh the possibility of harm to the child.

Section 49 of the Act as amended,[96] which relates to Youth Courts, now provides for an automatic ban on publishing certain identifying details relating to a juvenile offender, including his or her name and address, although the court can waive the ban. Under the Crime (Sentences) Act 1997, the court can lift reporting restrictions where it considers that a ban would be against the public interest.

The s 39 restrictions were extended under s 44 of the Youth Justice and Criminal Evidence Act 1999, which now covers children involved in adult proceedings. The 1933 Act did not cover the period before proceedings begin. The 1999 Act prohibits the publication once a criminal investigation has begun, of any matter relating to a person involved in an offence while he is under 18 which is likely to identify him. Thus, juveniles who are witnesses are also covered. Under s 44(4), the court can dispense with the restrictions if it is satisfied that it is in the public interest to do so. Thus, s 44 brings the restrictions relating to juveniles in adult proceedings into line with those under s 49 relating to youth proceedings, placing the onus on the court to find a good reason for lifting the restriction rather than having to find a good reason for imposing it. The discretion of the court is therefore more narrowly confined.[97] This is clearly an instance in which, as between the demands of press freedom and the interest in the protection of the privacy and reputation of juveniles, the latter interest has prevailed.

Victims of sexual offences

A number of special restrictions also apply to the victims of certain sexual offences. Under s 4(1)(a) of the Sexual Offences (Amendment) Act 1976, once an allegation of rape was made it was an offence to publish or broadcast the name, address or photograph of the woman who was the alleged victim. Once a person was accused of rape, nothing could be published by the media which could identify the woman. These restrictions were extended under s 1(1) of the Sexual Offences (Amendment) Act 1992 as amended by s 48 of the Youth Justice and Criminal Evidence Act 1999 and Sched 2. Section 1(1) covers a number of sexual offences as well as rape, and provides: 'where an allegation has been made that an offence to which the Act applies has been committed against a person,[98] no matter relating to that person shall during that person's lifetime be included in any publication.'

---

95   See *The Guardian*, 11 July 2001, p 2. See further guardian.co.uk/bulger.
96   As amended by Sched 2 to the Youth Justice and Criminal Evidence Act 1999.
97   See the discussion in *Lee* [1993] 1 WLR 103, pp 109–110.
98   Male victims are also covered under the CJPOA 1994, s 142.

This restriction, unlike those considered above, is not subject to any exception. Therefore, in that respect, it affords less recognition to freedom of speech, although it does not prevent the reporting of the case or discussion of it once it is over, so long as details likely to identify the victim are not revealed.

Impact of the HRA

The most important concern arising from the use of these reporting restrictions is the fear that they may create unacceptable curbs on the freedom of the press and broadcasters. The main safeguard for media freedom is the possibility that the restrictions – apart from that of anonymity in relation to certain sexual offences – may be dispensed with in the public interest. In the HRA era, Art 10 jurisprudence is likely to become an increasingly important influence upon development of the public interest test, so that it becomes the principal mechanism for a balanced resolution of rights to privacy (and, on occasion, to life) and to freedom of expression. It is apparent from Convention jurisprudence that, where two Convention rights come into conflict, some kind of balancing act between the two needs to be undertaken.[99] Although jurisprudence in this area is very limited, it appears that the margin of appreciation becomes particularly significant here, so that States have a fairly wide discretion in resolving the conflict.[100] Domestic courts will therefore have an appreciable degree of latitude in determining where to strike the balance between the two interests. Section 12 of the HRA, which enjoins the court to have 'particular regard' to Art 10 when making any order which might infringe it, would be relevant when civil matters, including wardship proceedings, or the doctrine of confidence, were in question. Since throughout this chapter the effect of s 12 and of public interest tests in relation to Art 8 rights is a central theme, the question of seeking to resolve the conflict between Arts 8 and 10 is considered fully in one section, below.[101]

Press self-regulation

The Press Council

The Press Council was created in 1953 with a view to allowing the press to regulate itself. It issued guidelines on privacy and adjudicated on complaints. It could censure a newspaper and require its adjudication to be published. In practice, however, a number of deficiencies became apparent: the Council did not issue clear enough guidelines, its decisions were seen as inconsistent and in any event ineffective: it had no power to fine or to award an injunction.[102] Moreover, it was seen as too lenient; it would not interfere if

---

99　*Otto-Preminger Institut v Austria* (1994) 19 EHRR 34, para 55. The two Convention rights in conflict there were free speech itself and – so the court found – the right to religious freedom, protected by Art 9.

100　*Ibid*. The restriction on Art 10 entailed by the seizure of an allegedly blasphemous film was justified by reference to the Art 9 right to freedom of religious belief. The Court applied a wide margin of appreciation, and simply said that 'the content of the film cannot be viewed as incapable of grounding' the conclusion of the national authorities that seizure was justified (para 56). Thus, the test applied was reminiscent of the narrow *Wednesbury* standard of unreasonableness. See also *Wingrove v UK* (1997) 24 EHRR 1. Both decisions are discussed in Chapter 6 pp 317–20.

101　See pp 617–30.

102　See further Levy, *The Press Council*, 1967.

the disclosure in question could be said to be in the public interest, and what was meant by the public interest was uncertain. Its inefficacy led the Younger Committee, convened in 1972, to recommend a number of proposals offering greater protection from intrusion by the press.[103] These proposals were not implemented but, by 1989, a perception had again begun to arise, partly influenced by *Kaye v Robertson*,[104] (discussed below) that further measures might be needed to control the press, although at the same time there was concern that they should not prevent legitimate investigative journalism. This perceived need led eventually to the formation of the Committee on Privacy and Related Matters chaired by Sir David Calcutt (hereafter 'Calcutt 1') in 1990[105] which considered a number of measures, some relevant to actual publication and some to the means of gathering information. The Committee decided that improved self-regulation should be given one final chance and recommended the creation of the Press Complaints Commission, which was set up in 1991 to police a Code of Practice for the press.

The Press Complaints Commission

After self-regulation by the Press Complaints Commission in accordance with the new Code of Practice had been in place for a year, Sir David Calcutt (hereafter 'Calcutt 2') reviewed its success[106] and determined that the Press Complaints Commission 'does not hold the balance fairly between the press and the individual (it is in essence a body set up by the industry (dominated by the industry'. He therefore proposed the introduction of a statutory tribunal which would draw up a revised code of practice for the press and would rule on alleged breaches of the code; its sanctions would include those already possessed by the Press Complaints Commission and in addition the imposition of fines and the award of compensation. When the matter was considered by the National Heritage Select Committee[107] in 1993, it rejected the proposal of a statutory tribunal in favour of the creation of another self-regulatory body to be known as the Press Commission, which would monitor a Press Code and which would have powers to fine and to award compensation. It also decided that a regulatory level beyond the commission was needed and recommended the setting up of a statutory Press Ombudsman.

However, the then Conservative Government did not respond to these proposals, making no move to appoint a new self-regulatory body or to give the Press Complaints Commission new powers. It responded to the National Heritage Select Committee in 1995,[108] stating that the system of voluntary self-regulation was to be preferred to statutory measures. It also noted various improvements in that system. The Commission itself had decided in January 1994 to appoint a Privacy Commissioner with the power to

---

103 The Committee considered the need for legal curbs on the press; it recommended the introduction of a tort of disclosure of information unlawfully acquired and a tort and crime of unlawful surveillance by means of a technical device. See Younger Committee, Cmnd 5012, 1972; criticised: MacCormick, *op cit*, fn 1.

104 [1991] FSR 62.

105 *Report of the Committee on Privacy and Related Matters*, Cm 1102, 1990 (Calcutt Report); for comment see Munro, C, 'Press freedom – how the beast was tamed' (1991) 54 MLR 104.

106 Review of Press Self-regulation, Cm 2135.

107 Fourth Report of the Committee 294–91, *Privacy and Media Intrusion*, Fourth Report, HC 291-1 (1993).

108 *Privacy and Media Intrusion*, Cm 2918, 1995.

recommend that newspaper editors should be disciplined for breaching the Press Code. In January 1995, Lord Wakeham was appointed Chairman of the Commission; he was strongly in favour of continued self-regulation and pointed to a number of improvements made in the system, including the fact that the Commission by that point had a strengthened lay majority. The government did, however, make some suggestions for improvement in the system, including the establishment of a press hotline whereby the PCC could warn editors, thought likely to publish a story in breach of the Code, of the consequences of so doing. It also proposed that a fund should be set up in order to compensate members of the public whose privacy has been invaded. Neither proposal has been implemented.

Policing the Code of Practice

The Press Complaints Commission agreed a Code of Practice in 1990, which the newspapers accepted. In 1997, the Code was made more restrictive.[109] The Commission can receive and pronounce on complaints of violation of the Code and can demand an apology for inaccuracy, or that there should be an opportunity for reply. However, almost all the clauses of the Code that relate to intrusion into private life are subject to exceptions in the public interest; this is defined non-exhaustively as including 'detecting or exposing seriously anti-social conduct, protecting public health or safety or preventing the public being misled by some statement or action of an individual or organisation'.

Code provisions

Clause 3(i) incorporates part of the wording of Art 8(1) into the Code; it provides: 'Everyone is entitled to respect for his or her private or family life, home, health and correspondence,' and that publications intruding into private life without consent must be justified. The Code makes special mention of hospitals and similar institutions in cl 9 and requires that the press must identify themselves and obtain permission before entering non-public areas. Intrusion into grief and shock must be done with sympathy and discretion under cl 5. Children receive special protection under cl 6: they must not be interviewed or photographed on subjects involving the welfare of the child or any other child in the absence of or without the consent of a parent or other adult who is responsible for the children. Children must not be approached or photographed at school without the permission of the school authorities. In 1999, Tony Blair complained to the PCC regarding a news story about Kathryn, his daughter.[110] The complaint was upheld. It was in fact the first complaint to be made under cl 6 regarding the privacy of the children of public figures at school. The PCC said: 'if every story about the PM's children which relates to their education is to be justified on the basis that he has made statements about education, then the Code provides no protection for his children or others in a similar position.' But the PCC also said that the press should be free to report on matters relating to children of public figures if such stories revealed hypocrisy or had an impact on policy. The child should only be identified if that child alone had to be the centre of the story.

---

109 The latest version of the Code was ratified by the PCC on 26 November 1997.
110 Press Complaints Report (1999). Complaint upheld: 17 July 1999.

Under cl 10, the press must avoid identifying relatives and friends of persons convicted or accused of crime without their consent. Clause 3(ii) provides that the 'use of long lens photography to take pictures of people in private places without their consent is unacceptable'. Private places are stated to be public or private property 'where there is a reasonable expectation of privacy'. The taking of photographs in private places, persistent phoning, questioning, photographing or pursuit of individuals after being asked to desist, or failing to leave private property after being asked to do so (cl 4(ii)), harassment (cl 4(i)), and the use of listening devices (cl 8), are also all proscribed. However, although all these rules, except that under cl 5, are subject to the public interest defence, it is notable that editors are enjoined in cl 4 – the harassment clause – not only to ensure that those working for them comply with the cl 4 requirements, but also not to publish material from other sources which do not meet those requirements. The requirement as regards other sources – usually freelance journalists – is not expressly included in the other privacy clauses, most notably cl 3.

Further provisions of the Code reflect certain of the reporting restrictions mentioned above, but go further than they do. Under cl 7, 'the press must not, even where the law does not prohibit it, identify children under 16 who are involved in cases concerning sexual offences, whether as victims or witnesses'. Equally, cl 12 provides that the press must not identify victims of sexual assault unless they are free to do so by law and there is 'adequate justification'.

Interpretation

The PCC's interpretation of the very significant privacy clause, cl 3, suggests that the non-consensual publication of specific identifying personal information, including addresses, is not necessarily a breach of the Code unless the person in question may be thereby put at risk from stalkers[111] or the person involved may be 'potentially vulnerable'.[112] If this is the case, it is suggested that it is not in accord with the principle of informational autonomy.

The interpretation of 'a reasonable expectation of privacy' is clearly a significant matter. Since the Press Complaints Commission, which monitors the Code and its interpretation, is a public authority under s 6 of the HRA, it is suggested that it should now adopt the Strasbourg interpretation of a reasonable expectation of privacy, thus extending it well beyond obviously private places. Strasbourg has been prepared to extend the notion of private space beyond obvious places such as the home; as Harris, O'Boyle and Warbrick put it: 'it is not enough just for the individual to be himself: he must be able to a substantial degree to keep to himself what he is and what he does ... the idea of private space need not be confined to those areas where the person has some exclusive rights of occupancy'.[113] In this respect, the Strasbourg approach may be developing in a direction which will take it away from the current UK statutory approach: 'the expanding understanding of private life set out in the *Niemetz* case indicates that a formal public/private distinction about the nature of the location will not

---

111 Complaint by a well known entertainer, complaint dated 16 July 2000.
112 Complaint of Mrs Renate John, adjudication, 2000.
113 Harris, O'Boyle and Warbrick, *op cit*, fn 27, p 309.

always be decisive'.[114] *Niemetz v FRG*[115] concerned office premises, making it clear that rights to respect for privacy are not dependent on an interest in property.

This identifiable general trend suggests that this is another instance in which the emphasis should be on the evolutive nature of the Convention[116] rather than on the outcome of particular applications to the Commission, such as that in *X v United Kingdom*.[117] The Commission found that the actions of the police in taking and filing photographs without consent of a woman arrested for taking part in a political demonstration disclosed no *prima facie* breach of Art 8. The reasoning was unclear, but a central factor appeared to be the public and voluntary nature of her activities. The decision has been viewed as out of line with the trend of Art 8 jurisprudence: 'In the opinion of some scholars, the ... decision may well be an outdated aberration in the case law of the Strasbourg organs'.[118]

The approach in other jurisdictions may indicate the direction in which the Strasbourg jurisprudence is likely to develop. In *Broadcasting Standards Commission ex p BBC*[119] it was found that privacy can be retained even in a place to which the public have access, such as a shop. The German Supreme Court[120] refused to follow the approach of the Appeal Court that privacy 'stopped at the doorstep' and that therefore no action lay for invasion of privacy in respect of events which had taken place outside the home or other clearly private spaces. The approach indicated was that one may still be entitled to respect for privacy in semi-public places if, as the court put it, it is clear by reference to 'objective criteria' that one wishes to 'left alone' so that one can, 'relying on the fact of seclusion, act in a way that [one] would not have done ... in public'. In other words, the interest in privacy was clearly distinguished from property interests. The Canadian Criminal Code also reflects such a stance.[121] Thus, it may be argued that public/private distinctions based on location are too simplistic and that a test of a reasonable expectation of privacy or, more broadly still, of control of private information would be more satisfactory.[122] On the basis of such a test, if, for example, one person engages in a whispered exchange with

---

114 Harris, O'Boyle and Warbrick, *op cit*, fn 27, p 309. *Niemetz v FRG* A 251-B (1992) concerned office premises, making it clear that rights to respect for privacy are not dependent on an interest in property.

115 A 251-B (1992).

116 The Convention must be given an 'evolutive' interpretation (*Johnstone v Ireland* A 112 para 53 (1986)), which takes account of current standards in European society (*Tyrer v UK* A 26 para 31 (1978)). These would be expected to include the presence of privacy laws across Europe.

117 Appl 5877/72; (1973) 16 YBCHE, 328.

118 Bygrave, LA, 'Data protection pursuant to the right to privacy in human rights treaties' [1999] 6(3) IJLIT 247, p 265. Bygrave notes: '... there are good grounds for holding that it ought to be accorded little weight in present and future interpretation of Article 8'. In spite of these comments, however, Bygrave concedes that in the later decision of *Friedl v Austria* (1995) A 305B (not treated by the Court on the merits due to friendly settlement), 'the Commission laid weight upon the same ... kind of factors as those mentioned in *X v United Kingdom*' (*ibid*, p 266). See also *Stewart-Brady v UK* (1999) 27 EHRR 284, in which a claim of an interference with Art 8 rights due to the taking of a photograph was declared inadmissible (although these findings were made in the context of positive State obligations and there was a conflict with Art 10).

119 [2000] 3 WLR 1327.

120 BGH, 19 December 1995 BGHZ 131, pp 322–46.

121 Section 487.01(4).

122 The Press Complaints Commission's Code of Practice defines 'private places [as] public or private property where there is a reasonable expectation of privacy'. Such a test was recommended by the Irish Law Reform Commission: *Privacy, Surveillance and Interception* (1996), Consultation Paper.

another in an almost empty street, and this exchange is recorded by means of a listening device, it is contended that an invasion of privacy has occurred which may fall within Art 8.

The interpretation of the public interest is also of crucial significance. In making a determination, the PCC takes into account the extent to which the material is already in the public domain, and the specific issues of public interest that are raised.[123] At present, despite the requirements of s 6 of the HRA, it is not apparent that it takes Art 8 or 10 jurisprudence into account in making its determinations.

Sanctions

The Commission does not require the complainant to waive any legal right of action as the Press Council was criticised for doing. However, it has the same limited sanctions as the Press Council: it has no coercive powers at all; it can do only what newspaper proprietors have agreed to allow it to do. At present, this is limited to adjudicating upon complaints received, making a public finding as to whether the Code was violated, and requesting newspapers to publish its adjudication – a request invariably complied with, to date. The Code preamble states that any publication criticised by the PCC must publish the adjudication 'in full and with due prominence'. Editors and publishers are required by the preamble to ensure that the Code is observed. The terms of the Code are incorporated into the conditions of employment of many members of the staff of newspapers, although not all. It still has no power to award fines, damages or prevent publication of offending items. It has not established a hotline, which – if editors were prepared to accept the PCC's implicit recommendation or advice not to publish – might have an effect similar to that of obtaining an *ex parte* injunction to prevent publication. No fund has been set up in order to compensate members of the public whose privacy has been invaded.

Conclusions

It is suggested that various fundamental problems are still apparent. Arguably, the PCC's own policing of the Code still errs on the side of generosity towards the newspapers. Employees of newspapers can on occasion simply ignore the Code. Or newspapers may publish material obtained by freelance journalists or others in breach of the Code. In particular, they continue to publish pictures of individuals in obviously private places (such as holiday villas), often taken with a long-range lens, without consent, even when it is virtually impossible to argue that a public interest in publication exists. An example of such flouting of the Code occurred in the case of *Holden (Amanda) v The Star*.[124] Holden, the star of a sitcom, was holidaying in a private villa in Italy when, without her consent, agency reporters took photographs of her sunbathing topless. One of the photographs was published in the Star. She obtained an *ex parte* injunction on grounds of breach of confidence, as interpreted in *Douglas and Others v Hello!*[125] preventing further publication

---

123 See PCC Report No 43 (1998), paras 3.0–3.2.
124 Unreported; see *The Guardian*, 2 July 2001; (2001) *The Observer*, 15 July.
125 [2001] 2 WLR 992.

of the photographs. Although the case was clearly covered by cl 3(ii) of the PCC's Code of Practice, she did not make a complaint, preferring – for obvious reasons – to go straight to the courts to obtain the injunction. She is claiming damages in respect of the publication which did occur.[126]

The PCC cannot prevent publication of material obtained even in gross breach of the Code and, ultimately, the PCC cannot enforce its adjudications. Absent radical changes to its powers, which would have to be agreed by the industry, it is contended that it cannot be regarded as providing an effective remedy for violations of privacy. This does not mean that it will have no role now that more effective remedies are being developed under the impetus of the HRA. It will continue to provide an alternative to using the law for those who cannot or do not wish to incur legal costs. It will continue, in conjunction with the National Union of Journalist's Code, to set benchmarking ethical standards for the profession. It also provides a means of appeasing and satisfying complainants, which may be less stressful and more speedy than court action.

Regulation of broadcasting

Introduction

Under s 142 of the Broadcasting Act 1990, the Broadcasting Complaints Commission (BCC) had a role similar to that of the PCC in adjudicating on complaints of infringement of privacy 'in or in connection with the obtaining of materials included in BBC or independent licensed television or sound broadcasts'. The term 'privacy' could receive quite a wide interpretation according to the ruling in *Broadcasting Complaints Commission ex p Granada Television Limited*.[127] Granada Television challenged a finding of the BCC that matters already in the public domain could, if republished, constitute an invasion of privacy. In judicial review proceedings, it was found that privacy differed from confidentiality and went well beyond it because it was not confined to secrets; the significant issue was not whether material was or was not in the public domain but whether, by being published, it caused hurt and anguish. There were grounds on which it could be considered that publication of the matters in question had caused distress, and therefore the BCC had not acted unreasonably in the *Wednesbury* sense in taking the view that an infringement of privacy had occurred. However, the alleged infringement of privacy could be found to have occurred only when the broadcast was over, and not earlier.[128] A broad view of privacy was also taken in *Broadcasting Standards Commission ex p BBC*;[129] it was found that a company – in this instance, Dixons – can complain of an invasion of privacy in respect of secret filming in one of its shops. The 'public' nature of the shop and the fact that the goods which were being filmed, with a view to showing that they were second-hand, were clearly on public display, did not affect this finding.

---

126 See *The Observer*, 15 July 2001.

127 (1993) *The Times*, 31 May; affirmed [1995] EMLR 163; (1994) *The Times*, 16 December, CA.

128 *Broadcasting Complaints Commission ex p Barclay and Another* (1997) 9 Admin LR 265; (1996) *The Times*, 11 October.

129 [2000] 3 WLR 1327.

The Broadcasting Standards Commission

The Broadcasting Complaints Commission was replaced by the Broadcasting Standards Commission (BSC) which was set up under s 106 of the Broadcasting Act 1996. The BSC is in a somewhat different position from that of the PCC since it is set up under statute and has certain statutory powers. This also means that such powers must all be interpreted compatibly with the Convention under s 3 of the HRA. The BSC was charged with the duty of drawing up a Code in respect of programme standards under s 107, which is based on s 152 of the 1990 Act, but for the first time the Code also had to cover matters of fairness and privacy.

Certain statutory limitations have been created. Under s 114, the BSC shall not entertain a fairness complaint (which includes a complaint regarding invasion of privacy) if the complainant already has another remedy. Under s 111, the complaint must be made by the person affected, which means that that person must have a direct interest in the subject matter of the treatment in question. The BSC adjudicates upon complaints received, makes finding as to whether the Code has been violated, and requests broadcasters to publish its adjudication. In this respect, s 119 of the 1996 Act affords the BSC a significant power, since it places the requirement to publish the BSC findings and a summary of the complaint on a statutory basis.

The Broadcasting Standards Commission's Privacy Code

This Code is similar to that of the PCC, but in certain respects, it is more extensive and offers greater guidance on the operation of the overriding public interest test. Under this test, an infringement of privacy can be justified on a number of grounds. They include revealing or detecting crime or disreputable behaviour, protecting public health or safety, exposing misleading claims made by individuals or organisations or disclosing significant incompetence in public office (cl 14).

Clause 18 provides that the use of hidden microphones must be justified by an overriding public interest. Under cl 19, if someone is inadvertently filmed, their identity should normally be obscured. Clause 25 provides that people who are currently in the news cannot object to interviewing in public places, but persistent questioning of individuals after being asked to desist can constitute an unwarranted infringement of privacy. Children receive special protection under cl 32. If under 16 they must not be interviewed without the consent of a parent or other adult who is responsible for them. If consent is refused a decision to go ahead must be justified by an overriding public interest and the child's appearance must be absolutely necessary. Persons suffering grief and shock must be approached with sensitivity and discretion under cl 28, and they should not be put under pressure to provide interviews. The Code makes special mention of agency operations in cl 33 (such as police investigations) and requires that the broadcasters must identify themselves and should leave private property if asked to do so unless there is an overriding public interest.

The role of the Independent Television Commission

The role of the Independent Television Commission (ITC) was considered in Chapter 6 and it was made clear that it has a number of significant sanctions to use against broadcasters who fail to adhere to the ITC Programme Code.[130] Although, as that chapter indicated, its role is likely to be taken over by a super-regulator, OFCOM, in 2003 or 2004, the model used for broadcasting regulation is unlikely to undergo radical change. The ITC's Programme Code has a section on privacy, also covering the gathering of information, which overlaps with the BSC Code on privacy. Clause 2.1 provides that the public interest may need to be balanced against individual privacy and states that the public interest includes detecting or exposing crime or a serious misdemeanour; protecting public health or safety; preventing the public from being misled by some statement or action of the individual or organisation concerned; exposing significant incompetence in public office. The Code echoes Art 8 in also providing that any act relying on the defence of public interest must be in proportion to the interest served.

Certain clauses are more specific and appear to be somewhat less generous to broadcasters than similar clauses in the BSC Code. For example, cl 2.7 of the ITC Code, dealing with children, goes into greater detail regarding what can be shown than does cl 32, the equivalent clause under the BSC Code. Clause 2.2(i) covers filming in institutions, such as hospitals, and requires that the broadcasters must obtain consent to transmit material when persons are shown in sensitive situations, such as in psychiatric hospitals, unless exceptions can be made in the public interest. Clause 2.2(ii) covers the filming of police operations or the investigations of similar bodies. It requires that the broadcasters must identify themselves and should normally leave private property if asked to do. Since a trespass may occur in such an instance, the licensee's most senior programme executive must be consulted before transmission and must be convinced that showing the material serves the public interest.

Clause 2.4 provides that the use of hidden microphones must not only be justified by an overriding public interest, they may only be used when it is clear that the material so acquired is essential to establish the credibility and authority of a story. Children receive special protection under cll 2.6 and 6.4. Clause 6.4 reminds broadcasters of regulations covering performances by children. Under cl 2.6, they must not be interviewed regarding private, family matters. This requirement is not subject to the public interest test. Clauses 5.8 and 2.7 remind broadcasters of the statutory reporting restrictions relating to reports on young offenders and to the reporting of sexual offences against children. The ITC Code, like the PCC Code, goes beyond what the law demands in disallowing broadcasting of the identity of children involved in a sexual offences. The privacy of persons suffering grief or distress must in particular be respected, under cl 2.5, and insensitive questioning should be avoided.

The impact of the HRA

It is suggested that the effect of the HRA on media bodies, and on the regulatory schemes in general, is already becoming apparent and is likely to be most significant as far as the PCC is concerned since, as indicated above, the problem of invasion of privacy by the press, not the broadcast media, is more pressing and the PCC has no statutory basis or powers. The most significant effect is likely to be that the PCC will be marginalised in

---

130 See p 304.

respect of its role in relation to privacy, since persons, particularly celebrities, whose privacy has been or is about to be invaded by the press will tend to seek *ex parte* injunctions and/or damages on grounds of breach of confidence, as discussed below, rather than complaining to the PCC, which has no such remedy at its command (and might be viewed, if it had, as reluctant to use it). If such a trend does become apparent, the PCC itself is likely to review its powers since otherwise, the self-regulation system is likely to become a dead letter. It may have to adopt some of the proposals it has at present rejected, such as the hotline system and the award of compensation to complainants.

Clearly, an *ex parte* injunction could also be obtained restraining the showing of a broadcast, on grounds of breach of confidence or, in the case of media bodies that are also public authorities, on grounds of invasion of privacy under Art 8, using s 7(1)(a) of the HRA. But it is suggested that marginalisation of the ITC and BSC as bodies charged, *inter alia*, with protecting privacy, is less likely to occur or likely to occur to a lesser extent, since the problem posed by invasion of privacy by the broadcast media does not seem to have reached the same proportions, and the sanctions available to the ITC, and to the lesser extent to the BSC, create greater confidence in the ability of those bodies to address it.

The BSC and ITC are subject to judicial review,[131] and this is also probably the case in respect of the PCC.[132] Therefore, as Chapter 4 indicated, it is almost certain that the BSC and ITC are functional public authorities, and this is probably also true of the PCC.[133] The BBC and possibly Channel 4, as bodies with a public service remit, will probably be public authorities.[134] Therefore, under s 6 of the HRA, these bodies are bound to comply with the Convention rights in exercising their functions. The duties of the ITC under s 6 of the HRA can be viewed as additional and complementary to those it has under s 6 of the Broadcasting Act 1990, while the BSC's duties under s 6 of the HRA are additional to those imposed under s 107 of the Broadcasting Act 1996. If these bodies fail to uphold complaints relating to invasion of privacy, proceedings could be brought against them under s 7(1)(a) of the HRA. In any such proceedings, a court would now have to satisfy s 12(4)(b) of the HRA, which would mean that the privacy Codes of these bodies would be admissible in evidence and would be considered. By this means, the PCC Code has acquired, it is suggested, a quasi-legal status. The ITC and BSC Codes already had such a status since they were set up under statute, but their status may now be viewed as enhanced, although the BSC Code was taken into account in any event in the pre-HRA ruling in *Broadcasting Standards Commission ex p BBC*.[135]

---

131 The bodies they replaced were so subject and this has already been found to be the case in respect of the BSC: see *R v BCC ex p Owen* [1985] QB 1153; *R v BSC ex p BBC* [2000] 3 WLR 1327; *R v IBA ex p Whitehouse* (1985) *The Times*, 4 April.

132 See *PCC ex p Stewart-Brady* (1997) 9 Admin LR 274.

133 See pp 157–59. See also fn 137 below.

134 There is a possible difficulty with this proposition which will have to be addressed by the courts. Arguably, the BBC (and Channel 4) may also, exceptionally, be viewed as both public authorities and victims for HRA purposes. They appear to satisfy the test for victims at Strasbourg, which is encapsulated under HRA 1998, s 7(7), since, although in a sense they are emanations of the State, they are editorially independent from it. It would of course be bizarre if they could not be viewed as victims since that would run contrary to the scrutinising role over the State that one would expect these bodies, especially the BBC, to exercise.

135 [2000] 3 WLR 1327.

In debate on the Human Rights Bill, a great deal of concern was voiced in Parliament about the possibility, as regards the PCC, that it would be a public authority for the purposes of the HRA. It was thought that it would be subject to judicial review for violation of the Convention in its rulings and therefore in some way in a position to threaten press freedom.[136] Although in theory this appears to be the case, it is unlikely in practice that this route will frequently be explored: it would be likely to provide, it is suggested, a merely paper remedy. Those expressing that concern appeared to overlook the fact that the PCC has no coercive powers. As far as both the PCC and BSC are concerned, it is also hard to see what impact a finding of breach of the Convention could have on the bodies they are regulating. If a finding was made that either body had violated the Convention rights, for example by finding that someone's privacy had not been invaded when, in the court's view, Art 8 required a contrary conclusion,[137] the very most that the court could do would be to quash the finding of that body by a quashing order (formerly *certiorari*) and require it to reconsider the case by a mandatory order (formerly *mandamus*). Damages could conceivably be awarded against it also. But this would not affect the newspapers or broadcasters themselves, in the sense that none of this would change the fact that the only 'remedies' they would be subject to would be those available at present: the publication of the BSC's adjudications and – although they could not be forced to do this – those of the PCC. However, an action brought directly against the ITC under s 7(1)(a) on grounds of failing to use sanctions in respect of an invasion of privacy in breach of its Privacy Code could lead to a mandatory order requiring the ITC to use the sanctions it has available, including, ultimately, withdrawal of its licence, against the broadcaster concerned. This possibility could have some impact, although it would apply post-broadcast; it would not prevent the broadcast of the material.

The only way in which the PCC could acquire greater powers than it has at present (for example, to levy fines against newspapers adjudged to have breached the Code) would be if the newspaper industry collectively agreed that it should have the power to demand fines and even then, it is hard to see what the sanction for non-payment would be, other than adverse publicity. It is possible that if actions are successfully brought against it, the PCC may seek agreement from the industry that breach of the PCC Code should lead to disciplinary action, including dismissal. But again, it could not enforce such action. Or it could ask newspapers to indemnify it against possible actions under the HRA. It goes without saying that the PCC, not having any statutory basis or powers, could not be given by the industry more than the power to request a newspaper not to publish a given article; it could never require non-publication. In short, therefore, the effect of the HRA on the PCC may be in the short term that a layer of judicial supervision will be added onto what will remain a mere self-regulatory body, with powers to do only that which the industry agrees voluntarily to submit to. In the longer term, the HRA may play a crucial part in the dismantling of the whole self-regulatory system – at least as far as privacy complaints are concerned.

---

136 See Hansard, HL Col 784, 24 November 1997.

137 Anna Ford, a BBC journalist, applied to the High Court for judicial review of the PCC's decision to reject her claim that the *Daily Mail* breached her right to privacy by publishing pictures of her on holiday with her partner (*The Observer*, 15 July 2001). The PCC's decision was vindicated.

4 LIABILITY FOR DISCLOSING PERSONAL INFORMATION

Introduction

This section will consider liability for publishing personal information outside reliance on s 7(1)(a) of the HRA. Its focus will be on the doctrine of confidence as by far the most apt cause of action for the protection of personal information from disclosure in the existing law. It will be argued that when the general principles and underlying values of the Convention – rather than the outcomes of particular applications – are examined, it can be discerned that the Convention does suggest that domestic law should provide a more effective remedy against invasions of privacy by publications, a view which is beginning to find judicial acceptance.[138]

The general thesis of this section is that the doctrine of confidence will be able to afford far more protection in this area than commonly thought, and that some recognition of its potential is already apparent,[139] but that an enormous amount of judicial labour will be required to flesh out and give definition to the current action which lacks at present a clear legal profile. It will be argued that any law protecting a person from unwanted publication of personal information must inevitably become 'a legal porcupine, which bristles with difficulties',[140] but that workable and principled solutions to the problems associated with the legal right to respect for privacy under Art 8 can be developed. In particular, it will be strongly contended that the perception of conflict between speech and privacy is often exaggerated and simplistic, and indeed that an examination of the values underlying each reveals them to be in many respects mutually supportive, rather than invariably antagonistic. In conclusion, it will be contended that the goals in view in developing a privacy law – the protection of human dignity and autonomy, the movement away from the demeaning and debasing pursuit of certain figures and the destruction of their privacy in order to sell newspapers, the consequent enhancement of the speech of the press and enrichment of our cultural life – should be sufficient to encourage the judiciary to grasp at the possibilities which the HRA offers to develop a privacy law in all but name.

Defamation and malicious falsehood

The law of defamation may offer some protection to an individual who has suffered from the unauthorised disclosure of private matters, but the interest protected by defamation – the interest of the individual in preserving his or her reputation – is far from coterminous with the interest in preserving privacy. A reputation may not suffer, but the fact that personal information is spread abroad may nevertheless be hurtful in itself for the

---

138 See p 581–83, below.

139 See the comments of Laws J in *Hellewell v Chief Constable of Derbyshire* [1995] 1 WLR 804, p 805 and the findings of the European Commission on Human Rights in *Spencer (Earl) v United Kingdom* (1998) 25 EHRR CD 105, discussed below. See also *Douglas and Others v Hello!* [2001] 2 WLR 992 and associated text.

140 The phrase is borrowed from *dicta* in an administrative law case: *Inner London Education Authority ex p Westminster CC* [1986] 1 WLR 28.

individual affected. Thus, no remedy was available in *Corelli v Wall*[141] which arose from publication by the defendants, without the plaintiff's permission, of postcards depicting imaginary events in her life. Such publication was not found to be libellous, and no remedy lay in copyright as the copyright was in the creator of the cards.

The ruling in *Kaye v Robertson and Another*[142] may be said to have made clear the inadequacy of defamation as a remedy for invasions of privacy. Mr Kaye, a well known actor, was involved in a car accident and suffered severe head injuries. While he was lying in hospital two journalists from the *Sunday Sport*, acting on Mr Robertson's orders, got into his room, photographed him and interviewed him. Owing to his injuries, he did not object to their presence and shortly after the incident had no recollection of it. The resultant article gave the impression that Mr Kaye had consented to the interview. His advisers sought and obtained an injunction restraining the defendants from publishing the photographs and the interview. On appeal by the defendants the Court of Appeal ruled that the plaintiff's claim could not be based on a right to privacy as such a right is unknown to English law. His true grievance lay in the 'monstrous invasion of privacy' which he had suffered but he would have to look to other rights of action in order to obtain a remedy, namely libel and malicious falsehood. The basis of the defamation claim was that the article's implication that Mr Kaye had consented to a first 'exclusive' interview for a 'lurid and sensational' newspaper such as the *Sunday Sport* would lower him in the esteem of right thinking people. The Court of Appeal held that this claim might well succeed, but that as such a conclusion was not inevitable it could not warrant grant of an interim injunction, basing this ruling on *Herbage v Times Newspapers and Others*.[143]

The court then considered malicious falsehood. First, it had to be shown that the defendant had published about the plaintiff words which were false. Their Lordships considered that any reasonable jury would find that the implication contained in the words of the article was false. As the case was, on that basis, clear cut, an interim injunction could in principle be granted. Secondly, it had to be shown that the words were published maliciously. Malice would be inferred if it was proved that the words were calculated to produce damage and that the defendant knew them to be false. The reporters clearly realised that Mr Kaye was unable to give them any informed consent. Any subsequent publication of the falsehood would therefore be malicious. Thirdly, damage must have followed as a direct result of the publication of the falsehood. The words had produced damage in that they had diminished the value of Mr Kaye's right to sell the story of his accident at some later date. That ground of action was therefore made out. Therefore, an injunction restraining the defendants until trial from publishing anything which suggested that the plaintiff had given an informed consent to the interview or the taking of the photographs was substituted for the original order. However, this was a limited injunction which allowed publication of the story with certain of the photographs, provided that it was not claimed that the plaintiff had given consent. Thus, it seemed that no effective remedy was available for the plaintiff. Legatt LJ

---

141 (1906) 22 TLR 532 (Ch).

142 [1991] FSR 62; (1991) *The Times*, 21 March; for comment, see Prescott, P, '*Kaye v Robertson*: a reply' (1991) 54 MLR 451; Bedingfield, D, 'Privacy or publicity: the enduring confusion surrounding the american tort of invasion of privacy' (1992) 55 MLR 111; Markesinis, BS, 'The Calcutt Report must not be forgotten' (1992) 55 MLR 118.

143 (1981) *The Times*, 1 May.

concluded his ruling by saying: 'We do not need a First Amendment to preserve the freedom of the Press, but the abuse of that freedom can be ensured only by the enforcement of a right to privacy.'[144]

Trespass

It has been suggested[145] that there are sufficient remedies in the common law of trespass to cover at least the kind of situation which arose in *Kaye v Robertson*.[146] The physical intrusion into the hospital involved trespass on to property (because the reporters, given their purpose, could have no implied licence to be there). Kaye obviously could not have brought an action on his own account as his property had not been trespassed upon, but the solution would have been to join the hospital as co-plaintiff in the action. Once trespass had been established, the court could exercise its equitable jurisdiction to grant an injunction to prevent the defendants from profiting from their own wrong by publishing the material obtained by the trespass for gain. The case of *Chappell and Co Limited v Columbia Gramophone Co*[147] was cited as support for this course of action. In that case, the defendants had wrongfully used the plaintiff's sheet music to make gramophone records. Although the making of the records themselves was not a violation of the plaintiff's legal rights, the court ordered their destruction on the grounds that the defendants should not be allowed to 'reap all the proceeds of their wrongdoing'. However, it is clear that there is no guarantee that possible co-plaintiffs (such as hotel owners) would agree to join in such actions.

Thus, the remedy available even in a case of physical intrusion onto private land would not be certain. Further, an action in trespass would be of limited application in relation to the interviewing of disaster or accident victims and their relatives generally: a person might be interviewed at or near the scene of a disaster in a public place or in a semi-private place, such as a shopping mall, which reporters could be viewed as having an implied licence to enter. Where, in such instances, victims of a disaster did not consent to be interviewed, it would not appear that interviewing them could found a cause of action in trespass. Further, it should be noted that if detailed information regarding Mr Kaye's condition had been obtained without physically entering the hospital – by photographing him with a long range lens or perhaps by interviewing him over the telephone – an action in trespass, as the cause of action is currently conceived, would not be possible. Specific remedies for invasion of privacy would be more appropriate, subject to a broad public interest defence.

However, although it is suggested that in the HRA era, the doctrine of confidence has developed into a privacy remedy, and that therefore there is less of a pressing need to look to trespass to provide such a remedy, it is possible that trespass will also show some development, under the impetus of the HRA. The findings in *Douglas and Others v Hello!*,[148] considered below, as to the effect of the Act on the common law, would be

---

144 [1991] FSR 621, p 104.
145 Prescott, op cit, fn 142.
146 [1991] FSR 62.
147 [1914] 2 Ch 745, pp 752, 754, 756, CA.
148 *Douglas and Others v Hello!* [2001] 2 WLR 992.

equally applicable to trespass. Arguably, a judge has a duty, under s 6 of the HRA and – where freedom of expression is in issue – s 12, to ensure that the common law reflects the Convention rights. In a case similar to that of *Kaye*, freedom of expression would be in issue and therefore, if a judge was faced with a plaintiff who was seeking to bring an action in trespass rather than in confidence, it is arguable that she should adapt the doctrine of trespass in order to provide a remedy for the invasion of privacy.

It is also possible, and perhaps more probable, that trespass will be developed under the HRA, not to provide a remedy in relation to the processing and publication of information, but in respect of the invasion of privacy which occurs due to an intrusion which is not a physical intrusion on property – for example, watching the home, using a long range lens to take photographs of persons on private property, etc. This is a matter which is considered in Chapter 12.

Causing harassment, alarm or distress, and anti-social behaviour

The Protection from Harassment Act 1997 (PHA) might offer a remedy in respect of some forms of repeated intrusions on privacy, although it was not aimed at persons such as reporters or photographers, but at 'stalkers'. Sections 1 and 2 make it an offence to pursue a course of conduct that amounts to harassment of another where the harasser knows or ought to know that this will be its effect. Apart from creating criminal liability for stalking, the Act also provides a civil remedy in s 3 in the form of damages or a restraining order. 'Conduct' includes speech (s 7(4)). The harassment must occur on more than one occasion (s 7(3)) and a defence of reasonableness is available (s 1(1)(c)).[149]

Since the remedies provided by the Act are statutory, s 3 of the HRA applies. The possibility that the Act could be used in respect of the invasion of privacy that occurs when a person – often a journalist – is seeking to obtain information about an individual by, for example, watching the home, interviewing neighbours, or planting bugging devices is considered in Chapter 12. But, it may be argued that s 3 of the PHA could also be used in respect of the publication of information. Bearing in mind the obligation of a court to interpret the PHA compatibly with Art 8 under the HRA, it could be argued that if on more than one occasion an article was published in a newspaper which caused profound distress to its subject due to its publication of private facts and to the indirect possibility of harassment or injury from members of the public who had read it, an injunction or damages could be obtained under s 3. An argument similar to this one was used successfully against the *Sun* newspaper in 2001. The *Sun* had published an article and, on a further occasion, readers' letters, attacking a black woman who was a civilian employee in a London police station. She had reported a racist incident relating to an asylum seeker, with the result that two police officers were disciplined. The *Sun*, in an article attacking 'political correctness gone mad' and omitting a number of key facts (including the fact that a white police officer had also reported the racist incident), identified her and the police station where she worked and invited readers to express their views as to her conduct. A number did so, in very hostile terms. She received hate

---

149 See further Chapter 9, pp 510–12.

mail and was also very distressed by the items; since she worked on the front desk she felt very vulnerable to attack from members of the public. She left her job as a consequence. Damages were awarded against the *Sun* under s 3 of the 1997 Act and the decision was affirmed on appeal.[150]

This was an interesting and entirely novel use of s 3 of the 1997 Act; it suggests that the judiciary are determined to find a remedy for the plaintiff who has suffered a gross breach of the right to respect for privacy under Art 8 even where no obvious remedy for the particular breach in question is available and despite the effect of s 12 of the HRA. However, had there been one item of publication only – in which identifying as well as distressing details were given – it is doubtful whether the 1997 Act could have been used, unless a particular article could be viewed as, say, being in two parts. This decision emphasises the need for specific remedies for invasion of privacy by the publication of identifying and distressing details. A similar example would arise where a tabloid newspaper published a story in sensationalist terms about a person who had been acquitted of a serious offence, or about a person bringing an action for race discrimination, identifying the individual involved and/or their place of work. He or she might suffer distress due to the articles themselves and also severe harassment from neighbours and others, which might make it impossible to avoid abandoning their home. It is arguable that a remedy should be available in such a situation, although it would have to be balanced against the right to freedom of expression of the newspaper, since s 12 of the HRA would be applicable and Art 10 would in any event be relevant, due to the effect of s 3 HRA. The defence of reasonableness could be used as the mechanism for recognising the value of freedom of expression.

Similar arguments could also be used in respect of the offences created under the 1997 Act and of the similar offences created under the Public Order Act 1986,[151] s 1 of the Crime and Disorder Act 1998 and s 41 of the Criminal Justice and Police Act 2001, all of which were discussed in Chapter 9,[152] although, of course, the police would have to take the initiative. All, except s 41 of the 2001 Act, contain similar defences which would allow for recognition to be given to freedom of expression under s 3 of the HRA, although s 12 of the HRA would not be applicable since the proceedings would be criminal. Methods of balancing expression and privacy rights are considered below.

Breach of confidence[153]

The common law doctrine of breach of confidence will protect some confidential communications and its breadth has for some time supported the view that it could

---

150 *Thomas (Esther) v News Group Newspapers* (2001) WL 753464; judgment of 18 July 2001.

151 See the use of the 1986 Act, s 5, in *Vigon v DPP* [1998] Crim LR 298; (1998) 162 JP 115. (The defendant had positioned a video camera in the changing room attached to his market stall, in which women were changing into swimming costumes. He was charged with the offence under s 5 since it was found that the switching on and use of the camera had caused the women harassment, alarm and distress, and his behaviour was insulting to them.) However, the requirement of immediacy which has been found to apply to s 4 of the 1986 Act and which therefore probably also applies to ss 5 and 4A may preclude the use of these provisions in the circumstances envisaged (see *R v Horseferry Road Metropolitan Stipendiary Magistrate ex p Siadatan* [1991] 1 All ER 324). See further Chapter 9, pp 506–10.

152 See pp 505–12.

153 See generally Dworkin, G, *Confidence in the Law*, 1971; Gurry, F, *Breach of Confidence*, 1991; Jones, G (1970) 86 LQR 463.

provide a general means of protecting personal information, although this area of law developed largely as a means of protecting commercial secrets. The Younger Committee, which was convened to report on privacy,[154] considered that confidence was the area of the law which offered the most effective protection for the privacy of personal information. However, less emphasis was placed on the ability of the doctrine to protect privacy in the discussions of both privacy and confidence which occurred following the *Kaye* case.[155] It can provide, it is suggested, protection from the invasion of privacy that occurs when personal information is published, causing distress, and probably from the invasion that can indirectly occur when the disclosure of information is likely to lead others to invade privacy. It cannot directly protect persons from invasions of privacy – such as persistent telephoning or the planting of bugs – created by information-seekers.

Elements of confidence

The House of Lords in *AG v Guardian Newspapers (No 2)*[156] found that the ruling in *Coco v AN Clark (Engineers) Limited*[157] conveniently summarised the three traditionally accepted key elements of the law of confidence: 'First the information itself ... must have the necessary quality of confidence about it. Secondly, that information must have been imparted in circumstances importing an obligation of confidence. Thirdly, there must be an unauthorised use of that information to the detriment of the party communicating it.' Even if these elements are made out, publication of the information may still be possible if the defence of public interest applies.

To satisfy the requirements of the first element, information must, it seems, not be in the public domain and must not be trivial.[158] The third element, unauthorised use of information, is fairly self-explanatory; as to detriment, it appears from the cases either that unwanted revelation of private facts *per se* may constitute detriment for the purposes of the law of confidence,[159] or, alternatively, that detriment might not always be necessary.[160] However, it is in the second element – the circumstances in which the courts will find an obligation of confidence to have been imposed – that the most radical development has occurred. Under the traditional model of confidence, one of two ingredients had to be satisfied for such an obligation to arise. The first was that, at least in cases involving personal, as opposed to commercial information, there had to be some identifiable pre-existing intimate or necessarily confidential relationship between confider

---

154 See *Report of the Committee on Privacy*, Cmnd 5012, 1972.

155 See the Calcutt Committee on Privacy and Related Matters (Cmnd 1102, 1990, para 32) and Wacks, *op cit*, fn 1, p 56); compare the earlier view of the Younger Committee (*Report of the Committee on Privacy*, Cmnd 5012, 1972, p 26).

156 [1990] 1 AC 109.

157 [1969] RPC 41, p 47.

158 Another change of note is that the courts now take a flexible approach to the form of the information; see Fenwick, H and Phillipson, G, 'Confidence and privacy: a re-examination' (1996) 55 CLJ 447, pp 449–50. See further below.

159 *AG v Guardian Newspapers (No 2)* [1990] 1 AC 109, p 265, *per* Lord Keith.

160 *Ibid*. Lord Goff explicitly left the point open (*ibid*, pp 281–82), while Lord Griffiths (*ibid*, p 270) thought that it was required. The remainder of the House did not address the point. In *X v Y* ([1988] 2 All ER 650, pp 651 and 657) it was held *per curiam* that actual or possible detriment to the plaintiff was 'not a necessary precondition to injunctive relief' ([1988] 2 All ER 650, pp 651 and 657). In the recent *Source Informatics* case [2000] 2 WLR 953, the Court of Appeal did not attempt to resolve the matter, but appeared to favour Lord Keith's view.

and confidant, such as a professional relationship of trust,[161] or marriage,[162] from which the obligation of confidence could be inferred, in the absence of an express agreement on the matter.

Development of the doctrine[163]

(1) The quality of confidentiality

Clearly, information is not confidential if it is already in the public domain. However, making a determination on this matter is often problematic. In *AG v Guardian Newspapers (No 2)*,[164] Lord Keith indicated that whether information is in the public domain will often be a matter of degree and therefore prior disclosure to a limited group of people might not rob the information of its confidentiality. His Lordship was referring to the possibility of publication abroad, but the principle behind his comments – that the true test is whether further and more serious damage will flow from the fresh disclosure contemplated[165] – could apply in a case in which the relevant information had been previously disclosed in this country but in such a manner or at such a distance in the past that the information could not fairly be characterised as being currently in the public domain. Probably, it has also been the case that confidence would not cover instances where the information was initially obtained through observation in a public place. However, the decision in *HRH Princess of Wales v MGN Newspapers Limited and Others*[166] casts some doubt on this contention, since the information in question was obtained in a gymnasium attended by other club members and therefore, clearly, it had been disseminated to an extent, albeit in a manner limited enough to prevent it from being viewed as in the public domain. An interim injunction to protect the information was nevertheless granted. Thus, information obtained by means of observation in similar semi-public places, such as restaurants, might now be found to retain the necessary quality of confidence. Where information conveys a particular message which is itself already in the public domain, the level of detail which accompanies it, which is not in the public domain, may allow the information to be termed confidential.[167] 'Public domain' has apparently become a rather more flexible – and imprecise – concept.

It is also apparent, it is suggested, that a contrary development is apparent in relation to government assertions of a breach of confidence. As Chapter 7 indicated, *AG v Times*, the Tomlinson case,[168] suggested that a tendency to find that information is already in the public domain even where it has been disseminated only to a small group of persons is apparent.[169] If it can eventually be said that the interpretation of public domain differs

---

161 See, eg, *W v Egdell* [1990] Ch 359 (doctor-patient); *X v Y (ibid)* ; *AG v Guardian Newspapers (No 2)* [1990] 1 AC 109 (both employer-employee).

162 As in *Duchess of Argyll v Duke of Argyll* [1967] 1 Ch 302.

163 This section is partly drawn from Fenwick and Phillipson, *op cit*, fn 158.

164 [1990] 1 AC 109, p 260.

165 Note the similar findings in the privacy context on this point in *Broadcasting Complaints Commission ex p Granada TV Ltd* (1993) *The Times*, 31 May; affirmed [1995] EMLR 163; (1994) *The Times*, 16 December, CA.

166 Transcript, Association of Official Shorthandwriters Limited, 8 November 1993. Discussed below.

167 See *Barrymore v NGN Ltd* [1997] FSR 600.

168 See Chapter 7, p 361.

169 See pp 361–62.

depending on whether the plaintiff is the government or a private individual, this would accord with the requirements of Strasbourg jurisprudence as recognised under s 2 of the HRA since in the former instance, the strong individual right under Art 8 is not also at stake. Section 12(4)(a)(i) of the HRA requires a court to 'have particular regard' to 'the extent to which the material has, or is about to become available to the public' when considering the grant of relief which, if granted, might affect the exercise of the Art 10 right (s 12(1)). If the development indicated becomes a settled one, this would mean that the courts had accepted that differing approaches should be taken to the interpretation of s 12(4)(a)(i) of the HRA, depending on whether Art 8 was or was not at stake. Moreover, the requirement to take into account the extent to which the material is about to become available (emphasis added) would have the effect of widening the public domain test in a manner reconcilable with the spirit of *AG v Times* (Tomlinson case), but arguably not with *HRH Princess of Wales v MGN Newspapers Limited and Others*.[170]

What is 'information' for the purposes of the law of confidence? It is suggested that both substance and form will be in question. The traditional view was that equity would not intervene to protect trivial information. However, there are signs that the categories of information capable of being accounted sufficiently substantial are widening: information concerning an individual's sexual orientation (*Stephens v Avery*)[171] and physical appearance (*HRH Princess of Wales*) has been found to merit protection.

A number of decisions suggest that the courts will also adopt a flexible approach to the form of the information. In *HRH Princess of Wales*, Drake J had no hesitation in granting interim injunctions to prevent the Daily Mirror and others from publishing photographs of the Princess exercising in a gymnasium, taken by the gymnasium owner without her knowledge or consent. The plaintiff's case was based both on breach of contract and on confidence, but Drake J appeared to take the view that although the contractual claim was more clearly made out, either limb of the claim would have justified the injunction.[172] Similarly, in *Shelley Films Limited v Rex Features Limited*[173] the defendant was restrained by injunction from publishing photographs, which had been taken without permission on the set of the film Frankenstein. The possibility that the taking of photographs can amount to the acquiring of confidential information was also expressly accepted by Laws J in *Hellewell v Chief Constable of Derbyshire*.[174] These three decisions go much further, it is suggested, than simply affirming that photographs can carry information for the purposes of the law of confidence.[175] A photograph is merely a record and as such may be treated as any other means of recording information. However, in these instances, the 'information' had not been captured and contained in any particular form until the defendant brought that about. It would seem to follow that had the gymnasium owner in the *HRH Princess of Wales* case merely observed Princess Diana's appearance in the gymnasium without recording it, he would have been in possession of 'information', and an interim injunction to restrain publication of the

---

170 Transcript, Association of Official Shorthandwriters Limited, 8 November 1993.
171 [1988] Ch 449.
172 *Ibid*, pp 4–5.
173 [1994] EMLR 134.
174 [1995] 1 WLR 804, p 807.
175 As earlier indicated by *Pollard v Photographic Company* (1888) Ch 345.

observations would have been available. Thus it appears, it is submitted, that a record of any matter of substance not already in the public domain may amount to confidential information for the purposes of the doctrine of confidence.

But it can be concluded that since most of the case law concerns commercial information,[176] the courts have not yet evolved any workable tests to decide what kinds of personal information should be protected, save for the requirement that the information must not be 'in the public domain' – a negative requirement considered below – and that it must not be mere trivial tittle-tattle. It appears from *Stephens v Avery*[177] and *Michael Barrymore*[178] that information relating to an individual's sexual life may merit protection,[179] a decision clearly in harmony with the approach of Strasbourg[180] and the DPA 1998.[181] The US 'private facts' tort requires that 'the matter made public must be one which would be offensive and objectionable to a reasonable man of ordinary sensibilities'.[182] However, if, as has been argued, protection for informational autonomy provides the theoretical underpinning of the action to protect privacy, objective notions of offensiveness should not be the essential issue, since it is a person's ability to apply their own standards of openness which should – within limits – be protected.[183]

A further potential problem concerns the possibly inadequate scope of the confidence action in this area. Confidence requires unauthorised use of personal 'information',[184] like many privacy torts which take as the root of the complaint the publication of 'private facts'.[185] On its face, therefore, it would not appear to encompass situations where there has clearly been some invasion of privacy, assessed intuitively, but where it is difficult to conceptualise what has occurred as concerning 'information'. An example would be a broadcast showing mourners at a funeral in acute emotional anguish.[186] The root of the complaint in such situations, it is suggested, is not that the 'fact' that a person is weeping,

---

176 In such cases, the issue of whether the information is 'confidential' may be readily resolved by reference to its potential or actual commercial value.

177 [1988] Ch 449.

178 [1997] FSR 600.

179 The decision in *HRH Princess of Wales* Transcript, Association of Official Shorthandwriters Limited, 8 November 1993 (which concerned photographs taken of the Princess exercising while wearing a leotard) gives some weak *prima facie* evidence that information regarding physical appearance may attract protection in some circumstances.

180 See *Lustig-Prean v UK* (1999) 29 EHRR 548; discussed in Chapter 16, pp 1056–57.

181 As indicated below, p 604, such information is classified as 'sensitive personal data' along with matters such as a person's religious and political opinions, and his physical and mental health (s 2). The processing of 'sensitive personal data' attracts a higher level of safeguards than normal data under Data Protection Principle 1(b) (Sched 1) as elucidated by Sched 3.

182 Prosser, D, 'Privacy' (1960) 48 Calif L Rev 383, p 396. The tort grew out of the Warren and Brandeis article (*op cit*, fn 8). The Restatement (Second) of the Law of Torts, 625D defines the tort as follows: 'One who gives publicity to a matter concerning the private life of another is subject to liability to the other for invasion of his privacy, if the matter publicised is of a kind that (a) would be highly offensive to a reasonable person and (b) is not of legitimate concern to the public.'

183 See above, pp 530–32.

184 See the definition in *Coco* [1969] RPC 41, fn 157 and associated text).

185 Privacy torts in the United States and New Zealand require the disclosure of identifiable private facts. A number of Canadian cases have also stressed this requirement, although it is not required by the strict words of the relevant section of the Canadian Charter: see Paton-Simpson, E, 'Private circles and public squares: invasion of privacy by the publication of "private facts"' (1998) 61 MLR 318.

186 *Ibid*, p 337.

or that details of their appearance in mourning have been disclosed, but rather of mass intrusion through unwanted attention into a highly personal situation.[187] Moreover, a requirement of identifiable 'information' may find it difficult to accommodate the importance of anonymity and context. For example, some people may be happy to appear on a public beach nude or topless when surrounded by others doing likewise, because in this situation their nudity becomes unremarkable and therefore un-remarked upon. If, however, a photograph is taken and given mass publicity through the pages of a newspaper, feelings of intrusion and violation justifiably arise.[188] The difficulty is that it might seem problematic to define such situations as involving protected information: the mere 'fact' that a person is weeping at a funeral seems too innocuous to count as 'personal information', while the normally private nature of the appearance of someone's unclothed body might appear to be lost by the voluntary public exposure of it on a beach.

Such an approach would be, we suggest, simplistic. Wacks has made the important point that 'any definition of 'personal information' must ... refer both to the quality of the information and to the reasonable expectation of the individual concerning its use'.[189] In other words, one cannot assess whether information is 'personal' or not, without looking at the use which the defendant has made or proposes to make of it. Can confidence accommodate such delicate assessments? It should be recalled that the doctrine protects against unauthorised use of information and so is capable of singling out particular actions of defendants as giving rise to liability. Moreover, there is no reason why the 'reasonable man' test it now employs to decide whether an obligation of confidentiality should be imposed could not be pressed into service to determine what is to count as protected information in the first place. A reasonable man might be expected to understand that the activities of mourners at a funeral, or nude sunbathers on a beach, can be seen as personal in so far as such people reasonably expected that their behaviour would not be subject to unwanted mass attention. Thus, contrary to the doubts expressed on this point,[190] it is suggested that a duty of confidentiality could attach in respect of particular uses of information, such as mass publicity.

Such an approach would also resolve a further objection to the use of confidence in privacy cases, namely the fear that precisely because the action – unlike the American privacy torts[191] – does not require wide publicity, but only 'unauthorised use' of information, it could in principle catch mere gossip between friends and neighbours. It has been argued that the intervention of the blunt tool of the law into the delicate area of social life and friendship which this would entail would both create intolerable legal uncertainty and also wrongly introduce the possibility of legal sanctions into an area which depends upon the unenforceable trust of one who confides for its moral

---

187 For the argument that such matters should be included within the definition of privacy, see Gavison, R, 'Privacy and the limits of law' (1980) 89(3) Yale LJ 421; Paton-Simpson, *ibid*, pp 337–38; Reinman, J, 'Driving to the Panopticon: a philosophical exploration of the risks to privacy posed by the highway technology of the future' (1995) 11 Computer & High Tech LJ 27, p 30. For a contrary view, see Parent, pp 306–07.

188 This example is used because of the propensity of tabloid photographers to take photographs of celebrities in such situations.

189 Wacks, *Personal Information: Privacy and the Law*, 1980, p 24.

190 Wacks, *op cit*, fn 1, p 56.

191 This applies to the US 'false light' and 'private facts' torts. See Wacks, *ibid*, pp 56–59, for an extended comparison of confidence with the American torts.

integrity.[192] The solution to this problem would be, we suggest, to adapt the rule from defamation for cases of personal, as opposed to commercial information and, as suggested by Warren and Brandeis,[193] to develop a rule that no cause of action would lie in respect of oral publication by private individuals in the absence of actual financial loss to the plaintiff.[194] Such a limitation is justifiable in principle, on the approach just indicated: our reasonable expectations as to the uses made of personal information probably encompass the possibility of a certain amount of social gossip, as part of the price of living within a relatively free society. On a more pragmatic level, such a limitation would be necessary in the interests of legal certainty. As Zimmerman points out: '... most courts limit the private facts tort's scope by requiring mass or widespread communication as an element of the cause of action. American judges either tacitly or expressly recognise that they would create an impossible legal tangle if they subjected back-fence and front-parlour gossip to liability.'[195]

(2) The obligation of confidentiality

Since *Stephens v Avery*,[196] the basic principle on which the doctrine of confidence has been based appears to be that confidentiality will be enforced if the information was received 'on the basis that it is confidential'.[197] This will depend on all the circumstances of the case, and the imposition of confidence is not limited (as had previously been thought) to instances in which there was a pre-existing relationship between the parties: 'The basis of equitable intervention to protect confidentiality is that it is unconscionable for a person who has received information on the basis that it is confidential, subsequently to reveal that information ... The relationship between the parties is not the determining factor.'[198] It is suggested that this explanation of the basis of the doctrine weakens the requirement to identify the public interest, such as the interest in preserving the stability of the family,[199] which would be served by protecting the information in question.

The fact that the information is given in confidence may be expressly communicated to the defendant (as in *Stephens v Avery*), but can be implied from the circumstances surrounding the communication. In *Fairnie (Dec'd) and Others v Reed and Another*[200] the confidential information (the format of a board game which the plaintiff wished to market) was mentioned by him incidentally during conversation with a virtual stranger about another matter; it was therefore transmitted only in passing, and the recipient was

---

192 Wilson, *op cit*, fn 1, p 56.

193 *Op cit*, fn 8, p 217.

194 Eg, where a friend or acquaintance disclosed the secret of a person's homosexuality to an employer where it was foreseen that this would probably damage the plaintiff's career. Publication by radio or television would not be counted as 'oral', for obvious reasons.

195 Zimmerman, D, 'Requiem for a heavyweight: a farewell to Warren and Brandeis's privacy tort' (1983) 68 Cornell L Rev 291, p 337; at note 246 she cites the decision in *La Fontaine v Family Drug Stores, Inc*, 33 Conn Supp 66, p 73; 360 A 2d 899, p 902 (Conn CP 1976) where the court commented that the abandonment of the mass publicity requirement 'would expand the concept of invasion of privacy beyond manageable limits'.

196 [1988] Ch 449.

197 *Ibid*, p 482.

198 *Ibid*.

199 As in *Duchess of Argyll v Duke of Argyll* [1967] 1 Ch 302.

200 20 May 1994, CA, transcript from LEXIS.

not told that it was given in confidence. The Court of Appeal found that there was an arguable case that the information had been transmitted in confidence, relying primarily on the fact that the information was of clear commercial value.[201]

It appears that an obligation of confidence may be imposed even where the information was not intentionally communicated to the defendant by the plaintiff. In *AG v Guardian Newspapers (No 2)*[202] Lord Goff suggested *obiter* that the nature of the information and the fact that it was not intended that the defendant should acquire it[203] could in itself impose the duty, using the example of '... an obviously confidential document ... dropped in a public place and then picked up by a passer-by ...'. He said, p 281: 'I start with the broad principle (which I do not in any way intend to be definitive) that a duty of confidence arises when confidential information comes to the knowledge of a person (the confidant) in circumstances where he has notice, or is held to have agreed, that the information is confidential, with the effect that it would be just in all the circumstances that he should be precluded from disclosing the information to others ... in the vast majority of cases ... the duty of confidence will arise from a transaction or relationship between the parties ... but it is well settled that a duty of confidence may arise in equity independently of such cases ...' *Francome v Mirror Group Newspapers*,[204] in which the information was obtained by means of a telephone tap, suggests that a duty of confidence may arise on the basis of such factors,[205] as does *Shelley Films Limited v Rex Features Limited.*[206]

These findings further confirm that the duty can still be imposed (or perhaps imposed *a fortiori*) where the defendant sets out deliberately to acquire the information without the plaintiff's knowledge, as opposed to stumbling across it inadvertently.[207] Presumably,

---

201 '[Plaintiff's counsel] submits that in the context [the plaintiff] disclosed to [the defendant] a confidential idea which he believed could be commercially successful, particularly with his endorsement. In my judgment, that is an arguable inference ... It all depends precisely on the language used, and the circumstances in which the conversation took place ... [defendant's counsel] points out that ... if the plaintiff simply blurted out or casually referred to the number one game ... then the defendant could not be taken as understanding that he was being given that information in confidence. That may be so, but in my judgment it is not possible to say ... precisely what inference should be drawn by the reasonable man who was the bystander and observer of the conversation', *per* Stuart Smith LJ, pp 7–8. The hearing was an appeal upon an application to strike out, so the court did not have to decide whether an obligation of confidence was in fact imposed.

202 [1990] 1 AC 109, p 281.

203 *Fairnie*, 20 May 1994, CA, transcript from LEXIS, suggests that it will not always be essential to show that this element is present.

204 [1984] 1 WLR 892.

205 *Cf* the *obiter* remarks in *Malone v Comr of Police of the Metropolis (No 2)* [1979] Ch 344, p 376, to the effect that those who spoke of confidential matters in situations in which it was foreseeable that they could be overheard (eg, on the telephone) could not claim that any eavesdroppers were bound by a duty of confidentiality. However, in *Malone v UK* (1984) 7 EHRR 14, the European Court of Human Rights reaffirmed (p 38) the place of telephone conversations within Art 8 and therefore must be taken to have rejected the notion that citizens assume a lack of confidentiality in communication by telephone.

206 [1994] EMLR 134, *per* Mr Mann QC (sitting as a deputy judge): '... [the photographer] was not an invitee and assuming that he saw the signs [forbidding photography] ... (I am not convinced that it would be fatal to Shelley's case if he did not) ... it is impossible ... not to conclude that what he saw and understood from his location might not have fully and sufficiently fixed him with knowledge [that the plaintiff wished to keep the appearance of 'the Creature' and its costume secret] according to any of the relevant standards ...' The Australian case of *Franklin v Giddins* [1978] 1 QdR 72 was relied upon as persuasive authority.

this would also be the case where the defendant acquired the information with the awareness, but without the consent of the plaintiff and where, as in *Hellewell v Chief Constable of Derbyshire*,[208] the defendant was acting under a legal power in acquiring the information for one specific purpose but wished to use it for another.[209] The decisions in *Rex Features, HRH Princess of Wales* and *Hellewell* also indicate that there need be nothing recognisable as a 'communication' from the plaintiff to any other person for the duty to arise,[210] although presumably the information concerned must in some sense emanate from the plaintiff. Thus, the obligation of confidence can now be imposed unilaterally; it is not founded on the express or implied agreement of the parties that the communication would be confidential.[211] In *Maudsley v Palumbo and Others*[212] Knox J said (*obiter*) that while the absence of actual belief on the part of the defendants that they were being given confidential information was 'quite capable of being significant', he '[did] not accept that ... a person who forms no belief on the question is thereby absolved from being found to have received information in confidence'.

It used to be thought that confidence was of limited value in protecting privacy, since it only covered those specific instances in which information was communicated in confidence. Thus, for example, it was not thought to cover situations where reporters took unauthorised photographs by means of telephoto lenses or surreptitiously recorded conversations with a view to publication. However, the developments described above significantly widen the circumstances in which the duty of confidence will be imposed, with the result, it is suggested, that many of the activities of reporters engaged in uncovering private facts may now be caught by the law of confidence. As Laws J remarked *obiter* in *Hellewell*:

> If someone with a telephoto lens were to take ... a photograph of another engaged in some private act, his subsequent disclosure of the photograph would in my judgment ... amount to a breach of confidence ... In such a case the law would protect what might reasonably be called a right of privacy, although the name accorded to the cause of action would be breach of confidence.[213]

Care must be taken in extrapolating general principles from some of the decisions discussed here, since a number of them concerned interim injunctions only[214] and therefore it was only necessary for the plaintiff to make out an arguable case. Others concerned appeals from applications to strike out[215] in which, as Stuart Smith LJ

---

207 For the contrary view that a duty will only be imposed where there is unlawful action by the taker of information, see Wei, G, 'Surreptitious takings of confidential information' (1992) LS 302. For critical discussion of Wei's view, see the articles cited by him, p 309.

208 The case concerned the taking of photographs under Code of Practice D (para 4) made under the Police and Criminal Evidence Act 1984 of a suspect in police custody. The police wished to allow a 'shop watch' scheme to use the photographs. An injunction was refused on the basis that the public interest was clearly served by the disclosure in question.

209 See also *Marcell and Others v Comr of Police of the Metropolis* [1992] Ch 224, esp pp 236–37.

210 See Thompson, *Confidentiality and the Law*, 1990, p 73.

211 An approach indicated earlier in *Coco v AN Clark (Engineers) Ltd* [1969] RPC 41, p 48.

212 (1995) *The Times*, 19 December, transcript from LEXIS; the case concerned an application for an injunction to restrain the defendants from making use of an idea for a dance club disclosed to them by the plaintiff.

213 [1995] 1 WLR 804, p 807.

214 *Rex Features; HRH Princess of Wales*, fn 166; *Francome v Mirror Group Newspapers Ltd*.

emphasised in *Fairnie*, the plaintiff must succeed unless his case is 'unarguable'.[216] Nevertheless, it is suggested that in the pre-HRA era, the courts were inclining towards a position regarding imposition of the duty to maintain confidence which may be indicated as follows. It is not necessary to establish a pre-existing relationship, an express imposition of the duty, an agreement between the parties or anything resembling a communication of the information by the plaintiff to the defendant or anyone else.[217] This ingredient can now be established in a number of ways. Since *Stephens v Avery*,[218] it appears that the existence of a formal relationship is 'not [now] the determining factor'.[219] Instead, confidentiality will be enforced simply on the basis that the information was received 'on the basis that it is confidential',[220] since to allow such a recipient to reveal the information would be 'unconscionable', an approach confirmed in a number of cases, including *Francome v Mirror Group Newspapers*,[221] *Shelley Films*,[222] *Creation Records*,[223] and *Hellewell*,[224] where no prior relationship was present.

Where there was no formal relationship, the alternative ingredient traditionally required for a duty of confidence to arise was an express or implied agreement between the parties, or promise by the defendant, that the information received would be treated as confidential.[225] The notion of 'implied agreement' denoted an agreement which, although unspoken, was in fact mutually assumed between the parties. Owing to this requirement, it was thought that the action caught only those specific instances in which information was (voluntarily) communicated in confidence. Thus, it was not thought to cover the paradigm example of an invasion of privacy where reporters surreptitiously took photographs by means of telephoto lenses or recorded private conversation, with a view to publication, because in such cases there is no possibility of agreement between the parties or a promise (express or implied) of confidentiality: it would be absurd to say that the defendant journalist had 'agree[d] to treat the information as confidential'[226] when his whole purpose was to publish it, while the plaintiff 'confider' was blissfully unaware that any communication of information was taking place at all. However, as a

---

215 *Fairnie*, 20 May 1994, CA, transcript from LEXIS, above; *Stephens v Avery* [1988] Ch 449.

216 *Ibid*, p 1.

217 Following *AG v Guardian Newspapers (No 2)* [1990] 1 AC 109; [1990] 3 WLR 776; [1988] 3 All ER 545, HL, the defendant need not be the person to whom the information was originally 'communicated'.

218 [1988] Ch 449: the plaintiff brought an action against a friend to whom she had confided that she had had a lesbian affair; the friend sold the story to a newspaper.

219 [1988] Ch 449, p 482, *per* Browne-Wilkinson VC.

220 *Ibid*.

221 [1984] 1 WLR 892. The information concerned (that the plaintiff, a well known jockey, had breached various rules of racing) was obtained by means of tapping the plaintiff's telephone; the tapes so made were sold to the press.

222 *Shelley Films v Rex Features Limited* [1994] EMLR 134. An injunction was granted to prevent the use of a photograph taken surreptitiously on the film set of Frankenstein.

223 *Creation Records Ltd v News Group Newspapers Ltd* [1997] EMLR 444; an injunction was granted against a newspaper to prevent it from publishing a photograph of a new album cover designed for the group Oasis which had been taken surreptitiously on the set where the album cover was being shot.

224 *Hellewell v Chief Constable of Derbyshire* ([1995] 1 WLR 804). The 'information' here was a 'mug'-shot of the plaintiff taken by the police which was later passed by them to local shopkeepers to aid the prevention of shoplifting.

225 See the Law Commission report, *op cit*, fn 2, para 6.11: for an obligation to be imposed, 'any confidant must agree to treat the information as confidential'.

226 The requirement which the Law Commission thought necessary (*op cit*, fn 2).

result of the successful actions in *Shelley Films*,[227] *Creation Records*[228] and *HRH Princess of Wales*[229] (all involving surreptitiously taken photographs), *Francome*,[230] (where information was obtained by a newspaper using a telephone tap) and *Lam v Koo and Chiu*[231] (involving the surreptitious obtaining of a document), any requirement for a communication between plaintiff and defendant seems to have disappeared, a development also supported by *dicta* of Lord Goff in *AG v Guardian Newspapers (No 2)*.[232] This has been possible because the requirement of an 'implied agreement' of confidentiality has been radically re-interpreted: the new approach of the courts is to imply the agreement of confidentiality into the dealings between the parties, not on the basis of any mutual agreement on the matter, but instead on the basis that the reasonable man in the position of the defendant would have assumed such an obligation.[233]

The test appears to be wholly objective.[234] What factors would lead a reasonable person to realise that the information is confidential? The authorities suggest that they would include the following: where it has clear commercial value, as in *Fairnie* and *Rex Features*, and where it is obvious that the plaintiff did not wish the information to be obtained (as in *HRH Princess of Wales* and *Rex Features*). Conversely, where the plaintiff deliberately refrains from mentioning confidentiality to the defendant, this may prevent the imposition of the duty, as in *Palumbo*.

This bold development, a clear departure from the view of the Law Commission on the matter,[235] has radically increased the potential scope of the confidence action: it may now cover cases where personal information is surreptitiously obtained by the media and then published without consent,[236] since in many such instances, it would be open to the court to say that the reasonable man would have assumed an obligation of confidence. This possibility has – as indicated above – recently received further clear recognition from

---

227 [1994] EMLR 134. The case was discussed extensively in the *Spencer* decision (1998) 25 EHRR CD 105.

228 *Creation Records Ltd v News Group Newspapers Ltd* [1997] EMLR 444.

229 *HRH Princess of Wales v MGN Newspapers Limited and Others* (1993) Transcript, Association of Official Shorthandwriters Ltd, 8 November 1993. Photographs of the plaintiff exercising in a private gymnasium taken by a hidden camera were sold to and published by a tabloid newspaper.

230 [1984] 1 WLR 892.

231 [1992] Civil Transcript No 116, CA (a Hong Kong case): a medical researcher accidentally or surreptitiously obtained a confidential research document produced by the plaintiff.

232 *AG v Guardian Newspapers (No 2)* [1990] 1 AC 109; [1990] 3 WLR 776; [1988] 3 All ER 545, HL. Lord Goff considered *obiter* that confidentiality would be imposed in instances where, eg, '... an obviously confidential document is wafted by an electric fan out of the window into a crowded street, or when an obviously confidential document ... is dropped in a public place and is then picked up by a passer-by ...' (*ibid*, p 281).

233 Thus, in *Creation Records* ([1997] EMLR 444), Lloyd J reasoned: '... the circumstances were such that any reasonable man in the shoes of [the photographer] would have realised on reasonable grounds that he was obtaining the information, that is to say the view of the scene, in confidence ...'.

234 In *Li Yau-wai v Genesis Films Limited* [1987] HKLR 711, a Hong Kong decision, an 'officious bystander' test was used to impose the duty of confidence (*per* Rhind J, p 719). An objective test was also employed in *Lam v Koo and Chiu* (1992) Civil Transcript No 116, see esp p 30 (Hong Kong Court of Appeal). See Wacks, *Privacy and Press Freedom*, op cit, fn 1, pp 62–63; Loh, E, 'Intellectual property: breach of confidence?' (1995) 17 EIPR 405–07.

235 'It would in our view, extend the idea of breach of confidence too far to cover situations where the potential defendant has not expressly or by inference accepted an obligation of confidence in respect of information which has come into his possession' (*op cit*, fn 2, para 6.11).

236 Provided that the information 'has the necessary quality of confidence about it' (*Coco* [1969] RPC 41). See discussion below.

the European Commission in *Spencer*[237] and in the now well known *Hellewell* case,[238] *per* Laws J: 'If someone with a telephoto lens were to take ... a photograph of another engaged in some private act, his subsequent disclosure of the photograph would in my judgment ... amount to a breach of confidence'.

When used in this way, the central interest served by protecting confidences ceases to be enforcing promise keeping, or preserving certain kinds of relationships; rather, it becomes simply that of preventing private or personal information entering the public domain without the plaintiff's consent. The action, therefore, while still termed 'breach of confidence',[239] becomes almost indistinguishable from a 'pure' privacy tort.[240] The Law Commission on breach of confidence explained the difference between confidentiality and privacy by saying that the former 'arises from the nature of the information itself: it would be based on the principle that certain kinds of information are categorised as private and *for that reason alone* ought not to be disclosed'.[241] The 'new' model of confidence outlined above allows a duty of confidentiality to be imposed solely on the basis of matters relating to the information: as noted above, it must be of substance and not already in the public domain; it must be such that the reasonable person standing in the defendant's shoes would have realised that it should be kept confidential. When the doctrine is dealing with personal information, this realisation can come purely from the nature of the information itself, coupled sometimes with the manner in which it was acquired: the fact that the defendant has had to intrude on the plaintiff in some way in order to gather the information is evidence to the defendant that the plaintiff regards what he is doing as private.[242]

One final aspect of the utility of confidence in this area should be mentioned: in many cases, newspapers obtain private information about the plaintiff from his or her friends and acquaintances, as in *Stephens v Avery*[243] and *Michael Barrymore v News Group Newspapers Ltd*.[244] In such a case, an obligation of confidence can be imposed upon the newspaper on the orthodox basis that they knew or ought to have known that they had

---

237 (1998) 25 EHRR CD 105. There is some recognition amongst the commentators as well; see, eg, Singh, Grosz and Braithwaite, Wright (all *op cit*, fn 1).

238 [1995] 1 WLR 804, p 807.

239 As Laws J remarked in *Hellewell*: 'In such a case the law would protect what might reasonably be called a right of privacy, although the name accorded to the cause of action would be breach of confidence' (*ibid*).

240 Confidence does, however have one limitation in such a guise: it cannot directly cover cases where there is intrusion but no information is gained or where information is gathered but never used (the Protection from Harassment Act 1997 might apply in cases of persistent intrusion). However, a reporter could be prevented by the terms of an injunction from passing any information gained on to anyone else in a newspaper, and presumably from processing and storing the information in the newspaper's archives (activities which might also engage the Data Protection Act 1998 (see below, pp 603–11). Moreover, the availability of a remedy in confidence against the publication of private information obtained by, eg, a bugging device, might give rise to a perception that such use was pointless if lawful publication of the material gained was not possible; it might thus come to have a 'chilling effect' upon this form of intrusion.

241 Law Commission Report No 110, *op cit*, fn 2, para 2.3 (emphasis added).

242 In *AG v Guardian Newspapers (No 2)* [1990] 1 AC 109, Lord Goff stated that the courts should take account of 'all the circumstances, including the manner in which the information was acquired' (at p 283).

243 [1988] Ch 449.

244 [1997] FSR 600. A man with whom Mr Barrymore had allegedly had a homosexual affair passed the details to *The Sun* newspaper.

received the fruits of a broken confidence;[245] alternatively, under the 'new' model of the doctrine, the obligation could be imposed upon the newspapers directly, on the basis that the reasonable man would have realised that the information received should be kept confidential, due its clearly private character.[246]

(3) Detriment arising from unauthorised use of the information

The third element identified as essential in *Coco v AN Clark (Engineers) Ltd* appears to require two ingredients – unauthorised use of the information and detriment arising from such use. This point was addressed by the House of Lords in *AG v Guardian Newspapers (No 2)*, but the Law Lords were divided as to the need to show detriment where a private individual was claiming a breach of confidence. Lord Griffiths considered that detriment had to be shown even in such a case;[247] Lords Brightman and Jauncey were silent as to the issue, while Lord Goff considered that the question should be left open.[248] Lord Keith, however, was of the view that in this respect a private individual should not be treated in the same way as a State body:

> The right to personal privacy is clearly one which the law should in this field seek to protect ... I would think it is sufficient detriment to the confider that information given in confidence is to be disclosed to persons who he would prefer not to know of it even though the disclosure would not be harmful to him in any positive way.[249]

Obiter dicta in *Shelley Films Limited v Rex Features Limited* appear to favour the position taken by Lord Goff,[250] while Lord Keith's view receives some support from the finding in *HRH Princess of Wales v MGN Limited and Others*[251] which suggests that in relation to private individuals, the courts may be prepared to assume the presence of detriment. The point remains unclear.

The public interest defence

Perhaps the most important concern relating to the development of confidence as remedy for invasion of privacy is the fear that the action will pose an unacceptable risk to media freedom. The main insurance against this possibility rests with the public interest defence, whereby disclosure of admittedly private or confidential information is permitted if this

---

245 See *AG v Guardian Newspapers* [1987] 1 WLR 1248, esp p 1265, *per* Lord Browne-Wilkinson, and the Law Commission report: 'The third party is liable to be restrained from disclosing or using information which he knows or it would seem, he ought to know, was subject to an obligation of confidence' (*op cit*, fn 2, para 4.11).

246 The successful use of either route would refute the view of the Law Commission (*ibid*, para 5.9) that cases such as *Fraser v Evans* [1969] 1 QB 349 mean that the doctrine can give no remedy to the 'owner' of personal information where the promise of confidentiality is given to another, as where a newspaper promises a journalist that information he obtains on a celebrity will not be published in her lifetime, and then breaches that promise, leaving, so the Commission thought, the celebrity with no remedy. See also the doubts of Wacks on this point (*Privacy and Press Freedom*, 1996, p 56).

247 [1990] 1 AC 109, pp 269–70.

248 *Ibid*, pp 281–82.

249 *Ibid*, pp 255–63.

250 10 December 1993, transcript from LEXIS, p 16.

251 Transcript, Association of Official Shorthandwriters Limited, 8 November 1993.

would serve the public interest.[252] None of the cases in which it has been discussed at length have concerned the paradigmatic privacy claim, and Art 10 of the Convention had little influence upon it prior to the inception of the HRA.[253]

Traditionally, confidential information will not be protected if the public interest served by disclosing the information in question outweighs the interest in preserving confidentiality. This aspect of the doctrine is often termed the 'public interest' defence. In *Woodward v Hutchins*,[254] intimate facts about Tom Jones and another pop star were revealed to the Daily Mirror by a former agent who had been their confidante. The plaintiffs sought an injunction on the ground of breach of confidence. There had been a confidential relationship and they claimed that the agent should not be able to take unfair advantage of that confidentiality. The Court of Appeal failed to uphold the claim on the basis that the plaintiffs had sought to publicise themselves in order to present a certain 'image' and therefore could not complain if the truth were later revealed. This decision has been criticised on the basis that a need to reveal the truth about the plaintiffs was irrelevant to the breach of confidence on the part of the agent,[255] but it has not been overruled. The public interest in knowing the truth about the plaintiffs seemed to rest on a refusal to use the law to protect their attempt to mislead the public.

It is sometimes said that there is no confidence in iniquity: the plaintiff cannot use the law of confidence to cover up his or her own wrong-doing and therefore the public interest in disclosure will prevail. However, it appears that the 'public interest defence' was not limited to cases of iniquity. The House of Lords found *obiter* in *British Steel Corporation v Granada Television*[256] that publication of confidential information could legitimately be undertaken only where there was misconduct,[257] but in *Lion Laboratories v Evans*[258] Stephenson LJ said that he would reject the 'no iniquity, no public interest rule' agreeing with Lord Denning's statement in *Fraser v Evans*[259] to the effect that 'some things are required to be disclosed in the public interest in which case no confidence can be prayed in aid to keep them secret and [iniquity] is merely an instance of just cause and

---

252 While originally only allowing disclosure if it would reveal wrongdoing on the part of the plaintiff (*Gartside v Outram* (1856) 26 LJ Ch 113, p 114 and in relation to copyright, *Glyn v Weston Feature Film Co* [1916] 1 Ch 261) the strength of the public interest in question rather than the individual wrongdoing of the plaintiff is now the determining factor: see *Fraser v Evans*, ([1969] 1 QB 349), *Schering Chemicals v Falkman* [1981] 2 WLR 848, esp p 869, *X v Y* ([1988] 2 All ER 648) and *AG v Jonathan Cape* [1976] 1 QB 752; *Lion Laboratories v Evans and Express Newspapers* [1984] 1 QB 530, *W v Egdell* ([1990] Ch 359) and *Hellewell* [1995] 1 WLR 804; *AG v Guardian Newspapers (No 2)* [1990] 1 AC 109, p 282, *per* Lord Goff, and p 268, *per* Lord Griffiths. Note that where disclosure has been said to be in the public interest because it exposes particular criminal or anti-social behaviour or reveals some specific risk to public health, it has been held this will not always justify disclosing the matter in the press: see *Francome* ([1984] 1 WLR 892); *Initial Services Ltd v Putterill* [1968] 1 QB 396, pp 405–06, *per* Lord Denning; *AG v Guardian Newspapers (No 2)* [1990] 1 AC 109, p 269, *per* Lord Griffiths; *ibid*, p 282, *per* Lord Goff; *ibid*, p 177, *per* Sir John Donaldson in the Court of Appeal.

253 Remarkably, Jacob J's quite recent pre-HRA judgment in *Michael Barrymore* [1997] FSR 600 – a case relating to the unauthorised disclosure of personal information and thus clearly raising both privacy and speech issues – does not once advert to the Convention.

254 [1977] 1 WLR 760, CA.

255 Wacks, R, *The Protection of Privacy*, 1980, p 85.

256 [1981] AC 1096; [1981] 1 All ER 417, HL.

257 See Cripps (1984) 4 OJLS 184 on the public interest defence.

258 [1985] QB 526, p 537.

259 [1969] 1 QB 349, p 362.

excuse for breaking confidence'. These rulings concerned confidential information held by private companies and seemed to leave open the possibility of the existence of a broad public interest defence which, it seemed from Woodward, might also sometimes apply in the case of public figures.

Where personal information relating to a private individual was in issue, the ruling in *X v Y*[260] suggested that the public interest defence was confined to cases of iniquity. On the other hand, *Lion Laboratories v Evans and Express Newspapers*,[261] *W v Egdell*[262] and *Hellewell* suggested that the defence had broadened its focus of concern with the result that the strength of the public interest in question rather than the individual wrongdoing of the plaintiff might tend to be the determining factor. In *W v Egdell*, no such wrongdoing was relied upon in finding that the medical report relating to the plaintiff's condition should be placed before the appropriate authorities where it was in the public interest to do so. It should be noted that this decision placed some limitations on the ability of the public interest defence to afford protection to press freedom: it might sometimes be appropriate to pass information to a particular body rather than disclosing it to the public at large. On the other hand, where the public itself had previously been misled by the plaintiff, it appeared that wide disclosure might be warranted.

The above discussion should not be taken as assuming that the public interest always required disclosure of information and would therefore invariably be in competition with the interest of the plaintiff in suppressing it. Clearly, there was a general public interest in allowing the transmission of information from one person to another without interference, and in certain circumstances such as those which arose in *X v Y*[263] there might be a further specific public interest in maintaining confidentiality. A newspaper wished to publish information deriving from confidential hospital records which showed that certain practising doctors were suffering from the AIDS virus. In granting an injunction preventing publication, Rose J took into account the public interest in disclosure, but weighed it against the private interest in confidentiality and the public interest in encouraging AIDS patients to seek help from hospitals, which would not be served if it was thought that confidentiality might not be maintained.

Where public bodies are in possession of personal information, their obligations in relation to disclosure may differ from those applicable in private law. In *Chief Constable of the North Wales Police ex p Thorpe*,[264] the police had confidential information to the effect that the occupants of a caravan on a particular site were paedophiles, with a number of convictions for sexual offences. They sought judicial review of the decision of the police to disclose their convictions to the owner of the caravan site. It was found by the Court of Appeal that the duty of the police in such a circumstance differs from that under private law. The police as a public authority were not free to publish the information despite the fact that it could be viewed as being in the public domain, but that the information could be used if that was what was required to protect the public, as in the instant case. Both Art

---

260 [1988] 2 All ER 648.
261 [1985] QB 526; [1984] 2 All ER 417, CA.
262 [1990] Ch 359; see also *X v Y* [1988] 2 All ER 658 and *dicta* of Lord Goff in *AG v Guardian Newspapers (No 2)*, p 659.
263 [1988] 2 All ER 648.
264 [1999] QB 396.

8 and English administrative law would accept that the police were entitled to use the information in such an instance.

The approach of domestic courts in the pre-HRA era was becoming very similar to that of the House of Lords in the important decision on defamation in *Reynolds v Times Newspapers*,[265] which concerned the proper balance to be struck between the individual right to reputation on the one hand and the freedom of the press on the other. The issue for determination was whether qualified privilege[266] should attach to good-faith political speech in the media. Their Lordships, while recognising for the first time that it could, showed a marked preference for the retention of a very broad and flexible test which asked simply whether, in all the circumstances, the public interest required publication of the material in question.[267] While Lord Nicholls showed some recognition of the possible 'chilling effect' which could arise if the imprecision of the test left the media uncertain as to the boundaries of permissible speech, he thought some uncertainty unavoidable and regarded its likely extent as relatively small in any case.[268] It thus seemed plausible to assume that a similar approach was likely to prevail in relation to the breach of confidence action,[269] as recommended by the Law Commission.[270]

It may be concluded that there were two key developments in the defence in the pre-HRA era. First, while originally only allowing disclosure if it would reveal wrongdoing on the part of the plaintiff,[271] the strength of the public interest in question rather than the individual wrongdoing of the plaintiff is now the determining factor.[272] Secondly, where disclosure has been said to be in the public interest because it exposes particular criminal or anti-social behaviour or reveals some specific risk to public health, it is now clear that this will not always justify disclosing the matter in the press.[273]

The public interest defence provided a means of reconciling the demands of speech and privacy. Under the impetus of the HRA, this balancing exercise is becoming, as indicated below, more sophisticated since it will largely be undertaken under s 12 of the HRA, and will therefore draw in Arts 10 and 8, with their associated jurisprudence and the PCC Privacy Code. The Strasbourg principles of necessity and proportionality will

---

265 [1999] 3 WLR 1010; [1999] 4 All ER 609.

266 If the defendant can establish the privilege, then even though he cannot prove the truth of the defamatory allegations, the plaintiff can succeed only if he can show that the defendant had known the allegations to be false or was indifferent to their veracity.

267 This approach was thought to be in harmony with Strasbourg jurisprudence on Art 10: see fn 60 above, p 610 (the head note) and p 625 (*per* Lord Nicholls), an issue discussed below.

268 *Ibid*, pp 623–24.

269 The defence will always involve somewhat different considerations: in privacy cases, matters concerning the defendant's attempts to verify the allegations and give a balanced account will be inapplicable.

270 The Commission considered that the courts should retain a 'broad power' to decide whether 'in the particular case' the public interest required disclosure (*op cit*, fn 2, para 6.77).

271 *Gartside v Outram* (1856) 26 LJ Ch 113, p 114 and in relation to copyright, *Glyn v Weston Feature Film Co* [1916] 1 Ch 261.

272 See *Fraser v Evans* [1969] 1 QB 349; *Schering Chemicals v Falkman* [1981] 2 WLR 848, esp p 869; *X v Y* [1988] 2 All ER 648 and *AG v Jonathan Cape* [1976] 1 QB 752; *Lion Laboratories v Evans and Express Newspapers* [1984] 1 QB 530, *W v Egdell* [1990] Ch 359; and *Hellewell* [1995] 1 WLR 804; *AG v Guardian Newspapers (No 2)* [1990] 1 AC 109, p 282, *per* Lord Goff, and p 268, *per* Lord Griffiths.

273 See *Francome* [1984] 1 WLR 892; *Initial Services Ltd v Putterill* [1968] 1 QB 396, pp 405–06, *per* Lord Denning; *AG v Guardian Newspapers (No 2)* [1990] 1 AC 109, p 269, *per* Lord Griffiths; *ibid*, p 282, *per* Lord Goff; *ibid*, p 177, *per* Sir John Donaldson in the Court of Appeal.

determine the balance between the conflicting demands of speech and privacy, as indicated below, but it is likely that these domestic decisions will nevertheless be drawn upon since they provide some useful guidance in making determinations as to the resolution of that conflict.

The effect of Art 8 and the HRA

What, then, is the role of Art 8 in the development of confidence, given that the judges already apparently had to hand a serviceable tool with which to tackle invasions of privacy? It is suggested that it performs two, linked functions. First, it provides the normative impetus for the consolidation of the radical developments outlined above. Secondly, given the somewhat inchoate nature of the new model of confidence, Art 8, together with s 12 of the HRA, provides an organising principle around which the uncertainties inherent in the action, particularly the conflict between the demands of privacy and press freedom, may be resolved, a matter addressed below. It is suggested that Art 8, together with s 12 of the HRA, performed the first of these functions and also gave indications as to the means of resolving that conflict in the important post-HRA decision of the Court of Appeal in *Douglas and Others v Hello! Ltd*.[274]

The magazine *OK!* secured an agreement with two celebrities, Michael Douglas and Catherine Zeta-Jones, eight days before their wedding under which it agreed to pay a very large sum of money to them in respect of rights to publish exclusive photographs of the wedding and an article about it. The couple trusted *OK!* to project only the images they wanted projected to the public. They also retained rights of approval in relation to anything that was to be published. Mr Douglas and Ms Zeta-Jones undertook to use their best efforts to ensure that: 'no other media (including but not limited to photographers, television crews or journalists) shall be permitted access to the wedding, and that no guests or anyone else present at it (including staff at the venues) shall be allowed to take photographs.' The rival magazine *Hello!* had tendered for the rights but had failed. *Hello!* clearly knew that exclusive rights were to be granted for coverage of the wedding, and that it had not secured them. However, the security operation at the wedding failed to prevent some unauthorised photos from being taken and *Hello!* obtained them. The couple were informed after the wedding that copies of *Hello!* were already in the UK with a photo of the wedding on the front cover and that they would be distributed very shortly. They rapidly obtained an *ex parte* injunction restraining publication.

The Court of Appeal had to decide whether an injunction restraining the publication should be continued in force until trial, thereby effectively 'killing' that issue of *Hello!*. The key issues were (a) the applicability of the law of confidence; (b) the relevance of the HRA 1998; (c) whether the injunction should be continued until the trial of the action or whether the claimants should be left to seek to obtain damages at the trial. The Court noted that the doctrine of confidence originally arose from the exercise of the equitable jurisdiction to restrain freedom of speech in circumstances in which it would be unconscionable to publish private material. It said that it was clearly established that where information was accepted on the basis that it would be kept secret, the recipient's

---

274 [2001] 2 WLR 992. See for discussion Moreham, N [2001] 64(5) MLR 767–74; Elliott, M [2001] CLJ 231–33.

conscience would be bound by that confidence, and it would be unconscionable for him to break his duty of confidence by publishing the information to others.[275]

Sedley LJ found that the law of confidence has developed to the point at which it can provide a right to privacy, in so far as a privacy right may be viewed as covering matters which are distinct from those which confidence has come to be viewed as capable of covering. He accepted that it might have reached that point even independently of the HRA. In particular, he found that it is arguable that confidence does not cover surreptitious takings of personal information by someone whose conscience cannot be said to be bound to maintain confidence – a 'stranger' – and that such takings are more readily covered by a right to privacy, albeit originating from confidence. His point appeared to be that although such takings could be covered by confidence, as indicated above,[276] the notion of an implied obligation to maintain confidence might be viewed as artificial, depending on the circumstances. In this instance the photographs might have been taken by a guest (who would come under an obligation of confidence since his or her conscience would be bound, in which case it would be immaterial whether the cause of action was called confidence or privacy). A cause of action would be available.

However, if the photos in the instant case had been taken by a 'stranger', the cause of action in his view could arguably be termed a right to privacy, and the HRA aided that conclusion since it provided a clear impetus to develop the law on the lines indicated obiter by Laws LJ in *Hellewell*.[277] Thus, the HRA gave a force to the above argument – that confidence has developed in such a way as to provide a right to privacy – which it might not otherwise have had. Sedley LJ made this clear: 'we have reached a point at which it can be said with confidence that the law recognises and will appropriately protect a right of personal privacy.' He based this finding in part on the coming into force of the HRA since it requires the courts of this country – as public authorities under s 6 of the HRA – to give effect to the right to respect for private and family life set out in Art 8 of the European Convention on Human Rights. He said that the jurisprudence of the Court and the common law 'now run in a single channel because, by virtue of s 2 and s 6 of the Act, the courts of this country must not only take into account jurisprudence of both the Commission and the European Court of Human Rights which points to a positive institutional obligation to respect privacy; they must themselves act compatibly with that

---

275 *Stephens v Avery* [1988] Ch 449, p 456. The court noted that in *Argyll v Argyll* [1967] Ch 302, 329f–330b it was said: 'It ... seems to me that the policy of the law, so far from indicating that communication between husband and wife should be excluded from protection against breaches of confidence given by the court in accordance with *Prince Albert v Strange* ((1848) 2 De Gex & Sm 652; on appeal 1 Mac & G 25), strongly favours its inclusion ...'. The court also relied on *Michael Barrymore v News Group Newspapers Ltd* [1997] FSR 600; Jacob J had followed those principles in a case in which a newspaper sought to publish information concerning an intimate homosexual relationship.

276 See *Francome v MGM* [1984] 1 WLR 892 and *dicta* in *AG v Guardian Newspaper (No 2)* [1990] 1 AC 109, p 281, discussed above.

277 In *Hellewell v Chief Constable of Derbyshire* [1995] 1 WLR 804 Laws LJ said: 'I entertain no doubt that disclosure of a photograph may, in some circumstances, be actionable as a breach of confidence. If someone with a telephoto lens were to take from a distance and with no authority a picture of another engaged in some private act, his subsequent disclosure of the photograph would, in my judgment, as surely amount to a breach of confidence as if he had found or stolen a letter or diary in which the act was recounted and proceeded to publish it. In such a case the law would protect what might reasonably be called a right of privacy, although the name accorded to the cause of action would be breach of confidence.'

and the other Convention rights. This, for reasons I now turn to, arguably gives the final impetus to the recognition of a right of privacy in English law.'

His key point in relation to a possible difference between confidence and privacy was: 'a concept of privacy does ... accord recognition to the fact that the law has to protect not only those people whose trust has been abused, but those who simply find themselves subjected to an unwanted intrusion into their personal lives. The law no longer needs to construct an artificial relationship of confidentiality between intruder and victim: it can recognise privacy itself as a legal principle drawn from the fundamental value of personal autonomy.' He pointed out that Art 8(1) of the Convention creates a right to respect for private and family life, although Art 8(2), and ss 6, 7 and 8 of the HRA, make it clear that these rights are enforceable only against public authorities. However, he noted that, as indicated above, the European Court of Human Rights has relied on the positive duty imposed on the Member States by Art 1 of the Convention,[278] and therefore found that Art 8 does recognise the applicability of its guarantee as between private parties.

Clearly, in an action between private parties – as in the instant case – it could not be said that the defendant is bound by the Convention since it is not a public authority under s 6 of the HRA. Sedley LJ found that the court, as itself a public authority under s 6, is obliged to give some effect to Art 8, among other provisions of the Convention. Its duty appears to allow it to 'take the step from confidentiality to privacy'.[279] Significantly, he found that in so far as there is doubt as to the scope of the duty of the court under s 6, s 12(4) makes the matter crystal clear where interference with the right to freedom of expression is in issue. Section 12(4) requires the court to have particular regard to the right to freedom of expression under Art 10. Therefore, it is clear that Art 10 is applicable as between one private party to litigation and another; in other words, it has indirect horizontal effect. However, Art 10(2) is qualified in respect of the reputation and rights of others and the protection of information received in confidence. Therefore, in having particular regard to Art 10, it is also necessary to have such regard to the other Convention rights including Art 8. Section 12(4) does not, therefore, merely give freedom of expression priority over the other rights. In weighing up the competing claims, the court also had to take the Code policed by the Press Complaints Commission into account under s 12(4)(b); it did not appear that the photographer had complied with the provision of cl 3 (which, as indicated above, provides, in part, that, 'A publication will be expected to justify intrusions into any individual's private life without consent ... The use of long lens photography to take pictures of people in private places without their consent is unacceptable.'). This clause is qualified by the exceptions where a public interest can be demonstrated to apply. That was not the case in this instance, since knowing of the details of the wedding could not serve a legitimate public interest. The court concluded that the claimants had an arguable case that they had suffered a breach of their privacy; this claim was based on the law of confidence, interpreted compatibly with Art 8, due to the requirements of s 12(4). Although the court was unanimous in reaching this conclusion, Sedley LJ differed from the other two judges in differentiating between confidence and privacy in respect of surreptitious takings of information.

---

278 See the judgment of the court in *A v United Kingdom* (1999) 27 EHRR 611.
279 He noted that this argument is supported by Hunt, in *op cit*, fn 52.

The court then considered whether the injunction against *Hello!* should be continued. Section 12(3) provides that prior restraint on expression should not be granted except where the court considers that the claimant is 'likely' to establish at trial that publication should not be allowed. Under s 3 of the HRA the court has a duty to construe all legislation, which must include the HRA itself, compatibly with the Convention rights 'so far as it is possible to do so'. Therefore, clearly, both sub-sections must be read in such a way as to ensure that all the rights are given full weight; s 12(3) must not accord more weight to Art 10 than to the other rights. The outcome, in any particular instance, would be determined, it found, principally by considerations of proportionality. Sedley LJ said that the court has to 'look ahead to the ultimate stage and to be satisfied that the scales are likely to come down in the applicant's favour. That does not conflict with the Convention, since it is merely requiring the court to apply its mind to how one right is to be balanced, on the merits against another right, without building in additional weight on one side.' Taking into account the fact that the claimants had in a sense already 'sold' their privacy, Sedley LJ found that their rights to privacy were outweighed by the right of publication and considered that they should be left to a claim for damages at the trial of the action.

But the court also had to consider the effects of leaving the claimants to a damages claim. In *American Cyanamid Company v Ethicon Ltd*[280] it was found that a judge must weigh the respective risks that injustice may result from his deciding one way or the other at the interim stage. If an injunction is refused, but the claimant does succeed in establishing his legal right at the trial which he sought to protect by means of the injunction, he might in the meantime suffer harm which could not adequately be compensated for by an award of money. On the other hand, there was the risk that if the injunction was granted, but the claimant failed at the trial, the defendant in the meantime might have suffered harm which was also irrecompensable. This weighing up is sometimes termed 'the balance of convenience'. Brooke LJ found that the balance of convenience appeared to favour leaving *OK!* to assert its legal rights at the trial of what he said was 'essentially a commercial dispute between two magazine enterprises'. Therefore, although the court found that the claim might succeed at trial and result in an award of compensation, it also found that the injunction should be discharged. Thus, Hello! could publish the issue which contained the wedding photographs.

The ultimate outcome of what was essentially a commercial case is of little interest in terms of future privacy claims; the case is of interest since it affords confirmation to the development of confidence, as discussed above, into a privacy remedy, a development which was accepted and relied upon in *Venables, Thompson v News Group Newspapers Ltd, Associated Newspapers Ltd, MGM.*[281] As indicated above, a number of newspapers made representations to the court, arguing that on grounds of press freedom, an injunction should not be granted to protect the claimants' identities. Dame Butler-Sloss P in the High Court found that the newspapers could not be said to be public authorities under s 6 of the HRA and therefore, the Convention rights were not directly applicable to them. But she said that the tort of breach of confidence is an established cause of action. She found,[282] taking into account the effect of the Convention on domestic law, that the law of

---

280 [1975] AC 396.

281 [2001] 1 All ER 908 Fam Div (High Court of Justice, Queen's Bench Division); discussed above, pp 547–48.

282 *Ibid*, pp 1064–65, paras 80–81.

confidence could extend to cover the injunctions sought in the instant case. She said that 'the common law continues to evolve, as it has done for centuries, and it is being given considerable impetus to do so by the implementation of the Convention into our domestic law'. Her view was that the duty of confidence could arise in equity independently of a transaction or relationship between the parties. She said that the duty of confidence placed upon the media arises when confidential information comes to their knowledge in circumstances in which the media have notice of its confidentiality. She further said that it is also recognised that it is just in all the circumstances that information known to be confidential should not be disclosed to others, in this case by publication in the press.[283] The issue in question was whether the information leading to disclosure of the claimants' identity and location comes within the confidentiality brackets. In answering that crucial question, she found that she could rely upon the European case law and the duty on the court, where necessary, to take appropriate steps to safeguard the physical safety of the claimants, including the adoption of measures even in the sphere of relations of individuals and/or private organisations between themselves. She said:

> Under the umbrella of confidentiality there will be information which may require a special quality of protection. In the present case the reason for advancing that special quality is that, if the information was published, the publication would be likely to lead to grave and possibly fatal consequences.

Therefore, since a case based on confidence might be made out, the court had to look at s 12. As indicated above, the court would then have to consider Art 10 and also the other Convention rights by virtue of the protection of the rights of others under Art 10(2). The court found, relying particularly on the findings in *AG v Guardian Newspapers (No 2)*,[284] discussed above, that the lack of a pre-existing relationship or agreement between the parties did not preclude the finding that the newspapers came under an obligation of confidence. But the public interest in preserving confidence could be outweighed by some other countervailing public interest favouring disclosure. Therefore, the court had to carry out a balancing operation, weighing the public interest in maintaining confidence against the interest in disclosure. However, s 12 of the HRA and Art 10(1) of the Convention give an enhanced importance to freedom of expression and so to the right of the press to publish. Therefore, under the HRA, a balancing exercise would no longer be appropriate.

The court went on to find that the freedom of the media to publish could only be restricted if the need for those restrictions could be shown to fall within the exceptions set out in Art 10(2). In considering the limits to the law of confidence, and whether a remedy is available to the claimants within those limits, it was found that the exceptions must be narrowly interpreted. The claimants' right under Art 2 (right to life), Art 3 (right to freedom from torture and inhuman and degrading treatment) and Art 8 (right to respect for private life) were in issue. The rights under Arts 2 and 3 are not capable of derogation. In *Osman v United Kingdom*,[285] the European Court held that the provisions of Art 2 enjoined a positive obligation upon Contracting States to take measures to secure the right to life. The case, discussed in Chapter 2,[286] concerned the failure of the police to act

---

283 She relied on Lord Goff in *AG v Guardian Newspapers Ltd (No 2)* [1990] 1 AC 109.

284 (1998) 29 EHRR 245.

285 [1999] 1 FLR 193.

286 See p 39.

to protect a family from criminal acts, including murder. The European Court said, paras 115–16:

> The court notes that the first sentence of Art 2(1) enjoins the State not only to refrain from the intentional and unlawful taking of life, but also to take appropriate steps to safeguard the lives of those within its jurisdiction ... it must be established that the authorities knew or ought to have known at the time of the existence of a real and immediate risk to life of an identified individual or individuals from the criminal acts of a third party and that they failed to take measures within the scope of their powers which, judged reasonably, might have been expected to avoid that risk.

Since in the instant case the court found that there was a real possibility that the claimants might be the objects of vigilante or revenge attacks, the potential breaches of Arts 2, 3 and 8 had to be scrupulously evaluated. Further, since a restriction on freedom of expression was in issue, all the criteria in Art 10(2), narrowly interpreted, had to be met. The court was satisfied that confidence could extend to cover the injunctions sought and that therefore, the restrictions proposed were in accordance with the law. It was found that the common law continues to evolve and was given 'considerable impetus' to do so by the implementation of the Convention into domestic law by the HRA. Also, it was a strong probability that on the release of the claimants there would be great efforts to find them and some of those seeking to do so would be determined upon revenge. The requirement in the Convention that there can be no derogation from the rights under Arts 2 and 3 provided strong support for the very pressing social need that their confidentiality should be protected. The provision of injunctions to achieve the object sought also had to be proportionate to the legitimate aims they pursued. The aim was to protect the claimants from serious and possibly irreparable harm. Dame Butler-Sloss noted that Lord Woolf said in *Lord Saville of Newdigate ex p A*:[287]

> ... when a fundamental right such as the right to life is involved, the options open to the reasonable decision-maker are curtailed. They are curtailed because it is unreasonable to reach a decision which contravenes or could contravene human rights unless there are sufficiently significant countervailing considerations. In other words it is not open to the decision-maker to risk interfering with fundamental rights in the absence of compelling justification ...

Bearing that finding in mind, Dame Butler-Sloss found that the appropriate measures to be taken were to grant the injunctions since they would substantially reduce the risk to each of the claimants. It was not thought that this extension of the law of confidence would lead to the granting of general restrictions on the media in cases where anonymity would be desirable since, under the strict application of Art 10(2), it would only be appropriate to grant injunctions to restrain the media where it could be convincingly demonstrated, within those exceptions, that it was strictly necessary. The court left open the question whether it would be appropriate to grant injunctions to restrict the press in this case if only Art 8, as opposed to Arts 2 and 3, had been likely to be breached. Although the breach of the claimants' right to respect for family life and privacy would have been likely to be serious, it might not have been sufficient to meet the importance of the preservation of the freedom of expression in Art 10(1).

---

287 [2000] 1 WLR 1885, p 1857.

In any event, the court was satisfied that there was a real and serious risk to the rights of the claimants under Arts 2 and 3 and it was found that, in principle, jurisdiction to grant the injunctions to protect the claimants was present. The court went on to assess the strength of the evidence relating to those risks; finding that a real risk existed and that the protection represented by the injunctions was proportionate to the need for confidentiality, the injunctions were granted. The injunctions are intended to last for their whole lives, although, as noted above, the existence of the internet makes their efficacy in practice doubtful.[288]

The decisions in *Douglas* and *Venables* were followed in *Mills (Heather) v News Group Newspapers Ltd*.[289] Mills was a well known and successful model who had, since 1999, been publicly associated with Sir Paul McCartney. She contracted to buy a property in Hove. In view of a number of very disturbing e-mails she received, and in the light of the circumstances surrounding the death of John Lennon, and the attack on George Harrison, she was anxious to ensure that details of her address were not given public circulation, since she feared that she might be subject to physical threats or even injury. She bought the property under an alias. However, the *Sun* was informed by a person, who had obtained the information from a friend who lived nearby, that she had information that Mills was buying a house. The editor of the *Sun* decided, owing to the good relationship of the newspaper with Sir Paul McCartney, not to run the story. He was asked for confirmation that the paper would not publish the address and/or a photograph and/or a description of the property in breach of the Code of Practice of the Press Complaints Commission (PCC). He would not confirm this in writing because he thought that other newspapers would run the story, and that were others to publish, he could not guarantee that the *Sun* would not publish it by way of 'secondary publication'. He said, however, that he could run it within the PCC Code but had decided not to. In view of this response there seemed to be a risk of publication; Mills then sought and obtained an *ex parte* injunction against the publishers of the Sun newspaper to restrain publication of material which might identify her new address.

The High Court had to consider whether to grant an interim injunction. It said that the starting point was s 12 of the HRA since it applies 'if a court is considering whether to grant any relief which, if granted, might affect the exercise of the Convention right to freedom of expression' (s 12(1)) and, in particular, provides that 'no such relief is to be granted so as to restrain publication before a trial unless the court is satisfied that the applicant is likely to establish that publication should not be allowed' (s 12(3)). The court also noted the provision of s 12(4):

The court must have particular regard to the importance of the Convention right to freedom of expression and, where the proceedings relate to material which the respondent claims, or which appears to the court, to be journalistic, literary or artistic material (or to conduct connected with such material), to

(a) the extent to which—

   (i)   the material has, or is about to, become available to the public; or

   (ii) it is, or would be, in the public interest for the material to be published;

(b) any relevant privacy code.

---

288 See above, pp 548–49.

289 [2001] EMLR 41, 4 June, High Court No HC 0102236, WL 720322. See also *A v B and C* (2001) WL 1251798.

The court went on to refer briefly to 'frequent and authoritative expressions of the importance of a free press and freedom of speech'. It noted that in *Reynolds v Times Newspapers Ltd*[290] the House of Lords stressed that there is a basic and fundamental right to freedom of expression, that freedom of expression would be buttressed by s 12 of the HRA, and that when the Act was fully in force the common law would have to be developed and applied in a manner consistent with Art 10. The court said that to be justified, 'any curtailment of freedom of expression must be convincingly established by a compelling countervailing consideration, and the means employed must be proportionate to the end sought to be achieved; and the interest of a democratic society in ensuring a free press weighs heavily in the balance in deciding whether any curtailment of this freedom bears a reasonable relationship to the purpose of the curtailment'.[291] Thus, it found that freedom of expression 'is the rule and regulation of speech is the exception requiring justification. The existence and width of any exception can only be justified if it is underpinned by a pressing social need.'[292] It relied on the findings of Hoffmann LJ in *Central Independent Television plc*:[293]

> Newspapers are sometimes irresponsible and their motives in a market economy cannot be expected to be unalloyed by considerations of commercial advantage. Publication may cause needless pain, distress and damage to individuals or harm to other aspects of the public interest. But a freedom which is restricted to what judges think to be responsible or in the public interest is no freedom. Freedom means the right to publish things which government and judges, however well motivated, think should not be published. It means the right to say things which 'right-thinking people' regard as dangerous or irresponsible. This freedom is subject only to clearly defined exceptions laid down by common law or statute ...

The court found that the combination of Art 10 and s 12 had a number of consequences. It was clear, relying on *Douglas v Hello! Ltd*[294] *per* Sedley LJ, that Art 10 is directly applicable as between the parties to private litigation. Further, it found that an injunction should not be granted to restrain publication before trial unless the court was satisfied that the applicant was likely to establish that publication should not be allowed. It said that s 12(3) makes it clear that the applicant must show more than the *American Cyanamid* threshold of a serious issue to be tried. It noted that in *Douglas v Hello! Ltd* Sedley LJ said, in applying the test set out in s 12(3), and taking s 3 of the HRA into account, that by virtue of s 12(1), (4) the qualifications set out in Art 10(2) are as relevant as the right set out in Art 10(1).[295] Therefore, the rights of others, including their Convention rights, are, it found, as material as the defendant's right of free expression and so is the prohibition on the use of one party's Convention rights to injure the Convention rights of others. He also found that the term 'likely' in s 12(3) should not be read as requiring simply an evaluation of the relative strengths of the parties' evidence.

---

290 [1999] 3 WLR 1010.

291 Referring to Lord Nicholls, p 1023.

292 Referring to Lord Steyn, pp 1029–39. The court also noted the findings in *McCartan Turkington and Breen v Times Newspapers Ltd* [2000] 3 WLR 1670, p 1686 (HL), where Lord Steyn said that the European Convention fulfilled the function of a Bill of Rights, and considered *Secretary of State for the Home Department ex p Simms* [2000] 2 AC 115, p 126.

293 [1994] Fam 192, pp 202–04.

294 [2001] 2 WLR 992, p 1027, para 133.

295 *Ibid*, p 1028, para 136.

He said that a wholly unjustifiable invasion of privacy is entitled to no less regard, by virtue of Art 10(2), than is accorded to the right to publish by Art 10(1): 'neither element is a trump card. They will be articulated by the principles of legality and proportionality which, as always, constitute the mechanism by which the court reaches its conclusion on countervailing or qualified rights.' The court also noted the findings of Keene LJ in the same case. He said that s 12(3) deals with the interlocutory stage of proceedings and requires the court to look at the merits of the case and not merely to apply the *American Cyanamid* test.[296] This meant that the court had to look ahead to the ultimate stage and be satisfied that the scales were likely to come down in the applicant's favour.

The court noted that the case for an injunction was on the ground of breach of confidence since, in general, the rights in the Convention, as incorporated by the 1998 Act, and in particular Art 8, do not justify the creation of new causes of action to give effect to them where the common law or statute law is deficient.[297] It said that the English courts have not, unlike the American courts which applied and developed the views expressed by Warren and Brandeis in their famous article in the *Harvard Law Review* in 1890,[298] developed a separate right of privacy prohibiting unreasonable and offensive intrusion on the interest of a person in solitude or seclusion, or objectionable publicity of private information about a person. However, it thought that this deficiency was being remedied, as was made clear by Sedley LJ in *Douglas v Hello! Ltd*.[299]

The Court pointed out that information which has entered the public domain is not subject to confidentiality; in other words, that there may be circumstances in which the information is so generally accessible that, in the circumstances, it cannot be regarded as confidential. Therefore, the fact that information may be known to a limited number of members of the public does not of itself prevent it having and retaining the character of confidentiality.[300] It also said that even if it has previously been very widely available, the restraint of further dissemination of the confidential material may be justified to prevent harm.[301]

Assuming that the information in question – Ms Mills' address, or information that would reveal it – was therefore confidential information, the question was whether it should be protected by an injunction. The court found that there was no evidence that the newspaper had learned of it from or through some person who learned of it through some confidential relationship or transaction. But, it said that it is no longer a necessary element of the cause of action that the information arises from a confidential relationship. In so finding it relied on the findings of Dame Elizabeth Butler-Sloss P in *Venables v News Group Newspapers Ltd*[302] to the effect that the court had jurisdiction to restrain the

---

296 [1975] AC 396, p 1032, para 150.

297 In so finding it relied on *Venables v News Group Newspapers Ltd* [2001] 2 WLR 1038, pp 1048–49, 1075, paras 24–25, 111, and disagreed with *Douglas v Hello! Ltd*, p 1026, para 129, *per* Sedley LJ.

298 Vol 4, p 193.

299 [2001] 2 WLR 992, p 1025, paras 125–26. Sedley LJ said: the 'two first-named clients have a right of privacy which English law will today recognise and, where appropriate, protect. To say this is in my belief to say little, save by way of a label, that our courts have not said already over the years ...'. Cf Brooke LJ, para 95; Keene LJ, paras 165–67. See further Jack J in *A v B and C* (2001) unreported, 30 April.

300 It referred to *Stephens v Avery*, p 454; *R v Broadcasting Complaints Commission ex p Granada Television Ltd* [1995] EMLR 163, p 168; *Creation Records Ltd v News Group Newspapers Ltd* [1997] EMLR 444, p 456.

301 *AG v Guardian Newspapers (No 2)*, p 260, *per* Lord Keith of Kinkel.

302 [2001] 2 WLR 1038.

publication of material about Venables and Thompson, to protect information about their identities and whereabouts, because the disclosure of the information would have disastrous consequences for them.

Thus, the court found that there is jurisdiction to restrain a newspaper from publishing the address of a person in certain circumstances. However, it said that the mere publication of an address may not be a breach of confidence, or an unwarranted invasion of privacy. It said that, as the *Venables* case shows, one of the necessary additional elements may be the risk of injury or death to the person involved. In so finding, the court noted the practice of the PCC in applying the privacy provision of its Code of Practice (cl 3) which it said indicated that the rationale for prohibiting newspapers from publishing the address of the home of a celebrity (or material which might enable people to find its whereabouts) is not simply that the address is protected information, but that a risk to the safety of the person might thereby be created.

It went on to note that cl 3 is plainly based on Art 8 of the Convention and that although Art 8 is not directly applicable in England in the sense of creating new causes of action, the English court (a) must, in determining a question which has arisen in connection with a Convention right, take into account, *inter alia*, the decisions of the European Court of Human Rights (under s 2(1) of the HRA) and (b) because the court is a public authority (s 6(3)(a) of the HRA), must not act in a way which is incompatible with a Convention right. The court went on to consider the exception under Art 10(2) in respect of 'the protection of the reputation or rights of others', which it said must include Convention rights such as Art 8 when being given effect by such means as the law of confidentiality; and also the exception 'for preventing the disclosure of information received in confidence'.

In applying the Convention jurisprudence under s 12(3) of the HRA, and bearing in mind that the qualifications in Art 10(2) are as relevant as the basic right of freedom of expression in Art 10(1), the court noted that the European Court of Human Rights has emphasised that the national court has to strike a fair and proportionate balance between the respective Convention rights, depending on such factors as the nature and seriousness of the interests at stake and the gravity of the interference. Further, one of the matters which the court has to take into account in deciding whether prior restraint is justified is 'any relevant privacy code', and the PCC Code of Practice is clearly such a code.[303] It noted that the rules on privacy under cl 3 are 'disarmingly simple' and found that the existence of the statutory provisions, coupled with the current wording of the relevant privacy code, meant that in any case where the court was concerned with issues of freedom of expression in a journalistic, literary or artistic context, it was bound to pay particular regard to any breach of the rules set out in cl 3 of the Code, especially where none of the public interest claims set out in the preamble to the Code was asserted.

It found that a newspaper which flouts cl 3 of the Code is likely in those circumstances to have its claim to an entitlement to freedom of expression trumped by

---

303 It noted that in *Douglas v Hello! Ltd* [2001] 2 WLR 992, Brooke LJ said (p 1018, paras 92–94): '... the Code of Practice ratified by the Press Complaints Commission in November 1997 states that all members of the press have a duty to maintain the highest professional and ethical standards, and that the code sets the benchmarks for those standards: it both protects the rights of the individual and upholds the public's right to know.'

Art 10(2) considerations of privacy, and it said that unlike the court in *Kaye v Robertson*,[304] Parliament had recognised that it had to acknowledge the importance of the Art 8(1) respect for private life, and it was able to do so untrammelled by any concerns that the law of confidence might not stretch to protect every aspect of private life. Therefore, in making a determination in the instant case, the court found that it was not necessary to go beyond s 12(3) of the 1998 Act and cl 3 of the Press Complaints Commission's Code to find the ground rules by which to weigh the competing considerations of freedom of expression on the one hand and privacy on the other.

However, the court had to be satisfied, if it was to restrain publication before trial, that the claimant was likely to establish that publication should not be allowed. In deciding not to grant the injunction, the court took into account the fact that the risk to personal safety which arose was only slight, and the fact that the Sun had repeatedly said that it would not publish the address and that it would abide by the PCC Code. It also found that whether or not the information appeared in the press, it would, at least to a limited extent, become available to the public, simply as a result of Ms Mills living in a busy and populous town. The court said that that was not in itself a reason for denying her a remedy, but that it was relevant both in assessing the degree to which publication should be restrained, and the impact of publication on her privacy and security. The court did not take account of the fact that Ms Mills had for several years courted publicity, and had herself stimulated public interest in her lifestyle, sex life, and her homes.

The Court noted that in *Venables v News Group Newspapers Ltd*[305] the President had held that the court has jurisdiction to grant an injunction against the world in order to protect individuals from the criminal acts of others. That jurisdiction, it said, has a wider and more direct effect than the decision in *AG v Times Newspapers Ltd*[306] that newspapers which know of an injunction against another newspaper would, if they were to publish the information, be guilty of contempt. The rationale of that decision was that publication of the material by other newspapers would nullify the purpose of the proceedings against the defendant by putting into the public domain material which the applicant claimed should remain confidential, and they would be in contempt by impeding or interfering with the administration of justice. In the instant case, the court found that it would not be right to grant an injunction against the world on the *Venables* basis because the balancing exercise would not support so doing, especially in view of the absence of evidence of the apprehended harm and the other relevant matters.

After these three decisions it can be said, with a certainty that was not previously appropriate, that the law recognises and protects a right of personal privacy. That right finds its roots in an existing cause of action, the doctrine of confidence. The HRA has, as commentators predicted, given the courts the impetus to develop confidence to this point. But it is important to be clear about the method of reaching this stage. The *Douglas* decision did not rely on the creation of so-called direct horizontal effect in the sense of the creation of a new free-standing cause of action: the HRA precludes an action directly against newspapers based on Art 8, since newspapers are not public authorities within the meaning of s 6 of the HRA. But, once the plaintiffs were in court presenting an

---

304 [1991] FSR 62.
305 [2001] 2 WLR 1038, p 1071, para 100.
306 [1992] 1 AC 191; see Chapter 5, p 249.

arguable case for an injunction on grounds of confidence, the court had a duty, under s 12(4) of the HRA (if not under s 6 as a public authority) to develop that action by reference to Art 10, which meant also giving full weight to Art 8 as a right recognised under Art 10(2). In taking Art 8 into account, the domestic courts have also now accepted that, as interpreted at Strasbourg, its guarantees clearly affect the relations between private parties. The most important aspect of the findings in *Douglas* relates to the possibility of a surreptitious taking of the photographs since that is the instance in which the doctrine of confidence as traditionally conceived gives way to privacy. In other words, where surreptitious takings of information are in question, privacy values can determine the issue, although both *Mills* and *Venables* consider that these values are reflected in an extension of the doctrine of confidence, not in a common law doctrine of privacy. As indicated above, this development was already occurring, but the reliance on privacy values gives it a grounding in case law and in principle which it previously lacked.

Where prior restraint is in question, s 12(3) requires consideration of the merits of the privacy right and of expression in the particular circumstances. Also, as the *Venables* case made clear, such prior restraint must be justified by a strict application of the tests under Art 10(2), in particular those of necessity and proportionality. The so called 'public interest defence' under the doctrine of confidence can no longer lead to a balancing of such interest against maintaining confidentiality: the tests under Art 10(2) have taken its place.

These three decisions provide a consolidation of the developments in the law of confidence described above, which was clearly needed. While, prior to the inception of the HRA, confidence had the potential to be applied in the archetypal privacy cases, the developments outlined above had a relatively slight grounding in authority: there were comparatively few cases involving personal, as opposed to commercial information; moreover, in those which dealt with such information, there was only one decision, at the interlocutory stage,[307] where the obligation of confidence was imposed without there being an express or implied promise that the information would be kept secret[308] or where there had not at least been a pre-existing relationship between confider and confidant.[309] All but one of the cases[310] involving surreptitious takings of information (where there was no pre-existing relationship or agreement of confidentiality) occurred in the commercial or professional context. It had been argued that in such cases, the courts were protecting the plaintiffs' rights to the fruits of their labour;[311] conversely, it was said that the basis of intervention in personal information cases had historically been to protect the integrity of certain kinds of relationship. Thus, where personal information was revealed in circumstances where there was no such prior relationship, it was argued that there was no clear social need to protect confidentiality[312] and in the absence of such

---

307 *Francome* [1984] 1 WLR 892.

308 As there was in *Stephens v Avery* [1988] Ch 449 and *HRH Princess of Wales*(1993) Transcript, Association of Official Shorthandwriters Ltd, 8 November 1993.

309 In *Duchess of Argyll v Duke of Argyll*[1967] 1 Ch 302, there was a prior relationship of husband and wife, in *HRH Princess of Wales* (1993) Transcript, Association of Official Shorthandwriters Ltd, 8 November 1993, a commercial relationship, and in *Michael Barrymore* ([1997] FSR 600), a close friendship and a sexual relationship (there was also a written agreement of confidentiality).

310 *Francome* [1984] 1 WLR 892 is the exception.

311 Wilson, *op cit*, fn 1, p 49.

312 This view ignored the argument, notably advanced by Feldman, that the right to privacy does serve a strong social function in protecting the integrity of the different spheres of business, social and personal life within which we operate as individuals ('Secrecy, dignity or autonomy: views of privacy as a civil liberty' (1994) 47(2) CLP 42, pp 51–53).

a need, the judges should not use the law to enforce 'free-standing' moral convictions,[313] such as a belief that private information should not be disclosed without consent. Moreover, Lord Bingham said of the claim that confidence could have been used to remedy the violation of privacy which occurred in *Kaye v Robertson*,[314] that such use would have done 'impermissible violence to the principles upon which that cause of action is founded'.[315]

Thus, had it not been for the advent of the HRA, a conservative appellate court, determined to restore the action to the founding principles which Lord Bingham invoked, could well have found that the use of confidence to protect privacy was weakly supported by authority, an illegitimate distortion of the law and lacking any underpinning in clear legal principle.[316] But, as *Douglas* demonstrates, now that the HRA is in force, the right to respect for privacy declared by Art 8 has become, as discussed above, an important legal value or principle, which may properly inform the direction of the common law. The Strasbourg jurisprudence examined above indicates that unremedied invasions of privacy by the media are in principle a violation of Art 8. Thus, the consolidation of the developments described above, far from being regarded as an illegitimate exercise in judicial activism, has now been underpinned by legal principle, and justified by the need identified at Strasbourg to answer to the requirements of Art 8 in this area through the common law.

Somewhat ironically, s 12 of the HRA, introduced after intense media lobbying to provide greater protection for the press to counterbalance the possible effect of Art 8, has in fact encouraged the courts to provide remedies against the worst excesses of intrusive journalism. In particular, it has afforded further status, as these three decisions emphasise, to the PCC Code, which is, as indicated above, quite extensively concerned with privacy.

Proposals for civil and criminal liability for invasion of privacy

Introduction

At present, aside from the development just discussed, no tort of invasion of privacy exists in the UK, as in the US,[317] to control the activity of the media or others in intruding on the privacy of individuals, obtaining information regarding an individual's private life and then publishing the details, perhaps in exaggerated, lurid terms. In the early 1990s, comprehensive legal controls were proposed, intended to be used against the media and others when private information was published. These controls were to affect both the publication of the information and the methods used to obtain it. When information such as a photograph is obtained, there may often be some kind of intrusion on property, albeit of a nebulous kind, such as long range surveillance. Proposals regarding legal controls

---

313 Wilson, *op cit*, fn 1, pp 54–55.

314 [1991] FSR 62. The argument is put in Fenwick and Phillipson, *op cit*, fn 158.

315 Bingham LJ, 'Should there be a law to protect rights of personal privacy?' (1996) 5 EHRLR 450, p 457.

316 See, however, the very recent Court of Appeal judgment in *Dept of Health ex p Source Informatics Ltd* [2000] 2 WLR 953.

317 US Restatement 2d Torts (1977) No 652A.

relevant to the publication of information will be considered first, followed by the legal control of intrusions.

Proposals

Proposals for the enactment of a tort of invasion of privacy in the UK centred around the protection of personal information. As indicated above, the HRA, as interpreted in *Douglas and Others v Hello!*,[318] has brought about development of the existing doctrine of breach of confidence, with the result that greatly increased protection for control of personal information has been created. However, such development is not yet certain and in any event, there is still an argument for providing further protection for privacy by means of a statutory tort balanced by wide ranging and carefully drawn specific public interest defences. Such a tort could provide a more comprehensive protection for privacy, including protection from intrusions.

Support for a statutory tort has, however, been far from unanimous in the relevant committees which have considered the issue. Thus, while the Younger Committee in 1972[319] recommended the introduction of a tort of disclosure of information unlawfully acquired, Calcutt 1[320] decided against recommending a new statutory tort of invasion of privacy relating to publication of personal information, although the Committee considered that it would be possible to define such a tort with sufficient precision. Calcutt 2[321] recommended only that the government should give further consideration to the introduction of such a tort, but the National Heritage Select Committee[322] recommended its introduction, as did the later Lord Chancellor's Consultation Paper, the Green Paper.[323] As indicated above, these proposals were abandoned in July 1995,[324] although they found some expression in the DPA 1998.[325] It may be noted that the Lord Chancellor's Paper did not propose an extension of legal aid to those seeking redress under the proposed new civil privacy liability. If, in future, a new tort is created without the provision of legal aid, it might merely be used – as arguably defamation has been – by powerful figures to protect their activities from scrutiny while the ordinary citizen might be unable in practice to obtain redress for invasions of privacy.

The possible definition of the proposed tort put forward by Calcutt 1 was designed to relate only to personal information which was published without authorisation. Such information was defined as those aspects of an individual's personal life which a reasonable person would assume should remain private. The main concern of the Committee was that true information which would not cause lasting harm, was already known to some, and was obtained reputably might be caught by its provisions. The Lord Chancellor's proposals were wider: there should be a new cause of action for

---

318 [2001] 2 WLR 992.

319 *Op cit*, fn 1.

320 *Op cit*, fn 1.

321 *Op cit*, fn 1.

322 *Op cit*, fn 1.

323 The paper was released on 30 July 1993 – CHAN J060915NJ.7/93. See 143 NLJ 1182 for discussion of these proposals.

324 The White Paper, *Privacy and Media Intrusion: the Government's Response*, Cmnd 2918, July 1995, found against creation of a statutory tort.

325 See below, pp 603–10.

'infringement of privacy causing substantial distress' (para 5.22). No definition of privacy was offered, although it was stated to include matters relating to health, personal relationships and communications, and freedom from harassment.

Legatt LJ asserted confidently in *Kaye* that a right to privacy exists in the US which will be enforced and suggested that such a right should be imported into UK law, but this proposition has come under attack,[326] on the basis that the scope of US privacy rights is limited by a general defence of 'newsworthiness'[327] which allows many stories disclosing embarrassing and painful personal facts to be published. This perhaps suggests that there is little value in looking to the US for a model if a UK right to privacy is to have any efficacy. The Calcutt Committee did not consider that liability should be subject to a general defence of public interest on US lines, although it did favour a tightly drawn defence of justified disclosure. Under Calcutt 2 (para 12.23) it was proposed that it would be a defence to show that the defendant had reasonable grounds for believing that publication of the personal information would contribute to preventing, detecting or exposing the commission of a crime or other seriously anti-social conduct; or to preventing the public from being misled by some public statement or action of the individual concerned; or that the defendant had reasonable grounds for believing that publication would be necessary for the protection of public health or safety. The Green Paper invited comments on these defences and in particular on the question whether the public interest defence should be defined in general terms or whether it should be more specific (para 5.62–5.67). The Green Paper proposed (para 5.45) that there should be a defence that the defendant had acted under any lawful authority. *Prima facie*, these defences seem to range widely enough to prevent public figures from being able to use the tort to stifle legitimate investigative journalism. The defence of seeking to prevent the public from being misled by some public statement or action of the individual concerned is, it is submitted, essential to draw a clear distinction between the private citizen and the public figure, and to ensure the accountability of the latter.

Further proposals for reform aimed at methods of obtaining information were also put forward. The Younger Committee proposed the introduction of a tort and crime of unlawful surveillance by means of a technical device, and both Calcutt Committees[328] recommended the creation of a specific criminal offence providing more extensive protection – a recommendation which was backed by the National Heritage Select Committee when it considered the matter.

The clause creating the offence under Calcutt 2 also offered the individual whose privacy has been invaded the possibility of obtaining injunctions in the High Court to prevent publication of material gained in contravention of the clause provisions; damages would also be available to hold newspapers to account for any profits gained through publication of such material. Criminal liability under the clause would be made out if the defendant did any of the following with intent to obtain personal information or photographs, in either case with a view to their publication: entering or remaining on private property without the consent of the lawful occupant; placing a surveillance device

---

326 Bedingfield, *op cit*, fn 142.

327 Bedingfield cites the example of *Kelley v Post Publishing Co Mass* [1951] 98 NE 2d 286. A father was unable to restrain publication of a picture of the severely injured body of his daughter due to the finding that the accident was newsworthy.

328 See above, p 535, fn 1.

on private property without such consent; using a surveillance device whether on private property or elsewhere in relation to an individual who is on private property without his or her consent; taking a photograph or recording the voice of an individual who is on private property without his or her consent and with intent that the individual should be identifiable. This clause seemed to specify the forbidden acts fairly clearly and to be aimed at preventing what would generally be accepted to be on the face of it undesirable invasions of privacy; it is worth noting that France, Germany, Denmark and the Netherlands all have similar offences on the statute books. (It should be noted that the offence would not cover persistent telephoning;[329] or photographing, interviewing or recording the voice of a vulnerable individual such as a disaster victim or a bereaved relative in a public place).

Calcutt 1 and the Green Paper[330] proposed defences to the proposed criminal offences which were wider than the defences suggested in relation to a tort of invasion of privacy. Calcutt 1 proposed (para 6.35) that it would be a defence to any of the actions above to show that the act was done:

(a) for the purpose of preventing, detecting or exposing the commission of a crime or other seriously anti-social conduct; or

(b) for the purpose of preventing the public from being misled by some public statement or action of the individual concerned; or

(c) for the purpose of informing the public about matters directly affecting the discharge of any public function of the individual concerned; or

(d) for the protection of public health or safety; or

(e) under any lawful authority.

Calcutt 1, 2 and the Green Paper were silent as to the mental element required with respect to the defences. There appear to be three possibilities here which, for the purposes of exposition, will be examined using the example of a claim of defence (a). First, the defence would succeed only if it was shown that the forbidden act actually could have led to the exposure of crime, so that if it turned out that in fact no criminal activity had been present – though perhaps a reasonable person would have thought that it was – the defence would fail. Secondly, the defence would succeed if the defendant could show that she honestly and reasonably believed that she was acting with the purpose of exposing crime. Thirdly, it would succeed if the defendant could show that she honestly believed that she was acting with this purpose. It is submitted that the first possibility would be undesirable for three reasons: first, it could lead to serious injustice where a reporter had a reasonable suspicion which turned out later to be untrue; secondly, it would offend against the principle of criminal law formulated in *DPP v Morgan*[331] that the defendant should be judged on the facts as she believed them to be, and thirdly, it could act as a serious deterrent to investigative journalism. The second possibility is an improvement, but it again falls foul of the *Morgan* principle; moreover, there would be a risk that judges might demand quite a high standard of reasonable belief so that journalists would have to

---

329 The Protection from Harassment Act 1997 might offer some protection in this area (see above, pp 564–65).

330 See above, p 535, fn 1.

331 [1976] AC 182.

produce substantial evidence justifying their suspicions in order to make out the defence – a burden which would again exercise a deterrent effect.

It is suggested that the third possibility is to be preferred; a journalist who honestly believes that she is acting in the public interest (within the terms of one of the defences) should not be criminalised. It may be feared that such a fully subjective test would always provide an escape from liability and thus render the offence useless. However, a journalist who merely asserted that she thought she was acting within the terms of one of the specific public interests, but was unable to adduce any grounds at all for her belief, would probably not be believed by the court. The other advantage of adopting this third possibility would be that it could come into play while the journalistic investigation was still at an inchoate stage so long as some evidence could be adduced supporting the necessary belief. On this basis, the proposed offence would provide a remedy against some unjustifiable invasions of privacy, but would be unlikely to deter serious journalism. However, the Lord Chancellor's consultation paper favoured narrowing the defences by omitting the words 'seriously anti-social conduct' from defence (a) and curtailing defences (b) and (c). If this occurred, the public lives of public figures such as ministers would be protected from scrutiny, an instance of curtailment of freedom of speech which would clearly prevent the full participation of the citizen in the democratic process.

Conclusions

As indicated above, these proposals were eventually abandoned. Obviously, there is now less need to create a new tort, since the doctrine of confidence has partially taken over the role such a tort would have had. Nevertheless, the development of the doctrine to cover the requirements of Art 8 of the Convention under the HRA 1998 may eventually prompt Parliament to introduce a new tort. It is possible that the uncertainties of using the doctrine of confidence as affected by s 12 of the HRA and Art 8 might lead the media to view the enactment of a tort of invasion of privacy along the lines of that proposed by Calcutt 2 as preferable (although it would presumably co-exist with the new-style confidence action and would also be affected by ss 3 and 12 of the HRA). It may also be desirable to enact certain very specific and narrowly defined areas of liability, relating to particularly intrusive invasions of privacy, including harassment.[332]

5 THE DATA PROTECTION ACT 1998

Introduction

Until 1998, there was no statute in the UK equivalent to the US Privacy Act 1974 which enables persons to obtain access to information held on them in government files. In the UK, certain categories of information covered by the Official Secrets Act 1989 could not be

---

332 The Protection from Harassment Act 1997, ss 1 and 2 make it an offence to pursue a course of conduct which amounts to harassment of another where the harasser knows or ought to know that this will be its effect. This offence is not aimed at reporters or photographers and is not dependent on acquiring or attempting to acquire information, but it might be applicable where individual reporters had pursued a particular individual on a number of occasions.

disclosed, but if personal information fell outside those categories there was still no general right of access to it. Central government and public authorities in general hold a vast amount of personal information in manual and computerised files. The police, for example, use a national system which stores an immense amount of personal information, as does the Inland Revenue. But private bodies, including the media, also process personal information. Until relatively recently, the citizen had no means of knowing what information was held on him or her by private or public bodies, and no control over the nature or use of such information. However, an inroad into the principle of secrecy was made in 1984 by the Data Protection Act 1984,[333] which was adopted in response to the Council of Europe Convention of 1980.[334] Once access to certain computerised files became possible, access rights to some manual files began to follow, although no general statutory rights of access to personal information or control over the processing of such information were created until the Data Protection Act 1998 (DPA) was passed, and therefore much personal information still remained inaccessible and its processing was uncontrolled. Such a right was proposed in the 1993 White Paper on freedom of information and open government,[335] but was not implemented. Prior to the passing of the 1998 Act, the access to information measures discussed below merely provided exceptions to the general denial of access. Therefore, the 1998 Act is of immense significance in terms of protecting the privacy of personal information by seeking to ensure that processing is conducted in accordance with the Data Principles.

The Data Protection Act 1984

Information held electronically[336]

In response to the steady computerisation of information, the government decided in 1975 that those who use computers to handle personal information cannot remain the sole judges of the extent to which their own systems adequately safeguard privacy. The Committee on Data Protection was therefore set up, but the final impetus came from the Council of Europe, which promulgated the Convention on Data Protection in 1980.[337] In response, the DPA 1984, applying to personal information in both the public and private sectors, was passed.[338] It was seen as a measure to protect privacy and a first step towards freedom of information. However, it must be questioned whether it was clear

---

333 The provisions of the 1984 Act were extended by the Data Protection (Subject Access Modifications) Health Order 1987, SI 1987/1903.

334 Convention for the Protection of Individuals with regard to the Automatic Processing of Personal Data, 17 September 1980.

335 Cm 2290. For further discussion of the Code of Practice on Access to Government Information, which was introduced in 1994 as promised in the White Paper, see Chapter 7, pp 372–78, above. The Code and the Freedom of Information Act 2000, which will take over its role, are not designed to protect personal information, except in the sense that it is exempted from the access.

336 General reading: see Lloyd, I, *Information Technology and the Law*, 3rd edn, 2000; Reed (ed), *Computer Law*, 1990, Chapter 9; Sieghart, P, *Privacy and Computers*, 1977; Tapper, C, *Computer Law*, 1989; Hewitt, P (ed), *Computers, Records and the Right to Privacy*, 1979; Wacks, *op cit*, fn 1, Chapter 6.

337 Convention for the Protection of Individuals with regard to the Automatic Processing of Personal Data, 17 September 1980.

338 For commentary see 'Confidential: computers, records and the right to privacy' (NCCL); Savage, N and Edwards, C, *A Guide to the Data Protection Act*, 1985.

that there was a pressing need to allow access to electronically held information as opposed to a need for access to all personal information. As indicated below, the DPA 1998 recognised that most of the argument regarding the electronic storage of information could also be applied to manual files.

It may be argued that the electronic storage of information presents a particular threat to privacy because computers exacerbate problems which also exist with respect to manual files. For example, an error may creep into information held on manual files, but where information is collated from a large number of sources, as may be more likely in respect of computerised files, an error may be more likely to occur. Moreover, once it does occur, the speed with which information can be retrieved and disseminated means that an error can reach far more persons and may do more damage than a record on a manual file. It is possible to transmit data from one data bank to another much more easily than can be done using manual files. Personal information gathered for a purpose acceptable to its subject may be transferred to another data bank without the subject's knowledge or consent. It may also be linked up with other information, thus creating what may be a distorted picture.

There is a danger that the confidentiality of information may be placed at risk. Information may be given to an employer by an employee on the understanding that because there is a confidential relationship between the parties it will go no further. If it is then stored in a data bank, there is a danger that the confidentiality will be lost. An action for breach of confidence could lie, but the individual affected would have to be aware of the breach. The retention of data may also create disadvantages. Although a person's circumstances or behaviour may change, old data may not be updated, but may follow him or her around with the result that (for example) he or she is refused credit. Manually held information is less likely to follow an individual so effectively.

The regime created by the DPA 1984

It may therefore be said that no difference in principle between problems associated with the storage of manually held and computerised information can be discerned, but that there is a difference of degree. The 1984 Act attempted to address these problems by placing certain obligations on persons storing personal data. Below, the key features of the regime created by the DPA 1984 are indicated; they will be compared with those of the regime created under the 1998 Act.

Any person using a computerised system in order to store data relating to people was designated the 'data user', while the person who was the subject of the data was the 'data subject'. Any data relating to a living person was termed 'personal data'.[339] The data user had to register with the Data Protection Registrar. Section 5 provided that the data user must not use the data for any purpose other than the one it was collected for and under Sched 1, it had to be kept up to date. Also, it had to be adequately protected; appropriate security measures were to be taken. Under ss 10 and 11, if the Data Registrar was satisfied that the data user was not complying with the Act, she could serve an enforcement notice, and if this measure was not adequate, she could serve a deregistration notice. It was a criminal offence for an unregistered person or body to store personal data.

---

339 These definitions are found in ss 4 and 5 of the Act.

Section 21 provided that if the data user was asked by the data subject whether personal data was held on her or him, that information had to be given and the data subject had to be allowed access to such data. Schedule 1 also provided that if the data was found to be inaccurate, the data subject could have it corrected or erased. If the data user did not comply, the subject could apply to court under s 24 for an order erasing or rectifying the data. Under s 22, compensation could be awarded if loss or damage had resulted from inaccurate data. However, compensation was available only if the data user compiled the inaccurate information, not if the data user compiled inaccurate material supplied by a malicious or careless third party. No compensation was available for circulating the inaccurate data; nor could the data subject know the third party's name.

Certain aspects of the 1984 Act attracted criticism, especially the wide subject access exemptions which included information relating to crime, national security, and a person's physical or mental health. A broad interpretation tended to be given to these exemptions; thus, the results of the lack of protection for privacy were unchecked in those categories. Moreover, there was still the possibility of transferring data to manual files and as provisions relating to manual files were narrow in scope, especially those under the Access to Personal Files Act 1987, it could well be the case that the manual file would not fall within any of the provisions affording access. The transfer of data from a registered data user such as the Department of Employment to an unregistered user, such as the Security Services, remained secret, and national security was exempt from the principle that data users could not allow data to be used for a purpose other than the original one.

Further, the budgetary restraint on the Data Protection Registry made it impossible to keep a check on all data users. In any event, it was considered relatively straightforward to devise an information retrieval system which only provided an incomplete copy of an individual's record. In such an instance, it appeared probable that no action for breach of the Act was likely to follow due to the inability of the Data Registrar Officer to check up on what had occurred. It would take a specialist a long time to work out what had happened, and, given the constraints on the Data Registrar, that time was unlikely to be available. Thus, it may be said that the Act was certainly a step in the direction of control over personal information, but it contained many loop-holes.

The Computer Misuse Act 1990

Unauthorised access to information electronically held falls within the Computer Misuse Act 1990[340] which criminalises such conduct whether or not the 'hacker' has a sinister purpose. It may be wondered why it should be an offence to access files held on an office computer, but not files held in the filing cabinet. One answer is that hacking presents a more widespread and pernicious danger: it is possible to access the files from a different part of the country – there is no need for the would-be hacker to break into the office, as in the case of the unauthorised seeker of information in manual files. Thus, the possibility that persons may gain unauthorised access to personal information may now be diminished, although use of the 1990 Act in practice has proved problematic.[341] Together,

---

340 For comment, see 'The Computer Misuse Act 1990' (1990) 140 NLJ 1117.
341 See Charlesworth, A, 'Between flesh and sand: rethinking the Computer Misuse Act 1990' (1995) 9 International Yearbook of Law, Computers and Technology 33.

the 1984 and 1990 Acts formed a code which until the inception of the 1998 Act provided a relatively comprehensive protection for privacy in relation to computerised files when compared with that available in respect of manually held files.

Protection for manually held files prior to the inception of the DPA 1998

In the wake of the DPA 1984, access rights to manual files were gradually extended under the influence of the Campaign for Freedom of Information, although without government support. The Access to Personal Files Bill was put forward as a Private Members' Bill and would have allowed access to a wide range of personal information. However, the government forced its proponents to accept an eviscerated Bill covering only housing and social security files. Thus, the Bill was restricted to local government because central government was resistant to any measure allowing individuals access to personal files. The Bill became the Access to Personal Files Act 1987. It allowed access to 'accessible information' and therefore provided for the rectification of errors. However, it was acknowledged in the passage of the Bill that there was nothing to prevent the keeping of a secret file behind the accessible file. Moreover, the Act does not have retrospective effect; thus, it does not apply to information collected before it came into effect.

The findings of the European Court of Human Rights in the *Gaskin* case[342] illustrated the inadequacy of the available measures. Graham Gaskin wanted to gain access to the personal files on his childhood in care kept by Liverpool City Council because he wanted to sue the council in negligence. He sought to invoke Art 8 and also Art 10. However, the files did not fall under the DPA 1984 since they were manually held; nor did they fall within the Access to Personal Files Act 1987 because they were collected before it came into force. The first question to be determined under Art 8 was whether it could apply to such a situation since it was considered that the essential object of Art 8 is to protect the individual from arbitrary interference by the authorities. However, the court found that there could also be a positive obligation on the authorities to act in certain situations. Here, the information consisted of the only coherent record of the whole of Gaskin's early childhood. It was therefore found that *prima facie* an obligation to protect privacy arose, because individuals should not be obstructed by the authorities from obtaining information so closely bound up with their identity as human beings. Thus, a positive obligation could arise although it was thought that Art 8 would not normally import such an obligation.

The Court then considered whether the exception under Art 8(2) in respect of the rights of others could apply. On the one hand, there was the need to demonstrate respect for Gaskin's privacy; on the other, the contributors of the information wanted it kept confidential. It was found that the two interests should be weighed against each other by invoking the principle of proportionality. However, the local authority had not put in place any means of independently weighing the two values; thus the preference would automatically be given to the interest in maintaining confidence. Therefore, the principle of proportionality was offended and a breach of Art 8 was found. Gaskin was awarded damages on the basis of the distress he had suffered. No breach of Art 10 was found. It

---

342 *Gaskin v UK* (1990) 12 EHRR 36.

was determined that the right to receive information protected by Art 10 meant that the government should not interfere if a willing speaker wished to impart information, but that there was no positive obligation on the government to impart it.

The government complied with this ruling by introducing the Access to Personal Files (Social Services) Regulations 1989, as amended,[343] which provides that social services departments must give personal information to individuals unless the contributor of the information can be identified and he or she does not consent to the access. Certain personal health information is also exempted. Thus, local authorities now have to weigh against each other the two values considered by the Court of Human Rights. One further possible result of the *Gaskin* case may be that test cases will be encouraged in relation to central government files where they are not covered by the DPA 1998 (see below).

A method of obtaining access to medical information relating to oneself arises under the Medical Reports Act 1988[344] which also started life as a Private Members' Bill. It provides for limited circumstances in which a person can obtain access to personal medical information: if an insurance company or prospective insurer asks for a medical report for employment purposes, the individual in question can see it beforehand to read it and check it for errors. An example was given in parliamentary debate on the Bill of a woman who had had mistakenly included in her medical record a sheet from another record indicating that she was dying of cancer. She was refused insurance and would never have been able to obtain insurance since she had no chance of putting the mistake right. Similarly a misdiagnosis might remain on a medical record and never be corrected. These possibilities are of particular significance because a medical record contains information on a person's sexual habits and family circumstances; it does not merely contain purely medical information.

The Act, however, creates only a limited right of access; it does not mean that a person has a general right of access to all his or her medical files. There is a view in the medical profession that patients who do not have medical knowledge will not be able to place medical notes in their context, and moreover that knowing of certain conditions may exacerbate their illness since they may worry and therefore come under greater stress. Concerns may also be raised that a general right of access might increase the likelihood of a negligence action; clearly such an action might fail, but they do not welcome the waste of time and energy which fighting an action, even successfully, would entail. The darker side to this argument is, of course, that lack of access rights might preclude a legitimate negligence action: in some instances a patient might never realise that a mistake had been made.

The Access to Health Records Act 1990, which came into force on 1 November 1991, took the principle of access in this area much further.[345] Since the introduction of the DPA 1984, patients had been entitled to have access to their computerised health records, but the 1990 Act was intended to provide an equivalent right of access to information recorded in manually held health records. The access to health records allows people to examine exactly what has been recorded about them – thus satisfying personal curiosity – but, more importantly, it will allow for mistakes to be noted and rectified. The emphasis

---

343 SI 1989/206, as amended by SI 1991/1587.
344 See also the Access to Health Records (Control of Access) Regulations 1993, SI 1993/746.
345 See 'Access to health records' (1990) 140 NLJ 1382.

of the Act is on an individual's control of personal and private information. However, several exceptions curb the actual scope of the access. First, as in the Access to Personal Files Act, no pre-commencement material must be shown, unless it is necessary for a full understanding of something which has been shown. It is clear that no right of access to pre-commencement material arises at common law.[346] Secondly, if the holder of the information – the doctor – considers that disclosure of information would result in serious physical or mental harm to the patient, access can be denied. Thirdly, patients need not be told when information is being withheld. Although the 1990 Act is a move in the direction of enabling individuals to enjoy a degree of control over personal medical information and should ensure higher standards of accuracy and objectivity on the part of doctors and other record holders, it remains the case that patients whose documents are held as computerised records enjoy greater legal protection.

In general, the anomalous situation whereby an individual has greater access to and control over his or her personal information held in computerised as opposed to manual files will change once the DPA 1998 is fully in force.[347]

The Data Protection Act 1998[348]

The DPA 1998 was passed in response to the European Data Protection Directive on the protection of individuals with regard to the processing of personal data and the free movement of such data.[349] The aim of the Directive is to ensure that the same level of data protection is established in all Member States in order to facilitate the transfer of personal data across national boundaries within the European Union. Once the DPA 1998 is fully in force in the UK,[350] it will create a far more comprehensive protection for personal information than has ever previously been available. The 1998 Act is based on the 1984 Act but it is far more extensive; in particular, unlike its predecessor, it covers both manual and computerised files. This follows from s 1(1), which defines data as information processed by equipment operating automatically or recorded with the intention that it should be processed by means of such equipment or recorded as part of a relevant filing system or which forms part of an accessible record. The most significant part of this definition refers to data recorded as part of 'a relevant filing system'. Such a system is defined in s 1(1) as any set of information relating to individuals that is structured by reference to individuals or by reference to criteria relating to individuals 'in such a way that specific information relating to individuals is readily accessible'. This

---

346 *Mid-Glamorgan Family Health Services and Another ex p Martin* (1993) *The Times*, 2 June.

347 See below, fn 350.

348 For a basic guide, see Carey, P, *The Data Protection Act 1998*, 1998; for discussion of the impact of the Act on the media see Tugendhat, M, 'The Data Protection Act 1998 and the Media' [2000] YBMCL 115; Rasiah and Newell, 'Data protection and press freedom' [1997–98] YBMEL 209.

349 Directive 95/46/EC of the European Parliament and of the Council of 24 October 1995 (1995) OJ L281/31, mainly Art 6.

350 Certain sections came into force on the date of the passing of the statute – 16 June 1998. Most of the provisions came into force in 1999. As indicated below, certain provisions came into force after the first transitional period, ending on 24 October 2001; further provisions will come into force after the end of the second transitional period, ending on 24 October 2007. Transitional provisions under Sched 14 provide for the transition from the regime of the 1984 Act to that of the 1998 Act while transitional relief from the full rigour of the new Act is provided in Sched 8. Schedule 16 will repeal the whole of the 1984 Act.

definition is clearly imprecise, but it seems that most, if not all, structured filing systems relating to paper-based materials containing personal information will be covered.

The following discussion is not intended as a comprehensive guide to the 1998 Act, something that would be out of place in a book of this nature. Instead, it will focus on certain specific privacy issues, and especially on their relationship with freedom of expression.

The Data Principles

The Data Principles, contained in Schedule 1 of the Act, form its central core. The rest of the Act elaborates on the system for ensuring that these principles are adhered to. The Principles set out a number of fundamental privacy rights which encapsulate the value of informational autonomy. They accept that personal information must be stored and used by others, but surround such use by safeguards intended to preserve informational autonomy so far as possible, consistent with such acceptance.

Data Principle 1 states that personal data must be processed fairly and shall only be processed if at least one of the conditions in Sched 2 is met. The conditions include the requirement that the data subject has given consent to the processing, or it is necessary for the administration of justice or for the exercise of statutory functions, of functions of a minister or government department or for the exercise of other functions of a public nature exercised in the public interest, or for the purposes of legitimate interests pursued by the controller or a third party, except where the processing is unwarranted by reason of prejudice to the legitimate rights or freedoms of the subject.

Especially intimate private information is classified as 'sensitive personal data'; this covers a person's sexual life, along with matters such as a person's religious and political opinions, and his or her physical and mental health (s 2). The processing of 'sensitive personal data' attracts a higher level of safeguards than normal data under Data Principle 1 (b) (Sched 1), as elucidated by Sched 3. Sensitive personal data must be processed fairly and must only be processed if at least one of the conditions in Sched 3 is met. The conditions include the requirement that the data subject has given her explicit consent to the processing, or the information has deliberately been made public by the subject, or it is necessary for medical purposes, or for the administration of justice, or for the exercise of statutory functions, of functions of a minister or government department, or for the purposes of legitimate interests pursued by certain non-profit-making bodies.

Data Principle 2 provides that the data may be obtained only for one or more specified purposes and shall not be processed in any manner incompatible with that purpose. Under Data Principles 4 and 5, data must be accurate and, where necessary, kept up to date; when it is kept for a specific purpose, it must not be kept for longer than is necessary for that purpose. Also, data must be processed in accordance with the rights of data subjects under Data Principle 6, and under Data Principle 7 it must be adequately protected; appropriate security measures must be taken.

A number of subject exemptions, however, allow certain activities to be exempted from a number of the new provisions. The Data Principles and most of the key provisions of the Act do not apply where the exemption is required for the purpose of safeguarding national security. Thus, the security and intelligence services will be exempt. Data related to the prevention and detection of crime are exempt from the first Data Principle and the subject access provisions in s 7. As indicated below, there is a special exemption for journalistic purposes; where the media exemption operates, the media will be exempt from a number of the provisions, including all the Data Principles, except the seventh.

Obligations of data controllers

Any person using a computerised system in order to store data relating to people is now designated the 'data controller' (s 1(1)), while the person who is the subject of the data remains the 'data subject'. However, the processing of personal data no longer requires the performance of operations by reference to a data subject (s 1(1)). Any data relating to a living person is still termed 'personal data'.[351] Personal data covers expressions of opinions about an individual, but now also covers indications of intentions in relation to that individual. This would include, for example, the intentions of a personnel manager regarding the promotion or demotion of an employee. Under s 17, the data controller must register with the Data Protection Registrar, now renamed the Data Protection Commissioner. The data controller must notify the holding of data to the Commissioner under s 17(1), who will then make an entry in the register maintained under s 19 unless, under s 17(3), processing is unlikely to prejudice the rights or freedoms of data subjects or unless, under s 23(1), the data controller has an approved in-house supervision scheme. However, the Act requires compliance with the Data Principles and therefore such compliance is not dependent on the registration of the data holder .

Section 7 provides that if the data controller is asked by the data subject in writing whether personal data is being processed by or on behalf of the data controller, that information must be given within 40 days. If such data is being processed, the data subject is entitled to a description of the data, of the purposes for which it is being processed and of the recipients to whom it may be disclosed. Also, the data subject is entitled to have the data communicated to her and any information available to the controller as to the source of the data, in a form which is capable of being understood. Under Sched 1, Part II in relation to the fourth principle it is provided that if the data is found to be inaccurate, the data subject can notify the controller of the fact, which should then be indicated in the data. If it is so indicated, the fourth principle is not contravened. If a court is satisfied on the application of a data subject that personal data of which the applicant is the subject is inaccurate the court under s 14 can make an order erasing, blocking, destroying or rectifying the data.

Under s 10, the data subject has a new right, enforceable by court order, to prevent the processing of data likely to cause substantial damage or distress, if that damage or distress is or would be unwarranted.

Enforcement

The enforcement mechanisms allow for the enforcement of privacy rights against a range of bodies including private ones, thus affording greater respect for Art 8 rights than is afforded under the HRA, since under it only public authorities are directly bound. The

---

351 The definition of personal data is found in s 1(1) of the Act.

Act creates a number of offences in relation to data processing and the Act's requirements. In particular, it is a criminal offence for an unregistered person or body to store personal data under s 21(1).

Under s 13, compensation can be awarded if damage has resulted from the contravention by a data controller of any of the requirements of the Act, including the requirement to rectify, destroy, block or erase inaccurate data. However, it is a defence for the controller to prove that he had taken such care as is reasonable in the circumstances to comply with the requirement.

The rights granted under the Act are largely enforceable by the Data Protection Commissioner. Importantly, the Commissioner has security of tenure, being dismissible only by the Crown following an address by both Houses of Parliament. Under s 47, a failure to comply with a ruling of the Commissioner is a criminal offence. But the Commissioner can only make such a ruling after serving an enforcement notice under s 40 and such a notice may only be served if one or more of the Data Principles has been breached. The enforcement mechanism under the 1998 Act is based on the serving of notices on data controllers. If a person thinks that data of which she is the subject is being processed in contravention of the Act she can apply to the Commissioner for an assessment as to whether this is the case (s 42). The Commissioner can serve an information notice under s 43 on a data controller requiring the controller to furnish information to her within certain time limits.

Where the Commissioner is satisfied that a controller is contravening the Act, she may ultimately force the controller to act by serving upon it an enforcement notice, which (under s 40(1)) requires the controller to take, within such time as may be specified in the notice, such steps as may be specified for complying with the requirements of the Act. The notice may either ask the controller to rectify, block, erase or destroy any inaccurate data or data containing an expression of opinion or take steps to check the accuracy of the data. If a controller fails to comply with an enforcement or information notice, it will commit a criminal offence.

Under s 48, an appeal lies from decisions of the Commissioner to the Tribunal which is made up of experienced lawyers and 'persons to represent the interests' of data subjects under (s 6(6)). This power of appeal is exercisable upon the broadest possible grounds. The Act provides that any person may appeal to the tribunal against an enforcement or information notice (s 48) either on the basis that the notice is not in accordance with the law, or that the Commissioner ought to have exercised her discretion (if any) differently' (s 49). The tribunal is also empowered to substitute such other notice as could have been served by the Commissioner. There is a further appeal from the tribunal to the High Court, but on a 'point of law' only (s 49(6)). In practice, this will probably be interpreted so as to allow review of the tribunal's decisions, not just for error of law, but also on the other accepted heads of judicial review.

Thus, the Commissioner's decisions can, in the final analysis, be enforced, just as can orders of the court. These powers are buttressed by powers of entry, search and seizure to gain evidence of a failure by the authority to carry out its obligations under the Act or of the commission of a criminal offence under the Act (detailed in Sched 9).

Impact on the media

The media will be regarded as data controllers under the DPA 1998 and this is a very significant matter, since personal information stored manually may now be covered. The Act, however, gives the media quite generous conditional exemptions from many of its provisions and protection from the possibility of interim injunctions to restrain publication. Where data is processed for the 'special purpose' of journalism[352] under s 32(1) and (2), the key protective provisions (including Data Principles 1 and 2 and s 10) do not apply at all if the processing is undertaken with a view to publication, the data controller reasonably believes that, having regard to the special importance of the public interest in freedom of expression, publication is in the public interest, and compliance with the protective principles is incompatible with journalistic activity.[353] In considering the belief of the data controller that publication is in the public interest, regard may be had under s 32(3) to his compliance with any relevant code of practice that has been designated by the Secretary of State for the purposes of the sub-section. Journalists are not exempt from Data Principle 7, which in essence requires that care must be taken of the personal data, but this provision alone does not provide a significant protection for privacy. Even if a journalist was found to have breached the Act due to a failure to take such care, no interim injunction could be granted – the most valuable remedy for the purpose of protecting privacy – under s 32.

Although the Act gives an individual the right to apply to the court for an order that a journalist, as a data controller, cease processing information about him which is causing or is likely to cause substantial, unwarranted distress (s 10), the mere claim that the processing is for the purposes of journalism with a view to publication stays the proceedings and the case is referred to the Data Commissioner for a determination on the point (s 32(4)). Thus, interim injunctions to prevent unfair processing by the press – a critical remedy in privacy cases – will not be available. Where the exemption applies, it may be said then that the DPA 1998 will probably have only a marginal impact on non-consensual media use of personal information.

The right under s 10 to demand that the data controller ceases processing and the right if they do not to seek a remedy in court is unlikely, in any event, to bite against the media since the data subject must first notify the data controller to require that she cease processing, and the controller has 21 days to reply stating the action she intends to take. In the case of the media it seems probable that if publication of the personal data was intended, the media body in question would publish it, if possible, within the 21 day period.

However, these protections for the media do have limits. If data is being processed for the special purposes without a view to publication – which could be the case if it has already been published – the exemption does not apply. Equally, it does not apply to unpublished personal information if no reasonable belief could be demonstrated that publication of the information would be in the public interest. Clearly, there would also be cases where it was uncertain whether that belief could be demonstrated. Thus, journalists would be subject to the requirements of the Act in certain circumstances. A key

---

352 Section 3.
353 For further discussion, see Carey, *op cit*, fn 348, pp 196–98.

question in relation to the First Data Protection Principle is, as indicated above, that of consent, since data cannot be processed unless one of the conditions in Sched 2, in relation to personal data, or Sched 3, in relation to sensitive personal data, is met. The obvious condition which would apply in relation to journalism would be that consent had been obtained, since in most circumstances it is unlikely that one of the other conditions could be met. Schedule 3 refers to explicit consent. Thus, in relation to non-sensitive personal data, implied consent is sufficient. In relation to sensitive data, it is sufficient if the information has deliberately been made public by the subject. The Act does not explain what is meant by consent.

It could be claimed – as it has been successfully both under the UK doctrine of confidence and under the American private facts tort – that the plaintiff has sought publicity in the past and therefore in some way has consented, or should be deemed to have consented, to a current publication of data to which he or she now objects.[354] English judges in breach of confidence cases have in the past shown some receptivity to this claim, although there has often been a tendency to conflate it with the different claim that the plaintiff's private life has *per se* lost its quality of confidentiality. For example, in *Woodward v Hutchins*,[355] the Court of Appeal denied the plaintiffs (pop singers) an injunction against a former employee in respect of a series of newspaper articles giving detailed accounts of the singers' private lives. Bridge LJ reasoned that: 'those who seek and welcome publicity of every kind bearing upon their private lives so long as it shows them in a favourable light are in no position to complain of an invasion of their privacy by publicity which shows them in an unfavourable light'.[356] A similar approach was taken in *Lennon v News Group Newspapers*[357] in which one party to a marriage was denied relief in respect of personal information concerning the relationship on the grounds that both had sought publicity about it on previous occasions. In a similar vein, Elwood argues in the American context that celebrities[358] may be seen to have waived their right to privacy so that a defence of implied consent may be used against any privacy actions they may bring.

However, in relation to specific disclosures of personal data, it would often be absurd for a newspaper to claim that the data subject would have given actual consent if asked. This might equally be said of the argument that a celebrity had deliberately revealed sensitive personal data, relating, say, to his sexuality and that therefore numerous details regarding his sexual partners or practices can now be published. This is particularly obvious where the information has been obtained surreptitiously, as is often the case. It

---

354 Reported remarks of Lord Wakeham, Chair of the Press Complaints Commission, to the effect that the former Princess of Wales had made herself 'fair game' for public analysis of her private life by discussing it herself on television, exemplify this attitude (*The Times*, 2 May 1996). A similar argument was also put forward in *Mills v News Group Newspapers* [2001] EMLR 41, 4 June, High Court No HC 0102236, WL 720322 by the *Sun*.

355 [1977] WLR 760.

356 *Ibid*, p 765. The decision is not clearly reasoned; Lord Denning also found (p 763): 'There is no doubt whatever that this pop group sought publicity ... [relating to] their private lives also.' But this finding may also have been directed towards the idea that, having sought publicity themselves, they had effectively placed their private lives in the public domain; the decision also seems to have motivated by the idea that it was in the public interest to correct the false favourable impression that early publicity had given (*ibid*, p 764).

357 [1978] FSR 573.

358 'Outing, privacy and the First Amendment' [1992] Yale LJ 747.

may be noted that this principle is encapsulated in the BSC Privacy Code which provides that 'even when personal matters become the proper subject of enquiry people in the public eye 'do not forfeit their right to privacy' (para 17). Moreover the claim that prior, voluntary revelations constitute some kind of generalised, all-purpose consent to future invasions of privacy is simply implausible: no-one can realistically suppose that when a certain celebrity gives, for example, an interview to a newspaper about particular problems in a past or current marriage, she thereby gives *carte blanche* to the media to publish any information relating to her personal life which they can obtain in future. Thus, as the quotation from *Woodward*[359] indicates, the consent terminology can be in reality merely a cloak for a purely normative argument: since in the past the plaintiff has sought publicity for personal information, she should not be allowed to complain about this publication.

This argument, although superficially more attractive, is also difficult to justify: it is wholly incompatible with the core privacy value – the individual's right to control over the release of personal information. All of us exercise this right to selective disclosure in our social lives. For example, a friend who is shown a highly personal letter on one occasion, does not assume that he has thereby acquired the right to read, un-invited, all other such letters. But when such selectivity is exercised in the context of disclosures to the media, it is unjustifiably viewed in an entirely different light. In contrast, if selectivity in disclosure had resulted in a public deception on a matter of importance, there would be a genuine public interest in correcting it by revealing the truth. However, while the presence of such an interest is an essential pre-condition for the exemption of journalists from the Data Principles, there is nothing in the Act to suggest that it could be a determining factor in finding that consent could be viewed as impliedly given, in an instance in which a journalist was not exempt.

The better approach, it is suggested, to the question of consent in such cases therefore would be simply to inquire whether the plaintiff has in fact robbed the information disclosed of its private quality through prior, voluntary publicity about matters of a similar kind.[360] It will be important to apply this test with some discernment.[361] The US courts have not always done so, on occasions drawing no distinction between voluntary and involuntary attainment of notoriety[362] or finding that once someone has achieved notoriety in one area, whole other areas of their lives are opened up to close scrutiny as a result.[363] As Wacks has remarked: 'It is in principle unacceptable that merely because an individual seeks favourable publicity ... his entire private life might be laid bare with

---

359 *The Times*, 2 May 1996.

360 This point leaves aside the quite separate issue as to whether the publication should be allowed on expression grounds, for which see discussion below.

361 Prosser suggests at least that consent is only impliedly given 'if the plaintiff has industriously sought publicity of the same kind' (*op cit*, fn 182, pp 420–21).

362 Thus in *Metter v Los Angeles Examiner* (1939) 35 Cal App 2d 304, a person committed suicide by jumping from a high building and the court found that the victim had made herself a public figure 'for a brief period' through her own actions. However, the same result – denial of any right to privacy – was reached in *Kelly v Post Publishing Co* (1951) 327 Mass 275, where there was no element of voluntariness at all, the victim having died in a car accident.

363 See, eg, the decision in *Ann-Margaret v High Society Magazine Inc* (1980) 498 F Supp 401 in which a well known actress was denied relief in respect of the publication of a nude photograph of her.

impunity'.[364] The notion of 'consent', then, should be used only where there is an arguable claim of actual consent to the publication in question, express in respect of sensitive personal data[365] or implied in respect of personal data.[366] An acceptance that implied consent could be given is clearly necessary since, in relation to personal data, it appears clear that implied consent is sufficient.

It is concluded, therefore, that the 1998 Act may have an impact on the media[367] since, except in a narrow range of instances, they are not exempt from the requirement to obtain consent where one or more of the conditions set out in s 32 do not apply. Although, from the point of view of protecting privacy, it may be argued that this is a welcome development, it may be suggested that the Act does not properly hold the balance between Arts 10 and 8. If so, since s 3 of the HRA applies, the courts will have to consider the scope within the Act for creating a fairer balance in accordance with the demands of both those articles. For example, s 10 speaks of unwarranted disclosures, a terminology which would appear to create leeway for arguments based on Art 10. Although publication or processing in the public interest is not a general defence under the Act there is, as indicated, scope for interpreting what is meant by the public interest in s 32 in order to create such a balance, a matter that is considered further below.[368]

Impact of the HRA

The DPA 1998 is precisely aimed, *inter alia*, at the preservation of informational autonomy in a very broad sense, going far beyond the obligations created by the HRA, under Art 8, which is directly applicable only to public authorities. The provisions of the 1998 Act will of course have to be interpreted compatibly with the Convention rights, including those under Arts 8 and 10, under s 3 of the HRA. But as Chapter 4 explained, s 3 is only an interpretative obligation, not a means of binding persons to abide by the rights. Thus, the 1998 Act is of immense significance as a privacy measure which reaches fully into the private sphere. In so far as they are reflected in the 1998 Act, the rights under Art 8 will bind private bodies.

If remedies are granted that might affect freedom of expression, s 12 of the HRA will also be relevant, whether the body against which relief is sought is a private body or a public authority under the HRA.[369] The 1998 Act has very significant implications for the media[370] and, in certain respects, it is suggested that, it has – in effect – favoured the

---

364 Wacks, *op cit*, fn 190, p 24.

365 Under the US tort, the test for actual consent is whether the complained of publicity differed 'materially ... in kind or extent' from the informational material in relation to which consent was actually given (Prosser, *op cit*, fn 182, p 420).

366 A realistic doctrine of implied consent is clearly necessary, so that, eg, there would be no question of photographs of the Queen appearing on the balcony of Buckingham Palace engaging liability since consent, although unspoken, would clearly be present. See the comments of the Major Government in *Privacy and Media Intrusion: The Government's Response*, Cm 2918, para 3.14 and the rejoinder by Bingham LJ (writing extra-judicially), (1996) 5 EHRLR 450.

367 See, for further discussion of the impact of the Act on the media, Tugendhat, 'The Data Protection Act 1998 and the media' [2000] YBMCL 115.

368 See pp 618 *et seq*.

369 Since, as pointed out above, s 12 is not limited in its application to public authorities; see p 583.

370 See further Tugendhat, *op cit*, fn 348; Rasiah and Newell, *op cit*, fn 348.

protection of Art 8 over Art 10 rights. Therefore, some tension between the DPA 1998 and the HRA may arise.

A number of the bodies processing data are public authorities and therefore will be bound to observe the Convention rights in relation to such processing, under s 6 of the HRA. The bodies charged with the enforcement of the 1998 Act are also public authorities, and therefore must abide by the Convention rights in relation to any adjudications. Since the 1998 Act implements an EU Directive, the obligation to take the Convention into account in relation to processing of data, and adjudications relating to such processing, stems not only from s 3 but from the reliance on the Convention as a source of principles informing EU legislation.[371] This could be a matter of significance, since articles of the Convention, in particular Art 13, that have not been received into domestic law under the HRA Sched 1, should be considered. Further, EU law can override domestic law and it has a greater impact than the HRA due to the possibility of bringing a *Francovich* action.[372] The Directive could override incompatible primary legislation; if it has been inadequately implemented, an action could be brought directly against the State, thereby extending the impact of the privacy rights it encompasses, which should reflect Art 8 principles. The 1998 Act therefore reflects an acceptance of the value and significance of privacy interests which was not previously present in domestic law. It also arguably affords those interests priority – in certain respects – over free expression interests – a priority which is further reinforced by the complex relationship between the HRA and other domestic provisions and between the HRA and EU law.

The Data Protection Commissioner and Tribunal operating under s 6 of the DPA 1998 are public authorities and therefore they are directly bound, under s 6 of the HRA, by the Convention rights. Both bodies would therefore be subject to judicial review for violation of the Convention in their rulings. Since under s 47 a failure to comply with a ruling of the Commissioner is a criminal offence, a significant possibility of enforcing Art 8 rights might appear to arise.

The exemptions under the Act are broad; where they apply to bodies that are public authorities under s 6 of the HRA, Art 8 could be relied upon to seek to prevent the unfair processing of data where an infringement of its guarantee had occurred or appeared likely to occur. This is a matter that is considered further in Chapter 11, but it may be noted here that Art 8 clearly views the processing of personal data as *prima facie* falling within para 1.[373]

---

371 See Chapter 3, pp 115–17.

372 *Francovich v Italy* [1993] 2 CMLR 66 (circumstances in which national governments have a duty to compensate individuals for loss caused by failure to implement Directives and for other breaches of EC law). See also Chapter 3, pp 115–16.

373 In *MS v Sweden* (1997) 3 BHRC 348, the applicant complained that disclosure of her medical records in respect of a compensation claim infringed Art 8. The Court found that disclosure was an interference with private life but justified – economic well being of State information relating to an individual's sexual life may merit protection, a decision clearly in harmony with the approach of Strasbourg.

6 ISSUES ARISING FROM THE IMPACT OF THE HRA

Introduction

Almost all the measures discussed above allow for a balancing of expression and privacy rights by means of some form of public interest or 'reasonableness' test. This is true, albeit to quite a limited extent, of the DPA 1998; it is true of the common law doctrine of confidence and of the Privacy Codes affecting broadcasting and the press, and it may be noted that the PCC code in particular has now been given added status since it (and the two broadcasting codes discussed above) are recognised in s 12(4)(b) of the HRA and in s 32(3)of the DPA.[374] Thus, the methods of resolving the conflict, relying on the Convention jurisprudence and, if necessary, jurisprudence from other jurisdictions, is crucial. Such methods are considered below.

In determining whether information is to count as private, Art 8 must now be viewed as a source of interpretation under s 3 of the HRA. This is made explicit in the PCC Code, cl 3, and is clearly the case in respect of all statutory provisions which mention personal information, including the DPA 1998. By virtue of ss 2 and 6 of the HRA, it is also the case in relation to the common law. But, in order to engage Art 8 at all, information must be viewed as private and either must not be fully or at all in the public domain, or must be capable of causing further harm by being re-publicised.[375] The balancing exercise between Arts 10 and 8 cannot occur until these matters are resolved and s 12(4)(a)(i) of the HRA makes it clear that the public domain issue is relevant in undertaking it. Therefore, the discussion below will begin by considering what constitutes personal information, and when it can be said to be in the public domain, two separate but linked issues.

Personal information

It is suggested that to introduce an element of objectivity into the test for personal information, the present requirement that the information should not be trivial could be developed into a requirement of reasonable foreseeability that publication of truthful matter relating to her private rather than public life would cause substantial distress to the individual concerned. This test would draw on WA Parent's proposed definition: '[personal] information about a person which most individuals in a given time do not want widely known' and 'facts which though not generally considered personal a particular person feels acutely sensitive about'. This test encapsulates the crucial distinction between breach of privacy and defamation, since the latter action is concerned with untruthful matter. The word 'private' is used in order to seek to make a distinction between information which a person wishes to keep secret because it is personal or intimate to her, and information (such as the fact that she had lied to Parliament) which raises no privacy issues, but which she wishes to conceal because it would hurt her reputation. Admittedly, there will be borderline cases in which it will not be possible to

---

374 If the Secretary of State designates the Code by order for the purposes of the sub-section, under s 32(3)(b).

375 See *Mills v News Group Newspapers* (2001) WL 720, p 322, above p 589 on this point.

determine whether information can be said to relate to a person's private or public life. In that case, the information could be viewed as private and the question of its public nature would be relevant in determining the public interest in disclosure – in other words, at the stage of balancing speech and privacy rights. This test would provide more satisfactory protection than is provided by the US private facts tort in covering those cases where the matter disclosed, although not ordinarily considered 'offensive', is of great import to the individual concerned. In the well known case of *Sidis v F-R Publishing Corporation*[376] the New York Times revealed the identify and history of a former mathematical genius, who had given up his research and retired into obscurity. The article had a devastating effect on Sidis, but despite the court's finding that the article was 'merciless in its dissection of intimate details of the subject's personal life',[377] his action for breach of privacy failed on the basis that nothing was revealed which would have been offensive to the reasonable man.

If this is accepted, problems may still arise relating to the requirement that a matter should be personal and that it should be sufficiently weighty to be regarded as information with which the law should be concerned. In respect of the first question, a particular problem arises where information, alleged to be personal, relates to a matter occurring within a public or semi-public environment and it is consequently argued that it cannot be seen as 'personal information'. Two basic approaches to this problem and other variants of it may be discerned concerning the borderline of the public/private divide.[378] The first is the straightforward approach adopted by the US courts, which hold, with apparent logic, that what takes place in 'public' cannot by definition be 'private'. As Prosser puts it: 'the decisions indicate that anything visible in a public place may be recorded and given circulation by means of a photograph [or] ... written description, since this amounts to no more than giving publicity to what is already public and what any one present would be free to see'.[379] The advantages of this approach in terms of legal certainty and predictability are apparent. However, it misses the point that privacy need not be an absolute state of affairs[380] to be valuable and that everyday lives are in fact a constant trade-off between human interaction and the formation of relationships on the one hand, and the maintenance of a reasonable degree – not an absolute state – of privacy on the other. The alternative approach is therefore more nuanced and recognises that a degree of privacy may be retained in a semi-public environment, such as a restaurant,[381] or gymnasium.[382]

English courts will find that Strasbourg jurisprudence provides little specific guidance on this particular matter, though it probably does not require the narrow approach

---

376 113 F 2d 806 (2d Cir 1940).

377 *Ibid*, p 807.

378 See below, p 615.

379 Prosser, *op cit*, fn 182, pp 394–95.

380 Gavison suggests that an individual 'enjoys perfect privacy when he is completely inaccessible to others' (*op cit*, fn 187, p 428) without suggesting that this is anything other than an unrealistic and undesirable scenario.

381 See the decision of the German Federal Court: BGH 19 December 1995 BGHZ 131, 322–46, discussed below.

382 The location where surreptitious photographs were taken of the former Princess of Wales in *HRH Princess of Wales*.

characterised by the US jurisprudence.[383] However, if judges are prepared to look further afield, they will find that a recent decision of the German Supreme Court[384] provides a useful contrast to the US approach. Princess Caroline of Monaco complained of photographs taken by the press of her having an intimate dinner with her boyfriend in a garden restaurant in France. The Supreme Court refused to follow the approach of the Appeal Court that privacy 'stopped at the doorstep': they found that the Princess had clearly 'retreated to a place of seclusion where [she wished] to be left alone' and that she was entitled to respect for that wish. The approach indicated was that one may still be entitled to respect for privacy in semi-public places, recognising, as the court put it, that people may 'transfer their private sphere of life to a place outside their home'. While the presumption will be that events taking place in such places do not attract privacy protection, this may be rebutted if, as the court put it, it is clear by reference to 'objective criteria' that one wishes to be 'left alone' so that one can, 'relying on the seclusion of the place, behave in a manner which [one] would not have done if ... in full view of the public'.[385] Thus, identifying such places of seclusion is not to be done simplistically by reference solely to locality,[386] an approach implicitly approved in a recent decision of the Canadian Supreme Court involving the publication, without consent, of a photograph of the plaintiff taken in public.[387]

This flexible attitude to privacy is indeed suggested by the Press Complaints Commission's Code of Practice drawn up by the press itself, to which, as noted above, the courts have to have regard under s 12(4) of the HRA. As indicated above, the Code defines 'private places [as] public or private property where there is a reasonable expectation of privacy'. The fact that an event takes place in a semi-public environment may, however, be a factor which can reasonably be used in assessing the 'weight' of the privacy claim, when and if it is placed in the balance against any public interest in disclosure, including the interest in media freedom, a matter discussed below. This flexible attitude to personal information is also reflected in the case law on the doctrine of confidence; as indicated above, the courts have been prepared to protect information already – in essence – in the public domain, such as the physical appearance of Princess Diana[388] or of Catherine Zeta-Jones.[389] In those instances, protection for the details of an individual's personal appearance on a specific occasion was available. It is also clear that the courts are prepared to view information already partly in the public domain as

---

383 The Commission found in *X v United Kingdom* ((1973) Appl 5877/72 16 YBCHE, p 328) that the actions of the police in taking and then filing photographs taken without consent of a woman arrested for taking part in a political demonstration disclosed no prima facie breach of Art 8, partly it seems because of what was described as the 'public and voluntary' nature of her activities (emphasis added). This decision has however, been described as 'an outdated aberration' in the case law of the Commission: Bygrave, 'Data protection pursuant to the right to privacy in human rights treaties' (1999) 6(3) IJLIT 247, 265; see also *Niemetz v Germany* (1992) 16 EHRR 97.

384 BGH 19 December 1995 BGHZ 131. See the discussion of this decision in Markesenis, B and Nolte, N, 'Some comparative reflections on the right of privacy of public figures in public places', in Birks, P (ed), *Privacy and Loyalty*, 1997, pp 118 *et seq*.

385 *Ibid*.

386 Feldman expresses strong support for this view: *op cit*, fn 23, pp 59–62.

387 *Les Editions Vice Versa Inc v Aubry* [1999] 5 BHRC 437 (appeal from decision of Quebec courts under the Charter of Rights and Freedoms which protects the right to privacy (s 5)). The photograph did not show the plaintiff engaged in any private act, or partially unclothed, but it was held that the right to privacy included the right to control over one's image.

388 See p 568.

389 See pp 581–82.

worthy of protection on the grounds that it can still be viewed as private.[390] In so doing it is arguable that they have shown some recognition for the underlying values of dignity and autonomy at stake.

It should be pointed out that the question whether information is personal can either pre-date the 'public domain' inquiry, considered below, or can be indistinguishable from it. Thus, one might have to consider whether information could be viewed as personal at all where it relates to an event occurring in a semi-public environment. If it is determined that it can be viewed as personal, a court would go on to consider whether nevertheless it had been disseminated to such an extent that it had lost the personal quality that it otherwise would have had. A different situation would arise where information clearly has a personal quality, such as information relating to a person's sexual life, but it has received such wide publicity that it has arguably lost that quality. This is a difficult issue since, depending on the circumstances, it is a point at which the difference between confidence and privacy emerges. Bearing in mind that confidence is a now a key mechanism to be used to prevent non-consensual disclosures of personal information, a tension between privacy values and confidence ones is likely to become apparent, suggesting that Sedley LJ's approach in *Douglas*[391] may be more satisfactory than that of Dame Butler-Sloss in *Venables*.[392] Where the claimant has deliberately placed her sexual life in the public domain and has profited from it (for, example, where it is part of a certain image that she wishes to project) it is suggested that in terms of privacy it has lost its personal quality and in terms of confidence it is no longer secret. This approach is, as noted above, consonant with that under the DPA since it is one of the conditions for processing sensitive personal data. But where others have placed her sexual life in the public domain it is suggested that in terms of privacy the information retains its personal quality in the sense that each re-revelation causes her distress, whereas in terms of confidence it is no longer secret despite her lack of acquiescence in the disclosures.[393]

Public domain issues

Under the law of confidence and under the American private facts tort, once it can be determined that information is in the public domain, through, for example, previous media attention or other participation in a public process, such as a trial, an individual is no longer able to protect it through legal action. This is confirmed by s 12(4)(a)(i) of the HRA under which courts must have regard to the extent to which the material has, or is about to, become available to the public. The BSC Privacy Code also impliedly adopts a nuanced approach, speaking of determining whether when filming events in public places it is clear that information is sufficiently in the public domain to make it justifiable to broadcast it without consent (para 16). The public domain issue is addressed only in a very limited fashion by the DPA, in Sched 3, para 5, which provides that one of the conditions for the processing of sensitive personal data is that the data subject has deliberately placed the information in the public domain.

---

390 See *Mills v News Group Newspapers* (2001) WL 720322, above p 589 on this point.
391 [2001] 2 WLR 992.
392 [2001] 1 All ER 908, Fam Div (High Court of Justice, Queen's Bench Division).
393 The difference between the two was encapsulated in *Broadcasting Complaints Commission ex p Granada Television* [1995] EMLR 163.

The public domain issue is especially problematic where the information now disclosed had previously been recorded in a public record or given some earlier publicity. Once again, the US courts have opted for an absolutist stance in such situations: the Second Restatement of Torts states: 'there can be no [privacy] liability for giving publicity to facts about the plaintiff's life which are matters of public record.'[394] Prior publicity also generally negatives liability.[395] In contrast, the English doctrine of confidence and s 12(4)(a)(i) of the HRA have adopted a more nuanced approach, whereby the existence of prior publicity is a relevant but not conclusive factor. Thus, in the leading decision, *AG v Guardian Newspapers Limited (No 2)*,[396] Lord Keith argued that whether information is in the public domain will often be a matter of degree and therefore prior disclosure to a limited group of people might not rob the information of its confidentiality, an approach which received general support in the case.[397] The Law Commission, in its final report on the doctrine of confidence,[398] decided not to follow its own earlier suggestion[399] that information should automatically be classified as in the public domain if it is on a register or other record required by law to be open to the public. This, it is suggested, reflects a realistic recognition of the fact that there is a world of difference between, as Ingber puts it, 'the disclosure of a personal fact in a dusty public record hidden somewhere in the bowels of a county courthouse and a similar disclosure disseminated through the mass technology of the modern press'.[400] This approach has been followed in recent cases involving disclosure of past criminal convictions, despite the fact that such convictions are arrived at and announced in open court.[401] While such approaches have been attacked,[402] it is notable that under the DPA 1998, information relating to a person's criminal record forms one of the seven categories of 'sensitive personal data',[403] the processing of which attracts a higher level of safeguards than normal data.[404] It should also be borne in mind that the public interest would often require disclosure in such cases, as it did in the two cases just cited.

---

394 Restatement, 625D.

395 See, eg, *Sidis* 113 F 2d 806 (2d Cir 1940) and *Forsher v Bugliosi* 26 Cal 3d 792, 608 P 2d 716, 163 Cal Rptr 628 (1980); cf the earlier decision in *Melvin v Reid* 112 Cal App 283 (1931).

396 [1990] 1 AC 109; [1990] 3 WLR 776; [1988] 3 All ER 545, HL.

397 *Ibid*, p 260. His Lordship was referring specifically to the possibility of publication abroad – *Spycatcher* had been published in the United States – but the principle is of general application. Sir John Donaldson in the Court of Appeal took the same approach, remarking that 'it is a matter of degree' (*ibid*, p 177), as did Scott J (*ibid*, p 149). See also *AG v Guardian Newspapers* [1987] 1 WLR 1248 (the first *Spycatcher* case).

398 *Op cit*, fn 2, para 6.74; see also para 6.68.

399 Set out in their Working Paper No 58, para 103.

400 Ingber, S, 'Rethinking intangible injuries: a focus on remedy' (1985) Cal L Rev 772, pp 848–49, cited in Paton-Simpson, E, 'Private circles and public squares: invasion of privacy by the publication of "private facts"' (1998) 61 MLR 318 p 327; see also pp 326–29.

401 *R v Chief Constable of North Wales Police ex p AB* [1997] 3 WLR 724, CA; in *Hellewell*, the applicant complained that his 'mug shot', lawfully taken by the police, had been passed on to local retailers as part of their own anti-crime efforts, thus revealing the fact of his arrest. Laws J treated the fact that the complainant had been involved with the police as 'not ... a public fact' but '*prima facie* at least ... a piece of confidential information' ([1995] 1 WLR 804, p 810).

402 See Thompson [1995] Conv 404, pp 406–07.

403 Along with matters such as a person's sexual life, religious and political opinions, and his physical and mental health (s 2).

404 Markesenis points out that the German courts have also afforded privacy protection to ex-criminals whose records are revealed, hampering their rehabilitation (*op cit*, fn 1, p 123).

Similarly, the Law Commission has found that prior publicity some time ago in local newspapers should not preclude later legal protection for such information. Instead, their recommendation was simply that information could be said to be in the public domain only if 'having regard to its nature and the circumstances of its disclosure, it is generally available to the public'.[405] They considered that information was not in the public domain if 'it is only accessible to the public after a significant contribution of labour, skill or money'.[406] Such a flexible definition would allow courts to draw distinctions both between readily accessible public records and those buried in obscurity,[407] and between matters reported some years previously in a local newspaper and the contemporary mass reporting of the same matter.[408]

It is suggested that such approaches are to be preferred to the more absolutist stance. While the latter has the advantage of making it relatively easy to predict in advance what can be disclosed with impunity, it relies, as Paton-Simpson has persuasively argued, on a simplistic and misleading attitude whereby privacy is treated as an all or nothing concept, rather than as a matter of degree.[409] Nevertheless, in rejecting this approach, it is stressed that s 12 of the HRA and Art 10 of the Convention require the judiciary to have regard to the possible impact on press freedom in developing remedies against privacy: this must be considered in terms of the certainty or otherwise of definitions of private facts, as well as the substance of those definitions. The courts must therefore seek to strike a balance between a definition which is sufficiently sophisticated not to do manifest injustice to the underlying values they are seeking to protect, but which yet allows editors and journalists to foresee to a reasonable extent whether given actions will result in liability. As Zimmerman notes, 'The [US Supreme] Court has stated repeatedly that vague proscriptions against speech may chill the willingness of individuals and the media to take part in those communicative activities that are clearly protected by the First Amendment'.[410]

Balancing privacy and speech rights

Introduction

As indicated throughout this chapter, the notion of the public interest has been the key domestic mechanism allowing for the balancing of speech and privacy rights. Under the

---

405 *Op cit*, fn 2, para 6.74(i).
406 *Ibid*, para 6.74(ii). They gave the example of a reporter who combs through the back copies of a local newspaper in order to find out information about a now famous person; she would be gathering information not in the public domain, as she is expending considerable labour in the task (para 6.67).
407 It is clear that if the controller of the record is under a statutory duty not to disclose it to others, for example under the Rehabilitation of Offenders Act 1974 or the Data Protection Act 1998, then the information should be regarded as prima facie confidential at common law also.
408 A similar approach was followed in the New Zealand case, *TW3 Network Services Ltd v Broadcasting Standards Authority* [1995] 2 NZLR (HC) 720, p 731: 'Although information has been made known to others, a degree of privacy, entitled to protection, may remain. In determining whether information has lost its private character it would be appropriate to look realistically at the nature, scale and timing of previous publications.'
409 See Paton-Simpson, *op cit*, fn 400.
410 Zimmerman, *op cit*, fn 195.

HRA, as *Venables*[411] and *Mills*[412] indicated, such balancing will occur in confidence actions under s 12 of the HRA which draws in Art 10 and therefore Art 8, and takes account of any relevant privacy codes. Common law speech jurisprudence is also taken into account. Where an action for breach of Art 8 is brought directly against a media body which is a public authority, the same mechanisms apply, albeit by a slightly different route. The public authority will be bound by Arts 8 and 10 under s 6 of the HRA. Therefore, Art 8 need not be drawn in via s 12 and Art 10(2). This may be of some significance in terms of the structure of the argument seeking to create the speech–privacy balance, which is considered below. In this instance, Arts 10 and 8 on the face of it compete more clearly on equal terms. Section 12 will be relevant as a means of creating a balance between the two rights, again taking into account any privacy code. Where a statute is in question, particularly the DPA 1998, ss 3 and 12 will be the significant provisions, unless the data controller is a public authority, in which case it will be directly bound by the Convention rights under s 6. Under s 3, leeway in the DPA can be explored, allowing consideration to be paid to Art 10, in particular the question of the public interest in s 32 and the notion of an 'unwarranted' invasion of privacy in s 10. If, having considered the application of the DPA, it seems that freedom of expression might be affected, s 12 will become the main balancing mechanism allowing for the resolution of conflict between Arts 10 and 8. The obligation to consider the privacy code will flow from both the DPA and the HRA. But s 12(3) will not be applicable since, as indicated above, the DPA does not appear in most circumstances to allow for the use of injunctions against the media.

In all those instances, then, the statutory scheme of the HRA, the Convention rights and the relevant privacy codes provide the ground rules for determining when material should be published despite the invasion of privacy which will occur. This scheme is affected by the importation of the Strasbourg concepts of necessity and proportionality as applied under the HRA, Arts 10 and 8. In making determinations as to the application of those concepts in a particular instance, a form of public interest test is drawn into the equation under s 12(4)(b) since the relevant privacy codes, in particular that of the PCC, are heavily influenced by the test. Therefore, when persons seek to protect privacy interests, this scheme provides the principal mechanism which seeks to create a balanced resolution of the two rights of privacy and speech.

If such a defence is to produce consistent, principled and reasonably foreseeable resolutions of the conflicting interests at stake, rather than amounting merely to an *ad hoc* exercise of judicial 'common sense', it is, it is suggested, essential that it be approached with an awareness of the values underlying both freedom of the press and privacy itself. In this section, therefore, principles are discussed which may be derived from an examination of the main free speech theories in the context of possible conflicts with privacy rights.

---

411 [2001] 1 All ER 908, Fam Div (High Court of Justice, Queen's Bench Division).
412 (2001) WL 720322.

Free speech theories and privacy

The theory that freedom of speech is necessary for the discovery of truth, discussed in the Introduction to Part II,[413] has been a strong influence in US jurisprudence[414] but not historically at Strasbourg[415] or in the UK courts.[416] It has been persuasively argued that this rationale has little application to the paradigm privacy case, in which intimate facts about an individual are revealed. Barendt has contended that 'Mill's argument ... applies more strongly to assertions of opinion ... than to ... propositions of fact'.[417] The argument is that since privacy actions attempt to prevent the publication of private facts only, and not general expressions of opinion, they will pose little threat to that free and unhindered public debate about matters of importance which Mill's argument seeks to protect. Moreover, as Schauer has argued,[418] on finding out a new fact, it may not replace a previously false belief, but merely add to what was previously 'epistemologically empty space'. Much intrusive journalism merely communicates a set of probably trivial facts about a given figure and it is very hard to maintain plausibly that the simple acquisition of such factual information has any inherent truth value. However, this is not the case in relation to some investigative journalism. For example, the revelation of the paedophile tendencies of a right wing evangelist leading a campaign against homosexual rights would contribute to various strands of public debate. Anonymity orders covering relatives of children involved in criminal proceedings may also indirectly stifle debate.

Similarly, the justification for speech which may be referred to as the argument from autonomy[419] arguably has minimal application in this area, and indeed the values it espouses actually point to a reasonable degree of privacy protection. The basic thesis is that matters of substantive moral choice must be left to the individual as an autonomous, rational agent (subject, of course, to his duty to respect the basic rights of others); therefore, the State offends against human dignity, or treats certain citizens with contempt, if the coercive powers of the law are used to enforce the moral convictions of some upon others by, say, banning certain kinds of pornography or extreme political discourse.[420] It is immediately apparent that much privacy-invading speech, by both directly assaulting informational autonomy and indirectly threatening the individual's freedom of choice over substantive issues,[421] far from being bolstered by the autonomy

---

413 See pp 202–03. The most famous exposition of the 'truth' argument is to be found in Mill's *On Liberty*, in Cowling (ed), *Selected Writings of John Stuart Mill*, 1968, p 121.

414 See the famous *dicta* of Judge Learned Hand in *United States v Associated Press* (1943) 52 F Supp 362, p 372; and of Holmes J, dissenting but with the concurrence of Brandeis J, in *Abrams v United States* (1919) 250 US 616, p 630.

415 The repeated reference by the ECtHR to freedom of expression being one of the 'basic conditions for [society's] progress' (see, eg, *Otto-Preminger Institut v Austria* (1994) 19 EHRR 34, para 49) could be seen as a reference to the justification.

416 But see, recently, *R v Secretary of State for the Home Department ex p Simms* [1999] 3 All ER 400, p 408, *per* Lord Steyn.

417 *Freedom of Speech*, 1985, p 191.

418 Schauer, F, 'Reflections on the value of truth' (1991) 41 Case Western Reserve L Rev 699, p 708. His other categories are: 'one's belief may be unjustified [though possibly true]; [and] one's belief can be false.'

419 The argument has been most recently and influentially put by writers in the revived tradition of deontological liberalism. See Chapter 1, p 6.

420 The particular concern of Thomas Scanlon's influential approach set out in 'A theory of freedom of expression' (1972) 1 Phil & Pub Aff 216.

421 See pp 530–33, above.

rationale, is in direct conflict with it. The State, in restricting what one citizen may be told about the private life of another, is not acting out of a paternalistic desire to impose a set of moral values thereby, but rather to assure an equal freedom to all to live by their own values.

The argument from self development – that the freedom to engage in the free expression and reception of ideas and opinions in various media is essential to human development[422] – has received some recognition at Strasbourg[423] and recently in the House of Lords.[424] As with the argument from autonomy, it is immediately apparent that this justification, since it seeks to facilitate human flourishing, far from inevitably opposing the right to privacy, must support it to some extent since, as argued above,[425] a reasonable degree of privacy is a requirement, not a threat to individual self-development, particularly the human capacity to form intimate relationships, without which the capacity for individual growth would be severely curtailed.

Moreover, as Barendt has argued,[426] it is implausible to view most newspaper reporters as freely serving their own human need for self-development. The focus must therefore be on the readers of such material. Joseph Raz has proposed a theory of freedom of expression which he argues provides a reader-based justification for expression and is concerned not with 'serious' public debate, but with the type of speech which is 'often overlooked' or seen as 'trivial'.[427] He points out that much public expression in the media portrays and expresses aspects of forms of different lifestyles[428] which, he argues, 'validate the styles of life portrayed'. Conversely, censorship is not only an 'insult' to the persons leading the lifestyle censored – a point which sounds very like Dworkin's argument for freedom of expression based on equal respect for citizens[429] – but it also, in a more instrumental vein, denies those living the lifestyle the opportunity for reassurance, the sense that they are not alone in their lifestyles and its problems, and also the chance for the public to learn about the widest possible range of lifestyles, thus maximising their freedom of choice.[430]

Raz considers that his argument does not in general justify revelations about particular individuals, but may do so in relation to 'individuals who have become symbols of certain cultures, or ideologies, or ... styles of life'.[431] It is clear, however, that if

---

422 See the Introduction to Part II, pp 204–05. Emerson, C, for example, argues that the right to free expression is justified as the right of the individual to realise his character and potentialities through forming his own beliefs and opinions: 'Towards a general theory of the First Amendment' (1963) 72 Yale LJ 877, pp 879–80; see also Redish, M, *Freedom of Expression*, 1984, pp 20–30.

423 One of the stock phrases of the European Court of Human Rights in relation the value of freedom of expression asserts that it is one of the 'essential foundations for the development of everyone' (eg, *Otto-Preminger Institut v Austria* (1994) 19 EHRR 34, para 49).

424 *Per Lord Steyn in R v Secretary of State for the Home Department ex p Simms* [2000] 2 AC 115, p 498.

425 See pp 530–31.

426 Barendt and Hitchens, *op cit*, fn 417, p 68; he concedes that such arguments may have some applicability to the writers of 'fringe or underground journals'.

427 Raz, J, 'Free expression and personal identification' (1991) 11(3) OJLS 303, p 310.

428 *Ibid*: 'Views and opinions, activities, emotions etc, expressed or portrayed are an aspect of a wider net of opinions, sensibilities, habits of action or dressing, attitudes etc which taken together form a distinctive style of form of life.'

429 Dworkin, *A Matter of Principle* 1985, esp pp 272–74.

430 Raz, *op cit*, fn 427, p 312.

431 *Ibid*, p 316.

speech which invades the privacy of such individuals is restricted, the 'message' sent by the State thereby, far from suggesting condemnation or contempt for the lifestyle revealed, in fact displays respect for the ability of the individual to decide for himself whether he wishes to share his life-decisions with the public at large. Moreover, the reassuring knowledge that control of such information rests with the individual will surely further the core aim of the self-fulfilment justification – the ability of persons to make free choices to experience and experiment with the widest possible range of lifestyles and activities. Conversely, the inability of the individual to exercise such control would, as argued above, amount to a significant 'chilling effect' upon the willingness of individuals to make controversial choices about their personal lives. On both deontological and consequentialist arguments, then, this justification tends to support a reasonable degree of protection for informational autonomy.

As the Introduction to Part II explained, the 'self-governance' or argument from democracy is viewed as 'the most influential theory in the development of 20th century free speech law',[432] an assertion supported by examination of the approach of UK and Strasbourg judges, discussed in the Introduction to Part II. Its basic thesis is that citizens cannot participate fully in a democracy unless they have a reasonable understanding of political issues; therefore, open debate on such matters is necessary to ensure the proper working of a democracy;[433] as Lord Steyn has put it, 'freedom of speech is the lifeblood of democracy'.[434] In so far as democracy rests upon ideas both of participation and accountability, the argument from democracy may be seen to encompass also the function which a free press performs in exposing abuses of power,[435] thereby allowing for their remedy and also providing a deterrent effect for those contemplating such wrong-doing.[436]

As has been indicated previously, it is a marked feature of the Strasbourg jurisprudence that clearly political speech receives a much more robust degree of protection than other types of expression.[437] Thus, the 'political' speech cases discussed in this book[438] all resulted in findings that Art 10 had been violated and all were marked by an intensive review of the restriction in question. In contrast, in cases involving artistic speech, supported by the values of autonomy and self-development rather than self-government, an exactly converse pattern emerges: applicants have tended to be unsuccessful and a deferential approach to the judgments of the national authorities as to

---

432 See pp 203–04.

433 See Meiklejohn, A, 'The First Amendment is an absolute' (1961) Sup Ct Rev 245 and *Political Freedom*, 1960, esp pp 115–24.

434 *R v Secretary of State for the Home Department ex p Simms* [2000] 2 AC 115, p 408.

435 See Blasi, V: 'The checking value in First Amendment theory' (1977) Am B Found Res J 521.

436 See Greenwalt, K, 'Free speech justifications' (1989) 89 Columb L Rev 119, p 143.

437 See Chapter 4, pp 209–10 above.

438 See, eg, *Jersild v Denmark* (1994) 19 EHRR 1; *Lingens v Austria* (1986) 8 EHRR 103, discussed above, p 209.

its obscene or blasphemous nature has been adopted.[439] As indicated in Part II a similar pattern may be discerned in the domestic jurisprudence: the most lofty rhetorical assertions of the importance of free speech and the strongest determination to protect it have been evident in cases where journalistic material raises political issues, broadly defined.[440] In such cases, the courts have either overtly adopted the Strasbourg principles described above[441] or have strongly emphasised the high status freedom of speech holds in the common law, as 'a constitutional right'.[442] Media freedom in relation to political expression has clearly been recognised as having a particularly high value in UK law and Convention jurisprudence. In contrast, when speech supported by the arguments from self-development or autonomy rather than self-government is in question, decisions have tended to be far more cautious.[443]

Two points emerge from this discussion. Where speech is supported mainly by arguments from autonomy, truth and self-development, there will in general be little or no justification at the level of principle for allowing it to override privacy; indeed, the discussion above reveals the truth of Emerson's remark that, far from being invariably in conflict, the twin rights to freedom of speech and to privacy 'are mutually supportive, in that both are vital features of the basic system of individual rights'.[444] In more practical terms, the type of speech which, as we have seen, receives the highest level of protection, namely political speech, is by its nature most unlikely to conflict with the right to privacy. In many cases it will not raise privacy issues, as where it consists of the discussion of political ideas, institutions, and policies. Where political speech does concern individuals, as where it reveals abuse of State power, the conflict is more likely to be with reputation than privacy.[445] Conversely, the paradigm cases of journalistic invasions of privacy which, by definition, involve the personal, not the public-political affairs of its subject, usually involve celebrities rather than public servants, and are driven by purely commercial considerations. Such publications simply do not engage core Art 10 values

---

439 See Chapter 6, pp 277–81, at which the following cases are discussed: *Müller v Switzerland* (1991) 13 EHRR 212; *Gibson v UK*, App No 17634 (declared inadmissible by Commission); *Handyside v UK*, A 24 (1976) (not a case involving artistic speech but where the issue was obscenity); *Otto-Preminger Institut v Austria* (1994) 19 EHRR 34; *Gay News v UK* (1982) 5 EHRR 123. In *Wingrove v UK* (1997) 24 EHRR 1, the Court remarked: 'Whereas there is little scope under Article 10(2) of the Convention for restrictions on political speech or on debate of questions of public ... a wider margin of appreciation is generally available to the Contracting States when regulating freedom of expression in relation to matters liable to offend intimate personal convictions within the sphere of morals or, especially, religion' (para 58). See Harris, O'Boyle and Warbrick, *op cit*, fn 27, pp 397 and 414.

440 *Reynolds v Times Newspapers; Derbyshire CC v Times Newspapers* [1993] AC 534; *R v Secretary of State for the Home Department ex p Simms* [2000] 2 AC 115. However, deference to widely drafted primary legislation (*Secretary of State for Home Affairs ex p Brind* [1991] 1 AC 696) or governmental arguments from national security (*AG v Guardian Newspapers* [1987] 1 WLR 1248) has resulted in the ready upholding of restrictions on directly political speech.

441 See the approach of the Court of Appeal in *Derbyshire (ibid)* and in *Ex p Leech* [1994] QB 198, of the House of Lords in *Reynolds*, pp 621–22, *per* Lord Nicholls, pp 628 and esp 635, *per* Lord Steyn, p 643, *per* Lord Cooke and *Ex p Simms*, p 407 *per* Lord Steyn and pp 419–20 *per* Lord Hobhouse.

442 *Reynolds v Times Newspapers*, pp 628–29 (Lord Steyn). In *Ex p Simms* (p 11), Lord Steyn described the right as 'fundamental', as did Lord Hoffman (*ibid*, p 412).

443 *Gibson* [1990] 2 QB 619; *Knuller v DPP* [1973] AC 435; *Lemon* [1979] AC 617.

444 Emerson, 'The right of privacy and the freedom of the press' (1979) 14(2) Harvard Civil Rights – Civil Liberties L Rev 329, p 331.

445 As in the recent case of *Reynolds v Times Newspapers* [1993] AC 534, in which the former Irish Taoiseach sued newspapers which published reports accusing him of lying to the Irish Dail; see also, eg, *Lingens* (1986) 8 EHRR 103 and *Thorgeirson* (1992) 14 EHRR 843.

such as the furtherance of a democratic society. Thus, it will only be in a fairly narrow category of cases that any real conflict will arise – those where the publication in question relates to the personal life of a particular figure,[446] but there is a serious argument that it serves a valuable purpose in revealing a matter relevant to that person's fitness for office, or in furthering public knowledge or debate about matters of serious public concern. The remainder of this section will consider approaches to the resolution of such hard cases.

Approaches to the speech-privacy balance: structure

It is apparent from Convention jurisprudence that, where two Convention rights come into conflict, some kind of balancing act between the two needs to be undertaken.[447] Although jurisprudence in this area is very limited, it appears that the margin of appreciation becomes particularly significant here, so that States have a fairly wide discretion in resolving the conflict.[448] Domestic courts therefore have an appreciable degree of latitude in determining where to strike the balance between the two interests. Section 12 of the HRA, which enjoins the court to have 'particular regard' to Art 10 when making any order which might infringe it, appears on its face to suggest a higher weighting for speech interests. Such imbalance is also *prima facie* suggested by the strength of the 'speech' jurisprudence at both the Strasbourg and domestic levels discussed above. In *Ex p Simms*,[449] Lord Steyn referred to free speech as 'the primary right ... in a democracy' and some commentators take the view that Art 10 attracts an especially high level of protection at Strasbourg.[450] The contrast with the meagre case law on privacy at the European level with its cautious approach to intervention between private individuals, and the historic failure of English judges to recognise such a right in the common law, might suggest that the twin rights to speech and privacy do not currently occupy an equal footing. It might therefore be feared – or hoped – that English law will come to replicate the position in the US where, as Wacks puts it, 'It is widely acknowledged that the ... "newsworthiness" defence has effectively demolished the private-facts tort'.[451]

Such fears would be, it is suggested, misplaced. Save for admitting the distinction between those rights stated in absolute terms, such as Arts 3, 4 and 7 and those subject to generalised exceptions (8–11), Strasbourg has never sought to establish a hierarchy of Convention rights. Rather, where rights collide, it has advocated a careful examination of the competing claims of each in the light of all the circumstances of the case.[452] There is

---

446 See the conclusions of the Calcutt Report on this point (*op cit*, fn 1, at paras 12.24–12.29).

447 *Otto-Preminger Institut v Austria* (1994) 19 EHRR 34, para 55. The two Convention rights in conflict there were free speech itself and – so the court found – the right to religious freedom, protected by Art 9.

448 *Ibid*. As Chapter 6 explained, the restriction on Art 10 entailed by the seizure of an allegedly blasphemous film was justified by reference to the Art 9 right to freedom of religious belief. The Court applied a wide margin of appreciation, and simply said that 'the content of the film cannot be viewed as incapable of grounding' the conclusion of the national authorities that seizure was justified (para 56). Thus the test applied was reminiscent of the narrow *Wednesbury* standard of unreasonableness.

449 [2000] 2 AC 115, p 407.

450 Leigh, I and Lustgarten, L, 'Making rights real: the courts, remedies, and the Human Rights Act' (1999) 58 CLJ 509, p 524 and note 79.

451 Wacks, *op cit*, fn 1, p 113.

452 See the views of Lord Steyn and Lord Cooke in *Reynolds* [1999] 4 All ER 609, pp 631 and 643.

no indication that Parliament, in passing the HRA, intended to alter this position and create a serious imbalance between the two rights;[453] rather, it is evident that the sponsors of the amendment which became s 12 saw it merely as a domestic reflection of the Strasbourg approach.[454] Moreover, the unbalanced American approach is out of line with other jurisdictions and flows from factors peculiar to that jurisdiction, namely the absolute nature of the First Amendment, and the fact that it is not balanced by any constitutional right to informational privacy.[455] Where privacy has such a status, as in Germany and Canada, courts have rejected any notion of establishing an *a priori* ranking of rights.[456]

The issue of balance arises in another, more subtle form: how should the courts structure the competing claims of speech and privacy? At present, speech considerations arise as a defence in common law and in statutory provisions protecting aspects of privacy – apart from the DPA, which contains no general defence, although the public interest is an important factor in the media exemption under s 32. In *Reynolds*, however, a libel case, where expression interests also function as a defence, the House of Lords took a different approach. 'The starting point,' Lord Steyn stated,[457] 'is now the right of freedom of expression, a right based on a constitutional or higher legal order foundation. Exceptions ... must be justified as being necessary in a democracy. In other words, freedom of expression is the rule, and regulation of speech is the exception requiring justification'.[458] These findings were echoed in the *Mills* case.[459] They are in line with the general Strasbourg approach which finds that in cases in which other interests potentially threaten free speech, the concern is not with 'a choice between two conflicting principles but with a principle of freedom of expression that is subject to a number of exceptions which must be narrowly interpreted'.[460] If this approach is applied in domestic privacy cases, as seems possible,[461] the result will be that privacy will lose its Convention status as a fully fledged right, becoming instead merely a narrowly interpreted exception to the right of freedom of expression.

This, however, would introduce a striking asymmetry: the protection of the right to privacy would have to be justified as necessary in a democratic society, while the claims of free speech would be simply assumed. This could not be right. While the European

---

453 An amendment providing that a court should 'normally' give precedence to Art 10 over Art 8 was rejected (HC Deb Vol 315 Cols 542–43, 2 July 1998).

454 See, eg, the speech of Jack Straw on new cl 12: HC Deb Vol 315 Cols 535–39, 2 July 1998.

455 The US Supreme Court has fashioned a constitutional right to what it has termed 'privacy', but by this it signifies choice over substantive matters, such as sexual activity and abortion: see, eg, *Griswold v Connecticut* (1965) 381 US 479 and *Roe v Wade* (1979) 410 US 113.

456 The German Supreme Court has remarked that the protection of personality [including privacy] and of free expression are both 'essential aspects of the liberal democratic order ... with the result that neither can claim precedence in principle over the other' (BVerfGE 35, 200) – we are indebted to Markesenis's translation (*op cit*, fn 1, p 123)). For an example of the Canadian approach, see *Hill v Church of Scientology* [1995] 2 SCR 1130, p 1179 and the recent decision in *Les Editions Vice Versa Inc v Aubry* [1999] 5 BHRC 437, which involved a careful balancing of the rights to privacy and speech.

457 An approach echoed by Lord Nicholls: 'My starting point is freedom of expression' (*Reynolds* [1999] 4 All ER 609, p 621).

458 *Ibid*, p 629.

459 See fn 289 above and associated text.

460 *Sunday Times v UK* A 30 (1979), para 65.

461 There were signs of this approach in *Mills v NGN* [2001] EMLR 41, 4 June, High Court No HC 0102236, WL 720322.

Court has not addressed the matter explicitly,[462] it must be the case that where a restriction on a Convention right is justified not as serving one of the societal interests the Convention enumerates,[463] such as economic well being or protection of morals, but as ensuring the protection of another Convention guarantee, a different approach must be followed. In cases where Convention rights have clashed, Strasbourg has still formally followed the standard approach, treating one right as primary, so that restrictions upon it by a competing right have to be justified as necessary in a democratic society. However, this is because when Strasbourg hears cases brought by individuals alleging a violation of a Convention right, other, competing rights, figure only as possible means of justification for the respondent State. By contrast, the position of a domestic court is fundamentally different: except in instances in which the media body is a public authority, both sides before it will be private bodies or individuals; both will claim that their rights are equally in issue. Even where a body, such as the BBC, is a public authority, it is suggested that, as argued above, it can exercise Convention rights.[464] It would therefore be quite perverse for such a domestic court, by a prior ordering, to assign one right (speech) a position as the primary norm, and the other (privacy) that of a mere exception to it.

The better approach, it is suggested, would be for the court to consider the issue from two perspectives. It might first be asked whether Art 10 was engaged, and, if so, s 12 of the HRA would apply. The standard Convention test would then be followed, asking whether the interference with the Art 10 guarantee proposed by the plaintiff would be necessary in a democratic society and proportionate to the legitimate aim of protecting private life. But since, under s 12, Art 10(2) is drawn into play, affording an equal status, according to the findings in *Douglas*[465] and *Mills*,[466] to Art 8 as one of the 'rights of others', the court should then consider the issue from the opposing perspective, with the rights reversed in position, so that the speech interest was treated as an exception to the primary right to respect for privacy under Art 8. The same inquiries as to necessity and proportionality could then be made from this opposing perspective. This is even more clearly the case where Art 8 must be considered due to the demands of ss 6 or 3 of the HRA. In this way, useful insights could be gleaned by asking, for example, both whether the publication in question was more intrusive than was necessary to its legitimate aim of provoking discussion on matters of public interest or revealing a lack of fitness for public office, and, conversely, whether the remedy sought by the plaintiff went further than was necessary in order to protect the legitimate privacy interest. In a manner reminiscent of the approach of the German[467] and Canadian courts,[468] the claims of both parties would thus be subject to a searching, but balanced examination.

---

462 There are relatively few cases where the issue has arisen. One of the most important is *Otto-Preminger*: see discussion in Chapter 6, pp 317–19.
463 See the second paragraph of Arts 8–11.
464 See fn 134, above.
465 [2001] 2 WLR 992.
466 [2001] EMLR 41, 4 June, High Court No HC 0102236, WL 720322.
467 See Markesenis and Nolte, *op cit*, fn 43, pp 122–24.
468 See fn 456, above.

Resolving the conflict: content and outcomes

In order to resolve a given case under this approach, a court would clearly have to make some assessment of the weight of the competing interests engaged, always a requirement when proportionality is in issue.[469] In assessing the gravity of the invasion of privacy involved, many of the considerations explored above would be of relevance. Thus, it could be asked: how intimate were the facts revealed; had they received some previous publicity; had the events reported happened in a very intimate setting (for example, the plaintiff's home) or in a more 'public' environment, such as a restaurant, a beach, or even the street; had particularly intrusive means, such as telephone tapping, been used to obtain the information; did the publication affect, or was it likely to affect, substantive privacy interests?[470]

In determining the strength of the opposing speech claim, the court could, as suggested, start by asking how far the expression in question was bolstered by any of the free speech justifications examined above, or indeed how far it opposed them. Thus, for example, mere reportage of a celebrity's sexual life would be likely to have little or no truth value, be actively opposed by autonomy and developmental considerations, and contribute little or nothing to debate on matters of substantive public interest. Conversely, a serious story concerning, say, the homosexual affairs of a well known politician who publicly advocated very conservative 'family values' would contribute to political discussion, influence the standing of the political party in question, and reveal a public deception, engaging the self-government and – to a lesser extent – the 'truth' justifications quite strongly.

In such 'fitness for office' cases, the status of the individual concerned would obviously be of some importance. In this respect, English courts could build on the US approach, which strives, as Prosser puts it, for a 'rough proportion[ality]', between the importance of the office or position the person holds and the amount and range of ordinarily protected information that may be revealed'.[471] Not only does the public have a greater need to know about more powerful figures, such individuals must have foreseen the close scrutiny that their lives would come under through accepting the basic duty of democratic accountability when taking up office, a factor regarded as relevant both in domestic law[472] and at Strasbourg.[473] Thus, where the plaintiff held elected position or was employed by the State to make decisions directly affecting the basic

---

469 See Craig, P, *Administrative Law*, 1999, p 591.

470 Dignity, substantive autonomy and the ability of the plaintiff to form intimate relationships with others (see pp 530–32 above).

471 Prosser, *op cit*, fn 182, p 417.

472 As the Court of Appeal put it in the *Reynolds* case ([1998] 3 WLR 862, p 910): '... those who engage in public life must expect and accept that their public conduct will be the subject of close scrutiny and robust criticism ...' Note that having regard to such a matter is not the same as the 'implied consent' argument earlier criticised. The foresight of risk of the person concerned becomes not a means of stripping away any prima facie claim to privacy that they may have, but rather as a means of adding weight to a speech argument in competition with an admitted privacy claim.

473 Thus, eg, in *Lingens v Austria* (1986) 8 EHRR 103, para 42, the Court remarked that: '... a politician ... unlike [a private individual] inevitably and knowingly lays himself open to close scrutiny of his every word and deed by both journalists and the public at large, and he must consequently display a greater degree of tolerance.'

interests of the citizenry,[474] there would in general be a stronger argument for the press under the self-governance justification. However, the courts should be astute to recognise that certain persons, who are celebrities or well known in some field, although formally mere private citizens, may nevertheless wield what Lord Cooke recently described as 'great practical power over the lives of people or great influence in the formation of public opinion ... [which] may indeed exceed that of most politicians'.[475] The distinction between the two should, nevertheless, still be recognised: the public, even if informed about distasteful aspects of a celebrity's private life, has no control by means of the democratic process over those with only *de facto* public power,[476] and thus, arguably, less need to know about them.

Some evaluation must also be made of the importance of the subject matter of the publication, a more difficult issue. Where it is claimed that it revealed matters relevant to an assessment of an individual's fitness for office, an immediate problem arises: who is to decide whether a given piece of conduct is relevant to such an assessment? Suppose, for example, that an article revealed the extra-marital affair of a government minister and the justification urged by the newspaper is the belief, held by some, that 'If the minister will lie to his wife about an affair, he will lie to the public about political matters'.[477] If the court decided that this belief was nonsense, and that the affair was not relevant to the minister's fitness for office, the judge would in effect be dictating to the public what it should and should not take into account in exercising its collective right to self-determination.[478] The exercise of this right surely involves the public not only in judging a politician's fitness for office, but also in being able to decide for itself what criteria to employ in making that assessment.

Real as this objection is, we suggest that it can be overcome. It is evident that the alternative would mean that judges would be forced to allow publicity about virtually any aspects of a public figure's life on the basis that it was not for her to say that such revelations could not be relevant to the views of some member of the public. Privacy for such figures would therefore be wholly destroyed, an outcome which must be wrong in principle under a system which, in accordance with the Convention, is committed to a

---

474 Eg, the Chairman of the Bank of England and other powerful central banks (eg, the Federal Reserve in America and the European Central Bank), persons such as Chief Constables of police, chairs of powerful quangos, etc.

475 *Reynolds* [1998] 3 WLR 862, p 640. In this respect it is, as Ivan Hare remarks, 'revealing that the US Supreme Court in the years after *Sullivan* ((1964) 376 US 254) expanded the scope of the "actual malice" rule [in defamation] from public officials to public figures' ('Is the privileged position of political expression justified?', *op cit*, fn 9).

476 Thus, revelations about the private lives of various Conservative MPs in the early 1990s and about the former Welsh Secretary, Ron Davies, in 1998, led directly to their falls from political life through the direct or indirect effect of public opinion. By contrast, even if the extensive and often adverse publicity given to the break-up of the marriage of Rupert Murdoch in 1998 changed public opinion about him, no direct consequences could flow from this.

477 Somewhat different issues would arise if the revelation revealed an active, public deceit, such as where one who has held himself out as a conservative moraliser is revealed as an adulterer. The principle of correcting a publicly created false impression appears as one of the defences to press intrusion in the various privacy measures suggested by the Calcutt Report (*op cit*, fn 1, para 12.23); it appears in the Code of the PCC (see pp 552–53 above); see also *Woodward v Hutchins* [1977] 1 WLR 760, p 764. The factor is also seen as relevant in the German courts: see BGH 5 May 1964, BGHZ NJW 1964.

478 This problem, adverted to in *Gertz* (1974) 418 US 323, p 346, has led US courts to allow press interests to prevail over privacy as a general rule.

sensitive balancing of the two rights.[479] In *Lingens*,[480] the Court remarked that the protection for reputation under Art 10(2) 'extends to politicians too, even when they are *not* acting in their private capacity'. As indicated above, this stance is accepted under the PCC Code, cl 3 and the BSC Code, cl 17. *A fortiori*, the right to privacy – unlike reputation, a primary right under the Convention – must encompass politicians when they are acting in such a capacity. Moreover, a judge making some assessment as to the relevance of the information to fitness for office would be making his judgment not out of contempt for the views of others, or paternalism, but simply because the rights of others demanded that some line be drawn.[481] Finally, the courts could employ some relatively weak test whereby the press would have to show merely that in the view of a rational person, the information could be of real relevance to an assessment of fitness for office. The rational person should, however, be taken to be reasonably broad-minded and tolerant, in line with the view of the European Court that such values are essential in a democratic society.[482]

In other cases, the justification for stories about an individual's private life will be, not that they are relevant to her fitness for office, but more generally, that they contribute to discussion of matters of general interest. The problem with this justification is that it can be used so broadly as to encompass almost any invasion of privacy, apart from pictures clearly designed merely to titillate. If its breadth and imprecision are not confronted head on, it could lead to the virtual abrogation of any privacy remedy which does develop. Where such speech is not directly political, it will not lie at the core of the self-governance justification. But, to quote Lord Cooke in *Reynolds*: 'Matters other than those pertaining to government and politics may be just as important in the community'.[483] Such speech which, as Zimmerman puts it, can 'inform the social, political, moral and philosophical positions of individual citizens'[484] could include revelations relating to matters as diverse as eating disorders, abortion, attitudes to sexuality, education and the like; it will often concern not politicians, but celebrities and their relatives[485] and those who, for a short time and for a particular reason only, are thrust into the public gaze.

It is suggested that the courts should be slow to accept that the use of a person's private life to provoke discussion, efficacious as it may be, is justified under Art 10 grounds. The example of so called 'outing' illustrates the objection: the argument in favour of such revelations is that if the public comes to learn that a person they admire or

---

479 It should be noted that the German Supreme Court has held that 'even politicians who are in the limelight are entitled to have their privacy respected' (BGHZ 72, pp 120, 122–23).

480 (1986) 8 EHRR 103, para 42 (emphasis added).

481 As Lord Nicholls put it in *Reynolds* [1999] 4 All ER 609, p 624: '... an outside body ... one other than the newspaper itself [must] decide ... This is bound to be so, if the decision of the press itself is not to be determinative ... The court has the advantage of being impartial [and] independent of government.

482 See, eg, *Otto-Preminger* (1994) 19 EHRR 34, para 47.

483 *Ibid*, p 640.

484 *Ibid*, p 346. Meiklejohn accepted a wide definition of protected speech: 'The First Amendment is an absolute' (1961) Sup Ct Rev 245, p 256.

485 The relatives of celebrities are increasingly becoming a focus for media attention: see the analysis of Natasha Walker, (2000) *The Independent*, 14 February, and the Spencer case itself, in which the stories complained of appeared under headlines such as: 'Di's sister-in-law in booze and bulimia clinic' (*News of the World*, 2 April 1995).

respect is homosexual, this may force them to re-examine their own prejudices against homosexuality.[486] The objection is that this justification is utilitarian to the point of ruthlessness. It amounts in effect to forcing a person to provide highly personal information for the purposes of fuelling public debate and therefore amounts to one of the clearest breaches one could imagine of the Kantian imperative to treat persons as ends in themselves. For example, the disputed article concerning the former child prodigy, in the American case of *Sidis*,[487] was 'a merciless' dissection of Sidis' life, which had a 'devastating effect' upon him, but was justified partly on the basis that, as Zimmerman puts it, it provided 'helpful insights into the problems experienced by gifted children',[488] or, as the court said, it was 'instructive'.[489] It is apparent that such an approach would have the effect, as in America, of virtually demolishing the right to privacy, since virtually all pieces of personal information about a person in the public view could be seen as relevant to some area of public debate.[490] Moreover, as argued above,[491] one of the principal justifications for open discussion of different lifestyles and the like is to promote autonomous choice and diversity: acts of intrusive journalism, likely to deter others from taking up controversial lifestyles, are in clear conflict with this aim.

In assessing the speech value of a given publication, the court should, as suggested above,[492] consider whether the restrictions which each party proposes to place upon the other are 'necessary in a democratic society'. The plaintiff's concerns might in some cases be sufficiently answered, not by injuncting the publication, but simply by requiring it to be anonymised. On the other hand, in relation to a publication which, it was claimed, contributed to public debate, it might be asked whether there was not another means of so contributing which would not have involved a violation of privacy. Given that in our contemporary, confessional culture, there are a large number of people, ranging from private individuals to celebrities, who are prepared to reveal intimate aspects of their lives in a wholly voluntary manner, it might be difficult to maintain that the invasion of privacy involved in publishing completely involuntary revelations was in any way necessary for that continuation of public debate which is admittedly valuable. Where, instead, it was claimed that a publication threw light on a particular person's fitness for office, if the court decided that the basic facts conveyed should be protected under Art 10, it could go on to consider whether the details of the publication went further than was necessary in informing the public. Thus, it has been said that while it is arguable that the public have a right to know about a Cabinet minister's adulterous affair, they do not need to know 'the content of such a person's intimate conversations or the details of his or her sexual activity'.[493] Thus, a court might make some attempt to sift out those aspects of

---

486 In *Sipple v Chronicle Publishing Co* (201 Cal Rpt 665 1984), an ex-marine foiled an assassination attempt upon President Ford, thereafter attracting great media interest. A Californian newspaper revealed that Sipple was homosexual, a matter which he had concealed from his relatives. The court decided the case partly on the basis that 'the exposure was motivated by the wish to combat the stereotyping of homosexuals as "timid, weak and unheroic"'.

487 113 F 2d 806 (2d Cir 1940).

488 Zimmerman, *op cit*, fn 195.

489 Zimmerman, *op cit*, fn 195, p 807.

490 See Zimmerman's defence of this position (*op cit*, fn 195, p 353).

491 See the discussion of Raz's views, pp 620–21 above.

492 Page 625.

493 National Heritage Select Committee, *op cit*, fn 1, para 5.

journalistic reportage which serve some serious function from those which, under the banner of promoting democratic accountability, merely peddle titillation or gossip. As was said in *Mills*, the freedom to publish only that which judges view as responsible is no freedom. Nevertheless, if the right to respect for privacy, now given clear recognition for the first time in domestic law, is to be afforded genuine weight, some consideration must be given to the genuine public interest value of privacy-invading speech, taking into account the factors discussed.

Remedies

The privacy measures considered in this chapter – apart from the 'powers' of the PCC in relation to the PCC Code – offer a variety of remedies. The ITC has a number of internal remedies at its command and since it is a public authority under s 6 of the HRA, it must act in accordance with Arts 10 and 8 in applying them. Various criminal offences arise under the DPA 1998, while reporting restrictions can be enforced in contempt proceedings. Compensation is available under s 13 of the DPA and journalists are subject to a less restricted liability to pay damages than other data controllers. However, as indicated above, it appears that interim injunctions are not obtainable under s 32 of the DPA unless the claimant is seeking to prevent re-publication of the material. If the doctrine of confidence is relied on, a number of civil remedies are available, and those remedies are presumably also available where an action is brought directly for invasion of privacy under Art 8 against a media body which is a public authority under s 7(1)(a) of the HRA.[494] Where an action was brought directly against a media body, either under the doctrine of confidence or, in the case of the BBC or Channel 4 under the HRA, the claimant would normally be seeking an injunction. In the case of the ITC, the order sought by the claimant could be a declaration or a mandatory order, since he or she would be asking the ITC to use its powers either to punish a broadcaster or to prevent a future broadcast. Orders against the BSC would presumably take the form of mandatory orders or declarations. These remedies are considered below, together with the impact on them of s 12 of the HRA.

An account of profits[495] is available in confidence cases. Damages are also available,[496] whether or not the court could also have ordered injunctive relief in the particular circumstances.[497] While there is, as yet, no authority for the award of damages

---

494 See further Chapter 4, pp 157–59.

495 The court will not award both, on the basis that this would compensate the plaintiff twice over. See the comments of the Law Commission in its Working Paper No 58, Cmnd 5012, 1972, para 123.

496 Under Lord Cairns' Act; see Wacks, *op cit*, fn 1, pp 149, 151, and fns 28 and 44.

497 Damages may be awarded in addition to, or substitution for, injunctive relief regardless of whether, in the particular circumstances of the case, a court would have chosen to grant injunctive relief provided the court has jurisdiction to grant an injunction: *Hooper v Rogers* [1975] 1 Ch 43, p 48, *per* Russell LJ. See also *Race Relations Board v Applin* [1973] 1 QB 815 and the views of Capper ('Damages for breach of the equitable duty of confidence' (1994) 14 LS 313) and Gurry, *op cit*, fn 153, Chapter 23. See Wacks, *op cit*, fn 1, p 151, note 46; cf the views of Megarry VC in *Malone v Comr of Police for the Metropolis (No 2)* [1979] 1 Ch 344.

for emotional distress, precedents exist in other areas of law.[498] However, the most important issue both for plaintiffs and for media freedom will be the question of the basis on which the courts will grant an interlocutory injunction to restrain publication. From the plaintiff's perspective, obtaining an injunction is vital in privacy cases, far more so than in defamation. This is because the damage done to reputation by initial publication can be subsequently restored by a public finding that the allegation was false. By contrast, if private information is made public, the law can compensate for this harm at final trial by awarding damages, but it cannot in any way cure the invasion of privacy: it cannot erase the information revealed from people's memories. From the defendant's perspective, on the other hand, if the story is topical, even an interim injunction might kill it off completely. Thus, as Robertson and Nichol put it: 'In breach of confidence ... the critical stage is usually the application for an interim injunction ... If the publisher is able to publish ... the action will often evaporate ... If the story is injuncted the publisher will often lose interest ...'.[499] Similarly, Leigh and Lustgarten comment: 'the interim stage is the critical one ... [it is] effectively the disposition of the matter'.[500]

Prior to the inception of the HRA it was only necessary for the plaintiff to make out an arguable case for confidentiality[501] in order to obtain an injunction; the courts then sought to maintain the status quo, on the basis that if the story was published, the material would lose its confidential character, and there would be nothing to have a final trial about.[502] However, this consideration could be outweighed by the defence of public interest at the interlocutory stage. The view of Lord Denning in *Woodward v Hutchins*,[503] that the mere fact that defendants intend to plead public interest at final trial should preclude interim relief, did not find wide support; instead, it appeared that, whilst a plea of public interest could defeat a claim for such relief, the defence had to be supported by evidence and have a credible chance of success at final trial.[504] However, that test was thought to be potentially unfavourable to the media because, in balancing the rights of the two parties, courts took the view that while the plaintiff's right to confidentiality would be wholly defeated by publication, the press could always still publish the story if

---

498 Examples include contract (*Jarvis v Swans Tours Ltd* [1973] 1 QB 233), copyright and under the Sex Discrimination Act 1975, which gives the courts power to award damages on the same basis as in tort and which under s 66 allows courts to award damages for injury to feelings alone. Space precludes full discussion of the point, but it is clearly, therefore, an area free of authority; to decide that as a blanket rule, such damages could never be available, by leaving the plaintiff potentially remediless, would be clearly out of line with the Convention notion of effective protection for rights; Strasbourg has recognised the need to compensate for 'moral damage', including emotional distress (see Van Dijk and Van Hoof, *op cit*, fn 46, pp 179–82).

499 *Media Law*, 1992, p 190.

500 *Ibid*, p 533 (referring to the granting of interim injunctions generally); see also p 551.

501 Eg, *HRH Princess of Wales; Shelley Films Limited; Francome.*

502 See *AG v Guardian Newspapers (No 2)* [1990] 1 AC 109. Thus in *Francome* [1984] 1 WLR 892, p 900, Fox LJ said: 'Unless Mr Francome is given protection until the trial, I think that a trial might be largely worthless from his point of view even though he succeeded.' Similarly, in *Lion Laboratories* [1984] 1 QB 530, p 551, Griffiths LJ said: 'there will usually be a powerful case for maintaining the status quo by the grant of an interlocutory injunction to restrain publication until trial of the action.'

503 [1977] 1 WLR 760, CA.

504 See *Lion Laboratories* [1984] 1 QB 530, pp 538 and 553, *per* Stephenson LJ (explicitly rejecting Lord Denning's approach in *Woodward*); *ibid*, p 548 *per* O'Connor LJ and p 553 *per* Griffiths LJ; similarly in *Hellewell*, where the public interest argument prevented the award of an injunction.

they won at trial; they were thus inclined toward protecting the more fragile right of the plaintiff.[505]

The HRA addresses this issue directly. In this context, s 12 is of interest in respect of injunctions or other orders granted under its own powers, contained in s 8,[506] and at common law, where freedom of expression would be affected. It will be recalled that s 12 applies (per sub-s (1)): '... if a court is considering whether to grant any relief which, if granted, might affect the exercise of the Convention right to freedom of expression'; it provides (per sub-s (3)) that: 'no such relief is to be granted so as to restrain publication before trial unless the court is satisfied that the applicant is likely to establish that publication should not be allowed'. Section 12(4) specifically instructs the courts that when they are dealing with, *inter alia*, journalistic material, they should consider the extent to which 'it is, or would be, in the public interest for the material to be published' and thus remove any lingering doubts as to whether the court should consider the strength of the public interest defence at the interim stage. Sub-section (3), in allowing the court to grant injunctions only where it believes that the plaintiff will succeed at trial, requires the court to undertake a substantial balancing test at the interim stage; it also makes it clear that the burden is on the plaintiff to show that the privacy interest would probably succeed at trial. Undertaking such an evaluation at the interlocutory stage is not proving to be a difficult task, as the findings in *Douglas*,[507] *Venables*[508] and *Mills*[509] suggested.[510] Since the judges have the confidential information in question before them at that stage, they may be able to find quite readily that the defence is made out (as Laws J did in *Hellewell*) or will probably succeed (as in *Lion Laboratories*) or that it does not justify publication at large (as in *Francome*). Since, as we have suggested above, the paradigmatic privacy claim will often involve speech of little or no value in public interest terms,[511] it might, at least in some cases, be fairly easy to determine that the publication in question raises no serious speech or public interest issue.

When undertaking this inquiry, the courts obviously have to take account of Art 10 jurisprudence on interim injunctions; indeed, as noted above, s 12 instructs them to have 'particular regard' to Art 10. The leading case on prior restraints is *Observer and Guardian v*

---

505 This will generally follow under the 'balance of convenience' test (*American Cyanamid Co v Ethicon* [1975] AC 396). See *AG v Guardian Newspapers* [1987] 3 All ER 316, which concerned an application for an interim injunction to restrain publication of confidential information (extracts from *Spycatcher*). Lord Brandon remarked (*ibid*, p 1292): 'the choice lies between one course [allowing publication] which may result in permanent and irrevocable damage to the cause of [the plaintiff] and another course which can only result in temporary and in no wary irrevocable damage to the cause of the newspapers ... it seems to me clear that the second ... course should ... be preferred ...'; see also the similar reasoning of Lord Ackner, *ibid*, p 1305.

506 See Chapter 4, pp 172–75.

507 [2001] 2 WLR 992.

508 [2001] 1 All ER 908, Fam Div.

509 [2001] EMLR 41, 4 June, High Court No HC 0102236, WL 720322.

510 The position in defamation, in which the courts refuse an interim injunction if the defendants intend to plead justification, may be distinguished: justification is a factual claim, the investigation of which will often require sifting through a mountain of evidence and so cannot be resolved at the interlocutory stage; by contrast, the defence in confidence cases generally requires not an empirical, but an evaluative judgment.

511 Eg, Russbridger (*op cit*, fn 9) instances a story in the *News of the World* in January 1999, in which a lap dancer gave full details of a recent sexual encounter with the singer Tom Jones.

UK,[512] in which the Court considered the compatibility with Art 10 of interim injunctions preventing those newspapers from publishing *Spycatcher* material. The Court laid down the basic principle that:

> while Article 10 does not in terms prohibit the imposition of prior restraints on publication ... the dangers inherent in [them] are such that they call for the most careful scrutiny on the part of the Court ... news is a perishable commodity and delay of its publication, even for a short period, may well deprive it of all its value and interest.[513]

While the court's actual decision in the case seemed to suggest that the need to preserve the plaintiff's rights will in itself point strongly towards the imposition of an interim injunction,[514] the relatively cautious approach adopted may have been influenced by the fact that the very sensitive issue of national security was at stake. It is suggested that the domestic judiciary should look rather to the general principle laid down in the case that the granting of interim injunctions is a particularly significant *prima facie* infringement of Art 10, given the perishable qualities of news. This factor would then have to be weighed against the strength of the privacy claim, in the manner suggested earlier and, in accordance with s 12, a court should award the interim injunction only if it considers that the privacy argument is the stronger one.

7 CONCLUSIONS

This chapter has considered the various methods of protecting personal information available in domestic law and has focused in particular on the impact of the DPA 1998 and the HRA. The HRA has, as indicated, not only created a new right of privacy enforceable against public authorities, it has had and will have an effect on existing common law and statutory provisions, including those of the DPA. Its effect is twofold. First, it has provided the impetus under ss 6, 2 and 12 to develop the existing common law so that it protects privacy, while ss 2 and 3 may arguably be used to influence statutes in order to develop such protection.[515] Secondly, it provides, where necessary, the means of balancing such increased protection against freedom of expression under ss 12, 6 and 3, but especially s 12.

Both these effects are especially apparent, as this chapter has sought to demonstrate, in relation to the common law action for breach of confidence. It is now developing into a privacy law in all but name, and may provide a more effective and subtle means of protecting privacy than commonly thought. Legitimisation of this judicial enterprise can

---

512 (1991) 14 EHRR 153; for comment see Leigh, I, '*Spycatcher* in Strasbourg' [1992] PL 200.

513 *Ibid*, para 60.

514 It was found that the initial injunctions, which prevented publication for over a year, had the aim of maintaining the Attorney General's ability to bring a case claiming permanent injunction, a case which would have been destroyed if *Spycatcher* material had been published before that claim could be heard. This factor was found to establish the existence of a pressing social need justifying the restriction of Art 10. The finding that the continuation of the injunctions after the book had been published in the US could not be justified was based simply on the fact that such publication had destroyed the confidentiality of the material, making it impossible to maintain the Attorney General's rights as a litigant.

515 See p 564 above.

now be found in the HRA: its introduction of the Convention into UK law allows the courts to draw upon the decisions discussed and, importantly, upon the general principles expressed in the Strasbourg jurisprudence. As the chapter has tried to demonstrate, such an enterprise may also be grounded in universal human rights values as expressed in other jurisdictions; case law from these jurisdictions may also point the way to resolution of some of the problems discussed above which the judiciary will need to confront as they engage in incremental development of the action.

The principal objection to the development of privacy rights has always been the perceived threat to media freedom. This chapter has argued that this fear is largely misplaced and indeed that the right to free speech and to protection for privacy are 'mutually supportive',[516] because, as the German Supreme Court has put it, both are 'essential aspects of the liberal democratic order'.[517]

The introduction of some legal protection for privacy might encourage a movement away from the prurient trivia currently infesting so many of our newspapers and therefore, far from threatening free speech in the press, could enhance it. It is essential, however, that the senior judiciary appreciate the need for a proper resolution of speech and privacy interests. In this regard, if Art 10 had not been introduced into UK law, and its importance highlighted by s 12 of the incorporating Act, the developments considered in this chapter would have been less opportune.

---

516 Emerson, C, 'The right of privacy and the freedom of the press' (1979) 14(2) Harvard Civil Rights – Civil Liberties Law Review 329.

517 BGH 19 December 1995 BGHZ 131, 322–46.

CHAPTER 11

POWERS OF THE SECURITY AND INTELLIGENCE SERVICES; STATE SURVEILLANCE; SEARCH AND SEIZURE OF PROPERTY

1 INTRODUCTION

Agents of the State frequently invade privacy. They may enter property, seize documents, intercept telephones and place persons under surveillance. The method of obtaining information creates an invasion of privacy; its use creates a further invasion. These actions are undertaken by the police, other law enforcement agencies and the security and intelligence services with the aim of promoting internal security or preventing and detecting crime. Such aims are clearly legitimate; the question is whether the safeguards against unreasonable or arbitrary intrusion are adequate. Under the requirements of the Human Rights Act (HRA), such safeguards should include a clear remedy for the citizen who has been the subject of unauthorised surveillance or other intrusion, and strict control over the power to effect such intrusion or issue authorisation for it. The latter safeguard is particularly crucial since the citizen may not even be aware that intrusion is taking place. This is particularly true of telephone tapping and the use of surveillance devices.

However, not only have legal developments failed to keep pace with technological ones, the principles which in a liberal democracy should inform the law governing such invasions of privacy have largely failed to find expression in it. It will be argued that the value of privacy still finds little place in it despite the fact that the central statute now governing this area, the Regulation of Investigatory Powers Act 2000, was introduced specifically in order to meet the demands of the European Convention on Human Rights.

The common law has always given a high priority to preventing interference with personal property[1] and therefore, prior to the inception of the HRA, privacy received some incidental protection. Remedies for intrusion on property are found in the torts of trespass and nuisance, while seizure of goods is also *prima facie* tortious.[2] Trespass is defined as entering on to land in the possession of another without lawful justification. It is confined to instances in which there is some physical entry; prying with binoculars is not covered and, obviously, nor is electronic eavesdropping. The limitations of the law have been determined in certain decisions. In *Hickman v Maisey*[3] the defendant, who was on the highway, was watching the plaintiff's land. It was found that the plaintiff owned the land under the highway and that the defendant was entitled to make ordinary and reasonable use of it. Such watching was held not to be reasonable; the defendant had gone outside the accepted use and therefore had trespassed. Thus, it was made clear that intention in such instances is all important, but that unless behaviour could be linked to some kind of physical presence on land, trespass would not provide a remedy.

---

1   See *McLorie v Oxford* [1982] 1 QB 1290.
2   Under the torts of trespass to goods and conversion.
3   [1900] 1 QB 752, CA.

This decision can be contrasted with that in *Bernstein v Skyviews and General Ltd*[4] in order to determine the limits of trespass. The defendants flew over the plaintiff's land in an aircraft in order to take photographs of it and the question arose whether the plaintiff had a right in trespass to prevent such intrusion. It was held that either he had no rights of ownership over the air space to that height or, alternatively, if he did have such rights, s 40 of the Civil Aviation Act 1942 exempted reasonable flights from liability. The court was not prepared to find that the taking of one photograph was unreasonable and a remedy could not be based solely on invasion of privacy as, of course, there is no such tort. The distinction between this decision and that in *Hickman* arises partly because the plaintiff could not show that he had an interest in what was violated – the air space – and so he fell outside the ambit of trespass.

The tort of nuisance has not provided a means of protecting privacy except in extreme instances. Liability for nuisance will arise if a person is disturbed in the enjoyment of his or her land to an extent that the law regards as unreasonable. There is a dearth of authority on the issue of straightforward surveillance but, in an Australian case, *Victoria Park Racing Company v Taylor*,[5] where a platform was erected in order to gain a view of a racecourse which diminished the value of the plaintiff's business, no remedy in nuisance was available. The activity was held not to affect the use and enjoyment of the land, but dicta in the case suggested that there would, in general, be no remedy in nuisance for looking over another's premises. However, *dicta* in *Bernstein* favoured the possibility that grossly invasive embarrassing surveillance would amount to a nuisance and that possibility was followed up (though not explicitly) in somewhat different circumstances in *Khorasandjian v Bush*.[6] An injunction was granted against the defendant restraining him from using violence to or harassing, pestering or communicating with the plaintiff, the child of the owner of the property in question. This decision, which sought to extend the tort to cover interference with rights to privacy, was criticised by the House of Lords in *Hunter v Canary Wharf*,[7] where it was confirmed that the tort is essentially concerned with injury to land. Thus, it is fair to conclude that trespass and nuisance offer only limited protection in this area from the crudest and most obvious forms of invasions of privacy.

Therefore, under the common law, when an invasion of privacy did not fall within these narrow areas of tortious liability, it did not require lawful authority. Thus police search and seizure of property required such authority, but the interception of communications and much state surveillance had no comprehensive legal basis. This chapter demonstrates that the European Convention on Human Rights, both before and after the inception of the HRA, has been the driving force for change. The state has been forced, incrementally, to accept that a legal basis for the invasion of privacy by state agents must be put in place. Such a basis is now in place, contained in a range of statutes of which the most recent and the most comprehensive is the Regulation of Investigatory Powers Act 2000. However, the creation of a legal basis for State invasion of privacy does not necessarily mean that the requirements of Art 8 have been met. The main concern of

---

4   [1978] QB 479; [1977] 2 All ER 902.
5   (1937) 58 CLR 479.
6   [1993] 3 All ER 669. For discussion of this decision see (1993) 143 NLJ 926 and (1993) 143 NLJ 1685.
7   [1997] AC 655, pp 691G–692B.

this chapter is to consider how far Art 8 principles are in actuality reflected in these statutes, a concern that has been given a sharper focus now that the HRA is in force.

2 POLICE POWERS OF ENTRY AND SEARCH[8]

In America, the Fourth Amendment to the Constitution guarantees freedom from unreasonable search and seizure by the police, thus recognising the invasion of privacy which a search of premises represents. A search without a warrant will normally[9] be unreasonable; therefore, an independent check is usually available on the search power.[10] In contrast, the common law in Britain, despite some rulings asserting the importance of protecting the citizen from the invasion of private property,[11] allowed search and seizure on wide grounds, going beyond those authorised by statute.[12] Thus, the common law did not provide full protection for the citizen and the Police and Criminal Evidence Act 1984 (PACE) went some way to remedy this by placing powers of entry, search and seizure on a clearer basis and ensuring that the person whose premises are searched understands the basis of the search and can complain as to its conduct if necessary. Whether the new procedures actually do provide sufficient protection for the privacy interests of the subject of the search is the question to be examined by this section.

Entry without warrant

The Police and Criminal Evidence Act (PACE)

The power to enter premises conferred by ss 17 and 18 of PACE is balanced in a manner similar to the method employed in respect of stop and search, which is discussed in Chapter 13. The power can be exercised under s 17 where: an officer wants to arrest a person suspected of an arrestable offence; in order to arrest for certain offences under the Public Order Act 1936 or the Criminal Law Act 1977; to recapture someone unlawfully at large such as an escapee from a prison, court or mental hospital; to save life or limb or prevent serious damage to property or to execute a warrant of arrest arising out of criminal proceedings. This last provision allows an entry to be made to search for someone wanted under a warrant for non-payment of a fine.

---

8   See generally Feldman, D, *The Law Relating to Entry, Search and Seizure*, 1986; Stone, RTH, *Entry, Search and Seizure*, 1989; Lidstone, K and Bevan, V, *Search and Seizure under the Police and Criminal Evidence Act 1984*, 1992; Clayton, R and Tomlinson, H, *Civil Actions Against the Police*, 2nd edn, 1999, Chapter 7.

9   *Coolidge v New Hampshire* (1973) 403 US 443: exception accepted where evidence might otherwise be destroyed.

10 For comment on the efficacy of this check, see Lafave, W, *Search and Seizure*, 1978.

11 See, eg, rulings in *Entinck v Carrington* (1765) 19 St Tr 1029; *Morris v Beardmore* [1981] AC 446; [1980] 2 All ER 753.

12 The ruling in *Ghani v Jones* [1970] 1 QB 693 authorised seizure of a wide range of material once officers were lawfully on premises. *Thomas v Sawkins* [1935] 2 KB 249 allowed a wide power to enter premises to prevent crime (see above, p 433).

A further power of entry arises under s 18 if a person has been arrested for an arrestable offence and the intention is to search the person's premises immediately after arrest:

> ... a constable may enter and search any premises occupied or controlled by a person who is under arrest for an arrestable offence, if he has reasonable grounds for suspecting that there is on the premises evidence, other than items subject to legal privilege, that relates:
>
> (a) to that offence; or
>
> (b) to some other arrestable offence which is connected with or similar to that offence.

Thus, the power is subject to some significant limitations; it does not arise in respect of an arrest under s 25. If a search was considered necessary in respect of a s 25 arrest, a search warrant would have to be obtained unless the provisions of s 32 applied. Section 32 allows a search of premises after arrest for any offence if the arrestee was arrested on those premises or was on them immediately before the arrest.

The Terrorism Act 2000

The provisions for warrantless search of premises under PACE after arrest are wide enough to cover many circumstances in which police officers might wish to search for items relating to a terrorist investigation. But, they are supplemented by special powers under warrant which are discussed below and also, in an emergency, by a power which arose under Sched 7, para 7(1) of the Prevention of Terrorism (Temporary Provisions) Act (PTA) 1989 allowing a police officer of at least the rank of superintendent to authorise a search by written order if there are 'reasonable grounds for believing that the case is one of great emergency and that in the interests of the State immediate action is necessary'. There is evidence that the use of special search powers without the need to rely on reasonable suspicion or on a warrant have some value in terrorist investigations.[13] Nevertheless, the use of such powers represents an invasion of liberty which requires a strong and clear justification rather than a reliance on an uncertain phrase such as 'the interests of the State'. The power is reproduced in the Terrorism Act 2000 in Sched 5 para 3.

A further power of search arose under s 16C and para 7 of Sched 6A which were added to the PTA by the Criminal Justice and Public Order Act 1994. Section 16C allow police officers of at least the rank of superintendent, engaged in a terrorism investigation, to establish in certain circumstances a police cordon around an area. Once the cordon is in place, para 7 of Sched 6A gave a power of search. The power was reproduced in ss 33–36 of the Terrorism Act 2000. It must be authorised in writing by an officer of at least the rank of superintendent who must have reasonable grounds for believing that material which would be of substantial value to the investigation, and which is not excluded or special material or material covered by legal privilege (see below), is on specified premises within the cordon. The power is exercised by a constable who may enter and search premises and may seize items not protected by legal privilege if he has reasonable grounds for believing that they will be of substantial value to the investigation.

---

13   See Walker, C, *The Prevention of Terrorism*, p 195.

The Police Act 1997

As discussed below, this Act places police powers of surveillance on a statutory basis. It also provides powers of entry, search and seizure. An authorisation may be issued if the search is believed to be necessary because it will be of substantial value in the prevention and detection of serious crime[14] and the objective cannot reasonably be achieved by other means (s 93(2)). As explained below,[15] the main check on these extensive powers is provided by the special commissioners appointed from the senior judiciary (s 91(1)). Where the entry and search contemplated is of a dwelling house, prior approval by the commissioner is necessary, but this requirement is waived where the authorising officer believes that the search is urgent. Since the belief does not need to be based on reasonable grounds, such a safeguard may have little impact in practice. These controversial extensions of the police powers of entry are therefore subject to very limited independent oversight and, unlike the s 18 power, they may be divorced from the needs of an immediate criminal investigation.

Search warrants

Searching of premises other than under ss 17 and 18 can also occur if a search warrant is issued under s 8 of PACE by a magistrate. A warrant under s 8 will only be issued if there are reasonable grounds for believing that a serious arrestable offence has been committed and where the material is likely to be of substantial value to the investigation of the offence. A large number of other statutes also provide for the issuing of warrants to the police and to other public officials. Special provisions arise, *inter alia*, under s 27 of the Drug Trafficking Act 1994, s 2(4) of the Criminal Justice Act 1987 (in relation to serious fraud) and, as discussed below, in relation to the security and intelligence services under the Intelligence Services Act 1994.

A wide power to search premises arose under Sched 7, para 2 of the Prevention of Terrorism (Temporary Provisions) Act 1989[16] which, in contrast to the warrant power under PACE, was not dependent on the need to allege a specific offence and could therefore take place at a very early stage in the investigation. This power was reproduced in the Terrorism Act 2000, Sched 5, which as Chapter 8 indicated, applies to a wider range of groups. A justice of the peace must be satisfied that a terrorist investigation is being carried out and that there are reasonable grounds for believing that there is material which is likely to be of substantial value to the investigation. Also, it must appear that it is impracticable to gain entry to the premises with consent and that immediate entry to the premises is necessary. A warrant could also be issued under s 15(1) of the PTA in order to allow entry to premises to effect an arrest under s 14(1)(b). This power was thought necessary since the general PACE powers would not be applicable due to the broad nature of s 14(1)(b).[17] It was continued in the Terrorism Act 2000, Sched 5.

---

14 For the definition of serious crime, see below, p 692.
15 See p 702.
16 See Walker, *op cit*, fn 13, pp 185–97.
17 See below, Chapter 13, pp 783–84.

A warrant authorising the police to search premises does not of itself authorise officers to search persons on the premises. The Home Office circular on PACE stated that such persons could be searched only if a specific power to do so arose under the warrant (for example, warrants issued under s 23 of the Misuse of Drugs Act 1971).

Applications for warrants by police officers and the execution of the warrant must comply with the procedures set out in ss 15 and 16 of PACE. The application for the warrant must be supported, under s 15(3), by an 'Information' in writing. It must specify the enactment under which it is issued, the premises to be searched[18] and the articles or persons to be sought (s 15(6)).

Section 16 governs the procedure to be followed in executing the warrant. The warrant must be produced to the occupier (although it seems that this need not be at the time of entry if impracticable in the circumstances)[19] and must identify the articles to be sought, although once the officer is on the premises, other articles may be seized under s 19 if they appear to relate to any other offence. Further, the warrant authorises entry to premises on one occasion only and does not allow for a general search of the premises[20] since the search must only be for the purpose for which the warrant was issued (s 16(8)).

Under s 16, if a search is under warrant, a copy of the warrant must be issued to the subject of the search. The warrant will identify the articles or persons sought and the offence suspected, but need not specify the grounds on which it was issued or give the name of the constable conducting the search. A warrant, like the Notice of Powers and Rights (discussed below) therefore provides the occupier with limited information. Moreover, as noted above, it need not be produced to the occupier before the search begins if the purpose of the search might be frustrated by such production.[21] However, within these limitations, the courts seem prepared to take a strict view of the importance of complying with this safeguard. In *Chief Constable of Lancashire ex p Parker and McGrath*[22] police officers conducted a search of the applicant's premises in the execution of a search warrant issued under s 8 of PACE. However, after the warrant had been signed by the judge, the police detached part of it and reattached it to the other original documents. In purported compliance with s 16 of PACE, the police produced all these documents to the applicants. Thus, the police did not produce the whole of the original warrant and moreover, did not supply one of the documents constituting the warrant. The applicants applied for judicial review of both the issue and the execution of the warrants. It was determined that s 16(5)(b) of PACE had been breached in that the warrant produced to the applicants was not the original warrant as seen and approved by the judge and a declaration was granted to that effect. The police had admitted that there was a breach of the requirement under s 16(5)(c) that a copy of the warrant should be supplied to the occupier of the premises.

---

18 *Southwestern Magistrates' Court ex p Cofie* [1997] 1 WLR 885.
19 *Longman* [1988] 1 WLR 619, CA; for comment, see Stevens, R, *Justice of the Peace*, 1988, p 551.
20 See *Chief Constable of Warwick Constabulary ex p Fitzpatrick* [1999] 1 WLR 564.
21 *Longman* [1988] 1 WLR 619, CA.
22 (1992) 142 NLJ 635.

Power to enter premises at common law

At common law, a power to enter premises in order to prevent crime arises from the much criticised case of *Thomas v Sawkins*.[23] Lord Hewart CJ contemplated that a police officer would have the right to enter private premises when 'he has reasonable grounds for believing that an offence is imminent or is likely to be committed'. This judgment may receive some endorsement from s 17(5) and (6), which provides that all common law powers on entry are abolished except to deal with or prevent a breach of the peace. However, this narrows down the power of entry, as it does not arise in respect of any offence. *Thomas v Sawkins* arose in the context of a public meeting held on private premises, but common law powers do not seem to be confined to such circumstances; in *McGowan v Chief Constable of Kingston on Hull*[24] it was found that police officers were entitled to enter and remain on private premises when they feared a breach of the peace arising from a private quarrel.

Voluntary searches

Code of Practice B made under PACE,[25] which governs powers of entry, search and seizure, makes special provision for voluntary searches. Paragraph 4 of Code B as originally drafted provided that a search of premises could take place with the consent of the occupier and provided under para 4(2) that he must be informed that he need not consent to the search; in requiring that the consent should be in writing, it recognised that there might sometimes be a doubt as to the reality of such consent and went some way towards resolving that doubt. After revision in 1991, para 4 went further in that direction. Under sub-para 4.1 the officer concerned must ensure that the consent is being sought from the correct person, whereas previously this problem was only addressed in a Note for Guidance (4A), and then only in respect of lodgings. Sub-para 4.3 provides that the search must cease if the consent is withdrawn during it and also contains an express provision against using duress to obtain consent.[26] However, it has been doubted whether these provisions have had much effect on ensuring that use of consensual search is not abused because it is not always made clear to occupiers that they can withhold consent.[27]

Power of seizure

At common law prior to PACE, a wide power of seizure had developed where a search was not under warrant. Articles could be seized so long as they either implicated the owner or occupier in any offence or implicated third parties in the offence for which the search was conducted.[28] However, the power of seizure under PACE is even wider than this. Under s 8(2), a constable may seize and retain anything for which a search has been

---

23 [1935] 2 KB 249; for criticism, see Goodhart (1947) 6 CLJ 222; see further Chapter 9, p 433.

24 [1968] Crim LR 34. But see the ruling in *McLeod v UK* (1998) 27 EHRR 493.

25 See Chapter 13, p 757 for discussion of the PACE Codes of Practice.

26 For criticism of these provisions see Bevan, K and Palmer, C, *Bevan and Lidstone's The Investigation of Crime*, 1996, pp 117–21.

27 See further Dixon, D, 'Consent and the legal regulation of policing' (1990) 17 JLS 345–62.

28 *Ghani v Jones* [1970] 1 QB 693; *Garfinkel v MPC* [1972] Crim LR 44.

authorised. The power of seizure without warrant is governed by s 18(2) which provides that: 'A constable may seize and retain anything for which he may search under subsection (1) above.' This power is greatly widened, however, by the further power of seizure arising under s 19:

The constable may seize anything which is on the premises if he has reasonable grounds for believing:

(a) that it has been obtained in consequence of the commission of an offence; and

(b) that it is necessary to seize it in order to prevent it being concealed, lost, damaged, altered or destroyed.

The constable may seize anything which is on the premises if he has reasonable grounds for believing:

(a) that it is evidence in relation to an offence which he is investigating or any other offence; and

(b) that it is necessary to seize it in order to prevent the evidence being concealed, lost, altered or destroyed.

Under s 22(1), anything which has been so seized may be retained 'so long as is necessary in all the circumstances'. It was made clear in *Chief Constable of Lancashire ex p Parker and McGrath*[29] that the above provisions assume that the search itself is lawful; in other words, material seized during an unlawful search cannot be retained and if it is, an action for trespass to goods may arise. It was accepted in this instance that the search was unlawful (see below), but the Chief Constable contended that the material seized could nevertheless be retained. This argument was put forward under the provision of s 22(2)(a), which allows the retention of 'anything seized for the purposes of a criminal investigation'. The Chief Constable maintained that these words would be superfluous unless denoting a general power to retain unlawfully seized material. However, it was held that the sub-section could not bear the weight sought to be placed upon it: it was merely intended to give examples of matters falling within the general provision of s 22(1). Therefore. the police were not entitled to retain the material seized.

Excluded or special procedure material or material covered by legal privilege

Under s 9, excluded or special procedure material or material covered by legal privilege cannot be seized during a search not under warrant and it is exempt from the s 8 search warrant procedure under s 8(1). However, the police may gain access to excluded or special procedure material by making an application to a circuit judge in accordance with Sched 1 or, in the case of special procedure material only, to a magistrate for a search warrant. Access to excluded material may only be granted where it could have been obtained under the previous law relating to such material. Excluded material is defined under s 11 to consist of material held on a confidential basis, personal records,[30] samples of human tissue or tissue fluid held in confidence and journalistic material held in confidence. Personal records include records held by schools, universities, probation officers and social workers. 'Special procedure material' defined under s 14 operates as a

---

29   [1993] 2 WLR 428; [1993] 1 All ER 56; (1992) 142 NLJ 635.
30   Defined in s 12.

catch-all category which is, it seems, frequently used[31] to cover confidential material which does not qualify as personal records or journalistic material.[32] A production order will not be made unless there is reasonable suspicion that a serious arrestable offence has been committed, the material is likely to be of substantial value to the investigation and admissible at trial. It should be noted that when inquiries relating to terrorist offences are made, Sched 7, para 3 of the Prevention of Terrorism (T.P.) Act 1989 allowed access to both special procedure and excluded material. This power is reproduced in Sched 5 of the Terrorism Act 2000. The judge only needs to be satisfied that there is a terrorist investigation in being, that the material would substantially assist it and that it is in the public interest that it should be produced. It may well be that once the first two requirements are satisfied, it will be rare to find that the third is not.

The ruling in *Guildhall Magistrates' Court ex p Primlacks Holdings Co (Panama) Limited*[33] made it clear that a magistrate must satisfy him or herself that there were reasonable grounds for believing that the items covered by the warrant did not include material subject to the special protection. The magistrates had issued search warrants authorising the search of two solicitors' firms. Judicial review of the magistrates' decision to issue a warrant was successfully sought; it was found that the magistrate had merely accepted the police officer's view that s 8(1) was satisfied rather than independently considering the matter.

The strongest protection extends to items subject to legal privilege, since they cannot be searched for or seized by police officers and therefore, the meaning of 'legal privilege' is crucial. Under s 10, it will cover communications between client and solicitor connected with giving advice or with legal proceedings. However, if items are held with the intention of furthering a criminal purpose they will not, under s 10(2), attract legal privilege. It seems that this will include the situation where the solicitor unknowingly furthers the criminal purpose of the client or a third party. In *Crown Court at Snaresbrook ex p DPP*[34] it was found that only the solicitor's intentions regarding the criminal purpose were relevant, but the House of Lords in Central Criminal Court *ex p Francis and Francis*[35] rejected this interpretation in finding that material which figures in the criminal intentions of persons other than solicitor or client will not be privileged. A judge must give full consideration to the question whether particular documents have lost legal privilege.[36]

This interpretation of s 10(2) was adopted on the basis that otherwise, the efforts of the police in detecting crime might be hampered, but it may be argued that it gives insufficient weight to the need to protect the special relationship between solicitor and client and, as argued below, may be vulnerable to challenge under the HRA.

---

31 See Lidstone, K (1989) NILQ 333, p 342.
32 For comment on these provisions see Stone [1988] Crim LR 498.
33 [1989] 2 WLR 841.
34 [1988] QB 532; [1988] 1 All ER 315.
35 [1989] AC 346; [1988] 3 All ER 375. For comment see Stevenson (1989) Law Soc Gazette 1 February, p 26.
36 *Southampton Crown Court ex p J and P* [1993] Crim LR 962.

New powers of seizure under the Criminal Justice and Police Act 2001

The Criminal Justice and Police Act 2001 (CJP) extends the power of seizure very significantly. The further powers of seizure it provides in s 50 apply to police powers of search under PACE and also to powers of seizure arising under a range of other statutes and applicable to bodies other than police officers, as set out in Schedule 1 of the CJP. The new power of seizure under s 50(1) depends on three conditions. The person in question must lawfully be on the premises. Once there, if he finds something which he has reasonable grounds for thinking is something he is authorised to seize, and it is not reasonably practicable at the time to determine whether what he has found *is* something he is authorised to seize, he can seize as much of it as is necessary to make that determination. A further new power of seizure under s 50(2) allows the person in question to seize material which he has no power to seize but which is attached to an object he does have the power to seize, if it is not reasonably practicable to separate the two.

This provision is significant since *inter alia* it allows police officers to remove items from premises even where they are not certain that – apart from s 50 – they have the power to do so. Thus a number of items can now be seized from premises although no power of seizure – apart from that now arising under s 50 – in fact arises.

As indicated above, the seizure of excluded or special procedure material is restricted, while material covered by legal privilege cannot be seized. Most significantly, s 50 may serve to undermine these protections for certain material since where such material is part of other material and cannot practicably be separated, it can be seized. It can also be seized where a police officer takes the view on reasonable grounds that it is something that he has the power to seize, although it turns out later that it falls within one of the special categories.

Special provisions are made for the return of excluded or special procedure material or material covered by legal privilege. For obvious reasons, these provisions are most significant in relation to material covered by legal privilege since they could aid in undermining the privilege. Under s 54 such material must be returned unless it falls within s 54(2). Section 54(2) covers a legally privileged item comprised in other material. Such an item will fall within that sub-section if the retention of the rest of the property would be lawful and it is not reasonably practicable to separate the legally privileged item from the rest of the property without prejudicing the use of the rest of that property. Section 57(3) provides that ss 53–56 do not authorise the retention of property where its retention would not be authorised apart from the provisions of Part 2 of the CJP. Under s 62 inextricably linked property cannot be examined or copied but under sub-section 4 can be used to the extent that its use facilitates the use of property in which the inextricably linked property is comprised.

The provisions of ss 57 and 62, taken together with the provisions of ss 54 and 55 appears to create two categories of property. Property within the first can be retained as it would have been but for the CJP. Property within the second is not subject to an obligation to return but cannot be treated as it would have been had it fallen within the first category. It can be used to a limited extent in accordance with s 62(4). Section 62 makes it clear that s 62(4) applies to excluded or special procedure material or material covered by legal privilege which has not been returned since it is compromised in other lawfully held property.

Thus, ss 50, 54 and 55 taken together do provide avenues to the seizure and non-return of the specially protected material. The new provisions thus circumvent the limitations placed on the seizure of excluded or special procedure material and, most importantly of all, provide an avenue to the seizure and use of legally privileged material. It can be said that for the first time legally privileged material has lost part of the protection it was accorded under the common law and under PACE.

These wide powers are 'balanced' by the provisions of ss 52–61 which provide a number of safeguards. Notice must be given to persons whose property has been seized under s 52, and under s 59 he or she can apply to the 'appropriate judicial authority' for the return of the whole or part of the seized property, on the ground that there was no power to seize, or that excluded or special procedure material, or legally privileged material, is not comprised in other property as provided for in ss 54 and 55. Under s 60 a duty to secure the property arises which includes the obligation under s 61 to prevent *inter alia*, copying of it. But despite these safeguards, it is unclear that the new powers, especially to seize and use legally privileged material, are compatible with the requirements of the Convention under the HRA.

Procedural safeguards under Code of Practice B

As revised in 1991 and 1995, Code of Practice B made under PACE provides for an increase in the amount of information to be conveyed to owners of property to be searched by use of a standard form, the Notice of Powers and Rights (para 5.7). It covers certain information including specification of the type of search in question, a summary of the powers of search and seizure arising under PACE and the rights of the subjects of searches. This notice must normally be given to the subject of the search before it begins, but under para 5.8 need not be if to do so would lead to frustration of the object of the search or danger to the police officers concerned or to others. These exceptions also apply under para 5.8 to leaving a copy of the warrant where the search is made under warrant. As explained above, s 18(4) provides that premises occupied or controlled by a person arrested for an arrestable offence may be searched after the arrest if an officer of the rank of inspector or above gives authority in writing. Under para 3.3, the authority should normally be given on the Notice of Powers and Rights. This clears up previous confusion[37] as to the form the authority should take.

Under original paras 4 and 5, the amount of information to be conveyed to the subject of a search depended on its status. Before any non-consensual search, an officer had to convey certain information orally to its subject: his identity, the purpose of the search and the grounds for undertaking it. In the case of a consensual search, it was only necessary to inform its subject of its purpose. Thus, the subject of an apparently consensual search dissatisfied with its conduct or intimidated by the officers concerned would have found it more difficult to make a complaint than would the subject of a non-consensual search. Under current paras 4 and 5 as revised, the subjects of all searches, regardless of the status

---

37 In *Badham* [1987] Crim LR 202 it was held that merely writing down confirmation of an oral authorisation was insufficient.

of the search, must receive a copy of the Notice of Powers and Rights and, under para 5.8 where a consensual search has taken place but the occupier is absent, the Notice should be endorsed with the name, number and station of the officer concerned. Oddly enough, it is not stated expressly that this information must be added to the Notice where the subject of a consensual search is *present*. Sub-paragraph 5.5 provides that officers must identify themselves except in the case of inquiries linked to terrorism, but this provision appears to apply only to non-consensual searches due to the heading of that section. It might be thought that a person who voluntarily allows police officers to come onto his or her premises does not need the information mentioned, but this is to ignore the possibility that such a person might wish to withdraw consent during the search but might feel too intimidated to do so.

The power to search and seize is balanced by the need to convey certain information to the subject of the search in question, thereby rendering officers (at least theoretically) accountable for searches carried out. However, it is arguable that the provisions are largely of a presentational nature: they ensure that a large amount of information is conveyed to the occupier and make an attempt to ensure that community relations are not adversely affected by the operation of the search power,[38] but have little to say about the way the search should be conducted. In other words, the regulation of the search power under Code B emphasises the provision of information to the owner of premises so that officers can be rendered accountable for searches made, rather than regulating circumstances relating to the nature of the search itself in order to minimise the invasion of privacy represented by such searches. In contrast, searches made in order to gain evidence relating to civil proceedings, under orders known as *Anton Piller* orders,[39] must observe a number of safeguards: they must be organised on weekdays in office hours so that legal advice can be obtained before the search begins; the defendant must be allowed to check the list of items to be seized before items can be removed and in some circumstances, an independent solicitor experienced in the execution of such orders must be present, instructed and paid for by the plaintiff.[40] It may be argued that there is a greater public interest in the prevention of crime than in ensuring that evidence is obtained by a party to civil proceedings and therefore the police need at times to make an immediate search of premises, but the power to do so without judicial intervention should, it is submitted, be narrowed down to instances where the urgency of the search was demonstrable, while Code B should contain clearer safeguards applicable to all searches, allowing, for instance, for a legal advisor to be present during a non-urgent search and including a clear prohibition on non-urgent searches at night. At present, searches should be conducted at 'a reasonable hour'[41] and under Note for Guidance 5A this is explained to mean at a time when the occupier or others are unlikely to be asleep. But, as discussed elsewhere,[42] the Notes for Guidance are not part of the Codes and are of

---

38 There is provision under para 2.5 for informing the local police community relations officer before a search of premises takes place if it is thought that it might adversely affect the relationship between the police and the community, subject to the proviso that in cases of urgency it can be performed after the search has taken place.

39 From *Anton Piller KG v Manufacturing Processes Ltd* [1976] Ch 55; [1976] 1 All ER 779, CA.

40 These conditions, and others, were laid down in *Universal Thermosensors Ltd v Hibben* (1992) 142 NLJ 195. For discussion of the concern created by such orders prior to this decision see (1990) 106 LQR 601.

41 Code B, para 5.2.

42 See Chapter 13, p 758.

very uncertain legal status: a prohibition on the non-urgent entry and search of property at night by State agents – perhaps one of the most unpleasant invasions of privacy possible – requires a more certain basis. The provision that an occupier may ask a friend or neighbour to witness the search unless there are reasonable grounds for believing 'that this would seriously hinder the investigation' would usually be inadequate to allow the occupier to obtain legal advice or the presence of a solicitor.[43]

Impact of the HRA and police accountability

The PACE search and seizure provisions are clearly intended to make lawful actions which would otherwise amount to trespass to property and to goods only in very specific circumstances and only where a certain procedure has been followed. Invasion of a person's home has traditionally been viewed as an infringement of liberty which should be allowed only under tightly controlled conditions and in the exercise of a specific legal power. The HRA affords specific expression to these values. The PACE provisions suggest some determination to strike a reasonable balance between the perceived need to confer on the police a general power to search property and the need to protect the privacy of the citizen. It is less clear that this is true of the TA and CJP provisions.

Breaches of Code of Practice B

Although Code B plays a part in creating safeguards for individual privacy, breaches of Code B will not attract tortious liability[44] and unlike Codes C, D and E (discussed in Chapters 13 and 14), exclusion of evidence will rarely operate as a form of redress because the courts are very reluctant to exclude physical evidence[45] and therefore it can have little impact on Code B provisions. Such reluctance may be justifiable since the significance of Code B can be attributed to their regulation of invasive procedures rather than to their concern to ensure the integrity of the evidence thereby obtained. As Chapter 13 demonstrates, Codes C, D and E, on the other hand, are arguably concerned more with outcome than with rights (with the exception of access to legal advice) which are fundamental in themselves. This difference is due partly to the nature of the rights involved: privacy of the home or of the person represents an important value in itself, unlike a person's right to the contemporaneous recording of an interview. However, this does leave something of a gap as far as a means of redress for breaches of Code B is concerned in comparison with the other three Codes, since the only means available will normally be by way of a complaint. The possibility of raising arguments in criminal proceedings under s 7(1)(b) of the HRA which might lead – in effect – to an enhancement of the status of the Codes of Practice is discussed in Chapter 14.[46]

Reliance on Art 8

Article 8 values might come to influence this scheme due to the use of arguments under s 7(1)(b) of the HRA, either raised in criminal proceedings, in civil actions against the

---

43 Paragraph 5.11.
44 PACE 1984, s 67(10).
45 See below Chapter 14, pp 890–96.
46 See Chapter 14, pp 851–54 and 902–07.

police for trespass, trespass to goods or for conversion, or as freestanding actions under s 7(1)(a) of the HRA. It could be argued that whether or not a basis in law for an entry to property is established, rendering the action non-trespassory, various features of the police actions amount to infringements of Art 8. Where it was clear that a legal basis for the entry itself was likely to be established, a freestanding action could be brought against the police as a public authority under s 7(1)(a), arguing that although the entry had such a basis, such features amounted to a breach of Art 8. The use of Art 8 arguments in criminal proceedings under s 7(1)(b) is discussed in Chapter 14.[47]

The European Court of Human Rights has found that entry, search and seizure can create interferences with all the Art 8 guarantees apart from that of the right to respect for family life.[48] Search for and seizure of documents is covered by the term 'correspondence' and the documents do not have to be personal in nature.[49] Such interferences can be justified only if they are in accordance with the law (Art 8(2)). This requirement covers not only the existence of national law, but its quality.[50] The statutory and common law powers probably meet this requirement[51] and have the legitimate aim of preventing crime or protecting national security.

It must further be shown that the interference 'corresponds to a pressing social need and, in particular, that it is proportionate to the legitimate aim pursued'.[52] It was found in the context of intercept warrants in *Klass v FRG*[53] that judicial or administrative authority for warrants would provide a degree of independent oversight: sufficient safeguards against abuse were available. This requirement was also stressed in *Kopp v Switzerland*.[54] It could be argued that the arrangements whereby magistrates issue search warrants might fail to meet this requirement since, although in appearance an independent judicial check is available before the event, the 'check' may be almost a formality in reality.[55] These provisions provide a scheme which is reasonably sound in theory, but which is dependent on magistrates observing its requirements. Research suggests that in practice, some magistrates make little or no attempt to ascertain whether the information a warrant contains may be relied upon, while it seems possible that magistrates who do take a rigorous approach to the procedure and refuse to grant warrants are not approached again.[56] It might be considered, therefore, that a breach of Art 8 might be established in respect of the practice of certain magistrates. It may be noted, however, that this argument failed in the Scottish case of *Birse v HM Advocate*.[57]

---

47   See pp 892–93, and also Chapter 13, pp 853–54.
48   See *Funke v France* (1993) 16 EHRR 297; *Mialhe v France* (1993) 16 EHRR 332.
49   See *Niemetz v Germany* A 251-B (1992).
50   *Kopp v Switzerland* (1999) 27 EHRR 91, paras 70–71.
51   In *McLeod v UK* (1998) 27 EHRR 493 powers to enter to prevent a breach of the peace were found to meet this requirement (paras 38–45).
52   *Olsson v Sweden* A 130 (1988), para 67.
53   (1978) 2 EHRR 214.
54   (1999) 27 EHRR 91.
55   See the comments of Feldman, D, *Civil Liberties and Human Rights in England and Wales*, 1st edn, 1993, p 414 and of Clayton, R and Tomlinson, H, *The Law of Human Rights*, 2000, p 863.
56   This point is made by Dixon, D (1991) 141 NLJ 1586.
57   Unreported, 13 April 2000.

It is also arguable that the decision of the House of Lords in *Central Criminal Court ex p Francis and Francis*[58] regarding material subject to legal professional privilege may require re-consideration in relation to Art 8. As indicated above, the House of Lords found that privilege is lost when the material is innocently held, but is for a third party's criminal purpose. The approach in *Niemetz v Germany*[59] was to the effect that a search of a lawyer's office had led to a breach of Art 8 since it was disproportionate to the aims of preventing crime and of protecting the rights of others. That decision also raises questions about the provisions of Part 2 of the CJP. Since the CJP was accompanied by a declaration of its compatibility with the Convention rights, legal advice to the government must have been to the effect that Part 2 was compatible with Art 8. Clearly, this advice could subsequently be found to be flawed; the judiciary remain entirely free (in the higher courts, as Chapter 4 explained) to make a declaration of incompatibility between one or more of the Part 2 provisions and Art 8.

Clearly it could be argued that the limitations placed on the seizure and the use of legally privileged material by Part 2 may represent a proportionate response to the aim of preventing crime under Art 8(2). In other words, an interference with the Art 8 rights represented by the existence of legislation or in any particular instance could be viewed as relatively minimal, consistent with the need to serve that aim. On the other hand, the use of Part 2 provisions in practice may undermine the relationship between client and solicitor. Probably the attitude of the courts will depend upon the facts of any instance which comes before them and upon the attitude of the particular court to the value of affording the convention rights real efficacy.

3 POWERS OF THE SECURITY AND INTELLIGENCE SERVICES

Introduction

Traditionally, the security and intelligence services were governed by informal non-statutory mechanisms. The Security Service (MI5) was governed by the unpublished Findlater-Stewart Memorandum and then by the Maxwell-Fyfe Directive published in 1952. The Intelligence Service (MI6) was governed by a Directive to 'C' – the title given to the Chief of the Service. Until 1994, MI6 'maintained [its] existence in legal darkness'.[60] After an existence which spanned almost all of the 20th century, it was only in 1989 that the Government admitted to the existence of the Security Service[61] and only in 1994 to the existence of the Secret Intelligence Service.[62] GCHQ, the signals intercept body, was also placed on a statutory basis in 1994.

---

58 [1989] AC 346; [1988] 3 All ER 375. For comment see Stevenson, *op cit*, fn 35.

59 A 251-B (1992).

60 Leigh, I and Lustgarten, L, 'The Security Service Act 1989' (1989) 52 MLR 801, p 802.

61 The Secret Service bureau was established in 1909 and became known as MI5 in January 1916.

62 See also Leigh, I and Lustgarten, L, *In From the Cold: National Security and Parliamentary Democracy*, 1994, *Coda* for discussion of the new statutory framework for MI6 and Wadham (1994) 57(6) MLR 916. For discussion of aspects of the new position of MI6 see Davies, P, 'Integrating intelligence into the machinery of British central government' (2000) 78(1) Public Administration 29.

The central impetus for change arose from the need to comply with the demands of the European Convention on Human Rights.[63] Once a model for the statutory framework of MI5 had been devised in the form of the Security Service Act 1989, based on the model used for the Interception of Communications Act 1985, also introduced to comply with the Convention, the model was extended to the Secret Intelligence Service and GCHQ in the Intelligence Services Act 1994. A complaints mechanism relying on deliberation in secret by a Commissioner and tribunals was created. At the same time, a level of parliamentary oversight of the agencies was added. Thus, in 1997, the Labour Government inherited a particular statutory framework. It largely adopted, it will be argued, the model it provided when it made changes to the agencies' accountability in the Regulation of Investigatory Powers Act 2000.

In the era of the Northern Irish peace process, fragile as it is, and of the HRA, with its guarantee of protection for individual privacy in Art 8, the powers of the three agencies raise a number of concerns. The Government considers that current levels of terrorist activity provide a justification for increasing the funding for the services. This view of the Government is reflected in the recent budgets for the three agencies and, as the Government puts it, it has 'set spending plans which will enable the agencies to face up to the formidable tasks, old, new and changing, which confront them'.[64] The Security Service has had a role in countering terrorist threats since the 1960s. But that role is likely to undergo some redirection in response to the redefinition of terrorism, discussed in Chapter 8,[65] which is now contained in s 1(1) of the Terrorism Act 2000. The Government and the parliamentary committee charged with oversight of the agencies, the Intelligence and Security Committee, agree in considering that such redirection aids in justifying the maintenance of the services: 'The [Intelligence and Security] Committee acknowledges the continued need for the intelligence and security agencies in a changed but still dangerous world and believes they must be maintained and funded in a sustainable way. The Government reached the same conclusions in the Comprehensive Spending Review.'[66]

But in its Third Report in 1998, the Committee raises concerns regarding the continued existence of the services in the current era:

> So far from being invented to justify the agencies' continued existence [new challenges to the services] are real enough, and the country rightly expects to be protected against them ... However, the agencies face these tasks in a new environment of greater openness and accountability. They also face them with new technologies available to bring new capacities for the collection of information in many forms, which may pose new challenges to ensuring that the privacy of law-abiding individuals is respected ... [in times of no grave national threat] public confidence can be very fragile. That is the inevitable consequence of operating within a 'ring of secrecy' which prevents a more balanced public view of their activities. The public must therefore be confident that there is adequate independent

---

63 See *Harman and Hewitt v UK* Appl No 1211 75/86; (1992) 14 EHRR 657.

64 *The Government Response to the Intelligence and Security Committee's Annual Report* Cm 4089, 1998, p 3, para 1. The figure for 1999/2000 was £743.2m for all three services; in 2000/2001 it was £745.0m: *The Intelligence and Security Committee Report 1997–98*, Cm 4073, p 9. Individual figures for the three services were not published.

65 Home Office and Northern Ireland Office, *Legislation against Terrorism: A Consultation Paper*, Cm 4178, 1998.

66 *Op cit*, fn 64.

scrutiny and democratic accountability on their behalf by people within that ring of secrecy. That is the task of this Committee.[67]

The Fourth Report, for 1998/99, also adopted a robust tone.[68] It took particular exception to the continuing refusal of the Government to publish a national audit office report on the excessive spending of the agencies on refurbishment. The Chairman, Tom King, said: 'The cloak of secrecy has been used to cover up inadequacies and serious lapses in expenditure control.' The Chairman of the Commons Public Accounts Committee endorsed this view on the day the Intelligence Committee's Fourth Report was published.

The Intelligence and Security Committee, in both its Third and Fourth Reports, is clearly signalling its concern at the probable tension between the continued existence of doubtfully accountable agencies, with an increasing remit, in an age when the expectations of accountability have never been higher. The implication is that the confidence in the balance supposedly struck by the statutory mechanisms between individual rights, especially to privacy, and the demands of secrecy, has never been more fragile.

While making gestures in the direction of openness and accountability, the statutory mechanisms, including the most recent one, the Regulation of Investigatory Powers Act 2000 (RIPA), are still, it will be argued, imbued with the culture of secrecy.[69] Therefore, it is questionable whether the more extensive statutory basis for the agencies' activities which is now available can create confidence in them. It has been shaken by a number of allegations from ex-MI5 or MI6 agents. *Spycatcher*, written by Peter Wright, a former member of MI5, alleged that MI5 had 'bugged and burgled its way around London', that the Service had tried to destabilise the Labour Government of Harold Wilson, and that the Director General from 1956–65, Roger Hollis, was a Soviet agent.[70] Richard Tomlinson, a former MI6 officer, was prosecuted in 1998, as was David Shayler, a former MI5 officer, in 2001[71] under the Official Secrets Act, in both instances for seeking to make public a number of grievances and concerns about the services. Concerns were also raised over MI5's and MI6's handling of the Vasili Mitrokhin affair in 1999[72] and regarding allegations of involvement in the attempt to assassinate Colonel Gadafy.

---

67 *Op cit*, fn 64, p vii.

68 Cm 4532, published on 25 November 1999.

69 Admittedly, the specifically operational aspects of the work of the security and intelligence services it covers would be secret anywhere in the world. But the tendency to curb the scrutinising role of the ordinary courts discussed in this chapter, especially in relation to the interception of communications, suggests that secrecy remains the dominant value.

70 See *AG v Times Newspapers Ltd* [1991] 2 All ER 398; [1992] 1 AC 191, discussed in Chapter 7. The last two allegations appear to be unreliable, see *MI5: The Security Service*, 3rd edn, 1998, pp 39–40; Mitrokhin, V and Andrew, C, *The Mitrokhin Archive*, 1999, confirmed that the allegation regarding Roger Hollis was untrue.

71 He was imprisoned in France pending determination of the extradition request which was so that he could face charges under the Official Secrets Act, s 1. France refused to extradite him. Once he returned to the UK, in August 2000, he was charged with an offence under s 1(1) of the Act: see *Shayler*, Transcript of the Preparatory hearing on 14 May 2001 and the judgment of the Court of Appeal on 28 September 2001. It was found that no defence to a charge under s 1(1) could arise by reliance on s 3 HRA, but that a defence of necessity could arise. See further Chapter 7, pp 349–51. For discussion of the background to the prosecution and the civil actions brought against Shayler, see Best, K, 'Implications of the Shayler affair' (2001) 6 J Civ Lib 18.

72 Mitrokhin was a KGB defector who identified Melita Norwood and others as Soviet agents in *the Mitrokhin Archive*, 1999 .

It will be contended below that ministerial responsibility, parliamentary oversight and the complaints and checking mechanisms of the relevant Commissioners and tribunals create only a limited and flawed control of the agencies. Although the changes to the tribunal system occurring under the Regulation of Investigatory Powers Act 2000 represent a step in the direction of greater accountability, they are, it will be argued, unlikely to have much impact in terms of creating stricter control, since in various respects, including the role of parliamentary oversight, the new tribunal system is based on the old model.[73] Without radical structural change to these methods, which will allow some breaching of the ring of secrecy, no real control will be achieved. The HRA may aid in providing some of the impetus for such change, but its direct impact on the agencies, in terms of ensuring protection for privacy, is likely to be minimal, for the reasons discussed below.

The framework for the agencies

The functions of MI5 are set out in s 1 of the Security Services Act 1989. Section 1(1) provides: 'the function of the Service shall be the protection of national security and, in particular, its protection against threats from espionage, terrorism and sabotage, from the activities of agents of foreign powers and from actions intended to overthrow or undermine Parliamentary democracy by political, industrial or violent means.' Section 1(3) adds the function of safeguarding 'the economic well-being of the UK' but only from external threats. The Act was amended to add ss 1(4) by s 1 of the Security Services Act 1996 in order to add to the two existing functions of the Security Service a third function: 'to act in support of the activities of police forces, [the National Criminal Intelligence Service (NCIS), the National Crime Squad and other law enforcement agencies in the prevention and detection of serious crime].' The words in square brackets were added by s 134(1), Sched 9, para 60 of the Police Act 1997. As indicated above, the definition of terrorism was greatly widened under the Terrorism Act 2000. This means that the functions of the Service have been widened quite significantly since the 1989 Act was passed. Sections 1(2) and 3(2) of the Intelligence Services Act 1994 provide that the function of MI6 and of GCHQ will be exercisable only in the interests of national security with particular reference to the defence and foreign policies of HM Government and in the 'interests of the economic well-being of the UK' and 'in support of the prevention and detection of serious crime'. MI6 is empowered under s 1(1) to obtain and provide information relating to the actions or intentions of persons outside the British Isles and perform tasks relating to such actions and intentions. Thus, MI6 is geared to external rather than internal security, in accordance with its traditional role, but this does not mean that it does not carry out operations on British soil. Targeted individuals may temporarily come to Britain and information relating to them may be found here. The police have pointed out that NCIS is a more open and accountable body than MI5 and, further, that there is little point in putting resources into a police intelligence body if MI5 then removes some of its main functions.

---

73   See below, pp 714 *et seq.*

In order to perform their functions, the agencies operate their broad powers under a secrecy and a lack of accountability which would not be acceptable in respect of the police or other law enforcement agencies. But under a model which gave a high priority to oversight and democratic accountability, it would be found that the agencies should carry out no function which could be carried out by a service, such as the police, which was more open to scrutiny. A confusion of functions between such services and MI5 is occurring due to the fact that this principle has not been followed, although given the secrecy surrounding the operations of the agencies, it is not possible to come to any conclusion as to the genuine necessity of affording them a serious crime function or of allowing them to investigate the activities of a wider range of groups by designating them 'terrorist'. MI5 is specifically empowered to function against terrorist groups. MI6 and GCHQ can operate against them, since part of their function is to further the interests of national security which terrorism is assumed to threaten. Thus, widening the definition of terrorism widens the function of all three agencies.

The Intelligence and Security Committee

The 1989 Act provided for no real form of parliamentary oversight of the Security Service.[74] But the 1994 Act set up, under s 10, the Parliamentary Committee, the Intelligence and Security Committee, to oversee the 'expenditure, administration and policy' of MI5, MI6 and GCHQ.[75] Operational matters were omitted from their remit. Thus, for the first time, all three services were made, to an extent, accountable to Parliament. The Committee's Report is not, however, presented directly to Parliament but to the Prime Minister, who may censor it before presentation on broad grounds – it need not be damaging to national security, merely to the continued discharge of the functions of the Services. Appointment to the Committee is by the Prime Minister. Since the Committee is not a Select Committee, it has no powers to compel witnesses to appear before it. The members of the Committee have been notified that s 1 of the Official Secrets Act will apply to them as though they were members of the services themselves and therefore, they will commit a criminal offence if they disclose any information or document they have obtained as a result of their work. They would have no defence that the disclosure revealed a serious abuse of power which could not be otherwise addressed, or that the information was already in the public domain. 'Sensitive' information can be withheld from the Committee by agency heads[76] and non-sensitive information can be withheld by the Secretary of State.[77]

It was clear at its inception that the extent to which the work of the Committee was likely to have a real impact on the agencies depended on its appointees and on the way they interpreted their role. The 1996–97 Report of the Intelligence and Security Committee made no recommendations as to independence at all, in quite strong contrast to the 1997–98 Report, which adopted a more adversarial approach. Tom King chaired the Committee over this period of time and appears to be adopting an increasingly robust

---

74 See further Leigh and Lustgarten, *op cit*, fn 60.

75 For discussion of the introduction of the Committee in 1994 see Leigh and Lustgarten, *op cit*, fn 62.

76 Schedule 3, para 3(2).

77 Schedule 3, para 3(4).

stance. The 1998 Report signalled a change of direction towards a more rigorous scrutiny, and this continued in the 1999 Report, also under his chairmanship.

The 1998 Report was completed after the system had been in place for four years. In its section on oversight, it looked especially at the oversight available in other countries, having talked in the past year to counterpart bodies. They found that other countries have 'more extensive forms of "independent" oversight'.[78] One feature of such 'more extensive' models of oversight is the Inspector General (IG), a full time appointment who has wide powers of access to operational and other information. The Commissioner for the Security Service has similar powers of access, but it is not his function to review operations and the tribunals only do so in response to a direct complaint. Clearly, many members of the public who might have grounds for complaint would not be able to bring one, since they would be unaware of the operation. An IG would be able to consider operational abuse of power without depending on a complaint. The Committee pointed out that it cannot 'investigate directly different aspects of the Agencies' activities' and it found that the Committee's reach should be extended by an additional 'investigative capacity'.[79] It considered that without this capacity, it cannot make authoritative statements and needed some reinforcement of authority. In its 'Future Programme of Work' it set forth a number of issues to be pursued in 1998 and 1999, including the question whether individuals should have rights in connection with the destruction or otherwise of any file held on them; protections against storage and use, against individuals' interests, of inaccurate information, and the implications of the European Convention. Following this Report, additional support was given to the Committee on a non-statutory basis, reflecting their interest in an 'Inspector General' model of accountability. This is a step forward in those terms, but since no powers are granted, the co-operation of the services will be on a consensual basis only.

Warrant procedure

The legal constraints on targets in the UK may be compared with those in Canada and the US. In the US, warrants are only issued if there is 'probable cause' that the target is a foreign power or agent of a foreign power and collection is for the purpose of obtaining foreign intelligence.[80] In Canada, warrants may be issued only if there are 'reasonable grounds' for believing that the warrant is required to investigate a threat to national security.[81] It is apparent that the constraints in these jurisdictions are narrower and, in particular, the serious crime work is not included. The functions of the agencies in assisting in preventing or detecting serious crime is likely to form a much smaller percentage of their work than will widening the definition of terrorism. The MI5 booklet published in 1998[82] mentions 'arrangements' governing the role of the Service in assisting in serious crime work and the need for a close working relationship with the other agencies in question.[83] The arrangements are not published. Therefore, two executive

---

78   See p 24, para 62.
79   See p 25, para 69.
80   Under the Foreign Intelligence Surveillance Act.
81   Under the Canadian Security Intelligence Service Act 1984, s 2.
82   *MI5: The Security Service* (*op cit*, fn 70).
83   *Ibid*, p 18.

bodies are left to determine, in a barely accountable and 'invisible' manner, the key issue of principle at stake here.

The warrant procedure for all three agencies is governed partly by ss 5 and 6 of the Intelligence Services Act 1994 and partly by Part II of RIPA. Under s 5(2) of the 1994 Act, the Home Secretary can issue a warrant authorising the 'taking of any such action as is specified in the warrant in respect of any property so specified or in respect of wireless telegraphy so specified'. In other words, members of the agencies can interfere in any way with property so long as it appears that the action would be of 'substantial value' to the agency in carrying out any of its functions.

The Security Services Act 1996 added sub-ss 3, 3A and 3B to s 5 of the 1994 Act. Section 5(3) provides that warrants issued to GCHQ and MI6 in respect of their 'serious crime' function 'may not relate to property in the British Islands'. Section 5(3A) provides that in respect of the Security Service's serious crime work a warrant may not relate to property within Britain unless s 3B applies. Section 3B applies if the conduct in question appears to constitute one or more offences and either involves the use of violence, results in substantial gain or is conduct by a large number of persons in pursuit of a common purpose or is an offence for which a person of 21 or over with no previous convictions could be expected to receive a sentence of imprisonment of three years or more.

The purpose of the 1996 Act was to allow the Security Service to aid the police in preventing and detecting serious crime, by which the Government stated that it meant organised crime. However, the terms of the Act do not limit its application to serious or organised crime. It could be used, for example, against persons engaging in public protest who might well (given the breadth and vagueness of some public order law), commit an offence, such as obstruction of the highway, and who can be said to be acting in pursuit of a common purpose. Thus, a distinction is created between the agencies in terms of what they may do in relation to property, and this is continued in Part II of the RIPA. But, clearly, all three were able to engage in other activities in relation to persons in the British Islands, whether under warrant or not, so long as, formally speaking, the activities were in accordance with their functions. This position became untenable under the HRA and therefore, in anticipation of its coming into force, such activities were provided with a statutory basis under the RIPA. 'Directed surveillance' and covert 'human intelligence sources' can be used by MI6 and GCHQ, but 'intrusive surveillance', which entails an intrusion onto 'residential premises', can normally be used only by MI5 in respect of its serious crime work.[84]

It was suggested in debate in Parliament that the 1994 Act should contain a clear set of principles which would govern and structure the operations of the services in carrying out these statutory functions. It was suggested that they should include the requirements that the more intrusive the technique, the higher the authority should be to authorise its use, and that except in emergencies, less intrusive techniques should be preferred to more intrusive ones.[85] The Government rejected these amendments to the 1994 Act on the ground that they were implicit in s 5 of the Act. Section 5 provides that the Secretary of State should be satisfied that 'what the action seeks to achieve cannot reasonably be

---

84   See RIPA 2000, s 42.
85   HC Standing Committee E, Col 72, 8 March 1994.

achieved by other means'. This imprecise requirement is clearly no substitute for the more detailed set of principles suggested. If a member of the Service wishes to intercept communications on the public telephone system, another level of control is imposed, since the procedure under the Interception of Communications Act 1985 applies (discussed below). The RIPA addressed the anomaly that members of the services could engage in various forms of surveillance in reliance merely on the procedure under the 1994 Act, but that in respect of this particular form, an extra layer of control was added.

The result of s 5 is that a private individual can have surveillance devices placed on his or her premises or can be subject to a search of the premises even though engaged in lawful political activity which is not intended to serve any foreign interest. An amendment to the Security Services Bill was put forward that would have exempted such a person from the operation of the legislation, but it was rejected by the Government.

The authorisation must be by the Home Secretary, personally, under s 6(1) of the 1994 Act, except in the case of emergency warrants which may be authorised by a senior official, with express authorisation from the Home Secretary. The arrangements for intrusive surveillance under the RIPA are similar, as explained below,[86] but no independent authorisation procedure is necessary in respect of the other two forms of surveillance. The s 6 warrant procedure begins with a letter from the agency to the Home Office. It is considered in the warrants division which may require further information in order to strengthen the application. As Leigh and Lustgarten point out, this process could be viewed as a gulling of their political master by collusion between 'the Security Service and its Whitehall counterpart', or it could be seen as 'conscientious control' over the requests, endowing stronger ones with greater credibility and rejecting weaker ones.[87] Under s 5 of the 1994 Act, the Home Secretary should then consider whether it is necessary for the action to be undertaken on the ground that 'it is likely to be of substantial value in assisting the agency in question in carrying out its function, as indicated above'. He must be satisfied that what is sought to be achieved could not be achieved by other means and as to the arrangements for disclosure of information obtained. It is not possible to ascertain how far each of these matters is subjected to serious scrutiny or how far, assuming that they were taken seriously, a Home Secretary would be able to detect weaknesses in the application. Obviously, these matters would depend partly on the particular Home Secretary in question. But applications are very rarely rejected and, as Lustgarten and Leigh point out, political considerations as well as legal ones enter into the approval.[88] The warrants are issued for six months initially by the Home Secretary and may be renewed by him for that period so long as it is thought necessary for them to continue. There is no overall maximum period and some warrants may therefore be, in effect, permanent. If issued by a senior official, the warrant ceases to have effect after two working days.

The warrant procedure has been compared unfavourably with that in other mature democracies. The Canadian Security Intelligence Service may only be granted warrants on the authorisation of a Federal Court judge, thus ensuring a measure of independent

---

86　See pp 697–98.
87　*Op cit*, fn 62, p 57.
88　*Ibid*, p 58.

oversight. Moreover, the warrant will not be issued unless the facts relied on to justify the belief that a warrant is necessary to investigate a threat to national security are set out in a sworn statement.[89] In the US, the warrants are authorised by special Foreign Intelligence Surveillance Act courts comprising selected federal judges, although in certain circumstances, the Attorney General can authorise searches or warrants by executive order only. These arrangements present a strong contrast with those in the UK, since there is no judicial involvement at all in the UK in the issuing of warrants under either the 1994 or 2000 Acts. Any judicial involvement can occur only after the warrant has been issued. Thus, the crucial stage of the procedure is entirely in executive hands – one part of the executive is authorising another to interfere with individual rights. The impact of judicial authorisation must not be overestimated; clearly, some judges may develop a tendency to rubber-stamp requests. But the fact of placing papers before a judge may foster internal scrupulousness in their preparation. Since many persons will have no means of knowing that they have been targeted and therefore will have no ability to make a complaint, judicial involvement at the complaints stage only is of marginal importance. The failure to allow such involvement in the warrant procedure may be viewed as one of the key weaknesses in the scheme.

The system for accountability therefore relies mainly on a level of ministerial control, but only as regards activities of the agencies which are under warrant or require ministerial authorisation under the RIPA. As indicated, a further, judicial level of control is then added which relates only to the warrant procedure. The Commissioner is supposed to provide oversight of the procedure, but only after the event. At present, the same Commissioner, Stuart-Smith LJ, operates as Commissioner in respect of all three agencies, and will be re-appointed to continue his role as 'the Intelligence Services Commissioner' under s 59 of the RIPA. The oversight is, however, limited. The Commissioner can only oversee the issuance of warrants under ss 5 and 6 of the 1994 Act; he cannot order that they should be quashed; nor can he order an operation against a particular group to cease. The Commissioner cannot address instances in which no warrant was necessary, since the procedure in question is not unlawful. The remit of the Commissioner precludes consideration of unauthorised actions since he can only consider whether a warrant was properly authorised. If an action does not require a warrant, such a question becomes irrelevant. This is also true of actions which are unlawful and unauthorised by warrant, such as burgling a property.

Personal files

The Intelligence and Security Committee has taken a particular interest in the creation and use of personal files stored by the agencies, particularly those on British citizens. A particular concern was to consider 'the protection for an individual against having information inappropriately or inaccurately gathered, stored and used against their interests.'[90] These files play a significant role in security vetting, which affects a wide

---

89 For discussion of the impact of this system in practice see Leigh, I, 'Secret proceedings in Canada' (1996) 34 Osgoode Hall LJ 113.

90 *Report of the Intelligence and Security Committee for 1997/98*, Cm 4073, p 16, paras 39 and 40.

range of jobs in the UK. It applies to senior staff in a range of government departments, to independent bodies such as the BBC and in the private sector.[91] Security checks will include consideration of information, if any, held on an applicant by MI5.

The Security Service currently holds 250,000 hard copy files on individuals and a further 4,000 are archived on microfiche. Of these, 17,500 are currently coded 'green'[92] or active, and 13,000 relate to British citizens. The Service is currently reviewing files for destruction by category. The Committee expressed concern that reviewing was restricted to individuals over 55. Thus, files may be retained on individuals under that age because they had 20 years ago joined an organisation then classed as subversive, whereas a file would not be opened on a person joining the same organisation today.[93] The Committee found: 'We believe ... that some form of independent check should be built into the process ...'[94] The Government response to this recommendation suggests that secrecy remains the overriding priority. 'The Government does not believe that the process of reviewing files for destruction would be assisted by independent scrutiny.'[95]

The Committee took a somewhat less robust view of the SIS and GCHQ records and data. SIS has 86,000 records, half of which relate to UK citizens. Many of them relate to the staff of the Agency and its contacts. Of these, 75% are closed and some relate back to 1909. Thus, it appears to have no destruction policy and of course no independent check that it is not holding files on British citizens needlessly. The argument for an independent check may not be as pressing as in respect of the Security Service, but it is clearly applicable, especially as internal procedures reveal an unawareness of the abuses which can arise if files are stored for many years without review.

Like SIS, GCHQ does not hold and create personal records in the same way that MI5 does. But its rationale is to hold personal data collected by intercepting communications. GCHQ informed the Committee that such data 'which may arise from collection under warrant *or otherwise* (emphasis added) is a necessary and sometimes key analytical tool'. GCHQ has a lawful basis for interception under s 5 of the 1994 Act and under s 3(2)(a)(i) of the 1985 Act. But these words imply that GCHQ is currently holding some personal data without a basis of legal authorisation. Since such holding of data was not a criminal offence or civil wrong, this practice of GCHQ could not be said to be unlawful until the HRA came fully into force. Assuming that it amounts to an infringement of Art 8, it is now unlawful, since it cannot be said to be in accordance with the law. As discussed below, it may well be the case that no avenue, other than the complaints mechanism, is available to an individual to challenge the holding of his or her personal information which has been obtained unlawfully. In future, such a matter could be brought before the

---

91 See First Report from the Select Committee on Defence, Session 1982–83, Positive Vetting Procedures in Her Majesty's Services and the Ministry of Defence HC (182/83) 242 and the Radcliffe Report, Cmnd 1681, 1962, Chapter 7; Linn, I, *Application Refused: Employment Vetting by the State*, London, 1990; Hollingsworth, M and Norton-Taylor, R, *Blacklist: The Inside Story of Political Vetting*, London, 1988. The current vetting guidelines are set out in a statement made at HC Deb Vol 251–766w, 15 December 1994.

92 This is part of the 'traffic lighting' process for files: 'green' files are active; 'amber' ones are closed but may have papers added; 'red' ones are closed and retained for research only.

93 *Ibid*, p 19, para 47.

94 *Ibid*, p 20, para 50.

95 *The Government Response to the Intelligence and Security Committee's Annual Report* Cm 4089, 1998, p 5, para 16.

new tribunal set up under the RIPA; this is discussed below. The Government has said that all GCHQ interception, use and retention of material is carried out only in accordance with the 1994 and, where appropriate, 1985 Acts and 'these arrangements are subject to continuing scrutiny by the Commissioners' under the two Acts.[96]

One means of allowing a check on the retention and use of personal information would be to allow some access, with use of editing, under the forthcoming Freedom of Information Act to the personal data held by all three agencies. However, the three agencies will all be excluded from the Act. They are also now fully exempt from the obligation to apply the data protection principles under the Data Protection Act 1998, on the basis that the files are held for national security purposes. Under the 1984 Act, personal data held on national security grounds was not exempt from the principles, although the agencies did not register under the Act on national security grounds. The protection is therefore weaker under the 1998 Act, although a person directly affected by the exemption can appeal against the issue of a national security certificate, under s 28 of the 1998 Act. Since the agencies, and MI5 in particular, have a role in relation to serious crime, this position is anomalous. As the Data Protection Registrar (now Commissioner) has argued, MI5 should be placed in the same position as the police in relation to this role.[97] The Commissioner has no general statutory remit to obtain access to files for monitoring purposes. But individual cases referred to him may raise general issues of file keeping. The position may be compared to that in Canada, where the agencies are subject to privacy and access to information legislation, although individuals have no right of access to their files and are not informed that the file exists. An edited version of the file may be made available which will be limited to information already in the public domain. The key point is that the *Commissioners* in Canada have access to the files. In the US, records may only be established and held if they are relevant to the conduct of authorised intelligence operations and they are subject to the Freedom of Information Act. Individuals can ask to see files; they may be given an edited version and the agency can choose neither to confirm nor deny that material has been withheld. These arrangements, qualified as they are, represent an improvement on the complete exclusion of the agencies from the relevant privacy and FoI legislation, as in the UK.

Complaints

Taking the Interception of Communications Act as a model, the 1989 Act set up a Commissioner under s 4 and a tribunal under s 5 as a means of oversight for MI5. The procedure for complaints and composition of the tribunal are dealt with in Scheds 1 and 2. The 1994 Act adopted the same model for MI6 and GCHQ under ss 8, 9 and Scheds 1 and 2.

No duty is imposed on the agencies to disclose the fact to an individual that an operation has occurred, after it is over. Most individuals will have no means of knowing

---

96   Government Response, p 6, para 19.

97   Our Answers: Data Protection and the EU Directive (95/46/EC), the Data Protection Registrar, July 1996. This position was also strongly criticised by Justice in its report *Under Surveillance: Covert Policing and Human Rights Standards*, 1998, p 90. For the position of the police under the 1998 Act, see Chapter 10, p 605.

that it has occurred and therefore will be unlikely to bring a complaint. If an individual brings a speculative complaint to the tribunal, uncertain whether surveillance or intrusion has occurred, the result may leave him or her none the wiser. The tribunals only reported that the result was unfavourable to the complainant, not whether an operation was indeed taking place, but was viewed as justified. The tribunals were not permitted to give reasons for their decisions.[98] Service personnel who felt that they had been required to act improperly in bugging or searching a person's property may not disclose the matter.

As discussed in Chapter 7, s 1 of the Official Secrets Act 1989 prevents members or former members of the security and intelligence services disclosing anything at all about the operation of those services. These provisions also apply to anyone who is notified that he or she is subject to the provisions of the section. Similarly, s 4(3) of the Act prohibits disclosure of information obtained by, or relating to, the issue of a warrant under the Interception of Communications Act 1985 or the Security Services Act 1989.

The 1989 and 1994 Acts provide no avenue for members of the agencies to complain to the Commissioner or Tribunals. Therefore, any disclosure of information to them or to the individual citizen concerned by such members would be a criminal offence under the Official Secrets Act. Thus, the persons who would be most aware of an abuse of power are denied this means of either supporting a complaint or enabling the individual concerned to instigate one. They can complain to the Security and Intelligence Services Staff Counsellor, appointed by the Prime Minister in 1987, but the office is, as Leigh and Lustgarten put it, 'a safety valve for conscience-troubled officials, rather than a form of oversight'.[99] The Reports of the Counsellor for the Prime Minister, Home Secretary and Foreign Secretary are unpublished and therefore there is no means of knowing whether his work has any benefit in terms of terminating unlawful or improper agency activities.

Under Sched 1, para 2 of the 1989 Act, the Security Service Tribunal could investigate two types of complaint: that the agency had instituted inquiries about the complainant and, if so, whether it had reasonable grounds for so doing. If the inquiries were due to a person's membership of a category of persons, the only question to be asked was whether there were reasonable grounds for believing him or her to be a member of that category, not whether the Service had reasonable grounds for investigating the group in question. Where information had been disclosed to an employer, the tribunal would investigate whether there were reasonable grounds for believing the information to be true. No inquiry is to be made into the misleadingness of the information or its factual truth. Nor can the tribunal consider the reasonableness of the categorisation of a particular group, or part of a group. The final ground for complaint was apparently wide: a person 'may complain to the tribunal if he is aggrieved by anything which he believes the Service has done in relation to him or any property of his'.[100] But the tribunal cannot investigate a complaint which relates to property and must pass it to the Commissioner who would utilise the principles applied by a court on an application for judicial review.[101]

---

98 Schedule 1, para 5(3) of the 1989 Act and Sched 1, para 6 of the 1994 Act.
99 *Ibid*, p 430.
100 1989 Act, Sched 1, para 1; 1994 Act, Sched 1, para 1.
101 1989 Act, Sched 1, para 4; 1994 Act, Sched 1, para 3(b).

The standard of scrutiny in the tribunals was unlikely to be rigorous: in *Secretary of State for Home Affairs ex p Ruddock*[102] (determined prior to the coming into force of the 1985 Act) the question was whether the decision of the Home Secretary in granting the warrant was 'so outrageous in its defiance of logic or accepted moral standards that no sensible person who applied his mind to the question to be decided could have arrived at it'. Since the tribunals can merely ask whether the agency had 'reasonable grounds' for its action, they cannot consider the questions whether the action was proportionate to the invasion of privacy and whether the action could have been carried out by the police. The tribunals both sit in secret and the complainant has no right to be informed of the findings of the investigation, only whether it is favourable or unfavourable. The Commissioner is operating under severe constraints, which arguably render his office a merely tokenistic one. He sits as a full time judge, has no staff and takes roughly two weeks' leave plus his own free time to carry out his role. He has been appointed to carry out his task in respect of all three agencies, and therefore he is expected to oversee bodies with, as noted, a combined budget of £747m and a staff of around 5,000.[103] In the US, Canada and Australia, the equivalent bodies have a full time staff.

Given these limitations, it is unsurprising to find that no complaint has ever been upheld by the tribunals or Commissioner. Between the introduction of the 1989 Act and the end of 1997, the tribunal set up under s 4 of the 1989 Act investigated 275 complaints; none was upheld.[104] The Report of the Security Services Commissioner presented to Parliament in June 1999[105] reports that the tribunal received 28 complaints in 1998, of which 18 were investigated and none was upheld. The Commissioner received 16 complaints and upheld none.[106] The Prime Minister has the power to censor the report before it is presented to Parliament, a power which is clearly exercised routinely. It appeared to be almost impossible, in practice, for a member of the public who was dissatisfied with the outcome of the complaints procedure to seek a remedy in the courts. The tribunals were set up as the only avenue of complaint and, under s 5(4) of the 1989 Act and s 9(4) of the 1994 Act, the decisions of the tribunals, including decisions as to their jurisdiction, were not questionable in any court of law.

Commentators have not viewed this system for complaints as a success and the Commissioner has implied that it was flawed from the outset. He has said that the limitations of the complaints mechanism are the fault of the 'architects' of the statutory provisions.[107] It has been said: 'A major cause for concern ... is the failure to confront adequately the need for accountability and review of the Services.'[108] John Wadham of *Liberty* described the Security Service Tribunal as 'useless'.[109] Gill found: 'this structure ... has been constructed neither for elegance nor impact'.[110] Lustgarten and Leigh sum up

---

102 [1987] 1 WLR 1482.

103 This is an estimate; the numbers have been censored from the Parliamentary Committee's Report 1998, pp 42 and 47.

104 *MI5: The Security Service, op cit*, fn 70, p 33.

105 Report of the Commissioner for 1998, Cm 4365.

106 *Ibid*, p 5.

107 Leigh and Lustgarten, p 438.

108 Ewing, KD and Gearty, CA, *Freedom under Thatcher*, 1989, p 178.

109 *Op cit*, fn 62, p 439.

110 Gill, P, *Policing Politics: Security Intelligence and the Liberal Democratic State*, 1994, p 295.

the problem: 'in so far as the government believed that by creating these new structures it would reassure the public that all is well it seriously miscalculated.'[111] As indicated below, a new complaints system has been established under the RIPA. A new tribunal has replaced the current ones and has also taken over the Commissioner's complaints' role. An Interception of Communications Commissioner as well as a Chief Surveillance Commissioner will be appointed under the RIPA. The remit of the new Commissioners will overlap with that of Stuart-Smith LJ, when he is re-appointed, since it will include some oversight of surveillance undertaken by the agencies.[112]

Impact of the HRA

Now that the HRA is fully in force, it can be said that the Convention represents a set of principles which may be read into the 1989, 1994 and 2000 Acts so long as no irremediable incompatibility between the statutory provisions and the rights exists.[113] Further, the three agencies in question, the relevant ministers and the oversight bodies (apart from the Parliamentary Committee)[114] as public authorities are bound by the rights under s 6 of the HRA. Although, formally, this is the legal position, the means whereby the Convention rights can be enabled to have a real rather than a theoretical impact on the agencies are highly circumscribed. They are discussed below, but although possible methods of bringing the HRA to bear on the agencies in court are considered, it is contended that the main impact of the HRA in this context will be an educative and cultural one: it will provide the openness the Parliamentary Committee currently favours with a clearer basis, and it may have an eventual, incremental impact on the work of the oversight bodies, in terms of the attitude they bring to their work. Most significantly, it may help to provide the impetus for the further evolution of the oversight.

Convention requirements

The Art 8(1) guarantees of respect for private life, the home and correspondence are clearly of most relevance to the activities of the agencies. The Introduction to Part III argued for a broad view of what constitutes invasion of privacy, based on the notion of control of personal information.[115] An interference with property will normally create an interference with one or more of the guarantees, as indicated above.[116] This would include planting a 'bug' on the premises in question, or entering them in order to remove property.[117] Less obvious invasions will also engage Art 8. The provisions of the Acts themselves may constitute a continuing invasion of privacy.[118] In *Harman and Hewitt v*

---

111 *Op cit*, fn 62, p 439.

112 See p 702. For the role of the Chief Surveillance Commissioner, see the same page.

113 The HRA, s 3.

114 Parliament itself is not a public body under s 6 and nor is a person exercising function in connection with proceedings in Parliament (s 6(3)(b)). It is probable that the Committee is not a public authority under this definition.

115 See pp 530–32.

116 See p 648.

117 See below, pp 703–06.

118 See *Klass v FRG* (1978) 2 EHRR 214.

UK,[119] the European Commission of Human Rights found that secret surveillance by MI5 of two former NCCL officers, Patricia Hewitt and Harriet Harman, had infringed Art 8(1), although they had not been subjected to direct intrusion. The intrusion was termed 'indirect' since information about them obtained from the telephone or mail intercepts of others had been recorded.

The use made of personal information, including disclosure to others, might also engage Art 8(1). In *MS v Sweden*,[120] the applicant complained that the use of medical records in respect of a compensation claim had infringed Art 8. The Court found that the disclosure did constitute an interference with the respect for private life, although it was found to be justified under Art 8(2).[121] The findings in *G, H and I v UK*[122] implied that the compiling and use of personal files by the Security Service might fall within Art 8, although they also raised questions regarding the onus placed on applicants to establish that they were likely to have been the victims of surveillance – in that instance of positive vetting for civil service posts. *Esbester v UK*[123] confirmed that a security check based on personal information would fall within Art 8. It may be concluded that many, if not almost all, activities of the agencies in obtaining, collecting, using and disclosing personal information are likely to engage Art 8.

Once Art 8(1) is engaged, the question is whether the interference can be justified under para 2. To be justified, State interference with the Art 8 guarantee must first be in accordance with the law. As indicated in Chapter 2, interpreting 'prescribed by law' (treated as an equivalent provision at Strasbourg), Strasbourg has asked first whether the interference has some basis in domestic law, and secondly whether it is of the right 'quality'.[124] In *Huvig v France*[125] and in *Kruslin v France*[126] the Court said that the requirement of quality means that the law 'should be accessible to the person concerned, who must moreover be able to foresee its consequences for him, and compatible with the rule of law'. The application in *Harman and Hewitt v UK*[127] was declared admissible since the activities of MI5 in placing the applicants under surveillance were not in accordance with the law. No sufficient basis in law existed at the time, and the successful application led to the passing of the 1989 Act. Although there is room for argument that certain of the terms used in the 1989 and 1994 Acts are too imprecise and broad to satisfy the 'in accordance with the law' requirement, it is unlikely that this would be found to be the case in respect of primary legislation in this context, unless the domestic courts are prepared to take a much stricter view of that requirement than that taken at Strasbourg. In *Christie v UK*,[128] the Security Service and Interception of Communications Acts were both found to meet this requirement and the Commission noted: 'the [Strasbourg] case law

---

119 Appl No 121175/86; (1992) 14 EHRR 657.
120 (1999) 28 EHRR 313.
121 On the grounds of being necessary in a democratic society to further the economic well being of the State.
122 15 EHRR CD 41.
123 18 EHRR CD 72. See also *Harman v UK* Appl No 20317/92 (1993) unreported.
124 See *Sunday Times v UK* A 30, para 49 (1979), discussed in Chapter 5, pp 229–30.
125 (1990) 12 EHRR 528, para 26.
126 (1990) 12 EHRR 547, para 27.
127 Appl No 121175/86; (1992) 14 EHRR 657.
128 78-A DR E Com HR 119.

establishes that the requirements of forseeability in the special context of sectors affecting national security cannot be the same as in many other fields'. Nevertheless, in criticising the provisions of the 1996 Act, Peter Duffy and Murray Hunt have argued that it breaches Art 8[129] since it probably does not pass the Convention requirement that an interference with private life should comply with rule of law principles. Executive discretion is so unfettered under the Act that any interference may not be 'in accordance with the law' as interpreted in *Huvig v France*[130] and *Kruslin v France*.[131] No application from the UK has been made since the passing of the 1996 Act and therefore, the 'in accordance with the law' question cannot be regarded as finally settled.

In *Esbester v UK*,[132] which concerned the alleged supply of information by MI5 regarding the applicant's membership of the Communist Party of Britain and of CND, leading to the revocation of a job offer, the Commission found that the 1989 Act complies with the 'in accordance with the law' requirement since the grounds under s 3 were expressed sufficiently precisely. This was a cautious, narrow application of the Convention requirements by the Commission. In *Leander v Sweden*,[133] which concerned the holding of information in a secret police register, the Court found that unpublished statements explaining the law could not meet the accessibility requirement. Since, as indicated above, vetting procedures are either unpublished or have not been placed on a statutory basis, it might have been expected that they would fail to meet this requirement. The Commission in *Esbester* seemed to fail to distinguish between the different invasions of privacy created by vetting, and to have failed to look for a satisfactory basis in law in relation to the interference created when the information is supplied. Possibly this is a context in which the Court will eventually allow a narrower margin of appreciation in scrutinising the quality of the domestic basis for vetting more rigorously, bearing in mind its deterrent effects which may undermine freedom of association. Chapter 8 contends that the Court's freedom of association jurisprudence in the context of membership of political groups has recently become somewhat more interventionist.[134] Since security vetting tends to raise issues under both Art 8 and Art 11, it is possible that such a stance may also become more evident under Art 8.

Any residual activities undertaken by the Security and Intelligence Services which at present are not covered by the procedures under the 1994 and 2000 Acts may not be in accordance with the law, assuming that the primary right under Art 8(1) is engaged. For example, at present, agents must acquire a warrant if they intend to enter property or interfere with it. They are also bound by the terms of Part I of the RIPA; under s 1, as discussed below, it is a criminal offence to tap into a public or private telecommunications system without authorisation. But certain surveillance techniques may not be covered by Parts I or II of the RIPA. Until the inception of the HRA, use of such techniques was lawful under civil or criminal law in the sense that since no law forbade them, they were

---

129 See (1997) 1 EHRR 11.
130 (1990) 12 EHRR 547.
131 (1990) 12 EHRR 528.
132 18 EHRR CD 72. See also *Harman v UK* Appl No 20317/92 (1993) unreported.
133 (1987) 9 EHRR 443.
134 See p 398.

assumed to be permitted. The Intelligence and Security Committee in its 1998 Report[135] spoke of 'executive and judicial checks that intelligence and security services are obeying the law, in particular on acts which would be unlawful but for express authorisation'.[136] The implied distinction is between acts which do not require such authorisation and acts which do. But under the HRA it is unlawful for a public authority to fail to abide by the Convention rights and therefore, as explained below, this distinction between acts which require express authorisation and those which do not will tend to break down. All these activities require a basis in law under the HRA since all, or almost all of them represent an infringement of privacy. Following the principle laid down in *Harman and Hewitt v UK*,[137] it is clear that placing the use of certain surveillance activities on a legal basis, which includes requiring warrant applications, is insufficient if others remain unregulated.

Christie v UK[138] concerned an interference, telephone tapping, which requires a warrant if it is not to amount to a criminal offence, as the Commission pointed out. No breach of Art 8 was found. It is unclear, but possible, that had the complaint concerned a procedure which did not require a warrant but which infringed Art 8, its basis in law might have been viewed as insufficient, given that no involvement of the Secretary of State in checking warrants or, under s 6 of the 1985 Act, in reviewing the use of resultant material, would have been necessary.

This contention must be put forward tentatively. It may be that activities which did not require authorisation until the inception of the HRA might be said to have a form of legal basis under the statutory provisions if they are carried out in accordance with the stated functions of the agencies in the 1989 and 1994 Acts. But it is suggested that this basis is so exiguous and leaves discretion so unfettered that it may in future be found to fail to satisfy the 'accordance with the law' requirement. The case of *G, H and I v UK*[139] raised questions concerning the efficacy of the 1989 Act, although the applications failed. As indicated above, the RIPA is intended to provide the necessary legal basis. Clearly, there may still be activities of the agencies which fall outside it. Further, it is questionable whether the RIPA itself provides a basis of sufficient quality, a matter that is discussed further below.

Assuming that an interference is 'in accordance with the law', under the 1989, 1994 or 2000 statutes, it must also, under Art 8(2), have a legitimate aim, be necessary in a democratic society and be applied in a non-discriminatory fashion (Art 14). In cases of invasion of privacy by the State, Strasbourg's main concerns have been with the requirements of 'in accordance with the law' and 'necessary in a democratic society'. In this context, the 'legitimate aim' requirement has always been found to be satisfied. This is unsurprising since the grounds available for interference are so broad. They are: the interests of national security, public safety or the economic well being of the country, the prevention of disorder or crime, the protection of health or morals, the protection of the rights or freedom of others. The provision against non-discrimination under Art 14 has not been so far a significant issue in the State invasion of privacy jurisprudence. The

---

135 Cm 4073.
136 *Ibid*, p 23.
137 Appl No 121175/86; (1992) 14 EHRR 657.
138 78-A DR E Com HR 119.
139 15 EHRR CD 41.

Court has interpreted 'necessary in a democratic society' as meaning: 'an interference corresponds to a pressing social need and, in particular, that it is proportionate to the legitimate aim pursued.'[140] As explained in Chapter 4, the doctrine of proportionality is strongly linked to the principle of the margin of appreciation. The width of that margin appears to depend partly on the aim of the interference in question and partly on its necessity. In relation to the aim of national security, the Court has allowed a very wide margin to the State.

In *Klass v Federal Republic of Germany*[141] the European Court of Human Rights found, bearing the margin of appreciation doctrine in mind, that German telephone tapping procedures were in conformity with Art 8 since, *inter alia*, they provided for compensation in proceedings in the ordinary courts for persons whose phones had been unlawfully tapped. The legality of such interceptions could be challenged in the ordinary courts. No such provision is available under the Security Services Act 1989 or the Intelligence Services Act 1994 in respect of analogous intrusions, although, theoretically, the old tribunals could award compensation, either of their own motion or on a reference from the Commissioner.[142] This system would appear to represent a significantly lower standard of accountability than the West German one in respect of phone tapping and it is at least possible that a breach of Art 8 would have been found in *Klass* had the margin allowed to Germany been narrower.

Leander v Sweden[143] concerned rather similar complaints mechanisms. Information on the applicant was stored on a secret police register for national security purposes and used for employment vetting. This created an interference with Art 8(1), but a wide margin was allowed to the State in choosing the means of protecting national security. The aggregate of remedies available, recourse to an independent Ombudsman and Chancellor of Justice, were found to be sufficient to satisfy Art 13. In *Harman v UK*[144] and *Esbester v UK*,[145] the Commission found that the 1989 Act complied with the procedural requirements of Art 8(2), at least in the national security context. In *Christie v UK*,[146] in respect of the almost identical mechanisms under the 1985 Act, the Commission found, 'having regard to the wide margin of appreciation in this area', the safeguards provided by the tribunal and the Commissioner were sufficient in the instant case.

These findings need not be taken to mean that the oversight mechanisms provided under the 1989 and 1994 Acts, and now under the 2000 Act, meet Convention requirements. They were made in relation to the particular case, not as abstract comment on such mechanisms in general, and they were heavily influenced by the margin of appreciation, especially wide where national security is in issue. As argued in Chapter 4, that doctrine is not available at national level and this, it is contended, means that it should not influence national decision makers. An activist domestic judge considering,

---

140 *Olsson* v *Sweden* A 130 (1988), para 67.

141 (1978) 2 EHRR 214.

142 Schedule 1, para 6(1) and para 7(2) of the 1989 Act. Schedule 1, para 8(1)(b) and para 8(2)(b) of the 1994 Act.

143 (1987) 9 EHRR 443.

144 Appl No 121175/86; (1992) 14 EHRR 657.

145 18 EHRR CD 72.

146 78-A DR E Com HR 119.

judicially or extra-judicially (assisting the new tribunal, or as a member of it, or on appeal) whether the domestic complaints or reference provisions meet Strasbourg standards, and untrammelled by the margin of appreciation doctrine, might conclude that the controls built into the UK system under the 1989, 1994 and 2000 Acts are insufficient to prevent abuse. The framework is largely based on scrutiny of the procedure after the event and in a manner which keeps most of its key aspects in the hands of the executive. In this respect it fails to accord with the rule of law, since a part of the executive is authorising another part to invade rights; the checking procedure which is then marginally available appears to provide a largely illusory protection and in respect of key aspects of it, the only recourse is to the executive again. Arguably, the safeguards would not appear to satisfy Art 8(2).

But it is more probable that the judiciary would find that traditional notions of deference in the national security context would yield the same result as the application of the margin of appreciation doctrine.[147] There are signs, however, that at Strasbourg, in its very recent decisions, the Court is becoming less deferential towards claims of national security, although admittedly they have been in the context of Art 6 rather than Art 8, a significant difference due to the qualifications under Art 8.[148] The question whether the new, single tribunal provides an effective remedy for the citizen is discussed below.[149]

Using the HRA in practice

Clearly, there have always been, theoretically, methods of seeking to curb the agencies' powers when they impinge on individual citizens. Agents could be prosecuted for burglary, for example, if the action was unauthorised or improperly authorised. Prosecution of agents is, however, highly unlikely, since no means of referring an investigation to the police is provided in the statutes; further, any risk of revealing secrets would probably be avoided simply by taking a decision not to prosecute. It would also be difficult to acquire evidence due to the provisions against providing evidence to complainants. Actions for trespass to property or other tortious liability could be brought against agents, although the secrecy of operations makes this very unlikely. Any such action brought in the post-HRA era would have to accord with the Convention. The HRA extends the theoretical protection available for the citizen since, under ss 6, 7 and 8, it creates civil liability where activities are carried out that were not previously unlawful, but which breach the Convention guarantees. However, allegations that such breaches have occurred would have to be brought in the new tribunal created under s 65 of the RIPA, not in the ordinary courts, as indicated below.[150]

The new tribunal has a duty under s 6 of the HRA to comply with the Convention in adjudicating on complaints and the Commissioner will have such a duty in overseeing not only warrants, but also the discharge of the duties of the Home Secretary and the agencies under the RIPA. The tribunal, Commissioner and Home Secretary are bound by the Convention under s 6; they are also providing oversight of bodies which are themselves so bound.

---

147 See further Chapter 4, pp 186–87. See also the *Rehman* case, discussed in Chapter 15, p 956.
148 *Tinnelly v UK* (1998) 27 EHRR 249 (discussed below, p 721); *McElduff v UK* Appl No 21322/92.
149 See pp 723–24.
150 See pp 714 *et seq.*

However, reliance on court action in efforts to secure the agencies' compliance with the guarantees will be very unlikely, largely due to the secrecy of the operations. Action in the ordinary courts at the citizen's instigation may in any event be almost entirely ruled out. As indicated above, ouster clauses contained in s 5(4) of the 1989 Act and s 9(4) of the 1994 Act barred the way to obtaining judicial review of the decisions of the Commissioner and tribunals. Both were post-*Anisminic*[151] ouster clauses in that they covered decisions of the tribunals and Commissioner as to their jurisdictions. The new tribunal will also be protected by such a clause, although there will also be a very narrow right of appeal. Judicial review of ministerial decisions in the ordinary courts appears to be ruled out since complaints should be brought to the relevant tribunal or Commissioner and now to the new tribunal. However, judicial review could be sought, it was made clear in the preparatory hearing in *Shayler*,[152] of the refusal of a minister or other person within s 12 of the Official Secrets Act 1989 to authorise a member of the agencies to disclose matters relating to the work of the services.[153] Any such refusal would have to comply with the Convention rights, and a court considering the matter would not merely consider whether the decision was reasonable, but whether it had so complied.

Security vetting in the UK, taking into account information held on an applicant by MI5, raises a number of Convention issues. The position of applicants who are dismissed or refused employment as regards obtaining recourse to industrial tribunals has recently improved due to the government response to the findings of the European Court of Human Rights in *Tinnelly v UK*.[154] The Court found that a ministerial certificate, stating that the reasons for the failure to employ the applicants were national security ones, effectively blocked the applicants' claim, since the judge could not go behind its terms and consider the claim, and therefore a breach of Art 6 had occurred. As a result of the ruling, the law as regards employment hearings in which national security is a factor was changed. Section 90 of the Northern Ireland Act 1998 provides for the creation of a tribunal, modelled on the Special Immigration Appeals Tribunal, to review the issue of ministerial certificates in Northern Ireland.[155] Thus, the issue of national security will be justiciable. However, the extent to which the evidence can be tested will be questionable. As White puts it: 'the central difficulty with the type of Tribunal set up by the 1998 Act is that it attempts to create an adversarial forum where one of the parties is severely hampered in presenting his or her case.'[156] This tribunal provided a model for the new tribunal to be set up under the RIPA; the discussion of its procedure and its compatibility with the Convention below are therefore of relevance. Section 193 of the Employment Rights Act 1996 and s 10 of the Employment Appeals Tribunals Act 1996 were amended[157] so that complaints of unfair dismissal cannot be dismissed on national

---

151 *Anisminic Ltd v Foreign Compensation Commission* [1969] 2 AC 147. See further p 719, fn 389.

152 Transcript of the Hearing of 14 May 2001, para 25.

153 Under the Official Secrets Act 1989, ss 7(3)(b) and s 7(5); see further Chapter 7, p 348.

154 (1998) 27 EHRR 249. For discussion, see McEvoy, K and White, C, 'Security vetting in Northern Ireland' (1998) 61 MLR 341, pp 349–54.

155 For discussion see White, C, 'Security vetting, discrimination and the right to a fair trial' [1999] PL 406–18.

156 *Ibid*, p 413.

157 By the Employment Rights Act 1999, Sched 8. Security and Intelligence service members may also have access to industrial tribunals, under Sched 8.

security grounds unless it is demonstrated that the reason for dismissal was on those grounds. All these tribunals, including the new one in Northern Ireland, are bound by s 6 of the HRA, and therefore their procedure must comply with the Convention, and the Convention points considered above could be raised before them. In industrial tribunals, under the previous position, the assertion of national security grounds would have precluded their consideration.

The possibility of further actions at Strasbourg in future cannot be ruled out, probably under Arts 8, 6 or 13, despite the fact that at the present time, as indicated below, the domestic arrangements probably satisfy the Convention requirements in a number of respects. As Chapter 2 points out, decisions of the Commission, taken some years ago and heavily influenced by the margin of appreciation, may not reflect the stance of the Court over the next few years, post-2000. Given the arguments canvassed here, it might be argued that no domestic remedy which must be exhausted, other than that represented by the new tribunal procedure exists; such absence would speed up the process of taking a case. In other fields, the HRA itself might offer such a remedy which would require exhaustion in the ordinary courts, but in this one that argument is much weaker owing to the provisions of ss 65 and 67(8) of the RIPA.

Conclusions

Consideration of the oversight and accountability system above indicates that no fundamental change has taken place and is unlikely to do so as a result of the inception of the HRA. There are signs of a strengthening accountability, taking into account the RIPA changes, particularly the introduction of the new tribunal, but the mechanisms are still, it is contended, too weak to live up to the expectations currently created in the new era of openness and accountability under the HRA. At the time when they were put in place, the mechanisms were viewed as a radical departure from the old order and all that could be expected of the governments in question. Now, although their inadequacies are apparent, they have provided the model for the mechanisms provided under the RIPA. In the current era, the assumptions underlying them look more questionable.

But the introduction of such mechanisms and the extension of a statutory basis for the agencies, under the RIPA, are first steps in a process. It is perhaps no longer likely, now that these first steps have been taken, that the impetus for greater accountability will come from Strasbourg, and the barriers in the way of using the HRA in the domestic courts to create more accountability look almost insurmountable, except, to an extent, in criminal proceedings. It has been suggested that the impetus is most likely to come from pressure from the current oversight mechanisms themselves, especially the Parliamentary Committee, from MPs and from commentators. It is possible that greater accountability will be achieved through the operation of the new tribunal but, as argued below, its efficacy is clearly open to question.

4 THE INTERCEPTION OF COMMUNICATIONS

Introduction

The interception of communications clearly presents a profound threat to the core value of privacy identified in the Introduction to Part III, informational autonomy. However, a State has a duty to preserve national security and to prevent and detect crime. But, as Leigh and Lustgarten put it: 'in attempting to protect democracy from threats such as terrorism there is the ever-present risk that ... that which was to be preserved has been lost.'[158] The approach which succeeds in preserving respect for democracy and for the value of individual privacy, as a hallmark of democracy, while affording respect to State interests, is one which is increasingly reflected in the jurisprudence of the European Court of Human Rights, even taking into account the wide margin of appreciation conceded in this particular area.[159]

Methods of communication and, in response, methods of interception have become increasingly sophisticated. Telephonic interception was possible for much of the 20th century, but its incidence and the interception facilities have recently increased.[160] In other words, its value in terms of combating crime and terrorism has long been recognised. But legal recognition of the harm interception causes, in terms of creating invasions of privacy, has lagged behind. Prior to 1985, there was no requirement to follow a particular legal procedure when authorising the tapping of telephones or the interception of mail. The tapping of telephones was neither a civil wrong[161] nor a criminal offence. Interference with mail was a criminal offence under s 58 of the Post Office Act 1953, but under s 58(1) such interference would not be criminal if authorised by a warrant issued by the Secretary of State. The conditions for issuing warrants for interception of postal or telephonic communications were laid down in administrative rules which had no legal force.[162] Under these rules, the interception could be authorised in order to assist in a criminal investigation only if the crime was really serious, normal methods had been tried and had failed, and there was good reason for believing that the evidence gained by the interception would lead to a conviction. If the interception related to security matters, it could be authorised only in respect of major subversion, terrorism or espionage, and the matters obtained had to be directly useful to the Security Service in compiling information allowing it to carry out its function of protecting State security.

The Interception of Communications Act 1985 was introduced as a direct result of the ruling in the European Court of Human Rights in *Malone v UK*[163] that the existing British warrant procedure violated the Art 8 guarantee of privacy. The Court held that UK domestic law did not regulate the circumstances in which telephone tapping could be

---

158 Leigh and Lustgarten, *op cit*, fn 62, p 41.

159 See, eg, the pronouncements of the Court in *Klass v FRG* (1978) 2 EHRR 214.

160 Report of the Commissioner under the Interception of Communications Act 1998, published June 1999, Cm 4364, p 2, para 13 and p 11.

161 *Malone v MPC (No 2)* [1979] Ch 344.

162 See Report of the Committee of Privy Councillors, Cmnd 283, 1957.

163 (1984) 7 EHRR 14; for comment see (1986) 49 MLR 86.

carried out sufficiently clearly or provide any remedy against abuse of the power. This meant that it did not meet the requirement of being 'in accordance with the law' under Art 8(2). The decision therefore required the UK Government to introduce legislation to regulate the circumstances in which the power to tap could be used.

Thus, the driving force behind the response of the UK Government in the Interception of Communications Act 1985 was the need to provide a statutory basis for interception. Nevertheless, it was an incomplete reform. Despite its misleading name, the 1985 Act only covered certain limited means of intercepting communications. It did not cover interception by means of listening devices or all forms of telephone tapping. It covered the interception of only one means of telephonic communication – communication via the public telecommunications system. This covered telephone, fax, telex and any other data transmission on the system, such as e-mail.[164] Given the immense increase in the use of mobile phones,[165] pagers, cordless phones, the potential for e-mail transmission outside the telecommunications system, and the growth of internal telephone systems over recent years, the Act became increasingly marginalised. Marginalisation was likely to increase since e-mails are likely to be sent more frequently via mobile phones, using satellites.[166] It was therefore apparent that the statutory basis for interception provided by the 1985 Act was inadequate and would probably be shown to be so in reliance on the HRA.[167] The Labour Government responded by introducing a far more comprehensive basis under the Regulation of Investigatory Powers Act 2000, Part I.

The Regulation of Investigatory Powers Act 2000, Part I (RIPA)

The intention of the Labour Government was to bring all forms of interception within the RIPA, Part I so that the 1985 Act would be superseded and could be repealed.[168] Under s 2(1) of the RIPA, the term 'public telecommunications system' used in s 2(1) of the 1985 Act, covers any system 'which exists (whether wholly or partly in the UK or elsewhere) for the purpose of facilitating the transmission of communications by any means involving the use of electrical or electro-magnetic energy'. This includes all such systems which provide or offer a telecommunications service to the public or part of it. This definition would cover all the forms of communication, including e-mail, mentioned above, provided by any private company.[169] Section 2(1) of the RIPA also covers private telecommunications systems – most obviously those confined to a particular company or

---

164 Prior to the inception of the RIPA 2000, the government maintained that some use of email was covered by the 1985 Act where public telephone lines were used.

165 Mobile to mobile communication would appear to fall outside the 1985 Act. Mobile communication which partially uses the telecommunications system (when a system such as BT Cellnet or Vodafone sends a signal to the telecommunications system) may be within it.

166 Possibly without use of a 'server' computer.

167 See the Consultation Paper 'Interception of Communications in the UK' (1999) Cm 4368.

168 Part I has repealed the key sections of the 1985 Act: ss 1–10, s 11(2)–(5), Sched 1.

169 These would include, eg, BT, Orange, Vodafone. It would also cover other providers of e-mail systems such as Freeserve or Yahoo. However, it is in fact unclear that the technology to intercept e-mails sent via the internet is available. Such e-mails are sent by so called 'split package' technology; the message is split into a number of different packages, sent by different global routes. If a hundred million messages are sent a day, split into tiny particles, interception of particular messages may be almost impossible.

body – although its coverage of private systems is limited to those which are attached to the public system directly or indirectly.[170] Its wording appears to be wide enough to cover most forms of telecommunication currently available, apart from entirely self-standing private systems,[171] although not necessarily those which may arise in the near future. Ironically, the point was made in parliamentary debate that 'the Bill does not recognise the changing technologies'.[172]

Issuance of warrants

The 1985 Act provided very wide grounds under s 2(2) on which warrants for the purposes of interception could be authorised by the Secretary of State, and the same grounds appear in the RIPA, with one addition. Under s 5(3), a warrant may be issued if necessary '(a) in the interests of national security'; '(b) for the purpose of preventing or detecting serious crime';[173] or '(c) for the purpose of safeguarding the economic well-being of the UK'. In relation to the third ground, the information must relate, under s 5(5), to 'the acts or intentions of persons outside the British Isles'. This wording almost exactly reproduces that used under s 2(4) of the 1985 Act. These grounds are significantly wider than those under the old Home Office guidelines previously relied upon in order to authorise warrants. The last ground falls under sub-para (d): 'in circumstances appearing to the Secretary of State to be equivalent to those in which he would issue a warrant by virtue of paragraph (b), for the purpose of giving effect to the provisions of any international mutual assistance agreement.' This ground relates to Art 16 of the EU draft Convention on Mutual Assistance in Criminal Matters.[174] Its purpose is to require satellite operators based in the UK to provide technical assistance to another Member State. The discussion below reveals that the safeguards relating to warrants issued on this ground are significantly weaker than those relating to the other three. This is an instance in which the EU's 'Third Pillar' policies relating to law and order and national security have allowed decisions to be taken on matters which may infringe human rights, possibly to the extent of breaching the Convention. Such decisions are taken within 'a framework where the EU's democratic deficit is most prominent'.[175]

Section 5(2) of the RIPA, however, contains a stronger proportionality requirement than that contained in s 2(3) of the 1985 Act. The Secretary of State 'shall not' issue an interception warrant unless he believes that the conduct it authorises 'is proportionate to what is sought to be achieved'. This includes asking, under s 5(4), whether the information which it is thought necessary to obtain under the warrant could reasonably be obtained by other means. This question also had to be asked under s 2(3). But s 5(2)

---

170 Its coverage of private systems is a direct response to *Halford v UK* [1997] IRLR 471.

171 Such as intranet systems not connected to any public system.

172 HC Deb Col 806, 6 March 2000.

173 Defined in s 81(3).

174 The EU draft Convention on Mutual Assistance in Criminal Matters (5202/98–C4-0062/98) was set out in the EU-FBI telecommunications plan adopted by the EU in January 1995. Under ENFOPOL, the information required includes e-mail addresses, credit card details, passwords, IP addresses, customer account numbers.

175 Norton-Taylor, in Blackburn and Plant (eds), *Constitutional Reform: The Labour Government's Constitutional Reform Agenda*, 1999, p 208. See also *Enhancing Parliamentary Scrutiny of the Third Pillar*, Select Committee of the European Communities, HL Session 1997–98, 31.7.97.

implies that further matters should be considered. For example, where the information *cannot* reasonably be obtained by other means, the proportionality of the particular interception warrant with its objective could still be considered. This might involve considering its contents and duration. Clearly, s 5(2) was introduced in an effort to meet the proportionality requirement under Art 8(2), discussed below. Under s 7(1) of the RIPA, the warrants must be personally signed by the Secretary of State or, under s 7(2) in urgent cases, or cases under the fourth ground, by 'a senior official' with express authorisation from the Secretary of State. A 'senior official' is defined in s 81(1) as 'a member of the Senior Civil Service' and under s 81(7) the Secretary of State 'may by order make ... amendments [to] the definition of "senior official"'. Under the 1985 Act the official had to be 'an official of his Department of or above the rank of Assistant Under Secretary of State'. In this respect, the requirements have been relaxed under the RIPA.

This new procedure is based on the model provided by the 1985 Act in that it allows for administrative oversight, but maintains executive authorisation of interception; it may therefore be contrasted with that in the US, where prior judicial authorisation is required,[176] and with that in Denmark where authorisation is by an investigating magistrate.[177] The Commissioner, appointed under s 8 of the 1985 Act, and re-appointed as the new Interception of Communications Commissioner under s 57(8) of the RIPA, has a role in overseeing the issuance of warrants, but this is a general review role, which occurs after the event. The possibility of replacing an executive with a judicial mechanism was entirely rejected by the Labour Government. In debate on the Bill, it received support only from the Liberal Democrats.[178] Judicial involvement only at the complaint stage (discussed below) is of little significance as a safeguard since many persons will have no means of knowing that tapping is occurring. Nevertheless, prior judicial involvement in authorising warrants cannot be said at present to be a requirement of Art 8.[179]

Under s 4(5) and (6) of the 1985 Act, the warrants were issued for an initial period of two months and could be renewed for one month in the case of the police and for six months in the case of the security and intelligence services. Under s 9(6) of the 2000 Act, warrants are issued for an initial period of three months if by the Secretary of State and can be renewed for six months if he states his belief that the grounds under s 5(3)(a) or (c) apply. If the other grounds apply, the renewal period is three months. If signed by a senior official, they can be issued initially for five working days but renewed for three months. In the case of all warrants, particularly those issued in respect of the prevention or detection of serious crime, to the police, these are significant increases. The period in respect of the serious crime ground may be compared with that in Denmark, which is four weeks, renewable.[180]

As was the case under the 1985 Act, there is no overall limit on renewals and it is likely to continue to be the case that some warrants will be very long standing. The number of interception warrants issued is also likely to increase. The Commissioners' Reports only cover the warrants authorised by the Home Office and Scottish Office. These

---

176 *Berger v NY* (1967) 388 US 41.
177 Code of Criminal Procedure, Art 126m.
178 HC Deb Col 8076, March 2000.
179 *Klass v FRG* (1978) 2 EHRR 214; *Mersch v Luxembourg* 43 D & R 34 (1985).
180 Code of Criminal Procedure, Art 126m.

figures show that at the end of 1989, 315 warrants were in force and 522 were issued during the year.[181] By 1993, a clear upward trend in the numbers of warrants issued was evident: in 1993, 1,005 warrants for telephone tapping and 115 for mail interceptions were issued; 409 warrants were in force at the end of the year.[182] The trend continued: in 1996 1,795 telecommunications warrants were in force or were issued during the year; by 1998, the figure had risen to 2,251.[183] As the Commissioner accepts, these figures do not provide a satisfactory guide as to the number of persons subject to interception, since a single warrant can cover a large organisation. The figures do not cover all the warrants authorised, since those authorised by other departments, including the Foreign Office, are viewed as too sensitive.

Section 8(1) of RIPA suggests that the warrants should be precise; they must specify a person or an address. However, a 'person' can equal 'any organisation and any association or combination of persons'.[184] Once a warrant is obtained, all communications to or from the property or 'person' specified must be intercepted, if that is what is required in order to give effect to the warrant.[185] Failure to comply with the warrant is an offence under s 11(7) carrying a maximum sentence of two years. Under s 11(4), telephone tapping and mail interceptions are conducted by Post Office or 'public telecommunications employees' or by persons controlling or partly controlling private systems wholly or partly in the UK.[186]

Under s 6(2), the request for the warrant may be made by a number of persons from a non-exhaustive list. They include: the Director General of the Security Service, the Chief of MI6, the Director of GCHQ, the Director General of the National Criminal Intelligence Service, the Commissioner of Police of the Metropolis; the Chief Constable of the RUC, Chief Constables in Scotland,[187] the Commissioners of Customs and Excise; the Chief of Defence; the relevant person for the purposes of any international mutual assistance agreement. The Bill originally provided: 'or any such other person as the Secretary of State may by order designate.' The Government was eventually persuaded to omit the last provision. A number of other such powers are, however, scattered throughout the Act, meaning that this statute, comprehensive as it is, leaves open a great deal of leeway for significant and more covert extension. On Second Reading of the Bill in the Commons this list was criticised on two grounds. The Conservative opposition considered that the list was not extensive enough and that, in particular, the Benefits Agency of the DSS[188]

---

181 Report of the Commissioner for 1989, Cm 1063, p 2. Similar figures are available for other years; see reports for 1986, Cm 108 and for 1987, Cm 351.

182 See Report of the Commissioner for 1993, Cm 2522.

183 The figure for postal interceptions rose from 115 in 1996 to 167 in 1998. Figures from the Report of the Commissioner under the Interception of Communications Act for 1998 published June 1999, Cm 4364, p 11.

184 RIPA 2000, s 78(1) which, with the addition of an 'association', reproduces s 10(1) of the 1985 Act.

185 Section 11(4).

186 Bearing in mind the range of companies which are affected and the difficulty of complying, especially in relation to the internet, a provision regarding practicality was necessary. Section 11(5) recognises that there may be circumstances under which it is not reasonably practicable to comply with the duty to implement the warrant. The prosecution must prove that it was practicable.

187 'Of any police force maintained under or by virtue of section 1 of the Police (Scotland) Act 1967.'

188 HC Deb Cols 778 and 831, 6 March 2000.

and the Inland Revenue[189] should be added to it. The Liberal Democrats, supported by Tom King, Chair of the Intelligence and Security Committee, argued that primary legislation, not a statutory instrument, should be used in order to add bodies to the list.[190]

Lawful interception without a warrant

Sections 3 and 4 of the RIPA allow for lawful interception without a warrant. Section 3(2) covers instances where it is reasonably believed that both parties to the communication have consented to the interception.[191] In such circumstances, the interception must also be authorised within Part II, s 26. This provision effects a compromise in relation to so called 'participant monitoring' (where one party is aware of the interception). It was pointed out in the leading Canadian authority[192] that the consent of one party does not affect the infringement of privacy suffered by the other. But s 3(2) does not demand that 'participant monitoring' should be subject to the controls necessary for other interceptions; it is subject only to the lesser controls for 'directed' surveillance, discussed below. Section 4 covers persons whose communications are intercepted who are believed to be outside the UK, instances where the Secretary of State has made regulations covering the interception for business[193] purposes (s 4(2)), and instances in psychiatric hospitals or prisons (within the relevant applicable statutes). These provisions may raise questions as to their compatibility with the Convention, which are considered below.

Use of the intercepted material

Section 15 provides safeguards regarding the use of the intercepted material. They are intended to limit the persons who can see the material and to ensure that it is destroyed once it is no longer necessary to retain it for the authorised purposes. However, the Act does not state how these objectives are to be achieved; it is left to the Secretary of State to put arrangements into place to secure them. Further, s 15 does not apply to material obtained without warrant, under ss 3 or 4. Since, as indicated below, personal criminal intelligence information obtained from interceptions and then stored and processed electronically is not subject to the stronger controls under the data protection regime of the 1998 Data Protection Act, it is clear that the controls created under s 15 are potentially crucial in protecting this aspect of privacy.

Unauthorised interceptions

Section 1 of the 1985 Act dealt with unauthorised interceptions and made it a criminal offence to intercept a postal communication or telecommunication intentionally without authorisation. It did not cover taps outside the public telecommunications system. So, for example, no criminal or even civil wrong was committed by the Chief Constable of Merseyside when a tap on the internal police phone system was used against Alison

---

189 HC Deb Col 821, 6 March 2000.
190 HC Deb Cols 768 and 831, 6 March 2000.
191 This provision is clearly more protective of privacy than its counterpart under the 1985 Act, s 1(2), which relied on the consent of one party only.
192 *Duarte* [1990] 53 CCC (3d) 1.
193 'Business' includes government departments.

Halford in order to seek to discredit her and undermine her sex discrimination claim against the police service.[194] The RIPA, which under s 1 reproduces the old s 1 offence with extensions, also covers interception of private systems, unless they are entirely freestanding. However, it is subject to an exception under s 1(6) which might have been applicable in the *Halford* case.[195] Section 1(6) provides that conduct is excluded from criminal liability if the interceptor 'is a person with a right to control the operation or the use of the system; or he has the express or implied consent of the [person intercepted]'. Section 1(3) creates civil liability in relation to unauthorised interception of a private, not a public system. Possibly in future, therefore, a person in a situation similar to that of Alison Halford might be able to bring a civil action only.

The role of the Commissioner

The Commissioner is a senior judge appointed by the Prime Minister on a part time basis to monitor the warrant procedure and to consider complaints. He had a duty under s 8(1)(a) of the 1985 Act, which will continue under s 57(2)(a) of the RIPA, to keep the warrant procedure under review. Apart from the statutory limitations of his powers, the practical constraints on them have been overwhelming. He had no staff and carried out the checking procedure personally on a part time basis. Clearly, as he accepts, these constraints precluded consideration of every warrant which is brought to his attention. His powers were very limited. He could not order that warrants should be quashed or that the material obtained should be destroyed; under s 8(9) he could merely report a contravention of ss 2–5 to the Prime Minister, which had not already been the subject of a tribunal report, or a contravention of s 6 which covered destruction of material, and he had to prepare an annual report for the Prime Minister under s 8(6). These arrangements regarding checking of warrants were largely continued under RIPA, under ss 57[196] and 58 when he became the Interception of Communications Commissioner, although staff may be appointed. His complaints role was taken over by the new tribunal.

The remit of the Commissioner gave him the opportunity to note that unauthorised tapping had occurred, but only when he was informed of it by the agencies concerned. Where he was so informed, he was told at the same time that the unauthorised action had been recognised, usually 'immediately', and all resultant material destroyed. His view was that these unauthorised actions, that is, criminal offences under s 1, termed 'errors' were 'comparatively few in number when considered in the context of the volume and complexity of the operations carried out'.[197] In his annual reports, the Commissioner found no instance in which a warrant was issued unjustifiably. Although Crown servants, telecommunications and postal workers were under a duty to provide the Commissioner with the information he required to carry out his task, under s 8(3) of the 1985 Act

---

194 See *Halford v UK* (1997) 24 EHRR 523.

195 *Ibid.*

196 Under s 57(2), 'Subject to subsection (5), the Interception of Communications Commissioner shall keep under review the exercise and performance by the Secretary of State of the powers and duties conferred or imposed on him by or under sections 1 to 11'.

197 Report of the Commissioner under the Interception of Communications Act 1998, published June 1999, Cm 4364, p 10.

(continued and extended to a wider range of people under the 2000 Act),[198] he had no effective means of checking that information had not been withheld. He received a list of warrants issued, renewed, modified or cancelled since the last visit, and checked a sample of them. He had no means of knowing whether the list was in fact complete, and unauthorised interception was not, unsurprisingly, recorded on it. If the Commissioner acquires staff to aid him in these tasks, when he carries them out under the RIPA, a greater proportion of warrants may be checked. But these basic limitations affecting his role remain unchanged under the RIPA arrangements. The key reform under the RIPA is to the tribunal system.

The old tribunal

Section 7 of the 1985 Act established a tribunal to consider complaints from people who believed that their telephone had been tapped or their mail intercepted. It should be noted that the statutory provisions had no retrospective effect. Thus, complaints could relate only to post-commencement activities. The RIPA sets up a new tribunal, under s 65, which will, as indicated above, replace the current one and those set up under the Security Services Act and the Intelligence Services Act. It will also take over the role of Commissioners in hearing complaints under s 102 and Sched 7 of the Police Act 1997, (discussed below) while it will have a new role in considering surveillance undertaken by other public authorities. It will be able to consider pre-commencement activity, within certain limitations. Thus, its role extends well beyond that of the old Interceptions of Communications Tribunal. It will therefore have immense significance as the central mechanism protecting citizens against abuse of State surveillance powers. The new tribunal is discussed fully below.[199]

The old tribunal set up under the 1985 Act (which consisted of five senior lawyers) had a duty under s 7(3) of that Act, on receiving a complaint, to investigate whether a warrant had been issued and if so, whether it was properly issued – whether there were adequate grounds for issuing it and whether statutory procedures were complied with. Under s 7(4), the tribunal applied 'the principles applicable by a court on an application for judicial review' to this exercise. The tribunal could only consider the matters referred to in ss 2–5 of the 1985 Act concerning the issuance of warrants; it could not consider the questions whether the action was proportionate to the invasion of privacy and whether the action could have been carried out by other means.

The Report of the Commissioner for 1998 states that the tribunal received 75 complaints in 1998, of which 72 were investigated and none was upheld.[200] The 1997 Report[201] states that since it was established in 1986, the tribunal has received 568 complaints and that none has ever been upheld. According to the Report, in only eight of these cases was interception being carried out by a government agency and in each case it was properly authorised. The possibility that in some of the other 560 cases, or in others,

---

198 See s 58(1), s 21(4) and s 49.

199 Pages 714 *et seq.*

200 Report of the Commissioner under the Interception of Communications Act 1998, published June 1999, Cm 4364, p 10.

201 Cm 4001.

unauthorised interception was occurring is seen in the Report as 'very remote' since it would involve a criminal conspiracy between the agency and the Public Telecommunications Operators. It may be noted that the Act did not provide any possibility of recognising that an invasion of privacy could occur due to the possibility that a phone had been tapped. The Court accepted in *Klass v Federal Republic of Germany*[202] that this possibility represented a continuing invasion of privacy, since conversations would be inhibited.

Parliamentary oversight

Under the 1985 Act, parliamentary oversight, such as it was, was limited to interceptions which fell within the statute. Under the new statute, the oversight is equally limited, but it will cover a far wider range of interceptions. Modelled on the old arrangements, the annual report of the new Commissioner must be presented to Parliament and published as a Command Paper, under s 58(6). The Prime Minister may censor the report under s 58(7) if it appears to him that it contains matter 'prejudicial to national security, to the prevention and detection of serious crime or to the economic well-being of the UK'. These grounds are the same as the previous ones under the 1985 Act. A new, broad one has been added: the matter may be excluded if it appears to be prejudicial to 'the continued discharge of the functions of any public authority whose activities include activities that are subject to review by that Commissioner'. It may be unnecessary, in any event, for the Prime Minister to censor the report; the practice has been for the Commissioner to designate the part to be withheld.

Thus, parliamentary oversight will continue to be highly circumscribed since no Committee is directly charged with monitoring State surveillance. Bearing in mind the brevity of the Commissioner's reports, the opportunity for Parliament to oversee these arrangements is very limited. The parliamentary oversight is clearly much weaker than that applicable in Germany, as considered in the *Klass* case[203] (below). The opportunity of enabling the new, comprehensive interceptions statute to reflect notions of openness and accountability to Parliament in the era of the Human Rights and Freedom of Information Acts has been lost.

The impact of the HRA

As indicated, Part I of the RIPA was intended to be compatible with the requirements of the Convention. Since it allows for State invasion of privacy, the Convention Article of most relevance is Art 8. The discussion below identifies some of the aspects of Part I which are arguably of doubtful compatibility with Art 8. It then goes on to consider the effect of the HRA in this context and the means available under it of seeking to ensure that the Convention rights are adhered to when interception is used.

---

202 (1978) 2 EHRR 214.
203 *Ibid.*

Interference with the primary rights

As indicated above, the interception of communications is likely to represent an interference with the Art 8(1) rights to respect for private life, the home and correspondence. The Court found in *Klass*[204] that the possibility that an interception was occurring could infringe Art 8, and this was also accepted in *Malone v UK*.[205] In *Klass*, the Court said: 'in the mere existence of the legislation itself there is involved, for all those to whom the legislation could be applied, a menace of surveillance; this menace necessarily strikes at freedom of communication between users of the postal and telecommunications services ...'[206] Thus, the provisions of the 1985 Act could be viewed as representing a continuing invasion of privacy, whether or not in any individual case an intercept had actually been used, and the same can now be said of Part I of the RIPA.

As the Court explained in *Halford v UK*,[207] under the Convention the issue would be whether, on the particular facts, the essence of the complaint concerned the actual application to her of the measures of surveillance or that her Art 8 rights were menaced by the very existence of the law and practice permitting such measures. *Halford v UK* concerned the tapping of the applicant's office telephone by the police at a time when she was bringing a claim of sex discrimination against the police authority in question. The Government argued that in using the private internal office system, the applicant could not expect to retain her privacy and that an employer should in principle be able to monitor calls made by an employee on the internal system without prior warning or consent.[208] The Court disagreed, finding that calls made from business premises as well as the home may be covered by the notions of 'private life' and 'correspondence' within the meaning of Art 8(1). This stance was also taken in *Kopp v Switzerland*.[209] The Court emphasised in that case that the interception of the telephone calls constituted the interference with the right under para 1; the fact that the recordings were not subsequently used was irrelevant. Thus, the Court has taken quite a broad approach, strongly protective of informational autonomy, to the meaning of the terms used in Art 8(1), thereby widening their application beyond obviously private spheres, including the home. The use made of material obtained from intercepts, including disclosure to others, may also fall within Art 8(1).[210]

In accordance with the law

As indicated above, State interference with the Art 8 guarantees must be in accordance with the law, under para 2, if it is to be justified and this requirement covers not only the existence of national law, but its quality. In *Halford v UK*,[211] the interception of the internal office telephone was clearly not in accordance with the law since domestic law provided no regulation at all of such interception, and therefore the Court found a breach of Art 8.

---

204 (1978) 2 EHRR 214.
205 (1984) 7 EHRR 14.
206 See p 21, para 41.
207 [1997] IRLR 471; (1997) 24 EHRR 523.
208 Para 43.
209 (1999) 27 EHRR 91, paras 70–71.
210 *MS v Sweden* (1999) 28 EHRR 313.
211 (1997) 24 EHRR 523.

Part I of the RIPA was introduced in response to the findings in *Halford v UK*[212] and, generally, to provide a statutory basis for interception outside the public telecommunications system. Thus, a basis in national law now exists. Once such a basis is found, its quality must be considered; it must be asked whether it is 'compatible with the rule of law ... there must be a measure of legal protection in domestic law against arbitrary interferences by public authorities with [the right to respect for private life under Art 8(1)]. Especially where a power of the executive is exercised in secret, the risks of arbitrariness are evident.'[213] In *Kopp v Switzerland*[214] the Court clearly stated that the essential requirements of a national legal basis are those of accessibility and foreseeability so that, in this context, the citizen is sufficiently aware of the circumstances allowing interception. It must be clear as to the 'circumstances in and conditions on which public authorities are empowered to resort to any such secret measures'.[215]

In *Christie v UK*,[216] the 1985 Act was found to meet this requirement in relation to the terms 'national security' and 'economic well being'. The Commission viewed those terms as sufficiently precise since they had been explained by 'administrative or executive statements'. The Interception of Communications Tribunal had investigated and had found no breach in relation to the warrant procedure; this could be taken to mean that no warrant had been issued, a matter outside the jurisdiction of the tribunal, or that one had been properly issued. The other issue concerned the retention of information collected through the tap by the Security Service. It is notable, however, that this was a decision of the Commission only, that it was influenced by the margin of appreciation doctrine and that it was not made in the context of the 'serious crime' provision under the Act.

In *Kruslin v France*,[217] a basis in law was found for interception but it was not found to be of sufficient quality owing to its imprecision, which was found to fail to satisfy the requirement of foreseeability.[218] Similarly, in *Kopp v Switzerland*, which was also concerned with crime, not national security, the Court said: 'interception ... constitutes a particularly serious interference with private life and correspondence and must accordingly be based on a "law" that is particularly precise.'[219] In another case outside the realm of national security or economic well being, *Valenzuela v Spain*,[220] the Court also found that the legal basis available for interception did not satisfy the requirements of foreseeability. In particular, the conditions necessary under the Convention to satisfy that requirement, including the nature of the offences which might give rise to an intercept order, were not included in the relevant provisions.[221] A development towards greater

---

212 *Ibid*.
213 *Malone v UK* A 82, para 67; 4 EHRR 330. The Court reaffirmed this in *Halford v UK* (1997) 24 EHRR 523 above: 'this expression ... relates to the quality [of domestic law], requiring it to be compatible with the rule of law' (para 49).
214 (1999) 27 EHRR 91, paras 70–71.
215 *Halford v UK* (1997) 24 EHRR 523, para 49.
216 78-A DR E Com HR 119.
217 (1990) 12 EHRR 528.
218 *Ibid*, para 30. See also *Huvig v France* (1990) 12 EHRR 528, para 29.
219 *Ibid*, para 44.
220 (1998) 28 EHRR 483.
221 *Ibid*, para 75.

stringency appears to be evident in the jurisprudence, at least within the 'prevention of crime' context.

It is arguable that the 1985 Act did not fully meet the 'in accordance with the law' requirement since, *inter alia*, the serious crime ground was not defined as *Valenzuela v Spain* requires. It is defined in the RIPA, albeit in broad terms.[222] The question whether Part I of the RIPA meets this requirement in all respects remains open, bearing in mind the possible future development of the Strasbourg jurisprudence on this matter. The grounds under s 5(3), including the 'mutual assistance' ground, are clearly ill defined.

The fact that the Act provides for authorisation by executive, rather than judicial warrant, is also relevant to the requirement of foreseeability. In *Kopp v Switzerland*, in finding a breach of Art 8 for failure to satisfy that requirement, the Court said: 'it is ... astonishing that this task should be assigned to an official of the Post Office's legal department, who is a member of the executive, without supervision by an independent judge.'[223]

The provision under s 3 of the RIPA allowing for interception with consent on the basis of reasonable belief may be questionable under Art 8, depending on the steps which must be taken in practice to establish the consent, especially in relation to the *recipient* of the communication.[224] Moreover, the authorisation procedure is less demanding than that in relation to interception by warrant and might appear, therefore, to be out of accord with the requirement of quality. However, at the present time the procedure is in principle in accordance with Art 8. The Court has found that where one party to the conversation had given consent under the equivalent provision of the 1985 Act, s 1(2), Art 8 was not breached since citizens would be sufficiently aware of the risk.[225]

Legitimate aims and necessity in a democratic society

If an interference is 'in accordance with the law', it must have a legitimate aim and be necessary in a democratic society. The legitimate aims under Art 8(2), set out above,[226] are very broad and echo those used under s 5(3), apart from the fourth one. But since the aim of that ground is to prevent crime, this aim would probably be viewed as legitimate. Thus, this requirement appears to be satisfied.

The Court has interpreted 'necessary in a democratic society' as meaning: 'an interference corresponds to a pressing social need and, in particular, that it is proportionate to the legitimate aim pursued.'[227] The doctrine of proportionality, as Chapters 2 and 4 indicated, is strongly linked to the principle of the margin of appreciation. The width of that margin appears to depend partly on the aim of the interference in question and partly on its necessity. In relation to the aim of national security, the Court has allowed a very wide margin to the State.

---

222 In s 81(3).

223 *Ibid*, para 46.

224 See *Lambert v France* (1999) 1 EHRLR 123. In *Kruslin v France* (1990) 12 EHRR 547, para 26, it was accepted that although the line of a third party had been tapped, an interference with the applicant's Art 8 rights had occurred, since his conversations on that line had been intercepted and recorded.

225 *Nadir Choudhary v UK* (1999) 1 EHRLR 522. See also *Smith v UK* [1997] EHRLR 277.

226 See p 665.

227 *Olsson v Sweden* A 130 (1988), para 67.

In *Klass v Federal Republic of Germany*[228] the European Court of Human Rights found, bearing the margin of appreciation doctrine in mind, that German telephone tapping procedures were in conformity with Art 8 since they contained a number of safeguards. An oversight body, a parliamentary board,[229] could consider, on an application from an aggrieved individual or *ex officio*, whether the interception had been authorised and its necessity. There was also quite a substantial degree of parliamentary scrutiny: the minister in question had to report to a parliamentary board and also to give an account of the interceptions ordered to a Commission. The possibility was available of compensation for persons whose phones had been unlawfully tapped and of challenges to interception in proceedings in the ordinary courts, and the individual warrants had to be reviewed by a Commission headed by a person qualified for judicial office.

The Court did not, however, state that these were the minimal safeguards necessary; it said:

> The Court considers that in a field where abuse is so easy in individual cases and could have such harmful consequences for democratic society as a whole, it is in principle desirable to entrust supervisory control to a judge. Nevertheless, having regard to the supervisory and other safeguards provided ... the Court concludes that the exclusion of judicial control does not exceed the limits of what may be deemed necessary in a democratic society. The Parliamentary Board and the ... Commission are independent of the authorities carrying out the surveillance, and are vested with sufficient powers and competence to exercise an effective and continuous control. Furthermore, the democratic character is reflected in the balanced membership of the Parliamentary Board. The Opposition is reflected on this body and is therefore able to participate in the control of the measures ordered by the ... Minister ...[230]

In *Christie v UK*,[231] the Commission found: 'having regard to the wide margin of appreciation in this area' the safeguards provided by the Interception of Communications Tribunal and the Commissioner were sufficient in the instant case where the applicant was a trade unionist with links with communist Eastern Europe and his phone was being tapped on the grounds of 'national security' and 'economic well-being'. The interception was proportionate to those legitimate aims, on the facts of the case. Similar findings were made, rather readily, by the Commission in *Remmers and Hamer v The Netherlands*[232] in the context of serious crime.

Bearing in mind the findings in *Klass*, the findings in Christie need not be taken as absolutely conclusive evidence that the oversight mechanisms provided by the 1985 Act, and maintained, with modifications, under Part I of the RIPA, meet Convention requirements. They were made in relation to the particular case, not as abstract comment on the mechanisms or on the warrant procedure in general, and they were heavily influenced by the margin of appreciation. As indicated in Chapter 4, that doctrine is not available at national level and this, it is contended, means that it should not influence national decision makers, including judges acting judicially or extra-judicially, and other

---

228 (1978) 2 EHRR 214.
229 Under Law G10.
230 *Ibid*, p 235.
231 78-A DR E Com HR 119.
232 (1999) 27 EHRR CD 168.

national bodies. The Government and the Commissioner have assumed that the decision in *Christie* closes the question as far as the 1985 Act is concerned and as the statement of compatibility accompanying it demonstrates, the Government takes this stance in respect of Part I, Chapter I of the RIPA as well. But in respect of interception under warrant, under the RIPA, the issue could be re-opened in future, under developments in the Court's jurisprudence, bearing in mind the possibility of changing standards in other Member States.

Therefore, a national judge (probably sitting in the new tribunal,[233] not in an ordinary court) would be free to take a more rigorous look at the safeguards provided by the RIPA and at the necessity of an interference. The approach taken in practice would depend on the tendency to follow the traditionalist model: it might be found that traditional notions of deference to the executive in this sensitive area would yield the same result as adherence to the margin of appreciation doctrine. But a judge might be prepared to depart from a deferential stance outside the national security context. As indicated above, it is a statutory requirement for the Secretary of State or Senior Official to consider proportionality[234] in issuing a warrant. Therefore, the new tribunal would be expected to consider whether the statutory requirements have been met, taking Strasbourg guidance into account, but adopting a more rigorous scrutiny. The continued lack of judicial authorisation under the RIPA should be considered, when looking at the necessity of an interference, bearing in mind the fact that the other safeguards available, including parliamentary oversight, are weaker than those considered in *Klass*.

*Obligations of oversight bodies, of those applying for warrants
and of those carrying them out*

As a public authority under s 6 of the HRA, the Interception of Communications Commissioner has a duty to abide by the Convention rights in discharging his oversight role. The Commissioner should ensure that the agencies he oversees are themselves ensuring Convention compliance. The members of the agencies and telecommunications and postal workers are bound by s 6 not to infringe the Convention in carrying out their work. In other words, all the public authorities involved should comply with the requirements of the Convention.

Parliament is not bound by s 6, but in considering reports of the Commissioner or in debating any issues arising from the operation of the RIPA, it would be expected that the Convention requirements would be strictly borne in mind, especially as a statement of compatibility accompanied the Act.

Raising Convention issues in court proceedings

Under s 7(1)(b) of the HRA, Convention issues could be raised in prosecutions against agency members, police officers, telecommunications or postal workers or other public authorities in respect of the various offences arising from non-co-operation with State interception created under the 2000 Act. But this would not normally involve

---

233 Note that tribunal members, apart from the President, need not be judges (see Sched 3).
234 Section 5(2).

consideration of the key issue – the invasions of privacy allowed for under the RIPA. Consideration of the compatibility of intercepts with Art 8 in court proceedings appears to be almost entirely precluded by s 17 of the RIPA. Section 17 is based on s 9 of the 1985 Act which provided: 'In any proceedings before any court or tribunal, no evidence shall be adduced and no question asked in cross-examination which ... tends to suggest that 'the offence under s 1 has been or is to be committed by postal or telecommunications workers or Crown Servants or 'that a warrant has been or is to be issued to any of those persons'.

Section 17 provides:

subject to s 18, no evidence shall be adduced, question asked, assertion or disclosure made or other thing done in, for the purposes of or in connection with any legal proceedings which (in any manner)–

(a) discloses, in circumstances from which its origin in anything falling within subsection (2) may be inferred, any of the contents of an intercepted communication or any related communications data; or

(b) tends (apart from any such disclosure) to suggest that anything falling within subsection (2) has or may have occurred or be going to occur.

Section 17(2) covers:

(a) conduct ... that was or would be an offence under s 1(1) or (2) of this Act or under s 1 of the ... 1985 Act;

(b) a breach by the Secretary of State of his duty under section 1(4) of this Act;

(c) the issue of an interception warrant or of a warrant under the ... 1985 Act;

(d) the making of an application by any person for an interception warrant, or for a warrant under that Act;

(e) the imposition of any requirement on any person to provide assistance with giving effect to an interception warrant.

This is clearly a far more comprehensive clause than s 9, although it is subject to certain exceptions under s 18, which may allow Convention points to be raised, in accordance with the courts' duty under s 6 of the HRA. This rule is clearly arbitrary, since material deriving from the use of bugging and other surveillance devices can be adduced, as discussed below.

Section 18(1) provides that s 17(1) does not apply in proceedings before the tribunal, for an offence under the RIPA, s 1 of the 1985 Act, s 4(3)(a) of the Official Secrets Act, and a number of other provisions relating to the secrecy of interceptions. Section 18(4), (6), (7) and (9) provides a number of very significant new exceptions. Section 18(4) applies *inter alia*[235] where the interception was by consent under s 3; s 18(6) provides that s 17(1)(b) does not prevent doing anything which discloses conduct for which a person has been convicted under ss1(1), 11(7), 19 or s 1 of the 1985 Act. Under s 18(7), s 17(1) does not prohibit disclosure of '(a) any information that continues to be available for disclosure' to

---

235 Section 18(4) also provides that s 16(1)(a) does not apply if the interception was lawful by virtue of s 1(5)(c) (relating to stored material obtained under another statutory power), or s 4(1) (persons believed to be outside UK). For discussion of ss 17 and 18, see Mirfield, P [2001] Crim LR 91.

the prosecution 'for the purpose only of enabling that person to determine what is required of him by his duty to secure [its] fairness' or (b) disclosure to a relevant judge[236] by order of the judge 'to be made to him alone'. Under s 18(8), a judge shall not order such a disclosure unless satisfied that 'the exceptional circumstances of the case make the disclosure essential in the interests of justice'. If disclosure is ordered, s 18(9) allows the judge, in 'exceptional circumstances', to 'direct the prosecution to make any admission of fact ... that the judge thinks is essential in the interests of justice'. But any such direction must not, under s 18(10), contravene s 17(1). Thus, where intercept material is still available, its disclosure to the judge or to the prosecution may be ordered. It may be noted that the material may still be in existence at the time of the trial, since it is preserved, for the benefit of the prosecution, under s 15(4)(d). Communications data (details of calls made) may be adduced in evidence, since it is not an intercepted communication as defined in s 17(4), so long as it does not suggest that the offences in question have been committed.[237]

Section 9 of the 1985 Act meant that if an intercept had been used to obtain material, whether unauthorised or not, the information gained would be inadmissible in evidence. But s 9 only applied to the forms of interception which the Act covered. Section 9 was considered in two House of Lords' decisions, which led to a bizarre and anomalous situation. In *Effick*,[238] the defendants were prosecuted for conspiracy to supply controlled drugs and police officers obtained part of the evidence against them by means of intercepting and taping their telephone calls. The offence under s 1 had not been committed since the calls taped were made on a cordless telephone which was not found to be part of 'a public telecommunications system' as required under s 1. The appellants were convicted, and appealed on the ground that the evidence deriving from the intercepted telephone calls should have been ruled inadmissible under s 9 of the Interception of Communications Act 1985, or under s 78 of the Police and Criminal Evidence Act 1984 (PACE), since they were made without a warrant for interception.

The House of Lords determined that argument under s 9 failed because its provisions were aimed at preventing disclosure of information which tended to suggest that the offence of unauthorised interception (under s 1(1) of the 1985 Act) had been committed by specified persons, or that a warrant had been or was to be issued to such persons. These matters were not in issue since the interception was not within the Act. Section 9 was not intended to render inadmissible evidence obtained which would not reveal such matters. Clear statutory language would have been needed to oust the principle that all logically probative evidence should be admitted. As this was not the case, and as the instance in question did not appear to fall within s 9, the evidence was admissible. The submission in respect of s 78 of PACE failed because it was not suggested that the police officers had deliberately contravened the 1985 Act. It was found that no unfairness to the defendants

---

236 *Inter alia*, a judge of the High Court or Crown Court. This provision will amend the Criminal Procedure and Investigations Act 1996, s 3(4).

237 This position continues that established under the 1985 Act in *Morgans v DPP* [2000] 2 WLR 386, HL; [1999] 1 WLR 968, CA in which it was found that s 9 of that Act does not preclude a court from receiving evidence of printouts obtained by a logging device.

238 [1994] 3 WLR 583; (1994) 99 Cr App R 312, HL; (1992) 95 Cr App R 427, CA. For criticism of the Court of Appeal decision, see Leigh, I (1992) 142 NLJ 944–45, 976–77; Smith, JC [1992] Crim LR 580. See generally Spencer (1999) 58 CLJ 43.

had occurred due to the admission of the evidence, but this begs the question whether the manner in which the evidence was obtained – on no legal basis and by means of a surreptitious act – could affect the fairness of the trial.

In *Preston*,[239] in contrast, a lawful intercept had occurred and the defence wanted admission of the material derived from it which, it was alleged, might have led to the acquittal of the defendants. In a decision which accepted somewhat reluctantly that the 1985 Act created a scheme designed to elevate the interests of secrecy above individual rights to privacy or to a fair trial, the House of Lords found that s 9 was designed to prevent information as to the manner of authorising and carrying out the intercepts from being uncovered at the trial. It was intended, *inter alia*, to prevent the defendant from seeking to uncover the source of information behind the decision to use an intercept. Thus, the defence had no right to obtain disclosure of the material deriving from the intercepts. Further, since on the proper interpretation of s 2(2) read in conjunction with s 6(3), destruction of material gained by the intercepts had to be undertaken once the criminal investigation (not the prosecution) was complete, such material would not be available.

The result of this decision was that although telephone tapping could be used as an investigative tool in the criminal process, material deriving directly from an intercept would not be admissible and the defence would not be allowed to ask any questions designed to discover whether an intercept was used. Thus, the prosecution might at times be disadvantaged, since some probative material would not be admissible,[240] but the other side of the coin was that material deriving from the intercept could not be disclosed to the defence even if (as the defence alleged in *Preston*) it might show the innocence of the defendants. One exception, favourable to the prosecution, to the rule deriving from s 9, as interpreted in *Preston*, was allowed in *Rasool* and *Choudhary*.[241] It was determined that where intercepts are consensual, material deriving from them will be admissible. The rule in s 9(1)(a) was not found to be sufficient to make consensual material inadmissible; it was found to be irrelevant to the question of admissibility that an offence had been committed in obtaining the evidence. Choudhary's appeal was dismissed while Rasool's was allowed on that ground. Similarly, in *Owen*,[242] the evidence deriving from an intercept was found to be admissible, on the basis that it did not suggest that the offence under s 1 had been committed. The defendant, in prison on remand, had admitted the offence with which he was charged in a phone call to his wife. He was deemed to have consented to the interception since notices warning of the likelihood of interception had been posted near telephones in the prison. The defendant claimed that he had not seen any such notice. But it was found that, on the basis that one of the parties had impliedly consented, the admission of the evidence would not suggest that the offence under s 1 of the Act had been committed.[243]

---

239 [1993] 4 All ER 638; (1994) 98 Cr App R 405, HL. For discussion, see Tomkins, A (1994) 57 MLR 941.

240 This factor influenced the Commission in declaring the application from Preston inadmissible: *Preston v UK*, 2 July 1997, Appl No 24193/94; available from the Commission's website.

241 [1997] 4 All ER 439. Choudhary applied, unsuccessfully, to Strasbourg: *Choudhary v UK* (1999) 1 EHRLR 522. For a further exception, see *Aujla* [1998] 2 Cr App R 16.

242 [1999] 1 WLR 949.

243 Since under s 1(2) of the Act, interceptions without warrant but with consent is not an offence.

The anomalous result of *Effick* and *Preston* was that in one, unlawfully obtained evidence, favourable to the prosecution, could be used as part of the prosecution evidence, while in another, lawfully obtained evidence could not be used at the behest of the defence. However, the decision in *Morgans*[244] addressed this anomaly. The House of Lords found that s 9 covers intercepts both with and without warrant. These decisions appear to have influenced Part I of the RIPA. Most obviously, the new statute covers most forms of communication so that the argument used in *Effick* regarding cordless phones could not be raised. Section 18(4), which refers inter alia to interceptions without a warrant where one party has consented to the interception (s 3), covers the findings from *Rasool* and *Owen*. Significantly, in certain imprecisely defined circumstances, disclosure relating to intercept material can be made to the prosecution and, if ordered, to the judge. But the defence may remain unaware of the source of the material. The fact that the use of the intercept led to the uncovering of other evidence, which is adduced, might be relevant to any challenge the defence could mount to the evidence. This position may not accord with the equality of arms principle under Art 6 of the Convention, since prosecution and defence may not be equally affected by the unavailability of the evidence.[245] The compatibility of ss 17 and 18 with the Art 6(1) guarantee of a fair trial may be raised. If the use of interception is lawful, and probative evidence is obtained, it is hard to identify the legitimate purpose of refusing to adduce it directly in court. Section 18 addresses the question of proportionality to a very limited extent, but the question arises whether the requirements of equality of arms can be satisfied by a provision which allows the intercept material to be disclosed to the prosecution but not to the defence. More generally, the question of the fairness of the trial arises in relation to the exclusion of probative evidence.

In circumstances similar to those in *Preston* in which the defence seeks disclosure of the evidence, whether or not it has been disclosed to the prosecution, the defence could make representations to the judge under s 18(9)(b), arguing that the term 'exceptional circumstances' must be rendered compatible with Art 6 under s 3 of the HRA, taking into account the requirements of fairness in the particular instance.[246] If the evidence is crucial to the defence, but the judge refuses to make an order, an appeal could be mounted on the basis that the judge had not complied with Art 6. Perhaps the most difficult situation would arise where, as in *Malone*, the defence suspected that an unauthorised intercept had been used. The defence might wish to mount an argument that evidence causally related to such use, rather than directly deriving from it, should be excluded since it would not have been obtained but for the illegality. Such exclusion could be argued for under s 78 of PACE, interpreted compatibility with Art 6.[247] But ss 18(10) and 17(1) stand in the way of obtaining an admission that an unauthorised intercept had been used. Possibly where an activist view of the exclusion of evidence requirement under Art 6 was taken, the only recourse would be to obtain a declaration of incompatibility between

---

244 [2000] 2 WLR 386. For an interesting application of the *Morgans* argument, see *Sargent* [2001] UKHL 54.

245 This could be argued by analogy with the decisions in *Windisch v Austria* (1990) 13 EHRR 281 and *Kostovski v Netherlands* (1989) 12 EHRR 434.

246 See pp 709–11. The findings in *Rowe and Davis v UK* (2000) 30 EHRR 1, although in a different context, which concerned unfairness arising from the non-disclosure of evidence, would be applicable.

247 See further Chapter 14, pp 892–906.

those provisions and Art 6(1) under s 4 of the HRA on the basis of unfairness under Art 6(1). However, if it was assumed that no appeal could succeed since those provisions would have to be applied, the defendants might view seeking such a declaration as worthless since it could not provide them individually with any redress. It appears therefore that although ss 17 and 18 show signs of seeking to escape from certain of the effects of s 9 of the 1985 Act, they nevertheless provide a scheme whose central aim is to preserve the secrecy surrounding interceptions, whether or not the interests of justice are thereby compromised.

Sections 17 and 18 are most likely to be relevant in criminal proceedings, but other proceedings are also affected. As discussed below, the route to judicial review of the decisions of the new tribunal may be barred by the ouster clause contained in s 67(8) of the RIPA[248] and based on s 7(8) of the 1985 Act. Section 65(2), which provides that the jurisdiction of the new tribunal is to be 'the only appropriate tribunal' for the purposes of s 7(1)(a) of the HRA, also stands in the way of review. Section 65 is discussed further below,[249] and it is suggested that judicial review of executive decisions in the ordinary courts is possible in respect of some surveillance. But in respect of the interception of communications, s 17 would also have to be circumvented. Since s 18(9) applies to criminal proceedings only, the way to judicial review in the ordinary courts appears to remain barred. The only, faint, possibility seems to be that eventually, a declaration of incompatibility under s 4 of the HRA between s 17 and Art 6 might eventually be made on appeal from proceedings for permission to seek review.

The possibility of a tort action, including that of a new cause of action based on breach of Art 8, is also probably ruled out on the same grounds. Where the existing law fails to cover interceptions which infringe Art 8, new tortious liability could have been created. Under the 1985 Act, the possibility would have been open of bringing an action once the HRA was fully in force in respect of forms of phone tapping outside the 1985 Act. This position was unsatisfactory and anomalous. But it did leave open the possibility, now probably closed down under Part I of the RIPA, of raising such matters in the ordinary courts. At present, apart from prosecutions for the offences created by the RIPA, or enforcement of interception in the civil courts, the new tribunal would probably provide the only judicial forum in which the Convention points discussed above could be raised.

Conclusions

The discussion suggests that court action as a method of seeking to ensure that the HRA is fully complied with in this context is highly circumscribed and uncertain. No clear and effective method is currently available, unless the new tribunal proves to be more effective than its predecessor. Parliamentary oversight is also limited. If the Convention rights are to have any real impact domestically in this context, this may be most likely to occur through incremental internal change in procedures, rather than through the courts or the complaints mechanisms.

---

248 Replacing s 7(8) of the 1985 Act and replacing s 91(10) of the 1997 Act in so far as complaints are concerned, and creating a new ouster clause in relation to complaints regarding surveillance by a range of other public authorities.

249 See pp 715–16.

It is notable that the inception of proceedings in the ordinary courts in relation to interception under Part I of the RIPA is at present a privilege intended to be accorded only to the State. The role of the judiciary in the ordinary courts in protecting individual citizens, at their instigation, from abuse of State power in conducting interceptions has been almost entirely removed. Instead, the intention is that the courts should be used only to seek to further State ends – as a means of enforcing the use of intercepts. Thus, civil or criminal proceedings can be used under ss 11(7) and (8) in order to compel private companies to intercept the communications of their customers. At the same time, a citizen whose communications appear to have been unlawfully intercepted has no means of challenging the interception in the ordinary courts, even assuming that she becomes aware of it. It is a criminal offence under s 19, a classic 'reverse onus' clause, for a telecommunications worker, for example, to inform a member of the public that her phone has been tapped under an unlawfully issued warrant. The unsatisfactoriness of this regime leads to the conclusion that further safeguards against arbitrary invasion of privacy by interception, and consequent modifications of Part I of the RIPA, may eventually be introduced as a result of Strasbourg findings or possibly as a result of relying on Art 8 under the HRA in applications to the new tribunal.

5 STATE SURVEILLANCE[250]

Introduction

The last 20 years have seen an immense and still increasing expansion in the availability and use of a range of highly sophisticated surveillance devices, and State surveillance has become more intensive since the Labour Government came to power in 1997.[251] The recent growth in State use of such devices as part of intelligence-led policing has received encouragement from official studies.[252] The growth in such policing, which involves using covert investigative techniques proactively to target suspects, is due, as the group *Justice* has pointed out, to the need to respond to organised crime, to the availability and efficacy of the new technology, and to the wider use of criminal intelligence following the growth of national and transnational agencies, including Europol and the National Criminal Intelligence Service,[253] and transnational agreements.[254] 'Bugging' equipment has become much more sophisticated in the last 20 years, with the result that it is now very powerful, readily concealable and relatively cheap.[255] The criminal intelligence

---

250 For discussion see Leigh, I, 'The security service, the press and the courts' [1987] PL 12–21.

251 See below, p 696.

252 Audit Commission, *Helping with Enquiries*, 1993; *Home Office Review of Police Core and Ancillary Tasks*, 1995. See Manwaring-White, S, *The Policing Revolution*, 1983; *Report of the Commissioner for 1993*, Cm 2522; *Security Services Work Against Organised Crime*, Cm 3065, 1996.

253 *Justice: Under Surveillance*, 1998, p 7. Walker and Taylor have pointed out that the use of surveillance techniques by police avoids adherence to the PACE interviewing rules and makes it less likely that evidence will be excluded: 'Bugs in the system' (1996) J Civ Lib 105, pp 107–08.

254 See the *Memorandum of Understandings on the Lawful Interception of Communications*, EU JHA-Council, 25.10.95.

255 See Taylor and Walker, *op cit*, fn 253.

information obtained can be matched and disseminated with increasing rapidity using the new technology.

Thus, surveillance devices and techniques offer an important weapon to the police and security services in the maintenance of law and order and the protection of national security. However, as the Supreme Court of Canada has said of them: '... one can scarcely imagine a State activity more dangerous to individual privacy than electronic surveillance.'[256] This was also the view of the Younger Committee, which considered the range of devices then in use.[257] The use by State bodies of surveillance techniques and their legal basis resembles the pattern considered above in relation to the interception of communications. Despite the development of such techniques and the increased use of them by the police and the security services, they had until recently no or a quasi-legal basis – a position which was possible under a constitution based on negative liberties since the State, like the ordinary citizen, was, according to a key decision, entitled to do anything which the law did not forbid.[258] They operated until recently outside the realms of parliamentary, judicial or administrative control. Bearing in mind the power of the State to conduct surveillance and its intrusiveness, this was an especially anomalous position.

Under administrative guidelines,[259] the use of listening devices could be authorised by Chief Constables in order to assist in a criminal investigation, if the crime was really serious, normal methods had been tried and had failed, and there was good reason for believing that the use of such equipment would lead to a conviction. Also, the authorising officer had to weigh the seriousness of the offence against the degree of intrusion necessary. When it became apparent in 1996 that this regime was inadequate, as explained below, since it did not meet the demands of the Convention, the use of certain surveillance techniques by the police was placed on a statutory basis in the Police Act 1997. Following the lead of the Interception of Communications Act 1985, it gives an impression of covering the use of surveillance devices by the police, while leaving many areas of their use outside its statutory framework.

The imminence of the HRA, and the effect of Art 8 in particular, was the driving force for change. The unsatisfactory nature of the arrangements was pointed out in 1998 by *Justice* in a report[260] which argued for integration of surveillance techniques with interception, in one comprehensive statute. The Regulation of Investigatory Powers Act provides that comprehensive basis. Overlapping with the 1997 Act, most of which it will not repeal, Part II of the RIPA covers a far wider range of both techniques and public authorities, including the police. It places the use of surveillance by the security and intelligence services on a clearer statutory basis, overlapping with the Intelligence Services Act 1994. By providing a comprehensive statutory basis that coincided (roughly) with the coming fully into force of the HRA, Part II sought to avoid the embarrassment of

---

256 *Duarte* (1990) 65 DLR (4th) 240.

257 *Report of the Committee on Privacy*, Cmnd 5012, 1972.

258 See Megarry VC in *Malone v MPC* [1979] Ch 344.

259 *Guidelines on the Use of Equipment in Police Surveillance Operations*, House of Commons Library, 19 December 1984.

260 See fn 253 above.

the findings in *Malone v UK*,[261] *Halford v UK*[262] and *Khan v UK*.[263] As indicated above, *Malone* led to the inception of the Interception of Communications Act 1985 since it was found at Strasbourg that the interference with privacy represented by telephone tapping was not in accordance with the law, as it had no satisfactory legal basis. In *Halford* it was found that the tapping of the applicant's internal office phone had no such basis, while the same finding was made as regards the use of 'bugging' devices in *Khan*. The finding in *Halford* was addressed in Part I of the RIPA, that in *Khan* in Part III of the 1997 Act.[264] Assuming that the forms of surveillance covered by Part II of the RIPA engage Art 8 in the sense that they represent an interference with the respect for private life guaranteed under that Article,[265] the Convention arguments raised in those cases would have been raised in the domestic courts under the HRA (under s 7(1)(a) or (b)) particularly in respect of forms of so called 'directed' surveillance (see below) if Part II of the RIPA had not been introduced. It also provides a fuller complaints mechanism, with a view to keeping most scrutiny of surveillance out of the ordinary courts, but nevertheless satisfying the demands of the Convention. In contrast with the position under Part I, it does not create a criminal offence of conducting unauthorised surveillance. Part II also seeks to deal with the problem of encryption by requiring disclosure of the key to information under s 49,[266] rendering refusal punishable under s 53, a classic 'reverse onus' clause.

Thus, for the first time a statutory basis for a number of investigative techniques has been created, clearly a welcome development. But it is questionable whether Part II is any more adequate at the level of principle than the previous scheme. It is clearly not as vulnerable to challenges under the Convention. Nevertheless, its compatibility with the Convention remains in doubt, as discussed below. The *Justice* Report (1998) influenced its introduction, but while the first of their key recommendations – that there should be an integrated, comprehensive statutory basis for surveillance – has largely been met, it is questionable whether this is true of the second – using a 'coherent set of principles as required by Art 8' to underpin the new scheme.[267]

The Police Act 1997 Part III

The House of Lords in *Khan*,[268] confronted with evidence obtained by police bugging involving trespass, recommended legislation, taking into account the fact that the regime

---

261 A 82 (1984), 7 EHRR 14.

262 [1997] IRLR 471.

263 (2000) 8 BHRC 310.

264 By the time that the European Court of Human Rights made this finding, Part III of the 1997 Act had already been passed. Nevertheless, at the time when the police used the bugging device to obtain evidence against Khan, no sufficient basis in law was available to meet the demands of Art 8.

265 The Strasbourg decisions, discussed pp 703–05, strongly suggest that this would be the case.

266 A s 49 notice requires service providers to disclose encryption keys and to keep secret the fact that a key has been disclosed. This provision may lead to adoption of a 'voluntary' key escrow system – a system whereby private encryption keys are deposited with a third party. Such a system would provide protection from prosecution for those who had genuinely lost or deleted their keys. But it clearly has significant privacy implications. See further Akedeniz, Y, 'UK Government policy on encryption' [1997] WSCL 1.

267 *Under Surveillance: Covert Policing and Human Rights Standards*, 1998; see Recommendation 1, p 107.

268 [1996] 3 All ER 289; [1996] 3 WLR 162; (1996) 146 NLJ 1024, HL; [1995] QB 27, CA.

governing the use of bugging devices was not on a statutory basis and therefore might not comply with the 'in accordance with the law' requirement under Art 8.[269] Their recommendation was one of the factors behind the passing of the Police Act 1997, which therefore represents another instance in which powers posing a grave threat to privacy and other individual rights were governed only by administrative guidelines until it became apparent that such a course could not be justified under the Convention.

The authorisation procedure

The Police Act, Part III placed the practice under the relevant Home Office guidelines[270] on a statutory basis, with certain changes. It only covers the installation of devices which could have attracted liability under trespass, criminal damage or unlawful interference with wireless telegraphy, under the Wireless Telegraphy Acts 1949 and 1967. Therefore, it does not cover 'stand off' devices. Also, it does not cover devices installed with the consent of the person able to give permission in respect of the premises in question.[271] The use of surveillance devices in a range of circumstances therefore falls outside it, as do a range of techniques, in particular the use of informants.[272] Such matters continued to be governed by the Guidelines until Part II of the RIPA (see below) came into force.

Part III of the Police Act is largely modelled on the Interception of Communications Act and therefore contains certain similar objectionable features. The basis for allowing the use of bugging is very broad. An authorisation may be issued if the action is expected to be of substantial value in the prevention and detection of serious crime and the objective cannot reasonably be achieved by other means (s 93(2)). Serious crime is defined under s 93(4) to include crimes of violence, those involving substantial financial gain, and those involving a large number of people in pursuit of a common purpose.[273] These definitions appear to be significantly wider than those under the old guidelines. The last possibility could allow bugging to be used against, for example, members of CND or anti-road protesters, if it was expected, *inter alia*, that their activities might infringe s 68 of the Criminal Justice and Public Order Act 1994.[274] The 1999 Code of Practice, however, adopted under s 101 of the Act, emphasises that the bugging powers must only be used in cases of serious crime such as drug trafficking.

---

269 See the comments of Lord Nolan [1996] 3 WLR 162, p 175 and Lord Slynn, p 166. See also the Home Affairs Select Committee 3rd Report for 1994–5, Organised Crime HC 18-1, which recommended a statutory basis. It may be noted that *Khan v UK* Appl No 35394/97 was declared admissible at Strasbourg: (1999) 27 EHRR CD 58, and the application was successful (Judgment of the Court of 12 May 2000, 8 BHRC 310) since at the time there was no sufficient basis in law for the interference with Art 8. See further Chapter 14, p 906.

270 HO Circular to Chief Constables, *Guidelines on the Use of Technical Equipment in Police Surveillance Operations.*

271 Under the Guidelines and the Code of Practice, Intrusive Surveillance. One example would be the placing of listening devices in a police station: see *Bailey and Smith* [1993] Crim LR 861; *Musqud Ali* [1966] QB 668.

272 See *H* [1987] Crim LR 47 and *Jelen and Katz* [1990] 90 Cr App R 456. The use of a wired informant may require permission under the HO Circular; Part II of the RIPA – provisions covering covert human sources – now applies.

273 Or the crime is one for which a person of 21 or over with no previous convictions could reasonably be expected to receive a prison sentence of three or more years.

274 See Chapter 9, pp 483–85.

Under s 93(5), an authorisation to interfere with property may be issued by the Chief Officer of Police or, if that is not practicable, by an officer of the rank of Assistant Chief Constable of the force in question (s 94), if s 93(2) applies. The authorisation will be given in writing, except in cases of emergency, when it may be given orally by the Chief Officer in person (s 95(1)). A written authorisation will last for three months, an oral one for 72 hours. Both forms may be renewed in writing for a further three months. The commissioners appointed under s 91(1) must be notified of authorisations as soon as they are made (s 96), but this does not prevent the police acting on the authorisation. There is no administrative check under the 1997 Act, as there is under the 1985 one: no minister is involved in the bugging authorisations. Apart from authorisations falling within s 97 (below), no other independent prior check is available although special Information Commissioners (to become Surveillance Commissioners under the RIPA, Part II) have an oversight role. As has been pointed out in relation to the checking procedure under the 1985 Act, subsequent independent checks are clearly not as effective as prior ones. Again, these arrangements may be compared with those in Denmark, where authorisation of the use of listening devices, wherever placed, and including 'participant monitoring', must be by an investigating magistrate.[275]

As initially drafted, the Bill made no provision for any prior independent scrutiny of the bugging warrants at all, thereby adopting the model used for the 1985 Act, but without even the intervention of Home Office officials. The warrants were to be issued by the Chief Constable of the force in question, continuing the old practice. Michael Howard, the then Home Secretary, considered that exclusion of an independent authorising body was necessary since the police must be able to react instantly to prevent crime. This proposal was severely criticised from various quarters[276] and amendments requiring prior independent approval were put forward by Labour and the Liberal Democrats.[277] The Labour amendment is reflected in s 97; prior approval of authorisation is not required in all instances. Under s 97(2), such approval by a Commissioner is required where the specified property is believed to be a dwelling, hotel bedroom or office premises. It is also needed where the authorising officer believes that information of a more sensitive nature may be acquired.

The involvement of special commissioners, even such a limited involvement, may provide a degree of independent oversight and scrutiny, although the commissioners will probably tend to accept and agree with police representations. Nevertheless, apart from other considerations, the involvement of Commissioners may mean that internal procedures will be tightened up before representations are made. No provision is made

---

275 Art 126 1 and Code of Criminal Procedure.

276 The criticism came from the pressure group, *Liberty*, and from some sections of the press, including sections of the tabloid press. It was argued that other countries accept prior judicial authorisation for bugging warrants and the UK accepts judicial involvement in other aspects of the policing process such as the authorisation of search warrants.

277 Labour proposed that an information commissioner appointed from the judiciary should be involved in checking the warrants, while the Liberal Democrats proposed that a judge acting in his or her capacity as a judge should undertake this role. See Standing Committee F Fifth Sitting Cols 131 *et seq*, 11 March 1997. The House of Lords accepted both amendments and Michael Howard then reached an agreement with Jack Straw, then the Shadow Home Secretary, that an information commissioner appointed from the judiciary should be involved in checking warrants if certain authorisations were in question.

under the Act for independent review of the authorisations in the ordinary courts. Nevertheless, under the Labour amendment, scrutiny of police practices will be, arguably, somewhat more effective than scrutiny of those of the Security Service, not weaker, as Michael Howard originally proposed. Clearly, this is a more satisfactory situation, since the arguments for excluding the judiciary from the process are weaker when matters pertaining to national security are not in question.

Various groups and bodies had put forward pleas for exemption from the provisions of the Bill. These included Catholic priests – who were afraid that the confessional would be bugged – doctors and solicitors. Section 97(2)(b) and the Code of Practice, *Intrusive Surveillance*, adopted under s 101 of the Act[278] reflect the concerns of these groups to an extent. Where the action authorised is likely to result in 'any person acquiring knowledge of matters subject to legal privilege, confidential personal information or confidential journalistic material', prior authorisation is required. Under s 98, 'matters subject to legal privilege' include communications between a professional legal advisor and his or her client connected with the giving of legal advice or relating to legal proceedings. Once approval for an authorisation has been given allowing, for example, for a solicitor's office to be bugged, all conversations between solicitors and clients would be recorded. Under s 99, 'confidential personal information' includes information relating to a person's physical or mental health or to spiritual counselling. But under s 97(3), even where s 97 applies, no approval is needed if the authorising officer 'believes that the case is one of urgency'. No requirement that the belief should be based on reasonable grounds is included. However, the Code of Practice provides that in all but exceptional cases the police must obtain prior approval of the authorisation where s 97 applies: the 'urgency' provision must not be used routinely. It may be noted, however, that s 101 is to be repealed by the RIPA and this Code will be replaced by a new Code to be issued under s 71 of that Act.

The Code of Practice: Intrusive Surveillance

The Code of Practice was revised in November 1999.[279] The revision appeared to be intended to limit further the power of intrusive surveillance in relation to the especially sensitive categories of information. Under the Code, surveillance operations will be banned in churches or temples where a minister of religion is giving spiritual counselling such as absolution. In order to use bugging equipment in such circumstances, not only will the provisions of the Act have to be complied with, but the police will also have to seek permission from the head of the appropriate church or faith. This provision brings the Church of England and other churches and faiths into line with the Roman Catholic Church: the sacramental confessional was given added protection under the original Code.

The relationship between the Code of Practice and the statute is significant. The Act grants broad discretionary powers to conduct intrusive surveillance and interfere with property to senior law enforcement officials, but seeks to constrain and structure these

---

278 It was issued on 27 October 1998.

279 The revised Code was published by the Home Office on 18 November 1999. As noted, it will be replaced under the RIPA.

powers in two main ways. First, there are general precedent conditions for the exercise of such powers, the most significant being the requirement that the action is likely to be of substantial value in preventing or detecting serious crime. Secondly, there are specific countervailing provisions intended to protect privacy and confidentiality. In this respect, s 97 is the key provision, but the Code of Practice, a set of quasi-legal rules, provides a due process underpinning. Section 97, with its ancillary statutory provisions, together with the Code provisions, could be viewed as providing a detailed domestic scheme satisfying the demands of Art 8. But this view fails to take account of the rule of law implications of placing a number of key protective provisions on a quasi-legislative basis within what Baldwin has termed 'tertiary rules', or government by circular.[280]

In common with many of the Codes accompanying 'State power' legislation discussed in this book,[281] the Code provisions are not on their face discretionary; they are in general phrased in the precise terms of mandatory instructions. Nevertheless, no formal sanction, apart from an internal disciplinary one, is provided for their breach. This is also true of the statutory provisions. However, they cloak otherwise tortious actions with authority, while the mere fact that they are statutory may appear to give them greater weight than the Code provisions in the eyes of those to whom they are directed, and of the judiciary. If the provisions were not followed, it would be, theoretically, an internal disciplinary matter and in practice, police officers might pay more attention to this than to the theoretical possibility of being sued. But, as Chapter 14 points out, the same sanction is used for breach of the PACE Codes and does not appear to be effective, taking into account the very few disciplinary charges laid for their breach.[282] Thus, senior law enforcement officials are in effect given at least a partial discretion as to whether to follow the Code rules and thus whether to respect the Art 8 rights which they reflect.[283] As pointed out in Chapter 1, the concept of a right precludes the idea of an open-ended discretion to infringe it in the pursuit of competing interests.[284]

Unless rigorous, independent review of rule-compliance and a clear remedy for breach are available, the Code rules will remain, in effect, largely discretionary, and the rights protected by them illusory. This is a concern in respect of the statutory provisions, including s 97, but it arises *a fortiori* in respect of the Code and will be equally true of the

---

280 See Baldwin, *Rules and Government*, 1995.

281 The Codes of Practice made under the Police and Criminal Evidence Act 1984 considered in Chapters 13 and 14 were the forerunners of the similar Codes considered in this book – the Codes adopted under the Terrorism Act 2000 and the Regulation of Investigatory Powers Act 2000.

282 See pp 915–20.

283 Ronald Dworkin has argued that if an official's decision whether to comply with a given rule is final and unreviewable, he is endowed with a form of discretion (*Taking Rights Seriously*, 1977, p 69). In practice, decisions taken by police officers in relation to the provisions of the Codes of Practice discussed in this book (see, in particular, Chapter 13) are in general unlikely to be considered in courts or in police disciplinary proceedings. In a minority of instances, however, such provisions may be considered in relation to exclusion of evidence. Even then, the 'sanction' of such exclusion is unlikely to be used in respect of most forms of non-confession evidence, the form of evidence to which the provisions of the RIPA Code are most likely to relate. See, generally, Davis, KC, *Discretionary Justice*, 1980, pp 84–88.

284 See pp 11–12. Dworkin argues that it only makes sense to denote an interest as a right if it will generally win any battle with competing societal considerations: see *op cit*, fn 695, p 191.

new Code to be introduced under s 71 of the RIPA, which will also be accompanied by no clear sanction for its breach (s 72(2)).[285] It is suggested below that the new tribunal system may prove ineffective, and that since no clear parliamentary or administrative means of seeking to enhance rule compliance is available, recourse to court-based remedies under the influence of the HRA would be of especial significance in this context if, which is very doubtful, they could find expression.

The Regulation of Investigatory Powers Act Part II[286]

Part II of the RIPA 2000 covers surveillance activities of immense potential to infringe privacy that previously had no – or only a narrow – basis in law. For the first time, a comprehensive statutory basis has been created for the expanding use of covert surveillance. The growth in proactive intelligence-led policing (targeting suspects using covert surveillance rather than investigating a crime after it has happened) and the proliferation of various forms of surveillance devices provided part of the impetus for reform.[287] Unlike Part III of the Police Act 1997 or s 5 of the Intelligence Services Act 1994 with which it overlaps,[288] Part II of the RIPA covers a very wide range of public authorities. It also covers a much wider range of circumstances. Prior to the introduction of Part II, invasions of privacy by means of covert surveillance falling outside the narrow scope of the 1997 or 1994 provisions were occurring, not on the basis of a legal power, but on the basis that the State is in the same position as the individual citizen in being free to do that which the law does not forbid. Since there was no legal right to privacy – in a broad, general sense – no legal power to invade it was needed.[289]

The pre-existing statutory provisions were mainly (although not exclusively) aimed at the form of surveillance termed 'intrusive' by Part II. Most significantly, a warrant or authorisation was required where there was a physical invasion of property by the police or security and intelligence services. So a wide area of surveillance fell outside those statutes and the need to cover this particular form of surveillance – in anticipation of the effects of the HRA – provided the immediate impetus for the introduction of Part II. Under the HRA it is clearly necessary for surveillance to be placed on a statutory basis even where previously it would not have attracted any form of liability, if it would amount to an invasion of privacy under Art 8 of the European Convention on Human

---

285 On the model provided by the PACE Codes (adopted for all the Codes mentioned in this book) it will be admissible in evidence under s 72(3). It should be taken into account by courts, the new tribunal and relevant Commissioners under s 72(4).

286 It may be noted that under s 46, there are restrictions on Part II authorisations extending to Scotland.

287 The use of covert surveillance together with other targeting methods, including the use of informers, has expanded rapidly and is seen as immensely useful by the police: see *Policing with Intelligence* HMIC Thematic Inspection Report, 1997/99.

288 Under the Police Act 1997, Part III, s 92: 'No entry on or interference with property or with wireless telegraphy shall be unlawful if it is authorised by an authorisation having effect under this Part'. Thus, forms of directed surveillance involving an actual interference with property (see below) – on non-residential premises – were covered by the Police Act 1997, Part III. Under the 1994 Act, s 5, the Home Secretary, on an application from a member of the Intelligence Service, can issue a warrant authorising the 'taking of any such action as is specified in the warrant in respect of any property so specified or in respect of wireless telegraphy so specified'.

289 See above, p 533; clearly, privacy received some protection in the pre-HRA era, especially under the doctrine of trespass.

Rights, since para 2 provides that an interference with individual privacy must be 'in accordance with the law'. The key aim of Part II is therefore to meet a central requirement under the Convention – that of legality.

It is clear that Part II has gone some way towards achieving this aim in the sense that it has provided a much more comprehensive statutory underpinning for covert surveillance than the pre-existing one. A basis in national law has been created which purports to meet the requirements of legality under the Convention. Below, it will be considered whether it has succeeded in meeting those requirements and whether the further Convention requirements of necessity and proportionality have been met. In order to do so, the new provisions governing so called 'intrusive' and 'directed' surveillance will be examined with a view to contending that when the two regimes are contrasted, the inadequacies of the latter, in Convention terms, are starkly revealed.

Intrusive surveillance

Under s 26(3) of the RIPA, 'intrusive' surveillance occurs when a surveillance device is used or an individual undertaking surveillance is actually present on residential premises, or in a private vehicle, or it is carried out by such a device in relation to such premises or vehicle without being present on the premises or vehicle. 'Residential' is defined in s 48(1) of the RIPA as premises used as living accommodation, while 'premises' includes movable structures and land. The definition expressly excludes common areas of residential premises and clearly does not cover office premises (s 48(7)(b)). Thus, covert surveillance of office premises falls within the term 'directed', rather than intrusive, surveillance.

Section 26(3), read with s 48(7), offers only a partial definition, since it would cover all forms of covert surveillance taking place in relation to residential premises. Some forms of such surveillance can be treated as directed surveillance, as indicated below, and it is in relation to residential premises that an area of uncertainty is created as to the category into which surveillance falls.

Under s 32(3) of the RIPA authorisation of intrusive surveillance is on the grounds of 'the interests of national security, for the purpose of preventing or detecting serious crime or of preventing disorder, in the interests of the economic well-being of the UK'. 'Serious crime' is defined in s 81(3)[290] in substantially the same terms as in s 93(4) of the Police Act 1997. Proportionality requirements are introduced under s 32(2): the authorising person must be satisfied that the action to be taken is proportionate to what is hoped to be achieved by carrying it out. Authorisations for such surveillance are granted by the Home Secretary under s 41 or, for police or customs officers, by senior authorising officers, who are the highest ranking police officers in Britain (see s 32(6)). There is also provision for

---

290 Section 81(2) provides that such crime satisfies the tests of sub-s 3(a) or (b). Under s 81(3), those tests are (a) that the offence is one for which a person of 21 with no previous convictions could reasonably expect a sentence of three years' imprisonment or more, or (b) that the conduct involves the use of violence, results in substantial financial gain, or is conduct by a large number of persons in pursuit of a common purpose.

the grant of authorisations in a case of urgency by persons of almost equally high rank, other than the senior authorising officer.[291]

The provisions for urgent and non-urgent authorisations under ss 33, 34, 35 and 36 mirror those under the Police Act, Part III in that, under s 35, notice must be given to a 'Surveillance Commissioner' and, under s 36, the authorisation will not take effect until it has been approved, except where it is urgent and the grounds for urgency are set out in the notice, in which case the authorisation will take effect from the time of its grant. Under s 38, senior authorising officers can appeal to the Chief Surveillance Commissioner against decisions of ordinary Surveillance Commissioners. The Commissioners have responsibility for the destruction of material obtained by surveillance, under s 37, but there is no requirement that material no longer needed for proceedings and no longer subject to an authorisation *must* be destroyed.

Under s 43, authorisations can be granted or renewed urgently orally by senior authorising officers or in writing by persons authorised to act on their behalf in urgent cases. If, under s 43(3)(a), an authorisation is granted or renewed by a person entitled to act only in urgent cases, or was renewed by such a person or orally, it ceases to take effect after 72 hours. Section 42 provides special rules for the intelligence services which overlap with those of s 5 of the Intelligence Services Act 1994. Under s 42, the security and intelligence services can undertake intrusive surveillance on grant of a warrant. The grounds are those under s 32(3). As far as intrusive surveillance is concerned, the function of the services in support of the prevention or detection of serious crime is excluded where the application is by a member of GCHQ or the SIS (under s 42(3)). Under s 44(3), a warrant authorising intrusive surveillance issued by a senior official, and not renewed under the hand of the Secretary of State, 'shall cease to have effect at the end of the second working day' after its issue. In the case of other such warrants, that point will be at the end of the period of six months from the day of issue or renewal.

This authorisation regime follows the model adopted for telephone tapping under the Interception of Communications Act 1985 and continued with minor modifications under Part I of the RIPA. That regime has been subjected to criticism on the basis that the mechanisms for creating executive accountability are so weak,[292] but it may meet Strasbourg requirements.[293] The regime for intrusive surveillance provides for independent checks and for the possibility that an authorisation will not be able to take effect if it does not satisfy the requirements, including those of proportionality. Clearly, the standard of scrutiny may be variable, but the very fact that an authorisation will be checked independently may tend to foster rigour in preparing the papers.

---

291 Under s 34(4), such persons are of a rank almost as high as such officers. In the case of police forces, this means a person holding the rank of Assistant Chief Constable or, in the case of the Metropolitan or City of London forces, of Commander.

292 See Lloyd (1986) 49 MLR 86; Leigh [1986] PL 8.

293 As discussed above, p 665, the regime created under the 1985 Act was considered in *Christie v UK* 78-A DR E Com HR 119; on the facts of the case no breach of Art 8 was found.

Directed surveillance

Under s 26(2) of the RIPA, all covert surveillance is directed surveillance if it is not intrusive and it is undertaken 'otherwise than by way of an immediate response to events or circumstances, the nature of which is such that it would not be practicable for an authorisation to be sought', and for the purposes of 'a specific investigation or ... operation', and 'in such a manner as is likely to result in the obtaining of private information about a person', even if he is not identified in relation to the investigation. If the device or person is not on the premises or in the vehicle, the surveillance is 'directed', not 'intrusive' unless 'the device is such that it consistently provides information of the same quality and detail as might be expected to be obtained from a device actually present on the premises or in the vehicle' (s 26(5)). The (draft) Code of Practice on Covert Surveillance (2000) made under s 71(3)(a) of the RIPA seeks to draw a distinction between general law enforcement functions and the systematic targeting of an individual; only the latter may amount to directed surveillance. Anomalously enough, the term 'directed surveillance' also covers an interception of communications in the course of its transmission that is consented to by the sender or recipient and in respect of which there is no interception warrant (s 26(4)(b) and s 48(4)).

From the above, it appears that directed surveillance would occur where a 'bugging' device is placed in the hallway of a block of flats that provides information of a lesser quality than would be obtained if the device was inside one of the flats. Intrusive surveillance would occur, for example, when a 'bugging' device is placed in a car parked near a private house that normally provides information of the same quality as would be obtained if the device was inside the house. These examples make it clear that very fine lines may be drawn between the two forms of surveillance, although, as indicated below, the two regimes differ so sharply. Moreover, the distinction between directed surveillance and 'general law enforcement' functions, such as observing persons entering or leaving a house, turns on the question whether or not the observation can be viewed as an immediate response – another instance in which fine lines may be drawn. If observation of a house occurs over a period of time, it can be argued that an invasion of privacy is occurring that can no longer be viewed as an immediate response and which requires therefore a statutory underpinning.[294]

Section 47(1) provides powers for the Secretary of State to extend or modify the authorisation provisions. He can provide for any directed surveillance 'to be treated for the purposes of this Part as intrusive surveillance'. Under s 47(2), this power is subject to the negative resolution procedure, but clearly that does not provide the same safeguards as the full parliamentary process.

'Directed' surveillance may be authorised on the grounds under s 28. The grounds include 'the interests of national security, for the purpose of preventing or detecting crime or of preventing disorder, in the interests of the economic well-being of the UK, in the interests of public safety; for the purpose of protecting public health; for the purpose of assessing or collecting any tax, duty ... or other ... charge payable to a government department'; or for any other 'purpose specified for the purposes of this subsection by an order made by the Secretary of State'. This order must be approved by Parliament.

---

294 Such an underpinning could be created, by order of the Secretary of State, under s 47.

Proportionality requirements are introduced under s 28(2) to the effect that the authorising person must believe that the authorisation or authorised conduct is 'proportionate to what is sought to be achieved by carrying it out'.

The authorisation for directed surveillance is granted by a 'designated person' under s 28. Under s 30, such persons are 'the individuals holding such offices, ranks or positions with relevant public authorities as are prescribed for the purposes of this subsection by an order' made by the Secretary of State. The Secretary of State can himself be a designated person under s 30(2). The 'relevant public authorities' (set out in Sched 1) include the police, the security and intelligence services, Customs and Excise, Inland Revenue, the armed forces, the Departments of Health; Social Security; Trade and Industry; Environment, Transport and the Regions. Further authorities can be designated by order of the Secretary of State. The prescribed persons in the relevant public authorities are now set out in The Regulation of Investigatory Powers Act 2000 (Prescription of Offices, Ranks and Positions Order 2000).[295] In police forces, the prescribed office is that of Superintendent; in urgent cases, that of Inspector. The draft Code of Practice, para 3.10 recommends that authorising officers should not 'ideally be responsible for authorising their own activities (emphasis added) ... however, it is recognised that this may sometimes be unavoidable ...'

Under s 43, written authorisations cease to have effect after three months, although they may be renewed for additional three month periods (security or intelligence service authorisations may be renewed for six months). Urgent authorisations cease to have effect after 72 hours unless they are renewed either orally (if the urgency subsists) by a person whose entitlement to act is not confined to urgent cases, or in writing. Authorisations cannot be granted orally except in urgent cases and by a person whose entitlement to act is not confined to such cases. Under s 43(3)(b) 'in a case not falling within paragraph (a) in which the authorisation is for the conduct or the use of a covert human intelligence source', the period is 12 months from its grant or last renewal. In a case falling outside s 43(3)(a) or (b), it is three months under s 43(3)(c). Under s 44(5)(a), when an authorisation for the carrying out of directed surveillance is granted by a member of any of the intelligence services and renewed by an instrument 'endorsed under the hand of the person renewing [it] with a statement that the renewal is believed to be necessary on grounds falling within section 32(3)(a) or (c), the authorisation (unless renewed again) shall cease to have effect at the end of the period of six months'.

A Chief Surveillance Commissioner, who may be assisted by Assistant Commissioners, has a general oversight role in relation to this regime, under s 62. But, this independent check occurs only after the event. Therefore, its impact on accountability may be minimal.

Other surveillance

Under s 47, the Secretary of State may also by order 'apply this Part, with such modifications as he thinks fit, to any ... surveillance that is neither directed nor intrusive'. The power is intended to afford, if necessary, a statutory basis for the use of other powers

---

295 SI 2000/2417.

which may be found to have fallen outside this Act. The compatibility of this basis with the Convention is questionable, partly because, it is suggested, the legal basis for the powers is so uncertain and so dependent on the exercise of executive power. The term 'such modifications' implies that lesser safeguards than those available for directed surveillance might be adopted, a possibility which would be likely to have Art 8 implications. These matters are considered below.

Confidential information

Certain safeguards relating to the type of information that can be gathered using directed or intrusive surveillance are created, but the relevant rules appear only in the draft Code of Practice, not in the Act itself. Para 2.3 relates to certain types of confidential information: confidential personal information (relating to physical or mental health or to spiritual counselling), matters subject to legal privilege and confidential journalistic material. Under para 2.10, if it is 'possible that a *substantial* proportion of the material acquired could be confidential material' (emphasis added), applications should be granted 'only in exceptional and compelling circumstances, with full regard to the proportionality issues'. Para 2.8 reminds those granting the authorisation that an undertaking has been given that material subject to the seal of the confessional will not be the subject of operations. General principles apply to confidential material, under para 2.11; they include the requirement to destroy the material 'as soon as it is no longer necessary to retain it for a specified purpose' and to refrain from dissemination of it unless 'an appropriate officer [having sought legal advice] is satisfied that is necessary for a specific purpose'. These rules fail to introduce any independent check into the process even where material is most clearly of a private nature. As far as directed surveillance is concerned, the question of acquiring and using confidential material is subject, in essentials, to the same regime as is available for non-confidential material.

The use and storage of information obtained by surveillance techniques is in general left to be governed by the Code of Practice to be made under s 71, although the Surveillance Commissioners also have power, when quashing authorisations of intrusive surveillance under s 37, to order the destruction of records. At present, storage and retention of police information are governed by a detailed ACPO Code[296] which instructs on the applicability of data protection principles to such information. As indicated above, concerns have been raised regarding record keeping by the Security Service, bearing in mind the fact that it does not have to comply with the Data Protection Act 1998, even in its criminal function.[297] Under the 1998 Act, in relation to personal information, the police do not have to comply with the fair and lawful processing provisions of the first data protection principle,[298] subject access requests, or restrictions on disclosure of personal information, if to do so would be likely to prejudice the prevention and detection of crime or the apprehension and prosecution of offenders. These are not blanket exemptions; they should be considered in their application to individual cases. But it is unclear that careful scrutiny on this basis occurs.[299] The RIPA Code of Practice will therefore be of

---

296 Code of Practice for Data Protection, 1995.

297 See p 604.

298 Except in relation to 'sensitive' data.

299 See the 1998 *Justice* report (*op cit*, fn 97) Chapter 4, esp pp 92–95.

significance since it could provide much greater clarity and safeguard a significant aspect of privacy. But, it is argued that such a significant task should not be undertaken by quasi-legislation.[300]

The oversight role of the Commissioners

The Police Act 1997 set up a complaints system which, apart from the lack of a special tribunal, strongly resembled that under the 1985 Act, considered above. The similarity was the more striking since the system related to ordinary crime, not necessarily to terrorism or other activities, having a potential impact on national security. This model has now been continued under s 62 of the RIPA which adds additional functions to those of the 'Chief Surveillance Commissioner', so that his role mirrors that of the Interceptions of Communications Commissioner. The office of Commissioner under s 91 of the 1997 Act is continued, but the Commissioners are re-designated 'Surveillance Commissioners' and their complaints role will be removed. Assistant Surveillance Commissioners may be appointed under s 63 of the RIPA to aid the Chief Surveillance Commissioner. Such aid will clearly be needed since he will provide oversight, not only of police surveillance, but also of surveillance carried out by all the persons covered by Part II of the RIPA. Thus, the oversight role of the Surveillance Commissioners is broader than their role in relation to authorisations, since the latter relates only to the police and customs, while the former covers other public authorities and the Home Secretary's authorising role under s 41. Thus, the role of the Surveillance Commissioners overlaps with that of the Intelligence Services Commissioner who has an oversight role which, as indicated above, covers, inter alia, surveillance carried out by those services.

Under s 107 of the Police Act 1997, the Chief Commissioner has reporting duties similar to those of the Intelligence Services Commissioner. (His duty under s106, to report to the Prime Minister if an appeal is allowed and where a finding in favour of a complainant is made by a Commissioner, was repealed under Sched 4 of the 2000 Act.) He must make an annual report on the discharge of his functions. The report must be presented to Parliament and published as a Command Paper. The Prime Minister may exclude matters from the report under s 107(4) of the Act if it appears to him that it contains matter 'prejudicial to the prevention and detection of serious crime' or to the discharge of the functions of a police authority, the service authorities for the National Criminal Intelligence Service or the duties of the Commissioner for Customs and Excise.

Closed circuit television

The increasing use by local authorities of closed circuit television as a form of visual surveillance is not regulated by RIPA 2000, Part II. It is not either directed or intrusive surveillance since it is not undertaken for a specific purpose. Section 163 of the Criminal Justice and Public Order Act 1994 clarifies the power of local authorities to install closed circuit cameras for surveillance purposes.[301] The fact of capturing the image of a person on CCTV may not, in all circumstances, in itself constitute an invasion of privacy,

---

300 See Chapter 13, pp 757–58 for analogous discussion in relation to the PACE Codes.
301 See *Brentwood Council ex p Peck* [1998] CMLR 697, now in the Strasbourg system. For further discussion see Norris, Moran and Armstrong (eds), *Surveillance, CCTV and Social Control*, 1999.

although the mere fact that a person is in a public place should not preclude that possibility.[302] Even where it is arguable that an invasion of privacy has not occurred, the use of the information later on may create one.[303]

Impact of the HRA

Interference with the guarantees of Art 8

A preliminary question in terms of the Convention requirements might, in this context, concern the status of the individual in question as a victim, where he or she was uncertain whether surveillance had occurred. The Court put forward the following reason in *Klass v Federal Republic of Germany*[304] for regarding the applicants as 'victims' under Art 25 despite the fact that they were uncertain whether or not their phones had been tapped: '[normally an applicant cannot challenge a law *in abstracto* ... the position is different [when] owing to the secrecy of the measures objected to, he cannot point to any concrete measure specifically affecting him'. Thus the existence of legislation permitting secret measures, including the RIPA and the Police Act 1997, may allow a person to claim to be the victim of a breach of Art 8 although she would also have to show a 'reasonable likelihood that surveillance had occurred'.[305] Given that the provisions in the HRA regarding the status of 'victims' rely on the Convention jurisprudence,[306] this finding would aid the claim of such a person in the ordinary courts. The remit of the new tribunal under s 65 RIPA, discussed below, might not allow it to consider such a claim, unless it interprets its jurisdiction more widely.

Assuming that there is a reasonable likelihood that surveillance had occurred, a key question for the new tribunal or court would be whether in the particular circumstances it fell within Art 8(1). The extent to which Art 8 provides protection from surveillance outside the home or other living accommodation such as hotel rooms might be considered. The principles at stake are similar to those discussed above in relation to interception: all these forms of surveillance interfere with informational autonomy. But while it is now clearly settled in the Strasbourg jurisprudence that in most circumstances interception (at least in the form of telephone tapping) creates an interference with Art 8 guarantees, this cannot be said with equal certainty of all the diverse forms of surveillance covered by Part II of the RIPA or Part III of the 1997 Act.

However, 'the State [has an obligation] to respect private life by controlling the activities of its agents [in collecting personal information]'.[307] It has been indicated that interference with property for surveillance purposes by the security and intelligence services has been found to fall within Art 8.[308] Collection and use of information derived from covert investigative techniques may do so unless the applicant is already involved

---

302 See below, pp 704–06.

303 See further the *Justice* Report, *op cit*, fn 97, p 31.

304 (1978) 2 EHRR 214.

305 *G, H and I v UK* 15 EHRR CD 41.

306 See Chapter 4, pp 164–65.

307 Harris, D, O'Boyle, K and Warbrick, C, *Law of the European Convention on Human Rights*, 1995, p 310.

308 See pp 662–65.

in criminal activity.[309] The acquiring of information represents one form of invasion of informational autonomy; further invasions may occur due to the storage and dissemination of the information. In a number of cases, Strasbourg has found that the collection of information about an individual by the State without his or her consent will, in principle, interfere with the right to respect for private life[310] and it has contemplated the possibility that compiling and retaining the information will also do so.[311] The use of listening devices has been found to create an interference with the Art 8(1) guarantee.[312] Systematic or even indirect targeting of an individual is also very likely to involve such an interference.[313]

The Strasbourg case law suggests that where an interference occurs in an obviously 'private' place, an infringement of the primary right will be found. The extent to which, outside such places, an invasion of privacy might be found in respect of surveillance is a matter which is subject to a developing jurisprudence at Strasbourg and nationally. An individual may expect to retain a degree of privacy in a semi-public environment, such as a restaurant,[314] gymnasium,[315] solicitor's office,[316] pub or shop.[317] Strasbourg has been prepared to extend the notion of private space beyond obvious places such as the home; as Harris, O'Boyle and Warbrick put it: 'it is not enough just for the individual to be himself: he must be able to a substantial degree to keep to himself what he is and what he does ... the idea of private space need not be confined to those areas where the person has some exclusive rights of occupancy'.[318] In this respect, the Strasbourg approach may be developing in a direction which will take it away from the current UK statutory approach: 'the expanding understanding of private life set out in the *Niemetz* case[319] indicates that a formal public/private distinction about the nature of the location will not always be decisive.'[320]

This identifiable general trend suggests that this is another instance in which the emphasis should be on the evolutive nature of the Convention[321] rather than on the

---

309 *Ludi v Switzerland* A 238 (1992).

310 See: *Murray v UK* A 300 (1994), paras 84, 85; *McVeigh v UK* (1981) 25 DR 15, p 49.

311 See *G, H and I v UK* 15 EHRR CD 41 (application of first and third applicants failed on the basis that they had not shown sufficient likelihood that such compiling or retention had occurred).

312 See *Govell v UK* (1997) 4 EHRLR 438; *Khan v UK* Appl No 35394/97 (declared admissible on 20 April 1999) (1999) 27 EHRR CD 58; Judgment of the Court: 8 BHRC 310.

313 *Harman and Hewitt v UK* (1992) 14 EHRR 657.

314 A situation considered in a decision of the German Supreme Court: BGH 19 December 1995 BGHZ 131, pp 322–46.

315 The location where surreptitious photographs were taken of the former Princess of Wales, in *HRH Princess of Wales v MGN Newspapers Limited and Others* (1993) Transcript, Association of Official Shorthand Writers, 8 November 1993.

316 See *Niemetz v FRG* A 251-B (1992).

317 See *R v Broadcasting Standards Council ex p BBC* [2000] 3 WLR 1327.

318 Harris, O'Boyle and Warbrick, *op cit*, fn 307, p 309.

319 *Niemetz v FRG* A 251-B (1992).

320 Harris, O'Boyle and Warbrick, *op cit*, fn 307, p 309. *Niemetz v FRG* A 251-B (1992) concerned office premises, making it clear that rights to respect for privacy are not dependent on an interest in property.

321 The Convention must be given an 'evolutive' interpretation (*Johnstone v Ireland* A 112 (1986), para 53), which takes account of current standards in European society (*Tyrer v UK* A 26 (1978), para 31). These would be expected to include the presence of privacy laws across Europe.

outcome of particular applications to the Commission, such as that in *X v United Kingdom*.[322] The Commission found that the actions of the police in taking and filing photographs without consent of a woman arrested for taking part in a political demonstration disclosed no *prima facie* breach of Art 8. The reasoning was unclear, but a central factor appeared to be the public and voluntary nature of her activities. The decision has been viewed as out of line with the trend of Art 8 jurisprudence: 'In the opinion of some scholars, the ... decision may well be an outdated aberration in the case law of the Strasbourg organs.'[323]

The approach in other jurisdictions may indicate the direction in which the Strasbourg jurisprudence is likely to develop. The German Supreme Court[324] refused to follow the approach of the Appeal Court that privacy 'stopped at the doorstep' and that therefore, no action lay for invasion of privacy in respect of events which had taken place outside the home or other clearly private spaces. The approach indicated was that one may still be entitled to respect for privacy in semi-public places if, as the court put it, it is clear by reference to 'objective criteria' that one wishes to be 'left alone' so that one can, 'relying on the fact of seclusion, act in a way that [one] would not have done ... in public'. In other words, the interest in privacy was clearly distinguished from property interests. The Canadian Criminal Code also reflects such a stance.[325] Thus, it may be argued that public/private distinctions based on location are too simplistic and that a test of a reasonable expectation of privacy or, more broadly still, of control of private information would be more satisfactory.[326] On the basis of such a test, if, for example, one person engages in a whispered exchange with another in an almost empty street, and this exchange is recorded by means of a listening device, it is contended that an invasion of privacy has occurred which may fall within Art 8(1). It may be noted that this test would bring some use of CCTV – where it captures private actions in semi-public or even public places – within Art 8(1).

As Leigh and Lustgarten observe: 'An atmosphere in which people practise self-censorship ... is stultifying and fearful ... Citizens should be able to assume that unless there are overwhelming reasons to the contrary, their thoughts and feelings will be communicated only to those to whom they choose to utter them.'[327] These comments clearly apply equally to conversations in the street, in a vehicle, in pubs, in hotel rooms. Obviously, there may be circumstances in which it is impossible to speak without

322 (1973) Appl No 5877/72 16 YBCHE, 328.

323 Bygrave, LA, 'Data protection pursuant to the right to privacy in human rights treaties' (1999) 6(3) IJLIT 247, p 265. Bygrave notes: '... there are good grounds for holding that it ought to be accorded little weight in present and future interpretation of Article 8'. In spite of these comments, however, Bygrave concedes that in the later decision of *Friedl v Austria* (1995) A 305B (not treated by the Court on the merits due to friendly settlement) 'the Commission laid weight upon the same ... kind of factors as those mentioned in *X v United Kingdom*' (*ibid*, p 266). See also *Stewart-Brady v UK* (1999) 27 EHRR 284, in which a claim of an interference with Art 8 rights due to the taking of a photograph was declared inadmissible (although these findings were made in the context of positive State obligations and there was a conflict with Art 10).

324 BGH 19 December 1995 BGHZ 131, pp 322–46.

325 Section 487.01(4).

326 The Press Complaints Commission's Code of Practice defines 'private places [as] public or private property where there is a reasonable expectation of privacy'. Such a test was recommended by the Irish Law Reform Commission Consultation Paper: *Privacy, Surveillance and Interception*, 1996.

327 *Op cit*, fn 62, p 40.

expecting to be overheard, as in a crowded train. But in other circumstances, this expectation would depend entirely on the circumstances. In a reasonably quiet street it would be viewed as socially and probably morally unacceptable to approach two persons speaking quietly together with the obvious intention of eavesdropping on their conversation, since the two would have a reasonable expectation of enjoying a degree of privacy. It follows, therefore, that the issue as to whether the respect for private life has been infringed by the secret recording of a communication should be resolved not by reliance on fine distinctions regarding the degrees of 'privacy' to be associated with different locations, but according to the intentions and reasonable expectations of at least one of the parties to it.[328] In other words, a shift in the meaning of 'privacy' would have to occur, one which appears to be in accordance with the notion of informational autonomy as the core privacy value and with changing perception of privacy at Strasbourg. Therefore, there is a sound argument that the use of surveillance devices or techniques in most circumstances will lead to findings that an interference with the rights to respect for private life and, where appropriate, to the home and correspondence, under Art 8 has occurred.

In accordance with the law

Once it is established that such an interference has occurred, it cannot be justified if it is not in accordance with the law. Until the 1997 Act and then the RIPA 2000, Part II were introduced, the use of various techniques had no sufficient basis in law.[329] Such a basis is now established, but it is questionable whether it is of sufficient quality.[330] The regimes governing the forms of surveillance show dissimilarities, especially between 'intrusive' and 'directed' surveillance. The position regarding the use of intrusive surveillance is broadly the same as that discussed above, in relation to interception, under Part I of the RIPA, since the provisions are equally foreseeable and accessible.[331] The same may be said of the regime under s 97 of the 1997 Act.

Bearing in mind the strictness of these requirements in this context, discussed above,[332] it is unclear that the requirement as to quality would be found to be satisfied in respect of certain of these provisions. This may be said in relation to the use of directed surveillance, and of listening devices within the 1997 Act, but outside s 97. The definition of directed surveillance is confusing and imprecise and creates an uncertain divide between directed and intrusive surveillance. Despite such uncertainty, the regime for intrusive surveillance is much stricter. This uncertainty creates, it is suggested, a fundamental flaw in RIPA 2000, Part II, which may mean that it cannot meet the requirement of quality, in that respect. As indicated above, ss 28, 29 and 30 allow the

---

328 This proposition finds support from the position in the US. The US Supreme Court has found: 'the Fourth Amendment protects people not places'; the significant issue was not the location of the covert device, but the existence of a reasonable expectation that privacy would be protected (*Katz v US* (1967) 389 US 347, pp 351–53).

329 See above, pp 690–1 and pp 696–7. See further *op cit*, fn 97, Chapter 7.

330 As indicated above, Art 8 may not be satisfied merely on the ground that interferences with privacy have a basis in primary legislation. See p 680.

331 See p 680.

332 See pp 680–81.

Secretary of State, by order, to make provision regarding 'designated persons', further grounds, and for allowing further bodies to engage in directed surveillance on the very broad grounds under ss 28 and 29. The extent to which, in all these instances, power is placed in executive hands so that it might be exercised in an unpredictable fashion calls into question the quality of the law, even accepting that in some, but not all, of these instances there is a lesser invasion of privacy, calling for less precision.[333] The accessibility of the law would also be questionable, bearing in mind the opportunities for its extension by executive order, albeit with the approval of Parliament. In respect of all these provisions, the means of keeping a check on their arbitrary use is in doubt due to the failure to include any independent check at all on authorisations of directed surveillance, outside the public authority in question.[334] No judicial or administrative check is necessary, in contrast to the provisions for intrusive surveillance and interception.

Legitimate aims

Assuming that an interference with the Art 8(1) guarantee occurs, which is found, in the particular circumstances which confront a court or the new tribunal, to be in accordance with the law, it must be shown that it had a legitimate aim. The 'legitimate aim' requirement would probably be readily satisfied in respect of intrusive surveillance and the use of surveillance devices under the 1997 Act since the grounds justifying interference under Art 8(2) correspond with the three grounds under s 32(3) of the RIPA and with the 'serious crime' ground under the 1997 Act. This is also probably true of the power to use CCTV under s 163 of the Criminal Justice and Public Order Act 1994.

There may be room for argument that certain of the grounds for the use of directed surveillance under s 28(3) are less clearly within para 2 since they cover, inter alia, the purpose of collecting any contribution due to a government department. However, they would probably fall within the 'economic well-being' exception.[335] The possibility is left open of including other grounds, by order of the Secretary of State. Any such further grounds would also have to fall within the para 2 aims. So far, under Art 8(2), the State has always satisfied the legitimate aim requirement.

Necessary in a democratic society

It must further be shown that the interference 'corresponds to a pressing social need and, in particular, that it is proportionate to the legitimate aim pursued'.[336] In assessing proportionality in relation to the aim of national security, the Court has allowed a very wide margin of appreciation to the State,[337] but it is less wide in relation to the prevention of crime and arguably also in respect of the other grounds. In any event, the margin of

---

333 This may be argued by analogy with the findings in *Malone v UK* (1984) 7 EHRR 14 regarding telephone metering as opposed to interception.

334 In *Leander v Sweden* (1987) 9 EHRR 433, the Court said: 'in view of the risk that a system of secret surveillance poses ... the court must be satisfied that there exist adequate and effective guarantees against abuse' (para 60).

335 *MS v Sweden* (1999) 28 EHRR 313, para 38.

336 *Olsson v Sweden* A 130 (1988), para 67.

337 *Leander v Sweden* (1987) 9 EHRR 433.

appreciation doctrine should be irrelevant in domestic decisions. In terms of the outcomes of applications, Strasbourg has not provided clear guidance on the question of when a pressing social need would be discerned in this context. In a number of key cases, including *Khan v UK*,[338] which concerned the use of a listening device, it was found that the interference had no basis in law.[339] In a further group of cases, it was found that the interference had such a basis and the safeguards available, particularly in the context of national security, were found to be sufficient, taking the margin of appreciation into account.[340] But some analogous jurisprudence is available.

As indicated above, it was found in *Klass v FRG*[341] that judicial or administrative authority for warrants would provide a degree of independent oversight. While the arrangements for intrusive surveillance under the RIPA 2000, Part II or under s 97 of the 1997 Act may meet this requirement, those under s 93 or for directed surveillance might fail to do so since no independent administrative or judicial check is available before the event. In this respect, the contrast with the arrangements for intrusive surveillance is very clear, bearing in mind the fact that directed surveillance is a means of acquiring large amounts of personal information; the only distinction between it and intrusive surveillance may be the quality of the sound or vision – the content of the information may be almost identical. Therefore, the strong distinction created between the two types of surveillance may be unwarranted. In particular, where a person has authorised himself to conduct surveillance, the requirement of independence could be said to be completely abrogated; it is hard to see that in such an instance, it can be said that a check on the requirements of proportionality is in place.

The key criticism of Part II is that a twin-track scheme is created under it whereby a much more rigorous regime is in place for intrusive as opposed to directed surveillance: intrusive surveillance requires authorisation at a higher level within the public authority and at an external level. Directed surveillance requires lower level internal authorisation and no external authorisation – merely review after the event by the Surveillance Commissioner. This markedly different regime leads to the suggestion that the new regime for directed surveillance fails to meet Convention requirements. The general principles espoused at Strasbourg may also be indicative. If it is accepted that informational autonomy lies in the 'core' of Art 8, as a value which a democratic society should respect,[342] interferences with it by a public authority should receive the strictest scrutiny. Such scrutiny would be of the arrangements for authorisation and their application in the particular instance. Even where the authorisation process itself was found to satisfy Art 8(2), a particular authorisation might be found to allow an interference disproportionate to the legitimate aim pursued. In particular, issues of proportionality might also arise where a listening device placed outside a house provided information of only a marginally lower quality than would be provided were it on the premises. The use of CCTV may be proportionate to the legitimate aim – of preventing

---

338 (2000) 8 BHRC 310.

339 Eg, *Malone v UK* (1984) 7 EHRR 14, *Halford v UK* [1997] IRLR 471; (1997) 24 EHRR 523.

340 Eg, *Christie v UK* 78-A DR E Com HR 119.

341 (1978) 2 EHRR 214.

342 See *Kjeldsen v Denmark* (1976) 1 EHRR 711, p 731.

crime – pursued, but the lack of regulation of the use of the information obtained may mean that there are insufficient safeguards available.

Using the HRA

Duties of Commissioners

All the Commissioners should comply with the Convention in relation to their reviewing functions under the 1997 Act and Part II of the RIPA. The position is very similar to that in respect of the Interception of Communications Commissioner, since all the Commissioners are bound by the Convention under s 6 of the HRA and are also providing oversight of bodies which are so bound. The Surveillance Commissioners are providing oversight of police officers and other 'public authorities' using surveillance while the Intelligence Services Commissioner is providing oversight of the Services' activities under the RIPA and the Intelligence Services Act.

Criminal proceedings

Significantly, there is no equivalent in the Police Act or Part II of the RIPA to s 17 in Part I of the RIPA, which, as indicated above, largely disallows reference to interceptions in any court or tribunal proceedings. Clearly, any such provision would be counter-productive in prosecution terms. But this does mean, depending on the extent of disclosure to the defence, that a defendant may become aware at some point during criminal proceedings that a surveillance operation has occurred, and therefore will be able to take any avenues of redress that may be open, including raising Convention arguments in the trial itself.

The issues of exclusion of evidence and of disclosure will be most significant. The duty of disclosure to the defence is restricted under the Criminal Procedure and Investigations Act 1996 and the residual common law rules on the public interest.[343] The fact that a particular surveillance technique has been used may not be disclosed on the basis that it is 'sensitive' material. Under that Act, the duty of the CPS is to disclose to the defence all material which it considers might undermine the prosecution case, except sensitive material which should not be disclosed in the public interest. The sensitivity of the material may be based on the need to use the technique in question in a future operation. If the prosecutor considers that the material is sensitive, an application to a court for a ruling to protect it on grounds of public interest immunity must be made.[344] It can be made *ex parte* with notice to the defence or, in an exceptional case, without notice. In any such application, a judge, bound by s 6 of the HRA, would have to consider Art 6 requirements in respect of such disclosure.[345]

---

343 The 1996 Act, s 21(2).

344 See ss 3(6) and 7(5).

345 These guidelines were provided in *Davis, Rowe and Johnson* [1993] 1 WLR 613. Now that the use of public interest immunity in that case has been found to breach Art 6 by the Court (*Rowe and Davis v UK* Appl No 28901/95; [1999] Crim LR 410; judgment of the Court of 16/2/00 (2000) 30 EHRR 1) they will have to be re-examined. The domestic courts will have the opportunity of doing so [contd]

If it is clear in criminal proceedings that surveillance has been used in order to obtain evidence against the defendant, the defence could seek to establish that it was unauthorised or improperly authorised or was not covered by Part III of the 1997 Act or Part II of the RIPA. The defence could also raise the argument, under s 7(1)(b) of the HRA, that therefore a breach of Art 8 had arisen or that, although the surveillance was properly authorised, a breach had nevertheless occurred since, for example, the requirements of proportionality under Art 8(2) had not been met. Assuming that the surveillance was not authorised, it would not be unlawful unless existing tortious liability had arisen and/or the public authority in question had incurred liability under s 6 of the HRA for breaching Art 8. In other words, surveillance which incurs no tortious or criminal liability, but only leads to a breach of Art 8, is unlawful only in the sense that the public authority using it (normally, of course, the police) has failed to abide by its duty under s 6 of the HRA. It should be noted that there is no offence of conducting unauthorised surveillance, in contrast to the position as regards unauthorised interception,[346] and, as indicated below, surveillance will not be unlawful solely on the ground that authorisation has not been sought. The court, as itself a public authority under s 6 of the HRA, is bound to offer redress for a breach of Art 8. The public authority using it would also have to provide such redress, but as explained below, owing to s 65 of the RIPA, this argument would usually be raised in the new tribunal where a complainant is seeking a remedy for breach of Art 8. But, in criminal proceedings, the redress sought could include exclusion of evidence. Thus, the defence could argue either that the evidence had been obtained unlawfully since, for example, the police had committed a trespass in obtaining it *and* had breached Art 8, or that it had been obtained unlawfully due to such a breach alone. In either instance, there might appear to be an argument, which is considered further in Chapter 14, that the evidence obtained should be excluded under s 78 of PACE. However, the courts are likely to be unreceptive to this argument.

The leading case of *Khan (Sultan)*[347] on exclusion of evidence obtained by the unlawful use of a listening device would apply, and at present it is clear that the stance taken will be continued in the post-HRA era since it has been re-affirmed by the House of Lords in *AG's Reference (No 3 of 1999)*.[348] In *Khan*, a listening device had been secretly installed on the outside of a house which Khan was visiting. The case against him rested solely on the tape recording obtained. The defence argued, *inter alia*, that the recording was inadmissible as evidence because the police had no statutory authority to place listening devices on private property and that therefore, such placement was a trespass,

---

345 [contd] now that Human Rights Act is fully in force. The findings in the same context in *Fitt and Jasper v UK* (1999) EHRLR 430 will be relevant. The Court said that in those instances, the judge had been able to consider the sensitive material in question and therefore was able to conduct a balancing act between fairness to the defence and to the prosecution. On that basis, no breach of Art 6 was found. The *Davis, Rowe and Johnson* guidelines may be compared with those adopted in other countries, particularly those used in Denmark after the *Van Traa Inquiry Report* (an inquiry which is generally viewed as an especially useful guide to the use of such methods in modern policing) into the use of covert methods, including particularly the use of informers and undercover officers. The new Danish law adopted in response sought to ensure that the trial judge or defence would not be subject to complete non-disclosure of evidence and of investigative methods.

346 Under RIPA 2000, s 1, it is an offence to intercept communications intentionally and without lawful authority.

347 [1996] 3 All ER 289; (1996) 146 NLJ 1024, HL; [1995] QB 27, CA.

348 [2001] 2 WLR 56.

and, further, that admission of the recording would breach Art 8. The House of Lords agreed with the Court of Appeal that the evidence was admissible, relying on the decision in *Sang*[349] to the effect that improperly obtained evidence other than 'involuntary' confessions is admissible in a criminal trial subject to a narrow discretion under s 78 of PACE to exclude it.[350] The decision in *Khan* not to exclude the evidence was found to accord with Art 6 at Strasbourg.[351] A Chamber of the Court found that, at the time, the interference with the Art 8 guarantees had no basis in law and therefore a breach of Art 8 was found. This breach was *not* found to necessitate exclusion of the evidence obtained on the basis that the assessment of evidence is a matter for the national courts, and therefore no breach of Art 6 was found. This issue is discussed further in Chapter 14.[352]

Thus, although arguments may be raised in court that Art 8 has been breached in conducting surveillance, it is unlikely that exclusion of any evidence obtained would follow. Thus, use of this avenue as a means of encouraging the police to respect the Art 8 guarantees has been at present almost entirely closed off.

Civil actions

Covert surveillance conducted without an authorisation is not unlawful on that basis alone. The (draft) Code of Practice on Covert Surveillance 2000 made under s 71(3)(a) of the RIPA makes this position explicit in para 2.1: 'There is no requirement on the part of a public authority to obtain an authorisation for a covert surveillance operation and the decision not to obtain an authorisation would not, of itself, make an action unlawful.' Intrusive surveillance involving an entry onto property and/or damage to it could be challenged in the ordinary courts since, if unauthorised, its use will amount to a crime or tort. Where directed, surveillance involves an entry on to non-residential premises or damage to them such actions would also be available.

Other forms of surveillance may breach Art 8, but will not be trespassory or attract any criminal liability. In such circumstance a complainant might, theoretically, have a remedy under the doctrine of confidence, assuming that some information was obtained and was used in some manner.[353] But, in such cases, the State body in question would normally be able to argue that the public interest defence applied.[354] Any court adjudicating on an action in confidence or trespass in this context would be bound by s 6 of the HRA to ensure that the Convention rights were complied with,[355] but the action would be based on the pre-existing common law, rather than on s 7(1)(a).[356] Where

---

349 [1980] AC 402; [1979] 2 All ER 1222, HL.

350 See Chapter 14, p 892.

351 *Khan v UK* Appl No 35394/97 (1999) 27 EHRR CD 58, Judgment of the Court (2000) 8 BHRC 310.

352 Pages 903–06.

353 See Chapter 10, pp 565–93.

354 This defence succeeded in *Hellewell* [1995] 1 WLR 804 in respect of unauthorised police use of a photograph of the defendant, who had been convicted of theft from shops, as part of a shopwatch scheme.

355 See Chapter 4, p 157.

356 The process of infusion of the rights into the common law may lead to the creation of new torts or at least a stretching of the boundaries of the old ones. See the comments of Sedley LJ in *Douglas and Others v Hello!* [2001] 2 WLR 992, Chapter 10, p 582.

surveillance attracts no existing criminal or civil liability, the position is more complex. The bodies or persons authorising and undertaking covert surveillance are all public authorities under s 6 of the HRA and therefore an action for breach of Art 8 could be brought against them under s 7(1)(a) of the HRA[357] where covert surveillance occurred but was not authorised, or improperly authorised, or properly authorised, but nevertheless in breach of Art 8. A s 7(1)(a) action, however, against the bodies most likely to use surveillance, in particular the police,[358] would have to be brought in the new tribunal set up under Part IV of the RIPA due to the provision of s 65(2)(a) of the RIPA, which is discussed below. Thus, in most circumstances a tort action in direct reliance on Art 8 would not be open.

It should be noted that persons engaged in all forms of surveillance under Part II are exempted from civil liability under s 27(2) in respect of conduct 'incidental' to authorised conduct and – in an opaquely worded provision – in relation to conduct to which the warrant or authorisation procedure under a 'relevant' Act[359] is inapplicable (not capable of being granted) and where it would not reasonably be expected to have been sought. This appears to cover forms of surveillance engaged in by public authorities which have no statutory basis and which, but for s 27(2), might attract liability under existing torts or under s 7 of the HRA in respect of a breach of Art 8. Since s 27(2) could, potentially, prevent a court from discharging its duty under s 6 of the HRA there is a case for suggesting that courts should restrict its ambit by using s 3 of the HRA to interpret the term 'reasonably' restrictively.

Actions under s 7(1)(a) of the HRA

The public authorities using forms of surveillance and authorising officers within the authorities are all, by definition,[360] subject to the Convention under s 6 of the HRA. The possibility of challenging decisions of such public authorities, as opposed to those of Commissioners, under s 7(1)(a), might appear to be available. However, s 65 of the RIPA stands in the way of Convention-based actions in the ordinary courts. Under s 65(2), the new tribunal will be the appropriate forum for the purposes of s 7(1)(a) of the HRA in relation to certain proceedings. These proceedings are indicated in ss 65(3) and (5). In essence, these provisions mean that s 65 stands in the way of challenges to actions of the security and intelligence services, or persons acting on their behalf, based on s 6 of the HRA (since s 7(1)(a) of the HRA is intended to provide for the bringing of proceedings where a public authority has acted unlawfully under s 6). Section 65(5) and (6) also bar

---

357 Under s 7(1)(a) 'a person who claims that a public authority has acted (or proposes to act) in a way that is made unlawful under s 6(1) may bring proceedings against the authority in the appropriate tribunal ...'. Under s 6(1) 'It is unlawful for a public authority to act in a way which is incompatible with a Convention right [unless the proviso of s 6(2) applies].

358 Section 65(6) provides: 'for the purposes only of subsection (3)', conduct to which Part II applies, an entry on or interference with property or an interference with wireless telegraphy is not conduct falling within sub-s (5) 'unless it is conduct by or on behalf of a person holding any office, rank or position with (a) any of the intelligence services; (b) any of Her Majesty's forces; (c) any police force; (d) the National Criminal Intelligence Service; (e) the National Crime Squad; or (f) the Commissioners of Customs and Excise ...'.

359 RIPA 2000; Intelligence Services Act 1994, s 5; Police Act 1997, Part III.

360 Section 81(1) provides that 'public authority' has the meaning given it by the HRA 1998, s 6.

the way to actions in the ordinary courts under s 7(1)(a) against the police, intelligence services, Customs and Excise, NCIS and the National Crime Squad in respect of surveillance under Part II of the RIPA or s 93 of the 1997 Act, which raises Convention issues under s 6 of the HRA. These s 7(1)(a) actions must be brought only in the new tribunal.

Judicial review

Scrutiny of the Commissioners' oversight function in the ordinary courts appears to be precluded. The 1997 Act contains an ouster clause in s 91(10) which is very similar to that contained in the Interception of Communications Act 1985. It provides: 'The decisions of the Chief Commissioner or ... any other Commissioner (including decisions as to his jurisdiction) shall not be subject to appeal or liable to be questioned in any court'. The inclusion of 'decisions as to his jurisdiction' was, of course, intended to make the Commissioners' decisions unreviewable. This ouster clause was not repealed by the RIPA, but it now no longer relates to the Commissioners' complaints' role, which was removed under s 70(2)(c) of that Act.[361]

Section 65 does not prevent challenges by way of judicial review or civil actions against public authorities other than the police or the intelligence and security services or other bodies listed in s 65(6) relating to surveillance.[362] Also, judicial review of decisions of those bodies listed could be sought without relying on s 7(1)(a) of the HRA. Any possibilities of bringing judicial review against the police or intelligence services which existed in the pre-HRA era still exist, due to s 11 of the HRA, so long as such possibilities do not depend on using s 7(1)(a) of the HRA. The ironic possibility arises, in relation to surveillance, that the development of judicial review taking Art 8 into account, as in the pre-HRA era,[363] might be more far-reaching and of greater significance than such development in reliance on s 7(1)(a), despite the fact that the review would be less intensive.[364]

Section 66 leaves open the possibility that the remaining jurisdiction of the ordinary courts in relation to surveillance (and, if necessary, to interception) will be partially ousted, by executive order, in providing: 'An order under section 65(2)(d) allocating proceedings to the Tribunal may (a) provide for the Tribunal to exercise jurisdiction in relation to that matter to the exclusion of the jurisdiction of any court or tribunal; but (b) if it does so provide, must contain provision conferring a power on the Tribunal, in the circumstances provided for in the order, to remit the proceedings to the court or tribunal which would have had jurisdiction apart from the order.' In other words, an avenue to court action would be left open if this course was taken in future.

---

361 Sections 106, 107(6) and Sched 7 of the 1997 Act will be repealed under the RIPA 2000.

362 This is of significance where, eg, a public authority not yet brought within the RIPA 2000, Part II used surveillance without falling within any existing liability, or where this occurred and the public authority, although within the Act, fell outside those listed in s 65(6).

363 See Chapter 3, pp 108–10.

364 See Chapter 4, pp 170–01.

Conclusions

The upshot, then, is that challenges by way of judicial review or tortious actions remain available against some public authorities, whether or not it is argued that the authority has breached s 6 of the HRA. Actions against the police or intelligence services in relation to surveillance operations, based on ss 6 and 7(1)(a) of the HRA, will have to be brought in the new tribunal only because of s 65 of the RIPA. It is notable that court action was not ruled out expressly under the Security Services Act 1989, the Intelligence Services Act 1994 or the Police Act 1997, although it was – in effect – under s 9 of the 1985 Act. In providing for complaint to be made to the old tribunal, s 5 of the 1989 Act and s 9 of the 1994 Act implied that complaint could not be made to a court. The same could be said of the Commissioner mechanism under the 1997 Act. But the provisions did not expressly exclude the jurisdiction of the courts since otherwise, the agencies would then have been placed, in effect, above the law. Section 65 does not exclude the courts' jurisdiction regarding surveillance by the police and intelligence services except in relation to breach of the Convention rights. Therefore, one purpose of the RIPA is to insulate all surveillance undertaken by the intelligence services, and much of that undertaken by the police, from the effects of the HRA, applied in the ordinary courts, except within prosecutions.

6 THE NEW TRIBUNAL

Introduction

This new tribunal, set up under s 65 of the RIPA,[365] has taken over from the Interception of Communications Tribunal and the Intelligence and Security Services Tribunals; it has also taken over the complaints role of the Commissioners set up under Part III of the 1997 Act.

It may be noted initially that in practice, applications to the tribunal will not be frequent since, as noted above, an individual has normally no means of knowing that an interception or surveillance has occurred; in contrast to the position in Germany[366] or Denmark,[367] the police and the other State agencies have no duty to inform him or her of the interception, after it is over. This position is contrary to the recommendation of the Data Protection Working Party for the European Commission which said in May 1999

---

365 Schedule 3 governs the membership of the new tribunal. Members, who are appointed for five years by the Lord Chancellor on behalf of the Queen, must have held 'high judicial office' or have a 10 year general qualification within the meaning of s 71 of the Courts and Legal Services Act 1990; in Scotland and Northern Ireland they must be practitioners of at least 10 years' standing. Thus, they need not be judges, although the President must be a judge. Its members will be remunerated by the Secretary of State, but can be removed from office only on an address to the Queen by both Houses of Parliament under Sched 3, para 1(5). These arrangements afford the tribunal a measure of independence from the executive.

366 See *Klass v Federal Republic of Germany* (1978) 2 EHRR 214. Germany's new bugging law contains this requirement.

367 Criminal Procedure Code, para 788.

that a 'person under surveillance [should] be informed of this as soon as possible'.[368] An individual will therefore normally be able to bring complaints or proceedings to the new tribunal only if she has become aware of the surveillance due to criminal proceedings. Section 17 of the RIPA will normally prevent this occurring in respect of interception and therefore complaints regarding interception are likely to be very rare. Police officers or other State agents who are aware that improperly authorised or unauthorised interception is occurring have no means of complaining to the new tribunal or the Commissioners.[369] Section 4(3) of the Official Secrets Act 1989, as amended by the 2000 Act,[370] is also available to punish such disclosures.

A further limitation is placed on complaints relating to interceptions. Section 67(5) provides that unless the tribunal in the circumstances considers it 'equitable' to do so, such complaints will not be considered if made more than one year after the conduct in question took place. Otherwise, conduct under s 65(5) can be considered whenever it occurred. Thus, pre-commencement surveillance can be brought before the tribunal.

Jurisdiction

Under s 65(2), the new tribunal will have three main functions and a potential fourth one. First, challenges to surveillance on Convention grounds by certain bodies or to interception by all bodies must be brought within it. In the words of the sub-section, 'it will be the only appropriate tribunal for the purposes of section 7 of the HRA 1998 in relation to any proceedings under subsection (1)(a) of that section (proceedings for actions incompatible with Convention rights) which fall within sub-section 3 of this section'. Under s 65(3), they are proceedings against any of the intelligence services '... or against any other person in respect of any conduct, or proposed conduct, by or on behalf of any of those services' or 'relating to the taking place in any challengeable circumstances of any conduct falling within subsection (5)'.

Section 65(5) applies to 'conduct ... (whenever it occurred) by or on behalf of any of the intelligence services; in connection with the interception of communications in the course of their transmission by means of a postal service or telecommunication system'; conduct to which ... Part II applies, any entry on or interference with property or any interference with wireless telegraphy'. Section 65(6) introduces a significant limitation in providing: 'for the purposes only of subsection (3)', conduct to which Part II applies, an entry on or interference with property or an interference with wireless telegraphy is not conduct falling within sub-s (5) 'unless it is conduct by or on behalf of a person holding any office, rank or position with (a) any of the intelligence services; (b) any of Her Majesty's forces; (c) any police force; (d) the National Criminal Intelligence Service; (e) the National Crime Squad; or (f) the Commissioners of Customs and Excise ...'. In other words, as indicated above, the intention is that surveillance by these bodies can be

---

368 See Statewatch (1999) Vol 9 Nos 3 and 4. The UK is the only Member State to have entered a derogation to Principle 2(2) of the Council of Europe Recommendation on the use of data in the police sector R(87)15.

369 Under RIPA 2000, s 19(4), any such disclosure would be an offence punishable on indictment by a maximum term of five years' imprisonment: s 19(4)(a).

370 Schedule 4, para 5.

challenged only in the tribunal where it is argued that they have breached a Convention right.

Secondly, the tribunal is the appropriate forum for complaints if, under s 65(4), 'it is a complaint by a person who is aggrieved by any conduct falling within subsection (5) which he believes to have taken place in relation to him, to any of his property, to any communications sent by or to him, or intended for him, or to his use of any postal service, telecommunications service or telecommunication system; and to have taken place in challengeable circumstances or to have been carried out by or on behalf of any of the intelligence services'. Sections 65(7) and (8) apply in relation to both ss 65(3) and (4). Section 65(7) defines 'challengeable circumstances' as conduct which '(a) takes place with the authority, or purported authority, of anything falling within subsection (8); or (b) the circumstances are such that (whether or not there is such authority) it would not have been appropriate for the conduct to take place without it, or at least without proper consideration having been given to whether such authority should be sought'.

Thus, in its complaints and 'proceedings' jurisdiction, the tribunal can consider unauthorised interception. In relation to complaints, the term used under s 67(3)(b) is 'investigate the authority' which does not appear to confine the tribunal, bearing in mind the meaning of challengeable circumstances', to merely considering whether the authority (if it exists) was properly given. Section 65(8) covers: interception warrants under the Acts of 1985 or 2000, an authorisation under Part II of the 2000 Act, a permission of the Secretary of State under Sched 2 (relating to powers to obtain data protected by encryption), or an authorisation under s 93 of the Police Act 1997.

Thirdly, the tribunal has jurisdiction (s 65(2)(c)) to determine a reference to them by a person that he has suffered detriment as a consequence 'of any prohibition or restriction' under s 17 (the exclusion of evidence section) on his relying on any matter in, or for the purposes of, civil proceedings. It is notable that no means is provided of seeking redress for detriment arising when evidence is excluded in *criminal* proceedings.[371] Finally, under s 65(2)(d), the Secretary of State can also, by order, allocate other proceedings to the tribunal but a draft of the order must have been approved by a resolution of each House of Parliament.[372]

Procedure

The new tribunal is modelled on the Special Immigration Appeals Commission (SIAC)[373] which in turn provided the model for the new tribunal set up under the Northern Ireland Act 1998.[374] The Investigatory Powers Tribunal Rules[375] came into force on the same date as the HRA – 2 October 2000. Under s 68, the tribunal is entitled to determine its own

---

371 See *R v Preston* [1993] 4 All ER 638 (above, p 686) in which the appellants may have suffered detriment due to the exclusion of material derived from phone tapping under the predecessor of s 17, s 9 of the 1985 Act.

372 Section 66(3).

373 Set up under s 1 of the Special Immigration Appeals Act 1997 in response to the findings in *Chahal v UK* (1997) 23 EHRR 413.

374 Under s 90. See also Chapter 15, pp 954–56.

375 SI 2000/2665.

procedure, subject to these rules. The new rules follow the old practices in various respects. Hearings will be secret.[376] The Rules envisage the possibility of an oral hearing, but there is no right to such a hearing.[377] The Rules allow for the possibility of separate oral hearings; the applicant and the representatives of the public authority will not confront each other.[378] Under s 68(6) and (7)(i) 'every person by whom or on whose application there has been granted any authorisation under Part II ... must disclose or provide to the Tribunal all such documents and information as the tribunal may require [in the exercise *inter alia* of its jurisdiction under s 65(2)(a)]'. But information given at the separate hearing can be withheld from the applicant unless the person providing it consents to its disclosure.[379]

The new tribunal, like the old one, will merely report its conclusion; it cannot report the reason for the decision.[380] If it finds that no warrant or authorisation exists and that apparently no surveillance or interception is occurring, or that proper authorisation occurred, it will merely inform the complainant that the complaint has not been upheld. The complainant who suspects, for example, that his or her phone or e-mails are being tapped is then left not knowing whether in fact tapping is occurring. But, if the complaint is upheld, she will know that tapping was occurring but unauthorised. This is, at least theoretically, an improvement on the old position since the fact that a complaint was not upheld could mean that unauthorised tapping was occurring. For example, on 6 December 1991, Alison Halford complained to the Interception of Communications Tribunal in respect of the suspected tapping of her home and office telephones.[381] From the circumstances, it appeared that tapping was probably occurring. She was informed on 21 February 1992, without any reason given, that the complaint had not been upheld: no contravention of ss 2–5 of the Act had been found. It later confirmed by letter that it could not specify whether any interception had in fact taken place. She was left in ignorance as to whether an intercept had indeed been authorised, whether one was in place, although unauthorised, or whether no interception was occurring.[382] Had it been authorised it is inconceivable, bearing in mind the circumstances, for it to have been authorised properly.

---

376 Rule 9(6): 'The Tribunal's proceedings, including any oral hearings, shall be conducted in private.'

377 Rule 9(2): 'The Tribunal shall be under no duty to hold oral hearings but may do so in accordance with this rule (and not otherwise).' Rule 9(3): 'The Tribunal may hold oral hearings at which the complainant may make representations, give evidence and call witnesses.'

378 Rule 9(4): 'The Tribunal may hold *separate* oral hearings which the person whose conduct is the subject of the complaint, the public authority against whom s 7 proceedings are brought ... may be required to attend and at which that person or authority may make representations, give evidence and call witnesses' (emphasis added).

379 Under Rule 2, the tribunal may not disclose to the complainant or any other person any information disclosed or provided to the tribunal in the course of [an oral hearing] without the consent of the person who provided it.

380 The 2000 Act, s 68(4). This matter was covered by the 1985 Act, s 7(4)(1) and Sched 1, para 4(2).

381 See the facts of *Halford v UK*[1997] IRLR 471; (1997) 24 EHRR 523, p 679 above.

382 Lord Nolan, the current Commissioner, has defended the failure to inform complainants as to whether an intercept has occurred on this basis: 'If the tribunal were able to tell a complainant that he or she had not been the subject of legitimate interception, silence or any equivocal answer on another occasion might be interpreted as an implication that interception had taken place. Furthermore a positive answer would allow criminals or terrorists to know whether they were subject to interception or not.' (Report of the Commissioner under the Interception of Communications Act 1998, Cm 4364, published June 1999, p 2, para 13 and p 11).

In its 'proceedings' under s 65(2)(a), the tribunal uses 'the principles applicable by a court on an application for judicial review'. Under the HRA it should therefore apply the principles a court bound by s 6 of the HRA would apply on such an application. The proportionality requirements under the RIPA should be strictly scrutinised. But one problem is, as Leigh and Lustgarten have argued, that the procedure may be unsuitable as a means of conducting such scrutiny due to its inefficacy in a fact finding role.[383] Clearly, this problem is likely to be exacerbated by the non-disclosure of relevant information.

So it appears likely that the determinations of the new tribunal will be as secretive as those of the old and the position of the complainant equally weak. Clearly, the difficulty with tribunals of this nature is that they may seek to give the appearance of adversarial proceedings, but the limitations under which they operate, which severely curtail opportunities of challenging evidence, undermine the potential benefits of such proceedings.[384]

Remedies

The remedial powers of the new tribunal will be similar to those of the old.[385] Under s 67(7), 'the Tribunal ... shall have power to make any such award of compensation or other order as they think fit; [subject to the power of the Secretary of State to make rules under section 69(2)(h)] ... and ... may make an order quashing or cancelling any warrant or authorisation; and an order requiring the destruction of any records of information which has been obtained in exercise of any power conferred by a warrant or authorisation; or is held by any public authority in relation to any person' (subject to s 69 orders). Thus the award of remedies continues to be discretionary; the successful complainant or applicant could be left remediless. The tribunal will not have the power to make a declaration of incompatibility.[386] If the new tribunal finds in favour of an applicant, a report would not automatically go to the Prime Minister under s 68(5); it would do so only if the Secretary of State bore some responsibility in the matter.

Recourse to the courts from the tribunal

At present, the RIPA seeks to make it impossible for a member of the public who is dissatisfied with the outcome of the tribunal procedure to seek a remedy in the courts. The Act, like the 1985, 1989, 1994 and 1997 Acts, contains a post-*Anisminic* ouster clause. Section 67(8) provides: 'Except to such extent as the Secretary of State may by order otherwise provide, determinations, awards, orders and other decisions of the tribunal (including decisions as to whether they have jurisdiction) shall not be subject to appeal or

---

383 See p 54. See Leigh, I and Lustgarten, L, 'Making rights real: the courts, remedies and the Human Rights Act' (1999) 158 CLJ 509.

384 See Walker, *op cit*, fn 13, p 82; he advocates an inquisitorial system for such tribunals; see also White [1999] PL 413, discussing the new tribunal set up under the Northern Ireland Act 1998.

385 Under the 1985 Act, s 7(5), the tribunal could order quashing of the warrant, destruction of material obtained and payment of compensation to the victim.

386 See the HRA 1998, s 4(5), discussed in Chapter 4, p 149.

be liable to be questioned in any court.' This leaves open the possibility that a tribunal or other body might be established to hear appeals.[387] Under s 67(9), the Secretary of State is under a duty to establish such a body to hear appeals relating to the exercise of the tribunal's jurisdiction under s 65(2)(c) or (d), but not, significantly, in relation to the broader and much more important jurisdiction under s 65(2)(a) or (b).

The upshot is, at present, that the citizen cannot challenge a finding as to interception rather than surveillance outside the tribunal since both s 17 and s 67(8) stand in the way of so doing. A citizen seeking to challenge a tribunal decision in respect of surveillance would be unaffected by s 17, but would have to seek to circumvent s 67(8).

Under s 3 of the HRA it is conceivable that s 67(8) could be interpreted in an application for leave under Order 53[388] in accordance with the Convention in such a way as to allow review. The argument for seeking to circumvent s 67(8) would depend upon the extent to which the tribunal appeared to meet Convention requirements, considered below. The courts have not so far circumvented such post-*Anisminic*[389] clauses. It could be argued that the wording of s 67(8) cannot be intended to be taken literally. The courts could rely on Anisminic itself in seeking to satisfy s 6 of the HRA, in that since the word 'decision' is used in relation to tribunal findings themselves, and in relation to its jurisdiction, the argument is open that any decision tainted by an error of law is a nullity; and therefore the ouster clause cannot bite on it.

Since the tribunal can determine its own jurisdiction under s 67(8), and it is bound by s 6 of the HRA, argument could also be raised before it that, at least in respect of the circumstances of certain claims, it does not provide a fair hearing under Art 6, due *inter alia* to orders made under s 69, and that therefore its duty under s 6 requires it to declare that its jurisdiction does not cover such claims. If the tribunal is unreceptive to such claims, which is, of course, likely, they may eventually have to be raised at Strasbourg.

The influence of the HRA

The tribunal is bound by all the rights, including Art 6, under s 6 of the HRA, but Art 6 will apply only if the tribunal hearings are within its field of application. The proceedings or determination of complaints in the new tribunal might be viewed as the 'determination of civil rights and obligations' under Art 6(1). The term 'civil' has, however, been taken to mean that these are rights in private rather than public law,[390] although it has been argued that: 'Recent jurisprudence by which more and more rights and obligations have been brought within Art 6, is not easy to explain in terms of any distinction between private and public law which is found in European national law'.[391]

---

387 Section 67(8) by an Order of the Secretary of State.

388 Of the Rules of the Supreme Court and the Supreme Court Act 1981, s 31.

389 In *Anisminic v Foreign Compensation Commission* [1969] 2 AC 147 the House of Lords refused to accept that the jurisdiction of the courts was entirely ousted on the basis that the Commission had acted outside its powers. Therefore, it had not made a determination; it had made a purported determination – ie, a nullity. The ouster clause under the RIPA seeks to avoid this possibility, since it provides that the jurisdiction of the tribunal cannot be questioned in any court.

390 *Ringeisen v Austria* A 13 (1971), para 94.

391 Harris, O'Boyle, Warbrick, *op cit*, fn 307, pp 174–75.

In its proceedings, it will be likely to inquire into breaches of Art 8, which represents a right binding on public authorities, including the agencies, under s 6 of the HRA. At Strasbourg, that in itself would not be sufficient to engage Art 6, while domestically, the guarantees may be viewed as operating in public law only, in which case Art 6 would not apply. On the other hand, certain of the rights claimed are private law rights, since where authorisation is not given, existing tortious liability may arise.[392] The term 'civil' has an autonomous Convention meaning and therefore cannot merely be assigned the meaning of 'private' as understood in UK administrative law. Whether a breach of the RIPA, which gives rise to liability only under Art 8, could be viewed as a matter of private law is debatable, although Strasbourg may be moving towards a position in which 'all those rights which are individual rights under the national legal system and fall into the sphere of general freedom ... must be seen as civil rights'.[393] Where it could be argued that breach of the RIPA did not give rise to liability under Art 8,[394] which may be the case in relation to some use of covert human sources, this question would be even more problematic.[395]

The better view is, it is contended, that the tribunal is bound by Art 6, at least in relation to its 'proceedings' jurisdiction, in which it is acting in a more judicial manner. It has potentially a pivotal role in upholding Convention rights in the face of the most significant assertions of State power. It would therefore be contrary to its role to find that it itself was not bound by the key due process guarantee. From a domestic standpoint, it would be anomalous in the extreme if were not so bound, bearing in mind its role in satisfying s 7(1)(a) of the HRA in respect of the obligations of a wide range of bodies, including, in particular, the police, under the RIPA. Whether it is within the field of application of Art 6 will be a matter which, initially, will be raised before the tribunal itself. If it considers that it is adjudicating on a public law matter, and is therefore outside Art 6, the matter will no doubt be raised at Strasbourg eventually.

Assuming that the tribunal is covered by Art 6(1) or, under the development of the Strasbourg jurisprudence may be found to be so covered in future, it is hard to see that it meets the Art 6 fair hearing requirements, bearing in mind the procedure it may follow, indicated above, since the complainant or applicant may be in such a weak position before it. As Chapter 2 indicated, since Art 6(3) contains *minimum* guarantees, the para 1 protection of a fair hearing goes beyond para 3.[396] In investigating a fair hearing, the domestic authorities are not confined to the para 3 guarantees; they can consider further requirements of fairness. If consideration is given to the procedures in question, it is apparent that, apart from any of the other requirements of fairness, the minimal safeguards of Art 6(3) may not be satisfied. In particular, as indicated above, the power to

---

392 See *Golder v UK* A 18 (1975).

393 *Bentham v UK* B 80 (1983), para 10, dissenting opinions of Mr Melchior and Mr Frowen.

394 See above, pp 703–06, for discussion as to invasions of privacy which are likely to engage Art 8.

395 But see *Fayed v UK* (1994) 18 EHRR 393, in which it was found that although, strictly speaking, there was no legal basis for the action and so no dispute to trigger Art 6, Art 6 applied to blanket immunities preventing access to a court.

396 See p 58.

limit or prevent cross-examination, or exclude the applicant[397] or her legal representative, or limit disclosure of evidence, may not comply with Art 6(1) or (3).[398]

As indicated, the tribunal will apply the principles of judicial review in its adjudications, which will include considering proportionality, since it is bound by s 6 of the HRA, and Art 8(2) requires such consideration. The problem will be, as Chapter 4 indicated, that in order to consider proportionality the tribunal may need to evaluate a number of factual matters. But it is bound, as indicated, by subordinate legislation and may have no discretion as to requiring cross-examination or disclosure of documents. Thus, the procedural limitations under which it operates may place even greater difficulties in its path in considering issues of proportionality than there would be in an ordinary court, in judicial review proceedings. If it therefore operates a very 'light touch' review, based in effect on *Wednesbury* unreasonableness, it will fail to satisfy the demands of Art 13, as recently interpreted at Strasbourg[399] and therefore *a fortiori* it will not satisfy Art 6. This will depend on its interpretation of the requirements of judicial review: under the HRA the use of judicial review principles by the tribunal should now include consideration of compliance with the Convention rights and therefore a more intensive review. If, despite the constraints it is under, it operates such review, at least in instances in which national security is not in issue, Art 13 may now be satisfied.[400] Its inability to give reasons or to take a binding decision may not render it ineffective.[401]

Following *Tinnelly v UK*,[402] if it is argued that documents or sources cannot be disclosed on grounds of national security or the prevention of crime under Art 8(2), the applicant could argue that the Art 6 requirements override such a claim. The success of such an argument would depend upon the particular circumstances of a claim and in particular the ground under the RIPA in question since, as the Court found in *Tinnelly*, proportionality should be found between the infringement of the rights of the claimant and the aim in question. Where the aim concerns, for example, one of the 'economic' grounds founding directed surveillance under the RIPA, the claim of the State would be less pressing and the question of proportionality should be more intensively scrutinised. If this was impossible due to the procedural constraints, the applicant could claim that the tribunal should consider whether its duty under s 6 of the HRA requires it to disapply the subordinate legislation in question, and conduct, in such circumstances, a more intensive inquiry. This possibility would be open to it since s 6(2)(b) of the HRA does not apply in respect of subordinate legislation, while it cannot be said that s 69 of the RIPA, which only

---

397 See, on this point, *Zana v Turkey* (1997) 27 EHRR 667, in which, in the context of terrorism, the applicant was not allowed to be present at the trial; a breach of Art 6 was found on this basis.

398 See further Chapter 14, pp 900–02.

399 *Smith and Grady v UK* (2000) 29 EHRR 493. The domestic court found that the continuance of the ban on homosexuals in the armed forces was not beyond the range of responses which was open to a reasonable decision maker. The Strasbourg Court considered that the threshold at which the domestic court could find the policy irrational was set so high that it effectively precluded consideration of the proportionality of the ban with the aim in view. Therefore judicial review was not found to satisfy the requirements of Art 13. The findings in *Smith and Grady v UK* on this point marked a departure from the stance preciously taken: see *Soering v UK* A 161 (1989). See also *Esbester v UK* 18 EHRR CD 72, on this point.

400 See further Chapter 2, pp 83–85 and Chapter 4, p 135.

401 *Esbester v UK* 18 EHRR CD 72.

402 (1998) 27 EHRR 249.

provides that the Secretary of State *may* make the orders in question, requires the tribunal to depart from Art 6.

In respect of the national security ground under the RIPA, the tribunal may take the view that it cannot consider the documents in question or other relevant matters in order to make a finding as to proportionality. In *Balfour v Foreign and Commonwealth Office*,[403] the court found that once an actual or potential risk to national security had been demonstrated by a public interest immunity certificate, the court should not exercise its right to inspect the documents. This view of national security as the exclusive domain of the executive was not adhered to in the robust approach taken to the concept in the context of deportation by the Special Immigration Appeals Commission (on which the new tribunal is partially modelled) in the case of *Secretary of State for the Home Dept v Rehman*.[404] However, the Court of Appeal overturned their ruling, finding that the threat to national security was for the government to determine and that it should be broadly defined to include the possibility of future threats, including those to the UK's 'allies'. The House of Lords confirmed that finding.[405]

These findings are not, it is argued, fully in accordance with the findings of the Strasbourg Court in *Tinnelly* or in *Chahal v UK*.[406] Both, particularly *Tinnelly*, took the view that the threat to national security should be demonstrated. Where Art 13, as opposed to Art 6, was in question, as in *Chahal*, the requirements thereby placed on the State would be weaker, since Art 13 must be read with Art 8(2).[407] But where Art 6 is engaged, as indicated, the requirements would be stricter. The tribunal may be placed in the difficult position of choosing between the domestic and the Strasbourg jurisprudence as to the stance it should take in respect of assertions of national security considerations. If so, the way would be open, under s 3 of the HRA, to depart from the former.

As indicated above, it could also be argued before the Tribunal (or, if necessary, at Strasbourg) that it ought to provide an effective remedy under Art 13. It may be noted that in *Khan v UK*[408] the Court found that exclusion of evidence under s 78 of PACE would not provide such a remedy,[409] so it must be provided – in respect of the surveillance of a number of public authorities – only in the tribunal. This is clear since ss 7 and 8 of the HRA are intended to take the place of Art 13 domestically and the tribunal is the 'appropriate forum' for s 7(1)(a) purposes. In *Khan v UK*, which also critiqued police disciplinary procedures, it was found that the procedures failed to meet Art 13 standards due to the influence of the Home Secretary. Although the arrangements for the new tribunal differ,[410] the strong influence of the Home Secretary in determining the procedure to be followed might be said to impair the tribunal's independence.

---

403 [1994] 2 All ER 588.
404 [1999] INLR 517.
405 [2001] 3 WLR 877, HL; [2000] 3 All ER 778, CA; for comment see Ryder [2000] J Civ Lib 358.
406 (1998) 27 EHRR 249 (in the context of Art 13).
407 *Leander v Sweden* (1987) 9 EHRR 433.
408 (2000) 8 BHRC 310.
409 Paragraph 44.
410 See fn 365.

The tribunal should play a part in providing an aggregate of remedies which, combined, would provide an effective remedy,[411] but the other potential remedies, such as raising complaints with an MP, are too ineffective to make much contribution. In *Harman and Hewitt v UK*,[412] a breach of Art 13 was found on the basis of the lack of an effective remedy. The 1989 Act was precisely intended to address this failure by creating the oversight mechanisms. In *Christie v UK*,[413] the Commission avoided the question whether the Interception of Communications Tribunal had provided an effective remedy since it found that the applicant did not have an 'arguable case' and that therefore Art 13 was inapplicable.[414] However, it found that it did provide such a remedy 'in principle'.[415]

In *Govell v UK*,[416] the use of a bugging device was the subject of an unsuccessful police complaint. The Commission found that the police investigative system did not meet the requisite standards of independence under Art 13 since, *inter alia*, the Home Secretary appointed and remunerated members of the Police Complaints Authority and the Home Secretary had a guiding role in determining the withdrawal of charges. In *Chahal v UK*, the Advisory Panel on deportation decisions was not found to satisfy Art 13 since it failed to offer sufficient safeguards for Art 13 purposes. The Court said that the remedy offered should be 'as effective as it can be' given the need, in the context in question, to rely on secret sources. In relation to the new tribunal, it might be argued that the Orders made by the Secretary of State may reduce its efficacy to the point where it no longer satisfies Art 13. While the tribunal's adjudications may appear adversarial in a superficial sense, the position of the applicant may be so weakened by the procedural limitations under which it operates that it cannot be said to be effective.

Unless a means of appeal from the tribunal is created in relation to its jurisdiction under s 65(2)(a), there will be no clear independent domestic means of determining whether the tribunal offers an effective remedy and whether it should abide by Art 6, which does not require that a court to which to appeal should be available. But it could be argued that Art 6 itself requires that the question of its own field of application should be able to be raised before an independent body.[417] While the Strasbourg jurisprudence would probably not support such an argument at present, it could be argued – somewhat less boldly – that Art 6 requires that the question whether a particular body provides an effective remedy under Art 13 should be able to be raised before an independent body and not merely in the disputed body itself. In principle, this is a strong argument, bearing in mind the fact that the new tribunal will be, in most circumstances arising under the

---

411 *Ibid.*

412 Appl No 121175/86; (1992) 14 EHRR 657.

413 Also, in *Christie v UK* 78-A DR E Com HR 119 the Commission found that the Interception of Communications Act 1985, the model for the 1989 and 1994 Acts, met the 'in accordance with the law' requirement of Art 8(2).

414 Similarly, in *Halford v UK* (1997) 24 EHRR 523, in respect of alleged tapping of the applicant's home phone, which was within the 1985 Act, the Court avoided this question in relating to the old tribunal since it found that the applicant did not have an 'arguable case' and that therefore, Art 13 was inapplicable.

415 See also *Esbester v UK* (1993) 1860/91; affirmed in *Matthews v UK* [1997] EHRLR 187.

416 (1997) 4 EHRLR 438.

417 See Van Dijk, P and Van Hoof, F, *Theory and Practice of the European Convention on Human Rights*, 1998.

Intelligence Services Act 1994, the Police Act 1997 and the RIPA, the only forum in which citizens will be able to raise the issue of violation of Art 8 rights.

The mere fact that a body termed a 'Tribunal' has been created should not obscure the possibility that it may have a merely cosmetic effect. Had a body been created which appeared to have even less credibility, such as a Panel of Advisors or Commission, or a body required to accept National Security certificates, the guarantee under Art 6 of access to a court[418] or, under Art 13, of providing an effective remedy, might have been found at Strasbourg to have been violated[419] and the domestic expectation would have been that this would eventually be the case. But the formal appearance of the new tribunal may be belied by the nature of its proceedings which may mean that, substantively, it is as ineffective as such bodies would have been.

7 CONCLUSIONS

The central value which is revealed by consideration of the statutory schemes governing the operation of the intelligence services and the State surveillance arrangements generally is secrecy, in the protection of State interests. The value of individual privacy is, it is argued, consistently and readily overcome, at almost every point in the arrangements at which a choice was made. The HRA had aroused the expectation not only that a new comprehensive statutory basis for invasion of privacy would be introduced, but that it would be underpinned by Convention principles.[420] While the introduction of such a basis in the RIPA is clearly a significant step forward in terms of protection of individual rights, there is little evidence of commitment to those principles despite the influence of the Convention on its inception. The same may be said of the Intelligence Services Act 1994 and of the Police Act 1997: both were introduced largely to meet the demands of Art 8 and both, it is argued, fail to show the respect for individual privacy which would therefore be expected. Perhaps ironically, the scheme enshrined in PACE 1984 for search and seizure does show such respect, to an extent, although it is only incidental to its traditional concern to protect the interest in property. Perhaps the contrast between PACE and the other statutory schemes considered reflects the lack of understanding of the value of individual privacy, as opposed to property, which has long influenced the common law and which, despite the reception of Art 8 into domestic law, continues to influence the regulation of secret investigatory powers.

The ability of the ordinary citizen to rely on Art 8 under the HRA in order to protect her privacy from State intrusion is highly circumscribed in a number of respects. A breach of Art 8 in searching for and seizing confidential documents is very unlikely to lead to their exclusion from evidence in court. Where there is doubt as to the standard of scrutiny applied by a magistrate in considering an application for a search warrant, again leading to a breach of Art 8, it is unclear that any redress is likely to be available. Perhaps the most striking feature of the RIPA is the determination evinced under it to prevent citizens

---

418 Such a guarantee has been implied into Art 6(1): see *Omar v France* (2000) 29 EHRR 210.
419 As in *Tinnelly* (1998) 27 EHRR 249 and *Chahal* (1997) 23 EHRR 413 respectively.
420 This was the expectation of the Justice report, *op cit*, fn 97.

invoking Convention rights in the ordinary courts against State bodies in respect of the profound threat to privacy represented by interception and surveillance.[421] The development of Convention jurisprudence in the ordinary courts in relation to such techniques has largely been prevented, before it had a chance to begin. A conflict is therefore revealed, it is contended, between the values underlying the RIPA and those underlying the HRA, despite their introduction by the same government.

The democratic values enshrined in the Convention demand that citizens in the democracy should be able to feel confident that surveillance and interception by the State is undertaken for appropriate ends, by proportionate means and with respect for privacy. The RIPA, like the Security Services Act, the Intelligence Services Act and the Police Act, pays lip service to proportionality while largely emasculating methods of scrutinising it. It is apparent that statutory schemes which hide the operations they empower largely from scrutiny, and which, for the most part, place power in the hands of the executive, while shrouding the citizen's complaints' mechanisms in secrecy, fail to reflect those democratic values.

---

421 For further discussion, see Akdeniz, Y, Taylor, N and Walker, C, 'RIPA (1): State surveillance in the age of information and rights' [2001] Crim LR 73.

CHAPTER 12

BODILY INTEGRITY AND AUTONOMY; SEXUAL EXPRESSION AND IDENTITY; FAMILY LIFE

1 INTRODUCTION[1]

This chapter is centrally concerned with personal autonomy in the sense of the ability of the individual to make decisions free from State interference regarding the most intimate aspects of her personal life. It also touches on the question of the positive obligations of the State in relation to furthering the ability to exercise autonomy. As a linked value, it considers the interest of the individual in freedom from humiliation, also in terms of both negative and positive obligations. It will be found that in some respects this area resembles that considered in Chapter 10 – the non-consensual disclosure of personal information. In both, domestic law showed a marked failure to recognise the value of autonomy at stake, which in the one instance may be termed informational and in the other, substantive.[2] As Chapter 10 demonstrated, it was only gradually, and ultimately under the impetus of the Human Rights Act (HRA), that personal information found legal protection from non-consensual publication. Similarly, it was the influence of the European Convention on Human Rights that, as this chapter will demonstrate, led to changes in domestic law to reflect respect for the sexual orientation of homosexuals.

However, there are a number of aspects of self-determination that are still unrecognised in domestic law and it is clear that individuals will seek to rely on Art 8 and other relevant Articles under the HRA in order to try to create such recognition. One such aspect is that of choice as to the manner and time of death. Another concerns rights of transsexuals over their own identity. Below, the extent to which UK law recognises the values of dignity and autonomy in the contexts in question and the possible influence of the HRA in improving such recognition are considered.

Recognition of the values of bodily integrity and autonomy, sexual identity, family life under the Convention

As the discussion of Art 8 in Chapter 2 indicated, a wide range of issues may be accommodated within the right to respect for private life. Other Convention guarantees, particularly those of Art 3, may also be relevant. The right to respect for family life, as the discussion below indicates, is a narrower concept, with which the right to respect for private life overlaps. The European Court of Human Rights has clearly recognised that private life covers individual, personal choices: *Dudgeon v UK*.[3] Equally, respect for family

---

1   See generally Feldman, D, *Civil Liberties and Human Rights in England and Wales*, 1993, Part 3; Markesinis, B (ed), *Protecting Privacy*, 1999; Clayton, R and Tomlinson, H, *The Law of Human Rights*, 2000, Chapters 12 and 13; Janis, M, Kay, R and Bradley, A, *European Human Rights Law: Text and Materials*, 2nd edn, 2000, Chapter 6; Feldman, D, 'The developing scope of Art 8 of the ECHR' [1997] EHRLR 265; Feldman, D, 'Secrecy, dignity or autonomy? Views of privacy as a civil liberty' (1994) 47(2) CLP 42, p 54; Warbrick, C, 'The structure of Article 8' [1998] EHRLR 32.

2   See discussion, pp 530–33.

3   (1982) 4 EHRR 149.

life covers freedom of parental choice,[4] within limits created by the opposing interests of the child.[5] Thus, the interest of individuals in exercising freedom of choice in decisions as to the disposal of or control over the body may be protected. Usually the individual is, in effect, asking the State to leave him or her alone to make such decisions in order to preserve autonomy. This is a negative obligation which is clearly within the scope of Art 8 where the interference can be viewed as arbitrary.[6]

In some instances, however, the individual will be requiring the assistance of the authorities in ensuring that he or she is able to exercise autonomy. The scope for the acceptance of positive obligations as an aspect of respect for private or family life is less wide. But the European Court has characterised claims that the State is under an obligation to provide such assistance, as necessary in order to demonstrate respect for private or family life.[7] In other words, the State may be obliged to provide legal protection for the individual even when the public authorities are not themselves responsible for an interference with the Art 8 right, although given that the State merely has to show 'respect', its discretion in determining the means of so doing tends to be increased.[8]

Where a positive obligation is claimed, Strasbourg will afford a wide margin of appreciation. The margin can widen or narrow depending on the circumstances of the case, resulting in a variation of the intensity of the Court's review of the States' actions. Two further factors may also be present in this context and may influence Strasbourg in conceding a particularly wide margin of appreciation where a complainant seeks to lay a positive obligation on the State. First, where the harm complained of flows from the action of a private party, rather than the State itself, so that the so-called 'horizontal effect' of the Convention is in issue and, secondly, where there is a potential conflict with another Convention right. Clearly, these factors may arise independently of each other. In a number of key decisions under Art 8 discussed in Chapter 10, all three were present,[9] which may explain the somewhat unsatisfactory and misleading nature of some of the judgments given. These factors may also arise in this context and may explain the cautious nature of certain of the decisions.

Horizontal effect under the HRA

As the discussion of horizontal effect under the HRA in Chapters 4[10] and 10 made clear, an individual who wishes to rely on Art 8 in respect of the privacy interests considered

4   See *Hoffman v Austria* (1993) 17 EHRR 293; *X v Netherlands* (1974) 2 DR 118.

5   See *Rieme v Sweden* (1992) 16 EHRR 155.

6   See *Belgian Linguistic (No 2)* (1968) 1 EHRR 252, para 7; *X and Y v Netherlands* (1985) 8 EHRR 235; *Hokkanen v Finland* (1994) 19 EHRR 139.

7   *X v UK* Appl No 7154/75; 14 D & R 31, p 32 (1978); *Marckx v Belgium* (1979) 2 EHRR 330, para 31. See also Chapter 2, p 68 and Chapter 10, pp 538–41.

8   See *JS v UK* Appl No 191173/91, 3 January 1993. The Commission rejected an application in which it was alleged that an insurance company had carried out a clandestine surveillance in investigating a claim.

9   All three were present in: *Winer v UK* (1986) 48 IR 154; *Spencer v UK* (1998) 25 EHRR CD 105, and *N v Portugal* Appl No 20683/92, 20 February 1995; however, the third was influential only in *Winer*.

10 See pp 161–64.

must identify the responsibility that a public authority bore in the matter in order to rely on the HRA under s 7(1)(a) or (b). But such a person could also rely on the courts' duty under s 6 of the HRA in respect of the development of the existing law, or on the interpretative obligation under s 3.[11]

2 BODILY INTEGRITY AND AUTONOMY

Introduction

Under Art 8, bodily privacy has a number of aspects. The European Court of Human Rights adopted a broad definition of privacy in *X and Y v Netherlands*:[12]

> ... [the concept of] private life ... covers the physical integrity ... of the person ... Art 8 does not merely compel the State to abstain from ... interference [with the individual]: in addition to this primarily negative undertaking, there may be positive obligations inherent in effective respect for private ... life.[13]

Thus, Art 8 recognises that individuals have an interest in preventing or controlling physical intrusions on the body and they may therefore lay claim to a negative right to be 'left alone' in a physical sense. Such a right might also encompass positive claims on the State to ensure that bodily integrity is not infringed. Thus, the State may fail to respect privacy if it fails to prevent infringement of it by others or if in itself it allows such infringement.

Bodily integrity

Interference with bodily integrity may breach the guarantee of freedom from degrading punishment under Art 3 of the European Convention on Human Rights and the guarantee of respect for privacy under Art 8. In general, any compulsory physical treatment of an individual will constitute an interference with respect for private life.[14] We will return below to the question as to the level of consensual bodily harm which will be forbidden.

Corporal punishment and discipline

Certain forms of physical punishment may be seen as an unjustified intrusion into bodily integrity. Corporal punishment was outlawed in UK State schools[15] after the decision of the European Court of Human Rights in *Campbell and Cosans v UK*,[16] which was determined not on the basis of Arts 3 or 8 but under Art 2 of the First Protocol, which protects the right of parents to have their children educated according to their own

---

11   See comment in Chapter 4, p 161, fn 137.
12   (1985) 8 EHRR 235.
13   *Ibid*, paras 22 and 23.
14   *X v Austria* 18 D & R 154 (1979).
15   Under the Education (No 2) Act 1986.
16   (1984) 2 EHRR 293.

philosophical convictions. However, corporal punishment in private schools was not outlawed, and in *Costello-Roberts v UK*[17] the European Court of Human Rights found that the UK had a responsibility to ensure that school discipline was compatible with the Convention even though the treatment in question was administered in an institution independent of the State. However, although the court considered that there might be circumstances in which Art 8 could be regarded as affording protection to physical integrity which would be broader than that afforded by Art 3, in the particular circumstances the adverse effect on the complainant was insufficient to amount to an invasion of privacy. The court took into account the 'public' context in which the punishment had occurred and its relatively trivial nature.

However, corporal punishment in both private and public sector schools has now been abolished.[18] Parents or persons with parental responsibility may still use reasonable force to discipline a child. So long as the force remains reasonable, the parent will have a defence to a charge of battery.[19] In *A v UK*[20] the applicant was a nine year old who had been beaten by his stepfather with a garden cane. The stepfather was acquitted of assault causing bodily harm after the jury was instructed that the crime did not include reasonable chastisement by a parent. It was found that the beating fell within Art 3 and that it was incumbent on States to take measures to ensure that individuals within their jurisdiction are not subject to Art 3 treatment. Had the beating been less severe, a breach of Art 8 rather than Art 3 might have been found. It is clear that, by definition, beating amounting to Art 3 treatment cannot be viewed as reasonable and therefore, in future, the defence of reasonable chastisement could not cover the degree of force used in *A*. Where a child has suffered punishment by a parent that fails to reach a level of severity which would fall within Art 3, he or she could rely on the criminal law of battery and use Art 8, under s 7(1)(b) of the HRA in arguing that the defence of reasonable chastisement should be narrowed down or abolished.

Intrusions on dignity in custody

Under Art 8, physical intrusions on the bodily integrity of individuals by State agents may be justified if the requirements of Art 8(2) are satisfied. Equally, UK law also recognises a need to create a balance between the interest of the State in allowing physical interference with individuals for various purposes, including the prevention of crime and the interest of the individual in preserving his or her bodily integrity. UK law determines that in certain circumstances, bodily privacy may give way to other interests. Articles 3 and 8 together provide substantive guarantees against certain types of custodial ill treatment. But, clearly, Art 3 will cover only the grossest instances of ill treatment. It is notable that the Convention contains no provision equivalent to that under Art 10 of the International Covenant on Civil and Political Rights which provides 'persons deprived of their liberty shall be treated with humanity and with respect for the inherent dignity of the human person'.

---

17 (1993) 19 EHRR 112; A 247-C.
18 Education Act 1996, s 548, as substituted by School Standards and Framework Act 1998, s 131.
19 *Hopley* (1860) 2 F & F 202.
20 (1999) 27 EHRR 611.

In the *Greek* case,[21] the conditions of detention were found to amount to inhuman treatment due to overcrowding, inadequate food, sleeping arrangements, heating, toilets and provision for external contacts. Failure to obtain medical treatment after a forcible arrest was found to infringe Art 3 in *Hurtado v Switzerland*.[22] Conduct which grossly humiliates is degrading treatment contrary to Art 3.[23] Art 8 may be viewed as overlapping, to an extent, with Art 3, but it also covers some matters which would not be serious enough to amount to Art 3 treatment.[24] As indicated in Chapter 11, its guarantee of a right to respect for privacy is subject to a number of exceptions in para 2, including for the prevention of crime. In order to bring Art 8 into play, it must be found that its protection extends to the matter in question – in this context, it would probably be that 'private or family life' is affected. Certain conditions or incidents of detention may fall outside Art 8, such as a failure to provide an interpreter. But a failure to allow a juvenile or a mentally disturbed person to consult privately with a member of his or her family, acting as an appropriate adult, might be viewed as an interference with either private or family life.

Code of Practice A made under the Police and Criminal Evidence Act 1984 (PACE), para 3.5, provides safeguards for a search by police officers of more than outer clothing which appear to be coterminous with the right to respect for privacy under Art 8. Strip and intimate searching would probably fall within Art 8 as well as – depending on the circumstances, including the use of force – Art 3.[25] Section 55 of PACE 1984, as amended by s 79 of the Criminal Justice and Police Act 2001, allows intimate searches, on the authorisation of an inspector, but recognises that the violation they represent may occur only in reasonably well defined circumstances. Examination may occur only if there is reasonable suspicion that drugs or implements which might be used to harm others may be found. The examination may only be carried out by a nurse (or a medical practitioner in respect of drugs or a weapon) or, if that is not practicable, it can be carried out by a police officer who must be of the same sex as the person to be searched. The provisions of s 55 are fleshed out in Annex A of Code of Practice C. Strip searches, as opposed to intimate searches, are covered only by part B of Annex A. It is notable that the authorisation of a strip search, prior to 1995, had to be by the custody officer, but that that requirement is no longer in place under the current Code of Practice C provisions.[26] If a violation of Art 8 was alleged in respect of a strip search, it might be found to be in

---

21 12 YB 1 (1969) Com Rep.

22 A 280-A (1994) Com Rep.

23 The *Greek* case, 12 YB 1 (1969) Com Rep.

24 See the findings in the corporal punishment case of *Costello-Roberts v UK* (1993) 19 EHRR 112 (above). The Court found that the treatment was not severe enough to fall within Art 3; in the particular circumstances it did not fall within Art 8, but the Court considered that there might be circumstances in which Art 8 could be viewed as affording a wider protection to physical integrity than that which is afforded by Art 3.

25 Violations of both Articles, together with Art 14, were argued for in *Wanyonyi v UK* (1999) 27 EHRR 195 in respect of racial abuse and humiliation during strip and intimate searching. The application was declared inadmissible for failure to exhaust domestic remedies.

26 Code C, Annex A, Part B.

accordance with the law since it is authorised under Code C[27] to have a legitimate aim (the prevention of crime), but to be disproportionate to the aim pursued and therefore unnecessary in a democratic society, since that element of independence has been removed. If so, the Code provision, which is not itself authorised by incompatible primary legislation as required under s 3(2)(c) of the HRA, could be struck down. Articles 8, 3 and 14 might also be engaged where the interrogation itself was of an especially intrusive nature, particularly where it could also be said to be discriminatory; this possibility is pursued in Chapter 13.

The question as to how far clothing could properly be removed for other purposes in police custody was considered in *Lindley v Rutter*,[28] and a general order to remove the bras of all female detainees in the police station was challenged. Justification was put forward for the order on the grounds that the detainees might otherwise injure themselves. However, it was found that such treatment constituted an affront to human dignity and therefore needed a clearer justification which could be derived only from the specific circumstances of the arrestee: something particular about the individual in question would be needed to support a suspicion that she might do herself an injury. It was found that in removing a detainee's bra where such specific justification did not exist, the police officer in question had acted outside her duty. Thus, the court evinced a reluctance to accept a generalised basis for invasion of privacy.

Bodily autonomy

Personal autonomy has been recognised for some time in the USA as strongly linked to privacy. In *Doe v Bolton*,[29] Douglas J said that 'the right to privacy means freedom of choice in the basic decisions of one's life respecting marriage, divorce, procreation, contraception, education and upbringing of children'. At Strasbourg, the value of personal autonomy has also received quite clear recognition.[30] Personal autonomy connotes an interest not only in preventing physical intrusion by others, but also with the extent to which the law allows an individual a degree of control over his or her own body. Domestically, recognition of the value of individual bodily self-determination has arguably become more prominent this century. Thus, abortion and suicide are no longer crimes under the Abortion Act 1967 and the Suicide Act 1961.

Control over the body: euthanasia

But the choice of adults as to the disposal of their own bodies is highly circumscribed. Although suicide is no longer a crime, aiding and abetting suicide has not been decriminalised. Thus, for example, a relation of a person who is unable to commit suicide

---

27 Arguably, the Code provisions satisfy this requirement. Interpreting 'prescribed by law' in *Sunday Times v UK* A 30 (1979), para 49, the European Court of Human Rights found: 'the law must be adequately accessible' and 'a norm cannot be regarded as a "law" unless it is formulated with sufficient precision to enable the citizen to regulate his conduct'. Where the Codes create an interference with suspects' rights, they are couched in reasonably precise language. See further Chapter 13, pp 757–58.

28 [1980] 3 WLR 661.

29 (1973) 410 US 179; (1973) 35 L E 2d 201.

30 *Dudgeon v UK* (1982) 4 EHRR 149; *Lustig-Prean v UK* (1999) 7 BHRC 65. For discussion, see Feldman, *op cit*, fn 1.

because she is incapacitated through illness cannot help her to die in order to avoid severe pain and suffering without risking prosecution for murder or manslaughter. Euthanasia is not recognised in UK law[31] except in the very narrow sense that allowing a patient in a persistent vegetative state to die will be acceptable if it can be said, objectively speaking, to be in his or her best interests because no improvement can be expected.[32] Also, under the so called 'double effect' doctrine, a doctor will not be guilty of murder if she administers a very high level of a pain-killing drug which she knows is likely to cause death so long as the primary intention is to relieve pain.[33] Clearly, as Chapter 2 indicated, a conflict with Art 2 might arise[34] if euthanasia was allowed in other situations; it has merely been found at Strasbourg that passively allowing a person to die need not attract criminal liability in order to satisfy Art 2.[35] The consent of the victim would be irrelevant; euthanasia is not covered by any of the Art 2 exceptions.

In 2001, an action was brought under the HRA against the Director of Public Prosecutions in relation to his decision that a husband who wishes to help his wife to die once her terminal Motor Neurone Disease reaches a certain stage would be liable to the risk of prosecution.[36] The woman wanted a declaration that her husband would not be prosecuted and argued that the State has a responsibility to make such a declaration since otherwise, Arts 3 and 8 would be breached. The claim was backed by the UK group *Liberty*. The claim was ultimately rejected by the House of Lords. A parallel action was brought in a Canadian case, *Rodriguez v British Columbia*.[37] A similar argument was received sympathetically; it was found that the Criminal Code prohibition on aiding and abetting suicide did infringe her right to security of the person. However, the application failed on the basis that it did not do so in breach of the principles of fundamental justice, the exception clause.

Since Art 3 is not qualified, it is possible that the claim under the HRA might succeed, although no decision at Strasbourg covers it. Moreover, if the declaration in question was made, it might be argued that the authorities were failing to fulfil their Art 2 obligations. On the other hand, it could be argued that homicide law would be unaffected by the declaration: euthanasia would continue to constitute murder, but in particular and rare instances on public policy grounds, no prosecution would be brought since there would be no, or an insufficient public interest in bringing one. Any such decision would obviously be controversial. Its effect might be to prompt Parliament to act to introduce a law similar to that operating in the Netherlands, which would arguably be the preferable course.[38]

---

31 For discussion, see Orst, S, 'Conceptions of the euthanasia phenomenon' [2000] JCIVLIB 155.

32 *Airedale NHS Trust v Bland* [1993] AC 789, HL.

33 *Cox* [1992] BMLR 38. In *Moor* (see [2000] J CIV LIB 155), a doctor who had administered a very high dose of diamorphine to an elderly patient who had pleaded with him for a speedy death was charged with murder. He was acquitted on the basis of evidence showing that the double effect doctrine applied, not on the basis of any right to be assisted to die.

34 See pp 40–1.

35 *Widmer v Switzerland*, No 20527/92 (1993), unreported. See also p 40.

36 The claim was rejected on appeal to the HL: *R (on the Application of Diane Pretty) v DPP and Secretary of State for the Home Dept* [2001] UKHL 61.

37 (1993) 85 CCC (3d) 15.

38 However, the law in The Netherlands has been severely criticised: see Keown, J, 'The law and practice of euthanasia in the Netherlands' [1992] 108 LQR 51–78. For discussion of the moral issues see Dworkin, R, *Life's Dominion*, 1993.

Control over the body: abortion

The European Court of Human Rights has so far avoided the question whether the foetus is protected by Art 2 – in other words, whether it would come within the term 'everyone'. In *Open Door Counselling v Ireland*, the Court deliberately left open the possibility that Art 2 might place some restrictions on abortion.[39] If it was to find that the foetus is protected, the result, in terms of changes to almost all the State parties' laws on abortion, would be immense, since only abortion falling within the exceptions to Art 2 would be permitted. There would be an immense increase in dangerous illegal abortions and women would travel outside the Member States for abortions, leading to an increase in later terminations. It has been found in the context of national legislation on abortion that the woman seeking abortion can rely on Arts 2 and 8, since her life and physical and mental health are in question.[40]

The Commission has, however, committed itself to the view that the foetus is not protected under Art 2. In *H v Norway*,[41] the Commission found that the lawful abortion of a 14-week foetus on social grounds did not breach Art 2. It took this stance partly on the basis that otherwise, a conflict with the mother's Art 8 rights might arise, and partly because, since the State Parties' laws on abortion differ considerably from each other, a wide margin of discretion should be allowed.

As argued in Chapter 4, there are strong reasons for considering that a question concerning an irreconcilable conflict of moral views should be left to the national legislatures.[42] The stance taken in a number of other jurisdictions suggests that where this human rights issue comes before the highest national courts, the woman's right to security of the person and to freedom of choice is viewed as paramount[43] and it has been found that the right to life does not extend to the foetus.[44]

Limitation of parental freedom of choice

Two specific limitations on parental freedom of choice are represented by the Prohibition of Female Circumcision Act 1985 and the Surrogacy Act 1985 (although it should be noted that surrogacy is only curbed by the Act, not outlawed: it only prevents the enforcement of commercial surrogacy arrangements). Carrying out female circumcision is a criminal offence unless it is performed for reasons of medical necessity. In deciding whether the operation is necessary for the mental health of the female, matters of custom and ritual cannot be taken into account: s 2(2) of the Act.

These two statutes place, it is argued, appropriate limits on parents' choice as to the welfare of children. It may be suggested that uncontrolled surrogacy arrangements may amount in themselves to an affront to human dignity. Female genital mutilation clearly

---

39   ECtHR, Judgment of 29 October 1992; (1992) 15 EHRR 244. For comment, see (1992) 142 NLJ 1696.

40   *X v UK*, Appl No 8416/78; 19 D & R 244 (1980).

41   Appl No 17004/90 (1992) 73 DR 155.

42   See pp 191–92. For discussion, see Dworkin, *op cit*, fn 38.

43   See the decision of the Canadian Supreme Court in *Morgentaler v R* [1988] 1 SCR 60; the decision of the US Supreme Court in *Planned Parenthood of Southeastern Pennsylvania v Casey* (1992) 505 US 833.

44   *Christian Lawyers Assoc of South Africa v The Minister of Health* 1998 (11) BCLR 1434; *Borowski v AG of Canada* (1987) 39 DLR (4th) 731.

represents an invasion of autonomy, since it is normally practised on girls who are far too young to give consent. It can also lead to life-long health problems. The practice almost certainly amounts to Art 3 treatment and therefore the UK authorities would fail to adhere to their obligations under the Convention if the law allowed the procedure to occur. The practice of female genital mutilation has been condemned by a number of international bodies including the World Health Organisation and under the International Covenant on Economic, Social and Political Rights.

In general, there is a presumption against allowing any procedure in respect of a child which is being carried out for a non-therapeutic purpose.[45]

Medical treatment

The notion of personal autonomy has arisen frequently in the context of allegedly negligent medical treatment, but the law has not so far made much progress in the direction of granting it recognition.[46] It was argued in *Sidaway v Board of Governors of the Bethlem Royal Hospital*[47] that a patient who was not fully informed as to the risks associated with the operation she was to undergo should be able to succeed against the doctor in negligence when one of those risks did materialise. However, it was found that so long as the doctor had acted in accordance with practice accepted as proper by a body of medical practitioners (the test deriving from *Bolam v Friern HMC)*[48] with regard to disclosure of risks, the action must fail. It may be argued that this stance fails to accord sufficient weight to the personal autonomy of the patient. The *Bolam* test was modified by the House of Lords in *Bolitho v Hackney Health Authority*.[49] The Lords considered that the Bolam test was still applicable, but that a court need not find that a doctor was not negligent merely because some medical experts had testified that the doctor's actions were in accord with accepted medical practice. The court had to be satisfied that the medical experts' opinion was reasonable, although in most instances the fact that the experts took a particular view would be in itself grounds for finding it to be reasonable.

The decision in *Bolitho* may accord greater weight to self-determination, in the sense that, in terms of information giving, accepted medical practice may be found occasionally to be negligent But the extent of the obligation to give information may still be unclear. Where a number of choices of treatment lie before a patient, how far might it be expected that he or she should participate in the decision making process? For example, if a patient had a serious cancerous condition, there might be two main options: radical treatment which would be disfiguring, but might prolong life, or conservative treatment which would not prolong life, but would not disfigure. Length of life would have to be weighed against quality of life. It might appear that only the patient who knows intimately which of the options fits with his or her own aspirations and lifestyle and who must live for the

---

45   See the Tattooing of Minors Act 1969, s 1; the Children Act 1989. See further Feldman, 1993, Chapter 4, pp 158–60.

46   See Teff, H, 'Consent to medical procedure: paternalism, self-determination or therapeutic alliance?' (1985) 101 LQR 432.

47   [1985] AC 871; [1985] 2 WLR 480, HL.

48   [1957] 2 All ER 118.

49   [1998] AC 232.

rest of his or her life with the decision taken, should make it and therefore all the risks and benefits of both courses of action should be disclosed.

Furthermore, it might be argued that the degree of self-determination allowable should be greater depending on the type of operation in question. For this purpose, treatment could be divided into three categories: it might be termed elective (sterilisation, cosmetic surgery), semi-elective (this would be a large category which would include on the one hand pain relieving operations and, on the other, operations in the face of life threatening conditions such as cancer) and non-elective (emergency operations where the patient, either due to unconsciousness or extreme pain, was unable to make a choice). It might be argued that self-determination should be complete in respect of purely elective operations and should be a highly significant factor in respect of semi-elective ones. In other words, the law should not impose or allow any further constraint on the patient's exercise of self-determination than is inherent in the situation already.

The law has not, however, recognised these distinctions or, indeed, any general right to bodily privacy in terms of the disclosure of risks. The *Sidaway* case concerned an operation which might be termed semi-elective in that it was aimed at pain relief, but where a purely elective operation was in question in *Gold v Haringey Health Authority*,[50] the same principles applied. Clearly, in order that a patient can exercise self-determination, he or she must know of the options for treatment and of the likely outcome in each instance. The patient can then give or withhold consent to the proposed course of treatment and, further, can question it. However, the test to be applied as to whether a doctor has been negligent in failing to inform the patient of certain possibilities – the *Bolam* test – does not lay a heavy burden upon doctors in terms of the amount of information which must be given. This test may be acceptable in respect of decisions as to diagnosis and treatment (although it may be argued that it puts the plaintiff in medical negligence cases in an extremely difficult position), but arguably it is unacceptable in respect of the duty to disclose information so that the patient can give an informed consent to the treatment proposed. It is arguable that judges have put their fear of defensive medicine and a flood of medical litigation before the need to uphold the right of the patient to control over his or her own body.

Given that positive obligations have been recognised as within the compass of Art 8, the argument could be raised in an action for negligence in circumstances similar to those of *Gold* or *Sidaway*, that the doctor or hospital had failed to respect personal autonomy as a value recognised under Art 8 by failing to furnish sufficient information relating to the risks of the operation. The tort of negligence might undergo development as a result, as did confidence as a result of the decision in *Douglas and Others v Hello!*.[51]

50   [1987] 2 All ER 888.
51   [2001] 2 WLR 992.

3 SEXUAL EXPRESSION AND IDENTITY

Introduction

In the UK, individuals enjoy a limited power of choice as to the expression of sexuality. At present, sexual freedom is restricted by the criminal law, which prohibits certain acts.[52] The rationale for such prohibition depends partly on use of the criminal law as the means of affirming and upholding a certain moral standard and partly on the need to prevent certain specific harms. The debate as to whether or not the proper function of the criminal law is to interfere in the private lives of adult citizens in order to enforce a particular pattern of behaviour where no clear harm will arise from the prohibited behaviour remains unresolved and is no doubt irresolvable.[53] However, the view put forward in the Wolfenden Report 1957,[54] to the effect that the criminal law should confine itself to prohibiting specific harms, has received quite widespread support.[55]

The use of Art 14 and of European Union law in relation to claims regarding employment detriment based on transsexuality and homosexuality are considered in Chapter 16.

Incest

Incest is punishable with a maximum sentence of seven years' imprisonment or with life imprisonment if with a girl under 13 years of age.[56] One justification for prohibiting incest is that the genetic risks associated with it appear to be high, but this argument could equally be extended to anyone affected by a hereditary disease who would then also be prohibited from intercourse. Moreover, the risk of producing children with genetic defects can provide only a partial rationale for the existence of the offence, since it may arise whether or not the man is sterile or the woman past child-bearing age or otherwise unable to have children.[57] On the other hand, the erosion of freedom created by this offence is limited, since it only prohibits acts with a certain group of persons. Following the principles put forward in the Wolfenden Report 1957, this offence should be abolished, although a more limited offence would have to replace it in order to protect younger members of families from the attentions of adult members.

---

52 For consideration of such offences, see Smith, JC and Hogan, J, *Criminal Law*, 8th edn, 1996, Chapter 14; Honore, T, *Sex Law*, 1978.

53 For discussion of the relationship between privacy and morality, see Leander, S, 'The right to privacy, the enforcement of morals and the judicial function: an argument' (1990) Current Legal Problems 115. See also the discussion of these issues in the leading case of *Dudgeon* (1982) 4 EHRR 737, especially the dissenting opinion of Judge Walsh, paras 9–23.

54 Cmnd 247. This view was challenged by Lord Devlin, *The Enforcement of Morals*, 1965.

55 See the *Dudgeon* judgment itself. In *Laskey, Jaggard and Brown v UK* (1997) 24 EHRR 39 (discussed below), the Court refused to rely on the protection of morality exception in Art 8(2), but looked only at the risk of physical harm. The stance taken by the Constitutional Court of South Africa in *National Council of Gay and Lesbian Equality v Ministry of Justice* (1998) (6) BCLR 726 (W) was opposed to the view that the criminal law should impose a view of morality on consenting adults wishing to express their sexuality in a particular manner. A stance similar to that in *Laskey* was taken by the Supreme Court of Canada in *R v Butler* [1992] 1 SCR 452.

56 Sexual Offences Act 1956, ss 10 and 11.

57 It may be noted that s 44 of the 1956 Act defines sexual intercourse as penetration without the need to show emission of seed.

Anal sexual intercourse

The offence of buggery consisted at common law of intercourse *per anum* by a man with a man or woman and intercourse *per anum* or *vaginam* with an animal and it could be committed by a husband with his wife.[58] The common law was enacted in s 12(1) of the Sexual Offences Act 1956. An exception was provided to the common law position by s 1 of the Sexual Offences Act 1967, which permitted consensual buggery between two males both of whom were 21 or over (the highest age of consent for homosexual intercourse in the European Community until 1994), done in private.

Under s 12(1) of the 1956 Act, a homosexual act done in 'public' will be an offence and this will include any place where anyone apart from the two parties is present. Thus, a homosexual act occurring in a house owned by one of the parties (known either as the 'agent' or the 'patient') would be criminalised if another person was in the same room, although unaware of what was occurring. If there is uncertainty as to whether a place is private or public it must be resolved by reference to all the facts, including the likelihood of a third person coming on the scene.[59] It is an offence under s 4 of the 1967 Act to procure another man to commit with a third man an act of buggery, while any agreement between two or more persons to facilitate homosexual activity may be caught by the common law offence of conspiracy to corrupt public morals. The existence of this offence was affirmed in *Knuller Ltd v DPP*[60] in which Lord Reid made clear the policy of the law regarding homosexual acts:

> I read the [1967] Act as saying that, even though [buggery] may be corrupting, if people choose to corrupt themselves in this way that is their affair and the law will not interfere. But no licence is given to others to encourage the practice.

He went on to equate homosexual connection with prostitution as an activity which was not in itself unlawful, but which was not 'lawful in the full sense'. Thus, it is fair to say that the legalisation of homosexual acts was effected in almost the narrowest conceivable manner and suggested a bare toleration of them.[61]

Dudgeon v UK[62] concerned the law in Northern Ireland (Offences Against the Person Act) 1861, which made buggery between consenting males of any age a crime. Dudgeon, who was suspected of homosexual activities, was arrested on that basis and questioned, but the police decided not to prosecute. He applied to the European Commission on the grounds of a breach of the right of respect for private life under Art 8. The European Court of Human Rights held that the legislation in question constituted a continuing interference with his private life, which included his sexual life. He was forced either to abstain from sexual relations completely, or to commit a crime. However, the court considered that some regulation of homosexual activity was acceptable; the question was what was necessary in a democratic society. The court took into account the doctrine of the margin of appreciation, as considered in the *Handyside* case,[63] where it was held that

58   *Jellyman* (1838) 8 C & P 604.
59   *Reakes* [1974] Crim LR 615.
60   [1973] AC 435; [1972] 3 WLR 143; (1972) 56 Cr App R 633, HL.
61   For discussion see Michael, J, 'Homosexuals and privacy' (1988) 138 NLJ 831.
62   (1982) 4 EHRR 149.
63   (1976) 1 EHRR 737.

State authorities were in the best position to judge the requirements of morals. However, the court found that the instant case concerned a very intimate aspect of private life. A restriction on a Convention right cannot be regarded as necessary unless it is proportionate to the aim pursued. In the instant case, there was a grave detrimental interference with the applicant's private life and on the other hand there was little evidence of damage to morals. The law had not been enforced and no evidence had been adduced to show that this had been harmful to moral standards. So the aim of the restriction was not proportional to the damage done to the applicant's privacy and, therefore, the invasion of privacy went beyond what was needed. In response to this ruling, Northern Irish law was changed under the Homosexual Offences (NI) Order 1982. *Dudgeon* demonstrates that the European Court of Human Rights is prepared to uphold the right of the individual to choose to indulge in homosexual practices[64] and suggests that the term 'private life' in Art 8 may be used to cover a wide range of situations where bodily or sexual privacy is in question.

In the European Community, Irish criminal law was until recently the most hostile to homosexuals; sexual acts between members of the same sex were outlawed in the Republic until June 1993, when the Irish Government introduced reform by lowering the age of consent for homosexual acts to 17, thus bringing it into line with the more progressive European countries. It was argued in *Dudgeon* that the age of consent should be lowered in order to ensure respect for the private life of homosexuals, but the European Court accepted that it was within the Member States' margin of appreciation to fix the age of consent at a level which would seem to protect the rights of others. It was recommended in 1984 by the Criminal Law Revision Committee that the age of consent should be lowered to 18, but this recommendation was not implemented. However, Parliament decided to include in the Criminal Justice and Public Order Bill 1994 a clause lowering the age of consent for male homosexuals to 18. Adoption of 16 as the age of consent was debated but rejected. The UK Government took the view, which it put forward in *Dudgeon*, that female homosexual activity does not present as great a danger to society, and particularly to young persons, as male homosexual activity. This may explain why the age of consent for lesbian acts remains the same as for heterosexual intercourse. That 16 is the age of consent is apparent on the basis that, although such acts may be capable of being indecent assaults,[65] they will normally be consented to and so will not be assaults. However, a girl under 16 cannot give the relevant consent and so any homosexual act done to or with a girl beneath that age would be unlawful, as would a heterosexual act. The reason given in *Dudgeon* for this apparent liberalism on behalf of the UK has been attacked as misleading; Edwards argues that its true basis lies in a traditional belief in the sexual passivity of females.[66] In its impact, this differentiation between male and female homosexuals was an instance of straightforward sexual discrimination working to the disadvantage of men.

Section 143 of the Criminal Justice and Public Order Act 1994 amended s 1 of the Sexual Offences Act 1967 to lower the age of consent to 18. The differential ages of consent

---

64 Cf the stance of the US Supreme Court in *Bowers v Hardwick* (1986) 478 US 186; for comment see (1988) 138 NLJ 831.

65 Under the Sexual Offences Act 1956, s 14.

66 Edwards, S, *Female Sexuality and the Law*, 1981, p 42.

under s 143 continued to allow discrimination between homosexuals and heterosexuals and between male and female homosexuals. In *Sutherland v UK*,[67] s 143 of the 1994 Act was successfully challenged under Art 8 in conjunction with Art 14 on the basis that it allowed discrimination between male and female homosexuals, since the age of consent for female homosexual intercourse is 16 under the criminal law as it stands at present, as indicated above. The Commission found by 14 votes to 4 that the fixing of a minimum age of consent at 18 as opposed to 16 was a violation of Art 8 and was discriminatory treatment under Art 14. It took into account the fact that many other States have equalised the ages of consent for homosexual and heterosexual acts and further found that the interference could not be justified on the grounds, including that of protecting public morality, put forward under Art 8(2). It appeared that the European Court of Human Rights was prepared to reconsider its remarks on the point in *Dudgeon* since, as indicated above, it tends to take the view that in sensitive matters of this nature, it should hold back until a clear European standard seems to be emerging; at the stage when a trend is clear, but no such standard has emerged, it will tend to invoke the margin of appreciation.[68] Given the changes in the law on this matter in the different Member States, it seemed that such a standard was emerging regarding equalisation of the ages of consent. The decision was postponed since the government assured the Commission that the Sexual Offences (Amendment) Bill would proceed equalising the age of consent.[69] This was eventually achieved under s 1 of the Sexual Offences (Amendment) Act 2000; the Government had to use the Parliament Act 1911 (as amended) procedure in order to pass the Bill against the opposition of the House of Lords.

Section 1 of the 1967 Act, as amended by s 1 of the 2000 Act, now lowers the age of consent for male homosexual intercourse to 16. Heterosexual buggery is decriminalised by s 1 so long as both parties are over 16. The act must still take place in private and s 12(1), (1B) provides that the act will not be in private if it takes place when two or more persons take part or are present, or it takes place in a public lavatory. Despite these changes, it is highly likely that the current law governing the sexual freedom of homosexuals is still not in accord with Art 8 due to the restrictions on homosexual intercourse which do not apply to heterosexuals. In particular, the law is almost certain to be changed so as to allow consenting homosexual intercourse in private between more than two men as a result of the *'Bolton Seven'* case brought against the UK.[70] The applicants were prosecuted in 1998 on the basis of a video which showed them engaging in consensual group sex. They were convicted of gross indecency. One of the men, Williams, and another, Connell, admitted to having had sex with one of the other five who was, at the time, six months under the then age of consent, 18. Williams was convicted of buggery, although his suspended sentence was later revoked by the Court of Appeal. At the time of the convictions, the court was warned that the prosecutions breached Art 8. Five of the men applied to the European Court of Human Rights and, in July 2001, in order to avoid defeat in the Court, the Government offered each of them compensation in an out of court settlement.

---

67   Appl No 25186/94; [1997] EHRLR 117.
68   See discussion on this point in relation to transsexuals, below, pp 743–4.
69   On 8 September 1999.
70   *ADT v UK* (2000) 2 FLR 697; see *The Guardian*, 27 July 2001.

By these incremental steps, legal acceptance of the sexual autonomy of homosexuals has almost been brought about, in the sense of achieving equality with heterosexuals, although the process will not be complete until the restrictions are equal. If the change in the law regarding the numbers of men who may engage in consensual sex fails to achieve equality, Art 8 and 14 arguments are likely to be raised in any domestic prosecutions under s 7(1)(b) of the HRA, and the same is true of other provisions of the criminal law which still enshrine inequality.[71]

Sado-masochism[72]

Most sado-masochistic acts are currently unlawful in the UK, regardless of the participants' consent to them. Following *Donovan*,[73] a person can consent to the infliction of minor or trivial injury, but not to 'any hurt or injury calculated to interfere with health or comfort ... it need not be permanent but must be more than merely transient or trifling'. *Donovan* appears to be incompatible with *Aitken*[74] in which it was found, in effect, that a person can consent to the risk of serious injury. However, in the leading case of *Brown*,[75] the House of Lords followed *Donovan* in finding that a person cannot consent to the infliction of harm amounting to actual bodily harm. However, consent to such harm may negate liability if there is good reason for the harm to be caused. There are a number of activities involving the causing of or the risk of consensual harm which have been found to be justified as in the public interest. These include rough horseplay,[76] organised games and some informal friendly athletic contests (although not prize fights).[77]

In *Brown*,[78] a group of sado-masochistic homosexuals had regularly over a period of 10 years willingly participated in acts of violence against each other for the sexual pleasure engendered in the giving and receiving of pain. They were charged with causing actual bodily harm contrary to s 47 and with wounding contrary to s 20 of the Offences Against the Person Act 1861 and were convicted. The convictions were upheld by the Court of Appeal which certified the following point of law of general public importance: 'Where A wounds or assaults B occasioning him actual bodily harm in the course of a sado-masochistic encounter, does the prosecution have to prove lack of consent on the part of B before they can establish A's guilt under s 20 and s 47 of the Offences Against the Person Act 1861.' The House of Lords, by a majority of three to two, answered this question in the negative, finding, therefore, that consent could operate only as a defence and would be allowed so to operate only where the public interest would thereby be served. It was found that in a sado-masochistic context, the inflicting of injuries amounting to actual bodily harm could not fall within the category of 'good reason' and therefore, despite the consent of all the participants, the convictions of the defendants were upheld.

---

71 See further Chapter 17, p 1068. For discussion, see Wintemute, R, *Sexual Orientation and Human Rights*, 1995, Chapter 4.

72 For discussion see Leigh (1976) 39 MLR 130.

73 [1934] 2 KB 498.

74 [1992] 1 WLR 1006.

75 [1993] 2 WLR 556; [1993] 2 All ER 75; for comment see (1993) 109 LQR 540; (1994) 20(3) JLS 356.

76 *Jones* (1986) 83 Cr App R 375.

77 *Coney* (1882) 8 QBD 534.

78 [1993] 2 WLR 556; [1993] 2 All ER 75, HL.

The judgments of the majority in the House of Lords are couched in terms which suggest that distaste for the activities in question was a significant influencing factor. Lord Mustill, in the minority in the House of Lords, considered each of the grounds considered by the majority to be in favour of criminalising the activities in question and discounted each of them. These included fear of the spread of AIDS and the possibility that things might get out of hand if activities such as these were allowed. AIDS, as Lord Mustill pointed out, may be spread by consensual buggery, which is legal, rather than by the activities in question. If a person consents to a lesser harm than that which is actually inflicted, the existing law could be used to punish the perpetrator.

It is unclear that any public interest was served by bringing the prosecution: the activities in question were carried on privately, and there was no suggestion that any of the 'victims' were coerced into consenting to them: all had apparently chosen freely to participate. No hospital treatment was needed and the police only discovered what had been occurring by chance. Thus, this decision may be criticised for its subjectivity; it is unclear why it is acceptable that boxing contests may be carried out which can result in serious permanent injury or even death, while activities such as those in *Brown* are criminalised although they may result in a lesser degree of harm.[79] Similarly, it is difficult to reconcile *Brown* with *Aitken*[80] and with *Wilson*.[81] In *Aitken*, a group of RAF officers, including G, at a party set fire to G's fire resistant suit, as a practical joke. G attempted to resist them, but was badly burned. The convictions of the officers for causing grievous bodily harm contrary to s 20 of the Offences Against the Person Act 1861 were quashed on appeal on the ground that the officers honestly believed that G had consented to their actions. In other words, it was found that G could consent to the risk of serious injury, injury of a more serious nature than that inflicted in *Brown*. In *Wilson*,[82] a husband branded his wife's buttocks with a hot knife at her request. The Court of Appeal found that consensual activity between husband and wife in the privacy of the matrimonial home was not a proper matter for criminal prosecution. An inference which may be drawn from the contradictory nature of decisions in this area is that while boxing, rough horseplay or private heterosexual activities are regarded by some members of the judiciary as acceptable and perhaps 'manly', they have little or no sympathy with or understanding of the value of some aspects of sexual expression, especially the sexual expression of homosexuals. The majority in the House of Lords did not appear to regard the decision as allowing an interference with private sexual activity between adults, but rather as an application of the criminal law to offences of violence which had a sexual motive.

Three of the men who were convicted in *Brown* applied to the European Commission on Human Rights, arguing that their convictions were in breach of Art 8 of the Convention,[83] since they constituted an interference with their private life. The Commission found that no violation of Art 8 had occurred and referred the case to the

---

79 See further on this point Roberts's discussion of the Law Commission, Consultative Paper No 139, *Consent in the Criminal Law*, 1995; (1997) 17(3) OJLS 389.

80 [1992] 1 WLR 1006.

81 [1996] 3 WLR 125.

82 *Ibid*.

83 *Laskey, Jaggard and Brown v UK* (1997) 24 EHRR 39 Appl No 21974/93. The case of *V, W, X, Y and Z v UK* Appl No 21627/93 raises the same issues.

Court, which came to the same conclusion: *Laskey, Jaggard and Brown v UK*.[84] The Court considered that the activities in question could be seen as occurring outside the private sphere: many persons were involved and videos had been taken. However, as the issue of privacy was not in dispute, the Court accepted that an interference with respect for the applicants' private life had occurred.

The question was whether the interference was necessary in a democratic society. It found that the harm was serious, since it concerned genital torture. The State is entitled to regulate the infliction of physical harm, and the level of harm to be tolerated by the State where the victim consents is in the first instance a matter for the State concerned. The activities had the potential to cause harm in the sense that if encouraged, harm, including the spread of AIDS, might occur in future. Was the interference proportionate to the aim pursued? Numerous charges could have been preferred, but only a few were selected. The level of sentencing reflected the perception that the activities were rendered less serious by the consent of the 'victims'. The Court, therefore, found that the State had not overstepped its margin of appreciation, taking into account the need for regulation of such harm and the proportionate response of the authorities. Thus, no violation of Art 8 was found. The partly dissenting judgment of Judge Pettiti is of interest. He reasoned that the case did not fall within Art 8 at all, since Art 8 provides protection for persons' intimacy and dignity, not for a person's baseness or criminal immorality. The wording of this judgment echoes the wording of parts of the majority judgments of the House of Lords in allowing distaste and lack of sympathy for the activities in question to have some bearing.

The judgment of the Court reflects, it is suggested, the tendency of the operation of the margin of appreciation to dilute the Convention standards. As suggested elsewhere in this book,[85] a strong justification for trusting human rights and freedoms to the judicial as opposed to the democratic process is that the interests of minorities (including sexual minorities) may thereby be safeguarded, whereas, if they were at the mercy of majoritarianism, they might be at risk. However, this judgment lends credibility to the arguments of those who view the Convention as ineffective as a protector of minorities who stray too far from conventional forms of sexual expression, even where all involved are consenting adults. Clearly, if a similar prosecution is brought in future, Art 8 arguments might be raised with more success, bearing in mind the fact that the margin of appreciation doctrine has no application in domestic law.

Sexual identity

UK law does not at present give full expression to the fundamental interest of individuals in determining their own identity. This significant aspect of private life has arisen in two cases brought under the European Convention on Human Rights against the UK by transsexuals. In *Rees v UK*[86] the applicant, who was born a woman but had had a gender re-assignment operation, complained that he could not have his birth certificate altered to

---

84   (1997) 24 EHRR 39.
85   See Chapter 4, p 180.
86   (1986) 9 EHRR 56.

record his new sex, thereby causing him difficulty in applying for employment. However, the court refused to find a breach of Art 8, because it was reluctant to accept the claim that the UK was under a positive obligation to change its procedures in order to recognise the applicant's identity for social purposes. It followed a similar route in *Cossey v UK*,[87] although it did consider whether it should depart from its judgment in *Rees* in order to ensure that the Convention might reflect societal changes. However, it decided not to do so because developments in this area in the Member States were not consistent and still reflected a diversity of practices. In *B v France*[88] it was found that although there had been development in the area, no broad consensus among Member States had emerged. Nevertheless, the civil position of the applicant in terms of her sexual identity was worse than that of transsexuals in the UK and on that basis, a breach of Art 8 could be found.

These decisions accept that sexual identity is an aspect of private life, although they do not afford full recognition to a right of individuals to determine both their own identity and the public expression of it. However, the Court appears to be coming closer to recognising a breach of Art 8 in such circumstances.[89] In his dissenting Opinion in *Sheffield and Horsham v UK*, Judge Van Dijk said: 'there has been a steady development in the direction of fuller legal recognition [of the status of transsexuals] and there is no sign of any retreat in this respect.'[90] It is possible that, under the HRA, the domestic courts will anticipate the position it seems likely, eventually, to take since the relevant legislation, s 1(1) of the Births and Deaths Registration Act 1953, could be reinterpreted under s 3. It can be changed if a 'factual' error is made. The question of what constitutes such an error is open to interpretation.

4 FAMILY LIFE

Introduction

Respect for family life and for private life can come into conflict with both competing individual and societal claims since it may allow restriction not only of activities of the State detrimental to individuals, but also of beneficial activity. Once a 'circle' has been drawn round the home or the family, privacy interests can be invoked to prevent action to benefit the weaker members within it.[91] Once the State has relinquished responsibility for the regime inside the circle, it will be regulated informally in a manner which may work unfairness for the weaker members within it. This statement from the Association of Chief Police Officers on domestic violence illustrates the danger: '... we are ... dealing with persons bound in marriage and it is important for a host of reasons to maintain the unity of the spouses.'[92] A similar view was expressed by the Home Office in 1975: '... the point

---

87 A 184; (1990) 13 EHRR 622. A similar application also failed in *Sheffield and Horsham v UK* (1999) 27 EHRR 163.

88 (1992) 13 HRLJ 358; for comment see [1992] PL 559.

89 *Sheffield and Horsham v UK* (1998) 27 EHRR 163, para 60.

90 *Ibid*, para 3.

91 For full discussion of this issue, see Donovan, K, *Sexual Divisions in Law*, 1985, Chapter 5.

92 HC Select Committee on Violence in Marriage Report, 1975, p 366.

at which the State should intervene in family violence should be higher than that which is expected in the case of violence between strangers.[93]

Such views are unlikely to be expressed at the present time, although the debate on marital rape[94] produced some of a similar nature; it was suggested by one commentator that marital rape should be equated with a trivial crime such as assault partly on the basis that otherwise, the marriage might not survive. The danger may be summed up as a desire on the part of the State to devote its energies to keeping the circle intact rather than trying to regulate what occurs within it.[95] Such informal withdrawal of regulation might be bolstered by the guarantee of respect for family life under Art 8. Of course, the danger of an assertion of individualism at the expense of social responsibility is not confined to feminist concerns. Socialist and Marxist theorists have argued that delineation of an area as private hampers State organisation of society for the benefit of weaker groups because intervention in housing or education policy in order to ensure equality can be met by a claim that it would fail to show respect for private or family life.[96]

However, there are signs that Art 8 jurisprudence recognises this danger and has rejected the notion that respect for family life, and perhaps for privacy generally, entails failure to interfere in the family when other rights or freedoms are in danger of abuse. In *Marckx v Belgium*,[97] the applicant complained under Art 8 in conjunction with Art 14 that an illegitimate child was not recognised as the child of his or her mother until the latter had formally recognised the child as such. Also, the child was treated under Belgian law as, in principle, a stranger to the parents' families. In finding that the State was under an obligation to ensure the child's integration in the family and therefore, that Art 8 applied, the court impliedly rejected the view put forward by the UK judge, Sir Gerald Fitzmaurice:

> It is abundantly clear that the main if not indeed the sole object and intended sphere of application of Art 8 was that of what I will call the 'domiciliary protection' of the individual. He (*sic*) and his family were no longer to be subjected to domestic. Such and not the internal regulation of family relationships was the object of Art 8 .

Now that Art 8 protection for the family is available in domestic law, it is reasonably clear that this notion of the meaning of respect for family life represents an impoverished view of the Convention requirements. Respect for family life means, negatively, that the State should abstain from interference except where to do so would mean failing to adhere to the requirements of respect for the private life of the child or to the requirements of another Convention Article.[98] The requirement of respect for family life also places positive obligations on the authorities to 'allow those concerned to lead a normal family life'.[99]

---

93 *Ibid*, p 418.

94 See Chapter 17, p 1064–65.

95 This argument is complicated, it has been suggested, by the 'male oriented' nature of the law; in other words, looking to the State for an objective source of control of the private sphere may be misguided (see MacKinnon, C, 'Feminism, Marxism, method and the State' (1982) 7 Signs 515).

96 See Unger, R, *Law in Modern Society*, 1976; Kamenka, 'Public/private in Marxist theory and Marxist practice', in Benn and Gaus (eds), *Public and Private in Social Life*, 1983.

97 (1979) 2 EHRR 330.

98 See *Riem v Sweden* (1992) 16 EHRR 155.

99 *Z and E v Austria* (1986) 49 DR 67.

The concept of 'family life'

This concept under Art 8 may encompass many types of 'family' – formal or informal – but if the 'family' in question might not fall within the term as, for example, a foster parent might not do, there might still be an interference with private life.[100] Generally, a close relationship falling within the term will be presumed where close ties such as those between parent and child exist; for other relations, the presumption will be the other way. In *X, Y and Z v UK*[101] the Court considered that no breach of Art 8 had arisen where the UK refused to recognise a female to male transsexual as the father of a child born after artificial insemination by a donor. The father had lived with the mother in a stable relationship for 10 years and acted as the child's father after the birth. Nevertheless, the Court did find that a family relationship existed between the 'father' and the child, taking into account his involvement with the child before and after the birth.

Respect for family life

Various aspects of family life have been in issue in cases brought against the UK.[102] *W, B v UK*[103] concerned a claim that access should be allowed to children in the care of the local authority. The court noted that Art 8 does not contain any explicit procedural requirements, but found that, in itself, that fact could not be conclusive. When the local authority made decisions on children in its care, the views and interests of parents should be taken into account and the decision making process should allow for this. If parents' views were not taken into account, then family life was not being respected. Therefore, a breach of Art 8 was found on the basis that there was insufficient involvement of the applicants in the process. This decision thus avoided a judgment on the substantive merits of denying parents a right of access to children in care. Had the parents been involved in the decision making process which had then led to the same conclusion, it would seem that no breach of Art 8 would have occurred.

Although the term 'family' may receive a broad interpretation, this has not consistently been the case with respect to the requirements arising from the need to respect family life. In *X v UK*,[104] which was found inadmissible by the Commission, it was determined that 'family life' cannot be interpreted so broadly as to encompass a father's right to be consulted in respect of an abortion. The Commission could have rested the decision on para 2 – the 'rights of others' exception – by taking the rights of the woman in question into account, but it preferred to interpret the primary right restrictively. Had it not adopted such an interpretation, 'family life' might have come into conflict with 'private life' since pregnancy and its management has been accepted as an aspect of a mother's private life, although not to be divorced entirely from consideration

---

100 See generally Liddy, J, 'The concept of family life under the ECHR' [1998] EHRLR 15; Kilkelly, U, *The Child and the ECHR*, 1999, Chapter 9.

101 (1997) 24 EHRR 143.

102 *Z and E v Austria* (1986) 49 DR 67.

103 Judgment of 8 July 1987, A 121; (1987) 10 EHRR 29.

104 Appl No 8416/78; 19 D & R 244 (1980).

of the life of the foetus.[105] Family life has also received a narrow interpretation in immigration cases in respect of a right to enter a country. In *Abdulaziz, Cabales and Balkandali v UK*[106] it was found that:

> The duty imposed by Art 8 cannot be considered as extending to a general obligation ... to respect the choice by married couples of the country of their matrimonial residence and to accept the non-national spouses for settlement in that country.

However, where an alien is in contrast faced with expulsion from a country in which he or she has lived for some time and where members of the family are established, the Court has recently shown itself willing to uphold the right to maintain family ties if satisfied that the ties are clearly in existence.[107]

---

105 *Brüggemann and Scheuten v Federal Republic of Germany* Appl No 6959/75, 10 D & R 100 (1975), Eur Comm HR, Report of 12 July 1977. See above, p 41 for possible conflict between Art 8 and Art 2 in respect of abortions. See above, p 745 for further discussion of the possible conflict between family life and private life.

106 Judgment of 28 May 1985, A 94; (1985) 7 EHRR 471. A breach of the Convention was found when Art 8 was read in conjunction with Art 14 (see above, p 957).

107 See *Moustaquim v Belgium*, A 193 (1991); (1991) 13 EHRR 802 and *Djeroud v France*, A 191-B, 1991; for comment see (1991) YBEL 554–56. See further Chapter 15, pp 957–58.

PART IV

PERSONAL LIBERTY

Part IV considers the extent to which agents of the State have the power to interfere with individual liberty and freedom of movement. Such interference occurs in the name of the prevention of crime, the preservation of national security or, in the case of curbing the entry of asylum seekers, in the interests of the economic well being of the country. In the case of police powers to arrest and detain, and of powers to remove persons from the country, complex statutory schemes put in place under the previous Conservative governments have been built upon by the current Labour Government in creating increasingly illiberal schemes. There remains the possibility that the Human Rights Act (HRA) may prove a corrective to the authoritarian tendency of the statutory schemes in this context. But, at the present time, its impact is already appearing uncertain, inconsistent and muted.

Clear tensions can be discerned between a number of the recent statutes considered in the three following chapters and the Human Rights Act. This is especially true of the Criminal Justice and Public Order Act 1994 (despite amendment), the Immigration and Asylum Act 1999, the Terrorism Act 2000 and the Criminal Justice and Police Act 2001. As will be indicated, the Anti-Terrorism, Crime and Security Bill 2001, which contains a clause allowing for detention without trial for non-British citizens suspected of terrorism, with appeal to the Special Immigration Appeals Tribunal (SIAC, discussed in Chapter 15) may be said to represent, at present, the culmination of this authoritarian tendency. The tension between the Bill and the Human Rights Act has reached a point at which it was only possible to declare the 2001 Bill compatible with the Convention by derogating from Article 5 in respect of the clause in question. It is doubtful, however, whether the derogation was justified since it is not clear that a state of emergency justifying it currently exists in the UK. However, the derogation cannot be questioned in court and would therefore have to be challenged at Strasbourg.

The legislation considered in these three chapters has, it is suggested, certain hallmarks, all of which are of doubtful legitimacy in Human Rights Act terms, There is a tendency to increase the discretion of the police and of other law enforcement officials, and, as discussed in Chapter 11, to seek to curb the ability of the ordinary courts to keep a check on the use of that discretion in the interests of protecting individuals from abuse of power. In so far as the ordinary courts can consider executive use of coercive power, either resulting from use of various legislative provisions or from their misuse, in judicial review proceedings or in the course of the criminal process, the judiciary has not shown a clear determination to use the Human Rights Act as a corrective. Thus they have not, Chapter 14 will argue, shown a willingness to rely on Article 6 to exclude evidence as a form of redress for police misuse of power which has resulted in the production of non-confession evidence. The weakness of the Strasbourg jurisprudence in this respect may have played a part in the adoption of this stance, but the far more likely explanation is that they have clung to their traditional common law-based fondness for retaining the maximum discretion for the judiciary. Where, in contrast, executive discretion is at stake, as in immigration decisions, they have, as Chapter 16 suggests, shown a preparedness, at times, to rely on the Human Rights Act to do precisely what s 6 of that Act allows them to do – to declare that a breach of the Convention rights by a public authority is unlawful. The Labour government has been gravely displeased by such uses of the Act which it itself introduced – a displeasure which, it is suggested, underlies some of the provisions of the new Anti-Terrorist Bill. Far from sympathising with activist interpretations of the Convention, or even with applications of the plain words of the HRA and the Convention, the government appears, in this crucial context, to want the judges to deliver less rights protection than Strasbourg does.

CHAPTER 13

FREEDOM FROM ARBITRARY SEARCH, ARREST AND DETENTION: SUSPECTS' RIGHTS IN CRIMINAL INVESTIGATIONS

1 INTRODUCTION[1]

The exercise of police powers such as arrest and detention represents an invasion of personal liberty which is tolerated in the interests of the prevention and detection of crime. However, the interest in personal liberty requires that such powers should be strictly regulated. One way of putting this is to say that due process requirements inevitably place curbs on police powers. Thus, the rights-based due process model seeks to recognise the 'primacy of the individual and the complementary concept of limitation of official power'.[2] It calls for the police to be subject to tightly defined and rigorous control and for clear, legally guaranteed safeguards for suspects, with clear remedies for abuse through the courts.[3] In contrast, the crime control model values a 'quick, accurate and efficient administrative fact-finding role ... over slow, inefficient, and less accurate judicial trials' in order to achieve 'the dominant goal of repressing crime'.[4]

Current analysis of aspects of the criminal justice system continues to rely quite heavily on the two familiar models of crime control and due process.[5] But while a rhetorical commitment to due process is still evident,[6] there is a clear perception that the law does not currently reflect this model. As Sanders and Young put it: 'Police and Court officials need not abuse the law to subvert the principles of justice; they need only use it.'[7]

1   For background reading, see: Hewitt, P, *The Abuse of Power*, 1982, Chapter 3; Lustgarten, L, *The Governance of Police*, 1986; Leigh, *Police Power*, 1985; Robilliard, J and McEwan, J, *Police Powers and the Individual*, 1986; Benyon and Bourn, *The Police: Powers, Procedures and Proprieties*, 1986; Newburn, T, *Crime and Criminal Justice Policy*, 1995, Chapter 3; Leishman, F, Loveday, B and Savage, S (eds), *Core Issues in Policing*, 1996; Morgan, R and Newburn, T, *The Future of Policing*, 1997. For early comment on the Police and Criminal Evidence Act, see [1985] PL 388; [1985] Crim LR 535. For current comment on the 1984 Act and on the relevant provisions under the Criminal Justice and Public Order Act 1994, see Feldman. D, *Civil Liberties and Human Rights in England and Wales*, 2nd edn, 2002, Chapters 5 and 9; Sanders, A and Young, R, *Criminal Justice*, 1994, 2000; Levenson and Fairweather, *Police Powers*, 1990; McConville, M, Sanders, A and Leng, R, *The Case for the Prosecution*, 1991; Bailey, SH, Harris, DJ and Jones, BL, *Civil Liberties: Cases and Materials*, 1995, Chapter 2; Zander, M, *The Police and Criminal Evidence Act 1984*, 1995; Lidstone, K and Palmer, C, *The Investigation of Crime*, 1996; Reiner and Leigh, 'Police powers', in McCrudden, C and Chambers, G (eds), *Individual Rights and the Law in Britain*, 1994; Klug, F, Starmer, K and Weir, S, *The Three Pillars of Liberty*, 1996.

2   Packer, H, *The Limits of the Criminal Sanction*, 1968. As Walker puts it: 'The primacy of individual autonomy and rights is central to the due process model', *Miscarriages of Justice*, 1999, p 39.

3   See further Baldwin, 'Taking rules to excess: police powers and the Police and Criminal Evidence Bill 1984' in Brenton and Jones (eds), *The Year Book of Social Policy in Britain 1984-85*, 1985, pp 9–29; Jones, P, 'Police powers and political accountability: the Royal Commission on Criminal Procedure'; Hillyard, P, 'From Belfast to Britain: some critical comments on the Royal Commission on Criminal Procedure', both in *Politics and Power*, Vol 4, 1981; Jefferson, T, 'Policing the miners: law, politics and accountability', in Brenton and Ungerson (eds), *The Year Book of Social Policy in Britain 1985-86*, 1986, pp 265–86.

4   Packer, *op cit*, fn 1.

5   Packer, *ibid*. Eg, the two models are extensively relied on in Walker, C and Starmer, K (eds), *Miscarriages of Justice*, 1999. For discussion and criticism of the two models see Sanders and Young, *Criminal Justice*, 2000, Chapter 1, Part 7.

6   See, eg, *Legislation Against Terrorism: A Consultation Paper*, Cm 4178, 1998, esp para 8 of the Introduction.

7   Sanders and Young, *op cit*, fn 1, p 20.

Further, as many scholars have argued, the impact of externally imposed rules on actual police practice is limited and uncertain;[8] in particular, researchers have highlighted the problems of rule-evasion – the avoidance of apparent safeguards through the use of informal practices[9] – and of deterrence.[10] There is general agreement that internal police governance and culture will be highly significant in determining the extent to which suspects' rights are delivered, but it should also be emphasised that that culture is itself likely to be influenced by enhanced possibilities of external review of internal police decisions. There appears to be academic agreement that the relationship between external rules and police culture is a complex one and that rather than tending merely towards straightforward evasion of the legal rules, the institutional culture may encourage the development of strategies intended to adapt and accommodate the rules within the practices it has already fostered.[11] But it is also suggested that enhanced external review of such practices under the Human Rights Act (HRA) may encourage a shift from the working rules formulated by the police towards an infusion of the legal rules into their informal counterparts. As Dixon puts it: '[Rule] compliance has to be sought by skilfully blending negotiation and imposition.'[12]

Before the inception of the Police and Criminal Evidence Act 1984 (PACE), the police had no general and clear powers of arrest, stop and search or entry to premises. They wanted such powers put on a clear statutory basis so that they could exercise them where they felt it was their duty to do so without laying themselves open to the possibility of a civil action. Thus, PACE was introduced in order to provide clear and general police powers, but these were supposed to be balanced by greater safeguards for suspects which took into account the need to ensure that miscarriages of justice, such as that which occurred in the *Confait* case,[13] would not recur. The Royal Commission on Criminal Procedure,[14] whose report influenced PACE, was set up largely in response to the inadequacies of safeguards for suspects which were exposed in the *Confait* report.[15]

The result was a scheme in which the broad discretionary powers granted were to be balanced by two central structuring constraints. First, there were general precedent

---

8   See: the PSI Report's distinction between Presentational, Inhibitory and Working Rules; Dixon, D, *Law and Policing: Legal Regulation and Police Practices*, 1997.

9   See, eg, Goldsmith, A, 'Taking police culture seriously: police discretion and the limits of the law' (1990) Policing and Society Vol 1, pp 91–114.

10 There is some evidence that use of exclusion of evidence may encourage police officers to observe suspects' rights. See Oldfield, 'The exclusionary rule and deterrence: an empirical study of Chicago narcotics officers' (1987) 54 U Chicago L Rev 1016–69. In the context of PACE, this finding receives some support from research by Sanders, Bridges, Mulvaney and Crozier entitled 'Advice and assistance at police stations', November 1989; it was thought that unlawful denials of legal advice had been discouraged by the ruling in *R v Samuel* [1988] 2 All ER 135. The research found that in 1987, before the ruling, delay was authorised in around 50% of applicable cases; in 1990–91, in only one case out of 10,000. Such evidence cannot, however, be treated as conclusive of the issue; apart from other factors, police officers will be aware that the question of exclusion of evidence is unlikely to arise since the case is unlikely to come to a full trial; even if it does arise, a conviction may still be obtained. Any deterrent effect is therefore likely to be undermined.

11 See Smith, DJ, 'Case construction and the goals of the criminal process' [1997] 37 Br Journal of Criminology 319; Ericson, RV, *Making Crime: A Study of Detective Work*, 1981.

12 In Walker and Starmer, *op cit*, fn 5, p 67.

13 See Report of the Inquiry by the Hon Sir Henry Fisher, HC 90 of 1977–78.

14 Royal Commission on Criminal Procedure Report, Cmnd 8092, 1981 (RCCP Report).

15 HC 90, *op cit*, fn 13.

conditions for the exercise of such powers, the most common and significant being the requirement of reasonable suspicion or belief. Secondly, there was the provision of specific countervailing due process rights, in particular a general right of custodial access to legal advice, in most cases laid down in, or underpinned by, quasi- and non-legal rules – the Codes of Practice and Notes for Guidance made under PACE.[16] Redress for breaches of the due process safeguards was largely to be within the disciplinary rather than the judicial sphere: breach of the Codes constituted automatically a breach of the police disciplinary Code.[17]

The driving force behind PACE may have been, despite concerns raised by the *Confait* case, much more to do with crime control than with due process, but it did not lose sight entirely of the reasons for adopting it. Post-PACE, the discovery of a number of miscarriages of justice – the cases of the *Birmingham Six*,[18] the *Guildford Four*,[19] *Judith Ward*,[20] *Stefan Kiszko*,[21] the *Tottenham Three*,[22] the *Maguire Seven*[23] – raised due process concerns again, although in only one of these instances was PACE applicable.[24] After the Birmingham Six were freed in 1992, the Home Secretary announced the setting up of another Royal Commission under Lord Runciman[26] in order to consider further measures which could be introduced, but although there appeared to be a link between the announcement of the Royal Commission and the *Birmingham Six* case owing to proximity in time, the Commission interpreted its remit as not requiring an analysis of the miscarriage of justice in that case. The remit was to examine the efficacy of the criminal justice system in terms of securing the conviction of the guilty and the acquittal of the innocent.[26] Once again, a Royal Commission was seeking to reconcile potentially conflicting aims – concern to protect due process, but also to further crime control. As a number of commentators have observed, however, not only was the former part of this remit largely swallowed up in the latter,[27] it failed to articulate a principled account of investigative procedures.

---

16   PACE 1984, s 66, Codes of Practice.

17   *Ibid*, s 67(8).

18   See *R v McIlkenny and Others* [1992] 2 All ER 417.

19   See May, J (Sir), *Report of the Inquiry into the Circumstances Surrounding the Convictions Arising out of the Bomb Attacks at Guildford and Woolwich in 1974, Final Report*, 1993–94 HC 449, Chapter 17.

20   *R v Ward* (1992) 96 Cr App R 1.

21   (1992) *The Times*, 18 February.

22   (1991) *The Times*, 9 December.

23   See *R v Maguire* [1992] 2 All ER 433.

24   The case of the *Tottenham Three* revealed flaws in the PACE scheme. It predated the introduction of PACE, but PACE was being used on a dry-run basis by the Metropolitan Police at the time. In the case of Winston Silcott, one of the Three, case notes of his confession, supposedly contemporaneous, were found under ESDA to have been tampered with, and his conviction was quashed in 1991; see (1991) *The Times*, 9 December.

25   Runciman Report, Cm 2263, 1993, Chapter 1, para 5; Royal Commission on Criminal Procedure chaired by Lord Runciman; it was announced by the Home Secretary on 14 March 1991, HC Deb Vol 187 Col 1109. It reported on 6 July 1993; see (1993) 143 NLJ 933–96 for a summary of its recommendations in respect of Police Investigations, Safeguards for Suspects, the Right to Silence and Confession Evidence.

26   Effectiveness in securing 'the conviction of those guilty of criminal offences and the acquittal of those who are innocent', Runciman Report, *ibid*, Chapter 1, para 5.

27   See Sanders and Young, 'The RCCJ' [1994] 14 OJLS 435; Walker and Starmer, *op cit*, fn 5, especially p 57.

After the Commission reported, the Major Government passed legislation, most notably the Criminal Justice and Public Order Act 1994 (CJPOA), which increased police powers significantly while removing a number of safeguards for suspects. In particular, the 1994 Act curtailed the right of silence, although the Runciman Royal Commission had recommended that the right should be retained since its curtailment might lead to further miscarriages of justice. Thus, there were significant developments in police powers during the Major years and the balance PACE was supposed to strike between such powers and due process was, it will be argued, undermined.

Since the Labour Government took office in 1997, there have been, apart from the passing of the HRA, no indications of attempts to break with the criminal justice legislative policies of the Conservative Party. Both before and after the general election of 2001, both major parties were seeking to outdo each other in encouraging and pandering to populist notions of crime control. One especially evident tendency has been the movement away from the need to show reasonable suspicion as a condition precedent for the exercise for police powers. Despite the fact that this condition appeared to offer little restraint in practice to police officers,[28] it may be said that its abandonment in the introduction of new arrest and detention powers is indicative of a formal acceptance of a less fettered police discretion, as opposed to the discretion developed *de facto* in police practice.

However, the UK now has a benchmark by which to measure standards of procedural justice. Given the current trend away from due process which this chapter will outline, the concomitant tendency to render police powers susceptible to subjective exercise, and the *de facto* discretion in respect of the delivery of due process rights which has developed, due at least in part to a largely unmet need for their enforcement, the HRA may be perceived as providing an opportunity to re-infuse due process into criminal procedure. It will be argued, however, that the impact of the HRA is likely to be diluted and unpredictable due to the weakness of the Strasbourg jurisprudence in certain key areas, areas in which the common law has traditionally failed to protect due process. Early decisions under the HRA indicate, this chapter and the next will argue, that the inception of the HRA will have little impact in such areas. More generally, judicial intervention and formal rules have always had, as indicated above, an uncertain impact on the institutional culture of the criminal justice system, and it would probably be unduly optimistic to predict a clear change of stance under the HRA.

In this chapter, the powers of the police and the safeguards which restrict the use of police powers are evaluated with a view to considering how far the suspects' rights granted by PACE have had an impact on police working practice and how far, if at all, change may occur in the light of the HRA. This is followed in Chapter 14 by a consideration of the value of the means of redress available, as affected by the inception of the HRA, if the police fail to comply with the rules.

---

28 See 'Arrest and reasonable suspicion' (1988) 85 Law Soc Gazette, 7 September, p 22, and see below, p 765.

2 THE STRUCTURE OF THE PACE RULES

At present, the rules governing the exercise of police powers are largely contained in the scheme created under PACE, as amended, which is made up of rules deriving from the Act itself, from the Codes of Practice made under it and the Notes for Guidance contained in the Codes. It is also influenced by Home Office circulars. The difference in status between these four levels and the significance of adopting this four tiered approach is considered below. A somewhat similar scheme has been created under the Terrorism Act 2000 with a view to creating at certain points a lesser level of protection for terrorist suspects.

PACE and the Codes

There are at present five Codes of Practice: Code A, covering stop and search procedures, Code B, covering searching of premises, Code C, covering interviewing and conditions of detention, Code D, covering identification methods and Code E, covering tape recording. Thus, each covers a particular area of PACE, although not all areas are covered: arrest, for example, is governed only by statutory provisions.[29] It may be asked why all of the stop and search rules, for example, were not merely made part of the Act. The answer may partly lie in the need for some flexibility in making changes: the Codes are quicker and less cumbersome to amend than statutory provisions. However, it is also possible that the government did not want to create rules which might give rise to liability on the part of the police if they were broken; rules which could operate at a lower level of visibility than statutory ones may have appeared more attractive.

Section 67(10) of PACE makes clear the intended distinction between Act and Codes in providing that no civil or criminal liability will arise from a breach of the Codes. This distinction is of significance in relation to the stop and search, arrest and detention provisions of Parts I to IV of PACE.[30] However, it does not seem to have any significance as far as the interviewing provisions of Part V are concerned. The most important statutory safeguard for interviewing, the entitlement to legal advice, has not been affected by the availability of tortious remedies.[31] Thus statutory and Code provisions concerned with safeguards for suspects are in an equally weak position in the sense that a clear remedy is not available if they are breached. The context in which breaches of the interviewing provisions have been considered is that of exclusion of evidence.[32] In that

---

29 HC 90, *op cit*, fn 13.
30 In that respect, such claims are becoming very significant; in 1991, the Metropolitan Police faced an increase in claims of 40% over 1990. See HC Deb Vol 193 Col 370w. For discussion of the use of tortious claims in this context, see Chapter 14, pp 909–15.
31 The question whether an unlawful denial of access to legal advice amounts to a breach of statutory duty has been considered in an unreported case, 26 October 1985, QB (Rose J), which is cited by Clayton, R and Tomlinson, H in *Civil Actions Against the Police*, 1st edn, 1992, p 359. It was held that the application would be refused even if jurisdiction to make the order sought existed as it would 'cause hindrance to police inquiries'.
32 Breach of a code provision is quite frequently taken into account in determining whether or not a confession should be excluded, usually under PACE, s 78. Breach of a code provision will not lead to automatic exclusion of an interview obtained thereby, but a substantial and significant breach may be the first step on the way to its exclusion (see *Walsh* [1989] Crim LR 822, CA, transcript from LEXIS).

context, the courts have not drawn a distinction between provisions of the Act or Codes except to require that breach of a Code provision should be of a substantial and significant nature[33] if exclusion of evidence is to be considered.

Notes for Guidance

The Notes for Guidance are contained in the Codes but are not part of them.[34] They were apparently intended, as their name suggests, to be used merely as interpretative provisions. However, as will be seen, they contain some very significant provisions, although it is unclear what the consequences of breach of a Note are. Evidence tainted by breach of a Note for Guidance is unlikely to be excluded since, unlike Code provisions, s 67(11) of PACE does not require a court to take the Notes into account in determining any question.[35] However, in *DPP v Blake*,[36] the Divisional Court impliedly accepted that a Note for Guidance will be considered in relation to exclusion of evidence if it can be argued that it merely amplifies a particular Code provision and can therefore be of assistance in determining whether breach of such a provision has occurred. Moreover, certain Notes need not merely be considered in conjunction with the paragraph they derive from; the ruling in *DPP v Rouse* and *DPP v Davis*[37] that they can sometimes be used as an aid to the interpretation of Code C as a whole extended their potential impact. Thus, it may be said that the Notes are of a very uncertain status but that their importance is beginning to be recognised in decisions as to admission of evidence.

Home Office circulars

There are a large number of such circulars dealing with disparate subjects relevant to the use of police powers; some of them are intended to work in tandem with a part of PACE as amplifying provisions and some operate in an area uncovered by the other provisions. They are in an even more equivocal legal position than the Notes. Their legal significance derives from their relevance to the obligations arising from the relationship between police forces and the Home Office and it is likely to be in that context rather than in relation to questions of admissibility that they will be considered.[38] Clearly, argument that a court may be disinclined to consider a Note for Guidance applies *a fortiori* to the

---

33   *Keenan* [1989] 3 All ER 598, CA.

34   This is provided for in the first paragraph of each Code; see, eg, Code C, para 1.3.

35   PACE 1984, s 67(11) provides: 'In all criminal and civil proceedings any such code shall be admissible in evidence; and if any provision of such a code appears to the court or tribunal conducting the proceedings to be relevant to any question arising in the proceedings it shall be taken into account in determining that question.'

36   [1989] 1 WLR 432, CA.

37   (1992) Cr App R 185.

38   See *Home Secretary ex p Westminster Press Ltd* (1991) *The Guardian*, 12 February; *Secretary of State for the Home Dept ex p Lancashire Police Authority* (1992) *The Times*, 26 May. They may also be relevant to issues arising under the Police Act 1996, s 89 (formerly the Police Act 1964, s 51). In *Collins and Wilcock* [1984] 3 All ER 374; [1984] 1 WLR 1172, Home Office circular 109/59 was wrongly interpreted by a police officer; her actions in reliance on the incorrect interpretation were held to be outside the execution of her duty. However, the question whether breach of provisions contained in a circular could lead to exclusion of evidence has not yet been determined.

circulars.[39] It also seems clear that a decision taken in breach of a circular will not be susceptible to judicial review.[40]

3 STOP AND SEARCH POWERS

The PACE stop and search powers were meant to maintain a balance between the interest of society, as represented by the police, in crime control and national security, and the interest of the citizen in personal liberty. Under the due process model, detention short of arrest – usually, although not invariably, exercised in the form of stop and search powers – should be based on reasonable suspicion relating to the specific actions of an individual. Under the crime control model, such detention is viewed as an investigative tool which should be based on general police experience; inhibitory rules should be kept to a minimum in order to allow police officers to act on instinct; police discretion should be the guiding principle. The use of such powers is currently viewed as a necessary part of effective modern policing. It has been argued that much policing is reactive; it is initiated by civilians[41] and therefore the nature of stop and search powers assumes less significance, but this argument is open to question.[42] However, at the present time the growth of intelligence-led policing[43] has led to a more proactive stance, which will tend to enhance the importance of stop and search. The powers represent less of an infringement of liberty than an arrest, but on the other hand their exercise may create a sense of grievance and of violation of personal privacy. Such feelings may contribute to the alienation of the police from the community, leading to a breakdown in law and order expressed in its most extreme form in rioting,[44] and otherwise in a general lack of co-operation with the police. Thus, the extensiveness of stop and search powers may tell us something about the extent to which UK society values individual liberty, but it is also clear that this is a complex issue: too great an infringement of liberty may be as likely to result ultimately in less effective crime control as in too great a restriction of police powers.

As this chapter will indicate, the grant of further powers has not been accompanied by a concomitant strengthening of the protection for the due process rights affecting arrest and detention. One of the key structuring constraints identified above as intended to protect due process under the Police and Criminal Evidence Act 1984 was the requirement of reasonable suspicion. This requirement has been eroded in the post-PACE

---

39 This point was made in Wolehover, D and Heaton-Armstrong, A, 'The questioning Code revamped' [1991] Crim LR 232, with reference to the revision of Code C.

40 See *Gillick v West Norfolk and Wisbech AHA* [1986] AC 112, HL (non-statutory administrative guidance by government departments to subordinate authorities is not as a general rule subject to judicial review). Applicability of this rule to circulars directed to the police was confirmed in *Home Secretary ex p Westminster Press Ltd* (1991) *The Guardian*, 12 February.

41 See Shapland, J and Vagg, J, *Policing by the Public*, 1988.

42 In 1993–94, 24% of arrests resulted from proactive policing including stopping and searching: Phillips and Brown, *Home Office Research Study No 185*, 1998. Sanders and Young, *op cit*, fn 1, 2000, p 70 argue that in future, stopping and searching may play a greater part in arrests.

43 See Chapter 11, p 696.

44 See, on this point, Lord Scarman, *The Brixton Disorders*, Cmnd 8427, 1981; McConville, M, 'Search of persons and premises' [1983] Crim LR 604–14.

developments; it has been dropped from the more recently introduced special powers and under the Terrorism Act 2000 it continues to be unnecessary in respect of terrorist suspects.

The use of these powers remains a contentious matter that continues to attract public attention, especially as it has frequently been suggested that they may be used in a discriminatory fashion. While it now appears incontrovertible that racial discrimination affects their use, the extent to which this is the case remains controversial.[45] Their recorded use has more than trebled since PACE came into force in 1986[46] and, as indicated below, a large number of further powers have been introduced in the post-PACE period. One factor influencing the rise in their use may have been the introduction of 'zero tolerance' policies in the mid-1990s. The efficacy of such powers is debatable. Only around 10%–14% of stops led to an arrest and only around 3% to a charge.[47] These figures do not include stops which did not lead to a search, or voluntary stops, and therefore the percentage of stops leading to a charge must be lower than this. There are, of course, other methods of measuring the crime control value of stop and search powers; in particular, they have some value in terms of information-gathering and, more controversially, as a means of asserting police authority on the streets.

This proliferation of usage and of powers was not accompanied by a full official review of their crime control value or adverse due process impact[48] until the issues were raised in relation to the *Lawrence* case in the MacPherson Report in 1999.[49] Owing to its remit, they did not form a central focus of the Report; in so far as powers to detain short of arrest were considered, the concern centred on the question of institutionalised racism in relation to their use. The part which such powers might play in miscarriages of justice and their general links with other aspects of policing, especially the interview, has hardly had an airing in recent official reports.[50] As discussed below, the possibility that informal street contacts may influence and structure the formal interview are especially significant in the post-HRA era.

The prevalence of voluntary searches also continues to undermine the reasonable suspicion requirement, and while this problem has been recognised post-PACE, no serious attempt has been made to address it. The apparently voluntary basis of a large number of searches has continued to be questionable.[51] Inconsistency of practice between forces is readily apparent.[52] Persons may be intimidated by police authority and may submit to a search where no power to search in fact exists. Such searches may come to light only if the suspect later raises the argument that the police were not entitled to

---

45   See fn 93, below.

46   Home Office Statistical Bulletin 21/93; Statistical Bulletin 27/97.

47   Home Office Statistical Bulletin 21/93.

48   They were outside the remit of the Runciman Royal Commission.

49   Cm 4262-I. (1999).

50   Eg, the *Consultation Paper on Terrorism*, Cm 4178, 1998, which recommended the retention of counter-terrorist stop and search powers, failed to consider these matters, and made no reference to research it might have been based on.

51   Dixon, D, Coleman, C and Bottomley, K, 'Consent and the legal regulation of policing' (1990) 17 JLS 345.

52   Certain forces such as Bedfordshire use a separate consent form for voluntary searches, but such practice is by no means universal. See 'Modernising the tactic: improving the use of stop and search', *Policing and Reducing Crime: Briefing Note No 2*, November 1999.

assume that he had consented or if, after initial compliance, the suspect resists and is charged with assaulting an officer in the course of his duty.[53]

The formal position remains unchanged – police officers have no right to detain and question a person in the absence of specific statutory powers allowing them to do so. Of course, society considers it desirable that the police should be able to make contact with citizens in order to make general inquiries without invoking any specific powers; on the other hand, citizens do not need to reply to such inquiries. A police officer can ask a citizen to refrain from doing something, but in general, the citizen may refuse if the action is not in itself unlawful. If this were not the case, there would be little need for other specific powers; an officer could, for example, merely ask a person to submit to a search and if he refused, warn him that he could be charged with obstruction. However, some otherwise lawful behaviour, including failure to obey a police officer, may bring a citizen within the ambit of the offence of obstruction of a constable which arises under s 89(2) of the Police Act 1996 (formerly under s 51(3) of the Police Act 1964), and therefore, the way it has been interpreted determines the borderline between legitimate and illegitimate disobedience to police instructions or requests.[54] Section 89(2) creates an area of liability independent of any other substantive offence. Behaviour is criminalised in relation to police officers which would not give rise to criminal liability if directed at any other group of persons. Thus, some contacts between police officer and citizen may result in the creation of liability where otherwise, none would have existed.[55]

Following *Rice v Connolly*,[56] three tests must be satisfied if liability for this offence is to be made out. First, it must be shown that the constable was in the execution of his or her duty. Actions outside an officer's duty would seem to include any action which is unlawful or contrary to Home Office circulars[57] or the Codes of Practice. However, some actions which may be termed unlawful may be found too trivial to take the officer outside the execution of his or her duty. In *Bentley v Brudzinski*[58] an officer laid a hand on the shoulder of the defendant in order to detain him so as to ask further questions. The court found that in trying to prevent the defendant from returning home, the officer was acting outside the execution of his duty, but considered that not all instances in which an officer used some physical restraint would be treated in the same way. Reference was made to *Donelly v Jackman*[59] in which, on very similar facts, it was found that an officer was not outside the execution of his duty. All that can be said, then, is that all the circumstances of the case must be considered in determining whether an officer is within the execution of his duty and that the more significant the restraint used, the more likely it is that the officer will be outside it. Does it follow that any action of an officer which is not unlawful

---

53 See *Osman v Director of Public Prosecutions* (1999) *The Times*, 29 September, Judgment of 1 July 1999, in which Sedley LJ indicated that an initial passive response to a search would not entitle officers to assume that the subject was consenting to it.

54 For discussion of the development of this offence see [1982] PL 558; (1983) MLR 662; [1983] Crim LR 29; [1983] Crim LR 21.

55 See further on this point [1983] Crim LR 21, p 36.

56 [1966] 2 QB 414; [1966] All ER 649; [1966] 3 WLR 17, DC.

57 In *Collins v Wilcock* [1984] 3 All ER 374; [1984] 1 WLR 1172 a police officer wrongly interpreted a Home Office circular; her actions in reliance on the incorrect interpretation were held to be outside the execution of her duty.

58 [1982] Crim LR 825; (1982) *The Times*, 3 and 11 March.

59 (1970) Cr App R 229; [1970] 1 WLR 562.

or contrary to official guidance will be within the execution of duty? It was found in *Coffin v Smith*[60] that any action within the officer's duty as a 'keeper of the peace' would be within his or her duty. Thus, an officer does not need to point to a specific requirement to perform a particular duty imposed by superiors, but equally, some actions which are not unlawful would seem to fall outside his duty.

Secondly, it must be shown that the defendant did an act which made it more difficult for the officer to carry out her or his duty. Physically attempting to prevent an arrest, as in *Hills v Ellis*,[61] will satisfy this test. This is not to imply that a physical act must occur, but that the police must actually be impeded in some way. In *Lewis v Cox*[62] a persistent inquiry as to where an arrested friend was being taken was held to amount to obstruction. The defendant opened the door of the police van, clearly preventing it from driving off, in order to make the inquiry after being told to desist. The ruling in *Ricketts v Cox*[63] that a refusal to answer questions accompanied by abuse was obstruction may delineate the lowest level of behaviour which may be termed obstructive. According to *Rice v Connolly*, a refusal to answer questions does not amount to obstruction; therefore, the abuse alone must have constituted the obstruction. This decision, which has been widely criticised,[64] is perhaps hard to reconcile with *Bentley v Brudzinski* and possibly interpreted the meaning of obstruction too widely.

It must, finally, be shown, following *Lewis v Cox*, that the defendant behaved wilfully in the sense that he acted deliberately with the knowledge and intention that he would obstruct the police officer. A defendant may be 'wilful' even though his purpose is to pursue some private objective of his own, rather than to obstruct the officer, so long as his act is deliberate and he realises that it will in fact impede the officer. This will be the case, according to *Hills v Ellis*, even if the purpose of the defendant is to help the officer.[65]

If a person physically resists an arrest or stop in the belief that it is unlawful, he may incur liability under the offence of assault on a constable which now arises under s 89(1) of the Police Act 1996. Liability may arise even though the defendant is unaware that the person he is assaulting is a police officer.[66] This is strange, since the only justification for creating an area of liability in addition to common law assault and battery would seem to be that there is greater culpability in striking an officer rather than any other individual owing to the officer's special position as keeper of the peace. However, if the defendant believes that unlawful force is being used against him, he can avail himself of the defence of self-defence, although according to *Albert v Lavin*,[67] the belief in the need to act in self-defence must be based on reasonable grounds. This limitation was not accepted by the Court of Appeal in *Gladstone Williams*:[68] it was found that an honest belief would be

60 (1980) Cr App R 221.
61 [1983] QB 680; [1983] 1 All ER 667.
62 (1985) Cr App R 1.
63 (1981) Cr App R 298; see commentary by Birch, D, 'Confessions and confusions under the 1984 Act' [1989] Crim LR 95; Smith, JC and Hogan, J, *Criminal Law*, 1988, p 394; Lidstone [1983] Crim LR 29, pp 33–35.
64 See Williams, *Textbook of Criminal Law*, 1983, p 204; Lidstone, K [1983] Crim LR 29, pp 33–35.
65 Cf *Wilmott v Atack* [1977] QB 498; [1976] 3 All ER 794.
66 *Forbes* (1865) 10 Cox CC 362; for criticism see Williams, *op cit*, fn 64, p 200.
67 [1982] AC 546; [1981] 3 All ER 878, HL. See (1972) 88 LQR 246 on the use of self-defence in these circumstances.
68 (1983) Cr App R 276; see commentary [1984] Crim LR 164.

sufficient. However, it appears that if the honest belief is arrived at through intoxication, the facts will be considered as an objective observer would have perceived them to be.[69] Apart from the assault, the other elements will be interpreted as for obstruction.

The PACE stop and search power

There was no general power at common law to detain without the subject's consent in the absence of specific statutory authority.[70] Instead, there was a miscellany of such powers, the majority of which have been superseded.[71] The Phillips Royal Commission, whose report influenced PACE,[72] recommended the introduction of a new general power, but accepted the need to maintain a balance between the interest of society as represented by the police in crime control, and the interest of the citizen in personal liberty and privacy. This balance was sought to be achieved partly by introducing a reasonable suspicion element into the PACE powers.

Under s 1 of PACE for the first time a general power to stop[73] and search persons (s 1(1)) or vehicles (s 1(2))[74] was conferred on police constables. It arises if the constable forms the reasonable suspicion that stolen goods, or prohibited articles (including offensive weapons)[75] will be found by searching the suspect. It may be that the suspect appears to be in innocent possession of the goods or articles; this does not affect the power to stop, although it would affect the power to arrest; in this sense, the power to stop is broader than the arrest power. Section 4 of PACE enables the police to use their powers under the Road Traffic Act 1988[76] to set up road blocks and to stop and search any vehicle to see whether it contains a wanted person.

Under s 1(6), if an article is found which appears to be stolen or prohibited, the officer can seize it. The s 1 power may be exercised in any place to which the public or a section of it, have access (s 1(1)(a)) or in any other place 'to which people have ready access at the time when [the constable] proposes to exercise the power but which is not a dwelling' (s 1(1)(b)). Powers to enter a dwelling arise under ss 17 and 18, but an officer can search a suspect in a garden or yard or other land 'occupied with or used for the purposes of a

---

69 See O'Connor [1991] Crim LR 135.

70 For a full list of the powers arising from 16 statutes see RCCP Report 1981.

71 A non-exhaustive list of current statutory stop and search powers to which Code A applies is given in Annex A to Code A (1999 version).

72 Op cit, fn 14.

73 It should be noted that the police do not need to search the suspect once he or she has been stopped; they may decide not to. Nevertheless, reasonable suspicion that stolen goods or articles are being carried must arise before the stop can be made.

74 A power to stop vehicles which is not dependent on reasonable suspicion arises under s 163 of the Road Traffic Act 1988. PACE 1984, s 4 regulates it when it is used as the basis for a general road check.

75 Under s 1(7), the articles are '(a) offensive weapons or (b) articles (i) made or adapted for use in the course of or in connection with an offence to which this sub-paragraph applies; or (ii) intended by the person having it with him for such use by him or by some other person'. Under s 1(8), the offences to which s 1(7)(b)(i) above applies are: '(a) burglary; (b) theft; (c) offences under s 12 of the Theft Act 1968; (d) offences under s 15 of that Act.' 'Section 1(8A) applies to [any article which falls within] s 139 of the Criminal Justice Act 1988'. Under s 1(9), offensive weapon means 'any article (a) made or adapted for use for causing injury to persons or (b) intended by the person having it with him for such use by him or by some other person'.

76 See fn 74 above.

dwelling' (assuming, of course, that the provision of s 1 as to reasonable suspicion are fulfilled) if it appears that the person does not reside in the dwelling or have the permission of the owner to be there (s 1(4)).

This general power to stop, search and seize is balanced in two ways. First, the concept of reasonable suspicion allows it to be exercised only when quite a high level of suspicion exists. Secondly, under s 2, the police officer must provide the person to be searched with certain information. These requirements are discussed below.

Power to search for drugs

Section 23 of the Misuse of Drugs Act 1971 provides a stop and search power which is frequently invoked. Under s 23, a constable may stop and search a person whom the constable has reasonable grounds to suspect is in possession of a controlled drug. This power may be exercised anywhere, unlike the power under s 1 of PACE; thus, persons on private premises may be searched once police officers are lawfully on the premises. The provisions as to reasonable suspicion will be interpreted in accordance with Code A. Code A and ss 2 and 3 of PACE apply to this as they do to other statutory stop and search powers unless specific exceptions are made (see below).

Reasonable suspicion

Reasonable suspicion is a flexible, broad and uncertain concept; para 1 of Code of Practice A on Stop and Search as revised in 1991, 1995, 1997 and 1999, applying to all statutory search powers dependent on reasonable suspicion, sets out to explain what it means. Paragraphs 1.6 and 1.7 provide that it is not enough for a police officer to have a hunch that a person has committed or is about to commit an offence; there must be a concrete basis for this suspicion which relates to the particular person in question and could be evaluated by an objective observer. When Code A was revised in 1997,[77] some departure from this stance was effected. Paragraph 1.6A allows an officer to take into account information that members of a particular gang habitually carry knives, other weapons or have drugs in their possession. Paragraph 1.7AA provides that if a person wears an item of clothing or other insignia suggesting that he belongs to such a gang, he may be stopped and searched. Paragraphs 1.6 and 1.7 explain the objective nature of reasonable suspicion and forbid stereotyping in arriving at such suspicion:

> 1.6 An officer will need to consider the nature of the article suspected of being carried in the context of other factors such as the time and the place and the behaviour of the person concerned or those with him. Reasonable suspicion may exist, for example, where information has been received such as a description of an article being carried or of a suspected offender; a person is seen acting covertly or warily or attempting to hide something; or a person is carrying a certain type of article at an unusual time or in a place where a number of burglaries or thefts are known to have taken place recently. But the decision to stop and search must be based on all the facts which bear on the likelihood that an article of a certain kind will be found.

---

77   SI 1997/1159.

1.7 ... a person's colour, age, hairstyle or manner of dress or the fact that he is known to have a previous conviction for possession of an unlawful article, cannot be used alone or in combination with each other as the sole basis on which to search that person. Nor may it be founded on the basis of stereotyped images of certain persons or groups as more likely to be committing offences.

The most significant change brought about when Code A was revised in 1991 was the omission of the requirement that the suspicion should be of the same level as that necessary to effect an arrest.[78] The original intention behind including this provision was to stress the high level of suspicion required before a stop and search could take place; this change, therefore, tends to remove some of that emphasis and could be taken to imply that there are two levels of suspicion, the level required under Code A being the lower. However, although this omission may convey such a message to police officers, it may not make much difference to the way the police actually operate stop and search.

In practice, there is little evidence that reasonable suspicion acts as a constraint if police officers wish to stop and search without it. Research in the area suggests that there is a tendency to view reasonable suspicion as a flexible concept which may denote a low level of suspicion.[79] Sanders and Young conclude, having reviewed the relevant research, that 'the legal understanding of reasonable suspicion plays little part in officers' thought processes or decision-making',[80] although they also suggest that PACE may be bringing about some change in 'cop culture'; young officers may be taught to act 'according to the book' as opposed to acting instinctively. The case law is meagre, but suggests that an imprecise and inconsistent standard is maintained. In *Slade*,[81] the suspect was close to the house of a well known drug dealer; on noticing the officer, he put his hand in his pocket and smiled. This constituted reasonable suspicion. However, in *Black v DPP*,[82] the fact of visiting a well known drug dealer was found to be insufficient as a basis for reasonable suspicion.

Counter-terrorist powers

The Prevention of Terrorism (Temporary Provisions) Act 1989, as amended (PTA) and the Northern Ireland (Emergency Provisions) Act 1996, as amended (EPA) contained special powers providing for the detaining, questioning and searching of pedestrians and vehicles for articles of use in carrying out acts of terrorism and to prevent terrorist attacks. The powers under ss 44–47 of the Terrorism Act 2000 (TA) are based on the PTA and EPA powers and, as Chapter 8 explains, they are applied to a far wider range of people under s 1 of the TA owing to the new and broad definition of 'terrorism'.[83] It may be noted that under s 116(2) of the TA, the powers conferred under the Act to stop persons are deemed to include powers to stop vehicles, and it is an offence to fail to stop a vehicle. Sections 15(3) and (4) of the PTA empowered a police officer to stop and search anyone who

---

78 Previously contained in Annex B, para 4 of Code A.
79 See Dixon (1989) 17 Int J Soc Law 185–206.
80 Sanders and Young, p 43.
81 LEXIS CO/1678/96 (1996).
82 (1995) unreported, 11 May.
83 See Chapter 8, pp 402–03.

appeared to him to be liable for arrest under s 14 of the Act and to search him for anything which might confirm the officer's suspicions as to his involvement in terrorism. Under s 14(1)(b), in order to arrest, a constable had to have reasonable grounds for suspecting that a person was 'concerned in the preparation or instigation of acts of terrorism connected with the affairs of Northern Ireland or any other act' of non-domestic terrorism.[84] The s 15 power was partially influenced by the reasonable suspicion requirement. It did not depend on the need to show reasonable suspicion that the suspect was carrying the items which might be searched for, but the officer had to have reasonable grounds for suspecting that the suspect was liable to arrest under s 14. These stop and search powers are reproduced, but broadened, under s 43 of the TA, which provides: 'A constable may stop and search a person whom he reasonably suspects to be a terrorist to discover whether he has in his possession anything which may constitute evidence that he is a terrorist.' 'Being a terrorist' is not in itself an offence under the TA (unless the 'terrorist' group in question is also proscribed), although some, but not all, actions falling within the definition of terrorism in s 1 of the TA are coterminous with existing offences; therefore, this power is not dependent on suspicion of commission of an offence or of carrying prohibited articles.

There were also powers in s 16 of and para 4(2) of Sched 5 to the PTA, which empowered the police and others to stop, question and search people, vehicles and unaccompanied freight, which were about to enter or leave Great Britain or Northern Ireland, to determine whether they had been concerned in the commission, preparation or instigation of acts of terrorism. These powers formed part of the 'ports and border controls' contained in the PTA. They are reproduced in Sched 7 of the TA and again, they are not dependent on showing reasonable suspicion.

Under the Major Government, additional stop and search powers were added to the PTA. These powers introduce a number of significant features. Not only do they arise independently of reasonable suspicion relating to objects suspected of being carried, but they make it an offence in itself to refuse to comply with the search. It is not an offence under PACE to refuse to comply with a s 1 search, or to obstruct it, although to do so would probably amount to the offence of obstructing a constable under s 89(2) of the Police Act 1996.[85]

Section 81(1) of the CJPOA 1994 amended the PTA by inserting into it a new s 13A which provides that an officer of the rank of Commander as regards the Metropolitan area or the City of London, or of the rank of Assistant Chief Constable as regards any other police area, can authorise officers to stop and search vehicles and their occupants within a particular locality if he or she considers that it is expedient to do so to prevent acts of terrorism. The authorisation must stipulate both the area to which it applies and the period, not exceeding 28 days, for which it will remain in force. Authorisations may be renewed for a further period or periods of up to 28 days at a time. If such an authorisation is in force, an officer may stop any vehicle within the specified locality in order to look for articles which could be used for the commission of acts of terrorism. Since the term 'expedient' is used, there is no requirement that the officer granting the

---

84 See below, p 783.
85 Reproducing the Police Act 1964, s 51(3).

authorisation should reasonably believe that it is necessary in order to prevent the commission of acts of terrorism. The term seems to connote a less rigorous requirement.

The PTA was further amended by the Prevention of Terrorism (Additional Powers) Act 1996 to include a number of new stop and search powers. The government considered that introduction of the new powers was necessary because of the threat of IRA activity on the British mainland in spring 1996. These include a power under s 1, which inserted s 13B into the PTA, to stop and search citizens in designated areas without reasonable suspicion.[86] The authorisation requirements were the same as those under s 13A but for the added requirement that the authorisation must be confirmed by the Secretary of State within 48 hours. If it was not so confirmed, it ceased to have effect (s 13A(8)), but if confirmed it remained in force, and subsisted for up to 28 days. Refusing to comply with the search is an offence carrying a penalty higher than those which could be used, if necessary, under the general offence of obstructing a constable.

The powers under ss 13A and B formed the basis for the powers arising under ss 44–46 of the Terrorism Act 2000, which replaced them. Authorisations apply to a specific area and are for a maximum of 28 days (although that period may be renewed). Reproducing ss 13A(4) and 13B(3), the new provisions expressly confirm that reasonable suspicion remains irrelevant. Section 45(1)(a) provides that the powers under s 44 'may be exercised only for the purpose of searching for articles of a kind which could be used in connection with terrorism' but in order to ensure that this is not interpreted as a limiting requirement, s 45(1)(b) provides that the powers 'may be exercised whether or not the constable has grounds for suspecting the presence of articles of that kind'.

One difference between the TA and PTA powers is that vehicle stop and search authorisations, as well as pedestrian ones, will have to be confirmed by the Secretary of State within 48 hours of their being made, or they will cease to have effect. This appears to be a gesture in the direction of due process, since it rectifies the anomaly of the difference between the exercise of the powers in respect of pedestrians and those in respect of vehicles, and provides, at least theoretically, a level of oversight in relation to both. An authorisation confirmed by the Secretary of State, can be renewed at the end of 28 days under s 46(7) which provides: 'An authorisation may be renewed in writing by the person who gave it or by a person who could have given it; and subsections (1) to (6) shall apply as if a new authorisation were given on each occasion on which the authorisation is renewed.' Thus, theoretically, authorisations could be continually renewed, depending on the intervention of the Secretary of State. The tendency of this provision may be in practice to leave the authorisation power largely in police hands alone.

If a person fails to stop when asked by a constable acting under s 44 of the TA to do so, or wilfully obstructs the constable in exercising these powers, he or she will be liable to a fine of £5,000 or a prison sentence of six months, or both, under s 47. Thus, if someone who is not involved in terrorism resists a search in a designated area, and is, for example, found to be carrying a small amount of cannabis, he or she might in theory face a prison sentence, although the offence committed – possession of cannabis – would not

---

86   The search only authorises a constable to require a person to remove headgear, footwear, outer coat, jacket or gloves (s 4A).

usually lead to the imposition of such a sentence and might well be dealt with by way of caution.

Special powers to prevent anticipated local violence

Section 60 of the CJPOA 1994, as amended by s 8 of the Knives Act 1997, provides police officers with a further stop and search power which does not depend on showing reasonable suspicion of particular wrongdoing on the part of an individual. An officer of at least the rank of inspector can authorise the stop and search of any person or vehicle within a particular locality if he or she reasonably believes that incidents involving 'serious violence' may take place in that area and that authorisation is expedient in order to prevent their occurrence. The authorisation may apply to a period not exceeding 24 hours, but it can be renewed for a further 24 hours if such an authorisation is in force. An officer may stop anyone within the specified locality in order to look for offensive weapons or dangerous instruments whether or not there any grounds for suspecting that such articles are being carried. In contrast to s 1 of PACE, failure to stop is an offence under s 60(8).

Section 60 was also amended by s 25 of the Crime and Disorder Act 1998 to provide a power under s 60(4A)(a) to demand the removal of a face covering 'if the constable reasonably believes that person is wearing [it] wholly or mainly for the purpose of concealing his identity'. Section 25 also amended s 60 to provide a further, separate, power under s 60(4A)(b) to 'seize any item which the constable reasonably believes any person intends to wear wholly or mainly for that purpose'. This is not, formally, a power to stop and search for face coverings. The constable must be acting under another power or the person must be carrying the covering (or item which could be used as a covering) openly. It is an arrestable[87] offence under the new s 60(8)(b) to fail to remove a face covering. These provisions have clear implications for public protest, which are discussed in Chapter 9.[88] While on their face they do not create a new power of stop and search, they may do so in practice since, once an authorisation is in force under s 60, a constable does not require reasonable suspicion that dangerous weapons or instruments will be found in order to stop and search.

Section 163 of the Road Traffic Act 1988

A very broad power to stop vehicles arises under s 163 of the Road Traffic Act 1988 (RTA). Its ambit remains unclear. Section 163 provides a constable in uniform with power to stop vehicles, which may be unqualified as to purpose[89] and does not depend upon reasonable suspicion. If s 163 is of general application, s 1(2) of PACE appears to provide a power to search a vehicle and to detain it for that purpose once it has been stopped under s 163.[90] If s 163 is concerned only with traffic offences, s 1(2) must contain an implied power to stop a vehicle in order to detain it for a search.

---

87   The 1998 Act, s 27(1) amends PACE 1984, s 24 for this purpose.
88   See p 430.
89   See HC Standing Committee E, Col 339, 13 December 1983.
90   This would confirm *Lodwick v Sanders* [1985] 1 All ER 577.

Use of the counter-terrorist, road traffic and special powers

It is notable that no judicial body is involved in the supervision of the counter-terrorist and special powers. All of them are subject to executive supervision only, either by the police themselves or, in the case of s 44 of the TA, by the Home Secretary. These powers discard a key due process safeguard and therefore might be justified only if they are likely to have real value in terms of curbing criminal or terrorist activity. In debate on the 1996 Bill, Michael Howard was asked how many arrests and convictions had followed use of the existing s 13A power to stop and search. In reply, he said that there had been 1,746 stops and 1,695 searches of vehicles, 2,373 searches of persons as occupants of vehicles in the five Metropolitan police areas and 8,142 stops and 6,854 searches of vehicles and 40 searches of persons as occupants of vehicles within the Heathrow perimeter. These had together led to two arrests under the PTA and to 66 other arrests.[91] These figures are clearly telling. They suggest that stopping and searching without reasonable suspicion leads to an extremely low level of arrests and therefore may not be the most effective use of police resources. This very low level of arrests may be compared with the general level flowing from stop and search with reasonable suspicion, which is now around 10%.[92] This figure itself is low (and may not be reliable), but nevertheless suggests that stop and search with reasonable suspicion (even though that concept may be interpreted very flexibly) is more productive on the face of it in crime control terms than stop and search without it. Howard, however, also made the point, although unsupported by specific evidence, that this does not represent the whole picture, since would-be terrorists may be diverted from their activities, information may be gathered and weapons may be found.

The figures given above also suggest that in so far as these powers do have a value, it lies partly in their (albeit low) level of apprehension of persons engaged in non-terrorist offences. If one of the objects of introducing the powers under ss 13A and 13B was in reality to curb drug trafficking, they should have been debated in Parliament on that basis. The 1999 revision of Code A introduced the requirement under para 1.16 that the ss 13A and B powers should 'not be used for stop and search for reasons unconnected with terrorism'. However, as indicated below, this provision is virtually unenforceable.

Since all these powers on their face allow for stop and search on subjective grounds, they may tend to be used disproportionately against the black community. Post-PACE research has consistently suggested that stop and search powers are used in a discriminatory fashion[93] and in response, a rather ambiguous anti-racism provision was introduced in the 1999 revision of Code A. Paragraph 1.16 gives an appearance of seeking to address the problem of racist stops in stating: 'officers should take particular care not to discriminate against members of ethnic minorities in the exercise of these powers.' But the paragraph continues: 'There may be circumstances, however, where it is appropriate for officers to take account of a person's ethnic origin in selecting persons to be stopped in response to a specific terrorist threat.' This hazily worded provision might be interpreted

---

91   HC Deb Col 211, 2 April 1996.

92   Wilkins and Addicot, *Home Office Statistical Bulletin 2/99*, 1999.

93   See Skogan, HO Research Study No 117, 1990 p 34; *Entry into the Criminal Justice System*, August 1998 and Statistics on Race and the Criminal Justice System, December 1998; MacPherson Report, 1999, Cm 4262-I. According to the report, in 1999 blacks were six times more likely than whites to be stopped; in 1998, blacks were five times more likely to be stopped than whites.

as legitimising racist stops and thereby undermining the preceding words. In 1995, Note 1A of Code A was revised to add the requirement that 'the selection of those questioned or searched is based upon objective factors and not upon personal prejudice'. In the 1999 revision, this requirement became part of Note 1AA and further requirements were added regarding the use of the power under s 25 of the Crime and Disorder Act 1998 (introducing new s 60(4A) and (B) into the CJPOA) to provide a power to demand the removal of a face covering. Note 1AA provides that if asking a Muslim woman to remove a covering, the officer should permit this to be done out of public view. Thus, as far as s 163 of the 1988 Act, s 60 of the CJPOA and s 44 of the TA are concerned, these requirements contained in quasi- or non-legal provisions are the only 'safeguards' against a racially stereotyped or insensitive use of these powers. As discussed below, this problem may be addressed under the HRA, while the amendments made to the Race Relations Act 1976 in 2000 by the Race Relations (Amendment) Act 2000 may have an impact on police practice since, as Chapter 16 explains,[94] discrimination on grounds of race in law enforcement is now covered by the 1976 Act.

This bundle of powers, which may allow near-random stopping once a designation is in force, may, as indicated, result not in arrests for terrorist offences or offences of serious violence, but for drug-related or other, more minor offences. It has often been observed that arrests may well be entirely unrelated to the reason for the original encounter with the police. These powers are therefore objectionable in the sense that they have been adopted apparently in response to near-crisis situations, whereas they may be used in situations which would not alone have justified their adoption. Since the wide powers under s 60 of the 1994 Act and s 44 of the Act of 2000 are not subject to limitation flowing from the concept of reasonable suspicion, they represent a departure from the principle that only an individual who has given rise to such suspicion due to his or her actions should suffer the infringement of liberty represented by a stop and search.

Special seizure powers

The Criminal Justice and Police Act 2001 (CJP) introduced certain new seizure powers. Under s 51(1) and (2) of the CJP, if an officer already has a power of search he or she can seize property which may not be covered by that power if it is not practicable to ascertain what the item is at the time or if it is attached to something that the officer does have the power to seize. This new provision is significant since *inter alia* it allows the police officers to remove items from persons even where they are not certain that – apart from s 51 – they have the power to do so.

This new power is 'balanced' by the provisions of ss 52–61 which provide a number of safeguards. Notice must be given to persons whose property has been seized under s 52, and under s 59 he or she can apply to the 'appropriate judicial authority' for the return of the whole or part of the seized property, on the ground that there was no power to seize it or that excluded or special procedure material or legally privileged material[95] is not comprised in other property as provided for in ss 54 and 55. Under s 60 a duty to secure the property arises which includes the obligation under s 61 to prevent *inter alia*

---

94 See p 991.
95 See Chapter 1, pp 642–43.

copying of it. Special provisions are made for the return of excluded or special procedure material or material covered by legal privilege, which are discussed in Chapter 11.[96] The property can be retained under s 56 if it appears to have been obtained in consequence of the commission of an offence and otherwise it might be lost, damaged, altered or destroyed. The idea behind these new powers is to allow the seizure of documents or computer discs which cannot readily be examined on the street. But despite the safeguards introduced, it is not clear that the new powers, especially to seize and use legally privilge material, are compatible with the requirements of the Convention under the HRA. For example, arguments could be raised at trial that Art 8 was breached due to the seizure of confidential material; it could be argued that due to the nature of these provisions they should be afforded a strict construction, using s 3 of the HRA if necessary.

Procedural requirements

Under s 2(1) of PACE, the procedural safeguards it sets out, together with those under s 3, apply to the PACE power and to powers under any other statutory provisions. Statutory powers of search are also subject to the same procedural requirements under Code A as those relating to the powers under s 1 of PACE, apart – where relevant – from the Code A provisions relating to reasonable suspicion (Code A, para 1.5(b)). The special counter-terrorism powers have been subject to such requirements but, in future, will be covered by a new TA Code of Practice.[97] An element of due process is introduced into all these statutory stop and search powers by the information giving and recording requirements under ss 2 and 3 of PACE and Code of Practice A, para 1.5(c) made under PACE or, in respect of the TA powers, by the equivalent TA Code provisions. Under s 2(3) of PACE, the constable must give the suspect certain information before the search begins, including 'his name and the name of the police station to which he is attached; the object of the proposed search; the constable's grounds for proposing to make it'. Under s 3, he or she must make a record of the search, either on the spot if that is practicable or as soon as it is practicable. The subject of the search can obtain a copy of the search record later on from the police station. General guidance as to the conduct of the search is contained in Code A, para 3; it requires the officer to complete the search speedily, to minimise embarrassment and to seek co-operation. Code A, para 4 fleshes out the recording requirements.[98]

Such requirements give the impression of due process-based control since they mean that the citizen can make a complaint and the police station will have a record of the number of stops being carried out. These procedural requirements are supposed to inject some accountability into stopping and searching, but in so far as they rely on Code A, they are effectively unenforceable, while they are entirely irrelevant to 'consensual' stops.

---

96 See pp 644–45.

97 PACE 1984, Code A was applied to the additional PTA powers introduced in 1996. The TA, ss 99 and 101 in respect of Northern Ireland and the new Code introduced under Sched 14, para 6 in respect of the UK generally will apply the TA Codes to the TA powers. Under Sched 14, para 5, 'An officer shall perform functions conferred on him by virtue of this Act in accordance with any relevant code of practice in operation under paragraph 6'. Paragraph 6(1) provides: 'The Secretary of State shall issue codes of practice about the exercise by officers of functions conferred on them by virtue of this Act.'

98 *Inter alia*, the record must include the name, address, date of birth and ethnic origin of the person searched (unless he or she is not willing to disclose the name and address).

Voluntary searches

Code A does not, in general, affect ordinary consensual contact between police officer and citizen; officers can ask members of the public to stop and can ask them to consent to a search and, at least theoretically, the citizen can refuse. However, the voluntariness of these contacts is frequently doubtful: some people might 'consent' to a search in the sense of offering no resistance to it owing to uncertainty as to the basis or extent of the police power in question.[99] The search could then be classified as voluntary and subsequently it would be difficult, if not impossible, to determine whether such classification was justifiable. Once a search is so classified, none of the statutory or Code A safeguards need be observed. Original Code A failed to recognise this problem, although a Home Office circular issued in December 1985[100] did make an effort to address it in para 1:

> ... The co-operation of the citizen should not be taken as implying consent ... Whilst it is legitimate to invite co-operation from the public in circumstances where there is no power to require it, the subject of a voluntary search should not be left under the impression that a power is being exercised. Voluntary search must not be used as a device for circumventing the safeguards established in Part I of the Act.

When the Codes were revised in 1991, the concerns articulated in the circular were given expression in new Notes for Guidance 1D(b) and 1E which created certain restrictions on voluntary searches. Under Note 1E, persons belonging to three of the vulnerable groups recognised throughout the Codes as requiring special treatment – juveniles, the mentally handicapped or mentally disordered – may not be subject to a voluntary search at all. The prohibition also applies to a range of other persons who do not appear capable of giving an informed consent to a search. This group may well include the hearing impaired or persons not proficient in English who are also recognised in the Codes as belonging to vulnerable groups,[101] but they should have been expressly included. Persons who do not fall within the above groups may be subject to a voluntary search under Note 1D(b) as revised in 1995, but the officer should 'always make it clear that he is seeking the consent of the person concerned to the search being carried out by telling the person that he need not consent and that without his consent, he will not be searched'.

These provisions represent a step towards dealing with this problem, but they are deficient in a number of respects.[102] No specific form of words need be used under Note 1D(b). A requirement that an officer issue a caution in similar terms to that used in Code B, para 4.2 in respect of searching of premises might have clarified matters, for example: 'You do not have to consent to this search but anything that is found may be used in evidence against you.' Further, under the 1995 revision, these important provisions continued to appear as Notes for Guidance only, when it might have been expected that because of their specific wording and prescriptive nature, they would have become part of Code A.

---

99 For further discussion of this point, see Dixon *et al*, 'Consent and the legal regulation of policing' (1990) 17 JLS 245–362.

100 Circular No 88/1985.

101 See, in particular, Code C, para 3(b), Detained Persons: Special Groups.

102 See Fenwick, H, 'Searching people and places under the revised PACE Codes' (1992) *Criminal Lawyer*, p 1.

Redress for breaches of the stop and search rules

If a search is conducted unlawfully, the citizen is entitled to resist and to sue for assault. But in many instances, and especially where a search is conducted under one of the provisions which do not require reasonable suspicion, the citizen has no means of knowing that the search is unlawful. A citizen who believed that there could be no grounds for a search and therefore resisted it would be taking a risk. Resistance to an authorised TA or CJPOA search, or a search under s 86 of the TA, would incur criminal liability, not only, in all probability, in respect of obstruction or assault of a constable,[103] but under the special TA or CJPOA search-related offences as well.

There is no provision under the TA, PACE or Code A to the effect that if the procedural requirements are not complied with, the search will be unlawful. As indicated, a number of due process requirements are contained only in Codes[104] and, therefore, their breach cannot give rise to civil liability,[105] although breach of certain of the *statutory* procedural requirements will render searches unlawful, as will breach of the statutory powers. It has been held that a failure to make a written record of the search in breach of s 3 will not render it unlawful,[106] whereas a failure to give the grounds for it will do so, following *Fenelley*[107] and *Samuel v Comr of Police for the Metropolis*,[108] as will a failure to comply with the duties to provide identification under s 2(3), following *Osman v Director of Public Prosecutions*.[109] In *Osman*, proper authorisation had been given for the police to search members of the public entering a park under ss 60(4) and 60(5) of the CJPOA 1994. When the defendant was searched, police officers failed to comply with s 2; the search was resisted and the defendant charged with assaulting an officer in the execution of his duty. It was found on appeal that it was plain from the mandatory words of s 2 that any search initiated without prior compliance with the duties set out in s 2 would mean that no officer was actually assaulted in the execution of his duty, since any search of a person might be a trespass requiring proper justification in law; the breach of s 2(3) meant that the search was unlawful and therefore not in the execution of their duty. The facts that the officers were clearly local and that numbers could have been obtained from their uniforms were found to be insufficient to avoid the finding of unlawfulness.[110] The strict

---

103 Offences arising under the Police Act 1996, s 89(1) and (2).

104 Code A made under PACE 1984, s 66 and the TA Code made under the TA, ss 96 and 98 in respect of Northern Ireland and the new Code introduced under Sched 14 in respect of the UK. See p 757 above.

105 Under PACE 1984, s 67(10). The TA Codes will have the same status as the PACE Codes; under Sched 14, para 6(2) 'The failure by an officer to observe a provision of a code shall not of itself make him liable to criminal or civil proceedings', but under sub-para (3) 'A code (a) shall be admissible in evidence in criminal and civil proceedings, and (b) shall be taken into account by a court or tribunal in any case in which it appears to the court or tribunal to be relevant'.

106 *Basher v DPP* (1993) unreported, 2 March.

107 [1989] Crim LR 142.

108 (1999) unreported, 3 March.

109 (1999) *The Times*, 29 September, Judgment of 1 July 1999.

110 The Crown Court had found that there had been a breach of the 1984 Act, s 2(3)(a), but given the fact that the officers were clearly local police officers policing a local event in broad daylight, as expeditiously as possible, and because numbers could readily be obtained from the officers' uniforms, the breach was not so serious as to render the search unlawful. These findings would clearly have undermined s 2(3).

interpretation of the information-giving duties evident in *Fenelley* and *Osman* was equally apparent in *Lineham v DPP*[111] in the context of a search of premises.

The PACE and TA Codes are admissible in evidence.[112] It may be necessary for a defendant who claims that a search was conducted improperly or unlawfully to seek the limited form of redress represented by exclusion of evidence which has been obtained as a result of a breach of PACE or Code A. A stop and search is most likely to produce physical evidence such as drugs or perhaps a weapon, but the courts are very reluctant to exclude such evidence unless there has been deliberate illegality because it is less likely to be unreliable than confession or identification evidence.[113] Thus, the mechanism of exclusion of evidence as a form of redress for breach of a Code provision which has operated to underpin Codes C and D is not as appropriate in relation to Code A, although an effective sanction is clearly needed.

This weakness is further exacerbated in relation to voluntary searches because provisions relevant to such searches are contained in Notes for Guidance rather than Code A itself, and since the Notes do not have the same legal status as Code provisions, they may be more likely to be ignored. The fact that provision for voluntary searches now appears in the Notes as opposed to the circular, but not in the Code itself, suggests that while the need for an important change has been recognised, there has been a failure to carry it through fully. What would be the position if, for example, a police officer persuaded a mentally handicapped person to 'consent' to a voluntary search in breach of Note for Guidance 1E? A judge might well be minded to view breach of a Note for Guidance as of insufficient significance to lead to exclusion of the products of the search, even if prepared to depart from the general presumption that physical evidence, however obtained, is admissible.

Disciplinary action, the other form of redress for breach of a Code provision, may be even less effective in relation to Code A than Codes C, D and E, which largely govern interrogation and identification, because stop and search powers are exercised away from the police station, at a low level of visibility. Moreover, if a police officer decides that a search can be called voluntary, he need not give his name or number and therefore it will be almost impossible to bring a complaint against him. Thus, it is fair to say that in so far as the balance between police powers and individual rights is supposed to be maintained by the Code A provisions, it is largely dependent on voluntary adherence to them.

Impact of the HRA

The lack of court-based accountability in enforcing the due process safeguards, especially in respect of consensual searches, encourages resort to the HRA, and in this context there are grounds for expecting that arguments raised under the Act may lead to judicial intervention in this largely unregulated area. As Chapter 14 will argue, Art 6 could be

---

111 (1999) unreported, judgment of 8 October. Laws LJ found that police officers who conducted a search under PACE 1984, s 18 had not been acting in the execution of their duty because they had failed to inform the appellant so far as possible as to the reason why they intended to search the premises.

112 PACE 1984, s 67(11); TA, Sched 14, para 6(3).

113 See the pre-PACE ruling of the House of Lords in *Fox* [1986] AC 281; also *Thomas* [1990] Crim LR 269 and *Khan* [1996] 3 All ER 289; cf *Fenelley* [1989] Crim LR 142. See further Chapter 14, pp 891–92.

relied upon where it was claimed at trial that a consensual search was in fact non-consensual or where breaches of Code A had occurred during the search, including breaches which might also amount to violations of Art 8.[114] Code A, para 3.5 provides safeguards for a search of more than outer clothing which appear to be coterminous with the right to respect for privacy under Art 8. However, Note 3A provides that there is nothing to prevent officers from asking a suspect to remove more than outer clothing in public. This Note is therefore of doubtful compatibility with Art 8, since persons who complied with such a 'request', believing that they had to, would suffer an interference with their Art 8 rights, which would not be in accordance with the law.

Article 6 arguments would also be available where a breach of Art 5 is alleged which might affect the fairness of the trial, and Art 5 arguments might be raised independently in a variety of contexts.[115] Article 5 provides a guarantee of 'liberty and security of person'. It appears that the short period of detention represented by a stop and search is sufficient to constitute a deprivation of liberty.[116] Deprivation of liberty can occur only on a basis of law[117] and in certain specified circumstances, including, under Art 5(1)(b), the detention of a person in order to secure the fulfilment of any obligation prescribed by law and, under Art 5(1)(c), the 'lawful detention of a person effected for the purpose of bringing him before the competent legal authority on reasonable suspicion of having committed an offence'. Both these provisions may cover temporary detention for the purposes of a search. The provision under Art 5(1)(b) raises difficulties of interpretation and is clearly not so straightforward as the form of detention permitted under Art 5(1)(c). On its face, its broad wording appears to allow arbitrary detention with none of the requirements of reasonable suspicion or authorisation which PACE and the TA (apart from the special Northern Ireland provisions) depend upon and without intervention by a court. It might even appear to allow preventive action before violation of a legal obligation. It gives the impression of representing a scheme which affords less weight to due process than the current domestic one.

However, para 5(1)(b) has received a restrictive interpretation at Strasbourg. In *Lawless*,[118] it was found that a specific and concrete obligation must be identified; once it has been, detention can in principle be used to secure its fulfilment. It is unclear that the term 'obligation' could apply to the current statutory provisions. The requirements are to submit to a search, and, apart from the power under s 163 of the Road Traffic Act, to remain under police detention for the period of time necessary to allow it to be carried out.[119] Following this interpretation, the PACE, CJPOA and TA stop and search provisions are of doubtful compatibility with Art 5(1)(b). In *McVeigh, O'Neill and Evans*[120]

---

114 Eg, regarding the requirements as to conduct of the search under Code A, para 3, including requirements as to removal of only outer clothing in public.

115 Most frequently in the context of a civil action for false imprisonment or assault, as Chapter 14 indicates, or at trial in respect of failing to stop, either under one of the specific offences under the relevant statute or under the Police Act 1996, s 89(1) or (2).

116 *X v Austria* (1979) 18 DR 154.

117 See discussion of this provision below, p 797.

118 Report of 19 December 1959, B1 (1960–61) p 64; Judgment of 1 July 1961, A 3 (1960–61); (1961) 1 EHRR 15.

119 See *McVeigh, O'Neill and Evans* (1981) 5 EHRR 71; the obligation imposed was a requirement to 'submit to examination'. In *Reyntjens v France* Appl No 16810/90 (1992) unreported, the obligation was to submit to an identity check.

120 (1981) 5 EHRR 71.

a requirement to submit to an examination on arrival in the UK was found not to violate Art 5(1)(b) since it was sufficiently specific and concrete, but the Commission emphasised that this was found on the basis that the obligation in question only arose in limited circumstances and had a limited purpose – to combat terrorism. The PACE powers, the Misuse of Drugs Act power and, arguably, the power arising under s 43 of the TA, which is a permanent power, not one adopted temporarily to meet an emergency as in *McVeigh*, could not readily be said to arise in limited circumstances. The CJPOA and other TA powers have more limited purposes in the sense that the place in which they can be exercised is circumscribed either by its nature (as in port or border controls) or by the authorisation given, which is based on the need for special powers. Whether any particular authorisation would be viewed as rendering the obligation in question sufficiently specific will be open to question, depending on the factual situation.[121]

The PACE powers, the powers under the 1971 Act and under s 43 of the TA are therefore fairly clearly of doubtful compatibility with Art 5(1)(b), while the compatibility of the other powers is uncertain. They may fall within Art 5(1)(c), which requires reasonable suspicion of the commission of an *offence*. This immediately calls into question s 43 of the TA, since no such suspicion is required. It also means that the exercise of the powers under PACE may, depending on the circumstances of a search, be of doubtful compatibility. Section 1 requires suspicion as to carriage of an article, not as to an offence; it is clearly aimed at gathering evidence of offences and its requirements are not fully coterminous with the relevant range of offences. Carrying certain of the articles which fall within s 1 of PACE is not an offence[1122] even if the carrier can be said to 'possess' them, although the officer also requires suspicion as to *mens rea*, while carriage of prohibited articles without sufficient 'possession' will clearly not constitute an offence. Code A, para 1.7A provides that where a police officer has reasonable grounds to suspect that a person is in innocent possession of a stolen or prohibited article, or other item for which he is empowered to search, the power of stop and search exists despite the absence of a power of arrest. That Code provision is clearly incompatible with Art 5(1)(c) and any stop undertaken in conformity with it would appear to be unlawful, unless in the circumstances it could be justified under Art 5(1)(b).

Article 5(1)(c) also requires that the detention should be for 'the purpose of bringing him before the competent legal authority'. It may be said that the powers under s 43 of the TA, the 1971 Act and PACE are exercised in order to determine whether sufficient evidence justifying an arrest is present or for general information-gathering purposes, and are therefore only indirectly aimed at the purpose Art 5 envisages. The exercise of the powers under s 60 of the CJPOA and ss 44 and 89 of TA may also be of doubtful compatibility with Art 5(1)(c). The Strasbourg Court indicated in *Murray v UK*[123] that the essential matter is the identification of objective grounds for suspicion in the particular instance, even where the domestic legislation allows for detention on subjective grounds. In order for stops under these provisions to comply with that finding, police officers would have to satisfy a requirement which is not present in the domestic legislation.

---

121 See further Reiner, R and Leigh, I, 'Police powers', in McCrudden and Chambers, *op cit*, fn 1, pp 93–94; Klug, Starmer and Weir argue in *op cit*, fn 1, that police stop and search powers may breach Art 5: pp 250–51.

122 Under s 1(7)(b), such articles could include credit cards or keys.

123 (1994) 19 EHRR 193.

The power under s 163 of the Road Traffic Act appears to fall outside both Art 5(1)(b) and (c), since it does not depend on reasonable suspicion of an offence and is not exercised in respect of a specific obligation, as explained in *McVeigh*. This is a matter of interpretation, since the obligation might be viewed as confined to one inherent in the use of a vehicle on the roads. But if the obligation it depends upon is not sufficiently specific, its use can be justified only if it does not amount to a deprivation of liberty. The power probably carries with it, impliedly, the power to detain for a short period.[124] The offence under the RTA of failing to stop would probably be committed if the response to the stop was to brake and pause for an instant before driving on. The person stopped may also be given the impression that she is obliged to remain during questioning. Therefore, it is suggested that Art 5 may be engaged by the use of this power, in which case incompatibility almost certainly arises.

Article 5 also imposes further, general requirements. The detention must not be arbitrary; this is implicit in the requirement of lawfulness.[125] A detention with the real purpose of searching for drugs, which had been authorised under s 44 of the TA in respect of terrorism, might be viewed as arbitrary in the sense that it was not proportionate to the purpose of ensuring the fulfilment of an obligation prescribed by the relevant law[126] – the TA. If such an argument was advanced at Strasbourg, involving, as it does, review of the proportionality of decisions taken by the State authorities, a certain margin of appreciation would be afforded to those authorities in respect of their assessment of the relevant circumstances.[127] But in the domestic courts, under the HRA, this approach would be inappropriate. Applying the notion of a discretionary area of judgment[128] would also arguably be inappropriate, since a search under terrorism legislation, but for a non-terrorist purpose, does not call for deference.

In appropriate cases, bearing in mind the recent evidence noted above of a police tendency to show racial bias in decisions to stop and search,[129] violation of Art 5(1)(b) or (c) might be found when read with the Art 14 guarantee of freedom from discrimination in the enjoyment of the Convention rights. This possibility may be of less significance given the amendments made to the Race Relations Act 1976 in 2000, allowing claimants to bring actions against the police in respect of direct or indirect discrimination in policing decisions, including decisions to stop and search. However, a defendant would also have the option of raising an Art 5 and 14 argument during the criminal process. It could be argued, for example, under Art 6(1) that if Art 14, read with Art 5, had been breached through a discriminatory search (one which would otherwise be lawful as in conformity with, for example, s 60 of the 1994 Act or s 44 of the TA), any products of the search should be excluded from evidence under s 78 of PACE, and in so far as the contact had influenced the subsequent investigation, evidence deriving from it should also be excluded. Such an argument would of course require recognition to be given to possible

---

124 This may be suggested by the findings in *Lodwick v Sanders* [1985] 1 WLR 382.
125 *Winterwerp v Netherlands* A 33 (1979), para 39.
126 *Ibid*; *Bouamar v Belgium* A 129 (1988), para 50.
127 *Ibid*, para 40.
128 See Chapter 4, p 186.
129 See fn 93, above.

racial stereotyping behind stop and search decisions, as opposed to imposing neutral explanations on them.[130]

The use of force in order to carry out a stop and search is permitted under s 117 of PACE, which provides: 'the officer may use reasonable force, if necessary, in the exercise of the [PACE] power.' The TA provides an equivalent provision in s 114(2). But, under Art 3, the use of force must be strictly in proportion to the conduct of the detainee; this is discussed further in respect of forcible arrest.[131] Under these provisions, the use of extreme force is permissible if necessitated by the conduct of the detainee, but if the use of such force causes death, it would appear to breach Art 2 which permits the use of lethal force to 'effect an arrest', not to effect a detention short of arrest. However, if the detainee sought to escape after being detained for the purposes of a stop and search, this might fall within the second limb of Art 2(2)(b): 'to prevent the escape of a person lawfully detained'. The lawfulness of the initial detention would then have to be considered, bearing in mind the arguments above.

4 POWERS OF ARREST

Arrest may often be the first formal stage in the criminal process. It does not need to be; the process could begin with a consensual interview with the suspect, perhaps in his or her own home, followed by a summons to appear at the magistrates' court. It appears that arrests are sometimes effected unnecessarily; this contention is supported by the pre-PACE variation in practice regarding arrest between police areas,[132] which does not seem to be explicable on the ground of necessity, but seems to be attributable to different policies in the different areas. Any arrest represents a serious curtailment of liberty; therefore, use of the arrest power requires careful regulation. An arrest, in common with the exercise of other police powers, is seen as *prima facie* illegal, necessitating justification under a specific legal power. If an arrest is effected where no arrest power arises, a civil action for false imprisonment will lie. Despite the need for clarity and precision, such powers were, until relatively recently, granted piecemeal, with the result that prior to PACE, they were contained in a mass of common law and statutory provisions. No consistent rationale could be discerned and there were a number of gaps and anomalies. For example, the Criminal Law Act 1967 gave a power of arrest without warrant where the offence in question arose under statute and carried a sentence of five years. Thus, no power of arrest arose in respect of common law offences carrying such a sentence. This situation was detrimental to civil liberties owing to the uncertainty of the powers, but it may also have been detrimental in crime control terms since officers may have been deterred from effecting an arrest where one was necessary. The powers are now contained

---

130 In the US context, AC Thompson argues that the tendency of the judiciary is to impose such explanations (based on the notion of police expertise in spotting criminal possibilities in neutral behaviour) on stop and 'frisk' decisions and to ignore, if possible, any racial element: 'Race and the Fourth Amendment' (1999) 74(4) New York UL Rev 956.

131 See pp 803–04.

132 Eg, in 1976 in Cleveland, 1% of persons were summonsed for an indictable offence, whereas in Derbyshire, 76% of suspects were, as were 40% of suspects in West Yorkshire and North Wales: Royal Commission Report 1981, Cmnd 8092, para 3.72. See further Bailey, SH and Gunn, MJ, *Smith and Bailey on the Modern English Legal System*, 1991, pp 630–32.

largely in PACE, but common law powers remain, while some statutes create a specific power of arrest which may overlap with the PACE powers.

The due process and crime control views of arrest and detention are diametrically opposed. Under the due process model, arrest should be based on strong suspicion that the individual has committed a specific offence, since arrest and subsequent detention represent a severe infringement of individual rights. Under the crime control model, arrest and detention need not be sanctioned merely in relation to specific offences, but should be both an investigative tool and a means of asserting police authority over persons with a criminal record or of doubtful character, with a view to creating a general deterrent effect. Under this model, reasonable suspicion is viewed as a needless irrelevancy, an inhibitory rule standing in the way of an important police function.

The body of research into the use of arrest and detention powers is to an extent conflicting, one school of analysis suggesting that the procedural due process elements which were supposed to create restraints on the powers largely fail to do so in practice in a number of respects.[133] A partially opposed view agrees as to 'the limited effectiveness of PACE's control mechanisms, including routinisation of supervisory controls', but suggests that 'the potential exists for [the PACE reforms] to be given more (or less) substance'.[134] It will be argued below that such potential may be realised under the impact of the HRA, but that its influence will be variable, especially as between the conventional and counter-terrorist schemes. While the conventional scheme shows a formal adherence to due process, which appears to have a subtle impact in practice, especially as regards controls on detention, the counter-terrorist scheme adheres, formally, to a lower standard, thereby providing greater leeway for departure from due process without necessarily breaching the rules.

At common law – power to arrest for breach of peace

PACE has not affected the power to arrest which arises at common law for breach of the peace. Factors present in a situation in which breach of the peace occurs may also give rise to arrest powers under PACE, but may extend further than they do owing to the wide definition of breach of the peace. The leading case is *Howell*,[135] in which it was found that breach of the peace will arise if violence to persons or property either actual or apprehended occurs. Threatening words are not in themselves a breach of the peace, but they may lead a police officer to apprehend that a breach will arise. A police officer or any other person may arrest if a breach of the peace is in being or apprehended,[136] but not when it has been terminated, unless there is reason to believe that it may be renewed.[137]

---

133 See Sanders and Young, *op cit*, fn 1, 2000, Chapter 3; McConville, Sanders and Leng, *op cit*, fn 1, esp p 189.

134 Dixon, in Walker and Starmer, *op cit*, fn 5, p 67.

135 [1982] QB 416; [1981] 3 All ER 383, CA; for comment see Williams (1982) 146 JPN 199–200, 217–19.

136 Following *Foulkes* [1998] 3 All ER 705, the breach must be imminent.

137 For commentary on this point and on breach of the peace generally see Williams [1954] Crim LR 578. The view that there is no power to arrest once a breach of the peace is over was put forward in the Commentary on *Podger* [1979] Crim LR 524 and endorsed *obiter* in *Howell* [1982] QB 416; [1981] 3 All ER 383, CA. See Chapter 9, pp 494–99 for full discussion of the use of breach of the peace.

Under PACE: power of arrest without warrant

PACE contains two separate powers of arrest without warrant, one arising under s 24 and the other under s 25. In very broad terms, s 24 provides a power of arrest in respect of more serious offences while s 25 covers *all* offences, however trivial (including, for example, dropping litter) *if* – and this is the important point – certain conditions are satisfied *apart from* suspicion that the offence in question has been committed. Thus, s 25 operates to cover persons suspected of offences falling outside s 24. The difference between ss 24 and 25 is quite significant because once a person has been arrested under s 24, he or she is said to have been arrested for 'an arrestable offence' and this may have an effect on his or her treatment later on. An 'arrestable offence' is therefore one for which a person can be arrested if the necessary reasonable suspicion is present without the need to demonstrate that any other ingredients were present in the situation at the time of arrest.

Arrest under s 24

Section 24 applies:

(1) (a) to offences for which the sentence is fixed by law;

(b) to offences for which a person of 21 years of age or over (not previously convicted) may be sentenced to imprisonment for a term of five years (or might be so sentenced but for the restrictions imposed by s 33 of the Magistrates' Courts Act 1980); and

(c) to the offences to which s 24(2) applies and in this Act 'arrestable offence' means any such offence.[138]

A police officer can arrest for one of the offences covered by s 24 if he or she has reasonable grounds to suspect that the offence is about to be, is being or has been committed. An ordinary citizen can arrest under s 24 in the same way with the omission of the possibility of arresting where the offence is about to be committed. Offences for which a person can be arrested under s 24 may also be classified as 'serious arrestable offences' under s 116. This does not affect the power of arrest, but it does affect various safeguards and powers which may be exercised during detention. The s 24 offences which may also fall into this category fall into two groups as defined under s 116 – first, those which are so serious (such as murder, manslaughter, and indecent assault which amounts to gross indecency) that they will always be serious arrestable offences and secondly, those which will be so classified only if their commission has led to certain specified consequences, namely, serious harm to the security of the State or public order, serious interference with the administration of justice or investigation of offences, death or serious injury, substantial financial gain or serious financial loss. This last possibility may considerably widen the category of serious arrestable offences in that whether or not a loss may be serious may need to be judged in relation to the financial consequences to the person suffering it: a loss of a small amount of money might be serious to a poor

---

138 Section 24(2) covers a miscellany of offences including offences under the Official Secrets Act 1989 and under the Theft Act 1968. It amends the Criminal Law Act 1967, s 2 and contains the powers of arrest which already existed.

person; someone arrested on suspicion of its theft could therefore be classified as in detention for a serious arrestable offence.

Arrest under s 25

The police acquired under s 25 the general power of arrest which they had lacked previously. However, as mentioned above, this power does not merely allow an officer to arrest for any offence so long as reasonable suspicion can be shown. Such a power would have been viewed as too draconian. It is balanced by what are known as the 'general arrest conditions' which must also be fulfilled. Therefore, in order to arrest under s 25, two steps must be taken: first, there must be reasonable suspicion relating to the offence in question; secondly, there must be reasonable grounds for thinking that one of the arrest conditions is satisfied. The need for the officer to have reasonable suspicion relating to the offence in question and to the general arrest conditions was emphasised on appeal in *Edwards v DPP*.[139]

A police constable (but not an ordinary citizen) can arrest if he or she has reasonable grounds to suspect the person of having committed or having attempted to commit the offence or of being in the course of committing or attempting to commit it. The general arrest conditions are:

(a) that the name of the relevant person is unknown to and cannot be readily ascertained by, the constable;

(b) that the constable has reasonable grounds for doubting whether a name furnished by the relevant person as his name is his real name;

(c) that:

   (i) the relevant person has failed to furnish a satisfactory address for service; or

   (ii) the constable has reasonable grounds for doubting whether an address furnished by the relevant person is a satisfactory address for service;

(d) that the constable has reasonable grounds for believing that arrest is necessary to prevent the relevant person:

   (i) causing physical injury to himself or any other person;

   (ii) suffering physical injury;

   (iii) causing loss of or damage to property;

   (iv) committing an offence against public decency; or

   (v) causing an unlawful obstruction of the highway;

(e) that the constable has reasonable grounds for believing that arrest is necessary to protect a child or other vulnerable person from the relevant person.

It can be seen that these conditions divide into two groups: those in which there is or appears to be a failure to furnish a satisfactory name or address, so that the service of a summons later on would be impracticable, and those which concern the immediate need to remove the suspect from the street, which would make it inappropriate to serve a summons later. The inclusion of these provisions implies that the infringement of civil

---

139 (1993) 97 Cr App R 301; (1993) *The Times*, 29 March.

liberties represented by an arrest should be resorted to only where no other alternative exists. In practice, however, arrest under s 25 may be resorted to quite readily; whether this will occur will depend on the interpretation given to 'reasonable grounds'. The phrase suggests that a clear, objective basis for forming the view in question should exist. However, in *G v DPP*[140] a belief that an address was false based on a general assumption that people who commit offences give false details was accepted as based on reasonable grounds. On this interpretation, the general arrest conditions would be unlikely to act as a limiting requirement: once an offence was suspected, it would seem that one of them would be almost automatically fulfilled. However, the decision in *Edwards v DPP*[141] suggests that the courts appreciate the constitutional significance of upholding the requirements under the general arrest conditions. In *Edwards*, an officer arrested the appellant in the course of a struggle, stating that the arrest was 'for obstruction'. Since no power of arrest arises in respect of obstruction, the arrest must have been under s 25. However, it was found to be necessary to demonstrate that the officer had the general arrest conditions in mind when arresting. This might have been inferred, but the express reference to obstruction was thought to preclude an inference that he had other matters in mind.

Counter-terrorist powers

The terrorist offences under the Terrorism Act 2000 (formerly contained in the Prevention of Terrorism (Temporary Provisions) Act 1989 (PTA)) are arrestable offences under s 24 of PACE. There was also a power of arrest under s 14 of the PTA itself. This power had two limbs. The first, s 14(1)(a), empowered a constable to arrest for certain specified offences under the PTA. As these offences were arrestable offences in any event, this power overlapped with that under s 24. However, if an arrest was effected under s 14 of the PTA, as opposed to s 24 of PACE, this had an effect on the length of detention. That power is reproduced in ss 41 and 40(1)(a) of the TA, which cover arrest in respect of certain TA offences.[142]

Part II of the EPA contained powers of arrest which were supplementary to those in s 14 of the PTA. They were applicable only in Northern Ireland and went further than those existing in the rest of the UK. Under s 18 of the EPA, a constable could arrest without warrant anyone whom he had reasonable grounds for suspecting of committing, having committed, or being about to commit, a scheduled offence or an offence under the EPA which was not a scheduled offence. Under s 19 of the EPA, a member of the armed forces on duty could arrest and detain a person for up to four hours on suspicion that he had committed, was committing or was about to commit any offence. The soldier was not required to inform the arrested person of the grounds of the arrest; and to effect the arrest he could enter and search any premises without a warrant. These powers are reproduced in ss 82 and 83 of the TA respectively. They continue to apply only in Northern Ireland,

---

140 [1989] Crim LR 150. For comment see [1993] Crim LR 567.

141 (1993) 97 Cr App R 301; (1993) *The Times*, 29 March.

142 The arrest under s 41 is in respect of reasonable suspicion of being a terrorist; under s 40(1)(a): 'In this Part "terrorist" means a person who has committed an offence under any of sections 11, 12, 15 to 18, 54, 56 to 63.' This definition is not exclusive; its other part, dependent upon s 40(1)(b), which is discussed below, covers the former s 14(1)(b) PTA arrest power.

but are based on the much wider definition of terrorism introduced under the TA. The continued absence of the need to give the grounds for arrest clearly raises the possibility that incompatibility with Art 5 will be found; this is discussed below.

Police discretion is particularly wide where no reasonable suspicion of any particular offence of any particular offence is necessary in order to arrest. Such a power is provided by s 41 of the TA read with s 40(1)(b), which largely reproduces s 14(1)(b) of the PTA. The continuation of this power is controversial, since it was adopted in the face of an emergency situation which is no longer in being and the arrest power will in future be applicable to a far wider range of groups under s 1 of the TA. Under s 14(1)(b), a constable had to have reasonable grounds for suspecting that a person was concerned in the preparation or instigation of acts of terrorism connected with the affairs of Northern Ireland or 'any other act of terrorism except those connected solely with the affairs of the UK or a part of the UK' in order to arrest. Under s 41 of the TA and s 40(1)(b), the qualifying words are omitted. Section 41 allows for arrest on suspicion of being a terrorist and s 40(1)(b) defines a terrorist as 'a person who is or has been concerned in the preparation or instigation of acts of terrorism'. In other words, the arrest power can now be applied to non-Irish UK domestic groups, such as environmental activists. In practice, since s 14(1)(b) did not require suspicion relating to an offence, it was used for investigation, questioning and general intelligence gathering which may be conducted, it has been said, for the purpose of 'isolating and identifying the urban guerrillas and then detaching them from the supportive or ambivalent community'.[143]

The Government, in its Consultation Paper on Terrorism,[144] acknowledged the criticisms which s 14(1)(b) had attracted: '... if the police have proper cause to suspect that a person is actively engaged in terrorism, they must have sufficient information to justify an arrest under PACE ... the absence of any requirement for reasonable suspicion of a specific offence effectively allows the police free rein to arrest whomsoever they wish without necessarily having good reason, including those who should not be arrested at all.'[145] However, the Government took the view that although the ordinary powers of arrest are extensive, they are insufficient to deal with the sophisticated evasion techniques of terrorists.[146] This claim might have been applicable to the well organised Irish groups which caused extensive and severe harm during 'the Troubles'. But in respect of the vast range of groups potentially covered by the new legislation, it is more doubtful, especially bearing in mind the wide range of TA offences, many based, as indicated in Chapters 8 and 9, on a minimal *actus reus* and requiring no proof of *mens rea*. The ordinary arrest powers under PACE or under the first power of s 41 of the TA, read with s 40(1)(a), would almost certainly cover arrests which could be undertaken under the second power covered by s 41 and s 40(1)(b). This second power is clearly aimed at allowing arrest as a stage in the investigation, not as the culmination of it, and it may therefore be said to be firmly based on the crime control model which views the purpose of arrest as a means of furthering general investigative goals. It therefore represents a clear departure from the

---

143 Lowry (1976–77) 8–9 Col *Human Rights L Rev* 185, p 210.

144 *Legislation Against Terrorism: A Consultation Paper*, Cm 4178, 1998.

145 *Ibid*, para 7.5.

146 Since they are 'skilled in, and dedicated to, evading detection ... terrorist crime is often quite different [from serious non-terrorist crime] both in terms of the sophistication of the techniques deployed and the (potential) harm caused'. *Ibid*, para 7.8.

traditional due process view of arrest taken by Phillips in 1981 as justified only after the investigation has uncovered sufficient evidence. The power was severely criticised when used in the context of Irish terrorism; it is likely to attract further criticism when transplanted into a completely different context and afforded a far wider application.

Owing to its departure from the due process principle in failing to require arrest for a particular offence, the reproduction of s 14(1)(b) of the PTA in ss 41 and 40(1)(b) of the TA renders the new power vulnerable to a challenge under Art 5 of the Convention, which in para 5(1)(c) encapsulates that principle. This possibility was recognised by Lord Lloyd, whose 1996 Report, prepared for Michael Howard, the then Conservative Home Secretary, underlies the new counter-terrorism Act.[147] He suggested that, in order to circumvent Art 5, a new offence of being concerned in the commission, preparation or instigation of acts of terrorism should be created. Having considered this suggestion, the Government rejected it, coming to the view, which is evaluated below, that this arrest power is compatible with Art 5(1)(c).[148]

Other statutory powers of arrest

If a statute creates an offence which is a serious offence falling within s 24 then obviously the arrest power under s 24 is applicable. If a statute creates a more minor offence then equally, the arrest power under s 25 is applicable so long as one or more of the general arrest conditions are satisfied. Section 11 of the Public Order Act 1986 and s 51 of the Police Act 1964 provide examples of such offences. However, certain statutes expressly create specific powers of arrest which are not dependent on ss 24 or 25, such as ss 12 and 14 of the Public Order Act. In such cases, the procedure under s 28 of PACE (which is discussed below) will still apply.

Reasonable suspicion

The powers discussed depend on the concept of reasonable suspicion. The idea behind it is that an arrest should take place at quite a late stage in the investigation;[149] this limits the number of arrests and makes it less likely that a person will be wrongfully arrested. It seems likely that it will be interpreted in accordance with the provisions as to reasonable suspicion under Code A although, as will be discussed below, the courts have not relied on Code A in ruling on the lawfulness of arrests. However, Annex B, para 4 of original Code A stated that the level of suspicion for a stop would be 'no less' than that needed for arrest. Although this provision is omitted from the revised Code A, it would seem that in principle, the Code A provisions should be relevant to arrests if the Codes and statute are to be treated as a harmonious whole. Moreover, it would appear strange if a more

---

147 Cm 3420.

148 *Ibid*, para 7.14. A further aspect of s 40 may raise issues under Art 5. Between the First and Second Readings of the Bill, s 40 was subtly changed to include reference to persons concerned in terrorism 'whether before or after the passing of this Act. Since the definition of terrorism in s 1 is much wider than that previously used in the PTA, s 20, s 40 allows arrest of a person for activity which would not have justified arrest (either under the PTA, s 14(1)(b) or at all) at the time when it was undertaken. The coverage of pre-commencement activity is confirmed in s 40(2).

149 See the Phillips Royal Commission Report, *op cit*, fn 14.

rigorous test could be applied to the reasonable suspicion necessary to effect a stop than that necessary to effect an arrest. If this is correct, it would seem that certain matters, such as an individual's racial group, could never be factors which could support a finding of reasonable suspicion. It would seem that a future revision of the Codes might usefully state that the concept of reasonable suspicion in Code A applies to arrest as well; if so, it would at least outlaw the use of such factors as the basis of reasonable suspicion.

The objective nature of suspicion required under Code A is echoed in various decisions on the suspicion needed for an arrest. In *Dallison v Caffrey*, Lord Diplock said the test was whether 'a reasonable man assumed to know the law and possessed of the information which in fact was possessed by the defendant would believe there were [reasonable grounds]'. Thus, it is not enough for a police officer to have a hunch that a person has committed or is about to commit an offence; there must be a clear basis for this suspicion which relates to the particular person in question and which would also be apparent to an objective observer. If an officer only has a hunch – mere suspicion as opposed to reasonable suspicion – he or she might continue to observe the person in question, but could not arrest until the suspicion had increased and could be termed 'reasonable suspicion'.

However, this still leaves a great deal of leeway to officers to arrest where suspicion relating to the particular person is at a low level but they want to further the investigation by gathering information. At present, the courts seem prepared to allow police officers such leeway and it should be noted that PACE endorses a reasonably low level of suspicion owing to the distinction it maintains between belief and suspicion, suspicion probably being the lower standard.[150] The decision in *Ward v Chief Constable of Somerset and Avon Constabulary*[151] suggests that a high level of suspicion is not required and this might also be said of *Castorina v Chief Constable of Surrey*.[152] Detectives were investigating a burglary of a company's premises and on reasonable grounds came to the conclusion that it was an 'inside job'. The managing director told them that a certain employee had recently been dismissed and that the documents taken would be useful to someone with a grudge. However, she also said that she would not have expected the particular employee to commit a burglary. The detectives then arrested the employee, having found that she had no previous criminal record. She was detained for nearly four hours and then released without charge. She claimed damages for false imprisonment and was awarded £4,500. The judge considered that it was necessary to find that the detectives had had 'an honest belief founded on a reasonable suspicion leading an ordinary cautious man to the conclusion that the person arrested was guilty of the offence'. However, the Court of Appeal overturned the award on the basis that the test applied by the judge had been too severe. It was held that the question of honest belief was irrelevant; the issue of reasonable suspicion had nothing to do with the officer's subjective state of mind. The

---

150 Section 17(2)(a) requires belief, not suspicion, that a suspect whom an officer is seeking is on premises; similarly, powers of seizure under s 19(2) depend on belief in certain matters. The difference between belief and suspicion and the lesser force of the word 'suspect' was accepted as an important distinction by the House of Lords in *Wills v Bowley* [1983] 1 AC 57, p 103, HL. See also *Johnson v Whitehouse* [1984] RTR 38, which was to the same effect.

151 (1986) *The Times*, 26 June; cf *Monaghan v Corbett* (1983) 147 JP 545, DC (however, although this demonstrated a different approach, the restriction it imposed may not be warranted: see *DPP v Wilson* [1991] Crim LR 441, DC).

152 NLJ 180, transcript from LEXIS.

question was whether there was reasonable cause to suspect the plaintiff of burglary. Given that certain factors could be identified, including inside knowledge of the company's affairs and the motive of the plaintiff, it appeared that there was sufficient basis for the detectives to have reasonable grounds for suspicion.

Purchas LJ also ruled that once reasonable suspicion arises, officers have discretion as to whether to arrest or do something else, such as making further inquiries, but that this discretion can be attacked on *Wednesbury* principles.[153] In making this ruling, Purchas J relied on the ruling of the House of Lords in *Holgate-Mohammed v Duke*.[154] The House of Lords had confirmed that in addition to showing that the relevant statutory conditions are satisfied, the exercise of statutory powers by officers must not offend against *Wednesbury* principles; officers must not take irrelevant factors into account or fail to have regard to relevant ones; an exercise of discretion must not be so unreasonable that no reasonable officer could have exercised it in the manner in question. Thus, an arrest will be found to be unlawful if no reasonable person looking at the circumstances could have considered that an arrest should be effected, if the decision is based on irrelevant considerations and if it is not made in good faith and for a proper purpose.[155] It was found in *Castorina* that no breach of these principles had occurred and, as reasonable grounds for making the arrest were found, the first instance judge had erred in ruling that further inquiries should have been made before arresting. Under the HRA, courts will have to consider whether the Convention rights have been adhered to; which would be expected to result in a more intensive scrutiny; this is discussed below. Thus, the need to make further inquiries would be relevant to the first stage – arriving at reasonable suspicion – but not to the second – determining whether to make an arrest. That it must be relevant to the first is axiomatic: an investigation passes through many stages, from the first, in which a vague suspicion relating to a particular person arises, up until the point when that person's guilt is established beyond reasonable doubt. At some point in that process, reasonable suspicion giving rise to a discretion as to whether to effect an arrest arises; thus, there must be a point in the early stages at which it is possible to say that more inquiries should have been made, more evidence gathered, before the arrest could lawfully take place. As the courts appear prepared to accept that arrest at quite an early stage in this process may be said to be based on reasonable grounds, and that the application of *Wednesbury* principles leaves little leeway for challenge to the decision to arrest, it may be said that the interest of the citizen in his or her personal liberty is not being accorded sufficient weight under the current tests.[156] As Sanders and Young observe, commenting on *Castorina*, 'The decision gives the police considerable freedom to follow crime control norms, in that it allows them to arrest on little hard evidence'.[157]

Under s 24(4), (5) and (7) it is not *always* necessary to show that reasonable suspicion exists. If an arrestable offence is *in fact* being committed or has been committed or is about

---

153 *Associated Provincial Picture Houses Ltd v Wednesbury Corpn* [1948] 1 KB 223; [1948] 2 All ER 680, CA.

154 [1984] 1 AC 437; [1984] 1 All ER 1054, HL.

155 For discussion of police discretion in this respect see [1986] PL 285.

156 See further as to reasonable grounds for suspicion Clayton, R and Tomlinson, H, 'Arrest and reasonable suspicion' (1988) Law Soc Gazette, 7 September, p 22; Dixon, D, Bottomley, K and Coleman, C, 'Reality and rules in the construction and regulation of police suspicion' (1989) 17 Int J Soc Law 185–206; Sanders and Young, *op cit*, fn 1, 1994, pp 85–98.

157 Sanders and Young, *ibid*, p 86.

to be committed, a constable can arrest even if he or she is just acting on a hunch which luckily turns out to be justified. Of course, if an officer arrests without reasonable suspicion, he or she is taking a risk. These provisions were included because it might seem strange if a person could found an action for false imprisonment on the basis that although he was committing an offence, he should not have been arrested for it. However, if it cannot be established that the offence was committed or was about to be committed, it is not enough to show that reasonable grounds for suspicion did in fact exist although the officer did not know of them. In *Siddiqui v Swain*[158] the Divisional Court held that the words 'reasonable grounds to suspect' used in s 8(5) of the Road Traffic Act 1972 include the requirement that the officer should actually suspect. This approach was also adopted in *Chapman v DPP*.[159] In *O'Hara v Chief Constable of the RUC*,[160] a decision on s 12(1) of the Prevention of Terrorism (TP) Act 1989, the House of Lords found that a constable could form a suspicion based on what he had been informed of previously as part of a briefing by a superior officer, or otherwise. The question to be asked was whether a reasonable man would personally have formed the suspicion after receiving the relevant information. It was not enough for the arresting officer to have been instructed by a superior officer to arrest; his own personal knowledge must provide him with the necessary reasonable suspicion. In the instant case, the arresting officer had sufficient personal knowledge of matters, which it was found provided a basis for reasonable suspicion. The House of Lords stated that these findings applied to arrest powers other than the one arising under s 12.

Research into the use of arrest suggests that in practice, the concept of reasonable suspicion is interpreted very flexibly by the police, as it is in respect of stop and search powers. A wealth of academic research and analysis has established that the need for reasonable suspicion provides little protection against wrongful arrest. Very doubtful grounds often appear to be sufficient to provide reasonable grounds to justify deprivation of liberty. Further, only in exceptional instances will an officer's use of this power be found to have been wrongful; the courts are quite ready to find that these somewhat hazy tests have been satisfied.[161]

Sanders and Young speak of appearing 'suspicious' as being 'a key working rule' in arrests and stops, and observe that association with other criminals is also often the basis for arrest even where the police are 'entirely without reasonable suspicion', since the object is to obtain statements against associates.[162] The courts appear to be reluctant to interfere with the police interpretation and use of the arrest power. Post-PACE decisions leave a great deal of leeway to officers to arrest where suspicion relating to the particular person is at a low level, but they want to further the investigation by gathering information.[163] These powers, especially the very broad power under s 25, mean that, as

---

158 [1979] RTR 454.

159 (1988) Cr App R 190; [1988] Crim LR 843.

160 [1997] 2 WLR 1; [1997] 1 All ER 129.

161 See McConville, Sanders and Leng, *op cit*, fn 1; Sanders and Young, *op cit*, fn 1, 1994, pp 92–98; Ryan, C and Williams, K, 'Police discretion' [1986] Public Law 285, and Clayton and Tomlinson, *op cit*, fn 156, p 22.

162 Sanders and Young, *op cit*, fn 1, 1994, p 92, based on research undertaken by Leng (Royal Commission on Criminal Justice Research Study No 10), 1993.

163 See *Ward v Chief Constable of Somerset and Avon Constabulary* (1986) *The Times*, 26 June; *Castorina v Chief Constable of Surrey* (1988) NLJ 180, transcript from LEXIS.

a number of commentators have pointed out, arrest became under PACE avowedly no longer the culmination of the investigative process but an integral part of it.[164] The strong evidence founding the charge which used to be obtained, it has been suggested,[165] prior to arrest, thus ensuring that innocent persons were unlikely to be arrested and that the infringement of liberty of a person innocent in the eyes of the law was kept to a minimum, tended after PACE to be found in the form of a confession, after arrest. PACE also confirmed the movement away from judicial supervision of arrest, by means of the warrant procedure, which had already begun.

Power of arrest with warrant

This power does not arise under PACE. There are a large number of statutory provisions allowing an arrest warrant to be issued of which the most significant is that arising under s 1 of the Magistrates' Courts Act 1980.[166] Under this power, a warrant may be issued if a person aged at least 17 is suspected of an offence which is indictable or punishable with imprisonment or of any other offence and no satisfactory address is known allowing a summons to be served. This provision therefore limits the circumstances under which a warrant can be sought as an alternative to using the non-warrant powers under PACE and as the police now have such broad powers of arrest under ss 24 and 25, arrest in reliance on a warrant is used even less under PACE than it was previously. The result is that judicial supervision of arrests is minimised.[167] This tendency leaves the operation of the arrest power to the discretion of the police and is part of a general move away from the judicial supervision of police powers.

Procedural elements of a valid arrest[168]

For an arrest to be made validly, not only must the power of arrest exist, whatever its source, but the procedural elements must be complied with. The fact that a power of arrest arises will not alone make the arrest lawful. These elements are of crucial importance owing to the consequences which may flow from a lawful arrest which will not flow from an unlawful one.[169] Such consequences include the right of the officer to use force in effecting it under s 117 of PACE or s 114 of the TA, if necessary, and the loss of liberty inherent in an arrest. If an arrest has not occurred, the citizen is free to go wherever she will and any attempt to prevent her doing so will be unlawful.[170] It is therefore important to convey the fact of the arrest to the arrestee and to mark the point at which

---

164 Sanders and Young, *op cit*, fn 1, 1994, p 70; Ewing, KD and Gearty, CA, *Freedom under Thatcher*, 1989, p 24.

165 Ewing and Gearty, *ibid*, p 25.

166 See [1962] Crim LR 520, p 597 for comment on these powers.

167 See *Criminal Statistics*, Cm 2680, 1993, Table 8.2, p 191.

168 The term 'valid arrest' is open to attack on the ground that there can be no such thing as an invalid arrest. However, a valid arrest may be contrasted with a purported arrest and this is the sense in which it is used in this section.

169 The question as to the difference between a valid and invalid arrest has been much debated; see Lidstone, KW [1978] Crim LR 332; Clark and Feldman [1979] Crim LR 702; Zander, M (1977) NLJ 352; Smith, JC [1977] Crim LR 293.

170 *Rice v Connolly* [1966] 2 QB 414; *Kenlin v Gardner* [1967] 2 QB 510 (see above, pp 761–62 in relation to obstruction of or assault on a police officer in the course of his duty).

the arrest comes into being and general liberty ceases. At common law, there had to be a physical detention or a touching of the arrestee to convey the fact of detention, unless he or she made this unnecessary by submitting to it;[171] the fact of arrest had to be made clear[172] and the reason for it had to be made known.[173]

The common law safeguards have been modified and strengthened by s 28 of PACE, which provides that both the fact of and the reason for the arrest must be made known at the time or as soon as practicable afterwards. However, an ordinary citizen is not under this duty if the fact of the arrest and the reason for it are obvious. Conveying the fact of the arrest does not involve using a particular form of words[174] but it may be that reasonable detail must be given so that the arrestee will be in a position to give a convincing denial and therefore be more speedily released from detention.[175] Given the infringement of liberty represented by an arrest and the need, therefore, to restore liberty as soon as possible, consistent with the needs of the investigation, it is unfortunate that s 28 did not make it clear that a reasonable degree of detail should be given.

However, the reason for the arrest need only be made known as soon as practicable. The meaning and implications of this provision were considered in *DPP v Hawkins*.[176] A police officer took hold of the defendant to arrest him, but did not give the reason. The youth struggled and was therefore later charged with assaulting an officer in the execution of his duty. The question which arose was whether the officer was in the execution of his duty since he had failed to give the reason for the arrest. If the arrest was thereby rendered invalid, he could not be in the execution of his duty, since it could not include effecting an unlawful arrest. It was determined in the Court of Appeal that the arrest became unlawful when the time came at which it was practicable to inform the defendant of the reason but he was not so informed. This occurred at the police station or perhaps in the police car, but did not occur earlier because of the defendant's behaviour. However, the arrest did not become retrospectively unlawful and therefore did not affect acts done before its unlawfulness came into being, which thus remained acts done in the execution of duty. Thus, the police have a certain leeway as to informing the arrestee; the arrest will not be affected, nor will other acts arising from it, until the time when it would be practicable to inform of the reason for it has come and gone. However, if there was nothing in the behaviour of the arrestee to make informing him or her impracticable, then the arrest will be unlawful from its inception. Following the decision in *Hawkins*, what can be said as to the status of the suspect before the time came and passed at which the requisite words should have been spoken? Presumably he was under arrest at that time. Where the procedural elements are not complied with but no good reason for such failure arises (or if no power to arrest arose in the first place), the arrestee will have grounds for

---

171 *Hart v Chief Constable of Kent* [1983] RTR 484.

172 *Alderson v Booth* [1969] 3 QB 216.

173 *Christie v Leachinsky* [1947] AC 573; [1947] 1 All ER 567, HL.

174 The Court of Appeal confirmed this in *Brosch* [1988] Crim LR 743. In *Abassey and Others v Metropolitan Police Comr* [1990] 1 WLR 385, it was found that there was no need for precise or technical language in conveying the reason for the arrest; the question whether the reason had been given was a matter for the jury. See also *Nicholas v Parsonage* [1987] RTR 199.

175 *Murphy v Oxford*, 15 February 1985, unreported, CA. This is out of line with the CA decision in *Abassey* [1990] 1 WLR 385, in which *Murphy* unfortunately was not considered.

176 [1988] 1 WLR 1166; [1988] 3 All ER 673, DC; see also *Brosch* [1988] Crim LR 743, CA.

bringing an action for false imprisonment. Moreover, if a false arrest occurs and subsequently physical evidence is discovered or the defendant makes a confession, the defence may argue that the evidence should be excluded owing to the false arrest. This is considered below and in Chapter 14.[177]

Consensual detainment

Apart from situations in which reasonable suspicion relating to an offence arises, there is nothing to prevent a police officer asking any person to come to the police station to answer questions. There is no legal power to do so, but equally, there is no power to prevent such a request being made. The citizen is entitled to ask whether he or she is being arrested and, if not, to refuse. However, if he or she consents, no action for false imprisonment can arise. This creates something of a grey area, since the citizen may not realise that he or she does not need to comply with the request.[178] The Government refused to include a provision in PACE requiring the police to inform citizens of the fact that they are not under arrest.

The requirement under s 29 that volunteers at police stations – those who are not under arrest – should be able to leave at will unless placed under arrest, does not appear to have much impact on police practice since many people may not realise that they can leave. Section 29 is backed up by para 3.15 of Code C, which requires that if a volunteer is cautioned, she must then be told that she may leave at will. However, this provision is less protective than it appears to be at first sight. A person need only be cautioned if there are grounds to suspect her of an offence. But if there are such grounds, she could probably be arrested, depending on the nature of the offence. Thus, para 3.15 would only come into play at the point when arrest could occur. It would only protect due process (assuming that it was adhered to) if it demanded cautioning on the arrival of a volunteer at a police station. Certain provisions included in Code of Practice C (see below) were intended to ensure that volunteers were not disadvantaged in comparison with arrestees.[179] Of course, such provisions do not affect the fact that some 'volunteers' might not have gone to the police station at all had they realised at the outset that they had a choice.

Use of force[180]

The police may use reasonable force so long as they are within one of the powers allowed under the PACE scheme. This is provided for under s 3 of the Criminal Law Act 1967 and s 117 of PACE 1984. Section 3 is in one sense wider than s 117, since it authorises the use of force by any person, although only in relation to making an arrest or preventing crime. The prevention of crime would include resistance to an unlawful arrest. Section 117 only applies to police officers and then only in relation to provisions under PACE which do not

---

177 See pp 875–85.

178 See McKenzie, I, Morgan, R and Reiner, R, 'Helping the police with their enquiries' [1990] Crim LR 22.

179 In particular, Code C, paras 3.15 and 3.16. See p 833 below for further discussion of the position of volunteers.

180 For consideration of the use of force, see [1982] Crim LR 475; *Report of Commissioner of Police of the Metropolis for 1983*, Cmnd 9268; Waddington, PAJ, *The Strong Arm of the Law*, 1991.

provide that the consent of someone other than a constable is required. Force may include as a last resort the use of firearms; such use is governed by Home Office guidelines,[181] which provide that firearms should be issued only where there is reason to suppose that a person to be apprehended is so dangerous that he could not be safely restrained otherwise. An oral warning should normally be given unless impracticable before using a firearm.[182] Under the 1967 Act, the force can only be used if it is 'necessary' and the amount of force used must be 'reasonable'. 'Reasonable' is taken to mean 'reasonable in the circumstances'[183] and, therefore, allows extreme force if the suspect is also using or appears to be about to use extreme force.

It may be argued that further guidance as to the meaning of 'reasonable' should be provided in PACE. Section 117 provides that 'the officer may use reasonable force, if necessary, in the exercise of the [PACE] power'. This could be taken to mean that any force used which was not, objectively speaking, absolutely necessary will be unreasonable or it might suggest that any force used which appeared necessary at the time will be reasonable, but it is likely that the courts will adopt the latter view. As Chapter 2 demonstrated, Art 2 of the European Convention allows the use of even lethal force which is 'absolutely necessary' in order to arrest;[184] therefore, UK law may not be in harmony with the Convention since a reasonableness test is used. This question is pursued below.

5 DETENTION IN POLICE CUSTODY

Time limits on detention after arrest

The position under the law prior to the 1984 Act with regard to detention before charge and committal before a magistrate was very uncertain. It was governed by s 43 of the Magistrates' Courts Act 1980, which allowed the police to detain a person in custody until such time as it was 'practicable' to bring him before a magistrate, in the case of a 'serious' offence. Since a person would be charged before being brought before the magistrate, this meant that the police had to move expeditiously in converting suspicion into evidence justifying a charge.[185] However, the common law had developed to the point when it could be said that detention for the purpose of questioning was recognised.[186] Thus, prior to PACE, the police had no clearly defined power to hold a person for questioning. The detention scheme governed by Part IV of PACE put such a power on a more certain basis in accordance with the Phillips recommendations,[187] that the purpose of the

---

181 The guidelines were reviewed in 1987 and reissued: see 109 HC Deb Cols 562–63, 3 February 1987; (1987) 151 JPN 146.
182 For comment on the use of firearms, see [1990] Crim LR 695.
183 See the ruling in *Farrell v Secretary of State for Defence* [1980] 1 All ER 166, HL.
184 See pp 38–41.
185 See *Holmes* [1981] 2 All ER 612; [1981] Crim LR 802.
186 *Holgate-Mohammed v Duke* [1984] AC 437; [1984] 1 All ER 1054, HL.
187 See Phillips Royal Commission, *op cit*, fn 14.

detention is to obtain a confession.[188] This was foreshadowed in the developing common law recognition that detention was for the purpose of questioning.[189]

Phillips did not, however, envisage the decision to arrest becoming, in effect, the decision to detain. This is reflected in the role of the custody officer under s 37 of PACE. In theory, he or she could refuse to accept the arrestee into detention. In practice this is extremely rare, if not unknown; the custody officer almost always simply rubber-stamps the arresting officer's decision that the suspect should be detained.[190] Thus, although s 37(3) appears to protect due process since it provides that the custody officer must be satisfied that there are reasonable grounds for the detention,[191] in practice it does not appear to affect police working practices.

Under s 41, the detention can be for up to 24 hours, but in the case of a person in police custody for a serious arrestable offence (defined in s 116) it can extend to 96 hours. Part IV of PACE does not apply to detention under the Terrorism Act 2000 (below) or to detention by immigration officers.[192] Under s 42(1), a police officer of the rank of superintendent or above can sanction detention for up to 36 hours if three conditions apply: he or she has reasonable grounds for believing that either the detention is necessary to secure or preserve evidence relating to an offence for which the detainee is under arrest or to obtain such evidence by questioning him; an offence for which the detainee is under arrest is a serious arrestable offence; and the investigation is being conducted diligently and expeditiously. After 36 hours, detention can no longer be authorised by the police alone. Under s 43(1), the application for authorisation must be supported by information and brought before a magistrates' court, which can authorise detention under s 44 for up to 96 hours if the conditions are met as set out above. Detention must be reviewed periodically;[193] in the case of a person who has been arrested and charged, the review must by the custody officer; in the case of a person arrested but not yet charged, by an officer of at least the rank of inspector. The detainee or his solicitor (if available) has the right to make written or oral representations.[194]

Research suggests, however, that these reviews are not treated as genuine investigations into the grounds for continuing the detention, but as routinised procedures requiring a merely formal adherence.[195] Perhaps in recognition of the need for rigour in relation to reviews, a proposal made in 1999 by the Chief Constable of Kent Police that detention review should be by video link in the majority of cases was rejected in judicial review proceedings on the ground, discussed below, that it might undermine the protection for liberty they are intended to offer, taking Art 5 into account.[196]

---

188 Part IV, s 37(2).

189 *Mohammed-Holgate v Duke* [1984] QB 209.

190 See Dixon, D *et al*, 'Safeguarding the rights of suspects in police custody', 1 Policing and Society 115, p 130.

191 Under s 37(2) they are: 'To secure or preserve evidence relating to an offence for which he is under arrest or to obtain such evidence by questioning him.'

192 PACE 1984, s 51.

193 Under s 40(1)(b).

194 Under s 40(12) and (13).

195 Dixon *et al*, *op cit*, fn 190, pp 130–31.

196 *R v Chief Constable of Kent Constabulary ex p Kent Police Federation Joint Branch Board and Another* (1999) *The Times*, 1 December, Judgment 18 November 1999. See further on this decision below, p 797.

However, the Government then brought forward legislation – s 73 of the Criminal Justice and Police Act 2001 (CJP) – to reverse the effect of this decision. Section 73 inserts new ss 40A and 45A into PACE to allow for the use of telephone and video links for reviews of detention. Section 40A allows for review by an officer of at least the rank of inspector by telephone where it is not reasonably practicable for the officer to be present at the station, and where the review is not one authorised to be carried out by video link under s 45A. Section 45A is an enabling section: it allows for the Secretary of State to make regulations to allow an officer to perform functions in relation to detainees when he or she is not present in the station but has access to a video link. The functions include carrying out the function of custody officer under ss 37, 38, 40 and the carrying out of a review under s 40(1)(b). The function of custody officer can only be carried out by a custody officer at a designated station (s 45A(4)). Clearly, these new provisions in relation to review of detention detract from the face to face confrontation that was originally envisaged.

The powers of detention are very significant, but they are intended to embody the principle that a detained person should normally be charged within 24 hours and then either released or brought before a magistrate. They are supposed to be balanced by all the safeguards created by Part V of PACE and Codes of Practice C and E. It may be noted that a person unlawfully detained can apply for a writ of habeas corpus in order to secure release from detention, and this remedy is preserved in s 51(d). Its usefulness in practice is, however, very limited since the courts have developed a practice of adjourning applications for 24 hours in order to allow the police to present their case. Thus, detention can continue for that time allowing the police to carry out questioning or other procedures in the meantime.

Detention under the Terrorism Act 2000

The detention scheme adopted in respect of terrorist suspects allowed for the suspect to be detained for longer periods and for a lower level of due process safeguards to be applicable during detention.[197] If a person was arrested under s 14 of the PTA as opposed to s 24 of PACE, whether the arrest was for an offence or on suspicion of being a terrorist, the detention provisions under PACE did not apply. The arrestee could be detained for up to 48 hours following arrest (s 14(4)) of the PTA) but this period could be extended by the Secretary of State by further periods not exceeding five days in all (s 14(5) of the PTA). Thus, the whole detention could be for seven days and, in contrast to the PACE provisions, the courts were not involved in the authorising process; it occurred at a low level of visibility as an administrative decision. The similar provision under the PTA 1984 was found to be in breach of Art 5(3) in *Brogan v UK*[198] on the ground that holding a person for longer than four days without judicial authorisation was a violation of the requirement that persons should be brought promptly before a judicial officer. The *Brogan* decision clearly presented the Government with a difficulty in formulating the Terrorism Act 2000. Although the HRA continued the derogation entered in *Brogan*, under s 14(1)(a)

---

197 See below, pp 804 *et seq* for discussion of such safeguards.
198 (1989) 11 EHRR 117.

HRA, for a time, it was vulnerable to challenge at Strasbourg at some future point, in the light of the new settlement in Northern Ireland. The Government put forward various justifications for producing new terrorist legislation in 2000, but it recognised that it might be in difficulties in arguing that a state of emergency sufficient to support the derogation could be said to exist post-2000.[199] Its solution, in the TA, was to make provision for judicial authorisation of detention, rather than to decrease the length of time during which terrorist suspects could be detained, harmonising it with the PACE period. In deciding on these arrangements, including the retention of the possibility of up to seven days' detention, the Government rejected the suggestion of Lord Lloyd that once there is a lasting peace in Northern Ireland, it ought to be possible to reduce the maximum period for which a suspect could be detained under the new legislation to a total of four days – two days on the authority of the police and two days with judicial authorisation.

The maximum period of detention, applicable to a person arrested under s 41 of the TA, continues to be seven days, but para 29, Sched 8 provides that it must be under a warrant issued by a 'judicial authority'.[200] Under para 32, the warrant may be issued if there are reasonable grounds for believing that 'the detention of the person to whom the application relates is necessary to obtain relevant evidence whether by questioning him or otherwise or to preserve relevant evidence'. The detainee or his solicitor has the right to make written or oral representations under para 33(1). Thus, authorisation may not be merely 'on the papers'. Such a possibility might not have satisfied the aim of achieving compliance with Art 5(3), despite the involvement of a judicial figure.

The police can detain a person on their own authority for 48 hours under s 41(3) which provides:

> *Subject to* subsections (4) to (7), a person detained under this section shall (unless detained under any other power) be released not later than the end of the period of 48 hours beginning –
>
> (a) with the time of his arrest under this section, or
>
> (b) if he was being detained under Schedule 7 when he was arrested under this section, with the time when his examination under that Schedule began (emphasis added).

These provisions differ quite significantly from those under the PTA. Section 14(4) of the PTA provided that the 48 hour period is subject *only* to sub-s 5, which allowed for extension of detention by the Secretary of State. Section 41(4)–(7) of the TA provide three possibilities of continuing the detention beyond 48 hours, over and above the possibility of extension under judicial authorisation. These possibilities represent, depending on the interpretation they are afforded, quite notable departures from the previous scheme. Section 41(6) provides that if an application for an extension of detention is made, or under s 41(5), it is intended that it will be made, detention can continue while it is pending. This impliedly means that the police can continue to detain for more than 48

---

199 See *op cit*, fn 144, para 8.2.

200 Paragraph 29(4) provides: 'In this Part "judicial authority" means (a) in England and Wales, the Senior District Judge (Chief Magistrate) or his deputy, or a District Judge (Magistrates' Courts) who is designated for the purpose of this Part by the Lord Chancellor, (b) in Scotland, the sheriff, and (c) in Northern Ireland, a county court judge, or a resident magistrate who is designated for the purpose of this Part by the Lord Chancellor.'

hours so long as an application is being made or is about to be made, even if it is subsequently refused. The application need not be made during the 48 hours; under Sched 8, Part III, para 30 it may be made within six hours of the end of that period.

The 48 hour period is also subject to s 41(4), which provides: 'If on a review of a person's detention under Part II of Schedule 8 the review officer does not authorise continued detention, the person shall (unless detained in accordance with sub-sections (5) or (6) under any other power) be released.' The reviews have to occur every 12 hours. This appears to mean that the review officer (this must be an officer of at least the rank of superintendent after the first 12 hours) can continue the detention periodically, at 12 hour intervals, so long as the review conditions (which are the same as the warrant conditions) continue to apply. No express time limit is placed on the total period which the review officer can authorise. On their face, the provisions suggest that there is a twin track system of detention, one dependent on the judicial authority and one on the police themselves. Clearly, s 41(4) should be interpreted strictly to mean that *within* the 48 hour period there must be periodic reviews (subject to the provisions for delaying reviews); the possibility of providing the police with a new power to extend detention beyond 48 hours under s 41(4) should be rejected, since it seems to be due to ambiguous drafting. The words 'subject to' the decision of the review officer to continue detention could be interpreted either way. The stricter interpretation appears to accord with the Government's intention as expressed in the Consultation Paper.[201] If, in practice, s 41(4) was interpreted to allow some detentions on the authority of the review officer only, beyond 48 hours, such detentions would obviously be more likely than those under the previous provisions to create breaches of Art 5(3).

As part of the port and border controls regime, Sched 5 of the PTA provided a further power of detention in allowing a person to be detained for 12 hours before examination at ports of entry into Britain or Northern Ireland. The period could be extended to 24 hours if the person was suspected of involvement in the commission, preparation or instigation of acts of terrorism. These provisions are partially reproduced in Sched 7 of the TA; they are modified to take account of the abolition of the exclusion power.[202]

Clearly, the PACE and TA detention schemes differ quite radically in due process terms, despite the fact that many of those who will be potentially subject to the new TA scheme are likely to represent a far more divergent group than the previous one which fell within the rubric of 'terrorist'. Even within that previous group, as a number of the most famous miscarriage of justice cases imply, those who were designated terrorist suspects, such as *Judith Ward*,[203] were often remarkably ill-suited to the draconian terrorist regime to which they were subject. The peace process presented an opportunity for the harmonisation of the PACE and counter-terrorist regimes that might have avoided the potential for future miscarriages which, it is suggested, is inherent in the TA scheme, bearing in mind the special propensity evidenced in the cases of the *Birmingham Six*,[204]

---

201 *Op cit*, fn 144.
202 See Chapter 15, pp 967–68.
203 *Ward* (1992) 98 Cr App R 1.
204 See *McIlkenny and Others* [1992] 2 All ER 417.

Guildford Four,[205] *Maguire Seven,*[206] *Ward,*[207] and *UDR Four,*[208] of terrorist cases to miscarry.

Searches of detained persons

Detained persons may not automatically be searched, but the power to search arrestees under s 32(1) of PACE is quite wide. It arises under s 32(1) if the suspect has been arrested somewhere other than a police station and a constable has reasonable grounds to suspect that an arrestee has anything on him which might be evidence relating to an offence or might be used to help him escape from custody or that he may present a danger to himself or others. The much wider power arises under s 32(2) and allows search, again on reasonable grounds, for anything which might be evidence of an offence or could help to effect an escape from lawful custody. The nature of the search must relate to the article it is suspected may be found; if it is a large item, the search may not involve more than removal of a coat. Such searching may occur routinely, but it must be possible to point to objectively justified grounds in each case which must not go beyond those specified.[209] A power of search also arises under s 54, as amended, allowing search to ascertain property the detainee has with him or her, which will apply if someone has been arrested at the police station or brought there after being arrested elsewhere. The custody officer must determine whether it is necessary to conduct a search for this purpose.

Impact of the HRA on arrest and detention

As discussed above in relation to detention short of arrest, Art 5(1) of the Convention provides a right to liberty subject to certain exceptions which must have a basis in law. Not only must an exception apply, the requirements under Art 5(2), (3) and (4) must also be met. The current domestic arrest and detention scheme for non-terrorist suspects is, as one would expect, largely coterminous, formally speaking, with these provisions, and in some respects may afford a higher – or, at least, clearer – value to due process. But the use of Art 5 as an interpretative tool may lead to a more rigorous judicial approach to the detention scheme. Breaches of Art 5 may be most likely to be established in respect of the special counter-terrorist arrest and detention powers available under the TA.

As discussed in Chapter 14, Art 5 arguments could be raised within the trial process, by means of a civil action or under the police complaints provisions. Judicial review, on Art 5 principles, of decisions within the police complaints process, or in respect of judicial authorisations within the PACE or TA schemes, or of proposals relating to detention practice would also be available under s 7(1)(a) of the HRA.

---

205 See May, *Report of the Inquiry into the Circumstances surrounding the Convictions Arising out of the Bomb Attacks at Guildford and Woolwich in 1974, Final Report,* 1993–94 HC 449, Chapter 17.

206 See *Maguire* [1992] 2 All ER 433.

207 *Ward* (1992) 98 Cr App R 1.

208 See [1988] 11 NIJB 1.

209 *Eet* [1983] Crim LR 806.

Detention in accordance with a procedure prescribed by law

The first and most essential requirement of Art 5 is that a person's detention is in accordance with a procedure prescribed by law. This means that the procedure should be in accordance with national law and with recognised Convention standards, including Convention principles, and is not arbitrary.[210] Thus, where one of the Art 5(1) exceptions applies to a person's detention, this requirement will also have to be satisfied. The procedure covers the arrest provisions[211] and the procedure adopted by a court in authorisations of detention.[212] The requirement that the detention should be in accordance with the law was given a robust interpretation based on due process norms in one of the first domestic decisions in the pre-HRA period to place a heavy reliance on Art 5. In *Chief Constable of Kent Constabulary ex p Kent Police Federation Joint Branch Board and Another*,[213] the court had to consider an application by Kent Police Federation Joint Branch Board, representing all ranks of the Kent Constabulary, for judicial review of the proposal by the Chief Constable of Kent that the conduct of reviews of police detention under s 40(1)(b) of the 1984 Act should be, in the majority of cases, by video link.

Lord Bingham referred to Art 5 and said that, although not yet part of domestic law, it embodied important and basic rights recognised and protected by English law. If citizens were to be deprived of their liberty, such deprivation had to be in accordance with the law. He found that the court was dealing with an area of extreme sensitivity, namely the circumstances in which, and the conditions on which, a citizen not convicted or even charged with crime might be deprived of his or her liberty. The Act and the Codes giving it effect represented, he said, a complex and careful balance between the obviously important duty of the police to investigate crime and apprehend criminals on the one hand and the rights of the private citizen on the other. Under s 37(5), a written record of the grounds of detention had to be made by the review officer 'in the presence of the person whose detention is under review'. He found that that condition was not met if the review officer was in one place and the person whose detention was under review was in another. Section 37(5) did not refer to physical presence, but 'presence' in ordinary parlance meant physical presence.

Lord Bingham concluded that Parliament had provided for a face to face confrontation between the review officer and the suspect and, if important rights enacted to protect the subject were to be modified, it was for Parliament after appropriate consultation so to rule and not for the courts. This decision indicated a determination to give real efficacy to Art 5, where a contrary interpretation, impliedly supported by a guiding note,[214] was readily available. Review by video link would have meant the intrusion of technology, controlled by the police, into the review process, leading arguably to a depersonalised confrontation and possibly to a further impression of tokenism.

---

210 *Winterwerp v Netherlands* A 33 (1979), para 39.

211 *Fox, Campbell and Hartley v UK* A 182 (1990); 13 EHRR 157.

212 *Weston v UK* 3 EHRR 402; *Van der Leer v Netherlands* A 170-A (1990).

213 (1999) *The Times*, 1 December, Judgment 18 November 1999.

214 He found that the provisions of Code C do not provide conclusive support for either construction. Note for guidance 15C permits review by telephone so long as the requirements of s 40 are met, but Lord Bingham had difficulty in seeing how a review conducted over the telephone could ever comply with those requirements, as that Note appeared to envisage.

The exception under Art 5(1)(c)

In considering the exceptional circumstances in which liberty can be taken away, the requirements connoted by the general provision that they must have a basis in law under Art 5(1) are also implied into the 'prescribed by law' rubric of each sub-paragraph.[215] Article 5(1)(c) of the Convention sets out one of the circumstances in which an individual can be detained. It permits the lawful arrest or detention of a person effected for the purpose of bringing him before the competent legal authority on reasonable suspicion of having committed an offence, or where it is reasonably considered that an arrest is necessary to prevent the person in question from committing an offence or fleeing after having done so. In requiring arrest only for specific offences and not for general crime control purposes, Art 5(1)(c) adheres closely to the due process model of arrest indicated above. Sections 24 and 25 of PACE and s 41 of the TA (in so far as it relates to certain specific terrorist offences under s 40(1)(a)) may *prima facie* comply with these provisions owing to their requirements of reasonable suspicion.

As indicated above, in what is usually regarded as the leading post-PACE case on the meaning of that requirement, *Castorina v Chief Constable of Surrey*,[216] the grounds for suspicion regarding a burglary of a firm were that the suspect was a former employee who appeared to have a grudge and the burglary appeared to be an 'inside job'. But, the suspect was not considered by the victim to be likely to commit burglary and she had no criminal record. Nevertheless, the court found that reasonable suspicion had been established. Clayton and Tomlinson criticised the decision in these terms: 'if the police are justified in arresting a middle-aged woman of good character on such flimsy grounds without even questioning her as to her alibi or possible motives, then the law provides very scant protection for those suspected of crimes.'[217] *Castorina* may be compared with the findings of the Strasbourg Court in *Fox, Campbell and Hartley v UK*.[218] The applicants had been arrested in accordance with s 11 of the Northern Ireland (Emergency Provisions) Act 1978 which required only suspicion, not reasonable suspicion. The only evidence put forward by the Government for the presence of reasonable suspicion was that the applicants had convictions for terrorist offences and that when arrested, they were asked about particular terrorist acts. The Government said that further evidence could not be disclosed for fear of endangering life. The Court found that although allowance could be made for the difficulties of evidence-gathering in an emergency situation, reasonable suspicion which 'arises from facts or information which would satisfy an objective observer that the person concerned may have committed the offence'[219] had not been established. Moreover, 'the exigencies of dealing with terrorist crime cannot justify stretching the notion of reasonableness to the point where the essence of the safeguard secured by Art 5(1)(c) is impaired'.[220] The arrests in question could not, therefore, be

---

215 *Winterwerp v Netherlands* A 33 (1979), para 39.
216 (1988) 138 NLJ 180.
217 (1988) Law Soc Gazette, 7 September, p 26.
218 A 182 (1990); 13 EHRR 157.
219 *Ibid*, para 32.
220 *Ibid*, para 32.

justified. In *Murray v UK*,[221] this test was viewed as a lower standard for reasonable suspicion, applicable in terrorist cases, but it was again emphasised that an objective standard of reasonable suspicion was required,[222] although the information grounding the suspicion might acceptably remain confidential in the exigencies of a situation such as that pertaining at the time of the arrest in question, in Northern Ireland.[223] It is debatable whether the UK courts are in general applying a test of reasonable suspicion under PACE or the PTA which reaches the standards which the European Court had in mind, especially where terrorism is not in question. The departure which the HRA brings about is to encourage stricter judicial scrutiny of decisions to arrest.

The *purpose* of the arrest should also be in compliance with Art 5(1)(c), even where reasonable suspicion is established, in that it should be effected in order to 'bring [the suspect] before the competent legal authority', although this does not mean that every arrest must lead to a charge.[224] In the individual circumstances of a case, a breach of Art 5(1)(c) might be found where, although reasonable suspicion was present on the facts, the arrest discretion was not exercised in accordance with Art 5(1)(c) since the purpose of the arrest was in reality for general information-gathering ends. This might occur where, although there were, objectively, reasonable grounds for suspicion, the police had no belief in the guilt of the suspect. In such an instance, the arrest would be unlawful under s 6 of the HRA, not merely *Wednesbury* unreasonable. A breach might also be established where the arrest was unnecessary in order to further the purpose in question. For example, if the suspect was co-operative, there would appear to be no need to arrest her since the purpose under Art 5(1)(c) could be served by interviewing her in her own home. That purpose would not appear to cover an arrest undertaken merely for the purpose of interviewing such a suspect in the police station.[225] It was found, however, in *Chalkley and Jeffries*,[226] that the existence of a collateral motive for an arrest would not necessarily render it unlawful. Under the HRA, a domestic court would have to consider whether Art 5 would be satisfied by an arrest with a 'mixed' purpose.

The test under Art 5(1)(c) relies on reasonable suspicion regarding an offence and therefore, as indicated above, calls into question s 41 of the TA, in so far as it relates to suspicion that a person is a terrorist in the sense of (under s 40(1)(b)) being concerned in the commission, preparation, or instigation of an act of terrorism. Section 41 therefore allows for arrest without reasonable suspicion that a particular offence has been committed. The compatibility of s 41 and Art 5(1)(c) depends on the interpretation afforded to *Brogan and Others v UK*.[227] The case concerned the EPA provision which was largely reproduced in s 41, read with s 40(1)(b). The Court applied two tests to the basis for the arrests in finding that the power of arrest was justified within Art 5(1)(c). First, the definition of acts of terrorism was 'well in keeping with the idea of an offence'.[228]

---

221 [1994] EHRR 193.
222 Paragraph 50.
223 Paragraphs 58–59.
224 *K-F v Germany* (1997) 26 EHRR 390.
225 Cf *Holgate-Mohammed v Duke* [1984] AC 437.
226 [1998] 2 All ER 155.
227 Judgment of 29 November 1988 (1989) Series A 145-B (1989) 11 EHHR 117.
228 Paragraph 51.

Secondly, after arrest, the applicants were asked about specific offences. Thus, 'the Court decided the point on the basis that involvement in "acts of terrorism" indirectly meant the commission of specific criminal offences under Northern Irish law, which would appear to be the better approach on the facts'.[229]

On either test, arrests under s 41 read with s 40(1)(b) might be in a more doubtful position. The definition of terrorism relevant in *Brogan* was identical to the s 20 PTA definition – the use of violence for political ends. The current definition under s 1 of the TA is far wider: it covers the use or threat, 'for the purpose of advancing a political, religious or ideological cause', of action, designed to influence the government or intimidate the public, which involves serious violence against any person or serious damage to property, or is designed to seriously disrupt an electronic system, or endangers life, or creates a serious risk to health or safety. Unlike the previous one, this definition may cover matters, such as threatening to hack into a computer system, or to destroy genetically modified crops, which do not clearly correspond to existing offences and therefore might not be viewed so readily as 'in keeping with the idea of an offence'. The application of the second test would partly depend in practice on the particular instance which arose before a domestic court. If a person was arrested under s 41 as part of an investigation and was not asked about specific offences on arrest, the connection with the basis of the arrest, bearing in mind the width of the s 1 TA definition, might be viewed as too tenuous to be termed an arrest on reasonable suspicion of an offence. Moreover, the purpose of such an arrest would not appear to be in accordance with the Art 5 requirement, since it would not be to 'bring [the suspect] before the competent legal authority'.

Article 5(1)(c) also calls into question the provision under s 24 of PACE allowing for arrest without reasonable suspicion so long as a 'hunch' turns out to be justified (s 24(4)(a), (5)(a) and (7)(a)). Sanders and Young call this possibility a 'classic crime control norm since the ends are regarded as justifying the means'.[230] Such an arrest would appear to be unlawful under s 6 of the HRA where effected by a police constable since no exception under Art 5 appears to allow for it.

Article 5(2)

Article 5(2), which provides that a person must be informed promptly of the reason for arrest, corresponds to s 28 of PACE. In *Fox, Campbell and Hartley v UK*[231] the applicants, who were arrested on suspicion of terrorist offences, were not informed of the reason for the arrest at the time of it, but were told that they were being arrested under a particular statutory provision. Clearly, this could not convey the reason to them at that time. At a later point, during interrogation, they were asked about specific criminal offences. The European Court of Human Rights found that Art 5(2) was not satisfied at the time of the arrest, but that this breach was healed by the later indications made during interrogation of the offences for which they had been arrested. In *Murray v UK*,[232] soldiers occupied a

---

229 Harris, D, O'Boyle, K and Warbrick, C, *Law of The European Convention on Human Rights*, 1995, p 116.
230 Sanders and Young, *op cit*, fn 1, 1994, p 76.
231 (1990) A 182; 13 EHRR 157.
232 *Murray v UK* (1994) 19 EHRR 193.

woman's house, thus clearly taking her into detention, but did not inform her of the fact of arrest for half an hour. The House of Lords had found that the delay in giving the requisite information was acceptable because of the alarm which the fact of arrest, if known, might have aroused in the particular circumstances – the unsettled situation in Northern Ireland.[233] The European Court of Human Rights found no breach of Art 5(2); Mrs Murray was eventually informed during interrogation of the reason for the arrest and, in the circumstances, it was found acceptable to allow an interval of a few hours between the arrest and the point when she was informed of the reason for it. The claim also made, that Art 8 had been breached, was dismissed. The violation of privacy fell within the exception under Art 8(2) in respect of the prevention of crime and was found to be necessary and proportionate to the aims of that exception.

The decisions in both *Fox* and *Murray* were influenced by the terrorist context in which they occurred, and provide examples of the Court's tenderness to claims of a threat to national security made by governments of Member States. In both, a very wide margin of appreciation was allowed. Probably as a result, both were influenced by the crime control consideration of allowing leeway to the police to resort to doubtful practices in relation to terrorist suspects and both exhibit a lack of rigorousness in relation to due process. Such lack of rigour might be acceptable if there was a real connection between a failure to give information to suspects and an advantage to be gained in an emergency situation, since proportionality might be satisfied. However, in Mrs Murray's case, once she was in detention, and her house in effect sealed off from the outside world, it is unclear that telling her of the fact of the arrest could create or exacerbate an unsettled situation. Giving the requisite information would not have raised an alarm which had not already been raised when the soldiers entered the house. Following these judgments it seems that, where special circumstances may be said to obtain, an arrest which does not comply with all the procedural requirements will still be an arrest, for a period of time, as far as all the consequences arising from it are concerned, under Art 5(2).

Under s 28 of PACE, the police also have a certain leeway as to informing the arrestee; the arrest will not be affected, nor will other acts arising from it, until the time when it would be practicable to inform of the reason for it has come and gone. However, if there is nothing in the behaviour of the arrestee or in the general situation to make informing him or her impracticable, then the arrest will be unlawful from its inception. If the word 'practicable' in s 28 is interpreted in accordance with the interpretation of Art 5(3) in both *Murray* and *Fox* it seems that, depending on the circumstances, a certain amount of leeway is created in respect of informing the arrestee. An arrest which fails to comply with the procedural requirements will be in a more precarious position than an arrest which, from its inception, complies with them, because it will cease to be an arrest at an uncertain point. On somewhat doubtful grounds, the Convention has allowed some departure from the principle that there should be a clear demarcation between the point at which the citizen is at liberty and the point at which her liberty is restrained. Sanders and Young observe, commenting on the House of Lords' decision in *Murray*, 'Even where the legislature, as in s 28 of PACE, appears to be creating strong inhibitory rules, the judiciary still manages to draw their due process sting by rendering them largely presentational'.[234] This might also be said of the decision of the European Court. A

---

233 *Murray v Ministry of Defence* [1988] All ER 521, HL; for comment see Williams (1991) 54 MLR 408.
234 Sanders and Young, *op cit*, fn 1, 1994, p 103.

domestic court in the post-HRA era might, however, be prepared to take a more activist approach to the application of Art 5(2), especially where a s 41 TA arrest, accompanied by delay in informing of the reason owing (apparently) to the terrorist context, occurred in circumstances which could not be compared in terms of volatility to the situation in Northern Ireland when *Murray* was decided.

As noted above, the temporary provision under s 83 of the TA allowing members of the armed forces to effect arrests, applicable only to Northern Ireland, does not provide that the grounds must be given. Section 83(2) provides: 'A person making an arrest under this section complies with any rule of law requiring him to state the ground of arrest if he states that he is making the arrest as a member of Her Majesty's forces'. Section 83(6) then appears to accept that s 83(2) will lead to findings that Art 5(3) has been breached in providing: 'The reference to a rule of law ... does not include a rule of law which has effect only by virtue of the HRA.' If a judge is confronted with an arrest under s 83 in which the arrestee merely stated that he was effecting it as a member of Her Majesty's forces, it would appear that the arrest would be likely to be found unlawful, unless in the circumstances, *Murray* could be applied. But the application of *Murray* might be viewed as inappropriate, given the influence of the margin of appreciation doctrine on the judgment.

Article 5(3)

Article 5(3) confers a right to be brought promptly before the judicial authorities; in other words, not to be held for long periods without a hearing. It covers both arrest and detention. There will be some allowable delay in both situations; the question is therefore what is meant by 'promptly'. Its meaning was considered in *Brogan v UK*[235] in relation to the arrest and detention of the applicants considered above, arising by virtue of the special powers under s 12 of the PTA. The UK had entered a derogation under Art 15 against the applicability of Art 5(3) to Northern Ireland, but withdrew that derogation in August 1984. Two months later, the Brogan case was filed. The applicants complained *inter alia* of the length of time they were held in detention without coming before a judge, on the basis that it could not be termed prompt. The Court took into account the need for special measures to combat terrorism; such measures had to be balanced against individual rights. However, it found that detention for four days and six hours was too long. The Court did not specify how long was acceptable; previously, the Commission had seen four days as the limit. The Government made no move to comply with this decision; instead, it entered a derogation under Art 15 to Art 5(3).

This derogation was challenged unsuccessfully in *Brannigan and McBride v UK*[236] as invalid. The European Court of Human Rights found that it was justified since the state of public emergency in Northern Ireland warranted exceptional measures. The Court found: 'a wide margin of appreciation [on the question] of the presence of an emergency ... and on the nature and scope of derogations necessary to avert it [should be allowed].'[237] Among the government contentions uncritically accepted by the Court was

---

235 Judgment of 29 November 1988; (1989) 11 EHRR 117; A 145.
236 Series A, 258-B (1993); (1993) 17 EHRR 594.
237 Paragraph 207.

one to the effect that in the particular situation, the judiciary should not be permitted a role in protecting the liberty of detainees. As Judge Walsh pointed out in his dissenting opinion, this was precisely a role which the public would expect a judge to have. *Brannigan* might appear a doubtful decision because the derogation was entered after the decision in *Brogan*, although it might also be said that States should not be encouraged to enter derogations too readily on 'insurance' grounds in order to pre-empt claims. Arguably, although there was a state of emergency in 1989, the UK had chosen not to enter a derogation even though one would have been warranted. Whatever the merits of this argument in the particular situation, it is questionable whether the exigencies of the situation did require detention of six days without recourse to independent review. Possibly it was assumed on insufficient grounds that such review would prejudice the legitimate purpose of the investigation.

In requiring judicial authorisation for detention for up to seven days under s 41 and Sched 7 of the TA, the Government has sought to ensure, as indicated above, that the new detention provisions comply with Art 5(3) as interpreted in *Brogan* and *Brannigan*, meaning that it became possible to withdraw the derogation and, once this was accomplished, the HRA was accordingly amended.[238] One question which will probably be raised eventually in the domestic courts or at Strasbourg will be whether allowing a detention for seven days, even with judicial authorisation, is in accordance with Art 5. Further, it appears that the new arrangements could allow for detention for longer than 48 hours with authorisation only by the police themselves. If, for example, towards the end of 54 hours in detention (a possibility under the TA, as indicated above) the police decided to apply for an extension of detention, they would have the power under s 41(5) to continue the detention while the application was being made and then under s 41(6) while the hearing was occurring. There is also the highly controversial possibility of continued 12-hourly extensions of detention on review by a superintendent under s 41(4); while it is unlikely that s 41(4) would be interpreted as allowing much leeway to continue to detain beyond 48 hours, the provision appears to detract from the certainty of the 48 hour deadline. Both these possibilities do not appear to accord with *Brogan* and *Brannigan* since neither provides for any possibility of judicial authorisation of detention. Bearing in mind the wide margin of appreciation allowed in *Brannigan*, a domestic court taking a more activist stance might be prepared to find a breach of Art 5(3) in respect of a s 41 detention, depending on its length, in the particular circumstances before it. One clear possibility would be to limit the application of s 41(4) in accordance with the Government's intention that the new detention regime should comply with Art 5(3) which allowed for the withdrawal of the derogation.

Article 2 and forcible arrest

Article 2 of the European Convention allows the use of force which is 'absolutely necessary' in order to arrest. The Convention requirements refer to the amount of force to be used, not to the question whether to use any force at all. But the Convention jurisprudence suggests that standards may differ in terms of planning operations[239] and

---

238 See further Chapter 2, p 55.

239 *McCann, Farrell and Savage v UK* (1995) 21 EHRR 97, A 324, Council of Europe Report. For further discussion of this issue see above, pp 42–43.

executing them in the immediate situation.[240] Section 117 of PACE and s 114 of the TA allow for the use of 'reasonable force', if necessary, in the exercise of the powers they provide. This wording could be taken to mean that any force used which was not, objectively speaking, necessary would be unreasonable, or it might suggest that any force used which appeared, subjectively, necessary at the time would be reasonable. Article 2 suggests that the latter test should be used.[241] Where lethal force has been used it is arguable that, under s 3 of the HRA, the term 'absolutely' should be implied into the domestic provisions.

Article 3, which provides a guarantee against torture or inhuman or degrading treatment,[242] may also be relevant where physical force is used in the course of an arrest and detention. In *Ribbitsch v Austria*[243] the Court said: 'any recourse to physical force which has not been made strictly necessary by his own conduct diminishes human dignity and is in principle an infringement of the right set forth in Article 3.'[244] Force may only be used where it is strictly required to restrain the detainee and the force used must go no further, in terms of causing injury or humiliation, than is strictly necessary to achieve the purpose of restraint. Thus, a strict proportionality test is applied and force outside the limits it sets will infringe Art 3. *A fortiori*, this must be the case under Art 2, where lethal force is used.[245]

6 SAFEGUARDS FOR DETAINEES

The role of the custody officer

The general use of custody officers provided for under s 36 is a key feature of the scheme for detention, treatment and questioning created under Parts IV and V of PACE. The custody officer's role is to underpin the other safeguards by ensuring that the suspect is treated in accordance with PACE and the Codes and by generally overseeing all aspects of his or her treatment.[246] Use of custody officers was intended to ensure that somebody

---

240 *Andronicou and Constantinou v Cyprus* (1996) 22 EHRR CD 18.84. See above, p 39.

241 See *Kelly v UK* (1985) 8 EHRR 45.

242 Article 3 treatment may be justifiable where its object is to satisfy the demands of Art 2, the right to life: *Herczegfalvy v Austria* A 244 (1992).

243 (1996) 21 EHRR 573.

244 See p 26. See *Selmouni v France* (2000) 29 EHRR 403 for an example of treatment in police custody found to amount to torture.

245 Article 2 therefore calls into question the recent cases of death caused by restraint during arrest. In 'Deaths in police custody: learning the lessons', Police Research Series Paper 26, 1998, Leigh, Johnson and Ingram found, in section 6, 13 cases of death in which police restraint may have been a factor. They found six cases where restraint may have led to 'postural' or 'positional asphyxia', leading to death. In two others, death was due to a neck-hold; in a further two, to force applied with a baton. They viewed these cases as having implications for training. *The Butler Report*, 1998, also considered a number of death in custody cases. In one of these, that of O'Brien, the arrestee, after being handcuffed, was held face down on the ground by at least four officers, one of whom knelt on his back, and one on his legs. The evidence was conflicting, but his family and a bystander stated that he was saying that he could not breathe. The post mortem found that he had died due to postural asphyxia and he had bruising to his head, shoulders and right arm. See Chapter 14, p 923 in relation to criticism of decisions of the CPS in relation to this case. It is suggested that *prima facie*, the force used went well beyond that which was absolutely necessary, and therefore it was not in accord with Art 2.

246 For discussion of judicial interpretation of the PACE provisions, see Feldman [1990] Crim LR 452.

independent of the investigating officer could keep a check on what was occurring. The scheme was not a new idea; in certain police stations an officer was already fulfilling this role, but PACE clarifies the duties of custody officers and ensures that most stations have one. Thus, best practice was placed on a statutory basis.

However, the efficacy of the custody officer scheme may be called into question. It may not always be in operation: in non-designated police stations, there must simply be someone who can act as custody officer if the need arises and in designated police stations, there need not always be a custody officer on duty. The ruling in *Vince and Another v Chief Constable of Dorset*[247] made it clear that s 36 does not require that a custody officer must always be present. The plaintiffs (acting for members of the joint branch board of the Police Federation of England and Wales of the Dorset Police) sought a declaration that by virtue of s 36(1) of PACE a custody officer should normally be available in a police station. However, it was found that s 36(1) clearly provided that the Chief Constable had a duty to appoint one custody officer for each designated police station and a power to appoint more in his discretion which had to be reasonably exercised. It was found that there had been no breach by the Chief Constable, implying that a decision that a custody officer need not always be on duty is a reasonable one. It may be argued that this case exposes a weakness in one of the central safeguards provided under PACE. This was referred to by Steyn LJ, who commented that the Royal Commission on Criminal Procedure[248] might wish to consider this loophole in the PACE provisions. As indicated above, s 45A of PACE, inserted by s 73 of the CJP 2001, allows for a custody officer at a designated police station to act as a custody officer for the purposes of ss 37, 38 and 40(1)(b) of PACE by video link.

The custody officer may not always be able to take a stance independent of that of the investigating officer.[249] This weakness in the scheme arises from the lowly rank of the custody officer; under s 38(3), the officer need only be of the rank of sergeant and may therefore be of a lower rank than the investigating officer, making it very difficult to take an independent line on the treatment of the suspect. If the two disagree, the custody officer must refer up the line of authority (s 39(6)); there is no provision allowing the custody officer to overrule the investigating officer. Thus, there is a danger that the custody officer will merely rubber-stamp the decisions of the investigating officer; whether this occurs in practice may largely depend on the attitude of the superior officers in a particular force to the provisions of the PACE scheme.

Caution and notification of rights

When the detainee arrives at the police station, he or she will be 'booked in'. The crucial nature of this stage in the proceedings is made clear below in relation to the discussion of the legal advice provisions. Under para 3 of Code C, a person must be informed orally and by written notice of four rights on arrival at the police station after arrest: the right,

---

247 (1992) *The Times*, 7 September.
248 Set up in 1992 after the miscarriage of justice which occurred in the case of the *Birmingham Six*. See p 755, fn 18 above.
249 See Sanders and Young, 2000, Chapter 4, p 189.

arising under s 65 of PACE, to have someone informed of his detention;[250] the right to consult a solicitor and the fact that independent legal advice is available free of charge; the right to consult Code C and the other Codes of Practice, and the right to silence as embodied in the caution. The caution is in the following terms: 'You do not have to say anything. But it may harm your defence if you do not mention when questioned something which you later rely on in court. Anything you do say may be given in evidence.'[251] Minor deviations do not constitute a breach of this requirement, provided that the sense of the caution is preserved. The caution must be repeated during the interview if there is any doubt as to whether the detainee realises that it still applies. If a juvenile or a person who is mentally disordered or mentally handicapped is cautioned in the absence of the appropriate adult, the caution must be repeated in the adult's presence.[252] The change to the caution which occurred to reflect s 34 of the CJPOA 1994, discussed further below, means that the suspect is warned that refusing to answer questions may lead to the drawing of adverse inferences in court.

The right of access to legal advice

There is general agreement that the most significant protection introduced for the first time by PACE[253] for due process was access to legal advice.[254] But this right is far from absolute. Interviews outside the police station continue to be unaffected by it, in the sense that notification of the right is reserved for the police station, thus disadvantaging the inexperienced suspect who is not already aware of it. The very significant reform of notification of legal advice on caution was omitted from all the Code C revisions, including the 1999 one, despite the fact of curtailment of the right to silence and of the strong possibility that questioning accompanied by the risk of drawing adverse inferences from silence without access to legal advice breaches Art 6(1).[255] The right is also subject to a number of formal exceptions, which are broader in terrorist cases, and is dependent on a formal request to exercise it. Encouragement to the police to seek to ensure that the suspect has access to legal advice was recently provided by s 58 of the Youth Justice and

---

250 Under para 5.1, if the person cannot be contacted, the person in charge of detention or of the investigation has discretion to allow further attempts until the information has been conveyed (see Notes 5C and 5D).

251 Paragraph 10.4. Modification to the caution occurred in order to reflect the CJPOA 1994, s 34. See further below, p 843.

252 Paragraph 10.6.

253 The Criminal Law Act 1977, s 62 declared a narrow entitlement to have one reasonably named person informed of the arrest. It did not provide that the arrestee must be informed of this right, nor did it provide any sanction for non-compliance by a police officer. That statutory form of this right gave it no greater force than the non-statutory Judges' Rules (rules of practice for the guidance of the police: see *Practice Note* [1984] 1 All ER 237; 1 WLR 152). The Judges' Rules upheld the right of the suspect/arrestee in the police station to communicate with/consult a solicitor, but permitted the withholding of such access 'lest unreasonable delay or hindrance is caused to the process of investigation or the administration of justice'. Any officer, in relation to a person detained for any offence, could deny access to legal advice on these broad grounds; see *Lemsatef* [1977] 1 WLR 812; [1977] 2 All ER 835.

254 See Dixon, *Miscarriages of Justice*, 1999, p 67. The research studies mentioned in this chapter do not question the value of the legal right of access, although they do question its quality and the responses of the police.

255 See further below, pp 855–57.

Criminal Evidence Act 1999. Section 58 inserted s 34(2A) into the CJPOA to provide that an adverse inference cannot be drawn from the suspect's silence unless he has had an opportunity to consult a solicitor before being questioned. This is a significant provision, but it can have a direct impact only on suspects who have not had such an opportunity, who then remain silent, are charged and plead not guilty. Nevertheless, it may have a general effect on police adherence to the legal advice scheme since the impact it may have in any particular instance will not normally be apparent at the relevant points in detention.

Both PACE and the TA entitle a suspect to consult an advisor privately[256] under a publicly funded scheme;[257] to be informed of this right;[258] given, if necessary, the name of the duty solicitor;[259] and be permitted to have the solicitor present during questioning.[260] In cases involving 'serious arrestable offences', however, there are certain saving provisions[261] allowing an officer of at least the rank of superintendent to authorise delay, and a further power to delay access arises under Code C.[262] The exceptions are, however, narrowly drawn and, as indicated below, have received a narrow interpretation. However, the factor which previously motivated the police to delay (or refuse) access to legal advice remains unchanged: the suspect still has the right to remain silent and the legal advisor may advise him or her to exercise it in the particular circumstances of the case, despite the risk that adverse inferences may be drawn later at court. Even if the solicitor does not advise silence, the police may think that they are more likely to obtain incriminating admissions from detainees in the absence of a solicitor and therefore at times may deny the access to one envisaged by s 58. Quite a large body of research suggests that the police continue to prefer to interview suspects who have not had advice and without an advisor present.[263] Research confirms that the possibility of formally delaying access to legal advice is almost certainly not as significant as the more informal police influence on the notification and delivery of advice and on securing the presence of the advisor.[264] This may be due in part to the determination shown by the Court of Appeal to protect this due process right by restrictive interpretation of the formal exceptions under s 58(8) of PACE in a key decision.[265] A number of formal and informal methods of evading the scheme are available and five such methods are identified below.

---

256 PACE, s 58(1): 'A person in police detention shall be entitled, if he so requests, to consult a solicitor privately at any time.' For TA suspects, this right also arises under the TA, Sched 8, para 7.

257 See the Legal Aid Act 1988, Sched 6.

258 Code C, para 3.1(ii).

259 Code C, Note 6B. The duty solicitor arrangements are governed by the Legal Aid Board Duty Solicitor Arrangements (1994).

260 Code C, para 6.8.

261 Under s 58(8).

262 Code C, para 6.3(b)(ii). Where a solicitor has agreed to attend, awaiting his arrival would cause unreasonable delay to the process of the investigation. See also Annex B.

263 The research undertaken by Sanders et al, Advice and Assistance at Police Stations, November 1989; Brown, PACE Ten Years On: A Review of the Research, Home Office Research Study 155, 1997, p 77.

264 The research undertaken by Sanders et al, ibid, put the figure at around 2%. In comparison, Brown found that approximately 35% of suspects may have been influenced against advice by the police. The government's Consultation Paper on Terrorism (1998) stated that it was not aware of any formal denial in terrorist cases over the last two years in Britain (para 8.31).

265 R v Samuel [1988] 2 All ER 135; [1988] 2 WLR 920.

(1) Delaying access

The most direct method of delaying legal advice involves invoking one of the s 58(8) exceptions. The exceptions come into operation if the suspect is in police detention for a serious arrestable offence[266] and the decision to invoke them must be taken by an officer of at least the rank of superintendent. If both these conditions are fulfilled, access, if requested, can be delayed for up to 36 hours Under s 58(8): 'An officer may only authorise delay where he has reasonable grounds for believing that the exercise of the right ... (a) will lead to interference with or harm to evidence connected with a serious arrestable offence or interference with or physical injury to other persons; or (b) will lead to the alerting of other persons suspected of having committed such an offence but not yet arrested for it; or (c) will hinder the recovery of any property obtained as a result of such an offence.' Under sub-s (8A), delay can also be authorised 'where the serious arrestable offence is a drug trafficking offence and the officer has reasonable grounds for believing (a) that the detained person has benefited from drug trafficking and (b) that the recovery of the value of that person's proceeds of drug trafficking will be hindered by the exercise of the right ...'. In other words, the officer must believe on reasonable grounds that exercise of the right at the time when the person in police detention desires to exercise it will lead to the solicitor acting as a channel of communication between the detainee and others – alerting them or hindering the recovery of stolen property or the products of drug trafficking.

The leading case determining the scope of the s 58 exceptions is *Samuel*.[267] The appellant was arrested on suspicion of armed robbery and, after questioning at the police station, asked to see a solicitor. The request was refused, apparently on the grounds that other suspects might be warned[268] and that recovery of the outstanding stolen money might thereby be hindered.[269] The appellant subsequently confessed to the robbery and was later convicted. On appeal, the defence argued that the refusal of access was not justifiable under s 58(8) and that therefore, the confession obtained should not have been admitted into evidence as it had been obtained through impropriety. The Court of Appeal considered the use of the word 'will' in s 58(8), which suggests that the police officer must be virtually certain that a solicitor, if contacted, will thereafter either commit a criminal offence or unwittingly pass on a coded message to criminals. It must be asked, first, whether he did believe this and secondly, whether he believed it on reasonable grounds. The court considered that only in the remote contingency that evidence could be produced as to the corruption of a particular solicitor would a police officer be able to assert a reasonable belief that a solicitor would commit a criminal offence. They went on to hold that showing a reasonable belief that a solicitor would inadvertently alert other criminals would also be a formidable task; such a belief could only reasonably be held if the suspect in question was a particularly resourceful and sophisticated criminal or if there was evidence that the solicitor sought to be consulted was particularly inexperienced or naive. It was found that as no evidence as to the naivety or corruption of

---

266 Defined in s 116. The Criminal Justice Act 1988, s 99 extends these exceptions to drug trafficking offences.

267 [1988] QB 615; [1988] 2 All ER 135; [1988] 2 WLR 920, CA.

268 Section 58(8)(b).

269 Section 58(8)(c).

the solicitor in question had been advanced it could not be accepted that the necessary reasonable belief had existed. The police had made no attempt to consider the real likelihood that the solicitor in question would be utilised in this way; in fact, it was apparent that the true motive behind the denial of access was a desire to gain a further opportunity to break down the detainee's silence. It should be noted that Code C[270] expressly disallows denial of access to a solicitor on the ground that he or she will advise the suspect to remain silent.[271]

This interpretation of s 58(8) greatly narrowed its scope, since it means that the police will not be able to make a general, unsubstantiated assertion that it was thought that others might be alerted if a solicitor was contacted. The authorising officer will have to show, on very specific grounds, why this was thought to be the case (the question of exclusion of the confession through this impropriety is considered below).[272] This decision may have prevented mere refusals to allow access to advice in some instances. However, there are a number of loopholes in the legal advice scheme which may allow for less formal methods of evading its provisions and it may be that the suspects who are thereby most disadvantaged are those most in need of legal advice. Further powers to interview the suspect without his having had legal advice arise under Code C.[273] All these provisions apply to all arrestees, but in terrorist cases there were further exceptions to the general right arising under Code C: the right could be delayed if a superintendent reasonably believed that communication with an advisor 'will lead to interference with the gathering of information about the commission, preparation, or instigation of acts of terrorism' or make it more difficult 'to prevent an act of terrorism or apprehend and prosecute the perpetrators of any such act'.[274]

Under the TA 2000, the access can be delayed for up to 48 hours (see Sched 8, para 8(2)) on the grounds for delay mentioned above, with additional ones relating to the recovery of the proceeds of crime, set out in Sched 8, para 8(4). The TA harmonises the arrangements for delay in Northern Ireland with those in England and Wales, in that once access has been granted, it will not then be withheld.[275] The arrangements in Scotland under the TA allow for delay under Sched 8, para 16(7) if, under para 17(3) delay is 'in the interests of the investigation or prevention of crime, or in recovering property criminally

---

270 In *Delaney* (1989) 88 Cr App R 338; (1988) *The Times*, 20 August, CA, the status of the Codes was considered. It was held that the mere fact that there had been a breach of the Codes of Practice did not of itself mean that evidence had to be rejected. Section 67(11) of the Act provides that '... if any provision of such Code appears to the court ... to be relevant to any question arising in the proceedings, it shall be taken into account in determining that question'.

271 Annex B, para 2.

272 See p 484.

273 Code C, para 6.5, 6.6 and Annex B. The para 6 provisions are not dependent on the offence in question being a serious arrestable one. Under para 6, a power to proceed with the interview, although the suspect has not had advice, arises if there are reasonable grounds for believing that delay would cause harm to persons or serious harm to property, or, where a solicitor has agreed to attend, awaiting his arrival would cause unreasonable delay to the process of the investigation, or the solicitor is unavailable.

274 Code C, Annex B. This applied to detention under the PTA, but will apply to the equivalent TA provisions. This provision is likely to appear in the new TA Code.

275 Under the EPA and its Codes, the powers to delay access were broadly the same as under the PTA, but also, once the police had allowed access, further delays could be imposed and there was no right to have advisors present in interviews. This right is not contained in the TA, but may appear in its accompanying Code, when promulgated.

obtained, or in confiscating the proceeds of an offence, or of the apprehension, prosecution or conviction of offenders'. In all three jurisdictions, when a review officer authorises continued detention under Sched 8 of the TA he must remind the detainee of his rights to contact a friend or relative and to consult a solicitor[276] and, if applicable, of the fact of their being delayed. The officer must also consider whether the reason or reasons for which the delay was authorised continue to subsist, and if not, he must inform the officer who authorised the delay of his opinion. However, there is no provision allowing the review officer to override the view of the officer who originally authorised delay. The TA provisions largely continue the old regime, and therefore do not address the concerns of those who view confessions obtained after 24 hours in detention as inherently fallible,[277] particularly where the detainee has also been held incommunicado.

Under this scheme, the power of delay in Scotland is wider and is less dependent than in the other jurisdictions on the interests of preventing or detecting acts of terrorism. This seems to be anomalous given that one of the aims of the TA is to harmonise the position of terrorist suspects throughout the UK. The changes under the TA also provide further grounds for delay in obtaining access to legal advice which also apply to a far wider group of persons than those covered by the PTA and EPA since, potentially, a far larger group may become 'terrorist' suspects in future. Within that group are persons who signally fail to fit the stereotype of the 'terrorist', and are therefore more in need of legal advice. The wider possibilities of delaying access under the TA in relation to the terrorist, as opposed to the conventional suspect, are therefore open to question under Art 6, as discussed below.

(2) Subverting notification

Notification of the right of access to legal advice under para 3.1 of Code C is still reserved for arrival at the police station, thus disadvantaging certain suspects not already aware of it at the point when admissions may be made.[278] It is probably fair to assume, first, that many suspects, including those who are criminally experienced,[279] are aware of the right to legal advice and, secondly, that the group who are not so aware would tend to include some of the more vulnerable members of society. It has already been noted above that there is leeway in the interviewing scheme to allow admissions to be made before notification of advice during 'booking in' at the police station. At the point of notification, the suspect not already aware of the right to advice is in a very vulnerable position since he is dependent for information on the very persons who have an interest in withholding it or misleading him. Research conducted by Sanders[280] has demonstrated that notification can be subverted by various methods, most commonly by ensuring that suspects never really take in what is on offer.[281] When Code C was revised in 1991 and in

---

276 Under para 27. These rights arise under paras 6 and 7 of Sched 8.

277 See, eg, Walker, *op cit*, fn 2, p 18.

278 Softley's research into the issue indicated that when suspects were informed of this right, requests for advice were three times as high as when they were not so informed (Softley, *Police Interrogations*, 1980).

279 The Sanders research, above, supports this suggestion; out of 60 suspects who knew that they had a right to legal advice, only 23.3% did not know this before informed of it by the police; p 46.

280 Op cit, fn 264.

281 Sanders found that the most popular ploy (used in 42.9% of the instances observed) was to read the rights too quickly or incomprehensibly or incompletely; *op cit*, fn 262, p 59.

1995, this problem was recognised and an attempt was made to address it. The requirement of notification under para 3.1 was backed up by new para 6.3, requiring that police stations display a prominent poster (under new Note 6H with ethnic translations if appropriate) advertising the right to have advice. However, it must be questioned whether the provision of posters will make much difference. The 'booking in' stage is likely to be one of the more traumatic points in the process, especially for the suspect who is inexperienced or in some way vulnerable. Whether he is likely to notice and take in a message conveyed in this way which is not specifically directed at him is open to question. If he remains silent in the face of a rapid notification, his silence can be taken as a waiver of advice when in actuality it merely denotes incomprehension. The requirement introduced in 1995 under para 6.5 that the suspect should be asked his reason for declining legal advice, and that this should be noted on the custody record, may go some way towards ensuring that suspects understand what is on offer and may curb 'ploys' (see below), as may the requirement to point out that the suspect may speak on the telephone with a solicitor. Nevertheless, the possibility of manipulation of the custody record remains, since the whole process of making the record remains in the hands of the custody officer.[282] Research conducted after the 1991 revision of Code C found that a higher proportion of suspects were being informed of the right to legal advice,[283] but that the information was given in a quarter of cases in an unclear or unduly rapid fashion.

(3) Encouragement to defer the decision

If the suspect does take in what is being offered, he may be encouraged not to exercise the right straight away. In fact, the Sanders research suggested that encouraging a suspect to defer the decision to have advice was quite popular.[284] The 1991 revision of Code C did address this problem. Paragraph 3.1 now provides that it is a 'continuing right which may be exercised at any stage' and under para 11.2, a suspect must now be reminded of the right before each interview in the police station. Although this change is to be welcomed, it should not obscure the value of having advice before any interviewing at all takes place.[285] It is therefore unfortunate that para 3.1 does not make this clear and could even be said to encourage the suspect to defer the decision. However, Note 3G seems designed to dissuade some suspects from deferring it by providing that a request for advice from a mentally disordered or handicapped person or a juvenile should be pursued straight away without waiting for the appropriate adult to arrive. It appears intended to prevent

---

282 It has been suggested (by Wolchover and Heaton-Armstrong (1990) 140 NLJ 320–21) that a requirement of an own hand declaration of waiver of advice would have represented an effective means of addressing the problem because it would have forced the custody officer to ensure that the suspect understood what was being offered and would require positive action on the suspect's part to refuse it.

283 Brown, Ellis and Lancombe, *Changing the Code: Police Detention under the revised PACE Codes of Practice* (research conducted for the Royal Commission on Criminal Procedure), 1993, Home Office Research Study 129. It found that 73% of suspects, as opposed to 66% prior to April 1991, received notification.

284 This 'ploy' was used in 8.2% of the cases observed. In a further 1.8% of cases, it was suggested that the suspect waited until after his transfer to another station before having advice and in a further 2.7% of cases that he waited until he got out of the police station; Sanders, *op cit*, fn 262, p 59.

285 Sanders found that suspects had often made admissions in the absence of the solicitor and that therefore 'the potential impact of the solicitor was neutralised in advance by the police'; *op cit*, fn 262, p 143. This finding arose in the context of informal questioning, but could be equally applicable to instances where the suspect defers the decision to have advice.

police officers playing off adult against suspect by telling the suspect to defer making a decision about advice until the adult arrives,[286] and then giving the adult the impression that the juvenile has waived advice or does not need it.[287] It appears that this provision has not had much impact,[288] which might be because it is contained in a Note and not in the Code itself. Provision aimed at preventing this ploy could have been taken further by including a requirement that even where a suspect had waived advice, suspect and adult should be left alone together for a few minutes after re-notification of the right.

(4) Encouragement to forgo advice

Suspects who are thinking of asking for legal advice straight away may still be persuaded out of doing so by various methods and the Sanders research found that such methods – termed 'ploys' – were most successful against least experienced suspects.[289] However, there has been some attempt to combat the use of such ploys. For example, suspects were supposed to be given a leaflet under original Note 3E explaining the arrangements for obtaining advice, including the fact that it was free, but in practice a number of suspects did not receive it or did not understand it, thereby enabling police officers to mislead them.[290] Under para 3.1(ii), the suspect must now be informed that advice is free[291] (although the posters need not carry this information). Further, general discouragement of ploys is articulated in new para 6.4, which provides that no attempt should be made to dissuade the suspect from having advice. The detainee who has decided to have advice can nevertheless change his or her mind; this is provided for by sub-para 6.6(d), if the consent is given in writing or on tape. However, there is some leeway allowing police officers to engineer a change of heart. No limitations were placed on the reasons for giving such consent, thus creating a serious flaw in the legal advice provisions. In particular, if the consent is based on a police misrepresentation, ought it to be treated as genuine? This question arises in part due to the lack of certainty as to the relationship between sub-para 6.6(d) and (c). Sub-paragraph 6.6(c) provides that the detainee can be interviewed without legal advice if the nominated solicitor is unavailable and notification of the duty solicitor scheme is given but the duty solicitor is unavailable or not required. The provisions under sub-paras 6.6(c) and (d) appear to be expressed as alternatives, but the drafter's intention must surely be that the police cannot obtain the detainee's consent to be interviewed merely by failing to inform him or her of the scheme.

The first instance decision in *Vernon*[292] suggested that the consent must be genuine; in other words, it must not be based on misleading information given by the police. The defendant consented to be interviewed under the misapprehension that if her own

---

286 This ploy was used in 5.4% of instances observed; *op cit*, fn 262, p 59.

287 This ploy was used in 2.4% of instances observed; *op cit*, fn 262, p 59.

288 Brown *et al*, *op cit*, fn 283; apart from this propensity, particular problems were found with the notification of this right to juveniles, with a wide variation in the number of juveniles requesting advice in the different stations: 7% to 58%.

289 The take-up rate for advice among suspects with no previous convictions 'declined sharply as more ploys were used'. This was contrasted with the smaller correlation between the use of ploys and take up rate among all suspects; *op cit*, fn 262, pp 57 and 61.

290 This ploy was used in less than 1.5% of the instances observed; *op cit*, p 59.

291 The research by Brown *et al* shows a dramatic improvement in the number of suspects informed that advice is free after the revision of the Codes: 73% compared with 5%.

292 [1988] Crim LR 445.

solicitor was unavailable, there was no alternative means of obtaining advice; the confession so obtained was excluded. Andrew J held that as her consent to the interview was given under the misapprehension that otherwise, the interview would be delayed till the morning, this could not be termed true consent: had she known of the availability of the duty solicitor, she would have withheld her consent. Thus, the exception under sub-para 6.3(d) (now para 6.6(d)) was not fulfilled: para 6.3 had been breached. This ruling suggests that although the exceptions under sub-paras 6.6(c) and (d) are expressed disjunctively, they should be read together; if a detainee has fallen within sub-para 6.6(c) by nominating a solicitor and being disappointed, he or she should then be informed of the alternative. It would not seem to accord with the drafter's intention to treat the consent of such a person in the same way as that of a detainee who has decided against having a solicitor at all.

The ruling of the Court of Appeal in *Hughes*,[293] however, suggested that if the police misled the suspect without bad faith, a resultant consent would be treated as genuine. The appellant, disappointed of obtaining advice from his own solicitor, inquired about the duty solicitor scheme but was informed, erroneously (but in good faith), that no solicitor was available. Under this misapprehension, he gave consent to be interviewed and the Court of Appeal took the view that his consent was not thereby vitiated. Sub-paragraphs 6.3(c) and (d) (now 6.6(c) and (d)) were to be treated as alternatives and the fact that the detainee was within (c) did not vitiate his consent under (d). Thus, no breach had occurred. The court did not advert to the difficulty that there can be no difference in principle between failing to inform a detainee of the scheme and informing him or her of it but stating wrongly that no solicitor is available. This ruling opens the possibility that the consent given in *Vernon* will in future be treated as true consent. The only distinction between the cases is that in *Hughes*, the misrepresentation was apparently made innocently, while in *Vernon*, the failure to give the information was deliberate: *Vernon* demonstrates a willingness to interpret Code C restrictively against the police if bad faith is demonstrated. The view was taken in *Hughes* that if the misrepresentation had been made negligently or deliberately, a different conclusion would have been reached. This seems to confuse the para 6.3(d) issue and the issue of fairness under s 78 (which will be considered fully below);[294] the judgment would have been clearer if the court had considered first whether a breach of para 6.3 had occurred and, secondly, whether the breach in the circumstances would have an adverse effect on the fairness of the trial. Innocence or bad faith on the part of the police has been determined to be relevant when considering s 78,[295] but there is nothing in Code C to suggest that these matters are relevant in relation to the narrow question of failure to fulfil a Code provision. Generally, consent to forgo a right should be treated with caution when the parties are on an unequal footing; and the possible unfairness is exacerbated when the party who will obtain an advantage from the consent gives false information in obtaining it. Had the Court of Appeal found itself able to hold that such consent is not true consent, the onus would have been placed on the police to ensure that administrative practice in relation to the duty solicitor scheme was tightened up. As it is, moves towards obtaining consent in similar circumstances may become more marked and it is likely to be the more suggestible detainee who suffers.

---

293 [1988] Crim LR 519, CA, transcript from LEXIS.
294 See Chapter 14, pp 880–83.
295 See *Alladice* (1988) 87 Cr App R 380, CA; [1988] Crim LR 608. See below, p 884.

Under the 1991 revision, once the suspect has changed his mind about having advice, the interview can proceed subject to the need to obtain the permission of an officer of the rank of inspector or above. This was the main change from the original Code and was obviously not a full safeguard against the possibility of pressure from the police considered above. Inclusion of a provision that a consent based on erroneous information given by the police could not be treated as true consent might have encouraged the police to tighten up administrative practices and perhaps avoided a recurrence of the *Hughes* type of situation. A provision included in the 1991 Home Office circular,[296] requiring a note to be made in the custody record of the reason for the suspect's change of heart, may allow a court to determine whether the consent was based on misleading information. This circular provision, in the form of a requirement to record the reason for the change of mind and repeat it on tape, became part of para 6.5 under the 1995 revision to Code C. This provision may allow a court to determine whether the consent was based on misleading information, but it leaves open the possibility of treating the consent as valid so long as such information was apparently given in good faith.

(5) Debarring solicitors' clerks

As already noted, s 58(1) entitles the detainee to consult a solicitor at any time. This provision does not extend to solicitors' clerks but, under Code C, para 6.9 (now para 6.12), if the solicitor who has been contacted decides to send a clerk, he or she should be admitted to the police station. After the decision in *Samuel*,[297] access to a solicitor can be delayed only in very specific circumstances. These exceptions do not apply to clerks but, since the decision of the Court of Appeal in *Chief Constable of Avon ex p Robinson*,[298] access to a clerk can be denied in a much wider range of circumstances. The Chief Constable had issued instructions that the character and antecedents of certain unqualified clerks employed by the applicant – a solicitor – were such as to make their presence at police interviews with suspects undesirable. The Chief Constable left the final decision on access to the officer in question, but gave his opinion that it would only rarely be appropriate to allow these particular clerks access to a suspect. The applicant sought judicial review of the instructions, contending that they were in breach of para 6.9.

The Court of Appeal considered the scope of the express exception to para 6.9: '... the clerk shall be admitted unless an officer of the rank of inspector or above considers that such a visit will hinder the investigation of crime.' (Similar wording is now used in para 6.12.) It was held that the investigating officers had been entitled in each instance to invoke the exception because they had known of the criminal activities of the clerks. They had been informed of such activities by the Chief Constable, but he had not imposed a blanket ban on the clerks; the discretion to debar the clerks had been left with the officers concerned. Accordingly, there had been no breach of para 6.9 and the application would therefore be refused. May LJ, in a lengthy *dictum*, also considered that there was an implied requirement under para 6.9 that a clerk be capable of giving advice on behalf of the solicitor and therefore a police officer would be entitled to exclude a clerk if he

---

296 When the revised PACE Codes came into force in April 1991, a Home Office circular was issued in conjunction with them by F2 Division, Home Office.
297 [1988] QB 615; [1988] 2 All ER 135; [1988] 2 WLR 920, CA.
298 [1989] All ER 15; [1989] 1 WLR 793.

appeared incapable of giving advice owing to his age, appearance, mental capacity or known background.

The concern as to the possible effects of employing these untrained clerks was understandable, but the result of this decision was to confer a very wide power on the police to exclude clerks, which potentially has unfortunate consequences. If a detainee asks for legal advice and a clerk arrives but is not admitted to the police station on one of the grounds considered above, or if he or she is not allowed to remain in the interview, the police, under Code C, para 6.14, must give the original solicitor the opportunity of making other arrangements. The Code is silent as to what should happen if the solicitor is unable to do so, although under para 6.10, if a solicitor is excluded from the station, the police must give the suspect an opportunity to consult another solicitor. Paragraph 6.12 now provides that para 6.10 applies to clerks and, therefore, in the circumstances described, the police as a last resort presumably ought to inform the detainee of the duty solicitor scheme. It is probably regrettable that the Court of Appeal suggested such wide grounds on which to exclude clerks. If the police take advantage of their width to exclude clerks rather too readily, some detainees may be likely to experience substantial delay in obtaining advice. There is always the danger when advice is delayed that a detainee will succumb to pressure to get the interview over with quickly and will consent to be interviewed without advice. The 1995 revision addressed this possibility to some extent: para 6.12 restricts the grounds for exclusion as far as clerks or other accredited representatives of solicitors are concerned, since it defines such persons as 'solicitors'. This means that the trainee, clerk or legal executive is 'accredited in accordance with the Law Society's scheme for accreditation'. Therefore, the more restrictive provisions relating to exclusion from the interview of solicitors, paras 6.9, 6.10 and 6.11, will apply. Under para 6.9, the solicitor may be excluded from the interview if his or her conduct is such that the investigating officer is unable properly to question the suspect. Under para 6.12, a non-accredited or probationary representative may be excluded from the police station if an officer of the rank of inspector or above considers that the visit would hinder the investigation of crime and directs otherwise. The factors influencing the discretion to exclude such advisors from the police station are set out in paras 6.12 and 6.13 and include taking account of 'any matters set out in any written letter of authorisation provided by the solicitor'. It is unclear that this discretion is markedly narrower than that indicated in Robinson and, therefore, it will be hard ever to challenge a decision to exclude such persons, leaving open the possibility that officers may at times exercise this power rather too readily. Once advice is delayed, a detainee may succumb to pressure to forgo it in order to speed matters up.

Value of legal advice and relationship with the right to silence

Access to legal advice has an impact in upholding due process which encompasses, but goes beyond, advising on making 'no comment' answers. How far it has such an impact in practice is debatable. The impact varies, depending on the contact with the suspect. The Sanders research in 1989 found that telephone advice alone had little impact on suspects: 50% of those who received telephone advice made admissions, as opposed to 59.6% of those who received no advice.[299] The research criticised the great variation in

---

299 Sanders *et al, op cit,* fn 262.

practice between advisors, and considered that too many duty solicitors gave telephone advice only, thereby depriving the client of most of the benefits of legal advice.[300] Subsequent research suggests that in 23% of cases when advice is requested, telephone advice only continues to be given, and only around 12–14% of suspects in police interviews have an advisor present.[301]

The relationship between access to legal advice and the right to silence is complex,[302] particularly in view of the curtailment of the right to silence under ss 34, 36 and 37 of the CJPOA 1994, which is discussed below. The available research lends some support to the following propositions. The suspect will probably be aware, if he has had advice, that he can keep silent and also that this may be a risky course of action. It was, however, clear, even prior to 1994, that advisors did not advise silence routinely.[303] Dixon found in 1991 that solicitors were likely to advise silence at least temporarily if the client was in a confused or emotional state[304] or had been bullied or deceived, or where the police had refused to disclose at least some of the evidence against the client to the advisor.[305]

The legal advisor may help the suspect to maintain silence where advice alone might not be enough. It should be recognised, however, that the key question is not whether the presence of a legal advisor means that the detainee remains silent, but whether it means that he is unlikely to make an unreliable confession. Further, assuming for the moment an inverse correlation between a legal advisor's presence and an unreliable confession, what contribution to it, if any, is made by the right to silence in its current modified form? Obviously, the detainee will not make such a confession if he remains silent, but this is a rather crude and, in any event, ineffective[306] way of tackling the risk of such confessions; the real concern here is with the question whether the legal advisor will enable the detainee to maintain a selective silence or refuse to depart from his version of events at key points in the interview.

Clearly, the curtailment of the right to silence discussed below is tending to affect the nature of custodial legal advice. It has affected the role of the legal advisor in the police station; that role was already, it seemed, interpreted in a variety of ways by advisors, but in circumstances where silence would previously have been advised by most of them it

---

300 The Sanders research found that only 50% of solicitors attended the police station: 25% gave advice over the telephone and 25% gave no advice. Even attendances at the police station were not always followed by attendance at the interview. A few solicitors merely put the police case to the suspect; *op cit*, fn 262, p 150. It appeared that some advisors who did attend the interview disadvantaged the client by seeming to give their imprimatur to improper police behaviour.

301 Brown, *op cit*, fn 263, pp 94–95.

302 The relationship is a matter of some controversy; the Home Office, *Working Group on the Right to Silence* (C Division, Home Office, London, 13 July 1989; see [1989] Crim LR 855 for comment) considered that there was a causal relationship between legal advice and silence, but this finding has been doubted by Dixon, D, 'Solicitors, suspects, runners, police' [1991] PL 233, p 251. However, the Sanders research (*op cit*, fn 262) found that suspects confess less often when they have advice: 35.8% of those whose solicitor was present at the interrogation confessed, as opposed to 59.6% of those who did not receive advice; *op cit*, fn 262, p 136). Confirmed by Bucke *et al*, *The Right of Silence: The Impact of the CJPOA 1994*, Home Office Research Study No 199, 2000.

303 See the research undertaken by Sanders *et al*, p 129, which found that out of 24 suspects, only two were advised to remain silent. Dixon's findings, *op cit*, p 243 were to the same effect.

304 See Dixon, D, 'Common sense, legal advice and the right to silence' [1991] PL 233, p 244.

305 *Ibid*, pp 246 and 247.

306 The Sanders research found that only 2.4% of suspects exercised their right to silence as against 54.1% who made admissions (the others denied the offence) (*op cit*, fn 262, p 136).

seems possible that, at present, it may not be.[307] Possibly the difficulty of advising the client as to when to remain silent and when not to take the risk of so doing may mean that some advisors tend to adopt the role of referee or counsellor rather than that of legal advisor. More experienced advisors will, however, be of great value to the client, since they will be able to advise on the risks of staying silent, which may be much greater in response to certain questions than to others.[308] The main studies in this area[309] recognised that interviews may be a means of constructing or creating truth rather than discovering it, but their concern was more with the causal relationship between the presence of a legal advisor and exercise of the right to silence than with the relationship between such presence and the making of an unreliable confession. This issue was touched on in the study by Dixon,[310] which found that legal advisors were more likely to advise silence at least temporarily if the client was in a confused or emotional state[311] or had been bullied or deceived.[312] A further study, conducted for the Royal Commission on Criminal Justice[313] found, not surprisingly, that the relationship between legal advice and the right to silence was affected by the quality of the advice given. The research found that many 'legal advisors' are clerks, secretaries and former police officers with no legal education or training in the provision of custodial legal advice. Such persons, it was found, often had little or no grasp of the case in question and little apparent understanding of the need, at times, for the client to maintain a selective silence. According to the research, 78% of the advisors counselled the client to co-operate with the police. Some recent research echoes these findings as to the quality of advice and suggests that advisors adopt a passive stance in interviews, failing to intervene where intervention is clearly called for.[314] Professor McConville found that the presence of some legal advisors in interviews may have had a detrimental impact on suspects: 'Lacking any clear understanding of their role in the process, some advisors simply become part of the machine which confronts the suspect.'[315] The suggestions that advisors are reluctant to adopt an adversarial stance were given credence by the two post-PACE cases of oppression which arose in respect of tape recorded interviews with an advisor present.[316] The advisors must operate on police territory and may, as Dixon puts it, deal with the resultant pressures by making 'some positive adaptation'.[317] However, more recent research has pointed out that intervention is not called for in around one-quarter of

---

307 See Bucke *et al*, *op cit*, fn 302.

308 For further discussion see Fenwick, H [1995] Crim LR 132; Jackson, M [1995] Crim LR 587.

309 The Sanders research, *op cit*, fn 262, the Home Office Study by Brown, *op cit*, fn 301 and the study by Bucke *et al*, *op cit*, fn 302.

310 *Op cit*, fn 304

311 *Op cit*, fn 304, p 244.

312 *Op cit*, fn 304, pp 246 and 247.

313 The study by Hodgson and McConville took place over an eight month period during which the researchers followed suspects and advisors into 180 interrogations; see (1993) 143 NLJ 659.

314 *The Role of Legal Representatives at Police Stations*, HMSO 1992 Research Study No 3, summarised at [1993] Crim LR 161. The approach of the research has been criticised: see Roberts [1993] Crim LR 368, with reply by Baldwin, p 371.

315 McConville, M and Hodgson, J, *Custodial Legal Advice and the Right to Silence*, Royal Commission Study No 13.

316 *R v Paris* (1993) 97 Cr App R 99; *Heron* (1993) unreported, judgment of Mitchell J, 1 November 1993.

317 Dixon, *op cit*, fn 304, pp 236–37.

interviews, that advisors usually intervene when it is called for but, in half of such cases, do not do so as often as is needed.[318]

Thus, despite the general perception that legal advice reduces the likelihood that unreliable confessions will be made, the available empirical evidence relating specifically to the issue allows only the tentative suggestion that the advisor may ensure that the client is aware of the right to silence and may sometimes advise that he exercises it, despite the risks, especially where the client does not seem able to cope with the interview.[319] In this context, it is worth bearing in mind that it tends to be a feature of cases in which a miscarriage of justice has occurred that the confessions were uttered in the absence of a legal advisor.[320] This has not invariably been the case; the confessions gained by oppression in the case of the *Cardiff Three* were obtained in the presence of a solicitor.[321] Of course, if an unreliable confession is made in the presence of a legal advisor, this may say much more about the quality of the advice given than it does about the principle of having legal advice. The presence of a solicitor can affect the reliability of the confession in other ways. The suspect may feel generally reassured by the presence of a person independent of the police who is undaunted by the interview process.

Moreover, his or her presence may sometimes be a potent factor discouraging use of improper tactics,[322] and may help to alter the balance of power between interviewer and interviewee, thus tending to create a climate in which an unreliable confession is less likely to be uttered. Reassurance deriving from the presence of a solicitor is not merely valuable in terms of the reliability of the confession; it may serve to make the whole experience of police detention less traumatic and daunting. In theory, the solicitor will intervene if the interview is conducted in an intimidatory fashion or if other improper tactics are used. Although it seems clear that the quality of legal advice improved over the 1990s, the availability of legal advice may not always have such effects, as indicated above. In other words, the mere fact that a person labelled a 'legal advisor' turns up at the police station and may be present at the interview may have little impact in terms of evening up the balance of power between suspect and police officer. Indeed, the presence of such a person may sometimes be to the disadvantage of the suspect, as it may offer a reassurance which it does not warrant.

---

318 Bridges, L and Choongh, S, *Improving Police Station Legal Advice*, 1998.

319 It is worth noting that the Court of Appeal has accepted as a general rule that most suspects, unless clearly experienced and independently minded, are less likely to make any confession in the presence of a solicitor (*Samuel* [1988] 1 QB 615; [1988] 2 All ER 135; [1988] 2 WLR 920, CA; *Dunford* (1990) 140 NLJ 517, CA).

320 Eg, the *Confait* case, see the *Report of an Inquiry by the Hon Sir Henry Fisher* (1977) HC 90; the case of the *Birmingham Six* (1991) *The Times*, 28 March; *Silcott* (1991) *The Times*, 8 December.

321 *Paris* (1993) 97 Cr App R 99; [1994] Crim LR 361, CA. This also occurred in *Heron* (1993) unreported, judgment of Mitchell J, 1 November 1993; the judge, Mitchell J, drew attention to the fact that only a legal executive was present during oppressive questioning and said that this was unacceptable.

322 One of the conclusions of the Sanders research, *op cit*, fn 262, p 150, was that suspects who did not receive advice or whose solicitors did not attend the interrogation would have been greatly assisted had the solicitor been present. Two examples are given, pp 138 and 139, of forceful or threatening questioning which produced a possibly unreliable confession from an easily intimidated suspect in the absence of a solicitor. This finding received some support from Dixon's study (*op cit*, fn 304). See also Bucke, *op cit*, fn 302.

Conclusions: improving the legal advice scheme

This discussion has suggested that the revisions of Code C in 1991 and 1995 tinkered with the problem of informal subversion of the right, but no radical change was undertaken. The 1999 revision signalled an abandonment of attempts to improve the scheme, despite the fact that after 1995, commentators had continued to point out its defects.[323] The fundamental problem is that the process of delivering advice remains in the hands of a body which has an interest in withholding it, while many suspects continue to need disinterested advice regarding the decision whether to have advice.[324]

The result is that the introduction of new provisions aimed at curbing informal subversion are unlikely to have much impact and police working practices of subverting the new provisions themselves will tend to develop. It has been found that 'in around 28% of cases prior to the 1991 revisions but in 35% afterwards suspects may have been influenced against seeking advice by the police'.[325] The percentage of suspects who receive advice remains relatively low and the research suggests that this continues to be due in part to subversion of notification and the responses of the police to requests for advice.[326] It is too early to predict the effect of s 34(2A) of the CJPOA (inserted by s 58 of the Youth Justice and Criminal Evidence Act 1999), although it would appear to be likely to encourage the police to afford access to legal advice. Whether it does so in practice will depend on the interpretation of the term given to the provision. It provides essentially that adverse inferences shall not be drawn from a suspect's silence under caution before or after charge at an authorised place of detention if he has not been allowed an 'opportunity' to consult a solicitor before that point (emphasis added). Clearly, the term 'opportunity' may be taken to mean that, formally, an opportunity had been offered, but the suspect had not availed himself of it. This would not curb the use of ploys as discussed above. The provision also excludes questioning under caution at somewhere other than an authorised place of detention. As explained below, Code C allows for informal interviews outside the police station. Theoretically, then, such an interview, in which a suspect had remained silent and clearly would not have had an opportunity to consult a solicitor, could be adduced in evidence and s 34(2A) would not prevent the drawing of adverse inferences. Such a possibility would not appear to accord with Art 6 jurisprudence, discussed below. But, at present, it may be argued that the reform effected by s 34(2A) is flawed and incomplete.

Exclusion of admissions obtained after a breach of the legal advice provisions may encourage police officers to adhere to the scheme. However, most of the methods of evading the legal advice provisions considered here tend to consist of rule evasion as opposed to rule breaking. Courts tend to prefer the defence to point to a specific breach of a Code provision before deciding whether to invoke s 78 to exclude admissions.[327]

---

323 See Brown, *op cit*, fn 263; Sanders, 'Access to justice in the police station: an elusive dream?', in *Access to Justice*, 1996.

324 The Sanders research found that suspects quite often asked officers whether or not they should have advice: *op cit*, fn 262, p 65.

325 Brown *et al*, *op cit*, fn 283.

326 Brown, *op cit*, fn 263, pp 94–95; Bucke, *op cit*, fn 302.

327 See, eg, *Keenan* [1989] 3 WLR 1193.

However, the disapproval of persuading an inexperienced suspect to forgo advice expressed in *Beycan*[328] suggests that there may be a willingness on the part of the judiciary to consider rule evasion in this context. Where it seems that such evasion has occurred, it could be characterised as general subversion of the legal advice scheme or perhaps as a breach of the para 6.4 provision that no attempt must be made to persuade the suspect to waive advice. There would be scope for such argument where, for example, a suspect who made admissions in an interview after he had waived his entitlement to advice stated that something an officer said (such as an overstatement of the time needed to contact a solicitor) or failed to say to him, persuaded him to that decision.

Although para 6.4 seems to be aimed at preventing such improper persuasion at the 'booking in' stage, it might also apply if it appeared that police officers had pressurised or misled a suspect into reversing the decision to have advice. For example, an untrue representation (even though made in good faith) that the duty solicitor was unavailable which had the effect of persuading the detainee to reverse the decision to have advice might be brought within para 6.4. If no reason for such a reversal was recorded as required by the 1991 Home Office circular, that might lend weight to the argument that the suspect was improperly persuaded to forgo advice. It is clear that although para 6.4 has not so far received much attention, it does open up a number of possibilities. This point will be returned to in Chapter 14 when exclusion of evidence as a form of redress for a breach of PACE is considered. However, it should be noted here that even if methods of evading the legal advice scheme could be given the character of a breach of PACE, exclusion of evidence would not inevitably follow. Thus, this 'sanction' remains extremely weak and is, of course, inapplicable to a suspect who is improperly denied advice or encouraged to forgo it, but later pleads guilty.

Various suggestions for reform of the legal advice scheme have already been made above which could bring about significant improvement without necessitating a radical change. There are other possibilities: ploys could be discouraged and untrue allegations by suspects of lack of notification of advice precluded if the 'booking in' stage were video or audio taped.[329] Such an innovation could be used in conjunction with the para 6.4 prohibition of attempts to dissuade the suspect to forgo advice. Inadequate notification of advice could be characterised as an attempt at persuasion to forgo it on the ground that it was intended to and did have that effect. Finally, and very importantly, notification of legal advice could take place on arrest or even on caution, thereby harmonising the position of all suspects. Clearly, such changes would not ensure that all suspects who needed it received advice.

Further, improvement in the quality and delivery of advice can be brought about only by an increase in funding for the scheme. It may be argued that only specially trained solicitors should offer advice, but until better funding is available, solicitors will delegate this function. The Royal Commission, in its 1993 report, proposed that the performance of solicitors should be monitored and that the police should receive training in the role solicitors are expected to play.[330] In a response to the available research and

---

328 [1990] Crim LR 185.

329 The suggestion of video taping was made by Fordham J (1991) 141 NLJ 677. He suggested that it could take place by means of a fixed camera focused on the 'booking in' desk. The Royal Commission Report 1993 also proposed (Proposal 57) that a waiver of advice at this point should be video taped.

330 Proposals 64–69.

recommendations of the Runciman Royal Commission,[331] the Law Society undertook a programme of training with a view to ensuring that clerks or other non-solicitor advisors are accredited in accordance with the Law Society's scheme for accreditation.[332] Thus, when non-solicitors give advice, they are normally accredited,[333] although it has been pointed out that firms can use untrained paralegals who are not trained and then replace them after six months with another untrained trainee.[334] But the quality of advice, although improving, remains variable: around 26% of those giving custodial legal advice are non-solicitors[335] and where an 'own' as opposed to a duty solicitor gives advice, there is no requirement that he or she should have specialist training in this area.

However, it may be that more radical action is necessary to address this problem. There are various possibilities; for example, suspects could routinely be offered the chance at booking in to speak to a duty solicitor on the phone regarding the question of having legal advice. More radically, and expensively, legal advisors (who might be trainee solicitors and should at least have some legal education) could be employed on a temporary basis to attend all interviews in police stations except where the suspect requested his own solicitor or a duty solicitor or specifically required that a legal advisor should not be present. Such advisors could receive some special training concerned specifically with advising the suspect in the police station.[336] Apart from such advisors, persons other than solicitors should not attend the suspect during interviews. Such a scheme would not only address most of the difficulties outlined here, but also the problems caused by the reluctance of solicitors to attend the police station[337] and the variation in the quality of the response of solicitors to the request for advice.[338]

Vulnerable groups

Throughout Code C, recognition is given to the special needs of certain vulnerable groups: juveniles, the mentally disordered or handicapped, those not proficient in English, the hearing impaired or the visually handicapped. Juveniles and the mentally handicapped or disordered should be attended by an 'appropriate adult'. Under para 1, the 'appropriate' adult in the case of a juvenile will be the parent or guardian, a social worker or another adult who is not a police officer. The suspect should be informed by the custody officer that the appropriate adult is there to assist and advise him and can be consulted with privately (para 3.12). However, research suggests that this requirement is not always observed and that in any event, appropriate adults often seem unclear as to

---

331 Runciman Report Recommendations 61–68. In response to the McConville study, reported at (1993) 143 NLJ 659, the Law Society and Legal Aid Board announced that from October 1993, legal aid would not be available for police station work unless advisors had been through a training course and passed a Law Society test.

332 See Shepherd, *Becoming Skilled*.

333 See further Cape, E, *Defending Suspects at Police Stations*, 1999.

334 Bridges and Choongh, *op cit*, fn 318.

335 Brown, *op cit*, fn 263, p 108.

336 Eg, the College of Law course: 'Advising the suspect at the police station'.

337 The Sanders research found that 25.6% of solicitors gave telephone advice only, which was less valuable for the suspect; *op cit*, fn 262, p 104.

338 The Sanders research found an enormous variation in the quality of service offered in this context, *op cit*, fn 262, pp 112–17.

the role they are supposed to play.[339] Under the revision of Code C in 1991 and 1995, the estranged parent of a juvenile can no longer be the appropriate adult,[340] if the juvenile 'expressly and specifically objects to his presence'. Previously this was possible and, in such instances, the parent was likely to collude with the police or generally show hostility to the juvenile rather than look after his or her interests.[341]

This change was probably prompted by the decision in *DPP v Blake*[342] that a confession obtained from a juvenile in the presence of an estranged parent acting as the appropriate adult may be excluded from evidence. Compliance with the original Note 13C (now sub-para 11.16), which indicated the respects in which the appropriate adult should look after the interests of the juvenile, could not be ensured if an estranged parent was present; now Note 1C may go some way towards ensuring that sub-para 11.16 can be given full effect. Under Note 1F, the solicitor should not be the appropriate adult; this provision was included in response to some evidence that the police had been treating the solicitor as the appropriate adult, thereby producing a conflict of interests.[343] It was thought that the roles of legal advisor and appropriate adult differed; the same person could not therefore fulfil both. It should be noted that the juvenile can be interviewed without the presence of an appropriate adult if an officer of the rank of superintendent or above considers that delay will involve an immediate risk of harm to persons or serious loss of or serious damage to property.[344] At various points to be discussed, the particular vulnerability of juveniles is recognised, but although this is to be welcomed, research suggests that the treatment of juveniles, particularly during interviews, is still at times unsatisfactory.[345]

In the case of a mentally disordered or handicapped detainee, the appropriate adult under para 1 will be a relative, guardian, other person responsible for his or her welfare or an adult who is not a police officer.[346] The custody officer must as soon as practicable inform the appropriate adult of the grounds for the person's detention and ask the adult to come to the police station to see him or her. If a person appears mentally ill, the custody officer must immediately call the police surgeon or, in urgent cases, send the person to hospital or call the nearest available medical practitioner.[347] The notification of rights must be given in the presence of the adult,[348] which may mean repeating the notification, but if the suspect wants legal advice, this should not be delayed until the adult arrives.[349] The appropriate adult who is present at an interview should be informed that he or she is not expected to act simply as an observer; and also that the purposes of

---

339 Brown, Ellis and Larcombe, *op cit*, fn 283.

340 Note 1C.

341 See Softley, 'Police interrogation: an observational study in four police stations' (1985) Policing Today 119.

342 [1989] 1 WLR 432, CA; this problem also arose recently at first instance in *Morse* [1991] Crim LR 195.

343 LAG Bulletin, November 1989.

344 See Annex C: urgent interviews.

345 Evans, R, 'The conduct of police interviews with juveniles' (1993) Home Office Research Study No 8. On the treatment of juveniles generally, see Dixon, D, 'Juvenile suspects and PACE', in Freestone, D (ed), *Children and the Law*, 1990, pp 107–29.

346 Paragraph 1.7(b).

347 Paragraph 9.2.

348 Paragraph 3.11.

349 Note 3G and Annex E, Note E2.

being present are, first, to advise the person being interviewed and to observe whether or not the interview is being conducted properly and fairly and, secondly, to facilitate communication with the person being interviewed.[350]

The Runciman Royal Commission Report 1993 recommended review of the role of appropriate adults with a view to considering their training and availability and the criteria employed by the police in order to determine when an adult was needed.[351] In response, the Home Office set up a review group which, in June 1995, made a number of recommendations. They included entitling appropriate adults to a confidential interview with the suspect, defining the role of appropriate adults in Code C, providing guidance for professionals and others likely to act in this role and setting up local appropriate adult panels.[352]

It will be found, in discussion in Chapter 14 of unreliable confessions, that mentally handicapped or disordered persons are very likely to make an untrue or exaggerated confession and therefore it is particularly important that all the safeguards available should be in place when such a person is interviewed. However, there is provision for urgent interviewing of such persons without the appropriate adult if an officer of the rank of superintendent or above considers that delay will involve an immediate risk of harm to persons or serious loss of or serious damage to, property.[353] The main defect in the provisions relating to the mentally handicapped or disordered is that they rely on the ability of officers who will have had little or no training in the field to make the judgment that a person is mentally disordered.[354] It would seem essential that custody officers at least should have special training in this regard. Various provisions are available for the protection of members of the other vulnerable groups mentioned. A blind or visually handicapped person must have independent help in reading documentation.[355] A deaf or speech-handicapped person, or someone who has difficulty understanding English, must only be interviewed in the presence of an interpreter,[356] but this may be waived in the case of urgent interviewing under Annex C.

Physical treatment

Physical treatment of detainees is governed by para 8 of Code C and it is intended that they should be provided with basic physical care. Paragraph 8 embodies the principle that the detainee's physical safety should be ensured and his physical needs met. It does, however, allow more than one detainee to be placed in the same cell if it is impracticable to do otherwise and although a juvenile must not be placed in a cell with an adult, it does

---

350 See para 11.16.

351 Proposal 72. For further discussion see Hodgson J [1997] Crim LR 785.

352 The Report is available from the Chairman of the Review Group: Mr Stephen Wells, F2 Division, Home Office.

353 See para 11.14 and Annex C.

354 Annex E, para 1 provides that if an officer 'has any suspicion or is told in good faith that a person of any age, whether or not in custody, may be suffering from medical disorder or is mentally handicapped or cannot understand the significance of questions put to him or his replies, then he shall be treated as a mentally disordered or mentally handicapped person'.

355 Paragraph 3.14.

356 Paragraph 13.

not make clear provision for frequent checks on juveniles in police cells. It provides that cells should be adequately heated, cleaned, lit and ventilated and that three meals should be offered in any 24 hour period. A juvenile will only be placed in a police cell if no other secure accommodation is available and the custody officer considers that it is not practicable to supervise him if he is not placed in a cell. Persons detained should be visited every hour but, where possible, juveniles should be visited 'more frequently';[357] those who are drunk should be visited every half hour. No additional restraints should be used within a locked cell unless absolutely necessary and then only suitable handcuffs. Reasonable force may be used if necessary (para 8.9), but only to secure compliance with reasonable instructions and to prevent escape, injury, damage to property or the destruction of evidence. Under para 9, if a person appears mentally or physically ill or injured, or does not respond normally to questions or conversation (other than through drunkenness alone) or otherwise appears to need medical attention, the custody officer must immediately call the police surgeon (or, in urgent cases, send the person to hospital or call the nearest available medical practitioner).

Intimate searches

Under s 55, an intimate search can only be ordered if an officer of the rank of superintendent or above has reasonable grounds for believing that an article which could cause physical injury to a detained person or others at the police station has been concealed or that the person has concealed a Class A drug which he intends to supply to another or to export. Even if such suspicion arises, the search should not be carried out unless there is no other means of removing the object. Before it can be carried out, the reasons for undertaking it must be explained to the suspect and a reminder given of the entitlement to legal advice.[358] An intimate search at a police station may only be carried out by a registered medical practitioner or registered nurse unless the authorising officer considers, in the case of a concealed object which could cause injury, that it is not practicable to wait, in which case a police officer of the same sex as the suspect can carry it out. An intimate search at a police station of a juvenile or a mentally disordered or mentally handicapped person must take place only in the presence of the appropriate adult of the same sex unless the suspect requests otherwise.[359]

7 QUESTIONING OF SUSPECTS

Introduction

In crime control terms, the police interview occupies a central position in the criminal justice system; it represents an effective use of resources, since if a confession becomes available, the criminal process is likely to be accelerated.[360] In particular, since *mens rea* is

---

357 Note 8A.

358 See Code C, para 4.1 and Annex A.

359 Under Annex A, para 5 in the case of a juvenile, the search may take place in the absence of the appropriate adult only if the juvenile signifies in the presence of the appropriate adult that he prefers the search to be done in his absence and the appropriate adult agrees.

360 See McConville, M (1993) RCCJ Research Study No 13, 1993; Baldwin (1993) 33 Br J Criminology 325.

a requirement of most offences, admissions provide the most readily available means of establishing the state of mind of the suspect at the relevant time. The interview may, in effect, replace the trial, since its results may play a key part in the pre-trial balancing and negotiating process in which the suspect decides whether to plead guilty. Clearly, the stronger the risk of a conviction which would be unaccompanied by a sentence discount, the less likely it is that he or she will plead not guilty.[361] If the suspect has confessed or made some admissions, he may feel that there is no point in pleading not guilty even if the admissions are false, exaggerated or misleading. The interview may also frequently play a part in general criminal intelligence gathering.[362] The crime control advantages of the interview are readily apparent.

From a due process perspective, on the other hand, the police interview is largely unjustifiable, since its *raison d'être* is to secure admissions which probably would not otherwise be secured; it therefore undermines the privilege against self-incrimination. This due process norm traditionally underpinned criminal justice practice,[363] but it was gradually abandoned until it became accepted in the pre-PACE years that the purpose of the interrogation was to obtain admissions.[364] The precarious position of the interview from this perspective explains, it is suggested, why it seemed necessary, when PACE placed police interrogations on a formal basis, to infuse due process elements into them. Such elements are intended to detract from any impression that the confession is involuntary. The police, however, remain the gatekeepers to these safeguards, which run counter to their crime control concerns, and therefore they may not be observed or, more subtly, the weaknesses and loopholes in the interviewing scheme will be discovered and explored.

PACE strongly reflects this uneasy compromise between crime control and due process: the detainee can be detained for the purposes of obtaining a confession under s 37(2), but a number of safeguards were created which are influenced by due process concerns to lessen the coerciveness of the interview and to ensure its integrity and reliability so that it can be used as evidence. The extensive and complex rules of Code C which appear to surround police interviews with a range of safeguards, including access to legal advice, afford the interview a due process appearance. A number of flaws, however, in due process terms, were built into the scheme when it was first introduced. Most significantly, there are no sanctions for breach of the interviewing rules, including those arising under PACE itself, apart from the possibility of disciplinary action;[365] virtually no guidance is given as to the acceptable limits of 'persuasive' interviewing; there is scope for interviewing away from the police station, thereby evading the most significant safeguards, the tape of exchanges between suspect and police will not record all exchanges between them at the police station and there is uncertainty as to when an exchange with police becomes an interview so as to attract all the safeguards.

---

361 See Sanders and Young, *op cit*, fn 1, 2000, Chapter 7, Part 2.

362 Maguire and Morris, RCCJ Research Study No 5, 1992.

363 The 1912 Judges' Rules did not allow police interrogation, although the police could invite and receive voluntary statements.

364 *Holgate-Mohammed v Duke* [1984] 1 AC 437; [1984] 1 All ER 1054.

365 This possibility became even more remote when PACE, s 67(8), rendering breach of the Codes automatically a breach of the police Disciplinary Code, was repealed in 1994 by the Police and Magistrates' Courts Act 1994, s 37 and Sched 9.

The original interviewing scheme under Code C was revised in 1991 and improved by the introduction of tape recording under Code E. That revision, was, it is suggested, concerned wholly with improving the scheme's due process elements, albeit in a manner best described as superficial: the rules became more complex in order to deal with police evasion of them, but their fundamental flaws were hardly addressed. Despite the relationship a number of commentators had observed to exist between coerced confessions and miscarriages of justice,[366] the recommendations made by the 1993 Runciman Royal Commission on Criminal Procedure, which might, minor as they were, have continued the improvements undertaken in 1991, were largely ignored.[367] Under the Major Government, the disciplinary sanction for breaching the Codes was removed under s 37(f) of the Police and Magistrates Court Act 1994, and the right to silence was curtailed under ss 34–37 of the CJPOA 1994. Largely as a consequence of the changes introduced under the CJPOA, the PACE Codes were revised once again in 1995; this revision, unlike the previous one, appeared to have a dual aim: it seemed to be intended to have some weak due process impact in eradicating loopholes, but it also introduced various provisions in order to give effect to the curtailment of the right to silence. These changes indicated a move away from the rather ineffectual attempts previously undertaken to protect the due process elements in the interviewing process.

Codes C and E were issued in revised versions which came into effect in 1999, but no radical change from the 1995 version was made. The opportunity presented by the 1999 revision of taking forward the improvements made in 1991 was therefore lost, as was the possibility of addressing some of the more fundamental flaws of Code C, in the light of the inception of the HRA. The failures to provide any sanction for breach of the Codes, to address the uncertainty as to the status of the Notes, which continue to contain significant protections for due process, to reduce the scope for out of station interviews and afford such interviews greater due process protection, or to remove provisions which themselves allow for breaches of the Convention rights, are all continued in the 1999 revision. These flaws, and their implications, are discussed at the relevant points, below.

The interviewing scheme had, from its inception, created a twin-track system under PACE, the counter-terrorist legislation and the Codes, that is, one in which terrorist suspects were exposed to a regime adhering to a lower level of due process than that applicable in respect of 'ordinary' suspects. This regime afforded the coercive elements of the scheme greater rein both formally and informally. Most obviously, as explained above, terrorist suspects could be exposed to a longer period of detention, which allowed greater scope for prolonged pressure during interrogation. The interviewing regime for such suspects was also less protective. The counter-terrorist scheme introduced by the Labour Government under the TA 2000, its Codes of Practice and the 1999 revision of Codes C and E not only confirms and extends the twin track system, but applies it to a much wider and more diverse range of suspects. The only concession to due process introduced under

---

366 See Walker, *op cit*, fn 5, p 54.

367 Eg, the Runciman Report Chapter 4, para 23 put forward a recommendation to retain the right to silence, in the context of improved safeguards for suspects, taking into account recommendations intended to lead to improvement in the quality of custodial legal advice. The Report made other proposals for improvement of the interviewing scheme including the video taping of a waiver of legal advice (Proposal 57) and a special warning to juries regarding uncorroborated confessions (Chapter 4, paras 56–87).

the TA is the possible extension of audio recording, already occurring on a voluntary basis, to interviews with terrorist suspects. The acceptance of the primacy of crime control values as underpinning police interviewing, reflected in the changes undertaken in the CJPOA, marked a turning point in criminal justice policies which was unaffected by the change of government in 1997.

This section does not concentrate only on questioning of suspects inside the police station because contact between police and suspect takes place a long time before the police station is reached, and this has been recognised in the provisions of Part V of PACE and Code of Practice C, which govern treatment of suspects and interviewing, but have some application outside as well as inside the police station. It should be noted that many of the key provisions relating to interviewing are contained in Code C rather than in PACE itself. The most crucial events during a person's contact with police will probably be the interviews and therefore, this section will concentrate on the safeguards available which are intended to ensure that interviews are fairly conducted and are properly recorded wherever they take place. Having considered the key features of both the terrorist and the conventional schemes, the discussion will go on to consider the influence that the HRA may have on them. The effect of flaws in the pre-trial procedures discussed here on the fairness of the trial is considered in Chapter 14.

This section examines the key aspects of the interviewing scheme in the following manner:

(a) identification of the points at which the various safeguards must be in place;

(b) the conduct of the interview;

(c) the means of recording the interview;

(d) the curtailed right to silence;

(e) relationship with the legal advice scheme.

The interviewing scheme: bringing the safeguards into play

Under the pre-PACE rules, safeguards for the interview were governed largely by the Judges' Rules and Administrative Directions to the Police[368] and s 62 of the Criminal Law Act 1977. The latter provided for access to a solicitor (although it was frequently ignored). The former provided, *inter alia*, for the issuing of cautions when a person was charged (not necessarily when he was arrested) and for the exclusion in evidence of statements and confessions which were not 'voluntary' (see below). Under PACE, those rules were replaced by new rules contained either in the Act itself or in Codes of Practice C or E. The interviewing rules form the most detailed and complex part of the whole scheme.

It might be expected that the distribution of the provisions governing the interviewing scheme would give some recognition to theoretical differences in status between PACE, the Codes, the Notes for Guidance and Home Office circulars, the most fundamental provisions being contained in the Act and so on. In fact, this is not the case: although the Act contains the right to legal advice, the other important features of the interviewing scheme, including the right to silence,[369] are governed by non-statutory

---

368 Eg, Home Office Circular 89/1978, Appendices A and B.
369 As contained in the caution: Code C, para 10.4.

provisions. Just as it cannot be assumed that Code provisions are less weighty than statutory ones, equally the Notes for Guidance and even the circulars[370] do not invariably contain less crucial provisions than the Codes. In other words, the distribution of provisions between the four tiers does not follow a consistent pattern: the source of a provision may possibly have an effect on the likelihood that it will be complied with, but does not necessarily say much about its significance.

The most significant safeguards available for interviews include contemporaneous noting down of the interview or tape recording, the ability to verify and sign the notes of the interview as a correct record, the legal advice provisions and, where appropriate, the presence of an adult. One of the most important issues in relation to these safeguards and reflected in the 1991 (and, to an extent, the 1995) revision of Code C, is the question when they come into play. There may be a number of stages in a particular investigation beginning with first contact between police and suspect and perhaps ending with the charge. At various points the safeguards mentioned have to come into play and two factors can be identified which decide which safeguards should be in place at a particular time. First, it must be asked whether an exchange between police and suspect can be termed an interview and secondly, whether it took place inside the police station or was lawfully conducted outside it.

Interviews and non-interviews[371]

The correct interpretation of the term 'interview' under the original Code C scheme was highly significant because the relevant safeguards were unavailable unless an exchange[372] between police officer and suspect was designated an interview. The term therefore tended to be given a wide interpretation[373] and eventually the definition given to it by the Court of Appeal in *Matthews*[374] – 'any discussion or talk between suspect and police officer' – brought within its ambit many exchanges far removed from formal interviews. It also covered many interviewees, as it spoke in terms of 'suspects' not arrestees. However, it was qualified by the ruling in *Scott*[375] that unsolicited admissions cannot amount to 'interviews' and by the ruling in *Marsh*[376] to the same effect as regards 'genuine requests' from the police for information. In *Marsh*, police officers investigating a burglary suddenly came across wraps of papers and asked the appellant about them; the questions and answers were admissible although no caution had been given because until that point, the officers had had no reason to suspect her of any drug-related offence. The

---

370 Eg, a provision in the 1991 circular required that where a suspect had changed his mind after requesting legal advice, a note should be made in the custody record of the reason for the change. The provision was presumably included with a view to discouraging police officers from providing misleading information which might induce the suspect to forgo legal advice.

371 See further Fenwick, H, 'Confessions, recording rules and miscarriages of justice' [1993] Crim LR 174–84.

372 'Exchange' will be used throughout this section to denote any verbal interaction between suspect and police officer, including unsolicited admissions.

373 The Court of Appeal in *Absolam* (1989) 88 Cr App R 332 defined it as 'a series of questions directed by the police to a suspect with a view to obtaining admissions'. This definition was quite wide in that it obviously included informal questioning.

374 [1990] Cr App R 43; [1990] Crim LR 190, CA, transcript from LEXIS.

375 [1991] Crim LR 56, CA. See also *Younis* [1990] Crim LR 425, CA.

376 [1991] Crim LR 455.

ruling in *Marsh* bears some resemblance to that in *Maguire*[377] which pre-dated *Matthews*. It was determined that questioning an arrestee near the scene of the crime apparently in order to elicit an innocent explanation did not constitute an interview. Thus, the original interpretation of an interview created some leeway – but not much – for gathering (or apparently gathering) admissions in informal situations before any safeguards were in place.

In one respect, distinguishing between interviews and non-interviews will not be as crucial under the current scheme as it was previously: under para 11.13 as revised, any comments relevant to the offence made by a suspected person outside the context of an interview must be accurately recorded[378] and then verified and signed by the suspect. However, making such a distinction will still be highly significant, because it remains the first step towards bringing the other safeguards into play.

A definition of the term 'interview' is now contained in para 11.1A Code C which reads:

> An interview is the questioning of a person regarding his involvement or suspected involvement in a criminal offence or offences which by virtue of Para 10.1 of Code C is required to be carried out under caution.

Paragraph 10.1 reads:

> A person whom there are grounds to suspect of an offence must be cautioned before any questions about it (or further questions if it is his answers to previous questions which provide the grounds for suspicion) are put to him regarding his involvement or suspected involvement in that offence if his answers or his silence (ie failure or refusal to answer a question or to answer satisfactorily) may be given in evidence to a court in a prosecution. He therefore need not be cautioned if questions are put to him for other purposes, for example, solely to establish his identity or his ownership of any vehicle or to obtain any information in accordance with any relevant statutory requirement ... or in furtherance of the proper and effective conduct of a search.

It may be noted that the list of examples of instances under para 10.1 in which no caution would be necessary is not exhaustive. No such definition appeared in the original Code, but Note 12A read: 'The purpose of any interview is to obtain from the person concerned his explanation of the facts and not necessarily to obtain an admission.' The new definition obviously differs from this considerably and differs even more from the definition of an interview contained in *Matthews*.[379] It echoes the rulings of the Court of Appeal in *Maguire*[380] and *Marsh*[381] in attempting to draw a distinction between questioning a person regarding suspected involvement in an offence and questioning for other purposes. It appears that cautioning would not be required if the information obtained is in fact relevant to the offence, but the questioning was not directed towards

---

377 (1990) 90 Cr App R 115; [1989] Crim LR 815, CA.

378 It may be noted that the weight actually given to this provision may depend on the question of whether its breach may be described as substantial and significant (see below, p 882); in this respect it is disturbing to note a first instance decision in which it was found that it should not be so described: *Oransaye* [1993] Crim LR 772.

379 [1990] Crim LR 190.

380 (1990) 90 Cr App R 115; [1989] Crim LR 815.

381 [1991] Crim LR 455.

uncovering such information. Such an interpretation would be in conformity with the ruling in *Marsh* that the level of suspicion excited in police officers present at the scene determines when an exchange becomes an interview. This approach is readily justifiable. However, para 11.1A combined with para 10.1 does not make it sufficiently clear that where an explanation of the facts does relate to suspected involvement in an offence and is either perceived to do so by the officer concerned or would be by the ordinary reasonable officer,[382] an interview will take place.

Thus, para 11.1A might on occasion act as an invitation to police officers to play down the level of suspicion excited by the circumstances in order to demonstrate that no interview took place. Such tactics might amount to a self-fulfilling prophecy in the sense that the officer concerned would have an interest in viewing the exchange as a non-interview requiring only accurate rather than contemporaneous recording; such recording would create more scope for giving the exchanges the character of a non-interview and it would therefore appear for future purposes that a non-interview did indeed take place. The only person able to impede this process would be the suspect, who must be asked to verify and sign the record of the exchanges; it is unlikely, however, that he would appreciate the implications of what had occurred.

The para 11.1A test must be qualified by the ruling of the Court of Appeal in *Weekes*.[383] Once an exchange becomes an interview, that fact will have a retrospective effect on earlier exchanges; if safeguards applicable to an interview were not available in respect of such exchanges, they will be excluded from evidence. It will not be possible to sever them from the 'interview'. This ruling seems to be in conflict with *Marsh*. However, as the *Weekes* ruling concerned a juvenile, it may be confined to such instances.

Where the level of suspicion clearly falls within para 10.1 as, of course, it will do after arrest, the use of the term 'questioning' in para 11.1A nevertheless impliedly excludes instances where nothing definable as questioning has taken place. This is the correct interpretation where the police have apparently merely recorded what was said, according to the Court of Appeal in *Menard*.[384] Paragraph 11.1A may also exclude chats or discussions between suspect and police officer or statements or commands which happen to elicit an incriminating response.[385] This interpretation seems to lead to a conflict between para 11.1A and the ruling from *Matthews*[386] which could be resolved by arguing that rulings of the Court of Appeal will prevail over a provision contained only in a Code provision.[387] This would be the more satisfactory result, as more likely to curtail opportunities for 'verballing' (concocting admissions). However, a possible response might be that the definition from *Matthews* is now enshrined in para 11.13 and is not

---

382 This qualification must be introduced to take account of the situation which arose in *Sparks* [1991] Crim LR 128; the officer who questioned the appellant apparently did not recognise the significance of the admissions made and therefore did not consider it necessary to caution him.

383 [1993] Crim LR 222; (1992) *The Times*, 15 May, CA.

384 [1995] Cr App R 306.

385 See *Absolam* (1989) 88 Cr App R 332.

386 If statements or commands eliciting a response from the suspect could be said to fall outside the *Matthews* ([1990] Crim LR 190) definition of an interview, which is unlikely, they could still constitute an interview according to the ruling in *Absolam, ibid*.

387 The Codes of Practice brought in by a resolution of both Houses of Parliament do not have statutory authority. It has, however, been held by the Court of Appeal that they can prevail over rules derived from case law (*McCay* [1990] Crim LR 338) although commentators have thought that the Court of Appeal was mistaken in this view (Birch, D [1990] Crim LR 340).

therefore inconsistent with para 11.1A. In other words, the *Matthews* definition applies to most exchanges between suspect and police officer, but para 11.1A applies to certain particularly important ones labelled 'interviews'. This interpretation is to an extent supported by the wording of para 11.13: 'a written record shall also be made of any comments made by a suspected person, including unsolicited comments which are outside the context of an interview but which might be relevant to the offence ...', thus implying that comments relevant to the offence other than unsolicited comments will not invariably be part of an interview. It also receives some support from the ruling in *Williams*,[388] which seems to have accepted impliedly that 'social visits' by police to suspects in the cells involving conversations relevant to the offence in question do not constitute interviews, although they are to be discouraged. This interpretation would mean that a number of exchanges which would previously have been interviews will no longer be so labelled and this is especially of concern owing to evidence that police officers tend to favour the informal chat in the police station.[389]

The improvement in the position of some suspects should not be allowed to obscure the fact that certain safeguards may now be triggered off only in a confined group of situations. Whether this will be the effect of para 11.1A is still unclear, but in *Cox*,[390] the Court of Appeal adopted what might be termed a 'purposive approach' to Note 11A (which previously contained the definition of an interview, under the 1991 revision) in finding that the intention of the 1991 revision was to increase rather than decrease protection for suspects and therefore, Note 11A should be interpreted in the light of previous decisions such as *Matthews* which broadened the definition of an interview. This was followed in *Oransaye*,[391] which suggested that the emphasis should not be placed on the form of the exchange – on whether or not questions were asked – but on whether what was said went to 'the heart of the matter'. If so, the exchange should be termed an interview.[392]

Interviews inside and outside the police station

Once an exchange could be called an interview, the safeguards applying to it under the original provisions differed quite markedly depending on where it took place. Those available *inside* the police station included contemporaneous recording[393] or tape recording,[394] the ability to read over, verify and sign the notes of the interview as a correct record,[395] notification of legal advice,[396] the right to have advice before

---

388 (1992) *The Times*, 6 February, CA.

389 See Holdaway, S, *Inside the British Police*, 1985; Sanders [1990] Crim LR 494, referring to his research on access to legal advice in police stations (research undertaken by Sanders, Bridges, Mulvaney and Crozier, entitled *Advice and Assistance at Police Stations*, November 1989) found that such practices were still continuing post-PACE.

390 [1993] Crim LR 382; see also *Goddard* [1994] Crim LR 46.

391 [1993] Crim LR 772.

392 For discussion of the meaning of 'interview' see Field, 13(2) LS 254.

393 Original para 11.3 provided that if the interview took place in the police station or at other premises, 'the record must be made during the course of the interview unless in the investigating officer's view this would not be practicable or would interfere with the conduct of the interview'.

394 Under original para 11.3.

395 Under Code E, para 3.

396 Under original para 12.12.

questioning[397] and, where appropriate, the presence of an adult.[398] If the interview took place on 'other premises', the same safeguards would apply apart from the requirements to *inform*[399] of the right to legal advice and to allow the suspect to verify and sign the record of the interview.

In the street, however, it was only necessary to ensure that an accurate record of the interview was made[400] and, where appropriate, an adult was present.[401] Thus originally, a minimum level of protection only was available creating scope for impropriety, including fabrication of confessions. In particular, it meant that only the experienced suspect interviewed outside the police station would be aware of the right to legal advice. Thus, however widely the term 'interview' was interpreted, it was of little use to suspects who made (or allegedly made) admissions outside the police station.

The 1991 revision reduced the significance of this factor to some extent. Provision for giving the suspect the record of the interview to verify and sign was moved out of para 12, applying only to interviews in the police station and into para 11,[402] which is headed 'Interviews general',[403] although this change was made less significant by the provisions of para 11.13. The verifying and signing rules were supplemented in 1995 by the requirement, imposed, however, only in a Note for Guidance, Note 11D, that the suspect should declare in his or her own hand on the interview record that it is correct. Such a provision clearly has more value than the requirement only to obtain a signature. Under para 11.5, the interview must be recorded contemporaneously wherever it takes place, unless this would not be practicable.

However, the unseasoned suspect interviewed outside the police station will still be unaware of the right to legal advice[4404] and it is also at present unlikely that the interview would be tape recorded: Code E does not envisage tape recording taking place anywhere but inside the police station.[405] In some circumstances suspects will not, however, be disadvantaged by these differences, thanks to the provisions of para 11.1, introduced by the 1991 revision, which reads:

---

397 Under para 3.1.

398 The Court of Appeal in *Absolam* (1989) 88 Cr App R 332 determined that no questioning could take place inside the police station before the suspect had been notified of the right to legal advice; answers allegedly made to questions put before such notification were thereby rendered inadmissible.

399 Under original para 13.

400 Section 58, governing the right of access to legal advice, is expressed to apply to persons in police detention but para 3.1, governing the right to be notified of the s 58 entitlement was (and is) expressed to apply only to those in the police station. However, volunteers under caution in the police station or on other premises had the right to be informed of the entitlement to legal advice under original para 10.2.

401 Original para 13 did not state expressly that an adult must be present during any interview whether conducted in or out of the police station when a juvenile was interviewed. However, this could be implied; the ruling in *Fogah* [1989] Crim LR 141 confirmed that this was the correct interpretation.

402 Paragraph 11.10.

403 The Court of Appeal determined in *Brezenau and Francis* [1989] Crim LR 650 that these provisions could only apply inside the police station; departure from the clear words of para 12 was not warranted.

404 This is governed by para 3.1, which is expressed to apply only to persons in the police station.

405 Code E, para 3.1 states: '... tape recording shall be used at police stations for any interview ...' Some police forces have experimented with hand held tape recorders used outside the police station, but at present this is by no means common practice.

> Following a decision to arrest a suspect he must not be interviewed about the relevant offence except at a police station [except in certain instances specified in 11.1(a), (b) and (c) which call for urgent interviewing]. For the definition of an interview see Note 11A.

Paragraph 11.1 could merely have read: 'A suspect must not be interviewed about the relevant offence except at a police station …'. Clearly, it was designed to allow some interviewing outside the police station owing to its requirement of a higher level of suspicion than that denoted by para 11.1A and para 10.1. It implies that a police officer should categorise someone either as possibly involved in an offence or as on the verge of arrest; so long as the first category is applicable, questioning can continue. This category was presumably intended to include persons under caution, because a caution must be given 'when there are grounds to suspect (him) of an offence'.[406] Obviously, these categories will tend to merge into each other. However, it will be difficult to be certain in retrospect as to which applied, although the police may find it difficult where there are very strong grounds for suspicion to support a claim that interviewing could continue because the decision to arrest had not been taken. It is clear that the problems associated with exchanges between suspect and officer still remain and it is evident that a significant number of suspects are still interviewed outside the police station.[407] The Runciman Royal Commission proposed that admissions made outside the police station should be seen as needing some form of corroboration such as their acceptance by the suspect on tape at the police station,[408] and this was implemented under the 1995 revision in para 11.2A. However, crucially, para 11.2A does not provide that admissions or silences made outside the police station will be inadmissible if *not* accepted on tape by the suspect at the police station. Therefore, presumably, if no breaches of Code C have occurred, they would be admissible even though uncorroborated, subject to the possibility of excluding them under ss 76 or 78 of PACE, as discussed in Chapter 14.

Original para 10.2 provided that a volunteer who was questioned under caution on 'other premises' had to be told of his right to legal advice. This placed such persons in a better position than arrestees and, therefore, tended to be evaded by bringing forward the moment of arrest. Current para 10.2 removes the special requirement for volunteers. However, in removing one loophole, another has been created: volunteers under caution outside the police station are disadvantaged because they can be questioned without notification of the right to legal advice, whereas once the decision to arrest has been made, a suspect should not normally be questioned before arrival at the police station, where he will be informed of the right. In other words, in the context of the current provision under para 11.1, the old requirement under para 10.2 would have had some value; had it been retained and extended to all volunteers under caution, it would have removed some of the incentive which now exists to delay, or apparently delay, the decision to arrest in order to interview outside the police station. Clearly, this would have been a radical move, but it might have been welcome as harmonising the position of such suspects with that of arrestees.

---

406 Paragraph 10.1.
407 Brown, Ellis and Larcombe, Home Office Research Study No 129. The study showed that questioning and/or unsolicited comments occurred in 24% of cases. Questioning occurred in 10% of cases.
408 Royal Commission Report 1993, Proposal 40.

Even more significantly, since suspects not at the police station can be interviewed, without having had an opportunity to consult a solicitor, they are not protected by the provision of s 34(2A) of the CJPOA: adverse inferences could be drawn if they remain silent. Further, s 34(2A) does not affect the position of suspects who make admissions despite not having had that opportunity.

Where the level of suspicion would obviously justify an arrest, a police officer who is eager to keep a suspect out of the police station for the time being might be able to invoke one of the more broadly worded exceptions allowing urgent interviewing in order to avert certain specified risks. The first exception under para 11.1(a), allowing interviewing to take place at once where delay might lead to interference with evidence, could be interpreted very broadly and could apply whenever there was some likelihood that evidence connected with any offence but not immediately obtainable was in existence. Even if there were no others involved in the offence who had not been apprehended, it could be argued that the evidence was at risk from the moment of arrest because news of the arrest might become known to persons with a motive for concealing it. This argument could also apply to the exception under (c) with the proviso that it will apply to a narrower range of offences. Once the arrest has occurred, s 30(1) of PACE provides that the suspect must be taken to the police station by the constable as soon as practicable. Under s 30(1)), the police can delay doing so if the suspect is needed elsewhere to carry out investigations which it is reasonable to carry out immediately. Thus, further leeway for informal interviewing *after* arrest is created.

Once the suspect is inside the police station under arrest or under caution,[409] any interview[410] (using this term to connote an exchange which falls within para 11.1A) should be tape recorded, but there are exceptions in respect of terrorist suspects, which are considered below.

Varying levels of protection for exchanges

It is now possible to identify the points at which the safeguards will be brought to bear and it is apparent that there are four levels of protection available:

(1) Inside or outside the police station, if the exchange cannot be (or at times is not) labelled an interview, even though it may be relevant to the offence, it seems that the level of protection provided by para 11.13 only will apply. This will be the case even where the suspect is an arrestee or a volunteer under caution.

(2) If an interview takes place outside the police station and falls outside the para 11.1 prohibition or within the leeway created by s 30(1), the verifying and recording provisions under paras 11.10 and 11.5 will apply with the proviso that contemporaneous recording is likely to be viewed as impracticable.[411] What is impracticable does not connote something that is extremely difficult, but must involve

---

409 Under para 3.4 of Code E, once a volunteer becomes a suspect (ie, at the point when he should be cautioned) the rest of the interview should be tape recorded.

410 Under para 3.1(a), an interview with a person suspected of an offence triable only summarily need not be taped.

411 The mere fact that an interview is conducted in the street may not be enough to support an assertion that it could not be contemporaneously recorded. This seems to follow from the decision in *Fogah* [1989] Crim LR 141.

more than mere inconvenience.[412] Where appropriate, an adult must be present.[413] Notification of the right of access to legal advice will not occur, although adverse inferences could be drawn if the suspect remains silent.

(3) Inside the police station, if the person in question is an arrestee or a volunteer under caution[414] and the exchange is an interview, all the available safeguards, including access to legal advice and tape recording, will apply.[415]

(4) If the conditions under (3) are satisfied but the person is suspected of involvement in terrorism under para 3.2 (or falls within one of the other exemptions from tape recording),[416] all the available safeguards except tape recording will apply.

Thus, wide but uncertain scope still remains for interviewing outside the police station and for gathering admissions outside the context of an interview. The main objection to this scheme, apart from its complexity,[417] is that the degree of protection available is too dependent on factors irrelevant to the level of suspicion in question. It may be pure chance, or something more sinister, which dictates whether a volunteer under caution is interviewed inside or outside the police station or whether or not an exchange with an arrestee can successfully be characterised or disguised as a non-interview. Bearing in mind that unreliable confessions may be most likely to emerge from informal exchanges, it is argued that the mechanisms triggering off the main safeguards – para 11.1A and para 11.1 – are deficient both in creating large areas of uncertainty as to the level of protection called for at various points and in allowing the minimal level of protection under para 11.13 to operate in too many contexts.

Conclusions

Street interviewing remains at quite a high level,[418] while the key due process safeguards of access to legal advice and audio recording continue to be reserved for formal interviews within the police station. The caution which, as suggested below, serves both crime control and due process purposes, can be, and in most instances should be, used outside the police station, with the result that the suspect is warned of the dangers of

---

412 *Parchment* [1989] Crim LR 290. Note-taking while the suspect was dressing and showing the officers round his flat was held to be impracticable.

413 Paragraph 11.14.

414 Under para 3.15, which largely reproduces original para 3.9, volunteers under caution have the right to be told that they may obtain legal advice. The other important Code C safeguards are contained in paras 11 and 12 and apply to arrestees and volunteers under caution. Under Code E, tape recording must be used for interviews with persons under caution in the police station (E 3.1(a)).

415 Unless under Code E, para 3.3, it would not be reasonably practicable to tape the interview owing to failure of the recording equipment or non-availability of an interview room or recorder. Note 3K of Code E provides that if necessary, an officer must be able to justify the decision not to delay the interview.

416 See fn 415, above.

417 The need to adopt a commonsense approach to the rules was expressed in *Marsh* [1991] Crim LR 455 by Bingham LJ in relation to the original scheme. However, the current scheme does not lend itself readily to a simple interpretation. See especially the comments of McCullough J in *Cox* [1993] Crim LR 382 regarding Note 11A.

418 See Brown, Ellis and Larcombe, *op cit*, fn 283; the study showed that questioning or unsolicited comment occurred outside the station in 24% of cases. The Runciman Royal Commission found that around 10% of interviews took place outside the police station: RCCJ Report, Cm 2263, 1993; see Sanders and Young, *op cit*, fn 1, 2000, pp 272–73A.

failing to speak before the key safeguards can be in place. Due process protection outside the police station is minimal; it consists only of contemporaneous note-taking under caution if an interview is occurring or accurate non-contemporaneous note-taking if the exchange is not an interview. Relevant non-interview exchanges with juveniles and mentally disordered persons may be admissible in evidence even though no adult is present.

Not only, therefore, is due process virtually abandoned in relation to out of police station exchanges and interviews, they may also have a structural formative influence on formal interviews and ultimately on the outcome of the process,[419] thereby undermining the protection available for such interviews. Suspects may feel, rightly or wrongly, that they have already prejudiced their position too far during informal exchanges to attempt to retrieve it in a formal taped interview; therefore, any confession made in such an interview – or any ill-considered silence – may not be truly voluntary. Thus, it is extremely important to determine how far the scheme leaves scope for exchanges to occur before the police station is reached.

From both a due process and a crime control perspective, it would not be appropriate to address the leeway in the scheme for informal interviewing by requiring that, where sufficient suspicion is present, suspects should always be arrested and taken to the police station before any exchange occurs. In crime control terms, this might not represent an efficient use of resources since some unnecessary arrests would be made. In due process terms, there are some disadvantages in police station interviewing: the element of detention is coercive and the fact of detention may lead suspects to make admissions in order to leave it. Rather, the due process 'deficit' in street exchanges may be addressed, to an extent, by applying stronger safeguards to such interviewing[420] and, as discussed in Chapter 14, by giving careful consideration, under Art 6, to the admission of such exchanges as evidence.

Interviewing techniques and recording methods

Audio recording

Section 60 of PACE allowed for the issuing of a Code of Practice in connection with tape recording of interviews, and this was accomplished by means of Code of Practice E. Once the suspect is inside the police station under arrest or under caution,[421] any interview (that is, an exchange which falls within para 11.1A of Code C) with a person who has been cautioned in respect of an indictable or 'either way' offence[422] should be audio recorded under Code of Practice E. Initial resistance by the police gave way to a recognition of the advantages of audio recording, which seems to be generally

---

419 See *James* [1996] Crim LR 650.

420 Using hand-held tape recorders and notifying the suspect of the right of access to legal advice as part of the caution.

421 Under para 3.4 of Code E (1999 version), once a volunteer becomes a suspect (ie, at the point when he should be cautioned) the rest of the interview should be tape recorded.

422 Under para 3.1(a), an interview with a person suspected of an offence triable only summarily need not be audio taped, although under Note 3A it can be recorded at police discretion.

accepted[423] as reflecting a truer picture of an interview than note-taking[424] and, thanks to recent developments, the jury are in one sense even *better* placed than they would have been had they been present at the interview because they may be allowed to take the tape recordings into the jury room[425] to replay as necessary.[4426]

However, exchanges may occur between formal interviews, when the tape is switched off, which affect the formal interview and although they should be recorded in writing under para 11.13, the record may not cover everything that was said and the facts recorded by the police officers may be disputed by the suspects. In other words, leeway for falsely imputing admissions to the suspect is created.[427]

Audio recording was not initially used in terrorist cases, under Code E, para 3.2, or in cases of espionage under s 1 of the Official Secrets Act 1989. This provision was clarified under Note for Guidance 3G of Code E; interviews with those suspected of terrorism solely connected with the affairs of the UK or any part of the UK other than Northern Ireland should be tape recorded. A written contemporaneous record could still be made of interviews which fell within Code E, para 3.2. This exemption was included because it was feared that the contents of tapes might become available to terrorist organisations. The Home Office reviewed it in 1990,[428] and although it did not introduce mandatory audio recording, police in Britain undertook it in terrorist cases on a voluntary basis. Since, under s 1 of the TA, terrorism is defined much more widely to include those covered by Note G, and the problem of Irish terrorism has diminished, the obvious step is to make audio recording of interviews with terrorist suspects mandatory. Under the original version of the Bill, this was accomplished by Sched 7, para 9 of the TA, which provided for the audio recording of any interview by a constable of a person detained under s 41 and Sched 7 of the TA, once a new Code of Practice had been introduced. This step would not have changed current practice, apart from that in Northern Ireland, but it would have afforded formal recognition to this due process safeguard. The current position is left unclear, since audio recording is to be dealt with by a Code of Practice to be issued by the Secretary of State and different provision may be made for different parts of the UK.[429]

---

423 See Wills, Mcleod and Nash, *The Tape recording of Police Interviews with Suspects*, 2nd Interim Report, Home Office Research Study No 97, 1988. The study found that police officers and prosecutors generally welcomed taping, since it is a faster recording method and renders them less vulnerable to allegations of 'verballing'.

424 Research conducted by Baldwin and Bedward of the Institute of Judicial Administration, University of Birmingham, on summaries made of tape recorded interviews found that the summaries were often of a very poor quality and presented a distorted picture of what occurred during the interview. However, they also found that the police were aware of this problem and were beginning to address it. See [1991] Crim LR 671.

425 *Emmerson* [1991] Crim LR 194. In *Riaz and Burke* [1991] Crim LR 366, the Court of Appeal held (in instances where the jury had not already heard the tapes) that better practice would be to reassemble the court and play the tapes in open court.

426 This permission was expressed to extend only to those parts of the tapes which had been heard in open court; other material would have to be edited out.

427 See *Dunn* (1990) 91 Cr App Rep 237.

428 HC Deb Vol 168 Col 273, 1 March 1990.

429 Schedule 8, para 3(1) and (7) .

Video recording

The recording of police interviews is one of the most rapidly developing areas of policing. The possibility that the introduction of tape recording,[430] replacing contemporaneous note-taking,[431] would eventually be overtaken by video taping has been under consideration for some time.[432] Video taping of police interviews was until recently at the experimental stage and the Home Office made it clear in 1991 that it supported its introduction[433] as a step in the direction of preventing miscarriages of justice. Section 60 of PACE has now been amended by s 76 of the CJP 2001 to insert s 60A, which provides the Secretary of State with the power to issue a new Code of Practice for the 'visual recording of interviews'. Commentators have given video taped interviews a cautious welcome;[434] criticism has largely been directed towards the difficulty of ensuring that they are not subverted by 'informal' contacts between police and suspect,[435] rather than at the quality of the recordings.[436] Arguably, such difficulties are endemic in the interviewing scheme as currently conceived, regardless of the recording technique used.

Interviewing techniques

There seems to be a tendency in some quarters to see developments in recording techniques as going a long way towards solving the problem of unreliable confessions.[437] However, there is a danger that other relevant issues will be obscured. It is important not to overemphasise the value of recording techniques at the expense of provisions which may have a more direct effect on their reliability. This danger was perhaps most readily apparent in the juxtaposition in the remit of the Royal Commission on Criminal

---

430 Governed by Code of Practice E, which came into force on 29 July 1988.

431 Originally governed by Code C, para 11.3 and under revised Code C by para 11.5. Tape recording has not entirely replaced contemporaneous note-taking, first because it does not apply to all interviews (see Code E, para 3) and secondly, because contemporaneous note-taking applies to interviews outside the police station where practicable, whereas tape recording is at present only required inside it (Code E, para 3.1).

432 Video taping of interviews as opposed to audio taping was one of the possibilities considered by the Royal Commission on Criminal Procedure chaired by Lord Runciman. See (1991) 141 NLJ 1512 for a brief interim report by John Baldwin of a study of video taping experiments currently taking place in four police stations. For some time, the police have been able to video tape a confession if they first obtained the consent of the accused: *Li Shu-Ling* [1989] Crim LR 58, PC. The Runciman Royal Commission proposed that further research into the use of video taping for interviews should be carried out (Proposal 70). However, the Home Office issued a circular on video recording of interviews which advised against moving quickly to introduce video recording owing to the cost of so doing (Circular 6/1993).

433 In response to a request from Sir John Farr MP for video taping of all police interviews in order to prevent miscarriages of justice, John Patten, then Secretary of State for the Home Office, indicated that this course would be considered after the results of a pilot project conducted for the Association of Chief Police Officers in conjunction with the Home Office were known. HC Deb Vol 200 Col 391, 5 December 1991.

434 See, eg, Barnes, M, 'One experience of video recorded interviews' [1993] Crim LR 444.

435 See McConville, M, 'Video taping interrogations: police behaviour on and off camera' [1992] Crim LR 532.

436 However, quality has been questioned: see John Baldwin's interim report of experiments with video taping of interviews, which found that there were fairly serious or very serious problems with video taping in over 20% of the recordings. These included poor picture or sound quality or camera malfunction. *Op cit*, fn 432.

437 When Kenneth Baker, the then Home Secretary, announced the inception of the Royal Commission on Criminal Procedure, he suggested that recent improvements in the provision for recording of police interviews would prevent miscarriages of justice in future: HC Deb Vol 187 Col 1109, 14 March 1991.

Procedure of the possibility of introducing video taping with that of abolishing the right to silence.[438] In this connection, it is instructive to compare the enthusiasm for video taping of interviews[439] with the decision to abolish the right to silence.[440] Probably video taping is to be welcomed, but arguably its value should not be over-stressed. Video taping might faithfully reflect the interview during which a confession was made,[441] but fail to affect the pressure likely to make it unreliable flowing from the suspect's perception that he must speak. The fact that it was video taped might give the confession a spurious credibility. This is not an argument against video taping in general, but against its use as part of the justification for failing to reverse the modification of the right to silence. It might be argued that unreliable confessions would be almost eliminated by the use of such advanced recording techniques, thereby providing a justification for increasing the pressure on the suspect to speak.

Improvement in the recording provisions is not aimed directly at promoting the reliability of a confession, but at allowing a court to consider an accurate record of it and to assess what occurred when it was made. There is clearly a difference between the reliability of admissions and the reliability of the *record* of them.[442] In contrast to the success of the scheme in this direction, there has been little development in the area of provisions able to *affect* what occurred; PACE does not attempt to regulate the conduct of the interview except in so far as such regulation can be implied from the provision of s 76 that confessions obtained by oppression[443] or in circumstances likely to render them unreliable will be inadmissible. Code C of PACE forbids oppressive interviewing in para 11.3[444] and gives some very general guidance as to interviewing mentally disordered or handicapped suspects in Code C, Note 11B, which is largely repeated in Note E3. Obviously, the provisions governing detention and the physical comfort of the detainee[445] have relevance in this context; they provide the setting for the interrogation and remove from the situation some of the reasons why a suspect might make an

---

438 In announcing the Royal Commission (see fn 437, above) the Home Secretary stated that part of its remit was to consider 'the extent to which the courts might draw proper inferences from any failure (on the part of the suspect) to take advantage of opportunities to state his position', at Col 1115. On 5 December 1991, John Patten, then Secretary of State for the Home Office, made it clear that the Royal Commission would be considering video taping of police interviews: *op cit*, fn 433.

439 See fns 432 and 433, above; see also Campbell, 'Videos of interviews "would help police"' (1991) *The Guardian*, 9 December.

440 The Home Office set up a working group in 1989 to consider the right to silence: see fn 302, above, after the right had already been modified in Northern Ireland by the Criminal Evidence (Northern Ireland) Order 1988. The group's recommendations assumed that abolition was necessary. For criticism see Greer, S (1990) 53 MLR 709 and Zuckerman [1989] Crim LR 855. Kenneth Baker signalled that interest in this possibility was still very much alive when announcing the remit of the Royal Commission on Criminal Procedure: *op cit*, fn 25. The Home Secretary announced in October 1993 that the right to silence would be abolished and this was brought about under the Criminal Justice and Public Order Act 1994, ss 34, 36 and 37.

441 But see John Baldwin's findings, *op cit*, fn 432.

442 See the discussion of *Paris* (1993) 97 CR App R 99 in Chapter 14, p 876.

443 Misleading statements made during an interview distorting the state of the evidence against the defendant or hectoring and bullying may well lead to exclusion of any confession obtained under either s 76 or s 78. See *Mason* [1987] Crim LR 119; [1987] 3 All ER 481, CA; *Beales* [1991] Crim LR 118; *Blake* [1991] Crim LR 119; *Heron* (1993) unreported, discussed in Chapter 14.

444 Code C, para 11.3 provides: 'No police officer may try to obtain answers to questions or to elicit a statement by the use of oppression.'

445 Paragraphs 8 and 9 of Code C; para 12.4 regulates the physical conditions in the interview room.

unreliable confession. But, once their limits have been set, they cannot influence what occurs next and it seems that the use of intimidation, haranguing and indirect threats is still quite common, especially in interviews with juveniles.[446] The Runciman Royal Commission, which reported on 6 June 1993, proposed that the role of the appropriate adult should be reviewed[447] and that officers should receive training in the role a solicitor would be expected to play,[4448] but did not make general proposals as to outlawing or regulating use of certain interviewing techniques.[449] Such proposals would be particularly relevant after the evidence of use of bullying techniques in interrogations which arose from the post-PACE case of *Paris, Abdullah and Miller* (the Cardiff Three).[450] In fact, such techniques may be in the process of being replaced by a more subtle 'investigative approach',[451] but this is no substitute for specific guidance under Code C as to improper techniques.

The right to silence

Introduction

There is general academic agreement that, as Sanders and Young have put it, 'it is over the right of silence that due process and crime control principles clash most fundamentally'.[452] The right to silence, in the sense of the immunity of an accused person from having adverse inferences drawn from failure to answer questions during police questioning, is central to the due process model. In contrast, adherence to crime control principles logically demands not only that such inferences should be drawn, but that in some or all circumstances, refusal to answer police questions should be an offence in itself, on the ground that innocent persons would not thereby be disadvantaged and the burden on the prosecution would be eased.

Within the due process camp, retention of the right to silence has been advocated on the grounds of its value in protecting suspects and also on the basis that it symbolises the presumption of innocence. One group of abolitionists departs from a classic crime control stance in arguing for an 'exchange' or trade-off between the PACE suspects' rights and the right to silence.[453] Since the inception of PACE, which adopted the due process stance,[454] there has been a clear movement towards the crime control position, on the basis of exchanging enhanced suspects' rights for curtailment of the right to silence. The

---

446 See Evans, 'The Conduct of Police Interviews with Juveniles', Home Office Research Study No 8, 1993. See (1994) 144 NLJ 120 and (1994) 144 NLJ 203 for criticism of a variety of interview techniques.

447 Proposal 72.

448 Proposal 64.

449 See Baldwin (1993) 143 NLJ 1194 for criticism of the failure of the Royal Commission in this respect. See also Reiner [1993] Crim LR 808.

450 (1993) 97 Cr App R 99.

451 Baldwin notes ((1993) 143 NLJ 1195 and 1197) that 1993 training manuals for police interviewers advocate this approach. It is advocated in the Interviewer's Rule Book.

452 *Criminal Justice*, 1st edn, 1994, p 191.

453 See Greer, *op cit*, fn 440.

454 The only recognition given to this right in PACE was in Code C, in the wording of the caution, para 10.4.

influence of the HRA on the position now reached in relation to the right is complex and is considered in a separate section, below.[455]

The right to silence was abrogated in 1988 in Northern Ireland in terms of allowing adverse inferences to be drawn from silence at trial.[456] But, post-PACE, the right was retained for most suspects, including terrorist suspects, in England and Wales until it was curtailed or undermined, although not abolished, under ss 34, 36 and 37 of the CJPOA 1994. The right, in the sense of an immunity from criminal sanctions due to a refusal to answer questions under suspicion, still exists as far as the majority of suspects are concerned.[457]

The majority of the Runciman Royal Commission agreed with the Phillips Commission in recommending that the right to silence should be retained, although it considered that provision to deal with so called 'ambush' defences (defences sprung on the prosecution at the last minute by a defendant who has hitherto remained silent as to his or her defence) should be introduced.[458] The Commission's recommendation was based not on a 'symbolic' but an 'instrumental retentionist' approach;[459] it arose from a concern that otherwise, a risk of miscarriages of justice might arise.[460] Given that the Commission was convened in the wake of a number of miscarriages of justice, it might have been expected that the Government would give these findings some weight.

The Home Secretary, however, took what could be termed an exchange abolitionist approach[461] – suspects have greater rights than they did in pre-PACE days and therefore do not need the right to silence. Since curtailment of the right was unlikely to have any effect at all on the crime rate, it seems most likely that it was undertaken not in order to gain genuine crime control advantage, but in order to give the impression that such advantage might be gained. The conviction rate was unaffected since the change had an impact only on the small number of criminals who are detected and who would otherwise have remained silent. While it may have had some influence on decisions to plead guilty, its main effect has probably been on that tiny percentage of cases which come to court[462] in which the defendant has remained silent and has pleaded not guilty. The academic consensus is that the advantages in terms of crime control are very doubtful, whereas the risk of miscarriages of justice has been increased.[463] At the same time it was acknowledged, prior to curtailment, that 'the reality of the right to silence is

---

455 See pp 854–57.

456 Criminal Evidence (Northern Ireland) Order SI 1988/1987 NI 20 1988.

457 See below p 858 for a number of statutory provisions which penalise silence.

458 RCCJ Report p 84, para 2. The proposal found effect in the Criminal Procedure and Investigations Act 1996, which imposes a duty of defence disclosure in most Crown Court cases. Michael Zander, a member of the RCCJ, considered that such disclosure would undermine the presumption of innocence (Zander, RCCJ Report, *A Note of Dissent*, p 22, paras 8 and 11). It may be found that the provisions of the 1996 Act are not fully in compliance with Art 6(2) of the Convention which guarantees the presumption of innocence. See below, pp 901–02.

459 See Greer, *op cit*, fn 440.

460 Runciman, RCCJ Report, p 55.

461 Greer, op cit, fn 440, p 719.

462 Over 90% of defendants to be tried in magistrates' courts plead guilty; for Crown Court defendants the figure is 65%. See further Sanders and Young, *op cit*, fn 1, 2000, Chapter 7.

463 See Zander, *op cit*, fn 1, pp 303–23; Fenwick, *op cit*, fn 308; Jackson, *op cit*, fn 308; Pattenden [1995] Crim LR 602–11.

much closer [in practice] to the crime control model than it might first appear',[464] partly due to informal inference drawing by juries and magistrates.[465]

Thus, it is fair to say that prior to the CJPOA changes, the right to silence did not necessarily have a significant impact on the conduct of the interview or ensure that a suspect had a bulwark against giving in to pressure to speak. In fact, few suspects refused to answer questions[466] and, as discussed above, silence is not routinely advised by solicitors. One of the key reasons for retaining the right to silence is that the suspect may be under stress and unable to assess the situation clearly; he or she may have a number of reasons for reluctance to speak, including fear of incriminating another and uncertainty as to the legal significance of various facts. It may also be argued that the right should be reinstated in full in order to guard against the possibility that the suspect will concoct a confession in order to escape the pressure of the interrogation. A juvenile suspect in the *Silcott* case,[467] questioned about the murder of police officer Blakelock by a riotous mob, made up a detailed confession based on suggestions put to him by police officers, although it was later found that he could not have been present at the scene. This suspect made the confession despite his right to exercise silence, suggesting that the right to silence alone will not benefit such suggestible detainees. However, as argued above, the right to silence in conjunction with advice from an experienced solicitor would seem to provide a surer safeguard against false confessions than either silence or legal advice alone. In other words, the pressure on the suspect in police interviews was already high and did not appear to be compensated for by other factors such as tape recording and access to legal advice. Thus, the large body of writing on the right to silence generally came down on the side of its retention.[468]

Drawing adverse inferences from silence

Section 34(1) of the CJPOA 1994 provides: 'where ... evidence is given that the accused ... (a) on being questioned under caution by a constable trying to discover whether or by whom the offence had been committed, failed to mention any fact relied on in his defence ... or (b) on being charged ... or on officially being informed that he might be prosecuted ... failed to mention any such fact, being a fact which in the circumstances existing at the time the accused could reasonably have been expected to mention when so questioned, charged or informed ... sub-ss(2) below applies'. Under s 34(2)(d), the court or jury 'in determining whether the accused is guilty of the offence charged may draw such inferences as appear proper'. The difference between sub-ss (1)(a) and (1)(b) is of interest. It is notable that sub-ss(1)(b) makes no mention of cautioning or of questioning. It implies that an inference of guilt may be drawn from the failure of the accused to volunteer information. Since it is not confined to the point at which the suspect is charged, it could,

---

464 Sanders and Young, *op cit*, fn 1, 1994, p 193.

465 Zander and Henderson, *Crown Court Study*, RCCJ Research Study No 19, 1993.

466 See Leng, *The Right to Silence in Police Interrogation*, Home Office Research Study No 10, 1993. Only 4.5% of suspects exercised their right to silence.

467 (1991) *The Times*, 9 December.

468 See *Report of the Home Office Working Group on the Right to Silence*, 1989 (in favour of modification of the right). For criticism of the report, see Zuckerman, *op cit*, fn 440. For review of the debate see Greer , *op cit*, fn 440; Coldrey (1991) 20 Anglo-Am L Rev 27. In favour of modification of the right see Williams (1987) 137 NLJ 1107; editorial (1988) Police Review, 29 April.

theoretically, apply at any point during the arrest and detention. Sections 36 and 37 of the 1994 Act provide that adverse inferences may be drawn from a failure to account for possession of substances or objects, or presence at a particular place. Under all these provisions, there is still a right to remain silent so long as the accused is prepared to take the risk that so doing may have an adverse impact on his defence, if the case comes to trial. The caution under para 10.4 Code C was accordingly revised in 1995 to read: 'You do not have to say anything, but it may harm your defence if you do not mention when questioned something which you later rely on in court. Anything you do say may be given in evidence.' In contrast to the old caution, the new one has a dual and contradictory effect: it can no longer be seen simply as a safeguard; it must also be seen as part of the coerciveness inherent in the police interviewing and detention powers. Further special cautions were adopted under para 10.5A and B of Code C in order to take account, respectively, of the provisions of ss 36 and 37 of the 1994 Act.

As indicated above, s 34(2A) was inserted into the CJPOA by s 58 of the Youth Justice and Criminal Evidence Act 1999. The amendments provide that if the defendant was at an authorised place of detention and had not had an opportunity of consulting a solicitor at the time of the failure to mention the fact in question, inferences cannot be drawn. This is a very significant change to the interviewing scheme, which was introduced as a direct response to the findings of the European Court of Human Rights in *Murray v UK*.[469] The implications of this change are considered in relation to the custodial right of access to legal advice, below.[470]

It is implicit in all three sections that inferences may only be drawn if a sound explanation for the silence is not put forward. Although staying silent carries risks, it may be, depending on the circumstances, less risky than making ill-considered admissions since silence, unlike admissions, must be corroborated.[471] However, as the Runciman Commission pointed out, the caution is likely to put most pressure on vulnerable suspects.[472] The suspect most likely to be unable to evaluate the riskiness of silence is precisely the type of suspect who needs the protection originally afforded by the right. Vulnerable persons interviewed outside the police station may be confused by the caution and without the benefit of legal advice may be pressurised into making inaccurate and ill-considered admissions and perhaps into mentioning matters they have not been questioned about.[473] Thus, although it may be argued that in a number of circumstances it may not be 'proper' for a jury to be directed to draw adverse inferences from silence or that it was not reasonable in the circumstances existing at the time to expect the suspect to speak, this will not benefit the suspect who does in fact speak in response to the current caution. Ironically, it is probably the seasoned criminal who understands the operation of s 34 of the CJPOA and may be able to predict that silence may not be a more risky strategy than it was previously, who has not been disadvantaged by the change.[474]

---

469 (1996) 22 EHRR 29. See below, pp 855–56.

470 See pp 856–57.

471 CJPOA 1994, s 38(3).

472 RCCJ Report, para 4.50.

473 It was found in *Nicholson* [1999] Crim LR 61 that if the police have not asked about facts, adverse inferences should not be drawn against the defendant if he does not state those facts.

474 See Moston, S and Williamson, T, 'The extent of silence in police stations', in Greer and Morgan (eds), *The Right to Silence Debate*, 1990.

The emerging case law on s 34 of the CJPOA suggests that the courts are not on the whole taking a restrictive approach, although it has been made clear that where the prosecution do not seek to rely on a silence, the judge should direct the jury positively not to draw inferences.[475] In *Murray v DPP*,[476] which was decided on the 1988 Northern Ireland Order, but is clearly applicable to s 34, the House of Lords found that silence allows the drawing not only of specific inferences from failure to mention particular facts, but also of the inference that the defendant is guilty. The decision in *Condron and Another*[477] also favoured a broad application of the provisions. The appellants were to be questioned by police at the police station on suspicion of being involved in the supply and possession of heroin. The police surgeon found that they were fit to be interviewed, but their solicitor considered that they were unfit, since they were suffering withdrawal symptoms, and so advised them not to answer any questions. They relied on that advice during the interview and remained silent. At trial, the defence involved reliance on facts which had not been mentioned in the course of the interview and thus potentially fell within s 34 of the CJPOA. The judge held a *voir dire* and rejected argument under s 78 that the no comment interview should be excluded as unfair because they were unfit to be interviewed. Argument that it would be improper to allow an inference to be drawn under s 34 because in making no comment they had only followed the bona fide advice of their solicitor was also rejected. The interviews were admitted and the prosecution then argued that they could reasonably have been expected to mention at interview the facts they now relied on in their defence; they were cross-examined on their failure to mention such facts. They gave the explanation that they had relied on the solicitor's advice. In summing up, the judge directed the jury that they must determine whether any adverse inferences should be drawn from the failure of the defendants to mention the facts in question during the police interview. The judge did not explain that the inferences could only be drawn if, despite the explanation, the jury concluded that the silence could only sensibly be attributed to the defendants having no satisfactory explanation to give. Thus, it is possible that the jury may have drawn adverse inferences despite accepting the defendants' explanations.

The appellants were convicted and argued on appeal that the jury should not have been directed that they could draw adverse inferences from the refusal to answer questions since they had followed the advice of their solicitor in so refusing. The Court of Appeal took into account an earlier case, *Cowan and Others*,[478] which concerned the position of defendants failing to testify in court under s 35, and applied the principles enunciated to police questioning. The principles were as follows. A jury cannot infer guilt from silence alone (s 38(3)), so that the jury should only consider drawing inferences if a *prima facie* case to answer has been made out by the prosecution. Also, the burden of proof remains throughout on the prosecution to prove their case; in effect, a silence will be only one factor which can be used to make out the case. Inferences can be drawn if the only sensible explanation of silence was that the suspect had no explanation, or none that would stand up to cross-examination. The judge's direction was criticised in that it did

---

475 *R v McGarry* [1998] 3 All ER 805.
476 [1994] 1 WLR 1.
477 [1997] 1 Cr App R 185.
478 [1996] QB 373; [1995] 4 All ER 939.

not make this clear. The court then considered the procedure to be followed in relation to s 34, where silence is on legal advice. The jury may draw an adverse inference from the failure unless the accused gives the reason for the advice being given. The reason for the advice is legally privileged, since it is part of a communication between solicitor and client, but once the client gives evidence of the nature of the advice, that will probably amount to a waiver of privilege so that the solicitor and/or client can then be asked about the reasons for the advice in court. The court found that if an accused gives as the reason for not answering questions in a police interview that he has been advised not to do so, this assertion without more will not amount to a sufficient reason for not mentioning relevant matters which may later be relied on in defence. The convictions were upheld on the basis of the overwhelming evidence of drug supply, despite the flaw in the summing up.

It was made clear in *Bowden*[479] that explaining the grounds for the advice will amount to a waiver of privilege. Therefore, the prosecution can cross-examine the advisor on what was said to the suspect with a view to discovering discrepancies between the grounds put forward at trial and those discussed in the police station. The effect of these two decisions is to place the defendant and advisor in an invidious position. The advisor may be reluctant to advise silence even where there seem to be good reasons for doing so.[480] If the advisor advises silence, it may well appear to the defendant that that in itself is a sound reason for remaining silent. But that reason will not be accepted by a court. The advisor can either refuse to waive legal privilege and accept that adverse inferences will be drawn from the silence, or he can waive it and hope that the reasons given for the advice will be accepted in order to discourage the drawing of inferences. There may also be other confidential matters which the advisor does not wish to be asked about. It has been pointed out that solicitors may breach their professional Code of Conduct if they act for a client when they may be a material witness in the court case.[481] But if there is an arguably sound reason for advising silence, the jury should be directed, following the findings of the Court of Appeal in *Condron*, that if they view the reason as sound, they should not draw adverse inferences.

In *Argent*,[482] the Court of Appeal found that when considering whether, in the circumstances existing at the time, the defendant could reasonably have been expected to mention the fact he now relies on, the court should take into account matters such as the defendant's age, health, experience, mental capacity, sobriety, tiredness, personality and legal advice. It is a matter for the jury to resolve whether, bearing these matters in mind, the defendant could have been expected to mention the fact in question, although the judge may give them guidance. Any restrictive impact of these findings is doubtful; in *R v Friend*[483] adverse inferences were drawn under s 35 against a defendant aged 14, with a mental age of 9.

---

479 (1999) *The Times*, 25 February.

480 See, as to the difficulties facing advisors, Cape, E, 'Advising on silence' (1999) LAG, 14 June.

481 Tregilgas-Davey, M, 'Adverse inferences and the no-comment interview' [1997] 141 SJ 500. *The Guide to the Professional Conduct of Solicitors*, 1996, para 21.12.

482 [1997] 2 Cr App R 27; (1996) *The Times*, 19 December. See Broome, K, 'An inference of guilt' (1997) 141 SJ 202.

483 [1997] 1 WLR 1433.

Under the Blair Government, the CJPOA provisions were retained and further provisions curtailing the right to silence in terrorist cases were introduced. Section 1 of the Criminal Justice (Terrorism and Conspiracy) Act 1998 inserted a new provision, s 2A, into the PTA, making further provision for the drawing of inferences from the suspect's silence. These provisions were reproduced in s 109 of the TA 2000, but applied only to Northern Ireland.[484] Section 109(2) of the 2000 Act (previously s 2A(5) of the PTA as inserted) provides that an inference that the suspect belongs to a proscribed organisation may be drawn at trial if the accused fails to mention, on being questioned by a constable under caution and before charge, a fact which is material to the offence and which he could reasonably be expected to mention. Under s 109(3) (previously s 2A(6)), an inference of guilt may be drawn at trial if the accused failed to mention, on being charged or informed by a constable that he might be prosecuted for the offence under s 11, a fact which is material to the offence and which he could reasonably be expected to mention. Theoretically, s 109(3) could apply even before a caution has been given, so long as the provisions in s 109 allowing access to legal advice are satisfied. Presumably, however, if no caution had been given, it could not be said that the accused could reasonably have been expected to mention the information in question.

These provisions are additional to the provision under the CJPOA for drawing adverse inferences from silence and it may be noted that s 34 of the CJPOA is narrower than s 109, since it refers only to matters which are later relied on *in defence*. As indicated, case law on s 34 of the CJPOA already establishes that inferences may only be drawn if a sound explanation for silence is not put forward. Applying this to s 109, it would appear that it cannot be inferred that the reason for silence was the need to concoct a false explanation of factors suggesting membership of a proscribed organisation if the real and innocent reason for silence is put forward. Following *Argent*, the jury should only consider drawing inferences under s 34 if there is a *prima facie* case to answer made out by the prosecution. Under s 38(4), the conviction cannot be based on silence alone; the position is the same under the TA, under s 109(4). Under s 109, the burden of proof remains throughout on the prosecution to prove its case; in effect, a silence will be only one factor which can be used to make out the case. However, s 109 leaves open the possibility that the conviction or committal for trial could be based on an inference of guilt from silence together with the opinion of a police officer (admissible in evidence under s 108). Moreover, the possibility may also be open of combining inferences drawn in reliance on ss 34, 35, 36 or 37 of the CJPOA with an inference *or* an opinion under ss 108 and 109 of the TA. Therefore, for example, the possibility is not ruled out of combining silence when questioned as to presence at a particular place (which is, or is near to, a meeting place of a proscribed organisation) with silence on being informed of the possibility of prosecution under s 109.

Penalising silence

Prior to the inception of the CJPOA, the right to silence was abolished in certain specific circumstances under a number of provisions which made failing to answer questions an offence. The provisions included: s 172 of the Road Traffic Act 1988; s 2 of the Criminal

---

484 Under the transitional provisions of the TA 2000, Part VII, ss 108 and 109.

Justice Act 1987; ss 177 and 178 of the Financial Services Act 1986; ss 236 and 433 of the Insolvency Act 1986; s 437 of the Companies Act 1985; the Banking Act 1987 and the Friendly Societies Act 1992. These provisions, apart from s 172 of the RTA, were amended in 1999, as explained below. Thus, in a number of instances, the right to silence had already been eroded until it reached the point where it could be said to have virtually disappeared.[485] If, for example, inquiries were made into a failed business, its owner could receive a 's 2 notice' from the Serious Fraud Office issued under the Criminal Justice Act 1987 which meant that a criminal offence would be committed if he or she did not attend for interview and answer questions (*Director of the Serious Fraud Office ex p Smith*).[486] Also, if the company was being investigated, a refusal to answer questions under s 432(2) of the Companies Act 1985 attracted criminal liability.

While the Conservative governments of 1989–97 were responsible for the shift towards the crime control position which occurred under these provisions and under the CJPOA 1994, the Blair Government was responsible for a further marked shift in that direction. The TA 2000 abolished the right to silence – in the sense of making it an offence to refuse to answer questions in defined circumstances – at certain points in the investigation of such cases. The Government raised the possibility of creating such an offence in the Consultation Paper on Terrorism in 1998. It noted that the recent Criminal Justice (Terrorism and Conspiracy) Act 1998 'extends the provisions by allowing inferences to be drawn in connection with membership of a specified proscribed organisation; but even there that is insufficient in itself to secure a conviction'. The intention was to take this provision further by creating an additional offence of refusing to answer questions, modelled on the power currently given to investigators in a range of cases such as serious fraud investigations, and customs and licensing inquiries. The Government recognised that there were what it termed 'serious ECHR constraints on this option'[487] and that, in order to circumvent these constraints, the resulting evidence, whether answers or silence, could not be used in a subsequent case against the individual concerned. The Government clearly had in mind the case of *Saunders v UK*,[488] which is considered below.

These considerations led to the inclusion of paras 13, 14 and 16 in Sched 5 of the 2000 Act. The provisions relate to terrorism generally, not merely to proscription, but their relatively limited nature indicates the influence the Convention is already having in tempering legislation in attempts to ensure that it is compatible with the Convention. The Government clearly did not wish to risk the political embarrassment which it would have incurred had it included provision allowing coerced statements to be included as evidence, provision which would have necessitated issuing with the Act a statement of incompatibility under s 19 of the HRA.

The provisions as they stand are, however, of doubtful compatibility. The requirements of para 13 represent a further infringement of the rights of the suspect, albeit of a relatively limited nature and subject to judicial authorisation. Under para 13 of

---

485 See *Re London United Investments* [1992] 2 All ER 842; *Ex p Nadir* (1990) *The Times*, 5 November; *Bishopsgate Investment Management Ltd v Maxwell* [1992] 2 All ER 856, CA.

486 [1993] AC 1; [1992] 3 WLR 66; see also *AT & T Istel Ltd v Tulley* [1992] 3 All ER 523, HL.

487 *Op cit*, fn 6, para 14.3.

488 (1997) 23 EHRR 313. See below, p 855.

Sched 5: 'a constable may apply to a circuit judge for an order ... requiring any person specified in the order to provide an explanation of any material – (a) seized in pursuance of a warrant under paragraph 1 or 11, or (b) produced or made available to a constable under paragraph 5'. This does not affect material protected by legal privilege, but under para 13(3) a lawyer may be required to provide the name and address of her client. Under para 13(5), para 10 applies to such orders: they will have effect as if they were orders of the Crown Court. Thus, a person who refused to comply could incur liability for contempt. But, any statement obtained cannot be used in evidence except on a prosecution for an offence under para 14. Paragraph 14(1) provides: 'a person commits an offence if, in purported compliance with an order under paragraph 13, he makes a statement which he knows to be false or misleading in a material particular', or recklessly makes such a statement. This offence is punishable by a maximum prison sentence of two years. Paragraph 16 is even more controversial; it provides a further possibility, untrammelled by judicial intervention, of punishing persons for failing to give explanations, or giving misleading ones. Paragraph 16(1) provides: 'if a police officer of at least the rank of superintendent has reasonable grounds for believing that the case is one of great emergency he may by a written notice signed by him require any person specified in the notice to provide an explanation of any material seized in pursuance of an order under paragraph 15.' Under para 16(3), in contrast to para 13, the suspect will commit an offence carrying a maximum prison term of six months if he fails to comply with a notice under the paragraph.

Both paras 13 and 16 allow for the admissibility of coerced statements, although in respect of the para 14 offence only. Thus, courts will have to consider whether admitting such statements in respect of that offence would be compatible with Art 6. Further, the paragraphs do not refer to silences which may be admissible in respect of other offences, as may evidence from the statement against another person. Also, the evidence from any statements made, while not directly available to the court, may nevertheless underpin the other prosecution evidence, thereby arguably undermining the right to freedom from self-incrimination (see below).[489]

The transitional provisions applying to Northern Ireland create a further erosion of the right to silence. Under s 89(2) of the TA it is an offence punishable by a fine not to stop when required to do so by an officer; it is also an offence to refuse to answer a question asked during the stop or to answer it inadequately, failing to answer 'to the best of his knowledge and ability'.

8 IDENTIFICATION OF SUSPECTS

Evidence obtained from the suspect himself or from witnesses can identify the suspect as the person who committed the offence in question, or can demonstrate that he is innocent of it. The identification procedure is largely governed by the provisions of Code D which has as its overall aim the creation of safeguards against wrongful identification, bearing in mind that mistaken identification can be a very significant cause of wrongful

---

489 See pp 854–55.

convictions.[490] It also contains provisions which are intended to safeguard vulnerable groups and to ensure that the invasion of privacy represented by some methods of identification is kept to a minimum consistent with the Code's overall aim. Many of the procedures will only take place with the suspect's consent, although if consent is not forthcoming, this may be used in evidence against him or her. In the case of a mentally handicapped or disordered person, consent given out of the presence of the 'appropriate adult' will not be treated as true consent while the consent of a juvenile alone will not be treated as valid if the adult does not also consent.[491] Identification can take place by various means which include by witness, by fingerprints and by the taking of samples from the body of the suspect.[492]

Witness identification

Methods

If identification is to be by witness, Code D, para 2.1 provides that the following methods may be used: a parade; a group identification; a video film; or a confrontation. A group identification consists of allowing the witness an opportunity of seeing the suspect in a group of people and it should, if practicable, be held in a place other than a police station (for example, in an underground station or shopping centre). The suspect will be asked to consent to a group identification, but where consent is refused, the identification officer has the discretion to proceed with a group identification if practicable. Under para 2.13, if neither a parade nor a video identification nor a group identification procedure is arranged, the suspect may be confronted by the witness and such a confrontation does not require the suspect's consent, but it may not take place if any of the other procedures are practicable.

Practicability

A parade must be used if the defendant requests it and it is practicable. A parade may also be held if the officer in charge of the investigation considers that it would be useful and the suspect consents. The aim is to use the best means of identification available; therefore, if it is impracticable to use a parade, the police may move on to a group identification; they cannot merely move straight to the last possible method – a confrontation.[493] However, there is uncertainty as to when it could legitimately be said to be impracticable to hold an identification parade. In *Ladlow, Moss, Green and Jackson*,[494] 20 suspects had been arrested and the confrontation method of identification was used, as otherwise it would allegedly have been necessary to hold 221 separate parades. Despite this, it was ruled that evidence derived from the parades would be excluded. However, in *Penny*[495] the police wrongly thought it impracticable to hold a parade, but the trial judge

---

490 The Criminal Law Revision Committee 1972 considered that wrongful identification was the greatest cause of wrongful convictions (para 196).

491 Paragraph 1.11.

492 Identification can also be by photographs under Code D, Annex D.

493 *Ladlow, Moss, Green and Jackson* [1989] Crim LR 219.

494 *Ibid.*

495 (1991) *The Times*, 17 October.

admitted the evidence and the Court of Appeal refused to interfere with the decision. It is unfortunate that the opportunity of clarifying the position was not taken when Code D was revised in 1991, especially as the uncertainty also affects the term 'practicable' used in para 2 with respect to video and group identification. However, where it is genuinely hard to assemble sufficient persons resembling the defendant to take part in the parade, owing perhaps to alienation of the particular group from the police,[496] video identification may provide a means of obtaining acceptable evidence. If group identification takes place in the street, the area in question may be relevant; if the defendant is of a certain race, a mixed race area should be chosen in order to increase the chances that someone of the same race might pass by.[497]

Safeguards

The officer in charge of the identification ('the identification officer') must not be below the rank of inspector and must not be involved with the investigation. No officer involved with the investigation of the case against the suspect may take any part in the procedures.[498] It is also important that witnesses should not be able to confer before the identification; if they do so confer, the identification may be excluded from evidence.[499]

When Code D was revised, various new safeguards for witness identification were introduced: under new para 2.15, the suspect must be reminded that free legal advice is available before taking part in the identification procedure and, under new para 2.16, the identification procedure and the consequences, if consent to taking part is not forthcoming, must be explained in a written notice which the suspect must be given reasonable time to read.

Under para 2.15, before the means of identification is arranged, the identification officer must explain a number of matters to the suspect orally and in writing: the fact that he is entitled to free legal advice and can have the advisor present; the fact that he does not have to take part in a parade or co-operate in a group identification or with the making of a video film and, if it is proposed to hold a group identification or video identification, his entitlement to a parade if this can practicably be arranged. However, he must also be told that if he does not consent to take part in a parade or co-operate in a group identification or with the making of a video film, his refusal may be given in evidence in any subsequent trial and police may proceed covertly without his consent or make other arrangements to determine whether a witness identifies him.

Identification by fingerprints or bodily samples

Under para 3 of Code D, a person over the age of 10 may be identified by fingerprints if he or she consents or without consent under ss 27 and 61 of PACE, which also allow the use of force. Section 61 was amended by s 78 of the CJP 2001 to insert s 61(3A) to allow for the re-taking of fingerprints without consent.

---

496 See *Campbell and Another* [1993] Crim LR 47, CA; the police had arranged a confrontation because they had not found sufficient Rastafarians to take part in a parade. Lack of co-operation between the police and the Rastafarian community was condemned by the Court of Appeal.

497 *Jamel* [1993] Crim LR 52.

498 *Gall* (1990) 90 Cr App R 64; *Jones* [1992] Crim LR 365.

499 *Finley* [1993] Crim LR 50, CA.

A person may also be identified by bodily samples, swabs and impressions, but only if the offence is a serious arrestable offence, the officer has reasonable grounds to believe that such an impression or sample will tend to confirm or disprove the suspect's involvement in the offence and with the suspect's written consent.[500] However, the Royal Commission proposed that these provisions should also apply in the case of all offences.[501] A juvenile has the right to have the appropriate adult present unless he or she requests otherwise in the presence of the adult.[502] The suspect will be warned that a refusal may be treated, in any proceedings against him, as corroborating relevant prosecution evidence.[503] The warning is set out in Code D, Note 5A. He must also be reminded of his entitlement to have free legal advice and the reminder must be noted in the custody record. Intimate samples[504] may only be taken under ss 62 and 63 PACE, as amended by s 80 Criminal Justice and Police Act (2001) (CJP) by a registered medical or dental practitioner or registered nurse, whereas non-intimate samples[505] may be taken by a police officer. They may be taken without consent if an officer of the rank of inspector or above has reasonable grounds for suspecting that the offence in connection with which the suspect is detained is a serious arrestable offence and for believing that the sample will tend to confirm or disprove his involvement in it.

9 IMPACT OF THE HRA

Introduction

As Chapter 14 will demonstrate, arrest and detention and, where relevant, treatment within that period may be considered under Art 6, whether or not a breach of Art 5 or any other Article is established.[506] Under Art 6, the Court has developed the concept of the fairness of the trial 'as a whole', allowing for consideration of custodial treatment in a broad sense. In *Saidi v France*[507] the Court said that its role was to determine 'whether the proceedings in their entirety ... were fair'.[508] In *Barbéra, Messegué and Jabardo*,[509] the trial taken as a whole could not be said to be fair. This was partly due to features of the treatment of the defendants pre-trial, taken cumulatively. They were held for a substantial period of time incommunicado and when they confessed to the police they did not have legal assistance. Nevertheless, their confessions were significant in later questioning by examining judges. The unfair pre-trial treatment clearly had a tendency to render the trial unfair, although it is improbable that such a tendency would have been found without

---

500 Under para 5.

501 Proposal 19.

502 Paragraph 5.12.

503 PACE 1984, s 62(10).

504 'Blood, semen or any other tissue fluid, urine, saliva or pubic hair or a swab taken from a person's body orifice' (PACE, s 65).

505 Including hair other than pubic hair or a sample taken from a nail or from under a nail or a skin impression (PACE, s 65, as amended by CJPOA 1994, s 80(5)(b)).

506 See pp 901–03.

507 (1994) 17 EHRR 251.

508 Paragraph 43.

509 A 14 6(2) (1989).

the unfairness at the hearing itself.[510] Nevertheless, the findings in *Barbéra* are significant, since they emphasise the need to consider the whole criminal process, including any custodial period, in determining fairness. It might be appropriate where the pre-trial custodial treatment, including the manner of questioning, had a cumulatively harsh effect, to stay the prosecution for abuse of process. In other circumstances, exclusion of evidence obtained during or as a result of a course of harsh or adverse treatment might be appropriate in order to satisfy Art 6. Civil actions may be brought against the police, including claims for damages in respect of breaches of the rights. These possibilities are discussed further in Chapter 14.[511]

Article 3 treatment in detention

Article 3 treatment may arise in respect of a number of aspects of detention. Failure to obtain medical treatment after a forcible arrest was found to infringe Art 3 in *Hurtado v Switzerland*.[512] In the *Greek* case,[513] the conditions of detention were found to amount to inhuman treatment owing to inadequate food, sleeping arrangements, heating and sanitary facilities combined with overcrowding and inadequate provision for external contacts. It was also found that conduct which grossly humiliates may amount to degrading treatment contrary to Art 3. Such treatment may include racially discriminatory and, probably, sexually discriminatory arrests and treatment in detention;[514] it might be found to fall more readily within Art 3 in a non-terrorist context.[515] Where discrimination is a factor, Art 14 would also be engaged.

The substantive criminal law would not be applicable in certain of these instances of Art 3 treatment. Art 3, therefore, provides guarantees against various forms of maltreatment in police detention, which are not currently duplicated in domestic statutory provisions, although the guarantees are limited since Art 3 demands that such maltreatment should be of a high level of severity. In so far as certain conditions of detention are relevant, domestic law currently reflects its guarantees in Code C alone. For example, the conduct of intimate searches is governed by s 55 of PACE, but its provisions are fleshed out in Annex A of Code C. Strip searches, as opposed to intimate searches, are covered only by part B of Annex A to Code C. The use of force to conduct them is authorised by s 117 of PACE.[516] The provisions governing the conditions of detention mentioned in the *Greek* case arise only in Code C, paras 8 and 9. Provisions in Code C, para 8 regarding the use of restraints, including handcuffs, in cells might be viewed as

---

510 There were 'unexpected changes' in the membership of the court, the hearing was brief; most importantly, there was a failure to adduce and discuss evidence orally in the accused's presence.

511 See pp 909–14.

512 A 280-A (1994) Com Rep.

513 12 YB 1 (1969) Com Rep.

514 *East African Asians* cases (1973) 3 EHRR 76. See also *Lustig-Prean and Beckett v UK* (1999) 29 EHRR 548, and *Smith and Grady v UK* (2000) 29 EHRR 493, which suggested that grossly humiliating, intrusive interrogation could, if of an extreme and prolonged nature, amount to a breach of Art 3 (discussed below, pp 853–54).

515 In *McFeeley v UK* (1980) 20 DR 44, intimate body searches in a terrorist context did not give rise to a breach of Art 3, but it has been suggested (see Harris, O'Boyle and Warbrick, *op cit*, fn 229, p 83) that this finding might not apply in a non-terrorist context.

516 Clearly, criminal law applicable to indecent assault would not be applicable where the search was properly authorised.

intended to ensure that Art 3 is not infringed. Bearing in mind the quasi-legal status of the Codes, such provisions might be afforded, indirectly, a higher status because of their role in relation to Art 3, under s 6 of the HRA.[517]

Assuming that the treatment arguably falls within Art 3, the burden of proof on the detainee is affected, following the decisions in *Tomasi v France*[518] and *Aksoy v Turkey*.[519] Once the detainee has shown that he was free of the injury or harm in question before arrest, the State will then bear the burden of providing a plausible explanation for it which is consistent with the evidence. If it does not do so, the domestic court should assume that the injuries in question were caused in the manner alleged by the complainant. It may be noted in this context that allegations of ill-treatment in police custody have recently raised grave concerns[520] which may now be addressed by the use of Art 3 in actions directly against the police under s 7(1)(a) of the HRA.

Oppressive and intrusive questioning

As indicated above, PACE and the TA make no provisions as regards interviewing techniques, and Code C of PACE hardly touches on this matter, except to forbid oppressive interviewing in para 11.3 and to give some very general guidance as to interviewing mentally disordered or handicapped suspects. No such provisions are duplicated in PACE itself although, as indicated above, oppression is defined under s 76(8) as including Art 3 treatment, and under s 76(2)(a) a confession obtained by oppression is subject to an absolute exclusionary rule. On its face, the Convention does not bear upon this issue, except in so far as Art 3 covers oppressive interviewing. But, as indicated above, the general requirements of fairness under Art 6 will allow consideration of interviewing techniques as part of the fairness of the criminal process as a whole. Arguments could also be raised regarding unethical, intrusive interviewing techniques under Arts 3, 8 and 14.

Articles 3, 8 and 14 might be engaged where the interrogation itself was of an especially intrusive nature, particularly where it could also be said to be discriminatory. Grossly humiliating treatment may breach Art 3, and this might include very intrusive, prolonged questioning. Where such questioning was accompanied by racist, sexist[521] or homophobic abuse, a breach might be found of Art 3 read with Art 14. Article 8 could also be considered where the questioning dealt, for example, with sexual matters. These possibilities were considered in *Lustig-Prean and Beckett v UK* and *Smith and Grady v UK*[522] in the context of an investigation by service police concerning their homosexuality, but by

---

517 See above, pp 757–58.

518 A 241-A (1992).

519 (1996) 23 EHRR 553. These decisions should also be taken into account where treatment in police custody results in death, engaging Art 2. See Chapter 14, p 923.

520 See the *Report of the European Committee for the Prevention of Torture and Inhuman or Degrading Treatment or Punishment*, based on a visit carried out from 8–17 September 1999. See also the Butler Report, 1998. *Inter alia*, the Report covers the case of Derek Treadaway (pp 37–38). He alleged that he had suffered ill-treatment, possibly amounting to torture, in police custody, and successfully sought judicial review (31 July 1997) of the decision of the CPS not to prosecute the officers involved. For relevant Convention jurisprudence, see above, Chapter 2, pp 44–45.

521 *East African Asians* cases (1973) 3 EHRR 76.

522 (1999) 29 EHRR 548, and (2000) 29 EHRR 493.

analogy, the findings of the court would appear to be applicable to police interviewing in certain circumstances. The Court considered the investigations, and in particular the interviews of the applicants, to have been exceptionally intrusive and to constitute especially grave interferences with their private lives, which could not be justified within the meaning of Art 8(2). It considered that treatment grounded upon a predisposed homophobic bias, as in the present case, could, in principle, fall within the scope of Art 3 and that the investigations were undoubtedly distressing and humiliating, but that in the circumstances of the case, the treatment did not reach the minimum level of severity which would bring it within the scope of Art 3. Having found a breach of Art 8, the court did not go on to consider Art 14 as a separate issue.

The failure to regulate interviewing techniques is a significant gap in the PACE and TA schemes, bearing in mind the established likelihood of a link between coercive questioning and unreliable confessions.[523] Although there has been a movement from such questioning towards so called ethical techniques,[524] it cannot be assumed that interviewing will not at times verge on the oppressive and abusive. Use of Art 8 as in *Lustig-Prean* may encourage a movement towards ethical interviewing and provide an avenue by which to challenge humiliating, discriminatory questioning under the HRA. As discussed above, the Race Relations Act 1976, after amendment in 2000, provides a means of redress in respect of racial abuse or racially discriminatory treatment by police, which will also cover interviewing. But, this possibility does not exist in respect of other forms of discriminatory treatment, including treatment which is gender-related or homophobic.[525]

Freedom from self-incrimination and the presumption of innocence

Article 6 of the Convention contrasts with Art 14(3) of the International Covenant on Civil and Political Rights and with Art 34(1) of the South African Bill of Rights in that it does not expressly forbid using compulsion to obtain confessions.[526] The expectation under Art 6(2) that the State bears the burden of establishing guilt impliedly requires that the accused should not be expected to provide involuntary assistance by way of a confession. Thus, the presumption of innocence under Art 6(2) is closely linked to the right to freedom from self-incrimination which the Court has found to be covered by the right to a fair hearing under Art 6(1).[527]

Article 6(2) further impliedly requires that when carrying out their duties, members of a court should not start with the preconceived idea that the accused has committed the

---

523 See Justice, *Unreliable Evidence? Confessions and the Safety of Convictions*, 1994.

524 Home Office Central Planning and Training Unit, The Interviewer's Rule Book, 1992; Home Office Circular 7/1993 'Investigative interviewing'.

525 The Sex Discrimination Act 1975 has not been amended in the same way as the Race Relations Act (under the Race Relations (Amendment) Act 2000) and therefore will not cover the actions of public authorities except in the contexts covered by s 6 of the Act. At present, no statute forbids discriminatory treatment on grounds of sexual orientation. Bearing in mind the 'dualist' impact of international law in the UK, this means that Protocol 12 (see Chapter 2, p 85) may not provide a remedy for such treatment domestically, even if it is received into domestic law under the HRA. See further Chapter 16, p 985.

526 It may be noted that the UN Human Rights Committee has already expressed concerns regarding the compatibility of the CJPOA 1994, ss 34, 36 and 37 with Art 14(3).

527 *Funke v France* (1993) 16 EHRR 297.

offence charged; the burden of proof is on the prosecution, and any doubt should benefit the accused. These matters are at issue when silence under interrogation by law enforcement bodies is penalised by a formal penalty or by drawing adverse inferences from it. The Court has drawn a distinction between these matters, although it recognised in *Murray (John) v UK*[528] that they were not entirely distinct, since adverse inference-drawing is clearly a form of penalty; it was termed 'indirect compulsion'.

It is possible that curtailment of the right to silence under ss 34, 36 or 37 of the CJPOA 1994 may, depending on the particular circumstances of a case, lead to a breach of Art 6 on the basis that it infringes the presumption of innocence under Art 6(2) and the right to freedom from self-incrimination.[529] Consideration of the judgments in *Saunders v UK*[530] and *Murray (John) v UK* reveals that it is only where a penalty formally attaches to silence, and the interview may then be used in evidence, that a breach of Art 6 is almost bound to be established, but that where adverse inferences can be drawn from the silence at trial, a breach may be established, taking into account the question whether the suspect has had access to legal advice. *Saunders v UK* concerned the sanction for refusing to answer questions in serious fraud investigations under s 437 of the Companies Act 1985. Acting under s 437, Inspectors of the Department of Trade and Industry had interviewed Saunders regarding allegations of fraud. He was forced to answer the questions put to him and therefore lost his privilege against self-incrimination, which he argued was unfair and amounted to an abuse of process. The interviews were admitted in evidence under s 431(5) of the Companies Act and he was convicted.[531] The Strasbourg Court found that the applicant's right to freedom from self-incrimination under Art 6(1) had been infringed due to the threatened imposition of a penalty for remaining silent and the subsequent admission of the interviews into evidence. This finding was based on the special compulsive regime applicable to Department of Trade and Industry inspections, but the key issue was the use made of the material obtained in court.

The decision in *Murray (John) v UK*[532] may be contrasted with that in *Saunders* since it suggests that, depending on the circumstances of a case, Art 6 takes a different stance towards imposing a formal penalty on silence and drawing adverse inferences from it. Murray was arrested under the Prevention of Terrorism (Temporary Provisions) Act 1989 and taken to the police station. A detective superintendent, pursuant to the Northern Ireland (Emergency Provisions) Act 1987, decided to delay access to a solicitor for 48 hours. While being interviewed, Murray repeatedly stated that he had 'nothing to say'. After he had seen his solicitor, he stated that he had been advised not to answer the questions. As indicated above, the Criminal Evidence (Northern Ireland) Order 1988 enables a court in any criminal trial to exercise discretion to draw adverse inferences from an accused's failure to mention a fact during police questioning. Such inferences were drawn from Murray's silence in the police interviews once the prosecution had established a *prima facie* case against him, and he was convicted. The Strasbourg Court

---

528 (1996) 22 EHRR 29. For comment, see Munday [1996] Crim LR 370.

529 See the comments of the Court of Appeal in *Birchall* [1999] Crim LR 311; see also the study by Bucke, *op cit*, fn 302.

530 (1997) 23 EHRR 313; Appl No 19187/91, Com Rep, paras 69–75.

531 His appeal on grounds of abuse of process and on the basis that the interviews should not have been admitted into evidence under s 78 was rejected: *R v Saunders and Others* [1996] 1 Cr App R 463.

532 (1996) 22 EHRR 29.

emphasised that its decision was confined to the particular facts of the case in finding that no breach of Art 6(1) or (2) had occurred where adverse inferences had been drawn at trial from the applicant's refusal to give evidence, taking into account the degree of compulsion exerted on the applicant and the weight of the evidence against him. The Court placed emphasis on the fact that he had been able to remain silent; also, given the strength of the evidence against him, the matter of drawing inferences was one of common sense which could not be regarded as unfair.[533] But, crucially, the Court did find that Art 6(1) and (3)(c) had been breached by the denial of custodial access to a lawyer for 48 hours since it found that such access was essential where there was a likelihood that adverse inferences would be drawn from silence. In effect, therefore, the Court adopted something close to an exchange abolitionist approach.[534] The distinction it drew, impliedly, between direct and indirect compulsion flowing from the risk of adverse inference drawing and criminal penalties respectively was not explicated and rests, it is suggested, on doubtful premises.

The regime under the 1988 Order is, in essentials, the same as that under s 34 of the CJPOA, which may therefore be vulnerable to challenge under the HRA. As indicated, the findings in *Murray* were carefully confined to the particular facts of the case, and therefore must be treated with caution. But it is clear that the right to freedom from self-incrimination cannot be viewed as absolute. Drawing adverse inferences from silence in police interviewing does not necessarily breach Art 6(2), but the greater the reliance placed on such inferences at the trial, the greater the likelihood that a breach will occur. The Court said that it would be incompatible with Art 6(1) and (2) 'to base a conviction solely or mainly on the accused's silence or refusal to answer questions'. Under s 38(3) of the CJPOA, a conviction cannot be based 'solely' on silence. Art 6(1) and (2) might therefore be found to be breached in circumstances differing from those applicable in *Murray*, including those in which the evidence against the defendant was less overwhelming. A domestic judge would not satisfy Art 6 if he directed a jury that the drawing of adverse inferences could play a major part in a conviction. Further, in *Murray*, there was no jury: the case was decided by a 'Diplock' court. Therefore, the evidence was weighed up by a professional who had the expertise to determine how much weight to give to aspects of it, including the 'no comment' interviews.

Murray makes it clear that drawing adverse inferences from silence when the defendant had not had access to legal advice prior to the failure to reply to questioning will breach Art 6. As indicated above, s 58 of the Youth Justice and Criminal Evidence Act addressed that finding by inserting s 34(2A) into the CJPOA. But it need not be assumed, conversely, that Art 6 will necessarily be satisfied where a defendant has had such access prior to that point. Cases such as *Condron* or *Bowden* (above), where the defendants had had legal advice and had acted on it in remaining silent, should be considered on their particular facts, in relation to the Art 6 requirements. Such cases differ from *Murray* on the issue of the relationship between silence and legal advice. In *Condron* the defendants acted on legal advice in refusing to answer questions; in *Murray* a breach of Art 6(1) was found on the basis of inference-drawing in the absence of legal advice (not on the basis of inference-drawing *per se*). In *Condron*, the fact of having legal advice was not to the

---

533 Paragraph 54.
534 See Greer, *op cit*, fn 440.

defendants' advantage, possibly the reverse, since in a sense they may have been misled into remaining silent. It is arguable that allowing adverse inferences to be drawn in that context – where the innocent explanation for silence was that it was on legal advice – could in certain circumstances be viewed as a breach of Art 6(1). For example, this might be argued where the advisor had failed to point out that adverse inferences might be drawn despite the advice and/or where the defendant could not be expected – due to his or her low intelligence, youth or other vulnerability – to decide to speak despite the advice. To hold otherwise might be viewed as undermining the value attached in *Murray* to granting access to legal advice where adverse inferences would be drawn from silence.[535] The principle from *Murray* clearly rests impliedly on the value of such advice, which the domestic decision in *Condron* appears to undermine. The possibility, therefore, arises that even where a suspect has had access to legal advice before taking a decision to remain silent, there may be circumstances, such as those arising in *Condron*, in which the jury should be directed that no adverse inferences should be drawn, or the interview should be excluded from evidence under s 78 if Art 6 is not to be breached.

It was found at Strasbourg that the applicants in *Condron v UK*[536] had failed to receive a fair trial under Art 6 on the basis that the appeal court should not have found that the conviction was safe, despite the erroneous direction of the judge to the jury. Since the Court could not know what part the drawing of adverse inferences played in the jury's decision, it should have allowed the appeal. That decision impliedly confirms that juries should be directed that they should not draw adverse inferences where they consider that there was a sound reason for advising silence. The decision affects the role of the Court of Appeal; it does not give guidance on, *inter alia*, the question when a no comment interview, based on legal advice, should be excluded from evidence, or as to the reasons which might be viewed as sound for advising a suspect to remain silent.

At present, therefore, the circumstances in which adverse inference drawing will amount to a breach of Art 6 remain uncertain,[537] except in the instance in which access to legal advice is also denied. In that instance under s 34(2A) of the CJPOA, no inferences may be drawn from silence. It is notable that s 34(2A) does not provide that such a silence will be *inadmissible*. Informal inference drawing, which appeared to occur prior to the introduction of ss 34, 36 and 37 of the CJPOA, could therefore still occur. Further, s 34(2A) of the CJPOA does not cover the defendant who has not had legal advice but makes admissions in response to the new caution or (*prima facie*) the defendant who fails to obtain advice, although no formal denial occurs. These very significant matters are discussed further below.

As *Saunders v UK*[538] establishes, the use of formal coercion to obtain statements from persons will clearly be incompatible with Art 6 if the statement is then used against him or her in criminal proceedings. In *R v Staines; R v Morrisey*[539] the Court of Appeal refused,

---

535 It may be noted that such a finding would involve a departure from the current position under UK law as set out in *Condron* [1997] 1 Cr App R 185 and confirmed in *Bowden* (1999) *The Times*, 25 February.

536 [2001] 31 EHRR 1, Appl No 35718/97; [2000] Crim LR 679.

537 See further Birch, D, 'Suffering in silence: a cost-benefit analysis of s 34 of the CJPOA' [1999] Crim LR 769.

538 (1997) 23 EHRR 313; Appl No 19187/91, Com Rep, paras 69–75.

539 [1997] 2 Cr App R 426.

despite the judgment in *Saunders*, to overturn a conviction although the trial judge had refused to exclude evidence under s 78 of PACE obtained in a similar manner to that adopted in Saunders. In the post-HRA era, such a response would not appear to satisfy the duty of the court under s 6 of the HRA or the interpretative obligation of the judiciary under s 3. As indicated above, a large number of statutes contain provisions broadly equivalent to the provisions of the Companies Act 1985 which were at issue in *Saunders*. The Attorney General has issued guidance to prosecutors with a view to ensuring that evidence gained under a number of those provisions should not be used in criminal proceedings. This issue may not, therefore, arise at present under certain of these statutory provisions – a significant instance in which primary legislation was rendered nugatory even before the HRA was in force. This matter was placed on a statutory basis in s 59 and Sched 3 of the 1999 Act. Schedule 3 lists the statutory provisions mentioned above,[540] apart from s 172 of the Road Traffic Act 1988, and provides that the coerced statements will be inadmissible.

Nevertheless, the Government appears to envisage that certain very significant statutory provisions allowing for coercion, including a number arising under the Terrorism Act 2000, will be used in the post-HRA era. Section 172 of the Road Traffic Act 1988 makes it an offence for motorists not to tell police who was driving their vehicle at the time of an alleged offence. The coerced statement can then be used in evidence at trial for the RTA offence in question. The provision clearly contravenes the right against self-incrimination, and this was found to be the case in Scotland in *Stott v Brown*[541] during the period of time when the Convention was in force in Scotland, but not in England.[542] The defendant encountered the police officers after parking her car and was suspected of driving while intoxicated; she was asked under s 172 to reveal the name of the person driving the car at the relevant time. On pain of the penalty under s 172 she did so, revealing that she had been driving, and was convicted of driving while intoxicated, after the coerced statement was admitted into evidence. Her conviction was overturned on appeal owing to the finding that s 172 contravened Art 6. The ruling of the Edinburgh High Court is of interest since the court rendered s 172, effectively, nugatory. This stance was taken on the basis of the requirements of the Scotland Act, which differ from those of s 6 of the HRA since they do not include the possibility envisaged under s 6(2)(b) that the authority was 'acting so as to give effect to or enforce those provisions [of incompatible primary legislation]'.

As Chapter 4 explained, the ruling of the Edinburgh High Court was overturned by the Privy Council: *Brown v Stott*.[543] The Privy Council did not find it necessary to declare that s 172 is incompatible with Art 6(1) or (2). They reached the decision that the two were compatible, despite the findings in *Saunders v UK*, on the basis that the requirements of Art 6 admit of implied restriction. The restriction, Lord Hope said, must have a legitimate aim in the public interest. It was found that this was the case, bearing in mind the need to promote road safety. If so, he went on to ask, 'is there a reasonable relationship of proportionality between the means employed and the aim sought to be realised?'[544] He

---

540 See pp 846–47.
541 2000 SLT 379; see [2000] J CIV LIB 193.
542 The Convention rights were brought into force in Scotland under the Scotland Act 1998, s 57(2).
543 [2001] 2 WLR 817. See Chapter 4, pp 144–45.
544 See, above, p 144.

found that the answer to the question, in terms of limiting the right not to incriminate oneself under Art 6(1), was in the affirmative since the section demands a response to a single question, and does not allow prolonged questioning, as in *Saunders*.

The decision in *Brown* rested on the finding that coercing a statement from the defendant was not a disproportionate response to the legitimate aim of seeking to address the problem of road safety. However, it is arguable that it re-opens the whole question of the compatibility of penalising silence in other contexts. If it can be argued that the requirement of s 172 is in proportion to the problem it seeks to address, it might be argued equally that where the legitimate aim in question is even more pressing, as in the case of combating terrorism, a more intrusive provision, allowing for more prolonged questioning, could be viewed as a proportionate legislative response.

Therefore, it can no longer be said with certainty that the decision in *Saunders v UK* calls into question the provisions allowing a limited use of coerced statements in evidence in terrorist investigations under Sched 5, paras 13 and 16 of the TA. Such statements may be admitted into evidence in order to convict of the offence under para 14 of making a statement which the defendant knows to be false or misleading in a material particular, or as to which he is reckless, in purported compliance with an order under para 13. Clearly, a misleading statement might not be made but for the pressure flowing from the penalties which para 13 and, to a greater extent, para 16, carry. Nevertheless, it is now debatable whether the possibility of admitting the statement is incompatible with the right against self-incrimination.

Further, despite the evident attempt in paras 13 and 16 to achieve Convention compliance, bearing *Saunders* in mind, the possibility of incompatibility remains, taking into account the broader implications of fairness in the trial as a whole under Art 6(1). If someone other than the person who had made the coerced statement was on trial and the prosecution wished to admit the statement in evidence, argument could be raised as to the fairness of so doing, bearing in mind the fact that the statement could not be used against its maker.[545] The issue of the fairness of the trial as a whole[546] could also be raised where the statement had influenced the prosecution or enabled the police to obtain evidence, since it could be argued that the statement had had an indirect impact in undermining the right against self-incrimination. Admittedly, there are precedents in current UK law for basing a prosecution on evidence uncovered in reliance on information from statements which are themselves inadmissible.[547] However, each of those precedents will need to be tested against Art 6 standards, taking into account all the circumstances applicable in an individual case.

The further question is whether Art 6 might be breached in an instance in which a silence in response to the threat of penalties under the paragraphs in question was admitted in respect of one of the other offences under Sched 5, or indeed any other

---

545 Analogy might be drawn with *Rowe and Davis v UK* (2000) 30 EHRR 1, in which statements made by accomplices were used against the accused, although the statements had been extracted on the basis of promise of immunity from prosecution and financial reward. These matters, which did not come to light at the trial, owing to the use of PII certificates, led the Court to find that the accused had not had a fair trial, in breach of Art 6.

546 The concept of the fairness of the trial taken as a whole was developed in *Barbéra, Messegué and Jabardo*, A 14 6(2) (1989).

547 PACE 1984, s 76(4). Impliedly under the Interception of Communications Act 1985, s 9.

offence. *Brown* and *Saunders* do not expressly address the question whether the admission into evidence of a no-comment interview (as opposed to admissions) in response to formal coercion would breach Art 6. Obviously, a situation can be envisaged in which the accused might decide to risk the imposition of the penalty in question. The prosecution might then put forward the interview in evidence for the purpose of drawing adverse inferences from it. On one view, the case for drawing such inferences might be strengthened on the argument that if the accused is prepared to risk the imposition of the penalty in question, he must have something very significant to hide. But equally, it might be argued that a vulnerable defendant who did not have legal advice (as a result of factors other than its formal denial) had made no comment, perhaps due to fear of retaliation from the real perpetrator of the offence. Such situations appear to fall more within the ruling from *Murray* than within that from *Saunders*; therefore, the factors identified here as relevant to arguments based on *Murray* would be applicable.

Section 89(2) of the TA, applicable only in Northern Ireland, raises similar issues. Section 89(2) provides that it is an offence punishable by a fine to refuse to answer a question asked during a stop or to answer it inadequately, failing to answer 'to the best of his knowledge and ability'. Evidence obtained under s 89 can be used to convict of the s 89 offence itself; further, the TA does not expressly provide that it cannot be used in respect of other TA offences, although in practice it would be unlikely that it would be so used, owing to the incompatibility of so doing with Art 6(1) and (2).

It may be noted that the PACE Code C provisions, paras 10.1 and 10.5C, which envisage the possibility of coercion under the statutory provisions mentioned, and make provision for it, may also be incompatible with Art 6. Paragraph 10.1 provides that there is no need to caution if information is to be obtained under a 'relevant statutory requirement', while para 10.5C provides that the suspect should be informed of the consequences of failing to co-operate in the interview, regardless of the caution, where a statutory requirement to provide information applies and may render him liable to conviction for an offence or arrest. These provisions should therefore have been omitted or modified in the 1999 revision of the Codes. As they stand, the relevant parts of the paragraphs appear to amount to incompatible subordinate legislation which can simply be rendered invalid, if necessary, under the HRA since, although they reflect primary legislation, it cannot be said that such legislation 'prevents the removal of the incompatibility'.[548]

Custodial access to legal advice

Article 6(3)(c) provides that everyone charged with a criminal offence has the right to defend himself through legal assistance of his own choosing.[549] Access to legal advice in pre-trial questioning, as opposed to such access for the purposes of the trial, is not expressly provided for in Art 6. However, some protection for such access can be implied into Art 6(1) and 6(3)(c). Where a violation of Art 6 is claimed in respect of a lack of access to legal advice in pre-trial questioning, a breach of both paras (1) and (3) will be in question.

---

548 See HRA 1998, s 3(2)(c).
549 See Chapter 2, pp 63–64.

The judgment in *Imbrioscia v Switzerland*[550] suggests that if either the accused or his lawyer requests that the latter should be present in pre-trial questioning, this should be allowed if the answers to questions would be likely to prejudice the defence; the ruling may be applicable to police interviews. As explained above, the Court went further than this in *Murray (John) v UK*[551] in finding that Art 6(1) and (3)(c) had been breached by the denial of custodial access to a lawyer for 48 hours, since such access was essential where there was a likelihood that adverse inferences would be drawn from silence. It found that Art 6 would normally require that the accused should be allowed to benefit from the assistance of a lawyer in the initial stages of police interrogation, although that right might be subject to restrictions for good cause.

In *Averill v UK*,[552] the applicant was denied access to a solicitor during the first 24 hours of interrogation; he was then allowed to consult a solicitor, but the solicitor was not allowed to be present during subsequent interviews. The provisions governing access to a solicitor were contained in s 45 of the EPA 1991. Adverse inferences were drawn from his silence at trial under Art 3 of the Criminal Evidence (Northern Ireland) Order 1988. The Court found that no breach of Art 6(1) had occurred; he had been subject to 'indirect compulsion', but that in itself was not decisive.[553] The drawing of adverse inferences, it was found, did not render the trial unfair since the presence of incriminating fibres found on his clothing called for an explanation from him. Further, the drawing of adverse inferences was only one factor in the finding that the charges were proved. However, the Court did find a breach of Art 6(3)(c) read with Art 6(1) on the basis – which it noted in *Murray* – that, bearing in mind the scheme contained in the 1998 Order, it is of 'paramount importance for the rights of the defence that an accused has access to a lawyer at the initial stages of police interrogation'.[554] This is because, under the scheme, the accused is confronted with a dilemma from the outset. If he remains silent, adverse inferences may be drawn. If he breaks his silence, his defence may be prejudiced. In order to deal with this dilemma, legal advice is needed at the initial stages of the interrogation.

Bearing in mind the scheme under ss 34, 36 and 37 of the CJPOA, which is similar to the scheme under the 1988 Order, the findings in *Murray* and *Averill* cover most or all police interviews under caution, since once the caution has been given, it is clear that adverse inferences may be drawn from silence. Thus, a right of access to legal advice in custodial questioning may be implied into Art 6(3)(c) when read with Art 6(1) where the drawing of adverse inferences is a relevant issue.

Such a right is already catered for, under s 58 of PACE and Sched 8, para 7 of the TA, but the formal and informal loopholes in the access discussed above appear not to accord with the requirements of Art 6(3)(c) in conjunction with Art 6(1) as interpreted in *Murray* and *Averill*. Clearly, s 34(2A) of the CJPOA, which was introduced in response to *Murray*, caters for this situation, but only to an extent.

Where access to legal advice has formally been delayed, and the suspect has stayed silent, s 34(2A) will not allow the drawing of adverse inferences. In such an instance, there

---

550 (1993) 17 EHRR 441; A 275 (1993).
551 (1996) 22 EHRR 29.
552 (2001) 31 EHRR 36; (2000) *The Times*, 20 June. See also *Magee v UK* (2001) 31 EHRR 35; (2000) *The Times*, 20 June.
553 Paragraph 48.
554 Paragraph 59.

would be no need to rely on arguments raised under s 7(1)(b) of the HRA. But, where access to legal advice has formally been delayed, particularly in the case of terrorist suspects, who can be denied access for up to 48 hours, and the suspect has not stayed silent, the grounds for denial will have to be subjected to strict scrutiny in the light of the requirements of Art 6. In particular, the good cause for the delay in obtaining advice required by *Murray* may not be satisfied by the grounds for proceeding with the interview, although advice has not been obtained under Code C, para 6, which includes the vague and broad test: where 'awaiting [the arrival of the solicitor] would cause unreasonable delay to the process of the investigation'.

A further, separate issue arises in situations in which the suspect does not receive legal advice, but in which s 34(2A) would seem to allow the drawing of adverse inferences. Section 34(2A) does not apply to silences occurring in out of police station interviews (which will be prior to the point of notification of the availability of legal advice). It is suggested that the objections, based on *Murray* and *Averill*, to the drawing of adverse inferences from such silences cannot be fully met by the provision of para 11.2A of Code C to the effect that any significant silence or statement outside the police station should be put to the suspect at the beginning of an interview at the police station. In such out of station interviews, the dilemma mentioned by the Court of Human Rights arises since the suspect should be under caution and therefore formally aware of the dangers of remaining silent. Street interviews or exchanges, of necessity without advice, may have an impact on later interviews even where para 11.2A is adhered to. In the light of these comments, it is perhaps surprising that the revision of Code C in 1999 did not respond to *Murray* by modifying paras 11.1, 11.1A, 11.13 and 3.1 which provide leeway for interviews to occur outside the police station without notification that access to legal advice is available.

A further significant question is whether Art 6 might be breached where legal advice is not *formally* denied to the defendant for a period of time, as in *Murray*, although he has not in fact received advice before being interviewed. This argument might be raised where a suspect has been influenced by police ploys in failing to obtain advice (whether due to inadequacies in the informing procedure or to direct or more subtle persuasion). The admission of a subsequent interview might be viewed as affecting the fairness of the trial, following *Murray*. This argument would be strongest where other adverse factors were also present, including a confession made after 24 hours or more in detention, or where the inexperienced, young, emotionally unstable or educationally sub-normal suspect could not be expected to make his or her own assessment as to the value of having legal advice and was therefore very vulnerable to police suggestions.

If Art 6 is concerned with the objective reliability of the interview in influencing the integrity and fairness of the trial, it can be argued that, unless the defendant made a clear, positive (albeit possibly misguided) decision not to have custodial advice, the admission into evidence of an interview under caution without such advice, whatever the reason for the failure, might affect the fairness of the trial. It is unclear that the fact that a vulnerable defendant (for example, on the verge of mental handicap) had waived advice or had received brief telephone advice only, would be relevant where it could be said that the trial, objectively speaking, might be rendered unfair by the admission of the interview. Similar arguments could perhaps also be raised where the advisor attends the station but the advice obtained is clearly inadequate. When the Strasbourg Court spoke of the need for legal advice where adverse inferences were to be drawn from silence, it may be suggested that it had in mind – taking into account the general need for the rights to be genuinely efficacious, not illusory – the notion of sound, adversarial advice.

It may finally be pointed out that there seems to be no reason in principle to confine the findings in *Murray* and *Averill* to a circumstance where the defendant in fact stayed silent. Rather, as the Court implied, it may be that the suspect who fails to remain silent is most in need of legal advice.[555]

Clearly, there will be uncertainty for a time as to the extent of the application of *Murray* to police interviews without advice, but the central point is clear: under the current domestic provisions there are instances when suspects will be interviewed in the knowledge that adverse inferences may be drawn from silence, but access to legal advice will not be available, although not formally denied. As Chapter 14 will point out, the Court in *Teixeira de Castro v Portugal*[556] found that certain pre-trial procedures render a fair trial almost impossible and therefore curb the discretion of the court in its response.[557] This finding was not made in the context of custodial legal advice but, together with the findings in *Murray*, could be applied to s 78 of PACE, in support of an argument that the exclusionary discretion embodied under the section may be narrowed almost to vanishing point where no access to legal advice was made available before or during the police interview which is proffered in evidence (possibly even if the lack of access was not due to a clear breach of statutory or Code provisions), although the suspect was aware that adverse inferences might be drawn from silence.[558] There would be a strong argument that such an interview should be excluded from evidence under s 78, following *Murray*, since otherwise Art 6 would not appear to be satisfied. Failing to do so would appear to breach the duty of the judiciary under s 6 of the HRA to abide by Art 6 and would arguably also fail to render s 78 compatible with Art 6(1) and 3(c).

An argument similar to this one did not receive much encouragement in one of the early decisions on the HRA, from Scotland.[559] In *Paton v Procurator Fiscal*,[560] the appellant was to be interviewed about attempted theft and at the police station he indicated that he wanted a solicitor to be informed of his detention. When he was interviewed, his solicitor was not present and he was not told that the police had a discretion to allow his solicitor to be present during the interview if he so wished. After caution, the appellant admitted that he was trying to break into the premises in question. When the charges were recited,[561] the appellant said that he had been merely passing by when the police chased him. The appellant argued that Art 6(1) and 6(3)(c) of the Convention had been

---

555 See further on this point Bucke, *op cit*, fn 302.

556 (1998) 28 EHHR 101.

557 *Ibid*, pp 904–06.

558 Under PACE 1984, Code C, this would include all interviews since, as indicated above, under para 11.1.A the definition of an interview is an exchange regarding involvement in criminal activity which is required to be under caution.

559 By virtue of the Scotland Act 1998, s 57(2), a Scottish court is required, *inter alia*, to take into account the various rights enshrined in the Convention. At the time, the Human Rights Act itself was not fully in force in Scotland.

560 Judgment of 24 November 1999 (unreported).

561 He was charged with attempting to break into premises with intent to steal and, in the alternative, that he was found at premises without lawful authority, the inference being that he might commit theft contrary to the Civil Government (Scotland) Act 1982, s 57(1).

contravened. The court took into account the fact that the appellant had not made a request for his solicitor to be present and that neither Scottish law nor the Convention required that in all cases a detained person should be afforded the opportunity to have a solicitor present. The court found that the question whether a fair trial could be achieved depended not simply upon what happened during the preliminary investigation, but on the whole proceedings, and a number of safeguards were accorded to the accused during the investigation and the trial process; on this basis, the appeal was refused and the case was remitted to the sheriff to proceed to trial. These findings do not appear to encourage the notion that certain rights, such as access to custodial legal advice, are of especial constitutional significance; they encourage a broad brush approach which appears to assume that a breach of suspects' rights may be cured by affording other rights. However, these findings may be based on the lack of a right to have a solicitor present in interview in Scotland and, it is suggested, on a doubtful, minimalist interpretation of Art 6.

It is notable that s 109 of the TA (formerly ss 2A(4)(b) and 2A(5)(b) of the PTA) constitutes a response to the findings in *Murray* similar to that under s 58 of the 1999 Act, since consultation with a legal advisor is essential if adverse inferences are to be drawn from silence. These two instances in which Convention compliance has been ensured by Parliament might encourage the courts to consider exclusion of the interview where a suspect who had not had legal advice had remained silent, or to make a finding that no adverse inferences should be drawn from the silence. Apart from the duty of courts under s 6, a further route to such a finding would mean interpreting the term 'circumstances' in ss 34, 36 and 37 of the CJPOA strictly to include a failure to have access to legal advice. The phrase 'had not been allowed to consult a solicitor' in s 58 of the Youth Justice and Criminal Evidence Act 1999 could also be construed broadly to cover informal denials or even informal encouragement to forgo advice. This would depend on how flexible judges and magistrates are prepared to be in respect of their interpretative obligation under s 3 of the HRA.

It is clear that the courts have the opportunity, if they are prepared to take an activist line in giving a wide interpretation to *Murray*, to curb the formally allowed and informally developed police discretion in affording access to legal advice which this chapter has discussed. Eventually, Code C may have to be revised to allow for notification of advice on caution, to clarify the provisions allowing for delays in access and to require a positive decision to refuse advice. Further moves towards improving the quality of advice may have to be undertaken.

CHAPTER 14

REDRESS FOR POLICE MALPRACTICE

1 INTRODUCTION[1]

Chapter 13 was concerned with the question of the balance to be struck between the exercise of powers by the police in conducting an investigation on the one hand and safeguards for the suspect against abuse of power on the other. As we have seen, the statutory rules, including in particular those under the Police and Criminal Evidence Act 1984 (PACE), the Criminal Justice and Public Order Act 1994 (CJPOA), the Criminal Justice and Police Act 2001 (CJP) and the Terrorism Act 2000 (TA) contain, on the one hand, provisions intended to secure suspects' rights, such as s 58 of PACE and Sched 8, para 7 of the TA, while on the other they create or extend a statutory basis for the exercise of police powers, which frequently enhances those powers.[2] Thus, the rules can be viewed as reflecting two different models – those of crime control and due process – and since the approach and aims of those models is conflicting, the statutes in question and their application in practice reflect the resulting inevitable tension. This may be said even of new provisions which appear to be intended, fairly obviously, to enhance police powers, such as ss 50 and 51 of the CJP. These provisions provide, as Chapters 11 and 13 indicated, new powers of seizure during searches of people or of premises. But they are 'balanced' by the provisions of ss 52–61 which, while affording new powers of retention of property seized a clear statutory basis, also provide for notice to persons whose property has been seized, and safeguard its use by various provisions.[3] It is not suggested that the balance struck is satisfactory, but it is clear that, although these CJP provisions are very much orientated towards crime control, they are limited by provisions reflecting due process concerns.

Thus, the relevant statutory provisions declare that certain standards for the conduct of criminal and terrorist investigations must be maintained; a complex, not to say cumbersome, domestic scheme is currently in place, part of it post-dating the Human Rights Act (HRA), creating such standards. Under the European Convention on Human Rights, another scheme setting standards for criminal justice is apparent. Clearly, the two schemes are very different. Not only is the domestic scheme far more detailed, they have different starting points. One – the domestic scheme – essentially sets out police powers and then provides for restrictions on them. The other – the Convention – sets out fundamental rights and then, in the case of the right to liberty under Art 5, the guarantees

---

1 Reading: Maher, G, *A Theory of Criminal Process*, 2000; Feldman, D, *Civil Liberties and Human Rights in England and Wales*, 1st edn, 1993, Chapters 5 and 9; Sanders, A and Young, R, *Criminal Justice*, 2nd edn, 2000; McConville, M, Sanders, A and Leng, R, *The Case for the Prosecution*, 1991; Bailey, SH, Harris, DJ and Jones, BL, *Civil Liberties: Cases and Materials*, 4th edn, 1995, Chapter 2; Zander, M, *The Police and Criminal Evidence Act 1984*, 3rd edn, 1995; Lidstone, K and Palmer, C, *The Investigation of Crime*, 2nd edn, 1996; Reiner, R and Leigh, I, 'Police powers', in McCrudden, C and Chambers, G (eds), *Individual Rights and the Law in Britain*, 1994; Klug, F, Starmer, K and Weir, S, *The Three Pillars of Liberty: Political Rights and Freedoms in the UK*, 1996; Sharpe, S, *Judicial Discretion and Criminal Investigations*, 1998; Clayton, R and Tomlinson, H, *The Law of Human Rights*, 2000, Chapter 11. See also Nobles, R and Schiff, D, *Criminal Appeals and the HRA*.
2 Such as PACE 1984, s 25 and TA, s 41.
3 Including the duty to secure the property arising under s 61 by preventing, *inter alia*, copying of it.

of a fair trial under Art 6 and the right to be free of torture, inhuman or degrading treatment under Art 3, leaves them unqualified or not materially qualified. Only Art 5 could be said to create exceptions which correspond to aspects of domestic police powers. Nevertheless, it can be said at a high level of generality that both schemes set standards for administering criminal justice. As explored in Chapter 13, the standards of the domestic scheme and those recognised under the Convention are not necessarily the same. Each scheme does two things – it sets certain standards for crime control and for suspects' rights; it then provides that there should be a means of redress if the standards are breached. The domestic scheme goes on to prescribe the remedies that should then be offered. In other words, it makes – as of course it has to – substantive choices, while as far as remedies are concerned, the international scheme confines itself to a procedural account.

The HRA brings the two schemes into juxtaposition, or perhaps confrontation, and demands under s 3(1) that, in so far as the domestic scheme is statute-based, it should, if interpretation will so allow, be compatible with the requirements of the other. The HRA also demands, under s 6, that each person or body administering the domestic scheme should, unless primary legislation using very clear words provides otherwise, abide by the Convention rights. It is not enough, it is contended, if the police do not adhere to the Convention but their mistakes (unlawful actions) are then 'rectified' in court so that in their entirety the pre-trial and trial process ultimately so adheres. Each actor in it should (since all are public authorities) adhere to the Convention in their own actions and decisions. Thus, although in practice a court may use the methods available to it to seek to ensure that despite such mistakes, the proceedings as a whole comply with Art 6, a remedy should still be available in respect of the failure of the police.

It may be said, then, that the HRA provides mechanisms for asking, first, whether the standards expressed by the domestic scheme are in conformity with the Convention rights. This was the question addressed by Chapter 13. Secondly, it ensures that the question is asked whether the means of redress provided are in conformity with what the Convention demands in terms of an effective remedy. This question is addressed in this chapter. This latter question has two facets. It asks (a) if the domestic standards *themselves* are not in conformity, what can be done to rectify that by reliance on the Convention and the HRA, and (b) whether or not the standards are in conformity, if the police do not abide by the standards set out in the domestic scheme, does the Convention add anything to what can be done under the domestic provisions to provide redress? I will suggest that this latter question is the more interesting, since it is in respect of redress that the domestic scheme is the most lacking.

As this chapter will explain, there are five domestic methods of providing redress: complaints about the police; prosecutions of the police; civil actions, appeals and trial remedies; exclusion of evidence; and stays for abuse of process. However, police complaints and exclusion of evidence have not been found to provide an effective remedy for breaches of the Convention rights at Strasbourg.[4] Civil actions (outwith s 7(1)(a) of the HRA) will provide such a remedy, but are not applicable to many breaches of the scheme. Stays for abuse of process are rarely used and would not be used in respect of some

---

4   In *Khan v UK* (2000) 8 BHRC 310, paras 44–47.

breaches of Convention rights – a matter that is explored below. Prosecutions are very rare and can only indirectly protect Convention rights.[5] Typically, the question of redress may arise as follows: an investigation may not, at certain points, reach the standards set by the statutory scheme and it may at the same time breach one or more of the Convention rights. The police may sometimes feel hampered by all the PACE and Code provisions; they may feel, for example, that they are close to obtaining a confession from a detainee, but that in order to obtain it, they need to bend the interviewing rules a little. Similarly, police officers may purport to act within a power, such as the power to arrest or search premises, where no power to do so arises.

In such circumstances, certain remedies are available: a civil action leading to an award of damages, if successful, or a complaint leading to disciplinary action against the officers involved, if upheld. However, as already noted, civil actions are not available for breach of the Codes and will be inapplicable to some breaches of PACE itself, such as improper denial of access to legal advice. Police disciplinary action is applicable to breaches of both PACE itself and the Codes, but at present it does not represent an effective remedy. Apart from these two remedies, a further means of redress exists, represented by the use of exclusion of evidence, and it is in this context that many breaches of PACE and the Codes have in fact been considered. Therefore, argument raised under s 7(1)(b) of the HRA is most likely to be raised in respect of exclusion of evidence. But, not only is such exclusion irrelevant in the vast majority of cases since the suspect will plead guilty, it too cannot be viewed as an effective remedy for breaches of Convention rights for reasons to be considered below, even where the case does come to trial. Possibly, it could be viewed as an effective remedy for breaches of the statutory and Code-based scheme itself that are not coterminous with breaches of the Convention.

Thus, s 7(1)(a) of the HRA fills a clear gap, since a remedy in damages for breach of Convention rights in the criminal justice system pre-trial is now available. If aspects of the domestic scheme, including Code provisions, are coterminous with the Convention rights, they have now received for the first time a remedial underpinning. However, that remedy may not be available in respect of some breaches of Art 6, including failures of access to custodial legal advice, since it might be assumed that the remedy would be provided in the trial itself.

The basis for this argument is that since Art 6 is concerned with the fairness of the trial, it only makes sense to consider the effect of a failure of such access within the context of the trial. It will be suggested below that this argument is flawed. But, assuming that it prevails, which is, in the author's view, likely, it can be said that even under the HRA there is no effective remedy domestically for breach of certain rights within the criminal justice system. This is a very serious matter, since the HRA should provide at least the same protection for rights as Strasbourg would.

The key contention of this chapter will therefore be that no sufficient or effective means of redress are available in respect of police abuse of power, although the HRA will enhance the remedial scheme to an extent. Therefore, the safeguards considered in Chapter 13 are not fully underpinned by such a scheme. Clearly, even if such a scheme were available in the form, for example, of a fully independent police disciplinary system,

---

5   Since no criminal liability is created under the HRA 1998.

police internal practices and culture would still have an impact on the delivery of the safeguards. But, as Chapter 13 argued, externally imposed rules can affect that culture.[6] If the enforcement of those rules is weak, as this chapter contends, this impact on institutional practices is likely to be lessened.

This reading of the domestic and Convention provisions addresses significant matters, and is the main concern of this chapter, but alone it would be, it is suggested, inadequate. At the end of the chapter it will be possible to discern that the Convention under the HRA is quite likely, depending on the attitude of the judiciary, to have at least some impact in terms of reviving and reaffirming a concern for due process which has gradually been eroded. In other words, a return to those values expressed quite strongly by PACE and less so in the later legislation might become apparent in the HRA era. But such an account would not be influenced by a victim-orientated or feminist perspective. By concentrating only on due process concerns, such perspectives would be ignored. The implication would be that where a choice had to be made legislatively, judicially or executively (and the latter term, of course, includes the police themselves), the demands of due process and crime control would provide the parameters of the debate. But, adoption of such a gender-neutral stance would ignore the gendered impact of the decision which would then be made, as well as the impact on victims. Thus, this chapter will argue for a more developed conception of the criminal justice system, one that recognises the values of privacy and equality as well as those of due process.

2 EXCLUSION OF EVIDENCE

Introduction: conflicting values

An example may illustrate the effect of exclusion of evidence. Assume that the police have arrested a man on suspicion of theft. They are fairly certain that he is guilty and think that they have a good chance of getting him to confess. However, he asks for legal advice. The police think that a solicitor may advise him not to answer some questions or may at least help him to withstand certain questioning techniques and so they tell him (untruthfully) that the duty solicitor is unavailable and that they might as well get on with the interview rather than prolong the process. They then question him for four hours without a break. Eventually, he succumbs to the pressure and makes a full confession to theft.

The police have breached PACE and Code C (s 58, paras 6.6 and 12.7); arguably, they have also breached a Convention right: Art 6(3)(c).[7] The suspect does have a means of redress. He could seek to bring an action against the police under s 7(1)(a). He can also make a complaint, but whether he pursues these remedies or not, the flawed interrogation may continue to produce consequences for him: it may lead to a trial, a conviction and possibly imprisonment. He may, of course, decide to plead guilty. But if he pleads not guilty, his counsel may ask the judge at the trial not to admit the confession in evidence on the basis that the interrogation which produced it was conducted unfairly.

---

6   See above, p 754.
7   See Chapter 13, pp 860 *et seq.*

The trial judge could then ensure that the original abuse of power on the part of the police produced no more consequences for the detainee. It may not lead to a conviction and imprisonment if the judge refuses to admit the confession in evidence (depending on any other evidence against the defendant). The judge can hold a *voir dire* (a trial within a trial) by sending out the jury and then hearing defence and prosecution submissions on admitting the confession. If it is not admitted, the jury will never know of its existence and will determine the case on the basis of any other available evidence. The judge is in a difficult position. On the one hand, it is apparent that the police have abused their powers; the judge does not want to condone such behaviour by admitting evidence gained thereby. On the other, the prosecution case may collapse and a possibly guilty man walk free from the court if the confession is excluded.

If the defendant did commit the theft, it might be said that the end in view – the conviction – justifies the means used to obtain it, but should the judge ignore the fact that the confession might not be before the court at all had the police complied with PACE and Code C? Should the judge merely consider the fate of one defendant in isolation? If the confession is admitted, the judge is in effect making a public declaration that the courts will not use their powers to uphold standards for police investigations. The result may be that in future, PACE standards are not adhered to and that occasionally, an innocent citizen is convicted after a false confession has been coerced from him. The multiplicity of issues raised by examples of this nature have provoked a long running debate among academics and lawyers as to the purpose of excluding evidence which has been obtained improperly, and a number of schools of thought have arisen advocating different principles on which evidence should be excluded. All are affected by the inception of the HRA, as indicated below.

The crime control position is that evidence should be excluded only if it appears to be unreliable, that is, in the case of a confession, false or inaccurately recorded.[8] Taken to its logical conclusion, this would mean that if a true confession has been extracted by torture, it should nevertheless be admitted. This is argued on the basis that the function of a criminal court is to determine the truth of the charges against the accused, not to inquire into alleged improprieties on the part of the police. It is not equipped to conduct such an inquiry; therefore, if evidence is excluded on the basis that impropriety occurred in the investigation, the reputation of the police officer in question will be damaged after a less than full investigation into his conduct. Also, even if impropriety did occur in the investigation, this should not allow an obviously guilty defendant to walk freely from the court. On this argument, the court in admitting evidence obtained by improper methods is not condoning them. It is acknowledging that it is not within its function to inquire into them.

It is suggested that in so far as this position reflects the current approach of domestic courts,[9] it has been called into question by the HRA. It implies, *inter alia*, that despite its duty under s 6 of the HRA, the court will simply ignore a breach of Convention rights which has occurred in the pre-trial or custodial procedures and which has been instrumental in obtaining evidence. In respect of non-confession evidence, this is the

---

8   See Wigmore, JH, *Treatise on Evidence*, 3rd edn, 1940, and Andrews [1963] Crim LR 15, p 77.
9   See *Chalkley* [1998] 2 Cr App R 79, discussed below, p 892.

current approach of the domestic courts. There is in fact an argument, considered below, that this position is sustainable to an extent under the HRA, but clearly it has now been placed under pressure.

From a due process stance, it has been argued that a court cannot merely inquire into the truth of the charges against a particular defendant: it must also play a part in maintaining standards in criminal investigations.[10] The court has one particular part to play in the processing of the defendant through the criminal justice system: it should not play its brief part and ignore what has gone before. If the courts are prepared to accept evidence obtained by improper methods, the police may be encouraged to abuse their powers to the detriment of the citizen. Exclusion of evidence should be used to punish the police by depriving them of the fruits of their impropriety and to deter them from using such practices. This principle – the disciplinary principle – may encompass either a deterrent or a punitive role for exclusion of evidence, although it is recognised that no clear-cut relationship between police behaviour and rejection of evidence should be envisaged.[11]

The use of exclusion of evidence to punish the police has come to be viewed by most commentators as a clumsy and possibly ineffective means of protecting due process, and this has led Ashworth to suggest a somewhat different principle, which he terms protective.[12] He contends that once a legal system has declared a certain standard for the conduct of investigations, the citizen obtains corresponding rights to be treated in a certain manner. If such rights are denied and evidence gained as a result, the court can wipe out the disadvantage to the defendant flowing from the denial by rejecting the evidence in question. If, for example, it appears that the defendant made the confession because the police failed to caution him or her, the judge could recreate the situation for the jury's benefit as it would have been had the caution been given, by excluding the confession. In the eyes of the jury, the position would be as if the right had never been denied; the judge would therefore have succeeded in protecting the defendant's right to silence in the interrogation. It must be pointed out that use of this argument in practice became more problematic when the caution became a warning that silence may be commented on adversely in court. If the new-style caution is not given, it might be argued that such a failure could not be causally related to the confession, since the defendant would have confessed in any event. This point will be returned to below.

An alternative but allied argument, also founded on due process values, may be termed the 'reputation' or 'integrity' principle. It can be argued that admitting the confession causes the trial to appear unfair because the court thereby appears to condone or lend itself to the original unfairness. The imprimatur of the court is necessary in order to allow the impropriety to bear fruit. If the trial is viewed, not as a separate entity, but as the culmination of a process in which the court and the police both play their part as emanations of the State, it can be argued that the court should refuse to lend itself to the unfairness which has gone before in order to ensure that the State does not profit from its own wrong. It cannot wipe out the unfairness, but it can wipe out its consequences, thereby ensuring that the reputation of the criminal justice system is not tarnished. But it

10   Eg Cross, R (Sir), *Cross on Evidence*, 5th edn, 1979, pp 318–28.

11   *Ibid*, p 328.

12   See Ashworth, A [1979] Crim LR 723.

need concern itself with the police unfairness only if that unfairness did have consequences. If it concerned itself with an inconsequential breach, the reputation of the criminal justice system would also suffer since the detriment caused to society in allowing someone who has perpetrated a serious crime to walk free from the court would be perceived as entirely outweighing the detriment to the defendant caused by the breach.[13] Ashworth has found, after surveying the position in a number of jurisdictions, that where the police have breached a convention right, evidence thereby obtained should be excluded partly to vindicate the right and partly to preserve the integrity of the criminal justice system.[14]

It might appear that the inception of the HRA lends force to arguments based on the protective principle since the citizen obtains rights not merely as an extrapolation from the standards declared in the statutory scheme, including that under PACE, but also under the Convention, on the basis that is unlawful for the public authority in question – the police – to breach them, under s 6 of the HRA. It might also be said that by giving further effect to the Convention rights, and placing a duty on the courts to uphold them, the HRA implies that the integrity of the criminal justice system would be compromised where evidence is admitted in breach of a right. However, although there are suggestions from the case law that the approach of the courts in the early post-PACE years bore a resemblance to this argument, that approach was hardly evident in the immediate pre-HRA period and the inception of the HRA did not affect that position.

The position in other common law jurisdictions

The US Supreme Court has taken the disciplinary and protective principles into account in determining that evidence obtained by improper methods should be excluded. For example, in *Mapp v Ohio*,[15] the police conducted an illegal search of Mrs Mapp's boarding house and seized certain obscene materials. The Supreme Court held that the evidence obtained in the course of the illegal search was inadmissible. The majority opinion gave two main reasons for reaching this conclusion: first, that the police should be discouraged from conducting illegal searches, and secondly, that the defendant's entitlement to freedom from such search and seizure should be recognised by excluding the evidence obtained thereby. The *Mapp* rule on searches was mirrored by the *Miranda* rule, that improperly obtained confessions would be inadmissible in evidence.[16] However, there has been some retreat recently from *Mapp* and *Miranda*, seen in decisions such as that in *Moran v Burbine*,[17] which have brought America somewhat closer to the position adopted under UK common law.[18]

The argument that evidence should be excluded if obtained through impropriety consisting of a fundamental breach of a constitutionally recognised right, has been accepted in New Zealand,[19] and receives explicit recognition under the Canadian

---

13 This argument was put forward in the second edition of this book.
14 See Clayton and Tomlinson, *op cit*, fn 1, p 1465.
15 (1961) 367 US 643.
16 Deriving from *Miranda v Arizona* (1966) 384 US 436.
17 (1986) 475 US 412.
18 See Stuntz, W, 'The American exclusionary rule and defendants' changing rights' [1989] Crim LR 117.
19 *R v Butcher* [1992] 2 NZLR 257; *R v Te Kira* [1993] 3 NZLR 257; *Simpson v AG* [1994] 3 NZLR 703.

Charter.[20] In Australia, evidence may be admitted although obtained by trickery and it has been found that the trial may still be viewed as fair.[21] In other words, by making a determination that admission of such evidence does not impair fairness, the finding was avoided that evidence was being admitted in breach of a fundamental right. However, it has been found that evidence obtained by secret recording will be excluded where unfairness has been caused to the accused.[22]

Requirements of the Convention

Article 6(1) is silent as to the admissibility of improperly obtained evidence. The Strasbourg Court has emphasised that the assessment of evidence is for the domestic courts[23] and that Art 6 does not require any particular rules of evidence. Thus, it has allowed the national authorities a wide margin of appreciation in this respect. In *Schenk v Switzerland*[24] the Court found no breach of Art 6(1) when an illegally obtained incriminating tape recording was admitted in evidence, and made it clear that unlawfully obtained evidence is not necessarily inadmissible. The Court found: 'While Article 6 guarantees the right to a fair trial it does not lay down any rules as to admissibility of evidence as such, which is therefore primarily a matter of regulation under national law'. The test is to ask whether the trial as a whole would be rendered unfair if the 'tainted' evidence was admitted.[25]

In the late 1990s, a change in the Court's stance occurred, although the *principle* deriving from *Schenk* remained unaffected. A much more interventionist approach was adopted in a number of judgments, including that in *Teixeira de Castro v Portugal*.[26] The applicant, who had no criminal record and was previously unknown to the police, was introduced by a third party to two undercover police officers who told him that they wished to buy 20 grams of heroin. He bought the drugs on their behalf at a price allowing him to take a profit. He was then tried and convicted on the evidence of the officers of drug dealing and sentenced to six years' imprisonment. The Court found, by 8 votes to 1, that the entrapment by the police officers in order to secure evidence had made a fair trial impossible: 'right from the outset the applicant was definitively deprived of a fair trial.'[27]

It might have been expected that where pre-trial impropriety consisted of a fundamental breach of another Convention right, the *Teixeira* approach would have been

---

20 Section 24(2). In *Feeney* [1997] 2 SCR 13, the Canadian Supreme Court said that admission of evidence obtained through a serious breach of the appellant's Charter rights would be more damaging to the reputation of the criminal justice system than would its exclusion. (See also *Burlingham* [1995] 2 SCR 206.) A more technical breach has not been found, however, to demand exclusion since to do so would cause greater affront to the system than its inclusion: *Belnavis* [1997] 3 SCR 341.

21 *Ridgeway v the Queen* (1995) 129 ALR 41.

22 *Swaffield, Pavic v R* (1998) 151 ALR 98.

23 *Edwards v UK* A 247-B (1992).

24 (1988) 13 EHRR 242.

25 A 140 (1988), para 46. This test was also used in *Khan v UK* (2000) 8 BHRC 310; see further below, pp 902–07.

26 (1998) 28 EHRR 101; [1998] Crim LR 751. See also *Van Mechelen v Netherlands* (1998) 25 EHRR 647; the findings of the Commission and Court in *Rowe and Davis* (2000) 30 EHRR 1; *Condron v UK* (2001) 31 EHRR 1.

27 *Ibid*, para 39.

followed. However, a Chamber of the Court did not adopt this stance in its important decision on admission of evidence under Art 6 in *Khan v UK*,[28] despite finding a breach of Art 8. A fundamental breach of Art 8 (secret recording which was not in accordance with the law)[29] had occurred in obtaining the only evidence against the defendant, but, following *Schenk*,[30] no breach of Art 6 was found, owing to the admission of the evidence. The Court said that it was not its role to determine whether unlawfully obtained evidence should be admissible. Thus, the Court appears to adhere to two, partly conflicting views. First, if the pre-trial behaviour is such that the trial is almost bound to be unfair, a breach of Art 6 will be found. The Court has not characterised this issue as one relating to exclusion of evidence. Secondly, where pre-trial practices, although consisting of a breach of another Convention right, are viewed as creating less unfairness to the accused, and the question of a breach of Art 6 arises in the form of a question of admissibility, the Court leaves the matter to the national courts. Possibly, the difference between these two positions is justifiable, but the Court has made little attempt to explain what those justifications are. These questions are returned to below.[31]

The traditional domestic stance

Thus, little guidance is available to domestic courts seeking to apply the Strasbourg jurisprudence under s 2 of the HRA unless the matter can be characterised as one falling within the ruling in *Teixeira*. It may therefore be argued that the domestic courts could look to other jurisdictions for guidance as to the requirements of Art 6. The counter-argument is that the HRA does not require them to do so, that other jurisdictions have developed their own rules, in accordance with their own traditions, for the assessment of evidence, as has Britain, and that therefore the domestic common law tradition should prevail in the HRA era. It is suggested that the early HRA cases demonstrate that this is the approach which will continue to be adhered to. Therefore, the discussion below will concentrate on the established domestic position.

The common law pre-PACE went some way towards endorsing the crime control 'reliability' principle. Illegally obtained evidence other than 'involuntary' confessions was admissible in a criminal trial. Involuntary confessions were inadmissible on the ground that if a defendant was in some way induced to confess during a police interrogation, his confession might be unreliable. A confession would be involuntary if it was obtained by oppression[32] or 'by fear of prejudice or hope of advantage exercised or held out by a person in authority'.[33] According to the Court of Appeal in *Isequilla*,[34] 'oppression' denoted some impropriety on the part of the police, but the House of Lords in *Ping Lin*[35] doubted whether such impropriety was necessary if the real issue was the reliability of

---

28 (2000) 8 BHRC 310; Commission decision: (1999) 27 EHRR CD 58.
29 See Chapter 11, pp 710–11.
30 (1988) 13 EHRR 242.
31 See pp 904–07.
32 *Prager* [1972] 1 All ER 1114, CA.
33 *Ibrahim* [1914] AC 599.
34 [1975] All ER 77.
35 [1976] AC 574.

the confession. Uncertainty as to the need for impropriety on the part of the police and as to the kind of impropriety which could amount to oppression, allowed cases such as the *Confait* case[36] to slip through the net. In that case, three young boys, one of them mentally handicapped, confessed to involvement in a murder they could not have committed after they had been denied both legal advice and the presence of an adult during the police interrogation. The confessions were admitted in evidence and led to the conviction of all three. They were finally exonerated seven years later.

The concept of fear of prejudice or hope of advantage was at one time interpreted strictly against the police and very mild inducements were held to render a confession involuntary. In *Zaveckas*,[37] for example, the Court of Appeal held that a confession had been rendered involuntary because the defendant had asked the police officer whether he could have bail if he made a statement. However, in the case of *Rennie*,[38] Lord Lane held that a confession need not be excluded simply because it had been prompted in part by some hope of advantage. This case paved the way for the relaxation of this rule which can be found in the PACE scheme on exclusion of evidence.

Physical evidence discovered as a result of an inadmissible confession was admissible;[39] the police witness would have to state at the trial that after interviewing the defendant, the evidence in question was discovered – in the hope that the jury would see the connection. Illegally or improperly obtained non-confession evidence, such as fingerprints, was admissible at common law unless the evidence had been tricked out of the detainee,[40] in which case there would be a discretion to exclude it. However, the House of Lords in *Sang*[41] re-affirmed the rule that non-confession evidence, however obtained, is admissible and there is no general discretion to exclude it.

Exclusion of evidence was largely placed on a statutory basis under PACE.[42] PACE contains four separate tests which can be applied to a confession to determine whether it is admissible in evidence. In theory, all four tests could be applied to a particular confession, although in practice it may not be necessary to consider all of them. The four are the 'oppression' test under s 76(2)(a), the 'reliability' test under s 76(2)(b), the 'fairness' test under s 78 and the residual common law discretion to exclude evidence, preserved by s 82(3). It will become apparent that there is a large area of overlap between all four tests. Section 78 could cover unreliable evidence and also evidence obtained by the use of improper methods, whether amounting to oppression or not. Equally, certain types of improper behaviour could be termed oppressive, thus falling within s 76(2)(a), but they could also be viewed as circumstances likely to render a confession unreliable, falling therefore within s 76(2)(b). The courts have gone some of the way towards creating a distinct role for each test, but not all the way.[43] In some circumstances, a confession will obviously fail one of the tests under s 76 and there will be no need to consider the other

---

36 See Price, C and Caplan, J, *The* Confait *Confessions*, 1976; Report of the Inquiry by the Hon Sir Henry Fisher, HC 90 (1977–79).

37 (1970) 54 Cr App R 202, CA.

38 [1982] 1 All ER 385, CA.

39 *Sang* [1980] AC 402; [1979] 2 All ER 1222, HL.

40 *Callis v Gunn* [1964] 1 QB 495.

41 [1980] AC 402; [1979] 2 All ER 1222, HL.

42 For general commentary see Birch, D, 'Confessions and confusions under the 1984 Act' [1989] Crim LR 95; Feldman, D [1990] Crim LR 452.

43 See Birch, *ibid*.

three. In other circumstances, it may be worth considering all four tests. The scheme in respect of non-confession evidence is less complex: only ss 78 and 82(3) are applicable. Significantly, physical evidence which is discovered as a result of an inadmissible confession will be admissible under s 76(4)(a).

Section 76(2)(a) of PACE: the 'oppression' test

Section 76(2)(a) provides that where:

> ... it is represented to the court that the confession was or may have been obtained by oppression of the person who made it ... the court shall not allow the confession to be given in evidence against him except in so far as the prosecution proves to the court beyond reasonable doubt that the confession (notwithstanding that it may be true) was not obtained as aforesaid.

This test derives from the rule as it was at common law: if the prosecution cannot prove beyond reasonable doubt that the police did not behave oppressively, the confession produced is inadmissible. The judge has no discretion in the matter. The idea behind this is that threats of violence or other oppressive behaviour are so abhorrent that no further question as to the reliability of a confession obtained by such methods should be asked. This rule appears to have the dual function of removing any incentive to the police to behave improperly and of protecting the detainee from the consequences of impropriety if it has occurred. Under this head, once the defence has advanced a reasonable argument (*Liverpool Juvenile Court ex p R*)[44] that the confession was obtained by oppression, it will not be admitted in evidence unless the prosecution can prove that it was not so obtained. The reliability of a confession obtained by oppression is irrelevant: it matters not whether the effect of the oppression is to frighten the detainee into telling the truth or alternatively into lying in order to get out of the situation.

The only evidence given in the Act as to the meaning of oppression is the non-exhaustive definition contained in s 76(8): 'In this section "oppression" includes torture, inhuman or degrading treatment and the use or threat of violence (whether or not amounting to torture).' The word 'includes' ought to be given its literal meaning according to the Court of Appeal in *Fulling*.[45] Therefore, it appeared that the concept of oppression might be fairly wide: the question was whether it encompassed the old common law rulings on its width. In *Fulling*, the Court of Appeal held that PACE is a codifying Act and that therefore, a court should examine the statutory language uninfluenced by pre-Act decisions. The court then proffered its own definition of oppression: '... the exercise of authority or power in a burdensome, harsh or wrongful manner; unjust or cruel treatment of subjects, inferiors, etc; the imposition of unreasonable or unjust burdens.' It thought that oppression would almost invariably entail impropriety on the part of the interrogator.

However, the terms 'wrongful' and 'improper' used in this test could cover any unlawful action on the part of the police. This could have been taken to mean that any breach of the Act or Codes could constitute oppression. This wide possibility was

---

44   [1987] All ER 688.
45   [1987] QB 426; [1987] 2 All ER 65, CA.

pursued at first instance,[46] but has been abandoned. The Court of Appeal in *Hughes*[47] held that a denial of legal advice, owing not to bad faith on the part of the police, but to a misunderstanding, could not amount to oppression. In *Alladice*[48] the Court of Appeal also took this view in suggesting, *obiter*, that an improper denial of legal advice, if accompanied by bad faith on the part of the police, would certainly amount to 'unfairness' under s 78 and probably also to oppression. In *Beales*,[49] rather heavy-handed questioning accompanied by misleading suggestions, although not on the face of it a very serious impropriety, was termed oppressive because it was obviously employed as a deliberate tactic. In *Paris*,[50] the case of the *Cardiff Three*, confessions made by one of the defendants after some 13 hours of highly pressured and hostile questioning were excluded on the ground of oppression. He was a man of limited intelligence, but the Court of Appeal thought that the questioning would have been oppressive even with a suspect of normal intelligence.

This emphasis on bad faith may be criticised because from the point of view of the detainee, it matters little if mistreatment occurs because of an administrative mix-up, an innocent misconstruction of powers or malice. Looking to the state of mind of the suspect rather than that of the oppressor would enable account to be taken of the very great difference in impact of certain conduct on a young, inexperienced suspect and on a hardened, sophisticated criminal. However, at present the courts have not shown much desire to import a subjective assessment of oppression into s 76(2)(a), although at common law such an assessment would have been warranted.[51]

On the other hand, it cannot be said that the Court of Appeal has consistently invoked s 76(2)(a) rather than s 78 when the police *have* deliberately misused their powers in obtaining a confession; in *Mason*,[52] for example, a trick played deliberately on the appellant's solicitor led to exclusion of the confession under s 78. In *Blake*,[53] misleading statements made to the detainee, presumably in bad faith, led to exclusion of the confession under s 76(2)(b) or s 78. Thus, apart from the requirement of bad faith, it also seems necessary to show that the improper behaviour has reached a certain level of seriousness in order to show oppression.[54] However, the case law does not yet clearly indicate the level of seriousness needed. All that can be said with some certainty is that the impropriety should be of a serious nature and that bad faith appears to be a necessary, but not sufficient condition for the operation of s 76(2)(a), whereas it will probably automatically render a confession inadmissible under s 78.[55]

Improper treatment falling outside s 76(8) and unaccompanied by bad faith could fall within s 76(2)(b) if the confession was likely to have been rendered unreliable thereby. The

---

46 In *Davison* [1988] Crim LR 442.
47 [1988] Crim LR 519.
48 (1988) 87 Cr App R 380, CA.
49 [1991] Crim LR 118. See to the same effect *Heron* (1993) unreported; forceful questioning was accompanied by lies as to the identification evidence.
50 (1993) 97 Cr App R 99; [1994] Crim LR 361, CA.
51 *Priestley* (1966) 50 Cr App R 183, CA.
52 [1987] Crim LR 119; [1987] 3 All ER 481, CA.
53 [1991] All ER 481, CA.
54 See *L* [1994] Crim LR 839.
55 For discussion of the effect of bad faith under s 78, see below, p 883.

emphasis on bad faith or the lack of it at least gives an indication as to when improper behaviour on the part of the police will lead to automatic exclusion of the confession under s 76(2)(a) and when it will merely suggest the likelihood of unreliability under s 76(2)(b). But, since the operation of s 76(2)(a) is unpredictable and since confessions will rarely be excluded under the sub-section, its ability to protect due process is very limited.

Section 76(2)(b): the 'reliability' test

Section 76(2)(b) provides that where a confession was or may have been obtained:

> ... in consequence of anything said or done which was likely in the circumstances existing at the time, to render unreliable any confession which might be made by him in consequence thereof, the court shall not allow the confession to be given in evidence against him except in so far as the prosecution proves to the court beyond reasonable doubt that the confession (notwithstanding that it may be true) was not obtained as aforesaid.

The 'reliability' test derives from the rule as stated in *Ibrahim*[56] on inducements to confess. However, as will be seen below, it represents a relaxation of that rule as it was applied in *Ibrahim*. It also works certain changes in the emphasis of the test. The test does not reflect the full rigour of the reliability principle, which requires that a confession extracted by torture but determined to be true should be admitted in evidence.[57] Instead it is concerned with objective reliability: the judge must consider the situation at the time the confession was made and ask whether the confession would be *likely* to be unreliable, not whether it is unreliable.

It must be borne in mind that if an offer of some kind is made to the detainee in response to an inquiry from him, this will not render the subsequent confession unreliable,[58] thus explicitly rejecting the *Zaveckas* approach. It is not necessary, under this section, to show that there has been any misconduct on the part of the police. In *Harvey*,[59] a mentally ill woman of low intelligence may have been induced to confess to murder by hearing her lover's confession. Her confession was excluded as being likely to be unreliable. In *Harvey*, the 'something said or done' (the first limb of the test under s 76(2)(a)) was the confession of the lover while the 'circumstances' (the second limb) were the defendant's emotional state, low intelligence and mental illness. The 'something said or done' cannot consist of the defendant's own mental or physical state, according to *Goldberg*.[60] In that case, the defendant was a heroin addict who confessed because he was desperate to leave the police station and obtain a 'fix'. The contention of the defence counsel that the defendant's decision to confess prompted by his addiction amounted to 'something said or done' was not accepted by the court.

In many instances, the 'something said or done' will consist of some impropriety on the part of the police and in such instances, a court will go on to consider whether any circumstances existed which rendered the impropriety particularly significant. The 'circumstances' could include the particularly vulnerable state of the detainee. In

---

56 [1914] AC 599; see fn 33, above.
57 As advocated by Andrews, *op cit*, fn 8, p 77; see p 869 above.
58 Code C, para 11.3.
59 [1988] Crim LR 241.
60 [1988] Crim LR 678.

Mathias,[61] the defendant was particularly vulnerable because he had not been afforded legal advice although an offer of immunity from prosecution had been made to him. The Court of Appeal held that the offer had placed him in great difficulty and that this was a situation in which the police should have ensured that he had legal advice. From the judgment, it appears that if an inducement to confess is offered to the detainee, the police should ensure that he or she can discuss it with a solicitor, even if the police are entitled to deny access to legal advice, on the ground that the detainee falls within s 58(8) (see above). Thus the 'circumstances' will be the lack of legal advice and the 'something said or done', the inducement.

The vulnerability may relate to a physical or mental state. In *Trussler*[62] the defendant, who was a drug addict, had been in custody 18 hours, had been denied legal advice and had not been afforded the rest period guaranteed by Code C para 12. His confession was excluded as likely to be unreliable. In *Delaney*[63] the defendant was 17, had an IQ of 80 and, according to an educational psychologist, was subject to emotional arousal which would lead him to wish to bring a police interview to an end as quickly as possible. These were circumstances in which it was important to ensure that the interrogation was conducted with all propriety. In fact, the officers offered some inducement to the defendant to confess by playing down the gravity of the offence and by suggesting that if he confessed, he would get the psychiatric help he needed. They also failed to make an accurate, contemporaneous record of the interview in breach of Code C, para 11.3. Failing to make the proper record was of indirect relevance to the question of reliability since it meant that the court could not assess the full extent of the suggestions held out to the defendant. Thus, in the circumstances existing at the time (the mental state of the defendant), the police impropriety did have the special significance necessary under s 76(2)(b). The decision in *Marshall*[64] was to similar effect, although it did not identify a specific breach of Code C: the defendant was on the borderline of sub-normality and therefore, after an interview accompanied by his solicitor, he should not have been re-interviewed unaccompanied about the same matters.

From the above it appears that the 'circumstances existing at the time' may be circumstances created by the police (as in *Mathias*) or may be inherent in the defendant (as in *Delaney*). Impropriety on the part of the police can go to either limb of the test, but a state inherent in the detainee (such as mental illness) can go only to the 'circumstances' limb. Thus, a single breach of the interviewing rules such as a denial of legal advice in ordinary circumstances would not appear, as far as the current interpretation of s 76(2)(b) is concerned, to satisfy both limbs of the test. On the other hand, a doubtful breach or perhaps no breach but, rather, behaviour of doubtful propriety, such as misleading the suspect as to the need to have legal advice, might satisfy the 'something said or done' test where special circumstances were also present.

So far, the courts have considered instances where something is said or done, in particularly significant circumstances, which increases the likelihood that a confession will be unreliable. However, it is arguable that s 76 might exceptionally be applicable

---

61 (1989) *The Times*, 24 August.
62 [1988] Crim LR 446.
63 (1989) 8 Cr App R 338; (1988) *The Times*, 20 August, CA.
64 (1992) *The Times*, 28 December.

where something is said or done which might affect a subsequent confession, but the circumstances are normal. The example was given above of a detainee who was deprived of sleep as a result of an administrative mix-up. Deprivation of sleep would be likely to render a confession unreliable, but which 'circumstances' could be pointed to as existing at the time – as required by the second limb of s 76(2)(b)? The answer could be that the ordinary police methods of interrogation, applied to a detainee who had been deprived of sleep, would amount to 'circumstances' falling within s 76(2)(b). Thus, this would be an impropriety which could go to both limbs of the test. Such instances of breaches of Code C could also fall within s 78, as will be seen below. However, defence counsel would be expected to argue the point first under s 76(2)(b) as the prosecution would then have the onus of proving beyond reasonable doubt that the deprivation of sleep did not take place.

It must now be apparent that s 76(2)(b) could be used to exclude all confessions obtained by oppression. It may then be wondered why s 76(2)(a) exists at all. The principle lying behind the two heads of s 76 appears to be that some types of impropriety on the part of the police are so unacceptable that it would be abhorrent in a court to go on to consider the reliability of a confession gained by such methods. In other words, s 76(2)(a) can speed up a process which could be carried out under s 76(2)(b).

Causation and the two heads of s 76

The words of s 76(2): ' [if] it is represented to the court that the confession was or may have been obtained' (by oppression or something conducive to unreliability) appear to import a causal link between the police behaviour (the 'something said or done' or the oppression) and the confession. Thus, if the police threaten the suspect with violence *after* he has confessed, this will clearly be irrelevant to admission of the confession. However, it is possible that under s 76(2)(a), the causal link will not be much scrutinised so long as the oppression precedes the confession. This receives some support from *dicta* in *Alladice*;[65] the Court of Appeal determined that the improper denial of legal advice had not caused the detainee to confess but still found that, had it been accompanied by bad faith, exclusion of the confession under s 76 might have been undertaken. The general rule appears, then, to be that where the causal link in question clearly does not exist, s 76(2)(a) cannot be invoked, but in all other instances the fact that the confession was made subsequent to the oppression may be sufficient.

The question of causation under s 76(2)(b) appears, on the face of it, complex. From the wording of the sub-section it appears to be necessary to adopt a two stage test, asking first whether something was said or done, likely in the circumstances to render any confession made unreliable – an objective test – and secondly, whether that something caused the detainee to confess – a subjective test.

The relationship between ss 76 and 78

In general, the s 76 tests for admissibility of confessions could work to the detriment of inexperienced and more vulnerable detainees. In *Canale*,[66] the police breached the

---

65 (1988) 87 Cr App R 380, CA.
66 [1990] All ER 187, CA.

recording provisions and allegedly played a trick on the appellant in order to obtain the confession. Ruling that the confession should have been excluded under s 78, the Court of Appeal took into account the fact that the appellant could not be said to be weak minded; it was therefore thought inappropriate to invoke s 76(2)(b).[67] Thus, the need to identify special factors in the situation in order to invoke either head of s 76 means that breaches of the interviewing rules unaccompanied by any such factor are usually considered under s 78. Furthermore, allegedly fabricated confessions cannot fall within s 76(2) owing to its requirement that something has happened to the defendant which caused him to confess; its terms are not therefore fulfilled if the defence alleges that no confession made by the defendant exists.

In practice, confessions are rarely excluded under either head of s 76, presumably because the judges strongly wish to retain a discretion as to admissibility. As indicated above, even where a confession is excluded, physical evidence found as a result of information given in it need not be, under s 76(4).[68] Therefore, it may be said that s 76 has had little impact in upholding due process and there is no reason to imagine that this stance will change under the HRA. Thus, s 78 has operated as a catch-all section, bringing within its boundaries many confessions which pass the tests contained in either head of s 76.

Section 78 is also likely to be invoked where police questioning meets with a no comment response from a defendant. Such an interview cannot be considered within s 76 because of the use of the word 'confession' within that section. It would seem to be straining statutory language too greatly to use the term 'confession' to cover a silence. If a silence is excluded from evidence under s 78, adverse inferences obviously cannot be drawn from it (unless the jury or magistrate becomes aware of it in the course of hearing other evidence) and therefore argument on this issue has arisen, although so far the courts have shown themselves reluctant to exclude no comment interviews.[69]

Section 78: the 'fairness' test[70]

Section 78 provides:

> In any proceedings the court may refuse to allow evidence on which the prosecution proposes to rely to be given if it appears to the court that, having regard to all the circumstances, including the circumstances in which the evidence was obtained, the

---

67 Section 76(2)(a) was not invoked, although apparently the police deliberately breached the recording provisions. Presumably, breaches of the interviewing rules were not seen as behaviour serious enough to be termed 'oppression'. However, if the defence makes a – contested – allegation that the police made threats or deliberately tricked the detainee into confessing, the prosecution might not be able to prove beyond reasonable doubt that the police had in fact behaved properly owing to the breach of the recording provisions. This alternative line of argument could have been considered in *Canale* [1990] All ER 187, CA.

68 See further Mirfield, P, *Silence, Confessions and Improperly Obtained Evidence*, 1997; Mirfield, P, 'Successive confessions and the poisonous tree' [1996] Crim LR 554; Sharpe, *Judicial Discretion and Criminal Investigation*, 1998.

69 See *Condron* [1997] 1 WLR 827.

70 For discussion of the operation of s 78 see Allen [1990] CLJ 80; Gelowitz (1990) 106 LQR 327; May [1988] Crim LR 722; Stone (1995) 3 Web JCL 1; Sanders and Young, *op cit*, fn 1, Chapter 11, Part 5; Choo, AL-T and Nash, S, 'What's the matter with s 78?' [1999] Crim LR 929–40.

admission of the evidence would have such an adverse effect on the fairness of the proceedings that the court ought not to admit it.

Section 78 confers an exclusionary *discretion* on a judge and appears to have been conceived to cover the very narrow function of the old common law discretion[71] to exclude improperly obtained non-confession evidence. Until the ruling in *Mason*,[72] it was uncertain whether s 78 also covered confessions. Section 78 can be used to exclude evidence if admitting it would render the trial unfair. In adopting this formula, it was clear that the Government did not wish to import into this country a USA-type exclusionary rule. The Home Secretary informed the House of Commons[73] that the function of exclusion of evidence after police misconduct must not be disciplinary, but must be to safeguard the fairness of the trial. The idea behind this was that non-confession evidence obtained by improper means could still be admitted on the basis that police misconduct could be dealt with by internal disciplinary procedures. Similarly, confessions obtained improperly in circumstances falling outside s 76 could nevertheless be admissible in evidence with the proviso that the trial should not thereby be rendered unfair. In fact, as will be seen, the courts have managed to create a role for s 78 which, as far as confessions are concerned, is probably rather far removed from the Government's original intention. The approach adopted to confessions tends to reflect the protective and integrity principles.

Section 78: excluding confessions

The courts have been very reluctant to lay down general rules for the application of s 78,[74] but the attempt will be made here, albeit tentatively, to identify some of the factors which tend to be taken into account. It may be noted that s 78 is not explicit as to who bears the burden of proof where a breach of the rules is alleged, but in *Vel v Owen*[75] the Divisional Court ruled that the defence should make good its objection. In *Anderson*,[76] however, the court said that it was not entirely clear where the burden of proof lay. If it is found that admission of an interview would render the trial unfair, then not only the interview affected, but possibly any interviews subsequent to that one[77] may be excluded from evidence under s 78.

The PACE interviewing scheme may be infringed or undermined in a variety of ways. In the paradigm case, there may be a clear failure to put in place one of the safeguards such as access to legal advice or tape recording. However, it is not always possible to identify such a clear breach of the rules. The failure to do so may have contributed to the

---

71 See *Sang* [1980] AC 402; [1979] 2 All ER 1222, HL.
72 [1987] Crim LR 119; [1987] All ER 481, CA.
73 1983–84, HC Deb Col 1012, 29 October 1984.
74 See the comments of Auld J in *Katz* (1990) 90 Cr App R 456, CA.
75 (1987) JP 510.
76 [1993] Crim LR 447.
77 *Ismail* [1990] Crim LR 109, CA; cf *Gillard and Barrett* (1991) 155 JP Rep 352 and *Y v DPP* [1991] Crim LR 917. Later interviews may be found to have been contaminated by earlier breaches if those breaches are of a fundamental and continuing character and the accused has not had sufficient opportunity of retracting what was said earlier: *Neill* [1994] Crim LR 441, CA.

decision in *Hughes*:[78] the misrepresentation as regards unavailability of legal advice made to the appellant did not involve breach of a specific Code provision and therefore, may have led to reluctance to exclude the confession. Similarly, in *Khan*[79] it was found that while s 30(1) of PACE allowed officers to keep a suspect out of the police station for a time in order to make investigations, including a search, questioning during that time should be limited, since otherwise the provisions of the interviewing scheme would be subverted. Some of the questions which had in fact been asked went beyond what was needed for the search; however, they should not have been excluded, as the matter was 'a question of degree', although officers did not have *carte blanche* to interview suspects in such circumstances.

In contrast to this approach, there has been some willingness at first instance to consider situations where the PACE scheme seemed to have been infringed, although it was impossible to point to a clear breach.[80] The interviewing scheme lends itself to many methods of infringement, some of which may occur at a low level of visibility, but which may nevertheless be of significance. For example, there may be breach of a rule contained in an instrument other than PACE itself or Code C;[81] there may be evasion or bending of a rule as opposed to breaking it and instances where the interviewing scheme itself leaves it unclear whether or not a particular safeguard should have been in place at a given stage in the process.[82] Of course, a court may never have an opportunity to hear such argument. Infringement of this type is difficult to detect; for example, a suspect who is persuaded to forgo legal advice at the 'booking in' stage may be unaware that something has occurred to his disadvantage, unlike the suspect who has been straightforwardly refused advice. Even assuming that the suspect pleads not guilty, defence counsel may be reluctant to argue for exclusion of a confession if unable to point to a clear breach of the rules.

In *Keenan*,[83] the Court of Appeal ruled that once a breach of the rules can be identified, it will be asked whether it is substantial or significant. It found that a combination of breaches of the recording provisions satisfied this test. In contrast, a breach of para 10.2 requiring a police officer to inform a suspect that he is not under arrest, is free to go and may obtain legal advice has been held to be insubstantial.[84] This view of para 10.2 also seems to have been implicit in the ruling of the Court of Appeal in *Joseph*,[85] although a breach of para 10.5 in contrast was clearly found to be substantial and significant in order to merit exclusion of the confession. In *Walsh*,[86] the Court of Appeal held that what was significant and substantial would be determined by reference to the

---

78   [1988] Crim LR 519. See Chapter 13, p 813 for discussion of the decision.

79   [1993] Crim LR 54, CA.

80   See, eg, *Vernon* [1988] Crim LR 445; *Woodall and Others* [1989] Crim LR 288.

81   The Notes for Guidance, which are not part of the Codes (see Code C, para 1.3 – the provision to the same effect is the first paragraph of each Code) and therefore may in effect be said to form part of a separate instrument; Home Office circulars; Force Standing Orders.

82   This may be said in particular of Code C, para 11.1A and para 10.1 which determine when the safeguards surrounding interviews should be in place. See above, pp 828–31 (discussed in Fenwick, 'Confessions, recording rules and miscarriages of justice' [1993] Crim LR 174).

83   [1989] 3 WLR 1193; [1989] All ER 598, CA.

84   *Rajakuruna* [1991] Crim LR 458.

85   [1993] Crim LR 206, CA.

86   [1989] Crim LR 822; (1989) 19 Cr App R 161.

nature of the breach except in instances where the police had acted in bad faith: '... although bad faith may make substantial or significant that which might not otherwise be so, the contrary does not follow. Breaches which are themselves significant and substantial are not rendered otherwise by the good faith of the officers concerned.'

This test has so far been applied only to Code provisions. It seems likely that breach of rules contained in Notes for Guidance or Home Office circulars would fail it – assuming that a court was prepared to consider such breaches at all – but this hypothesis has not yet been tested because the courts have been reluctant to take such rules into account in the context of exclusion of evidence or, as far as the Notes are concerned, in any other context. This was the approach taken in *DPP v Billington*;[87] the Court of Appeal preferred not to consider Note 6C of Code C despite its relevance to the question before it. However, there are some signs that the judiciary are beginning to react to the Notes differently, perhaps owing to a perception that their legitimacy derives from their nature as opposed to their source. In *DPP v Blake*[88] the Divisional Court impliedly accepted that a Note for Guidance will be considered if it can be argued that it amplifies a particular Code provision and can therefore be of assistance in determining whether breach of such a provision has occurred. The question arose whether an estranged parent could be the appropriate adult at the interview of a juvenile under Code C, para 13.1;[89] that provision was interpreted in accordance with Note 13C, which describes the adult's expected role,[90] and it was then found that para 13.1 had been breached.[91] A variation on this view of the Notes, which nevertheless supports the argument that they are unlikely to be considered in their own right, has been expressed recently by the Court of Appeal in relation to one of the most significant Notes, Note 11A. It was taken into account on the basis that it could be seen as part of para 11.1 and could thereby acquire the status of a paragraph.[92]

Once a court has identified a significant and substantial breach of the interviewing rules, it may then take some account of the function of the rule in question. Rules governing access to legal advice and the right to silence provide rights which are valuable in themselves, since they tend to place the suspect on a more even footing with police officers during the interview. These rights are also reflected in the Convention in Art 6(2) and 6(3)(c).[93] An innocent detainee who is confused and upset by the interrogation may

---

87 (1988) Cr App R 68; [1988] 1 All ER 435. The court had to consider whether a desire to consult a solicitor first could properly found a refusal to furnish a specimen of breath under the Road Traffic Act 1972, s 8(7). Para 6 of Code C provides that a person who has requested legal advice may not be interviewed until he has received it. Note 6C provides that the s 8 procedure does not constitute an interview, but Lloyd LJ preferred not to take it into account while reaching a conclusion which was nevertheless in accordance with it. Thus, the issue which fell to be determined did not concern the question of exclusion of evidence, but has a bearing upon the general question whether courts are prepared to place any reliance upon the Notes.

88 [1989] 1 WLR 432, CA.

89 Now para 11.14 under the revised Code.

90 This role is now described in para 11.16; this provision has therefore been elevated in status, indicating its importance. The decision in *DPP v Blake* found recognition in Note for Guidance 1C.

91 This decision was followed in the first instance decision of *Morse* [1991] Crim LR 195; see also *DPP v Rouse* and *DPP v Davis* (1992) 94 Cr App R 185.

92 *Cox* (1993) 96 Cr App R 464; [1993] Crim LR 382; (1992) *The Times*, 2 December.

93 See Chapter 13, pp 854–64.

be less likely to make false admissions if a legal adviser is present at the interview.[94] In contrast, the verifying and recording rules may be said to be concerned mainly with the evidential integrity of the evidence rather than with providing rights valuable in themselves. Categorising the interviewing rules in this way – by means of their dominant function – may be useful as a means of determining the type of unfairness which may flow from their breach. However, occasionally, what may be termed the *subordinate* function of a rule may be relevant to the question of fairness with the result that, for example, breach of a recording rule could be treated in the same way as breach of the legal advice provisions.

In *Samuel*,[95] the Court of Appeal found that the confession should have been excluded under s 78 because it was causally linked to the police impropriety – a failure to allow the appellant access to legal advice. In order to establish this point, the solicitor in question gave evidence that had he been present, he would have advised his client to remain silent in the last interview, whereas in fact Samuel made damaging admissions in that interview which formed the basis of the case against him. It could not be said with certainty that he would have confessed in any event: he was not, it was determined, a sophisticated criminal who was capable of judging for himself when to speak and when to remain silent. Thus – although this was not made explicit – the Court of Appeal was prepared to make the judgment that a trial would be rendered unfair if a court associated itself with a breach of the PACE interrogation procedure. The Court of Appeal in *Alladice*,[96] also faced with a breach of s 58, accepted that the key factor in exercising discretion under s 78 after a breach of the interrogation procedure was the causal relationship between breach and confession (and, by implication, between breach and fairness at the trial). On the basis of this factor, it was determined that the confession had been rightly admitted despite the breach of s 58 because no causal relationship between the two could be established. This finding was based partly on the defendant's evaluation of the situation (that he only wanted the solicitor to see fair play and did not require legal advice) and partly on the fact that he had exercised his right to silence at certain points. Therefore, it was determined that he would have made the incriminating admissions in any event – even with the benefit of legal advice. Possibly this was surprising in view of the fact that the appellant, as the court itself accepted, was an unsophisticated criminal who did in fact make admissions in the absence of a solicitor which formed the basis of the case against him.[97]

In the early post-PACE years, there was a tendency for judges to move rather rapidly from a finding that the police had breached Code C to a determination that s 78 should be invoked, without explicitly considering whether a causal relationship between the breach

---

94 As pointed out at a number of points in Chapter 13, the evidence as to the advantage to the detainee of having the advisor present at the interview is of a rather mixed nature; see, eg, comment on the solicitor's role at [1993] Crim LR 368.

95 [1988] QB 615; [1988] 2 All ER 315; [1988] 2 WLR 920, CA.

96 (1988) 87 Cr App R 380. The Court of Appeal appeared to have a similar test in mind in relation to a failure to caution in *Weerdesteyn* (1995) 1 Cr App R 405; [1995] Crim LR 239, CA.

97 See also *Dunford* (1990) 91 Cr App R 150; (1990) 140 NLJ 517, CA: the Court of Appeal determined that the criminally experienced appellant had made his own assessment of the situation in deciding to make certain admissions and legal advice would not have affected his decision; the failure to allow legal advice was not therefore causally linked to the confession.

and the confession existed.[98] Such a tendency can be discerned in the case of *Absolam*[99] in which the Court of Appeal, in finding that 'the prosecution would not have been in receipt of these admissions if the appropriate procedures had been followed', seemed to assume that the causal relationship between the impropriety[100] and the admissions did exist. The chain of causation would have been fairly long – had the detainee been informed of his right to legal advice, he would have exercised it; had he exercised it, he would not have made the incriminating admissions – but the Court of Appeal did not make much attempt to scrutinise its links.[101] However, in *Walsh*,[102] the Court of Appeal reaffirmed the need to identify the causal relationship between the breach in question and the confession.

Deciding that an impropriety is causally linked to the confession does not of itself explain why admission of the confession will render the trial unfair, although it is perhaps reasonable to conclude that admission of a confession which is not so linked will not render the trial unfair. The necessary unfairness must arise through admission of the confession, in other words *after* its admission; the unfairness in the interrogation cannot therefore without more satisfy this requirement; instead, the unfairly obtained confession must be the agent which somehow creates unfairness at the trial. It has to be said that at present, the courts have not addressed this question. In *Samuel*, for example, the Court of Appeal merely stated:

> ... the appellant was denied improperly one of the most important and fundamental rights of the citizen ... if [the trial judge] had found a breach of s 58 he would have determined that admission of evidence as to the final interview would have 'such an adverse effect on the fairness of the proceedings' that he ought not to admit it.[103]

Broadly, it could be argued that if the court refuses to take the opportunity afforded by s 78 to put right what has occurred earlier in the process, this will give an appearance of unfairness to the trial. This argument is based on the 'protective principle':[104] if admissions gained in consequence of denial of a right (in the broad sense of an entitlement) are excluded, the particular right is being protected in the sense that the defendant is being placed at trial – as far as the jury is concerned – in the position he or she would have been in had the right not been denied. If s 78 is, at least in part, concerned with ensuring fairness to the defence, it is arguable that the court should take the opportunity offered to it of upholding the standards of fairness declared by PACE. However, following an argument based on the reputation or integrity principles, if the police unfairness has had no consequences for the defendant, the court need not exclude the confession since to do so would place him in a more favourable position than he would have been in had the proper standard of fairness been observed.

---

98 See *Williams* [1989] Crim LR 66 and *Mary Quayson* [1989] Crim LR 218.

99 (1989) Cr App R 332.

100 A failure to inform Absolam of his right to legal advice in breach of Code C para 3.1(ii).

101 Possibly, this may have arisen because the defendant had denied making the admissions in question; the court was therefore placed in the position of accepting the word of the police officer against that of the defendant – precisely the problem which Code C was designed to prevent. The Court of Appeal, while speaking in the language of causation, may simply have had a doubt as to whether the admissions were made at all.

102 [1989] Crim LR 822.

103 [1988] 2 WLR 920, p 934.

104 See Ashworth, *op cit*, fn 12.

Admittedly, both these arguments assume that the court will appear to be associating itself unfairly with the prosecution, rather than dealing even-handedly, if it admits the evidence in question and that therefore, the court should refuse to do so. They therefore seem to beg the very question to which s 78 demands an answer. If admitting the confession despite the breach *could* be seen as fair, the court would not be associating itself with unfairness and could not be seen as lacking even-handedness. But bearing in mind the balance PACE is supposed to create between increased police powers and safeguards for suspects, it can perhaps be argued that to accept evidence deriving from an interview in which the police were able to use their powers to the full, but the defendant was unable to take advantage of an important safeguard, would not be perceived by most reasonable people as fair. The findings of the Privy Council in *Mohammed (Allie) v State*[105] in respect of a denial of custodial access to legal advice adopted this stance: 'The stamp of constitutionality on a citizen's rights is not meaningless: it is clear testimony that added value is attached to the protection of the right ... Not every breach will result in a confession being excluded. But their Lordships make clear that the fact that there has been a breach of a constitutional right is a cogent factor militating in favour of the exclusion of the confession. In this way the constitutional character of the infringed right is respected and accorded a high value ...' This stance receives clear, albeit indirect support from Strasbourg, as will be indicated below.[106]

In this context, the curtailment of the right to silence under the CJPOA is particularly significant. One result of its curtailment may be that it becomes harder to establish that an improper denial of access to legal advice should lead to exclusion of evidence under s 78. This is because the main basis for excluding confessions gained after denial of legal advice may disappear. The courts have been excluding them mainly on the ground that had the legal adviser been present, he or she would probably have advised the client to remain silent, but if this cannot be contended, the causal relationship between breach and confession is destroyed. Whether this will happen depends, of course, on the general readiness of legal advisers to advise their clients to remain silent in the face of the knowledge that such silence may be commented on in court. At present, it is unclear that legal advisers are less disposed than they were previously to advise silence.[107] However, if such a tendency did become apparent, a number of consequences might follow. The police may have been encouraged to afford access to a legal adviser but, on the other hand, any disincentive to deny access – the result of such decisions as *Samuel* and *Absolam* – has been undermined. The balance still comes down in favour of discouraging, delaying or denying access.[108] If, on a *voir dire*, a court has to consider such a denial, it may be harder to contend confidently that the legal adviser would have advised the client to remain silent, with the result that in future, the courts will find themselves less able to uphold this particular safeguard for the suspect. Of course it might be said, in the light of a large amount of research,[109] that it was, even prior to the inception of the CJPOA, *already* becoming difficult to contend confidently that a legal adviser would have advised

105 [1999] 2 WLR 552 (Trinidad and Tobago); judgment delivered by Lord Steyn on 8 December 1998.
106 See also Chapter 13, pp 860–64.
107 See Chapter 13, pp 816–18.
108 See Chapter 13, pp 810–13.
109 See, eg, McConville, M and Hodgson, J, *Custodial Legal Advice and the Right to Silence*, 1993, Royal Commission Study No 16. See further Chapter 13, pp 816–19.

silence, except perhaps in cases where the client was under very obvious pressure.[110] However, that problem could be addressed by means of better training in the provision of custodial legal advice. The effect of curtailment of the right to silence, however, will probably be in the long run to undermine the main prop holding up the legal advice scheme.

Breach of rules aimed at ensuring that the record of an interview can be relied on at trial need not be considered under s 78 in terms of their impact on the defendant. Once such a breach, of a substantial nature, has been identified, a court will be likely to react by excluding the confession on the basis that it is impossible to be sure of its reliability[111] and therefore its prejudicial quality may outweigh its probative value. In other words, a jury may place reliance on an inaccurate record or believe a fabricated confession which clearly has no evidential value at all. An obvious example of such a breach is a failure to make contemporaneous notes of the interview in breach of Code C, para 11.5, allowing a challenge to the interview record by the defence on the basis that the police have fabricated all or part of it. The court then has no means of knowing which version of what was said is true, precisely the situation which Code C was designed to prevent. In such a situation, a judge may well exclude the interview record on the basis that it would be unfair to allow evidence of doubtful reliability to go before the jury. If, however, as in *Dunn*,[112] the defence has an independent witness to what occurred – usually a solicitor or solicitor's clerk – the judge may admit the confession as the defence now has a proper basis from which to challenge the police evidence.

It is fairly clear that allowing a confession which may have been fabricated to go before the jury may render a trial unfair: on the one hand, the jury may rely on a confession which may be entirely untrue, while on the other, if the defendant alleges that the police fabricated the confession, the prosecution can then put his character in issue and the jury may hear of his previous convictions. The jury may then tend to rely on his convictions in deciding that his guilt is established on this occasion. In both circumstances, the defendant is placed at a clear disadvantage.

When a breach of Code C has occurred which casts doubt on the accuracy of the interview record, the defence may not necessarily submit that the police have fabricated admissions; the judge may merely have to determine whether the trial will be rendered unfair if a possibly inaccurate record of an interview is admitted in evidence. There is authority to suggest that a judge in such circumstances will exclude the record,[113] presumably owing to the chance of a risk that the jury will rely on fabricated admissions.

As noted above, identifying the dominant function of the interviewing rule in question need not circumscribe the inquiry into the unfairness caused by its breach. Although identifying the dominant function of a rule may simplify this task in most circumstances, it is suggested that a court may sometimes focus on its subordinate function. For example, a breach of the recording provisions would be directly relevant to

---

110 See Dixon's findings in this respect: [1991] PL 233, p 244: '... silence may be advised ... when the suspect is confused or highly emotional ... several solicitors stressed that their clients are under great pressure.'

111 See, eg, *Keenan* [1989] 3 WLR 1193; [1989] 3 All ER 598, CA.

112 (1990) 91 Cr App R 237; [1990] Crim LR 572, CA. See also *Heslop* [1996] Crim LR 730.

113 *Foster* [1987] Crim LR 821; *Keenan* [1989] 3 All ER 598.

placing the suspect in a disadvantageous position at interview where there was no dispute between defence and prosecution as to the admissions made (although the defence may be alleging that they are untrue), but there was an allegation that the breach had allowed some impropriety to occur which had pressurised the suspect into making admissions. It may now be impossible to determine whether the defence or prosecution version of events during the interview is correct because of the defective record. Equally, access to legal advice can affect the evidential integrity of a confession: the legal adviser can give evidence in court as to what occurred during the interview and, if the interview record is defective, can support the defendant's version of what was said, thus lending support to the argument that the interview should be admitted. Conversely, if in such circumstances legal advice had been improperly denied, but the defendant was able to cope without advice, the unfairness would arise out of the inability of the defence to challenge the defective interview record rather than to the adverse effect of lack of advice.[114] In such instances, the subordinate function of the rule should determine the test to be applied. Thus, in the first example given, the only question would be whether the causal relationship between impropriety and confession could be established, assuming that it was impossible to determine the truth or otherwise of the allegation of impropriety.

In the cases considered above, it was not clear that the police had *deliberately* failed to comply with the rules; the failures in question may have arisen out of a mistake as to the application of PACE or because of an administrative error. It seems that if the police have acted deliberately, the exercise under s 78 will be far less complex. Lord Lane CJ in *Alladice*[115] stated that he would not have hesitated to hold that the confession should have been excluded had it been demonstrated that the police had acted in bad faith in breaching s 58. The lack of emphasis he thought should in general be placed on the causal relationship in question, if bad faith on the part of the police could be demonstrated, was the most striking feature of this decision. His approach appears to involve asking only whether a breach was accompanied by bad faith. If so, that would appear to be the end of the matter: exclusion of the confession would follow almost automatically. If the breach occurred in good faith, however, a close scrutiny of the causal relationship should follow.

Using the questions of bad faith and causation as alternatives to keep a check on a too ready exclusion of confessions can be criticised because it is hard to see why an instance of bad faith on the part of the police which is not causally linked to the confession should be considered in relation to its admissibility. Deliberate denial of rights certainly gives a greater appearance of unfairness to the interrogation than an innocent denial, but if the detainee is unaffected by it, why should it affect the trial? It cannot be said that the court is associating itself with or condoning the bad faith displayed by the police in the interrogation because the link between the two – the admissions arising from the denial of rights – is missing. If, in future, the situation which arose in *Alladice* recurs, but with the added ingredient of bad faith, it is hard to see why the consequences for the future defendant should differ so greatly. The only justification appears to be that the police are

---

114 This occurred in *Dunn* (1990) 91 Cr App R 237; [1990] Crim LR 572, CA. Ironically, the confession was admitted into evidence owing to the fact that the defendant's legal adviser had been present and could support his assertion that it had been fabricated; the jury presumably disbelieved her and convicted on that basis.

115 (1988) 87 Cr App R 380.

'punished' for their deliberate impropriety, but the disciplinary approach has been explicitly repudiated, in *Delaney*[116] and *Chalkley*,[117] on the basis that it is not part of the proper purpose of a criminal trial to inquire into wrongdoing on the part of the police. Nevertheless, at present, deliberate breaches of Code C will almost certainly lead to exclusion of evidence under s 78 whether the breaches were linked to the confession or not. The Court of Appeal in *Walsh*[118] confirmed that this was the correct approach and suggested that it would be followed even if the breach was of a trivial nature. In fact, the dearth of cases on this point suggests that courts are reluctant to accept that a breach of PACE may have been perpetrated deliberately.

It may be noted that a judge may exceptionally admit the confession after deciding to exclude it because some particular feature of the trial proceedings makes it necessary to do so in order to maintain the balance of fairness between prosecution and defence.[119] In other words, if it was clear that in some way the prosecution is at a disadvantage which could be seen as equal to that experienced by the defendant, the judge might allow the confession to be admitted. This flows from the concern of s 78 with the fairness of the proceedings rather than simply fairness to the defence. Reconsidering the decision to admit the confession could not occur under s 78, since it only operates *before* evidence is admitted (although s 82(3) might be invoked – see below).

Section 78: exclusion of non-confession evidence[120]

The arguments above have concentrated on exclusion of admissions, but it must be borne in mind that non-confession evidence can also be excluded under s 78 (or s 82(3)), although not under s 76. Where non-confession evidence is concerned, the courts have taken a stance which differs strongly from that taken to admissions obtained in police interviews which breach PACE. The general stance taken is that improperly obtained evidence is admissible in a criminal trial subject to a discretion to exclude it. Except in one instance – that of identification evidence – the discretion is viewed as very narrow, although where the impropriety consists of some forms of trickery, it may be wider. The courts have shown little inclination to take a different stance where the impropriety consists of a breach of a Convention right,[121] although that approach might change under the HRA.

---

116 (1989) 88 Cr App R 339; (1988) *The Times*, 20 August, CA.

117 [1998] 2 All ER 155.

118 [1989] Crim LR 822.

119 See *Allen* [1992] Crim LR 297: having decided to exclude a conversation between police officers and the defendant because of breaches of the recording provisions, the judge reconsidered when the nature of the defence case became apparent; it placed prosecution witnesses at an unfair disadvantage if they were unable to refer to the excluded conversation. Thus, it appears that in such circumstances the original unfairness caused to the defendant may be outweighed by unfairness to the prosecution if the confession is not admitted.

120 For discussion see Gelowitz, *op cit*, fn 70; Choo (1989) 9(3) LS 261; Allen, *op cit*, fn 70; Choo (1993) Journal of Crim Law 195; Choo and Nash, *op cit*, fn 70; Sharpe, (1998) Chapter 2.

121 See the judgment of the House of Lords in *Khan* [1997] AC 558.

Identification evidence

Identification evidence has been seen as particularly vulnerable and may therefore be treated in the same way as a confession obtained in breach of PACE. Arguments can be raised as to the reliability of identification evidence and also as to police impropriety in conducting identification. For example, if no reminder as to the availability of legal advice were given (para 2.15(ii)) before an identification was arranged, it could be argued that the form of the identification used prejudiced the position of the defendant, who would have asked for a different form had he had advice. It could be argued that no identification would have been made had the other form been used and that therefore, the failure to remind of the right to advice was causally linked to the identification evidence obtained. If some doubt is raised as to the reliability of the identification owing to delay[122] or to a failure to hold an identification parade where one was practicable,[123] the identification evidence is likely to be excluded. However, in the leading decision on identification evidence, *Forbes*,[124] the House of Lords found that despite a breach of Code D, para 2.3, there had been no need to exclude the evidence.

Thus, following this decision, each case must turn on its own facts except where bad faith is shown in conducting the identification procedure. In such an instance, it seems that the courts will react to it as they would in relation to confessions.[125] It will mean that no causal relationship between the breach and the evidence obtained need be shown and, possibly, that the breach need not be substantial and significant. It may be argued that there is a stronger case than that considered above in relation to confessions for treating bad faith shown during the identification process with particular stringency owing to the appearance of unfairness created to the defendant who may think that there has been collusion between witnesses and the police.

Other non-confession evidence

On due process grounds, the argument accepted in *Samuel*[126] as to the causal relationship between an impropriety and a confession (where bad faith is not shown) should be applied to non-confession evidence, such as a weapon or drugs found on the suspect or his premises during an improper or unlawful search. However, where such evidence is in question, the discretion under s 78 is applied narrowly. The first instance decision in *Fennelly*[127] in which a failure to give the reason for a stop and search led to exclusion of the heroin found is out of line with the later decisions. Indeed, even if the principles developed under s 78 with respect to confession evidence were generally applied to other evidence, *Fennelly* would still be a doubtful decision since, on the facts, no causal relationship could exist between the impropriety in question and the evidence obtained.

---

122 *Quinn* [1990] Crim LR 581, CA; (1990) *The Times*, 31 March.
123 *Ladlow* [1989] Crim LR 219.
124 [2001] Crim LR 649.
125 *Finley* [1993] Crim LR 50, CA.
126 [1988] QB 615.
127 [1989] Crim LR 142.

According to *Thomas*[128] and *Quinn*,[129] physical evidence will be excluded only if obtained with deliberate illegality; the pre-PACE ruling of the House of Lords in *Fox*[130] would also lend support to this contention. In *Fox*, the police made a *bona fide* mistake as to their powers in effecting an unlawful arrest and the House of Lords, in determining that the physical evidence obtained was admissible, considered that the unlawful arrest was merely part of the history of the case and not the concern of the court. This stance is in accord with that taken in *Sang*[131] and confirmed as correct in *Khan (Sultan)*.[132] It appears to be in accord with the general PACE scheme, since evidence obtained as a result of an inadmissible confession will be admissible under s 76(4).

Zander has pointed out,[133] citing, *inter alia, Sharpe v DPP*,[134] that the courts have rejected the 'real' evidence of intoxication in certain drink-driving cases under s 78 owing to the way in which the evidence was obtained, even where bad faith may not have been present. Zander views the Divisional Court decision in *Sharpe*, along with the decisions in cases such as *Samuel* and *Gall*[135] (on identification evidence) as affirming an abandonment of 'the amoral common law tradition of receiving non-confession evidence regardless of how it was obtained'.[136] However, it may now be said with some certainty that the amoral common law tradition will continue to prevail.

The position as regards unlawfully obtained evidence, which reflects a crime control stance, is as stated by the House of Lords in *Khan (Sultan)*,[137] now the leading case on s 78. It suggests that a narrow exclusionary discretion only is available under s 78, save where a confession may be said to be involuntary (in which case it would be excluded under s 76). A bugging device had been secretly installed on the outside of a house which Khan was visiting. Khan was suspected of involvement in the importation of prohibited drugs and the tape recording obtained from the listening device clearly showed that he was so involved. The case against him rested wholly on the tape recording. The defence argued, first, that the recording was inadmissible as evidence because the police had no statutory authority to place listening devices on private property and that therefore, such placement was a trespass and, further, that admission of the recording would breach Art 8 of the European Convention on Human Rights, which protects the right to privacy. Secondly, it was argued that even if the recording was admissible, it should be excluded from evidence under s 78 because of the unfairness of admitting the evidence so. It was accepted in the Court of Appeal that trespass to the building had occurred as well as some damage to it and that there had been an invasion of privacy. However, the Court of Appeal found,[138] supporting the trial judge, that these factors were of slight significance

---

128 [1990] Crim LR 269. See to the same effect *Wright* [1994] Crim LR 55.

129 [1990] Crim LR 581, CA.

130 [1986] AC 281; see to the same effect *DPP v Wilson* [1991] Crim LR 441. On similar facts, in *Matto v Wolverhampton Crown Court* [1987] RTR 337, physical evidence was excluded since the police had acted with *mala fides*.

131 [1980] AC 402; [1979] 2 All ER 1222, HL.

132 [1997] AC 558; [1996] 3 All ER 289.

133 Zander, *op cit*, fn 1, pp 236–37.

134 (1993) JP 595.

135 (1990) 90 Cr App R 64.

136 Zander, *op cit*, fn 1, p 236.

137 [1996] 3 All ER 289; (1996) 146 NLJ 1024. For comment see Carter (1997) 113 LQR 468.

138 *Khan* [1996] 3 All ER 289; (1996) 146 NLJ 1024, HL; [1995] QB 27, CA.

and therefore were readily outweighed by the fact that the police had largely complied with the Home Office guidelines and that the offences involved were serious. The court found that since the Convention is not part of UK law, it was of only persuasive assistance.

The House of Lords upheld the Court of Appeal. The Lords relied on the decision in *Sang*[139] to the effect that improperly obtained evidence other than 'involuntary' confessions is admissible in a criminal trial. Involuntary confessions were inadmissible on the ground that if a defendant was in some way induced to confess during a police interrogation, his confession might be unreliable. It was argued for the appellant that the recording fell within the category of involuntary confessions and therefore was outside the rule from *Sang*. The House of Lords disagreed and went on to find that *Sang* would be inapplicable only if there were a right to privacy in UK law and breach of such a right could be treated as a form of impropriety different in kind from that covered by *Sang* and so serious that it would render evidence thereby obtained inadmissible. Neither of these two new principles was accepted; therefore, the recording was admissible.

Should the recording have been excluded under s 78, taking Art 8 into account? The House of Lords found that although a judge in exercising discretion under s 78 might take Art 8 into account; or any relevant foreign law, an apparent breach of Art 8 would not necessarily lead him or her to conclude that the evidence in question should be excluded. The key question would be the effect of the breach upon the fairness of the proceedings. The House of Lords concluded that the circumstances in which the evidence was obtained, even if they involved a breach of Art 8, were not such as to require exclusion of the evidence.

This decision confirms that, apart from admissions falling within s 76 of PACE (which has partly replaced the common law concept of involuntariness), improperly obtained evidence is admissible in criminal trials subject to a discretion to exclude it. Thus, it fails to take a stance which protects due process. The House of Lords was only prepared to find that the Convention would be 'relevant' to the exercise of discretion under s 78 and further found that where a breach of the Convention was found, this would not necessarily lead a judge to conclude that evidence should be excluded.

In *Chalkley*,[140] the same stance was taken. The evidence consisted of incriminating statements made by the accused which were secretly recorded by the police. Despite the impropriety of the police actions, it was found that the evidence was rightly admitted. This stance did not change with the inception of the HRA. In *AG's Reference (No 3 of 1999)*,[141] a rape case, DNA evidence against the suspect should have been destroyed but had not been, in breach of s 64 of PACE. The evidence was not admitted under s 78 and the defendant was acquitted. On a reference of the Attorney General, it was found by the House of Lords, following the *Sang* principle, that the evidence could have been admitted, despite the breach of PACE. It was not found that Art 6 affected the position, since the Court has left the assessment of evidence to the national courts.

---

139 [1980] AC 402; [1979] 2 All ER 1222.

140 [1998] 2 Cr App R 79.

141 [2001] 2 WLR 56.

Thus, it may be said that the common law, post-HRA, continues to adhere to the crime control values implicit in the reliability principle. *Khan* may be consistent with the decisions on evidence obtained in breach of the interviewing or identification rules since, in such instances, it may be said that the evidence is unreliable.[142] Thus, it seems that improperly obtained non-confession evidence, apart from identification evidence, will be admissible subject to a very narrow discretion to exclude it. This stance seems to afford encouragement to police officers to disregard suspects' rights in the pursuit of such evidence and amounts to a declaration by the courts that a conviction may be based on evidence which would not be before a court had police officers not acted unlawfully. In due process terms, a principled justification for creating a distinction between improperly obtained, but probably reliable, confession evidence and improperly obtained physical evidence is not apparent. The due process argument, to the effect that certain types of impropriety should lead almost automatically to exclusion of the evidence affected by them, has so far been rejected. However, the courts have not yet been faced, post-HRA, with non-confession evidence obtained through a breach of a Convention right. There are indications in *Khan* that in such circumstances, it might be excluded, on the basis of the integrity principle.

Evidence obtained by tricks and undercover work[143]

As indicated, *Sang*[144] stated the general rule that improperly obtained evidence other than 'involuntary' confessions is admissible in a criminal trial subject to a very narrow discretion to exclude it. The fact that the police have acted as agents provocateurs, entrapping the defendant into a crime he would not otherwise have committed, was not found in *Sang* to mean that the evidence gained thereby should be excluded. The current position as regards tricks or undercover work by police was stated by the Court of Appeal in *Smurthwaite*.[145] The mere fact that the evidence has been obtained in the course of an undercover operation, of necessity involving deceit, does not of itself require a judge to exclude it. Everything will depend on the particular circumstances in question. For example, how active or passive was the officer's role in obtaining the evidence? What is the nature of the evidence and is it unassailable? If the officer's role is active, the evidence will be viewed as having been obtained by entrapment or by an agent provocateur and will probably be excluded. *Smurthwaite* suggests that the discretion to exclude 'unfair' evidence is of a somewhat wider scope than that indicated in *Sang*.

However, in the majority of cases, evidence obtained by a deception has been admitted,[146] but where the deception 'creates' the evidence and it is not possible to say that the defendant has applied himself to the ruse, the courts will tend to exclude it.[147] In

---

142 See the comments of the Court of Appeal in *Bray* (1998) 31 July, unreported, to the effect that where the impropriety does not affect the quality of the evidence, it should be admitted.

143 For discussion see Sharpe [1994] Crim LR 793; Robertson, Crim LR 805; Heydon [1980] Crim LR 129; Birch (1994) CLP 73.

144 [1980] AC 402; [1979] All ER 1222, HL.

145 [1994] All ER 898; (1994) 98 Cr App R 437, CA.

146 See, eg, *Maclean and Kosten* [1993] Crim LR 687; *Gill and Ranuana* [1991] Crim LR 358; *Edwards* [1991] Crim LR 45, CA.

147 See *Colin Stagg* (1994) unreported, but see national newspapers 15 September 1994; *H* [1987] Crim LR 47.

Williams and O'Hare v DPP,[148] police officers set up a 'virtue-testing' operation in order to see who might succumb to temptation. An insecure vehicle apparently loaded with cigarettes was left in a high crime area in order to catch would-be thieves. The resultant evidence was not excluded, since it was not found that it had been obtained by means of entrapment. The stance taken in *Smurthwaite* was confirmed by the House of Lords in *Shannon*[149] although the Lords took, it is suggested, a narrower view of practices amounting to entrapment. Reporters rather than undercover officers carried out a 'sting' operation in which evidence of drug dealing was obtained. Although it was arguable that the accused had, to an extent, been enticed into incriminating himself, the Lords found that the evidence thereby gained could rightly be viewed as admissible. It is suggested below that this stance is not fully in accord with that taken at Strasbourg.

In *Mason*,[150] the defendant had been tricked into confessing to damaging his neighbour's car by the police, who had falsely informed him and his solicitor that his fingerprints had been found on incriminating evidence. The Court of Appeal held that the confession should have been excluded under s 78: the trial judge had erred in omitting to take into account the deception practised on D's solicitor. The court appeared to view the deliberate deception practised by the police as the most significant factor without making it clear why the trial would be rendered unfair by admission of the confession gained thereby. It might have been better to have shown explicitly that the confession should be excluded on the basis that the police had acted improperly in deceiving the solicitor; the deception of the solicitor had resulted in receipt of the confession and the failure to exclude it meant that the court of first instance had, in effect, condoned the impropriety involved.

However, although deliberate impropriety may lead to the exclusion of evidence, it must, of course, be determined whether certain techniques will be designated improper. This issue has arisen particularly in the context of undercover police operations and secretly taped conversations. In *Bailey*,[151] investigating officers and the custody officer put on a charade intended to convince the suspects who had been charged that they did not wish to place them both in the same cell, which was bugged. This fooled the suspects who made incriminating admissions. It was submitted that the admissions should not have been admissible as undermining the spirit of Code C and especially the right to silence, since the men could not have been questioned by police at that point. However, the Court of Appeal rejected this argument on the basis that the evidence was reliable and that the conversation between the suspects could not be equated with a police interview. In other words, although there was a deception, and therefore the police could be viewed as passively recording a conversation that would have occurred anyway, that fact had no influence on the decision.

---

148 [1993] Crim LR 775.

149 [2001] 1 WLR 51.

150 [1987] Crim LR 119; [1987] 3 All ER 481, CA; see also *Woodall and Others* [1989] Crim LR 288 in which the 'trick' consisted of allowing the detainee to think that an off-the-record interview could take place in the police station.

151 (1993) *The Times*, 22 March; [1993] 3 All ER 513.

In *Christou*,[152] undercover police set up a jeweller's shop purporting to be willing to deal in stolen property and transactions with customers were recorded by means of recording equipment hidden in the shop. The police officers engaged in conversation with the defendants who came to sell recently stolen jewellery and asked them questions. They also asked the defendants to sign receipts for the jewellery. The defendants were convicted of handling stolen goods and appealed on the basis that all the evidence against them gained through the undercover operation should have been excluded either at common law under the principles enunciated in *Sang*[153] or under s 78 as obtained by deception: they would not have entered the shop had they known its true nature. This submission was rejected on the basis that the appellants had not been tricked, but had 'voluntarily applied themselves to the trick'; although specific deception had occurred, such as the request to sign the receipts, that was to be treated as part of the general deceit concerning the dishonest jeweller's shop. Therefore, the trick had not resulted in unfairness. The test for unfairness was the same at common law and under s 78.

It was also submitted that the conversations were an interview within the purview of Code of Practice C; the provisions applying to interviews should, therefore, have been followed. This submission was rejected on the basis that the Code provisions were intended to apply only where police officer and suspect were on an unequal footing because the officer was perceived to be in a position of authority. However, this was not to be taken as encouragement to officers to use undercover operations as a method of circumventing the Code provisions. In saying this, the court clearly recognised the danger that this ruling might encourage plain clothes police officers to operate secretly using hidden tape recorders to tape admissions, in preference to arresting openly and administering a caution. However, their remarks left open the possibility that such action, if cleverly enough disguised as a genuinely necessary undercover operation, could lead to circumvention of Code C and consequent erosion of the privilege against self-incrimination.

In *Bryce*,[154] the Court of Appeal was clearly fully alive to this danger. An undercover police officer posed as the buyer of a stolen car and, in conversation with the appellant, asked him questions designed to show that the car in question was stolen. The appellant allegedly gave incriminating replies. He was then arrested, refused to comment during the tape recorded interview, but allegedly made further admissions after the tape recorder had been turned off. He appealed against conviction on the ground that the evidence of the conversations and the interview was inadmissible under s 78. On the issue as to the admissibility of the conversation with the undercover officer, it was determined that the case differed from that of *Christou* on the following grounds: first, the questions asked went directly to the issue of dishonesty and were not necessary to the undercover operation; secondly, the possibility of concoction arose, whereas in *Christou* the conversations were taped. As to the unrecorded interview, the possibility of concoction clearly arose, owing to the suspicious willingness of the appellant to make admissions after refusing to do so during the recorded interview. Therefore, the judge at trial should

---

152 [1992] QB 979; [1992] 4 All ER 559, CA. See also *Williams and O'Hare v DPP* [1993] Crim LR 775; *Smurthwaite* [1994] 1 All ER 898, CA.
153 [1980] AC 402; [1979] 2 All ER 1222, HL.
154 [1992] 4 All ER 567; (1992) Cr App R 230; (1992) 142 NLJ 1161, CA.

have exercised discretion to exclude both the conversation and the unrecorded interview. Difficulty will arise after these two cases where it appears possible that a purported undercover operation has been used to circumvent the provisions of Code C, especially the need to caution, but the possibility of concoction does not arise, owing to the use of a hidden tape recorder. A court may have to draw a very fine line between questions asked going directly to the issue of guilt and those touching obliquely on it.

The common theme running through the cases considered is the use of a deception of one sort or another. The courts have had to draw fine lines between degrees of deception in determining whether or not admission of the evidence obtained would render the trial unfair. A rather different stance is taken, as indicated above, towards instances of secret recording in which no positive deception occurs, those in which it may be said that the role of the police is confined only to recording a conversation which would have taken place in any event. In such instances, it cannot be said that the police deception is instrumental in obtaining the evidence except in the hypothetical sense: had the defendant applied his mind to the possibility of secret recording, he might not have made the admissions in question. Passive secret recording may thus be contrasted with instances in which the police, or someone acting on their behalf, have created a situation which makes it likely that admissions will be made where otherwise they would not have been. This distinction may have led the courts to accept evidence derived from secret recordings[155] (except in the case of telephone tapping, where special rules apply)[156] more readily than evidence deriving from a 'positive' deception, since in comparison with other forms of deception, secret recording seems to be at the lower end of the scale. Moreover, although evidence obtained from secret recordings may have the same inculpatory effect as a confession made in police custody, the courts seem to view the two methods of obtaining admissions differently. The tendency, which reflects the reliability principle, is to view secretly recorded evidence as unaffected by the manner of its acquisition, unlike admissions made to the police in an interview conducted in breach of PACE. However, although secret recording may be regarded as less improper than the use of a positive deception, it may involve other forms of impropriety. Thus, in focusing only or mainly on the reliability of evidence obtained, the courts have demonstrated a clear preference for crime control over due process.

Section 82(3): the common law discretion

Section 82(3) provides:

> Nothing in this part of the Act shall prejudice any power of a court to exclude evidence (whether by preventing questions from being put or otherwise) at its discretion.

This provision presumably preserves the whole of the common law discretion to exclude evidence, thanks to inclusion in it of the words 'or otherwise'. In practice, its role as regards exclusion of evidence is likely to be insignificant, owing to the width of s 78.

---

155 See, eg, *Shaukat Ali* (1991) *The Times*, 19 February; *Chief Constable of West Yorkshire Police ex p Govell* (1994) transcript from LEXIS; *Effick* (1992) 95 Cr App R 427, CA; [1994] 3 All ER 458, HL; *Roberts* (1997) 1 Cr App R 217.

156 See *Preston* [1993] 4 All ER 638; (1994) 98 Cr App R 405, HL. See now the scheme under RIPA 2000, s 17; discussed in Chapter 11, pp 684–88.

However, a distinct function for s 82(3) was suggested in *Sat-Bhambra*;[157] it was held that ss 76 and 78 only operate before the evidence is led before the jury, but that s 82(3) can be invoked after that point. Similarly, Zander[158] argues that the common law discretion to exclude evidence is covered by both s 78 and s 82(3). Thus at present, s 82(3) may have a significant role to play only in preserving the judicial function of the judge in protecting witnesses or asking the jury to disregard evidence. The judge can at any point direct the jury to disregard evidence which has already been admitted and which may be unreliable.

In *O'Leary*,[159] May CJ expressed the view that s 82(3) rather than s 78 preserves the common law discretion to exclude unreliable evidence (presumably in circumstances falling outside s 76(2)(b)). However, it is hard to see how to separate the questions of the admissibility of unreliable evidence and of unfairness at the trial. Admission of unreliable evidence will always affect the trial. In *Parris*,[160] evidence which may have been fabricated by the police was excluded under s 78, not s 82(3). It appears likely that s 78 will continue to be used as a means of excluding unreliable evidence if s 76(2)(b) cannot be invoked.

Mentally handicapped defendants: special rules

As noted above, the confession of a suspect who is mentally disordered or of low intelligence may be rendered inadmissible under s 76(2)(b) if the interrogation is not conducted with particular propriety.[161] However, special rules will apply in the case of some mentally handicapped defendants. The confession of a mentally retarded defendant must be treated with particular caution. Under s 77, in such an instance, if the confession was not made in the presence of an independent person and if the case depends largely on the confession, the jury must be warned to exercise particular caution before convicting. (This does not apply to the mentally ill although the Royal Commission has recommended that it should be extended to cover all categories of mentally disordered suspects.)[162]

In some such instances, s 77 need not be invoked because the judge should withdraw the case from the jury. In *McKenzie*[163] the appellant, who was of subnormal intelligence and had sexual problems, was arrested and questioned about arson offences and about the killing of two elderly women. He made detailed admissions as to the arson offences and the two killings in a series of interviews. He also admitted to 10 other killings which he had not committed. He appealed against his conviction for manslaughter and arson and it was held on appeal that where the prosecution case depends wholly on confession evidence, the defendant is significantly mentally handicapped and the confessions are

---

157 (1988) JP Rep 365; (1988) Cr App R 55.
158 Zander, *op cit*, fn 1, p 210. Case law has not identified a distinction between the functions of the two sections (see, eg, *Christou* [1992] 4 All ER 559).
159 [1988] Crim LR 827, CA.
160 (1989) 9 Cr App R 68, CA.
161 See above, p 878.
162 Report Proposal 85.
163 [1993] 1 WLR 453; (1992) 142 NLJ 1162, CA.

unconvincing, the judge should withdraw the case from the jury. When these three tests were applied in the instant case in respect of the confessions to the killings, it was found that they were satisfied, the third largely by the doubt cast on the appellant's credibility owing to his confessions to killings he could not have committed. However, the first test was not satisfied in respect of the convictions for arson. Those convictions could therefore stand, but those for manslaughter were quashed. These rules are clearly of value as a means of affording protection to a group of persons who are least able to withstand pressure from the police and most likely to make a false confession. However, it is suggested that the second test could usefully be broadened so that it includes all those suffering from significant mental impairment at the time when the offences took place.

Abuse of process

If malpractice by police or prosecutors reaches a certain level of seriousness, the trial can halted on the basis that to do otherwise would be an abuse of process. The House of Lords found in *Latif*[164] that in considering whether to stay the proceedings for abuse of process, the judge should weigh the public interest in ensuring that those accused of serious crimes are brought to trial against the public interest in avoiding giving the impression, based on classic crime control norms, that courts are prepared to find that the end justifies the means. This balancing of interests may be termed the *'Latif* test'. The stance taken in *Latif* may be compared with that taken in *Mullen*[165] in which the Court of Appeal said: 'the need to discourage [blatant and very serious malpractice] ... is a matter of public policy to which ... very considerable weight should be attached'. However, these remarks do not suggest that an absolute test is in contemplation and in so far as there is a difference between the approaches of *Mullen* and *Latif* it is probable that the *Latif* test will prevail, since it derives from a House of Lords decision and is more in harmony with the approach taken to improperly obtained evidence under s 78, as indicated above.

In *Chalkley*,[166] Auld LJ stated that the issue of exclusion of evidence is distinct from the question whether the prosecution should be stayed for abuse of process. He said that while the discretion to declare an abuse of process would be governed by the balancing test referred to above, the discretion under s 78 would be governed almost entirely by the question whether the impropriety of the police or prosecutor had affected the reliability of the evidence. In other words, in exceptional circumstances, the trial might be halted to mark the court's disapproval of pre-trial malpractice; he considered that this would virtually never occur in respect of exclusion of evidence, except in the case of confessions.

3 TRIAL REMEDIES: EFFECTS OF THE HRA

Duties of the courts

Theoretically, a defendant could be convicted after a trial which failed to meet Art 6 standards, where the unfairness was due to incompatible domestic legislation. This is

---

164 [1996] 1 All ER 353.
165 [1999] 2 Cr App R 143, p 157.
166 [1998] 2 Cr App R 79.

allowed for under s 6(2)(b), as Chapter 4 points out.[167] If so, the conviction would have to stand and therefore, in general, there would appear to be no benefit in appealing to a higher court which could issue a declaration of incompatibility. But, there would be an incentive to appeal where there was leeway for the higher court to take a different view on incompatibility by finding a way of reconciling the domestic legislation with Art 6[168] or if there were grounds for expecting the higher court, once it had made the declaration, to award a lower sentence. In practice, however, it is likely that the domestic courts will be determined to avoid convicting and perhaps imprisoning a defendant under legislation which breaches the Convention, by declaring an abuse of process.[169]

The domestic courts will, save for the s 6(2) HRA proviso concerning incompatible legislation, fail to satisfy s 6 of the HRA if they act incompatibly with the Convention rights, since they are themselves public authorities. The position appears to be that wherever a court has a discretion in the course of criminal procedure, a decision regarding its use of that discretion will amount to an 'act' within the meaning s 6 of the HRA.[170] If a court does violate the rights in taking decisions as to, *inter alia*, exclusion of evidence or abuse of process, ss 7 and 8 of the HRA will be relevant. As Chapter 4 explains, s 7 allows a victim of an alleged violation, or proposed violation, of a Convention guarantee to rely on the right in litigation, and to argue in particular that he would be a victim of an unlawful act if the act proposed is undertaken. Section 8 allows courts to grant such remedies as seem to them just and convenient for such violations.

The view might be taken that breaches of Convention rights by courts should be remedied through the appeal process and that s 6 alone, rather than ss 7 and 8, is therefore relevant during the trial process. This view would not accord, however, with the stance of the House of Lords in the leading pre-HRA decision, *R v DPP ex p Kebilene and Others*.[171] In considering Art 6, the House of Lords pointed out, the domestic court is not, of necessity, in the same position as the Strasbourg court: 'it was inevitable that the European Court would conduct a retrospective review of [whether a trial was fair or unfair in Art 6(1) terms] in the national court', but that in the domestic court, this matter could be considered before completion of a trial. In other words, the Strasbourg Court could consider the whole pre-trial and trial process and come to a determination as to its fairness under Art 6(1). The domestic court would have to consider, during pre-trial hearings, the trial process, or on appeal, not only whether an actual or potential breach had occurred, but also whether Art 6 would be breached owing to its own regulation of the process. *Ex p Kebilene* suggests that appeals will not provide the only means of enforcing the Convention against courts. The better view, therefore, is that all three sections may be relied upon during the trial as well as on appeal.

The defendant might, for example, raise the argument that if the court failed to exclude evidence, Art 6(1) would be breached and that therefore, ss 7 and 8 require that the evidence should be excluded in order to avoid the breach. Section 8, as indicated, appears to afford some discretion to a court as to awarding the remedy, but it is almost

---

167 See p 156.
168 *Brown v Stott* [2001] 2 WLR 817.
169 See the judgment of Lord Steyn in *Ex p Kebeline* [1999] 4 All ER 801.
170 This is the stance of the Strasbourg Court: see *Z v Finland* (1997) 25 EHRR 371.
171 [1999] 3 WLR 972.

inconceivable that a court during a trial would accept the argument that it was about to act unlawfully, within s 6, but then, although it found leeway to do so and was not therefore affected by s 6(2), fail to provide a remedy by resiling from the threatened unlawfulness. A court might, of course, find, erroneously, that its particular decision during the criminal procedure would not breach Art 6, in which case the issue would have to be raised on appeal. A court adjudicating on the current grounds for allowing an appeal would itself be bound by s 6, but would theoretically also retain a discretion under s 8 as to the award of a remedy.

In accordance with the Strasbourg jurisprudence and s 6 of the HRA, the appeal court is itself bound by Art 6.[172] The test for criminal appeals from the Crown Court is simply whether the conviction is 'unsafe'.[173] In *Mullen*,[174] the Court of Appeal said that an abuse of process, or, equally, material irregularities at the trial would empower the court to find that a conviction was unsafe. If the Court of Appeal considered that despite a pre-trial breach of the Convention, a conviction was safe, this view could be challenged as itself – in the particular circumstances – contrary to Art 6. If Art 6 was itself breached owing to the effect of pre-trial improprieties, which were not cured at trial, it is hard to see that the conviction could be regarded as 'safe'.

This is broadly the stance, with a narrow caveat, currently taken by the Court of Appeal. In *Pearson*,[175] the Court of Appeal said: 'where this court takes the view that an appellant did not receive a fair trial this court would not, save in the most exceptional circumstances, reach the view that the conviction was nevertheless safe'. Now that Art 6 is binding on the Court of Appeal, the exception mentioned would cease to apply since otherwise, that court would be declaring, in effect, its intention to breach the Convention guarantee of a fair trial, contrary to s 6 of the HRA.

Requirements of Art 6

As Chapter 2 indicated, Art 6 is seen as a central Convention Article which holds a pre-eminent position in the Convention jurisprudence since the right it protects is so fundamentally important in a democratic society.[176] It expresses a 'fundamental principle of the rule of law'[177] and is to be interpreted broadly.[178] The Court has tended to take an increasingly interventionist stance towards the right to a fair trial. Such a stance was evident in *Teixeira v Portugal*,[179] *Van Mechelen v Netherlands*,[180] *Saidi v France*[181] and *Rowe*

---

172 *Delcourt v Belgium* A 11 (1970).

173 The Criminal Appeals Act 1968, s 2(1), as amended by the Criminal Appeals Act 1995. This provision, which allows the conviction to stand despite, eg, a misdirection of the judge, may require modification owing to the findings of the European Court in *Condron v UK* (2001) 31 EHRR 1; see (2000) J Civ Lib 253.

174 [1999] 2 Cr App R 143.

175 (1998) *The Times*, 20 February.

176 See pp 57–58.

177 *Salabiaku v France* (1988) 13 EHRR 379.

178 *Delcourt v Belgium* (1970) 1 EHRR 355.

179 (1998) 28 EHHR 101; [1998] Crim LR 751.

180 (1998) 25 EHRR 657.

181 (1994) 17 EHRR 251.

and Davis v UK[182] although the Court continues to adhere to the principle that the assessment of evidence is for the national court.[183] Apart from the right to be presumed innocent under Art 6(2), the guarantee of the access to legal advice and the other minimal guarantees of para 6(3),[184] the Court has found that a number of rights are implicit in the term a 'fair hearing'.[185] The principle of 'equality of arms' – equality between defence and prosecution – arising from Art 6(1) affects all aspects of a hearing, therefore overlapping with its expression under Art 6(3).[186]

Instances in which a trial remedy may be required

The key question that a number of commentators have emphasised is whether the requirement of fairness under Art 6(1) is likely to add anything to the possibilities of creating police accountability by excluding evidence or staying the proceedings that already existed pre-HRA, domestically.[187] In particular, where the police have not adhered to the statutory safeguards for suspects, is it more likely under s 8 of the HRA that evidence thereby obtained will be excluded, possibly providing greater protection for suspects? As indicated above, Art 6(1) allows each Member State to determine its own rules of evidence. Nevertheless, the admission of evidence obtained in certain ways has been found to infringe Art 6. In these situations, the duty of the court under s 6 of the HRA requires it to exclude the evidence or stay the proceedings. Thus, in certain circumstances, Art 6 is likely to create greater accountability.

It was argued in Chapter 13 that where access to legal advice has been delayed, and the accused has remained silent in interviews without having had access to legal advice, a breach of Art 6(3)(c) and possibly of Art 6(1) is likely to occur if adverse inferences are then drawn at trial.[188] One method of preventing this, which has not been catered for under domestic law,[189] would be to exclude the interviews. A similar argument could also be put forward where, in the same circumstances, the accused had in fact made admissions in the interviews.

A similarly strong argument for exclusion of evidence under Art 6(1) could be raised where the evidence of informers, although not illegally obtained, might affect the fairness of the trial,[190] particularly where part of the evidence and/or the identity of the informer

---

182 (2000) 30 EHRR 1.

183 *Khan v UK* (2000) 8 BHRC 310.

184 See Chapter 2, pp 63–64; Chapter 13, pp 860–64.

185 For general discussion see Harris, D, O'Boyle, K and Warbrick, C, *Law of The European Convention on Human Rights*, 1995, Chapter 6; Ovey, C, 'The ECHR and the criminal lawyer: an introduction' [1998] Crim LR 4; Clayton and Tomlinson, *op cit*, fn 1, Chapter 11.

186 The principle is fully established and long standing in the Art 6 jurisprudence: see *X v FRG* (1963) 6 YB 520, p 574. See further Chapter 2, p 62.

187 See, eg, Clayton and Tomlinson, *op cit*, fn 1, p 1465.

188 See pp 860–64. This argument is based on *Murray v UK* (1996) 22 EHRR 29, *Averill v UK* (2001) 31 EHRR 35, and *Magee v UK* (2001) 31 EHRR 35.

189 The Youth Justice and Criminal Evidence Act 1999, s 58, only provides that in such circumstances adverse inferences may not be drawn.

190 For detailed discussion see Justice, *Under Surveillance: Covert Policing and Human Rights Standards*, 1998, Chapter 2, especially pp 37–51 and Chapter 3, especially pp 70–74.

is not disclosed to the defence.[191] The rules on disclosure under the Criminal Procedure and Investigations Act 1996 create a regime which allows sensitive material to be withheld by the prosecution so that neither the court nor the defence is aware of its existence.[192] Where this has occurred, argument for exclusion of evidence could be raised under Art 6 at first instance or on appeal, based on the general requirements of fairness and on the 'equality of arms' principle.[193] The domestic courts would be expected to test issues of admissibility of evidence and of disclosure more directly against the requirements of Art 6 than has generally occurred at Strasbourg, owing to the effect of the margin of appreciation doctrine.

It was found in an early decision, *Austria v Italy*,[194] that maltreatment with the aim of extracting a confession created a breach of Art 6(2). This argument can be applied where 'compelled' admissions, including those obtained by treatment falling within s 76, and those obtained on pain of a penalty under the TA,[195] while not themselves used in evidence, had led to the uncovering of other evidence. It could be argued, in furtherance of a fair procedure under Art 6, that that other evidence should be excluded under s 78. The question of pressure on the applicant in the interview was taken into account by the Court in reaching its conclusion that Art 6 had been breached in *Saunders v UK*[196] by the admission in evidence of the coerced admissions, and the argument could be extended to encompass other evidence uncovered as a result of such admissions. Clearly, the decision in *Brown v Stott*[197] has, however, weakened this argument to an extent, since the courts in future are likely to consider the legitimate aim of the compulsion and the question whether the compulsion is in proportion to the aim in creating a minimal impact on the accused's Art 6 rights.

The general stance regarding police impropriety

Thus, there are certain instances in which the Strasbourg jurisprudence would support excluding evidence or staying the proceedings in order to meet the requirements of Art 6. But, aside from such instances, the general question of using exclusion of evidence or a stay where police impropriety has occurred arises, and Strasbourg has not offered much guidance as to the requirements of Art 6. Even in such instances, the stance of the domestic court cannot be predicted with any certainty. The domestic courts are not bound by the Strasbourg jurisprudence under s 2 of the HRA and may consider even in such instances that a trial remedy is not required. As indicated below, the domestic courts are

---

191 Eg, the evidence might be tainted owing to the motivation of the informer. In *Windisch v Austria* [1990] 13 EHRR 281 the Court said: 'the Convention does not preclude reliance, at the investigation stage, on sources such as anonymous informants. However, the subsequent use of their statements by the trial court to found a conviction is another matter.' But see *Edwards v UK* (1992) 15 EHRR 417 (it was found that the hearing in the CA remedied the failure of disclosure). These issues were, however, raised successfully under Art 6 in *Rowe and Davis v UK* (2000) 30 EHRR 1.

192 For discussion see *Archbold: Criminal Pleading, Practice and Evidence*, 1999, para 12-52.

193 In *Jespers v Belgium*, the Commission found that under Art 6(3), the accused has the right 'to have at his disposal ... all relevant elements that have been or could be collected by the relevant authorities': App no 8403/78, 27 DR 61.

194 Appl No 788/60 4 YB 112 (1961).

195 See Chapter 13, pp 846–48.

196 (1997) 23 EHRR 313. *Saunders* is discussed in Chapter 13, p 855.

197 [2001] 2 WLR 817.

likely to concentrate on the particular facts of each case and, in particular, on the question of the reliability of the evidence, in relation to the question of its exclusion. In contrast, a stay may occasionally be determined upon, even where the evidence may be reliable.

Clearly, in the case of very serious malpractice, including breaches of Convention rights, the court would view it as impossible to sustain the view that Art 6 would not be breached if the trial went ahead or if, depending on the circumstances, evidence was not excluded. As indicated, the statutory provisions leave this matter open; the only instance in which it is not a matter either of statutory interpretation under s 76, or a matter of discretion under s 78 or in respect of staying the proceedings, is in the case of confessions obtained in breach of Art 3, under s 76(2)(a). The discussion has shown that the courts have continued the common law tradition within the PACE scheme of excluding confessions tainted by impropriety, but they have shown great reluctance to exclude other evidence which is equally tainted. A stay will be used only in relation to certain instances of gross malpractice.

In practice, bearing in mind their previous tendency to exclude such evidence where impropriety or unlawfulness has occurred in the investigative or custodial process, domestic courts will probably exercise discretion in such a way as to ensure that admissions and, probably, silences are excluded under s 78 in compliance with Art 6(1). The domestic jurisprudence is far more extensive on this matter than that regarding confessions under Art 6, and, despite the reluctance of the judiciary to lay down guiding principles for the application of s 78, academics in an extensive literature have identified some indications of adherence to such principle.[198] The effect of Art 6 may be to encourage some clearer statements of principle.

But the stance currently taken towards *non-confession* evidence, including evidence obtained from informers and from other forms of surveillance, may not satisfy Art 6(1). As indicated, under domestic practice, evidence gained through a very serious impropriety, including a breach of a Convention right, is admissible, as is, under s 76(4) of PACE, physical evidence uncovered through an inadmissible confession gained as a result of impropriety, not excluding Art 3 treatment. The discretion to exclude non-confession evidence is very narrow and the impact which s 78 has had in encouraging adherence to due process may be diminishing at the present time. As L-T-Choo observes: 'recent decisions of the Court of Appeal signal a movement away from focusing on the nature of the breach [of PACE or the Codes] and towards an approach which takes the nature of the evidence as its central consideration'.[199] In other words, the movement is away from due process values and towards acceptance of the crime control norm that the end – a conviction – justifies the means. Until recently, there were expectations that such movement could be reversed under Art 6 following an interpretation of the *Teixeira* approach to the effect that some forms of evidence gathering would almost automatically render the trial unfair.

From a due process perspective, such an activist interpretation of Art 6 has been urged, and some commentators argued for a near-absolute rule requiring exclusion of evidence where it has been obtained in breach of a fundamental constitutional right or

---

198 See Allen, *op cit*, fn 70; Gelowitz, *op cit*, fn 70; May, *op cit*, fn 70; Stone, *op cit*, fn 70; Sanders and Young, *op cit*, fn 1, Chapter 11, Part 5.

199 Choo and Nash, *op cit*, fn 70.

where its admission would breach the right to a fair trial.[200] Clearly, it was tempting to argue that Art 6 requires that a court should not merely inquire into the truth of the charges against a defendant: it should also play a part in maintaining standards in criminal investigations, in discouraging police abuse of power and upholding the due process elements within the investigative process which correspond to the rights of the detainee recognised under PACE and the TA.

Clearly, the requirements placed on the domestic courts depend on the view taken of the meaning of fairness under Art 6. Strasbourg and the domestic courts have united in finding that a breach of another Convention right, perpetrated pre-trial, does not automatically render the trial unfair.[201] Therefore, the fact that such a breach has occurred is part of the history of the case which can be taken into account in considering the proceedings as a whole, but which, except in the case of a breach of Art 3 in order to obtain a confession,[202] is not conclusive of the issue regarding fairness. The same argument applies to findings that flaws in the custodial and investigative procedures, including breaches of the PACE or TA Codes of Practice, not amounting in themselves to breaches of Convention rights, have occurred. They could be addressed, under ss 6 and 7 of the HRA, by means of exclusion of evidence or a stay for abuse of process, in order to avoid breaching Art 6(1), but only if the trial would otherwise be unfair. The discussion below will consider the general Strasbourg stance in relation to improperly obtained evidence and its probable impact on domestic practice under the HRA.

The domestic response to Teixeira v Portugal: the narrow view

As discussed above, *Teixeira de Castro v Portugal*[203] laid down quite a strict test in relation to evidence obtained by entrapment. Where there had been enticement by undercover officers to supply drugs, the applicant was found to have been 'definitively deprived of a fair trial'.[204] The case could be distinguished from *Ludi v Switzerland*,[205] in which no breach of Art 6 was found where a police officer had posed as a buyer in a drug deal which was already under way. The Court, therefore, did not find that undercover work of this type would inevitably affect the fairness of the trial. The test was whether the defendant could be said to be 'predisposed' to commit the offence in question. If so, unfairness would not be established. This test arguably differs slightly from the current one under UK law. As indicated above, if undercover officers give the defendant an *opportunity* to commit the offence where it appears that he would have committed it had the opportunity been offered by someone else, that is not entrapment; but it will amount to entrapment if they impliedly persuade him into it or otherwise can be said to instigate it. It is suggested that while *Smurthwaite*[206] is probably in harmony with the test as laid down by the Court in *Teixeira, Williams and O'Hare v DPP* is not, since it was not certain

---

200 See, eg, Ashworth, A, 'Article 6 and the fairness of trials' [1999] Crim LR 261, p 271.

201 *Khan* [1997] AC 558 and *Khan v UK* (2000) 8 BHRC 310.

202 Under s 76(2)(a).

203 (1998) 28 EHHR 101; [1998] Crim LR 751. See also *Van Mechelen v Netherlands* (1998) 25 EHRR 647; the findings of the Commission and Court in *Rowe and Davis* (2000) 30 EHRR 1; *Condron v UK* (2001) 31 EHRR 1.

204 *Ibid*, para 39.

205 (1993) 15 EHRR 173.

206 [1994] 1 All ER 898.

that the particular offences in question would have been committed without the intervention of those conducting the 'sting'.

However, the first domestic decision to apply *Teixeira*, *Nottingham CC v Mohammed Amin*,[207] gave it a restrictive interpretation in distinguishing it on somewhat narrow grounds. The respondent, who was driving an unlicensed motor vehicle, responded to a flagging down by two constables posing as members of the public; he took them to their destination, where the fare was paid over. He contended that the constables had not confined themselves to passive investigation but had incited him to commit the offence, thereby rendering the proceedings as a whole unfair. Lord Bingham found that he had not been pressured or incited into committing an offence. The basis on which it was found that flagging him down – a positive action – was not incitement to commit the offence is, it is suggested, unclear. The respondent had turned off his light, thereby indicating that he was not for hire.[208] Similarly, in *Shannon*,[209] the Court of Appeal was unwilling to characterise the behaviour of the reporters as being that of *agents provocateurs*. But it was also found that even if their behaviour had crossed the borderline into that of an agent provocateur, it would not have been viewed as right to disturb the discretion of the judge to admit the evidence.[210] This stance was confirmed in *AG's Reference (No 3 of 2000)*[211] in which, on facts bearing quite a strong resemblance to those of *Teixeira*, it was found that the judge should not have stayed the trial, applying *Teixeira*, on the basis that the defendant had been encouraged to commit the offence in question by the undercover officers. Instead, it was found that the fact of enticement to commit the offence was not enough: a number of questions should have been asked concerning the defendant's freedom of choice and the extent to which he had been pressured into supplying drugs.

Thus, the key question appears to be whether the courts are prepared to express disapproval of certain evidence gathering techniques by excluding the evidence in question, as *Teixeira* arguably appears to require. In *Shannon*, the Court of Appeal appeared to be determined to view *Teixeira* as an abuse of process case rather than as applicable to exclusion of evidence, on the basis that to find otherwise would create a conflict with the finding of the Court in *Schenk*.[212] On this basis, the courts are able to disregard possible conflicts between the domestic basis for excluding evidence obtained by *agent provocateurs* and the Strasbourg basis, as expressed in *Teixeira*. It is suggested that determination to retain and maximise judicial discretion, allowing for the pursuit of crime control aims untrammelled by due process constraints imported from Strasbourg, provides the true reason for taking this view of *Teixeira*.

---

207 [2000] 1 WLR 1071; [2000] Crim LR 174.
208 Leave to appeal to the House of Lords was granted, but it is suggested that the Lords are likely to agree with Lord Bingham.
209 [2001] 1 WLR 51.
210 *Ibid*, p 73, para 50.
211 [2001] Crim LR 645.
212 (1988) 13 EHRR 242.

Reconciling Teixeira v Portugal *and* Khan v UK: *the broad view*

The current narrow interpretation of s 78 of PACE[213] indicated above means that improperly obtained non-confession evidence will not be excluded, whether or not the impropriety also amounted to a breach of a Convention right. In other words, the admission of evidence in such circumstances need not amount to a breach of Art 6. The findings in *AG's Reference (No 3 of 1999)*[214] suggest that at present, there is a tendency to reject the possibility of using exclusion of evidence to uphold fundamental rights. This seems to be the case even where such rights are recognised within a statutory scheme; and possibly also where the breach is of a Convention right. The case of *Khan v UK*[215] will be utilised by the courts to support this probability, despite the inception of the HRA. It was found in *Khan* that the admission of evidence obtained in breach of Art 8 did not create a breach of Art 6. It could be argued on a broad view of the decision that *Teixeira de Castro* is apparently out of accord with *Khan* since, in so far as the effect of the impropriety at issue in *Teixeira* might have been cured by exclusion of the evidence, the Court implied that there would be virtually no judicial discretion left to exercise to admit it.

Of course this is not the reading of *Teixeira* that the courts are adopting, as indicated above. But it is a possible reading. It is unfortunate that the Court did not address the question whether excluding the evidence obtained by entrapment would have rendered the trial fair. In the particular circumstances, the trial would probably have collapsed and therefore that question was of little import. But presumably, the Court itself wished to characterise the matter as one that did not reach into the question of exclusion of evidence since otherwise, it would have had to take a stance on the question of the assessment of evidence which it prefers to leave to the national court. But since it deliberately avoided the question of exclusion of evidence, it is arguable that in some circumstances the principle from *Teixeira* could be utilised to argue, not for the abandonment of the trial, but for exclusion of the evidence tainted by the unfairness. Moreover, there is a readily apparent argument to the effect that *Khan v UK* does not in fact imply that the failure to exclude evidence obtained in breach of a fundamental right meets nationally accepted standards of procedural justice, since Strasbourg merely decided that the assessment of evidence was for the national court. In other words, it conceded a margin of appreciation to the national court, leaving it free to take a different stance as to the exclusion of improperly obtained evidence.

A robust interpretation of the Art 6 guarantee of fairness, bearing *Teixeira* in mind, would support a requirement that an impropriety or illegality in the custodial or investigative procedures would tend to tip the scales towards exclusion of the evidence obtained as a result, including non-confession evidence.[216] The very significant difference between the positions of the Strasbourg and the national courts would support such an

213 See *Chalkley* [1998] 2 All ER 155; *Khan* [1997] AC 558 and *Shannon* [2001] 1 WLR 51.
214 [2001] 2 WLR 56, p 64, *per* Lord Steyn, and p 65, *per* Lord Cook of Thorndon.
215 (2000) 8 BHRC 310.
216 In this context, the decision of the Court of Appeal in *R v Radak and Others* [1999] 1 Cr App R 187; (1999) *The Times*, 7 October should be noted. The decision related to admission of a written witness statement pursuant to the Criminal Justice Act 1988, ss 23, 25 and 26, and was concerned with prosecution rather than police impropriety. But the decision is of interest since the court relied heavily on Art 6(1) and (3)(d) in finding that the judge's discretion under s 26 had been wrongly exercised, since he had failed to safeguard the defendants' rights in accordance with the Art 6 requirements.

interpretation. In particular, it might be found that breach of the Convention guarantees in the pre-trial procedures would make it virtually inevitable that the trial would be rendered unfair if evidence deriving from the breach were not excluded.

If this interpretation is adopted, which currently appears to be very unlikely, it would mean that in so far as certain of the due process rights enshrined in PACE, the TA and their associated Codes reflect certain of the principles enshrined in Arts 3, 5, 6 or 8, their status might be enhanced. One particular effect would be that the PACE or TA Code provisions in question, as the detailed domestic embodiment of those rights, would be accorded *de facto* a higher value than their legal status would appear to warrant.

Moving beyond due process and crime control

It was argued in the Introduction to this chapter that a more developed conception of criminal justice would take into account the interests of victims in dignity and in equality as well as the requirement of fairness to the accused. The issues of exclusion of evidence and of staying the proceedings provide a forum for considering what such a more developed conception might mean. Rape cases in particular highlight the problem of concentrating only on a gender-neutral account of the requirements of fairness to the accused, although the issues they raise also have a wider application.

It could be argued that where evidence which is reliable is crucial to the case, the Convention rights of the victim should be taken into account in making a determination as to its admittance or exclusion. If the accused walks free from court, the victim's life may be profoundly disrupted owing to psychological disturbance, fear, and physical constraints, such as feeling forced to move to a different area. She is likely to be profoundly affected in the free ordering of her life by the knowledge that the rapist is at large. These experiences may occur in any event, but there is a large body of evidence to the effect that the victim's recovery is affected by the conviction of the attacker,[217] while her physical security at the point at which she is psychologically most vulnerable will be affected by the fact that he has been imprisoned. Thus, it is argued that a developed conception of criminal justice would allow such considerations to be taken into account, under the rubrics of Arts 8, 14 and 3. The issue might be put squarely before the court if, for example, a women's campaigning group was allowed to intervene in order to argue that the courts' duty under s 6 of the HRA required it to take the victims' Convention rights into account.

Similar considerations apply in respect of the victims of many offences. The victim of a serious violent offence may be said to suffer a violation of his or her right to security of the person and possibly to privacy and freedom of movement if an offender is acquitted, not on the basis of doubts about his or her guilt, but as a result of police impropriety. The victim of a racial attack, or the family of the victim, may experience a similar restriction. Article 2 might also be engaged. To take an extreme example: if, in the case of a trial for attempted murder, a court excluded, owing to a serious breach of Art 8, tape recorded evidence linking a defendant with a history of domestic violence to the attempted murder

---

217 See, eg, Lees, S, *Ruling Passions, Sexual Violence, Reputation and the Law*, 1997; *Sexual Violence: The Reality for Women*, 1999.

of his wife, the possibility of her subsequent murder could be viewed as engaging the duty of the court under s 6 of the HRA to abide by Art 2.[218]

Such arguments clearly look like crime control arguments and they may well lead to the same outcome. However, feminist and victim-orientated arguments should not merely be co-opted by advocates of crime control.[219] The difference is that such arguments may be viewed as based on principle, while crime control arguments are purely consequentialist. While the crime control model would not allow for a nuanced, proportionate approach to exclusion of evidence since it would merely ask whether it was reliable, the approach which takes account of the victims' interests can be more nuanced since in some instances, the victims' interests could not be said to be engaged. The question is whether to elevate the concerns of Art 6 above those of Arts 8 or 3 or 14, which are, or may be, it is argued, engaged by the issues in question. Clearly, the court has a public duty to uphold standards of criminal justice which go beyond the interests of the victim.[220] However, strands of Convention jurisprudence are emerging which may allow for those interests to be taken into account in adoption of a nuanced approach.[221] The Convention provides a growing recognition of victims' rights.[222] In particular, there is now a significant body of jurisprudence recognising rights of victims and victims' families within the criminal justice system where the State is the 'attacker'.[223] Thus, there is a case for arguing, under the HRA, that the impact of a decision to exclude evidence or stay the proceedings should be considered from a perspective which is not bounded by Art 6 concerns alone.

Conclusions

While due process demands that improperly obtained evidence should be excluded, that the police officers involved should be disciplined or prosecuted, and, where appropriate, that compensation should be available, it is unclear that it demands, in principle, that a person who is factually guilty of an offence should be acquitted. If evidence is excluded and, as a result, the burden of proof cannot be discharged, acquittal must clearly follow. But methods of escaping from the conflicts of interest indicated inherent in such exclusion should be sought. Such acquittals uphold the integrity of the criminal justice system since they demonstrate a refusal of the courts to associate themselves with a fundamental breach of rights, but they profoundly fail to address the interests of victims, also recognised at Strasbourg, their relatives, and the general societal interest in the prevention of crime. Moreover, although exclusion of evidence may have symbolic value in terms of integrity, it has not been viewed at Strasbourg as providing an effective remedy for breach of a Convention right,[224] and it clearly can have no impact on the overwhelming majority

---

218 See *Osman v UK* (2000) 29 EHRR 245, discussed in Chapter 2, pp 39 and 60.

219 For discussion, see Whitty, N, Murphy, T and Livingstone, S, *Civil Liberties Law*, 2000, p 194; Young, J, *The Exclusive Society: Social Exclusion, Crime and Difference in Late Modernity*, 1999.

220 See Fenwick, H, 'Procedural rights of victims of crime: public or private ordering of the criminal justice process?' (1997) 60 MLR 317–33.

221 See further Chapter 2, pp 39–40.

222 See *X and Y v Netherlands* (1985) 8 EHRR 235.

223 *Kaya v Turkey* (1998-I) ECtHR 297; *Akdivar v Turkey* (1997) 23 EHRR 143; *Mentes v Turkey* (1997) 27 EHRR 595; *Gulec v Turkey* (1999) 28 EHRR 121; *Cetin v Turkey* (unreported); *Tekin v Turkey* RJD 1998-IV 53.

224 *Khan v UK* (2000) 8 BHRC 310, paras 44–47.

of cases in which the defendant pleads guilty. Given that, increasingly, the police know that the case is unlikely to come to trial,[225] the deterrent effect of exclusion, such as it is, may be diminishing. Even in cases that do come to trial, exclusion of evidence can have no impact where there is other evidence which can support the conviction. Stays for abuse of process are rarely used and arguably their use is arbitrary; therefore, they are unlikely to have a significant impact on police practice.

These arguments strengthen the case for further, more radical reform of the police complaints and disciplinary system and of CPS decision making, since so doing would tend to discourage illegality and impropriety and enhance levels of adherence to the PACE rules, including the Code provisions. Arguments for exclusion of evidence on the basis of police impropriety might be raised less frequently. There is a further pragmatic reason for adopting this approach. The judges have made it clear that despite the inception of the HRA, they are wedded to the common law tradition of admitting evidence even if it has been obtained improperly. If anything, decisions such as *Forbes* and *Shannon* suggest that their determination to adhere to this tradition has been *strengthened* by the inception of the HRA. Possibly, this is another example of the common law resisting or subsuming the influence of the Convention. Maintenance of judicial discretion to react to the facts of particular cases remains the overwhelming priority and, in furtherance of this aim, the requirements of Art 6 have been minimised. Given that this clear pattern is now emerging, remedies must be sought elsewhere, while at the same time failures of police accountability should be used to press for organisational reforms.[226] The efficacy of such other remedies is considered below.

4 TORTIOUS REMEDIES[227]

Tort actions

Tort damages will be available as a result of some breaches of PACE, the TA and other relevant statutes. For example, if a police officer arrests a citizen where no reasonable suspicion arises under ss 24 or 25 of PACE, an action for false imprisonment will be available. Equally, such a remedy would be available if the Part IV provisions governing time limits on detention were breached[228] or if a detention review failed to occur for a period of time.[229] Trespass to land or to goods will occur if the statutory provisions governing search of premises or seizure of goods are not followed. Malicious prosecution will be available where police have abused their powers in recommending prosecution to the Crown Prosecution Service. Also, one of the ancient 'malicious process torts' may be

---

225 See further Sanders and Young, *op cit*, fn 1, Chapter 7.

226 See Sanders and Young, *op cit*, fn 1, pp 724–30.

227 See Clayton, R and Tomlinson, H, *Civil Actions Against the Police*, 3rd edn, 1999, Sweet & Maxwell for a list of examples of recent damages awards. See also Sanders and Young, *op cit*, fn 1, Chapter 11, Part 3.

228 Eg, *Edwards v Chief Constable of Avon and Somerset* (1992) 9 March, unreported; the plaintiff was detained for 8 hours, 47 minutes following a lawful arrest. The detention was wrongful because it was 'unnecessary'; compensation was awarded.

229 In *Roberts* [1999] 1 WLR 662 the review took place two hours after it should have done. The Court of Appeal found that Roberts had been falsely imprisoned during those two hours even though it was found that, had the review taken place, he would have remained in detention.

available where a malicious search or arrest has occurred, although in fact these actions are extremely rare and their continued existence is in doubt.[230] Such actions may not be brought because a claim of false imprisonment is preferred, but there is a distinction between malicious process torts and false imprisonment in that in the former case, but not the latter, all the proper procedural formalities will have been carried out. Actions for malicious prosecution are quite common, but the plaintiff carries quite a heavy burden in the need to prove that there was no reasonable or probable cause for the prosecution.[231] It may be that if the prosecution is brought on competent legal advice, this action will fail, but this is unclear.[232]

Almost the whole of the interviewing scheme, which is contained mainly in Codes C and E rather than in PACE itself, is unaffected by tortious remedies. Section 67(10) of PACE provides that no civil or criminal liability arises from breaches of the Codes of Practice. The same is true of the TA Codes under Sched 12, para 6 of the TA. This lack of a remedy also extends to some statutory provisions, in particular the most significant statutory interviewing provision, the entitlement to legal advice, arising under both PACE and the TA.[233] There is no tort of denial of access to legal advice; the only possible tortious action would be for breach of statutory duty. It might have been expected that an action for false imprisonment might lie where gross breaches of the questioning provisions had taken place, such as interviewing a person unlawfully held incommunicado: a detention in itself lawful might thereby be rendered unlawful. However, although the ruling in *Middleweek v Chief Constable of Merseyside*[234] gave some encouragement to such argument, it now seems to be ruled out by the decision in *Weldon v Home Office*[235] in the context of lawful detention in a prison. It seems likely, therefore, that access to legal advice, like the rest of the safeguards for interviewing, will continue to be unaffected by the availability of the pre-HRA tortious remedies although, as discussed below, action under s 7(1)(a) of the HRA might be possible.

Where actions in tort *are* available against the police, they may be of particular value owing to the willingness of the courts to accept that exemplary or punitive damages may sometimes be appropriate. Such damages are awarded to punish the defendant and will be available only in two instances:[236] where there has been 'oppressive, arbitrary or unconstitutional behaviour by the servants of the government' or where the profit accruing to the defendant through his conduct may be greater than the compensation awarded to the plaintiff. Only the first of these two categories will be relevant in actions against the police, and in order that such damages should be available, the term 'servant of the government' has been broadly interpreted to include police officers.[237]

---

230 See Clayton, R and Tomlinson, H, *Civil Actions Against the Police*, 1st edn, 1987, p 284. For discussion see Winfield, *History of Conspiracy and Abuse of Legal Process*, 1921.

231 See *Glinskie v McIver* [1962] AC 726.

232 *Abbott v Refuge Assurance Co Ltd* [1962] 1 QB 632.

233 See Chapter 13, pp 806–07.

234 [1992] AC 179; [1990] 3 WLR 481.

235 [1991] WLR 340, CA.

236 This limitation was imposed by the House of Lords in *Rookes v Barnard* [1964] AC 1129, p 1226. Note that the Law Commission, *Consultation Paper on Punitive Damages*, Consultation No 132, 1993, advocates, in its provisional conclusion, retention of such damages, but that they should be placed on a more principled basis.

237 *Broome v Cassell and Co* [1972] AC 1027, p 1088.

If a civil action is brought against an officer on the basis that he or she has acted *ultra vires* and the officer shows that the statutory conditions for the exercise of power were present, the onus lies on the plaintiff to establish the relevant facts (*Greene v Home Secretary*).[238] In *Holgate-Mohammed v Duke* (1984),[239] the House of Lords confirmed that, in addition to showing that the relevant statutory conditions are satisfied, the exercise of statutory powers by officers must not offend against *Wednesbury* principles; officers must not take irrelevant factors into account or fail to have regard to relevant ones; an exercise of discretion must not be so unreasonable that no reasonable officer could have exercised it in the manner in question. In *Ministry of Defence ex p Smith and Others*,[240] the Court of Appeal affirmed that in judging whether the decision-maker had decided unreasonably, the human rights context was important; the more substantial the interference with human rights, the more the court would require by way of justification before it was satisfied that the decision was reasonable. Under s 6 of the HRA, the question (which would arise under s 7(1)(b)) is whether, in the exercise of discretionary powers, whether or not statute-based, the police breached a Convention right. Section 3 of the HRA is also relevant. This question is returned to below.

Quantum of damages

Civil actions against the police have in the past attracted high levels of damages. One of the highest awards was made in *White v Metropolitan Police Comr*.[241] Police officers unlawfully entered the home of a middle aged black couple at night and attacked the plaintiffs. The police then charged both plaintiffs with various offences in order to cover up their own conduct. The plaintiffs were awarded £20,000 exemplary damages each and, respectively, £6,500 and £4,500 aggravated damages. One of the highest awards was made in *Treadaway v Chief Constable of West Midlands*:[242] £50,000, which included £40,000 exemplary damages, was awarded in respect of a serious assault perpetrated in order to obtain a confession. In 1996, a number of very high awards were made against the Metropolitan Police. In *Goswell v Comr of Metropolitan Police*[243] the plaintiff was awarded £120,000 damages for assault, £12,000 for false imprisonment and £170,000 exemplary damages for arbitrary and oppressive behaviour. Mr Goswell, who is black, was waiting in his car when a police officer approached. Goswell complained about the lack of police activity over an arson attack on his home. He was handcuffed to and then struck by the officer; the blow left a permanent scar. Goswell was then arrested for assault and threatening behaviour. He was cleared of these charges and then brought the successful civil action.

In *Hsu v Comr of Metropolitan Police*,[244] the plaintiff won £220,000 damages for assault and wrongful arrest at his home. In *Kownacki v Comr of Metropolitan Police*,[245] actions for

---

238 [1942] AC 284, HL.
239 [1984] AC 437; [1984] 1 All ER 1054, HL.
240 [1996] 1 All ER 257; [1996] ICR 740.
241 (1982) *The Times*, 24 April.
242 (1994) *The Times*, 25 October.
243 (1996) *The Guardian*, 27 April.
244 [1997] 2 All ER 762.
245 (1996) *The Guardian*, 30 April.

false imprisonment and malicious prosecution against the Metropolitan Police were successful; 200 police invaded the plaintiff's pub and charged him with supplying cannabis and allowing the premises to be used for drug dealing. When the case came to trial, the prosecution offered no evidence and he was acquitted. As a result, he suffered depression and paranoia, which affected his work. The jury found that the officers had failed to prove that they had seen cannabis being openly smoked and sold on the premises during the surveillance operation; £108,750, including £45,000 of punitive damages, were awarded to reflect the jury's disapproval.

However, these high awards are no longer available. The question of the appropriate level of damages was addressed by the Court of Appeal in *Thompson v Comr of Police for the Metropolis*.[246] The court laid down guidelines for the award of damages which took as a starting point a basic award of £500 for the first hour of unlawful detention, with decreasing amounts for subsequent hours. It was found that aggravated damages could be awarded where there were special features of the case, such as oppressive or humiliating conduct at the time of arrest. Such damages would start at around £1,000 but would not normally be more than twice the level of the basic damages. Exemplary damages should only be awarded where aggravated and basic damages together would not appear to provide a sufficient punishment. Exemplary damages would be not less than £5,000, but the total figure awarded as exemplary damages would not be expected to amount to more than the basic damages multiplied by three. The overall award should not exceed £50,000. In accordance with these guidelines, the award made in *Hsu* was reduced to £50,000.

Impact of the HRA

Sections 6 and 8 of the HRA requires the courts to offer a remedy where a public authority violates the Convention rights,[247] unless in so doing it is acting in accordance with incompatible legislation.[248] As Chapter 13 indicated, Arts 3, 5, 8 and 14 potentially cover certain pre-trial rights of suspects, regardless of the trial context. Tortious liability would arise and damages could be awarded under s 8 of the HRA if one or more of these Articles were found to have been breached in respect of police treatment of suspects. As indicated, some custodial treatment in breach of these Articles is already tortious under domestic law, and civil actions against the police have provided an increasingly significant means of creating some police accountability,[249] but this possibility would clearly be of particular significance where domestic law currently fails to provide a tortious remedy in respect of maltreatment of detainees.

---

246 [1997] 2 All ER 762.

247 Sections 6(1), 7 and 8. For discussion, see Chapter 4, p 156 *et seq*.

248 Section 6(2). Section 3 requires that the legislation should rendered compatible with the Convention rights 'so far as it is possible to do so'.

249 See the Home Affairs Committee First Report 1997–98, *Police Disciplinary and Complaints Procedures* printed 16.12.97, which noted (para 32) the 'striking' rise in the cost of civil settlements for the Metropolitan Police, from £0.47m in 1991 to £2.69m in 1996. (This figure may decline owing to the decision in *Thompson*, [1997] 2 All ER 762.) The Police Action Lawyers Group and the Commission For Racial Equality attributed the rise to disillusionment with the complaints process.

The domestic courts may have to reconsider their current approach to conditions of detention in terms of tortious liability. Prior to the inception of the HRA, so long as existing torts or offences, such as assault, were not committed in detention, it followed from the findings in *Weldon v Home Office*[250] that no means of redress in respect of adverse conditions, other than a complaint, was available. The possible creation of liability[251] under the Convention by means of a creative interpretation of the guarantee under Art 8 would not only fill a gap in domestic law, it would fill the gap in the Convention which, as noted above, does not on its face cover most conditions of detention. Such a course would not necessarily involve departing from the findings in *Weldon v Home Office*, since the liability would be for breach of a Convention right under s 6, using s 7(1)(a) of the HRA, not for false imprisonment. In any event, departure from case law is clearly possible under the HRA, relying on the duty of the court under s 6 and the effect of the Strasbourg jurisprudence under s 2.[252]

Where an existing tort action is brought which relates to the exercise of discretionary powers by the police, it could be argued under s 7(1)(b) that the officer had breached a Convention right in their exercise and had therefore acted unlawfully. This would be in essence a question of proportionality in relation to Art 8 or a question of the content and requirements of the right in relation to Arts 2, 3, 5 and 6.[253] Unless s 6(2) applied, the action would succeed if the breach could be established, whether or not the exercise of the power appeared to have a statutory or common law basis. Alternatively, s 3 of the HRA could be relied on where the power was statute-based in order to show that once the provision in question was interpreted compatibly with the relevant Convention right(s), it did not provide the power to act as the officer did. This is clearly a significant matter since it requires more of a police officer than the *Wednesbury* test did, even in its stricter, more recent manifestations.[254]

As indicated in Chapter 13, a breach of the Code-based safeguards applying to the exercise of a *prima facie* tortious power will not deprive it of lawful authority owing to the provision against civil liability for such a breach under s 67(10) of PACE and Sched 12, para 6 of the TA. This will also be the case, *a fortiori*, where a police action which does not require lawful authority in order to avoid such liability breaches a Code provision. But where provisions of Arts 3, 8, 5 or 14 are coterminous with Code safeguards, liability to pay damages under the HRA for breach of the Convention guarantees might provide the Code provisions with a form of indirect protection, as the more detailed embodiment of the Convention requirements. Chapter 13 identified, at the relevant points, Convention guarantees, including aspects of the Art 3 requirements, which have no domestic statutory basis, but are recognised only in certain Code provisions.[255] The creation of new tortious liability indirectly protective of such provisions under the HRA would be a very significant matter, since it might lead to a regulation of police interviewing practices and techniques which has been largely absent from UK law.

---

250 [1990] 3 All ER 672.
251 Under HRA 1998, ss 6 and 7. The HRA does not allow for the creation of new criminal liability.
252 See, in a different context, *Douglas v Hello!* [2001] 2 WLR 992.
253 See further Chapter 2, p 66.
254 See Chapter 4, p 106.
255 See pp 852–53.

However, at present it is very doubtful whether Art 6 itself could be viewed as providing free-standing rights. Breaches of Art 6 are clearly most likely to be addressed within the criminal process itself. The Strasbourg jurisprudence does not cover instances in which the pre-trial procedure is flawed in a manner which might be viewed, potentially, as infringing the Art 6(1) guarantee of a fair trial, but where no court action in fact occurs. However, given that certain of the rights, and in particular the implied right of access to custodial legal advice under Art 6(3)(c), clearly have value outside the trial context, an action based on s 7(1)(a) or on a breach of the statutory duty under s 58 of PACE, but raising Art (3)(c) arguments under s 7(1)(b), might resolve this issue in favour of the complainant, domestically.

The quantum of damages must be determined in accordance with the provisions of s 8 which include the requirement, under s 8(4) of the HRA, that the court should take into account the principles applied by the European Court of Human Rights in relation to the award of compensation.[256] As indicated in Chapter 4, reliance on such principles means that the level of damages awarded may be fairly low;[257] in particular, the Court has not, formally, awarded exemplary or aggravated damages[258] and it is probably the case that exemplary damages are not available under the HRA.[259] But where the applicant has a coterminous tort action, such as false imprisonment, s 8 should not be used to detract from the level of damages which would have been awarded prior to enactment of the HRA.[260] It may be noted that Art 5(5) provides an independent right to compensation if Art 5 is breached, but this does not appear to add anything to the damages already available for false imprisonment.

Conclusions: value of civil actions

The value of civil actions against the police in terms of ensuring police accountability is limited for a variety of reasons.[261] The cost factor will deter most potential plaintiffs from suing the police, especially now that legal aid is unavailable for an increasing section of the population.[262] There is a strong tendency to settle actions, which means that the police do not admit liability. Even where a civil action is successful, disciplinary charges are unlikely to be brought against the officers concerned. This has been justified by the police in the past on the basis of the differing standards of proof: civil claims need only be proved on the balance of probabilities while, until recently, disciplinary charges had to be

---

256 See further Leigh, I and Lustgarten, L, 'Making rights real: the courts, remedies and the Human Rights Act' [1999] CLJ 509; Feldman, D, 'Remedies for violations of human rights under the Human Rights Act' (1998) EHRLR 691; Amos, M, 'Damages for breach of the Human Rights Act' (1999) EHRLR 178.

257 Non-pecuniary damages are likely to be in the range of £10,000–15,000: see *Johnson v UK* (1997) 27 EHRR 296.

258 *B v UK* A 136-D (1988), paras 7–12.

259 See Clayton and Tomlinson, *op cit*, fn 1, p 1437.

260 This follows from the HRA 1998, s 11.

261 It may be noted that if a civil action against a police officer is successful, he or she will not be personally liable. The Police Act 1964, s 48, provides that a chief constable will be vicariously liable in respect of torts committed by constables under his direction or control in the performance or purported performance of their functions.

262 See *Legal Action*, April 2000, p 34; for discussion see Hansen, O, 'A future for legal aid?' (1992) 19 JLS 85; see also Sanders and Young, *op cit*, fn 1, p 680.

proved beyond reasonable doubt. This is no longer the case, as explained below. Therefore, disciplinary action might be expected to follow a successful civil action, although there is no statutory requirement that it must do so, even in particularly serious cases. The high jury awards of damages in 1996 may reflect a growing public perception that the police are insufficiently accountable. If nothing else, a continuing propensity to make such awards might have helped to draw public and parliamentary attention to an unsatisfactory situation. However, the decision of the Court of Appeal in *Thompson* will make this less likely.

The HRA is unlikely to affect the quantum of damages or the practical problems of suing the police. But, it may have a significant effect. There is clearly something rather strange about creating a vast, complex statutory edifice (PACE, the TA, the CJP) which governs police powers and suspects' rights, but then failing to provide a remedy if those rights are breached, except where that breach is coterminous with an existing area of tortious liability. Thus the HRA can, in theory, have a significant impact in respect of civil liability, since it has created for the first time under ss 7(1)(a) and 8 a remedy in damages where Convention rights are breached in custody by the police, whether or not existing tortious liability would arise. Moreover, the Convention rights now provide the parameters within which discretionary powers must be exercised, under s 6 of the HRA.

5 COMPLAINTS AGAINST THE POLICE AND DISCIPLINARY ACTION[263]

Introduction

Clearly, the police complaints and disciplinary system provides a potential method of ensuring that the police adhere to the safeguards created by PACE, as amended, and the TA. PACE set up the Police Complaints Authority (PCA) as an independent body with an involvement in the complaints and disciplinary system, replacing the Police Complaints Board (PCB), which was set up under the Police Act 1976.[264] The idea was to afford an appearance of independence to the system. The scheme set up by PACE for dealing with complaints, contained in ss 83–106, was repealed and re-enacted in the Police Act 1996.[265] Under s 67(2) of the Police Act 1996, a complaint will go in the first instance to the Chief Officer of Police of the force in question, who must determine by reference to the section whether or not he is the appropriate person to deal with it and whether it, in fact, constitutes a complaint about 'the conduct of an officer' and not about 'the direction or

---

263 See Maguire, M, 'Complaints against the police: the British experience', in Goldsmith, A (ed), *Complaints Against the Police: A Comparative Study*, 1990; Greaves [1985] Crim LR; Khan (1984) 129 SJ 455; Williams [1985] Crim LR 115; Lustgarten, L, *The Governance of Police*, 1986, pp 139–40. The Runciman Commission considered that the existing arrangements probably do not command public confidence: Cm 2263, p 46; Harrison, J, *Police Misconduct: Legal Remedies*, 1987; Triennial Review of the PCA 1991–94, HC 396 (1994–95); Home Affairs Committee Fourth Report, HC 179 (1991–92); Sanders, A and Young, R, *Criminal Justice*, 2nd edn, 2000, Chapter 11, Part 4, pp 400–15; House of Commons Home Affairs Select Committee, Police Disciplinary and Complaints Procedure, First Report, HC-258-1 (1998).

264 The operation of the PCB did not create confidence in the complaints system: see Brown, *Police Complaints Procedure*, Home Office Research Study No 93, 1987.

265 Which came into force on 1.4.99, replacing PACE 1984, Part IX.

control' of a police force.[266] The decision as to the side of the dividing line on which a particular complaint falls is made by the police force complained about. Therefore, at the very outset, 'an issue of independence arises'.[267]

A complaint must be referred to the PCA if it concerns serious misconduct.[268] Under s 75(3) of the 1996 Act, if the Chief Officer determines that the report on the complaints investigation indicates that a criminal offence may have been committed, he must send a copy of it to the DPP. In addition, there is a discretionary power to refer complaints to the PCA. It does not carry out the investigation itself in such cases, but supervises it and receives a report at the end of it under s 72. Thus, its role in relation to complaints is very limited.

Failures of the complaints and disciplinary system

The overwhelming majority of complaints do not result in disciplinary proceedings: as many as 30% of complaints are dealt with by informal resolution[269] and 50% of complaints are withdrawn.[270] Clayton and Tomlinson noted that the 16,712 complaints dealt with in 1990 led to 305 criminal or disciplinary charges and advice or admonishment in 573 cases; thus, less than 2% of complaints led to any disciplinary action.[271] The PCA Report of 1995 reported that out of 245 complaints of serious assault by police officers, eight led to disciplinary charges; none led to dismissal of an officer from the service. Out of 6,318 complaints of assaults, disciplinary charges were preferred in 64 cases; none led to dismissal of the officer.[272] The PCA Report of 1998 stated that 141 complaints concerned serious assaults; 8% of those fully investigated led to disciplinary action. A total of 16,550 complaints were received in 1998–99; 317 were fully investigated, a figure of approximately 2%.[273] In 1997, the Home Affairs Committee considered the figures for the outcome of complaints and found that over the previous two years, 2% of all recorded complaints were substantiated following a formal investigation and less than half of 1% of complaints led to disciplinary or criminal charges.[274] The record for 1998–99 suggests that the figures would be approximately the same. While the figures may be, to an extent, misleading,[275] they strongly suggest that the system is not operating fairly and effectively.

---

266 PACE 1984, s 84(4) and (5). The requirement regarding 'the conduct of a police officer' now arises under s 65 of the 1996 Act.

267 Home Affairs Committee First Report (1997–98), para 47.

268 Police Act 1996, s 70, formerly PACE 1984, s 87(4).

269 PCA Triennial Review, HC 466 (1985–88), para 1.14, p 8.

270 See Triennial Review of the PCA 1991–94, HC 396, 1994–95; Clayton, R and Tomlinson, H, *Civil Actions Against the Police*, 2nd edn, 1992, p 13.

271 Clayton and Tomlinson, *ibid*, p 13.

272 See Triennial Review of the PCA 1991–94, HC 396, 1994–95.

273 The 1998–99 Annual Report of the PCA, Table 5: 2,415 complaints concerned assaults; 81 disciplinary charges were preferred. 203 complaints concerned racially discriminatory behaviour; 3 charges were preferred. The Report does not give the figure for disciplinary action as a percentage of fully investigated complaints.

274 Home Affairs Committee First Report (1997–98), *Police Disciplinary and Complaints Procedures*, printed 16 December 1997, para 27.

275 See Lersch and Mieczkowski (2000) 23(1) Policing. They considered arguments that the numbers of complaints may not be indicative since citizens may under-complain for various reasons, including lack of confidence in the process. They also looked at the possibility of over-complaint.

The Committee found 'perhaps the most telling evidence that all is not well ... comes from the opinion of almost all the parties involved';[276] they concluded: 'there is a great deal of justified dissatisfaction with elements of the disciplinary and complaints system.'[277] These criticisms echo those which have, for a number of years, been directed against the whole police disciplinary process, including the hearings, and it is generally agreed that the present system is defective as a means of redress.[278] Maguire and Corbett conducted a review of the operation of the complaints system from 1968–1988[279] which found that the majority of complainants were dissatisfied and that the public did not have confidence in the system. The Runciman Commission considered that the existing arrangements probably do not command public confidence.[280] The Home Office Consultation Paper *Complaints against the Police*, issued in 2000,[281] accepted that the system had failed to win public confidence.

There is a disparity between successful civil actions against the police and disciplinary action or prosecution.[282] For example, in the *Hsu* case,[283] it was found that Mr Hsu was assaulted, racially abused and falsely arrested. It was accepted that the police officers in question had lied on oath and fabricated note-book entries. Mr Hsu was awarded £200,000 damages (reduced on appeal to £35,000), but no officer was disciplined.[284] Where officers are placed under investigation with a view to disciplinary charges, they may take early retirement or resign on medical grounds. After the MacPherson Report[285] into the *Stephen Lawrence* case, disciplinary charges were recommended against five officers involved. All, however, retired and therefore could not face charges. The Home Office is currently considering the possibility of disciplinary action up to five years after

---

276 Paragraph 35.

277 Paragraph 40.

278 See Greaves, *op cit*, fn 263; Khan, *op cit*, fn 263; Williams, *op cit*, fn 263; Lustgarten, *op cit*, fn 263, pp 139–40; Harrison, *op cit*, fn 263; Harrison and Cragg (1993) 143 NLJ 591; Maguire, *op cit*, fn 263; RCCJ Report, Cm 2263, p 46; Kennedy, H, in Walker, C and Starmer, K (eds), *Miscarriages of Justice: A Review of Justice in Error*, 1999, Blackstone, p 374; Goldsmith, A, *External Review and Self Regulation: Complaints Against the Police – The Trend to External Review*, 1988; Harrison, J and Cuneen, M, *An Independent Police Complaints Commission*, 2000.

279 *A Study of the Police Complaints System*, 1991.

280 RCCJ Report, Cm 2263, p 46.

281 London, Home Office, 2000.

282 *The Butler Report*, 1998, criticised the CPS for its decision making in the *Treadaway* case; Derek Treadaway was awarded £50,000 in damages in respect of a serious assault by police officers while he was in custody: *R v DPP ex p Treadaway* (1997) *The Times*, 18 November. The CPS decided not to prosecute the officers. Treadaway successfully sought judicial review of this decision and the case was remitted for re-consideration by the CPS.

283 *Thompson v Comr of Police for the Metropolis, Hsu v Comr of Police for the Metropolis* [1997] 2 All ER 762.

284 See further the Home Affairs Committee First Report (1998), Section B: 'The evidence from civil actions'. A further example, in which the disciplinary sanction was, in effect, rescinded, is provided by *Goswell v Comr of Metropolitan Police* (*The Guardian* Report, 27 April 1996). The officer who was found in that case to have perpetrated a serious assault, PC Trigg, was dismissed as a result of a complaint from Goswell. In the civil action Goswell had been awarded £120,000 for assault, £12,000 for false imprisonment and £170,000 for arbitrary and oppressive behaviour. Trigg appealed against his dismissal and was reinstated by the Home Secretary, Michael Howard. On the face of it, his reinstatement after it had been proved beyond reasonable doubt (in the disciplinary proceedings) that Trigg had perpetrated the assault in question appeared highly questionable.

285 Cm 4262-I, 1999.

retirement.[286] In the wake of the MacPherson Report, racist police behaviour may begin to lead more frequently to disciplinary charges,[287] although such a trend cannot yet be discerned.[288]

Independence

There appears to be a strong consensus that the independent element in the complaints and disciplinary process is too weak and is the key factor in the inefficacy of the system.[289] Maguire and Corbett commented in their 1991 review that an independent system might lead to an improvement in public confidence in the system, although they expressed doubts about its efficacy in other respects.[290] The MacPherson Report recommended that there should be an independent tribunal for serious complaints.[291] Morgan and Newburn find: 'The fact that most complaints ... continue to be investigated exclusively by the police themselves is almost certainly an important factor in explaining why so few complaints are made compared with the proportion of members of the public who report having felt like making a complaint.'[292] The Police Action Lawyers Group has stated: 'the fundamental problem ... is the lack of independence in the system.'[293] The House of Commons Home Affairs Committee found that the introduction of an independent element is desirable in principle.[294] Doubts have been expressed, however, taking into account experience from other jurisdictions, about the efficacy of a completely independent investigatory body,[295] but prior to the issuing of the Consultation Paper in 2000, there appeared to be a degree of consensus regarding the need for a stronger element of independence which could be achieved through the co-operation of police and expert civilian investigators, drawn from the ranks of bodies such as lawyers and customs officials.

Reform

The changes to the complaints procedure which occurred in the mid-1990s, partly in response to the Runciman Royal Commission Report, did not involve any radical reform. In particular, they did not include the introduction of a new, independent element into the process. The Police and Magistrates' Courts Act 1994, which was then consolidated in the Police Act 1996, made only limited changes to the functions and powers of the PCA.

---

286 MacPherson Report, Recommendations 55–57.
287 Eg, in February 2000 a police officer, PC Hutt, was disciplined and dismissed from the force for oppressive, racist behaviour (news report 22 February 2000).
288 See fn 273, above.
289 Sanders and Young, *op cit*, fn 1, p 702; Kennedy, *op cit*, fn 278, p 374.
290 *A Study of the Police Complaints* System, 1991.
291 Cm 4262-I, 1999, Recommendation 58.
292 *The Future of Policing*, 1997, p 53; finding based on Skogan, *Contacts between Police and Public: Findings from the 1992 British Crime Survey*, HO Research Study No 134, 1994.
293 Home Affairs Committee Report, para 43.
294 Home Affairs Committee, HC 258-I (1997–98), Recommendation 11.
295 See Goldsmith, *op cit*, fn 278; Loveday, B, 'Police complaints in the USA' (1988) 4 Policing 172.

Under s 37(a) of the 1994 Act, a breach of the PACE Codes became no longer automatically a breach of the Police Discipline Code.[296] This change may be seen merely as legitimising police working practices, since it appeared that very few complaints in respect of breaches of the Codes were made; those that were rarely led to disciplinary proceedings. Unsurprisingly, this trend continued after the 1994 Act came into force.[297] As indicated above, Part IV of the Police Act 1996, which now governs complaints and discipline, was merely a consolidating, not a reforming, measure.

The 1997 Report of the Select Committee on Home Affairs[298] made a number of recommendations, reflecting certain of the criticisms noted above, and the Home Secretary, Jack Straw, said that he had accepted the case for speedy reform. But the initial proposals for reform[299] mirrored the moderate changes proposed by the Conservative Government in 1993.[300]

New procedures were introduced in April 1999[301] which reflected certain of those proposals, including in particular abolition of the criminal standard of proof in disciplinary proceedings.[302] Under the new procedure, the hearing will be private, but the complainant can attend the proceedings, although not before his evidence is given,[303] and he may be allowed to cross-examine witnesses.[304] A number of provisions, however, allow for the exclusion of the complainant.[305] Racist language and behaviour is now a breach of the police code of conduct, but it is not yet possible to determine how far reaching such change might be.

The PCA in its 1998–99 Report noted that further, more radical changes, in particular the 'use of non-police investigators in exceptional cases', although accepted by the Home Secretary in principle, had been relegated to future legislation. The PCA concluded that there was no prospect of early legislation and mentioned its unsuccessful attempts to make the more non-controversial changes by means of Private Members' Bills.[306] In 2000, the Government commissioned a feasibility study into the practicality of using

---

296 Section 37(a) repealed PACE 1984, s 67(8).

297 Eg, the PCA Report for 1998–99 showed that there were 107 complaints relating to breach of Code A, governing stop and search in the period. One led to disciplinary charges (Table 5, p 13).

298 HC 258-I (1997–98).

299 HC 683 (1997–98).

300 The Government issued a consultation paper in April 1993 which included various proposals, including abolition of the criminal standard of proof in discipline cases and the double jeopardy rule, which means that criminal proceedings against officers are not followed by disciplinary proceedings. See 143 NLJ 591; in its Triennial Review 1988–91, HC 352, 1991, the PCA also made this proposal. The Labour proposals also address the tendency of police officers who are facing disciplinary charges to take extended sick leave and/or early retirement, thereby evading the disciplinary process.

301 The Police (Conduct) Regulations 1999. The new procedures operated alongside the 1995 ones until March 2000, when the transitional arrangements ended; all cases are now being dealt with under the new procedures.

302 *Ibid*, reg 23(3).

303 *Ibid*, reg 25(3).

304 *Ibid*, reg 25(4).

305 Under reg 25(5) the complainant can be removed if he interrupts. Under reg 27 he can be excluded if matters arise which it would not be in the public interest to disclose to him.

306 PCA Report (1998–99), p 53.

independent investigators in exceptional cases,[307] and put proposals to use such investigators to the annual Police Federation Conference in May 2000.[308] The Government issued a Consultation Paper in 2000 which proposed importing greater independence into the system, by means of a new body, the Independent Police Complaints Commission,[309] but made it clear that in the vast majority of cases, a full independent investigation would not occur, owing to cost. Once the system contains this independent element, a number of problems may remain even in relation to those exceptional cases in which independent investigation by civilian investigators occurs. Institutional factors, including obstruction of the system by the police and the possibility that civilian investigators will be affected by police culture, may continue to hamper the system; the success rate may remain low.[310]

Thus, despite evidence of police malpractice from miscarriage of justice cases such as that of the *Birmingham Six*[311] and the subsequent indications discussed above of poor practice and deliberate wrong-doing within the police service, the system for accountability remained, in essentials, the same. The new element of independence is unlikely to have any impact in the majority of instances. The system raises various serious issues under the HRA. It does not generate confidence that it will play a significant part in ensuring that police officers and forces act in compliance with the Convention. In so far as the Convention rights are reflected in the safeguards for suspects contained in PACE, the TA and their associated Codes, it is not apparent that it is likely to ensure adherence to them.

Impact of the HRA

The police complaints mechanism potentially provides a means of creating police accountability, both in terms of underpinning the balance apparently struck by PACE, and in ensuring compliance with the Convention under the HRA. The bodies administering the mechanism, the Police Complaints Authority (PCA), Chief Police Officers, and police disciplinary tribunals are all bound by the Convention as public authorities under s 6 of the HRA. They are also in the position of hearing complaints regarding police officers who are themselves so bound. Both aspects should inform their work and could be raised as issues by way of judicial review. Further, the statutory provisions governing police complaints should be interpreted compatibly with the Convention under s 3 of the HRA.

It is possible, although doubtful, that police disciplinary hearings fall within the field of application of Art 6. Under Art 6, the hearing might be viewed, first and foremost, as forming the determination of a 'criminal charge' against the officer concerned, although this is uncertain. Military and prison disciplinary proceedings fall within the term, owing to the severity of the possible penalty, which includes the possibility of imprisonment.

---

307 The study was conducted by the consultants KPMG. They reported on 17 May 2000; their report was accompanied by an independent report by Liberty, recommending the setting up of an independent body to hear police complaints.

308 On 17 May 2000. For comparative discussion of this possibility, see Goldsmith, A and Lewis, C (eds), *Civilian Oversight of Policing*, 2000.

309 *Complaints against the Police: A Consultation Paper*, 2000. See proposals: HL Deb, Vol 620, Col WA45, 19.12.00.

310 See Harrison and Cuneen, *op cit*, fn 278; Goldsmith, A and Faran, S, 'Complaints against the police in Canada: a new approach' [1987] Crim LR 615.

311 See *R v McIlkenny and Others* [1992] 2 All ER 417.

The position regarding disciplinary proceedings carrying the possibility of lesser, albeit quite severe, penalties, such as dismissal or the loss of pension rights, is not yet clearly settled, although there are indications that the Court would view proceedings carrying the possibility of lesser penalties as falling outside the meaning of criminal charge.[312] Disciplinary proceedings and hearings might also be viewed as the determination of the 'civil rights and obligations' of the complainant under Art 6(1), since they may frequently involve inquiry into breaches of such rights, including breaches of the Convention itself. The term 'civil' has, however, been taken to mean that these are rights in private rather than public law,[313] although a clear distinction between rights in private as opposed to public law is not apparent in recent Strasbourg jurisprudence. Possibly, complaints proceedings might be found to fall within this term at Strasbourg, or domestically, in future. This view might be encouraged since, as indicated above, the proceedings became more court-like after the 1999 reforms.

On the basis that disciplinary proceedings and the occasional disciplinary hearings ordered by the PCA might be found in future to fall within Art 6, it is arguable that they fail to comply with its requirements since the complainant is in such a weak position in them. They appear to fail to provide a fair hearing for the complainant, bearing in mind the procedure they follow. In investigating a fair hearing, the domestic authorities may take into account the Art 6(3) guarantees even in respect of civil determinations, since they are viewed as minimum guarantees which are covered by the wider para (1) protection of a fair hearing. If consideration is given to the procedures in question it is apparent that, apart from any of the other requirements of fairness, the minimal safeguards of Art 6(3) may not be present, depending on the application of the new Regulations in any particular case.[314] The system does not allow for the complainant or her legal representative to attend the full disciplinary proceedings or hearings. The independence and impartiality of the hearing may also be questioned, particularly as the vast majority of hearings are not ordered or supervised by the PCA. No compensation can be awarded to the complainant.

There is also be the possibility of considering whether the disciplinary system affords the complainant an effective remedy for breach of his or her Convention rights. This argument could be raised under Art 13 which, while omitted from the rights given further effect under the HRA, has some effect in domestic law.[315] It is debatable whether the police complaints and discipline process should be seen as being the appropriate forum for s 7(1)(a) HRA purposes, since breach of Convention rights by police officers could be raised in the ordinary courts under that sub-section. But, in any event, the Art 13 issue could be raised in, for example, a challenge to a breach of a Convention right in judicial review proceedings, if the applicant had made an unsuccessful complaint. In *Govell v UK*,[316] the Commission found that the police investigative system did not meet the requisite standards of independence under Art 13 since the Chief Constable can appoint a member of the same force to investigate; the Home Secretary appoints and remunerates members of the Police Complaints Authority and has a guiding role in

---

312 See *Demicoli v Malta* A 210 (1991) and *Ravnsborg v Sweden* A 283-B (1994).

313 *Ringeisen v Austria* A 13 (1971), para 94.

314 See further Chapter 2, pp 63–64.

315 See Chapter 4, p 135.

316 (1997) 4 EHRLR 438. See also *Khan v UK* (2000) 8 BHRC 310, paras 45–47.

determining the withdrawal of charges. The rules considered in *Govell* were the PACE rules, but the new rules maintain the same system. In *Khan v UK*,[317] the Court also found that the police disciplinary system failed to satisfy Art 13 because of the lack of independence. The remuneration system is still under the control of the Home Secretary,[318] and under s 83 of the Police Act 1996, his guiding role is retained. Under s 69(5),[319] a member of the force which is the subject of the complaint can conduct the investigation.

A further issue may arise in respect of public interest immunity attaching to documents coming into existence during a police complaints investigation. The position of the parties to court actions in relation to disclosure of material relating to a complaint was placed on a more equal basis as a result of *Chief Constable of West Midlands Police ex p Wiley; Chief Constable of Nottinghamshire Police ex p Sunderland*.[320] All the parties concerned argued that public interest immunity did not attach, on a class basis, to documents coming into existence during a police complaints investigation. The House of Lords had to consider whether *Neilson v Laugharne*[321] and the decisions following it were wrongly decided. In *Neilson*, Lord Oliver had determined that a class immunity should attach to police complaints documents on the basis that the police complaints procedure would be placed in jeopardy if that was not the case. However, the House of Lords considered that there was insufficient evidence to support Lord Oliver's conclusion as to the need for a new class claim to public interest immunity. Thus, it was found that *Neilson* must be regarded as wrongly decided, but that did not mean that public interest immunity would not attach to police complaints documents: whether it did or not would depend on the nature of the particular document or documents in question. This decision emphasises that a clear case must be made out for use of a broad class claim to public interest immunity. It is in the interests of a fair hearing under Art 6(1) and 6(3)(d), since it goes some way towards ensuring that, in actions against the police, or in prosecutions where previous disciplinary findings may be relevant, both parties have access to the same information. However, it leaves open the possibility of a contents claim or of a class claim in relation to specific groups of documents, although a strong justification would be required to establish such a claim. In *Taylor v Anderton*,[322] the Court of Appeal found that the reports prepared by investigating officers were entitled to class immunity, but that a litigant might nevertheless obtain disclosure of part or all of a report if the judge could be persuaded that the public interest in disclosure outweighed the interest in immunity.

It is debatable whether the current position would satisfy the findings as to the duty of disclosure to the defence in *Rowe and Davis v UK*[323] or in *Tinnelly and McElduff v UK*,[324] depending on the particular circumstances of a case. In *Tinnelly*, the Court found that the

---

317 *Ibid*, paras 44–47; [2000] Crim LR 684.
318 See PCA Report 1998–99 Appendix C, para 5.
319 Which has replaced PACE 1984, s 105(4).
320 [1995] AC 274; [1994] 3 All ER 420; (1995) 1 Cr App R 342, HL.
321 [1981] QB 736.
322 [1995] All ER 420, CA. See also *Kelly v Comr of Police of the Metropolis* (1997) *The Times*, 20 August in which it was found that PII attaches to certain of the new forms which are sent to the CPS by police forces.
323 (2000) 30 EHRR 1; (1998) 25 EHRR CD 118 (admissibility decision).
324 (1998) 27 EHRR 249.

use of a conclusive certificate preventing disclosure of the reasons for a decision[325] breached Art 6, since it prevented the tribunal from effectively reviewing the facts. Any judge determining the imposition of a contents immunity, whether in a civil action against the police or in a prosecution, would have to take the jurisprudence regarding the equality of arms provision arising both under Art 6(1) and 6(3) into account, as well as the general requirements of a fair trial. The latter requirement is ultimately the overriding one, since merely placing both parties in an equally disadvantageous position would not necessarily satisfy it.

6 PROSECUTION OF THE POLICE

Introduction

Police actions that are unauthorised may create criminal as well as civil liability. For example, the use of force in effecting an unlawful arrest would be an assault. The use of lethal force in such circumstances might give rise to liability for murder or manslaughter. Equally, excessive force used to effect a lawful arrest or to restrain a suspect lawfully detained might give rise to criminal liability. In practice, successful prosecutions of police officers are very rare.[326] A number of high profile cases have failed to lead, ultimately, to successful prosecutions. The Home Affairs Committee noted that no convictions of police officers had arisen from the recent miscarriage of justice cases despite strong evidence of fraud or perjury on the part of some of the officers involved.[327] The number of deaths annually in police custody remains high; between January 1990 and December 1996, 380 such deaths were reported to the Home Office,[328] and the failure of disciplinary charges or prosecutions in relation to complaints arising from such deaths has attracted quite severe criticism.[329] In 1997, the Home Affairs Committee considered evidence from the organisation Inquest which submitted 11 case studies, in certain of which no prosecution or disciplinary action had been taken against officers, despite apparently substantial evidence against them.[330]

---

325 This was not a PII certificate, which would not be conclusive, but a certificate provided for under the Fair Employment Act 1976 in Northern Ireland.

326 Only about 1.5% of cases concerning the police referred to the DPP are prosecuted. See Hyder, 'Cause for complaint' (1990) *New Statesman and Society,* 12 January.

327 *Ibid,* para 24.

328 Leigh, Johnson and Ingram, *Deaths in Police Custody,* Police Research Series Paper 26 (1998).

329 See *The Butler Report,* 1998; Kennedy, *op cit,* fn 278, p 374. Note the report in June (1999) LAG 21 regarding the inquest into the death of N Delahunty due to cocaine intoxication aggravated by police restraint. See also November (1999) LAG 6 regarding the acquittal of police officers for the death of a Mr O'Brien in custody after a restraint by a number of police officers. His death was considered in *The Butler Report,* s 6. In s 8, the report criticised the CPS system for considering prosecutions in respect of deaths in custody (including that of O'Brien) as 'inefficient and fundamentally unsound'. See above, Chapter 13, p 804, fn 245.

330 *Ibid,* para 25.

Crown Prosecution Service decision making

The Crown Prosecution Service take the decision as to prosecution, but their impartiality and independence have been questioned. It appears that the issue of independence arises at every stage in the decision making process of the CPS in relation to the question whether to prosecute police officers where complaints appear to disclose criminal offences. The CPS is, of course, independent of the police, but 'the issue is whether it exercises this independence properly'.[331] Evidence submitted in 1997 to the Home Affairs Committee regarding the matter indicated a 'lack of willingness' on the part of the CPS and DPP to prosecute. 'There is clearly bias which pervades both the police and the CPS preventing viable prosecutions through nonsensical analysis of evidence.'[332] The issue of the quality of CPS decision making in this context clearly raises a number of Convention-based arguments.

The Butler Report (1998) made a number of recommendations designed to improve the quality of CPS decisions as to prosecution. They included sending every death in custody case for a decision as to whether or not to prosecute to the Assistant Chief Prosecutor and instituting a compulsory training programme for all those employed in central casework at the CPS.[333] The Report also expressed unease with the system whereby the police themselves investigate and report to the CPS on a death in custody. It also suggested that where such a death had occurred and an inquest jury returned a verdict of unlawful killing, the reason for the decision not to prosecute should be given.[334]

Impact of the HRA

No criminal liability is created under the HRA, so that a breach of, for example, Art 3 or 8, non-coterminous with existing offences, could not found a prosecution. But, decisions as to prosecutions of the police raise a number of Convention issues which are likely to be addressed in proceedings for judicial review of a decision not to prosecute. The burden of proof would be affected where it was alleged that Art 3 had been breached by custodial maltreatment, or, under Art 2, where a death had occurred in custody. Once it was shown that the detainee was free of the injury in question[335] or was not already in a life threatening condition, before arrest, the State would bear the burden of exculpating the officers involved. This test appears to differ from that currently used by the CPS, which was criticised in *The Butler Report*.[336] The Butler recommendations, which were largely concerned with procedural matters, including clarification of the system of decision making in the CPS, did not, it is argued, fully address these Convention matters. Possibly it will become apparent that reforms based on a greater awareness of the demands of the Convention in this context are necessary, now that the HRA is fully in force.

---

331 See Home Affairs Committee First Report (1997–98), para 88.

332 *Ibid*, para 90.

333 *Ibid*, pp 53–54.

334 *Ibid*, p 55.

335 *Tomasi v France* A 241-A (1992). See also Chapter 2, p 46.

336 *Ibid*.

7 CONCLUSIONS

A recurring theme throughout this chapter and Chapter 13 has concerned the extent to which a 'balance' is struck between suspects' rights and police powers. The dual themes of the need for enhanced police powers but also for the introduction of rules to protect due process, are only clearly evident in the piece of legislation which is still central to police powers – the Police and Criminal Evidence Act 1984. The notion of achieving in PACE what Reiner has called 'a fundamental balance'[337] has some foundation. It may be said that on the face of it, the balance struck by PACE is fairly acceptable, at least in relation to the non-terrorist suspect, despite the increased powers of arrest and stop and search which PACE confers. Concern may be expressed as to the uncertainty of the concept of reasonable suspicion on which these powers depend but, nevertheless, taking PACE and the Codes at face value, a concern to protect the rights of suspects appears to be evident. It is, however, less clear that the later legislation, the Criminal Justice and Public Order Act 1994, the Terrorism Act 2000 and the Criminal Justice and Police Act 2001, reflects such a concern.

The post-PACE legislation, then, has effected continued extensions of police powers, but has brought about only minor increases in safeguards for suspects. Those increases, including the use of judicial authorisation for the lengthy detention of terrorist suspects[338] and the requirement of access to legal advice if adverse inferences are to be drawn from silence,[339] were in effect imposed on the Government by decisions of the European Court of Human Rights. The later legislation made no attempt to address one of the central problems inherent in PACE, the lack of sanctions for its breach.

This was a recurring theme in this chapter. It is particularly true of Code C; it creates a scheme which seems to make every effort to ensure fair treatment in custody and in the interview, but which operates outside the realm of general legal sanctions since breaches may be remedied (in the accepted sense of that word) only in internal disciplinary proceedings and only very rarely then. The right to legal advice, although on a statutory basis, is an equally weak position. The Notes for Guidance, which occupy key points in the interviewing scheme, appear intended to have no legal status at all. Since no other effective means is available of ensuring that the rules are adhered to, the courts have stepped into the breach and have developed complex rules for the exclusion of confessions obtained in breach of the interviewing rules. Thus, in effect, exclusion of confession evidence has become the main method of upholding the rights of the suspect while in custody and in the interview.

However, the use of exclusion of evidence as a means of redress leads to very uncertain protection for suspects' rights since it can only operate where the case comes to court and the suspect pleads not guilty. Thus, the police may still be inclined to break the rules in the hope of obtaining a guilty plea and therefore, many interviews may be conducted which fall below the TA or PACE standard. If, in particular instances, this does not come to light, a doubtful guilty plea may be accepted, or a false confession may be admitted, leading to a miscarriage of justice, while on the other hand such failures may

---

337 Reiner, R, 'The politics of the Act' [1985] PL 394, p 395.
338 See Chapter 13, p 794.
339 See Chapter 13, p 843.

sometimes mean that reliable confession evidence cannot be accepted in court, although it would have been had the rules been observed. If confession evidence would not have been available but for oppressive questioning, it is suggested that the energies of the police should have been devoted to uncovering other evidence. Curtailment of the right to silence has merely exacerbated the situation, since it is likely in itself to increase the pressure on the suspect to speak and it may also undermine the safeguard which it is suggested has most real value in the interview: the provision of legal advice from an experienced solicitor. Where non-confession evidence is obtained in breach of the PACE or TA standards, it appears increasingly likely, as *Forbes*[340] and *AG's Reference (No 3 of 1999)*[341] indicated, that the courts will admit it, thereby possibly encouraging laxity in adhering to the rules.

There is the further problem that, as this chapter and Chapter 11 have shown, the Code C and statutory safeguards can be evaded by operating entirely outside the PACE and TA schemes, using secret surveillance techniques, as occurred in *Khan*[342] and *Chalkley*,[343] or operating undercover, as in *Amin*.[344] Thus, the safeguards for suspects can be marginalised. While such techniques are effective in crime control terms,[345] the concern must arise that they may be used deliberately in some instances rather than arresting and interviewing a suspect, thereby triggering off all the safeguards. As Chapter 11 explained, such techniques are now regulated by the Police Act 1997 and the Regulation of Investigatory Powers Act 2000 (RIPA). But a breach of either statute does not in itself give rise to liability unless the action, if unauthorised, would create existing tortious or criminal liability. As seen in *Chalkley*, the courts are not willing to use exclusion of evidence as a means of upholding the integrity of the criminal justice system where such liability could have been incurred in the gathering of evidence. Further, following *Chalkley*, they are unlikely to do so, even under the HRA, where no existing liability could have been incurred, but a breach of Art 8 has been caused. This latter instance is clearly of particular importance, not only because it would mean that the courts are prepared to receive evidence obtained in breach of a fundamental human right, but also because no other remedy would be available, apart from the possibility of mounting a challenge to the police operation in the tribunal set up under the RIPA.[346]

Thus, it is fair to conclude that while the PACE and TA schemes themselves have not been upheld where non-confession evidence is obtained, it is also apparent that when the police operate outside those schemes, and act unlawfully, the courts are not prepared to exclude the evidence thereby obtained in order to vindicate the rights violated. As argued above, the use of exclusion of evidence in this fashion can ignore the interests of victims. But to argue for a nuanced approach which would allow consideration of such interests and of due process, depending on the particular circumstances of a case, is to demand a theorised and developed approach which it is currently almost impossible to discern in

---

340 [2001] Crim LR 649.
341 [2001] 2 WLR 56.
342 [1996] 3 All ER 289; (1996) 146 NLJ 1024.
343 [1998] 2 Cr App R 79.
344 [2000] 1 WLR 1071; [2000] Crim LR 174.
345 See Chapter 11, pp 689–90.
346 See Chapter 11, pp 714 *et seq.*

decision-making based almost entirely on crime control values. In other words, the trend away from due process evident in the legislative developments is echoed in the current judicial tendencies. As indicated, the other possible remedies available have had little impact in creating police accountability, either in terms of upholding suspects' rights generally, or in respect of the statutory and Code-based safeguards.

However, the same government that introduced the TA and the CJPOA introduced the HRA. One might have expected that the HRA would prove a corrective to the dominance of crime control values evident in criminal justice policies and in judicial decisions. In the pre-HRA period and in the period immediately after the HRA came into force, there was a view that the Act might allow for a 'reinvigoration of fundamental values' in the criminal justice system.[347] These two chapters have sought to suggest that, despite unfavourable statutory provisions, particularly those of the TA, the Convention offers some possibilities of curbing police discretion in the interests of due process values since it does allow domestic judges to look more closely and directly at standards of fairness in the criminal justice system. It appeared possible that the inception of the HRA might herald a return to an emphasis on such values which has not been evident since the early 1990s. But this chapter has suggested that the early decisions on the Convention, in particular *Brown v Stott*[348] and *Shannon*,[349] do not suggest that such a return is probable, although there have been decisions in the field of stop and search which suggest otherwise.[350] Also, where conditions of detention or secret police operations do not infringe existing tortious liability, the HRA provides the only method, under s 7(1)(a), of challenging the police, although, as explained in Chapter 11 in respect of surveillance, such a challenge would have to be brought in the new tribunal set up under the RIPA, not in the ordinary courts.

It appears likely that the HRA will have a diffuse and patchy effect; it will not have a radical impact on the use of the current repressive legislation or the further powers to be introduced under Part 10 of the Anti-Terrorism, Crime and Security Bill 2001, assuming that they become law. It may itself be manipulated either by the judiciary or the legislature in the sense that in court, the rights it affords can be 'read down' in order to preserve the effect of such legislation, while the use of s 19 statements of compatibility may provide such legislation with a spurious appearance of rectitude. MPs may accept that a process of human rights auditing has occurred, allaying concerns about the provisions. A blending of the Convention values with those of the common law is becoming especially apparent in this field, but it is suggested that those of the Convention will only attain an appearance of gaining greater respect owing to the HRA, where they harmonise with values *already* held dear by the common law. It may be said that where the judiciary have traditionally established a firm opposition to due process values, as they have in respect of the admission of improperly obtained non-confession evidence, the HRA is likely to have little impact, although it may do so where they have traditionally been sympathetic to due process, as they have been in relation to the deprivation of liberty in police detention.[351] Possibly the difference of attitude is

---

347 Walker, C, in Walker and Starmer, *op cit*, fn 278, p 62.
348 [2001] 2 WLR 817.
349 [2001] 1 WLR 51.
350 See Chapter 13, pp 773–74.
351 See *Roberts v Chief Constable of Cheshire* [1999] 1 WLR 662.

attributable to a traditional common law acceptance and understanding of certain basic human rights, including the right to liberty, but not of more sophisticated and nebulous ones such as rights to be free from humiliating treatment or invasion of privacy. Thus, both the creation of greater police accountability and the tempering of the effects of repressive legislation that could have occurred under the HRA are likely to be muted and inconsistent.

The legislation discussed in these chapters reflects the change in the political climate that became evident in the mid-1990s. As Dixon puts it, 'The political and professional consensus about the need for criminal justice reform [in the face of discovery of a number of miscarriages of justice] had broken down ... the new Home Secretary encouraged renewed populist obsession with law and order ...'.[352] At the time, the Conservative Party had a Home Secretary, in Michael Howard, who was perceived in many quarters as long on right wing law and order rhetoric, and tabloid appeal, but short on measured criminal justice policies.[353] The aims of crime control were furthered, so Howard claimed, by ensuring an enormous increase in the prison population, by increasing, on pain of penal sanctions, the number of instances in which the citizen must take orders from the police,[354] and by abolishing or undermining the rights of suspects, in particular the right to silence.[355] The stance taken was well summed up in Howard's own words as seeking to redress 'the balance in our criminal justice system which has tilted much too far in favour of the criminal and away from the protection of the public'.[356]

From the mid-1990s, once Tony Blair became Shadow Prime Minister and Jack Straw Shadow Home Secretary, the Labour Party in opposition adopted a very similar crime control stance to that of the Conservative Party. Since the Labour Government took office in 1997 there have been, apart from the passing of the HRA, no indications of attempts to break with the criminal justice legislative policies of the Conservative Party. Post-2000, both major parties were seeking to outdo each other in encouraging and pandering to populist notions of crime control. The attack on the World Trade Centre in New York in September 2001 has fostered the production of further counter-terrorist legislation in the UK which will continue the trend away from due process in terrorist investigations. The Anti-Terrorism, Crime and Security Bill 2001 includes a number of further police powers relating to identification in Part 10 and a power to detain non-national terrorist suspects without trial.[357] It requires derogation from Art 5 since otherwise, the new provisions would be found to be incompatible with its requirements. It is probably safe to predict that the election in 2001 of Iain Duncan-Smith as the leader of the Conservative Party is also likely to aid in confirming the continuing devaluation of due process in criminal justice policies. The HRA, together with improvement in the police disciplinary system, is, as indicated, likely to have a countering effect, but it is unlikely to be of the radical nature previously predicted.

---

352 In Walker and Starmer, *op cit*, fn 278, p 73.

353 Maguire, M, 'The wrong message at the wrong time?', in Morgan, D and Stephenson, G (eds), *Suspicion and Silence*, 1994, p 48.

354 In the CJPOA 1994, especially ss 71 and 68.

355 In the CJPOA 1994, ss 34, 36, 37; see Chapter 13, pp 842–43.

356 HC Deb Col 211, 2 April 1996.

357 The new Bill was passed in the Commons by 323 votes to 79, but it may well be amended in the Lords in December 2001.

CHAPTER 15

FREEDOM OF MOVEMENT

1 INTRODUCTION[1]

There is no general enforceable right to enter, remain in or move freely about in the UK or travel abroad except in so far as the freedom of movement provisions of EU law apply, and therefore this freedom is in a vulnerable position. International instruments providing rights to freedom of movement have not been ratified by the UK. As explained below, the UK has not ratified the freedom of movement Protocols of the European Convention. Article 12 of the International Covenant on Civil and Political Rights 1976 provides protection for freedom of movement, but the UK entered a number of important reservations to this right on ratification. In any event, unlike the Convention, it is not enforceable as far as the UK is concerned by means of individual petition.

In practice, the government has not generally tended to interfere with freedom of movement as far as British citizens are concerned, although they can be extradited. Further, this chapter charts a number of instances in which British citizens can be prevented from travelling abroad. However, non-British citizens born in or resident in the UK may not be allowed to remain or enter and may, therefore, be separated from their families. Asylum seekers who have a claim to enter the UK may not find that the claim receives full consideration, while persons may be expelled from the UK who have a claim to remain. Obviously, such expulsion represents one of the clearest possible infringements of freedom of movement and, although it must be weighed against the accepted right of every nation to place limits on those who can enter or remain within its boundaries,[2] the mechanism for balancing the two interests should in principle allow them to be fully and fairly weighed against each other.

The extent to which UK law allows determinations as to extradition or deportation and the claims of asylum seekers to be fairly and clearly made is the main issue addressed by this chapter. Thus, it concentrates on the circumstances in which a person can be required to leave the country, although it also considers the freedom to travel abroad. But apart from examining the position of asylum seekers, which raises a number of human rights issues, it does not consider the general claims of those wishing to enter the country, apart from those of asylum seekers, since the main focus of the chapter is on the freedom to remain in the country. Further, this choice is made on the basis that the complex

---

1   General reading: Evans, *Immigration Law*, 1983; Grant and Martin, *Immigration Law and Practice*, 1982 and supplements; MacDonald, I and Blake, N, *Immigration Law and Practice*, 5th edn, 2001; Supperstone, M, *Immigration Law*, 1988; Dummett, A and Nichol, A, *Subjects, Citizens, Aliens and Others – Nationality and Immigration Law*, 1990; Supperstone and Cavanagh, *Immigration*, 1992. See also Harlow, C and Rawlings, R, *Law and Administration*, 1984, Chapters 16 and 17; Reports of the Commission for Racial Equality, *Immigration Control and Procedures, Report of a Formal Investigation*, 1985 and the Select Committee on Home Affairs, *Immigration from the Indian Subcontinent* (1981–82, HC 90-1); Papademetriou, G, *The European Union's Struggle with Immigration and Asylum*, 1996; Jackson, D, *Immigration: Law and Practice*, 2nd edn, 1999.

2   Recognised by the European Court of Human Rights; see the *East African Asians* cases (1973) 3 EHRR 76.

provisions of immigration law are a matter more appropriately covered in a number of specialist texts. Full and detailed consideration of the lengthy and complex provisions relating to asylum seekers is also outside the scope of this book.

This chapter begins by looking at the position of asylum seekers in a separate section and considers the relevance of the Human Rights Act (HRA) to their position. It then considers the mechanisms which can be used to expel a person from the country. In a further section, it considers the issues that may be raised under the HRA in respect of such expulsion, matters that might also be raised in respect of asylum seekers. It moves on to consider recent curtailments of the freedom to travel abroad.

At present, the influence of the HRA on freedom of movement is limited. Despite the inception of the HRA, freedom of movement remains in a very precarious position since the routes allowing recourse to the domestic courts under the HRA or to the European Court of Human Rights are unavailable. The UK has so far failed to ratify Protocol 4[3] of the European Convention on Human Rights which, under Art 2, protects freedom of movement within a State's boundaries and the freedom to leave the state. Article 3 of Protocol 4, which contains no exceptions, guarantees the right of persons not to be expelled from the State of which they are nationals and to enter that State, while Art 4 prohibits the collective expulsion of aliens.

The UK has also failed to ratify Protocol 7,[4] which goes further than Art 4 of Protocol 4 since it prohibits the expulsion of an alien unless he or she has been given an opportunity to submit reasons against expulsion and have the case reviewed by the 'competent authority'. The authority need not be a judicial body which complies with Art 6 of the Convention, and compliance with Art 4 of the Protocol would be achieved if that authority merely reconsidered the matter. Thus, this guarantee is of a limited and circumspect nature.

The domestic reception of the Convention under the HRA did not affect the availability of these guarantees to UK citizens, since these later Protocols were not received with the rest of the Convention into domestic law. The Government has reconsidered the question of incorporating the Fourth and Seventh Protocols. It has decided at present to ratify the Seventh Protocol[5] although it has not yet done so, but has not yet decided to ratify the Fourth, which would require changes to immigration legislation or the entry of a reservation.[6] It must be noted that European Union nationals have the right to freedom of movement subject to limited exceptions under the Treaty of Rome 1957 and the Treaty of European Union,[7] as amended by the Amsterdam Treaty, which will be interpreted in accordance with Protocol 4, and Art 1 of Protocol 7.[8]

Breaches of other Convention rights attendant upon infringements of freedom of movement can be brought before the domestic courts, under the HRA, or ultimately

---

3   The Protocol came into force on 2 May 1968.
4   It came into force in November 1988.
5   This will require legislative change to certain family law principles creating inequalities between husband and wife.
6   See Home Office Review of Human Rights Instruments (amended) 26 August 1999.
7   The EC Treaty, Art 48 protects the free movement of workers while the TEU, Art K1 relates to asylum and immigration policy.
8   See further below, pp 946–48.

determined at Strasbourg. Argument that separation from family or from a particular community amounts to a violation of the Art 8 guarantee of privacy remains a possibility.

2 ASYLUM SEEKERS[9]

Introduction

The UK accepts certain international treaty obligations in respect of asylum seekers under the United Nations Convention Relating to the Status of Refugees 1951, as amended by the 1967 Protocol relating to the Status of Refugees. These are reflected in the Immigration Rules and given statutory recognition under s 1 of the Asylum and Immigration Appeals Act 1993, as regards appeals, although neither the Treaty nor the Protocol have been enacted directly into UK law. Thus, there is no right to asylum under domestic law. The scheme instead determines when refoulment (return of the asylum seeker to the country of origin) can occur. But, as indicated below, the maze of complex provisions have little to say about the grounds for the grant of asylum. They concern the methods of removing the asylum seeker from the country and dealing with the application as speedily as possible.

The current (cumbersome and complex) domestic scheme is governed by the Asylum and Immigration Appeals Act 1993, the Asylum and Immigration Act 1996 and the Immigration and Asylum Act 1999. The 1996 Act amended the 1993 Act and both the 1993 and 1996 Acts were amended and partly repealed by the 1999 Act.[10] A number of statutory instruments also affect the position of asylum seekers, including the Immigration Rules[11] and the Asylum Appeals (Procedure) Rules 1996,[12] which were superseded by the Immigration and Asylum Appeals (Procedure) Rules 2000.[13] The thrust of the changes to the scheme has been to seek to limit the ability to appeal, to speed up the procedure, to minimise the benefit entitlements consistent with enhancing its deterrent quality, and to enhance the possibilities of removing asylum seekers from the UK (to 'safe' third countries or to countries of origin deemed to be safe).

Under Art 1A(2) of the Convention, asylum should not be refused if the only country to which the person could be removed is one to which he is unwilling to go owing to a well-founded fear of being persecuted for reasons of race, religion, nationality, membership of a particular social group or political opinion. A duty to grant asylum is

---

9   See, generally, Burgess (1991) 141 NLJ 50; Bhaba, J, 'Deterring refugees' (1992) Imm & Nat LP 133; Stanley, A, 'The legal status of international zones: the British experience with particular reference to asylum seekers' (1992) Imm & Nat LP 126; with reference to EU migration control: Grant (1993) 143 NLJ 608; Bernstein, 'Political asylum' (1992) 142 NLJ 1097; on the 1993 Act, Munir (1993) 143 NLJ 1149 and Chowdhury (1994) 144 NLJ 207; *The Detention and Imprisonment of Asylum Seekers in the UK*, Amnesty International British Section, 1996; Goodwin-Gill, GS, 'Who to protect ... how and the future' (1997) 9(1) Int Journal of Refugee Law 1; Shah, P, *Refugees, Race and the Legal Concept of Asylum in Britain*, 2000; Harvey, C, *Seeking Asylum in the UK – Problems and Perspectives*, 2000.

10   The 1999 Act repealed ss 1–4, 7, 9 and 10 of the 1996 Act. It also repealed ss 3–12 and Scheds 1 and 2 to the 1993 Act.

11   Issued as HC 725 (1993) amending the previous restatement of the Rules; they were then incorporated in another restatement, HC 395 (1994).

12   SI 1996/2070.

13   SI 2333/L21.

not directly imposed, but if no safe alternative destination can be found for the asylum seeker, the country in question will have to grant asylum.

Rule 334 of the Immigration Rules provides that asylum will be granted if the Secretary of State is satisfied that: the applicant is in the UK; he is a refugee as defined in the Convention; 'refusing his application would result in his being required to go in breach of the Convention and Protocol to a country in which his life or freedom would be threatened on account of his race, religion, nationality, political opinion or membership of a particular social group'. It would appear that Rule 334 goes further than the Convention in requiring a threat to life or freedom. These appear to be more stringent requirements than those denoted by a well founded fear of persecution owing to membership of a particular social group.

At the present time, 78% of asylum applications are initially turned down by asylum case workers, but one-third of those decisions are reversed on appeal. Contrary to popular belief, asylum applications have not been constantly increasing. Between 1995 and 1996 the numbers declined from 40,000 to 20,000. However, between 1999 and 2000, the number increased to 76,000.[14] At present, the numbers are double what they were three years ago. The UK is perceived by some asylum seekers as having a more relaxed regime than some other European countries and as giving a broader definition to the meaning of persecution.[15] Also, a number of asylum seekers speak English and have family connections in Britain. At the initial stage of claiming asylum, certain asylum seekers are selected as appropriate for detention at centres such as the one at Oakington, where their claims can be fast tracked; they may receive an answer in seven days, but will lose their freedom during that time. As indicated below, the practice of detaining asylum seekers may be in breach of Art 5, although the House of Lords considers that the practice can be reconciled with Art 5.

The legal and political context

Commentators tend to agree that the Conservative Governments of 1989 to 1997, especially the Major Government, demonstrated an illiberal and mean-minded attitude towards asylum seekers.[16] The lengths to which the Government was prepared to go were demonstrated in 1996. The Social Security (Persons from Abroad) Miscellaneous Amendment Regulations 1996[17] removed all entitlement to income-related benefit from asylum seekers who failed to claim asylum immediately upon arrival in the UK and from those who were pursuing appeals. Thus, some genuine asylum seekers were faced with the choice of staying in the UK awaiting determination of their claims while homeless and destitute, or abandoning their claims and returning to face persecution. In *Secretary of State for Social Security ex p Joint Council for the Welfare of Immigrants; Secretary of State for Social Security ex p B*[18] the applicants sought judicial review of the regulations on the

---

14   Home Office, Immigration Research and Statistics Directorate.

15   See below, fn 46 and associated text.

16   See Robertson, G, *Freedom, the Individual and the Law*, 7th edn, 1993, p 407; *The Detention and Imprisonment of Asylum Seekers in the UK*, Amnesty International British Section, 1996; Harvey, *op cit*, fn 9.

17   SI 1996/30.

18   [1996] 4 All ER 385; (1996) 146 NLJ 985. For comment see Harvey [1997] PL 394. See also *The Royal Borough of Kensington and Chelsea ex p Kihara* (1996) *The Times*, 10 July.

ground that they were *ultra vires* the Asylum and Immigration Appeals Act 1993, the enabling Act, since, *inter alia*, they created interference with the exercise of rights under the Act.

The Court of Appeal found that the *Leech* principle was of assistance to the applicants. *Secretary of State for Home Affairs ex p Leech (No 2)*[19] concerned the right of prison governors to open and read letters to a solicitor and a right exercisable on grounds of prolixity or objectionability to stop them (Rule 33(3)) unless a writ had already been issued. The opening and reading of such letters was challenged by way of judicial review. The Court of Appeal found that it was a principle of great importance that every citizen had an unimpeded right of access to a court and that this was buttressed by the principle of legal professional privilege. A common law privilege of this nature could openly be taken away by subordinate legislation only where that was expressly authorised by the enabling legislation (s 47 of the Prison Act 1952). Section 47 might authorise some screening of correspondence, but it must be strictly construed in accordance with the presumption against statutory interference with common law rights. The court found that the instant case involved taking the *Leech* principle a step further. *Leech* had concerned a direct interference with basic rights. The instant case concerned an indirect interference with such rights. However, the Court of Appeal considered that the step in question should be taken. Simon-Brown LJ found that the rights conferred on asylum seekers under the 1993 Act would be rendered nugatory for some of them by the impact of the 1996 Regulations. The only alternative would be for them to experience a destitution which no civilised nation could tolerate. Simon-Brown LJ said: 'Parliament cannot have intended a significant number of genuine asylum seekers to be impaled on the horns of so intolerable a dilemma: the need either to abandon their claims to refugee status or to maintain them as best they can but in a state of utter destitution.' On these grounds, the 'uncompromisingly draconian' regulations were held to be *ultra vires*.

The Social Security Secretary, Peter Lilley, then decided to reverse the decision of the Court of Appeal by means of primary legislation. An amendment to the Asylum and Immigration Bill 1996 was therefore rushed through Parliament. When the 1996 Act came into force, many asylum seekers were placed in the situation described by Simon-Brown LJ as one which 'no civilised nation can tolerate' (under s 11 and Sched 1 of the 1996 Act). The asylum seekers in question were helped by voluntary and church groups, but such groups were placed under a great strain as a direct result of the government policy. It became hard, if not impossible, for many asylum seekers to pursue the legal right to claim asylum. However, the asylum seekers' lawyers discovered that the National Assistance Act 1948 obliges local authorities to provide temporary accommodation for those in need. Obviously, the doctrine of implied repeal would have been expected to mean that the 1948 Act was repealed to the extent of its inconsistency with the 1996 Act. It was very difficult to argue with credibility that the Conservative-dominated Parliament had not intended that asylum seekers should be rendered destitute under the terms of the 1996 Act, since that was clearly what it had intended. Nevertheless, when the issue was considered in the High Court (*Hammersmith and Fulham LBC ex p M*),[20] Collins J found 'it was impossible to believe that an asylum seeker who was lawfully here and could not

---

19   [1993] 4 All ER 539.
20   (1996) *The Times*, 10 October.

lawfully be removed from the country should be left destitute, starving and at grave risk of illness and even death'. This judgment was upheld on appeal in February 1997 by a court headed by the Master of the Rolls, Lord Woolf.[21] Thus, at present, withdrawal of accommodation is no longer used to deter asylum seekers and encourage them to abandon their claims.[22]

The intention of the Labour Government on taking office in 1997 was apparently to uphold Britain's obligations under international law and to make a fresh start with asylum policy.[23] In 1995, Jack Straw called the introduction of the 'white list' (see below) 'the most crude playing of the race card I have ever seen and we are going to resist it. We will have no truck with the crude racist legislation which Mr Howard is proposing.'[24] So far, however, it has shown no preparedness to dismantle some of the more draconian asylum rules. The 1998 White Paper accepted that asylum seekers could not be left destitute, but worked on the premise that those who had not established their right to be in the UK were not entitled to the same benefits as those who had.[25] The main aim of the government appeared to be to maintain benefits at a minimal level in order to create deterrence.

It is fair to say that the policies of the current Labour Government have not been marked by greater liberality than those of its predecessor. The statutory framework it introduced – the Immigration and Asylum Act 1999 – introduced a range of measures designed to deter entry, to speed up the procedure for determining the claim and to deal with the accommodation of asylum seekers while the claim is being heard. The 1999 Act in particular introduced a dispersal policy and gave recognition to the practice of detaining asylum seekers under para 16(1), Sched 2 of the Act which was already apparent.[26]

The practice of detaining asylum seekers was challenged, in 2001, by action taken under the HRA, relying on Art 5. Collins J found that none of the exceptions under Art 5 applied to such detention and, therefore, the practice was unlawful under s 6 of the HRA.[27] The decision caused an outcry in the national press and an attack on the judge from the Home Office. However, it merely depended on a straightforward application of s 6 of the HRA and Art 5. The judgment was then over-turned by the Court of Appeal[27a] on the ground that the short period of detention in question (10 days) was justified in order to ensure the speedy resolution of the many claims. This was, it is suggested, an executive - friendly ruling which has created a worrying exception to Article 5.

Thus, a pattern similar to that apparent in the Conservative years is emerging, in the sense that the Government answers to popular opinion by producing extensive and draconian laws aimed at asylum seekers, which are then subject to challenge on human

---

21 *Hammersmith and Fulham LBC ex p M* (1997) *The Times*, 19 February.

22 See further Cholewinski, 'Enforced destitution of asylum seekers in the UK: the denial of fundamental rights' (1998) 10(3) Int Journal of Refugee Law 462–99.

23 Government White Paper, *Fairer, Faster, Firmer – Modern Approach to Immigration and Asylum*, Cm 4018, July 1998.

24 BBC Radio 4 'Today' programme, 26 October 1995.

25 *Ibid*, para 8.17.

26 Under ss 148–57. In 1999, 1,000 detention places were available, three-quarters of which were used for asylum seekers (Home Office, Immigration Research and Statistics Directorate, July 1999).

27 *R (on the Application of Saadi and Others) v Secretary of State for the Home Dept.* Judgment of 10 September 2001.

27a (2001) *The Times*, 22 October; (2001) 145 SJLB 246; (2001) 151 NLJ 1573; [2001] EWCA Civ 1512.

rights grounds in the courts. The difference is that under the HRA, the judiciary have a clearer mandate for intervention. This does not imply that they will use it; the above judgment of the Court of Appeal suggests that under pressure from the executive, they may decline to do so.

EU policy on asylum

In June 1997, a proposed revision to the Treaty of Rome was considered at the Amsterdam summit meeting and included in the Treaty of Amsterdam, which came into force in May 1999. It allows the European Commission to make proposals for harmonisation of asylum policy which require only qualified majority voting rather than unanimity. The revision is intended to address the lack of uniformity in EU policy on asylum. Some areas are governed by EU standards, but others are the preserve of the individual States. This leaves some areas uncoordinated, including the length of time an asylum seeker might wait in order to hear whether a third country – the one in which he or she should have claimed asylum – will take him or her back. Minimum standards for the reception of asylum seekers are also left to be determined by the individual countries, as are the procedures for dealing with the applications. Harmonisation of policy in the EU may lead to improved standards in relation to some aspects of asylum seeking, although previous harmonisation has probably led to a general lowering of standards. For example, the British rule that asylum must be sought in the first 'safe' country of arrival is now part of EU policy. It may be noted that, as part of the reforms, Spain wishes to amend the EU Treaty so that nationals from one EU country cannot seek asylum in another EU country. However, such an amendment would override the 1951 Convention and would fail to take account of possible future human rights abuses in EU countries.[28]

Grounds for the grant of asylum

The Treaty and Protocol are concerned only with *political* asylum seekers and this is reflected in the ambit of Rule 334, so that those fleeing from natural disasters or economic crises are not covered. Clearly, sometimes it may be hard to make this distinction when persons leave a country which is in the middle of a civil war. The applicant must belong to a group which is likely to be persecuted and this will include a 'social group'. The meaning of this term of Rule 75 (now Rule 334) was considered in *Secretary of State for Home Affairs ex p Binbasi*:[29] it was held to mean that a group of persons could be identified as sharing fundamental unchangeable characteristics or as sharing characteristics to which they had an overriding moral commitment on religious or other grounds.[30] However, even where the applicant can be viewed as being a member of such a group, he or she will fail in a claim for asylum on the basis of religious persecution unless an element of discrimination is also present. In *Omoruyi v Secretary of State for the Home Dept*[31] the applicant, a Nigerian Christian, claimed asylum on the basis that he feared

---

28   See further Alston, P, *The EU and Human Rights*, 1st edn, 1999.

29   [1989] Imm AR 595.

30   For discussion of the meaning of this term as applied to homosexuals, see Bamforth [1995] PL 382.

31   (2000) *The Times*, 3 November.

death since he had defied a Nigerian cult in refusing to submit the corpse of his father to them for ritual mutilation, in accordance with his Christian beliefs. It was found that no element of discrimination was present, since he was under the threat of death for defying the cult, not on the basis of discrimination because of his beliefs. This decision fails to appreciate that the applicant had been *indirectly* discriminated against, since he had been subjected to a threat which bore unequally on persons depending on their religious beliefs. Possibly, the decision to refuse asylum could also have been challenged by basing his argument on Art 9 read with Art 14 of the European Convention, since Art 14 may recognise indirect discrimination.[32]

An asylum seeker may well enter the country without a valid passport or without other documents establishing his or her identity or nationality. However, the House of Lords has ruled that such a person cannot be treated as an illegal entrant under the Immigration Act 1971.[33] If a person seeks asylum, the case must be referred by the immigration officer to the Home Office for decision even though it appears that the claim is unjustified. The Home Office will consider the case in accordance with the provisions of the Convention and Protocol Relating to the Status of Refugees, and the claimant will not be removed until such consideration is completed.

The term 'persecution' has been interpreted fairly restrictively as meaning 'to oppress for holding a heretical opinion or belief';[34] under this strict interpretation, 'harassment' will not always be sufficient.[35] The House of Lords in *Secretary of State for Home Affairs ex p Sivakumaran*[36] laid down the test for determining whether the fear of persecution is well founded. Once it appears that the applicant genuinely fears persecution, the Secretary of State is required to ask himself on the basis of all the available information whether there has been demonstrated a 'real likelihood' or 'reasonable chance' of persecution.[37] The applicant has the burden of proving that there are grounds for thinking that persecution may occur. However, information may be taken into account of which he or she is unaware. Thus, the fear must be based on reasonable grounds, objectively assessed. It therefore appears that the question is not whether a person in possession of the information known to the applicant would have feared persecution, but whether such fear would have been felt by an objective observer in possession of *all the available information*.

The emphasis of this test differs from that put forward by the High Commissioner, which involves asking whether, subjectively, a real fear of persecution is present and then considering whether it is a fear no one would reasonably hold. The test put forward by the House of Lords therefore provides less protection for refugees and, moreover, the imprecise nature of expressions such as 'real likelihood' leaves considerable latitude for differences of opinion as to the severity of the risk of persecution. The House of Lords' decision in *Ex p Sivakumaran* to uphold the Secretary of State in refusing asylum applications of the six applicant Tamils from Sri Lanka differed from that of the

---

32 See Chapter 16, p 984.

33 *Nailie and Kanesarajah* [1993] AC 674; [1993] 2 WLR 927, HL.

34 See *Immigration Appeal Tribunal ex p Jonah* [1985] Imm AR 7, *per* Nolan J.

35 *Secretary of State for Home Affairs ex p Yurekli* [1990] Imm AR 334, QBD.

36 [1988] AC 958; [1988] 1 All ER 193.

37 See Lord Diplock's judgment in *Fernandez v Government of Singapore* [1971] 2 All ER 691, p 697.

adjudicator who later heard the appeals of the Tamils from abroad and found that there was a sufficient risk of persecution based upon race, religion and political opinion.[38] The fact that all the available information must be considered may also, of course, work to the advantage of the applicant since it will mean that a court cannot disregard any piece of information: this will include what has happened in the past which should be related to any current events,[39] although the mere fact that an asylum seeker has been persecuted in the past will not raise a presumption in his favour that he is a refugee.[40] However, in determining the well-foundedness of the fear, the fact that the applicant has not been singled out for persecution will not be conclusive of the issue.[41]

It may be noted that gender is not included expressly in the Convention, but that women may, in certain circumstances, form a persecuted group. There seems to be an increasing possibility that women who are subject to barbaric practices and grossly unequal treatment owing to their gender in certain countries (such as beheading on suspicion of adultery in some Islamic countries, denial of freedom of movement or education under some fundamentalist regimes, genital mutilation in India) may be able to seek asylum on those grounds.[42] The House of Lords in *Islam v Sec of State for the Home Dept; R v IAT and Another ex p Shah (Consolidated Appeals*[43] recognised that in some circumstances, women can be viewed as a persecuted group. The Lords found that women in Pakistan can be viewed as a particular social group who are persecuted merely through membership of that group, since they are at risk of flogging or death if accused of adultery by their husbands.

Thus, the rights of women and girls may be recognised and declared through the medium of asylum seeking in a manner which, it is suggested, gives the lie to cultural relativism. Such asylum seeking may lead to a greater recognition in the West that unequal practices in some cultures cannot be defended as forming part of a strong cultural tradition, since they merely reflect long standing male dominance in the particular culture.

If the test as to persecution is satisfied and if, as in *Bugdaycay*, the refugee cannot be returned to another safe country, he or she can settle in the UK, but the United Nations Convention requires under Art 2 that measures relating to public order must be observed. If they are not observed, the refugee can be removed, but not back to the country he or she originally fled from or any other where persecution would be likely to arise.[44]

Third country rules

However, it will be irrelevant that an applicant may have a genuine case for refugee status if the 'third country' rule applies. This rule was enshrined in Rule 354 of the 1994 Rules. If an applicant has had an opportunity to seek asylum in a safe third country en

---

38 *Immigration Appeal Tribunal ex p Secretary of State for Home Affairs* [1990] 3 All ER 652, CA; for comment see Blake, N (1989) 4(1) Imm & Nat LP 7; Burgess, D (1991) 141 NLJ 50.

39 *Secretary of State for Home Affairs ex p P* [1992] COD 295.

40 *Secretary of State for Home Affairs ex p Direk* [1992] Imm AR 330.

41 *Secretary of State for Home Affairs ex p Gulbache* [1991] Imm AR 526.

42 See, eg, *IAT ex p Shah* (1996) *The Times*, 12 November.

43 [1998] 1 WLR 270; [1999] 2 All ER 545; for discussion, see July (1999) J Civ Lib 243.

44 Immigration Rule 173.

route to the UK, he or she will be sent back to that country to seek asylum there. If this appears to be the case, the Secretary of State need not give substantive consideration to the claim and need not contact the authorities in the third country in order to make a judgment as to the likely response to the asylum seeker's application. This can mean that where a plane has simply touched down briefly in a third country, the asylum seeker will be returned to that country. It may also mean that he or she may be returned to a country which can only doubtfully be regarded as safe and which may return the asylum seeker to the original country, as occurred in *Bugdaycay*, below.[45]

Under s 2(2) of the Asylum and Immigration Act 1996, an applicant for asylum could be removed to a third country if, *inter alia*, the government of that country would not send him to another country otherwise than in accordance with the Convention. In *Secretary of State for the Home Dept ex p Adan*[46] the House of Lords found that proposals to remove a Somali citizen to Germany and an Algerian citizen to France were contrary to the 1996 Act. Both France and Germany interpret the expression 'fear of persecution' as relating to conduct that can be attributed to a State, a narrower meaning than that adopted in many other States. Since in both Somalia and Algeria the applicants were not protected from threats from private citizens, France and Germany might view them as not being subject to persecution. Therefore, since the expression in the Convention had only one autonomous meaning and France and Germany were not applying that proper interpretation, they were not countries to which the asylum seekers could be returned.

However, the position has now changed under the Immigration and Asylum Act 1999. Under s 11, Member States of the EU are *deemed* to be places from which the asylum seeker would not be sent to another country otherwise than in accordance with the Convention. This provision runs contrary to the findings in *Adan*. A decision based on s 11 could only be challenged on the basis that the applicant's Convention rights might be breached as a result.

Appeals

If leave to enter was refused to a claimant to refugee status, he used to be in the same position as other persons seeking entry: under s 13 of the 1971 Act, he had no right of appeal while in the UK. The Asylum and Immigration Appeals Act 1993, however, provided for the first time a statutory right of appeal in limited circumstances to a Special Adjudicator under s 8. The Asylum and Immigration Appeals Act 1993 was amended by the Asylum and Immigration Act 1996. It was then amended as part of the broad changes to the rules introduced by the Immigration and Asylum Act 1999. The Immigration and Asylum Appeals (Procedure) Rules 2000 Pt III, para 3,[47] makes provision for the procedure to be followed. An appeal lies to a Special Adjudicator; leave to appeal to the Immigration Appeals Tribunal may be granted, by the tribunal, and there is the further possibility of leave to appeal from the tribunal on a point of law to the Court of Appeal. This scheme is considered below.[48]

---

45   See also *Secretary of State for Home Affairs ex p Mehari* [1994] 2 WLR 349.
46   (2000) *The Times*, 20 December; see *Adan v Secretary of State for the Home Dept* [1999] 1 AC 293.
47   SI 2000/2333 (L21).
48   See pp 954–56.

The right of appeal was balanced under the 1993 Act by a short cut procedure for claims for asylum which the Home Secretary considered to be without foundation. Under the fast track procedure, many asylum applicants have to submit their appeal against refusal of refugee status within 48 hours and it would be heard and decided within seven days. Those who arrive from countries officially designated as ones from which asylum applications will be presumed to be unfounded (countries on the official so called 'white list')[49] will also be dealt with by this procedure, which may mean that their personal circumstances, which do place them in danger, are not considered. The Asylum and Immigration Act 1996 extended the fast track method; the procedure to be followed is laid down in the Asylum Appeals Procedure Rules 1996.[50] Sections 2 and 3 of the 1996 Act removed the 'in country' right of appeal in third country cases. Under s 11 of the Immigration and Asylum Act 1999, Member States of the EU which are parties to the Dublin Convention of 1990 (making provision for the question of which State should deal with asylum claims of those arriving from outside the EU) are deemed to be safe countries. A decision based on s 11 can only be challenged on the basis that the applicant's Convention rights might be breached as a result.

Section 12 of the 1999 Act creates two categories of safe countries. Certain other countries can be certified as 'safe' by the Secretary of State. Section 1(2) of the Asylum and Immigration Act 1996 placed the notion of the white list on a statutory basis, although the designated countries were set out in the Asylum (Designated Countries of Destination and Designated Safe Countries) Order 1996.[51] Those countries are also designated safe under the 1999 Act. That category of countries also includes those members of the EU which have not signed the Dublin Convention. The second category covers all other countries. The Home Secretary must designate them as safe. However, a person cannot be removed to a country in this category if an appeal under s 71 of the 1999 Act is pending. An appeal can be mounted under s 71 to the issue of a certificate under ss 11 or 12, but unless the country falls into the second category under s 12, there is no right to remain in the UK while the appeal is being heard.

Appeals against removal under ss 11 or 12 on the basis that the removal would be unlawful under s 6 of the HRA can be made to an adjudicator under s 65, but the Secretary of State can, under s 72(2), certify that the appeal is manifestly ill-founded. The applicant could challenge the certificate by way of judicial review, but would not have the right to remain in the country while the review was being heard.

Challenges to executive decisions; impact of the HRA

Prior to the inception of the HRA, decisions of the Home Secretary regarding asylum seekers were normally challenged on the basis that they were unreasonable. However, as the following discussion demonstrates, this set the threshold for challenge very high. In particular, it meant that the mere fact that the applicant's Convention rights had been violated by a decision did not in itself provide a ground for review, so long as the decision

---

49   For the countries designated by Michael Howard, the then Home Secretary, as safe for white list purposes see HC Deb Vol 268 Col 703.

50   SI 1996/2070.

51   SI 1996/2671.

maker had acted reasonably. However, under the HRA, the decision maker is bound by s 6. Therefore, if one or more of the Convention rights are breached, the decision will be unlawful unless s 6(2) applies.

Wednesbury *unreasonableness*

In making a decision as regards the grant of asylum, the Home Secretary may take into account guidance given by the advisory Executive Committee to the High Commissioner for Refugees as to the interpretation of the Treaty and Protocol.[52] If an interpretation of the Immigration Rules is adopted which does not conform with the Convention, the decision may be quashed for 'illegality' or 'irrationality' as occurred in *Bugdaycay v Secretary of State for Home Affairs*.[53] The applicant was a Ugandan refugee whose father and cousins had been killed by the secret police and who therefore feared for his life if he should return to Uganda. He had lived in Kenya and the Home Secretary, in rejecting his claim for asylum, determined to deport him there regardless of the fact that Kenya had been known to return such refugees to Uganda. The House of Lords found that when the Immigration Rules were interpreted in accordance with Art 33 of the Convention, it could then be found that the decision to deport him would contravene it, because although deportation to Kenya would not directly threaten his life, it might lead to such a threat owing to the probability that Kenya would deport him.

However, the Court of Appeal in *Munongo v Secretary of State for Home Affairs*[54] confirmed that the courts would not interfere with the Home Secretary's decision as long as he had followed the correct procedure and his decision was not *Wednesbury* unreasonable – tainted by illegality or irrationality. They would not, therefore, question the basic credibility of the Home Secretary's decision as long as there was some evidence to support his findings. The arbitrariness of an executive decision in respect of asylum seekers will be irrelevant to its reasonableness according to the High Court in *Special Adjudicator ex p Kandasamy*.[55] The applicant, a Tamil, left Sri Lanka, travelled to Sweden and from there to the UK with the intention of claiming asylum in Canada. He and another person in the same circumstances, S, were detained in the UK and then claimed political asylum. Substantive consideration of their applications was refused, but then S's application was substantively considered. The applicant sought judicial review of the decision of the Special Adjudicator to refuse substantive consideration of his application on the ground that the adjudicator's findings were perverse in failing to acknowledge the fact that the situations of S and the applicant were identical or flawed in failing to make plain the respects in which they differed. The fact that an applicant had been treated differently from another in very similar circumstances was not found to provide a ground for review. Public law acknowledged no general principle of consistency. The application therefore failed.

---

52 See *Miller v Immigration Appeal Tribunal* [1988] Imm AR 358, CA; *Bugdaycay v Secretary of State for Home Affairs* [1987] AC 514, HL; *Immigration Appeal Tribunal ex p Yassine* [1990] Imm AR 354, QBD.

53 [1987] AC 514; [1987] 1 All ER 940.

54 [1991] Imm AR 616, CA.

55 (1994) *The Times*, 11 March.

If an asylum seeker applies for leave to move for judicial review of the decision not to grant asylum, it would be expected that he or she would not be removed from the UK pending the further hearing. If he or she is so removed, an injunction may be issued ordering the minister in question to return him or her to the jurisdiction of the court. If that injunction is breached, the minister may be in contempt of court. The House of Lords so held in *M v Home Office*;[56] the case concerned defiance of a court order by the then Home Secretary, Kenneth Baker. Immigration officials had placed a refugee from torture in Zaire back on a plane to that country despite the order prohibiting this. In making the finding of contempt, the House of Lords affirmed the fundamental constitutional principle of obedience of the executive to the law. This contempt conviction of a Cabinet minister persuaded the Government to enshrine in law the principle that refugee claimants have a right to remain in the country until a decision is made on their claim (s 6 of the 1993 Act). This provision is now enshrined in s 15 of the 1999 Act. However, as indicated, the 1999 Act provides for the removal of the applicant in a number of circumstances even before an appeal is heard.

The Human Rights Act

As indicated above, the courts can now find that a decision relating to an asylum seeker is simply unlawful, following the wording of s 6 of the HRA, on the basis that the decision maker has breached one or more of the Convention rights. The most relevant Articles are likely to be Arts 2, 3, 5 and 6. An example was given above of a straightforward finding that Art 5 had been breached by the detention of asylum seekers. Argument could be raised that Art 6 has been breached by the certification of the Home Secretary under s 72(2) of the 1999 Act that an appeal would be manifestly ill-founded, followed by removal of the applicant to another country, since it could be said that the right of access to a court is so fundamentally impaired.[57]

The determination that a country may be viewed as safe has been of especial significance. The courts have allowed the Home Secretary a wide discretion in making such a determination. In *Secretary of State for Home Affairs ex p Canbolat*[58] it was found that the Home Secretary was entitled to decide that France was a safe third country, despite evidence to the contrary. The Special Adjudicator had considered that France was not a safe country. However, it was found that the Home Secretary was entitled to form a contrary opinion which could not be challenged on its merits. In *Secretary of State for Home Affairs ex p Abdi; Secretary of State for Home Affairs ex p Gawe*,[59] the applicants appealed to the Special Adjudicator regarding certificates issued by the Home Secretary to the effect that their claim to asylum was without foundation. The applicants, Somalian nationals, had flown to Spain; they had not claimed asylum there, but had claimed it in the UK. The Home Secretary considered that there was no reason to believe that Spain would not comply with its obligations under the Convention. It was found that the Home Secretary was not obliged to reveal all the material on which he had based the 'without foundation' certificates. Further, the Home Secretary's letters of decision alone were sufficient as a

---

56 (1993) 143 NLJ 1099; [1993] 3 All ER 537, HL; [1992] 1 All ER 75, CA; for comment on this decision see [1993] PL 586.

57 See *Omar v France* (2000) 29 EHRR 210.

58 [1998] 1 WLR 269.

59 (1996) *The Times*, 17 February.

basis on which the Adjudicator could uphold the decision. This decision in particular affords judicial review a very narrow role in rendering the Home Secretary accountable for decisions regarding the safety of third countries. Similar leeway was also allowed to the Home Secretary in *Secretary of State for Home Affairs ex p Chahal*.[60]

However, these decisions may be contrasted with that in *R v Secretary of State for the Home Dept ex p Javed*,[61] in which it was found that the minister had erred in law in arriving at the view that Pakistan could be considered a safe country. The judge, Rose J, reviewed the evidence in coming to the conclusion that women and religious minorities faced persecution in Pakistan.

If decisions, such as those in *Javed* and that of Collins J on Art 5,[62] which apply s 6 of the HRA at its face value without showing the deference previously accorded to ministers, continue to occur, it will be possible to say in this context that the HRA has had a real impact in counteracting the effects of repressive legislation. The further possibilities of raising Art 3 and 8 arguments are considered below, in relation to deportation, as is the possibility of arguing that the right of appeal has been impaired beyond a point which can be tolerated under the Convention.

Conclusions

The system continues to be very heavily weighted against a successful claim by means of the application of the third country rule, the use of the white list, the conditions and length of detention awaiting resolution of the claim[63] and the limitations placed on rights of appeal. Amnesty estimates that only about six in every 100 applications to the UK are successful.

The current climate in Parliament and in the country is unconducive to the development of a more humane policy towards asylum seekers, and the attacks on New York and the Pentagon on 11 September 2001 are likely, however illogical this may seem, to serve to increase the hostility currently shown towards them, and to encourage the introduction of ever more draconian legislation. If the current politically courageous attitude of certain judges in this context continues to be evident, they will be placed in an increasingly invidious position, one that places them at odds with the executive, with much of the media, and with public opinion, as they use the HRA as a counterbalance. At present, the Labour Government is being embarrassed by the straightforward effects of the legislation it itself introduced. Section 6 of the HRA does not provide that the judiciary should show deference to the executive in respect of asylum seekers and, therefore, appears to demonstrate a desire on the part of Parliament to bring about a break with the previous position. It appears possible that the Government will react by seeking to limit the possibility of bringing proceedings under s 7(1)(a), as it has done under the RIPA[64] and in respect of deportation, as considered below.

---

60 (1993) *The Times*, 12 March.

61 (2001) *The Times*, 9 February; see also *R v Secretary of State for the Home Dept ex p Turgut* [2001] 1 All ER 719.

62 See fn 27, above.

63 See *The Detention and Imprisonment of Asylum Seekers in the UK*, Amnesty International British Section, 1996.

64 See Chapter 11, pp 712–13.

3 DEPORTATION

Deportation represents the clearest infringement of freedom of movement and, therefore, should be used only where there is clear justification and where there are mechanisms allowing careful scrutiny of the decision to deport.[65] Deportation is available only in respect of persons who are not British citizens. The position as regards citizenship is governed by the Immigration Act 1971, which, as amended, is the current governing legislation replacing the Commonwealth Immigrants Acts.

Prior to 1962, all UK and Commonwealth subjects had the same freedom of movement in terms of entering and remaining in the UK. Immigration controls under the Immigration Act 1962 extended control beyond aliens for the first time.[66] The 1962 Act was intended to impose control on the numbers of entrants except for those possessing personal or ancestral connections with the UK itself. It therefore marked the development of a policy allowing persons from the mainly white Old Commonwealth to enter while restricting entrants from the mainly black New Commonwealth, which was to continue in subsequent enactments.

However, the 1962 Act did not cover many would-be entrants. In particular, many Asians in Kenya chose, when Kenya became independent in 1963, to opt for retaining their citizenship of the UK and Colonies rather than becoming Kenyan citizens. They would, therefore, have been able to enter the UK under the terms of the 1962 Act and to curb this, the Commonwealth Immigrants Act 1968 was passed. It imposed controls to cover holders of UK passports issued outside the UK, unless such persons could show parental or grandparental links with the UK itself (patriality). This test appeared neutral on its face, but in fact discriminated against black Commonwealth citizens in favour of white ones. It also meant that some citizens who now lost UK entry and settlement rights had no such rights in the countries from which they sought entry and so found themselves unable to enter either country.

The 1968 Act thus avoided making an overt affirmation that the UK was prepared to operate arbitrary distinctions between would-be entrants but, in fact, created hardship for particular groups. Eventually, it was condemned as racially motivated by the European Commission of Human Rights in the *East African Asians* cases[67] on the basis that it had subjected them to racial discrimination which, in the circumstances of the case, could be termed 'degrading treatment' within Art 3. However, well before that ruling, the concept of partiality had become the basis of the main immigration measure, the Immigration Act 1971.

The 1971 Act was amended by the British Nationality Act 1981 which attempted to simplify matters by defining the categories of citizens who would be subject to controls and those who would not. 'British citizens', as defined under the Act, are immune from controls, while all others are subject to control including those within the new categories of 'British Dependent Territories Citizens' and 'British Overseas Citizens', a category

---

65   For criticism of the procedure see Zellick [1973] Crim LR 612; Robertson, *op cit*, fn 16, pp 322–28.
66   For background to this Act and the 1968 Act which followed it, see Steel, *No Entry*, 1969; Bevan, *The Development of British Immigration Law*, 1986; Dummett and Nichol, *op cit*, fn 1.
67   (1973) 3 EHRR 76.

covering UK and Colonies citizens resident in independent Commonwealth countries without citizenship of those countries. The first category includes residents of Hong Kong. However, these new categories cannot be relied on without reference to the 1971 Act in order to determine whether a person is immune from immigration controls because the concept of British citizen is itself defined to include all those who had such immunity when the 1981 Act came into force in 1983.

Thus the 1971 Act created two groups of people: those who have the 'right of abode'; and those who do not, and are therefore subject to controls.

The right of abode is governed by s 2 of the 1971 Act as amended, which provides:

(1) A person is under this Act to have the right of abode in the United Kingdom if:

   (a) he is a British citizen; or

   (b) he is a Commonwealth citizen who –

      (i) immediately before the commencement of the British Nationality Act 1981 was a Commonwealth citizen having the right of abode in the United Kingdom by virtue of s 2(1)(d) or s 2(2) of this Act as then in force; and

      (ii) has not ceased to be a Commonwealth citizen in the meanwhile.

(2) In relation to Commonwealth citizens who have the right of abode in the United Kingdom by virtue of subsection (1)(b) above, this Act, except this section and s 5(2), shall apply as if they were British citizens; and in this Act (except as aforesaid) 'British citizen' shall be construed accordingly.

In general terms, the Act largely placed Commonwealth citizens in the same position as aliens in respect of the right of abode, apart from EEA citizens, who have special rights of entry (see below). Therefore, two categories of citizens had the right of abode: those who had acquired rights before commencement of the Act; and those who were British citizens.

British citizens

Obviously, only the category of British citizens is ongoing; therefore, it is important to consider the mechanisms by which a person can become a British citizen. Citizenship can be acquired by birth, although not by birth alone, adoption, descent, registration and naturalisation. In practice, the relevant group will largely consist of Commonwealth immigrants who were born in the UK, have a UK-born parent or, in some cases, grandparent, or have been settled in the UK for some time.

After 1983, when the 1981 Act came into force, merely being born in the UK was not enough to acquire British citizenship of the United Kingdom and Colonies; the further requirement was imposed that the child's father or mother be, at that time, either a British citizen or 'settled' in the UK.[68] The meaning of 'settled' is considered above. If the child was illegitimate, however, the question of settlement would only be relevant in relation to the *mother*.[69] This discriminates against the father and although the Family Law Reform Act 1987 has equated the positions of legitimate and illegitimate children in a number of

---

68   The 1981 Act, s 1(1).
69   See s 50(9)(b).

respects, it has not done so in this one despite a recommendation to do so by the Law Commission.[70] If a child is born outside the UK after 1983 and either parent is a British citizen, the child will acquire citizenship,[71] but again the father is discriminated against if the child is illegitimate, since he will not be able to pass on his right to British citizenship.

One fundamental problem arising from the provisions relating to those born in the UK after 1983 is that it may not be clear whether the parent is 'ordinarily resident' (settled). Much will depend on the residence intentions of the parents at the time of the birth. A person's citizenship entitlement may therefore remain uncertain for a substantial period. However, if the parent is not a British citizen or settled at the time of the birth, but becomes so before the child is 18, he or she can still become a British citizen. Alternatively, he or she can become a British citizen if until the age of 10, in any one year for all those 10 years, the number of days on which he or she was absent from the UK did not exceed 90.[72] The Home Secretary has a discretion to register even where the 90 day period has been exceeded in any or all of those first 10 years under s 1(7).

Various other persons have the right to be registered as British citizens, including certain former citizens of the UK and Colonies who did not become British citizens under the 1981 Act and have remained in the UK for five years without breach of the immigration laws and have been accepted for settlement.[73] The Home Secretary can also register certain persons such as minors as citizens at his discretion.[74]

Naturalisation is at the discretion of the Home Secretary under s 6 of the 1981 Act. The Home Secretary may 'if he thinks fit' grant a certificate of naturalisation to a person who appears to him to satisfy the requirements of Sched 1 of the Act. These requirements relate to past residence in the UK, intention to remain there, good character and knowledge of the language.

Before 1981, wives of citizens of the UK and Colonies acquired on marriage the right to obtain citizenship by registration. In contrast, husbands of citizens of the UK and Colonies could only apply for naturalisation. This distinction was, however, removed by the 1981 Act which took away the registration rights of wives and made the grant of citizenship discretionary in both cases. The Immigration Act 1988 placed a further restriction on wives, who could acquire the right of abode. A polygamous wife used to be able to claim the right under s 2(2) of the 1971 Act (before amendment), but it is now provided that the first polygamous wife to exercise such right, by entry or by obtaining a certificate of entitlement shall, by so doing, exclude the rights of others.

Citizenship can be acquired by naturalisation but, in contrast to the right of certain persons considered above to citizenship by registration, citizenship by naturalisation is only at the discretion of the Home Secretary. In exercising this discretion, he will take into account the requirements of Sched 1.[75] The requirements include past residence in the

---

70 Law Com No 118, para 11.20.

71 The 1981 Act, s 2.

72 Sections 1(3) and (4).

73 The 1981 Act, s 4(2).

74 See the 1981 Act, s 3(1): power to register any minor; and under ss 1(7), 3(4) and (5), 7(6) and (8): persons who have not fulfilled certain requirements which, if fulfilled, would have placed the Home Secretary under a duty to register them.

75 The 1981 Act, s 6.

UK, good character, knowledge of language and intention to remain; they may not be so stringently applied where the applicant is married to a British citizen.

The position of EU and EEA nationals[76]

European Union nationals have enforceable rights to freedom of movement under the Treaty of Rome[77] and these were extended to nationals of Austria, Finland, Iceland, Norway and Sweden under the Immigration (European Economic Area) Order 1994 SI 1994/1895. Prior to 1994, the Immigration Rules could only affect EU nationals to the extent permitted by Community law.[78] It was clear that any conflict between the Rules and EU provisions had to be resolved in favour of the latter.[79] The position of EU nationals was strengthened when s 7(1) of the Immigration Act 1988 was brought into force in July 1994: 'A person shall not "require leave to enter or remain" in any case in which he is entitled to do so by virtue of an enforceable Community Right ...' Thus, EEA nationals must be viewed as entering as of right rather than falling into categories of persons who need administrative permission to enter. This does not mean that EEA nationals may not be subject to border controls. In *Secretary of State for Home Affairs ex p Flynn*,[80] the applicant sought judicial review of the decision of the Home Secretary to maintain border controls affecting the free movement of persons between Member States of the EU. He relied on Art 7(a) of the EC Treaty (inserted by Art 13 of the Single European Act 1986 and renumbered by Art G(9) of the Treaty on European Union 1992), which provides that the Community shall adopt measures with 'the aim of progressively establishing the internal market over a period expiring on December 1992 ... The internal market shall establish an area without internal frontiers in which the free movement of goods, persons ... is ensured.' The appellant argued that Art 7(a) required the abolition of border controls by that date and that he had been detrimentally affected since he had been subjected to such controls. In Case 44/84 *Hurd v Jones*,[81] the ECJ had found that a provision produces direct effects between the Member States and their subjects only if it is clear and unconditional and not contingent upon any discretionary implementing measure. Article 7(a) did not satisfy those requirements, since no clear and precise obligation was imposed by Art 7(a): the establishment of the internal market was not an obligation but an aim. Article 7(a) was therefore not of direct effect so that individuals could invoke it.

Article 48 is the principal provision governing the free movement of workers and it is supplemented by implementing secondary legislation. The fact of employment brings the provisions into play as regards the worker and his or her family and this has been interpreted, at least in the English courts, to mean that a person divorced from a worker is

---

76 See, generally, Evans (1982) 45 MLR 97; (1984) American Journal of Comparative Law 679; Steiner, J, *Textbook of EC Law*, 1998, Chapter 18 for further reading in respect of the relevant EU provisions.

77 See rr 68–70; acceptability of discrimination between EU nationals and non-EU nationals reiterated in *Immigration Appeal Tribunal ex p Al-Sabah* [1992] Imm AR 223, CA.

78 Council Regulations (EEC) 1612/68, (EEC) 1251/70; Council Directives (64/221 EEC), (68/360 EEC), (72/194 EEC), (73/148 EEC), (75/34 EEC), (75/35 EEC); Council Declaration (EEC) 1451/68.

79 See *Giangregorio v Secretary of State for Home Affairs* [1983] 3 CMLR 472; *Monteil v Secretary of State for Home Affairs* [1974] 1 CMLR 265; *Rubruck v Secretary of State for Home Affairs* [1984] 2 CMLR 499.

80 (1995) *The Times*, 20 July.

81 [1986] ECR 29.

no longer entitled to remain in the UK.[82] The free movement to work may include the right to seek work,[83] although it may be necessary to show that the person has a genuine chance of obtaining work,[84] while the term 'worker' includes persons working to fulfil some economic purpose even though the work is part time and the worker must partly rely on public funds for support.[85]

These rights do not extend to those wishing to enter and remain to exercise civil or political rights.[86] Moreover, they are not absolute; EU law permits a Member State to refuse a Community national permission to enter and remain on various grounds. States can deny these rights to workers on the grounds of 'public policy, public security and public health' (Art 48(3)).[87] This principle has been enshrined in Directive 64/221. Public policy is the most uncertain term and potentially very wide; however, it has been held by the European Court of Justice (ECJ) in *Van Duyn v Home Office (No 2)*[88] that Member States are not free to interpret it unilaterally, although it has been accepted that the concept of public policy will vary from State to State, and so States will have an area of discretion within the limits defined by the Treaty. In *Rutili v Ministre de l'Intérieur*,[89] the ECJ found that restrictions on the free movement of EU nationals could be imposed only where an individual's presence constituted a 'genuine and sufficiently serious threat to public policy'. The court considered that this principle embodied the principle applied to the restrictions on the rights under the European Convention that restrictions should be accepted only when necessary. Thus, the test of proportionality must be applied to restrictions on movement on grounds of public policy. In *Bouchereau*,[90] the concept of public policy was further narrowed, the ECJ holding that it connoted a threat 'affecting one of the fundamental interests of society'.

Under Art 3(1) of the Directive, moreover, the power to restrict movement by deportation or otherwise may only be exercised on grounds of personal unacceptability.[91] Thus, if the *sole* reason relied upon to justify exclusion or deportation is past membership of an undesirable organisation, the exclusion or deportation will not be lawful. It is necessary to show that there is something substantively undesirable about the specific individual in question. Reliance on the commission of a criminal offence *simpliciter* to justify exclusion or deportation would be contrary to the Directive. Thus, the EU national would retain his or her rights to enter and stay if re-offending was not anticipated or the crimes committed were fairly trivial, because the 'public policy' condition would not be satisfied.[92] The ruling in *Bouchereau* gave some guidance as to the factors to be taken into

---

82 *Secretary of State for Home Affairs ex p Sandhu* [1983] 3 CMLR 131.

83 *Hoth v Secretary of State for Home Affairs* [1985] Imm AR 20; *Bouanimba v Secretary of State for Home Affairs* [1986] Imm AR 343, IAT (Arts 48–51).

84 *Immigration Appeal Tribunal ex p Antonissen* [1992] Imm AR 196: appeal against a deportation order failed as the applicant, who had served a prison sentence for a serious crime, was thought to have no chance of finding employment.

85 *Kempf v Staatssecretaris van Justitie* [1987] 1 CMLR 764.

86 See *Levin v Secretary of State for Justice* [1982] ECR 1035; and *Re a Belgian Prostitute* [1976] 2 CMLR 527.

87 For consideration of Art 48, see O'Keeffe [1982] 19 CMLR 35.

88 [1974] ECR 1337.

89 [1975] ECR 1219; [1976] 1 CMLR 140.

90 [1977] ECR 1999.

91 *Van Duyn v Home Office (No 2)* [1974] ECR 1337.

92 See *Bonsignore v Oberstadtdirektor of the City of Cologne* [1975] ECR 297.

account in making a determination as to the relevance of criminal activity; the relevant factors included the type of offence, the defendant's assumed propensity to re-offend and the seriousness of the offence if recommitted.[93] In *Escuriaza*,[94] the Court of Appeal considered that these tests are the same as those which will generally be applied in order to deport an alien, but it is suggested that cases may arise of a less clear cut nature than *Escuriaza* in which it will be important to apply the more stringent Community test.

Grounds for deportation

Broadly, a person who is not a British citizen can be deported under s 3(5) of the 1971 Act, as amended by the Immigration and Asylum Act 1999. The 1999 Act amendments cover those who do not observe conditions attached to a limited leave to enter or persons who remain or stay beyond the time limited by the leave. The effect is that those in breach of conditions of entry or overstayers are now subject to removal (rather than deportation) on receipt of directions given by an immigration officer. In practice, this distinction is of significance only in that rights of appeal are restricted in respect of such persons.

A person is liable to deportation under s 3(5) of the 1971 Act as amended, on three grounds: the Secretary of State deems his deportation to be conducive to the public good; or a court recommends deportation after his conviction for a criminal offence. A person may also be deported on other than personal grounds if he or she belongs to a family of which the wife or husband is deported. This rule arises under s 5(4) and is overtly discriminatory in that a wife will normally be deported with her husband, whereas a husband may remain when his wife is deported. The wife will not, however, be automatically deported with the husband: rr 365 and 367 of the 1994 Rules provide that various circumstances should be taken into account, including her own wishes and her ability to maintain herself, without charge on the public funds for the foreseeable future. A wife will not normally be deported with the husband under r 365 of the 1994 Rules where she qualifies for settlement in her own right or where she is living apart from the husband. However, the bland assumption that all husbands, whatever their actual circumstances, should be treated differently from all wives is unjustifiable.

In considering the merits of the decision to deport, r 364 provides guidance as to the factors to be taken into account:

> ... the public interest will be balanced against any compassionate circumstances of the case. While each case will be considered in the light of the particular circumstances, the aim is an exercise of the power of deportation which is consistent and fair as between one person and another, although one case will rarely be identical with another in all material respects.

---

93 See also *Puttick v Secretary of State for Home Affairs* [1984] Imm AR 118; *Immigration Appeal Tribunal ex p Tamdjid-Nezhad* [1986] Imm AR 396.

94 [1989] 3 CMLR 281. For further discussion of deportation of EU nationals see Vincenzi [1994] Crim LR 163.

Deportation after conviction

Deportation owing to conviction of a criminal offence is fairly readily resorted to but, as the Court of Appeal held in *Nazari*,[95] it should not be undertaken without full inquiry into all the circumstances. It should not be done, as has sometimes happened in the past, 'as if by an afterthought at the end of observations about any sentence of imprisonment'. A number of factors were identified which a court might bear in mind when considering deportation: the long criminal record of the accused; the seriousness of the offence bearing in mind the circumstances surrounding it, not merely its nature;[96] the effect that an order recommending deportation will have on others who are not before the court and who are innocent persons, in terms of hardship and breaking up of families. The court should not, however, take into account the nature of the regime to which the deportee will return.

An important circumstance will be the likelihood of the repetition of the offence; where this factor is present, it may aggravate an otherwise trivial offence; where it is absent, it may have a mitigating effect on a serious offence.[97] This seems to have been accepted in *Serry*:[98] one offence of shoplifting did not support deportation, presumably because there were no particular aggravating circumstances.

Deportation for the public good

This head of deportation, which is the most contentious in civil liberties terms, can cover a number of factors, but it seems reasonably clear that the decision to deport should be based on all the circumstances relevant to the particular evil in question and the consequences flowing from the deportation. Thus, in *Immigration Appeal Tribunal ex p (Mahmud) Khan*,[99] the applicant successfully challenged the IAT's dismissal of his appeal against deportation, on the ground that the tribunal's reasons for its decision – that he had entered into a marriage of convenience – failed to show that it had properly considered whether the couple did intend to live as man and wife. In other words, grounds which might raise an inference that the marriage was merely one of convenience were not examined to see whether this was actually the case.[100] Similarly, it is not enough to show that a person has behaved in an anti-social manner in the past; it must be considered whether future wrongdoing is likely.[101] In considering circumstances flowing from the deportation, it would appear that detriment as well as good flowing from it to the public or part of the public may be considered: the two may be balanced against each other. Thus, in *Singh v Immigration Appeal Tribunal*[102] the House of Lords held that the immigration adjudicatory authorities ought to have taken into account the detrimental

95   [1980] 3 All ER 880, CA.

96   See Sachs LJ in *Caird* (1970) 54 Cr App R 499, p 510.

97   See *Tshuma* (1981) 3 Cr App R (S) 97.

98   (1980) 2 Cr App R (S) 336.

99   [1983] QB 790.

100 The ruling in *Immigration Appeal Tribunal ex p Ghazi Zubalir Ali Khan* [1983] Imm AR 32 was reached on similar grounds.

101 *Malik v Secretary of State for Home Affairs* [1981] Imm AR 134; *Immigration Appeal Tribunal ex p Ullah* (1983) *The Times*, 14 January.

102 [1986] 2 All ER 721, HL.

effect on the Sikh community in the UK which deportation of the applicant would have. The applicant was a valued member of that community by virtue of his religious, charitable and cultural activities.

The 'conducive to public good' ground for deportation can be used where a person is convicted of an offence, but the court does not recommend deportation, and also, most controversially, against individuals who have engaged in some form of undesirable political activity.[103] The use of this power to exclude people on political rather than criminal grounds has attracted most criticism. For example, the student activist Rudi Dutschke was deported back to West Germany in 1969, on the basis that he might 'become a focus for student unrest'.[104] Similarly, the journalists Agee and Hosenball were deported on national security grounds, Agee presumably because of the damage he might have done to the CIA in writing books exposing certain of their activities.[105] It was unclear, however, that damage to the public good would be averted by the deportation. Similarly, rather flimsy grounds were relied on in deciding to deport a number of Iraqi or Kuwaiti residents during the Gulf War 1991. For example, a Lebanese citizen, Cheblak – a known pacifist who had lived and worked as an academic in the UK for 15 years, had two children who were British citizens and who had campaigned for an Iraqi withdrawal from Kuwait – was ordered to be deported on national security grounds.

Cheblak sought leave to apply for judicial review of the Home Secretary's decision, partly on the basis that it was irrational or that all relevant circumstances had not been taken into account. In *Secretary of State for Home Affairs ex p Cheblak*[106] the Court of Appeal, however, preferred not to make any inquiry into these possibilities on the basis that national security matters are the sole preserve of the executive.[107] However, it seems to follow from dicta in that case that although the decision to deport was effectively excluded from review, there could be some review of preconditions and procedures.[108] The deportation notice informed the applicant that he could make representations to an independent panel who would advise the Secretary of State. Lord Donaldson MR said, in relation to this panel, 'I have no doubt that the advisory panel is susceptible of judicial review if, for example, it could be shown to have acted unfairly within its terms of reference'.[109] However, so long as a fair procedure seems to have been followed, bearing in mind the constraints on the disclosure of the case against him to the applicant, it seems that no redress will be available if the Secretary of State decides to ignore the advice of the adviser or if the grounds for exclusion are flimsy or based on error. This is because the courts tend to view decisions taken on national security grounds as purely a matter for the executive despite their impact on civil liberties.[110]

Ultimately, Cheblak was not deported after his case was considered by the advisory panel set up to replace a statutory right of appeal. However, 14 persons were deported

---

103 See *Martinez-Tobon v Immigration Appeal Tribunal* [1988] Imm AR 319, CA.

104 For discussion, see Hepple (1971) 45 MLR 501.

105 See *Secretary of State for Home Affairs ex p Hosenball* [1977] 1 WLR 766; [1977] 3 All ER 452, CA.

106 [1991] 1 WLR 890; [1991] 2 All ER 319, CA. For comment see [1991] PL 331.

107 *Secretary of State for Home Affairs ex p Cheblak* [1991] 1 WLR 890. See below, p 952. For discussion see [1991] PL 333.

108 See Walker, C, *The Prevention of Terrorism in British Law*, 1st edn, 1986, pp 90–92.

109 [1991] 1 WLR 890, p 907.

110 See *Council of Civil Service Unions v Minister for the Civil Service* [1985] AC 374, p 412.

and, of these, it is not known whether the panel advised revocation of the order or whether the grounds on which it was ordered were as doubtful on the face of it as those which applied in *Cheblak's* case.

The purpose of deportation on this ground should be clear: that removal of the deportee is necessary for the public good and that even if this is not the only purpose, it should be the dominant one.[111] However, in a number of rulings, courts have not applied a 'dominant purpose' test in considering the relevance of other purposes which may have influenced the Secretary of State's decision to deport. In *Brixton Prison Governor ex p Soblen*,[112] a deportation order was challenged on the grounds that the Secretary of State had allegedly acted for an improper purpose – in order to comply with a request from the US for S's return made in order to circumvent the non-availability of extradition proceedings which were not possible owing to the nature of S's offences. The Court of Appeal upheld the deportation order on the basis that the Secretary of State could act for a plurality of purposes. The fact that this might be termed extradition by the back door did not affect the validity of the order. The court considered that the need to serve the public good by the removal of S need not be the dominant motive in making the order, although the minister must have a genuine belief that removal was necessary on that basis. It did not matter if the minister's main motive for acting might have been to comply with the request from the US.

The danger in this approach is clearly that the individual circumstances of the person in question may become much less significant than the political expediency of falling in with the wishes of particular governments. However, there are signs that this approach may not be sustained. In subsequent cases it has been accepted that there may be a 'plurality of purposes', but that it should be shown that the same decision would have been reached even in the absence of consideration of the 'improper' purpose.[113]

Appeals

Certain appeals against deportation may be brought to the Immigration Appeal Tribunal under s 63 of the Immigration and Asylum Act (IAA) 1999. The tribunal can consider the determinations of both facts and law under the Sched 4, para 21 of the IAA 1999, and there is a right of appeal on a point of law to the Court of Appeal under Sched 4, para 23 of the IAA 1999. Arguments based on the Convention, raised under s 7(1)(a) of the HRA, must be brought in the tribunal under s 65.

The position as regards the more controversial deportation decisions is rather different. If the decision to deport has been taken for reasons of 'public good', on grounds of 'national security', 'diplomatic relations' or for 'reasons of a political nature', the ordinary right of appeal was excluded unless the deportee was an asylum seeker, in which case Sched 2 para 2(a) of the Asylum and Immigration Appeals Act afforded him or her the right to appeal to a special adjudicator. Similarly, a person refused entry on grounds of public good (without anything more specific as to reason) had no right of

---

111 See, in another context, *Westminster Corporation v London and North Western Rly Co* [1905] AC 426.
112 [1963] 2 QB 243.
113 See *Inner London Education Authority ex p Westminster CC* [1986] 1 All ER 19; *Broadcasting Complaints Commission ex p Owen* [1985] QB 1153; and *Lewisham LBC ex p Shell UK Ltd* [1988] 1 All ER 938.

appeal (ss 15(3), (4), (5) and 14(3)). In such cases, there was a right to an *ex gratia* hearing before three advisors. The procedure was described by the then Home Secretary as follows:

> The person concerned ... will be given ...such particulars of allegations as will not entail disclosure of sources of evidence. He will be notified that he can make representations to the three advisors ... The advisors will ... allow him to appear before them, if he wishes ... As well as speaking for himself he may arrange for a third party to testify on his behalf. Neither the sources of evidence nor evidence that might lead to disclosure of sources can be revealed to the person concerned but the advisors will ensure that the person is able to make his points effectively ... Since the evidence against a person necessarily has to be received in his absence, the advisors in assessing the case will bear in mind that it has not been tested by cross-examination and that the person has not had the opportunity to rebut it ... On receiving the advice of the advisors the Secretary of State would reconsider his original decision but the advice given to him would not be revealed.[114]

Thus, a person could be deported after a hearing in which he was unable to challenge the case against him, in which evidence which he was unable to contest was given in his absence and in which he could not call witnesses or have legal representation. He was not informed of the decision taken by the advisors, did not know whether it was complied with or why it was not complied with and could not appeal from it.

Mark Hosenball challenged this procedure in respect of the decision to deport him on grounds of national security (see *Secretary of State for Home Affairs ex p Hosenball* above) on the basis that it did not comply with the principles of natural justice since he had not been given adequate particulars of the allegations against him. The Court of Appeal, while acknowledging that the principles of natural justice would normally require that such particulars would be given, said that in cases where national security is involved, 'the rights of the individual (including his entitlement to natural justice) must be subordinated to the protection of the realm' (*per* Geoffrey Lane LJ). Lord Denning considered that in such cases it was not the proper role of the courts to attempt to determine the proper balance between the requirements of national security and the claims of the individual; this role fell correctly within the ambit of the Home Secretary's responsibilities. Similarly, in *Ex p Cheblak*,[115] the applicant complained that the reasons given for the decision that his deportation would be for the public good were wholly insufficient to enable him to challenge the order. Lord Donaldson MR referred to Geoffrey Lane LJ's comments in *Secretary of State for Home Affairs ex p Hosenball* and said:

> In accepting, as we must, that to some extent the needs of national security must displace civil liberties ... it is not irrelevant to remember that the maintenance of national security underpins and is the foundation of all our civil liberties.[116]

He used the analogy of a person who is detained pending trial and then found innocent. However, he did not address the flaw in the analogy: there must be reasonable suspicion that the person remanded in custody has committed the offence, whereas in the case of the deportee, there may be a very insufficient objective basis for determining that

---

114 HC Deb Vol 819 Col 376, 15 June 1971.

115 [1991] 1 WLR 890; [1991] 2 All ER, CA. See also *Secretary of State for Home Affairs ex p Chahal* [1995] 1 All ER 658; (1993) *The Times*, 12 March.

116 [1991] WLR 890, p 907.

deportation is in the public good. Nevertheless, no check existed which could prevent the deportation if the Home Secretary's personal decision was that it should be carried out. Thus, civil liberties were severely infringed in a manner arguably unwarranted by the needs of national security.

This was eventually found to be the case by the European Court of Human Rights in *Chahal v UK*.[117] Originally an illegal immigrant, Mr Chahal obtained leave to remain in Britain indefinitely in 1974. In 1984, he visited the Punjab for a family wedding and met the chief advocate of creating an independent Sikh state to be carved out of India. Later, he was arrested by the Indian police and allegedly tortured. He escaped from India and became the founder of the International Sikh Youth Federation in the UK. After a fight at a Sikh temple, he was arrested and convicted of assault and affray, but his conviction was overturned by the Court of Appeal. In 1990, he was arrested after a meeting at a Southall temple. The Home Office accused him of involvement in Sikh terrorism; the Secretary of State made a determination that deportation of the applicant would be conducive to the public good and therefore he was liable to be deported under s 3(5)(b) of the Immigration Act 1971. However, the applicant claimed asylum in the UK on the basis that he was a refugee within the meaning of the Convention relating to the Status of Refugees 1951 as recognised in r 173 of the Immigration Rules 1990. He claimed that he would be tortured if sent back to India. The Secretary of State maintained that the question whether he was a refugee was irrelevant once the decision to deport had been made. The applicant sought judicial review of the decision to deport him on the basis that his status as a refugee should have been taken into account.[118]

The main question at issue was whether a balancing exercise between the threat to the security of the UK posed by the applicant and the threat to the life or freedom of the applicant if deported to the country in question (India) should have been carried out. It was found that the combined effect of the Convention and the 1990 Rules required that it should have been. However, although the Secretary of State had not deemed such an exercise necessary, there was no evidence that it had not been carried out. The court was not able to determine whether, after carrying out such an exercise, the Secretary of State's decision could be called irrational, since while there was a great deal of evidence as to the risk to the applicant, there was none as to the risk to national security in the UK which he posed. However, the court could consider whether the Secretary of State had been correct in his assessment of the risk to the applicant if returned to India. The Secretary of State had observed that under the Indian Constitution, the applicant could come to harm only if convicted of a crime by due process and in accordance with the law. That still left open the possibility of informal ill-treatment; nevertheless, there were not considered to be sufficient grounds for finding that the Secretary of State had made an irrational or perverse decision in determining that the applicant's claim for asylum status was not made out. The application therefore failed.

Mr Chahal was then imprisoned while he pursued an application to the European Commission of Human Rights, alleging a breach of Art 3, which guarantees protection from torture and from inhuman and degrading treatment, and of Art 5, which guarantees judicial control over loss of liberty. The European Court of Human Rights noted that the

---

117 (1997) 23 EHRR 413.
118 *Secretary of State for Home Affairs ex p Chahal* [1995] 1 All ER 658.

protection of Art 3 of the Convention is absolute (no derogations are provided or allowed) and found that there were strong grounds for believing that Mr Chahal would indeed have been tortured had he been returned to India. Thus, had the order to deport been implemented, a breach of Art 3 would have occurred. Article 5(1) not only provides that deprivation of liberty is only permitted within the specified exceptions, it also requires that it should be 'in accordance with a procedure prescribed by law'. In *Winterwerp v Netherlands*[119] the court found that this meant that the procedure in question must be in accordance with national and Convention law and it must not be arbitrary. In the instant case, the applicant complained, *inter alia*, that he had been detained although there had been no court hearing. The court found that a breach of Art 5 had occurred, since his detention should have been subject to scrutiny in court. It had been considered by the advisory panel, but that did not provide sufficient procedural safeguards to qualify as a court. Further, a breach of Art 5 read in conjunction with Art 13 had occurred, since effective remedies did not exist before the courts in England.

The judgment in *Chahal v UK* now stands in stark contrast to the executive-minded judgments in *Secretary of State for Home Affairs ex p Hosenball* and indicates the failure of the domestic judiciary to maintain human rights standards as high as those maintained by the European Court of Human Rights. As regards decisions to detain persons who are alleged to pose a risk to national security, it was apparent that methods of disclosing to a court some of the material on which that claim was based had to be put in place. Both aspects of this decision are to be welcomed as enhancing the role of the judiciary in relation to persons who are often in an extremely vulnerable position. At the same time, it should be borne in mind that Mr Chahal was detained for six years in breach of Art 5 of the Convention. Thus, his fundamental rights were violated for all that period of time.

The Labour Government implemented the ruling of the European Court of Human Rights in *Chahal v UK*[120] by creating the Special Immigration Appeals Commission (SIAC) set up under s 1 of the Special Immigration Appeals Act 1997 (SIACA). SIACA provides under s 4 that the tribunal can hear an appeal on a point of law or on the basis that the discretion exercised should have been exercised differently. Under amendment by the 1999 Act s 2A of the SIACA now provides that the tribunal will be the appropriate forum for actions under s 7(1)(a) of the HRA. There is also a right of appeal on a point of law to the Court of Appeal. The SIAC will now deal with the most controversial cases, as indicated above, in particular those where deportation is deemed to be for the public good.

The Rules governing the procedure have been issued which prescribe the forms of hearing adopted by the tribunal in relation to particular proceedings,[121] and which allow for hearings in the absence of the person bringing the proceedings and his or her legal representative. In such instances, a special advocate will be appointed who has had security clearance. It appears possible that the position of the complainant in the determinations of the new tribunal will be quite weak in some instances, depending on the circumstances and the national security issues. The difficulty with tribunals of this nature is that the limitations under which they operate, which limit the opportunities of the defence to challenge evidence, tend to detract from the benefits of such

---

119 A 33; (1979) 2 EHRR 387.
120 (1997) 23 EHRR 413.
121 SI 1998/1881.

proceedings.[122] The tribunal can allow the appeal. If it finds a breach of a Convention right owing to the effect of incompatible legislation, it will not have the power to make a declaration of incompatibility.

Convention rights under the HRA

All the persons administering deportation decisions are public authorities under s 6 of the HRA and therefore must abide by the Convention rights. As indicated, under the Immigration and Asylum Act 1999, Convention-based arguments must be raised in one of the two tribunals. Argument below will concentrate on the SIAC, since it deals with the more contentious claims.

The SIAC is bound by s 6 of the HRA, since it is a public authority. Thus argument could be raised before it that, at least in respect of the circumstances of certain claims, it does not provide a fair hearing under Art 6. However, Art 6 will apply only if the Commission hearings are within its field of application. The proceedings of the SIAC might be viewed as the 'determination of civil rights and obligations' under Art 6(1). The term 'civil' has, however, been taken to mean that these are rights in private rather than public law,[123] although a clear distinction between rights in private as opposed to public law is not apparent in its recent jurisprudence. The role of the Commission under s 7(1)(a) of the HRA as providing a remedy against public authorities in respect of alleged breaches of Convention rights may suggest that it need not satisfy Art 6 on the basis that the rights cannot be viewed as private, depending on the sense in which such rights are viewed as 'private'.[124] They cannot merely be assigned the meaning of 'private' as understood in UK administrative law. Whether it falls within Art 6 is likely to be a matter which, initially, will be raised before the Commission itself.

Assuming that the tribunal is covered by Art 6(1) or, under the development of the Strasbourg jurisprudence, may be found more clearly to be so covered in future, it is hard to see that it is likely to provide a fair hearing for the applicant, bearing in mind the procedure it may follow, indicated above, since the complainant or applicant may be in such a weak position before it. As Chapter 2 indicated, since Art 6(3) contains *minimum* guarantees, the para 1 protection of a fair hearing goes beyond para 3.[125] In investigating a fair hearing, the domestic authorities are not confined to the para 3 guarantees; they can consider further requirements of fairness. If consideration is given to the procedures in question it is apparent that, apart from any of the other requirements of fairness, the safeguards of Art 6(1) and Art 6(3) may not be satisfied, depending on the use of the power to exclude the applicant[126] or her legal representative, or limiting disclosure of evidence.[127]

---

122 See Walker, *op cit*, fn 108, p 82; he advocates an inquisitorial system for such tribunals; see also White, C, 'Security vetting, discrimination and the right to a fair trial' [1999] PL 406, p 413, discussing the new tribunal set up under the Northern Ireland Act 1998.

123 *Ringeisen v Austria* A 13 (1971), para 94.

124 See Chapter 2 for discussion of the public law/private law issues; p 59. It must be borne in mind that the term 'civil' has an autonomous Convention meaning.

125 See p 58.

126 See, on this point, *Zana v Turkey* (1997) 27 EHRR 667, in which, in the context of terrorism, the applicant was not allowed to be present at the trial; a breach of Art 6 was found on this basis.

127 See further Chapter 14, pp 900–02.

The Commission should, in any event, provide an effective remedy in order to answer to the demands made clear in *Chahal*. In *Chahal*, the Advisory Panel on deportation decisions failed to satisfy Art 13 since it failed to offer sufficient safeguards for Art 13 purposes. In particular, it lacked the ability to take a binding decision. The Court said that the remedy offered should be 'as effective as it can be' given the need, in the context in question, to rely on secret sources. The Commission can take binding decisions, but its efficacy in other respects is questionable.

In making determinations as to alleged breaches of Art 8 the Commission will have to consider proportionality, since Art 8(2) requires such consideration. In order to do so it may need to evaluate a number of factual matters. But the procedural limitations under which it will be likely to operate may place even greater difficulties in its path in considering the question of proportionality than there would be in an ordinary court, in judicial review proceedings. It may be argued that documents or sources cannot be disclosed on grounds of national security or the prevention of crime. If as a result it operates a 'light touch' review, based in effect on *Wednesbury* unreasonableness, it will fail to satisfy the demands of Art 13 as recently interpreted at Strasbourg[128] and therefore, *a fortiori*, it will not satisfy Art 6.

In *Balfour v Foreign and Commonwealth Office*[129] the court found that once an actual or potential risk to national security had been demonstrated by a public interest immunity certificate, the court should not exercise its right to inspect the documents. This view of national security as the exclusive domain of the executive was not adhered to in the robust approach taken to the concept in the context of deportation by the SIAC in the case of *Secretary of State for the Home Dept v Rehman*.[130] However, the Court of Appeal overturned their ruling, finding that the threat to national security was for the government to determine and that it should be broadly defined to include the possibility of future threats, including those to the UK's 'allies', and their findings were confirmed by the House of Lords.[131] These findings are not fully in accordance with the findings of the Strasbourg Court in *Tinnelly* or in *Chahal v UK*.[132] Both, particularly *Tinnelly*, took the view that the threat to national security should be demonstrated.

Since there is a means of appeal from the Commission and the tribunal, there is an independent domestic means of determining whether the tribunal offers an effective remedy and whether it should abide by Art 6.

Article 3

Applicants may raise Art 3 arguments before the Immigration Adjudicator, Commission or the Immigration Appeals Tribunal, or in proceedings for judicial review, based on a

---

128 *Smith and Grady v UK* (2000) 29 EHRR 493. The domestic court found that the continuance of the ban on homosexuals in the armed forces was not beyond the range of responses which was open to a reasonable decision maker. The Strasbourg Court considered that the threshold at which the domestic court could find the policy irrational was set so high that it effectively precluded consideration of the proportionality of the ban with the aim in view. Therefore, judicial review was not found to satisfy the requirements of Art 13.

129 [1994] 2 All ER 588.

130 [1999] INLR 517.

131 [2000] 3 WLR 1240, CA; [2000] 3 WLR 877, HL.

132 (1998) 27 EHRR 249 (in the context of Art 13).

number of Convention decisions. In *MAR v UK*,[133] for example, the applicant argued that if deported to Iran, he would be likely to meet with Art 3 treatment owing to his drug convictions. The application was declared admissible. *D v UK*[134] also concerned the risk of Art 3 treatment after deportation. The European Court of Human Rights found that removing a drug courier in an advanced stage of AIDS to his country of origin, St Kitts, would expose him to Art 3 treatment there. In St Kitts, much less effective treatment for AIDS was available; he would had have no accommodation and no means of support. A similar stance may be taken where, if deported, the applicant would be likely to be subject to criminal proceedings which could lead to a disproportionate or unjust sentence.[135]

Article 8

Argument could also be raised based on Art 8, on the basis that removal from the country would adversely affect private and family life. However, as Chapter 12 indicated, the Strasbourg jurisprudence has afforded a wide margin of appreciation to the State in relation to deportation and immigration decisions, on the basis that it is accepted in international law that the State has the right to control the entry of non-nationals onto its territory. Thus, in *Abdulaziz, Cabales and Balkandali v UK*,[136] it was found that the duty imposed by Art 8 did not extend to creating a general obligation to respect the choice by married couples of the country of their matrimonial residence. Therefore, Art 8 did not require the UK to accept the non-national spouses for settlement in that country.

However, in contrast, where a non-national is faced with expulsion from a country in which he or she has lived for some time and where members of the family are established, the Court has shown itself willing to uphold the right to maintain family ties if satisfied that the ties are clearly in existence.[137] In *Beldjoudi v France*,[138] the European Court of Human Rights found that the right to family life under Art 8 encompasses the right of an alien to remain in a Convention State if it has been demonstrated that he or she has a long established and settled family life there.[139] In *Nasri v France*[140] the applicant, who had committed serious crimes, was threatened with expulsion from France to Algeria. He had lived in France almost all his life and was deaf and dumb. The Court considered that the impact of expulsion on his family life would be particularly severe, bearing the effect of his handicap in mind. He was able to maintain a 'minimum

---

133 Unreported.

134 (1998) 24 EHRR 423; (1997) *The Times*, 12 May.

135 *Altun v Germany* (1983) 36 DR 209.

136 Judgment of 28 May 1985, A 94 (1985); (1985) 7 EHRR 471. A breach of the Convention was found when Art 8 was read in conjunction with Art 14 (see above).

137 In *Moustaquim* A 193; (1991) 13 EHRR 802 it was found that deporting the applicant to Morocco from Belgium where his family lived would entail a breach of Art 8; this claim outweighed the claim of the Belgian state that expelling Moustaquim was necessary for the 'prevention of disorder and crime'. Of course, had his expulsion been characterised as necessary on grounds of national security, the outcome would probably have been different. The European Court of Human Rights tends to show timidity in the area of national security on the ground that the Member State is best placed to determine its needs (see *Leander v Sweden* (1987) 9 EHRR 443) and see further Chapter 2. See also *Djeroud v France*, A 191-B (1991); for comment see (1991) YBEL 554–56.

138 A 234-A; (1992) 14 EHRR 801.

139 See also the opinion of the European Commission of Human Rights in *Uppal v UK (No 2)* (1981) 3 EHRR 399.

140 (1995) 21 EHRR 458.

psychological and social equilibrium only within his family'.[141] His family had no close ties to Algeria. On this basis, a breach of the right of respect for family life was found. A similar decision was reached in the *Berrehab* case,[142] in which the Netherlands wished to deport the father of a small child resident there with her mother. The father could not be expected to travel frequently between the Netherlands and Morocco and therefore would be unable to maintain family ties. A breach of Art 8 was found.

A key factor in these decisions was the extent to which the applicant could be viewed as having close ties with the country of origin. A breach of Art 8 is more likely to be found where he or she had left that country at an early age and could not be viewed as having such ties. These factors have to be balanced against factors of immigration control, where there have been breaches of immigration law, or, where relevant, public order. In *Poku v UK*,[143] the balance came down against family life. The applicant came from Ghana and was an illegal overstayer. She had a husband and young child in the UK and a child by a former husband, a British citizen. She argued that her deportation would interfere with the rights of her children, husband and former husband. But, taking into account the extent of the disruption of family life and the question whether the family could live in Ghana, and balancing these factors against her breaches of immigration law, it was found that the application was manifestly ill-founded. The Commission reiterated the finding in *Abdulaziz, Cabales and Balkandali v UK*[144] to the effect that Art 8 does not create a general obligation to respect the choice by married couples of the country of their matrimonial residence.

Given that this is an instance in which a wide margin of appreciation has been conceded to the State, it is suggested that these decisions should not merely be applied domestically without taking into account the effect of that doctrine. If immigration officials or ministers have breached Art 8, they have acted unlawfully under s 6 of the HRA. It is not apparent that deference is called for. However, it does not appear that the courts are applying this standard of review. In *Secretary of State for the Home Dept ex p Mahmood*,[145] the applicant sought judicial review of the decision of the Home Secretary to remove him from the UK as an illegal entrant. He had been married for less than two years to a woman resident in the UK who had borne him two children. On the assumption that the HRA applied (the decision had been made in 1999), the court applied a low standard of review. It asked whether the decision maker could reasonably have concluded that the interference with family life was necessary to achieve one or more of the legitimate aims of the Convention. Taking into account the relevant Strasbourg jurisprudence, the court found no breach of Art 8.

It is suggested that the court applied the wrong standard of review. It should have asked whether the tests under Art 8(2) were satisfied: was the decision necessary and proportionate to the end in view? In other words, the court should have addressed itself to those questions rather than asking whether the response of the decision maker could

---

141 Paragraph 46.

142 (1988) 11 EHRR 322.

143 (1996) 22 EHRR CD 94.

144 Judgment of 28 May 1985, A 94 (1985); (1985) 7 EHRR 471. A breach of the Convention was found when Art 8 was read in conjunction with Art 14 (see above, Chapter 2, p 86).

145 (2001) *The Times*, 9 January.

be viewed as reasonable in the light of that end. The test used appeared to represent a standard of review indistinguishable from that denoted by the *Wednesbury* test. A rather different standard was applied in *R v Secretary of State for the Home Dept ex p R*.[146] The court found that a decision to remove R which might break his close ties with his ex-wife and children would risk a breach of Art 8 on the basis of failing to respect his family life. The Secretary of State gave an undertaking not to remove R until his wife's application to remain in the UK had been determined. Arguably, this was a somewhat more generous interpretation of the requirements of Art 8 than accorded to them at Strasbourg. Further, the court did not appear to ask whether the decision was one of those reasonably open to the decision maker as furthering the aims recognised in Art 8(2); the court merely asked whether there was a risk of that the decision would breach Art 8.

It may be concluded that the HRA is showing its potential to have a tempering effect on deportation decisions, and is imposing a human rights dimension on them which was not previously apparent and was infrequently imposed upon them through the medium of the *Wednesbury* test. But clearly, the standard of review which becomes the accepted one under s 6 of the HRA will remain the crucial issue.

At the time of writing, the Government, with strong support from the Conservative Party led by Iain Duncan-Smith, has introduced a new Bill dealing with terrorism in the wake of the attacks on the Pentagon and on the World Trade Centre in New York in September 2001, the Anti-Terrorism, Crime and Security Bill 2001. A power of detention without charge or trial for non-British citizens suspected of terrorism who cannot be deported is included. This power infringes certain of the Convention rights, most notably Arts 6 and 5, under the HRA but the government has entered a derogation to Art 5. Under (current) clause 29 the judiciary would be prevented from hearing challenges to certain of the new counter-terrorist powers.

At the present time, the Home Secretary, David Blunkett, has spoken of changing the balance between human rights and such powers. The leader of the Conservative Party, Iain Duncan-Smith, agrees with him as to the need to change the balance. The possibility that the HRA may be amended or that challenges under the HRA to the new counter-terrorist powers, can be heard only by Special Commissioners or Advisors, not in the ordinary courts, arises.

4 EXTRADITION

Introduction

The law of extradition is concerned mainly with persons who are alleged to have committed a crime in one country but are currently in another country, whether because they normally reside there or because they have escaped to that country. It is a procedure that creates a very significant infringement of freedom of movement and potentially of other human rights. It will therefore be suggested that there is a tension between the European Convention on Human Rights on the one hand and the European Convention on Extradition 1984 on the other. Extradition is also anomalous in the sense that the level

---

146 (2001) *The Times*, 29 November.

of suspicion required of an offence in order to extradite a person is lower than that which would be required to convict him of an offence in the UK. Thus, a person may be punished by being extradited to a country in which he might arguably receive a trial of a lower level of fairness than he would have received in the UK; he may receive a longer prison sentence and harsher treatment during it than he would have received and he may be imprisoned away from his family so that he cannot readily receive visits. This may all occur on the basis of a fairly low level of suspicion. These possibilities, and certain of their implications under the HRA, are considered further below.

The extradition procedure allows for the expulsion of British citizens from their own country; since it represents such a serious invasion of freedom of movement and of liberty, a number of procedural barriers have been created. Owing to the formality of the procedure, attempts are sometimes made to circumvent it by using deportation as a disguised form of extradition. In particular, this may occur where, in reality, the suspect is wanted for a 'political' offence. As indicated above, this was alleged in *Brixton Prison Governor ex p Soblen*.[147] It was argued that the US had requested S's return in order to circumvent the non-availability of extradition proceedings, which were not possible owing to the nature of S's offences.

Elements of extradition

The most significant statute governing extradition is currently the Extradition Act 1989. Under s 1(1) and (2), the State requesting extradition must be one with which the UK has an extradition agreement or must be a Commonwealth State. There is also provision for special extradition arrangements made in relation to specific cases with States which do not have an extradition agreement with the UK. The crime must be committed within the territory of the requesting country. In *Al Fawwaz v Governor of Brixton Prison*[148] the US sought the extradition of A, who was alleged to have conspired with terrorists to plant bombs in various US installations and to murder US citizens. A argued that he had never been to the US and that he could not be extradited, since the offences in question had taken place outside that country. It was found that the required territorial jurisdiction could be established on the basis of certain acts of A, including purchasing a satellite phone system in the US and setting up a secure telephone line.

Section 2 defines the crimes which are 'extradition crimes'. The term means conduct which, had it occurred in the UK, would have constituted an offence carrying a sentence of at least 12 months' imprisonment. The conduct must have constituted such an offence at the time when it was committed, according to the House of Lords in *Bow Street Magistrates' Court ex p Pinochet Ugarte (No 3)*.[149] However, there is a very significant exception to these rules. The offence must not, under s 6, be of a political character. It has been found that the offence must be political in relation to the requesting State, not another State. Thus, the attempted assassination of the vice-premier of Taiwan in New York, not in Taiwan, by a member of an opposition organisation, was not viewed as political since the applicant had no political grudge against the US. Had it occurred in

---

147 [1963] 2 QB 243.
148 (2000) *The Times*, 2 December.
149 [1999] 2 All ER 97.

Taiwan, it might have been viewed as falling within the political offence exception. There must be a close link between the crime and the political motive. The killing of civilians, although from a political motive, was not found to fall within the exception in *T v Secretary of State for the Home Dept*,[150] since the explosion which caused the deaths occurred at an airport, not at a military installation or government building.

Under s 9(8) of the Extradition Act, a magistrate must be satisfied that there is a *prima facie* case against the accused. In other words, extradition will not be possible unless the requesting State has quite a strong case against him. However, s 9(8) is subject to an exception which renders it almost valueless as a procedural safeguard. If there is an Order in Council giving effect to extradition arrangements with the requesting State, which provides that there is no need for evidence of a *prima facie* case, the magistrate need be satisfied merely that conduct alleged against the accused amounts to an extraditing crime. This arrangement is in accordance with the European Convention on Extradition. An interesting situation might arise where a *prima facie* case was required and the evidence supporting it had been obtained in breach of a Convention right. It would seem, according to the ruling of the Divisional Court in *Re Proulx*,[151] that even in such circumstances, and where the evidence was confession evidence, it might not be appropriate for the magistrate to refuse to admit it since the admissibility of the evidence would eventually be considered in the requesting State. The decision implied that even though the evidence might normally have been inadmissible, it would not be in an extradition case. It is unclear, it is suggested, that this decision is in accordance with the duties of the court and of the magistrate under s 6 of the HRA and Art 6.

Where a *prima facie* case is not needed, it is arguable that a magistrate, bound by s 6 of the HRA, should still consider the effect of extradition on the applicant's Convention rights, owing to the requirements of s 6. If the magistrate or a higher court, on appeal, considered that extradition, although otherwise warranted, would create a breach of the rights, it would seem to be consonant with the courts' duty under s 6 to refuse to commit. However, so doing might appear to be contrary to the relevant Order in Council. If so, a higher court could make a declaration of incompatibility between the Order and the right in question.[152] This would not, of course, benefit the applicant.

State immunity

A country may seek the extradition of a former Head of State in order to stand trial for crimes committed during his period of office for which he appears to bear responsibility. The questions which will arise in such an instance were extensively considered by the House of Lords in *Bow Street Magistrates' Court ex p Pinochet Ugarte (No 3)*.[153] The case concerned an extradition request from Spain to the UK that Senator Pinochet should be extradited to stand trial for conspiracy to murder, conspiracy to torture and hostage-taking. Pinochet was in the UK at the time for medical treatment. He had been in power in Chile between 1973 and 1990; the House of Lords considered that there was little

---

150 [1996] 2 All ER 865, HL.

151 [2001] 1 All ER 57.

152 Since Orders in Council fall within the meaning of primary legislation under the HRA; see Chapter 4, p 139.

153 [1999] 2 All ER 97.

dispute that appalling human rights abuses, including murder and torture, had occurred during his time in power.

The first ruling of the House, to the effect that Senator Pinochet could be extradited, was set aside because a member of the House of Lords, Lord Hoffman, had connections with Amnesty International, which was a party in the case.[154] A differently constituted appeal committee of seven Law Lords re-heard the appeal.

The key question concerned the extent of State immunity. Heads of State have immunity for all actions while in office and retain it after leaving office in relation to activities carried out in an official capacity while in office. However, the question was whether that immunity could extend to 'crimes against humanity' including torture (an international crime by virtue of the 'Torture' Convention of 1984). It would be anomalous if the immunity covered such crimes since the their target is, precisely, the officials likely to carry them out, acting in an official capacity. However, it was necessary that the crimes in question were criminal in UK law at the time when they were allegedly carried out. The Torture Convention was ratified in UK law on 8 December 1988. Therefore, it was found, the crimes of torture in question were not recognised in UK law before that date. The House of Lords found that Pinochet lost his immunity on that date in relation to such crimes once he was no longer in power. Therefore, he had no immunity in relation to the crime of conspiracy to torture which he was alleged to have committed after that date. In the event, it was decided, controversially, by the Home Secretary, that he was too ill to stand trial and he returned to Chile.

This was clearly a significant decision of the House of Lords since it means that former Heads of State may not be able to escape responsibility for the commission of crimes against humanity while they were in power, committed in their official capacity. It means at the very least that the number of countries they can travel to are limited, depending on the crimes in question and the point at which, if at all, a country recognised those crimes in its own law. Clearly, if such recognition only occurred after the commission of the crimes, extradition would not be possible. Thus, there are limitations on the use of extradition in this respect. Nevertheless, this was a significant decision in terms of creating accountability for human rights abuses perpetrated by the State.

Challenges to extradition: impact of the HRA

Procedures

A person can challenge an extradition committal in various ways. He or she could seek *habeas corpus* – the ancient writ which can be used to challenge detention on any ground.[155] It is sought in the High Court by means of an *ex parte* application and must take precedence over all other business. The court will, if it thinks that there is a case for the issuance of the writ, adjourn the proceedings and hold an *inter partes* hearing. If the writ is issued, it will mean that the person detaining the applicant must immediately release him or her. Under s 6 of the HRA, a court considering a writ for *habeas corpus* must ensure that it discharges its duty to abide by the Convention rights.

---

154 *Bow Street Magistrates' Court ex p Pinochet Ugarte (No 2)* [1999] 1 All ER 577.
155 The person must be notified of this possibility: Extradition Act 1989, s 11.

Thus, although the scope for review was quite limited in a *habeas corpus* application, it is suggested that it has now widened; apart from considering procedural issues, the court should also consider whether it itself, as a public authority, would ensure that no breach of the rights would occur if it intervened to prevent return of the applicant, unless in so doing it was acting within the terms of s 6(2) of the HRA to enforce incompatible legislation. For such an argument to succeed, it would have to be found that sections of the Extradition Act are irretrievably (taking s 3 of the HRA into account) incompatible with one or more of the requirements of the Convention rights. At present, it is suggested that a court would be unlikely to take such a stance, but would instead read down the legislation or the Convention right in question in order to avoid having to make a declaration of incompatibility.[156] Thus, it appears that the courts have a more substantive supervisory jurisdiction in hearing a *habeas corpus* application in relation to extradition, owing to the HRA, than they considered that they had previously.[157] Clearly, the Home Secretary, also a public authority under s 6 of the HRA, should already have discharged his or her duty not to breach the Convention rights in taking an extradition decision. But, the mere fact that this ought to be the case would not absolve the court from taking a fresh decision on the matter since each public authority has a separate responsibility for ensuring that it does not breach the Convention rights.

The applicant can also make representations to the Secretary of State within 15 days of receiving notice that the Secretary of State is minded to issue an order of return.[158] Since, as mentioned above, the Home Secretary is a public authority under s 6 of the HRA, the possibility, which may not have been brought fully to his or her notice, that such an order would lead to a breach of the applicant's Convention rights, could be put forward, with substantiating evidence.

The applicant could seek judicial review of the decision to extradite, but it might seem most fruitful to seek to challenge the decision under s 7(1)(a) of the HRA, which would of course be possible since the bodies involved in making decisions in relation to extradition are all public authorities. The use of s 7(1)(a), as opposed to non-HRA judicial review, would be a better option, since the standard of review should be stricter. However, alternatively, judicial review could be sought on the basis that the decision was unreasonable, and HRA arguments could also be raised under s 7(1)(b). The question should be, straightforwardly, has the decision maker breached one of the applicant's Convention rights in the sense that, if the decision is carried out, a breach is very likely or almost bound to follow? The breach could be a direct consequence of the extradition or it could be indirect, in the sense that it would occur as a result of the treatment the applicant would receive in the requesting State. Thus, a direct breach might occur of Art 8 or possibly Art 12, while an indirect breach of Arts 2, 3, 5, 8 or 6 or of Art 1, Protocol 6 might be likely. It may be noted that no derogation or reservation may be made in relation to Protocol 6.[159]

It should be pointed out that under the new anti-terrorism legislation, introduced into the Commons in October 2001, the procedures described are to be speeded up and appeal

---

156 See Chapter 4, pp 143–45.
157 See *Schmidt v Federal Government of Germany* [1994] 3 All ER 65.
158 Extradition Act 1989, s 13(1), (2).
159 Protocol, Arts 3 and 4.

rights are to be removed. The new legislation may well, therefore, be of doubtful compatability with Art 6 of the Convention.

Convention rights

The most relevant rights are those of Arts 8, 3, 5, 2, 14 or Protocol 6. As Chapter 2 explained, a violation of Art 3 may occur because of the treatment a person may receive when returning to his or her own country having been expelled or refused admission. It will have to be clearly established that the danger of such treatment is really present. The question arose in *Soering v UK*[160] whether expulsion to a country (the US) where the applicant risked the death penalty would be compatible with Art 3 because it would subject him to conditions on Death Row likely to cause him acute mental anguish. It was found that the conditions on Death Row would expose the applicant to Art 3 treatment.

Now that the UK has ratified Protocol 6 and included it in Sched 1 of the HRA, the possibility that an extradition will lead to the use of the death penalty against the applicant would create a violation of Art 1 of Protocol 6. Thus, the duty of the Home Secretary under s 6 of the HRA means that persons can no longer be extradited to the US if they would be very likely, owing to the nature of the alleged crimes, to face the death penalty there,[161] regardless of the question of possible Art 3 treatment. This means that if a person who was allegedly part of the terrorist organisation which conspired to hijack planes in order to fly into the World Trade Centre in New York on 11 September 2001, murdering over 5,000 people, was apprehended in the UK, he could not be extradited to the US.

Arguments similar to those considered above in relation to deportation could be raised under Art 8 regarding the effect of extradition on family life. Since the person in question may be a British citizen, the arguments could have, in one respect, more weight. However, given that it will be alleged that he or she has committed a criminal offence, such arguments would probably be outweighed.

Argument could be raised under Arts 5 and 14 that although a breach of Art 5 alone would not occur, owing to the prison sentence likely to be received in the requesting State, evidence of discriminatory sentencing affecting the group to which the applicant belongs might demonstrate that a breach of the two Articles read together would occur if he or she is extradited. A similar argument could be made in relation to the right to a fair trial under Art 6.[162]

---

160 Judgment of 7 July 1989, A161; (1989) 11 EHRR 439. For discussion see Schabas (1994) 43 ICLQ 913.

161 See *Aylor-Davis v France* (1994) 76-A DR 164; *Raidl v Austria* (1995) 82-A DR 134.

162 A similar argument, but not based on the Convention, was put forward, but failed, in *Re Ramda* (1997) *The Independent*, 27 June.

4 EXCLUSION ORDERS[163]

Power of exclusion

Apart from extradition, there are now no general powers to exclude British citizens from the country. Until recently, however, exclusion orders could be made under s 5 of the Prevention of Terrorism (Temporary Provisions) Act (PTA) 1989 in respect of a British citizen (as defined under the British Nationality Act 1981) who had been ordinarily resident in Britain for three years or less, although he or she could not be excluded from Britain altogether, only moved from one part of it to another. In practice, this meant that persons were excluded from England to Northern Ireland. It was irrelevant whether the person excluded to Northern Ireland was born in Britain and had family there so long as he or she had only been ordinarily resident in Britain for three years or less.[164] The order prevented the citizen being in or entering Britain; an order under s 6 prevented the citizen being in or entering Northern Ireland. A s 7 order excluded a non-British citizen from either Britain or Northern Ireland. In effect, these powers meant that Northern Irish citizens could be forced to go back to Northern Ireland; there was little reciprocity in terms of excluding Irish citizens to Britain.[165]

An order could be made if the person was suspected of involvement in acts of terrorism or was attempting or might attempt to enter Britain with a view to being concerned in such an offence. The Home Secretary had to be 'satisfied' that the person in question is so involved. The decision to exclude took place secretly and was often based on material of doubtful worth.[166] If an order was served on a person, he or she had the right within seven or 14 days to make written representations to the Secretary of State and to have a personal interview with an adviser nominated by the Secretary (Sched 2, para 4 of the PTA). There was no requirement for the Secretary of State to give reasons for making an order. Once the order was made, the excludee could not re-enter the forbidden territory at all until it was revoked; there was no power to suspend the order for a short period of time in order to allow the excludee to attend family occasions such as funerals. Exclusion orders expired in three years and this meant that the case would be reviewed every three years, but a fresh order could be issued before the end of the three year period.

These provisions were reviewed by Lord Jellicoe in 1983;[167] he concluded that they were of some value in curbing terrorism, but accepted that dumping the problem in Northern Ireland as opposed to Britain was merely transferring it from one area to another. He also accepted that by this means, the whole problem of political terrorism

---

163 Reading: (for background) Laquer, *The Age of Terrorism*, 1987; Wilkinson, P, *Terrorism and the Liberal State*, 1995; Gearty, CA, *Terror*, 1991; in relation to Ireland: Townshend, *Political Violence in Ireland*, 1983; on exclusion orders specifically: Walker, C, *The Prevention of Terrorism in British Law*, 2nd edn, 1992, Chapter 6; Bonner, D, *Emergency Powers in Peacetime*, 1985, Chapter 4; Ewing, KD and Gearty, CA, *Freedom under Thatcher*, 1990, Chapter 7, pp 217–21; Bonner, D, 'Combating terrorism in the 1990s: the role of the prevention of Terrorism Act 1989' [1989] PL 440, pp 452–56; on application of exclusion orders to MPs, see Walker [1983] PL 537.

164 This occurred in *Mathews* (1993) unreported, 7 July.

165 Walker, *op cit*, fn 163, pp 84–85; only four persons have been excluded to Britain.

166 Lord Shackleton, in his review of the PTA, warned that some of the material had no evidential value and had to be treated with great caution (para 41 of the review). See also Ewing and Gearty, *Freedom under Thatcher*, p 218.

167 *Report on the Operation of the Prevention of Terrorism (Temporary Provisions) Act 1978*, 1983.

might be exacerbated owing to the alienation the suspected terrorist would feel in being uprooted. In accordance with his Report, the period of ordinary residence for s 5(4) purposes was reduced to three years from 20 with a view to bringing within the net only those who might well have come to Britain specifically with the idea of perpetrating terrorist offences. The Report concluded that the exclusion power should be allowed to lapse as soon as circumstances suggested that it was not strictly necessary.[168]

Safeguards

The safeguards available were of limited scope: the individual concerned could write to the Home Secretary requesting an interview, the interview would be with an adviser appointed by the Home Secretary and accountable to him. It hardly amounted, therefore, to an independent review of the decision. Moreover, there was no need for the Home Secretary to give reasons for the order and therefore the individual concerned could not challenge it effectively. Detention could be based on an exclusion order even where the grounds for the order were flimsy or non-existent. In *Breen v Chief Constable for Dumfries and Galloway*,[169] police detained Breen while an exclusion order was being made. When the detention was challenged, it was found that the police can detain on this basis so long as they are unaware that there may be no grounds for the order. Thus, police accountability for such detention was extremely limited.

Decisions to exclude appeared to be subject to extremely limited judicial review. In *Secretary of State for Home Affairs ex p Stitt*,[170] it was found that considerations of national security and confidentiality meant that the Secretary of State need not give any reasons at all for the decision to exclude. Some progress was made towards less restricted review in *Secretary of State for Home Affairs ex p McQuillan*.[171] The applicant applied for judicial review of the Home Secretary's decision to exclude him from Great Britain and the subsequent refusal to reconsider that decision in spite of the changed circumstances of the applicant. Evidence was adduced by the applicant to show that he had not at any time been involved in any terrorist activity and also that his life would continue to be endangered if he was forced to remain in Northern Ireland. It was found that the case raised human rights issues and that therefore, the order required close scrutiny. However, it was found that on national security grounds, the Home Secretary's decision must stand: he could not be required to give any reasons for it and thus the court was unable to assess its rationality. The argument that the human rights context requires close scrutiny of a decision was confirmed as correct in *Ministry of Defence ex p Smith and Others*.[172] The Court of Appeal found that: '... the more substantial the interference with human rights, the more the court will require by way of justification before it [will be] satisfied that the

---

168 *Ibid*, para 200; however, the review by Lord Colville recommended on this basis that power to make exclusion orders should be repealed (*Report on the Operation in 1990 of the Prevention of Terrorism Act 1989*).
169 (1997) *The Times*, 24 April.
170 (1987) *The Times*, 3 February.
171 [1995] 3 All ER 400; (1994) *The Independent*, 23 September.
172 [1996] 1 All ER 257; [1996] ICR 740; (1995) *The Times*, 6 November. See also *Cambridge HA ex p B* [1995] TLR 159, CA; [1995] 1 WLR 898 pp 904–05; *Secretary of State for Home Affairs ex p McQuillan* [1995] 3 All ER 400; (1994) *Independent*, 23 September, in which Laws J's approach was expressly followed. Sedley J was unable to find for the applicant owing to the particular statutory framework in question.

decision was reasonable.'[173] However, the national security justification normally put forward in exclusion cases was likely, in the pre-HRA era, to satisfy even this more stringent requirement of reasonableness.

It should be noted, however, that it is a fundamental principle of English law that the courts always have a duty to ensure that a body exercising power does so within the parameters set for it by the primary legislation. In *Anisminic*,[174] it was held that this power of the court to keep the deciding body within the remit defined in the Act which gave it its powers could not be excluded, despite clear words in a statute to the contrary. To allow the court's supervisory jurisdiction to be ousted would be to accede to the proposition that the body in question had arbitrary powers and the courts are not prepared to believe that such powers are ever granted, since the grant of them would undermine the basic principle of the rule of law. However, in the area of exclusion orders, since the courts had decided that the minister was not obliged to give them reasons for his decisions, they had made it effectively impossible for them to determine whether the minister had acted within his powers. In practice, therefore, though not in theory, review by the courts was limited to cases in which the order given was bad on its face, because, for example, it purported to exclude a suspect for more than three years contrary to Sched 2, para 2. To assert that the courts would not have had the power to quash such an order through the writ of certiorari would have been tantamount to asserting that the minister had been endowed with an unlimited and arbitrary power in which case, by definition, the power would not be a legal one. It is submitted, therefore, that the courts retained the power of supervisory review of exclusion orders but that in practice, review was impossible except in the improbable case of an order which palpably purported to exceed the powers given to the minister under the Act.

Abolition

The powers were used with increasing infrequency: there were 248 orders in force in 1982; by the end of 1996 there were 24. In 1997, the Home Secretary considered that they were no longer effective in combating terrorism and revoked the 12 which remained. The exclusion powers were lapsed with effect from midnight on 21 March 1998. Thus, under the Labour Government, exclusion orders were not used, although until repeal of the PTA by the Terrorism Act 2000, they could have been reactivated.

The power of exclusion was abolished under the Terrorism Act 2000 in the sense that the PTA was repealed and the powers were not included in the new Act. These powers would clearly be entirely irrelevant in relation to the new domestic groups to be designated as terrorist[175] and probably largely irrelevant to the small Irish splinter groups, such as the Real IRA. They would be extremely complex to operate in respect of 'international terrorists'. Thus, even if they were retained, these powers would probably remain largely unused under the new statute. Nevertheless, their repeal is to be welcomed on the principle that such laws should be repealed rather than left to lie on the statute book with the possibility that they could be arbitrarily reactivated in future.

---

173 [1996] 1 All ER 257, p 263.
174 [1969] 2 AC 147, HL.
175 See Chapter 8, pp 402–03.

Conclusions

There may be some value in exclusion orders; they may have the effect of disrupting lines of communication and breaking up terrorist units. Also, they can prevent terrorists travelling freely between Britain and other countries. Obviously, imprisonment would be a more effective way of achieving these objects, but if evidence had to be produced in court, it might endanger informers and witnesses. Also, such orders allow preventive action before a group can become established in the UK; they may also be useful where a terrorist is currently imprisoned, but it is clear that he or she will return to terrorism on release. They can even be used where a person has been acquitted of terrorist offences,[176] where the evidence, while failing to connect the defendant beyond reasonable doubt to particular offences, does suggest that there may be some involvement in terrorism. This has also occurred where a person has been arrested but not charged.[177]

However, it is unclear that the serious infringement of civil liberties which these orders represent can be justified by reference to their value. The power to exclude a person from a particular place where he or she may be surrounded by friends and family to a place where he or she may be a target for terrorists on grounds which may have not been fully tested represents a gross infringement of personal liberty which requires a very strong justification and should be balanced by effective safeguards. Such justification would be shown if exclusion orders had a clear effect on terrorism and the individuals affected were unlikely to engage in terrorist activities in the place to which they were excluded. However, it is not possible to be sure that these conditions are met, especially as, by its nature, the exclusion process allows persons to be excluded of whom it cannot be said that they are clearly implicated in terrorism.

6 FREEDOM TO TRAVEL ABROAD[178]

United Kingdom law has traditionally presumed that UK citizens would be free to travel abroad, but this freedom is in practice dependent on the possession of a valid passport, although in law it is possible to enter or leave Britain without one. A passport was defined in *Brailsford*[179] as a 'document issued in the name of the Sovereign ... to a named individual ... to be used for that individual's protection as a British subject in foreign countries'. As this definition suggests, passports grew up not as a restriction on freedom of movement, but as an affirmation of it, but the position today hardly reflects such an affirmation. Passports are issued by the Passport Office, a department of the Home Office, under the royal prerogative. Thus, the Home Secretary can exercise a discretion to withhold a passport where a person wishes to travel abroad to engage in activities which are politically deplored, although legal. Because these powers arise under the royal prerogative, it was thought that they would not be open to review until the ruling in

---

176 The cases of *McBrearty* (1990) *The Times*, 9 January, p 2 and *Ellis* (1991) *The Times*, 31 October, p 3.

177 Eg, *Hagan* (1987) *The Times*, 20 May.

178 For comment, see Williams, DW, 'British passports and the right to travel' (1974) ICLQ 642; Jaconelli, J (1975) 38 MLR 314.

179 [1905] 2 KB 730, p 745.

Council for Civil Service Unions v the Minister for the Civil Service (the *GCHQ* case)[180] in which the House of Lords determined that the mere fact of the power deriving from the prerogative as opposed to statute was not a sufficient reason why it should not be open to review. Lord Roskill said that the executive may act under statute which has, by necessary implication, replaced a former prerogative power or may act under the prerogative alone, but that in either case it would be an archaism to talk of the act of the executive as the act of the sovereign. This decision was applied in *Secretary of State for Foreign and Commonwealth Affairs ex p Everett*,[181] the Court of Appeal holding that review was available of a refusal to issue a passport to a British citizen living in Spain. Thus, refusal or withdrawals of passports must be made fairly and reasonably, although the merits of such decisions cannot be considered.

Recently, certain restrictions on travel have been imposed in respect of two groups of persons – those suspected of football hooliganism and those convicted of drug trafficking offences. Section 33 of the Criminal Justice and Police Act 2001 provides a court with power, on sentencing the offender in respect of certain drug trafficking offences, to impose a travel restriction order. If it does not do so, it must state its reason for that decision, under s 33(2)(c). The order must continue for not less than two years after the offender's release from custody, under s 33(3). It may include a direction to surrender the offender's passport, under s 33(4).

The Government sought to deal with the problem of football hooliganism abroad by introducing the Football (Disorder) Act 2000, Sched 1 of which amends the Football Spectators Act 1989 in order to curb the freedom of movement of football supporters in certain circumstances. Section 14e of the 1989 Act provides power for a court to remove a person's passport after he has been convicted of certain offences.

The most significant powers arise under s 21. Section 21A of the 1989 Act, as amended, provides a power for a constable in uniform, with permission from an inspector, to detain a person for up to six hours where reasonable suspicion relating to certain offences arises. Section 21B(2)(c) provides a power, with the authorisation of an officer of at least the rank of inspector, to order the detainee not to leave England and to surrender his passport on the basis of suspicion that he may commit certain offences. This power is therefore not subject to supervision by the courts. Under the Football (Disorder) Duration of Powers Order 2001, the powers under s 21 have been extended for a further year, from 28 August 2001 to the same date in 2002.

These new provisions strike directly at freedom of movement, but it appears that they are not directly affected by the HRA or the European Convention, as an international instrument, since Protocol 4 guaranteeing freedom of movement is not included in Sched 1 of the HRA and has not been ratified by the UK. If it is eventually included in Sched 1, Art 2 – which provides that everyone shall be free to leave any country – would appear to be in conflict with the new provisions. However, it is subject to para 3, which provides that infringement can be justified to allow restrictions necessary in a democratic society for the prevention, *inter alia*, of crime or disorder. It may well be that s 21 of the 1989 Act, as amended, is incompatible with Protocol 4, Art 2, on the basis that preventing a person

---

180 [1985] AC 374; [1985] 3 WLR 1174; [1984] 3 All ER 935, HL.
181 [1989] QB 891; [1989] 1 All ER 655, CA.

from travelling abroad on the grounds merely of the suspicion of a police officer, with no judicial oversight, is disproportionate to the aim in view.

It would be possible for a person to seek judicial review of a decision to remove his passport. As far as the substantive right to freedom of movement is concerned, the review would be based, however, not on the Convention, but on the pre-HRA grounds. Therefore, so long as the discretion of the officers in question had been exercised in a reasonable manner and within the s 21 powers, the fact that Protocol 4, Art 2 would have been breached would be irrelevant. But once judicial review proceedings had been brought, the applicant could raise the question of the effect of Art 6 under s 7(1)(b) of the HRA. It could be argued that the ban on travelling amounted to a penalty similar to a criminal sanction and that therefore, it should not be possible for it to be ordered by a police officer, without the possibility of a fair hearing before a court or tribunal. At Strasbourg, the fact that national law classifies an act as non-criminal is relevant, but not conclusive. In *Benham v UK*,[182] the leading case on 'criminal charge', the Court found that although the legislation in question[183] clearly did not create a criminal offence in UK law, it should be accounted criminal for Art 6(1) purposes. The proceedings against the applicant[184] had been brought by the public authorities; the proceedings had some punitive elements and the bringing of them implied fault on the part of the applicant. Further, the penalty was severe (committal to prison for up to three months).[185]

Under the HRA the national court, however, may be placed in a difficulty where an act is impliedly classified as non-criminal, but Art 6 suggests that it is criminal. Owing to the provision of s 3(2) of the HRA, it would appear that a national court could not merely re-define s 21 as creating a criminal offence if that involved finding that Art 6 and s 21 were incompatible. The court would have to issue a declaration of incompatibility if it found that s 21 should be so viewed, since there would be no means of interpreting the provisions in order to create compatibility. The fact that the Football (Disorder) Act 2000 was declared to be compatible with the Convention rights under s 19 of the HRA should not (and would be unlikely to) deter a judge from making a declaration of incompatibility, since the legal advice behind the s 19 declaration might have been flawed.

7 CONCLUSIONS

A recurring theme throughout this chapter has concerned the balance struck by the relevant rules between the rights of those who wish to remain in this country, or travel abroad, and societal interests. Such interests are, of course, the proper concern of EU governments. They are also affected by popular perceptions of the nature of the threats to such interests and their impact on society. Such perceptions focus the debate on certain threats in a manner which may obscure other methods of serving the public interest. A

---

182 (1996) 22 EHRR 293. See also *Lauko v Slovakia* [1999] 1 EHRLR 105 in which it was found that a penalty for anti-social behaviour was inherently criminal in nature.

183 Community Charge (Administration and Enforcement) Regulations, reg 41.

184 In respect of default on payment of the community charge or poll tax.

185 The magistrates could only exercise their power of committal on a finding of wilful refusal to pay or culpable neglect (para 56 of the judgment).

government may well feel disinclined to provide benefits for asylum seekers in the knowledge that funds are thereby being redirected away from matters of legitimate domestic concern, such as the provision of education or housing, which are also far more popular with voters. Speedy extradition and deportation procedures can be used to tackle the international problems of terrorism and drug trafficking. The more minor problem of football hooliganism abroad is nevertheless a problem that attracts immense media attention, and the measures adopted to curb it can be viewed as a test of a government's general preparedness and ability to adopt tough measures to tackle crime and disorder.

It is suggested that the later legislation discussed in this chapter shows a tendency to display an increasingly authoritarian trend, although it has been tempered by the need to import procedures imposed on the UK by Strasbourg. The Government which introduced the Immigration and Asylum Act 1999 and the Football (Disorder) Act 2000 also introduced the Human Rights Act 1998. The HRA may prove to be a corrective to the introduction of unbalanced measures unduly interfering with freedoms in the name of curbing entry into the country or removing persons from it in order to enhance State security or prevent crime or for economic purposes. As indicated, the HRA has had a certain counterbalancing effect, not on freedom of movement, but on rights-infringing measures incidental to its curtailment.[186] Clearly, the effect of the HRA is impaired by the failures so far to introduce Protocols 4 and 7 into Sched 1. But, although it is not possible to rely on those Protocols, other rights, in particular those guaranteed under Arts 3 and 8 and Protocol 6, can be relied upon, and provide, as they should do, a set of values which determine the parameters within which decisions to remove persons from the country have to be taken.

Perhaps the key concern of the civil libertarian at the present time is that the corrective effect of the HRA in this context, fragile, precarious and partial as it is, will be curbed almost to vanishing point. In the aftermath of the attack on the World Trade Centre in New York in September 2001, the Government decided to introduce three new anti-terrorism Bills.[187] The measures to be introduced include the introduction of faster deportation procedures for asylum seekers and speedier extradition procedures which would prevent or curb the use of appeals. As indicated above, a legal power to detain a suspected terrorist indefinitely until a country is found to which he can be deported is being introduced. The power is likely to require amendment of the HRA in order to derogate from Article 5. Clearly, the HRA itself provides a basis for intervention in such instances and also – on its face – demands a more intensive scrutiny of executive actions under s 6. One method of importing such faster procedures could be modelled on the arrangements put in place by the RIPA for the new tribunal which considers allegations of unlawful actions by the police and security and intelligence services.[188] As Chapter 11 explained, challenges to those bodies under the HRA must be brought in the tribunal and recourse to the ordinary courts thereafter is minimal. Any such move in the context of removal from the UK may be accompanied by further powers afforded to the Home Secretary to issue certificates preventing even such recourse on various grounds. If the

---

186 See p 942.
187 They were announced by Tony Blair at the beginning of the Labour Party Conference in Brighton, on 30 September 2001.
188 See Chapter 11, pp 714 *et seq.*

counter-terrorist measures to be put in place proved effective, there would be less cause for complaint, since terrorism presents in itself one of the greatest possible threats to civil liberties, both in terms of actual and feared effects, regardless of the government response. But the concern is that far reaching repressive measures which have been waiting for some time to get on to the statute book will be introduced on the basis that this is an opportune moment. They will then remain there, whether or not the terrorist threat eventually subsides, and the victims may be those weak and unpopular groups in society who have been the main subjects of this chapter.

PART V

EQUALITY AND THEORIES OF
ANTI-DISCRIMINATION LAWS

One of the main themes in human rights jurisprudence concerns the duty of States to treat citizens with equal concern and respect. This does not mean that no differentiation between citizens may occur, but that inequality of treatment should not be based on factors which do not justify it. Thus, discrimination may be defined as morally unjustifiable as opposed to justifiable differentiation.[1] It may be said that the latter occurs when a difference in treatment is accorded owing to behaviour which is the result of voluntary choice, the former when it is based on an attribute over which the individual has no control, such as sex or skin colour. Thus, in a society that allows or imposes discrimination in this sense, the groups affected will be entirely frustrated in pursuing their objectives in all areas of life because the disadvantage they are under cannot be removed. These statements alone, however, are inadequate as failing to deal with behaviour which may in a sense be the result of voluntary choice, but might also be said to be determined by social conditioning. Further, they do not explain whether differentiation would be justified if based on behaviour to which a person is morally committed owing to her membership of a certain group. Thus, it should also be argued that morally unjustifiable differentiation would also occur, at least presumptively, if different treatment was based on behaviour over which the individual had little real choice. Finally, this argument should encompass the notion that the physical attribute or behaviour in question may, exceptionally, be objectively relevant to the differential treatment and thereby could justify it. As Chapter 16 will demonstrate, anti-discrimination schemes tend to begin by outlawing discrimination on the basis of sex, race or skin colour. They then move on to a more developed conception of equality, which understands that discrimination occurs on the basis of a number of other factors, including sexual orientation, transsexuality, religion or disability.

Once factors which do not justify differentiation are identified, the State can be said to be under a duty to ensure that unequal treatment on the basis of such factors does not occur, at least in spheres under its control. However, at different times and according to different schools of thought, the scope of the duty varies. Under early classic liberal rights theory, the State came under a duty to ensure that no formal discriminatory mechanisms were in place, but once that was done, it was thought that individuals would have equal freedom to exercise their talents.[2] However, this theory came to encompass the notion of State intervention in order to ensure that some individuals did not prevent others from exercising their talents. This is the dominant theory underpinning the UK legislative policy on equality: it assumes that once people have equal freedoms, they will have equal opportunities and thus all that is needed is to ensure such freedoms. Some egalitarians would go further, insisting that persons should be placed in a similar position, even if in order to do so they are treated unequally. Some forms of liberal thought[3] would now also

---

1   See Wallman, 'Difference, differentiation, discrimination', 5 New Community 1.
2   See Mill, JS, *On the Subjection of Women*, 2nd edn, 1869.
3   See Raz, J, *The Morality of Freedom*, 1986; Dworkin, R, *Taking Rights Seriously*, 1978, p 272.

support treating persons unequally in order to ensure equality of opportunity. However, broadly, liberals view equality as formal, while egalitarians, including socialists or communitarians, view it as substantive. Formal equality[4] (or treating like as like) is the limitation placed upon equality legislation by liberalism; its drawback is that it puts the protection of such legislation beyond the reach of those who are differently situated.[5] If women's domestic and parental roles[6] tend to differ from those of men, and those roles interfere with women's role as (cost efficient) workers, in a formal equality model, which takes the male as the norm and assumes that a woman is like a man, the employer may justifiably treat women differently. If some persons from minority groups are educationally or socially disadvantaged, their difference of situation cannot be addressed by means of legislation based on a formal equality model.

This argument does not imply that the imposition of formal equality has *no* impact on the distribution of social benefits. In particular, formal equality affects the market by inducing it not to act in an arbitrary and ultimately inefficient fashion. Formal equality, if fully established, disallows the individual biases of employers to feed into the market,[7] and may therefore promote genuine competition based on individual merit, thereby preventing the unwarranted under- or over-advantaging of certain groups. Perpetuation of an unequal pay policy may not seem to lead clearly and immediately to an inefficient operation of the market. If a certain group can be treated disadvantageously in terms of pay, this may appear in some respects to benefit the market, since the availability of cheap labour may lead to increased productivity and market expansion. Nevertheless, unequal pay may eventually distort the operation of market forces, creating dysfunction in the market, since certain professions and certain specialities within professions may be shunned by advantaged groups because of the low pay they offer, with the result once again that genuine competition is not fostered within them.

Thus, it may be argued that formal equality 'perfects' the market: rather than allowing bias to benefit certain individuals at the expense of others, it forces the market to treat every employee or would-be employee as an autonomous individual having made a free choice as regards position in the market. Further, it can force the market to treat each individual as an equivalent 'unit of production'.[8] Beyond that it will not go, and therefore it is not ultimately gravely disruptive of market forces. Once a formal equality regime is established and internalised by the market, market forces can have free rein.

---

4   Under classic liberalism as expressed by Mill, *op cit*, fn 2.

5   Several feminist writers have pointed out that the principal limitation of the formal equality principle is that it assumes that the male is the norm. MacKinnon puts it particularly aptly, 'Why should you have to be the same as a man to get what a man gets simply because he is one?' See MacKinnon, C, 'Difference and dominance: on sex discrimination', in Bartlett, K and Kennedy, R (eds), *Feminist Legal Theory*, 1991; see also MacKinnon, C, 'Reflections on sex equality under law' (1991) 100 Yale LJ 1286–93.

6   Matters belonging to the 'private' sphere, in a liberal conception. Mill's view, as expressed in *op cit*, fn 2, was that formal equality operates in certain 'public' spheres, such as franchise, employment and education.

7   This argument is put forward by Weiler in 'The wages of sex: the uses and limits of comparable worth' (1986) 99 Harv L Rev 1728, p 1762: '... real world labour markets leave a good deal of leeway for countless managerial judgments about how to classify, value and pay certain jobs in comparison to others.'

8   In other words, formal equality requires in general that one employee should not be perceived as more expensive than another and therefore the market need not accommodate the cost of individuals who are given unnecessary special protection such as, eg, barring women from night work during pregnancy.

Substantive equality, on the other hand, demands not merely that persons should be judged on individual merit, but that the real situation of many women and/or members of minority groups which may tend to place them in a weaker position in the market should be addressed by a variety of means, including anti-discrimination legislation. Proponents of this argument recognise that the achievement of substantive equality involves more than a few discrimination claims. Such claims can only have limited impact in bringing about social change; far reaching structural changes can be achieved only as a result of government policy and changed social expectations. Nevertheless, under a substantive equality model, equality legislation would attempt to reflect and further the societal movement towards equality which is taking place in the Member States of the EU. Thus, legislation enshrining anti-discrimination measures may move beyond seeking to ensure formal equality and may encompass a more sophisticated notion of equality, requiring understanding of the differential impact of certain measures on certain groups, and of the value of positive action.

FROM INEQUALITY TO NEUTRALITY, FROM FORMAL TO SUBSTANTIVE EQUALITY

During the 20th and 21st centuries in Western democracies, it has been possible to discern a pattern in the landscape of 'equality' law. There has been a clear movement, reflected in the law, towards acceptance of the equal treatment of persons, and towards a more developed conception of equality, and away from the acceptance of unjustifiable differentiation, which reflects to an extent the different theories considered above. In the first phase such differentiation, based on particular protected grounds expressly enshrined in the law, is gradually removed; in the second, there may be a hiatus during which the law is neutral and there is freedom to discriminate; in the third, the law may be used to try expressly to prevent discrimination, or at least certain aspects of it, on such grounds. In the fourth, a more developed conception of equality may become apparent: in this phase, the law will tend to *permit* discrimination – termed positive or affirmative action – on the ground that it is morally justified as a temporary measure intended to combat the effects of previous discrimination.

However, although this general pattern can usually be identified, it may well be that particular aspects of the 'first phase' discrimination which for various reasons – usually associated with religion or with the armed forces – are especially resistant to change, are still in existence during the third phase. Such aspects will still tend to follow the general trend, but more slowly, and will themselves almost certainly move eventually from one phase to another.[9] In other words, some specific inequalities may still be enshrined in law in the third or fourth phases. Moreover, *within* each phase there may be movement; in the first, legislation may enshrine gross and absolute inequality, which gradually gives place to a lesser and more pragmatic inequality. An example is afforded by the legal regulation of sexual acts between consenting males: until 1967 these were merely forbidden, on the

---

9   An example is afforded by the exclusion of women from the Anglican priesthood, an instance of 'first phase' discrimination which survived until 1994. 'First phase' discrimination in this context, although almost squeezed out of existence, will subsist: under the current arrangements, women priests cannot become bishops.

ground that sexual satisfaction gained in this manner was inimical to the moral basis of society. The removal of this barrier but the fixing of the age of consent for male homosexuals at 21, and then at 18, suggested a retreat from an absolutist position, but a disinclination to carry through such a retreat fully.

Since slavery was abolished at the beginning of the 19th century, generalised racial inequality has never been enshrined in law in the UK in the way that sexual inequality has been until relatively recently. People from certain ethnic backgrounds have not been prevented from voting, from holding civic office, from owning property or from forming contracts. The legal scheme which until quite recently governed sexual inequality in the UK would probably find parallels in terms of racial inequality only under regimes such as that in South Africa during the apartheid years.

The movement towards equality on the grounds of sexual orientation is still poised between the first and second phases, although a few instances of legally enshrined inequality remain. In the UK, there are signs at present that its entry into the third phase is imminent; it seems highly probable that it will do so sometime within the next few years. The signs that this is likely to occur are already in place: the existence of pressure groups operating within the UK and abroad; and official recognition afforded to such groups in some other Western democracies coupled with instances in which their policies have been afforded a degree of legal recognition.[10] Moreover, instruments which are capable of affecting law and policy in the UK already enshrine guarantees of freedom from discrimination on this ground, including the European Convention on Human Rights and the International Convention on Civil and Political Rights. Recently, more far reaching European legal instruments have been introduced, at international level, which could be used to address discrimination on this ground. Arguments in favour of discrimination on the ground of sexual orientation in various spheres such as employment may now be viewed as rooted only in prejudice: the social need to retain such discrimination is not apparent.[11] At present, such prejudice is allowed relatively free rein and therefore can affect every area of life from employment to expressions of sexuality, and since the UK does not, in general, recognise same-sex partners, they suffer in comparison with heterosexual couples in relation to immigration,[12] pensions and inheritance rights.

ANTI-ASSIMILATIONISM

Although this chapter concentrates on the extent to which the law has influenced equality of opportunity, it does not imply that all members of the groups in question will

---

10 Eg, the armed forces in Belgium, Denmark, The Netherlands and Spain are all open to homosexuals. See further Homosexuality: A Community Issue, 1993, a report compiled by the European Human Rights Foundation.

11 Some Conservative opinion takes the view that homosexuality is a form of immorality which should be suppressed in order to uphold the moral bonds which keep society together. This view may derive from that expressed by Lord Devlin (The Maccabaean Lecture, The Enforcement of Morals, 1959, reprinted in 1965). It seems likely that this body of opinion would not support legislation aimed at preventing discrimination in, eg, employment on grounds of sexual orientation. For discussion of Lord Devlin's view see Chapter 5, p 269.

12 See Chapter 15, p 945, and below, pp 1052 et seq.

necessarily *want* the opportunity to adopt the way of life of the dominant group. Some women and some members of ethnic minorities believe that true equality means accepting and respecting different values rather than trying to extinguish them.[13] The notion of 'assimilationism' has come particularly under attack[14] in various writings on feminist legal theory, which have advocated the 'feminism of difference' and rejected the rights analysis of the liberal feminist.[15] Of course, there is a crucial difference here between the assertion of the values of groups of persons belonging to ethnic minorities and those of women, in that women will be committed to an enormous and disparate range of values and will therefore behave as differently from each other as men do.[16] However, assuming for the purposes of the argument that a body of values of a more nurturing, caring, conscience-based kind can be associated with women, just as certain values and beliefs can be associated with groups such as Sikhs or Muslims, it could be argued that such values are not necessarily opposed in their entirety to those of the dominant group and, in any event, need not be rejected in seeking to overcome disadvantage. In suggesting this, the danger should be borne in mind that extreme forms of 'celebration of difference' may be merely another route to economic and political subjugation; history does not afford many examples of groups who overcame disadvantage by rejoicing in their rejection of the whole body of values which originally placed them in that position. In any event, despite a difference of emphasis, there is a measure of harmony between moderate anti-assimilationist theory and liberal rights theory as regards the need to protect people from discrimination on unjustifiable grounds by outlawing sex- and race-based disadvantages, so that women or members of ethnic minorities can choose whether or how far to accept – while perhaps working to modify – the lifestyle associated with the dominant group.

DISCRIMINATION AND THE LAW

This part begins, in Chapter 16, by considering and evaluating the domestic and European legislation aimed specifically at preventing discrimination based on certain protected grounds including those of race, sex and disability. The anti-discrimination scheme adopted in respect of disability is compared with those applicable to discrimination on grounds of sex or race. The chapter considers the means used in the legislation of distinguishing between relevant and irrelevant factors founding

---

13 Eg, MacKinnon, C, 'Toward feminist jurisprudence', 34 Stanford L Rev; Littleton, CA, 'Reconstructing sexual equality', in Bartlett, *op cit*, fn 5.

14 See Gilligan, C, *In A Different Voice: Psychological Theory and Women's Development*, 1982. It should be noted that the 'feminism of difference' has itself come under attack from postmodern feminists as impoverished and limited in its assumption that there is essential commonality between all women. See Cain, 'Feminist jurisprudence: grounding the theories', in Bartlett and Kennedy, *op cit*, fn 5, pp 265–68.

15 'Feminist rights analysis generally pretends that there are no differences between men and women and attempts to advance women by giving them the rights men have': Olsen, F, 'Statutory rape: a feminist critique of rights analysis', in Bartlett and Kennedy, *op cit*, fn 5, p 312.

16 The argument that women can and should be viewed as a homogeneous group has been put by Martha Minow: 'cognitively we need simplifying categories and the unifying category of "woman" helps to organise experience even at the cost of denying some of it' (Minow, M, 'Feminist reason: getting it and losing it', 38 J Legal Educ 47, p 51).

differentiation, since only the former provide a morally justifiable basis for different treatment. The legal means of ensuring that such distinctions can be made can then be contrasted with the failure so far to ensure that homosexuality *per se* is not regarded by the law as an irrelevant factor on which to base differentiation in such spheres as employment, housing and education.

Broadly, the legislation embodies two methods of challenging direct discrimination and discriminatory practices: under the first, the 'individual' method, the responsibility lies mainly with the victim of discrimination to bring an action against the discriminator, while under the second, termed the 'administrative' method, an institution or body uses various methods of seeking to ensure that discrimination is prevented. Chapter 16 moves on to consider the efficacy of the current legal model in practice.

The main emphasis of this chapter will be on the tensions placed on the interpretation of the legislation, not only as claimants have sought to use it, to do more than merely bring about formal equality, but also as they have sought to bring further grounds within the category of those that are protected. It will be apparent that a number of further grounds have received protection – the anti-discrimination schemes, both domestic and European, have widened their scope and are currently under pressure to widen still further. The potential of the Human Rights Act (HRA) to influence the domestic scheme in both respects is quite a significant theme, although, owing to the influence of EC law, the HRA is likely to have less influence in this context than in others considered by this book.

The anti-discrimination legislation focuses on certain specific and limited areas of activity, in particular that of employment. However, discrimination affects all areas of life and certain areas of law, especially of criminal law, may embody and reinforce it, subsisting alongside specific anti-discrimination laws in other spheres. Therefore, Chapter 17 goes on to consider the effect in this area of criminal law and the criminal process as positively or negatively influencing the achievement of substantive equality on certain grounds. Many aspects of discrimination on grounds of race have now, in a very significant reform, been brought within the race discrimination scheme by its amendment in 2000. The analysis of civil anti-discrimination legislation undertaken in Chapter 16 will focus on its efficacy in identifying, compensating for or preventing unjustifiable differentiation and this will also be the case in relation to the criminal law and the criminal justice system: consideration will be given to the role of the criminal law in preventing certain expressions of discrimination which are unaffected by the civil anti-discrimination legislation but which have a severe impact on the lives of certain groups, while the extent to which the criminal justice system positively seeks to eliminate discriminatory behaviour by those who administer it will be explored. However, the criminal law and the criminal justice system will also be considered in another light; it will be considered how far they may be said to contain provisions which themselves discriminate on the basis of morally irrelevant factors. Such provisions may be particularly significant, since they amount to a denial of moral autonomy and may also be said to signal the acceptance of some forms of discrimination as part of British culture.

CHAPTER 16

ANTI-DISCRIMINATION LEGISLATION

1 INTRODUCTION[1]

The discussion of anti-discrimination law in England and Wales below will show that a similar, but far from identical, model is used in respect of the protected grounds. It concentrates heavily on an individualistic remedial model, that is, one that relies on the aggrieved individual to seek a remedy. Obviously, this model is found throughout tort law but, in this instance, depending on trade union involvement, it may be especially indefensible since it may mean that a member of an already weak and disadvantaged group may find that their disadvantage is exacerbated by the process of bringing an action.[2] The significant differences between the schemes will be indicated, especially where they represent a weakness.

The model is, it is suggested, complex, tortuous and formalistic. Its expression in the various anti-discrimination measures also provides a protection against discrimination, which has often been found to be patchy, inconsistent and ineffective.[3] Nevertheless, it has also often been said that there is 'too much law' in this area. It is suggested that this is for two reasons. In the UK, there are three strands of law, deriving from the domestic schemes and those of the European Community and the European Convention on Human Rights. The Human Rights Act (HRA) has complicated the issue since it has introduced a form of anti-discrimination law into domestic law – Art 14 – but has given it a lesser status than has EC law. At the same time, at the international and domestic level, the Convention is a source of general principles for EC law. This complex web of law will soon affect a number of protected grounds.

The further reason for the over-abundance of law is that a struggle is evident at every point in the schemes to take account of the needs of employers and others, bearing in mind that the private sector is affected, while affording some recognition to the detriment that discrimination creates. Thus, measures have been carefully tempered by exception clauses, which have then in turn gathered complex legal accretions. In other words, there are strong indications, especially in the scheme relating to disability, of reluctant and timid reform. Nowhere is such reluctance more evident, it will be argued, than in relation to the nature of the remedies and their delivery.

---

1   Reading on race and sex discrimination: Gregory, J, *Sex, Race and the Law: Legislating for Equality*, 1987; Feldman, D, *Civil Liberties*, 1st edn, 1993, Chapter 18; Dine, J and Watt, B (eds), *Discrimination Law*, 1996; Palmer, *Discrimination at Work*, 3rd edn, 1996; McCrudden (ed), *Anti-Discrimination Law*, 1991; Hepple, B and Szyszczak, E (eds), *Discrimination and the Limits of the Law*, 1992; von Prondzynski, F and Richards, W, 'Tackling indirect discrimination' [1995] PL 117; Gardner, J, 'Discrimination as injustice' (1996) 16(3) OJLS 353; Clayton, R and Tomlinson, H, *The Law of Human Rights*, 2000, Chapter 17; McColgan, A, *Discrimination Law: Text, Cases and Materials*, 2000; Ewing, KD, Bradley, A and McColgan, A (eds), *Labour Law: Text and Materials*, 2001; Livingstone, S, 'Article 14 and the prevention of discrimination in the ECHR' (1997) EHRLR 25; Ewing, KD, 'The HRA and labour law' (1998) 27 ILJ 275; Deakin, S and Morris, J, *Labour Law*, 2nd edn, 1998, Chapter 6; Bindman, *Discrimination Law*, 2000; Hepple, B, Coussey, M and Choudhury, T, *Equality: A New Framework*, 2000.

2   See, especially, pp 1047–48, below.

3   See the criticisms in Hepple, Coussey and Choudhury, *op cit*, fn 1.

Nevertheless, the law acts as a symbolic affirmation of society's disapproval of discrimination and arguably provides a focus for challenge that, it is suggested, fuels determination to seek change rather than distracting attention away from more fruitful avenues.

Flawed as the schemes are, it will be found that they only apply arbitrarily to certain protected grounds. Others, including that of sexual orientation, are not yet within them, although attempts have been made through the courts to obtain legal recognition for such other grounds for discrimination. The net result is, this chapter will suggest, that a mass of complex and, in some respects, unsatisfactory law has gathered round certain protected grounds, while in respect of others the strong possibility of discrimination leads the individual concerned to seek to conceal the potential basis for discrimination from others, thereby in turn obscuring the true nature of the problem.

European Community law

Sex discrimination law in the UK cannot be studied without taking into account European Community law, which has been a highly significant influence (race discrimination provisions have also been influenced indirectly). Article 119 of the Treaty of Rome, which was signed by Britain in 1973, governs the principle of equal pay for equal work. It is now Art 141 of the EC Treaty. It is amplified by the Equal Pay Directive 75/117, while the Equal Treatment Directive 76/207 and the Pregnancy Directive 92/85 govern other aspects of sexual discrimination. Treaty Articles have both direct and horizontal effect and, therefore, Art 141 can be enforced in domestic courts against private and State bodies through the vehicle of the Equal Pay Act (below).[4] In other words, the provisions of the Act can be ignored or twisted out of their natural meaning in order to give effect to Art 141.[5] Directives, in contrast, only have vertical effect; they can, if sufficiently precise, clear and unconditional, be enforced against State bodies – emanations of the State.[6] Also, they can have indirect horizontal effect against private bodies through interpretation.[7] They can also by this means have indirect vertical effect (the interpretative obligation can be employed in an action in reliance on the domestic implementing legislation where the respondent is a State body).

There have been a number of significant recent developments.[8] Directive 97/80, the Burden of Proof Directive,[9] implemented in SI 2001/2660, affects the anti-sex discrimination scheme, as indicated below. The Race Directive,[10] extending beyond the employment field, which is to be implemented by July 2003, will bring race discrimination within the direct coverage of EC law for the first time. The Framework Directive[11] on equal opportunities in employment, adopted, like the Race Directive,

---

4   See *Biggs v Somerset CC* [1996] IRLR 203.
5   See *Worringham v Lloyds Bank plc* Case C-69/80 [1981] ECR 767; for the CA decision see [1982] IRLR 84.
6   See fn 13, below.
7   Through s 2(4) of the European Communities Act 1972.
8   For discussion, see Lord Lester of Herne Hill QC, 'New European equality measures' [2000] PL 562.
9   The Sex Discrimination (Indirect Discrimination and Burden of Proof) Regulations 2001, in force from 12 October 2001. For discussion, see Guild (2000) 29 ILJ 416.
10 Com 2000 328 (01), adopted in June 2000 by the Council of Ministers. The 'Race Directive' came into force on 19 July 2000 and has to be implemented by Member States within three years of this date (for comment, see Lord Lester of Herne Hill QC, *op cit*, fn 8).
11 Adopted under Art 13 of the Treaty Establishing the European Community (TEC).

under Art 13 of the EC Treaty,[12] will allow for the extension of anti-discrimination measures into new areas, in particular that of discrimination on grounds of sexual orientation. Thus, there is clear pressure emanating from the EC to develop a broad anti-discrimination programme domestically. The reforms could have two effects. First, the depth and impact of the current domestic provisions relating to discrimination on grounds of sex, gender reassignment, race and disability, could be strengthened. Second, the anti-discrimination programme is likely to broaden so that discrimination on new bases, in particular that of sexual orientation, but also that of transsexuality *per se*, is recognised within the law as unjustifiable.

The HRA and the European Convention on Human Rights

The EC provisions are in some respects more valuable than the guarantee of freedom from discrimination under Art 14 of the European Convention, partly because they may override domestic statutory provisions in domestic courts,[14] and partly because, as Chapter 2 explained, Art 14 only covers areas falling within the scope of the other Articles.[14] This limitation was highlighted in *Botta v Italy*.[5] The European Court of Human Rights considered a claim that the lack of disabled facilities at a seaside resort violated the applicant's right to equal enjoyment of his right to respect for private life under Art 8 read together with Art 14. The claim was rejected on the basis that 'social' rights, such as the participation of disabled people in recreational facilities, fall outside Art 8. Therefore, Art 14 did not apply.

Even where Art 14 may apply, Strasbourg has been very reluctant to afford it separate consideration, if a breach of another Convention right is established.[16] Where Art 14 has been considered, it has been afforded a narrow interpretation by the Commission. For example, in *Stedman v UK*[17] a requirement to work on a Sunday led to the dismissal of the applicant, who had religious objections to Sunday working. It was found by the Commission that a general requirement that has a disproportionate impact on one group is not discriminatory. This decision suggests that Art 14 does not recognise indirect discrimination and that, as Ewing puts it, 'the Convention rights can be qualified by contract'.[18] This does not mean, however, that Art 14 is of no value in this area. The Court may eventually adhere to a more developed conception of discrimination and may depart, as it has done in some other contexts, from the stance taken by the Commission.

---

12 For discussion of Art 13, which was added by the Amsterdam Treaty, see Bell [1999] 6 Maastricht J of European and Comp Law 5.

13 In general, EU directives are enforceable in national courts only against the State or against bodies under the control of the State (*Foster v British Gas plc* [1990] 3 All ER 897) but not against private bodies. However, it was found in *Francovich v Italy* [1992] 21 IRLR 84; [1991] ECR I-5357; [1995] ICR 722 that an individual who suffers loss at the hands of a private body owing to the State's failure to undertake full implementation of a directive may have a claim against the State. See further Ellis, E, *European Community Sex Equality Law*, 2nd edn, 1998, Chapter 4. For discussion of the influence of EU equality laws, see McCrudden (1993) 13 OJLS 320; Ellis [1994] 31 CMLR 43.

14 See Chapter 2, pp 85–86.

15 (1998) 26 EHRR 241.

16 See *Dudgeon v UK* (1982) 4 EHRR 149, para 69; discussed in Chapter 12, pp 738–39.

17 (1997) 23 EHRR CD 168.

18 Ewing, *op cit*, fn 1, p 288.

In *Schuler-Zgraggen v Switzerland*[19] the Court said: 'the advancement of the equality of the sexes is today a major goal in the Member States of the Council of Europe and very weighty reasons would have to be put forward before such a difference of treatment [as occurred in the instant case] could be regarded as compatible with the Convention.'[20] The Court has recognised that positive discrimination may be appropriate in some circumstances; it has said that the guarantee under Art 14 will be violated where persons in analogous situations are treated differently where there is no objective and reasonable justification, but also where States without such justification fail to treat differently persons whose situations are significantly different.[21]

Further, Art 14 covers discrimination on a wide range of bases and therefore, combined with Art 8 or, in some circumstances, Arts 9, 10 or 11 can be used to address discrimination that is currently outside the EC or domestic anti-discrimination schemes. For example, it can be used to attack discrimination on the grounds of sexual orientation or of religion, which are not covered under the schemes discussed below, or under the current EC schemes. It can also, very significantly, cover discrimination in contexts not covered by the domestic or EC schemes and can fill gaps in those schemes even within the contexts they do cover. But the HRA itself will curb the effect of the Convention since it only binds public authorities under s 6. Since it currently appears that the HRA does not create direct horizontal effect,[22] its impact in this area is subject to certain limitations.

If a public authority discriminates in a manner that could be addressed by Art 8 in conjunction with Art 14, or Art 8 alone, a free standing action could be brought against it under s 7(1)(a) of the HRA. If anti-discrimination measures are statutory, s 3 of the HRA applies if it appears that there is a potential conflict between the provisions and Arts 14 and 8. Since this area of law is largely (although not wholly) covered by statute, Art 14 may have quite a wide ranging indirect horizontal effect. As discussed below, this may open the possibility of bringing some forms of discrimination within the Sex Discrimination Act that are not currently covered by it. The problem is that the statutory scheme is limited to discrimination on certain grounds and it may not be possible to interpret the provisions widely enough to cover other forms of discrimination. But, by this route, it is possible that gaps in the statutory schemes, including the scheme relating to disability, could be narrowed.

Thus, unless the courts eventually take the view that they themselves, as public bodies, must seek to ensure that an applicant obtains his or her Convention rights, Arts 14 and another Article (usually Art 8) combined will not be directly justiciable against private bodies except as a matter of interpretation where a statute applies and s 3 of the HRA has an impact. It is hard to see that indirect horizontal effect could be created by seeking to develop the existing common law under the impetus of s 6 of the HRA[23] since

---

19   (1993) 16 EHRR 405, para 22; see also *Van Raalte v Netherlands* (1997) 24 EHRR 503, para 39.

20   See further Livingstone, *op cit*, fn 1; Ewing, *op cit*, fn 1, p 288; Clayton and Tomlinson, *op cit*, fn 1, Chapter 17.

21   *Thlimmenos v Greece*, Judgment of 6 April 2000.

22   See Chapter 4, pp 161–2 and Chapter 10, pp 542–43.

23   As occurred in *Douglas v Hello!* [2001] 2 WLR 992; see Chapter 10, pp 581–86.

the common law has failed so far to develop any anti-discrimination remedies. Thus, the potential of Art 14 domestically is doubly limited – first by its own inherent limitation, since it is non-free standing, and second by the lack of direct horizontal effect under the HRA. In general, therefore, it is not expected that at present the impact of the HRA in this context will be very great, although in respect of certain currently unprotected grounds it may be of great value, while it may also be valuable in extending the meaning of statutory provisions, by considering the effect of Arts 8 and 14 read together.

Where another Article and Art 14 combined cover the same area as EC provisions, they can be used as a source of general principles for the interpretation of the EC law, under Art 6 of the Treaty of Rome (now Art 13, as amended by the Amsterdam Treaty). The EC provisions can override domestic law and, therefore, by this means those Convention Articles could be given, in a sense, further effect than the HRA allows them to have. Thus, for example, an applicant bringing an action against a private body and seeking to rely on the Sex Discrimination Act in respect of discrimination on grounds of gender reassignment in a context excluded from the Act, could begin by arguing that s 3 of the HRA should be used to broaden the meaning of the Act in reliance on Arts 8 and 14. If this failed, on the basis that such an interpretation would amount to legislating, the applicant could rely on s 2(4) of the European Communities Act 1972[24] in arguing that the interpretation in question should be adopted in order to satisfy the demands of Equal Treatment Directive.[25] At that stage, in order to determine the requirements of the Directive, Strasbourg jurisprudence on Arts 8 and 14 could re-enter the argument. Once (and if) domestic measures are adopted in response to the Framework and Race Directives, this possibility may become even more significant.

As Chapter 2 explained, Protocol 12 provides a free standing right to freedom from discrimination.[26] Protocol 12 is evidence of a clear recognition of the weakness of the anti-discrimination measures under the Convention and its existence may perhaps prompt the European Court of Human Rights to move away from its previous stance under Art 14 in favour of a more developed and determined position on anti-discrimination, even prior to the ratification of Protocol 12. If Protocol 12 is ratified by the UK and then included in Sched 1 of the HRA, it will have a far reaching impact in this context, since a free standing right to non-discrimination on a wide range of grounds, including those of sexual orientation or religion, would then be created, which would have direct effect as against public authorities. It might also have an impact on the currently protected grounds since it could be relied upon in an attempt to extend or fill gaps in the legislation. Thus, it would create new rights against public authorities. At present, Protocol 12 has not been ratified and the Government is opposed to ratification.

---

24 See Chapter 3, p 130.
25 See p 989, below.
26 See p 85 for further discussion see Khaliq, V, 'Protocol 12 to the ECHR: a step forward or a step too far?' [2001] PL 457.

2 DOMESTIC ANTI-DISCRIMINATION MEASURES

The Sex Discrimination Act 1975[27]

At common law and under statute, women were historically subject to a number of legal disabilities, but the end of the 19th and the beginning of the 20th century saw the gradual removal of such disabilities by statute. Women obtained the right to sign contracts, to own property irrespective of their marital status, to vote and to stand for Parliament. The Sex Disqualification (Removal) Act 1919 removed any disqualification by way of sex or marriage for those who wished to exercise a public function, hold a civil or judicial office, enter any civil profession or vocation or be admitted to any incorporated society. However, the marriage bar continued to operate in many jobs until the Second World War.[28] Once these disabilities had been removed there was opposition to further legislation.[29] It was thought that the barriers preventing women entering public life were down and therefore further measures were unnecessary. However, the fact that women were, for the first time, able to enter the public domain did not mean that they were accepted there. Theoretically, women had the same opportunities as men but, in practice, since there were no formal barriers to discrimination by employers and others, these practices continued. It may be assumed that this was due in part to prejudice and in part to the operation of the market which had no interest in ensuring better treatment for a group of employees who could traditionally be treated badly. Employers openly paid the 'women's' rate for the job,[30] a lower rate than that for men, and openly refused to appoint women above a certain level or to do certain jobs.[31] Under the common law, it was immaterial that the grounds for such decisions might be capricious or reprehensible.

The view taken in the 1974 White Paper on Sex Discrimination preceding the 1975 Act was that women were being held back in employment and other fields because they were

---

27 General reading: Atkins and Hoggett, *Women and the Law*, 1984, pp 1–63 for background; Pannick, D, *Sex Discrimination Law*, 1985; Bourne, C and Whitmore, J, *Anti-discrimination Law in Britain*, 3rd edn, 1996; Townshend-Smith, R, *Sex Discrimination in Employment*, 1989; Honeyball, *Sex, Employment and the Law*, 1991; McCrudden, *op cit*, fn 1; Rhode, D, *Justice and Gender: Sex Discrimination and the Law*, 1989; Fenwick, H and Hervey, T, 'Sex equality in the Single Market: new directions for the European Court of Justice' [1995] 32 CMLR 443–70; Hervey, T, *Justifications for Sex Discrimination in Employment*, 1993; Ellis, 'The definition of discrimination in EC sex equality law' (1994) 19 EL Rev 563; Millar and Phillips, 'Evaluating anti-discrimination legislation in the UK: some issues and approaches' (1983) 11 Int J Soc Law 417; McGinley, 'Judicial approaches to sex discrimination in US and UK – a comparative study' (1986) 59 MLR 413, p 415; on pregnancy, see Conaghan (1993) 20 JLS 71. Current reading: Fredman, S, *Women and the Law*, 1997, esp Chapters 5, 7, 9; Deakin and Morris, *op cit*, fn 1, Chapter 6; von Prondzynski and Richards, *op cit*, fn 1; Barnard, C and Hepple, B, 'Substantive equality' (2000) 59(3) CLJ 562; Hepple, Coussey and Choudhury, *op cit*, fn 1; Clayton and Tomlinson, *op cit*, fn 1, Chapter 17; McColgan, *op cit*, fn 1; McGlynn, C, 'Reclaiming a feminist vision: the reconciliation of paid work and family life in EU law and policy' (2001) 7 Columbia Journal of European Law 241.

28 The 1919 Act was found to mean only that the employers must lift restrictions on women; it did not prevent particular employers imposing restrictions on women and it gave rise to no right of litigation: see *Price v Rhondda Urban Council* [1923] 2 Ch 372.

29 Atkins and Hoggett note the lack of parliamentary concern about women at work and failure to debate the problem: *op cit*, fn 27, p 19.

30 In 1970, women's average pay was 63.1% that of men (EOC, 1988b, p 45).

31 The study by National Segregation 1979 showed that by 1971, over half of all men were in occupations where they outnumbered women by at least 9 to 1 and 77% worked in occupations which were at least 70% male.

not being judged on their individual merits, but on the basis of a general presumption of inferiority. It was apparent that the common law was not going to bring about change, partly because the judiciary saw the creation of a comprehensive anti-discrimination code as the province of Parliament but also because, even in the 1970s, sympathy with discriminatory practices was evident among certain judges. In *Morris v Duke-Cohen*,[32] for example, a judge was prepared to find a solicitor negligent for taking advice from a wife when a husband was available, on the basis that a sensible wife would expect her husband to make the major decisions.

Formal and substantive equality

The legislation affords recognition to two competing views as to the most effective means of securing equality: the so called formal equality approach and the pluralist approach.[33] The former, which, as mentioned above, is based on classic liberalism and is the dominant approach, assumes that in a just society, the sex of a person would carry no expectations with it; it would be as irrelevant as their eye colour. It takes the view that women and men are equally able to take advantage of opportunities and that therefore, if a man would have been expected to satisfy the same conditions as the woman, no discrimination has occurred. Thus, once specific instances of differential treatment based on sex are prevented or addressed, women will no longer be placed at a disadvantage. The pluralist approach, on the other hand, which was imported from the US,[34] takes a number of factors, such as past discrimination or social conditioning, into account and asks whether policies and practices which are neutral on their face actually have an adverse impact on women owing to factors which particularly affect them. It accepts that there may be differences between the situations of men and women, but holds that penalties should not inevitably attach to the recognition of those differences. This approach derives from the Supreme Court decision in *Griggs v Duke Power Company*;[35] when the defendant company administered an aptitude test to all job applicants it was shown that significantly fewer blacks than whites passed the test and that the skills examined by the test were not particularly relevant to the jobs applied for. In these circumstances, it was held that the test was discriminatory.[36] In the context of sex discrimination, the use of aptitude or other tests would be unlikely to disadvantage women. But past discriminatory practices – although their effects are becoming less apparent – might do so,[37] as might the effect of caring responsibilities: for example, currently more women than men are single parents.

The two methods of securing equality embodied in the legislation – the individual approach and the general administrative approach – need not entirely be considered in isolation from each other. The weakness of the first is that specific instances of

---

32 (1975) 120 SJ 826.

33 See Gardner (1989) 9 OJLS 1 and Brest (1976) 90 Harv LR 1 on the different philosophies apparent in the legislation.

34 For a comparative discussion of the approaches to UK and US discrimination, see McGinley, *op cit*, fn 27.

35 (1971) 401 US 424.

36 For further discussion in the US context see Wilborn, 'The disparate impact model of discrimination: theory and limits' (1985) 34 American University L Rev 799.

37 See *Steel v Post Office* [1977] IRLR 288.

discrimination may be addressed only if the individual concerned is prepared to take on the burden of a legal action. Such an approach is clearly only capable of bringing about slow and piecemeal change, especially as the two parties concerned – usually the woman and her employer – are clearly not confronting each other on equal terms; the lack of legal aid exacerbates this situation. However, apart from bringing about general change by addressing itself to institutionalised discrimination, the administrative body created by the legislation can aid the individual and can undertake the investigation triggered off by an individual action.

Field of Application of the Sex Discrimination Act

The Sex Discrimination Act 1975 (SDA) covers discrimination on a number of protected grounds: of sex, of marital status and of gender reassignment. The protection on grounds of sex applies equally to men. Section 3 covers discrimination on the grounds of marital status, but in this instance the comparison is between a single person and a married person of the same sex. The provision against marital discrimination is more circumscribed: it is confined to the employment field only and discrimination on the grounds of divorce or of being unmarried is not covered. Section 2A, which now prohibits discrimination on grounds of gender reassignment, is even more circumscribed; it only covers direct (not indirect) discrimination in employment and training and in relation to barristers (in Scotland, advocates). Pay-related discrimination on this ground is dealt with under the SDA, although such discrimination on grounds of sex is dealt with in the Equal Pay Act 1970 (EPA). In other words, the SDA covers only the non-pay-related aspects of employment discrimination on grounds of sex – the pay-related aspects fall within the EPA. As will be seen, this separation has added to the complexity of the substantive law, although the two statutes are intended to work together as a complete code.

The Act does not make discrimination on the three protected grounds generally illegal; it only outlaws it in the contexts in which it operates. Thus, a two-stage approach has been created; first, discrimination must be shown, and then that it falls within one of the contexts covered by the Act. The contexts are: employment (s 6), education (s 22) and the provision of goods and services (s 29). Section 29 was found to have a narrow application to public bodies by the House of Lords in *Amin*.[38] A number of public functions, including policing decisions, were excluded.

The prohibition of discrimination on grounds of gender reassignment arose from the findings of the ECJ in Case 13/14 *P v S and Cornwall CC*.[39] P had been dismissed from her employment on the ground that she was a transsexual. Her application under the Sex Discrimination Act failed as it was found that transsexuals were outside the terms of the Act. It was argued in the European Court of Justice that her case fell within the Equal Treatment Directive. The decision of the European Court of Human Rights in *Rees v UK*[40] was relied upon by the European Court of Justice in deciding that transsexuals fall within the Directive. This was found on the basis that the Directive is simply the expression of

---

38 [1983] 2 AC 818 HL. The decision partly relied on interpreting RRA 1976, s 75 as intended to limit the application of the Act in respect of public authorities.

39 Judgment of 30 April 1996; [1996] ECR I-2143; [1996] IRLR 347.

40 (1986) 9 EHRR 56.

the principle of equality, which is one of the fundamental principles of European Union law. It was found that where a person is dismissed on the basis that they have undergone or are about to undergo gender reassignment, he or she is being discriminated against in comparison with persons of the sex to which he or she was deemed to belong before undergoing gender reassignment. This ruling was given domestic effect in the Sex Discrimination (Gender Reassignment) Regulations 1999, which brought direct discrimination on grounds of gender reassignment within the SDA 1975 by introducing s 2A.[41]

However, the domestic implementation may be inadequate. In particular, the exclusion of indirect discrimination may mean that s 2A does not do enough to comply with the Equal Treatment Directive. As indicated above, an argument that the provisions of the SDA should be extended by purposive interpretation in order to comply with the Directive could be strengthened by taking account both of s 3 of the HRA and of the general requirement under EC law to use the Convention as a source of general principle. Further, since Directives have vertical effect, they can, if sufficiently precise, clear and unconditional, be enforced against State bodies – emanations of the State. Thus, if necessary, a claim for indirect discrimination on this ground could be brought against such a body relying only on the Directive.

Discrimination on grounds of race[42]

It was apparent that the common law would not provide a sufficient remedy for racial discrimination. For example, in *Constantine v Imperial Hotels*[43] nominal damages only were awarded in respect of clear racial discrimination although the applicant had attempted to claim exemplary damages. However, the discriminatory effect of a contract or covenant could be taken into account by a court as a matter of public policy in reaching a decision,[44] while discriminatory words contained in a trust might, under certain circumstances, be struck out, although the courts have tended to be reluctant to do this.[45] The discriminatory nature of foreign legislation might also be considered in determining its impact,[46] and this possibility still exists, although it is not of great significance. There

---

41 SI 1999/1102; see the Government's Consultation Paper *Legislation Regarding Discrimination on Grounds of Transsexualism in Employment*; for discussion see McColgan, *op cit*, fn 1, pp 382–86 and see further Griffiths, E (1999) J Civ Lib, July, p 230.

42 General reading: Bailey, SH, Harris, DJ and Jones, BL, *Civil Liberties: Cases and Materials*, 4th edn, 1995, Chapter 10; Lustgarten, L, *The Legal Control of Racial Discrimination*, 1980; Gregory, *op cit*, fn 1; Bourne, C and Whitmore, J, *Race and Sex Discrimination*, 1993; Feldman, *op cit*, fn 1, pp 874–79; Lustgarten, L, 'Racial inequality and the limits of law' (1986) 49 MLR 68–85; Bindman, 'Reforming the Race Relations Act' (1985) 135 NLJ 1136–38 and 1167–69; Clayton and Tomlinson, *op cit*, fn 1, Chapter 17; McColgan, *op cit*, fn 1; Millar and Phillips, *op cit*, fn 27; Deakin and Morris, *op cit*, fn 1, Chapter 6; von Prondzynski and Richards, *op cit*, fn 1; Barnard and Hepple, *op cit*, fn 27; Hepple, Coussey and Choudhury, *op cit*, fn 1.

43 [1944] KB 693.

44 On public policy at common law see Cretney (1968) 118 NLJ 1094; Garner (1972) 35 MLR 478.

45 *Re Lysaght* [1966] Ch 191 (in order to qualify for a scholarship under the trust a student had to be male, British and could not be Catholic or Jewish; this was not found contrary to public policy, but as the college which was to be a trustee refused to discriminate on religious grounds, those words were struck out); for comment see (1966) 82 LQR 10.

46 See *Oppenheimer v Cattermole* [1975] 2 WLR 347.

seemed to be a clear need for further measures and, therefore, the first Race Relations Act (RRA) was passed in 1965, although it was soon superseded by the 1968 Act and then by the 1976 Act. The 1976 Act is much more far reaching than its predecessors; under the 1968 Act, an individual had to complain to the Race Relations Board rather than take the complaint to court. The 1976 Act was modelled on the Sex Discrimination Act; it makes discrimination a statutory tort, follows the same pattern as regards direct and indirect discrimination and sets up the Commission for Racial Equality with a similar role to the Equal Opportunities Commission,[47] set up under the 1975 Act. It also operated initially in the same contexts and uses the same terms; therefore, decisions under one of the two statutes affect the other. The Act provides a remedy for direct or indirect discrimination on the grounds of colour, race, nationality or ethnic or national origins.

The discrimination must occur within the areas covered by the Act: employment, education, housing or the provision of goods and services. Section 20 of the RRA, which covers the provision of goods and services, was found to have a narrow application to public functions owing to the decision in *Amin*.[48] Thus, areas of governmental activity were excluded from the ambit of the Act. The prison service was not covered, nor were a number of police activities such as exercising stop and search powers or investigating offences. Thus the RRA, like the SDA, had an inconsistent and arbitrary application to the police. Until its amendment in 2000, the RRA could not be used to challenge allegedly discriminatory practices in the criminal justice system except in the sphere it covered, including employment. Thus, for example, racial discrimination in a prison resulting in refusal of employment would be covered,[49] but other discriminatory practices within the criminal justice system, such as racially discriminatory arrests or stops and searches, fell outside the Act.

However, the decision in *Farah v Comr of Police of the Metropolis*[50] made it clear that racial bias in policing decisions will fall within the Act although, importantly, it did not create vicarious liability in respect of such decisions. Farah, a Somali citizen and refugee who was 17 at the time, was attacked by a group of white teenagers who set a dog on her and injured her. She summoned police help by telephone; when the police arrived, they made no attempt to arrest her attackers, but arrested her and charged her with affray, assault and causing unnecessary suffering to a dog. No evidence was offered when she appeared to answer the charges, and she was acquitted. She brought an action for damages against the Commissioner of Police of the Metropolis, alleging false imprisonment, assault and battery and malicious prosecution. She included in the statement of claim an allegation that the conduct of the police officers amounted to unlawful racial discrimination. Judge Harris refused to strike out the allegation of racial discrimination. He also allowed her to amend that part of her claim, so that she alleged that the officers were acting as the commissioner's agents and had discriminated against her on grounds of race in both failing to afford her the protection which would have been afforded to white victims of crime and in bringing the proceedings against her. The

---

47 See below, pp 1049–52 for consideration of the role of both bodies.

48 [1983] 2 AC 818 HL. The decision partly relied on interpreting RRA 1976, s 75 as intended to limit the application of the Act in respect of public authorities.

49 RRA 1976, Part II; in *Alexander v Home Office* [1988] 1 WLR 968, CA (the plaintiff, a prisoner, was refused work in prison kitchen owing to racial stereotyping).

50 [1997] 1 All ER 289.

commissioner appealed against the refusal to strike out the allegation of racial discrimination.

The Court of Appeal found that two important issues fell to be determined. First, whether a police officer came within s 20 of the RRA 1976, which prohibits racial discrimination in the provision of services and, secondly, if he did, whether his Chief Officer of Police would be answerable in law for any breaches of the Act he might have committed. The court held that an officer providing protection to a citizen was providing a service within the section. Policy reasons against such a conclusion, including the possibility that the police would have to face numerous claims of race discrimination, were rejected as outweighed by the need to provide a remedy for a citizen who had suffered discrimination in a situation where she was in dire need of protection. Moreover, nothing in the Act made police officers immune from claims of racial discrimination. However, the court found that the Commissioner was not vicariously liable for the acts of the officers. Section 53 appeared to deny vicarious liability except in so far as provided for by the Act. Her claim against the individual officers for discrimination was out of time. The appeal was allowed and therefore her claim of discrimination had to be struck from the statement of claim. This decision was to be welcomed as making it clear that the possibility of compensation for racially discriminatory police actions and decisions was available. However, it also hedged this possibility around with restrictions, since it denied the possibility of vicarious liability.

However, after amendment by the Race Relations (Amendment) Act 2000 (which inserted s 19B into the 1976 Act), discrimination (direct or indirect) by a public authority in carrying out its functions is brought within the ambit of the Act. This amendment of the RRA was effected to implement Recommendation No 11 of the MacPherson Report into the death of Stephen Lawrence,[51] after the MacPherson inquiry found 'institutional racism' in the Metropolitan Police, which had resulted in significant failures in the investigation of his death at the hands of racists. The term 'public authority' is to be interpreted consistently (although not identically) with the interpretation afforded to the same term under the HRA.[52] Law enforcement by public authorities is now brought within the statutory framework for the prohibition of discrimination, thus closing the gap that was dramatically and disturbingly highlighted by the Stephen Lawrence case. Thus, the actions of the police in investigating crime are now covered by the RRA, as are other functions of public authorities. Section 4 of the 2000 Act inserts ss 76A and B into the RRA, providing that chief officers of police will be vicariously liable for the actions of their officers.

However, there are still exceptions to the coverage of the Act, created by the amendments. Section 19D exempts 'any act done for the purpose of making a decision about instituting criminal proceedings'. This formulation leaves open the possibility that acts remote from that decision, including the uncovering of evidence, are covered by the RRA.

The amendments to the RRA now represent one of a number of important differences between the statutory scheme covering discrimination on grounds of sex and that

---

51 Cm 4262-I. For discussion of the amendments, see O'Cinneide, C, 'The Race Relations (Amendment) Act 2000' [2001] PL 220.

52 See Chapter 4, pp 157–61.

covering the ground of race. The RRA creates the most comprehensive domestic scheme that this chapter considers since the provisions under the RRA outlawing discrimination in private clubs of 25 members or more, segregation and 'transferred discrimination' – discrimination on the grounds of another's race – have no counterparts under the SDA. The 'functions of a public authority' head is not replicated in the SDA. Employment covers 'pay', thus ensuring a less complex scheme than that applying in respect of sex discrimination claims. The influence of the EU is less important, although rulings of the European Court of Justice and of the domestic courts taking EU provisions into account affect concepts under the RRA. It should be noted that the EU has not ignored race discrimination and has passed a number of resolutions and declarations giving guidance to Member States,[53] but its influence in this area, although beginning to develop, is at a much earlier stage than its influence on sex discrimination. As indicated above, the Race Directive will bring race discrimination directly within the ambit of EU law. And aside from EU provisions, the UK is a party to a number of international declarations on race discrimination and xenophobia which, although not part of UK law, may influence it.[54]

The Disability Discrimination Act 1995[55]

The Disability Discrimination Act 1995 (DDA) is modelled to an extent on the SDA and RRA schemes; the DDA adopted the concepts of direct discrimination and victimisation used in the SDA and RRA and a body was set up to promote and monitor the scheme, although it initially had an advisory role only. But the DDA scheme differs in some important respects from the earlier schemes. In general, it is narrower in scope than the earlier legislation, in terms both of its application and of the forms of discrimination covered. Originally, the Act only applied to employers who employ more than 20 people. It is now applicable to those employing more than 15 (s 7(1)).[56] Thus, many small businesses will still fall outside its scope. Most significantly, the Act does not import the concept of indirect discrimination in its full sense, although, as indicated below, the concept of direct discrimination is broader than that used in the SDA and RRA. Also, direct discrimination can be justified; this is understandable, within limits, in this context. Unlike the provisions against race and sex discrimination, the Act is incomplete – it relies on being fleshed out by non-statutory rules.[57] Under one of the more significant SIs, tribunals are bound to take into account the Disability Discrimination Code of Practice, which came into force in December 1996.[58]

---

53 See Resolutions, Reports and Declarations of the Council of the EC: Resolution of 16 July 1985 (OJ C186 26.7.85, p 3); Declaration of 11 June 1986 (OJ C158 25.6.86, p 1); Resolution of 24 May 1988 (OJ C177 6.7.88, p 5); Council Decision 88/348/EEC (OJ L158 25.6.88); Eurigenis Report 1991. For criticism of the EU stance on racism, see Bindman (1994) 144 NLJ 352; see also Lester, *op cit*, fn 8.

54 European Convention on Human Rights, Arts 3 and 14; International Labour Organisation; International Covenant on Civil and Political Rights; the International Covenant on Economic, Social and Cultural Rights, para 2; International Convention on the Elimination of All Forms of Racial Discrimination.

55 For discussion, see McColgan, *op cit*, fn 1, Chapter 8; 'Interpreting the Disability Discrimination Act (1998) 80 EOR 14; Doyle, B, 'Enabling legislation or dissembling law? The DDA 1995' (2001) 64 MLR 7; *Butterworth's Discrimination Law Handbook*, 2000; Clayton and Tomlinson, *op cit*, fn 1, pp 1230–33.

56 By 2004, this figure is to be reduced to apply to employers who employ more than two employees.

57 See SI 1996/1996; SI 1996/2793; SI 1996/1836.

58 Under SI 1996/1996.

The Act adopts what may be termed a 'medical' as opposed to a 'social' model of discrimination. Under a medical model, the impairment is located in the person in question; he or she must claim to be significantly impaired in his or her ability to perform certain tasks in order to come within the scope of the legislation. Under a social model, the impairment depends on the attitudes of others as reflected in the arrangements for, for example, access to buildings. Thus, a person who has, for example, muscular dystrophy and has as a result significant mobility difficulties might well have no difficulty in performing a managerial job which depends on skills unrelated to mobility, so long as no obstacles are placed in her way in the form, for example, of steps which make it difficult for her to enter her own workplace. If a lift or other means of access were provided, she would not be impaired in her ability to perform the job. Thus, the impact of her disability would be determined by social factors such as the willingness of the management to install a lift, rather than by the inherent nature of her disability.

Field of application

The DDA 1995 does not make discrimination on the ground of disability generally illegal; as with the sex and race legislation, it only outlaws it in the contexts in which it operates: employment (Part II), disposal of premises (s 22) and the provision of goods and services (s 19). The Act was also amended and extended by the Special Education Needs and Disability Act 2001 to place duties on schools and on the providers of post-16 education and related services. The Act applies to all employers who have 15 or more employees, but it excludes a number of occupations, including the police, firefighters, barristers, prison officers, the armed forces, and those working on ships or aircraft.[59] Unlike the provisions in respect of employment, which do not apply at present to businesses with fewer than 15 staff, the service provisions apply across the board. These provisions require traders not to refuse service to disabled people or to offer an inferior service. The Special Education Needs and Disability Act 2001, which adds s 28A to the DDA, covering schools, and s 28R covering further and higher education, leaves the full field of application to orders made by the Secretary of State in respect of coverage of certain educational institutions under s 28R(6)(c) and in respect of the services covered within schools under s 28A(3).

The Act creates complex definitions as to those who are covered by it. Under s 1(1) the person concerned must have 'a physical or mental impairment which has a substantial and long term adverse effect on his ability to carry out normal day to day activities'. The definition includes within its scope progressive diseases such as multiple sclerosis or forms of dystrophy which may not currently be of great significance in terms of impairment, but are likely to become so. The DDA also covers those who have had a disability in the past, whether or not they have recovered (s 2(1)). Thus a three stage approach has been created; first it must be shown that the applicant is 'disabled' within the definition, then discrimination must be shown, and then that it falls within one of the contexts covered by the Act. Further, as discussed below,[60] a duty of adjustment is placed on various bodies under the Act.

---

59 See below for consideration of certain exclusions.
60 See pp 1043–45.

Coming into force in stages

The employment-related provisions came into force in December 1996. The first part of Part III of the Act, the provision of access to goods, facilities and services, also came into force in December 1996. The second part of Part III of the Act, the duty to make reasonable adjustments in the context of the provision of access to goods, facilities and services, did not come into force until 1 October 1999. The third stage of Part III will not come into force until 2004 and will require traders to make physical alterations to premises to facilitate equal service, typically by installing lifts or ramps. The provisions regarding education added to the DDA in 2001 will come into force as appointed by the Secretary of State.

3 DIRECT DISCRIMINATION ON GROUNDS OF SEX, MARITAL STATUS, GENDER REASSIGNMENT, RACE OR DISABILITY

Sex discrimination

The concept of direct discrimination on grounds of sex governed by s 1(1)(a) of the Sex Discrimination Act 1975 embodies the formal equality approach. It involves showing that the applicant has been less favourably treated than a man has been or would be treated. There is little guidance in the Act as to the basis for comparison; s 5(3) merely provides that there must be no material difference between the situations of the man and the woman. Thus, the comparison is between a woman and a comparable man. It should be noted that it is possible for the applicant to compare herself with a hypothetical man; the issue is not whether a man or a woman receives a benefit, but whether the woman would have been better treated if she had been a man.

The test can be broken down into three stages. First, the woman must show that there has been differentiation in the treatment afforded to herself and a man (or a hypothetical man). Motive is irrelevant; the question at this stage is merely whether a woman has been treated one way and a man another. Secondly, she must show that her treatment has been less favourable and thirdly, following the ruling of the House of Lords in *James v Eastleigh BC*,[61] that there is a causal relationship between her sex and the treatment; in other words that but for her sex, she would have been treated as favourably as a man was or would have been. Following *Birmingham CC ex p EOC*[62] it is not necessary to show that the less favourable treatment is accorded through an intention to discriminate: motive is irrelevant.

The plaintiff bears the burden of showing that the differential treatment was on grounds of sex and not for some neutral reason. She is always likely to find difficulty in discharging this burden of proof, as the ruling in *Saunders v Richmond-upon-Thames LBC*[63] suggests. The applicant applied for a job as a golf professional and was asked questions at

---

61 [1990] AC 751; [1990] 2 All ER 607; [1989] IRLR 318; [1989] 3 WLR 122; the 'but for' test applied in James was put forward by Lord Goff in the House of Lords in *Birmingham CC ex p EOC* (1989) 18 ILJ 247; for comment, see Ellis (1989) 52 MLR 710.

62 [1989] AC 1155; [1989] 1 All ER 769.

63 [1978] IRLR 362.

the interview which were *prima facie* discriminatory. She was asked, for example, whether she thought she would be able to control unruly male players and whether she considered the job unglamorous. She was not appointed, although she was somewhat better qualified than the man who was. The Employment Appeal Tribunal (EAT) held that had her qualifications been substantially better than those of the appointee, that would have raised a *prima facie* inference of discrimination which the employer would have had to rebut by giving a satisfactory explanation. It was found that the nature of the questions, taking all the circumstances into account, did not of themselves raise a sufficient inference.

In *Khanna v MOD*[64] it was found that the evidential burden would shift only when the evidence was all on one side, but this was clarified by the finding in *Dornan v Belfast CC*[65] that once the woman has raised a *prima facie* inference of discrimination, the burden will shift to the employer to show that the differentiation occurred on non-discriminatory grounds. In other words, although the plaintiff began the case bearing the burden of proof, it might shift to the defendant once a certain stage is reached. Thus, the formal burden of proof remained on the plaintiff, but once it appeared that a minimum threshold of proof of discrimination is established, the burden shifted to the defendant. Now, under the Sex Discrimination (Indirect Discrimination and Burden of Proof) Regulations 2001 the complainant need not prove her case, merely the facts of the case, from which the court of tribunal should draw inferences of discrimination if the employer does not provide a satisfactory explanation.[66]

Dismissals and other detrimental action on the ground of pregnancy might appear to be discriminatory, but the wording of s 1(1) may not allow such action to fall readily within the scope of direct discrimination because in making the comparison between a woman and a man it is required under s 5(3) that 'the relevant circumstances in the one case are the same or not materially different in the other'. Dismissal on grounds of pregnancy was covered by s 60 of the Employment Protection (Consolidation) Act 1978, which provided that if a woman were dismissed because she was pregnant then the dismissal was automatically unfair, but in order to rely on this an employee had to have been employed for two years; where this was not the case, the employee had to seek to show that the 1975 Act applied. Pregnancy dismissals were regulated from October 1994 by ss 23–25 and Scheds 2 and 3 of the Trade Union Reform and Employment Rights Act (TURERA) 1993,[67] and now are regulated by s 99 of the Employment Rights Act 1996. Under s 99, such dismissal will be unfair from the date on which employment begins. Further, under s 47C of the 1996 Act, as amended by the Employment Relations Act 1999, an employee has the right not to be subjected to a detriment done for a prescribed reason. Such reason is prescribed by regulations made by the Secretary of State and relates to pregnancy, maternity, childbirth, and maternity leave.

Since pregnancy dismissals were therefore only recently addressed under other legislation, applicants sought to rely on the SDA.[68] The decisions discussed below could now be relied upon in an action in which it was argued that other employment discrimination based on maternity had arisen. Section 47 of the 1996 Act would provide a

---

64   [1981] ICR 653, EAT.

65   [1990] IRLR 179. See, further [1990] IRLR 161.

66   See fn 9, above. The Regulations came into force on 12 October 2001.

67   The TURERA sections mentioned implemented the EC Pregnancy Directive 92/85.

68   See Fredman, S, 'A difference with distinction: pregnancy and parenthood re-assessed' (1994) 110 LQR 106.

further possible argument in such circumstances. A pregnancy dismissal was at issue in *Turley v Allders*;[69] since the applicant did not have the requisite period of continuous employment, she sought to rely on the SDA. The EAT held that there was no male equivalent to a pregnant woman and therefore, as no comparison could be made, the action must fail. However, a method of making the comparison was found in a later EAT decision, *Hayes v Malleable WMC*;[70] it was found that it could be made between a pregnant woman and a man with a long term health problem. Thus, it would be direct discrimination if a woman was dismissed on grounds of pregnancy where a man needing the same period of absence through illness would not have been dismissed. This analogy has not been well received;[71] it has been pointed out that pregnancy is a healthy, normal state, not an illness;[72] moreover, it may be planned, unlike an unexpected illness, and in any event there will normally be far more notice before the absence takes place than there would be in a case of illness. Commentators have found the comparison between a pregnant woman and a diseased man inherently distasteful. It is also highly disadvantageous to women, a very high percentage of whom may become pregnant at some time during their working life and in particular between the ages of 20 and 35 (the time when women are most likely to become pregnant), while the percentage of men likely to take around two or more months off work during those years owing to an illness or accident is likely to be far lower.

The *Hayes* approach will no longer be followed after certain decisions of the European Court of Justice. In *Dekker v VJV Centrum*[73] the court found that a woman who was not appointed to a post because she was pregnant at the time of the interview, although she was considered to be the best candidate, was the victim of direct discrimination. *Webb v Emo Air Cargo (UK) Ltd*[74] concerned the dismissal of the claimant after it was found that she was pregnant. She had been recruited to replace an employee going on maternity leave, but had then discovered herself to be pregnant and therefore (it seemed) unavailable for duties in the period required. The question was whether her dismissal constituted direct discrimination within the terms of s 1(1)(a) of the Sex Discrimination Act 1975, in the light of Community law. The Court of Appeal continued the *Hayes* approach in determining that if a man with a medical condition as nearly comparable as possible (with the same practical effect upon availability to do the job) with pregnancy would also have been dismissed, then the dismissal of the woman was not sex discrimination. Thus, the plaintiff who was, owing to pregnancy, unavailable for duties in the period required, could be dismissed without infringing the SDA because a diseased man who was similarly unavailable at the relevant time would also have been dismissed. The argument was therefore rejected that since only a woman can be pregnant, it followed that a woman who is dismissed for any reason related to her pregnancy is dismissed because of her sex and thus discriminated against. The House of Lords favoured the approach of the Court of Appeal, but since it considered that the relevant

---

69   [1980] ICR 66.

70   [1985] ICR 703. See also *Brown v Rentokil Ltd* [1992] IRLR 302; *Shomer v B and R Residential Lettings Ltd* [1992] IRLR 317. It may be noted that dismissal on grounds of pregnancy seems to be increasing. The EOC cited a number of such instances in its 1991 report.

71   See *Proposals of the Equal Opportunities Commission: Equal Treatment for Men and Women*, 1988, Chapter 2.

72   Lacey (1987) 14 JLS 411, p 417.

73   [1991] IRLR 27; [1990] ECR I-3941.

74   [1993] 1 WLR 49, HL; [1992] 1 CMLR 793, CA.

rulings of the European Court of Justice did not indicate clearly whether the dismissal would be regarded as based on pregnancy or on unavailability at the relevant time, it referred the following question to the court:

> Is it discrimination on grounds of sex contrary to the Equal Treatment Directive for an employer to dismiss a female employee:
>
> (a) whom it engaged for the specific purpose of replacing another female employee during the latter's forthcoming maternity leave,
>
> (b) when very shortly after appointment the employer discovers that the appellant herself will be absent on maternity leave during the maternity period of the other employee and the employer dismisses her because it needs the jobholder to be at work during that period, and
>
> (c) had the employer known of the pregnancy of the appellant at the date of appointment she would not have been appointed, and
>
> (d) the employer would similarly have dismissed a male employee engaged for this purpose who required leave of absence at the relevant time for medical or other reasons?

The European Court of Justice found that the plaintiff should not be compared with a man unavailable for work for medical or other reasons, since pregnancy is not in any way comparable with pathological conditions. The court then found that, since the plaintiff had been employed permanently, her dismissal could not be justified on the ground of inability to fulfil a fundamental condition of her employment contract because her inability to perform the work was purely temporary. In other words, it could not be said that she had been taken on solely to cover a maternity leave. The court further found that the protection of Community law for pregnant women could not be dependent on the question whether the woman's presence at work during the maternity leave period is essential to the undertaking in which she is employed. Thus, dismissal of the plaintiff clearly constituted sex discrimination, contrary to the Equal Treatment Directive. (When the House of Lords reconsidered the case in the light of these findings, it allowed the appeal and remitted the case to the IT to consider the award of compensation to the applicant (*Webb (No 2)*).[75]

In a similar decision, *Habermann-Beltermann*,[76] rather than relying directly upon unavailability, the employer sought to rely upon the statutory exclusion (with criminal sanctions)[77] of pregnant women from night work, which 'caused' Habermann-Beltermann's temporary unavailability for work. The court's decision that the statute could not justify Habermann-Beltermann's dismissal, or the termination of her contract, reflects a refusal to focus upon a male norm or to pander to the argument that the continuation of the employment relationship in such circumstances produces undue financial burdens upon the employer.[78] However, in both *Habermann-Beltermann* and

---

75 [1994] QB 718; [1994] 4 All ER 115; [1994] 3 WLR 941. *Webb* was applied in *O'Neill* (1996) *The Times*, 7 June in relation to a pregnancy dismissal. Following *Webb*, the dismissal was found to be unlawful.

76 [1994] ECR I-1657.

77 The German *Mütterschutzgesetz* (MSchG), para 8(1), which prohibits the employment of pregnant or breast-feeding women on night work.

78 See the Opinion of the Advocate General, para 16.

Webb, the court refused to confront clearly the question whether any adverse treatment of women connected with pregnancy amounts to sex discrimination. In both judgments, the crucial fact upon which the court relied was that the employment contracts in question were of a permanent and not fixed term nature. The decision of the court in both cases was based upon the mismatch between the period for which the employee would be unavailable and the period for which she had been employed (indefinitely). This was a very significant development from the stark statement of principle in *Dekker.* The court's conclusion that the termination of Habermann-Beltermann's contract was not 'on the ground of pregnancy' but by reason of the statutory provision in the MSchG, opens the door to a narrower interpretation of the *Dekker* ruling than that ruling seemed at first to promise.[79] The result was that the court, unlike the Advocate General,[80] was able to avoid making explicit the point that a justification based on availability, with reference to market cost to the employer, would be by definition excluded in a case of direct discrimination on grounds of pregnancy, thereby, by implication, leaving it open in future cases.

Likewise, the ruling in *Webb* is not ultimately fully supportive of substantive equality since it leaves open the possibility of an apparently neutral explanation for pregnancy dismissals: that a pregnant woman recruited on a temporary basis may justifiably be dismissed if unable through unavailability to fulfil the purpose for which she was recruited. The argument is therefore left open that if a temporarily employed man or hypothetical man would have been dismissed, if unable through unavailability to satisfy a purpose for which he was employed, a woman so unavailable through pregnancy, who has been dismissed, has not been discriminated against. Therefore, by the recruitment of temporary staff, the employer can safeguard its market position. Elements of the ruling, however, suggest a desire to go further and it is in this sense internally inconsistent: it asserts that in general, to dismiss a pregnant woman through unavailability at a time when she is essential to a purpose of the undertaking can never be justifiable, but it leaves open the possibility that the employer can do just that so long as she was recruited on a temporary basis specifically for that purpose.

Thus, both judgments impliedly accept that adverse treatment flowing from pregnancy is susceptible to justification. Therefore, an employer may be able to contend successfully that not only market costs associated with unavailability but also other costs arising from pregnancy,[81] not the pregnancy itself, were the 'cause' of the dismissal of a pregnant woman. It is even possible that such an argument could be used in relation to a *permanently* employed woman, since the court's mismatch argument is not so readily applicable to a justification based on the other costs associated with pregnancy. This is not to contend that the court would necessarily accept such assertions by employers, merely to note that, in principle, the judgments leave open these possibilities. The effect of the

---

79 This part of *Habermann-Beltermann* is similar to the court's ruling in *Hertz* that dismissal through absences caused by illness, where those absences arise outside the protected period of maternity leave, is permissible, even where the illness is pregnancy-related. See Shaw, J, 'Pregnancy discrimination in sex discrimination' (1991) 16 EL Rev 313–20.

80 Opinion of the Advocate General, para 16.

81 Eg, adjustment of working conditions, time off for ante-natal examinations, removal of hazardous substances from the working environment or other measures of special protection for pregnant workers required, eg, by the Pregnancy and Maternity Directive, Council Directive 92/85/EEC.

judgments may be to disadvantage women doubly: they may have to take the risk that they will have no remedy if employed on a temporary basis, but dismissed for reasons connected with pregnancy,[82] and they may tend to find that they are more likely to be offered temporary contracts, thereby undermining their bargaining power in the market still further.

In both judgments, the court could have rejected a formal equality interpretation of the legislation in favour of completely excluding the use of unavailability through pregnancy or the cost of pregnancy as a justification,[83] thereby affording recognition to the real situation of women. In support of this, it should be pointed out that the real situation of women which may mean that they are unavailable for work for a period is only biologically determined in so far as the bearing of children is concerned; in terms of caring for children, it is legally and socially determined. The legal and social factors in question which found the perception that pregnancy, maternity leave and child care are to be viewed as one single indivisible burden to be shouldered by women alone, arise, it is submitted, from a sexually stereotyped view of the child care responsibilities of males and females. Thus, unavailability for work arising, or apparently arising,[84] from pregnancy, maternity leave and child care is not a sex neutral justification for adverse treatment.

At the least, the court could have achieved a compromise somewhat more satisfactory in terms of promotion of substantive equality than the one it does achieve, by framing its judgment in terms of the proportion of the period for which the woman was employed during which she would be unavailable. Thus, a woman employed, for example, on a temporary three year contract in order to fulfil a particular purpose who would be unavailable for three months on maternity leave and therefore unable to fulfil it would be said nevertheless to be available for a substantial part of the period. Instead, the court chose to confine its ruling to those employed for an indefinite period.

As indicated above, under s 99 of the Employment Rights Act 1996 (ERA) a woman is protected from dismissal on grounds of pregnancy and under s 71 of the ERA, as amended, all women have an automatic right to 18 weeks' maternity leave. If a woman has one year's continuous service, she has a right to an additional period of leave which ends after the 29th week after the start of the week in which birth occurred.[85] Compensation under the ERA is much lower than that which was available under the SDA.

---

82 So long as the context allows the dismissal to be characterisable as owing to unavailability and therefore inability to satisfy a particular purpose.

83 The argument for so doing was put succinctly by Stevens J in a dissenting US judgment: commenting on a rule allowing adverse treatment of women for reasons connected with pregnancy, he said: 'By definition such a rule discriminates on grounds of sex, for it is the capacity to become pregnant which primarily differentiates the female from the male.' *General Electric Co v Gilbert* (1976) 429 US 126, pp 161–62.

84 It appeared that no attempt was made to ascertain the period for which the plaintiff would actually be unavailable. See *Webb v EMO Air Cargo* [1992] 4 All ER 929, HL, p 932, *per* Lord Keith. It is not mandatory that employees should be absent from work for the whole period of maternity leave or that, during maternity leave, they should be out of communication with the workplace.

85 ERA, s 73 and the Parental Leave and Maternity etc. Regulations 1999, regs 5 and 7. Previously, she had a right to return to work within 29 weeks of the birth under the Employment Protection Consolidation Act 1978, s 39(1)(b). For further discussion of the current position see McColgan, A, 'Family friendly frolics' (2000) 29 ILJ 125.

Detrimental action on grounds of pregnancy other than dismissal (such as demotion or failure to appoint or to promote) will fall within the *Webb* approach and it is therefore unfortunate that the European Court of Justice failed to rule clearly that such action would be direct sex discrimination. A possible approach would be to treat detrimental action on grounds of pregnancy as indirect rather than direct discrimination on the ground that a condition is being applied to all employees not to need certain periods of time off work. As argued above, this is very likely to have an adverse impact on women and arguably cannot be justified using the current tests for justification (see below). This is not to suggest that this would be a satisfactory approach: the use of equality law in relation to pregnancy is flawed since it relies on comparisons with men rather than simply acknowledging, as pregnancy-related legislation does, that proper provision for maternity is good employment practice. As will be seen below, there have been a number of instances in which women, especially single parents, have been forced to address the issue of flexible working – in the sense of working hours that fit in with child care – by seeking to use the concept of indirect discrimination. In many ways this attempt has highlighted the problem of using this concept in the way that the early (and, to an extent, also the later) decisions on pregnancy-as-direct-sex-discrimination did.

In discussing pregnancy, it must be borne in mind that the legislation relating to maternity leave enshrines straightforward direct discrimination on grounds of sex since it relates only to women. A preferable approach would be to offer a more generous parental leave entitlement to parents rather than only to mothers, to be divided between the partners as they saw fit. Parental leave has been available in most of the EU Member States[86] prior to the implementation of the Parental Leave Directive, implemented by the Parental Leave and Maternity etc Regulations.[87] The Regulations allow for three months' unpaid leave for any person having responsibility for a child until it is five. This is in addition to maternity leave provision. Section 57A of the ERA also allows for reasonable time off for carers. The take up of parental leave is clearly likely to be low since it is unpaid, while take up under s 57A will be slow, although it will increase since it applies only to children born after 19 December 1999. The five-year cut off point under s 57A is also very grudging.

At present, women are doubly disadvantaged: on becoming parents they have in effect no choice but to be the partner that takes leave, but they may be viewed by employers as less reliable or less committed owing to this fact. Even women who do not wish to have children may experience discrimination on this ground since, at the point of appointment to a post, the possibility that they may have children and therefore take leave may be covertly, even unconsciously, held against them. At present, as indicated by the provision for parental leave, recognition, of a slow and reluctant nature, of the responsibilities of fathers is occurring[88] and if flexible working hours are eventually

---

86 For details see McColgan, *op cit*, fn 1, pp 378–79.

87 The Parental Leave and Maternity etc Regulations 1999 SI 1999/3312 were passed to implement the Directive.

88 The proposals under the Green Paper on Parental Rights 2001 which propose the introduction of paid paternity leave and 26 weeks' adoptive leave are limited to parents of disabled children and adoptive parents. The Government still opposes paid parental leave.

introduced as a right they are likely to be applicable to both parents.[89] Without further change in this direction the problems associated with the legally enshrined expectation that some women will damage their career for their home life, while some men will conversely damage their home life to further their career, will continue. These include the likelihood that some women will forgo having children, and that some of those who do may suffer employment detriment, including periods without work, leading to poverty and insecurity for themselves and their children, and severely affecting them after they reach pensionable age.[90] At present, some employers recognise that many employees have children and that seeking to enable them to continue at work without suffering stress is good practice that makes business sense, since skills and training are not lost to the company and productivity is enhanced. A company which could only or mainly rely on those without parental responsibilities would clearly be impoverished in terms of the pool of talent it could rely on. But the stance of the current government in seeking to enhance opportunities to achieve work/family balance, while showing greater imagination and far-sightedness than the previous one, has so far been hesitant and reluctant. This issue is considered further below, in relation to indirect discrimination on grounds of sex.

Discrimination on grounds of marital status

The concept of direct discrimination on grounds of marital status is governed by s 3(1)(a) of the SDA 1975. Under s 3(1)(a), the applicant must show that he or she has been less favourably treated on grounds of marital status than a single person of the same sex has been or would be treated. There is little guidance in the Act as to the method of making the comparison; s 5(3) merely provides that there must be no material difference between the situations of an unmarried and a married person. As with discrimination on grounds of sex, it is possible for the applicant to compare him or herself with a hypothetical single person. The test can be broken down into three stages. First, the married person must show that there has been differentiation in the treatment afforded to him or herself and a single person (or a hypothetical single person). Motive is irrelevant. Secondly, he or she must show that the treatment has been less favourable and thirdly, following the ruling of the House of Lords in *James v Eastleigh BC*,[91] that there is a causal relationship between his or her marital status and the treatment; in other words that but for her marital status, she would have been treated as favourably as a single person was or would have been. The plaintiff bears the burden of showing that the differential treatment was on grounds of marital status and not for some neutral reason.

---

89 The proposals under the Green Paper on Parental Rights 2001 include the possibility of an entitlement to reduced hours working for both parents. See below, pp 1014–15 for discussion of some of the current measures relating to the work/life balance.

90 See TUC Submissions to the House of Commons Social Security Committee, June 1999 (see TUC website: www.tuc.org.uk).

91 [1990] AC 751; [1990] 2 All ER 607; [1989] IRLR 318; [1989] 3 WLR 122; the 'but for' test applied in James was put forward by Lord Goff in the House of Lords in *Birmingham CC ex p EOC* (1989) 18 ILJ 247; for comment, see Ellis, *op cit*, fn 61.

Discrimination on grounds of gender reassignment

Under s 2A(1) of the SDA 'person A discriminates against another person B if he treats B less favourably than he treats or would treat other persons, and does so on the ground that B intends to undergo, is undergoing, or has undergone gender reassignment'. This provision is based on the models already considered relating to discrimination on grounds of sex and marital status. Thus, the same steps must be taken and the plaintiff bears the burden of showing that the differential treatment was on grounds of gender reassignment. It must be pointed out that s 2A does not prohibit discrimination on grounds of transsexuality in a general sense[92] and that therefore, there is a significant gap in the legislation which possibly could be filled by the use of purposive interpretation, as discussed above.[93]

Race discrimination

Direct discrimination arises under s 1(1)(a) of the RRA and the test to be applied mirrors that under the SDA except that the unfavourable treatment in question must be on 'racial grounds'. This means that discrimination on the grounds of someone else's race is covered (transferred discrimination).[94] For example, if a waitress disobeyed an instruction to serve whites only and was dismissed for serving black customers, that would be discrimination on racial grounds.[95] The applicant must show that the group falls within the definition of racial grounds in s 3(1) of the Act which covers 'colour, nationality, ethnic or national origins' and a racial group is defined by reference to the same. Employment of the concept of ethnic origins widens the meaning of racial group and means that some religious groups may fall within it even though discrimination on the grounds of religion is not expressly covered. The leading case on the meaning of 'racial group' is *Mandla v Dowell Lee*.[96] The House of Lords had to consider whether Sikhs constituted an ethnic group and defined the term 'ethnic group' as one having a long shared history and a cultural tradition of its own, often, but not necessarily, associated with religious observances. On that definition Sikhs were a racial group and fell within s 3(1). This does not mean that a purely religious group will fall within s 3(1).

Using this definition it was found in *CRE v Dutton*[97] that gipsies, who have a shared history going back 700 years, may be termed a racial group and the definition was considered further in *Dawkins v Department of Environment*[98] in relation to the claim that Rastafarians constitute a racial group. It was found that the group in question must regard itself and be regarded by others as a distinct community by virtue of certain

---

92 See *Bavin v The NHS Trust Pensions Agency and Secretary of State for Health* [1999] ICR 1192.

93 See pp 982–85.

94 It was confirmed in *Showboat Entertainment Centre v Owens* [1984] 1 WLR 384 that dismissal for refusal to obey an unlawful discriminatory instruction would fall within s 1(1)(a). See, to the same effect, *Zarczynska v Levy* [1979] 1 WLR 125.

95 See *Zarczynska v Levy* [1979] 1 WLR 125.

96 [1983] All ER 1062; [1983] 2 AC 548; for comment, see Beynon and Love (1984) 100 LQR 120; McKenna (1983) 46 MLR 759; Robilliard [1983] PL 348; Pagone (1984) 43 CLJ 218.

97 [1989] WLR 17; [1989] 1 All ER 306, CA. See also *Souster v BBC Scotland* [2001] IRLR 150.

98 [1993] ICR 517; for comment, see Parpworth (1993) 143 NLJ 610.

characteristics. The two essential characteristics were: a long shared history of which the group was conscious, and a cultural tradition of its own including family and social customs. Lord Fraser considered that there could be other relevant, but not essential characteristics such as a common geographical origin, a common language, literature and religion. It was found that Rastafarians did have a strong cultural tradition which included a distinctive form of music and a distinctive hair style. However, the shared history of Rastafarians as a separate group only went back 60 years; it was not enough for them to look back to a time when they, in common with other Africans, were taken to the Caribbean. That was not sufficient to mark them out as a separate group since it was an experience shared with other Afro-Caribbeans. It appears, then, that this first step is complex and, it might seem, not entirely free from ambiguity. The exclusion of religious groups such as Muslims from the scope of the legislation is a matter which, it is suggested, should be reviewed, although they may fall within the indirect discrimination provisions, as indicated below. It should be noted that religious (but not racial) discrimination in employment may give rise to liability in Northern Ireland under the Fair Employment (NI) Act 1976.

A decision made on racial grounds means that the alleged discriminator made a decision influenced by racial prejudice, but according to the ruling in *CRE ex p Westminster Council*,[99] this does not mean that the discriminator must have a racial motive. The council wanted to employ a black man as a refuse collector, but withdrew the offer after pressure from the all-white work force. The Commission for Racial Equality (CRE) initiated a formal investigation and served a non-discrimination notice on the council. The council challenged the service of the notice by means of judicial review and sought certiorari on the basis that the CRE's findings were perverse – a finding that the CRE could not reasonably make. However, it was held that the decision was made on racial grounds, although it was found that the employer was not motivated by racial prejudice, but by the desire to avoid industrial unrest. Nevertheless, that was irrelevant; the decision was influenced by racial prejudice, although it was not the prejudice of the respondent.

Often, the hardest task in a direct discrimination case will be proving that unfavourable treatment was on grounds of race. However, the decision in *Dornan*[100] will apply in race discrimination cases and will mean that once an inference has been raised that discrimination has occurred, the burden of proof will shift to the employer to prove that the decision in question was made on other grounds. Raising such an inference may involve obtaining statistical material from the employer. In *West Midlands Passenger Transport Executive v Jaquant Singh*[101] the applicant, who believed that he had been racially discriminated against in being refused promotion, wanted an order of discovery in respect of specific material held by his employers indicating the number of whites and non-whites appointed to senior posts. He claimed that if he were able to obtain access to the material, he would be able to invite an inference of direct racial discrimination. The employers resisted discovery. The Court of Appeal held that discovery would be ordered only where it could be termed necessary, but that it could be so termed since the

---

99 [1984] IRLR 230, QBD.
100 [1990] IRLR 179. See above, p 995.
101 [1988] WLR 730.

employee had to establish a discernible pattern of treatment towards his racial group and there was no other way of raising the necessary inference.

Under s 1(2) of the Act it will be direct discrimination to maintain separate facilities for members of different races, even though they are equal in quality. However, if segregation grows up because of practices in the workforce, the employer will not come under an obligation to prevent it according to the ruling in *Pel Ltd v Modgill*[102] although this seems to be in conflict with s 32 of the Act which provides that an employer will be liable for acts done by employees in the course of employment unless he or she has taken reasonable steps to prevent such acts. It would seem that the employer should come under some obligation to prevent segregation even if he or she did not instigate it. Moreover, even if segregation in itself is not unlawful, it may be that once a black/white divide in the workforce is established, a practice of treating the black group differently may develop, which will raise an irresistible inference of direct discrimination even though such treatment might not raise such an inference if applied to an individual black worker.[103]

Disability discrimination

The concept of direct discrimination within the DDA 1995 involves showing, in relation to the fields covered, that the applicant has been less favourably treated for a reason related to her disability than a non-disabled person has been or would be treated. No guidance is given in the Act as to the basis for making a comparison between the two persons. It should be noted that it is possible for the applicant to compare herself with a hypothetical person; the issue is not whether a disabled or non-disabled person receives a benefit, but whether the disabled person would have been treated more favourably if she had not been disabled.

The test can be broken down into five stages. First, the applicant must show that she is disabled within the meaning of the Act. Then she must show that there has been differentiation in the treatment afforded to herself and a non-disabled person (or a hypothetical person). Third, she must show that her treatment has been less favourable. Fourth, the applicant can rely on the ruling of the House of Lords in *James v Eastleigh BC*,[104] the sex discrimination case mentioned above, in showing that there is a causal relationship between her disability and the treatment; in other words that but for her disability she would have been treated as favourably as a non-disabled person was or would have been. Following *Birmingham CC ex p EOC*[105] it is not necessary to show that the less favourable treatment is accorded by an intention to discriminate: motive is irrelevant. Fifth, the alleged discriminator can seek to justify the treatment.

The plaintiff bears the burden of showing that the differential treatment is on grounds of disability and not for some neutral reason. Discharging this burden of proof may be

---

102 [1980] IRLR 142.

103 See John Haggas plc (1993) *The Guardian,* 29 May: different, less favourable treatment of the black group was found to be direct discrimination.

104 [1990] AC 751; [1990] 2 All ER 607; [1989] IRLR 318; [1989] 3 WLR 122; the 'but for' test applied in James was put forward by Lord Goff in the House of Lords in *Birmingham CC ex p EOC* [1989] 18 ILJ 247; for comment, see Ellis, *op cit,* fn 61.

105 [1989] AC 1155; [1989] 1 All ER 769.

problematic, although it may sometimes be clearly apparent that the employment detriment was on grounds of disability, and attention will shift to considering whether the disability fell within the Act and whether the detriment can be justified. The decision in *Dornan*[106] will probably, however, apply in disability discrimination cases and will mean that once an inference has been raised that discrimination has occurred, the burden of proof will shift to the employer to prove that the decision in question was made on other grounds.

As indicated above, the DDA does not cover indirect discrimination, but the requirements regarding unfavourable treatment bear some resemblance to the indirect discrimination provisions relating to the other protected grounds, discussed below. The idea is to outlaw practices which, while neutral on their face as between disabled and non-disabled people, place some disabled people at a substantial disadvantage. The test under the DDA differs from that of the RRA or SDA in that the less favourable treatment can be justified. This is inevitable, since otherwise a mentally handicapped person with severe learning difficulties could win an action under the DDA in respect of failure to appoint her to, for example, a post as a teacher. Under s 5(3) of the DDA, the adverse treatment is justified only if the reason for it is material to the circumstances of the case and is substantial. Similar wording is used in s 28S(8) in relation to higher or further education, but the treatment can also be justified if it is to maintain academic standards or other 'prescribed' standards under s 28S(6). Under s 28S(7), less favourable treatment can also be justified if it is of a prescribed kind, and/or it occurs in prescribed circumstances. This was explained in Parliament as allowing for the making of rules which would have the effect of excluding a disabled person from a course where they would be unable because of their disability to undertake a profession which the course is designed to lead to.[107] Wording similar to that of s 5(3) is used in s 28B(7) in relation to schools, but less favourable treatment can also be justified if it is the result of a 'permitted form of selection' as defined in s 25 of the 2001 Act, inserting s 28Q(9) and (10) into the DDA. Essentially, this means that where a school operates a form of selection, either as a private school or under the relevant legislation (on grounds of ability or special aptitude), that may justifiably preclude the admission of a disabled pupil. The Code of Practice explains that less favourable treatment will be justified only if the reason for it relates to the individual circumstances in question and is not trivial or minor.[108]

The test for justification in respect of the provision of goods and services differs from the key test in relation to employment or education. It consists of a list of instances in which the unfavourable treatment will be justified, under s 20(4). They include treatment necessary not to endanger health or safety, treatment necessary since otherwise the service could not be provided to members of the public, and differences in the cost of providing the service to the disabled person and to members of the public.

The test under s 5(3) (and the equivalent tests in relation to education) bears some similarity to the need to show justification for an indirectly discriminatory requirement under s 1(1)(b) of the SDA or RRA. But it is not as strict a test as that of objective

---

106 [1990] IRLR 179. See above, p 995.

107 *Per* Margaret Hodge, Parliamentary Under-Secretary for Education and Employment, Standing Committee B, Sixth Sitting, Col 206, 3 April 2001.

108 Paragraph 4.6.

justification laid down in *Bilka-Kaufhaus GmbH v Weber von Hartz*,[109] which is discussed below. Under the *Bilka* test, conditions creating disparate impact will be justifiable if they amount to a means chosen for achieving an objective which correspond to a real need on the part of the undertaking, are appropriate to that end and are necessary to that end. It was found that the DDA test differed from that in *Bilka*, and the difference between the tests was made clear by the EAT in *Baynton v Saurus*.[110] It was determined that the individual circumstances in question must relate to both employer and employee and that a balancing of those circumstances can be carried out. In *Heinz v Kendrick*,[111] the EAT followed *Baynton*, but made it clear that once the test was satisfied, the disadvantage must be justified, even though this meant that justification could readily be found. It criticised the lowness of the threshold, but considered that Parliament alone could remedy it. In *Jones v Post Office*[112] Arden LJ said *obiter* that the term 'substantial' in s 5(3) of the DDA (equivalent to s 28S(8) of the DDA) means that the reason given by the employer (or educational institution) must carry real weight, but this does not mean that the employer must take into account all the latest research on the subject. The Court of Appeal in that case gave further elucidation. It was found that the reason given by the employer (or other) must fall within the band of reasonable responses of a reasonable employer.[113]

Section 5(5) of the DDA provides that if an employer is under a duty to make reasonable adjustment under s 6 (see below), but fails without justification to make any such adjustment, his treatment of that person cannot be justified, unless it would have been justified even if he had complied with the duty. This requirement is reiterated, with examples in the Code.[114] Clearly, s 5(5) also implies that if the failure is justifiable or that the adjustment is made, but unfavourable treatment occurs, it is *a fortiori* possible to find that the treatment is justifiable.

It is suggested that, contrary to the findings of the EAT above, the *Bilka* test could be imported by interpretation of the meaning of both 'material circumstances' and 'substantial'. As it is, it is unclear how the test is to be applied. For example, a requirement to drive on a daily basis in a job description or advertisement would not affect some disabled people, but would probably discourage a candidate with epilepsy. The employer would be under a duty to make reasonable adjustment under s 6 (see below). Assuming that the employer had failed to make any such adjustment, the question would then be first whether that failure was justified and, secondly, whether, once it was justified, or even if it was unjustified, the requirement to drive would have been justifiable even after the adjustment was made. In the circumstances, it might be possible to make adjustment by organising another person to drive the disabled person or by enabling her to use public transport. If such adjustment was not possible or would have placed an unreasonable burden on the employer, it would be justifiable not to make it. Alternatively, it might be possible to make some such adjustment which the employer refused to make,

---

109 [1986] IRLR 317; [1986] CMLR 701.
110 [1999] IRLR 604.
111 [2000] IRLR 141.
112 [2001] IRLR 384.
113 That test was also accepted as the proper one in *Foley v Post Office* [2000] ICR 1283.
114 Paragraph 4.7.

such as employing a person to drive the disabled person part of the week. In either circumstance, if the requirement to drive a car on a daily basis was found to be essential to the job, the less favourable treatment – not offering the job – would not breach the Act.

But, the questions to be asked in arriving at the conclusions that a failure to make reasonable adjustment was justified and that the unfavourable treatment was justified are unclear. In the circumstances envisaged, taking into account the employer's needs, it is unclear that it would be necessary to ask, for example, whether the undertaking had a real need, for instance, to broaden the geographical area which its sales executives could cover, or to ask whether the means used to answer to that need were appropriate or whether the requirement was necessary. The extent to which other means of achieving the same objective would have to be considered is also unclear. If such other means of achieving the objective were available or feasible, it could be seen as unnecessary to impose the condition that applicants have a driving licence. However, this fairly strict test for justification, based on *Bilka*, seems to have been rejected.

Harassment[115]

It has become clear under the SDA and RRA that if the employer subjects the applicant to employment detriment arising from harassment, such as a transfer from one establishment to another, this will be direct discrimination.[116] Moreover, sexual or racial harassment appears to be a detriment in itself[117] if it is discriminatory under s 6(6)(b) of the Sex Discrimination Act or s 4 of the Race Relations Act which speak of 'or subjecting [the employee] to any other detriment', even though it does not lead to other unfavourable action, so long as some employment disadvantage arises. In *De Souza v Automobile Association*[118] the Court of Appeal found that racial abuse in itself is not enough to cause an employee detriment within the meaning of s 4 of the RRA. The court must find that by reason of the act complained of, a reasonable worker would or might take the view that he had thereby been disadvantaged in the circumstances in which he had thereafter to work. Such disadvantage may be interpreted quite broadly. In *Hereford and Worcester CC v Clayton*,[119] firefighters were informed of the 'bad news: the new firefighter is a woman'. This was found to be a sexist insult capable of detrimental consequences. It sent the wrong signal to the firefighters and might have been likely to cause victimisation. This was less favourable treatment on the grounds of sex and amounted to unlawful sex discrimination.

There seems to be some uncertainty as to whether 'detriment' should be interpreted subjectively or objectively and a tendency to adopt the latter approach where the applicant is perceived as particularly sensitive[120] and the former where he or she is

---

115 See generally Hadjifotiou, *Women and Harassment at Work*, 1983; MacKinnon, C, *Sexual Harassment of Working Women*, 1979; Mullender, R, 'Racial harassment, sexual harassment and the expressive function of law (1998) 61 MLR 236.

116 *Porcelli v Strathclyde Regional Council* [1986] ICR 564.

117 Although see (1985) 101 LQR 471 on this point.

118 [1986] ICR 514.

119 (1996) *The Times*, 8 October.

120 *Wileman v Minilec Engineering Ltd* [1988] ICR 318; for criticism see Gay (1990) 19 ILJ 35, who considered this ruling to be an 'example of judicial insensitivity'.

thought to be more robust.[121] This mixed approach may render the test for harassment under-inclusive and it is therefore suggested that an objective test should be used, involving asking only whether the offending behaviour had reached a level at which reasonable people would term it humiliating.

The problem inherent in viewing harassment as discrimination is that the judicial inquiry necessarily focuses on the question of equal treatment rather than on the nature of the treatment. In other words, where a man or other comparator was or would also have been subjected to the behaviour in question, experienced by the applicant as humiliating or degrading, the claim may fail.[122] This problem was illustrated by the findings in *Stewart v Cleveland Guest Ltd*.[123] The claim was brought by a woman who had been subjected to a display of sexually explicit pictures of women in the workplace. She had also been subjected to sexual assault and to sexual harassment at work, although these incidents were not included in her claim. She had eventually got the pictures removed, when her union intervened, but the management had allowed the workers to know who was to blame for their removal, and she had felt unable to return to the workplace. The tribunal found that the display was sexually neutral (despite the fact that the pictures were only of women and women were in the minority in the workplace), although it also found that her objections to the pictures were reasonable. It reached the decision to dismiss her claim on the basis that other women in the workplace did not object and, therefore, it could be said that, objectively, the pictures were not offensive or created humiliating conditions of work. However, taking into account all the circumstances of the case, it could be argued that there was sufficient evidence that the pictures were, objectively, offensive and degrading and that the other women had been, as was argued, desensitised by the male-orientated general ethos. The EAT upheld the tribunal but left open the possibility that apparently neutral general treatment which had a particular impact on women could be viewed as discrimination.

However, in a later decision, *Sidhu v Aerospace Composite Technology Ltd*,[124] a different approach was taken. The plaintiff had been subject to racial abuse and an assault. He and the racist workmates were dismissed because of his violent reaction to the assault. The racist element in it was disregarded by the employers in taking the decision to dismiss him. It was found in the EAT that to disregard this element was a 'race-specific' decision having a 'race-specific' effect. The nature and effect of the decision was found to amount to treatment on racial grounds amounting in itself to racial discrimination under s 1(1)(a) of the RRA, and it was not found necessary to consider whether a person of a different racial group or a white person would have been treated differently. Clearly, the claim might have failed had the employer been allowed to rely on the argument that a white person who had reacted to a racist assault in the same way would have been treated in the same way. Thus, at present it appears that two different approaches are emerging. In applying these findings to allegations of harassment under the SDA as amended, the RRA

---

121 *Snowball v Gardner Merchant* [1987] ICR 719.

122 For criticism of this approach, which compares it with the evolving stance in US law away from the requirement to prove differential treatment and towards emphasis on the question whether there had been creation of a hostile working environment, see Dine, J and Watt, B, 'Sexual harassment: moving away from discrimination' (1995) 58 MLR 343.

123 [1996] ICR 535.

124 [1999] IRLR 683.

and the DDA, it is clear that behaviour that can reasonably be viewed as humiliating or degrading will not necessarily amount to discrimination: all will depend on the specific circumstances.

Section 41(1) of the SDA states that an act done by an employee in the course of employment shall be treated as done by the employer as well as by him or her, whether or not it was done with the employer's knowledge or approval. There are equivalent provisions in s 32 of the RRA and s 58 of the DDA. Thus, a harassment claim on the protected grounds may be brought where the employer had made little or no effort to curb the harassment.[125] In *Tower Boot Co v Jones*,[126] the Court of Appeal adopted a purposive approach to the legislation in finding that employers must take steps to make themselves aware of harassment in the workplace and must take further steps to prevent it. It was not sufficient for employers simply to argue that the harassment did not take place in the course of employment:[127] this would create an obvious anomaly, since gross harassment (which occurred in *Jones*) could never be said to take place in the course of employment. The decision reaffirmed a broad liability of employers for racial abuse, and in *Burton and Another v De Vere Hotels*[128] it was found that the employer will be liable if it allows employees to be subject to racial abuse where it could have been prevented. On this principle, an action might be brought successfully where the employer did not know of the harassment but should have known, thus placing a duty upon employers to be aware of what is occurring in the workplace.[129] These decisions were made in the employment field, but would be applicable to the fields of education and housing. For example, under s 17 of the RRA, which provides that discrimination by bodies in charge of educational establishments may occur if a person is subjected 'to any other detriment', an action might be successful against school administrators who failed to prevent racial harassment of a pupil.

The European Commission has defined sexual harassment as 'conduct of a sexual nature or other conduct based on sex affecting the dignity of men and women at work'.[130] This clearly covers verbal or physical conduct. The Commission has published a Code of Practice[131] on sexual harassment based on the definition above, which has been supported by the Council of Ministers,[132] giving guidance to employees and employers and stating that harassment 'pollutes the working environment and can have a devastating effect upon the health, confidence, morale and performance of those affected by it'.[133] The Commission has recommended that the Code should be adopted by

---

125 See *Enterprise Glass Co Ltd v Miles* [1990] Ind Relations Review and Report 412–15C.

126 [1997] ICR 254; [1997] IRLR 168.

127 This had been accepted by the EAT: see [1995] IRLR 529.

128 (1996) *The Times*, 3 October.

129 This has been accepted in the US: *Continental Can Co v Minn* 297 NW 2d 241.

130 OJ C157/2. See Employment Law Review for 1992, below.

131 Commission Recommendation of 27 November 1991 on the Protection of the Dignity of Men and Women at Work OJ L49 3, 1992. This followed a report by Rubenstein, M, *The Dignity of Women at Work: A Report on the Problem of Sexual Harassment in the Member States of the European Communities*, 1987. See above, fn 130. For criticism of the Code, see (1993) 143 NLJ 1473.

132 In a Declaration (see (1992) 217 European Industrial Relations Review 21; see also Rubenstein, M (1992) 21 ILJ 70).

133 See OJ 4.2.1992.

Member States,[134] which should also take other action to address this problem, but the UK Government has not yet shown any inclination to respond. However, industrial tribunals faced with an allegation of sexual harassment as a form of direct discrimination should have regard to the guidance offered by the Code.[135] The new Race Discrimination Directive[136] defines discrimination so as to include harassment where the behaviour in question creates an 'intimidating, hostile, degrading or offensive, humiliating or offensive environment' and has the purpose or the effect of violating a person's dignity. Thus, it is clear that the harasser need not appreciate the effect of his or her behaviour.

4 INDIRECT DISCRIMINATION ON GROUNDS OF SEX OR RACE[137]

Sex discrimination

The concept of indirect discrimination was imported into the SDA under s 1(1)(b) with a view to outlawing practices which, while neutral on their face as between men and women, have a disproportionately adverse impact on women. It was intended to outlaw not only isolated acts of discrimination, but also institutionalised discrimination. This reflects the pluralist approach; it takes account, for example, of past discrimination against women. In asking not whether a woman can, in theory, comply with a condition, but whether she can do so in practice, it broadens the area of morally unjustifiable differentiation.

There are four stages in operating this concept. First, it must be shown that a condition has been applied to the applicant. It might be to be of a certain seniority, height or type of experience. Secondly, it must be shown that the condition is one which will have a disproportionate impact on women; in other words, considerably fewer women than men will be able to comply with it. For example, fewer women than men might have a certain type of experience owing to a now outlawed system of keeping women at a certain level and thereby preventing them gaining the experience in question. Thirdly, once the claimant has proved these two requirements, the burden of proof shifts to the employer to show that the condition is justifiable regardless of sex. For example, there are fewer women engineering graduates than men; therefore, a requirement that applicants have a degree in engineering hits disproportionately at women. However, the employer will normally be able to show that a degree in engineering is genuinely needed for the job. Fourthly, if the employer cannot show that the requirement is genuinely needed for the job, the woman must show that it is to her detriment because she cannot comply with it. This requirement was included because it was thought necessary that the woman should be the victim rather than allowing anyone to bring a claim in respect of a discriminatory practice operating at her place of employment.

---

134 Commission Recommendation of 27 November 1991.

135 *Wadman v Carpenter Farrer Partnership* (1993) *The Times*, 31 May, EAT.

136 Directive 2000/43/EC.

137 See Byre, *Indirect Discrimination*, 1987; McGinley, 'Judicial approaches to sex discrimination in US and UK – a comparative study' (1986) 49 MLR 413, pp 427–35; Hunter, *Indirect Discrimination in the Workplace*, 1992; von Prondzynski and Richards, *op cit*, fn 1; Gardner, J, 'Discrimination as injustice' (1996) 16(3) OJLS 353; Townshend-Smith, R, 'Justifying indirect discrimination in English and American law: how stringent should the test be?' (1995) 1 Int Journal of Discrimination and the Law 103.

Two early decisions made clear the grounds for including this second type of discrimination in the Act and demonstrated the way in which it would operate. The case of *Steel v the Post Office*,[138] which concerned the allocation of postal walks to postmen or women, illustrated the operation of the four stages. Certain walks were more in demand than others and the walks were allocated on the basis of the seniority of the employee. Ms Steel made a bid for a walk, but lost it to a younger man. She had worked for the Post Office much longer than he had, but she had only been accepted into the permanent grade in 1975 when the SDA came into force. Before 1975, the Post Office had directly discriminated against women by refusing to allow them to enter the permanent grade. Ms Steel's seniority had been calculated from that point. The practice in question was interpreted as a 'requirement', thereby widening the meaning of the term. It had a disparate impact on women because fewer of them could comply with it than men because of the past discrimination and the requirement as to seniority could not otherwise be justified. 'Justified' was strictly interpreted as meaning 'necessary'. Finally, the requirement was clearly to her detriment, as she could not comply with it.

The application of the phrase 'can comply' was considered in *Price v Civil Service Commission*.[139] The Civil Service had a rule that applicants had to be under 28. Mrs Price, who was 35, applied but was rejected and claimed sex discrimination. It was found that owing to the prevailing social conditions, more men than women could comply with the requirement because at the time, there was a general expectation that women would rear a family and so would be less likely to be available in the job market at that age than men. However, women could theoretically comply with a requirement to be 28 and available in the job market; they could choose not to have children. The words 'can comply' were interpreted to mean that in practice, fewer women could comply with the condition. The court also considered the means of identifying a group of men and women to be looked at in order to see whether fewer women could comply with the condition. It found that the group to be considered would be the pool of men and women with the relevant qualifications; it would not include the whole population.[140] The applicant's case, therefore, passed all four tests and succeeded, with the result that the Civil Service altered the age bar.

The main difficulties in the operation of indirect discrimination have arisen in three areas: the finding of a disparate impact, involving identification of the correct 'pool', the meaning of justifiability and the determination as to the meaning of 'a requirement or condition'. The current position as regards disparate impact may be summed up in the following manner, which is based on the ruling of Mustill LJ in *Jones v Chief Adjudication Officer*:[141]

(a) identify the criterion for selection (the condition);

(b) identify the relevant population, the 'pool', comprising all those who satisfy the other criteria for selection and ignoring the allegedly discriminatory condition;

---

138 [1977] IRLR 288.

139 [1977] 1 WLR 1417.

140 See *Jones v Manchester University* (1993) *The Times*, 12 January, CA, which reaffirmed this approach to the 'pool', holding that the applicant could not redefine its parameters, which would be fixed by the relevant advertisement.

141 (1990) EOR 1991.

(c) divide the relevant population into groups representing, first, those who satisfy the allegedly discriminatory criterion and secondly, those who do not;

(d) ascertain what are the actual male/female balances in the two groups;

(e) if women are found to be under-represented in the first group, it is proved that the criterion creates disparate impact.

Choosing the appropriate 'pool' is crucial to the plaintiff's chances of success; the tribunal may decide that she has chosen the wrong pool and that therefore, the statistical evidence she has prepared showing disparate impact relates to the wrong groups of persons.[142] However, a more relaxed approach was evident in *London Underground v Edwards (No 2)*[143] (discussed further below) in which the Court of Appeal accepted that the tribunal could take into account the common knowledge that there are more female than male lone parents. Once the calculation has been completed, it will be possible to determine the proportions of women and of men affected by the disputed requirement. But, it must be found that the proportion of women who can comply is 'considerably smaller' than the equivalent proportion of men.

In *Secretary of State for Employment ex p Seymour-Smith and Perez*[144] a challenge was mounted against the increases in the qualifying period for redundancy from one to two years in 1985. It was argued that a considerably smaller proportion of women than of men could comply with it and that therefore, it breached the Equal Treatment Directive. In 1985, 77.4% of men and 68.9% of women fulfilled the condition. On a reference to the ECJ, it was found that such figures would not reveal that a considerably smaller proportion of women than men could fulfil the requirement. However, the ECJ also pointed out that a less than considerable differential, which persisted over a long period, could satisfy the requirement of indirect discrimination. The House of Lords considered the position as at 1991, not 1985, since both parties accepted that 1991 was the relevant date. Looking at the years between 1985 and 1991, there was a constant disparity between men and women: the ratio of men to women who qualified was 10:9. Given the persistence of this disparity it could not, it was found, be brushed aside as inconsiderable, bearing in mind the context of equality of treatment.

It is clear from this decision that determining the relevant proportions of men and women who can comply with a condition is not necessarily a straightforward matter that can be resolved by a 'snap-shot' approach. Further guidance was given in *Barry v Midland Bank*,[145] in which it was found that since the smaller the disadvantaged group in proportionate terms, the narrower the differential, a better guide may be to consider expressing the proportions as ratios of each other. Lord Nicholls explained that therefore, in a workforce of 10,000 employers of which 10% work part time, where 90% of the part timers are women, a requirement that disadvantages part timers will disadvantage 0.2% of males and 1.8% of women. Those proportions would not appear to satisfy the 'considerably smaller' requirement. But if the proportions are expressed as ratios of each

---

142 See *Pearse v City of Bradford MC* [1988] IRLR 379.

143 [1998] IRLR 364.

144 [2000] IRLR 263, HL.

145 [1999] 1 WLR 1465.

other it will be found that the ratio of women who cannot comply to that of men who cannot is 9:1.

The meaning of 'justifiable' has undergone considerable change since the ruling in *Ojutiku v Manpower Services Commission*[146] in which, departing from the *Steel* interpretation, it was held to mean 'reasons which would appear sound to right thinking people'. This obviously widened its meaning and would have allowed a great many practices to be justified, greatly undermining s 1(1)(b). However, in *Clarke v Eley IMI Kynoch Ltd*,[147] its meaning was somewhat narrowed. The company had a policy of always selecting part time workers for redundancy first, regardless of their length of service, although for full time workers a 'last in, first out' system was in operation. Therefore, the requirement to work full time so as not to be made redundant hit disproportionately at women, as more women than men worked part time. The employer argued that the practice could be justified because it was long standing and the workforce liked it, but it was found that this was not sufficient to render it 'justifiable', and the claimant therefore succeeded. This was clearly in accord with the policy of including indirect discrimination in the statutory scheme in order to outlaw long standing discriminatory practices.

The test for the meaning of justifiable[148] was more precisely defined by the European Court in *Bilka-Kaufhaus GmbH v Weber von Hartz*.[149] Under this test, conditions creating disparate impact will be justifiable if they amount to a means chosen for achieving an objective which correspond to a real need on the part of the undertaking, are appropriate to that end and necessary to that end. So this test would be fulfilled if, for example, an undertaking had a real need to increase its scientific expertise in a certain area. The means used to do so would have to be appropriate, such as asking that applicants have a degree in a certain science. If other means of increasing its expertise were not available, it would be seen as necessary to impose the condition that applicants have a science degree. This approach was taken in *Hampson v Department of Education and Science*,[150] and means that s 1(1)(b) has been brought into line with the 'material difference' defence under s 1(3) of the Equal Pay Act 1970 (see below).

The *Bilka* decision narrowed the defence available to employers, but the findings in *Perera v Civil Service Commission*[151] (a race discrimination case) meant that a number of requirements or conditions creating disparate impact will fall outside the Act and will obviously not require application of the *Bilka* test because they will not support an indirect discrimination claim at all. It was held in *Perera* that a condition must amount to an absolute bar in order to be termed a requirement or condition. If the employer has only taken the factor into account as one among others, it will not fall within s 1(1)(b). This is very restrictive, as non-absolute criteria could clearly be used and could have an adverse impact on an applicant. For example, an unjustifiable height bar might normally be

---

146 [1982] ICR 661; [1982] IRLR 418.
147 [1983] ICR 703.
148 For discussion of the test see Leigh (1986) 49 MLR 235.
149 [1986] IRLR 317; [1986] CMLR 701; see also *Rinner-Kuhn v FWW Spezial-Gebäudereinigung* [1989] IRLR 493.
150 [1991] 1 AC 171; [1990] 2 All ER 513, HL; on the Court of Appeal decision see Bourn (1989) 18 ILJ 170; Napier (1989) 48 CLJ 187.
151 [1983] ICR 428; [1983] IRLR 166.

operated, but the employer might be prepared on occasion to consider people under it. Nevertheless, the bar could have a significantly adverse effect on women. Thus, the development of indirect discrimination has been constrained and the EOC has therefore argued for reform of the meaning of the term 'condition'.[152] The decision in *Perera* may be out of accord with the ruling of the European Court of Justice in *Enderby v Frenchay*,[153] which is discussed below. In *Falkirk Council v Whyte*,[154] the decision was found to be out of accord with the purposive approach to legislation that implements a Directive, which has been adopted in a number of equal pay cases. It was found that the term 'a requirement or condition' should not be afforded a restrictive interpretation; the proper test, it was said, was to ask whether the 'factor' hindered women as opposed to men in the particular context. Under the Burden of Proof Directive, (implemented in SI 2001/2660) a similar approach will prevail, since the terms used are 'provision, criterion or practice', which appear to cover non-absolute criteria.

One of the key issues which has arisen over the last 10 years is that of flexible working. The term 'flexible' can be used in two senses. First, it can relate to the need of parents or other carers to work hours which do not impinge too greatly on their caring responsibilities – a matter forming one aspect of the 'work/life' balance. Secondly, it can refer to the preference of some employers to demand that employees work hours which suit the changing needs of the business or concern in question. These matters are increasingly becoming the subject of indirect discrimination claims. In *London Underground v Edwards (No 2)*[155] the plaintiff, a woman train driver, brought an indirect discrimination claim after the employer imposed shift changes in accordance with its new business plan. She could not comply with the changed shifts because of her responsibilities as a single parent. It was found that out of the pool of train drivers there were 2,000 men, all of whom could comply with the new shift arrangements. There was a component of only 21 women in the pool. Out of that number, one woman – the applicant – could not comply. Thus, 95.2% of women could comply and 100% of men could comply. In determining that a 'considerably' smaller proportion of women could comply, the Court of Appeal took into account the small number of women in the pool, suggesting that women already found it hard to comply with the requirements of the job. Further, if one more woman had been unable to comply, that would have had a significant effect on the proportion of women who could not comply, whereas if one man had not been able to comply, that would have had little effect on the male figures. On the issue of justification, the Court of Appeal found that employers should recognise the need to take a reasonably flexible attitude to accommodating the needs of their employees. They considered that London Underground could have quite readily accommodated the needs of a good employee (she had worked for them for 10 years and there had been no complaints about her work) which would not have been damaging to their business plan.

A different attitude was evident in *Clymo v Wandsworth LBC*[156] which concerned the employee's need to adopt a different pattern of working. The plaintiff had returned to

152 See Proposals of the EOC: Equal Treatment for Men and Women, p 9.
153 [1994] 1 All ER 495; [1993] ECR I-5535, ECJ; [1992] IRLR 15, CA.
154 [1997] IRLR 560.
155 [1998] IRLR 364.
156 [1989] ICR 250.

work after childbirth and found she could not comply with a requirement to work full time; she wished to work part time. The EAT found that no *requirement* to work full time had been applied. In any event, it was found, she could comply with it – she merely had to make a choice between her childcare responsibilities and full time working. This was a very technical approach to the statute, which gave priority to the employer's autonomy in choosing to impose full time working rather than to the employee's choices. It appears to be out of accord with the approach taken in *Edwards* and that taken in other, later decisions,[157] although it cannot be assumed that it has been entirely discarded.

A number of measures emanating from the EC have had some effect on the work/life balance, including the Working Time Directive,[158] which was implemented in the Working Time Regulations 1998.[159] But, it is generally accepted that while the Regulations have had some impact on the long hours culture of the UK,[160] it has not been of a radical nature, partly because of the possibilities of opting out of the provisions.[161] The Part-Time Workers Directive[162] was implemented in the Part-Time Workers (Prevention of Less Favourable Treatment) Regulations 2000.[163] The Regulations prohibit discrimination against part time workers. But the employee must point to a comparator under the Regulations, although possibly to a hypothetical comparator under the Directive, and must show that he or she has been treated unfavourably in comparison with a comparable employee working full time, on the ground of part time working. The unfavourable treatment can be justified. Thus, the scheme is likely to be limited in its effects; it has been estimated that, owing to the need to find an appropriate comparator, it is likely to affect only about 7% of UK part time workers.[164] The Regulations do not provide a right to work part time or to work flexible hours to accommodate caring responsibilities or to job-share. In order for employees to seek to assert such rights, they must use, as indicated above, the difficult route provided by the SDA. Thus, although social patterns are changing, and men increasingly have responsibilities as carers, the current gendered divide in caring responsibilities has not elicited a legislative response that recognises that divide, thus sometimes forcing women into a dependency on men which may result in a blighting of their lives and those of their children.[165] Use of the indirect discrimination route in efforts to avert these possibilities is, as indicated, burdensome and fraught with pitfalls.

---

157 See *Zurich Insurance Co v Gulson* [1998] IRLR 118.

158 Directive 93/104/EC.

159 SI 1998/1833.

160 See the TUC Report, March 2001 'Burnout Britain' factsheet, www.tuc.org.uk.

161 See further Ewing, Bradley and McColgan, *op cit*, fn 1, Chapter 4, pp 411–13.

162 Directive 96/34/EC.

163 SI 2000/1551.

164 Government's Regulatory Impact Assessment.

165 See Cabinet Office *Briefing Women's Incomes Over the Lifetime and Women and Men in the UK: Facts and Figures* (www.women.unit.gov.uk/publications.htm).

Race discrimination

The tests to be applied to establish indirect discrimination under s 1(1)(b) of the 1976 Act are identical to those arising under the Sex Discrimination Act, apart from the need to show that the requirement or condition which has been applied adversely affects persons of a particular racial group. Thus, the first step in a case of indirect discrimination on racial grounds is for the applicant to define which racial group he or she belongs to. For example, an individual could be defined as non-British, non-white, Asian or a sub-group of Asian. The choice of group is important, since discrimination affects racial groups differently. For example, a requirement to be clean-shaven might discriminate against Sikhs, but might not affect West Indians. Therefore, if in such circumstances the applicant chose 'non-white' as his group, the claim would fail. However, if he chose Sikh and non-Sikh, it would be more likely to succeed. The applicant should argue all possible groups in the alternative.

The next step, according to *Perera v Civil Service Commission*,[166] is for the applicant to show that an absolute condition has been applied to him or her. In *Perera* this concerned a requirement that a candidate for the Civil Service had a good command of English. This requirement was sometimes waived; it was determined that it could not, therefore, amount to a 'requirement or condition' for indirect discrimination purposes. As noted above in relation to indirect sexual discrimination, this decision placed a brake on claims of indirect discrimination[167] although that approach was being abandoned even prior to implementation of the Burden of Proof Directive. It was pointed out in *Meer v Tower Hamlets*[168] by Balcombe LJ in the Court of Appeal that it allows discriminatory preferences free rein, as long as they are not expressed as absolute requirements. In that case, a candidate who had previous experience working in the local authority was preferred although such experience was not absolutely required, and this had a tendency to debar non-British applicants. The Commission for Racial Equality has recommended that this interpretation should be abandoned so that non-absolute criteria can be considered.[169] Once the Race Directive is implemented, it will be reasonably clear that indirect discrimination can be found to exist where a non-absolute requirement is applied to the applicant. The Directive uses the same wording as that adopted in the Burden of Proof Directive.[170]

If a condition can be identified, the applicant must show that a 'considerably smaller proportion of his or her group can comply with it', and the approach adopted in sex discrimination cases, discussed above, will be used, although where indirect discrimination is based on nationality and affects an EC national it will be sufficient to establish a risk that the group of workers in question is unable to comply with the requirement.[171] This approach would obviate the need to produce statistical evidence proving the effect of the requirement in practice. This approach would not apply in other

166 [1983] ICR 428; [1983] IRLR 166.
167 For criticism of the decision see Mead (1989) 18 ILJ 59.
168 [1988] IRLR 399, p 403.
169 CRE, *Second Review of the Race Relations Act*, 1991.
170 See above, p 1014.
171 *O'Flynn v Adjudication Officer* Case C-237/94 [1996] All ER (EC) 541.

instances of indirect discrimination, but it may be introduced under the Race Discrimination Directive, which requires the applicant to show that the provision or practice in issue 'would put persons of a racial or ethnic group at a *particular disadvantage* compared with other persons' (emphasis added). That approach may appear to allow for consideration of a risk of inability to comply, although the use of the word 'would' as opposed to 'could' does not make this interpretation certain.

Once the applicant has established a *prima facie* case of indirect discrimination, the burden of proof shifts to the employer to show that the requirement or condition is justifiable.[172] In *Ojutiku v Manpower Services Commission*[173] two African students obtained places on a polytechnic management course, but were refused grants by the Manpower Services Commission since they lacked industrial experience. They claimed that this requirement was indirectly discriminatory as it was more difficult for African applicants to show that they had previous management experience. However, the claim failed on the basis that the requirement could be justified. The test for justification was determined to be somewhat short of 'necessary', connoting a belief which would be justifiable if held on reasonable grounds, and this was reiterated in *Singh v British Railway Engineers*.[174] The applicant, who wore a turban in accordance with his religious beliefs, could not comply with a requirement to wear protective headgear and therefore had to take a less well paid job. It was found that while the requirement did have an adverse impact it was justifiable, partly because the other employees would resent exceptions being made. However, the term 'justifiable' is now to be interpreted in accordance with the *Bilka* test,[175] which is applicable in sex discrimination cases and should therefore, by extension, apply to the equivalent provision under the RRA according to *Hampson v DES*.[176] This accords with the ruling in *Rainey v Greater Glasgow Health Board*[177] that the *Bilka* test would be applicable in sex discrimination and equal pay cases in respect of the grounds on which differential treatment could be justified. This is an important instance of the indirect influence of EU law on national provisions against racial discrimination.

The Commission for Racial Equality has, for a number of years, criticised the interpretation of indirect discrimination and has proposed a new definition: any practice or policy which is continued or allowed should be unlawful if it has a significant adverse impact on a particular racial group and is not necessary. It has further proposed that significant adverse impact should mean a 20% difference in impact between groups.[178] These proposals are now, broadly, encapsulated in the Race Directive, which must be implemented by July 2003.

---

172 For discussion of the justification defence see Lustgarten, L (1983) 133 NLJ 1057 and (1984) 134 NLJ 9.
173 [1982] IRLR 418.
174 [1986] ICR 22.
175 Above, fn 149.
176 [1991] 1 AC 171; [1990] 2 All ER 513, HL.
177 [1986] 3 WLR 1017, HL.
178 See the CRE Consultative Paper, *Second Review of the Race Relations Act 1976*, 1991. The 20% notion derives from US civil rights law.

5 EQUAL PAY[179]

The Equal Pay Act 1970 governs the contractual aspects of a woman's employment. It is anomalous in that it is separate from the SDA; there is no good reason for having two separate instruments and it merely introduces further complexity and technicality into an already complex scheme. The Act received the royal assent in 1970, but it did not come into force until 1975; the idea was that employers would voluntarily remove sexual discrimination in pay. In fact, as the TUC warned the government would happen, employers moved women off the 'women's grade' on to the lowest grades with a view to minimising their statutory obligations and made sure that men and women were not working on comparable jobs.

The aim of the Act is to prevent discrimination as regards terms and conditions of employment between men and women and, to this end, it employs the device of an equality clause. If certain conditions are satisfied, the terms of the woman's contract are deemed to include such a clause. Under the original provisions, the equality clause only operated in two circumstances: that the woman was employed on like work with men in the same employment under s 1(2)(a) or on work rated by a job evaluation scheme as equivalent to that of a man in the same employment under s 1(2)(b). The latter provision was not of much value as it was voluntary and it was, therefore, left to the woman to persuade her employer to undertake such a scheme. In practice, this meant that women were left with the like work provisions. Owing to sexual segregation in the job market, women were concentrated in certain occupations, such as cleaning or cooking, and were unable to point to a man doing like work even where he was in the same employment.

Thus, the Act had little impact on women's lower pay since it could only be used against the most gross forms of pay discrimination. However, in 1982 the European Commission brought an action against the UK (*Commission of European Communities v UK*)[180] on the basis that the UK was in breach of its obligations under the Equal Pay Directive owing to the narrow application of the equality clause. In response, the UK Government was forced to amend the 1970 Act in order to include the possibility of making an equal value claim. It did so very reluctantly and this was reflected in the response. The amendment (new s 1(2)(c)) was effected by statutory instrument, thereby curtailing debate on the new provisions, and the new regulations were intended to operate only as a last resort: the other two possibilities had to be tried first. Moreover, an attempt was made to widen the defences available to employers by using a different wording for equal value claims.

---

179 General reading: Townshend-Smith, *op cit*, fn 27, Chapter 9; Bourne, C and Whitmore, J, *Discrimination and Equal Pay*, 1989, Chapter 7; Arnull, A, 'Article 119 and equal pay for work of equal value' (1986) Eur L Rev 200; 'Pay inequalities and equal value claims' (1985) 48 MLR 560; 'Courts, community law and equal pay' [1988] PL 485; Edwards, 'Equal pay: the European dimension' (1990) BLR July 177; Bourne, 'Equal pay' (1990) 140 NLJ 1284; Fenwick, H, 'Indirect discrimination in equal pay claims' (1995) 3 European Public Law 331; McColgan, *op cit*, fn 1, Chapter 10.
180 [1982] ICR 578; [1982] 3 CMLR 284.

Choice of comparator

The first step under the Act is for the woman to choose a comparator. This might have caused difficulty where the woman was employed doing like work with a few men but wanted to compare herself with a man doing work of equal value; however, the issue was resolved in favour of claimants by the House of Lords in *Pickstone v Freemans*.[181] Mrs Pickstone and other warehouse operatives were paid less than male warehouse checkers, but a man was employed as an operative. The defendants therefore argued that the claim was barred owing to the wording of s 1(2)(c): '... where a woman is employed on work which, *not being work to which (a) or (b) applies,* is "of equal value"' (emphasis added). Paragraph (a) did apply because one man was employed doing the same work and therefore it could be argued that a like work claim arose, but not an equal value one. The House of Lords considered that allowing this argument to succeed would mean that Parliament had failed once again to implement its obligations under Art 119 and it could not have intended such a failure. In such circumstances, any interpretation should take into account the terms in which the amending regulations were presented to Parliament; in other words, a purposive approach should be adopted. Using this approach, the defendants' argument could be rejected on the basis that the claimant should be able to choose her comparator, rather than allowing the employer to impose one on her. This ruling put an end to what has been termed the 'token man loophole':[182] had it gone the other way, employers might have been encouraged to employ one man alongside a large number of women in order to bar equal value claims.

'Same employment'

Once a claimant has chosen a comparator, it must be shown that they are in the same employment. The meaning of this provision was considered by the House of Lords in *Leverton v Clwyd CC*.[183] A nursery nurse who wished to compare her pay with that of clerical staff was not employed in the same establishment as they were. Under s 1(6), 'the same employment' is defined as meaning at the same establishment or by the same employer and that the same conditions of employment are observed. The claimant and comparators were employed by the same employer and, although there were some differences in the individual terms of employment, it was still possible for the House of Lords to find on a broad view of the agreement governing the terms of employment of claimant and comparator that they were sufficiently similar to satisfy the s 1(6) test.

Clearly, it would be possible to frame legislation allowing equal value claims so that it would operate in one of three circumstances: it could apply to all employees who could point to any other employee, wherever employed, doing work of equal value; it could apply to employees employed by the same employer governed by roughly similar terms of service – the position taken under the UK legislation – or it could apply to employees working under the same roof as their comparators. In making it clear that a broad middle

---

181 [1988] AC 66; [1988] 2 All ER 803; for comment see: (1988) 51 MLR 221; [1988] PL 483.
182 See Napier, 'Julie Hayward and the continuing saga of equal pay' (1998) 138 NLJ 341.
183 [1989] 2 WLR 47; [1989] 1 WLR 65, HL.

way is open to such claims, the House of Lords gave encouragement to them and followed a policy which seems to be in tune with that underlying the legislation.

However, it is worth considering the advantages of the first and least restrictive method which was omitted from the legislation in order to minimise disruption to existing pay structures. If, in principle, a person doing work of equal value to that of another worker should be paid an equal wage, if the inequality is attributable to sex discrimination, then it ought to be immaterial that the two workers are employed by two different employers. It might be said that an employer cannot be expected to take responsibility for the wage policies of other concerns, but can only be expected to remove pay discrimination within the sphere he or she is able to affect. However, on a broader view, it might be argued that an employer has a duty to ensure that his or her own concern is not operating a discriminatory wage scheme whatever the basis of comparison. In closing off that broad possibility, the legislation leaves intact the grossest pay disparities arising from establishments with low paid all-female workforces, because they cannot point to a male comparator. This aspect of the legislation may even encourage sexual segregation in employment because if no male is employed (other than those prepared to work for the same low wages as the women) – at least in any post conceivably comparable with that of the majority of the workforce – equal value claims are precluded. The result in some occupations may be the encouragement of a low paid all-female workforce overseen by a few men in managerial positions.

The term by term approach

Assuming that a claimant can point to a comparator in the same employment, the industrial tribunal will appoint an independent expert in order to determine whether the two jobs are of equal value under such heads as responsibility, skill, effort, qualifications and length of training. The expert's report is not conclusive of the issue, but the tribunal is unlikely to reject it. If the jobs are of equal value, then a term of the claimant's contract which is less favourable than a term of her comparator's will be compared. It is now clear after the ruling of the House of Lords in *Hayward v Cammell Laird*[184] that the term by term approach – as opposed to consideration of the contract as a whole – is correct. The defendants had resisted the plaintiff's claim on the ground that her contract and that of the male comparators must each be looked at as a whole, in which case her perks – such as free lunches and two additional days' holiday – equalled the £25 per week extra which the men received. The House of Lords found that the word 'term' in s 1(2) was to be given its natural and ordinary meaning as a distinct part of a contract and, therefore, it was necessary to look at one term of the claimant's contract; if there was a similar provision in the comparator's contract which was found after they had been compared to be less favourable to the woman than the term in the comparator's, then the equality clause would operate to make that term equally favourable to her.

Obviously, this ruling prevented employers claiming that fringe benefits equalled pay. Such a claim might have been advantageous to an employer who might be able to provide a benefit at little real cost, such as free meals for a cook. Moreover, previously,

---

184 [1988] WLR 265; [1988] 2 All ER 803; for comment, see Ellis (1988) 51 MLR 781; Napier, *op cit*, fn 182.

employers might have provided a 'protective package' for female employees which included less pay but more time off or more sick benefits. All women, whether desirous of such a package or not, would receive it whether or not they would have preferred to be paid more. Employers, however, feared that the *Hayward* ruling would lead to 'leap frogging'; women would receive the male higher pay; the men would then claim the women's old fringe benefits and all employees would level up to the detriment of the company, which would be faced with a great increase in costs. However, employers may be able to avoid this by gradually modifying practices on pay and fringe benefits. There would also be the possibility – mentioned only as *dicta* in *Hayward* – that certain fringe benefits might be used to found a defence to an equal value claim (see below).

The 'material factor' defence

Even if a woman is able to show that she is doing like work, work rated as equivalent or work of equal value to that of her comparator, the claim will fail if a s 1(3) defence operates:

> ... an equality clause shall not operate in relation to a variation between the woman's contract and the man's contract if the employer proves that the variation is genuinely due to a material factor which is not the difference of sex and that factor:
>
> (a) in the case of an equality clause falling within subsection (2)(a) or (b) above, must be a material difference between the woman's case and the man's; and
>
> (b) in the case of an equality clause falling within subsection (2)(c) above, may be such a material difference.

This is known as the 'material factor defence'. The difference in wording for equal value claims was intended to mean that a 'material factor' could be interpreted more widely in such claims. In fact, as will be seen, the width of the interpretation given to the defence in all three types of claim means that this possibility is of less significance than was expected. The defence will operate if a material difference between the cases of the woman and the man can be identified which is not the difference of sex – such as additional payment for the geographical difference in the location of two parts of the same concern. As the 1970 Act must be construed in harmony with the SDA, the variation in pay must be genuinely due to the factor in question; otherwise it may be discriminatory. Therefore, in *Shields v E Coomes*,[185] the difference in pay was apparently due to the protective function exercised by the male employees in a betting shop. However, not all the men discharged such a function, but all received the higher pay and, therefore, allowing the protective function to operate as a material factor would have been directly discriminatory because a woman who exercised no protective function would not receive the higher pay, while a man in the same position would.

In *Leverton v Clwyd CC*[186] the House of Lords found that different hours and holidays could amount to a material factor under s 1(3) if pay could be broken down into a notional hourly income. If, once this was done, the pay of claimant and comparator were found to be equal, the claim would fail on the basis that the difference in salaries was due

---

185 [1978] WLR 1408, CA.
186 [1989] WLR 47.

to the difference in hours and not to the difference of sex. This point was touched on *obiter* in *Hayward*, but in *Leverton* it was made clear that a s 1(3) defence might be available where a man and a woman had different contractual packages so long as the packages did not contain any element of direct or indirect discrimination. It may be noted that more than one material factor may be identified; if so, it is not necessary for the employer to establish the proportion which each factor contributes to the difference in pay.[187]

The most far reaching and controversial argument under s 1(3) has been termed the 'market forces argument',[188] since it allows the employer to argue that because the market may favour some employees more than others, they must be paid more, and that to fail to do so would be to disrupt normal market forces.[189] In other words, if a woman is willing to work for less than a man, this provides a reason for paying her less. The early cases rejected this argument;[190] in *Jenkins v Kinsgate*,[191] for example, a part time worker was paid at a different hourly rate from the full time workers. The employer tried to use the s 1(3) defence in answer to her claim for equal hourly pay in arguing that part time workers have less bargaining power and therefore the market demanded that he should pay full time workers more. The argument was that this was a genuine difference between the two cases which was not sex-related; any part time worker, male or female, would have been paid less. However, the part timers were all female and so the practice had a disparate impact on women. Construing the EPA in accordance with the SDA, the EAT concluded that a practice which had a disparate impact on women could not sustain a s 1(3) defence, as to allow it to do so would be indirectly discriminatory.

However, this approach was not followed in *Rainey v Greater Glasgow Health Board*,[192] which concerned a comparison between female and male prosthetists working in the NHS. The men were receiving higher pay, but the defendants argued that this was due to the need to attract them from the private sector in order to set up the prosthetist service. This argument entailed consideration not just of factors relating to the personal attributes of the claimant and comparator, such as length of experience, but also the difference in their individual positions in the market. In other words, it widened what could be considered as a material factor. The relevant circumstances were that those from the private sector had to be paid above the normal rate to attract them. However, the House of Lords held that although taking this into account as a material factor was acceptable, it must be objectively justified – no element of discrimination must have crept into the circumstances. In order to ensure this, the House of Lords used the same test as for justification under indirect discrimination – the *Bilka* test laid down by the European

---

187 *Calder v Rowntree Macintosh Ltd* [1993] IRLR 27.
188 Townshend-Smith, *op cit*, fn 27, p 175.
189 The US doctrine of 'comparable worth' has also been attacked as disruptive of market forces: see, eg, Weiler, 'The wages of sex: the uses and limits of comparable worth' (1986) 99 Harv L Rev 1728.
190 *Clay Cross v Fletcher* [1978] 1 WLR 1429; [1979] 1 All ER 474.
191 [1981] IRLR 388, p 390.
192 [1987] AC 224; [1987] 1 All ER 65; [1986] 3 WLR 1017, HL. It may be that the reasoning in *Rainey* will be applied only where indirect discrimination can be identified affecting the factor in question: *Strathclyde Regional Council v Wallace* [1996] IRLR 672, noted (1997) 26(2) ILJ 171. If this is correct, the factor need not be objectively justified: it need only be genuinely necessary and material, ie, relevant. One problem with this approach is that it may lead to failures to recognise the existence of indirect discrimination affecting material factors.

Court of Justice.[193] Here, the objective was setting up the NHS prosthetist service which entailed attracting sufficient experienced prosthetists. The means chosen involved attracting persons from the private sector which involved paying them more. It was accepted that this was both appropriate and necessary. So the material factor passed the *Bilka* test and further, because this was a like work case, the factor *had* to be a difference between comparator and claimant. The difference was that she was from the public sector, while he was from the private sector.

Thus, this ruling broadened what could be termed a material factor and allowed market forces to defeat equal pay claims so long as no indirect discrimination was shown. Clearly, the danger of the market forces argument is that employers will often argue that business will suffer if a group of women are paid more. What are sometimes termed 'women's jobs' have traditionally been undervalued by the market; the equal pay legislation was specifically aimed at breaking down traditional pay hierarchies and, therefore, this argument, if allowed too wide a scope, could completely undermine it. However, the Rainey ruling does appear to an extent to be trying to keep the argument in check in finding that only in objectively justified circumstances should more be paid to a certain group; this is not the same as allowing the market generally to set the rate. The effect of this argument was further curbed in *Benveniste v University of Southampton*;[194] it was found that although particular constraints might affect pay and might lead to a pay differential between a man and a woman, they could do so only while the constraint was in operation. Once it had ceased to apply, the lower pay should be raised to the level it would have been at had it not been affected by the constraint.

A variation on the market forces argument was put forward in *Enderby v Frenchay*.[195] Speech therapists wished to compare their pay with that of clinical psychologists and pharmacists who were paid at much higher rates. The employers denied that the work of the two groups was of equal value, but argued that in any event, a material factor justified the difference: it had emerged as a result of different pay negotiations and, moreover, the pharmacists were in demand in the private sector and this had influenced pay. The employers further argued that the speech therapists could not assert that the material factor was tainted by indirect discrimination without first showing that a condition had been applied to employees which had an adverse impact on women. The employer thus had two arguments: first, no condition could be identified which had been applied; secondly, if it had been, it could be justified by the factors mentioned: the separate pay processes in conjunction with market forces.

The claimant, however, argued that the salaries of the therapists were low because the profession was predominantly female and that whether a condition could be identified or not was immaterial: in practice, one type of work was largely done by women and another largely by men and, although of equal value, the men's work attracted a higher salary. These factors, it was claimed, gave rise to a presumption of discrimination which could not be objectively justified because the reason for the difference was that the profession in question was staffed by women. This argument, if accepted, would have distinguished the claim from that in *Rainey*.

193 In *Bilka-Kaufhaus GmbH v Weber von Hartz* [1986] IRLR 317; [1986] CMLR 701. See above, p 1013.
194 [1989] IRLR 122.
195 [1994] 1 All ER 495; [1993] ECR I-5535, ECJ; [1992] IRLR 15, CA.

1023

The EAT found for the employers, ruling that the pay was the result of different bargaining processes which, looked at separately, were not indirectly discriminatory. Therefore, a material factor could be identified which was influenced by market forces. Further, even if the factor identified did not justify all of the difference in pay, that did not matter because it was impossible to say how much was needed above normal rates to attract and retain certain staff. It was clear that the case raised difficult issues, and so at the Court of Appeal stage three questions were referred to the European Court of Justice:

(1) If there is a difference in pay between two jobs assumed to be of equal value, of which one is carried out almost exclusively by women and the other predominantly by men, must the difference be objectively justified by the employer? Does this mean that all the steps needed to show indirect discrimination should be taken, including identifying a particular barrier?

(2) Are separate bargaining processes a sufficient justification for a variation in pay if they are not internally discriminatory?

(3) If there is a need to pay men more to attract them, but only part of the difference in pay is for that purpose, then does that justify all of the difference?

The first question relates to the determination of a *prima facie* case of indirect sex discrimination; is it necessary to be able to identify a 'barrier' or 'condition' which it is more difficult for women to meet than men (or vice versa) in order to show indirect discrimination? The second and third questions relate to justifications for indirect discrimination. First, is the use of separate sex-neutral collective bargaining systems sufficient justification for indirect sex discrimination? Secondly, will the more favourable market position of certain employees justify unequal pay? In other words, can the overt operation of market forces justify indirect sex discrimination?

Assuming that the jobs compared were of equal value, the Court of Justice held,[196] reiterating the well established principle of reversal of the burden of proof in indirect sex discrimination cases (citing Case C-33/89 *Kowalska v Freie und Hansestadt Hamburg*[197] and Case C-184/89 *Nimz v Freie und Hansestadt Hamburg*[198] concerning measures distinguishing between employees on the basis of their hours of work, including equal pay cases) that '... it is for the employer to prove that his practice in the matter of wages is not discriminatory, if a female worker establishes, in relation to a relatively large number of employees, that the average pay for women is less than that for men'.

Applying these rulings by analogy to this equal value claim, the court concluded that there is a prima facie case of sex discrimination, where the pay of speech therapists is significantly lower than that of clinical psychologists and pharmacists and speech therapists are almost exclusively women. The 'factual' considerations as to whether the jobs are indeed of equal value and whether the statistics adduced support the required disparities are questions for the national court. At this point, the burden of objective justification shifts to the employer.

The court replied in the negative to the question whether separate collective bargaining processes, which are each, in themselves, non-discriminatory, constitute

---

196 *Enderby v Frenchay* [1994] 1 All ER 495; [1993] ECR I-5535, ECJ; [1992] IRLR 15, CA.
197 [1990] ECR I-2591.
198 [1991] ECR I-297.

sufficient objective justification for the differences in pay. The fact that the different wages are reached by separate processes of collective bargaining does not of itself justify the discrimination, since it is a merely descriptive explanation. It fails to explain why one process produced a more favourable result for the employees than the other. Moreover, allowing that justification would enable employers to circumvent the principle of equal pay very readily by using such separate processes.

In contrast to its answer to the second question, the court accepted 'the state of the employment market' in its answer to the third as a possible justification for indirect discrimination. The market forces concerned here were the shortage of candidates for the more highly paid job and the consequent need to offer higher pay in that job in order to attract candidates. The court repeated that it is the duty of the national courts to decide 'questions of fact' such as this and reiterated from its previous case law[199] some forms of 'needs of the employer' which may constitute justification for indirect sex discrimination.[200]

While the questions referred to the ECJ were unanswered, the issue raised in (2) was resolved in *Barber and Others v NCR (Manufacturing) Ltd*[201] using a completely different approach from that of the EAT in *Enderby* and one which seems to be more in harmony with the policy of the Act and with the *Bilka* test. Indirect clerical workers, who were mainly women, wanted to claim equal pay with direct clerical workers who were mainly men (the women's work was 'indirect' as not directly related to shop floor production). The direct workers negotiated a new agreement regarding hours and moved to a shorter week. Thus, the hourly rates of the two groups now differed although it had been the same. The EAT considered whether the employer had established that because the difference arose from different collective bargaining agreements untainted internally by discrimination this could found a s 1(3) defence. In putting forward this argument, the employers had relied on *Enderby* where the EAT had held that this was possible. The EAT said that the correct question to be asked must first be identified. It could be asked whether the cause of the variation in pay was free from sex discrimination, or it could be asked whether the variation was itself genuinely due to a material factor other than the difference of sex. The second question was the right one because the cause – separate collective bargaining processes – might be free from discrimination, but the result might not be. In this instance, the evidence showed why the difference had been arrived at, but did not show any objective factor which justified it. Thus, there was a pay difference which was not based on a material factor. The equality clause therefore operated, meaning that although the claimants did not obtain the same pay as the comparators because of the difference in hours, the hourly rates were equalised. The EAT considered that it did not need to refer to the ECJ or await the decision in *Enderby*, since the proper result could be arrived at under domestic law.

---

199 Case 170/84 *Bilka* [1986] ECR 1607, Case C-184/89 *Nimz v Freie und Hansestadt Hamburg* [1991] ECR I-297 and Case 109/88 *Danfoss* [1989] ECR 3199; [1989] IRLR 532.

200 In 1997, the Government conceded the equal value issue and settled the claim: see April 1997 IRLB No 567.

201 [1993] IRLR 95. Cf the decision in *British Coal Corporation v Smith* [1993] IRLR 308.

This ruling was foreshadowed in *Handels-og Kontorfunktionaerernes Forbund i Danmark v Dansk Arbejdsgiverforening* (the *Danfoss* case),[202] which was a Danish reference to the ECJ. The Court did not need to consider the question as to the relevance of two separate collective agreements, one for women, one for men, but when the Advocate General addressed this point he determined that the existence of such agreements would not exclude the operation of the Equal Pay Directive although it would not inevitably be unlawful to have two separate agreements; it would be the manner of the agreements which would be relevant.

This approach should prevail, it is submitted, because merely to ask whether arriving at two levels of pay was due to the operation of two different bargaining processes would be to obscure the discriminatory nature of the result.[203] It is necessary to look behind the bargaining processes and to ask why one was able to arrive at a more favourable result. This might be because unions have traditionally been more effectual in obtaining better pay for men than for women and in itself this may be due to the fact that men's work has traditionally been valued more highly by the market than women's. Thus, to use different agreements as a material factor in themselves would be to cloak the discriminatory forces which lie behind them.

The main issue in the *Danfoss* case arose because the Danfoss Company paid the same basic wage to all employees, but also an individual supplement based on factors such as mobility and training. The result was that a somewhat lower average wage was paid to women and it was therefore claimed that the system was discriminatory. The Court determined that because the system lacked transparency, once a woman had shown that the average wage of women and men differed, the burden of proof would shift to the employer to prove that the wage practice was not discriminatory. It would have been unfair to expect the woman to prove that the system was discriminatory since she would not have been able to work out which factors had been taken into account. The Court considered that even if the application of criteria such as the need to be mobile worked to the detriment of women, the employer could still use them in relation to specific tasks entrusted to the employee so long as the *Bilka* test was satisfied.

Conclusions

The *Enderby* approach in the European Court of Justice obviously eases the task of the claimant in showing that a material factor is tainted with indirect discrimination in order to shift the onus onto the employer and determines that asking an employee to identify a specific requirement or condition where it is alleged that a material factor is so tainted is misconceived. Sometimes, it may be possible to identify a condition such as a need to be mobile in order to attract higher pay. However, and this seems to be the basis of the decision in *Enderby*, in many instances it may not be possible to identify any such condition with sufficient specificity. Instead, it would seem that where two jobs are of equal value, but that held by the woman attracts lower pay, the suggestion is that the

---

202 [1989] ECR 3199; [1989] IRLR 532.
203 For comment on this issue, see 'Equal value claims and sex bias in collective bargaining' (1991) 20 ILJ 163; see, also (1989) 18 ILJ 63.

market has allowed differentiation because of the traditional expectation that a woman would not be the breadwinner and would therefore work for less.

Thus, the 'condition' which has been applied, in a general sense, is for a woman to work in a traditionally 'male' occupation, such as lorry driving, rather than in one of a traditionally 'female' nature, such as cooking, in order to obtain the higher pay. Obviously, some women can do so, but such a requirement hits disproportionately at women since, in practice, they will be less likely to enter the 'male' occupation owing to tradition, discrimination against them – perceived and real – in such occupations and social conditioning. Identifying such a 'condition' should suffice to raise an inference of indirect discrimination which, of course, would be open theoretically to rebuttal by an objective justification. To go further as the EAT appeared to do in *Enderby* and require identification of some specific condition which the particular employer has imposed is to misunderstand the nature of equal pay claims and the scheme of the Act which is predicated on the assumption that it is not pure coincidence that some jobs done predominantly by women are paid less than those done predominantly by men. In other words, the 'condition' should be assumed to apply to a largely female profession; the question is whether the difference in pay can be justified and it may be argued that where a particular occupation is staffed predominantly by women and is of equal value to one staffed predominantly by men but there is a wide disparity in pay, it would be hard for the employer, if not impossible, to show that the difference arose from anything other than the mere fact that one occupation was female dominated. In any event, it is clear that the fact of separate bargaining processes merely amounts to a smoke screen obscuring the traditional operation of market forces founding the difference in pay and therefore clearly should not be able to justify it, given that the legislation was introduced in order to interfere with, rather than bow to, market forces.

The material factor defence could potentially be seen as operating at three different levels of generality. First, it might only arise where a difference in the 'personal equation' of the man and the woman, such as length of experience or qualifications, could be identified. This was the approach rejected in *Rainey*. Secondly, a factor might be identified going beyond the personal equation of the complainant, but still amounting to a non-sex-based difference between her and her comparator. At the present time this is the predominant approach. The most significant factor of this type and the one most likely to undermine the equal pay scheme is the 'market forces' factor, which received some endorsement from the ECJ in *Enderby*. This factor is, however, subject to a rigorous application of the *Bilka* test; it does not mean that the laws of supply and demand can simply determine the rates of pay in question. Nevertheless, adoption of this approach may tend to undermine the aim of the Act as removing pay discrimination. Thirdly – and this defence would be available only in respect of equal value claims because of the wider wording applicable – there might be scope for a number of market-based arguments not based on a difference between the man's and the woman's case, such as using the leap frogging argument from *Hayward* as being in itself a material factor, although arising only from the general operation of the concern in question. This possibility has not yet been put forward; it would, of course, be out of harmony with the policy of the Act and arguably could not be termed an 'objectively justified reason' under the *Bilka* test. The complexities of the second approach, which the courts are currently trying to get to grips with, illustrate the difficulty adverted to at the beginning of this chapter of ensuring that only morally justifiable differentiation occurs.

6 VICTIMISATION[204]

Under the relevant statutes, victimisation occurs when a discriminator treats a person less favourably for taking action or aiding in an action under the RRA or SDA or EPA or DDA – for doing a 'protected act'. The provisions under s 2 of the RRA and s 55 of the DDA are almost identical to the equivalent 'victimisation' provisions under s 4 of the SDA and have the same aim – to deter employers and others from dismissing or treating adversely someone who undertakes a 'protected act' or aids another in doing so.

In order to determine whether the unfavourable treatment is linked to the protected act, it is necessary to ask whether the claimant would have been subjected to the treatment but for performing the protected act. In order to decide this question, it must be asked how a comparable person would have been treated. According to the findings in *Aziz v Trinity St Taxis*[205] the comparison must be between a person who has done the act and a person who has not, not between a person who has done the act and a person who has taken action under other legislation. This stance was confirmed by the Court of Appeal in *Brown v TNT Express Worldwide (UK) Ltd*[206] and by the House of Lords in *Chief Constable of West Yorkshire Police v Khan*.[207]

Following *Aziz v Trinity St Taxis*[208] there has to be a clear causal relationship between the action brought and the unfavourable treatment. Aziz, a taxi driver and a member of Trinity Street Taxis (TST), thought that TST were unfairly treating him and made a tape recording of a conversation to prove it. He took his claim of race discrimination to an industrial tribunal, but it failed. He was then expelled from TST and claimed victimisation. The Court of Appeal considered the question of causation: had TST treated him less favourably by reason of what he had done in making the tapes with a view to bringing a race discrimination case, or had it expelled him because of the breach of trust involved in making the tapes? It was found that the necessary causal relationship was not established; it was not apparent that TST were influenced in their decision to expel him by the fact that the tapes were made in order to bring a race relations case; they would have expelled him anyway because of the breach of trust. This was a fine distinction to make and it is arguable that once a plaintiff has shown that unfavourable treatment has prima facie some causal relationship with a protected act, some causal potency, the burden of proof should shift to the employer to show that it was entirely unrelated to that act.

Under s 4(1) of the SDA, less favourable treatment of someone because she has done a 'protected act' – brought an action or intends to do so or has assisted in such action under

---

204 For discussion of the victimisation provisions see Ellis, E and Miller, CJ, 'The victimization of anti-discrimination complainants' [1992] PL 80.

205 [1988] WLR 79; [1988] 2 All ER 860.

206 [2001] ICR 182.

207 (2001) *The Times*, 16 October, HL; [2000] IRLR 324; [2000] ICR 1169, CA.

208 [1988] WLR 79; [1988] 2 All ER 860.

the 1975 Act or the EPA – amounts to victimisation. The usefulness of this provision has been diminished owing to the need to show that the unfavourable treatment is solely due to the protected act and not in part for some other reason.[209] It may often be hard to prove that this is the case and this is particularly unfortunate owing to evidence which is beginning to emerge in both race and sex discrimination cases that in respect of certain professions, including in particular the police, those in authority are becoming more likely to respond to a protected act by bringing disciplinary proceedings which might not otherwise have been undertaken. This occurred when Alison Halford brought discrimination proceedings against, *inter alia*, Merseyside Police Authority and was probably a factor in her decision to settle the discrimination claim rather than pursue it to a conclusion.[210] A further barrier to victimisation claims was identified in *Wales v Comr of Police for the Metropolis;*[211] it was found that unless the first action complained of amounts to actionable discrimination (the action would have succeeded had it been brought), further unfavourable acts occurring owing to the complaint do not fall within s 4(1). This decision may be incorrect and the decision of the Court of Appeal in *Tower Boot Co v Jones*[212] may ameliorate its impact (since many victimisation claims could be brought as harassment claims), but it does narrow down one avenue leading to possible redress.

Under the DDA, victimisation occurs when a discriminator treats a person, disabled or non-disabled, less favourably for complaining that the DDA has been breached or aiding in that complaint. Following *Aziz v Trinity St Taxis,*[213] there has to be a clear causal relationship between the action brought and the unfavourable treatment.

The approach in victimisation cases may, however, change somewhat as a result of the findings of the House of Lords in *Nagarajan v London Regional Transport.*[214] The Lords found that the alleged discriminator need not have the protected act consciously in mind; all it is necessary to show is that an important or significant cause of the less favourable treatment is the fact that he or she had knowledge of the fact that the applicant had done a protected act. Such a formulation of the test, which echoes the test under s 1(1)(1)(a) of the RRA and SDA, might have led to a different result in *Aziz* since it could have been argued that the employer had the protected act subconsciously in mind. At the least, it makes it clear that the alleged discriminator need not have a conscious motive connected with the relevant legislation and that there may be more than one cause of the unfavourable treatment. Thus, this decision and that in *Aziz* regarding the choice of comparator afforded greater force to the anti-victimisation provisions of the RRA, which will also extend to the equivalent provisions of the SDA and DDA. However, the decision of the House of Lords in *Chief Constable of West Yorkshire Police v Khan*[215] signalled, to an extent, a change of direction which may detract from that impact. The Lords found that

---

209 *Aziz v Trinity St Taxis* [1988] 2 All ER 860, CA.

210 A similar conclusion was reached in a race discrimination case which was settled in May 1993. Joginder Singh Prem claimed that Nottinghamshire Police had discriminated against him in failing to promote him. They responded by bringing disciplinary charges which were later dismissed. He was awarded a payment of £20,000 in respect of the discrimination and an ex gratia payment of £5,000 in respect of the victimisation, although it was denied. See (1993) *The Guardian*, 5 May.

211 [1995] IRLR 531. For discussion, see (1997) 26(2) ILJ 158.

212 [1997] ICR 254; [1997] IRLR 168. See above, p 1009.

213 [1988] WLR 79; [1988] 2 All ER 860.

214 [1999] 4 All ER 65; [1999] 3 WLR 425.

215 (2001) *The Times*, 16 October, HL; [2000] IRLR 324; [2000] ICR 1169, CA.

where a person who has made a claim to a tribunal alleging discrimination subsequently applies for another job, it is not victimisation for the current employer to refuse to provide a reference, citing the claim as the reason. The Chief Constable of Khan's force had stated in response to the reference request that he could not comment as to the reference for fear of prejudicing his own case before the tribunal. The Lords reached their conclusion on the ground that although Khan had been unfavourably treated by comparison with other employees who had not done a protected act (in respect of such persons, the reference would have been sent), the treatment was not by reason of his having done the protected act; it was due to the existence of the proceedings which made it reasonable for the Chief Constable to seek to preserve his position. The proper question to be asked was not merely 'But for the protected act would the adverse treatment have occurred?', but to inquire into the motivation of the alleged discriminator. In this instance, the motive concerned the need to preserve his position in relation to the legal claim; he did not, according to the House of Lords, act as he did in refusing to give the reference for the reason that Khan had done a protected act.

The problem with this approach is that it means that initiating a protected act is likely or bound to set in motion a chain of events, allowing an alleged discriminator to claim that it was one of those events, not the act itself, which led to the unfavourable treatment. If the focus of the inquiry is on the motivation of the alleged discriminator and not on the causal relationship between the unfavourable treatment and the protected act, the claim of victimisation may fail where the alleged discriminator can plausibly (and even with factual correctness) argue that he or she was motivated by one of the events set in motion by the doing of the protected act, not the act itself. In relation to this point it can be argued that two persons may be placed in a very difficult position by reason of the doing of the protected act – the alleged discriminator and the alleged victim. In the instant case, the Chief Constable might have prejudiced his position by writing the reference. Equally, Khan may have been adversely affected by the fact that it was not written. He did have an interview for the other post, but was eventually rejected. It is impossible to say whether the rejection was due at least in part to the lack of a reference and to the fact that he was known to be bringing a discrimination claim. Therefore, there is a choice in such instances before the courts. Should the position of the alleged discriminator or that of the alleged victim be protected? If a test of a straightforward causal relationship is used, the latter is likely to be protected. If a subjective test is used, the position of the former will be protected. The policy of the legislation appears to be to protect the position of the latter and, therefore, a causal relationship test should have been used.

But, in future, a person who has brought a discrimination claim will have to suffer the detriment of knowing that while the claim is pending, he or she is in difficulties in applying for another post, thus possibly missing significant opportunities and also being forced to stay in the same workplace in which he has made the claim, which may well be very unpleasant. Thus, the decision of the House of Lords allows a person who has done a protected act to suffer some detriment which is causally linked to the doing of the act. The decision may deter some claimants, precisely the outcome that the legislation appeared to be designed to prevent. In the instant case, it would not have seemed too onerous to expect the police force in question to have put a procedure in place designed to cope with this very situation, such as devolving the writing of the reference to a person not directly implicated in the discrimination claim. If that had any effect on the position of the Chief Constable in relation to the claim, that might be viewed as an inevitable consequence of seeking to protect the position of persons who undertake protected acts. In any event, it is hard to see that it would have such an effect since the person writing the reference would presumably rely on personnel records in order to do so which presumably would be disclosed in any event to the tribunal hearing the claim. But, the net result of the decision in *Khan* is to allow some detrimental action against persons who have done protected acts.

Flawed as these provisions are, it should be pointed out that they do not appear to cover the employee who is victimised for taking any form of legal action; nor do they apply to post-employment victimisation.[216] Thus, where a police officer brought an allegation of rape and buggery against a colleague in respect of an alleged off-duty attack, her subsequent vicious and prolonged victimisation at work could not, it was found, be addressed under the anti-victimisation provisions of the SDA,[217] although it might be said that a clearer example of gross discrimination on grounds of sex could hardly be found. She was, for example, threatened with violence by her Chief Superintendent, forced to undergo psychological analysis, advised to leave the force, harassed, and denied time off work.

This might be an instance in which action under the HRA would provide an alternative possibility. Indeed, the HRA may provide the possibility of curbing victimisation in relation to the taking of legal action in situations ranging far outside the employment context, although admittedly not where the responsibility lies with a private body. Where an applicant has been victimised in a work-related situation, or indeed in any situation for which a public authority has responsibility, such as in an educational institution, as a result of instigating legal action, whether against a colleague or the employer, or perhaps against any person or body, it would be arguable that Art 6 has been breached on the basis that the victimisation is intended to force her to drop the action, thus impairing her exercise of her Art 6 rights.[218] It could also be argued that where a person has been victimised post-employment on the basis of taking action under the RRA, SDA, or DDA, or on the basis of alleged employment detriment under other legislation on other unprotected grounds, Arts 6 and 14 could be engaged.[219] The same argument could be made on any protected ground within Art 14, including on the grounds of race, sex or disability, outside the contexts and/or grounds covered by the anti-discrimination legislation. Where victimisation reaches the level of viciousness found in the instance given above, an action based on Art 3 or Art 8[220] could be brought. In all these instances, assuming that the body responsible, directly or indirectly for the victimisation, was a public authority, the action could be brought directly against it under s 7(1)(a) of the HRA. This is clearly a very significant possibility, and since one might have

---

216 *Adekeye v Post Office (No 2)* [1997] IRLR 105.

217 *Waters v Comr of Police of the Metropolis* [1997] IRLR 589.

218 See the discussion in Chapter 2, pp 60–61.

219 On the basis that Art 14 encompasses a number of protected grounds in a non-exhaustive list; see Chapter 2, p 85.

220 Arguably, the treatment to which the woman police officer was subjected could be viewed as analogous to that suffered by the applicants in *Lustig-Prean v UK* (1999) 7 BHRC 65; *Smith and Grady v UK* (2000) 29 EHRR 493. Indeed, it is suggested that it might, unlike the treatment in those instances, fall within the boundaries of Art 3.

expected the courts, under the impetus of the HRA, to seek to prevent victimisation by private bodies with a view to punishing persons for or preventing them from taking legal action, it is at least possible that eventually a right to take legal action free from victimisation will be discovered to exist arising from common law principle.[221]

7 LAWFUL DISCRIMINATION

Exclusions from the Sex Discrimination Act[222]

A large number of exclusions were embodied in the Sex Discrimination Act and therefore discrimination in such circumstances was lawful under domestic legislation. Certain occupations were excluded under s 19, which covers employment for the purpose of organised religion, and s 21, which covers mine workers. The armed forces were also excluded under s 85(4), but this exclusion was abolished under ss 21–28 of the Armed Forces Act 1996. Acts safeguarding national security were exempted (s 52), as were acts done under statutory authority (s 7 and s 51). This last provision means that the 1975 Act is of lower status than other statutes, since it is unable to prevail over other statutory provisions relating to the protection of women even though they were passed before it. Thus, statutes intended to enshrine discrimination in their provisions, such as tax, immigration or social security statutes, were not affected by the 1975 Act.[223] These exceptions have tended to be narrowed owing to the impact of the Equal Treatment Directive. For discussion of lawful discrimination under EU law see below.[224]

A general exception to provisions against discrimination in the employment field also arises where sex can be said to be a genuine occupational qualification (GOQ) under one of the s 7 provisions.[225] This arises in a number of contexts, including those where the job appears to call for a man for reasons of physiology (excluding physical strength or stamina)[226] or for reasons of authenticity in respect of plays or other entertainment, or to preserve decency or privacy, or where the job involves dealings with other countries where women are less likely to be able to carry them out effectively because of the customs of that other country. MacKinnon has argued that these exceptions are too broad as extending some way beyond biological differences and accepting differential treatment based solely on social categorisation.[227] On this basis, it is arguable that they are due to be

---

221 There are recent indications that the common law is showing a robustness in providing for protection against discrimination which was not previously evident: see *Matadeen and Another v Pointu and Others, Minister of Education and Science and Another* [1999] 1 AC 98, but there would be the grave problem of finding an existing cause of action. The alternative is that direct horizontal effect will at some future point be found to arise under the HRA on the basis that a court is a public authority under s 6; see Chapter 4, p 157.

222 For discussion, see Pannick, *op cit*, fn 27, pp 255–70; McColgan, *op cit*, fn 1, Chapter 6, pp 346–54.

223 Section 51 was substituted by the Employment Act 1989, s 3, which is of narrower scope. For discussion of provisions intended to protect women, especially in relation to reproductive risks, see Kennedy (1986) 14 IJSL 393.

224 See pp 1037–38. See, particularly, the discussion of *Johnston v Chief Constable of the RUC* [1986] ECR 1651.

225 For analysis of s 7 see Pannick, D (1984) OJLS 198.

226 For criticism of this provision see Pannick, *op cit*, fn 27, p 238.

227 MacKinnon, *op cit*, fn 115, pp 121, 180.

overhauled and narrowed down, particularly the last-mentioned, on the ground that the UK should not bow to discriminatory practices in other countries.

The existing GOQs under s 7 of the SDA are also applied under s 7A in respect of discrimination on grounds of gender reassignment. Further GOQs are applied under s 7B where (a) the job involves the likelihood of performing intimate physical searches pursuant to statutory powers or (b) living in a private home where objection might reasonably be taken to allowing the person in question 'the degree of physical or social contact with a person living in the home' or 'knowledge of intimate details of the person's life', or (c) it is necessary to live on premises provided by the employer since it is impracticable for the holder of the job to live elsewhere and objection could be taken to the job holder sharing accommodation with persons of either sex while undergoing gender reassignment; or (d) the job holder provides personal services to vulnerable individuals and the employer reasonably believes that they cannot be effectively provided by a person while undergoing gender reassignment. The GOQs under paras (c) and (d) do not apply to persons whose gender reassignment is complete. It is arguable that the width of these GOQs means that the SDA is not in compliance with the Equal Treatment Directive, in which case, as argued above, the Directive itself could be relied upon or a purposive approach could be adopted to the SDA. If neither the SDA or ETD could be found to apply, the HRA could be relied upon if the action was against a public authority, using ss 6, 7(1)(a) and relying on Art 8.[228]

Exclusions from the Race Relations Act[229]

Like the SDA, the RRA cannot affect (a) discrimination which falls outside its scope or (b) discrimination enshrined in other statutes, even those which predate it (s 41(1))[230] or (c) discrimination occurring within the scope of a specific exception. In respect of (a) this includes not only racist behaviour falling outside the contexts covered by the Act, but also such behaviour occurring within those contexts but unable to find a legal niche within them owing to the particular wording of the Act. For example, it was found in *De Souza v AA*[231] that racial insults, as such, do not amount to 'unfavourable treatment' within employment.

Alternatively, one of the exceptions may apply. Exceptions in respect of small premises or partnerships with less than six partners are provided by s 10 and s 32. Under s 75, restrictions on employment in Crown Service are permissible, although the Government has accepted that this provision should be narrowed down.[232] Section 42 provides that nothing in the RRA 'shall render unlawful an act done for the purpose of safeguarding national security'. Prior to the passing of the Race Relations (Amendment)

---

228 See further on this point below, in relation to discrimination on grounds of sexual orientation; pp 1057–58.

229 For discussion see McColgan, *op cit*, fn 1, Chapter 7, pp 433–45.

230 The scope of s 41 was narrowed by the House of Lords in *Hampson v DES* [1990] 2 All ER 513 to cover only acts done in necessary performance of an express statutory obligation, not acts done in the exercise of a discretion conferred by the statute.

231 [1986] ICR 514; for comment see Carty (1986) 49 MLR 653; see also *Khan v GMC* (1993) *The Times*, 29 March.

232 Government Response to the CRE's Reform of the RRA 1976 (1998); available at http://195.44.11.137/coi/coipress.nsf.

Act 2000, s 69(2)(b) provided for the use of ministerial certificates as conclusive evidence that acts or arrangements specified were done for that purpose. Section 7 of the 2000 Act amends s 42 to add the words 'if the doing of the act was justified for that purpose', and repeals s 69(2)(b).

The Act employs the concept of a genuine occupational qualification (GOQ) under s 5, but the GOQs are of much narrower scope than those arising under the 1975 Act. They come down to two. First, that for reasons of authenticity, a person of a particular racial group must be employed. This might cover plays and restaurants or clubs with a particular national theme. Secondly, the services being provided are aimed at persons of a specific racial group and can most effectively be provided by persons of that same racial group. In *Lambeth BC v CRE*[233] it was determined that this requirement would be interpreted restrictively: a managerial position which involved little contact with the public would not fulfil it.

8 POSITIVE ACTION[234]

The theoretical basis

A significant divergence within equality theory lies between belief in equality of outcome and belief in equal treatment. The two views appear to diverge, since achieving an equal outcome may mean treating persons unequally for a time, as opposed to treating them equally even if that produces unequal results. Nevertheless, it may be argued that such divergence is to an extent more apparent than real, since the underlying aim of providing equal treatment may be to ensure, ultimately, an equal outcome. The conflict between ensuring equality of treatment and furthering equality of outcome by means of positive action appears to be founded on the perception that such action means treating two likes unalike and thereby creating a denial of formal equality. In espousing a very significant principle, equal treatment of two likes or formal equality has a clear, simple and, to an extent, warranted appeal. But, positive action cannot be accommodated within a formal equality model, since such a model only permits unlike (and, presumptively, unfavourable) treatment if difference is identified. In terms of pure theory, positive action has no place within a formal equality model either as an aspect of the equality principle or as an exception to it. In practice, an unsatisfactory compromise may be reached whereby positive action is viewed as an exception to the equality principle. Once that principle has been abandoned, unequal treatment may be meted out. But, apart from the conceptual incoherence of this position, it is suggested that it is unsatisfactory in that it does not readily provide a means of recognising the convergence between equality of outcome and of treatment which is not apparent within the other exceptions to the equality principle.

---

233 [1990] IRLR 231, CA.

234 For general discussion, see Edwards, *Positive Discrimination*, 1987; Sacks, V, 'Tackling discrimination positively in Britain', and Parekh, B, 'The case for positive discrimination', in Hepple and Szyszczak, *op cit*, fn 1.

However, it may be possible to escape from the constraints of formal equality by adopting a substantive as opposed to a formal equality model. Substantive equality recognises that men and women, whites and blacks, may be differently situated, but seeks to prevent both perpetuation of such difference and disadvantage flowing from it. In particular, substantive equality recognises that merely treating like as like, while ignoring the context within which such treatment is meted out, fails to understand the disadvantages certain groups may be under because of past discrimination, social attitudes and unequal distribution of social benefits. One factor both springing from and underpinning such a situation appears to be a lack of women or blacks in more advantageous and influential employment. Thus, use of positive action may be accommodated within a substantive equality model, since an outcome which both countered prior disadvantage and tended to change the context within which women or members of ethnic minorities take part in employment would be in accordance with such a model.

Forms of positive action and their recognition in national law

Four types of positive action may be identified:[235]

(1) reverse discrimination, which in its most absolute form would mean favourable treatment of a woman or a member of an ethnic minority on the ground of gender or race despite inferior qualification for a job or an inferior claim (in terms of criteria other than race or gender) to a facility such as housing;

(2) adopting a presumption in favour of appointing a candidate from the disadvantaged group if his or her qualifications were roughly equal to those of a person from the non-disadvantaged group;

(3) action to promote opportunities for members of the disadvantaged group in order to ensure that its members were in a strong position to compete for employment; or (in its weakest form)

(4) adoption of equal opportunities policies particularly affecting advertising and recruiting.

At present, there is no scope for positive action in the first two forms under the SDA and RRA, while scope for the third form is extremely limited. Acts done to meet the special needs of certain racial groups (such as by the provision of English language classes) in regard to education, welfare and training are permissible, but such provision can only be made available where there were no or very few members of the group in question doing that work in the UK at the time.[236] Also, under s 37 of the RRA, employers can encourage applications from members of particular racial groups which are under-represented in the workforce. Similarly, s 47(3) of the SDA permits the restriction of access to training facilities to those 'in special need of training by reason of the period for which they have been discharging domestic or family responsibilities'. It should be noted that employers and others are under no duty to make such provision. But, general positive action is unlawful under the wording of s 1(1) of both statutes. Thus, employers can pursue equal opportunities policies such as stating in job advertisements that applications from certain

---

235 For discussion of forms of positive action see McCrudden (1986) 15 ILJ 219.
236 RRA 1976, ss 35–38.

groups will be welcomed, but in general cannot appoint a less well qualified black[237] or woman in order to address under-representation of black people or women caused by past discrimination. Nor can they import a general presumption that a woman or black with roughly equal qualifications to those of other candidates should be appointed.

A particular type of positive action known as 'contract compliance', which fell within the third and fourth forms of action identified above and had the potential to produce quite far reaching beneficial effects, was outlawed by the then Conservative Government.[238] Under this method, organs of the State such as local authorities produced a 'check list' of equal opportunities policies and asked the companies with which it was thinking of dealing to show evidence of compliance with such policies. If the company could not show in response that certain procedures were in place intended to combat racism or sexism, it lost business. Parliament has, however, left intact a limited power to vet potential contractors as regards their race relations record,[239] presumably because the previous government viewed race discrimination as more serious or politically contentious than gender discrimination.

The RRA, after amendment by the Race Relations (Amendment) Act 2000 (which inserted a new s 71 into the 1976 Act), places a general duty on public authorities to 'eliminate unlawful racial discrimination' and to 'promote equality of opportunity and good relations between persons of different racial groups'. This general duty will be supported by specific duties set out in subordinate legislation and those specific duties will be enforceable by the CRE. The specific duties appear to allow for positive action of types (3) and (4), indicated above. Guidance will be offered by Codes of Practice to be promulgated by the CRE under s 71C. The CRE can seek to enforce the specific duties by issuing a compliance notice under s 71D. It will require the person in question to comply with the specific duty and can also require the person to furnish the CRE with information in order to verify that the duty has been complied with. A court order can be obtained under s 71E to force the public authority to furnish the information and to comply with any requirement of the notice.

Positive action favouring women under EU law

Given the recent increase in the use of positive action within some Member States of the Community and the acceptance of the need for such action by the European Council and Parliament (see Council Recommendation 84/635 EEC, below, and para 26 of the Advocate General's Opinion in *Kalanke* below) and in much of the relevant literature[240] the decision in Case 450/93 *Kalanke v Freie Hansestadt Bremen*[240a] was highly significant in terms of its ability to affect an emerging tendency.

Within the Equal Treatment Directive positive action is viewed, under Art 2(4), as a derogation from the equal treatment principle which must, it seems, be looked at in the same light as the other derogations from that principle under Art 2(2) and (3). The

---

237 In *Riyat v London Borough of Brent* (1983) (cited in IDS *Employment Law Handbook* 28, 1984, p 57) it was held that discrimination in favour of black job applicants was unlawful.

238 Under the Local Government Act 1988, s 17; for criticism, see Townshend-Smith, *op cit*, fn 27, pp 237–38.

239 The 1988 Act, s 18.

240 See, eg, Morris G, and Deakin, S, *Labour Law*, 1995, Chapter 6, p 589.

240a [1995] IRLR 660. For discussion see Shiek, D (1996) 25 ILJ 239.

exception under Art 2(2) is applicable to occupations in which the sex of the worker is a determining factor; Art 2(3) covers the provision of special protective measures for women, particularly those relating to pregnancy and maternity. The conceptual similarity between the derogations was confirmed and made explicit by the Advocate General and, to a lesser extent, by the Court of Justice in *Kalanke*; the decisions in Case 318/86 *Commission v France*[241] and Case 222/84 *Johnston v Chief Constable of the RUC*[242] on Art 2(3) and (4) are therefore relevant for comparative purposes.

The decision in Case 318/86 *Commission v France* concerned in part a quota system used to allot only 10–30% of posts to women in the French national police and prison service, regardless of their performance in the recruitment competition. The system was therefore intended to ensure that men overwhelmingly outnumbered women in these services. The French Government sought to justify this policy within Art 2(2) on the ground that appointing an 'excessive proportion of women' would 'seriously damage the credibility' of the police corps since it would have difficulty in maintaining public order. The Court of Justice found that certain activities within the police service could properly be performed by men only, but that this could not provide justification for a system of recruitment which left it unclear whether the quotas operating for each sex actually corresponded to the specific activities for which the sex of the person in question constituted a determining factor. The lack of transparency – the fact that no objective criteria determining the quotas laid down were available – made it impossible to verify such correspondence. This part of the Court's decision, therefore, left open the possibility of allocating men and women to different specific activities and thereby excluding women from certain areas of employment on grounds which, it would appear, were in themselves non-transparent, since the assumption that women police officers would be unable to carry out effectively activities intended to maintain public order was in itself untested. In effect, one non-transparent factor – the system of recruitment – cloaked another; the first such factor was rejected, but the second accepted. The other part of the decision concerned direct discrimination within the system of promotion to the post of head warder within the French prison corps. The Court found that 'having regard to the need to provide opportunities for promotion within the corps of warders' (p 3580, para 17) justification for the discrimination could be found. This finding was made despite acceptance by the Court that sex was not a determining factor for the appointment of governors owing to the administrative nature of the job.

A similar position was taken in Case 222/84 *Johnston v Chief Constable of the RUC* in which the Court found that Art 2(2) might in principle allow a wide derogation from the principle of equal treatment since 'in a situation characterised by serious internal disturbances the carrying of firearms by policewomen [in the Royal Ulster Constabulary (RUC)] might create additional risks of their being assassinated and might therefore be contrary to the requirements of public safety' (para 16). Thus, the sex of the worker could be a 'determining factor' in making appointments to posts which necessitated carrying arms. However, the national court might only rely on this derogation if it ensured compliance with the proportionality rule. It was for the national court to determine whether proportionality had been observed and therefore the Court did not give an

---

241 [1989] 3 CMLR 663; [1988] ECR 3559.
242 [1986] ECR 1651.

opinion on the matter (para 9). In contrast to this stance, the Court took a narrow view of Art 2(3), finding that it would not allow a reduction of the rights of women on the basis of a need for protection 'whose origin is socio-cultural or even political' (p 1659, para 8). It thereby created an appearance of accepting substantive equality arguments, but abandoned them in favour of focusing on special female vulnerability in relation to Art 2(2), readily accepting the assumption that women were more at risk than men and that women police officers could therefore be confined to other duties of a narrower, family-oriented nature. In a manner recalling the position taken in *Commission v France,* the Court did not appear to recognise that there was a contradiction in rejecting a potential basis for derogation on the ground that it was founded on socio-cultural considerations, but opening the way to acceptance of another which appeared to be equally open to such criticism.

The decision in *Kalanke v Freie Hansestadt Bremen* concerned a quota system which was in a sense the converse of that in question in *Commission v France* in that it ensured positive action in favour of women. In the German public services, an appointing procedure had been adopted whereby women with the same qualifications as men had to be given automatic priority in sectors in which they were under-represented. In evaluating qualifications family, work, social commitment or unpaid activity could be taken into account if relevant to the performance of the duties in question. Under-representation was deemed to exist when women did not make up at least half the staff in the individual pay brackets in the relevant personnel group or in the function levels provided for in the organisation chart. Mr Kalanke was not approved for promotion under this procedure and sought a ruling from the *Bundesarbeitsgericht* that the quota system was incompatible with the German basic law and the German civil code. The *Bundesarbeitsgericht* considered that no such incompatibility arose since the system only favoured women where candidates of both sexes were equally qualified and, further, that the quota system was interpreted in accordance with German basic law which meant that although in principle priority in promotions should be given to women, exceptions must be made in appropriate cases. However, since the national court was uncertain whether the system was in accord with the Equal Treatment Directive, it referred to the European Court of Justice questions relating to the scope of the derogations permitted to the principle of equal treatment under the Directive.

The court found that the quota system created direct discrimination within Art 2(1) but that it might be permissible under Art 2(4), basing this finding on the ruling from *Commission v France* cited by the Advocate General (para 18). It approved the finding of the Council in the third recital in the preamble to Recommendation 84/635/EEC of 13 December 1984 in relation to positive action (OJ 1984 L331, p 34) that 'existing legal provisions on equal treatment ... are inadequate for the elimination of all existing inequalities unless parallel action is taken by government ... and other bodies ... to counteract the prejudicial effects on women in employment which arise from social attitudes, behaviour and structures' (para 20). It then went on to find, citing *Johnston*, that derogations from the equality principle must be narrowly construed and that national rules which guarantee women 'unconditional priority' go beyond promoting equal opportunities and overstep the limits of the exception in Art 2(4). Although the Court found that Art 2(4) permits 'national measures relating to access to employment, including promotion, which give a specific advantage to women with a view to improving their ability to compete on the labour market' (para 19), it did not find that the promotion scheme at issue fell within the exception. This conclusion was apparently founded on the distinction it drew between equality of opportunity and equality of outcome in finding that the quota system 'substitutes for equality of opportunity the result which is only to be arrived at by providing such equality of opportunity'. It therefore found that national rules of the type in question are precluded by Art 2(1) and (4).

As this ruling and the Opinion of the Advocate General make clear, the Equal Treatment Directive encapsulates a view of equality under Art 2(1) which impliedly finds inequality of outcome acceptable so long as equal treatment is accorded. Positive action aimed at reducing such inequality must be seen as an exception to the equal treatment principle: the relationship between the two can be viewed only in negative terms under Art 2(4). The Directive therefore creates a conceptual separation between positive action and the equality principle which necessitates characterising such action as direct discrimination which may be susceptible to justification only within the specified exception.[243] There is therefore, it seems, no room for an argument from principle in favour of equality of outcome as an aspect of the equality principle encapsulated under the Directive. (It may be noted that this stance is out of accord with the UN Convention on the Elimination of All Forms of Discrimination Against Women 1979 Art 4(1), which provides that 'the adoption of temporary special measures aimed at accelerating *de facto* equality between men and women shall not be considered discrimination'.)

As the Advocate General observed, the stance of the Directive under Art 2(1) reflects a formal equality position. A formal equality model only permits unlike (and, presumptively, unfavourable) treatment if difference is identified. Nevertheless, as the Advocate General pointed out, positive action may be viewed as furthering substantive as opposed to formal equality. However, the Advocate General appeared to view substantive equality measures as confined to those which would allow individual women to compete with men on a formal equality basis. He did not appear to recognise that furtherance of substantive equality demands that the context within which such competition takes place must change. As MacKinnon has argued,[244] substantive equality recognises that the context within which women take part in employment may place them under a disadvantage owing to past discrimination, social attitudes and a gendered social situation. Positive action may be viewed not as compensating women for historical disadvantage, but as an effective means of allowing its effects to be more rapidly overcome in future. In finding that the quota system could not fall within Art 2(4), the court and the Advocate General failed to give weight to the substantive equality argument that the social context within which women undertake employment, which is influenced by the imbalance between women and men in senior or more influential posts, tends to perpetuate inequality. Although the Court found that certain measures giving a specific advantage to women would be permissible within Art 2(4), it considered that measures used to address such an imbalance could not be seen as a means of creating a

---

243 See Ellis, 'The definition of discrimination in European Community sex equality law' (1994) 19 EL Rev 563–80, pp 567–68; Hepple, B, 'Can direct discrimination be justified?' (1994) 55 EOR 48.

244 MacKinnon, C, *Towards a Feminist Theory of the State*, 1989; MacKinnon, C, 'Reflections on sex equality under law' (1991) 100 Yale LJ 1281.

reduction in the 'actual instances of inequality which may exist in the reality of social life'. The position adopted appeared to be contradictory since it accepted that ensuring equality of 'starting points' would not lead to achieving substantive equality and yet viewed substantive equality as the ultimate objective of providing equal opportunities (para 14).

The Opinion of the Advocate General and the judgment of the Court also reveal, it is suggested, a contradiction in the application of the proportionality principle. The Court, unlike the Advocate General, did not expressly apply that principle in finding that the limits of Art 2(4) had been overstepped. However, that finding in itself involved, it is suggested, *application* of the proportionality principle: the quota system appeared to fall within the Court's interpretation of Art 2(4) but created, in the view of the court, too great an offence to the equality principle owing to its unconditional nature. In *Johnston*, in contrast, the Court found that the national court might only rely on the derogation under Art 2(2) if it ensured compliance with the proportionality rule, but that ensuring such compliance was a matter for the national court to decide and therefore the Court did not give an opinion on the matter (para 9). However, it also found that in determining the scope of the derogation, proportionality must be observed (para 38), implying that making such a determination would not be a matter solely within the jurisdiction of the national court. Comparing the findings within these two lines of case law, it is suggested that the point at which the Court of Justice accepts that the principle of proportionality allows a derogation to apply, thereby leaving the determination as to compliance with proportionality in the particular instance to the national court, is unclear; the two exercises of jurisdiction are in danger of being unclearly demarcated, laying the court open to the charge that the principle is being used to excuse either intervention or failure to intervene in national policies in a non-transparent and subjective fashion.

If the findings in *Kalanke* and *Johnston* are inconsistent as regards the demarcation between the point at which proportionality becomes a matter for the national court and the point at which it remains a matter for the Court of Justice, it is suggested that the use made of the proportionality principle in *Kalanke* to find that the derogation under Art 2(4) did not apply is also incompatible with the view taken in *Johnston* that proportionality would be sufficiently adhered to in allowing the policy in question to fall within the Art 2(2) derogation. This may also be said, it is suggested, of the ruling in *Commission v France* in so far as aspects of the systems at issue in that case were found to fall within Art 2(2). It is contended that it would have been open to the court in *Kalanke*, basing itself on the previous line of case law, to find that proportionality would be sufficiently observed in bringing the quota system within the scope of the derogation and, further, that the case for so doing was stronger than in either of the other two instances. This is contended taking into account the extent to which the policies at issue in *Johnston* and *Commission v France* created inequality of treatment and the extent to which they were found to be subject to justification

The German quota system was dependent on equality of qualifications and, according to the national court, would not be rigidly adhered to. In contrast, the policy considered in Johnston operated on the same basis as reverse discrimination since it was unable to take account of the fact that the qualifications of women applicants might be superior to those of male applicants. That policy created a greater affront to the equality principle than the German system in that it aimed at creating a complete imbalance between men and women in the body of police in question, thereby ensuring inequality of treatment and of outcome, whereas under the German system it seemed probable that ensuring equality of outcome would have led eventually to equality of treatment, once the imbalance in certain sectors of the German Civil Service had been corrected. Moreover, in contrast to the position in Johnston and in relation to the post of governor under the French system, the German quota rules did not preclude applications from men for the posts in question.

The justification underpinning the French public service quota system arose from the view that disorder would be less readily contained if an imbalance between men and women in the police service was not maintained, basing this view on an untested assumption regarding the possibility that the presence of a certain number of female police officers might detrimentally affect the power of the police to control disorder. This assumption was accepted by the Commission (p 3581, para 23) and the Court in relation to specific activities, but it is suggested that the means adopted were not clearly an appropriate means of achieving the end in question or necessary to that end (the test for proportionality from Johnston, para 38). The same criticism may be levelled, it is submitted, at the justification advanced to defend the UK policy for the RUC, namely that reserving posts exclusively for men would ensure that persons in those posts would be subject to a lesser risk of assassination. In contrast, it is suggested that adoption of positive action in Kalanke would have been likely to contribute to achieving the desired outcome: as the Advocate General accepted, the imposition of quotas 'is an instrument which is certainly suitable for bringing about a quantitative increase in female employment' (para 9).

It is further suggested that if one applies the 'very logic underlying the derogations', which according to the Advocate General is aimed at 'ensuring the efficacy of the principle of equal treatment' (para 17) to the German quota system, it may be found to cause less affront to that principle than the systems at issue in the other two rulings. As argued above, the German system was in accordance with substantive equality in that it sought to achieve an outcome which would counter past disadvantage and it recognised the real and gendered situation in which women take part in employment. In contrast, it is suggested that in both Johnston and Commission v France the Court allowed the national authorities some discretion as to permitted exceptions from the equality principle on grounds which failed to further either formal or substantive equality. Thus, acceptance of positive action could have been seen merely as a means of moving more speedily towards a desired outcome and therefore, in contrast to the position taken in both the previous decisions, the offence to the equality principle could have been viewed as less significant. By this means, the Court could have recognised the distinction between the exception under Art 2(4) and the other two exceptions. Once the offence to the equality principle created by the German quota system is balanced, as indicated here, against the underlying justifications for it, it is suggested that scope can be created for finding that Art 2(4) was applicable.

However, in Case C-409/95 Marschall v Land Nordrhein-Westfalen[245] the Court found that a quota system allowing affirmative action was lawful on the basis that it was

---

245 [1995] IRLR 39, Judgment of 11 November 1997.

conditional (para 33 of the judgment). The Court said (para 29) 'even where male and female candidates are equally qualified males tend to be promoted ... particularly because of prejudices and stereotypes concerning the role and capacities of women in working life ...'. So a rule can fall within Art 2(4) if it counteracts the prejudicial effect on women of those prejudices (para 31). But since it is a derogation, it must be strictly construed, and so it must contain a proviso (as did the scheme at issue) allowing men to be promoted or employed if special circumstances apply (paras 32 and 33). In taking this stance, the Court appears to have adopted the course the Court left open to it (as argued above) in *Kalanke*. Similarly, in *Badek and Others v Landesanwalt bein Staatgerichtshof des Landes Hessen*[246] the Court found that the ETD does not preclude a rule applying in public service sectors where women are under-represented which gives priority to women where male and female candidates are equally qualified so long as an objective assessment of the candidates is carried out which takes account of their specific personal situations.

Article 141 of the Treaty, as amended by the Amsterdam Treaty, replaced Art 119, which provided for equal pay for work of equal value. Article 141 makes the same provision, but para 3 empowers the Council to adopt measures to ensure the application of the principle of equal opportunities and equal treatment including (emphasis added) the equal pay principle. Thus, measures may be adopted going beyond the provision of equal pay. Paragraph 4 provides:

> ... the principle of equal treatment shall not prevent any Member State from maintaining or adopting measures providing for specific advantages in order to make it easier for the under-represented sex to pursue a vocational activity or to prevent or compensate for disadvantages in their professional careers.

This wording differs from that used in Art 2(4) of the Equal Treatment Directive since, *inter alia*, the word 'opportunities' which was central to the findings in *Kalanke* is not used: it speaks instead of making it easier for the under-represented sex to pursue a 'vocational activity' or preventing or compensating for disadvantages in professional careers. But the term 'specific advantages' is reminiscent of the terms used by the Advocates General in *Kalanke* and *Marschall*, and may imply that covert disadvantages are outside the scope of the provisions. Indeed, the paragraph could be interpreted simply as seeking to ensure equality of starting points in the manner of para 2(4) as interpreted in these two instances. But it seems to have been adopted in response to *Kalanke*, and wording which is deliberately different from that used in Art 2(4) has been used. Thus, Art 141 appears to be in accordance with the findings of the Court in *Marschall* and may even go beyond them.

Thus, forms of positive action, in the sense in which that term is usually understood, are lawful in the Community so long as provisos apply. Positive action in the form of training opportunities may also be lawful within Art 2(4), but since, in referring to the areas covered in Art 1(1), Art 2(4) covers training in apparent contradistinction to access to employment and promotion, it would appear that measures going beyond allowing special training opportunities should be covered. The Advocate General mentioned positive action in the form of the development of child care structures, but this begs the question why such measures should be viewed as positive action, as opposed to being

---

246 Case C-158/97 [2000] All ER (EC) 289.

offered to all carers of children, men and women. Offering such measures only to women reinforces the perception not only that they are more expensive employees, but also that they should shoulder the main burden of responsibility in caring for children.

The main barrier to acceptance of positive action within the Equal Treatment Directive is created by its restrictive approach, which allows such action to be scrutinised only as an exception to the equality principle. Nevertheless, adoption of a broad approach to Art 2(4), similar to that taken in relation to Art 2(2) in *Johnston* and *Commission v France*, allowed the accommodation within the Directive of forms of positive action in *Marschall*. Such an approach can be justified in relation to Art 2(4), although not in relation to Art 2(2), on the basis that it provides a means of recognising the limitations of the formal equality approach.

Goals and timetables in the UK

The Government has not committed itself to the establishment of quotas on the lines of that considered in *Marschall*; it has instead preferred an approach relying on 'goals and timetables'. In July 1998, a target of a 50:50 male/female appointment ratio for men and women in public life, based on merit, was established.[247] In its White Paper *Modernising Government* it committed itself to a pro rata representation of ethnic minority groups in public appointments and to targets of 35% women in the top 3,000 Civil Service posts and 25% in the top 600. It also committed itself to a target of 3.2% of ethnic minority post-holders in the top 3,000 posts and stated that an equivalent target would be set for disabled persons.

In one context – the crucial one of parliamentary representation – the current Labour Government has gone further than merely setting non-statutory, voluntary goals. The Government brought forward legislation to amend the SDA to allow for all-women short lists in order to increase the representation of women in Parliament to a ratio of 50:50 women MPs.[248] The Conservative Party, although concerned at the gross under-representation of women in its group of MPs, has made no proposal likely to have any significant impact in changing the representation, while the Liberal Democrats voted against introducing all-women short-lists in their Autumn 2001 conference. They are therefore likely to remain in the same position as the Conservative Party in this respect.

The duty of reasonable adjustment under the DDA

The DDA does not cover indirect discrimination, but the duty of reasonable adjustment bears some resemblance to the indirect discrimination provisions discussed. It also represents a form of positive action, since the duty creates obligations to take positive steps to seek to remedy certain disadvantages that disabled persons might be under. The duty is placed on employers, on providers of services and on providers of education at all

---

247 Press release of a speech by Joan Ruddock, *Minister for Women*, at a TUC Conference, 9 July 1999 – www.dss.gov.uk/hq/press/1998/july98/186. htm.

248 The Sex Discrimination (Election Candidates) Bill 2001, which received its first reading in the Commons on 17.10.01.The intention is to reverse the decision in *Jepson and Dyas-Elliott v the Labour Party* [1996] IRLR 116, in which it was found that the use of all-women short-lists created unlawful discrimination against men.

levels. The idea is to outlaw practices which, while neutral on their face as between disabled and non-disabled people, place some disabled people at a substantial disadvantage.

Under s 5, the DDA will be breached if the employer fails to comply with a duty of reasonable adjustment and it cannot show that the failure to comply is justified. Section 6 provides that if arrangements made by the employer or physical features of the employer's premises 'place the disabled person at a substantial disadvantage in comparison with persons who are not disabled, it is the duty of the employer to take such steps as it is reasonable in the circumstances of the case for him to take to prevent the arrangements or feature having that effect'.

Under s 6(3), a non-exhaustive list of examples of adjustments is given. Such adjustment might include, for example, making adjustments to premises, making alterations to working procedures or hours, allowing absence for rehabilitation, assessment or treatment. In practice, such adjustments might mean providing Braille keyboards, installing ramps or lifts, or sanitary facilities with disabled access. In *Morse v Wiltshire CC*[249] it was made clear that the duty of the employer involves the taking of a number of sequential steps. It must first be asked whether there is a duty to adjust. Secondly, it must be considered whether the employer has taken reasonable steps to make the adjustment, and thirdly, whether any failure to take the steps can be justified.

A duty of adjustment also arises under s 19 in relation to the provision of goods and services. Under s 19, a service provider discriminates under the Act if he refuses to provide to the disabled person a service he provides to other members of the public. Section 21 provides that if the service provider has a practice that makes it impossible or unreasonably difficult for disabled persons to make use of a service which he provides to other members of the public, it is the duty of the provider to take such steps as it is reasonable in the circumstances of the case for him to take to prevent the practice having that effect. This means adjustment to current means of service provision, including provision of auxiliary aids and availability of alternative means of delivering a service. Unlike the provisions in respect of employment, which do not apply to businesses with fewer than 15 staff, the service provisions apply across the board. However, this requirement is qualified by the need to make only 'reasonable' adaptation. Thus, for example, a large restaurant chain might be expected to provide menus in Braille, but a small high street café might satisfy this requirement by having a waiter read out the menu.

Thus, the DDA will also be breached if the provider of services fails to comply with the duty of reasonable adjustment, depending on what is reasonable in the circumstances. A shop owner who refused to allow guide dogs on the premises would breach the DDA, although she could refuse to allow all other animals to enter. The duty might also mean that a café should display a price list in large type, an estate agents or bank might need to install an induction loop for those with impaired hearing. It might mean merely ensuring that a member of staff was available to open a door to a disabled person or to retrieve articles from high shelves.

---

249 [1998] ICR 1023; [1998] IRLR 352.

There is quite a lot of evidence suggesting that these requirements have not been brought to the attention of service providers. The Chairman of the National Disability Council, the official advisory body on disability (now replaced by the Disability Rights Commission),[250] has expressed concern that many businesses, especially small ones, were not aware of the requirements of the Act.[251] For example, a survey commissioned by the Guide Dogs for the Blind Association found in October 2001 that thousands of pubs and restaurants continue to refuse to accept guide dogs; only two respondents to the survey of 500 publicans and restaurateurs said that they were aware of the law.[252] Companies such as large supermarket operators are aware of the law, but tend to under-enforce it. For example, supermarkets provide disabled parking, but clearly prefer to use persuasive ('talking' spaces) rather than coercive means (wheel clamps) to prevent non-disabled drivers using the disabled spaces.

Under ss 28C and 28T the DDA, as amended by the 2001 Act, will be breached if the provider of education in question fails to comply with a duty of reasonable adjustment and he cannot show that the failure to comply is justified. Sections 28C and T provide that if arrangements made by the provider for admission to the institution in question and in relation to the services provided 'place the disabled person at a substantial disadvantage in comparison with persons who are not disabled', it is the duty of the provider to take such steps as it is reasonable for it to have to take to prevent that effect from occurring. The steps that should be taken do not require schools, under s 28C(2), to alter or remove a physical feature or provide auxiliary aids or services; the precise steps to be taken in schools will be determined by regulations to be made under s 28C(3). Examples of adjustments to be made in schools would include timetabling lessons on the ground floor if there is no lift and bringing library books to a disabled pupil if the library is inaccessible.[253] No provision states that higher or further educational institutions need not make physical alterations or provide auxiliary aids, which suggests that their duty of reasonable adjustment may be more far reaching than that placed on schools. In determining the steps to be taken the institution must, under s 28T(2), have regard to a code of practice issued under s 53A of the DDA.

It is suggested that the duties placed on educational institutions by the 2001 Act, while closing a significant gap in the DDA provision, are of quite a qualified and indeterminate kind. In this respect the 2001 Act continues the stance adopted by the DDA itself.

9 EFFICACY OF THE INDIVIDUAL METHOD

Remedies

The main weakness of the individual method arises from the various remedies available in discrimination cases which (apart from an award of equal pay) are generally perceived

---

250 See below, p 1049.
251 See *The Guardian*, 29 September 1999.
252 See *The Guardian*, 3 October 2001.
253 Standing Committee B Fourth Sitting Col 151, 29 March 2001.

as inadequate,[254] as are the means of enforcing them. Under the RRA, SDA and DDA a tribunal can award a declaration which simply states the rights of the applicant and the respect in which the employer has breached the law. It can also award an action recommendation which will be intended to reduce the effect of the discrimination. However, the EAT in *British Gas plc v Sharma*[255] held that this could not include a recommendation that the applicant be promoted to the next suitable vacancy since this would amount to positive discrimination. It has, however, been pointed out that this would merely be putting the person in the position he or she should have been in rather than giving them a special preference.[256] The tribunal can also award compensation which will be determined on the same basis as in other tort cases. It will be awarded for pecuniary loss and injury to feelings; exemplary damages will not be available. Awards have tended to be low,[257] but they have risen since the decision in *Noone*[258] in which a consultant who was not appointed on grounds of race was awarded £3,000 for injury to feelings. In *Alexander*, some guidance as to awarding compensation for injury to feelings was given by May LJ:

> ... awards should not be minimal because this would tend to trivialise or diminish respect for the public policy to which the Act gives effect. On the other hand ... awards should be restrained.

He considered that they should not be set at the same level as damages for defamation and awarded £500 for injured feelings owing to racial discrimination.[259] The legislation placed an upper limit on awards which was equivalent to that payable under the compensatory award for unfair dismissal. However, the upper limit on damages in respect of sex discrimination was challenged before the European Court of Justice in *Marshall (No 2)*.[260] The ECJ found that the award of compensation in sex discrimination cases brought against organs of the State should be set at a level which would allow the loss sustained to be made good in full. Thus, the Court found that the fixing of an upper limit of this nature was contrary to the principle underlying the Equal Treatment Directive since it was not consistent with the principle of ensuring real equality of opportunity. In response to this decision, the upper limits for compensation under the SDA and RRA were abolished.[261] The result has been a dramatic increase in the size of awards. For example, in *Johnson v HM Prison Service and Others*,[262] an award of £28,500 was upheld on appeal. It was found that the award was not excessive in the circumstances; severe victimisation on racial grounds had occurred. It may be noted that this is currently the highest UK award made in a racial harassment case. No compensation is payable in respect of indirect discrimination unless there has been an

---

254 See Lustgarten (1980), *op cit*, fn 42, pp 225–28; Cotterrell [1981] PL 469, p 475; McColgan, *op cit*, fn 1, Chapter 5, pp 280–88.
255 [1991] ICR 19; [1991] IRLR 101.
256 See Rubenstein [1991] IRLR 99.
257 Gregory notes that in 40% of cases, the award was less than £200 and in only 29% did it exceed £1,000 (Gregory, *op cit*, fn 1, pp 80–81).
258 [1988] ICR 813; [1988] 83 IRLR 195.
259 [1988] 1 WLR 968, CA.
260 [1993] QB 126; [1993] 3 WLR 1054; [1993] 4 All ER 586; [1993] IRLR 445, ECJ; [1994] 1 All ER 736, HL.
261 SI 1993/2798; Race Relations Remedies Act 1994.
262 (1996) *The Times*, 31 December. In a race discrimination case, *Virdi v MPS* (see (2001) *The Guardian*, 14 February) Virdi received £350,000 compensation.

intention to discriminate; this exclusion from the compensation scheme has been much criticised[263] and may contravene European law.[264] It seems fairly clear that awards made at the levels mentioned prior to the *Marshall (No 2)* decision were unlikely to deter employers from discrimination or to affect deeply rooted discriminatory ideologies in institutions.

It is fairly common for the defendant to fail to comply with the award[265] and, if so, the applicant must return to court in order to enforce it. If an action recommendation has not been complied with, the tribunal will award compensation, but only if compensation could have been awarded at the original hearing. As this is unlikely to be the case in an indirect discrimination claim, no remedy will be available except to apply to the CRE or the EOC alleging persistent discrimination.

Success rate of applications

The individual method has so far had only limited success in bringing about change. Gregory notes that in 1976, only 40% of applications in respect of sex discrimination were heard and 10% were successful, while in the same year 45% of applications in respect of race discrimination were heard and 3.4% were successful.[266] The number of applications began to decline from 1976 onwards, although it rose again in the 1990s.[267] Possibly, the decline may have occurred because the success rate was so low that applicants were deterred from bringing a claim in the first place. In other words, the number of applications may have been self-limiting: only the very determined applicants would pursue cases all the way to a hearing. Of course, the decline in the rate of applications may have been partly attributable to the initial rush to attack very blatant examples of sexism and racism, which died away as employers and others began to ensure that policies enshrining such values were either abolished or made less overt.

Less than half of the applications are heard; there is obviously a strong tendency to give up a claim half way through. There may be a number of reasons why cases are not brought, why they are abandoned and why the success rate is so low. Obviously, the applicant is in a very vulnerable position; the position of the parties is usually unequal, especially if an applicant is bringing the claim against his or her employer. The applicant will be afraid of being labelled a troublemaker, perhaps of being sacked or of losing promotion prospects. There may be continual pressure not only on the applicant but on any workmates who have consented to act as witnesses in the claim and they may withdraw their consent to act. The weakness of the remedies is unlikely to encourage claims and the complexity and technicality of the substantive law may also act as a deterrent. It may do so in any event, but coupled with the lack of legal aid, the task facing the applicant may appear overwhelming.

---

263 See, eg, Townshend-Smith, *op cit*, fn 27, p 206.

264 In *Von Colson v Land Nordrhein-Westfalen* [1984] ECR 1891 the Court held that any sanction must have a real deterrent effect. See also *Marshall (No 2)*, fn 260, above.

265 Leonard, *Judging Inequality*, 1987, found that almost 50% of applicants reported delay in getting the employer to pay the compensation (pp 27–29).

266 Gregory, *op cit*, fn 1, pp 87–88.

267 *The Equality Challenge*, EOC Annual Report for 1991; it showed an increase of 40% in applications in that year.

These two factors are exacerbated by and also contribute to the lack of experience tribunal members have of discrimination cases. The applicant may be aided by the Equal Opportunities Commission or the Commission for Racial Equality of the Disability Rights Commission. However, the EOC and CRE have had to refuse the majority of applications owing to their lack of funds. This leads to a poor quality of decision making and to the charge that the employers' lawyers may manipulate the members of the tribunal because of their lack of experience in the area. Thus, a vicious circle is set up. The tribunals need more experience in these cases, but do not receive it because of the factors mentioned here; when a tribunal does hear such a case, there may be flaws in its handling of it, thereby having some effect in terms of deterring future applicants and ensuring that tribunals do not gain more experience.[268]

Reform

The CRE has proposed that there should be a discrimination division of industrial tribunals dealing only with discrimination claims.[269] Such tribunals would gather expertise in such cases and could be equipped with powers to order higher levels of compensation. Legal aid could then be made available in this specialist division even though it remained unavailable in respect of other tribunal cases. The EOC has recommended that equal pay and sex discrimination provisions should be combined in one statute and that the distinction between indirect and direct discrimination as regards compensation should be abolished. Thus, where a person had acted in an indirectly discriminatory fashion, although unmotivated by sexism, compensation would still be payable. This is desirable because there is some evidence that some employers have deliberately failed to conduct a review of working practices so as to be able to put forward a convincing argument that they did not appreciate the discriminatory affect of certain practices. Both bodies have put forward proposals, which are considered below, to strengthen the individual method of challenging discriminatory practices by allowing it to work in tandem with the general, administrative method to a greater extent. Owing to their levels of funding, both bodies have to refuse many applications from individuals asking for help in bringing cases; such under-funding suggests that there is at present a lack of genuine commitment in government to ending discriminatory practices. The new European measures discussed above may aid change since they take a broader, less formulaic approach.

---

268 For early comment on sex discrimination claims, see Leonard, *op cit*, fn 265; on race claims, see Lustgarten (1986), *op cit*, fn 42. See, too, generally, Honeyball, *op cit*, fn 27, Chapter 1 and McColgan, *op cit*, fn 1, Chapter 5.

269 Review of the Race Relations Act 1976: Proposals for Change, Proposal 10.

10 THE COMMISSION FOR RACIAL EQUALITY; THE EQUAL OPPORTUNITIES COMMISSION AND THE DISABILITY RIGHTS COMMISSION

Introduction

Apart from the individual method of bringing about change, the RRA and SDA also contain an administrative method which was included with the aim of relieving the burden on individual applicants.[270] The Disability Discrimination Commission introduced under the DDA represented a much weaker form of administrative method since the Commission had an advisory capacity only. It did not have the power to issue a non-discrimination notice in respect of discriminatory practices. However, the Disability Rights Commission Act (DRCA) 1999 brought counter-disability discrimination powers in this respect into line with those under the RRA and SDA, by creating the Disability Rights Commission (DRC) while effecting certain improvements. The Special Educational Needs and Disability Discrimination Act 2001 amended the DDA to extend the role of the DRC to discrimination in education.

The administrative method represents a more coherent approach than the piecemeal method of bringing individual cases. The aim was to bring about general changes in discriminatory practices rather than waiting for an individual to take on the risk and the burden of bringing a case. Both the CRE and the EOC have three main powers. They can assist and advise claimants, they can issue Codes of Practice and they can conduct formal investigations or general investigations and issue a non-discrimination notice in respect of discriminatory practices. The RRA, after amendment by the Race Relations (Amendment) Act 2000 (which inserted a new s 71 into the 1976 Act) provided new powers for the CRE, as indicated above. It can seek to enforce specific duties on public authorities intended to create equality of opportunity for persons of different racial groups by means of a compliance notice backed up by a court order. Its general duty, extended to further functions by the Race Relations (Amendment) Act 2000, to 'eliminate unlawful racial discrimination' in public authorities was not backed up by any new powers, but is subject to the powers discussed below.

Investigative and remedial powers

An investigation into apparently discriminatory practices where there may be no known victim who wants or is prepared to bring a claim might arise because the company or institution had effectively deterred certain people from coming forward with applications for a job. In such circumstances, if indications of discrimination became apparent – if, for example, it seemed that very few of a certain group were employed – then first a formal investigation (ss 48–50 of the RRA) would be conducted. This decision might be taken if, for example, the workforce was only 1% black although the company was in a racially mixed area in which the black group comprised about 30% of the population. It might be

---

270 For discussion of the role of these two bodies see Lustgarten, L, 'The CRE under attack' [1982] PL 229; Lacey, 'A change in the right direction? The CRE's consultative document' [1984] PL 186; Lustgarten (1983), *op cit*, fn 172. For the EOC, see Sacks, V, 'The EOC – 10 years on' (1986) 49 MLR 560.

found that the recruiting policy was indirectly discriminatory; for example, it might largely be by word of mouth and therefore the existing workforce might tend to reproduce itself. If discriminatory practices were found, a non-discrimination notice would be issued and the CRE might apply for an injunction to enforce it under s 62(1).

However, the CRE has had the use of the power to issue a non-discrimination notice curbed by the House of Lords' decision in *CRE ex p Prestige Group plc*.[271] It was found that the CRE was not entitled to investigate a named person or company unless it already had a strong reason to believe that discrimination had occurred. This meant that where such suspicion did not exist, the CRE could embark on a general investigation only, meaning that it could not subpoena evidence or issue a non-discrimination notice. Thus, the CRE and the EOC are now confined to a more reactive approach; they can only react to very blatant forms of discrimination rather than investigating the more subtle and insidious instances of discrimination, which may be the more pernicious. After this decision, the CRE had to abandon a number of investigations which it had already begun and those formal investigations that it or the EOC did undertake took much longer.[272] There has, therefore, been a tendency for subtle institutionalised racism or sexism to continue unchecked,[273] although more blatant racism, such as the phrase 'no blacks' – which used to appear in advertisements – has now disappeared.

The DRC has powers similar to those of the other two bodies, but s 3 of the DRCA appears to have been included with a view to curbing or excluding a *Prestige* interpretation of the provisions. Nevertheless, it is unclear that the wording will prevent emasculation of the provisions by the judiciary.[274] Under s 53A of the DDA, as amended by s 36 of the 2001 Act, the DRC can issue Codes of Practice giving guidance to employers, service providers, educational bodies and others as to the avoidance of discrimination on grounds of disability.

Judicial review

Although the investigative powers of the EOC have been curbed, it may be able to bring about general changes in discriminatory practices by seeking a direct change in domestic law in reliance on European Community law. In *Secretary of State for Employment ex p EOC*[275] it was found that the EOC can seek a declaration in judicial review proceedings to the effect that primary UK legislation is not in accord with EU equality legislation. Certain provisions of the Employment Protection (Consolidation) Act 1978 governed the right not to be unfairly dismissed, compensation for unfair dismissal and the right to statutory redundancy pay. These rights did not apply to workers who worked less than the specified number of hours a week. The Equal Opportunities Commission considered that since the majority of those working for less than the specified number of hours were women, the provisions operated to the disadvantage or women and were therefore

---

271 [1984] 1 WLR 335; [1984] ICR 473.
272 See Sacks, *op cit*, fn 270.
273 For criticism of *Prestige* see Ellis and Appleby (1984) 100 LQR 349; Ellis and Appleby [1984] PL 236.
274 For discussion, see McColgan, *op cit*, fn 1, pp 307–09.
275 [1994] All ER 910; [1994] ICR 317.

discriminatory. The EOC accordingly wrote to the Secretary of State for Employment expressing this view and arguing that since the provisions in question were indirectly discriminatory, they were in breach of EU law.

The Secretary of State replied by letter that the conditions excluding part timers from the rights in question were justifiable and therefore not indirectly discriminatory. The EOC applied for judicial review of the Secretary of State's refusal to accept that the UK was in breach of its obligations under EC law. The application was amended to bring in an individual, Mrs Day, who worked part time and who had been made redundant by her employers. It was found that Mrs Day's claim was a private law claim which could not be advanced against the Secretary of State, who was not her employer and was not liable to meet the claim if it was successful.

The Secretary of State further argued that the EOC had no *locus standi* to bring the proceedings. However, the House of Lords found that since the EOC had a duty under s 53(1) of the SDA to work for the elimination of discrimination, it was within its remit to try to secure a change in the provisions under consideration and therefore the EOC had a sufficient interest to bring the proceedings and hence *locus standi*. The Secretary of State also argued that no decision or justiciable issue susceptible of judicial review existed. However, the House of Lords found that although the letter itself was not a decision, the provisions themselves could be challenged in judicial review proceedings. In other words, the real question was whether judicial review was available for the purpose of securing a declaration that certain UK primary legislation was incompatible with EU law and, following *Secretary of State for Transport ex p Factortame*, it would appear that judicial review was so available.

As regards the substantive issue – whether the provisions in question, while admittedly discriminatory, could be justified – the House of Lords thought that in certain special circumstances an employer might be justified in differentiating between full and part time workers to the disadvantage of the latter, but that such differentiation, employed nationwide, could not be justified. Thus the EOC, but not an individual applicant, was entitled to bring judicial review proceedings in order to secure a declaration that UK law was incompatible with EU law. Declarations were made that the conditions set out in the provisions in question were indeed incompatible with EU law.

This was a very far reaching decision: it means that where UK legislation is incompatible with EU law, a declaration can be obtained to that effect more rapidly than if it was necessary to wait for an individual affected to bring a case against the particular person or body who was acting within the terms of the UK legislation in question. The decision may not directly have an effect on race discrimination, but it opens the possibility that the EOC may challenge other provisions of UK law and where such provisions have an equivalent under the RRA they will, therefore, also be affected. Further, once the Race Discrimination Directive is implemented, the same route would be available to the CRE.

Reform

On a number of occasions, the CRE and the EOC have made proposals for reform which would strengthen the administrative method[276] and allow it to work more closely in harmony with the individual method. The CRE wants to try to narrow the gap between individual cases and what can be achieved by a formal investigation and has proposed that in order to do this, it should be able to join in the individual's case as a party to the action so as to draw attention to the likelihood of further discrimination occurring. Thus, the individual would receive the remedy, but the general effect of discrimination in the defendant body would be addressed by issuing a non-discrimination notice at the same time. This might be supported on the ground that if one individual brings a successful case against an employer, it is probable that discrimination in that concern is quite widespread. In particular, both the EOC and the CRE have proposed that legislation should be passed to reverse the *Prestige* decision since they consider that they need to be able to launch investigations into a named person or company even when there is no initial strong evidence of discrimination.[277]

11 DISCRIMINATION ON GROUNDS OF SEXUAL ORIENTATION[278]

Introduction

At present, a person who is refused promotion, dismissed from a job or refused an offer of housing, or in other respects adversely treated on grounds of sexual orientation, is in the same position as a woman so treated would have been before 1975, in the sense that at present, no anti-discrimination legislation specifically covers his or her situation. Indeed, far from seeking to outlaw discrimination on this ground, certain legal provisions, discussed below and in Chapter 17, imply that such discrimination is approved of by the law and therefore by society. However, the situation is rapidly changing, largely as a result of the election of the Labour Government in 1997, but also because of developments in EC law. Owing to the current gap in the law, leaving discrimination on

---

276 See the two CRE reviews of the 1976 Act, 1985 and 1991. See the EOC document, *Equal Treatment for Men and Women: Strengthening the Acts*, 1988.

277 See the reviews of the Race Relations Act by the CRE – reform proposals of 1992 and 1998 and the EOC 1988 proposals.

278 Reading: see Cane, *Gays and the Law*, 1982; Feldman, *op cit*, fn 1, pp 525–29; Hewitt, P, *The Abuse of Power*, 1982, Chapter 9; Wintemute, R, *Sexual Orientation and Human Rights: The US Constitution, the ECHR and the Canadian Charter*, 1995; Hervey, T and O'Keeffe, D (eds), *Sex Equality Law in the European Union*, 1996, Chapter 17; Wilkinson, B, 'Moving towards equality: homosexual law reform in Ireland' (1994) 45 NILQ 252; Wilets, *The Human Rights of Sexual Minorities*, 1996; Heinze, *Sexual Orientation: A Human Right: An Essay on International Human Rights Law*, 1995; Wintemute, R, 'Recognising new kinds of direct sex discrimination: transsexualism, sexual orientation and dress codes' (1997) 60(3) MLR 334; Bamforth, *Sexuality, Morals and Justice*, 1997; Skidmore (1997) 26(1) ILJ 51; Pannick, D, 'Homosexuals, transsexuals and the law' [1983] PL 279. For discussion from a non-liberal standpoint, see Stychin, C, *Law's Desire: Sexuality and the Limits of Justice*, 1995. See also: Rubin, G, 'Section 146 of the Criminal Justice and Public Order Act 1994 and the decriminalisation of homosexual acts in the armed forces' [1996] Crim LR 393; Smith, AM, *New Rights Discourses on Race and Sexuality*,1994; Skidmore, *ibid*; Wintemute, *ibid*; Duffy, P, 'A case for equality' (1998) EHRLR 134; Wintemute, R, 'Lesbian and gay inequality 2000: the potential of the HRA and the need for an Equality Act 2002' (2000) 6 EHRLR 603.

this ground to go relatively unchecked, the HRA may be looked to as a method of providing some protection for the rights of homosexuals.

The discussion below considers the provisions that can be utilised to seek to provide protection from discrimination on this ground in the various fields that would normally appear in anti-discrimination legislation. As will be indicated, the HRA may be able to provide such protection in a number of these fields, where a public authority has some responsibility for the discrimination in question.[279]

Clearly, merely offering a remedy where discrimination has occurred is only part of the answer to the problems caused where persons discriminate on this ground. Many homosexuals 'choose' discrimination-avoidance or harassment-avoidance by concealing their homosexuality. It has been found in a survey of 2,000 lesbians and gay men at work that 56% concealed their sexuality in all jobs and 33% concealed it in some.[280] A number of surveys have found evidence of widespread discrimination against persons on grounds of sexual orientation and a high incidence of harassment.[281] Offering a remedy in such instances must be a last resort and one that many persons would be unwilling to take. The discussion above as to claims based on the other protected grounds has sought to indicate that seeking to address discrimination through legal claims is fraught with difficulties and may leave a vulnerable person in a more vulnerable position. Thus, while anti-discrimination legislation is clearly needed, it would have a dual function. First, it would offer a remedy which is only doubtfully currently available. Secondly, it would affirm symbolically the abhorrence of society for homophobic attitudes and behaviour. It would be likely, eventually, to have the effect of indicating to persons inclined to homophobic views that those views are as unacceptable in society as racist or sexist ones.

Employment

Provisions against unfair dismissal

If a lesbian or homosexual has been employed for at least two years before dismissal, the provisions against unfair dismissal under the Employment Rights Act 1996 (previously contained in the Employment Protection (Consolidation) Act 1978) may offer some protection, although a dismissal will be fair if it is for 'some other substantial reason of a kind to justify dismissal', provided that the employer acts reasonably. Where dismissal is on grounds of sexual orientation, a wide interpretation has been given to the meaning of 'reasonable' in the older decisions. In *Saunders v Scottish National Camps*,[282] the applicant, who was employed as a maintenance handyman at a boys' camp, was dismissed on the grounds of homosexuality although his duties did not ordinarily bring him into contact with the boys. His dismissal was nevertheless held to be fair on the ground that many other employers would have responded in the same way. The decision is clearly open to

---

279 See Wintemute, *ibid*.

280 See Palmer, *A Survey of Lesbians and Gay Men at Work*, 1993.

281 'Equality for lesbians and gay men in the work place' (1997) Equal Opportunities Review 20.

282 (1981) EAT 7/80, judgment delivered 14 April 1980; for criticism, see quoted comments of Levin in Beer *et al*, *Gay Workers, Trade Unions and the Law*, 1981, p 27. See to similar effect *Boychuk v Symons Holdings Ltd* [1977] IRLR 395, but cf *Bell v Devon and Cornwall Police Authority* [1978] IRLR 283, McColgan, *op cit*, fn 1, Chapter 6, pp 387–97.

attack on the ground that even when his duties brought him into contact with the boys, there would have been no more reason to believe that they would have been in danger from him than would girls from a male heterosexual. Similarly, it has been found that the dismissal of a homosexual from GCHQ as a threat to national security was not unreasonable despite the fact that he had been open about his homosexuality and therefore could not be blackmailed.[283]

In the late 1990s, there was some recognition that discrimination on grounds of sex orientation was unacceptable. In *O'Connor v Euromoney Publications Inc*[284] the defendants admitted that O'Connor had been subjected to 'unacceptable and offensive' comments and had been discriminated against on the ground of his sexual orientation. He had also been dismissed from his job with the company. The respondents apologised and, in an out of court settlement, paid a large sum of damages in respect of the dismissal.

In *Lustig-Prean v UK*[285] and *Smith and Grady v UK*[286] the European Court of Human Rights found that the applicants had been subjected to treatment in breach of Art 8 when they were dismissed from the armed services on grounds of their sexual orientation. The UK Government has responded to the ruling, as discussed below. But, it has further implications. Under the HRA, a public authority which dismissed a homosexual on grounds of sexual orientation could be challenged in the courts under ss 6 and 7(1)(a) of the Act, relying on Art 8. Where a private body was the employer, the applicant could rely on s 3 of the HRA in seeking to persuade a tribunal to afford an interpretation to the unfair dismissal provisions which would allow a remedy to be offered. This possibility would, of course, also be available in unfair dismissal proceedings against a public authority.

The Sex Discrimination Act, Art 141 of the EC Treaty, and the Equal Treatment and Equal Pay Directives

Prior to the inception of the HRA, it was clear that a homosexual applicant could not fall within the SDA unless he or she could show that someone of the opposite sex would have been treated more favourably. In other words, where a lesbian woman or gay man would be subjected to equal and unfavourable treatment, no action would lie since s 1 of the SDA is concerned with grounds of sex, not sexual orientation. In the UK courts it was also found in 1996 that applicants treated unfavourably because of their sexual orientation are not covered by the Equal Treatment Directive.[287]

However, in 1997, it appeared that the weak position of homosexuals who are dismissed from employment or otherwise detrimentally treated might be about to change under the influence of EU law. In Case 13/14 *P v S and Cornwall CC*,[288] P was dismissed from her employment on the ground that she was a transsexual. Her application under the SDA 1975 failed as it was found that transsexuals were outside the terms of the Act.

---

283 *Director of GCHQ ex p Hodges* (1988) COD 123; (1988) *The Times*, 26 July.
284 (1999) *The Guardian*, 6 June.
285 (1999) 29 EHRR 548; (1999) 7 BHRC 65.
286 (2000) 29 EHRR 493.
287 *Smith v Gardner Merchant* [1996] ICR 790; [1996] IRLR 342, noted [1996] 67 EOR 48.
288 Judgment of 30 April 1996; [1996] ECR I-2143; [1996] IRLR 347.

As indicated above, it was found that her case fell within the Equal Treatment Directive on the basis that the Directive is simply the expression of the principle of equality, which is one of the fundamental principles of European Union law. Once it was found that transsexuals were within the Directive, it appeared probable that it would also cover homosexuals. The words 'on grounds of sex' within the Directive could be found to relate, *inter alia*, to the sex of the partner. Thus, where a man was in a partnership with a woman, he would not be likely to experience adverse treatment on that ground. But, where a woman was or was potentially in partnership with a woman, she might experience discrimination on that ground. In that respect, discrimination 'on grounds of sex' could include discrimination on grounds of sexual orientation. In other words, if discrimination occurs due to the fact that a person's partner is or is potentially of the 'wrong' gender, the Directive could, in principle, cover such a situation.

This argument was considered in *Secretary of State for Defence ex p Perkins*,[289] which also concerned the ban on homosexuals in the armed services, and it was determined that owing to the *P v S* decision, the case must be referred to the ECJ. In Case 249/96, *Grant v South West Trains Ltd*,[290] it was argued that a refusal to allow a lesbian partner the same employment perks as those which would be allowed to a heterosexual partner is discrimination contrary to the Directive and Art 119 (as it was). The Advocate General gave his Opinion that discrimination contrary to the Equal Pay Directive and Art 119 had occurred. However, the Court failed to decide in the same way, taking the view that discrimination on grounds of sexual orientation is not covered, with the result that lesbians and homosexuals are unable to claim in the domestic courts any pay or fringe benefits currently only available to heterosexuals. Thus, the Court refused to take this step forward in terms of outlawing discrimination on grounds of sexual orientation. Currently, the most pressing need is to outlaw discrimination on grounds of sexual orientation within decisions as to dismissal and appointment. Article 6a of the Amsterdam Treaty, signed by the Member States on 19 June 1997, provides that the Council can adopt provisions intended to combat discrimination on grounds of sexual orientation and the Framework Directive makes provision in this respect.

Smith v Gardner Merchant[291] followed *Grant*; the Court of Appeal found that a male homosexual could bring a claim under the SDA, but only if he could show that a female homosexual would have been treated more favourably. In other words, the claim would have to be based on grounds of gender and not on grounds of sexual orientation. However, it appeared possible, once the HRA was in force, that a different interpretation of the SDA could be adopted, and that it would be possible to find that discrimination on grounds of sexual orientation can be covered. This interpretation was adopted in *MacDonald v MOD*,[292] a Scottish case relying on the Convention. It was found that a creative interpretation of s 1 of the SDA would allow sexual orientation to fall within the Act. This decision was, however, overturned by the Court of Sessions, which followed *Smith v Gardner Merchant*.

---

289 [1997] IRLR 297.
290 [1998] IRLR 206.
291 [1998] 3 All ER 852.
292 [2001] 1 All ER 620. On appeal: 2001 SLT 819.

At present, there seem to be two possibilities which would bring about change. First, a court might take the view that since the *MacDonald* case was not decided under the HRA, a different approach could be adopted, using s 3 of the HRA to interpret s 1 of the SDA purposively in order to give effect to the protection for sexual orientation within Art 8, relying on *Lustig-Prean v UK* and *Smith and Grady v UK*. In taking this radical approach, such a court could find support from the House of Lords' decision in *R v A*[293] in which the Lords went so far as to read words into a statute in order to achieve a result that they viewed as in compliance with the Convention.

The further possibility is that the ECJ will reconsider its approach in *Grant*, perhaps in an instance in which the employment detriment in question was more profound. It is suggested that since, owing to *Grant*, EU law is out of harmony with ECHR law, as interpreted in *Lustig-Prean v UK* and *Smith and Grady v UK*, the two should be harmonised, if possible, by providing protection for persons discriminated against on grounds of sexual orientation.

Judicial review and the HRA

The guarantee of freedom from discrimination under Art 14 of the Convention, received into domestic law under the HRA, covers discrimination on grounds of sexual orientation through its use of the words 'without discrimination on any ground such as ...'.[294] Therefore, a number of possibilities are open. As indicated above and in Chapter 2, Art 14 only operates in conjunction with another Convention Article. But even where that other Article is not itself breached, a breach may be found when it is read with Art 14.

Prior to the inception of the HRA, judicial review provided a means of challenging decisions or policies having a discriminatory effect, but until the HRA came into force, the threshold for challenge was set so high that it provided an ineffective remedy. This was made clear in the case discussed below.

In the UK until recently, homosexuals were barred from the merchant navy and the armed forces, where homosexual acts were classed as 'disgraceful conduct',[295] although the armed forces in Belgium, Denmark, France, The Netherlands and Spain are all open to homosexuals. The legality of the policy of the Ministry of Defence in maintaining the ban was challenged in *Ministry of Defence ex p Smith and Others*.[296] The applicants, homosexuals who had been dismissed owing to the existence of the ban, applied for review of the policy. Their application was dismissed at first instance in the Divisional Court and the applicants appealed. Rejecting the argument of the MOD that it had no jurisdiction to review the legality of the policy in question, the court applied the usual *Wednesbury* principles. This meant that it could not interfere with the exercise of an

---

293 See Chapter 4, pp 142–44.

294 *Salgueiro da Silva Monta v Portugal* [2001] 1 FCR 653. In *Dudgeon* (1982) 4 EHRR 149 the Court of Human Rights was asked to consider the application of Art 14 read in conjunction with Art 8. It appeared to assume that Art 14 did cover discrimination on this ground, although it found that it did not need to consider the application of Art 14 in the instant case since a breach of Art 8 had been found.

295 See the Army Act 1955, s 66; the Sexual Offences Act 1967, ss 1(5) and 2.

296 [1996] 1 All ER 257; [1996] ICR 740. Noted: Skidmore (1995) 24 ILJ 363; (1996) 25 ILJ 63. For discussion, see Rubin, *op cit*, fn 278; Skidmore, *op cit*, fn 278.

administrative discretion save where it was satisfied that the decision was unreasonable in the sense that it was beyond the range of responses open to a reasonable decision maker. But, in judging whether the decision maker had exceeded that margin of appreciation, the human rights context was important: '... the more substantial the interference with human rights, the more the court will require by way of justification before it will be satisfied that the decision was reasonable.'[297] Applying such principles and taking into account the support of the policy in both Houses of Parliament, it could not be said that the policy crossed the threshold of irrationality, although it was criticised.

The applicants applied to the European Commission on Human Rights and the case was referred to the Court. It may be noted that previously, the Commission had rejected a challenge to the provision relating to the army as inadmissible on the argument that there is a special need to prevent disorder in the armed forces.[298] However, the Court found that the ban infringed Art 8 and Art 13. Its absolute nature meant that it could not be viewed as being in proportion to a legitimate aim. Not only the ban itself, but the intrusive questioning of the applicants after their homosexuality was suspected, was found to constitute an interference with the respect for their private life under Art 8. The applicants also argued that Art 3 had been infringed but, although the Court considered that this was a possibility in respect of discrimination on grounds of sexual orientation, it did not consider that the strict Art 3 test had been met in the circumstances of the case. As a result of this ruling, discharges from the armed services on grounds of sexual orientation have now ceased.

But, as indicated above, the ruling of the Court could be relied upon when seeking review of a decision or policy of a public authority which is discriminatory on grounds of sexual orientation. This route could be used in respect of dismissal and where employment detriment other than dismissal had occurred.

A number of possibilities are readily apparent. For example, a large number of posts in the Home Civil Service[299] are subject to positive vetting (PV). In 1982, the Security Commission recommended[300] that male homosexuality should be dealt with on a case by case basis in relation to PV clearance, but that it should be refused if the individual's practice of his homosexuality placed any doubt upon his discretion or reliability. PV clearance for the Diplomatic Service or armed forces was automatically refused. If security clearance for any governmental post is refused on the ground of sexual orientation, a challenge could be mounted using s 7(1)(a) of the HRA, which would mean that the court's review of the action or decision would be more intensive than that undertaken in *Smith*. It is no longer necessary to rely on seeking to show that in discriminating on this ground, a public body has acted unreasonably. Nevertheless, where national security appeared to be at stake, the courts are likely to afford the body in question a 'discretionary area of judgment' and as a result the review, even under ss 6 and 7(1)(a) of the HRA and Art 8 is unlikely to be intensive. But where national security is not a factor, this route appears to offer quite a strong possibility of success.

---

297 *Ibid*, p 263.
298 *B v UK* 34 D & R (1983); (1983) 6 EHRR 354.
299 In 1982, PV covered 68,000 posts (Cmnd 8540, p 5).
300 Cmnd 8540, 1982.

So long as the alleged discriminator is a public authority under s 6 of the HRA, there are a number of other possibilities, not all of which depend on using Art 8 (which has already shown its potential in this area read alone), but there might also be instances in which, although an invasion of privacy grounded on homosexuality fell within one of the exceptions, it could nevertheless be established taking Art 14 into account owing to its discriminatory nature. Article 10 read in conjunction with Art 14 might offer protection to expressions of the homosexual way of life such as the wearing of badges or even some physical gestures.[301] In *Salgueiro da Silva Mouta v Portugal*[302] the court relied on Art 14 in finding that a breach had occurred where a parent was denied contact with his child on the ground of sexual orientation.

Education

Discrimination against homosexuals in the field of education is enshrined in s 2A of the Local Government Act 1986, inserted by s 28 of the Local Government Act 1988 amended by S 104 of the Local Government Act 2000; it prohibits the deliberate promotion of homosexuality by local authorities or the teaching of 'the acceptability of homosexuality as a pretended family relationship'. Thus, local authorities may still fund certain groups so long as this is aimed at benefiting the group rather than at promoting homosexuality. Robertson argues that s 28 will not have a significant effect in schools, as local authorities do not directly control the curriculum[303] (and this is particularly the case under local management of schools). However, s 28 may serve to ratify and legitimise intolerance of homosexuals in education and outside it. In opposition, the Labour Party pledged to abolish s 28 and in government it brought forward a Bill in order to do so in 2000. The Bill was defeated in the House of Lords, but the intention of the Government continues to be to repeal s 28. The Scottish Parliament has already repealed s 28 as far as Scotland is concerned in 2000 under ss 25–26 of the Ethical Standards in Public Life (Scotland) Act 2000.

A person discriminated against in the field of education, such as a pupil forced – in effect – to leave a school or other institution owing to homophobic bullying which appeared to be condoned by the authorities could consider bringing an action in negligence against the institution in question or the education authority. But he or she could also bring an action under s 7(1)(a) of the HRA, relying on the Art 8 argument indicated above, so long as the institution was a public authority. Article 2 of the First Protocol might be used to argue that education in accordance with one's own philosophical convictions must include the need to allow some teaching about the homosexual way of life. If necessary,

---

301 In *Masterson v Holden* [1986] 3 All ER 39; [1986] 1 WLR 1017 the Divisional Court found that magistrates were entitled to view the behaviour of two homosexuals in kissing and cuddling as insulting for the purposes of the Metropolitan Police Act 1839, s 54(13). This approach might also be taken under the Public Order Act 1986, s 5, but such a wide interpretation of 'insulting' could allow many restrictions on the public expression of homosexuality, which might be in breach of Art 10, either read alone or in conjunction with Art 14. It appears that Art 10 does not cover homosexual intercourse *per se*, but may cover the physical as well as verbal expression of homosexual love: *X v UK* (1981) 3 EHRR 63.

302 [2001] 1 FCR 653, Judgment of 21 December 1999.

303 Robertson, G, *Freedom, the Individual and the Law*, 7th edn, 1993, p 382.

this guarantee could be used in an attempt to challenge any use of s 2A of the Local Government Act 1986.

Housing

Housing legislation tends to enshrine and rely on a limited notion of the 'family', and therefore it has led to discrimination against homosexuals living in a settled partnership. In *Fitzpatrick v Sterling Housing Assoc*[304] the Court of Appeal had to consider whether the homosexual partner of a deceased tenant could take over the tenancy under the Rent Act 1977, which limited such succession to persons who had lived with the original tenant 'as wife or husband' or were a member of his 'family'. The court, by a majority, found that the term 'family' was to be construed in the conventional sense, bearing prevailing social attitudes in mind. It was found that a 'family' was an entity which consisted of 'persons of the opposite sex cohabiting as man and wife'. Ward LJ, dissenting, pointed out that a number of other European countries had begun to allow same-sex couples to enter into property agreements on the same basis as unmarried heterosexual couples and that the US Supreme Court had recently found that a family should include 'two adult lifetime partners whose relationship is long term and characterised by an emotional and financial commitment and interdependence'. He found that 'the trend is to shift the focus ... from structure and components to function and appearance'. In other words, if a group acts as society expects a family to act, it is a family. He found that the exclusion of same-sex couples from the protection of the Rent Act which would follow from the preferred interpretation of the majority amounted to an assertion by society that their relationships are judged to be 'less worthy of respect, concern and consideration than the relationship between members of the opposite sex'.

On appeal, a bare majority of the House of Lords, in a landmark decision,[305] found that the term 'family' could be taken to include a cohabiting couple of the same sex. If it could be taken to include a cohabiting heterosexual couple, it was found that the term could be taken to include a homosexual one since, in principle, it was the bond and commitment between the two persons, not their sexual orientation, which was significant. The Lords did not consider, however, that a person could live with another of the same sex as his 'husband or wife'.

The future[306]

The potential of the HRA in this area has not yet been realised. It could range far outside the contexts covered by the discussion above. Article 6 might be used where a homosexual was refused a hearing in, for example, a child care or adoption case where a heterosexual would not have been so refused. Further possibilities are considered in Chapter 17. If the UK continues to resist the introduction of anti-discrimination

---

304 [1998] 2 WLR 225.
305 [1999] 3 WLR 1113.
306 See Wintemute, *op cit*, fn 278.

legislation, s 7(1)(a) of the HRA may provide quite an important substitute means of obtaining a remedy, at least where the other party is a public authority. The anomalies thereby created may eventually prompt the Government to introduce such legislation.

There is clearly a growing recognition in Europe that discrimination on grounds of sexual orientation amounts to a general problem which should be addressed. A report compiled for the Commission of the European Communities in May 1993[307] on discrimination against homosexuals found that the UK was one of the worst offenders and was one of only four Member States which provided no legal protection against discrimination. The report also criticised the Commission, which has argued that homosexuality is a matter to be left to individual governments. It recommended that human rights for homosexuals should be enshrined in European Community law.

The EOC, in the wake of the *Lustig-Prean* case, proposed that there should be a statutory provision outlawing discrimination in employment and other fields on the ground of sexual orientation. At present the Labour Government has, however, responded only by introducing an unenforceable Code of Practice covering such discrimination.[308] A Code of Practice is clearly unlikely to have much influence. It cannot outlaw discrimination on grounds of sexual orientation and is likely to be ignored by many employers. The very fact that a Code rather than a statute has been introduced signals to employers and others that this is not a significant matter.

Currently, pressure is coming from Europe, within the EC and Convention systems, for the introduction of measures to combat discrimination on this ground. The Framework Directive[309] on equal opportunities in employment allows for the extension of anti-discrimination measures to cover the ground of sexual orientation and, as Chapter 2 explained, Protocol 12 provides a free standing right to freedom from discrimination.[310] However, as indicated above, the domestic response to Protocol 12 is at present not very favourable.

---

307 By Peter Ashman, Director of the Independent European Human Rights Foundation.

308 In February 2000, the Government asked the EOC to draw up a Code governing this area: *Daily Telegraph*, 18 February 2000.

309 Adopted under the Treaty Establishing the European Community (TEC), Art 13.

310 See Chapter 2, p 85; for further discussion see Khaliq, *op cit*, fn 26.

CHAPTER 17

DISCRIMINATION AND EQUALITY IN THE CRIMINAL LAW AND THE CRIMINAL JUSTICE PROCESS

1 INTRODUCTION[1]

This chapter will consider evidence of discrimination on three of the protected grounds – those of race, sex and sexual orientation – within the criminal law and the criminal justice process. The areas considered are outside the anti-discrimination legislation considered in Chapter 16. As that chapter demonstrated, many aspects of discrimination on grounds of race have now been brought within the Race Relations Act (RRA) after its amendment in 2000 and, therefore, those aspects will not be considered here.

Consideration will be given below to the role of the criminal law in preventing certain expressions of discrimination which are unaffected by the civil anti-discrimination legislation, but which have a severe impact on the lives of certain groups. It will also consider the extent to which the criminal justice system positively seeks to eliminate discriminatory behaviour by those who administer it. But, the chapter will also consider how far the criminal law and criminal process may be said to contain provisions which themselves discriminate or allow for discrimination on the basis of the protected grounds covered. Bearing in mind the fact that discrimination against women in the criminal justice process does not fall within the Sex Discrimination Act, since no amendments equivalent to those made to the RRA in 2000 have been introduced, it is possible that the Human Rights Act (HRA) could be used instead. As Chapter 16 explained, arguments based on Arts 14 and another Article (usually Art 8), or on Art 8 alone, could be raised under s 7(1)(a) or (b) of the HRA.[2] This route could also be used in respect of discrimination on the ground of sexual orientation.[3]

2 RACIAL DISCRIMINATION

Criminal law

The criminal law does not overtly enshrine discrimination on grounds of race as it does on grounds of sex or sexual orientation. Instead, it contains some specifically anti-racist measures – although not many – intended to combat expressions of racial discrimination largely arising in the public order context. In general, however, it has only a very narrow role to play in fighting racial discrimination, due to the policy decision taken when the relevant legislation was being drawn up to leave the individual to pursue his or her individual remedy by means of a tort action. Even gross racial discrimination evinced by an employer, including racial harassment or absolute segregation, can be addressed only

---

1 For reading: Whitty, N, Murphy, T and Livingstone, S, *Civil Liberties: The Human Rights Act Era*, 2001, Butterworths, Chapter 8 (general reading); Clayton, R and Tomlinson, H, *Human Rights Law*, 2000, OUP, Chapter 17.
2 See pp 984–85.
3 See p 1054.

by a civil remedy if the individual chooses to seek it – unless it falls within the ambit of one of the general offences such as assault.

But racial harassment of individuals in certain areas of the UK can be addressed by the normal criminal measures and the offences in question exist, under provisions introduced in s 28 of the Crime and Disorder Act 1998, in an aggravated form where there is an added element of racism. Thus, an assault which is clearly racially motivated is classed as an aggravated assault. Those under ss 4, 4A and 5 of the Public Order Act 1986[4] can occur in a racially aggravated form, as can assaults under the Offences Against the Person Act 1861, and criminal damage and harassment under the Protection from Harassment Act 1997.[5] Section 153 of the Powers of Criminal Courts (Sentencing) Act 2000 provides for increases in sentences for racial aggravation. The Anti-Terrorism, Crime and Security Bill 2001 contains clause 39 which provides that these offences can also be 'religiously aggravated' while sentences can be increased under the 2000 Act for religious aggravation. However, at present, there seems to be no prospect of creation of a specific offence of racial attack. The case for creating such an offence, and perhaps a general offence of racial victimisation, is quite strong, given that it could be worded in such a way as to avoid colliding with other civil liberties as the incitement to racial hatred provision, considered in Chapter 6, potentially does.[6]

Criminal justice

As Chapter 16 showed, aspects of racial discrimination in the criminal justice system are now covered by the RRA, after its amendment in 2000. However, even prior to that point, a degree of official recognition was given to fighting or preventing racial, as opposed to sexual, discrimination in the criminal justice system, at least at the investigation stage. These provisions will now work alongside the RRA provisions and, if afforded respect by the police, will still be of relevance, since they do not depend on individual action by the victim of racial discrimination, action which he or she may sometimes be reluctant to take owing to fear or suspicion of the police.

Section 101(b) of the Police and Criminal Evidence Act 1984 (PACE) provides for regulations to make racially discriminatory behaviour a specific disciplinary offence. Whether the regulations deter the use of racist remarks or racial harassment of offenders is open to doubt, especially in the face of some evidence that officers may display racism to their own black colleagues.[7] Guidance is given under the PACE Codes of Practice as to interviewing practices to be adopted with detainees not proficient in English. Code A of PACE enjoins officers not to stop and search on the basis of a person's colour,[8] and by implication this may also apply to arrests. It is unclear whether this has had any effect on the arrest rates of blacks who have been found in various studies to be over-represented

---

4   See Chapter 6, pp 506–10.
5   See Chapter 9, pp 510–11.
6   See Chapter 5, pp 327–29. For discussion of these possibilities see Hare (1997) 17(3) OJLS 415.
7   On 4 May 1993, Joginder Singh Prem was awarded £25,000 damages for racial discrimination and victimisation in settlement of his claim after the force had admitted discrimination (see (1993) *Guardian*, 5 May).
8   Paragraph 1.7; see further Chapter 13, p 765.

in each offence group.[9] One possible conclusion which could be drawn is that the police are more ready to arrest blacks because of a stereotypical assessment of their propensity to commit offences, but doubt has been cast on this assumption in a study[10] by Jefferson and Walker, which suggested that when blacks were compared with whites living at a similar level of social deprivation, as opposed to comparing them with the white population generally, the difference in arrest rates between the two groups largely disappeared. The study also found a wide variation in the experience of blacks and Asians in the criminal justice system, blacks having consistently a less favourable attitude to the police,[11] while Asians had a more favourable attitude than whites. Under the RRA, a victim of a racially discriminatory offence could now receive compensation in respect of discriminatory arrests or stops so long as he or she was prepared to take on the burden of bringing a claim.

Evidence as to discrimination at the court hearing and in the outcome of arrests is mixed, despite quite a large body of work in the area.[12] The Jefferson and Walker study found that although the cautioning rates of Asians and blacks differed significantly, it was not possible to find a clear difference in sentencing policy.[13] A study of contested bail applications found no racial bias in the remand decisions of magistrates,[14] although some difference as to conditions of bail was found between Afro-Caribbean and white defendants.[15] Although the evidence of racial bias seems to be mixed, it is appropriate to try to remove any appearance of unfairness from the criminal justice system and, to this end, it may be argued that certain practices should change; for example, juries should contain some members from ethnic minority groups in cases where this was particularly appropriate. However, this possibility is not, according to the ruling in *Ford*,[16] available under any residual discretion of the judge. This decision of the Court of Appeal brought an end to the practice of some judges who had managed to achieve a racially mixed jury in certain cases.[17] An appearance of unfairness in the criminal justice system and perhaps the reality of it may also be created by the lack of black judges (in 1991, 1% of judges were black) and exacerbated by the failure of the law society to adopt an anti-discriminatory practice – both matters which have recently been the subject of concern.[18]

---

9 Crime statistics from the Metropolitan Police District by ethnic group for 1987, victims, suspects and those arrested: Home Office Statistical Bulletin 5/89. Blacks comprised 16% of those arrested in 1987, but only 5% of the population of London.

10 See Jefferson and Walker, 'Ethnic minorities in the criminal justice system' [1992] Crim LR 83.

11 *Op cit*, p 92.

12 McConville, M and Baldwin, 'The influence of race on sentencing in England' [1982] Crim LR 652–58; Crow and Cove, 'Ethnic minorities and the courts' [1984] Crim LR 413–17; Walker, *The Court Disposal and Remands of White, Afro-Caribbean and Asian Men*, 1983; Brown and Hullin, 'The treatment of ethnic minority and white offenders' (1992) 32 Br J Criminal Law 41–53.

13 *Op cit*, p 90.

14 Brown and Hullin, 'Contested bail applications: the treatment of ethnic minority and white offenders' [1993] Crim LR 107, p 111.

15 *Op cit*, p 110.

16 [1989] QB 868, CA. The Society of Black Lawyers in 'A time for freedom and a time for justice' has suggested that the practice of allowing a racially mixed jury in certain cases should be enshrined in statute. See (1993) 143 NLJ 837 (editorial).

17 Eg, *Bansal* [1985] Crim LR 151.

18 See (1991) 141 NLJ 1692 and (1991) 143 NLJ 1376. It should be noted that s 64(1) of the Courts and Legal Services Act 1990 made special provision for amending the SDA and RRA in order to ensure that discrimination against barristers fell within their ambit.

As Chapter 16 indicated, the application of the new s 19B of the RRA is limited in respect of criminal investigations. Moreover, under s 19C, s 19B does not apply to 'any judicial act' or 'act done on the instructions or on the behalf of a person acting in a judicial capacity'. Thus, while some law enforcement functions including arrest, bail detention and search by police officers and officers with similar powers are brought within the RRA, allegations of discrimination in the judicial process cannot be addressed under the Act.

3 GENDER DISCRIMINATION[19]

Criminal law

Until the late 19th century and, in one respect, until 1991, the criminal law enshrined and perpetuated gross sexual discrimination. Violent or indecent behaviour in the form of assault, battery, procuring sexual intercourse by threats, false imprisonment, indecent assault or rape was, it seems, lawful[20] if perpetrated against a married woman by her husband. The respect in which such discrimination survived was, until very recently, to be found in the law of rape: wives were deemed to have given an irrevocable consent to sexual intercourse within marriage. Hale's law on marital rights[21] is credited with creating immunity for a husband from a rape conviction and, therefore, the law was that by marrying her, a man acquired the right to 'rape' a woman without being convicted of rape. Hale also considered whether concubines should be able to withdraw consent to sex and determined that they should,[22] a liberal view at that time which ran counter to the previous position.[23] The marital immunity was favoured in some quarters because it was thought that the criminal law should not violate the privacy of the home, as it might endanger the continuance of family life. However, the argument that wives must not have the full protection of the criminal law, because if they invoke it the marriage is unlikely to survive,[24] fails to recognise that in itself it is helping to perpetuate their suffering by refusing to offer a sufficient deterrent to their husbands. It seems reasonable to assume that the 'ordinary raping husband'[25] was encouraged to rape by an exemption which declared, in effect, that he had a right to do so.

---

19 Reading: McCrudden, C (ed), *Anti-discrimination Law*, 1991; Rhode, D, *Justice and Gender: Sex Discrimination and the Law*, 1989; Clayton, R and Tomlinson, H, *The Law of Human Rights*, 2000, Chapter 17; McColgan, A, *Discrimination Law: Text, Cases and Materials*, 2000; Fredman, S, *Women and the Law*, 1997; Silberman, 'Equality, human rights, women and the justice system' (1994) 39 McGill LJ 489.

20 Until *Jackson* (1891) 1 QB 671 it was thought that a husband could forcefully imprison and (probably) chastise his wife in order to enforce the right to cohabitation. See *Atwood v Atwood Finch's Chancery Precedents* 492 and *Re Cochrane* 8 Dowl 630 in which Coleridge J said 'the husband may keep her by force ... and may beat her'. Under the Criminal Law Amendment Act 1885, s 3, a husband who forced his wife by threats to have sex with another incurred no liability. As late as 1984 in *Caswell* [1984] Crim LR 111 it was found that a husband could incur no liability in respect of what would otherwise have been an indecent assault on his wife. Marital rape was lawful until 1991, below fn 28.

21 Sir Matthew Hale CJ, *History of the Pleas of the Crown*, 1736.

22 1 PC 628–29.

23 In the 13th century it seems to have been the case that if a man had had consensual sex with his victim previously, he would be acquitted of rape. *Crown Pleas of the Wiltshire Eyre* 1249; Stenton, *Rolls of the Justice in Eyre for Yorkshire*, 1218–19.

24 Put by Glanville Williams (1992) 142 NLJ 11. For reply by the author, see (1992) 142 NLJ 831–32, 870–71.

25 (1991) NLJ 206.

The marital immunity created some interesting anomalies such as that found in the ruling of the Court of Appeal in *Kowalski*.[26] A husband who forced his wife to have oral sex with him as a preliminary to forced sexual intercourse was convicted of indecent assault although no liability could arise in respect of the sex act itself. It also seemed that a husband could be liable as an accessory to rape,[27] but not as a principal.

The House of Lords in *R*[28] finally swept away the marital exemption. However, it is still possible that husbands will be sentenced more lightly than other rapists because some judges appear to see cohabitation as a mitigating factor. In *Berry*,[29] a man raped his former cohabitee after some years had passed; the factor of cohabitation played a part in the decision to award a sentence of four years. That this policy may be pursued after the decision in *Billam*[30] that a sentence of five years would normally be appropriate for a rape without aggravating or mitigating features, is suggested by the decision of the Court of Appeal in *AG's Reference (No 7 of 1989)*[31] in which, again, a sentence of four years as opposed to five was awarded, possibly – although this was not made explicit in the judgment – because the man had cohabited with his victim. The ruling in *Stockwell*[32] suggests that the length of cohabitation will also be considered relevant; in reducing a sentence of three years to two, the Court of Appeal took into account the 10 years that the wife and husband had lived together. However, if a judge is able to look at all the circumstances of a rape without being expected to give the factor of cohabitation undue prominence, the domestic and stranger rapist will be punished on roughly the same scale bearing in mind the specific circumstances of each case. This is not merely a matter of proper sentencing policy, but of a declaration that women have the right to full protection from violation whatever the status of the attacker.

A number of areas of criminal law remain, enshrining gender-based differentiation on grounds which, it is submitted, are not objectively justifiable. These include the anomalous defence of coercion available to married women under s 47 of the Criminal Justice Act 1925, which assumes that wives are under the subjection of their husbands and the offences relating to abduction of a woman under the Sexual Offences Act 1956 – in particular the offence under s 19 of abducting a girl under 18 (whether or not with her consent), which assumes that such girls are to a greater extent than boys in the possession of their parents. The offences relating to prostitution under the 1956 Act and the Sexual Offences Act 1985 are, it is suggested, unnecessarily sexually segregated; if such offences are to exist, there seems to be no good reason why all of them should not apply equally to women and men.

---

26 (1988) 86 Cr App R 339.
27 *Cogan and Leake* [1976] QB 217.
28 [1991] 4 All ER 481; [1991] 3 WLR 767; [1992] Fam Law 108; [1992] Crim LR 207. For comment see 55 MLR 386.
29 [1988] Crim LR 325.
30 [1986] 1 All ER 985.
31 (1990) 12 Cr App R (S) 1.
32 (1984) 6 Cr App R (S) 84.

Criminal justice

There is quite a large body of literature postulating and analysing institutionalised sexist ideologies in the criminal justice system,[33] but this does not seem to have brought about sweeping changes, although it is fair to say that in one area – the management of a rape allegation – there have been improvements at the investigation stage, such as the introduction of 'rape suites' and questioning by female officers. Only the barest indication of the findings of this body of work can be given here, but it is clear that it has been wide ranging, considering the perceptions of female offenders held by magistrates, judges, police officers, prison officers and probation officers. A common theme seems to be that the treatment of female offenders may be affected by the private sexist ideologies of such persons, male or female, but that this factor is not as significant as the effect of such ideologies enshrined in the administrative and organisational context of the occupations in question.

A recurring theme concerns the treatment of victims of rape. Disquiet as to their treatment in the 1970s led to the setting up of the Heilbron Committee in 1975 whose recommendations were, in part, enshrined in the Sexual Offences (Amendment) Act 1976. This provides under s 2 that the victim should not be questioned as to her sexual experience except at the judge's discretion. It seems that a judge will not allow a complainant to be cross-examined as to sexual experience in order to suggest that for that reason alone she should not be believed,[34] but if her past sexual experience can be made to relate in some way to the issue of consent, leave should be given to cross-examine her on it.[35] Rape is the only crime in which a corroboration warning has to be given before allowing the jury to rely on the adult victim's evidence. Thus, the possibility of casting serious doubt on the credibility and veracity of the victim[36] and of indirectly blackening her character subsisted into the early 1990s.

Section 41 of the Youth Justice and Criminal Evidence Act was introduced, after a long campaign by women's groups, in order to prevent the cross-examining of victims about sexual experience, except in a very narrow range of circumstances – where the issue of consent relates to sexual behaviour taking place at about the same time as the event which is the subject matter of the complaint (s 41(3)(b)) or where consent is in issue and the sexual behaviour of the complainant taking place at about the same time is so similar to the behaviour relating to that issue (s 41(3)(c)). However, in R v A,[37] the House of Lords found a method of undermining the effect of s 41. The Lords used an extremely bold interpretative technique – that of reading words into s 41(3) in order to render it compatible with Art 6, under s 3 of the HRA. It may be suggested that in so doing, they went beyond using interpretative techniques and rewrote part of the legislation, thus

---

33 See Edwards, *Policing Domestic Violence*, 1989 and *Female Sexuality and the Law*, 1981, especially Chapters 2 and 5; Dunhill (ed), *The Boys in Blue: Women's Challenge to the Police*, 1989; Gelsthorpe, *Sexism and the Female Offender*, 1989 (which criticises the other writings, but seems to arrive at similar conclusions regarding the institutions under scrutiny).

34 *Viola* (1982) 75 Cr App R 125.

35 *SMS* [1992] Crim LR 310.

36 Judge Sutcliffe gave this corroboration warning in 1976: 'It is known that women in particular and small boys are liable to be untruthful and to invent stories', Old Bailey, 18 April 1976.

37 [2001] 2 WLR 1546; [2001] UKHL 25.

allowing the admission of relevant evidence relating to a previous sexual relationship between defendant and complainant, at the trial judge's discretion. The Lords did not appear fully to recognise the role of the legislation in protecting the Art 8 rights of the complainant. The Lords had to strike a balance between the fair trial rights of the defendant and the rights of the victim. They chose to strike a balance that differed from that which Parliament had determined upon. Given the Lords' acceptance of judicial deference to the executive in other spheres covered by this book, it is a matter of concern that in this instance they were not prepared to defer to Parliament.

The effect of this decision is likely to be to the detriment of women in general (since it will not aid in improving the rate of conviction in rape cases) and of rape complainants in particular. It means that if a man alleges that he had had sexual intercourse with the woman complainant on a previous occasion and that this relates to the issue of consent, she can be questioned, at the discretion of the judge, regarding that incident. Bearing in mind that most rapists are known to their victims, it may, depending on the circumstances, be relatively easy for the man to allege that sexual intercourse had occurred on a previous occasion, even where that was not the case. The Lords were concerned about a rape allegation against a cohabitee, and considered it bizarre that the woman could not, except in very limited circumstances, be asked about the cohabitation. However, the fact that a man and woman had been cohabitees would be bound to become apparent from the evidence. Further, nothing under s 41 would prevent the fact from being adduced by the defence in relation to the man's belief in consent. Thus, given that s 41 did not create an absolute bar and that the harm to a fair trial which concerned the Lords was very unlikely to arise, it is suggested that the Lords should have accepted that the section is designed to ease the burden on rape complainants and does not, in furtherance of that aim, create a disproportionate interference with a fair trial. It is suggested that a woman who is subjected to intrusive questioning during a rape trial whether as a result of this ruling or otherwise, has the basis for a claim that Art 8 has been breached which would, however, have to be pursued at Strasbourg,[38] unless a court was prepared to hear argument on the issue during a rape trial, under s 7(1)(b) of the HRA.

Policies and perceptions underlying investigation, prosecuting policy, sentencing and judicial pronouncements in passing sentence in rape and indecent assault cases are still, it is submitted, a matter of concern in so far as they reflect a perception that women are not all equally worthy of protection by the criminal law.[39] Prostitutes, promiscuous women, women who are out on the streets at night or who accompany a man to a house after an

---

38 Since HRA 1998, s 9(1) limits the right to bring proceedings under s 7(1)(a) in respect of judicial acts and also under s 9(3) precludes an award of damages in respect of a judicial act done in good faith. It may be noted that a complaint under Art 3 in respect of degrading treatment of a woman in a UK rape trial has been declared admissible at Strasbourg: *JM v UK* (2001) 2 EHRLR 215. The woman was subjected to prolonged cross-examination – over a period of days – by the rapist himself, who was deliberately wearing the clothes in which he had raped her. The experience, which was extremely humiliating and distressing, could no longer recur thanks to the provision of the Youth Justice and Criminal Evidence Act 1999, s 34, introduced as a result of that case.

39 See the analysis of the response of the criminal justice system to the rape victim by Temkin, J, *Rape and the Legal Process*, 1987, Chapter 1.

evening out may be seen as to different degrees blameworthy[40] and this may be reflected in the nature of the sentence and in the likelihood that the allegation of rape will be rigorously pursued. It seems that factors such as being out on the street at night tend to be seen as of less relevance in relation to male victims of serious crime.

4 SEXUAL ORIENTATION[41]

The criminal law and the criminal process

As Chapter 12 and the discussion below indicate, the criminal law and the criminal process can work in concert to allow for homophobic bias in the criminal justice system. The very existence of certain offences creates leeway for homophobic investigative methods. However, the position has improved, largely as a result of the influence of the Convention jurisprudence. Chapter 12 considered the changes to the age of consent for homosexual intercourse; they have meant that investigation and arrest or harassment of gays on suspicion of intercourse with young men is now much less likely since the age of consent is now 16.[42] However, as that chapter indicated, a position of full equality with heterosexuals has not yet been reached, allowing and encouraging the continuance of homophobic bias both in investigative techniques and in the substantive effect of the criminal law. For example, s 13 of the Sex Offences Act 1956 creates an offence of gross indecency in respect of homosexual acts. The 1967 Sex Offences Act qualifies this by providing that homosexual acts in private are decriminalised if no more than two persons are present, and as Chapter 12 explained, the age of consent to those acts is now 16. But the offence of gross indecency can still be charged where these conditions are not met; it was recently found to create a breach of Art 8 at Strasbourg in *ADT v UK*[43] in respect of charges brought against a man in respect of consensual oral sex and masturbation with more than one other man. A narrow margin of appreciation only was conceded to the State in finding that prosecution and conviction were disproportionate to the aims in question. Article 14 was not considered.

---

40 In a 1986 case, the Court of Appeal drastically reduced the sentences of a group of men convicted of indecent assault, Watkins LJ commenting that the victim was 'dissolute and depraved': (1986) *The Times*, 28 February. It may be of interest to note that in less liberal countries than Britain, such as Turkey, it is official policy to sentence rape of a prostitute much less heavily than rape of other women.

41 Reading: Feldman, D, *Civil Liberties in England and Wales*, 1993, pp 525–29; Hewitt, P, *The Abuse of Power*, 1982, Chapter 9; Wintemute, R, *Sexual Orientation and Human Rights: The US Constitution, the ECHR and the Canadian Charter*, 1995; Wilkinson, B, 'Moving towards equality: homosexual law reform in Ireland' (1994) 45 NILQ 252; Wilets, *The Human Rights of Sexual Minorities*, 1996; Heinze, E, *Sexual Orientation: A Human Right: An Essay on International Human Rights Law*, 1995; Wintemute, R (1997) 60(3) MLR 334; Bamforth, N, *Sexuality, Morals and Justice*, 1997; Skidmore (1997) 26(1) ILJ 51; Pannick, D, 'Homosexuals, transsexuals and the law' [1983] PL 279. Stychin, C, *Law's Desire: Sexuality and the Limits of Justice*, 1995; Rubin, 'Section 146 of the CJPOA 1994 and the decriminalisation of homosexual acts in the armed forces' [1996] Crim LR 393; McNorrie, K, 'Constitutional challenges to sexual orientation discrimination' 49(4) ICLQ 755; Wintemute, R, 'Lesbian and gay inequality 2000: the potential of the HRA and the need for an Equality Act 2002' (2000) 6 EHRLR 603.

42 See Chapter 12, p 740.

43 (2001) 31 EHRR 33.

Studies of discrimination against homosexuals in the criminal justice system have tended to concentrate on the investigation stage and methods of enforcing certain areas of the criminal law such as s 13 or s 32 of the Sexual Offences Act 1956.[44] Section 32 provides that it is an offence 'for a man to persistently solicit or importune in a public place for immoral purposes'. Research suggests that this section is used by police officers engaged in surveillance in public lavatories to trap gay men into some behaviour which might be said to come within the terms of the section.[45] It seems that almost any behaviour, 'any physical gesture or words' in context may fulfil its terms. Thus, homosexuals can be criminalised in respect of trivial behaviour which would not have occurred had a police officer not trapped them into it. Judgments under this section appear to reflect the bare tolerance of homosexuality mentioned above since, in determining what is meant by the term 'immoral' as used in the section, the assumption has been made that a jury would inevitably decide that homosexual behaviour is immoral,[46] and therefore, there is nothing to encourage police officers to adopt different investigative methods. Such assumptions made by judges imply that the homosexual way of life is contemptible and mean that the coercive force of the law may be used to impose a view of 'normal' behaviour on a minority, thereby failing to treat a group of citizens with equal concern and respect.

Potential impact of the HRA

As Chapters 12 and 16 explained, the HRA has potential as a means of improving the position of homosexuals. Its potential is highly relevant to discrimination on this ground in the criminal justice system, since all those involved in that system are public authorities and therefore can be sued directly under s 7(1)(a) of the HRA in respect of discriminatory practices such as, for example, arresting or stopping or searching a person on a homophobic basis. Moreover, since the criminal justice process is covered by a number of Convention Articles, as Chapter 13 demonstrated, the weakness of Art 14 would be less significant in this context than in those covered by Chapter 16. It would normally be possible to find that Art 5 or 6 (or Arts 8 or 3) was applicable. All these possibilities offer homosexuals avenues of challenge to discrimination practised against them in the criminal justice system, while s 3 of the HRA may provide a means of curbing the ambit of statutory offences which have a homophobic bias.

5 CONCLUSIONS

These two chapters have shown that, domestically, there is in place a complex anti-discrimination scheme which is, however, riddled with gaps and which covers only certain protected grounds. The strongest protection lies in the area of sex discrimination in employment, owing to the effect of EC law. The most comprehensive protection is available in respect of race discrimination. But in respect of the protected grounds, there

---

44 See Cane, *Gays and the Law*, 1982; Campaign for Homosexual Equality: evidence to the Royal Commission on Criminal Procedure 1981, Cmnd 8092; 'Soliciting by men' [1982] Crim LR 349; Power, 'Entrapment and gay rights' (1993) 143 NLJ 47–49 and 63.

45 See Power, *ibid*.

46 Eg, Gray [1981] 74 CAR 324; Kirkup (1992) *The Guardian*, 10 November; for comment, see Power, *ibid*.

are a number of anomalous gaps. No protection from indirect discrimination on grounds of gender reassignment or on the ground of transsexuality *per se* is provided. Discrimination on grounds of sex within the criminal justice system is not covered. Discrimination on grounds of sexual orientation, religion or age is not covered at all by specific statutory schemes (except in Northern Ireland), although the existing schemes covering the other protected grounds provide some incidental coverage of these other areas.

Clearly, addressing sometimes deep-rooted prejudice by individual legal action is an inherently flawed response.[47] Using anti-discrimination law at all can be profoundly inadequate because of the need to make comparisons with another person, as Chapter 16 pointed out. Clearly, disadvantage can often be addressed more effectively by changes in economic policies and through publicity campaigns. However, the law itself plays an educative role, since it symbolically affirms that some forms of behaviour are not countenanced by society. It can be very effective in addressing specific instances of discrimination, as the *Smith and Grady* case demonstrated.[48] Thus, examination of the available legal measures and their potential for development remains a legitimate avenue of inquiry.

Chapter 16 considered the potential of a number of EC measures in addressing some of these anomalies. Further, on the face of it, it is at least possible that the HRA could be used not only to fill gaps in the current schemes, but also to create remedies in respect of discrimination on the largely unprotected grounds. However, apart from the weaknesses of the Convention and the Strasbourg jurisprudence, there is also the problem of the generally unsympathetic attitude of the domestic judiciary. In a number of instances, explored in these chapters, they have curbed and limited the effects of the existing provisions. They are likely to find that this is a context in which they should leave the creation of a more extensive anti-discrimination scheme to Parliament, and the Strasbourg jurisprudence tends to leave them sufficient leeway to take this minimalist approach.

---

47   See Hepple, B and Szyszczak, E (eds), *Discrimination and the Limits of the Law*, 1992.
48   See Chapter 16, p 1054.

BIBLIOGRAPHY

Abel, R, *Speech and Respect*, 1994, Sweet & Maxwell

Adjei, C, 'Human rights theory and the Bill of Rights debate' (1995) 58 MLR 17

Akdeniz, Y, Walker, C and Wall, D (eds), *The Internet, Law and Society*, 2000 Longman/Pearson

Akendiz, Y, 'To link or not to link?' (1997) 11(2) International Review of Law, Computers and Technology 281

Alkema, EA, 'The third party applicability or *drittwirkung* of the ECHR in protecting human rights', in *The European Dimension*, 1988

Allan, TRS, 'Public interest immunity and ministers' responsibility' (1993) CLR 661

Allan, J, 'Bills of Rights and judicial power – a Liberal's quandary' (1996) 16(2) OJLS 337–52

Allan, TRS, 'Constitutional rights and common law' (1991) 11 OJLS 453–60

Allan, TRS, 'Legislative supremacy and the rule of law' (1985) 44 CLJ 111

Allan, TRS, 'Procedural fairness and the duty of respect' (1988) 18 OJLS 497

Allen, MJ and Cooper S, 'Howard's way: a farewell to freedom?' (1995) 58 MLR 364

Alston, P, *The EU and Human Rights*, 1st edn, 1999, OUP

Amnesty International, *The Detention and Imprisonment of Asylum Seekers in the UK*, 1996, Amnesty International British Section

Amos, M, 'Damages for breach of the Human Rights Act' (1999) EHRLR 178

Aquinas, '*Summa theologica*', in d'Entreves, P (ed), *Selected Political Writings*, 1970

Archbold: Criminal Pleading, Practice and Evidence, 1999, Sweet & Maxwell

Arlidge, A and Eady, D, *Contempt of Court*, 1982, Sweet & Maxwell

Arlidge, A and Smith, ATH, *Arlidge, Eady and Smith on Contempt*, 2nd edn, 1999, Sweet & Maxwell

Arnull, A, 'Article 119 and equal pay for work of equal value' (1986) Eur L Rev 200

Ashworth, A, 'Article 6 and the fairness of trials' [1999] Crim LR 261

Ashworth, A, 'The European Convention on Human Rights and English criminal justice: ships which pass in the night?', in Andenas, M (ed), *English Public Law and the Common Law of Europe*, 1998, Keyhaven

Austin, R, 'Freedom of information: the constitutional impact', Chap 12, pp319- 371 in Jowell, J and Oliver, D (eds), *The Changing Constitution*, 4th edn, 2000, OUP

Bailey, SH and Gunn, MJ, *Smith and Bailey on the Modern English Legal System*, 2nd edn, 1991

Bailey, SH, Harris, DJ and Jones, BL, *Civil Liberties: Cases and Materials*, 4th edn, 1995 (5th edn, forthcoming 2002), Butterworths

Bamforth, N, 'The application of the Human Rights Act 1998 to Public Authorities and Public Bodies' (1999) 58 CLJ 159–70

Bamforth, N, 'The scope of judicial review: still uncertain' [1993] PL 239

Barendt, E and Hitchens, L, *Media Law: Cases and Materials*, 2000, Longman

Barendt, E, *Broadcasting Law: A Comparative Study*, 1995, OUP

Barendt, E, 'Freedom of assembly', in Beatson, J and Cripps, Y (eds), *Freedom of Expression and Freedom of Information: Essays in Honour of Sir David Williams*, 2000, OUP

Barendt, E, 'Freedom of speech in the universities' [1987] PL 344

Barendt, E, 'Libel and freedom of speech in English law' [1993] PL 449

Barendt, E, 'Prior restraints on speech' [1985] PL 253

Barendt, E, '*Spycatcher* and freedom of speech' [1989] PL 204

Barendt, E, 'The First Amendment and the media', in Loveland, I (ed), *Importing the First Amendment, Freedom of Expression in Britain, Europe and the USA*, 1998, Hart

Barendt, E, *Freedom of Speech*, 1987, Clarendon

Barnard, C and Hepple, B, 'Substantive equality' (2000) 59(3) CLJ 562

Barnes, M, 'One experience of video recorded interviews' [1993] Crim LR 444

Barnum, DG, 'The constitutional status of public protest activity in Britain and the US' [1977] PL 310

Baxter, JD, *State Security, Privacy and Information*, 1990

Beatty, D, 'The Canadian Charter of Rights: lessons and laments' (1997) 60(4) MLR 487

Beckett, S and Clyde, I, 'A Human Rights Commission for the UK: the Australian experience' (2000) 2 EHRLR 116

Beddard, R, 'The rights of the criminal under Article 7 ECHR' (1996) ELR 3

Beddard, R, *Human Rights and Europe*, 3rd edn, 1980, Cambridge UP

Bedingfield, D, 'Privacy or publicity: the enduring confusion surrounding the american tort of invasion of privacy' (1992) 55 MLR 111

Bennion, F, 'What interpretation is possible under s 3(1) of the Human Rights Act?' [2000] PL 77

Betten, L and Grief, N, *EU Law and Human Rights*, 1998, Longman

Bevan, K and Palmer, C, *Bevan and Lidstone's The Investigation of Crime*, 1996

Bevan, VT, 'Protest and public disorder' [1979] PL 163

Beyleveld, D, 'The concept of a human right and incorporation of the European Convention on Human Rights' [1995] PL 577

Bhaba, J, 'Deterring refugees' (1992) Imm & Nat LP 133

Birch, D, 'Confessions and confusions under the 1984 Act' [1989] Crim LR 95

Birch, D, 'Suffering in silence: a cost-benefit analysis of s 34 of the Criminal Justice and Public Order Act' [1999] Crim LR 769

Birkinshaw, P and Parry, N, 'Every trick in the book: the Freedom of Information Bill 1999' (1999) 4 EHRLR 373

Birkinshaw, P, 'An "All singin' and all dancin'" affair: New Labour's proposals for FoI' [1998] PL 176

Birkinshaw, P, *Freedom of Information: The Law, the Practice and the Ideal*, 2nd edn, 1996; 3rd edn, 2001, Butterworths

Birkinshaw, P, 'I only ask for information – the White Paper on open government' [1993] PL 557

Birkinshaw, P, *Reforming the Secret State*, 1990, Hull University Press

Birtles, W, 'Big brother knows best: the Franks Report on section 2 of the Official Secrets Act' [1973] PL 100

Blackburn, R, 'A Parliamentary Committee on Human Rights', in Blackburn, R and Plant, R (eds), *Constitutional Reform: The Labour Government's Constitutional Reform Agenda*, 1999, Longman

Blasi, V, 'The checking value in First Amendment theory' (1977) Am B Found Res J 521

Bonner, D and Stone, R, 'The Public Order Act 1986: steps in the wrong direction?' [1987] PL 202

Bonner, D, 'Combating terrorism in the 1990s: the role of the prevention of Terrorism Act 1989' [1989] PL 440

Bonner, D, 'The Baker Review of the Northern Ireland (Emergency Provisions) Act 1978' [1984] PL 348

Bourne, C and Whitmore, J, *Anti-discrimination Law in Britain*, 3rd edn, 1996, Sweet & Maxwell

Boyle, A, 'Freedom of expression as a public interest in English law' [1982] PL 574

Boyle, K, 'Religious intolerance and the incitement of hatred', in Coliver, S (ed), *Striking a Balance: Hate Speech, Freedom of Expression and Non-discrimination*, 1992, ARTICLE 19

Bradley, AW and Ewing, K *Constitutional Law*, 12th edn, 1997, Longman/Pearson

Bradley, AW, 'Courts, community law and equal pay' [1988] PL 485

Bradley, AW, 'Justice, good government and public interest immunity' [1992] PL 514

Bradley, AW, 'Police powers and the prerogative' [1988] PL 298

Bratza, N and O'Boyle, M, 'Opinion: the legacy of the Commission to the new Court under the 11th Protocol' (1997) EHRLR 211

Brazier, R, 'The judiciary', in Blackburn, R and Plant, R (eds), *Constitutional Reform: The Labour Government's Constitutional Reform Agenda*, 1999, Longman

Brewry, G, 'The *Ponting* case' [1985] PL 203

Bridges, L and Choongh, S, *Improving Police Station Legal Advice*, 1998, Law Society

Briggs, A, *The History of Broadcasting Vols 1 and 2*, 1961 and 1965

Brown and Hullin, 'Contested bail applications: the treatment of ethnic minority and white offenders' [1993] Crim LR 107

Brown and Hullin, 'The treatment of ethnic minority and white offenders' (1992) 32 Brit J Criminal Law 41–53

Brownlie, I and Supperstone, M, *Law Relating to Public Order and National Security*, 2nd edn, 1981, Butterworths

Bryan, MW, 'The Crossman Diaries: developments in the law of breach of confidence' (1976) 92 LQR 180

Bryant, B, *Twyford Down: Roads, Campaigning and Environmental Law*, 1996, E & FN Spon

Butler, A, 'Why the New Zealand Bill of Rights is a bad model for Britain' (1997) 17 OJLS 332

Butterworth's Discrimination Law Handbook, 2000, Butterworths

Buxton LJ, 'The Human Rights Act and private law' (2000) 116 LQR 48

Bygrave, LA, 'Data protection pursuant to the right to privacy in human rights treaties' (1999) 6(3) IJLIT 247

Cain, P, 'Feminist jurisprudence: grounding the theories', in Bartlett, K and Kennedy, R (eds), *Feminist Legal Theory: Readings in Law and Gender*, 1991, Westview

Calcutt, Sir D, *Review of Press Self-regulation*, Cm 2135, 1993

Campbell, T and Sadurski, W (eds), *Rationales for Freedom of Communication*, 1994, Dartmouth

Carey, *Media Law*, 2nd edn, 1999, Sweet & Maxwell

Carey, P, *Blackstone's Guide to The Data Protection Act 1998*, 1998, Blackstone

Charlesworth, A, 'Between flesh and sand: rethinking the Computer Misuse Act 1990' (1995) 9 International Yearbook of Law, Computers and Technology 33

Chesterman (1997) 'OJ and the dingo: how media publicity for criminal jury trials is dealt with in Australia and America' 45 Am Jo Comp Law 109

Childs, M, 'Outraging public decency – the offence of offensiveness'[1991] PL 20–29

Cholewinski, R, 'Enforced destitution of asylum seekers in the UK: the denial of fundamental rights' (1998) 10 (3) Int Journal of Refugee Law 462–99

Choo, AL-T and Nash, S, 'What's the matter with s 78?' [1999] Crim LR 929–40

Clapham, A, 'The privatisation of human rights' (1995) EHRLR 20

Clapham, A, *Human Rights in the Private Sphere*, 1993, Clarendon

Clayton, R and Tomlinson, H, *Civil Actions Against the Police*, 1st edn, 1987, 2nd edn, 1992, 3rd edn, 1999, Sweet & Maxwell

Clayton, R and Tomlinson, H *The Law of Human Rights*, 2000, OUP

Clayton, G, 'Reclaiming public ground: the right to peaceful assembly' (2000) 63 MLR 252

Clements, B, 'Defining "religion" in the First Amendment: a functional approach' (1989) 74 Cornell LR 532

Cohen, M (ed), *Ronald Dworkin and Contemporary Jurisprudence*, Duckworth, 1984

Coleman, F, 'All in the best possible taste – the Broadcasting Standards Council 1989–1992' [1992] PL 488

Coppel, J and O'Neill, A 'The European Court of Justice: Taking Rights Seriously?' [1992] 29 CMLR 669

Cotterell, R, 'Prosecuting incitement to racial hatred' [1982] PL 378

Cotterell, R, *The Politics of Jurisprudence*, 1989, Butterworths

Craig, P and De Burca, G, *European Law: Text and Materials*, 2nd edn, 1998, OUP

Craig, P, *Administrative Law*, 4th edn, 1999, Sweet & Maxwell

Craig, P, *Public Law and Democracy in the United Kingdom and the United States of America*, 1990

Cram, I 'Automatic reporting restrictions in criminal proceedings and Article 10 of the European Convention on Human Rights' [1998] EHRLR 742

Cripps, Y, 'Breach of copyright and confidence: the *Spycatcher* effect' [1989] PL 13

Cripps, Y, 'Disclosure in the public interest: the predicament of the public sector employee' [1983] PL 600

Cumper, P, 'The protection of religious rights under s 13 of the HRA' [2000] PL 254

Curtis, LJ, 'Freedom of information in Australia' (1983) 14 Fed LR 5

Davies, P, 'Integrating intelligence into the machinery of British central government' (2000) 78(1) Public Administration 29

Deakin, S and Morris, G, *Deakin and Morris, Labour Law*, 2nd edn, 1998, 3rd edn, 2001, Butterworths

Devlin P (Lord), *The Enforcement of Morals*, 1965, OUP

Dhavan, R, 'Contempt of court and the Phillimore Committee Report' (1976) 5 Anglo-Am L Rev 186–253

Dicey, AV, *Introduction to the Study of the Law and the Constitution*, 10th edn, 1965, Macmillan

Dickson, B, 'The common law and the European Convention', in Dickson (ed), *Human Rights and the European Convention*, 1997, Sweet & Maxwell

Dickson, B, Connelly, A, *Human Rights and the European Convention*, 1997, Sweet & Maxwell

Dine, J and Watt, B (eds), *Discrimination Law: Concepts, Limitations and Justifications*, 1996, Longman

Dine, J and Watt, B 'Sexual harrassment: moving away from discrimination' (1995) 58 MLR 343

Dixon, D *et al*, 'Safeguarding the rights of suspects in police custody' 1 Policing and Society 115

Dixon, D 'Common sense, legal advice and the right to silence' [1991] PL 233

Dixon, D 'Solicitors, suspects, runners, police' [1991] PL 233

Dixon, D, 'Juvenile suspects and PACE', in Freestone, D (ed) *Children and the Law*, 1990, pp 107–29

Dixon, D, Bottomley, K and Coleman, C, 'Reality and rules in the construction and regulation of police suspicion' (1989) 17 Int J Soc Law 185–206

Dixon, D, Coleman, C and Bottomley, K, 'Consent and the legal regulation of policing' (1990) 17 JLS 345–62

Dixon, D, *Law and Policing: Legal Regulation and Police Practices*, 1997, Clarendon

Donovan, K, *Sexual Divisions in Law*, 1985 Weidenfeld & Nicholson

Donson, F, 'Can the common law really protect rights?' in Leyland, P and Woods T (eds), *Administrative Law Facing the Future:Old Constraints and New Horizons*, 1997, Blackstone

Doyle, B, 'Enabling legislation or dissembling law? The Disability Discrimination Act 1995' (2001) 64 MLR 7

Duffy, P 'A case for equality' (1998) EHRLR 134

Dummett, A and Nichol, A, *Subjects, Citizens, Aliens and Others – Nationality and Immigration Law*, 1990, Butterworths, Law in Context Series

Dutton, D, *British Politics since 1945*, 2nd edn, 1997, Blackwell

Dworkin, R, 'Do we have a right to pornography?', in *A Matter of Principle*, 1985, Clarendon

Dworkin, R, 'Liberalism', in *A Matter of Principle*, 1985, Clarendon

Dworkin, R, *Life's Dominion*, 1993, HarperCollins

Dworkin, R, *Taking Rights Seriously*, 1978, Duckworth

Dworkin, R *Law's Empire* 1986, Fontana

Dworkin, R, 'Is there a right to pornography?' (1981) 1 OJLS 177

Eady, D, 'A statutory right to privacy' (1996) 3 EHRLR 243

Eckersley, R, 'Whither the feminist campaign?: An evaluation of feminist critiques of pornography' 15 Int J Soc of Law 149

Edwards, M, 'Equal pay: the European dimension' (1990) BLR July 177

Edwards, S, *Female Sexuality and the Law*, 1981, Martin Robertson

Elliott, M, '*Lightfoot*: tracing the perimeter of constitutional rights' [1998] JR 217

Ellis, 'The definition of discrimination in European Community sex equality law' (1994) 19 EL Rev 563–80

Ellis, E and Miller, CJ 'The victimization of anti-discrimination complainants' [1992] PL 80

Ellis, E, *European Community Sex Equality Law*, 2nd edn, 1998, OUP

Emerson,C 'Towards a general theory of the First Amendment' (1963) 72 Yale LJ 877

Emerson, C, 'The right of privacy and the freedom of the Press' (1979) 14(2) Harvard Civil Rights – Civil Liberties L Rev 329

Ericson, RV, *Making Crime: A Study of Detective Work*, 1981, Butterworths

Evans, M and Morgan, R, *Preventing Torture: A Study of the European Convention for the Prevention of Torture*, 1998, OUP

Ewing, KD and Gearty, CA, 'Rocky foundations for Labour's new rights' (1997) 2 EHRLR 149

Ewing, KD and Gearty, CA, *Freedom Under Thatcher*, 1990, OUP

Ewing, KD and Gearty, CA, *The Struggle for Civil Liberties: Political Freedom and the Rule of Law in Britain 1914-1945*, 1999, Clarendon

Ewing, KD, 'Freedom of association and the Employment Act 1999' (1999) 28 ILJ 283

Ewing KD, 'Freedom of association', in McCrudden, C and Chambers, G (eds), *Individual Rights and British Law*, 1994, Clarendon

Ewing, KD, 'Social rights and constitutional law' [1999] PL 104

Ewing, KD, 'Social rights and human rights: Britain and the Social Charter – the Conservative legacy' [2000] 2 EHRLR 91

Ewing, KD, 'The Human Rights Act and labour law' (1998) 27 ILJ 275

Ewing, KD, 'The Human Rights Act and parliamentary democracy' (1999) 62(1) MLR 79

Ewing, KD, Bradley, A and McColgan, A (eds), *Labour Law: Text and Materials*, 2001, Hart

Fairley, D '"D" Notices, Official Secrets and the Law' (1990) 10 OJLS 430

Feingold, C, 'The *Little Red Schoolbook* and the European Court of Human Rights' (1978) Revue des Droits de l'Homme 21

Feintuck, M, *Media Regulation, Public Interest and the Law*, 1999, Edinburgh UP

Feldman, D, 'Content neutrality', in Loveland, I (ed), *Importing the First Amendment, Freedom of Expression in Britain, Europe and the USA*, 1998, Hart

Feldman, D, 'Remedies for violations of human rights under the Human Rights Act' [1998] EHRLR 691

Feldman, D, 'Secrecy, dignity or autonomy? Views of privacy as a civil liberty' (1994) 47(2) CLP 41

Feldman, D, 'The developing scope of Article 8 of the ECHR' [1997] EHRLR 265

Feldman, D, 'The Human Rights Act 1998 and constitutional principles' (1999) 19(2) LS 165

Feldman, D, 'The roots and early development of binding over powers' (1988) 47 CLJ 101–28

Feldman, D, *Civil Liberties and Human Rights in England and Wales*, 1st edn, 1993 (2nd edn, forthcoming 2002), OUP

Feldman, D, *The Law Relating to Entry, Search and Seizure*, 1986, Butterworths

Fenwick, 'Confessions, recording rules and miscarriages of justice' [1993] Crim LR 174–84

Fenwick, H and Hervey, T, 'Sex equality in the Single Market: new directions for the European Court of Justice' [1995] 32 CMLR 443–70

Fenwick, H and Phillipson,G, 'Direct action, Convention values and the Human Rights Act' (2001) 21(4) LS 535–68

Fenwick, H and Phillipson, G, 'Public protest, the Human Rights Act and judicial responses to political expression' [2000] PL 627–50

Fenwick, H and Phillipson, G, ' The doctrine of confidence as a privacy remedy in the Human Rights Act era' (2000) 63(5) MLR 660

Fenwick, H and Phillipson, G, 'Confidence and privacy: a re-examination' (1996) 55 CLJ 447

Fenwick, H and Phillipson, G, *Sourcebook on Public Law*, 1st edn, 1997 (2nd edn, forthcoming 2002), Cavendish Publishing

Fenwick, H, 'Indirect discrimination in equal pay claims' (1995) 3 European Public Law 331

Fenwick, H, 'Procedural rights of victims of crime: public or private ordering of the criminal justice process?' (1997) 60 MLR 317–33

Fenwick, H, 'The right to protest, the Human Rights Act and the margin of appreciation' (1999) 62(4) MLR 491

Fenwick, H, *Civil Rights: New Labour, Freedom and the Human Rights Act*, 2000, Pearson Education

Fiddich, P, 'Broadcasting: a catalogue of confrontation', in Buchan, N and Sumner, T (eds), *Glasnost in Britain: Against Censorship and in Defence of the Word*, 1989

Finnis, J, *Natural Law and Natural Rights*, 1979, Clarendon

Fitzpatrick, B and Taylor, N, 'Trespassers *might* be prosecuted: the European Convention and restrictions on the right to assemble' [1998] EHRLR 292

Fordham, M, 'What is anxious scrutiny?' [1996] JR 81

Fortin, J, 'Rights brought home for children' (1999) 62 MLR 350

Fredman, S and Morris, G, 'The costs of exclusivity: public and private re-examined' [1994] PL 69

Fredman, S, 'A difference with distinction: pregnancy and parenthood re-assessed' (1994) 110 LQR 106

Fredman, S, 'Bringing rights home' (1998) 114 LQR 538

Fredman, S, *Women and the Law*, 1997, OUP

Ganz, G, 'Matrix Churchill and public interest immunity' (1993) 56 MLR 564

Gardner, J, 'Discrimination as injustice' (1996) 16(3) OJLS 353

Gavison, R 'Privacy and the limits of law' (1980) 89(3) Yale LJ 421

Gearty, C, 'The European Court of Human Rights and the protection of civil liberties: an overview' (1993) 52 CLJ 89

Gearty, CA, 'Democracy and human rights in the European Court of Human Rights: a critical appraisal' [2000] 51(3) NILQ 381

Gearty, CA, 'Freedom of assembly and public order', in McCrudden, C and Chambers, G (eds) *Individual Rights and the Law in Britain*, 1994, OUP

Gearty, CA, 'Terrorism and human rights: a case study in impending legal realities' (1999) 19(3) LS 367

Gearty, CA (ed), *Terrorism*, 1996, Dartmouth

Ghai, Y, 'Sentinels of liberty or sheep in Woolf's clothing? Judicial politics and the Hong Kong Bill of Rights' (1997) 60 MLR 459

Ghandi, S and James, J, 'The English law of blasphemy and the European Convention on Human Rights' [1998] EHRLR 430

Gibbons, T, 'Aspiring to pluralism: the constraints of public broadcasting values on the deregulation of British media ownership' [1998] 16 Cardozo Arts and Entertainment Journal 475

Gibbons, T, 'Impartiality in the media' (1985) Archiv für Rechts- und Sozialphilosophie, Beiheft, Nr 28 pp 71–81

Gibbons, T, Regulating the Media, 2nd edn, 1998, Sweet & Maxwell

Gill, P, Policing Politics: Security, Intelligence and the Liberal Democratic State, Frank Cass, 1994

Goldberg, D, Prosser, T and Verhulst, S, Regulating the Changing Media: A Comparative Study, 1998, OUP

Goldsmith, A and Faran, S, 'Complaints against the police in Canada: a new approach' [1987] Crim LR 615

Goldsmith, A, External Review and Self-Regulation: Complaints Against the Police – The Trend to External Review, 1988, OUP

Goldsmith, A, 'Taking police culture seriously: police discretion and the limits of the law' (1990) 1 Policing and Society 91–114

Goodhart, AL 'Thomas v Sawkins: A Constitutional Innovation' [1936–38] CLJ 22

Goodhart, AL 'Newspapers and contempt of court in England' (1935) 48 Harv LR 885

Goodwin-Gill, GS, 'Who to protect ... how and the future' (1997) 9(1) Int Journal of Refugee Law 1

Gordon, R and Wilmot-Smith, R (eds), Human Rights in the UK, 1997, OUP

Graber, CB and Teubner, G, 'Art and money: constitutional rights in the private sphere?' (1998) 18(1) OJLS 61

Grant, A, 'Pre-trial publicity and fair trial' (1976) 14 Osgoode Hall LJ 275

Gray, K and Gray, S 'Civil rights, civil wrongs and quasi-public places' (1999) 1 EHRLR 46

Gray, K and Gray, S Elements of Land Law, 3rd edn, 2000, Butterworths

Greenwalt, K, 'Free speech justifications' (1989) 89 Columbia L Rev 119

Greer, S, 'The right to silence: a review of the current debate' (1990) 53 MLR 719

Grief, N, 'The Domestic Impact of the European Convention on human rights as mediated through Community law' [1991] PL 555

Griffiths, J, 'The Official Secrets Act 1989' (1989) 16 JLS 273

Griffiths, J and Lewis, T, 'The Human Rights Act s 12 – press freedom over privacy' (1999) 10(2) Ent LR 36

Griffiths, J, 'The brave new world of Sir John Laws' (2000) 63(2) MLR 159

Grosz, S Beatson J and Duffy, P Human Rights: the 1998 Act and the European Convention 2000, Sweet & Maxwell

Grosz, S and Braithwaite, N, 'Privacy and the Human Rights Act', in Hunt, M and Singh, R (eds), A Practitioner's Guide to the Impact of the Human Rights Act, 1999, Hart

Gurry, F, Breach of Confidence, 1984, Clarendon

Halsbury's Laws of England, 4th edn, Vol 34, Butterworths

Hanbury, W, 'Illiberal Reform of s 2' (1989) 133 SJ 587

Hansen, O, 'A future for legal aid?' (1992) 19 JLS 85

Harlow, C and Rawlings, R, *Law and Administration: Text and Materials,* 2nd edn, 1997, Butterworths

Harris, D, O'Boyle, K and Warbrick, C, *Law of the European Convention on Human Rights,* 1st edn, 1995 (2nd edn, forthcoming 2002), Butterworths

Harrison, J and Cuneen, M, *An Independent Police Complaints Commission,* 2000, Liberty

Harrison, J, *Police Misconduct: Legal Remedies,* 1987, LAG

Hart, HLA, 'Between utility and rights', in Cohen, M (ed), *Ronald Dworkin and Contemporary Jurisprudence,* 1984, Duckworth

Hart, HLA, 'Positivism and the separation of law and morals', in *Essays in Jurisprudence and Philosophy,* 1983, Clarendon

Hart, HLA, 'Social solidarity and the enforcement of morality', in *Essays in Jurisprudence and Philosophy,* 1983, Clarendon

Hart, HLA, *Essays in Jurisprudence and Philosophy,* 1983, Clarendon

Hart, HLA, *Law Liberty and Morality,* 1963, Clarendon

Hart, HLA, *The Concept of Law,* 2nd edn, 1994, Clarendon

Hartley, T and Griffiths, J, *Government and Law,* 2nd edn, 1981

Harvey, C and Livingstone, S, 'Human rights and the Northern Ireland peace process' [1999] EHRLR 162

Harvey, C, *Seeking Asylum in the UK – Problems and Perspectives,* 2000, Butterworths

Hepple, B and Szyszczak, E (eds), *Discrimination: the Limits of the Law,* 1992, Mansell

Hepple, B, 'Can direct discrimination be justified?' (1994) 55 EOR 48

Hepple, B, Coussey, M and Choudhury, T, *Equality: A New Framework* (Report of the Independent Review of the Enforcement of UK Anti-Discrimination Legislation, July 2000), 2000, Hart

Herman, D, 'Beyond the rights debate' (1993) 2 Social and Legal Studies 25

Hervey, T and O'Keeffe, D (eds), *Sex Equality Law in the European Union,* 1996, Kluwer

Hervey, T, *Justifications for Sex Discrimination in Employment,* 1993, Butterworths

Hewitt, P, *The Abuse of Power: Civil Liberties in the UK,* 1982, Martin Robertson

Hillyard, P, 'From Belfast to Britain: some critical comments on the Royal Commission on Criminal Procedure', in *Politics and Power,* Vol 4, 1981

Hitchens, LP, 'Approaches to broadcasting regulation: Australia and the UK compared' (1997) 17(1) LS 40

Hitchens, LP, 'Media Ownership and Control: A European Approach' (1994) 57 MLR 585

Hoffman (Lord), 'Human rights and the House of Lords' (1999) 62(2) MLR 159

Hoffman (Lord), 'The Human Rights Act and the House of Lords' (1999) 62(2) MLR 159

Hogg, PW, *Constitutional Law of Canada*, 1997, Carswell

Hollingsworth, M and Norton-Taylor, R, *Blacklist: The Inside Story of Political Vetting*, 1988

Home Office Central Planning and Training Unit, *The Interviewer's Rule Book*, 1992

Horwitz, P, 'Jury selection after *Dagenais*: prejudicial pre-trial publicity' (1996) 42 CR 220

Hoskyns, 'Women, European law and transnational politics' (1986) 14 Int J Soc Law 299–315

Hume, D, *Political Discourses*, 1906 (first published 1752)

Hunnings, N, 'Video censorship' [1985] PL 214

Hunt, M, 'The "horizontal effect" of the Human Rights Act' [1998] PL 423

Hunt, M, Singh, R and Demetriou, M, 'Is there a role for the 'margin of appreciation', in national law after the Human Rights Act?' (1999) 1 EHRLR 15

Hunt, M, *Using Human Rights in the English Courts*, 1997, Hart

Hyder, K, 'Cause for complaint' (1990) New Statesman and Society, 12 January

Ingber, S, 'Rethinking intangible injuries: a focus on remedy' (1985) Cal L Rev 772

Itzin, C (ed), *Pornography: Women, Violence and Civil Liberties*, 1992, OUP

Jackson, D, *Immigration: Law and Practice* 2nd edn, 1999, Sweet & Maxwell

Jackson, E, 'Catherine MacKinnon and feminist jurisprudence: a critical appraisal' (1992) 19 JLS 195–213

Jacobs, FG, 'From privileged crown to interested public' [1993] PL 121

Jacobs, FG, *The European Convention on Human Rights*, 1st edn, 1975, OUP

Jacobs, FG, and White, R *The European Convention on Human Rights*, 2nd edn, 1996, OUP

Jaconelli, J, 'The "D" Notice system' [1982] PL 39

Jaconelli, J, *Enacting a Bill of Rights*, 1980, Clarendon

Janis, M, Kay, R and Bradley, A, *European Human Rights Law: Text and Materials*, 2nd edn, 2000, OUP

Janisch, HN, 'The Canadian Access to Information Act' [1982] PL 534

Jefferson and Walker, 'Ethnic minorities in the criminal justice system' [1992] Crim LR 83

Jefferson, T, 'Policing the miners: law, politics and accountability', in Brenton and Ungerson (eds), *The Year Book of Social Policy in Britain 1985–6*, 1986

Jennings, WI, *The Approach to Self-Governance*, 1958, CUP

Jones, G, 'Breach of confidence – after *Spycatcher*' (1989) 42 CLP 49

Jones, P, 'Police powers and political accountability: the Royal Commission on Criminal Procedure'; in *Politics and Power*, Vol 4, 1981

Jones, T, 'The deregulation of broadcasting' (1989) 52 MLR 380–88

Jones, T, 'The devaluation of human rights under the European Convention' [1995] PL 430

Jowell, J and Lester, A, 'Beyond *Wednesbury*: substantive principles of judicial review' [1987] PL 369

Justice, *Unreliable Evidence? Confessions and the Safety of Convictions*, 1994

Kalven, H, 'The concept of the public forum' (1965) Sup Ct Rev 1

Kamenka, E, 'Public/private in Marxist theory and Marxist practice', in Benn and Gaus (eds), *Public and Private in Social Life*, 1983

Karst, 'Equality as a central principle in the First Amendment' 43 University of Chicago L Rev 20

Kearns, P, 'Obscene and blasphemous libel: misunderstanding art' [2000] Crim LR 652

Kennedy, H, in Walker, C and Starmer, K (eds), *Miscarriages of Justice: A Review of Justice in Error*, 1999, Blackstone

Kenny, CS, 'The evolution of the law of blasphemy' (1992) 51 CLJ 127–42

Keown, J, 'The law and practice of euthanasia in The Netherlands' (1992) 108 LQR 51–78

Kerrigan, K, 'Breach of the peace and binding over – continuing confusion' (1997) 2(1)J Civ Lib 30

Khaliq, V, 'Protocol 12 to the ECHR: a step forward or a step too far?' [2001] PL 457

Kilkelly, U, *The Child and the European Convention on Human Rights* 1999, Ashgate

Klug, F and Starmer, K 'Incorporation through the back door' [1997] PL 223

Klug, F and Wadham, J, 'The democratic entrenchment of a Bill of Rights: Liberty's proposals' [1993] PL 579

Klug, F, Starmer, K and Weir, S, *The Three Pillars of Liberty: Political Rights and Freedoms in the UK*, 1996, Routledge

Labour Party, *The Charter of Rights: Guaranteeing Individual Liberty in a Free Society*, 1990, Labour Party

Lacey, N, 'A change in the right direction? The CRE's consultative document' [1984] PL 186

Law Commission, *Offences Against Religion and Public Worship*, Report No 145, 1985

Laws LJ, 'The limitations of human rights' [1999] PL 254

Laws LJ, 'Wednesbury', in Forsyth, C and Hare, I (eds), *The Golden Metwand and the Crooked Cord: Essays in Honour of Sir William Wade QC* , 1998, Clarendon

Laws, J (Sir), 'Is the High Court the guardian of fundamental constitutional rights?' [1993] PL 67

Laws, J (Sir), 'The limitations of human rights' [1998] PL 254

Laws, J (Sir) 'Problems in the law of contempt' (1990) CLP 99

Le Sueur, AP and Sunkin, M, 'Application for judicial review' [1992] PL 102

Le Sueur, AP and Sunkin, M, *Public Law*, 1997, Pearson

Leander, S, 'The right to privacy, the enforcement of morals and the judicial function: an argument' (1990) CLP 115

Lees, S, *Ruling Passions, Sexual Violence, Reputation and the Law*, 1997, OU Press

Leigh, D, *Betrayed: The Real Story of the Matrix Churchill Trial*, 1993

Leigh, D, *The Frontiers of Secrecy – Closed Government in Britain*, 1980

Leigh, I and Lustgarten, L, *In From the Cold: National Security and Parliamentary Democracy*, 1994, OUP

Leigh, I and Lustgarten, L, 'Making rights real: the courts, remedies and the Human Rights Act' (1999) 58 CLJ 509

Leigh, I and Lustgarten, L, 'The Security Services Act 1989' (1989) 52 MLR 801

Leigh, I, 'Horizontal rights, the Human Rights Act and privacy: lessons from the Commonwealth?' (1999) 48 ICLQ 57

Leigh, I, 'Matrix Churchill, supergun and the Scott Inquiry' [1993] PL 630

Leigh, I, 'Reforming public interest immunity' (1995) 2 Web JCL 149–71

Leigh, I, 'Secret proceedings in Canada' (1996) 34 Osgoode Hall LJ 113

Leigh, I, '*Spycatcher* in Strasbourg' [1992] PL 200–08

Leigh, I, 'The security service, the press and the courts' [1987] PL 12–21

Leishman, F, Loveday, B and Savage, S (eds), *Core Issues in Policing*, 1996

Lester of Herne Hill (Lord) and Pannick, D (QC), *Human Rights Law and Practice*, 1999, Butterworths

Lester of Herne Hill (Lord), 'First steps towards a constitutional Bill of Rights' [1997] 2 EHRLR 124

Lester of Herne Hill (Lord), 'Interpreting statutes under the HRA', 20(3) Statute L Rev 218

Lester, A, 'Fundamental rights: the United Kingdom isolated?' [1984] PL 46

Lester, A, 'The judges as law-makers' [1993] PL 269

Lester, A, *Democracy and Individual Rights*, 1968

Lester of Herne Hill (Lord), 'New European equality measures' [2000] PL 562

Lester of Herne Hill (Lord), 'The European Convention in the new architecture of Europe' [1996] PL 5

Liddy, J, 'The concept of family life under the ECHR' [1998] EHRLR 15

Lidstone, K and Bevan, V, *Search and Seizure under the Police and Criminal Evidence Act 1984*, 1992

Lidstone, K and Palmer, C, *The Investigation of Crime*, 2nd edn, 1996, Butterworths

Lightman, G and Bowers, J, 'Incorporation of the ECHR and its impact on employment law' [1998] EHRLR 560

Linn, I, *Application Refused: Employment Vetting by the State*, 1990

Littleton, CA, 'Reconstructing sexual equality', in Bartlett, K and Kennedy, R (eds), *Feminist Legal Theory: Readings in Law and Gender*, 1991, Westview

Livingstone, S, 'Article 14 and the prevention of discrimination in the ECHR' (1997) EHRLR 25

Lloyd (Lord), 'Do we need a Bill of Rights?' (1976) 39 MLR 121

Lloyd, I, *Information Technology Law*, 3rd edn, 2000, Butterworths0

Locke, J, *The Second Treatise of Government*, 1698

Loh, E, 'Intellectual property: breach of confidence?' (1995) 17 EIPR 405–07

Loughlin, M, *Public Law and Political Theory*, 1992, Clarendon

Loveday, B, 'Police complaints in the USA' (1988) 4 Policing 172

Loveland, I (ed), *Importing the First Amendment, Freedom of Expression in Britain, Europe and the USA*, 1998, Hart

Loveland, I, *Constitutional Law: A Critical Introduction*, 2nd edn, 2000, Butterworths

Lowe, N and Willmore, 'Secrets, media and the law' (1985) 48 MLR 592

Lowe, N and Sufrin, B, *Borrie and Lowe: The Law of Contempt*, 3rd edn, 1996, Butterworths

Lustgarten, L, 'Racial inequality and the limits of law' (1986) 49 MLR 68–85

Lustgarten, L, 'The CRE under attack' [1982] PL 229

Lustgarten, L, *The Legal Control of Racial Discrimination*, 1980

Lustgarten, L, *The Governance of Police*, 1986

MacCormick, DN, 'A note on privacy' (1973) 84 LQR 23

MacDonald, I and Blake, N, *Immigration Law and Practice*, 5th edn, 2001, Butterworths

Mackie, 'The third theory of the law', in Cohen, M (ed), *Ronald Dworkin and Contemporary Jurisprudence*, 1984, Duckworth

MacKinnon, C, 'Difference and dominance: on sex discrimination', in Bartlett, K and Kennedy, R (eds), *Feminist Legal Theory: Readings in Law and Gender*, 1991, Westview

MacKinnon, C, 'Reflections on sex equality under law' (1991) 100 Yale LJ 1281

MacKinnon, C, 'Feminism, Marxism, method and the State' (1982) 7 Signs 515

MacKinnon, C, 'Feminism, Marxism, method and the State', in Bartlett, K and Kennedy, R (eds), *Feminist Legal Theory: Readings in Law and Gender*, 1991, Westview

MacKinnon, C, *Only Words*, 1993 HarperCollins

MacKinnon, C, *Sexual Harassment of Working Women*, 1979, Yale UP

MacKinnon, C, *Feminism Unmodified: Discourses on Life and Law*, 1987, Harvard UP

MacKinnon, C, *Towards a Feminist Theory of the State*, 1989, Harvard UP

Maguire, M, 'Complaints against the police: the British experience', in Goldsmith, A (ed), *Complaints Against the Police: A Comparative Study*, 1990, OUP

Maguire, M, 'The wrong message at the wrong time?', in Morgan, D and Stephenson, G (eds), *Suspicion and Silence: The Right to Silence in Criminal Investigations*, 1994, Blackstone

Maher, G, *A Theory of Criminal Process*, 2000, Hart

Mahoney, P, 'Marvellous richness or invidious cultural relativism?' (1998) 19 Human Rights LJ 1

Mallender, R, 'Judicial review and the rule of law' (1996) 112 LQR 182–86

Manchester, C, 'Criminal Justice and Public Order Act 1994: obscenity, pornography and videos' [1995] Crim LR 123

Mann, FA, 'Britain's Bill of Rights' (1978) 94 LQR 512

Markesenis, B (ed), *Protecting Privacy*, Clarendon, 1999

Markesenis, B and Nolte, N, 'Some comparative reflections on the right of privacy of public figures in public places', in Birks, P (ed), *Privacy and Loyalty*, 1997, Clarendon

Markesenis, B, 'Privacy, freedom of expression, and the horizontal effect of the Human Rights Bill: lessons from Germany' (1999) 115 LQR 47

Markesinis, B, 'The right to be let alone versus freedom of speech' [1986] PL 67

Markesinis, BS, 'The Calcutt Report must not be forgotten' (1992) 55 MLR 118

Marshall, G, 'Press freedom and free speech theory' [1992] PL 40

Martens, S, 'Incorporating the Convention: the role of the judiciary' (1998) 1 EHRLR 5

McBride, T, 'The Official Information Act 1982' (1984) 11 NZULR 82

McCabe, S and Wallington, P, *The Police, Public Order and Civil Liberties: Legacies of the Miners' Strike*, 1988, Routledge

McColgan, A, 'Family friendly frolics' (2000) 29 ILJ 125

McColgan, A, *Discrimination Law: Text, Cases and Materials*, 2000, Hart

McColgan, A, *Women under the Law: The False Promise of Human Rights*, 2000, Pearson

McConville M and Baldwin, 'The influence of race on sentencing in England' [1982] Crim LR 652–58

McConville, M and Hodgson, J, *Custodial Legal Advice and the Right to Silence*, 1993, Royal Commission Study No 16

McConville, M, 'Search of persons and premises' [1983] Crim LR 604–14

McConville, M, 'Video taping interrogations: police behaviour on and off camera' [1992] Crim LR 532

McConville, M, Sanders, A and Leng, R, *The Case for the Prosecution*, 1991, Routledge

McCrudden, C, 'The Effectiveness of European Equality Law: National Mechanisms for enforcing Gender Equality Law in the light of European Requirements' (1993) 13 OJLS 320

McCrudden, C (ed), *Anti-discrimination Law*, 1991, Dartmouth

McCrudden, C, 'A common law of human rights? Transnational judicial conversations on constitutional rights' (2000) 20(4) OJLS 499–532

McCrudden, C and Chambers, G (eds), *Individual Rights and the Law in Britain*, 1994, OUP

McDonald, RJ, 'The margin of appreciation in the jurisprudence of the European Court of Human Rights', in *International Law and the Time of its Codification*, 1987

McEvoy, K and White, C, 'Security vetting in Northern Ireland' (1998) 61 MLR 341

McGinley, 'Judicial approaches to sex discrimination in US and UK – a comparative study' (1986) 49 MLR 413

McKenzie, I, Morgan, R and Reiner, R, 'Helping the police with their enquiries' [1990] Crim LR 22

McNorrie, K, 'Constitutional challenges to sexual orientation discrimination' 49(4) ICLQ 755

Mead [1998] Crim LR 870

Meiklejohn, A 'The First Amendment is an absolute' (1961) Sup Ct Rev 245

Merrills, J and Robertson, A, *Human Rights in Europe, A Study of the European Convention on Human Rights*, 3rd edn, 1993, Manchester University Press

Michael, J, 'Spycatcher's end?' (1989) 52 MLR 389

Miles, J, 'Standing under the Human Rights Act: theories of rights enforcement and the nature of public law adjudication' (2000) 59 CLJ 133

Mill, JS, 'On Liberty', in Cowling, M (ed), *Selected Writings of John Stuart Mill*, 1968, CUP; 1972, Everyman

Mill, JS, *On the Subjection of Women*, 2nd edn, 1869, Longman

Millar and Phillips, 'Evaluating anti-discrimination legislation in the UK: some issues and approaches' (1983) 11 Int J Soc Law 417

Miller, A, *Assault on Privacy*, 1971

Miller, CJ, *Contempt of Court*, 2nd edn, 1999, OUP

Miller, CJ, 'The Sunday Times case' (1974) 37 MLR 96

Milne, AJM, 'Should we have a Bill of Rights?' (1977) 40 MLR 389

Minow, M, 'Feminist reason: getting it and losing it' 38 J Legal Educ 47

Mirfield, P, 'Successive confessions and the poisonous tree' [1996] Crim LR 554

Mirfield, P, *Silence, Confessions and Improperly Obtained Evidence*, 1997, Clarendon

Moon, G, 'The Draft Discrimination Protocol to the European Convention on Human Rights: a progress report' (2000) 1 EHRLR 49

Morgan, R and Newburn, T, *The Future of Policing*, 1997, OUP

Morrisson, CC, 'The Margin of appreciation in human rights law' (1973) 6 Human Rights J 263

Moston, S and Williamson, T, 'The extent of silence in police stations', in Greer, S and Morgan, R (eds), *The Right to Silence Debate*, 1990, University of Bristol

Mowbray, A, 'The European Court of Human Rights' approach to just satisfaction' [1997] PL 647

Mowbray, A, 'The role of the European Court of Human Rights in the promotion of democracy' [1999] PL 703

Mullender, R, 'Racial harrassment, sexual harrassment and the expressive function of law' (1998) 61 MLR 236

Munday, R, 'Inferences from silence and European human rights law' [1996] Crim LR 370

Munro, C, 'Press freedom – how the beast was tamed' (1991) 54 MLR 104

Munro, C, *Studies in Constitutional Law*, 2nd edn, 1999, Butterworths

Myron, W Oldfield (Jr), 'The exclusionary rule and deterrence: an empirical study of Chicago narcotics officers' (1987) 54 U Chicago L Rev 1016–69

Naismith, S, 'Photographs, privacy and freedom of expression' (1996) 2 EHLR 150

Nardell, G 'The Quantock Hounds and the Trojan Horse' [1995] PL 27

Nelken, D, 'Disclosing/invoking legal culture: an introduction' (1995) 4 SLS 435

Neuwahl, N and Rosas, A, *The European Union and Human Rights*, 1995, Martinus Nijhoff

Newburn, T *et al*, 'Increasing public order' (1991) 7 Policing 22

Newburn, T *et al*, 'Policing the streets' (1990) 29 HORB 10

Newburn, T, *Crime and Criminal Justice Policy*, 1995, Longman (Social Policy in Britain Series)

Nicol, D, 'Limitation periods under the HRA and judicial review' (1999) 115 LQR 216

Nimmer, MB, 'The meaning of symbolic speech under the First Amendment' (1973) 21 UCLA L Rev 29

Norton-Taylor, R, in Blackburn, R and Plant, R (eds), *Constitutional Reform: The Labour Government's Constitutional Reform Agenda*, 1999, Longman

Nozick, R, *Anarchy, State and Utopia*, 1974, Blackwell

O'Donell, T, 'The margin of appreciation doctrine: standards in the jurisprudence of the European Court of Human Rights' (1982) 4 Human Rights Q 474

O'Leary, S, 'Accession by the EC to the European Convention on Human Rights' (1996) 4 EHRR 362

Oliver, D, 'The frontiers of the State: public authorities and public functions under the HRA' [2000] PL 476

Oliver, D, 'The Human Rights Act and public law/private law divides' (2000) 4 EHRLR 343

Olsen, F, 'Statutory rape: a feminist critique of rights analysis', in Bartlett, K and Kennedy, R (eds), *Feminist Legal Theory: Readings in Law and Gender*, 1991, Westview

Orst, S, 'Conceptions of the euthanasia phenomenon' (2000) J Civ Lib 155

Ovey, C, 'The European Convention on Human Rights and the criminal lawyer: an introduction' [1998] Crim LR 4

Palmer, S, 'The government proposals for reforming s 2 of the Official Secrets Act 1911' [1988] PL 523

Palmer, S, 'Tightening secrecy law' [1990] PL 243

Palmer, S, 'Wilfully obstructing the freedom to protest?' [1987] PL 495

Pannick, D and Lester of Herne Hill (Lord), *Human Rights Law and Practice*, 1999, Butterworths

Pannick, D, 'Homosexuals, transsexuals and the law' [1983] PL 279

Pannick, D, 'Principles of interpretation of Convention rights under the Human Rights Act and the discretionary area of judgment' [1998] PL 545

Pannick, D, 'Religious feelings and the European Court' [1995] PL 7

Pannick, D, 'Who is subject to judicial review and in respect of what?' [1992] PL 1

Papademetriou, G, *The European Union's Struggle with Immigration and Asylum*, 1996, International Migration Policy Programme, Carnegie Endowment for International Peace

Parent, WA, 'A new definition of privacy for the law' (1983) 2 Law and Philosophy 305, 326

Parekh, B, 'The case for positive discrimination', in Hepple, B and Szyszczak, E (eds), *Discrimination: the Limits of the Law*, 1992, Mansell

Paton-Simpson, E, 'Private circles and public squares: invasion of privacy by the publication of "private facts"' (1998) 61 MLR 318

Penner, R, 'The Canadian experience with the Charter of Rights' [1996] PL 125

Phillipson, G, 'The Human Rights Act, "horizontal effect" and the common law: a bang or a whimper?' (1999) 62 MLR 824

Pleming, N, 'Assessing the Act: a firm foundation or a false start?' (2000) 6 EHRLR 560–79

Poulter, S, 'Towards legislative reform of the blasphemy and racial hatred laws' [1991] PL 85

Prescott, P, '*Kaye v Robertson*: a reply' (1991) 54 MLR 451

Price, 'Taking rights cynically' (1989) 48 CLJ 271

Prosser, D, 'Privacy' (1960) 48 California L Rev 383

Rasaiah, S, 'Current legislation, privacy and the media in the UK' (1998) 3(5) Communications Law 183

Rasaiah, S and Newell, 'Data protection and press freedom' [1997–98] YBMEL 209

Rawls, J, *A Theory of Justice*, 1973, Clarendon

Raz, J, 'Free expression and personal identification' (1991) 11(3) OJLS 303

Raz, J, *The Morality of Freedom*, 1986, Clarendon

Redish, M, *Freedom of Expression*, 1984, Michie

Reiner, R, 'The politics of the Act' [1985] PL 394

Reiner, R and Leigh, I, 'Police powers', in McCrudden, C and Chambers, G (eds), *Individual Rights and the Law in Britain*, 1994, OUP

Reinman, J, 'Driving to the panopticon: a philosophical exploration of the risks to privacy posed by the highway technology of the future' (1995) 11 Computer & High Tech LJ 27

Reville, N, *Broadcasting Law and Practice* 1997, Butterworths

Rhode, D, *Justice and Gender: Sex Discrimination and the Law*, 1989, Harvard UP

Rhode, D, 'Feminist critical theories' (1990) 42(3) Stanford Law Review 634–38

Richardson, J and Thomas, D (eds), *Archbold: Criminal Pleading, Practice and Evidence*, 1999, Sweet & Maxwell

Richardson, J, 'Discretionary life-sentences and the ECHR' [1991] PL 34

Roberts, N, 'The Law Lords and human rights: the experience of the Privy Council in interpreting Bills of Rights' (2000) EHRLR 147

Robertson, G and Nichol, AGL, *Media Law*, 2nd edn, 1992, 3rd edn, 1999, Sweet & Maxwell

Robertson, G, *Freedom, the Individual and the Law*, 7th edn, 1993, Penguin

Robertson, K, *Public Secrets*, 1982, Basingstoke

Robilliard, F, *Religion and the Law: Religious Liberty in Modern English Law*, 1984, Manchester University Press

Robillard, St J, 'Offences against Religion and Public Worship'(1981) 44 MLR 556

Rolph, CH, *Books in the Dock: The Trial of Lady Chatterley*, 1969, Andre Deutsch

Rubin, G, 'Section 146 of the Criminal Justice and Public Order Act 1994 and the decriminalisation of homosexual acts in the armed forces' [1996] Crim LR 393

Ryan, C and Williams, K, 'Police discretion' [1986] PL 285

Sacks, V, 'The Equal Opportunities Commission – 10 years on' (1986) 49 MLR 560

Sacks, V, 'Tackling discrimination positively in Britain', in Hepple, B and Szyszczak, E (eds), *Discrimination: the Limits of the Law*, 1992, Mansell

Sadurski, W, 'On "Seeing speech through an equality lens": a critique of egalitarian arguments for suppression of hate speech and pornography' (1996) 16(4) OJLS 713

Sanders, A and Young, R, 'The Royal Commission on Criminal Justice' (1994) 14 OJLS 435

Sanders, A, 'Access to justice in the police station: an elusive dream?', in *Access to Justice*, 1996, Blackstone

Sanders, A and Young, R, *Criminal Justice*, 1st edn, 1994, 2nd edn, 2000, Butterworths

Sands, P, 'Human rights, the environment and the *Lopez Ostra* case' (1996) EHRLR 597

Scanlon, T, 'A theory of freedom of expression' (1972) 1 Phil & Public Affairs 204

Scarman (Lord), *English Law – The New Dimension*, 1974, Stevens

Schabas, W, *International Human Rights Law and the Canadian Charter*, 1991, Carswell

Schauer, F, 'Reflections on the value of truth' (1991) 41 Case Western Reserve L Rev 699

Schauer, F, 'The political incidence of the free speech principle' (1993) 64 US Colorado LR 935

Schauer, F, *Free Speech: A Philosophical Enquiry*, 1982, CUP

Schermers, H, 'Adaptation of the Eleventh Protocol to the European Convention on Human Rights' (1995) 20 ELR 559

Schwartz, H, 'The short and happy life and tragic death of the New Zealand Bill of Rights' [1998] NZLR 259

Seipp, D, 'English judicial recognition of the right to privacy' (1983) 3 OJLS 325

Seldon, A, 'The consensus debate' (1994) 14 Parliamentary Affairs 512

Shah, P, *Refugees, Race and the Legal Concept of Asylum in Britain,* 2000, Cavendish Publishing

Sharpe, S, *Judicial Discretion and Criminal Investigations,* 1998, Sweet & Maxwell

Shaw, J, 'Pregnancy discrimination as sex discrimination' (1991) 16 EL Rev 313–20

Sherr, A, Freedom of Protest, Public order and the Law' 1989, OUP

Shetreet, S (ed), *Free Speech and National Security,* 1991, Dordrecht

Sieghart, P *The Lawful Rights of Mankind,* 1986, Clarendon

Silberman, R, 'Equality, human rights, women and the justice system' (1994) 39 McGill LJ 489

Simmonds, N, 'Imperial visions and mundane practices' (1987) 46 CLJ 465

Simmonds, N, 'Between positivism and idealism' (1991) 50 CLJ 308

Simmonds, N, *Central Issues in Jurisprudence: Justice, Law and Rights,* 1986, Sweet & Maxwell

Simon, 'Does the court's decision in *Nebraska Press Association* fit with the research evidence on the impact on jurors of news coverage?' (1978) Stanford L Rev 515

Singh, R, 'Privacy and the media after the Human Rights Act' (1998) EHLR 712

Singh, R, 'The indirect regulation of speech' [1988] PL 212

Smart, C, *Feminism and the Power of Law,* 1989, Routledge

Smart, JJC and Williams, B *Utilitarianism: For and Against,* 1973, CUP

Smith, JC and Hogan, J, *Criminal Law,* 9th edn, 1999, Butterworths

Smith, ATH, 'The Public Order Act 1986 Part I' [1987] Crim LR 156

Smith, DJ, 'Case construction and the goals of the criminal process' (1997) 37 Br Journal of Criminology 319

Spencer, S, 'A Human Rights Commission', in Blackburn, R and Plant, R (eds), *Constitutional Reform: The Labour Government's Constitutional Reform Agenda,* 1999, Longman

Squires, N, 'Judicial review of the prerogative after the HRA' (2000) 116 LQR 572–75

Stanley, A, 'The legal status of international zones: the British experience with particular reference to asylum seekers' (1992) Imm & Nat LP 126

Steiner, J, *Textbook of EC Law,* 1998, Blackstone

Steyn, K and Wolfe, D, 'Judicial review and the Human Rights Act: some practical considerations' (1999) EHRR 614

Straw, J and Boateng, P, *Bringing Rights Home: Labour's Plans to Incorporate the ECHR into UK Law: A Consultation Paper,* 1996

Stuntz, W, 'The American exclusionary rule and defendants' changing rights' [1989] Crim LR 117

Stychin, C, *Law's Desire: Sexuality and the Limits of Justice,* 1995, Routledge

Sufrin, B and Lowe, N, *The Law of Contempt,* 3rd edn, 1996, Butterworths

Supperstone, M and Coppel, J, 'Judicial review after the Human Rights Act' (1999) 3 EHRLR 301–29

Supperstone, M and O'Dempsey, D, *Supperstone and O'Dempsey on Immigration and Asylum*, 4th edn, 1996, Sweet & Maxwell

Supperstone, M, *Brownlie's Law of Public Order and National Security*, 2nd edn, 1981, Butterworths

Szyszczak, E, 'Pay inequalities and equal value claims' (1985) 48 MLR 139

Taggart, M, 'Tugging on Superman's cape: lessons from the experience with the New Zealand Bill of Rights' [1998] PL 266

Tapper, C, *Cross and Tapper on Evidence*, 9th edn, 1999, Butterworths

Taylor, N and Walker, C, 'Bugs in the system' (1966) 1 J Civ Lib 105

Teff, H, 'Consent to medical procedure: paternalism, self-determination or therapeutic alliance?' (1985) 101 LQR 432

Tierney, S, 'Devolution issues and s 2(1) of the Human Rights Act' [2000] 4 EHRLR 380–92

Tomkins, A, 'Public interest immunity after *Matrix Churchill*' [1993] PL 530

Tomkins, A, *The Constitution Unwrapped: Government after Scott*, 1998, Clarendon

Tomuschat, C, 'Freedom of association', in Macdonald, R St J, Matscher, F and Petzold, H (eds), *The European System for the Protection of Human Rights*, 1993, Nijhoff

Townhend-Smith, R, 'Justifying indirect discrimination in English and American law: how stringent should the test be?' (1995) 1 Int Journal of Discrimination and the Law 103

Travis, A, *Bound and Gagged – A Secret History of Obscenity in Britain*, 2000, Profile Books

Tregilgas-Davey, M, 'Adverse inferences and the no-comment interview' (1997) 141 SJ 500

Tregilgas-Davey, M, '*Ex parte Choudhury* – an opportunity missed' (1991) 54 MLR 294–99

Tugendhat, M, 'The Data Protection Act 1998 and the media' [2000] YBMCL 115

Tushnet, M, 'An essay on rights' (1984) 62(8) Texas Law Review 1363

Van Dijk, P and Van Hoof, F, *Theory and Practice of the European Convention on Human Rights*, 3rd edn, 1998, Kluwer

Vincent, D, *The Culture of Secrecy, Britain 1832–1998*, 1998, OUP

von Prondzynski, F and Richards, W, 'Tackling indirect discrimination' [1995] PL 117

Wacks, R (ed), *Privacy*, 1993, Dartmouth

Wacks, R, 'The poverty of privacy' (1980) 96 LQR 73

Wacks, R, *Personal Information, Privacy and the Law*, 1993, Clarendon

Wacks, R, *Privacy and Press Freedom*, 1995, Blackstone

Wacks, R, *The Protection of Privacy*, 1980, Sweet & Maxwell

Waddington, PAJ, *Liberty and Order*, 1994

Waddington, PAJ, *The Strong Arm of the Law: Armed and Public Order Policing*, 1991, Clarendon

Wade, William (Sir), 'Horizons of horizontality' (2000) 116 LQR 217

Wade, William (Sir), 'The United Kingdom's Bill of Rights', in Beatson, J, Hare, I and Forsyth, C (eds), *Constitutional Reform in the United Kingdom: Practice and Principles*, 1998, Hart

Wadham, J and Mountfield, H, *Blackstone's Guide to The Human Rights Act*, 1999, Blackstone

Waldron, J, 'A rights-based critique of constitutional rights' (1993) 13 OJLS 18

Walker, C, 'Fundamental rights, fair trials and the new audio-visual sector' (1996) 59 MLR 517

Walker, C, 'Scandalising in the eighties' (1985) 101 LQR 359

Walker, C, Cram, I and Brogarth, D 'The reporting of Crown Court Proceedings and the new Contempt of Court Act 1981' (1992) 55 MLR 647

Walker, C and Starmer, K (eds), *Justice in Error: A Review of Miscarriages of Justice*, 1999, Blackstone

Walker, C, *The Prevention of Terrorism in British Law*, 1st edn, 1986, 2nd edn, 1992, Manchester UP

Walker, S, 'Freedom of speech and contempt of court: the English and Australian approaches compared' (1991) 40 ICLQ 583

Wallington, P, 'Injunctions and the right to demonstrate' (1976) 35 CLJ 82

Wallington, P, 'Policing the miners' strike' (1985) 14 ILJ 145

Wallman, S, 'Difference, differentiation, discrimination', 5 New Community 1

Warbrick, C, 'Federalism and free speech', in Loveland, I (ed), *Importing the First Amendment*, 1998, Hart

Warbrick, C, 'The structure of Article 8' [1998] EHRLR 32

Warren S, and Brandeis, L 'The right to privacy' (1890) 4 Harv L Rev 193

Wasik, M and Taylor, R *Blackstone's Guide to the Criminal Justice and Public Order Act 1994*, 1995, Blackstone

Watson, A, *Legal Transplants in Comparative Law*, 2nd edn, 1993, Georgia UP

Wei, G, 'Surreptitious takings of confidential information' [1992] LS 302

Weiler, 'The wages of sex: the uses and limits of comparable worth' (1986) 99 Harv L Rev 1728

Westin, AF, *Privacy and Freedom*, Athenaeum, 1967

White, C, 'Security vetting, discrimination and the right to a fair trial' [1999] PL 406–18

Whitty, N, Murphy, T and Livingstone, S, *Civil Liberties: The Human Rights Act Era*, 2001, Butterworths

Wilborn, S, 'The disparate impact model of discrimination: theory and limits' (1985) 34 American University L Rev 799

Wildhaber, L, 'Right to education and parental rights', in Macdonald, R St J, Matscher, F and Petzold, H (eds), *The European System for the Protection of Human Rights*, 1993, Nijhoff

Wilkinson, B, 'Moving towards equality: homosexual law reform in Ireland' (1994) 45 NILQ 252

Wilkinson, P, *Terrorism and the Liberal State*, 1995, Macmillan

Williams Committee, *Obscenity and Film Censorship: Committee Report*, 1979, Cmnd 7772, HMSO

Williams, DGT, 'Contempt and the Thalidomide Case' (1973) 32 CLJ 177

Williams, DGT, 'The Crossman Diaries' (1976) 35 CLJ 1

Williams, DGT, *Keeping the Peace: The Police and Public Order*, 1967, Hutchinson

Williams, DGT, *Not in the Public Interest: The Problem of Security in Democracy*, 1965, Hutchinson

Williams, DW, 'British passports and the right to travel' (1974) ICLQ 642

Williams, G, 'Preventive justice and the rule of law' (1953) 16 MLR 417

Wilmo, P and Rodgers, W (eds), *Gatley on Libel and Slander*, 9th edn, 1998, Sweet & Maxwell

Wilson, 'Confidence, privacy and press freedom: a study in judicial activism' (1990) 53 MLR 43

Wintemute, R, 'Lesbian and gay inequality 2000: the potential of the Human Rights Act and the need for an Equality Act 2002' (2000) 6 EHRLR 603

Wintemute, R, 'Recognising new kinds of direct sex discrimination: transsexualism, sexual orientation and dress codes' (1997) 60(3) MLR 334

Wintemute, R, *Sexual Orientation and Human Rights: The US Constitution, the ECHR and the Canadian Charter*, 1995, Clarendon

Wolchover, D and Heaton-Armstrong, A, 'The questioning code revamped' [1991] Crim LR 232

Wolffe, W, 'Values in conflict: incitement to racial hatred and the Public Order Act 1986' [1987] PL 85

Woolf (Lord), Jowell, J and Le Sueur, A, *De Smith, Woolf and Jowell's Principles of Judicial Review*, 1999, Sweet & Maxwell (student edition)

Wright, J, 'How private is my private life?', in Betten, L (ed), *The Human Rights Act 1998: What It Means*, 1999, Martinus Nijhoff

Yang, TL (1966) 15 ICLQ 175

Young, J, *The Exclusive Society: Social Exclusion, Crime and Difference in Late Modernity*, 1999, Sage

Zander, M, *A Bill of Rights*, 4th edn, 1996, Sweet & Maxwell

Zander, M, *The Police and Criminal Evidence Act 1984*, 3rd edn, 1995, Sweet & Maxwell

Zellick, G, 'Fair trial and free press' [1982] PL 343

Zimmerman, D, 'Requiem for a heavyweight: a farewell to Warren and Brandeis's privacy tort' (1983) 68 Cornell L Rev 291

Zuckerman, AAS, 'Public interest immunity – a matter of prime judicial responsibility' (1994) 57 MLR 703

INDEX

E

M

O